KU-157-369

ECONOMICS
SECOND EDITION

MICHAEL PARKIN
UNIVERSITY OF WESTERN ONTARIO

DAVID KING
UNIVERSITY OF STIRLING

▲
ADDISON-WESLEY PUBLISHERS LIMITED
WOKINGHAM, ENGLAND • READING, MASSACHUSETTS • MENLO PARK, CALIFORNIA • NEW YORK • DON MILLS, ONTA
AMSTERDAM • BONN • SYDNEY • SINGAPORE • TOKYO • MADRID • SAN JUAN • MILAN • PARIS • MEXICO CITY • SEOUL

© 1995 Addison-Wesley Publishers Ltd.
© 1995 Addison-Wesley Publishing Company Inc.

All rights reserved. No part of this publication may be reproduced, stored in a retrieval system, or transmitted, in any form or by any means, electronic, mechanical, photocopying, recording or otherwise, without the prior written permission of the publisher.

Many of the designations used by manufacturers and sellers to distinguish their products are claimed as trademarks. Addison-Wesley has made every attempt to supply trademark information about manufacturers and their products mentioned in this book.

First printed 1995.

ISBN 0-201-59397-1

British Library Cataloguing in Publication Data
A catalogue record for this book is available from the British Library.

EDITOR-IN-CHIEF: **Tim Pitts**
PRODUCTION MANAGER: **Stephen Bishop**
PRODUCTION EDITOR: **Susan Keany**
PRODUCTION CONTROLLER: **Jim Allman**
COPY-EDITOR: **Penelope Williams**
PROOFREADER: **Lynne Balfe**
DEVELOPMENT ASSISTANT AND
PERMISSIONS COORDINATOR: **Davina Arkell**
SALES TEAM ADVISER: **Richard Beaumont**
COVER AND TEXT DESIGN: **Anthony Leung**
Designers and Partners
TYPESETTER: **Express Graphics**
PRINTER: **R.R. Donnelley & Sons**

Index compiled by Indexing Specialists, Hove, East Sussex.

Art developed by RWP Graphics, London, Ontario.

ABOUT THE AUTHORS

MICHAEL PARKIN was educated at the University of Leicester. Currently in the Department of Economics at the University of Western Ontario, Professor Parkin has held faculty appointments at the Universities of Sheffield, Leicester, Essex and Manchester, and has lectured extensively throughout Canada, the United States, Europe, Australia and Japan. He has served as managing editor of the *Canadian Journal of Economics* and on the editorial boards of the *American Economic Review* and the *Journal of Monetary Economics*. Professor Parkin's research on macroeconomics, monetary economics and international economics has resulted in 160 publications in the *American Economic Review*, the *Journal of Political Economy*, the *Review of Economic Studies*, the *Journal of Monetary Economics*, the *Journal of Money, Credit and Banking* and dozens of other journals and edited volumes.

DAVID KING took his first degree at the University of Oxford and his D.Phil. at the University of York. He spent six years at Winchester College before moving to the University of Stirling where he is a senior lecturer. His chief interest is in the economics of local government. He is a consultant on state and local finance for the OECD, spent two years seconded to the United Kingdom government advising on local finance, and has also been consulted by governments and officials in over a dozen other countries including many in eastern Europe. His numerous books and papers include *Fiscal Tiers: the Economics of Multi-level Government* which has also been published in Spanish. He has twice been invited as a visiting fellow to the Australian National University in Canberra.

BRIEF CONTENTS

*Summary, Key Elements, Review Questions and
Problems appear at the end of each chapter.

PART 4

FACTOR MARKETS
TONY ATKINSON   **371**

PART 7

MACROECONOMIC PROBLEMS AND POLICIES
WYNNE GODLEY **778**

PART 8

THE GLOBAL ECONOMY
JEFFREY SACHS   950

CREDITS

The publisher would like to thank the following for permission to use material in this book.

CHAPTER 1: Cartoon, Drawing by Modell, ©1985 **The New Yorker Magazine, Inc.** Pin factory, **Culver Pictures**. Woman with silicon wafer, **Tony Stone Images**. Adam Smith, **The Bettman Archive**.

PART 2: David Laidler, **Courtesy of John Tamblyn Inc**.

CHAPTER 4: The railroad suspension bridge near Niagra Falls, Anonymous, **Gift of Maxim Karolik for the M. and M. Karolik Collection of American Paintings, 1815–1865, Courtesy of the Museum of Fine Arts, Boston**. Concorde and other aircraft, **The Royal Aeronautical Society**. Antoine-Augustin Cournot and Alfred Marshall, **Stock Montage**.

CHAPTER 6: Boston Tea Party, **Courtesy American Antiquarian Society**. Petrol Pump, **Davina Arkell, Addison-Wesley**. Fleeming Jenkin, **Mary Evans Picture Library**.

CHAPTER 7: Canning peaches in Liby McNeal Cannery, **Selma, Fresnofactory, Keystone Mast, California Museum of Photography, University of Carolina, Riverside**. Woman executive, **Davina Arkell, Addison-Wesley**. Jeremy Bentham, **Mary Evans Picture Library**. William Stanley Jevons, **Macmillan Press**.

CHAPTER 10: Ford assembly line, **Brown Brothers**. Michael Dell, **Dell Computers**. Jacob Viner, **Archives of the University, Department of Rare Books and Special Collections, Princeton University Library**. Ronald Coase, **David Joel Photography**.

CHAPTER 12: Cartoon, **Culver Pictures**. Installing a satellite dish, **Courtesy of AlphaServe Ltd, Guildford**. Joan Robinson, **Ramsey and Muspratt Archives**.

PART 4: Anthony Atkinson, **Carlo Faulds Photography**.

CHAPTER 14: Manchester in 1914, **Local Studies Unit, Manchester Central Library**. Stacked cars, **Robert Hunt**. Harold Hotelling, **Wootten-Moulio**. Thomas Robert Malthus, **Mary Evans Picture Library**.

CHAPTER 18: Homeless, **Sparham/Network**. Frankfurt Crowd **Mike Mazzaschi/Stock Boston**. Simon Kuznets, **Harvard University, Office of News and Public Affairs**.

CHAPTER 19: Lake pollution, **Image Finders**. Fishing on the River Thames, **Mick Rouse/Angling Times**. James Buchanan, **George Mason University**. Arthur Cecil Pigou, **National Portrait Gallery**.

CHAPTER 22: Car wash, **Davina Arkell, Addison-Wesley**. Sir William Petty, **The Bettman Archive**.

CHAPTER 24: Couple in kitchen, **Davina Arkell, Addison-Wesley**. Student in shop, © **John Coletti/ The Picture Cube**. John Maynard Keynes, **Stock Montage**.

CHAPTER 27: Woman burning marks and David Hume, **The Bettman Archive**. Man at cash dispenser, **Davina Arkell, Addison-Wesley**.

CHAPTER 31: Cartoon, © **Ron Tandberg**. The Stock Exchange **The Bettman Archive**. Boarded up shop, **Davina Arkell, Addison-Wesley**. Robert Lucas Jr, **Marshall Heinrichs, Addison-Wesley**.

CHAPTER 32: Harold Wilson, **National History of Labour Party**. Hans Tietmeyer, **Bundesbank, German Embassy**. Milton Friedman, **Marshall Heinrichs, Addison-Wesley**.

PART 8: Jeffrey Sachs, **Courtesy of Hank Morgan**.

CHAPTER 34: Clipper ship, **Museum of the City of New York, Gift of Edward D. Thurston Jr**. Container ship, **Sealand Services Inc**. David Ricardo, **Mary Evans Picture Library**.

CHAPTER 36: Chinese peasant farmers and affluent Chinese couple, **Sally and Richard Greenhill**. Karl Marx, **The Bettman Archive**.

Acknowledgement is made to **Datastream International** for the use of material in figures and tables from the OECD and World Bank, and to the **Central Statistical Office**.

PREFACE

To change the way students see the world: this is our aim in teaching economics and in writing this book. Nothing gives a teacher of economics more satisfaction than to share the joy of students who begin to think like economists. But economics is not easy to master, and every day we remember the challenges facing those who seek to gain the insights we call the economist's way of thinking, and we remember our own early struggles with the discipline. In preparing this edition, we have drawn on our own experience and also on the experiences of instructors and students who have used the first edition.

Three assumptions guided the choices we faced in writing this book. First, students are eager to learn but have many claims on their time. They want to see the relevance of what they are studying to their own everyday experiences. Second, students want straightforward and logical explanations. Third, students want to be equipped for tomorrow's world. They want to learn the economics of the 1990s and the relevant lessons of the past so that they will be able to understand the world of the twenty-first century.

Approach

The core economic principles have been around for more than one hundred years and other important elements, especially parts of the theory of the firm and Keynesian macroeconomics, have been with us for more than fifty years. However, economics has also been developing and changing rapidly during the past few decades. All texts on economics principles pay some attention to these more recent developments, but they have not succeeded in integrating the new and the traditional. Our aim has been to incorporate new ideas – such as game theory, the modern theory of the firm, information, public choice, and the real business cycle – into the body of timeless principles.

The presence of modern topics does not translate into 'high level' or into 'bias'. We make recent developments in economics thoroughly accessible to beginning students. Where modern theories are controversial, alternative approaches are presented, evaluated and compared. For example, all the macroeconomics 'schools' – Keynesian, monetarist and New Classical – are given a thoughtful and even-handed treatment.

But this book does have a point of view. It is that economics is a serious, lively and evolving science – a science that seeks to develop a body of theory powerful enough to explain the economic world around us and that pursues its tasks by building, testing and rejecting economic models. In some areas the science has succeeded in its tasks, but in others controversy persists. Where matters are settled, we present what is known; where controversy persists, we present the alternative viewpoints. This positive approach to economics is, we believe, especially valuable for our students as they prepare to function in a world in which simple ideologies have become irrelevant and in which familiar patterns in the economic landscape have shifted and become blurred.

Microeconomics and Changes in the Second Edition

The structure of microeconomics remains consistent with the first edition but we have made many important changes. We have simplified but vastly increased the range of applications of the demand and supply model (Chapter 6) to handle such issues as who pays taxes on expenditure, trading in illegal goods, and agricultural policies. We have expanded the treatment of the marginal utility theory of consumer choice (Chapter 7) to give a stronger graphical derivation of consumer equilibrium and the demand curve. The modern theory of the firm, including principal and agent issues, is given a much simplified treatment in Chapter 9, and isoquants are covered in an appendix to Chapter 10. Our presentation of the game theory approach to understanding oligopoly (Chapter 13) has been well received by students and teachers for its simple yet serious treatment. In revising the oligopoly chapter, we have recognized that students can gain additional insights from the traditional oligopoly models. A new chapter (Chapter 17) deals with the issues arising from uncertainty and incomplete information and illustrates these issues with examples drawn from markets for used cars, insurance and risky assets. Our approach in this chapter is the same as in the rest of the book: to explain difficult (and in this case relatively new) topics in a clear and accessible way

that fits naturally into the core principles sequence. Finally, we have brought together market failure and public choice in Chapter 19.

Macroeconomics and Changes in the Second Edition

Our goals in revising the macroeconomics coverage have been to extend and improve the positive, fact-driven approach of the first edition; to make the complexities of macroeconomic models and events relevant and understandable to students; and to address the global macroeconomic issues of the 1990s.

We have changed the balance of the national income accounting material (Chapter 22) to give greater prominence to a discussion of the validity of GDP as a measure of economic well-being. We have simplified and streamlined the initial presentation of aggregate demand-aggregate supply (Chapter 23) so that students can make effective and immediate use of this model.

In the light of the 1991–1992 recession, the re-emergence of a large government deficit, and the experiences of the European Union's Exchange Rate Mechanism, it is apparent that a clear understanding of fiscal policy and monetary policy is essential. The role of fiscal policy is thoroughly discussed throughout the text (especially in Chapters 23, 25, 28 and 31), and is illustrated through issues drawn from the 1991–1992 recession. The presentation of monetary theory and policy has been reorganized to parallel that of expenditure theory and fiscal policy. Chapter 26 now covers the demand for and the supply of money and the determination of interest rates, and Chapter 27 explains how the central bank influences the economy by manipulating interest rates.

Open economy issues are introduced as briefly as possible, and a full explanation of the balance of payments and exchange rate appears in Chapter 35. This chapter can be covered much earlier if desired.

Our coverage of aggregate supply and unemployment has been thoroughly revised. We have more on productivity and growth and on alternative theories of unemployment in Chapter 29. The theory of inflation is now treated separately from theories of expectations (Chapter 30). The coverage of stabilization policy has been revised and extended to include a discussion of the political business cycle.

Finally, the problems faced by economies making the transition from planned to market economy has been completely revised. Chapter 36 provides a framework for understanding events in Eastern Europe, the former Soviet Union, and China as these countries change their economic systems and open their markets to international influences.

Changes in the European Union

As in the first edition, we make numerous references to the European Union. On 1 January 1995, the European Union was enlarged with the joining of Austria, Finland and Sweden. It now contains 15 member countries rather than 12. However, our text was written before 1 January 1995, and as a result we refer only to the previous twelve members.

Flexibility

We have chosen to present microeconomics first, but the book has been written to accommodate courses that put macroeconomics first. The microeconomics and macroeconomics chapters do not depend on each other; concepts and terms are defined and ideas are developed independently in each of the two halves.

We have accommodated a wide range of teaching approaches by building flexibility into the book. The core chapters (see p.xxix) can form the basis of a one-year course that covers both macro and micro. Non-core chapters may be omitted with no loss of continuity. And the *AD–AS* model can be covered later in the macro sequence than it appears in the book (see p. xxix).

Special Features

The second edition, like its predecessor, is packed with special features designed to enhance the learning process.

Art Program

A highly successful feature of the first edition was the outstanding art. The art was not only visually attractive and engaging, but also communicated economic principles clearly. We received enormously positive feedback about the art, which confirmed our belief that one of the most important tools for economists is

graphical analysis. Also, this is an area that gives many students much difficulty. In the second edition we have refined the data-based graphs and have devised a style that clearly reveals data and trends.

Our goal in the model-based art is to show clearly 'where the economic action is'. To do so, we use a consistent format which includes:

◆ Highlighting shifted curves, points of equilibrium and the most important features in red.

◆ Using arrows in conjunction with colour to lend directional movement to what are usually static presentations.

◆ Pairing graphs with data tables from which the curves have been plotted.

◆ Using colour consistently to emphasize the content, and referring to the colour in the text and captions.

◆ Labelling key pieces of information in graphs with boxed notes.

◆ Rendering each piece electronically, so that precision is achieved.

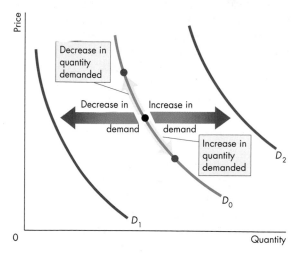

The entire art program has been developed with students' study and review needs in mind. We have retained the following features:

◆ Marking the most important figures and tables with a red 'key' ◆ and listing them at the end of the chapter as 'Key Figures and Tables'.

◆ Using complete, informative captions that encapsulate the major points in the graph, so that students can preview or review the chapter by skimming through the art.

The Interviews

Interviews with distinguished economists created another popular feature of the first edition which we have retained. But we have talked with an entire new cast of economists who have contributed significantly to advancing the thinking and practice in our discipline. The interviews help students to see the human face of economists as they discuss the areas of their specialization, their unique contributions to economics, and their general insights which are relevant to beginning students.

Each part of the book opens with an interview which covers topics that are developed in the following chapters. Students can use the interviews to preview the issues and the terminology they are about to meet. A more careful reading afterwards will give a fuller appreciation of the discussion. Finally, the whole series of interviews can be approached as an informal symposium on the subject matter of economics as it is practised today.

Reading Between the Lines

Another feature of the previous edition that was well received was 'Reading Between the Lines'. This feature helps students to develop critical thinking skills and to use economic principles in interpreting daily news events and their coverage in the media.

We have updated all the news articles and have deliberately selected topics that appeal to students. Each 'Reading Between the Lines' spread contains three passes at a story. It begins with a facsimile of an actual (usually abbreviated) newspaper or magazine article. It then presents a digest of the article's essential points. Finally, it provides an economic analysis of the news story, based on the economic models presented in that chapter.

Our Advancing Knowledge

The feature essays entitled 'Our Advancing Knowledge' have been revised to help students trace the evolution of path-breaking economic ideas and recognize the universality of their application, not only to the past but also to the present. For example, Adam Smith's powerful ideas about the division of labour apply to the creation of the computer chip with even more force than to the pin factory of the eighteenth century. And Dionysius Lardner's 1850s application of demand and supply theory to railway pricing applies with equal force to airline pricing today. A new visual design brings excitement and a new vitality to these essays, much in the way that the ideas they cover brought excitement and a new vitality to economics.

Mathematical Boxes

Mathematical Boxes are a new feature in this edition. Their purpose is to enable students who enjoy a rigorous mathematical approach to learning to use basic mathematical tools to explore fundamental relationships and principles in economics. The boxes do not assume a great deal of mathematical sophistication. But they do not *teach* mathematics. They *use* mathematics to deepen the student's understanding of economics. Students who do not find the mathematical approach illuminating should ignore these boxes. They contain no *economic* ideas that are not explained in non-mathematical language in the text and figures.

Learning Aids

We have refined our careful pedagogical plan to ensure that this book complements and reinforces formal teaching. Each chapter contains the following pedagogical elements:

Objectives   A list of objectives is given at the beginning of each chapter to enable students to set their goals before embarking on the chapter.

Chapter openers   Puzzles, paradoxes or metaphors are presented to frame the important questions which are unravelled as the chapter progresses.

Highlighted in-text reviews   Succinct summaries are interspersed through the chapter for review at the end of the main sections.

Key terms   Highlighted within the text, these concepts form the first part of a three-tiered review of economic vocabulary. These terms are repeated with page references at the end of the chapter and they are compiled in the end-of-book glossary.

Key figures and tables   These are identified with a 'key' logo ◆ and are listed at the end of each chapter.

End-of-chapter study material   Summaries organized around major headings; a list of key terms with page references; a list of key figures and tables with page references; review questions; and problems.

The Teaching and Learning Package

Our fully integrated text and supplements package provides students and instructors with a seamless learning and teaching experience. The authors of these components are outstanding educators and scholars who have used their own human capital (and that of their students!) to the task of improving the quality and value of the ancillaries for the second edition.

Study Guide   This was prepared by Brian Atkinson of the University of Central Lancashire. It has been carefully coordinated with the main textbook. Each chapter of the Study Guide contains: Chapter in Perspective (a brief summary of key definitions, concepts and material in the textbook chapter), Helpful Hints (to help students avoid common mistakes and to help them understand the most important concepts, graphs, equations, and techniques for problem solving); an explanation of Key Figures and Tables; and a Self-Test (to allow students to practise exam-style questions). Each Self-Test has a Concept Review, some True/False questions, some Multiple-Choice questions (mainly five choices per question), some Short-answer Questions, some Problems (graphical, numerical, analytical and policy-oriented) and some Data Questions. Each chapter also contains Answers to Self-Test.

Instructor's Manual   This was prepared by Brian Atkinson of the University of Central Lancashire. Each chapter of the Instructor's Manual includes an outline of the corresponding chapter in the textbook, teaching suggestions, a list of acetates in the full colour acetates and answers to all the review questions and problems in the textbook.

Full Colour Acetates   This contains full colour masters of 86 of the figures in the book. The figures selected include many key figures and many figures illustrating real-world data. The pack is available to qualified adopters of the textbook by contacting Addison-Wesley.

Updates in Economics   This is a yearly supplement edited by Brian Atkinson of the University of Central Lancashire. It contains topical articles linking important news items with the theory in the textbook. It is copyright free to allow instructors to copy and circulate the articles to students for private study or seminar use. It is available to qualified adopters of the textbook by contacting Addison-Wesley.

Test Bank   Thoroughly revised test items were prepared by Harvey B. King of the University of Regina. The Test Bank includes over 4,600 multiple-choice questions, over one-third of which are new to this edition. All questions have been reviewed carefully for accuracy. All Multiple-Choice questions in the Study Guide are identified by the symbol (SG).

Computerized Test Bank   Testing software with graphics capability is available to qualified adopters for IBM-PC and compatible PCs.

Economics in Action Software   New to this edition is a truly interactive tutorial software available for IBM compatible computers, adapted for this text by Robin Bade. The software includes modules on core concepts such as graphing, production possibilities and opportunity cost, demand and supply, elasticity, utility and demand, product curves and cost curves, perfect competition, monopoly, macroeconomic performance, aggregate demand and aggregate supply, expenditure multipliers, money and banking and international trade.

Four interactive modes take full advantage of the computer's capability to facilitate critical thinking skills. First, a tutorial mode walks students through the central concepts. Second, a quiz mode enables guided self-testing. Third, a free mode enables students and professors to interact with economic models by changing parameters and observing the effects on the graphs. Fourth, an evaluation mode allows students to construct and complete a multiple-choice test and keep a (read-only) record of their score.

In addition to its emphasis on interaction, the software is also closely integrated with the text. The art style is the same, the terminology is consistent, and supporting material in the text is cross-referenced in the software. The software has a user's manual and has been tested and reviewed for accuracy.

WinEcon This edition of Parkin and King has been indexed into the WinEcon tutorial software.

Acknowledgements

One of the great pleasures of writing an introductory text is the opportunity it affords to learn from so many generous friends and colleagues. Although the extent of our debts cannot be fully acknowledged here, it is nevertheless a joy to record our gratitude to the many people who have helped, some without realizing just how helpful they were.

Michael Parkin, in the Preface to his second US edition of *Economics*, acknowledged the generous colleagues and friends from around the world whose advice and suggestions were invaluable. He paid particular tribute to Robin Bade who was almost a co-author of that edition and who is co-author of the first and second Canadian editions. Both the authors of the present edition wish to acknowledge Robin's assistance and record that, once again, she made extraordinary contributions to this book.

David King is also grateful to his colleagues at Stirling for discussing many points with him. He is particularly indebted to Dipak Ghosh for suggesting many of the economics cartoons from his extensive collection.

Both authors would also like to acknowledge the skilful help they have received from Richard Parkin who managed the data files and who created all of the figures. They are indebted, too, to Wyn Morgan of the University of Nottingham for adapting the 'Our Advancing Knowledge' features and for the interviews to Robert Ackrill, also of the University of Nottingham, who assumed responsibility for the 'Reading Between the Lines' features.

Both of us acknowledge the debt we owe to the several thousand students to whom we have been privileged to teach introductory economics, especially students on the Economics 20 course at the University of Western Ontario and students on the Economics 4111 course at the University of Stirling. The enthusiasm and care with which they have used the book have been an inspiration to us, and we have benefited greatly from their comments, criticisms and suggestions. We dedicate this edition to them.

Finally we thank the editorial and production team at Addison-Wesley (UK). Tim Pitts, our editor, helped us to shape and craft this edition, ably assisted by Davina Arkell; they were a constant source of good judgement and good humour. Stephen Bishop managed and directed the production team, the key member of which was Susan Keany. Susan's skills, warmth, vitality and energy helped to keep us on track and ensured that the book finally appeared on time. It has been a great pleasure to work with this outstanding team and our gratitude is unbounded.

The empirical test of this textbook's value will be made by its users. We would appreciate hearing from instructors and students about how we might improve the book in future editions.

Michael Parkin
Department of Economics
University of Western Ontario
London, Ontario N6A 5C2
Canada

David King
Department of Economics,
University of Stirling
Stirling FK15 9PT
Scotland

Core Chapters and Flexibility

T he following chapters cover the core material and can form the basis of a one-year course in micro and macro. Any chapter not listed below may be added as time permits.

Core Chapters

Introductory Core	1. What Is Economics? 3. Production, Special- ization and Exchange 4. Demand and Supply
Micro Core	5. Elasticity 7. Utility and Demand 9. Organizing Production 10. Output and Costs 11. Competition 12. Monopoly 14. Pricing and Allocating Factors of Production 19. Market Failure and Public Choices
Macro Core	21. Unemployment, Inflation, Cycles and Deficits 22. Measuring Output and Price Level 23. Aggregate Demand and Aggregate Supply 24. Expenditure Decisions and GDP 25. Expenditure Fluctuations and Fiscal Policy 26. Money, Banks and Interest Rates 27. Central Banking and Monetary Policy 32. Stabilizing the Economy
International Core	34. Trading with the World

Flexibility Chapters

AD–AS Flexibility	
We do *AD–AS* early. But some lecturers prefer to develop the Keynesian expenditure system and monetary theory *before* deriving the *AD* curve. We have written the macro chapters so that this alter-native sequence can be used. The sequence on the right presumes that *AD–AS* will be done *after* the core Keynesian theory.	24. Expenditure Decisions and GDP (omit 'Real GDP and the Price Level', pp. 690–692) 25. Expenditure Fluctuations and Fiscal Policy (omit 'Multipliers and the Price Level', pp. 710–712) 26. Money, Banks and Interest Rates 27. Central Banking and Monetary Policy (omit 'Money, Real GDP, and the Price Level', pp. 766–773) 23. Aggregate Demand and Aggregate Supply **NOTE: Return to the omitted parts of Chapters 24 and 25.**
AD–AS Optional Chapter	28. Fiscal and Monetary Influences on Aggregate Demand (omit 'Real GDP, the Price Level and Interest Rates', pp. 803–805)

Reviewers

Addison-Wesley Publishers would like to express appreciation for the invaluable advice and encouragement they have received from many educators in the United Kingdom and elsewhere in Europe for this edition. We are specially appreciative of the help given by Wyn Morgan, of the University of Nottingham, who was asked to undertake an exceptional burden and who was referred to by the authors and the production team as the 'super reviewer', Robert Ackrill, of the University of Nottingham, and we also wish particularly to thank the following people for their comments and suggestions:

Dr John Struthers, University of Paisley
Professor Gavin C. Reid, University of St Andrews
Professor P.C. Stubbs, University of Manchester
Dr Søren Iversen, HHS Sonderborg
Dr Henning Jorgensen, HHS Esbjerg
Professor Dr Bernhard Gahlen, Univeisataer Augsburg
Dr R.A. Somerville, University of Dublin
Mr Francois D'Anethan (MBA) Dean, United Business Institute, Brussels
Professor Mitsutu Suzuki, Växjö University

Dr M.J. McCrostie, University of Buckingham
Dr Hilary Ingham, UMIST
Professor G. Norman, University of Edinburgh
Mr John Heaman, London Guildhall University
Dr Philippe Kirsch (PhD) Professor, United Business Institute, Brussels
Mr Chris Hicks, London Guildhall University
Mr Ken Heather, University of Portsmouth
Dr J. Tomlinson, Brunel, The University of London
Dr N.F.B. Allington, Cardiff Business School
Mr Michael Wood, South Bank University
Mr Mike Ashcroft, School of Economics and Business Studies
Dr Simon Price, University of Essex
Mr Andreas Kyriacou, Thames Valley University
Mr Darron Otter, Leeds Business School
Professor Dennis Swann, University of Loughborough
Mr David R. Claridge, Stoke on Trent College
Mr Martin Emmett, Chichester College of Art and Science and Technology

Professor C. Heady, University of Bath
Dr R.J.S. Kimmerling, Aston University
Dr S. Hill, University of Wales
Mr Peter Andersson, Universitetet Linköping
Markopoulos-Rantos Athanassios, South Bank University (Student)

PART 1

INTRODUCTION

**Talking
with
Frances
Cairncross**

Frances Cairncross has been environment editor of *The Economist* since the post was created in 1989. Before that she held posts as principal economic columnist on *The Guardian* newspaper, and as editor of *The Economist's* UK section. She was educated at Oxford University and at Brown University, Rhode Island. In 1992, she was editor of the World Bank's *World Development Report*. She has written two books on the environment: *Costing the Earth: the challenge for governments, the opportunities for business* and *Green Ink* to be published in 1995.

What originally attracted you to the study of economics?

I studied history as an undergraduate and came to economics only when I went to the United States to do graduate work. They seemed to me the ideal pair of disciplines to combine: one encourages you to look for explanations in the past, and in the way cultures and institutions evolve, while the other gives you an analytic approach that is – or tries to be – profoundly rational. I remember being enormously excited by the fact that concepts such as diminishing marginal returns and comparative advantage could be used to explain people's everyday behaviour. The mixture of relevance and rationality sums up the appeal of economics to me.

Who were the greatest influences on your study of the subject?

It may sound trite, but the main influence has been my father.[1] He came to economics after growing up in the years of the Depression, and saw it as a way to discover what might make people better off and more secure. I have learnt a great deal from his instinctive liberalism, and his view of economics as a tool to create a better and fairer society.

1

What are the main challenges an economics journalist faces?

The most difficult thing is to explain complicated concepts clearly and entertainingly. Nobody is forced to read a newspaper; people will read to the end of an article only if they are interested in it and enjoying it. It is never possible to explain an idea clearly unless you first understand it. Journalists therefore have to be like teachers – but teachers who earn only what the class will pay at the end of the lesson.

How easy is it to reconcile objective, positive economics with economics journalism?

I don't know that I would recognise 'objective' economics if I saw it. Most people who think that they are being objective are putting their own points of view. Just as two good economists can have an honest disagreement on an economic issue, two good economic journalists can argue two different points of view without misusing their disciplines. Economies are such complex, multifaceted things that it is always possible to find an example somewhere to buttress almost any point of view. Take a basic issue: that of government intervention. I have always tended to argue that economies are more likely to prosper if governments leave them alone as far as possible. But almost any point made to attack intervention (drawing on the experience of postwar Britain, for instance) can be countered with a point from one of the economies of South-east Asia. Good journalism needs to explain such quandaries, but it also needs to suggest to the reader where the balance of the argument lies.

Good economics should surely try to do the same.

Are economists too interested in market variables to have something positive to say about environmental issues?

Economists have plenty to say about environmental issues. The main problem is one of quantification, but that is a problem that arises in many other areas where economists have views. It is difficult to put a price on a human life or on the harm pollution does to a river. But there are techniques that help to get around such problems. More important are the sort of questions economists ask, such as 'If you spend £xx million on cleaning up the environment, will the benefits really be greater than the bill?' They can remind people that each extra step towards getting rid of pollution is likely to cost a little more and deliver a little less. They can point out that regulations to prevent pollution have a cost, even if they are imposed on companies rather than individuals. They can talk about the effects of environmental regulation on international competitiveness: a fashionable (non-economic) view is that tighter environmental regulation will help countries to compete. All these are important points to raise if society is to make sensible decisions about environmental protection.

Can 'positive economics' deal with the ethical and moral issues surrounding environmental concerns?

Economics is often a way of justifying an existing set of ethical assumptions. Environmental economics is especially subject to this view because it poses some questions to which answers can

be given only in ethical terms. They include: How should you put a value on benefits that arise far into the future? How should you weigh the interests of future generations compared with those of the present generation? How should you treat a decision whose consequences may be irreversible? It is extremely difficult for economists to use the conventional tools of the trade to decide how much society should spend today to avert climate change. The benefits of taking action now will exceed the costs only after a century or so. Some economists argue that we have a duty to posterity to err on the side of preventing climate change. Others, more rationally in my view, argue that the best thing we can do for posterity is to take decisions that will leave future generations better off – in a broad sense – and therefore better able to afford to tackle climate change, if it happens, in the way that seems appropriate at the time. I also believe that it would be better to spend money on preventing habitat loss and other kinds of environmental damage that are happening today than to spend it with uncertain results in the future.

Can markets really provide a mechanism that will help to protect the environment?

Markets can be the environment's enemy or its friend. If property rights are weak, then resources that are owned in common may be damaged by the unfettered operation of the market, as Joan Robinson implied in her famous question: 'Why is there litter in the public park but no litter in my back yard?' Remember that common resources include the earth's atmosphere and the ocean; rain forests and much natural habitat are often owned by the state, which may not protect them as well as a private owner would do.

Markets can be made to work for the environment if governments harness them properly. For example, taxing the use of energy is a much better way to reduce its use than imposing regulations on the energy efficiency of cars (as the United States does). Even if regulations lead to the production of more energy-efficient cars, people may simply drive more miles. And the efficiency of the existing car fleet will be unaltered. Manufacturers have no incentive to make a Fiat Panda if a Ford Escort meets the regulations. If taxes are high enough, people can make bigger savings by driving smaller and smaller cars.

Is more free trade bad for the environment?

Environmentalists worry that trade liberalization will make it harder for individual countries to set their own environmental standards. They are right in several respects. First, the rules of world trade discourage countries from setting rules on how imported products are produced. Countries cannot ban imports of tuna from countries which fish with driftnets and catch lots of dolphins in the process; they cannot insist that all tropical timber should be labelled to show whether or not it comes from a sustainably managed forest. The argument is that tuna looks and tastes the same, whether it has been caught with a rod or a driftnet, and so such a rule is unenforceable.

Second, countries with high environmental standards cannot impose a retaliatory tax on products produced in other countries with lower standards. Environmentalists in 'green' countries worry that the high cost of environmental standards will therefore encourage companies and jobs to move abroad, to dirtier places. In fact there is little evidence that such a thing has happened much yet; companies care more about labour costs and being near a market.

Environmentalists also fear that trade encourages economic growth and that growth is bad for the environment; they fret about all those extra lorries carrying goods back and forth across frontiers; and they dislike the fact that the rules of world trade discourage the use of trade sanctions to back up international environmental agreements. On the other hand, precisely because trade makes countries richer, it may encourage them to introduce better environmental policies. The really polluted countries are not the rich ones (like Germany or Denmark) but the poorish ones (like southern China or Thailand). As countries grow richer, they spend more on cleaning up pollution. Moreover, freer trade encourages the more efficient use of natural resources. If farm subsidies were scrapped (as free traders would like), less land in the rich countries would be used for intensive agriculture. Instead, more food would be grown in parts of the world which are appropriate for extensive farming, and where less fertilizer and pesticide would be needed.

Does protection of the environment imply fewer jobs and slower growth? As George Bush said, is it 'jobs not owls'?

Environmental protection does not necessarily cost jobs, indeed, it may create jobs: one of the fastest growing areas of employment in parts of the United States and eastern Germany is the clean-up of contaminated land. And nature conservation is a fast-growing employer in parts of rural Britain. But some of those jobs are, of course, paid for by the state, and money spent cleaning up contaminated land may come from companies which would otherwise use it in more conventional sorts of investment.

A more important question is whether environmental protection reduces economic growth. Often it will: if forests cannot be chopped down because they are full of spotted owls, GNP figures will not capture the value of protected trees but they will measure the loss of revenue to the logging companies. Pollution often occurs because polluters fail to pay the full costs of their dirty activities. These may be borne by the rest of society (if a river, say, is contaminated with factory waste) or by foreigners (if fumes from a chimney blow across borders) or left for posterity (if untreated chemical waste is left lying about). If polluters are made to carry more of these costs, economic growth will appear to suffer. As so often, GNP is an inadequate measure of welfare.

What advice do you have for anyone thinking of starting a career in economics journalism?

Read the newspapers. Learn to write well. Be a journalist at university. Remember that radio and television news will need good economists just as much as the newspapers.

[1] Sir Alex Cairncross

CHAPTER 1

WHAT IS ECONOMICS?

After studying this chapter you will be able to:

- ◆ State the kinds of questions that economics tries to answer

- ◆ Explain why all economic questions and economic activity arise from scarcity

- ◆ Explain why scarcity forces people to make choices

- ◆ Define opportunity cost

- ◆ Describe the function and the working parts of an economy

- ◆ Distinguish between positive and normative statements

- ◆ Explain what is meant by an economic theory and how economic theories are developed by building and testing economic models

IF YOU WANTED TO WATCH A FILM IN YOUR HOME IN 1975, YOU HAD TO HIRE A projector and screen – as well as the film itself. The cost of such entertainment was as high as that incurred by a cinema showing the same film to several hundred people. Only the rich chose to watch films in the comfort of their own homes. ◆ ◆ In 1976, the video cassette recorder (VCR) became available to consumers. Its typical price tag was £1,000, (£4,000 in today's pounds). Even at such a high price, the VCR slashed the cost of home film watching. Since that time, the price of VCRs has steadily fallen, so that today you can buy a reliable machine for £300. A video can be rented for £1 a day and can be bought for less than £15. In just a few years, watching a film at home has changed from a luxury available to the richest few to an event enjoyed by millions. ◆ ◆ Advances in technology

Choice and Change

affect the way we consume. We now watch far more films at home than we did a decade ago because new technologies have lowered the cost. ◆ ◆ We hear a great deal these days about lasers. Their most dramatic use is in weapons systems such as those used in 'Desert Storm' in 1991. But lasers affect us every day: they scan prices at the supermarket checkout; they create holograms on credit cards, making them harder to forge; neurosurgeons and eye surgeons use them in our hospitals.

◆ ◆ ◆ ◆ These examples show how new technologies affect both what we consume and the way that we produce goods and services.

Ever changing technology raises our first big economic question:

How do people choose what to consume and how to produce, and how are these choices affected by the discovery of new technologies?

Wages and Earnings

On a summer's afternoon a student spends three hours picking strawberries, and for this backbending work is paid £8. On the same day, Conchita Martinez spends little over an hour winning the women's singles championship at Wimbledon and wins £310,000.

One evening a music teacher gives instruction to a young pianist who never does any practice. For this unrewarding work the teacher is paid £10 an hour. In that same evening a professional singer has an enjoyable time singing in an opera to a full and appreciative opera house. For this immensely satisfying evening the singer is paid £5,000.

In the headquarters of many large companies, the chief executives work no harder, and in some cases less hard, than the people immediately below them. But the chief executives receive far higher salaries.

Situations like these raise our second big economic question:

What determines people's incomes and why do some people receive much larger rewards than others whose efforts appear to be similar?

Governments, the Environment and Economic Systems

Taking the central government along with local authorities, there are many governments in the United Kingdom. The European Union also has a parliament and forms another level of government. These authorities touch many aspects of life. The European Union operates policies for industry, including the notorious Common Agricultural Policy (CAP). The central government maintains the armed forces, the main roads and the National Health Service. Local governments provide most schools, the police, minor roads and fire services. Moreover, all levels of government make laws, and governments regulate matters as diverse as fishing policy, mergers between large firms and pollution levels.

The scale of government activity has increased dramatically over the years in most countries. A century ago the central government in the United Kingdom employed about 50,000 civil servants but in recent years it has employed over 10 times as many. Government activity costs money and, today, taxes amount to about 41 per cent of every pound earned in the United Kingdom.

Also, over the years, we have become more aware of our fragile environment. Chlorofluorocarbons (CFCs), used in a wide variety of products from coolants in refrigerators and air conditioners to plastic phones and cleaning solvents for computer circuits, are believed to damage the atmosphere's protective ozone layer. Burning fossil fuels – coal and oil – adds carbon dioxide and other gases to the atmosphere, which prevents infra-red radiation from escaping, resulting in what has been called the 'greenhouse effect'.

We have been hearing a lot recently about alternative economic systems and the proper role of government in economic life. The former Soviet Union and the countries of Eastern Europe have been shaking off decades of central economic planning and public ownership of their farms and factories. Bit by bit, they are moving towards the type of economic system and organization that is familiar to us in Western Europe – an economic system in which the government does not plan all the details of what is produced and does not own the nation's farms and factories. Instead, each individual farm and business decides what to produce.

These facts about government, the environment, and the dramatic changes taking place in Eastern Europe raise the third big economic question:

What is the most effective role for government in economic life, and can government help us protect our environment and do as good a job as private enterprise at producing goods and services?

Unemployment

During the worst years of the Great Depression, from 1929 to 1933, unemployment afflicted almost one-fifth of the labour force in the industrial world. For months on end, and in some cases years on end, many families had no income other than meagre payments from the government or private charities. In the 1950s and 1960s, the unemployment rate stayed below 5 per cent in most countries. Some countries even enjoyed rates below 2 per cent. During the 1970s and early 1980s, unemployment steadily increased. In the United Kingdom the peak year was 1986 when nearly 12 per cent of the labour force was looking for work. Unemployment rates peaked at even higher levels in some other countries. For instance, they exceeded 17 per cent in Ireland in 1985–87 and they exceeded 21 per cent in Spain in 1985. Unemployment rates then fell for a few years and in the United Kingdom they dipped below 6 per cent; but they rose again after 1989 and peaked at 10.6 per cent in 1993 before starting to fall again.

Unemployment hurts different groups unequally. When the average unemployment rate in the United Kingdom is 10 per cent, the unemployment rate among young people 16 to 19 years old is close to 20 per cent. The unemployment rate has a large regional variation as well, being especially high in Northern Ireland and northern England. These facts raise our fourth big economic question:

What are the causes of unemployment and why are some groups more severely affected than others?

Inflation

Between August 1945 and July 1946, prices in Hungary rose by an average of 20,000 per cent per month. In the worst month, July 1946, they rose 419 quadrillion per cent (a quadrillion is the number 1 followed by 15 zeros).

In 1985, the cost of living in Bolivia rose by 11,750 per cent. This meant that in central La Paz, a McDonald's hamburger that cost 20 Bolivianos on 1 January cost 2,370 Bolivianos by the end of the year. Inflation in the United Kingdom has been much lower than that. In the peak year of 1975, the rise in prices was just 27 per cent, but if that rate had continued, prices would have doubled in a mere three years. By 1993 the rate was down to around 2.5 per cent but even at that rate prices would double in 35 years. These facts raise the fifth big economic question:

Why do prices change, and why does the price level increase rapidly in some countries while remaining very stable in others?

International Trade

In the 1950s, almost all the cars and lorries on the roads of the United Kingdom were made in the United Kingdom. By the 1990s, domestic car manufacturers had only a minority of the market. Cars are not exceptional. The same can be said of television sets, watches and motor bikes. Central government is very concerned about international trade. Together

with other EU countries it imposes taxes, called tariffs, on some imports, and it has established quotas, which restrict the quantities that may be imported, on some others. These facts raise our sixth big economic question:

What determines the pattern and the volume of trade between nations, and what are the effects of tariffs and quotas on international trade?

Wealth, Poverty and the Environment

At the mouth of the Canton River in south-east China is a small rocky peninsula and a group of islands with virtually no natural resources. But this bare land supports more than five million people who, though not excessively rich, live in rapidly growing abundance. They produce much of the world's fashion goods and electronic components. They are the people of Hong Kong.

On the eastern edge of Africa bordering the Red Sea, a tract of land a thousand times larger supports a population of 34 million people – only seven times that of Hong Kong. The region suffers such abject poverty that in 1985 rock singers from Europe and North America organized one of the most spectacular worldwide fund-raising efforts ever seen – Live Aid – to help them. These are the desperate and dying people of Ethiopia.

Hong Kong and Ethiopia, two extremes in income and wealth, are not isolated examples. The poorest two-thirds of the world's population consumes less than one-fifth of all the goods and services produced. A middle-income group accounts for almost one-fifth of the world's population and consumes almost one-fifth of the world's output. A final one-fifth of the world's population – living in high-income countries such as North America, Western Europe, Japan, Australia and New Zealand – consumes almost two-thirds of the world's output.

These facts raise the seventh big economic question:

What causes differences in living standards among nations, making the people in some countries rich and in others poor; and will increases in living standards necessarily damage the environment and cause us to run out of resources?

These seven big questions provide an overview of economics. They are *big* questions for two reasons. First, they have an enormous influence on the quality of human life. Second, they are hard to answer. They generate passionate argument and debate, and almost everyone has an opinion about them. One of the hardest things for students of economics, whether beginners or seasoned practitioners, is to stand clear of the passion and emotion and to approach their work with the objectivity and rigour of a scientist.

Later in this chapter, we'll explain how economists try to find answers to economic questions. But before doing that, let's go back to the big questions. What do these questions have in common? What makes them *economic* questions? What distinguishes them from non-economic questions?

Scarcity

All economic questions arise from a single and inescapable fact: you can't always get what you want. We live in a world of scarcity. An economist defines **scarcity** to mean that the amount of goods and services that people would like to consume far exceeds the amount that can be produced.

One way of observing scarcity is to notice that none of us can afford all the things we would like to have. This is obvious in the case of homeless people sleeping in cardboard boxes on London's streets. But it also applies to a student who finds, shortly before Christmas, that she does not have enough money to buy Christmas presents for her parents if she buys a ticket for a disco; and it applies to people on average incomes who would like to have the sort of cars, houses, holidays and lifestyle enjoyed by the rich. It even applies to the mega-rich who may seem to have all the comforts money can provide, for they would like to have more of some items, such as holidays and works of art, than they can afford. Shortages of purchasing power even apply to the government, which has a far larger budget than any individual but can never spend as much on items such as the National Health Service or better roads as voters would like. Even parrots face scarcity – there just aren't enough crackers to go around.

Wants go even further than consuming goods and services. People want long and healthy lives, peace and security, and an awareness and understanding of themselves and their environment. Yet not even the wisest and most knowledgeable scientists or philosophers know as much as they would wish.

We can perhaps just imagine a world that satisfies people's material wants, though people always seem capable of wanting more. But we cannot imagine a

'Not only do I want a cracker–we all want a cracker!'
Drawing by Modell; © 1985 The New Yorker Magazine, Inc.

world in which people live for as long as they want in perfect health and security. Nor can we imagine people having all the time and energy to enjoy all the sports, travel, holidays and art that they would like.

Certainly, the world has huge resources. There are natural resources, such as minerals and fertile soil; there are human resources in the form of time, muscle-power and brain-power; and there are capital resources such as all the industrial plant and factories, all the roads and buildings, and all the vehicles and machinery that have been built by past human efforts. All these resources amount to an enormous heritage, but they are limited, and the amount they can produce is limited. In contrast, our wants are unlimited and will always outstrip the extent to which our time and resources are available to satisfy them.

Economic Activity

The confrontation of unlimited wants with limited resources results in economic activity. *Economic activity* is what people do to cope with scarcity. **Economics** is the study of how people use their limited resources to try to satisfy unlimited wants. Defined in this way, economic activity and economics deal with a wide range of issues and problems. The seven big questions posed earlier are examples of the more important problems economists study. Let's see why those questions would not arise if there were no problem of scarcity. We have to imagine a world in which, miraculously, all commodities are like clean air used to be – instantly available in whatever quantities we wish with no effort required in their production. And we also have to imagine that somehow people can have as much time as they want!

In such a world there would be no need to devise better ways of producing more goods and services.

Studying how we spent our time and effort would not be interesting because we would simply do what we enjoyed without restriction. People would not need any earnings. Unemployment would not be an issue because no one would work – except for people who wanted to work simply for the pleasure that it gave them. Inflation – rising prices – would not be a problem because everything would be free. Questions about government intervention in economic life would not arise because there would be no need for government-provided goods and services and so no need for taxes. There would be no international trade since, with complete abundance, it would be pointless to transport things from one place to another. Finally, differences in wealth among nations would not arise because we would all have as much as we wanted. All countries would be infinitely wealthy.

You can see that this science-fiction world of complete abundance would have no economic problems. It is the universal fact of scarcity that produces economic problems.

Choice

Let us return to our own planet. Faced with scarcity, people must make choices. When we cannot have everything that we want, we have to choose between the available alternatives. Because scarcity forces us to choose, economics is sometimes called the science of choice – the science that explains the choices that people make and predicts how changes in their circumstances affect their choices.

To make a choice, we balance the benefits of having more of some things against the costs of having less of something else. Balancing benefits against costs and doing the best within the limits of what is possible is called **optimizing**. There is another word that has a similar meaning – *economizing*. **Economizing** is making the best possible use of the resources available. Once people have optimized, they cannot choose to have more of *everything*: if they want to get more of one particular thing, then they will have to end up with less of something else. Let's put this in another way: in making choices, we face costs. Whatever we choose to do, we could always have chosen to do something else instead.

Opportunity Cost

Economists use the term 'opportunity cost' to emphasize that making choices in the face of scarcity

implies a cost. The **opportunity cost** of any action is the best alternative forgone. If you cannot have everything that you want, then you have to choose between the alternatives. The best action that you choose not to do – the best alternative forgone – is the cost of what you choose to do. Let's look at a few aspects of opportunity cost.

Money Cost We often express opportunity cost in terms of money. But this is just a convenient unit of measure. The pounds you spend on a book are not available for spending on a meal in a restaurant which might have been what you would have most liked instead of the book. The opportunity cost of the book is not the pounds spent on it but the restaurant meal forgone.

Time Cost The opportunity cost of a product includes the value of the time spent obtaining it. If it takes you an hour to visit your hairdresser, the value of that hour must be added to the amount you paid your hairdresser. We can convert time into a money cost by using a person's hourly wage rate. If you take an hour off work to visit your hairdresser, the opportunity cost of that visit (expressed in money) is the amount that you paid to your hairdresser plus the wages that you lost by not being at work. Again, it's important to keep reminding yourself that the opportunity cost is not the pounds involved but the best alternative item that you could have bought with those pounds.

External Cost We said that the opportunity cost of any action is the best alternative forgone. Not all of the opportunity costs that you incur are the result of your own choices. Sometimes others make choices that impose opportunity costs on you. And your own choices can impose opportunity costs on others. For example, when you take a ride on a bus, train, or car, part of the opportunity cost of the ride is the increased carbon dioxide in the atmosphere resulting from the burning of fuel used to power the bus, train, or car. Thus part of the opportunity cost of your ride is borne by other people, it arises because one of the things that is forgone by your action is a slightly less polluted atmosphere.

Best Alternative Forgone It's important, in measuring opportunity cost, to value only the *best* alternative forgone. To make this clear, consider the following example. You are supposed to attend a lecture at 9.00 on a Monday morning. There are two appealing alternatives to attending this lecture. One is to stay in bed for an hour and the other is to go jogging for an hour. You cannot, of course, stay in bed and go jogging for that one same hour. The opportunity cost of attending the lecture is not the loss of an hour in bed *and* the benefits derived from jogging for an hour. If these are the only two alternatives that you would contemplate, you must decide which one you would do if you did not go to the lecture. The opportunity cost of attending the lecture for a jogger is an hour of exercise; the opportunity cost of attending a lecture for a late sleeper is an hour in bed.

In a world of scarcity, everything we do and everything we consume has an opportunity cost. In choosing one activity, an individual decides that the cost of that activity – the activity forgone – is worth paying. Now scarcity not only implies cost, it also implies one other fundamental feature of human life – competition.

Competition and Cooperation

Competition   If wants exceed the amount that the world's resources can produce, then our wants must compete against each other for what is available. *Competition* is a contest for command over scarce resources. In the case of the student who wants to buy her parents Christmas presents and who also wants to go to a disco, the presents and the disco compete for her money. For the London Underground, new trains and refurbished stations compete for limited funds. For the government, new hospitals and roads compete with each other for limited tax revenue.

Scarcity also implies competition between people. If it is not possible to have everything that you want, then you must compete with others for what is available. In modern societies, competition is organized within a framework of almost universally accepted rules that have evolved over time. This evolution of rules is itself a direct response to the problem of scarcity. Not all societies, even modern societies, employ identical rules to govern competition. For example, the way that economic life is organized in the countries that belong to the European Union differs greatly from that in China. In Chapter 36, we examine these differences and compare alternative economic systems. For now,

we will restrict our attention to competition in the European Union.

A key rule of competition is that individuals are allowed to own anything that they have acquired through voluntary exchanges with other people. Individuals can compete with other people by offering more favourable terms – for example, by selling something for a lower price or by buying something for a higher price – but they are not allowed to compete with other people by simply taking things from them.

Cooperation   Perhaps you are thinking that scarcity does not make competition inevitable and that cooperation would solve economic problems more satisfactorily. *Cooperation* means working with others to achieve a common end. If we cooperated with each other instead of competing, wouldn't that ease our economic problems? Unfortunately, cooperation does not eliminate economic problems, because it does not eliminate economic scarcity. But cooperation is part of the best response to scarcity. We cooperate, for example, when we agree to rules of the game that limit competition to avoid violence and when we agree to participate in an economic system based on the rule of law and voluntary exchange.

Other examples of solving economic problems through cooperation abound. Marriage partners cooperate. Most forms of business also involve cooperation. In a small partnership, the partners cooperate with each other. In a large company, workers cooperate with each other on the production line, executives cooperate with each other to design, produce and market their products, and management and workers cooperate.

Common as it is, cooperative behaviour neither solves the economic problem nor eliminates competition. Almost all cooperative behaviour implies some prior competition to find the best individuals with whom to cooperate. Marriage provides a good example. Although marriage is a cooperative affair, unmarried people compete intensely to find a marriage partner. Similarly, professionals such as lawyers and doctors compete with each other for the best business partners. Likewise firms compete for the best workers while workers compete for the best employers.

Competition does not end when a partner has been found. Groups of people who cooperate together compete with other groups. For example, although a group of lawyers may have formed a partnership and may work together, they will be in competition with other lawyers.

R E V I E W

Scarcity is the problem that arises when unlimited wants confront the amount that can be produced by limited resources. Scarcity forces people to make choices. To make choices, people evaluate the costs of alternative actions. We call these opportunity costs, to emphasize that doing one thing removes the opportunity to do something else. Scarcity also implies that people must compete with each other. Economics studies the activities arising from scarcity. ◆

You now know the types of questions that economists try to answer and that all economic questions and economic activity arise from scarcity. In the following chapters, we are going to study economic activity and discover how a modern economy such as that of the United Kingdom works. But before we do that, we need to stand back and take an overview of the economy. What exactly do we mean by 'the economy'?

The Economy

The words 'the economy' are words we hear or read almost every day. For example, we may be told that 'the world economy is in the doldrums', or 'the European economy is making little progress out of recession', or 'the UK economy is beginning to recover', or 'the Scottish economy has held up relatively well during the recent recession'. But what is meant by 'the economy'? What is an economy? What happens in one? How does an economy work?

What is an Economy?

An **economy** comprises a set of scarce resources capable of producing a finite quantity of goods and services, a population with effectively unlimited

wants, and a social mechanism that allocates the resources among their competing possible uses. This social mechanism achieves three things that can be summarized as the answers to these three questions:

◆ What?
◆ How?
◆ For whom?

1. *What* goods and services will be produced and in *what* quantities? How many new homes will be built and how many eggs will be produced? Will people with rising incomes spend their extra money on high-performance cars or foreign holidays? How often will the streets be cleaned and how many home-helps will there be for the aged?

2. *How* will the various goods and services be produced? Will chickens be kept in battery cages or on free ranges? Will cars be made mostly by people or mostly by robots? Will streets be swept by people wielding brushes or will they be cleaned by special vehicles?

3. *For whom* will the various goods and services be produced? The amounts that different individuals consume depend greatly on the distribution of income and wealth. Those with high incomes and great wealth consume more goods and services than those with low incomes and little wealth. The mechanism of the UK economy decides that the tennis star can consume more than the strawberry picker and that the opera singer can consume more than the piano teacher.

The Economy's Working Parts

To understand how an economy works, we must identify its major working parts and see how they interact with each other. The main working parts of an economy fall into two categories:

◆ Decision makers
◆ Markets

Decision makers These are the economic actors. They make the economizing choices. We'll start with a very simple economy in which there are only two groups of decision makers – households and firms. Such an economy is depicted in Fig. 1.1. When we have finished looking at this simple economy we'll move on to an economy like the one we live in, where there is another group of decision makers – governments.

A *household* is any group of people living together

FIGURE 1.1

A Picture of an Economy with Households and Firms

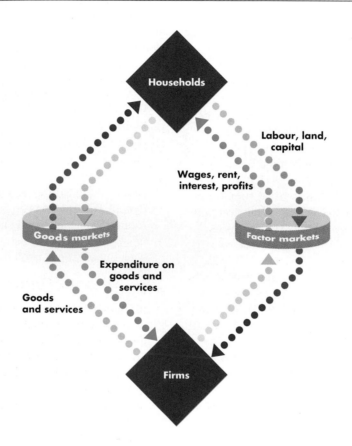

In this economy the only economic decision makers are households and firms. Households decide how much of their labour, land and capital to hire, sell or rent in exchange for wages, rent, interest and profits. They also decide how much of their income to spend on the various types of goods and services available. Firms decide how much labour, land and capital to hire, buy and rent and how much of the various types of goods and services to produce. These decisions by households and firms are coordinated in goods markets and factor markets. In these markets, prices constantly adjust to keep buying and selling plans consistent.

as a decision-making unit. For our purposes we regard all individuals in the economy as belonging to households – even if they live in caravans or cardboard boxes. Some households comprise a single person while others comprise families or groups of unrelated individuals, such as students sharing a flat.

A *firm* is an organization that produces and sells goods and services. All such producers are called firms, no matter how big they are or what they produce. Firms range from giants like the Post Office and Shell to farms and window cleaners. It is useful

to note that all firms are established and owned by people who live in households.

You can see these two groups of decision makers in Fig. 1.1. On the left-hand side of this figure you can see that households spend money buying products from firms. These products include goods such as bread and VCRs and services such as hairdressing and car repairs. The blue arrow shows the flow of money from households to firms while the red arrow shows the flow of goods and services from firms to households.

On the right-hand side of Fig. 1.1 you can see that

to produce their goods and services, firms need factors of production. **Factors of production** are the economy's productive resources, usually classified under three headings:

◆ Labour
◆ Land
◆ Capital

Labour is the brain-power and muscle-power of human beings; **land** is a term used to cover natural resources of all kinds; **capital** covers all the plant, buildings, vehicles and machinery that can be used in production. As it is households who own the firms, so it is ultimately the households who supply firms with the factors of production they need.

Households supply firms with all the labour they need by hiring out labour to them; in return, households are paid wages (and salaries). Households also ensure that firms are supplied with all the land and capital that they use. Households can do this in various ways. They may hire out land and buildings that they own, in which case they will be paid rent in return. Or they may buy land and capital and make it available for firms that they own, in which case they will be entitled to some of the firms' profits. Or they may lend money to firms so that they can buy some land and capital, in which case households will be paid interest on their loans. On the right-hand side of Fig. 1.1 you can see a blue arrow representing the flow of money spent on factors by firms, and a red arrow representing the flow of factors from households to firms.

Markets   In addition to two groups of decision makers and the flows between them, Fig. 1.1 shows two groups of markets. In ordinary speech, the word 'market' means a place where people buy and sell goods such as fish, meat, fruit and vegetables. In economics, 'market' has a more general meaning. A **market** is any arrangement that facilitates buying and selling. Examples of markets would include the hotel market in London, the UK milk market or the world insurance market. None of these markets has a single trading centre. Thus the world insurance market is not a place. It is the arena in which the many firms and households who buy insurance interact with the insurance companies and insurance brokers who sell it. In this market, decision makers do not always meet physically. They can make deals by telephone, fax and direct computer link.

The two groups of markets shown on Fig. 1.1 are:

◆ Goods markets
◆ Factor markets

Goods markets are those in which goods and services are bought and sold. Usually products are bought and sold, as with bread or VCRs, but sometimes they are hired or let, as with hired cars and rented student accommodation. **Factor markets** are those in which factors of production change hands. Factors may be bought, hired or rented. For instance, a garden centre may rent the land it uses, own the buildings it erects on the land and hire the labour that works there.

There are in fact other types of market which are omitted in our simple figure. These include markets in second-hand goods, for example homes bought and sold between households, and markets in raw materials and other items traded between firms, for instance iron ore.

Households' and Firms' Decisions

Households and firms make decisions that result in the transactions in the goods markets and factor markets shown in Fig. 1.1. Households decide how much of their labour, land and capital to hire, sell or rent on factor markets. They receive incomes in the form of wages, interest, rent and profits from these factors of production. Households also decide how to spend their incomes on goods and services produced by firms.

Firms decide the quantities of factors of production they will use, how to use them to produce goods and services, what goods and services to produce, and in what quantities. They sell their output in product markets.

Governments

Now let's turn to Fig. 1.2 which shows an economy like the United Kingdom's with a third group of decision makers – governments. A *government* is an organization that provides goods and services and redistributes income and wealth. Perhaps the most basic service provided by government is a framework of laws and a mechanism for their enforcement (courts and police forces). But governments also provide such services as national defence, health services and education.

In Fig. 1.2 you will see that all the flows between

FIGURE 1.2

A Picture of an Economy with Households, Firms and Governments

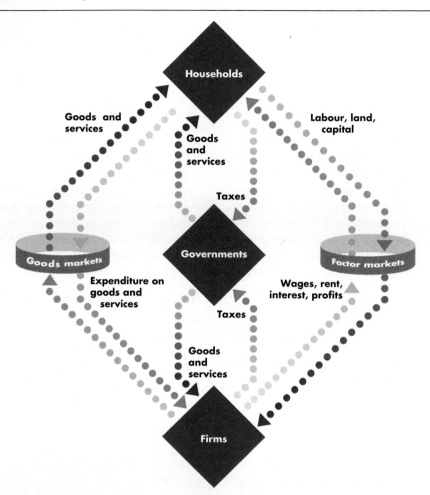

In this economy the economic decision makers include governments as well as households and firms. Households decide how much of their labour, land and capital to hire, sell or rent in exchange for wages, rent, interest and profits, and they decide how much of their income to spend on the various goods and services available. Firms decide how much labour, land and capital to hire, buy and rent, and how much of the various goods and services to produce. Governments decide which goods and services they will provide and the taxes that households and firms will pay. Many decisions are coordinated in the factor markets and goods markets, but some decisions are based on government command.

households and firms which we showed in Fig. 1.1 are shown again, but Fig. 1.2 has more flows that arise with the introduction of governments. Governments raise taxes from households and firms, and they also give money to households in the form of transfers – such as state pensions and student grants – and they give money to some firms in the form of subsidies. One blue arrow on Fig. 1.2 shows the net flow of money from households to governments – that is taxes minus transfers – and another blue arrow shows the net flow of money from firms to the government – that is taxes minus subsidies. The government uses the income it receives in this way to provide goods such as roads and services such as the police. On Fig. 1.2 you can see two red arrows showing the goods and services which it supplies to households and firms. These goods and services are supplied free of charge and so no payments are made for them in markets.

We have now added our third decision makers – governments. Governments decide what goods and services they will provide to households and firms, as well as the rates of taxes that create the funds to pay for them.

Coordination Mechanisms

Perhaps the thing that strikes you most about the choices made by households, firms and governments is that they must surely come into conflict with each other. For example, when it comes to goods and services that change hands in the goods markets, households choose the types and quantities of goods and services to buy while firms choose the types and quantities to sell. Moreover, the decisions made by firms and households are affected by government decisions. One reason for this is that these decisions regarding taxes, benefits and subsidies affect the amount of income that households and firms have available to spend. Another reason is that government decisions to provide more goods and services such as roads and the police may affect the quantity of cars and burglar alarms that households buy.

Conflict also seems likely in the factor markets. For example households choose how much work to do and what types of work to specialize in, but firms and governments choose the types and quantities of labour to employ in the production of various goods and services. In other words, households choose the types and quantities of labour to sell while firms and governments choose the types and quantities of labour to hire.

How is it possible for the millions of individual decisions taken by households, firms and governments to be consistent with each other? What makes households want to sell the same types and quantities of labour that firms want to buy? What happens if the number of households wanting to work as economists in universities exceeds the number that universities want to hire? How do firms know what to produce so that households will buy their output? What happens if firms want to sell more hamburgers than households want to buy?

A **coordination mechanism** can achieve a coordination of individual economic choices. There are two possible coordination mechanisms that can be used to decide how resources will be allocated:

◆ Market mechanism
◆ Command mechanism

Market mechanism   A **market mechanism** is a method of determining *what*, *how* and *for whom* goods and services are produced that involves using markets. Markets coordinate individual decisions through price adjustments. To see how, think about the market for hamburgers in your local area. Suppose that the quantity of hamburgers being offered for sale is less than the quantity that people would like to buy. Some people who want to buy hamburgers will not be able to do so. At the same time, suppliers of hamburgers find queues forming outside their premises. To make the choices of buyers and sellers compatible, buyers will have to scale down their purchases of hamburgers and more hamburgers will have to be offered for sale. An increase in the price of hamburgers will produce these results. A higher price will encourage producers to offer more hamburgers for sale. It will reduce the number of hamburgers that consumers wish to buy as some consumers will decide to buy hot dogs or other alternatives instead. So what is needed is a rise in price – and raising the price is exactly what producers are likely to do when they see the queues.

Now imagine the opposite situation where more hamburgers are available than people want to buy. Suppliers find that many of the hamburgers they produce are unsold and have to be thrown away. In this case a lower price is needed to make the decisions of suppliers and buyers compatible. A lower price will discourage the production and sale of hamburgers and it will also encourage their purchase and consumption. Now cutting the price is exactly what suppliers are likely to do when they find they are not selling all the hamburgers they produce.

The decisions of individual buyers and suppliers tend to change fairly frequently. But the decisions of the suppliers and buyers in any market can be kept compatible over time by adjustments in prices. Also, in many markets, producers are able to keep stocks so that it is not necessary for the amounts that buyers want to buy and suppliers want to sell to match every minute of the day – stocks can rise and fall a little as time passes. But suppliers are likely to raise prices if there is a sustained fall in stocks and vice versa.

We have now seen how the market mechanism can solve the question of *what* quantity of any item will be produced, such as how many hamburgers will be produced in your area. The market mechanism can also solve the question of *how* items will be produced. For example, hamburger producers can use gas, electric power or charcoal to cook their hamburgers. Which fuel they use depends in part on the flavour that they want to achieve. It also depends on the cost of the different fuels. Hamburger suppliers do not make hamburgers for the love of their trade but in order to make a living, and they will want to keep costs down in order to make as good a living as they can. So if one fuel becomes very expensive, as oil did in the 1970s, then less of it will be used and more of other fuels will be used in its place. Changes in methods of production are almost always made in response to changes in the costs of the different methods.

Finally, the market mechanism can help solve the question of *for whom* items are produced. A key factor which helps some people to secure a higher income than others is if they have a higher wage. Wages are prices for different types of labour and these prices are fixed in labour markets. Various factors explain why the wages in some labour markets are higher than those in others. One factor which helps some workers to secure high rates of pay is if they have a skill that is scarce: tennis stars are highly paid because people like to see tennis played at the highest level and few people have the skill needed. Of course, people also like freshly picked strawberries, but no rare skill is needed for strawberry picking so it tends to be poorly paid. Another factor that explains different earnings is the pleasantness or unpleasantness of different jobs requiring the same skill. Employers have to pay higher wages to persuade people to do dirty, dangerous or uncomfortable jobs.

Command mechanism   The market mechanism is one of two alternative coordination mechanisms: the other is a command mechanism. A **command mechanism** is a method of determining *what*, *how* and *for whom* goods and services are produced that is based on the instructions of a ruling body.

Types of Economy

An economy that relies on the command mechanism is called a **command economy**. Examples of command economies in the modern world are those of China, North Korea and Vietnam. There were important command economies in the former Soviet Union and Eastern Europe before these countries began

reform programmes late in the 1980s. In command economies, a central planning bureau makes decisions about *what* will be produced, *how* it will be produced and *for whom* it will be produced. We will study command economies and compare them with other types of economies at the end of our study of economics, in Chapter 36.

In contrast to a command economy, an economy which relies exclusively on markets to coordinate individual decisions about *what*, *how* and *for whom* goods and services are produced is called a **market economy**.

An economy which uses both market and command mechanisms to coordinate economic activity is called a **mixed economy**. The UK economy, like most other economies, relies extensively on the market mechan-ism for coordinating the plans of individual households and firms. There is, however, an element of the command mechanism in the UK economy. For instance, decisions over the level and type of defence are taken by the central government, while decisions over the level and type of rubbish disposal are taken by local governments. These decisions are not taken in markets.

Governments can also affect what does happen in markets. They act as buyers in some markets – for example the EU has built up its famous beef and butter mountains and its wine lakes by buying agricultural products. They act as suppliers in others – for example local authorities supply almost all school places. They affect some markets with taxes – for example the markets for alcoholic drinks – and they affect other markets with subsidies. They also make laws and regulations which affect decisions about what is produced. Note that laws can affect factor markets as well as goods markets – for example with rules over working conditions and equal pay for men and women doing the same jobs. Governments also affect decisions about for whom products are made by taxing the rich and giving benefits to the poor, thereby redistributing purchasing power.

The Global Economy

If any country decided to sever all links between its economy and other economies, that economy would be a **closed economy**. In practice, no country has a closed economy, though some countries have come close to this, as happened in Albania between World War II and 1991. The only truly closed economy is the global economy of the entire world. The UK economy is an open economy. An **open economy** is one that has economic links with other economies.

The UK economy is just one small part of the global economy. In 1993, the UK's 55 million people produced goods and services valued at over £627 billion. But in the global economy during 1993, some 5 billion people produced goods and services valued at more than £13 trillion. And today, an increasing proportion of each country's production is exchanged for the production of other countries. The world is evolving into a closely integrated economic machine that links the economies of the individual nations.

The economic links between the UK economy and the rest of the world are illustrated in Fig. 1.3. Firms in the UK economy sell some of the goods and ser-

vices they produce in world goods markets. Also, firms, households and governments in the United Kingdom buy goods and services from firms in other countries. These purchases are the UK's imports. These export and import transactions take place in the world goods markets which are illustrated in the figure.

The total values of exports and imports are not necessarily equal to each other. When a country's exports exceed its imports, it has a surplus. When its imports exceed its exports, it has a deficit. A country with a surplus lends to the rest of the world and a country with a deficit borrows from the rest of the world. These international lending and borrowing transactions take place on the world financial markets and are also illustrated in Fig. 1.3.

The United Kingdom has had a large deficit in recent years. As a consequence, it has borrowed from the rest of the world. Other countries, notably Germany and Japan, have had surpluses and these countries use their surpluses to lend to the rest of the world.

During the 1980s, the global economy became a highly integrated mechanism for allocating scarce resources and deciding *what* will be produced, *how* it will be produced and *for whom* it will be produced. The global economy is also a mechanism deciding *where* the various goods and services will be produced and consumed.

FIGURE 1.3

International Linkages

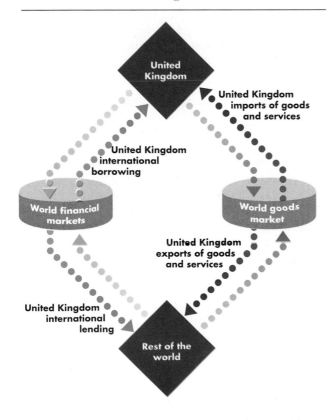

The UK economy buys and sells goods and services on world goods markets. What it buys are UK imports, and what it sells are UK exports. The UK economy also borrows from and lends to the rest of the world. These transactions take place on the world financial markets.

REVIEW

An economy is a mechanism that determines what is produced, how it is produced and for whom it is produced. Choices are made by households, firms and governments. Their choices are coordinated through markets – for both goods and services and factors of production – and through command mechanisms. The UK economy relies mainly on markets but it also relies to some extent on command mechanisms. Governments introduce command mechanisms in various ways, for instance by taxing, subsidizing, regulating and law-making. All countries have open economies, with more or less extensive links with other economies. The global economy became increasingly integrated during the 1980s. ◆

Economic Science

A science is an attempt to find a body of natural laws or principles that enables us to make predictions. This applies not only to economic science but also to the other social sciences, such as political science and psychology, and to the natural sciences, such as physics and biology. Economic science seeks to understand the laws or principles which determine the behaviour of households and firms – and, if possible, governments – when they take decisions in the economy. All sciences have two components:

1. Careful and systematic observation and measurement
2. Development of a body of theory to direct and interpret observations

All sciences are careful to distinguish between two types of statements:

◆ Statements about what *is* or *was* or *will be*
◆ Statements about what *ought* to be

What Is, Was, Will Be or Ought To Be

Statements about what *is*, *was* and *will be* are **positive statements**. Statements about what *ought* to be are **normative statements**. Let's illustrate the distinction between positive and normative statements with three examples.

'Our planet is warming because of an increased carbon dioxide build-up in the atmosphere' is a positive statement. 'We ought to use less carbon-based fuels such as coal and oil' is a normative statement. 'VAT (value added tax) was not cut during the recession' is a positive statement. 'VAT should have been cut during the recession' is a positive statement. 'Less generous social security will make people work harder' is a positive statement. 'Social security payments ought to be cut' is a normative statement.

Positive statements may be right or wrong. It is the job of scientists – whether natural, social, or economic – to discover true positive statements that are consistent with observations. Normative statements are matters of opinion. You agree or disagree with them. Science is silent on normative questions. It is not that such questions are unimportant. On the contrary, they are often the most important ques-

tions of all. Nor is it that scientists as people do not have opinions on such questions. It is simply that the activity of doing science cannot settle a normative matter, and the possession of scientific knowledge does not equip a person with superior morals or norms. A difference of opinion on a positive matter can ultimately be settled by careful observation and measurement. A difference of opinion on a normative matter cannot be settled in that way. We settle normative disagreements in the political and legal arenas, not in the scientific arena. The scientific community can, and often does, contribute to the normative debates of political life. But even though scientists have opinions about what ought to be, those opinions have no part in science itself.

Now let's see how economists attempt to discover and record positive statements that are consistent with their observations and that enable them to answer economic questions such as the seven big questions we reviewed earlier.

All sciences share two features:

◆ Observation and measurement
◆ The creation of theories

Observation and Measurement

Economic phenomena can be observed and measured in great detail. For example, we can record the amounts and locations of natural and human resources. We can describe who does what kind of work, for how many hours and how they are paid. We can record the things that people produce, consume and store, and their prices. We can describe in detail who borrows and who lends and at what interest rates. We can also record the taxes that governments raise and at what rates, and the services that governments provide and at what costs. This list is not exhaustive, but it gives a flavour of the array of things that economists can describe through careful observation and measurement of economic activity.

In today's world, computers have given us access to an enormous volume of economic description. Government agencies around the world, international and national statistical offices, private economic consultants, banks, investment advisers and research economists working in universities and colleges generate an astonishing amount of information about economic behaviour.

But economists do more than observe and measure economic activity, crucial as that is. Describing something is not the same as understanding it. You can describe your digital watch in great detail, but that does not mean you can explain what makes it work. Understanding what makes things work requires the discovery of natural laws or principles. That is the main task of economists – the discovery of laws or principles that govern economic behaviour.

Economic Theory

We can describe in great detail the ups and downs, or cycles, in unemployment, but can we explain *why* unemployment fluctuates? We can describe the fall in the price of computers and the dramatic increase in their use, but can we explain *why* their price has fallen and use has increased? Did the fall in the price lead more people to use computers, or did increased sales and production lower the costs of production and make it possible to lower the price? Or did something else cause both the fall in the price and the increase in use?

Questions like these can be answered only by developing a body of economic theory. An **economic theory** is a reliable generalization that enables us to understand and predict the economic choices that people make and the economic effects of their choices. How do economists develop theories? The answer to this question is that we develop economic theories by building and testing economic models. So let us explain what an economic model is.

Economic Model

Actually we have already presented one economic model. To explain what happens in an economy we built a model of an economy. We did not describe in full detail all the economic actions that take place in the economy. We concentrated our attention only on those features that seemed most important for understanding the economy and we ignored everything else. It may help you to appreciate what we mean by an economic model if you think about more familiar models. For example, we have all seen model trains, cars and aeroplanes, and we know that architects make models of buildings and that biologists make models of DNA (the double helix carrier of the genetic code).

The most important thing that all these models have in common is that they show less detail than their counterparts in reality. So, while they all resemble the real thing in *appearance*, they do not work like the real thing that they represent. Thus the architect's model of a new office block shows us what the building will look like and how it will fit in with the buildings around it – but it does not contain plumbing, telephone cables, lift shafts or central heating equipment. We can say that the models represent something that is real, but they lack some key features. They include only those features needed for the purpose at hand and they leave out the unessential or unnecessary. What a model includes and what it leaves out is not arbitrary: it results from a conscious and careful decision.

The models that we have just considered are all 'physical' models. We can see the real thing and we can see the model. Indeed, the purpose of those models is to enable us to 'visualize' the real thing. Some models, including economic models, are not physical. We cannot look at the real thing and look at the model and simply decide whether the model is a good or bad representation of the real thing. But the idea of a model as an abstraction from reality still applies to an economic model.

An economic model has two components:

◆ Assumptions
◆ Implications

Assumptions form the foundation on which a model is built. They indicate which things are relevant and need to be included in the model. *Implications* are the outcome of a model. The link between a model's assumptions and its implications is a process of logical deduction.

Let's illustrate these components of a model by building a simple model of a student's daily bus journey to college. The purpose of this model is to find the latest time the student can catch a bus to be on time for lectures. There are four relevant assumptions:

1. Lectures begin at 9.00 a.m.
2. Buses leave from the student's home bus stop at 10, 30 and 50 minutes past each hour.
3. The bus ride takes 30 minutes.
4. The walk from the bus to the college takes five minutes.

The implication of this model is that to be on time for lectures, the latest bus the student can catch is the 08.10 a.m.

The assumptions made when constructing a model depend on the model's purpose. The purpose of the model we have just described was to see the

Understanding the Sources of Economic Wealth

> **'It is not from the benevolence of the butcher, the brewer, or the baker, that we expect our dinner, but from their regard to their own interest.'**
>
> ADAM SMITH
> *The Wealth of Nations*

Adam Smith speculated that one person, working hard, using the hand tools available in the 1770s, might possibly make 20 pins a day. Yet by using those same hand tools but breaking the process into a number of individually small operations in which people specialize – by the division of labour – he observed that 10 people could make a staggering 48,000 pins a day. One draws out the wire, another straightens it, a third cuts it, a fourth points it, a fifth grinds it. Three specialists make the head and a fourth attaches it. Finally, the pin is polished and wrapped in paper.

In 1776, new technologies were being invented and applied to the manufacture of cotton and wool, iron, transportation and agriculture in what came to be called the 'Industrial Revolution'.

Adam Smith was keenly interested in these events. He wanted to understand the sources of economic wealth, and he brought his acute powers of observation and abstraction to bear on this question. His answer was:

◆ The division of labour
◆ Free domestic and international markets

Smith identified the division of labour as the source of 'the greatest improvement in the productive powers of labour'. The division of labour became even more productive when applied to creating new technologies. Scientists and engineers, trained in extremely narrow fields, became specialists at inventing. Their powerful skills speeded the advance of technology so that by the 1850s we could make machines that could make consumer goods and other machines by performing repetitive operations faster, more accurately, and for longer than people.

But, said Smith, the fruits of the division of labour are limited by the extent of the market. To make the market as large as possible, there must be no impediments to free trade both within a country and among countries. Smith argued that when each person makes the best possible economic choice based on self-interest, that choice leads as if by an 'invisible hand' to the best outcome for society as a whole.

Memory chips give your computer its instant-recall ability, logic chips provide its number-crunching power, and custom chips make your camera idiot-proof. The computer chip is an extraordinary example of the productivity of the division of labour. Designers, using computers (made from microchips), create the chip's intricate circuits. Machines print the design on paper and photograph it on glass plates called masks that work like stencils. Workers prepare silicon wafers on which the circuits are printed. Some slice the wafers, others polish them, others bake them, and yet others coat them with a light-sensitive chemical. Tech-

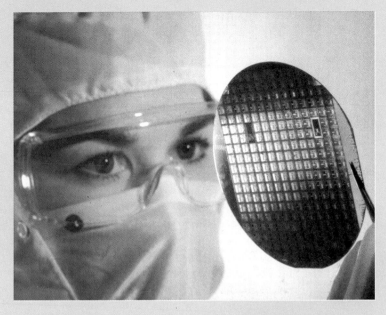

nicians put masks and wafers into a machine that shines light through the mask, imprinting a copy of the circuit on to the wafer. Chemicals eat the unexposed portion of the wafer. A further series of passes through gas-filled ovens deposits atoms that act as transistors. Aluminium is deposited on the wafer to connect the transistors. Finally, a diamond saw or laser separates the hundreds of chips on the wafer.

ADAM SMITH

Adam Smith and The Wealth of Nations

Adam Smith, born in 1723 in Kirkcaldy, a small fishing town near Edinburgh, Scotland, and only child of the town's customs officer (who died before his son was born), was a giant of a scholar who made extraordinary contributions in ethics and jurisprudence as well as economics.

His first academic appointment, at age 28, was as Professor of Logic at the University of Glasgow. He subsequently became tutor to a wealthy Scottish duke whom he accompanied on a two-year European grand tour, following which he received a pension of £300 a year – 10 times the average income at that time.

With the financial security of his pension, Smith devoted 10 years to writing the treatise that founded economic science, *An Inquiry into the Nature and Causes of The Wealth of Nations*, which was published to great acclaim in 1776.

Many had written on economic issues before Adam Smith, but it was he who made economics a science. His account of what was then known was so broad and authoritative that no subsequent writer on economics could advance his own ideas while ignoring the state of general knowledge.

latest time the student could catch a bus. The assumptions isolated the relevant factors and ignored irrelevant ones such as what the student likes to have for breakfast.

The purpose of an economic model is to understand how people make choices in the face of scarcity. So in building an economic model, we abstract from the detail of human life and focus only on behaviour that is relevant for coping with scarcity. Economists know that people fall in love and that they can experience great joy and great pain; but economists assume that in seeking to understand economic behaviour, they may build models that ignore many aspects of life. They focus on the fact that people have wants that exceed the amounts that their resources can produce and so, by their choices, have to make the best of things.

Assumptions of an Economic Model   Many economic models include four key assumptions:

1. *People have preferences.* Economists use the term **preferences** to denote people's likes and dislikes and the intensity of those likes and dislikes.

2. *At any one time people are endowed with a fixed amount of resources and a given technology that can use those resources to produce goods and services.* Economists use the term *endowment* to refer to the resources that people have and the term **technology** to describe the methods of using those endowments to produce goods and services.

3. *People economize.* They choose how to use their endowments and technologies to make themselves as well-off as possible. We use the term **rational choice** to describe the best possible choice from the point of view of the person making the choice *given the information available to that person at the time.* In an economic model, each choice is interpreted as a rational choice, no matter how foolish it may seem to an observer. With hindsight, when they have more information, people may feel that some of their own past choices were bad ones. But this does not mean their choices were irrational, because they were the best possible course of action from their point of view with the information available to them at the time.

4. *People's choices are coordinated.* One person's choice to buy something must be matched by another person's choice to sell that same thing.

One person's choice to work at a particular job must be matched by another person's choice to hire someone to do that job. The coordination of individual choices is made by either a market mechanism or a command mechanism or a mix of the two.

Implications of an Economic Model   There are many types of economic model that have been developed for different purposes, but all models seek to explain the equilibrium values of something which can vary. For example, the price and quantity of hamburgers sold in your area can vary, but economists might use an economic model to try to find the equilibrium values of price and quantity. An **equilibrium** value is the one which will emerge when everyone has economized – that is, when all individuals have made the best possible choices in the light of their own preferences and given present resource endowments, technologies and information – and when those choices have been coordinated and made compatible with the choices of everyone else.

The term *equilibrium* conjures up the picture of a balance of opposing forces. For example, a balance scale can be said to be in equilibrium if a kilogram of beans is placed on one side of the balance and a one kilogram weight is placed on the other side. The two weights exactly equal each other and so offset each other, leaving the balance arm horizontal. A soap bubble provides another excellent physical illustration of equilibrium. The delicate spherical film of soap is held in place by a balance of forces of the air inside the sphere and the air outside it.

This second physical analogy illustrates a further important feature of an equilibrium. An equilibrium is not necessarily static but may be dynamic – constantly changing. By squeezing or stretching the bubble, you can change its shape, but its shape is always determined by the balance of the forces acting upon it, including the forces that you exert upon it. Many economic equilibrium values are constantly changing. For example, the equilibrium price and quantity of hamburgers sold in your area may change if people move in and out of the area, or if new cafes are opened or simply if changes in the weather alter people's eating habits.

Notice that an economic equilibrium does not mean that everyone is happy and prosperous. In your area there may be some students whose parents are meant to contribute to their maintenance but do not do so. These students may well consume far fewer hamburgers than they would like to do. All we claim of an economic equilibrium is that given their preferences, endowments, the available technologies and the actions of everyone else, each person has made the best possible choice and sees no advantage in modifying his or her current action.

Microeconomic and Macroeconomic Models

Most economic models fall into two categories: microeconomic and macroeconomic.

Microeconomics is the branch of economics that studies the decisions of individual households and firms. Microeconomics also studies the way that individual markets work and the detailed way that government activities such as regulations and taxes affect individual markets. Much of microeconomics focuses on trying to understand what factors affect the prices and quantities traded in individual markets.

Macroeconomics is the branch of economics that studies the economy as a whole. It seeks to understand the picture as a whole rather than small parts of it. In particular, it studies the overall values of output as a whole, of unemployment and of inflation.

Of the seven big questions, those dealing with technological change, production and consumption, and wages and earnings are microeconomic. Those dealing with unemployment, inflation and differences in wealth among nations are macroeconomic.

Model, Theory and Reality

People who build models often get carried away and start talking as if their model *is* the real world – as if their model is reality! No matter how useful it is, there is no sense in which a model can be said to be reality. A model simply lists assumptions and their implications. When economists talk about people who have made themselves as well-off as possible, they are not talking about real people. They are talking about imaginary people in an economic model. Do not lose sight of this important but easily misunderstood fact.

Economic theory is the bridge between economic models and the real world. Economic theory is a catalogue of models that seem to work – that seem to enable us to understand and interpret the past and to predict some aspects of the future. Economic theory evolves from a process of building and testing economic models.

The process of using models to develop economic theories is illustrated in Fig. 1.4. We begin by building a model. This involves making some assumptions and then working out some implications. We then make some predictions about the world. At this stage we have a theory about the real world. The predictions can now be tested by comparing them with reality – with some observations we wish to

FIGURE 1.4

How Theories are Developed

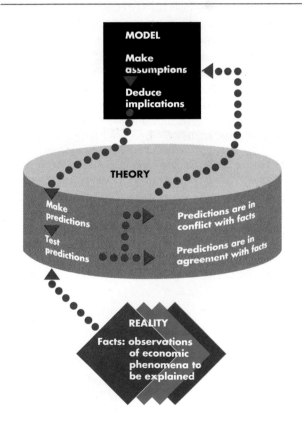

Economic theories are developed by building and testing economic models. An economic model makes a set of *assumptions* about what is important and what can be ignored and it tries to work out the *implications* of those assumptions. These implications are used to develop a theory about how the real world works and predictions about the real world are made. These *predictions* are tested by being checked against the facts. If the predictions are in conflict with the facts, then the theory is checked to see if it is making the most plausible predictions from the theory. If it is not, then we develop a better theory and test that. If it is, then we have to start again by making a new model which is based on revised assumptions. It is only when we start making predictions that are in agreement with the facts that we can believe we may have a useful theory.

explain. If the predictions are consistent with the facts we observe in the real world, we are inclined to think the theory is a good one – though it is possible that it is a bad theory which by fluke predicted well in our test! If the predictions are inconsistent with the real world, we have two choices. One is to discard the theory in favour of a superior alternative based on the same assumptions. The other is to return to the model-building stage, modify our assumptions and create a new model. Economics itself provides guidance on how we might discover a better model. It prompts us to look for some aspect of preferences, endowments, technology, or the coordination mechanism that has been overlooked.

One further point to note about testing models is that we can never hope to produce a model that will predict perfectly what will happen in the real world. This is because models are always simpler than the real world. So we do not necessarily reject a model because it predicts imperfectly. At the same time, there is always room for improving those models which seem to predict quite well.

Economics is a young science and is a long way from achieving its goal. Its birth can be dated fairly precisely in the eighteenth century with the publication of Adam Smith's *The Wealth of Nations* (see Our Advancing Knowledge, pp. 20–21). In the closing years of the twentieth century, economic science has managed to discover many useful generalizations. In some areas of the subject, however, we are still going around the circle – changing our assumptions, performing new logical deductions, making new predictions and getting wrong answers yet again. The gradual accumulation of correct answers gives most practitioners some faith that their methods will, eventually, provide usable answers to all the big economic questions.

◆ ◆ ◆ In the next chapter, we will study some of the tools that economists use to build economic models. Then, in Chapter 3, we will build an economic model and use that model to start to answer some of the big economic questions.

S U M M A R Y

Scarcity

All economic questions arise from the fundamental fact of scarcity. Scarcity means that our wants exceed the amount that our resources can produce. Human wants are effectively unlimited but the resources available to satisfy them are finite.

Economic activity is what people do to cope with scarcity. Scarcity forces people to make choices. Making the best choice possible from the options available is called optimizing. To optimize, a person must weigh up the costs and benefits of the alternatives. We say that the opportunity cost of the option that is selected is the best alternative that is forgone.

Scarcity forces people to compete with each other for the output of scarce resources. People may cooperate in certain areas, but all economic activity ultimately results in competition between individuals acting alone or in groups. (pp. 8–11)

The Economy

Any geographical area where production and consumption take place has an economy. The economy is a mechanism that allocates scarce resources among competing uses, determining *what*, *how* and *for whom* the various goods and services will be produced.

Every economy has two key components: decision makers and markets. Economic decision makers are households, firms and governments. Households decide how much of their factors of production to supply to firms and governments, and what goods and services to buy from firms. Firms decide what factors of production to hire and which goods and services to produce. Governments decide how much to raise in taxes, how much to give in transfers and subsidies, what goods and services to provide to households and firms, and what laws and regulations there should be.

There are two types of coordination mechanism: the market mechanism and the command mechanism. The UK economy relies primarily on the market mechanism in which prices adjust to keep buying plans and selling plans consistent. But the actions taken by governments create an element of a command mechanism and these actions do modify the allocation of scarce resources. Like most economies, the UK economy is therefore a mixed economy. (pp. 11–17)

Economic Science

Economic science, like the natural sciences and the other social sciences, attempts to find a body of natural laws or principles. Economic science seeks to understand what *is*, *was* and *will be* but cannot say what *ought* to be. Economists try to find economic principles by building models. The predictions of the models form the basis of economic theories.

The theories can be tested by comparing the predictions of the models with the facts of the real world. Economic models are abstract, logical constructions that contain two components: assumptions and implications.

Many economic models have four key assumptions:

1. People have preferences.
2. At any time people have a given endowment of resources and technology.
3. People economize.
4. People's choices are coordinated through market or command mechanisms.

The implications of an economic model are the equilibrium values of something which can vary, such as a price or a quantity. These equilibrium values are the ones which will arise when each individual is doing the best that is possible, given the individual's preferences, endowments, information and technology, and given the coordination mechanism. (pp.18–24)

KEY ELEMENTS

Key Terms

Key Figure

REVIEW QUESTIONS

1   Give your own examples to illustrate some of the seven big economic questions.

2   Why does scarcity force us to make choices?

3   What do we mean by 'rational choice'? Give examples of rational and irrational choices.

4   Why does scarcity force us to economize?

5   Why does optimization require us to calculate costs?

6   Why does scarcity imply competition?

7   Why can't we solve economic problems by cooperating with each other?

8   Name the main economic decision makers.

9   List the main economic decisions made by households, firms and governments.

10 What is the difference between a command mechanism and a market mechanism?

11 Distinguish between positive and normative statements by listing three examples of each type of statement.

12 What are the four key assumptions made by all economic models?

13 Explain the difference between a model and a theory.

PROBLEMS

1   You plan to travel round mainland Europe this summer. If you do you won't be able to take your usual job that pays £1,500 for the summer and you won't be able to live at home free. The cost of your trip will be £2,000. What is the opportunity cost of the trip?

2   On Valentine's Day Stephen and Trudy exchanged gifts: Stephen sent Trudy some red roses and Trudy bought Stephen a box of chocolates. They each spent £10. They also spent £30 on dinner and split the cost evenly. Did either Stephen or Trudy incur any opportunity costs? If so, what were they? Explain your answer.

3   Helen asks Vicky to be her bridesmaid at her wedding. Vicky accepts. Which of the following are part of her opportunity cost of being Helen's bridesmaid? Explain why they are or are not.

  a The £150 she spent on a new outfit for the occasion

  b The £50 she spent on a party for Helen's friends

  c The money she spent on a haircut a week before the wedding

  d The weekend visit she missed for her grandmother's 75th birthday which was on the same day as the wedding

  e The £10 she spent on lunch on the way to the wedding

4   The local shopping centre has free parking, but the shopping centre is always very busy and it usually takes 30 minutes to find an empty parking slot. Today when you found an empty slot, you just beat your friend Donald who also wanted it. Is parking really free at this shopping centre? If not, what did it cost you to park today? When you parked your car today did you impose any costs on Donald? Explain your answers.

5   Which of the following statements are positive and which are normative?

  a A cut in wages will reduce the number of people willing to work.

  b High interest rates make many young people delay buying their first home.

  c No family ought to be made to pay more than 25 per cent of its income in taxes.

  d The government should reduce its expenditure on roads and increase its expenditure on railways.

e The government ought to raise the level of student grants.

6 You have been employed by a company that makes and markets tapes, records and compact discs (CDs). Your employer is going to start exporting these products to a country with 100 million people. A survey has suggested that 40 per cent of the people in this country buy only popular music and 5 per cent buy only classical music. No one buys both types of music. The average income of the pop music fan is £10,000 a year and that of the classical fan is £20,000 a year. The survey also suggests that people with low incomes spend one quarter of 1 per cent of their income on tapes, records and CDs, while those with high incomes spend 2 per cent of theirs. You have been asked to predict how much is likely to be spent in this market on pop music and classical music in one year. Build a model to answer that question. In doing so:

a List your assumptions.

b Work out the implications of your assumptions.

c Highlight the potential sources of errors in your predictions.

CHAPTER 2

MAKING AND USING GRAPHS

After studying this chapter you will be able to:

◆ Make and interpret a scatter diagram, a time-series graph, and a cross-section graph

◆ Distinguish between linear and non-linear relationships and relationships that have a maximum and a minimum

◆ Define and calculate the slope of a line

◆ Graph relationships between more than two variables

THERE ARE THREE KINDS OF LIES, SAID BENJAMIN DISRAELI, A NINETEENTH century British prime minister: lies, damned lies and statistics. One of the most powerful ways of conveying statistics is in the form of a picture – a graph. And like statistics, graphs can lie. But the right graph does not lie. It reveals a relationship that would otherwise be obscure. ◆ ◆ Graphs are a modern invention. They first appeared in the late eighteenth century, long after the discovery of logarithms and calculus. But today, in the age of the personal computer and video display, graphs have become as important as words and numbers. ◆ ◆ How do economists use graphs? What types of graphs do economists use? What do economic graphs reveal and what can they hide? ◆ ◆ It is often said that in economics, everything depends on everything else. Variations in the quantity

Three Kinds of Lies

of ice cream bought are caused not only by variations in the temperature but also by variations in the price of cream and many other factors as well. How can we make graphs of relationships of several variables? How can we interpret such relationships?

◆ ◆ ◆ ◆ In this chapter, we look at the kinds of graphs that economists use. We are going to learn how to make them and read them. We are going to look at examples of useful graphs as well as misleading graphs. We are also going to study how we can calculate the strength of the effect of one variable on another. If you are familiar with graphs, you may want to skip (or skim) this chapter. Whether you study this chapter thoroughly or give it a quick pass, you can use it as a handy reference.

Graphing Data

Graphs represent a quantity as a distance. Figure 2.1 gives two examples. Part (a) shows temperature, measured in degrees Celsius, as the distance on a scale. Movements from left to right represent increases in temperature. Movements from right to left represent decreases in temperature. The point marked zero represents zero degrees Celsius. To the right of zero, the temperatures are positive. To the left of zero, the temperatures are negative (as indicated by the minus sign in front of the numbers).

Figure 2.1(b) provides another example. This time altitude, or height, is measured in thousands of metres above sea level. The point marked zero represents sea level. Points to the right of zero represent metres above sea level. Points to the left of zero (indicated by a minus sign) represent depths below sea level.

There are no rigid rules about the scale for a graph. The scale is determined by the range of the variable being graphed and the space available for the graph.

The two graphs in Fig. 2.1 show just a single variable. Marking a point on either of the two scales indicates a particular temperature or a particular height. Thus the point marked *a* represents 100°C, the boiling point of water. The point marked *b* represents 4,807 metres, the height of Mont Blanc, the highest mountain in Europe.

Graphing a single variable as we have done does not usually reveal much. Graphs become powerful when they show how two variables are related to each other.

Two-variable Graphs

To construct a two-variable graph, we set two scales perpendicular to each other. Let's continue to use the same two variables as those in Fig. 2.1. We will measure temperature in exactly the same way, but we will turn the height scale to a vertical position. Thus temperature is measured exactly as it was before but height is now represented by movements up and down a vertical scale.

The two scale lines in Fig. 2.2 are called *axes*. The vertical line is called the ***y-axis*** and the horizontal line is called the ***x-axis***. The letters *x* and *y* appear on the axes of Fig. 2.2. Each axis has a zero point

FIGURE 2.1

Graphing a Single Variable

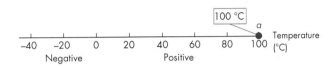

(a) Temperature

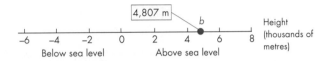

(b) Height

All graphs have a scale that measures a quantity as a distance. The two scales here measure temperature and height. Numbers to the right of zero are positive. Numbers to the left of zero are negative.

shared by the two axes. The zero point, common to both axes, is called the **origin**.

To represent something in a two-variable graph, we need two pieces of information. For example, Mont Blanc is 4,807 metres high and, on a particular day, the temperature at its peak is –20°C. We can represent this information in Fig. 2.2 by marking the height of the mountain on the *y*-axis at 4,807 metres and the temperature on the *x*-axis at –20°C. We can now identify the values of the two variables that appear on the axes by marking point *c*.

A point in a graph, such as point *c*, is identified by its coordinates. **Coordinates** are distances running from a point on a graph perpendicularly to an axis. The distance from *c* to the *x*-axis is the ***y-coordinate***, because its length is the same as the value marked off on the *y*-axis. Similarly, the distance from *c* to the vertical axis is the ***x-coordinate***, because its length is the same as the value marked off on the *x*-axis.

Now let's leave the top of Mont Blanc, at 4,807 metres and –20°C, and take a trip on a submarine. You are exploring the depths of the ocean, 2,000 metres below the sea at a sweltering 40°C. You are at point *d* in the figure. Your *y*-coordinate is –2,000 metres and your *x*-coordinate is 40°C.

FIGURE 2.2

Graphing Two Variables

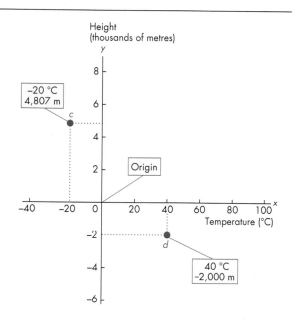

The relationship between two variables is graphed by drawing two axes perpendicular to each other. Height is measured here on the *y*-axis and temperature on the *x*-axis. Point *c* represents the top of Mont Blanc, 4,807 metres above sea level (measured on the *y*-axis), with a temperature of −20°C (measured on the *x*-axis). Point *d* represents the inside temperature in a submarine, 40°C, exploring the depths of the ocean, 2,000 metres below the sea.

Economists use graphs similar to this one in a variety of ways. Let's look at three examples:

◆ Scatter diagrams
◆ Time-series graphs
◆ Cross-section graphs

Scatter Diagrams

Economists use graphs to reveal whether a relationship exists between two economic variables. They also use graphs to describe such a relationship. The most important type of graph used for these purposes is the scatter diagram. A **scatter diagram** plots the value of one economic variable associated with the value of another. It measures one of the variables on the *x*-axis and the other variable on the *y*-axis.

The Relationship Between Consumption and Income

Figure 2.3 uses a scatter diagram to show the relationship between consumption and income. The *x*-axis measures income, and the *y*-axis measures consumption. Each point represents aggregate consumption and aggregate income in the United Kingdom in a given year between 1980 and 1992. The points for all 13 years are 'scattered' within the graph. Each point is labelled with its year. For example, in 1987, consumption was ₤187 billion and income was ₤250 billion.

This graph reveals that a relationship *does* exist between income and consumption. The pattern formed by the points in Fig. 2.3 tells us that when income increases, consumption also increases.

FIGURE 2.3

A Scatter Diagram: Consumers' Expenditure and Income

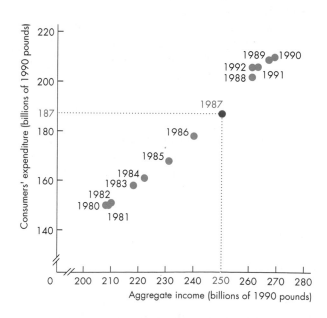

A scatter diagram shows the relationship between two variables. This scatter diagram shows the relationship between consumers' expenditure and aggregate income during the years 1980 to 1992. Each point shows the values of the two variables in a specific year. For example, in 1987 consumption was £187 billion and income was £250 billion. The pattern formed by the points shows that as income increases, so does consumption.

Breaks in the Axes   Notice that each axis in Fig. 2.3 has a break in it – illustrated by the small gaps. The breaks indicate that there are jumps from the origin, 0, to the first values recorded. The breaks are used because in the period covered by the graph consumption was never less than £150 billion and income was never less than £208 billion. With no breaks in the axes of this graph, there would be a lot of empty space, all the points would be crowded into the top right corner, and we would not be able to see whether a relationship existed between these two variables. By using axis breaks we are able to bring the relationship into view. In effect, we use a zoom lens to bring the relationship into the centre of the graph and magnify it so that it fills the graph.

The range of the variables plotted on the axes of a graph are an important feature of a graph, and it is a good idea to get into the habit of always looking closely at the axis values – and labels – before you start to interpret a graph.

Other Relationships   Figure 2.4 shows two other scatter diagrams. In part (a), the *x*-axis shows the percentage of households owning a video cassette recorder (VCR) and the *y*-axis shows its average price. Each point represents a year. Thus in 1985 the average price of a VCR was £300 and VCRs were owned by 20 per cent of all households. The pattern formed by the points in part (a) tells us that as the price of a VCR falls, a larger percentage of households own one.

In part (b), the *x*-axis measures UK unemployment, and the *y*-axis measures UK inflation. Again, each point represents a year. In 1987, unemployment was 10.2 per cent and inflation was 4.2 per cent. The pattern formed by the points in part (b) does not reveal a clear simple relationship between the two variables. But the graph does inform us, by its lack of a simple pattern, about the relationship between these two variables.

A scatter diagram enables us to see the relationship between two economic variables. But it does not give us a clear picture of how those variables evolve over time. To see the evolution of economic variables, we use a different but common kind of graph – the time-series graph.

Time-series Graphs

A **time-series graph** measures time (for example, years or months) on the *x*-axis and the variable or

FIGURE 2.4

More Scatter Diagrams

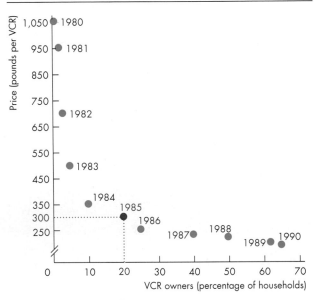

(a) VCR ownership and price

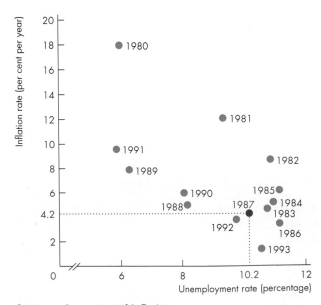

(b) Unemployment and inflation

Part (a) is a scatter diagram showing the relationship between the percentage of households owning a VCR and the average price of a VCR. It shows that as the price of a VCR has fallen, the percentage of households owning a VCR has increased. Part (b) is a scatter diagram showing inflation and unemployment. It shows that there is no clear relationship between these two variables.

variables in which we are interested on the y-axis.

Figure 2.5 illustrates a time-series graph. Time is measured in years on the x-axis. The variable that we are interested in – the UK unemployment rate (the percentage of the labour force unemployed) – is measured on the y-axis. The time-series graph conveys an enormous amount of information quickly and easily:

1. It tells us the *level* of the unemployment rate – when it is *high* and *low*. When the line is a long way from the x-axis, the unemployment rate is high. When the line is close to the x-axis, the unemployment rate is low.

2. It tells us how the unemployment rate *changes* – whether it *rises* or *falls*. When the line slopes upward, as in the early 1980s, the unemployment rate is rising. When the line slopes downward, as in the early 1940s, the unemployment rate is falling.

3. It tells us the *speed* with which the unemployment rate is *changing* – whether it is rising or falling *quickly* or *slowly*. If the line rises or falls very

steeply, then the unemployment rate is changing quickly. If the line is not steep, the unemployment rate is rising or falling slowly. For example, unemployment increased very quickly from 1930 to 1932. Unemployment went up again in 1933 but more slowly. Similarly, when unemployment was decreasing between 1987 and 1990, it fell quickly in 1989, but then it began to fall much more slowly in 1990.

A time-series graph can also be used to depict a trend. A **trend** is a general tendency for a variable to rise or fall. You can see that unemployment had a general tendency to rise from 1960 to the 1990s. That is, although there were ups and downs in the unemployment rate, there was an upward trend.

Graphs also allow us to compare different periods quickly. It is apparent, for example, that the 1920s and 1930s were different from any other period in the twentieth century because of exceptionally high unemployment.

FIGURE 2.5

A Time-series Graph

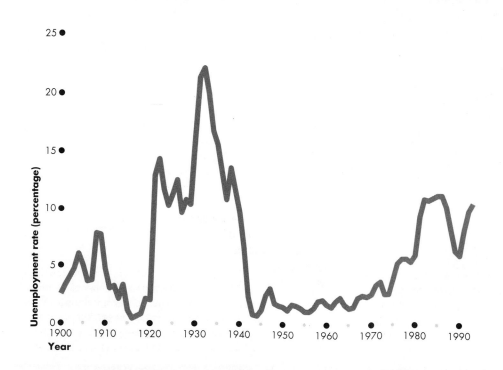

A time-series graph plots the level of a variable on the y-axis against time (day, week, month or year) on the x-axis. This graph shows the UK unemployment rate each year from 1900 to 1993.

Thus we can see that Fig. 2.5 conveys a wealth of information, and it does so in much less space than we have used to describe only some of its features.

Comparing Two Time-series   Sometimes we want to use a time-series graph to compare two different variables. For example, suppose you wanted to know how the unemployment rate fluctuated and how those fluctuations compared with changes in the inflation rate. You can examine two such series by drawing a graph of each of them in the manner shown in Fig. 2.6(a). The scale for the unemployment rate appears on the left side of the figure, and the scale for the inflation rate appears on the right. The red line shows the unemployment rate and the blue line shows the inflation rate. You can probably see in Fig. 2.6(a) that there is a tendency for the unemployment rate to fall when the infla-

tion rate rises – the blue line goes upward when the red line goes downward. In other words, it seems as if these two variables have a tendency to move in opposite directions.

In a situation such as this, it is often more revealing to flip the scale of one of the variables over and graph it upside-down. Figure 2.6(b) does this. The unemployment rate in part (b) is graphed in exactly the same way as in part (a). But the inflation rate has been flipped over. Now, instead of measuring an increase in inflation in the up direction and a decrease in the down direction, we measure an increase in the down direction and a decrease in the up direction. Now you can 'see' very clearly the relationship between these two variables. There is indeed a tendency for the inflation rate to decrease when the unemployment rate increases. But the relationship is by no means an

---

FIGURE 2.6

Relationships in Time-series

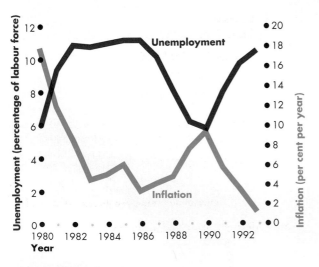

(a) Unemployment and inflation

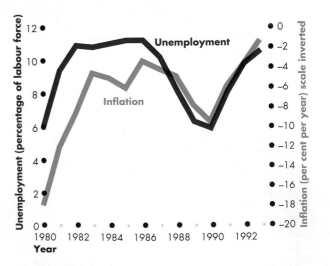

(b) Unemployment and inflation with scale inverted

A time-series graph can be used to reveal relationships between two variables. These two graphs show inflation and unemployment between 1980 and 1993. The unemployment line is identical in the two parts. In part (a), inflation is shown measuring increases upward and decreases downward on the right scale. It looks as if unemployment decreases when inflation increases. Part (b) inverts the scale

on which inflation is measured. Now an increase in inflation is measured in the down direction and a decrease in inflation is in the up direction on the right scale. The relationship between inflation and unemployment is now clearer. There is a tendency for the unemployment rate and inflation rate (as plotted) to move together. That is, unemployment tends to decrease when inflation increases.

exact one. There are significant periods, clearly revealed in the graph, when the unemployment rate and the inflation rate move apart. You can 'see' these periods as those in which the gap between the two lines widens.

Cross-section Graphs

The final type of data graph we'll consider is the cross-section graph. A **cross-section graph** measures the value of an economic variable on one axis and different members of a population on the other axis. An example of a cross-section graph is shown in Fig. 2.7(a). Output per person in 1992 relative to its level in 1980 is the economic variable of interest in this graph. And the population across which the variable is examined is the big seven industrial countries (called G-7 for the Group of Seven). This figure shows quickly and effectively that output growth has been largest for Japan and smallest for the United States. It also shows that the variation across the countries is not large, the range from the highest to the lowest being about 20 per cent.

Misleading Graphs

Graphs are powerful communicators and they can be used to distort rather than to clarify the situation. *All* types of graphs can lie, but the cross-section graph is the one that is most frequently distorted. Figure 2.7(b) shows a graph that distorts the facts. In this graph, the origin has been omitted from the axis that measures production per employee and the scale begins at 100 instead of 0. This graph creates the appearance that Japan has had output growth about four times larger than that of the United States and that even the United Kingdom has outgrown the United States almost threefold. Of course, the lie is easily detected. You simply have to pay attention to the numbers on the axes. But a quick glance certainly gives the wrong impression. Reading Between the Lines on pp.40–41 also considers a number of ways of presenting data, including misleading graphs.

Now that we have seen how we can use graphs in economics to represent economic data and to show the relationship between variables, let us examine how economists use graphs in a more abstract way to construct and analyse economic models.

FIGURE 2.7

Cross-section Graphs

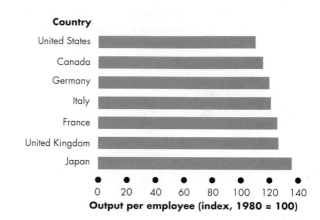

(a) Revealing graph with origin

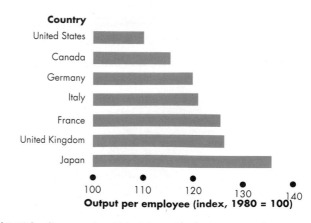

(b) Misleading graph with origin omitted

In part (a) a cross-section graph shows the way in which output per employee has grown between 1980 and 1992 across the G-7 countries. In all countries, output grew by a similar amount. In part (b) the growth rates are distorted and made to appear much larger than they have in fact been.

Graphs Used in Economic Models

The graphs used in economics are not always designed to show data. Instead their purpose is to illustrate the relationships among the variables in an economic model. Although you will encounter many different kinds of relationships in economic models, there are some patterns and, once you have learned to recognize them, they will instantly convey to you the meaning of a graph. There are graphs that show each of the following:

◆ Variables that go up and down together
◆ Variables that move in opposite directions
◆ Variables that are not related to each other at all
◆ Variables that have a maximum or a minimum

Let's look at these four cases.

Variables That Go Up and Down Together

Graphs that show the relationship between two variables shown in Fig. 2.8. The relationship between two variables that move in the same direction is called a **positive relationship**. Such a relationship is shown by a line that slopes upward.

Part (a) shows the relationship between the number of kilometres travelled in 5 hours and speed. For example, the point marked *a* tells us that we will travel 200 kilometres in 5 hours if our speed is 40 kilometres an hour. If we double our speed and travel at 80 kilometres an hour, we will cover a distance of 400 kilometres. The relationship between the number of kilometres travelled in 5 hours and speed is represented by an upward-sloping straight line. A relationship depicted by a straight line is called a **linear relationship**. A linear relationship is one that has a constant slope.

Part (b) shows the relationship between distance sprinted and recovery time (recovery time being measured by the time it takes the heart rate to return to normal). This relationship is an upward-sloping one depicted by a curved line that starts out with a gentle slope but then becomes steeper as we move along the curve away from the origin.

Part (c) shows the relationship between the number of problems worked by a student and the amount of study time. This relationship is illustrated by an

---

FIGURE 2.8

Positive Relationships

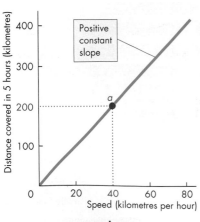

(a) Positive constant slope

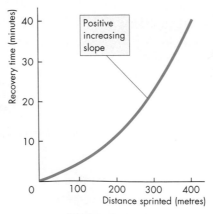

(b) Positive increasing slope

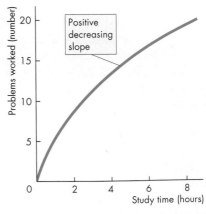

(c) Positive decreasing slope

Each part of this figure shows a positive relationship between two variables. That is, as the value of the variable measured on the x-axis increases, so does the value of the variable measured on the y-axis. Part (a) illustrates a linear relationship – a relationship whose slope is constant as we move along the curve. Part (b) illustrates a positive relationship whose slope becomes steeper as we move along the curve away from the origin. It is a positive relationship with an increasing slope. Part (c) shows a positive relationship whose slope becomes flatter as we move away from the origin. It is a positive relationship with a decreasing- slope.

upward-sloping curved line that starts out with a steep slope but then becomes more gentle as we move away from the origin.

There are three types of upward-sloping lines in the graphs in Fig. 2.8, one straight and two curved. But they are all called curves. Any line on a graph – no matter whether it is straight or curved – it is called a **curve**.

Variables That Move in Opposite Directions

Figure 2.9 shows relationships between variables that move in opposite directions. A relationship between variables that move in opposite directions is called a **negative relationship**.

Part (a) shows the relationship between the number of hours available for playing squash and the number of hours for playing tennis. One extra hour spent playing tennis means one hour less playing squash and vice versa. This relationship is negative and linear. Part (b) shows the relationship between the cost per kilometre travelled and the length of a journey. The longer the journey, the lower is the cost per kilometre. But as the journey length increases,

the cost per kilometre decreases at a decreasing rate. This feature of the relationship is illustrated by the fact that the curve slopes downward, starting out steep at a short journey length and then becoming flatter as the journey length increases.

Part (c) shows the relationship between the amount of leisure time and the number of problems worked by a student. If the student takes no leisure, 25 problems can be worked. If the student takes 5 hours of leisure, only 20 problems can be worked (point a). Increasing leisure time beyond 5 hours produces a large reduction in the number of problems worked and, if the student takes 10 hours of leisure a day, no problems are worked. This relationship is a negative one that starts out with a gentle slope at a low number of leisure hours and becomes increasingly steep as leisure hours increase.

Relationships That Have a Maximum and a Minimum

Economics is about optimizing, or doing the best with limited resources. Making the highest possible profits or achieving the lowest possible costs of production

---

FIGURE 2.9

Negative Relationships

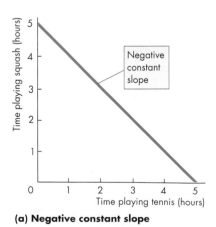

(a) Negative constant slope

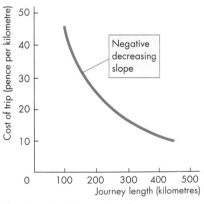

(b) Negative decreasing slope

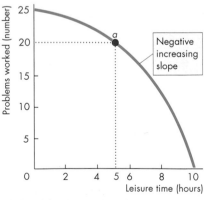

(c) Negative increasing slope

Each part of this figure shows a negative relationship between two variables. Part (a) shows a linear relationship – a relationship whose slope is constant as we travel along the curve. Part (b) shows a negative relationship of decreasing slope. That is, the slope of the relationship becomes less steep as

we travel along the curve from left to right. Part (c) shows a negative relationship of increasing slope. That is, the slope becomes steeper as we travel along the curve from left to right.

are examples of optimizing. Economists make frequent use of graphs depicting relationships that have a maximum or a minimum. Figure 2.10 illustrates such relationships.

Part (a) shows the relationship between rainfall and wheat yield. When there is no rainfall, wheat will not grow, so the yield is zero. As the rainfall increases up to 10 days per month, the wheat yield also increases. With 10 rainy days each month, the wheat yield reaches its maximum at 400 kilograms per hectare (point a). Rain in excess of 10 days per month starts to lower the yield of wheat. If every day is rainy, the wheat suffers from a lack of sunshine and the yield falls almost to zero. This relationship is one that starts out positive, reaches a maximum, and then becomes negative.

Part (b) shows the reverse case – a relationship that begins with a negative slope, falls to a minimum, and then becomes positive. An example of such a relationship is the petrol cost per mile as the speed of travel varies. At low speeds, the car is creeping along in a traffic snarl-up. The number of

miles per litre is low so the petrol cost per mile is high. At very high speeds, the car is operated beyond its most efficient rate and, again, the number of miles per litre is low and the petrol cost per mile is high. At a speed of 55 miles per hour, the petrol cost per mile travelled is at its minimum (point b).

Variables That are Independent

There are many situations in which one variable is independent of another. No matter what happens to the value of one variable, the other variable remains constant. Sometimes we want to show the independence between two variables in a graph. Figure 2.11 shows two ways of achieving this. In Fig. 2.11(a), your grade in economics is shown on the vertical axis against the price of bananas on the horizontal axis. Your grade (75 per cent in this example) does not depend on the price of bananas. The relationship between these two variables is shown by a horizontal straight line. In part (b), the output of French wine is shown on the horizontal axis and the

---

FIGURE 2.10

Maximum and Minimum Points

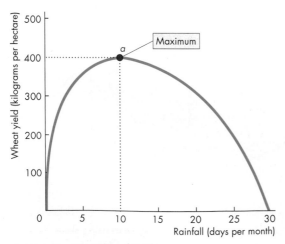

(a) Relationship with a maximum

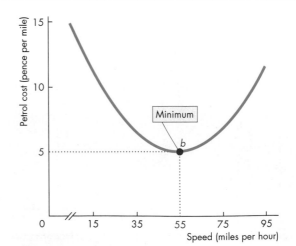

(b) Relationship with a minimum

Part (a) shows a relationship that has a maximum point, a. As rainfall increases up to 10 days a month, the wheat yield increases, but as rainfall increases above 10 days a month, the wheat yield decreases. The maximum wheat yield is 400 kilograms per hectare. Part (b) shows a relationship with a minimum

point, b. As speed increases up to 55 miles per hour, the petrol cost decreases, but as the speed increases above 55 miles per hour, the petrol cost increases. The minimum petrol cost is 5 pence per mile.

number of rainy days per month in Wales is shown on the vertical axis. Again, the output of French wine (15 billion litres per year in this example) does not change when the number of rainy days in Wales changes. The relationship between these two variables is shown by a vertical straight line.

Figures 2.8 to 2.11 illustrate 10 different shapes of graphs that we will encounter in economic models. In describing these graphs, we have talked about curves that slope upward or slope downward and slopes that are steep or gentle. The concept of slope is an important one. Let's spend a little time discussing exactly what we mean by slope.

The Slope of a Relationship

The **slope** of a relationship is the change in the value of the variable measured on the y-axis divided by the change in the value of the variable measured on the x-axis. We use the Greek letter *delta* (Δ) to represent 'change in'. Thus Δy means the change in the value of the variable measured on the y-axis, and Δx means the change in the value of the variable measured on the x-axis. Therefore, the slope of the relationship is:

$$\Delta y / \Delta x$$

If a large change in the variable measured on the y-axis (Δy) is associated with a small change in the variable measured on the x-axis (Δx), the slope is large and the curve is steep. If a small change in the variable measured on the y-axis (Δy) is associated with a large change in the variable measured on the x-axis (Δx), the slope is small and the curve is flat.

We can make the idea of slope sharper by doing some calculations.

Calculating the Slope of a Straight Line

The slope of a straight line is the same regardless of where on the line you calculate it. Thus the slope of

---

FIGURE 2.11

Variables with No Relationship

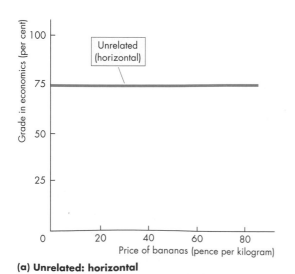

(a) Unrelated: horizontal

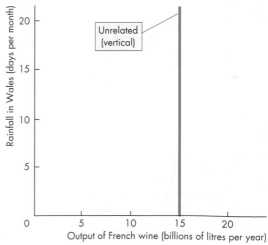

(b) Unrelated: vertical

This figure shows how we can graph two variables that are unrelated to each other. In part (a), a student's grade in economics is plotted at 75 per cent regardless of the price of bananas on the x-axis. In part (b), the output of the vineyards of France does not vary with the rainfall in Wales.

Graphs in Action

FINANCIAL TIMES, 14 JULY 1994

Inflation and average earnings unchanged

Philip Coggan and Gillian Tett

Two important measures of price pressure were unchanged yesterday, providing good economic news for the government.

The annual rate of headline inflation in June was 2.6 per cent, the same as in May, the Central Statistical Office said yesterday. But underlying inflation, which excludes mortgage interest payments, fell to 2.4 per cent, from 2.5 per cent in May.

Average earnings across the economy rose at an underlying rate of 3.75 per cent in May, the same as in April, the Department of Employment said.

A complex set of factors left the retail prices index unchanged in June. Price rises included 2p per pint on draught bitter, and there were some increases in bus and rail fares.

Inflation rate: +2.6%		RPI: 144.7 in June
Food (seasonal) (20)	+8.9%	
Food (non-seasonal) (142)	+0.1%	
Catering (45)	+3.8%	
Alcoholic drink (76)	+2.2%	
Tobacco (35)	+7.5%	
Housing (158)	+4.1%	
Fuel & light (45)	+6.4%	
Household goods (76)	+0.3%	
Household services (47)	+1.2%	
Clothing & footwear (58)	+0.7%	
Personal goods & services (37)	+3.5%	
Motoring expenditure (142)	+2.4%	
Fares & travel costs (20)	+2.1%	
Leisure goods (48)	–0.3%	
Leisure services (71)	+3.9%	Source: CSO

Figures in brackets are weights in retail prices index in parts of 1,000
Percentage represents annual % change to June 1994

Seasonal food prices, which rose sharply in May, failed to fall by as much as expected in June – a month-on-month fall of 0.5 per cent compared with a 4.6 per cent fall in June last year. Onions, cauliflowers and cucumbers all saw higher prices.

Retailers' summer sales have started later and have yet to see such sharp price cuts as last year. Nevertheless, the sales still put downward pressure on the RPI, as did cuts in the prices of personal articles, such as umbrellas, spectacle frames and clocks.

The annual growth in prices of non-seasonal food remained very low.

Second-hand car prices fell by about 0.4 per cent, the first time they had declined in June since 1982. The effect was to offset a 1p a gallon rise in the cost of four-star petrol and to leave motoring costs unchanged between May and June.

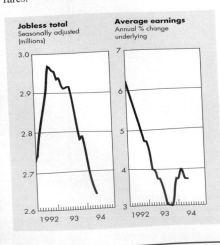

Jobless total
Seasonally adjusted (millions)

Average earnings
Annual % change underlying

The annual headline inflation rate to June 1994 was unchanged from the previous month.

Underlying inflation for the same period fell slightly.

The components of inflation, measured by the Retail Prices Index (RPI), showed conflicting movements to result in an unchanged rate of inflation.

Average earnings rose at the same rate in May 1994 as in the previous month.

The total jobless number is falling.

© The Financial Times. Reprinted with permission.

Background and Analysis

Inflation was unchanged in June 1994. The table and bar chart in the article show the composition of the overall price rise.

Prices for seasonal food, tobacco, and fuel and light rose by above-average amounts in the year to June but carry low weights. Prices for non-seasonal food, motoring expenditure and household goods rose by less than the average, but carry greater weights.

A graph showing inflation over time would give less information. A graph of all the information in the table, showing each element over time, would not be clear.

The graphs for total jobless and percentage change in average earnings in the article both show a decline. By omitting the origin and all data before 1992, it appears that both variables are at low levels.

Graphs of these variables over a number of years would show whether unemployment levels and increases in earnings were low historically, or simply slightly less high than in the previous few months.

The current jobless total is also divided up between regions within the United Kingdom. This lets us see which regions have higher rates of unemployment in June 1994, but does not show how these figures have changed over time.

A graph of regional unemployment over time would show if certain regions have consistently higher unemployment, or if today's low unemployment regions were yesterday's unemployment black-spots.

A graph drawn using annual data means month to month changes are lost, but it allows an analysis of whether the fall in unemployment indicates a healthy economy or merely the beginning of a recovery.

The graph in the figure shows annual average unemployment from 1979 to 1994 (except for 1994 which is the average of January to June). This allows recent unemployment rates to be put into their historical context for the period since the Conservative government last regained power.

Unemployment during the period 1992–1994 (the period covered by the graph in the article) is historically quite high. In the context of the current recession which started towards the end of 1989, unemployment is falling but is still much higher than in 1989 and 1990.

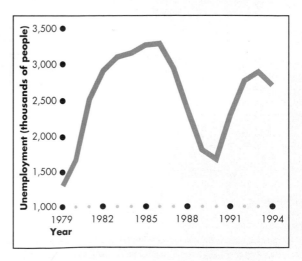

a straight line is constant. Let's calculate the slopes of the lines in Fig. 2.12. In part (a), when x increases from 2 to 6, y increases from 3 to 6. The change in x is +4 – that is, Δx is 4. The change in y is +3 – that is, Δy is 3. The slope of that line is

$$\frac{\Delta y}{\Delta x} = \frac{3}{4}$$

In part (b), when x increases from 2 to 6, y decreases from 6 to 3. The change in y is *minus* 3 – that is Δy is –3. The change in x is *plus* 4 – that is, Δx is +4. The slope of the curve is

$$\frac{\Delta y}{\Delta x} = \frac{-3}{4}$$

Notice that the two slopes have the same magnitude (3/4), but the slope of the line in part (a) is positive

(+3/+4 = 3/4), while that in part (b) is negative (−3/+4 = −3/4). The slope of a positive relationship is positive; the slope of a negative relationship is negative.

Calculating the Slope of a Curved Line

Calculating the slope of a curved line is trickier. The slope of a curved line is not constant. Its slope depends on where on the line you calculate it. There are two ways to calculate the slope of a curved line: you can calculate the slope at a point on the line or you can calculate the slope across an arc of the line. Let's look at the two alternatives.

Slope at a Point   To calculate the slope at a point on a curved line, you need to construct a straight line that has the same slope as the curve at the point in question. Figure 2.13(a) shows how such a calculation is

---

FIGURE 2.12

The Slope of a Straight Line

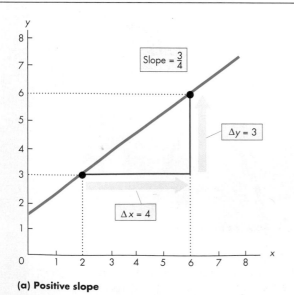

(a) Positive slope

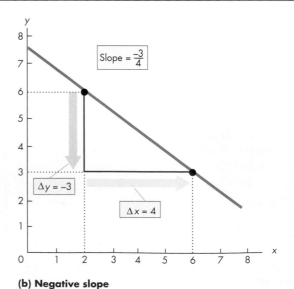

(b) Negative slope

To calculate the slope of a straight line, we divide the change in the value of the variable measured on the *y*-axis by the change in the value of the variable measured on the *x*-axis. Part (a) shows the calculation of a positive slope – where both *x* and *y* go up together. When *x* goes up from 2 to 6, the change in *x* is 4 – that is, Δx equals 4. That change in *x* brings about an increase in *y*

from 3 to 6, so that Δy equals 3. The slope ($\Delta y / \Delta x$) equals ¾. Part (b) shows a negative slope (when *x* goes up, *y* goes down). When *x* goes up from 2 to 6, Δx equals 4. That change in *x* brings about a decrease in *y* from 6 to 3, so that Δy equals –3. The slope ($\Delta y / \Delta x$) equals – ¾.

made. Suppose you want to calculate the slope of the curve at the point marked a. Place a ruler on the graph so that it touches point a and no other point on the curve, then draw a straight line along the edge of the ruler. Such a straight line is called a *tangent*. The red line in part (a) is such a line. If the ruler touches the curve only at point a, then the slope of the curve at point a must be the same as the slope of the edge of the ruler. If the curve and the ruler do not have the same slope, the line along the edge of the ruler will cut the curve instead of just touching it – the line will not be a tangent.

Having now found a straight line with the same slope as the curve at point a, you can calculate the

slope of the curve at point a by calculating the slope of the straight line. We already know how to calculate the slope of a straight line, so the task is straightforward. In this case, as x increases from 0 to 4 ($\Delta x = 4$), y increases from 2 to 5 ($\Delta y = 3$). Therefore, the slope of the straight line is

$$\frac{\Delta y}{\Delta x} = \frac{3}{4}$$

Thus the slope of the curve at point a is 3/4.

Slope Across an Arc   Calculating a slope across an arc is similar to calculating an average slope. An arc of a

---

FIGURE 2.13

The Slope of a Curve

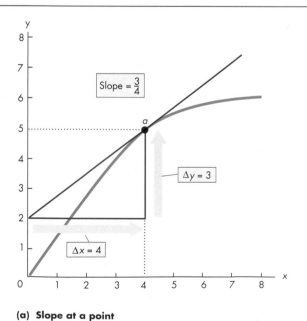

(a) Slope at a point

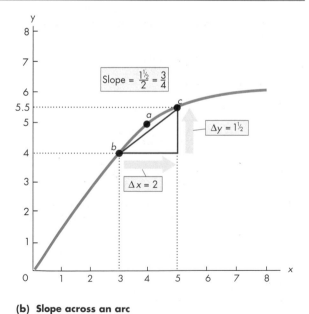

(b) Slope across an arc

The slope of a curve can be calculated either at a point, as in part (a), or across an arc, as in part (b). The slope at a point is calculated by finding the slope of a straight line that touches the curve only at one point. To calculate the slope of the curve at point a draw a straight line such that it touches the curve at point a. The slope of that straight line is calculated by dividing the change in y by the change in x. When x increases from 0 to 4, Δx equals 4. That change in x is associated with an increase in y from 2 to 5, so Δy equals 3. So the slope of

the line at point a is ¾. To calculate the slope across an arc, we place a straight line across the curve from one point to another and then calculate the slope of that straight line. To calculate the slope of the arc bc draw a straight line from b to c in part (b). The slope of the straight line bc is calculated by dividing the change in y by the change in x. In moving from b to c, x increases by 2 (Δx equals 2) and y increases by 1½ (Δy equals 1½). The slope of the line bc is 1½ divided by 2, or ¾. So the slope of the curve across the arc bc is ¾.

curve is a piece of the curve. In Fig. 2.13(b), we are looking at the same curve as in part (a) but instead of calculating the slope at point a, we calculate the slope across the arc from b to c. Moving along the arc from b to c, x increases from 3 to 5 and y increases from 4 to 5½. That is, the change in x is +2 ($\Delta x = 2$), and the change in y is 1½ ($\Delta y = 1½$). Therefore, the slope of the line is

$$\frac{\Delta y}{\Delta x} = \frac{1½}{2} = \frac{3}{4}$$

This calculation gives us the slope of the line between points b and c. The actual slope calculated is the slope of the straight line from b to c. This slope approximates the average slope of the curve along the arc bc. In this particular example, the slope across the arc bc is identical to the slope of the curve at point a in both part (a) and part (b). But the calculation of the slope does not always work out so neatly. You might have some fun constructing examples that do not give such an outcome. Box 2.1 provides an algebraic explanation of how the slope is calculated.

Graphing Relationships Between More Than Two Variables

We have seen that we can graph a single variable as a point on a straight line and we can graph the relationship between two variables as a point formed by the x and y coordinates in a two-dimensional graph. You may be suspecting that although a two-dimensional graph is informative, most of the things in which you are likely to be interested involve relationships among many variables, not just two.

Relationships between more than two variables abound. For example, consider the relationship between the price of ice cream, the air temperature and the amount of ice cream eaten. If ice cream is expensive and the temperature is low, people eat much less ice cream than when ice cream is inexpensive and the temperature is high. For any given price of ice cream, the quantity consumed varies with the temperature, and for any given temperature, the quantity of ice cream consumed varies with its price.

Other Things Being Equal

Figure 2.14 illustrates such a situation. The table shows the number of litres of ice cream that will be eaten each day at various temperatures and ice cream prices. How can we graph all these numbers? To graph a relationship that involves more than two variables, we consider what happens if all but two of the variables are held constant. This device is called *ceteris paribus*. **Ceteris paribus** is a Latin phrase that means 'other things being equal'. For example, in Fig. 2.14(a) you can see what happens to the quantity of ice cream consumed when the price of ice cream varies while the temperature is held constant. The line labelled 20°C shows the relationship between ice cream consumption and the price of ice cream when the temperature stays at 20°C. The numbers used to plot that line are those in the third column of the table in Fig. 2.14. For example, when the temperature is 20°C, 5 litres are consumed when the price is 30 pence a scoop and 10 litres are consumed when the price is 20 pence. The curve labelled 30°C shows the consumption of ice cream when the price varies and the temperature is 30°C.

Alternatively, we can show the relationship between ice cream consumption and temperature while holding the price of ice cream constant, as is shown in Fig. 2.14(b). The curve labelled 30 pence shows how the consumption of ice cream varies with the temperature when ice cream costs 30 pence a scoop, and a second curve shows the relationship when ice cream costs 15 pence. For example, at 30 pence a scoop 5 litres are consumed when the temperature is 20°C and 10 litres when the temperature is 30°C. Part (c) shows the combinations of temperature and price that result in a constant consumption of ice cream. One curve shows the combination that results in 10 litres a day being consumed and the other shows the combination that results in 7 litres a day being consumed. A high price and a high temperature lead to the same consumption as a lower price and lower temperature. For example, 7 litres are consumed at 10°C and 20 pence per scoop and at 20°C and 25 pence per scoop.

◆ ◆ ◆ With what you have now learned about graphs, you can move forward with your study of economics. There are no graphs in this book that are more complicated than those that have been explained here.

FIGURE 2.14

Graphing a Relationship Between Three Variables

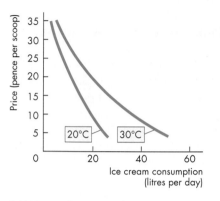

**(a) Price and consumption at
a given temperature**

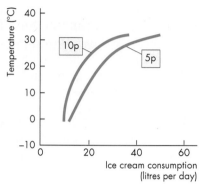

**(b) Temperature and consumption
at a given price**

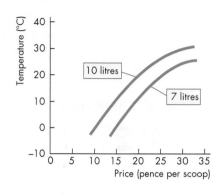

**(c) Temperature and price at
a given consumption**

Price (pence per scoop)	Ice cream consumption (litres per day)			
	0°C	10°C	20°C	30°C
5	12	18	25	50
10	10	12	18	37
15	7	10	13	27
20	5	7	10	20
25	3	5	7	14
30	2	3	5	10
35	1	2	3	6

The quantity of ice cream consumed (one variable) depends on its price (a second variable) and the air temperature (a third variable). The table provides some hypothetical numbers that tell us how many litres of ice cream are consumed each day at different prices and different temperatures. For example, if the price is 15 pence per scoop and the temperature is 10°C, 10 litres of ice cream will be consumed. In order to graph a relationship between three variables, the value of one variable must be held constant.

Part (a) shows the relationship between price and consumption, holding temperature constant. One curve holds temperature constant at 30°C and the other at 20°C. Part (b) shows the relationship between temperature and consumption, holding price constant. One curve holds the price at 10 pence the other at 5 pence. Part (c) shows the relationship between temperature and price, holding consumption constant. One curve holds consumption constant at 10 litres and the other at 7 litres.

S U M M A R Y

Graphing Data

There are three main types of graphs used to represent economic data: scatter diagrams, time-series graphs and cross-section graphs. A scatter diagram plots the value of one economic variable associated with the value of another. Such a diagram reveals whether or not there is a relationship between two variables and, if there is a relationship, its nature.

A time-series graph plots the value of one or more economic variables on the vertical axis (y-axis) and time on the horizontal axis (x-axis). A well-constructed time-series graph quickly reveals the level, direction of change and speed of change of a variable. It also reveals trends. Graphs sometimes mislead, especially when the origin is omitted or when the scale is stretched or squeezed to exaggerate or understate a variation.

A cross-section graph shows how the value of an economic variable changes across the members of a population. (pp. 30–35)

Graphs Used in Economic Models

Graphs are used in economic models to illustrate relationships between variables. There are four cases: positive relationships, negative relationships, relationships that have a maximum or a minimum, and variables that are not related to each other. Examples of these different types of relationships are summarized in Figures 2.8 to 2.11. (pp. 36–39)

The Slope of a Relationship

The slope of a relationship is calculated as the change in the value of the variable measured on the y-axis divided by the change in the value of the variable measured on the x-axis – $\Delta y/\Delta x$. A straight line has a constant slope, but a curved line has a varying slope. To calculate the slope of a curved line, we either calculate the slope at a point or across an arc. (pp. 39–44)

Graphing Relationships Between More Than Two Variables

To graph a relationship between more than two variables, we hold constant the values of all the variables except two. We then plot the value of one of the variables against the value of another. Holding constant all the variables but two is called the *ceteris paribus* assumption – other things being equal. (pp. 44–45)

K E Y   E L E M E N T S

Key Terms

Key Figures

R E V I E W   Q U E S T I O N S

1 Why do we use graphs?

2 What are the two scale lines on a graph called?

3 What is the origin on a graph?

4 What do we mean by the y-coordinate and x-coordinate?

5 What is a time-series graph?

6 List three things that a time-series graph shows quickly and easily.

7 What do we mean by trend?

8 What is a scatter diagram?

9 Sketch some graphs to illustrate the following:

  a Two variables that move up and down together

  b Two variables that move in opposite directions

  c A relationship between two variables that has a maximum

  d A relationship between two variables that has a minimum

10 Which of the relationships in Question 9 is a positive relationship and which a negative relationship?

11 What is the definition of the slope of a curve?

12 What are the two ways of calculating the slope of a curved line?

13 How do we graph relationships between more than two variables?

P R O B L E M S

1 The inflation rate in the United Kingdom between 1980 and 1993 was as follows:

Year	Inflation rate (per cent per year)
1980	18.0
1981	11.9
1982	8.6
1983	4.6
1984	5.0
1985	6.1
1986	3.4
1987	4.1
1988	4.9
1989	7.8
1990	9.5
1991	5.9
1992	3.7
1993	1.3

Draw a time-series graph of these data and use your graph to answer the following questions:

  a In which year was inflation highest?

  b In which year was inflation lowest?

  c In which years did inflation rise?

  d In which years did inflation fall?

  e In which year did inflation rise/fall the fastest?

  f In which year did inflation rise/fall the slowest?

  g What have been the main trends in inflation?

2 Interest rates on treasury bills issued by the United Kingdom government between 1980 and 1993 were as follows:

Year	Interest rate (per cent per year)
1980	13.6
1981	15.4
1982	10.0
1983	9.0
1984	9.3
1985	11.5
1986	10.9
1987	8.4
1988	12.9
1989	15.0
1990	13.5
1991	10.5
1992	6.4
1993	4.95

Use these data together with those in Problem 1 to draw a scatter diagram showing the relationship between inflation and the interest rate. Use this diagram to determine whether there is a relationship between inflation and the interest rate and whether it is positive or negative.

3 Use the following information to draw a graph showing the relationship between two variables x and y.

x	0	1	2	3	4	5	6	7	8
y	0	1	4	9	16	25	36	49	64

  a Is the relationship between x and y positive or negative?

  b Does the slope of the relationship rise or fall as the value of x rises?

4 Using the data in Problem 3:

   a Calculate the slope of the relationship between x and y when x equals 4.

   b Calculate the slope of the arc when x rises from 3 to 4.

   c Calculate the slope of the arc when x rises from 4 to 5.

   d Calculate the slope of the arc when x rises from 3 to 5.

   e What do you notice that is interesting about your answers to (b), (c), and (d), compared with your answer to (a)?

5 Calculate the slopes of the following two relationships between two variables x and y:

   a

x	0	2	4	6	8	10
y	20	16	12	8	4	0

   b

x	0	2	4	6	8	10
y	0	8	16	24	32	40

6 Draw a graph showing the following relationship between two variables x and y:

x	0	1	2	3	4	5	6	7	8	9
y	0	2	4	6	8	10	8	6	4	2

   a Is the slope positive or negative when x is less than 5?

   b Is the slope positive or negative when x is greater than 5?

   c What is the slope of this relationship when x equals 5?

   d Is y at a maximum or at a minimum when x equals 5?

7 Draw a graph showing the following relationship between two variables x and y:

x	0	1	2	3	4	5	6	7	8	9
y	10	8	6	4	2	0	2	4	6	8

   a Is the slope positive or negative when x is less than 5?

   b Is the slope positive or negative when x is greater than 5?

   c What is the slope of this relationship when x equals 5?

   d Is y at a maximum or at a minimum when x equals 5?

1. Linear Relationships

The equation for a linear relationship is:

$$y = a + bx$$

where y is the value of the variable on the y-axis, x is the value of the variable on the x-axis, and a and b are constants. If b is positive, the line for this equation slopes upward and if b is negative, the line slopes downward, and b is the slope. To see this fact, look at what happens to y is x changes by an amount we'll call Δx. Such an increase in x will increase y by an amount that we'll call Δy and the relation between x and y will now be:

$$y + \Delta y = a + b(x + \Delta x).$$

Subtract the original equation from this to get:

$$\Delta y = b\Delta x.$$

Divide Δy by Δx to find the slope and you have:

$$\Delta y/\Delta x = b.$$

2. Non-linear Relationships

In the non-linear case, we write the relationship as:

$$y = f(x)$$

which is just a convenient way of expressing y as a *function* of x. The slope of the function $f(\ )$ depends on the value of x and is called the *derivative* of y with respect to x. That is, the slope is given by:

$$dy/dx = f'(x).$$

where dy is the change in y, dx is the change in x, and dy/dx is the *rate of change of* y *with respect to a change in* x. Calculus is used to find the derivative of a function. The simplest type of non-linear relation is a quadratic, a relation that involves the square of a variable. An example is

$$y = 5 + 3x^2.$$

The rule for finding the derivative of y with respect to x is to ignore the constant amount 5 because it does not vary as x varies, and to multiply the coefficient 3 by the power 2 and decrease the power by 1. That is:

$$dy/dx = 6x.$$

The rate of change of y with respect to a change in x increases as x increases. Draw a graph of the equation above and convince yourself of this fact.

A quadratic equation is a special case of a more general type of non-linear relation called a *polynomial*, the equation for which is:

$$y = a + bx^n.$$

In words, y equals a constant amount a plus a variable amount x raised to the power n multiplied by b. The rule for finding the derivative (the slope at a point) of such a function is: ignore the a because it is a constant and so does not affect the *change* in y; multiply the coefficient b by the power n and decrease the power by 1. That is:

$$dy/dx = nbx^{n-1}.$$

For the linear case, $n = 1$ so $n - 1$ is zero and $dy/dx = b$, the slope you've just seen – recall from your school mathematics that $x^0 = 1$.

For a quadratic function, $n = 2$, that is:

$$y = a + bx^2$$

and the derivative is:

$$dy/dx = 2bx.$$

In the example we worked through, $b = 3$, so $2b = 6$, as we have already seen.

CHAPTER 3

PRODUCTION, SPECIALIZATION AND EXCHANGE

After studying this chapter, you will be able to:

◆ Define the production possibility frontier

◆ Calculate opportunity cost

◆ Explain why economic growth and technological change do not provide free gifts

◆ Explain comparative advantage

◆ Explain why people specialize and how they gain from trade

◆ Explain why property rights and money have evolved

W E LIVE IN A STYLE THAT MOST OF OUR GRANDPARENTS COULD NOT HAVE imagined. Advances in medicine have cured diseases that terrified them. Our parents are amazed at the matter-of-fact way we handle computers. We casually use products such as microwave ovens, graphite tennis rackets and digital watches that didn't exist in their youth. Economic growth has made us richer than our parents and grandparents. ◆ ◆ But economic growth and technological change have not liberated us from scarcity. Why not? Why, despite our immense wealth, must we still make choices and face costs? Why are there no 'free lunches'? ◆ ◆ We see an incredible amount of specialization and trading in the world. Each one of us specializes in a particular job – as lawyer, plumber, or homemaker. Only one in four UK workers are employed in manu-facturing. Over half of all UK workers are employed in wholesale and retail trade, bank-ing and finance, government and other services. ◆ ◆ Why do we specialize? How do we benefit from specialization and exchange? Over many centuries, institutions and social arrangements have evolved that we take for granted. One of them is property rights. Another is money. Yet another is government and a legal system that enforces contracts and that protects property rights. Why have these institutions evolved? And how do they extend our ability to specialize and increase production?

◆ ◆ ◆ ◆ This chapter explains why specialization and exchange occur and arise as a consequence of people's attempts to cope with scarcity. It also shows how differences in opportunity costs explain why people and countries specialize and why huge gains arise from specialization and trade.

Making the Most of It

The Production Possibility Frontier

What do we mean by production? **Production** is the conversion of *land*, *labour* and *capital* into goods and services. We defined the factors of production in Chapter 1. Let's briefly recall what they are.

Land is all the gifts of nature. It includes the air, the water and the land surface, as well as the minerals that lie beneath the surface of the earth. *Labour* is all the muscle-power and brain-power of human beings. The voices and artistry of singers and actors, the strength and coordination of athletes, the daring of astronauts, the political skill of diplomats, as well as the physical and mental skills of the many millions of people who make cars and cola, gum and glue, wallpaper and watering cans, are included in this category.

Capital is all the goods that have been produced and can now be used in the production of other goods and services. Examples include motorways, the fine buildings of great cities, dams and power projects, airports and jumbo jets, car production lines, shirt factories, and shoe shops. A special kind of capital is called human capital. **Human capital** is the accumulated skill and knowledge of human beings, which arise from their training and education. Human capital is not a separate entity like a bridge or a road. It is an integral part of *labour* and it affects the productivity of labour.

Goods and services are all the valuable things that people produce. Goods are tangible – cars, spoons, VCRs and bread. Services are intangible – haircuts, amusement park rides and telephone calls. There are two types of goods: capital goods and consumption goods. **Capital goods** are goods that are used in the production process and can be used many times before they eventually wear out. Examples of capital goods are buildings, computers, cars and telephones. **Consumption goods** are goods that can be used just once. Examples are pickled onions and toothpaste. **Consumption** is the process of using up goods and services.

The amount that we can produce is limited by our resources and the technologies available for transforming those resources into goods and services. That limit is described by the production possibility frontier. The **production possibility frontier** (PPF) marks the boundary between those combinations of goods and services that can be produced and those that cannot. It is important to understand the production possibility frontier in the real world, but in order to achieve that goal more easily, we will first study an economy that is simpler than the one in which we live – a model economy.

A Model Economy

Instead of looking at the real-world economy with all its complexity and detail, we will build a model of an economy. The model will have features that are essential to understanding the real economy, but we will ignore most of reality's immense detail. Our model economy will be simpler in three important ways:

1. Everything that is produced is also consumed so that in our model, capital resources neither grow nor shrink. (Later we will examine what happens if we consume less than we produce and add to capital resources.)

2. There are only two goods, corn and cloth. (In the real world we use our scarce resources to produce countless goods and services.)

3. There is only one person, Jane, who lives on a deserted island and has no dealings with other people. (Later we will see what happens when Jane's island economy has links with another economy. Also, we'll extend our view to the real world with its five billion people.)

Jane uses all the resources of her island economy to produce corn and cloth. She works 10 hours each day. The amount of corn and cloth that Jane produces depends on how many hours she devotes to producing them. Table 3.1 sets out Jane's production possibilities for corn and cloth. If she does no work, she produces nothing. Two hours a day devoted to corn farming produces 6 kilograms of corn per month. Devoting more hours to corn increases the output of corn, but there is a decline in the extra amount of corn that comes from extra effort. The reason for this decline is that Jane has to use increasingly unsuitable land for growing corn. At first, she plants corn on a lush, flat plain. Eventually, when she has used all the arable land, she has to start planting on the rocky hills and the edge of the beach. The numbers in the second

TABLE 3.1

Jane's Production Possibilities

Hours worked (per day)		Corn grown (kilograms per month)		Cloth produced (metres per month)
0	either	0	or	0
2	either	6	or	1
4	either	11	or	2
6	either	15	or	3
8	either	18	or	4
10	either	20	or	5

If Jane does no work, she produces no corn or cloth. If she works for 2 hours per day and spends the entire amount of time on corn production, she produces 6 kilograms of corn per month. If that same time is used for cloth production, 1 metre of cloth is produced but no corn. The last four rows of the table show the amounts of corn or cloth that can be produced per month as more hours are devoted to each activity.

column of the table show how the output of corn rises as the hours devoted to cultivating it rise.

To produce cloth, Jane gathers wool from sheep that live on the island. As she devotes more hours to collecting wool and making cloth, her output rises. The numbers in the third column of Table 3.1 show how the output of cloth rises as the number of hours devoted to this activity rises.

If Jane devotes all her time to growing corn, she can produce 20 kilograms of corn in a month. In that case, however, she cannot produce any cloth. Conversely, if she devotes all her time to making cloth, she can produce 5 metres a month but will have no time left for growing corn. Jane can devote some of her time to corn and some to cloth but not more than 10 hours a day total. Thus she can spend 2 hours growing corn and 8 hours making cloth or 6 hours on one and 4 hours on the other (or any other combination of hours that add up to 10 hours).

We have defined the production possibility frontier as the boundary between what is attainable

and what is not attainable. You can calculate Jane's production possibility frontier by using the information in Table 3.1. These calculations are summarized in the table in Fig. 3.1 and graphed in that figure as Jane's production possibility frontier. To see how we calculated that frontier, let's concentrate first on the table in Fig. 3.1.

Possibility *a* shows Jane devoting no time to cloth and her entire 10-hour working day to corn. In this case, she can produce 20 kilograms of corn per month and no cloth. For possibility *b*, she spends 2 hours a day making cloth and 8 hours growing corn, to produce a total of 18 kilograms of corn and 1 metre of cloth a month. The pattern continues on to possibility *f*, where she devotes 10 hours a day to cloth and no time to corn. These same numbers are plotted in the graph shown in Fig. 3.1. Metres of cloth are measured on the horizontal axis and kilograms of corn on the vertical axis. Points *a* to *f* represent the numbers in the corresponding row of the table.

Of course, Jane does not have to work in blocks of 2 hours, as in our example. She can work 1 hour or 1 hour and 10 minutes growing corn and devote the rest of her time to making cloth. All other feasible allocations of Jane's 10 hours enable her to produce the combinations of corn and cloth described by the line that joins points *a, b, c, d, e* and *f*. This line shows Jane's production possibility frontier. She can produce at any point on the frontier or inside it, within the orange area. These are attainable points. Points outside the frontier are unattainable. To produce at points beyond the frontier, Jane needs more time than she has – more than 10 hours a day. By working 10 hours a day producing both corn and cloth, Jane can produce at any point on the frontier. And by working less than 10 hours a day or by not putting her resources to their best possible use – by wasting some of her resources – she can produce at a point inside the frontier.

Technological Efficiency

Technological efficiency occurs when no resources are wasted. Equivalently, technological efficiency occurs when an economy is on its production possibility frontier. Jane produces corn and cloth, not for the fun of it, but so that she can eat and keep warm. She wants much more corn and cloth than she can produce, and the more of

FIGURE 3.1

Jane's Production Possibility Frontier

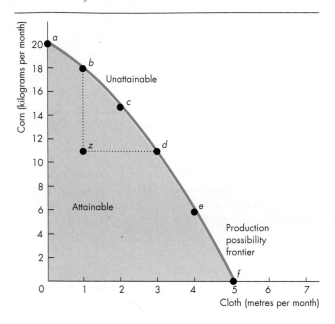

Possibility	Corn (kilograms per month)		Cloth (metres per month)
a	20	and	0
b	18	and	1
c	15	and	2
d	11	and	3
e	6	and	4
f	0	and	5

The table lists six points on Jane's production possibility frontier. Row *e* tells us that if Jane produces 6 kilograms of corn, the maximum cloth production that is possible is 4 metres. These same points are graphed as points *a, b, c, d, e* and *f* in the figure. The line passing through these points is Jane's production possibility frontier, which separates the attainable from the unattainable. The attainable orange area contains all the possible production points. Jane can produce anywhere inside this area or on the production possibility frontier. Points outside the frontier are unattainable. Jane prefers points on the frontier to any point inside. She prefers points between *b* and *d* on the frontier to point *z* inside the frontier because they give Jane more of both goods.

each she has, the better she likes it. Because Jane wants as much as possible of both corn and cloth the best she can do is to produce – and therefore consume – at a point *on* her production possibility frontier. To see why, consider a point such as *z* in the attainable region. At point *z*, Jane is wasting resources. She may be taking time off work, but leisure time on the island is not worth anything to Jane. Or she may not be using her sheep and her cornfields as effectively as possible. Point *z* is not a point of *technological efficiency*. Jane can improve her situation at *z* by moving to a point such as *b* or *d* or to a point on the frontier between *b* and *d*, such as point *c*. Jane can have more of both goods on the frontier than at points inside it. At point *b*, she can consume more corn and no less cloth than at point *z*. At point *d*, she can consume more cloth and no less corn than at point *z*. At point *c*, she can consume more corn and more cloth than at point *z*. Jane will never choose inefficient points such as *z* because efficient points, such as *b, c* and *d*, are available to her. That is, Jane prefers some point on the frontier to a point inside it.

We have just seen that Jane wants to produce at some point on her production possibility frontier, but she is still faced with the problem of choosing her preferred point. In choosing between one point and another, Jane is confronted with opportunity costs. At point *c*, for example, she has less cloth and more corn than at point *d*. If she chooses point *d*, she does so because she figures that the extra cloth is worth the corn forgone. Let's go on to explore opportunity cost more closely and see how we can measure it.

REVIEW

T he production possibility frontier is the boundary between the attainable and the unattainable. There is always a point on the frontier that is preferred to any point inside it. But moving from one point on the frontier to another involves an opportunity cost – having less of one good to get more of another. ◆

Measuring Opportunity Cost

We've defined opportunity cost as the best alternative forgone: for a late sleeper, the opportunity cost of attending an early morning class is an hour in bed; for a jogger, it is an hour of exercise. The concept of opportunity cost can be made more precise by using a production possibility frontier such as the one shown in Fig. 3.1. Let's see what that curve tells us.

The Best Alternative Forgone

The production possibility frontier in Fig. 3.1 traces the boundary between attainable and unattainable combinations of corn and cloth. Since there are only two goods, there is no difficulty in working out what is the best alternative forgone. More corn can be grown only by paying the price of having less cloth, and more cloth can be made only by bearing the cost of having less corn. Thus the opportunity cost of an additional metre of cloth is the amount of corn forgone, and the opportunity cost of producing an additional kilogram of corn is the amount of cloth forgone. Let's put numerical values on the opportunity costs of corn and cloth.

Opportunity Cost Calculation

We are going to calculate Jane's opportunity cost by using her production possibility frontier. We will work out how much cloth Jane has to give up to get more corn and how much corn she has to give up to get more cloth.

If Jane uses all of her 10 hours to produce corn, she produces 20 kilograms of corn and no cloth, at point a on her production possibility frontier in Fig. 3.2. If she decides to produce 1 metre of cloth, how much corn does she have to give up? To produce 1 metre of cloth, Jane moves along her production possibility frontier from a to b and gives up 2 kilograms of corn. Thus the opportunity cost of the first metre of cloth is 2 kilograms of corn. If she decides to produce an additional metre of cloth, how much corn does she give up? This time, Jane moves from b to c and gives up 3 kilograms of corn to produce the second metre of cloth.

These opportunity costs are set out in the table of Fig. 3.2. The first two rows set out the opportu-

nity costs that we have just calculated. The table also lists the opportunity costs of moving from c to d, d to e, and e to f on Jane's production possibility frontier. You might want to work out another example to be sure that you understand what is going on. Calculate Jane's opportunity cost of moving from e to f.

Increasing Opportunity Cost

As you can see, opportunity cost varies with the quantity produced. The first metre of cloth costs 2 kilograms of corn. The next metre of cloth costs 3 kilograms of corn. The last metre of cloth costs 6 kilograms of corn. Thus the opportunity cost of cloth increases as Jane produces more cloth. Figure 3.2(b) illustrates the increasing opportunity cost of cloth.

The Shape of the Frontier

Pay special attention to the shape of the production possibility frontier in Fig. 3.1. When a large amount of corn and not much cloth is produced – between points a and b – the frontier has a gentle slope. When a large amount of cloth and not much corn is produced – between points e and f – the frontier is steep. The whole frontier bows outward. These features of the production possibility frontier are a reflection of increasing opportunity cost. You can see the connection between increasing opportunity cost and the shape of the production possibility frontier in Fig. 3.2(a). Between points a and b, 1 metre of cloth can be obtained by giving up a small amount of corn. Here the opportunity cost of cloth is low and the opportunity cost of corn is high. Between points e and f, a large amount of corn must be given up to produce 1 extra metre of cloth. In this region, the opportunity cost of cloth is high and the opportunity cost of corn is low.

Everything Has an Increasing Opportunity Cost

We've just worked out the opportunity cost of cloth. But what about the opportunity cost of corn? Does it also increase as more of it is produced? You can see the answer in Fig. 3.2. By giving up 1 metre of cloth to produce some corn, Jane moves from f to e and produces 6 kilograms of corn. Thus the opportunity cost of the first 6 kilograms of corn is 1 metre of

FIGURE 3.2

Jane's Opportunity Cost of Cloth

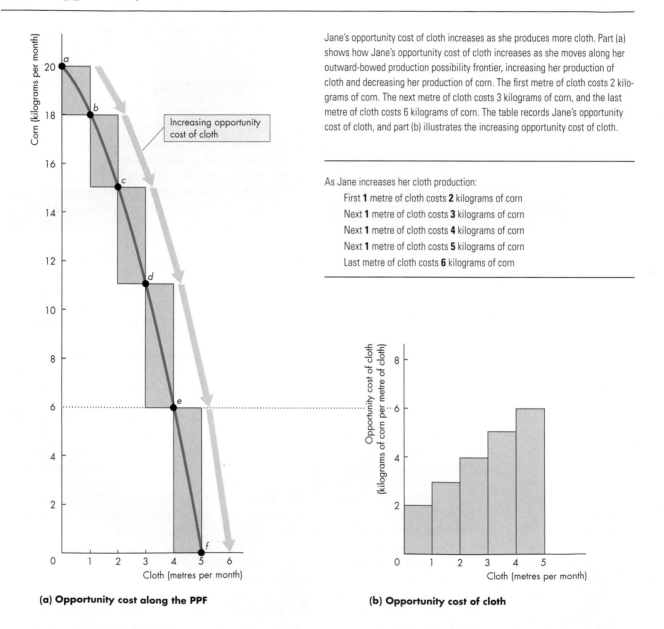

Jane's opportunity cost of cloth increases as she produces more cloth. Part (a) shows how Jane's opportunity cost of cloth increases as she moves along her outward-bowed production possibility frontier, increasing her production of cloth and decreasing her production of corn. The first metre of cloth costs 2 kilograms of corn. The next metre of cloth costs 3 kilograms of corn, and the last metre of cloth costs 6 kilograms of corn. The table records Jane's opportunity cost of cloth, and part (b) illustrates the increasing opportunity cost of cloth.

As Jane increases her cloth production:

First **1** metre of cloth costs **2** kilograms of corn
Next **1** metre of cloth costs **3** kilograms of corn
Next **1** metre of cloth costs **4** kilograms of corn
Next **1** metre of cloth costs **5** kilograms of corn
Last metre of cloth costs **6** kilograms of corn

(a) Opportunity cost along the PPF

(b) Opportunity cost of cloth

cloth. Moving from e to d, you can see that the next 5 kilograms of corn cost 1 metre of cloth. Thus the opportunity cost of corn also increases as Jane makes more corn.

Increasing opportunity cost and the outward bow of the production possibility frontier arise from the fact that scarce resources are not equally useful in all activities. For instance, some of the land on Jane's island is extremely fertile and produces a high crop yield, while other land is rocky and barren. The sheep on the island, however, prefer the rocky, barren land.

Jane uses the most fertile land for growing corn and the most barren areas for raising sheep. Only if she wants a larger amount of corn does she try to cultivate relatively barren areas. If she uses all her time to grow corn, she has to use some very unsuitable, low-yielding land. Devoting some time to making cloth, and reducing the time spent growing corn by the same amount, produces a small drop in corn production but a large increase in the output of cloth. Conversely, if Jane uses all her time to make cloth, a small reduction in the amount of time spent raising sheep yields a large increase in corn production.

Production Possibilities in the Real World

Jane's island is dramatically different from the world that we live in. The fundamental lesson it teaches us, however, applies to the real world. The world has a fixed number of people endowed with a given amount of human capital and limited time. The world also has a fixed amount of land and capital equipment. These limited resources can be employed, using the available but limited technology to produce goods and services. But there is a limit to the goods and services that can be produced, a boundary between what is attainable and what is not attainable. That boundary is the real-world economy's production possibility frontier. On that frontier, producing more of any one good requires producing less of some other good or goods.

For example, if the government makes available more child care services, it must at the same time cut the scale of spending on other programmes, increase taxes or borrow more. Higher taxes and more government borrowing mean less money left over for holidays and other consumption goods and services. The cost of more child care services is less of other goods. On a smaller scale but equally important, each time you decide to rent a video you decide not to use your limited income to buy pizza, chocolates, or some other good. The cost of one more video is one less of something else.

On Jane's island, we saw that the opportunity cost of a good increased as the output of the good

increased. Opportunity costs in the real world increase for the same reasons that Jane's opportunity costs increase. Consider, for example, two goods vital to our well-being: food and health care. In allocating our scarce resources, we use the most fertile land and the most skilful farmers to produce food. We use the best doctors and the least fertile land for health care. If we shift fertile land and tractors away from farming and ask farmers to do surgery, the production of food drops drastically and the increase in the production of health care services is small. The opportunity cost of health care services rises. Similarly, if we shift our resources away from health care towards farming, we have to use more doctors and nurses as farmers and more hospitals as hydroponic tomato factories. The drop in health care services is large, but the increase in food production small. The opportunity cost of producing more food rises.

This example is extreme and unlikely, but these same considerations apply to any pair of goods that you can imagine: guns and butter, housing for the needy and Rolls-Royces for the rich, wheelchairs and golf clubs, television programmes and breakfast cereals. We cannot escape from scarcity and opportunity cost. Given our limited resources, more of one thing always means less of something else, and the more of anything that we have or do, the higher is its opportunity cost. Reading Between the Lines on pp. 66–67 shows how opportunity cost relates to everyday household activities.

REVIEW

O pportunity cost is the value of the best alternative forgone. It is measured along the production possibility frontier by calculating the number of units of one good that must be given up to obtain one more unit of the other good. The production possibility frontier is bowed outward because not all resources are equally useful for producing all goods. The most useful resources are employed first. Because the frontier is bowed outward, the opportunity cost of each good increases as more of it is produced. ◆

Economic Growth

Although the production possibility frontier defines the boundary between what is attainable and what is unattainable, that boundary is not static. It is constantly changing. Sometimes the production possibility frontier shifts *inward*, reducing our production possibilities. For example, droughts or other extreme climatic conditions shift the frontier inward. Sometimes the frontier moves outward. For example, excellent growing and harvest conditions have this effect. Sometimes the frontier shifts outward because we have a new idea. It suddenly occurs to us that there is a better way of doing something that we never before imagined possible – we invent the wheel.

Over the years, our production possibilities have undergone enormous expansion. The expansion of our production possibilities is called **economic growth**. As a consequence of economic growth, we can now produce much more than we could a hundred years ago and quite a bit more than even ten years ago. By the late 1990s, if the same pace of growth continues, our production possibilities will be even greater. By pushing out the frontier, can we avoid the constraints imposed on us by our limited resources? That is, can we get our free lunch after all?

The Cost of Shifting the Frontier

We are going to discover that although we can and do shift the production possibility frontier outward over time, we cannot have economic growth without incurring costs. The faster the pace of economic growth, the less we can consume at the present time. Let's investigate the costs of growth by examining why economies grow and prosper.

Two key activities generate economic growth: capital accumulation and technological progress. **Capital accumulation** is the growth of capital resources. **Technological progress** is the development of new and better ways of producing goods and services. As a consequence of capital accumulation and technological progress, we have an enormous quantity of cars and aircraft that enable us to produce more transport than when we had only horses and carriages; we have satellites that make transcontinental communications possible on a scale much larger than that produced by the ear-

lier cable technology. But accumulating capital and developing new technology is costly. To see why, let's go back to Jane's island economy.

Capital Accumulation and Technological Change

So far, we've assumed that Jane's island economy can produce only two goods, corn and cloth. But let's now suppose that while pursuing some of the sheep, Jane stumbled upon an outcrop of flint and a forest that she had not known about before. She realizes that she can now make some flint tools and start building fences around the corn and sheep, thereby increasing production of both of these goods. But to make tools and build fences, Jane has to devote time to these activities. Let's continue to suppose that there are only 10 hours of working time available each day. Time spent making tools and building fences is time that could have been spent growing corn and making cloth. Thus to expand her future production, Jane must produce less corn and cloth today so that some of her time can be devoted to making tools and building fences. The decrease in her output of corn and cloth today is the opportunity cost of expanding her production of these two goods in the future.

Figure 3.3 provides a concrete example. The table sets out Jane's production possibilities for producing capital – tools and fences – as well as current consumption goods – corn and cloth. If she devotes all her working hours to corn and cloth production (row *e*), she produces no capital – no tools or fences. If she devotes enough time to producing one unit of capital each month (row *d*), her corn and cloth production is cut back to 90 per cent of its maximum possible level. She can devote still more time to capital accumulation and, as she does so, her corn and cloth production falls by successively larger amounts.

The numbers in the table are graphed in Fig. 3.3. Each point, *a* to *e*, represents a row of the table. Notice the similarity between Fig. 3.3 and Fig. 3.1. Each shows a production possibility frontier. In the case of Fig. 3.3, the frontier is that between producing capital equipment – tools and fences – and producing current consumption goods – corn and cloth. If Jane produces at point *e* in Fig. 3.3, she produces no capital goods and remains stuck on the production possibility frontier for corn and cloth shown in Fig. 3.1. But if she

FIGURE 3.3

Economic Growth on Jane's Island

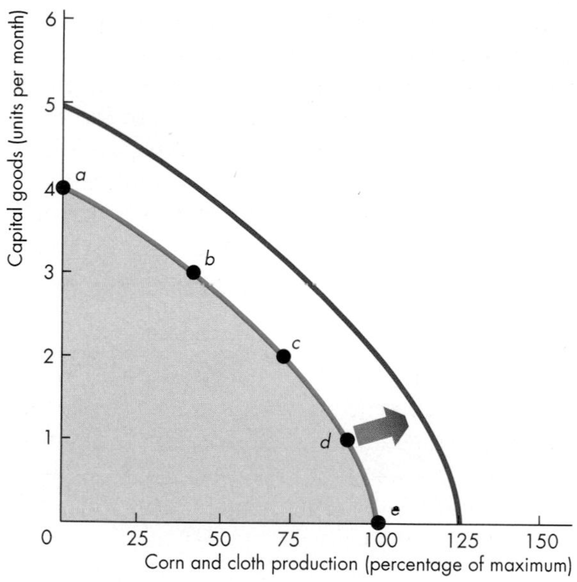

Possibility	Capital (units per month)	Corn and cloth (production per cent of maximum)
a	4	0
b	3	40
c	2	70
d	1	90
e	0	100

If Jane devotes all her time to corn and cloth production, she produces no capital equipment (row *e* of the table). If she devotes more time to capital accumulation, she produces successively smaller amounts of corn and cloth. The curve *abcde* is Jane's production possibility frontier for capital and consumption goods (tools and fences versus corn and cloth). If Jane produces no capital (point *e*), her production possibility frontier remains fixed at *abcde*. If she cuts her current production of corn and cloth and produces one unit of capital (point *d*), her future production possibility frontier lies outside her current frontier. The more time Jane devotes to accumulating capital and the less to producing corn and cloth, the farther out her frontier shifts. The decreased output of corn and cloth is the opportunity cost of increased future production possibilities.

moves to point *d* in Fig. 3.3, she can produce one unit of capital each month. To do so, Jane reduces her current production of corn and cloth to 90 per cent of what she can produce if all her time is devoted to those activities. In terms of Fig. 3.1, Jane's current production possibility frontier for corn and cloth shifts to the left as less time is devoted to corn and cloth production and some of her time is devoted to producing capital goods.

By decreasing her production of corn and cloth and producing tools and building fences, Jane is able to increase her future production possibilities. An increasing stock of tools and fences make her more productive at growing corn and producing cloth. She can even use tools to make better tools. As a consequence, Jane's production possibility frontier shifts outward as shown by the shift

arrow in Fig. 3.3. Jane experiences economic growth.

But the amount by which Jane's production possibility frontier shifts out depends on how much time she devotes to accumulating capital. If she devotes no time to this activity, the frontier remains at *abcde* – the original production possibility frontier. If she cuts back on current production of corn and cloth and produces one unit of capital each month (point *d*), her frontier moves out in the future to the position shown by the red curve in Fig. 3.3. The less time she devotes to corn and cloth production and the more time to capital accumulation, the farther out the frontier shifts.

But economic growth is not a free gift for Jane. To make it happen, she has to devote more time to producing tools and building fences and less to producing corn and cloth. Economic growth is no magic formula for abolishing scarcity.

Economic Growth in the Real World

The ideas that we have explored in the setting of Jane's island also apply to our real-world economy. If we devote all our resources to producing food, clothing, housing, holidays and the many other consumer goods that we enjoy, and none to research, development and accumulating capital, we will have no more capital and no better technologies in the future than we have at present.

Our production possibilities in the future will be exactly the same as those we have today. If we are to expand our production possibilities in the future, we must produce fewer consumption goods today. The resources that we free up today will enable us to accumulate capital and to develop better technologies for producing consumption goods in the future. The cut in the output of consumption goods today is the opportunity cost of economic growth.

The recent experience of the European Union and Japan provides a striking example of the effects of our choices on the rate of economic growth. In 1965, the production possibilities per person in the European Union (which was then

---

FIGURE 3.4

Economic Growth in Europe and Japan

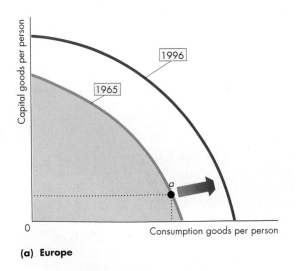

(a) Europe

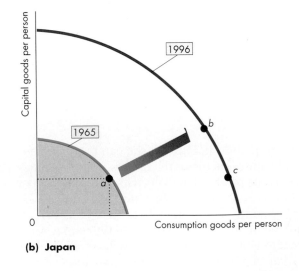

(b) Japan

In 1965, the production possibilities per person in the European Union (which was then the EEC), part (a), were much larger than those in Japan, part (b). But Japan devoted one-third of its resources to producing capital goods, while the European Union devoted only one-fifth – point *a* in each part of the figure. Japan's more rapid increase in capital resources resulted in its production possibility frontier shifting out more quickly than that of the European Union. The two production possibilities per person in 1996 are similar to each other. If Japan produces at point *b* on its 1996 frontier, it will continue to grow more quickly than the European Union. If Japan increases consumption and produces at point *c* on its 1996 frontier, its growth rate will slow down to that of the European Union.

the EEC) were much larger than those in Japan (see Fig. 3.4). The European Union devoted one-fifth of its resources to producing capital goods and the other four-fifths to producing consumption goods, as illustrated by point *a* in Fig. 3.4(a). But Japan devoted one-third of its resources to producing capital goods and only two-thirds to producing consumption goods, as illustrated by point *a* in Fig. 3.4(b). Both the European Union and Japan experienced economic growth, but the growth in Japan was much more rapid than the growth in the European Union. Because Japan devoted a bigger fraction of its resources to producing capital goods, its stock of capital equipment grew more quickly, and its production possibilities expanded more quickly. As a result, Japanese production possibilities per person are now so close to those in the European Union that it is hard to say which has the larger per person production possibilities. If Japan continues to devote one-third of its resources to producing capital goods (at point *b* on its 1996 production possibility frontier), it will continue to grow much more rapidly and its frontier will move out beyond that of the European Union. If Japan increases its production of consumption goods and reduces its production of capital goods (moving to point *c* on its 1996 production possibility frontier), then its rate of economic expansion will slow down to that of the European Union.

R E V I E W

Economic growth results from the accumulation of capital and the development of better technologies. To reap the fruits of economic growth, we must incur the cost of fewer goods and services for current consumption. By cutting the current output of consumption goods, we can devote more resources to accumulating capital and to the research and development that lead to technological change – the engines of economic growth. Thus economic growth does not provide a free lunch. It has an opportunity cost – the fall in the current output of consumption goods. ◆

The Gains From Trade

No one excels at everything. One person is more athletic than another; another person may have a quicker mind or a better memory. What one person does with ease, someone else may find difficult.

Comparative Advantage: Jane Meets Joe

Differences in individual abilities mean that there are also differences in individual opportunity costs of producing various goods. Such differences give rise to **comparative advantage** – we say that a person has a comparative advantage in producing a particular good if that person can produce the good at a lower opportunity cost than anyone else.

People can produce for themselves all the goods that they consume or they can concentrate on producing one good (or perhaps a few goods) and then exchange some of their own products for the output of others. Concentrating on the production of only one good or a few goods is called **specialization**. We are going to discover how people can gain by specializing in that good at which they have a comparative advantage and trading their output with others.

Let's return again to our island economy. Suppose that Jane has discovered another island very close to her own and that it too has only one inhabitant – Joe. Jane and Joe each have access to a simple boat that is adequate for transporting themselves and their goods between the two islands.

Joe's island, too, can produce only corn and cloth, but its terrain differs from that on Jane's island. While Jane's island has a lot of fertile corn-growing land and a small sheep population, Joe's island has little fertile corn-growing land and plenty of hilly land and sheep. This important difference between the two islands means that Joe's production possibility frontier is different from Jane's. Figure 3.5 illustrates these production possibility frontiers. Jane's frontier is labelled 'Jane's PPF', and Joe's frontier is labelled 'Joe's PPF'.

Jane and Joe can be self-sufficient in corn and cloth. **Self-sufficiency** is a situation in which people produce only enough for their own consumption. Suppose that Jane and Joe are each self-sufficient. Jane chooses to produce and consume 3 metres of

FIGURE 3.5

The Gains from Specialization and Exchange

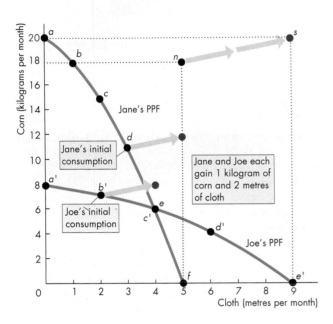

When Jane and Joe are self-sufficient, Joe consumes 7 kilograms of corn and 2 metres of cloth (point *b'*), and Jane consumes 11 kilograms of corn and 3 metres of cloth (point *d*). Their total production is 18 kilograms of corn and 5 metres of cloth (point *n*). Joe and Jane can do better by specialization and exchange. Jane, whose comparative advantage is in corn production, specializes in that activity, producing 20 kilograms a month (point *a*). Joe, whose comparative advantage is in cloth production, specializes in that activity, producing 9 metres of cloth a month (point *e'*). Total production is then 20 kilograms of corn and 9 metres of cloth (point *s*). If Jane gives Joe 8 kilograms of corn in exchange for 5 metres of cloth, they each enjoy increased consumption of both corn and cloth. They each gain from specialization and exchange.

cloth and 11 kilograms of corn a month, point *d*. Joe chooses to produce and consume 2 metres of cloth and 7 kilograms of corn a month, point *b'*. These choices are identified on their respective production possibility frontiers in Fig. 3.5. (Each could have chosen any other point on their own

production possibility frontier.) Total production of corn and cloth is the sum of Jane's and Joe's production: 18 kilograms of corn and 5 metres of cloth. Point *n* in the figure represents this total production.

Jane's Comparative Advantage In which of the two goods does Jane have a comparative advantage? We have defined comparative advantage as a situation in which one person's opportunity cost of producing a good is lower than another person's opportunity cost of producing that same good. Jane, then, has a comparative advantage in producing whichever good she produces at a lower opportunity cost than Joe. What is that good?

You can answer the question by looking at the production possibility frontiers for Jane and Joe in Fig. 3.5. At the points at which they are producing and consuming, Jane's production possibility frontier is much steeper than Joe's. To produce one more kilogram of corn, Jane gives up less cloth than Joe. Hence Jane's opportunity cost of a kilogram of corn is lower than Joe's. This means that Jane has a comparative advantage in producing corn.

Joe's Comparative Advantage Joe's comparative advantage is in producing cloth. His production possibility frontier at his consumption point is flatter than Jane's. This means that Joe has to give up less corn to produce one more metre of cloth than Jane does. Joe's opportunity cost of a metre of cloth is lower than Jane's, so Joe has a comparative advantage in cloth production.

Achieving the Gains from Trade

Can Jane and Joe do better than be self-sufficient? In particular, what would happen if each were to specialize in producing the good at which each has a comparative advantage and then trade with the other?

If Jane, who has a comparative advantage in corn production, puts all her time into growing corn, she can grow 20 kilograms. If Joe, who has a comparative advantage in cloth production, puts all his time into making cloth, he can make 9 metres. By specializing, Jane and Joe together can produce 20 kilograms of corn and 9 metres of cloth (the amount labelled *s* in the figure). Point *s* shows the production of 20 kilograms of corn (all produced by Jane) and 9 metres of cloth (all produced by Joe). Clearly, Jane and Joe produce more cloth and corn at point s than they were producing at point n, when each took care only of his or her own requirements. Jane and Joe prefer point s to point n because, between them, they have more of both corn and cloth at point s than at point n. They have an additional 2 kilograms of corn and 4 metres of cloth.

To obtain the gains from trade, Jane and Joe must do more than specialize in producing the good at which each has a comparative advantage. They must exchange the fruits of their specialized production. Suppose that Jane and Joe agree to exchange 5 metres of cloth for 8 kilograms of corn. Jane has 20 kilograms of corn and Joe has 9 metres of cloth before any exchange takes place. After the exchange takes place, Joe consumes 8 kilograms of corn and Jane 12 kilograms of corn; Joe consumes 4 metres of cloth and Jane 5 metres of cloth. Compared to the time when they were each self-sufficient, Jane now has 1 extra kilogram of corn and 2 extra metres of cloth, and Joe has 1 extra kilogram of corn and 2 extra metres of cloth. The gains from trade are represented by the increase in consumption of both goods that each obtains. Each consumes at a point outside their individual production possibility frontier.

Productivity and Absolute Advantage

Productivity is defined as the amount of output produced per unit of inputs used to produce it. For example, Jane's productivity in making cloth is measured as the amount of cloth she makes per hour of work. If one person has greater productivity than another in the production of all goods, that person is said to have an **absolute advantage**. In our example, neither Jane nor Joe has an absolute advantage. Jane is more productive than Joe in growing corn, and Joe is more productive than Jane in making cloth.

It is often suggested that people and countries that have an absolute advantage can outcompete others in the production of all goods. For example, it is often suggested that the European Union cannot compete with Japan because the Japanese are more productive. This conclusion is wrong, as you are just about to discover. To see why, let's look again at Jane and Joe.

Suppose that a volcano engulfs Jane's island, forcing her to search for a new one. And suppose

TABLE 3.2

Jane's New Production Possibilities

Possibility	Corn (kilograms per month)	Cloth (metres per month)
a	40	0
b	36	2
c	30	4
d	22	6
e	12	8
f	0	10

further that disaster leads to good fortune. Jane stumbles onto a new island that is much more productive than the original one, enabling her to produce twice as much of either corn or cloth with each hour of her labour. Jane's new production possibilities appear in Table 3.2. Notice that she now has an absolute advantage.

We have already worked out that the gains from trade arise when each person specializes in producing the good in which he or she has a comparative advantage. Recall that a person has a comparative advantage in producing a particular good if that person can produce it at a lower opportunity cost than anyone else. Joe's opportunity costs remain exactly the same as they were before. What has happened to Jane's opportunity costs now that she has become twice as productive?

You can work out Jane's opportunity costs by using exactly the same calculation that was used in the table of Fig. 3.2. Start by looking at Jane's opportunity cost of corn. The first 12 kilograms of corn that Jane grows cost her 2 metres of cloth. So the opportunity cost of 1 kilogram of corn is ⅙ of a metre of cloth – the same as Jane's original opportunity cost of corn. If you calculate the opportunity costs for Jane's production possibilities a to f, you will discover that each of them has remained the same.

Since the opportunity cost of cloth is the inverse of the opportunity cost of corn, Jane's opportunity costs of cloth also have remained unchanged. Let's work through one example. If Jane moves from *a* to *b* to make 2 metres of cloth, she will have to reduce her corn production by 4 kilograms – from 40 to 36 kilograms. Thus the first 2 metres of cloth cost 4 kilograms of corn. The cost of 1 metre of cloth is therefore 2 kilograms of corn – exactly the same as before.

When Jane becomes twice as productive as before, each hour of her time produces more output, but her opportunity costs remain the same. One more unit of corn costs the same in terms of cloth forgone as it did previously. Since Jane's opportunity costs have not changed and since Joe's have not changed, Joe continues to have a comparative advantage in producing cloth. Both Jane and Joe can have more of both goods if Jane specializes in corn production and Joe in cloth production.

The key point to recognize is that it is *not* possible for a person having an absolute advantage to have a comparative advantage in everything.

REVIEW

G ains from trade come from comparative advantage. A person has a comparative advantage in producing a good if that person can produce the good at a lower opportunity cost than anyone else. Thus differences in opportunity cost are the source of gains from specialization and exchange. Each person specializes in producing the good at which they have a comparative advantage and then exchanges some of that output for the goods produced by others. ◆ ◆ If a person can produce a good with fewer inputs than someone else – is more productive – that person has an absolute advantage but not necessarily a comparative advantage. Even a person with an absolute advantage gains from specialization and exchange. ◆

Specialization and Exchange in the World Economy

I n the real world, countries can gain by specializing in the production of those goods and services at which they have a comparative advantage. But to obtain the gains from trade in the real world, where billions of people specialize in millions of different activities, trade has to be organized. To organize trade, we have evolved rules of conduct and mechanisms for enforcing those rules. One such mechanism is property rights. Another is the institution of money. In the island economy of Jane and Joe, direct exchange of one good for another is feasible. In the real-world economy, direct exchange of one good for another would be very cumbersome. To lubricate the wheels of exchange, societies have created money – a medium that enables indirect exchange of goods for money and money for goods. Let's examine these two aspects of exchange arrangements in more detail.

Property Rights

Property rights are social arrangements that govern the ownership, use and disposal of property. **Property** is anything of value: it includes land and buildings – the things we call property in ordinary speech; it also includes stocks and bonds, durable goods, plant and equipment; it also includes intellectual property. **Intellectual property** is the intangible product of creative effort, protected by copyrights and patents. This type of property includes books, music, computer programs and inventions of all kinds.

What if property rights did not exist? What would such a social science fiction world be like?

A World Without Property Rights Without property rights, people could take possession of whatever they had the strength to obtain for themselves. In such a world, people would have to devote a good deal of their time, energy and resources to protecting what they had produced or acquired.

In a world without property rights, it would not be possible to reap all the gains from specialization and exchange. People would have little incentive to specialize in producing those goods at which they each had a comparative advantage. In fact, the more of a particular good someone produced, the bigger the chance that others would simply help themselves to it. Also, if a person could take the goods of others without giving up something in exchange, then there would be no point in specializing in producing something for exchange. In a world without property rights, no one would enjoy the gains from specialization and exchange, and everyone would specialize only in unproductive acts of piracy.

It is to overcome the problems that we have just described that property rights have evolved. Let's examine these property rights as they operate to govern economic life in the United Kingdom today.

Property Rights in Private Enterprise Capitalism

The UK economy operates for the most part on the principles of private enterprise capitalism. **Private enterprise** is an economic system that permits individuals to decide on their own economic activities. **Capitalism** is an economic system that permits private individuals to own the capital resources used in production.

Under the property rights in such an economic system, individuals own what they have made, what they have acquired in a voluntary exchange with others, and what they have been given. Any attempt to remove the property of someone against that person's will is considered theft, a crime punished by a sufficiently severe penalty to deter most people from becoming thieves.

It is easy to see that property rights based on these ideas can generate gainful trade: people can specialize in producing those goods that, for them, have the least opportunity cost. Some people will specialize in enforcing and maintaining property rights (for example, politicians, judges and police officers) and all individuals will have the incentive to trade with each other, offering the good in which they have a comparative advantage in exchange for the goods produced by others.

The UK economic system is based on private property rights and voluntary exchange. But there are important ways in which private property rights are modified in the United Kingdom.

Taxes Modify Private Property Rights

Taxes on expenditure, income and wealth transfer property from individuals to governments. Such transfers limit people's efforts to create more property and reduce their gains from specialization and exchange.

But the taxes themselves are not arbitrary. Everyone faces the same rules and can calculate the effects of their own actions on the taxes for which they will be liable.

Regulation Modifies Private Property Rights

Some voluntary exchanges are prohibited or regulated. For example, food and drug manufacturers cannot place a product on the market without first obtaining approval from a government agency. The government controls or prohibits the sale of many types of drugs, and also restricts trading in human beings and their component parts – that is, it prohibits the selling of slaves, children and human organs.

These restrictions on the extent of private property and on the legitimacy of voluntary exchange, though important, do not, for the most part, seriously impede specialization and gainful trade. Most people take the view that the benefits of regulation – for example, prohibiting the sale of dangerous drugs – far outweigh the costs imposed on the sellers.

Let's now turn to the other social institution that permits specialization and exchange – the development of an efficient means of exchange.

Money

We have seen that well-defined property rights based on voluntary exchange allow individuals to specialize and exchange their output with each other. In our island economy, we studied only two people and two goods. Exchange in such a situation was a simple matter. In the real world, however, how can billions of people exchange the millions of goods that are the fruits of their specialized labour?

Barter   Goods can be simply exchanged for goods. The direct exchange of one good for another is known as **barter**. However, barter severely limits the amount of trading that can take place. Imagine that you have roosters, but you want roses. First, you must look for someone with roses who wants roosters. Economists call this a *double coincidence of wants* – when person A wants to sell exactly what person B wants to buy, and person B wants to sell exactly what person A wants to buy. As the term implies, such occurrences are coincidences and will not arise frequently. A second way of trading by barter is to undertake a sequence of exchanges. If you have oranges and you want apples, you might have to trade oranges for plums, plums for pome-

The Opportunity Cost of a Wife

THE TIMES, 3 MARCH 1993

Wives are valued at £349 a week

Lindsay Cook, Money Editor

THE value of a wife and mother has almost doubled to £349 a week in the past 12 years, according to Legal & General, the life insurance company. That is the amount it would cost to replace a wife with paid cooks, child carers, cleaners, gardeners and chauffeurs. In 1981 the company put the price of a wife at £204 a week.

At £18,150 a year, the cost of replacing a wife is more than what three-quarters of the working population receives in wages. For the mother with a child under one, her efforts would cost £457 a week or £23,764 a year, Legal & General says, because of the extra hours of child care.

Legal & General says that the unpaid work done by women with dependent children contributes £100 billion a year to the economy. It says that housewives spend an average 71 hours a week on domestic chores and a woman with a part-time job still works an average 59 hours at home. Even those with a full-time job have an average domestic working week of 49 hours. Those with children aged under one spend 90 hours a week working at home.

The average housewife spends 17.9 hours a week as a nanny, which would cost £5.90 an hour if replaced by a professional, she cooks for 12.2 hours (£5.35 an hour replacement cost), cleaning 12.2 hours (£5.35), laundry 9.3 hours (£3.80), dishwashing without a machine 5.7 hours (£3.80), driving children about 2.6 hours (£4.50), gardening one hour and 24 minutes a week (£5.90), sewing 1.7 hours (£3.60).

The company surveyed 1,001 women, 47 per cent of whom were housewives, 35 per cent worked part time and 18 per cent full time.

Helen Matthews, Legal & General's life and pensions marketing controller, said: 'It is easy to underestimate the contribution that women make to the family economy. Very few working fathers could bring up a family without paid help, especially if the children are young.'

© The Times. Reprinted with permission.

The life insurance company Legal & General has estimated that if wives were not to perform any of the domestic activities they currently do, it would cost an average of £349 per week to pay specialists to carry out each activity.

This amount is based on hourly rates of pay for professionals carrying out such tasks as cleaning, cooking, gardening and so on.

The survey finds that even when wives have a job (part-time or full-time), they still spend considerable periods each week carrying out these activities.

The economic activities of a wife do not have a direct money value as she does not get paid for what she does.

In order to try and estimate this value, the study found out what the average housewife does each week and compared this with the cost of buying in specialists to carry out each task.

The survey reveals that even when wives work they still spend some time doing household tasks, so that taking on a part-time job means only 12 hours less are spent on domestic tasks, and a full-time job only 22 hours less.

If we assume the figures presented are correct and all embracing, then so long as the wife earns less than £3.60 an hour, she should not work, but specialize in domestic production instead.

If, however, she earns over £5.90 per hour, she should enter the labour market and hire domestic help. If her earnings are between £3.60 and £5.90 an hour, she could enter the labour market, but still carry out the higher cost domestic tasks herself.

In reality, however, there are a number of factors that mean the figures are probably incomplete.

The mother will derive a direct utility from being with and bringing up her children, rather than paying someone to do it for her (although she may of course be willing to share this task with her husband!).

There may be an emotional and intellectual benefit to the children from being brought up by their parents rather than a nanny or baby-sitter. The mother may derive benefit indirectly from this.

Activities such as gardening, sewing and cooking are, for many people, hobbies rather than domestic chores, from which utility is derived.

The analysis also overlooks the transaction costs associated with a large number of economic transactions. For example, 5.7 hours spent dishwashing each week averages out at about 50 minutes per day. The family may therefore consider it easier to do such tasks themselves rather than buy in somebody for such a short period each day.

The figure illustrates the trade-off faced by a wife between paid work and leisure time, out of which is taken time to perform domestic tasks.

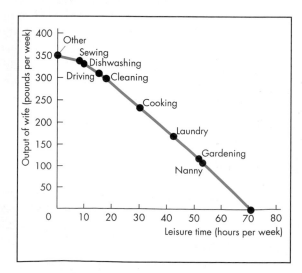

granates, pomegranates for pineapples and then eventually pineapples for apples.

Cumbersome though it is, quite a large amount of barter trade does take place. For example, when British rock star Rod Stewart played in Budapest, Hungary, in 1986, he received part of his £20,000 compensation in Hungarian sound equipment, electrical cable and the use of a fork-lift truck. And before the recent changes in Eastern Europe, hairdressers in Warsaw, Poland, obtained their barbershop equipment from England in exchange for hair clippings that they supplied to London wigmakers.

Although barter exchange does occur, it is an inefficient means of exchanging goods. Fortunately, a better alternative has been invented.

Monetary Exchange An alternative to barter is **monetary exchange** – a system in which some commodity or token serves as the medium of exchange. A **medium of exchange** is anything that is generally acceptable in exchange for goods and services. **Money** can also be defined as a medium of exchange – something that can be passed on to others in exchange for goods and services.

Money lowers the cost of transacting and makes millions of transactions possible that simply would not be worth undertaking by barter. Can you imagine the chain of barter transactions you'd have to go through every day to get your coffee, sandwiches, textbooks, professor's time, video and all the other goods and services you consume? In a monetary exchange system, you exchange your time and effort for money and use that money to buy the goods and services you consume, cutting out the incredible hassle you'd face each day in a world of barter.

Metals such as gold, silver and copper have long served as money. Most commonly, they serve as money by being stamped as coins. Primitive societies have traditionally used various commodities, such as seashells, as money. During the American Civil War and for several years after, people used postage stamps as money. Prisoners of war in German camps in World War II used cigarettes as money. But don't confuse cigarettes as a medium of exchange with barter. When cigarettes play the role of money, people buy and sell goods by using cigarettes as a medium of exchange.

In modern societies, governments provide paper money. The banking system also provides money in the form of current accounts. Current accounts can be used for settling debts simply by writing an instruction – writing a cheque – to the bank requesting that funds be transferred to another current account. Electronic links between bank accounts, now becoming more widespread, enable direct transfers between different accounts without any cheques being written.

◆ ◆ ◆ ◆ You have now begun to see how economists go about the job of trying to answer some important questions. The simple fact of scarcity and the associated concept of opportunity cost allow us to understand why people specialize, why they trade with each other, why they have social conventions that define and enforce private property rights, and why they use money. One simple idea – scarcity and its direct implication, opportunity cost – explains so much!

SUMMARY

The Production Possibility Frontier

The production possibility frontier is the boundary between what is attainable and what is not attainable. Production can take place at any point inside or on the production possibility frontier, but it is not possible to produce outside the frontier. There is always a point on the production possibility frontier that is better than a point inside it. (pp. 52–54)

Measuring Opportunity Cost

The opportunity cost of any action is the best alternative action forgone. The opportunity cost of acquiring one good is equivalent to the amount of another good that must be given up. The opportunity cost of a good increases as the quantity of it produced increases. (pp. 55–58)

Economic Growth

Although the production possibility frontier marks the boundary between the attainable and the unattainable, that boundary does not remain fixed. It changes over time, partly because of natural forces (for example, changes in climate and the accumulation of ideas about better ways of producing) and partly by the choices that we make (choices about consumption and saving). If we use some of today's resources to produce capital goods and for research and development, we will be able to produce more goods and services in the future. The economy will grow. But growth cannot take place without incurring costs. The opportunity cost of more goods and services in the future is consuming fewer goods and services today. (pp. 58–61)

Gains From Trade

A person has a comparative advantage in producing a good if that person can produce the good at a lower opportunity cost than anyone else. People can gain from trade if they each specialize in the activity at which they have a comparative advantage. Each person produces the good for which his or her opportunity cost is lower than everyone else's. They then exchange part of their output with each other. By this activity, each person is able to consume at a point *outside* his or her individual production possibility frontier.

When a person is more productive than another person – is able to produce more output from fewer inputs – that person has an absolute advantage. But having an absolute advantage does not mean there are no gains from trade. Even if someone is more productive than other people in all activities, so long as the other person has a lower opportunity cost of some good, then gains from specialization and exchange are available. (pp. 61–64)

Specialization and Exchange in the World Economy

Exchange in the real world involves the specialization of billions of people in millions of different activities. To make it worth while for each individual to specialize and to enable societies to reap the gains from trade, institutions and mechanisms have evolved. The most important of these are property rights, with a political and legal system to enforce them, and a system of monetary exchange. These institutions enable people to specialize, exchanging their labour for money and their money for goods, thereby reaping the gains from trade. (pp. 64–68)

K E Y   E L E M E N T S

Key Terms

Key Figures

R E V I E W   Q U E S T I O N S

1 How does the production possibility frontier illustrate scarcity?

2 How does the production possibility curve illustrate opportunity cost?

3 Explain what shifts the production possibility frontier outward and what shifts it inward.

4 Explain how our choices influence economic growth. What is the cost of economic growth?

5 Why does it pay people to specialize and trade with each other?

6 What are the gains from trade? How do they arise?

7 Why do social arrangements such as property rights and money become necessary?

8 What is money? Give some examples of money. In the late 1980s, people in Romania could use Kent cigarettes to buy almost anything. Was this monetary exchange or barter? Explain your answer.

9 What are the advantages of monetary exchange over barter?

P R O B L E M S

1 Suppose that there is a change in the weather conditions on Jane's island that makes the corn yields much higher. This enables Jane to produce the following amounts of corn:

Hours worked (per day)	Corn (kilograms per month)
0	0
2	60
4	100
6	120
8	130
10	140

Her cloth production possibilities are the same as those that appeared in Table 3.1.

a What are six points on Jane's new production possibility frontier?

b What are Jane's opportunity costs of corn and cloth? List them at each of the five levels of output.

c Compare Jane's opportunity cost of cloth with that in the table in Fig. 3.2. Has her opportunity cost of cloth gone up, down or remained the same? Explain why.

2 Amy lives with her parents and attends the local university. The university is operated by the government, and tuition is free. Jobs that pay £5 an hour are available in the town. Amy's mother takes a part-time job so that Amy can go to university. Amy's textbooks cost £140, and Amy gets an allowance of £40 a month from her mother. List the items that make up the opportunity cost of Amy attending the university.

3 Suppose that Leisureland produces only two goods – food and suntan oil. Its production possibilities are:

Food (kilograms per month)		Suntan oil (litres per month)
300	and	0
200	and	50
100	and	100
0	and	150

Busyland also produces only food and suntan oil, and its production possibilities are:

Food (kilograms per month)		Suntan oil (litres per month)
150	and	0
100	and	100
50	and	200
0	and	300

a What are the opportunity costs of food and suntan oil in Leisureland? List them at each output given in the table.

b Why are the opportunity costs the same at each output level?

c What are the opportunity costs of food and suntan oil in Busyland? List them at each output level given in the table.

4 Suppose that in Problem 3 Leisureland and Busyland do not specialize and trade with each other – each country is self-sufficient.

Leisureland produces and consumes 50 kilograms of food and 125 litres of suntan oil per month. Busyland produces and consumes 150 kilograms of food per month and no suntan oil. The countries begin to trade with each other.

a What good does Leisureland export, and what good does it import?

b What good does Busyland export, and what good does it import?

c What is the maximum quantity of food and suntan oil that the two countries can produce if each country specializes in the activity at which it has the lower opportunity cost.

5 Suppose that Busyland becomes three times as productive as in Problem 3.

a Show, on a graph, the effect of the increased productivity on Busyland's production possibility frontier.

b Does Busyland now have an absolute advantage in producing both goods?

c Can Busyland gain from specialization and trade with Leisureland now that it is three times as productive? If so, what will it produce?

d What are the total gains from trade? What do these gains depend on?

6 Andy and Bob work at Mario's Pizza Palace. In an eight-hour day, Andy can make 240 pizzas or 100 ice cream sundaes, and Bob can make 80 pizzas or 80 ice cream sundaes. Who does Mario get to make the ice cream sundaes? Who makes the pizzas? Explain your answer.

PART 2

HOW MARKETS WORK

Talking
with
David
Laidler

David Laidler was born in Tynemouth, England. He was an undergraduate at the London School of Economics. After obtaining an MA at Syracuse University, he went to the University of Chicago where he obtained his PhD in 1964.

Professor Laidler has taught at the University of California, Berkeley and the Universities of Essex and Manchester. Since 1975, he has been at the University of Western Ontario. He is the author of numerous books and articles on a wide range of topics that include the history of monetary theory and Canadian economic policy.

Why and how did you get into economics?

During my last three years at school, I took a course in the economic history of modern Britain. Unlike anything else I had studied, this was about places I knew and events that had been relevant to shaping the lives of the people around me. I applied to the London School of Economics under the impression that economics would be like economic history. It was not, of course, and the abstract nature of economic theory came as quite a shock; but after about two years I began to understand how I could use that theory to develop a richer understanding of the history that had attracted me to the subject in the first place. After that, I was hooked.

Although you are best known for your work on money and inflation, your earliest research was on housing. What was that work about and what did you discover?

My earliest research was on the demand for owner-occupied housing in the United States. You can think of buying a house in which to live as an investment that yields an income that you then spend on renting the house from yourself. That income – called an

'The main impetus to my research was a desire to see if microeconomic theory did produce predictions that were borne out by the facts.'

income-in-kind – is not taxed. If you put money in the bank and use the interest to pay rent, you have to pay income tax on that interest. If you use the money to buy a house in which to live, there is no associated income-tax liability; and in the United States, if you have a mortgage, the interest is tax deductible, too. In effect, this is a hidden subsidy that makes it cheaper than it otherwise would be, and ought, according to economic theory, to lead to more owner-occupied housing being demanded than would otherwise be the case. I investigated this phenomenon using both microeconomic analysis and statistical techniques and showed that the predictions of economic theory did indeed hold good in the light of the data.

And, of course, the problem is a socially important one. Owner-occupiers tend to be relatively richer than renters and it is somewhat anomalous that, in the United States, their housing is subsidized more heavily than the housing of renters. But I must admit that the main impetus to my research was a desire to see if microeconomic theory did produce predictions that were borne out by the facts.

There's a close connection, isn't there, between this work on the demand for housing and your subsequent work on the demand for money. Can you tell us about this connection?

Housing is a durable good, and its income tax treatment is a subsidy – a 'negative tax'. A good first approximation to use when modelling the role of money in the economy is to treat it as a durable good which yields 'liquidity services' to the people who hold it. We can also treat inflation as a (positive) tax on those services. The model that I used to analyse the owner-occupied housing market is exactly the same model that I later used to analyse money and inflation. Modern monetary economics has gone far beyond this point, but I still think that it provides a marvellous example of the generality and power of simple economic theory.

You have always been interested in and have made important contributions to our knowledge of the *history* of economic ideas. What does the history of ideas teach us that is useful for students today?

There are two important reasons for studying the history of economic ideas. The first is that, quite simply, good ideas tend to get lost with the passage of time if the problems with which they deal are not pressing ones. Again, take the example of inflation. The textbooks that I was brought up on in the 1950s and early 1960s had largely been written under the influence of the Great Depression when inflation was no problem at all. These textbooks contained next to nothing that was useful to help us understand inflation when it emerged in the 1960s and 1970s. But the literature of the nineteenth century was full of good analyses and important insights into inflationary mechanisms. People who had studied that literature had a head start in understanding what was happening in the 1960s and 1970s.

There is another point to be made here, in some respects a more important point. Economic agents, both policy makers and people working in the private sector, use economic ideas when they make their plans. As economic ideas change, so do economic policy and private sector behaviour. The history of economic thought studied along with economic history allows us to see this process in action. That is surely an important part of the education of any well-rounded economist.

At a time when the countries of Eastern Europe and China are turning to the market mechanism to allocate scarce resources, here in the United Kingdom, many people distrust 'naked market forces'. Why is 'the market' both necessary and unpopular?

It is hard to see how complex modern economies could be organized without markets. No economic planner could possibly have all the necessary information about people's tastes and about available technology, not to mention available resources, to produce a coherent economic plan. Market institutions provide society with a decentralized planning mechanism that enables society to cope with the problem of scarcity. I stress 'cope', however; I do not like to use the word 'solve' in connection with the scarcity problem. Scarcity will always be with us, it will always have to be tackled, and there is nothing we can ever do to eliminate it. We will always have to live with scarcity, and the idea that there is some political trick that will rid us of it is dangerous Utopian nonsense.

I think that people fear the market for three reasons. First, there is an intuitive understanding, which is surely correct, that when markets are competitive they promote social good. But monopoly power in the market place can be socially harmful, even offensive.

Second, markets tend to reward people in accordance with the prices they can get for the resources they own, and skills they possess and are able to sell. That often produces considerable inequality in the distribution of income. When the distribution of income becomes very unequal, people at the bottom begin to feel that they have no particular stake in the society to which they belong. That can be politically dangerous. So, perhaps the market should not be left 'naked'. Perhaps it needs to be dressed up a little with social programmes that ensure that a 'decent' minimum standard of living is available to everyone. 'Decent' has to be defined relative to the particular society you are discussing.

A final point that should be stressed is that the market mechanism provides a means for society to adapt to changes in technology – changes in taste, and so on. By and large, people seem to fear change and, to the extent that the market mecha-

nisms bring news of change, there is always the temptation to blame the message on the messenger.

What are the lessons from history and the history of ideas about the preconditions for a successful market?

The classical economists, particularly John Stuart Mill, stressed the importance of security of property rights to ensure that market mechanisms would function. After all, what we trade in markets are not so much goods and services as our property rights in those goods and services. If those rights are not secure, it is difficult to trade them and market mechanisms begin to break down.

An important element in ensuring secure property rights is stability in the purchasing power of money. Any property rights in income streams which are fixed in nominal terms – that is, in units of current purchasing power – can be severely eroded by even 'a little bit' of inflation. For example, a mere 4 per cent inflation rate would pretty much halve the value of a fixed money income in 15 years or so. Once again, the classical economists stressed the importance of saving as a factor driving economic growth; and to the extent that inflation deters saving (because it erodes the value of savings), it inhibits economic growth.

> '**A**s economic ideas change, so do economic policy and private sector behaviour.'

You seem to be saying that even a little bit of inflation is harmful. Can you elaborate and tell us why you support the goal of price stability for monetary policy? In particular, how would price stability help markets do their job?

All of our accounting conventions and our tax laws are drawn up on the assumption that the purchasing power of money is stable. When the purchasing power of money varies over time, it becomes difficult to value inventories of goods in hand and, hence, to calculate profits and losses. As a consequence, variable inflation distorts the incentives which firms have and prevents them from making wise economic decisions. Variable inflation also leads to arbitrary changes in the way in which the burden of taxation is spread across the economy. Worse still, coping with inflation uses up real resources. Intelligent people become tax lawyers and accountants and make a good living helping firms deal with the problems brought about by inflation. These activities are privately profitable for firms and their lawyers and accountants, but from a social

point of view they are a waste of resources. If there was no inflation, these intelligent people could be engaged in socially productive activities like designing new products, developing new marketing techniques, and so on. To put it in a nutshell, for market mechanisms to work efficiently, we need clear signals from the behaviour of prices. Inflation distorts these signals and leads to wrong decisions being made about the allocation of scarce resources.

What other subjects should students combine with their economic courses if they want to pursue a career as an economist? And why?

First and foremost, I would have to say mathematics. That is not because economics is mathematics, but rather because mathematics makes economic theory clearer and more precise. Take demand theory for example. It's all based on the assumption that households try to make the best use of their incomes. But that down-to-earth idea can be reformulated mathematically as 'maximizing satisfaction subject to not exceeding the household budget'.

Calculus, such as you might learn in sixth form or first year university, yields results that you cannot obtain through common sense alone. Mathematics also enables us to develop better statistical techniques for analysing data.

But I think that students should study some history as well. It is platitudinous, but true, that history is the source of all our economic data; and if we want our economic theory to be empirically relevant we must continuously test it against these data. To do that intelligently, we must understand the sources of the data.

CHAPTER 4

DEMAND
AND
SUPPLY

After studying this chapter you will be able to:

◆ Construct a demand schedule and a demand curve

◆ Construct a supply schedule and a supply curve

◆ Explain how prices are determined

◆ Explain how quantities bought and sold are determined

◆ Explain why some prices rise, some fall and some fluctuate

◆ Make predictions about price changes using the demand and supply model

S LIDE, ROCKET AND ROLLER-COASTER – FUNFAIR RIDES? YES, BUT ALSO things that prices do. The price of the CD player has been on a 10-year slide. In 1983, when the CD player first became available, its price tag was more than £600 in today's money. Now you can buy a CD player for less than £100. During the time that the CD player has been with us, the quantity bought has increased steadily. Why has there been a slide in the price of CD players? Why hasn't the increase in the quantity bought kept its price high? ◆ ◆ The prices of concert and theatre tickets have been rocketing. Why? And why, despite their rocketing prices, do people continue to clamber for seats in such large quantities? ◆ ◆ The prices of coffee, strawberries and other agricultural commodities follow a roller-coaster. Why does the price of coffee roller-coaster even when people's taste for coffee hardly changes at all?

Slide, Rocket and Roller-coaster

◆ ◆ ◆ ◆ We'll discover the answers to these and similar questions in this chapter by studying the theory of demand and supply. In the previous chapter, we learned about the tremendous benefits that result from specialization and exchange. But most exchange takes place in markets at prices determined by the interactions of buyers and sellers. By studying demand and supply, you will learn what determines prices and quantities in markets – markets for everything from CD players to strawberries to shares and bonds and foreign currency. The tools of demand and supply are so fundamental that you will find yourself using them repeatedly in economics and in your everyday attempts to cope with uncertainty and predict prices. Let's begin by studying demand.

Demand

The **quantity demanded** of a good or service is the amount that consumers plan to buy in a given period of time at a particular price. Demands are different from wants. **Wants** are the unlimited desires or wishes that people have for goods and services. How many times have you thought that you would like something 'if only you could afford it' or 'if it weren't so expensive'? Scarcity guarantees that many – perhaps most – of our wants will never be satisfied. Demand reflects a decision about which wants to satisfy. If you demand something, then you've made a plan to buy it.

The quantity demanded is not necessarily the same amount as the quantity actually bought. Sometimes the quantity demanded is greater than the amount of goods available, so the quantity bought is less than the quantity demanded.

The quantity demanded is measured as an amount per unit of time. For example, suppose a person consumes one cup of coffee a day. The quantity of coffee demanded by that person can be expressed as 1 cup per day or 7 cups per week or 365 cups per year. Without a time dimension, we cannot tell whether a particular quantity demanded is large or small.

What Determines Buying Plans?

The amount that consumers plan to buy of any particular good or service depends on many factors. The main ones are:

◆ The price of the good
◆ The prices of related goods
◆ Income
◆ Expected future prices
◆ Population
◆ Preferences

The theory of demand and supply makes predictions about prices and quantities bought and sold. Let's begin by focusing on the relationship between the quantity demanded and the price of a good. To study this relationship, we hold constant all other influences on consumers' planned purchases. We can then ask: how does the quantity demanded of the good vary as its price varies?

The Law of Demand

The law of demand states:

Other things being equal, the higher the price of a good, the lower is the quantity demanded.

Why does a higher price reduce the quantity demanded? Because of substitution. The key to the answer lies in *other things being equal*. Because other things are being held constant, when the price of a good rises, it rises *relative* to the prices of all other goods. Although each good is unique, it has substitutes – other goods that serve almost as well. As the price of a good climbs higher, relative to the prices of its substitutes, people buy less of that good and more of its substitutes.

Let's consider an example – blank cassette tapes, which we'll refer to as 'tapes'. Many different goods provide a similar service to a tape, for example, records, compact discs, prerecorded tapes, radio and television broadcasts and live concerts. Tapes sell for about £1.20 each. If the price of a tape doubles to £2.40 while the prices of all the other goods remain constant, the quantity of tapes demanded decreases. People buy more compact discs and prerecorded tapes and fewer blank tapes. If the price of a tape falls to 40 pence while the prices of all the other goods stay constant, the quantity of tapes demanded increases and the demand for compact discs and prerecorded tapes decreases.

Demand Schedule and Demand Curve

A **demand schedule** lists the quantities demanded at each different price, when all the other influences on consumers' planned purchases – such as the prices of related goods, income, expected future prices, population and preferences – are held constant.

The table in Fig. 4.1 sets out a demand schedule for tapes. For example, if the price of a tape is 40 pence, the quantity demanded is 9 million tapes a week. If the price of a tape is £2.00, the quantity demanded is 2 million tapes a week. The other rows of the table show us the quantities demanded at prices between 80 pence and £1.60.

A demand schedule can be illustrated by drawing a demand curve. A **demand curve** graphs the relationship between the quantity demanded of a good and its price, holding constant all other influences on consumers' planned purchases. The graph in Fig. 4.1 illustrates the demand curve for tapes. By convention, the quantity demanded is always measured on the horizontal axis, and the price is measured on the vertical axis. The points on the demand curve labelled *a* to *e* represent the rows of the demand schedule. For example, point *a* on the graph represents a quantity demanded of 9 million tapes a week at a price of 40 pence a tape.

Willingness to Pay

Another way of looking at the demand curve is as a willingness-to-pay curve. It tells us the highest price that will be paid for the last unit available. If a large quantity is available, that price is low; if a small quantity is available, that price is high. In Fig. 4.1, if 9 million tapes are available each week, the highest price that consumers are willing to pay for the 9 millionth tape is 40 pence. But if only 2 million tapes are available each week, consumers are willing to pay £2.00 for the last tape available.

To understand this view of the demand curve, think about your own demand for tapes. If you are given a list of possible prices for tapes, you can write down alongside each price your planned weekly purchase of tapes – your demand schedule for tapes. Alternatively, if you are told that you can buy just one tape a week, you can say how much you would be willing to pay for it. The price you would be willing to pay for one tape is the same as the price at which your quantity demanded is one tape per week. If you are then told you can buy a second tape, you can say how much you would be willing to pay for that tape. The amount you would be willing to pay is the same as the price at which you would buy two tapes a week. This process can continue – you are asked how much you are willing to pay for one more tape – and the resulting list of quantities of tapes and maximum prices you would be willing to pay is the same list as your demand schedule.

A Change in Demand

The term **demand** refers to the entire relationship between the quantity demanded and the price of a good. The demand for tapes is described by both the demand schedule and the demand curve in Fig. 4.1.

FIGURE 4.1

The Demand Curve

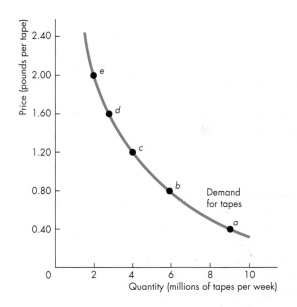

	Price (pounds per tape)	Quantity (millions of tapes per week)
a	0.40	9
b	0.80	6
c	1.20	4
d	1.60	3
e	2.00	2

The table shows a demand schedule listing the quantity of tapes demanded at each price if all other influences on buyers' plans are held constant. At a price of 40 pence a tape, 9 million tapes a week are demanded; at a price of £1.20 a tape, 4 million tapes a week are demanded. The demand curve shows the relationship between quantity demanded and price, holding everything else constant. The demand curve slopes downward: as price decreases, the quantity demanded increases. The demand curve can be read two ways. For a given price it tells us the quantity that people plan to buy. For example, at a price of £1.20 a tape, the quantity demanded is 4 million tapes a week. For a given quantity, the demand curve tells us the maximum price that consumers are willing to pay for the last tape bought. For example, the maximum price that consumers will pay for the 6 millionth tape is 80 pence.

To construct a demand schedule and demand curve, we hold constant all the other influences on consumers' buying plans. But what are the effects of each of those other influences?

1. Prices of Related Goods The quantity of tapes that consumers plan to buy does not depend only on the price of tapes. It also depends in part on the prices of related goods. These related goods fall into two categories: substitutes and complements.

Two goods are **substitutes** if the demand for one of the goods increases when the price of the other good increases. More loosely, a substitute is a good that can be used in place of – can be *substituted* for – another good. For example, a bus ride substitutes for a train ride; fish and chips substitute for chicken and salad; a pear substitutes for an apple. As we have seen, tapes have many substitutes – records, pre-recorded tapes, compact discs, radio and television broadcasts, and live concerts. If the price of one of these substitutes increases, people economize on its use and buy more tapes. For example, if the price of a record rises, more tapes are bought – the demand for tapes increases – and there is more taping of other people's records.

The effects of a change in the price of a substitute occur no matter what the price of a tape. Whether tapes have a high or a low price, a change in the price of a substitute encourages people to make the substitutions that we've just reviewed. As a consequence, a change in the price of a substitute changes the entire demand schedule for tapes and shifts the demand curve.

Two goods are **complements** if the demand for one of the goods *decrease*s as the price of the other good increases. More loosely, a complement is a good used in conjunction with – to *complement* – another good. Some examples of complements are hamburgers and chips, party snacks and drinks, spaghetti and Bolognese sauce, training shoes and track suits. Tapes also have their complements: Walkmans, tape recorders, and stereo tape decks. If the price of one of these complements increases, people buy fewer tapes. For example, if the price of a Walkman rises, fewer Walkmans are bought and, as a consequence, fewer tapes are bought – the demand for tapes decreases.

2. Income Another influence on demand is consumer income. Other things remaining the same, when income increases, consumers buy more of most goods, and when income decreases, they buy less of most

goods. Consumers with higher incomes demand more of most goods. Consumers with lower incomes demand less of most goods. Rich people consume more food, clothing, housing, art, holidays and entertainment than do poor people.

Although an increase in income leads to an increase in the demand for most goods, it does not lead to an increase in the demand for all goods. Goods that increase in demand as income increases are called **normal goods**. Goods that decrease in demand when income increases are called **inferior goods**. Examples of inferior goods are minced meat and potatoes. These two goods feature prominently in the diets of low-income people but hardly feature at all in the diets of the wealthy. As incomes increase, the demand for mince and potatoes declines as more expensive meat and poultry are substituted for them.

3. Expected Future Prices If the price of a good is expected to rise, it makes sense to buy more of the good today and less in the future when its price is higher. Similarly, if its price is expected to fall, it pays to cut back on today's purchases and buy more later when the price is expected to be lower. Thus the higher the expected future price of a good, the larger is today's demand for the good.

4. Population Demand also depends on the size of the population. Other things being equal, the larger the population, the greater is the demand for all goods and services, and the smaller the population, the smaller is the demand for all goods and services.

5. Preferences Finally, demand depends on preferences. *Preferences* are an individual's attitudes towards goods and services. For example, a rock music fanatic has a much greater taste for tapes than does a tone-deaf workaholic. As a consequence, even if they have the same incomes, their demands for tapes will be very different. Preferences are not observed. But preferences *change* slowly and so have little influence on *changes* in demand.

A summary of influences on demand and the direction of those influences is given in Table 4.1.

Movement Along Versus a Shift in the Demand Curve

Changes in the influences on buyers' plans cause either a movement along the demand curve or a shift in it. Let's discuss each case in turn.

TABLE 4.1

The Demand for Tapes

THE LAW OF DEMAND

The quantity of tapes demanded

Decreases if:

◆ The price of a tape rises

Increases if:

◆ The price of a tape falls

CHANGES IN DEMAND

The demand for tapes

Decreases if:

◆ The price of a substitute falls

◆ The price of a complement rises

◆ Income falls*

◆ The price of a tape is expected to fall in the future

◆ The population decreases

Increases if:

◆ The price of a substitute rises

◆ The price of a complement falls

◆ Income rises*

◆ The price of a tape is expected to rise in the future

◆ The population increases

*A tape is a normal good

FIGURE 4.2

A Change in Demand

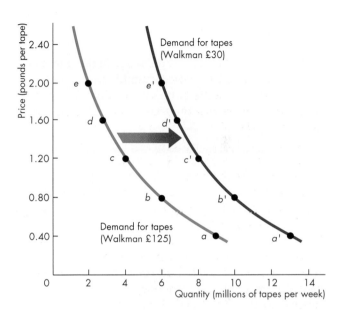

	Original demand schedule (Walkman £125)			New demand schedule (Walkman £30)	
	Price (pounds per tape)	Quantity (millions of tapes per week)		Price (pounds per tape)	Quantity (millions of tapes per week)
a	0.40	9	*a'*	0.40	13
b	0.80	6	*b'*	0.80	10
c	1.20	4	*c'*	1.20	8
d	1.60	3	*d'*	1.60	7
e	2.00	2	*e'*	2.00	6

A change in any influence on buyers other than the price of the good itself results in a new demand schedule and a shift in the demand curve. Here, a fall in the price of a Walkman – a complement of tapes – increases the demand for tapes. At a price of £1.20 a tape (row c of table), 4 million tapes a week are demanded when the Walkman costs £125 and 8 million tapes a week are demanded when the Walkman costs only £30. A fall in the price of a Walkman increases the demand for tapes. The demand curve shifts to the right, as shown by the shift arrow and the resulting red curve.

Movement Along the Demand Curve   If the price of a good changes but everything else remains the same, there is a movement along the demand curve. For example, if the price of a tape changes from £1.20 to £2.00, there is a movement along the demand curve, from point *c* to point *e* in Fig. 4.1.

A Shift in the Demand Curve   If the price of a good remains constant but some other influence on buyers' plans changes, we say that there is a change in demand for that good. We illustrate the change in demand as a shift in the demand curve. For example, a fall in the price of the Walkman – a complement of tapes – increases the demand for tapes. We illustrate this increase in demand for tapes with a new demand schedule and a new demand curve. Consumers demand a larger quantity of tapes at each and every price.

The table in Fig. 4.2 provides some hypothetical numbers that illustrate such a shift. The table sets out the original demand schedule when the price of a Walkman is £125 and the new demand schedule when the price of a Walkman is £30. These numbers record the change in demand. The graph in Fig. 4.2 illustrates the corresponding shift in the demand curve. When the price of the Walkman falls, the demand curve for tapes shifts to the right.

A Change in Demand versus a Change in the Quantity Demanded A point on the demand curve shows the quantity demanded at a given price. A movement along the demand curve shows a **change in**

FIGURE 4.3

FIGURE 4.3

A Change in Demand versus a Change in the Quantity Demanded

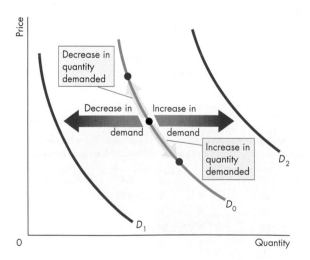

When the price of a good changes, there is a movement along the demand curve and *a change in the quantity of the good demanded*. For example, if the demand curve is D_0, a rise in the price of the good produces a decrease in the quantity demanded and a fall in the price of the good produces an increase in the quantity demanded. The blue arrows on demand curve D_0 represent these movements along the demand curve. If some other influence on demand changes, which increases the quantity that people plan to buy, there is a shift in the demand curve to the right (from D_0 to D_2) and an *increase in demand*. If some other influence on demand changes, which reduces the quantity people plan to buy, there is a shift in the demand curve to the left (from D_0 to D_1) and a *decrease in demand*.

---

the quantity demanded. The entire demand curve shows demand. A shift in the demand curve shows a **change in demand**.

Figure 4.3 illustrates and summarizes these distinctions. If the price of a good falls but nothing else changes, then there is an increase in the quantity demanded of that good (a movement down the demand curve D_0). If the price rises, but nothing else changes, then there is a decrease in the quantity demanded (a movement up the demand curve D_0). When any other influence on buyers' planned purchases changes, the demand curve shifts and there is a *change* (an increase or a decrease) *in demand*. A rise in income (for a normal good), in population, in the price of a substitute, or in the expected future price of the good or a fall in the price of a complement shifts the demand curve to the right (to the red demand curve D_2). This represents an *increase in demand*. A fall in income (for a normal good), in population, in the price of a substitute, or in the expected future price of the good or a rise in the price of a complement shifts the demand curve to the left (to the red demand curve D_1). This represents a *decrease in demand*. For an inferior good, the effects of changes in income are in the opposite direction to those described above.

R E V I E W

T he quantity demanded is the amount of a good that consumers plan to buy in a given period of time. Other things being equal, the quantity demanded of a good increases if its price falls. Demand can be represented by a schedule or curve that sets out the quantity demanded at each price. Demand describes the quantity that consumers plan to buy at each possible price. Demand also describes the highest price that consumers are willing to pay for the last unit bought. Demand increases if the price of a substitute rises, if the price of a complement falls, if income rises (for a normal good), or if the population increases; demand decreases. ◆ ◆ If the price of a substitute falls, if the price of a complement rises, if income falls (for a normal good), or if the population decreases. ◆ ◆ If the price of a good changes but all other influences on buyers' plans are held constant, there is a change in the quantity demanded and a movement along the demand curve. All other influences on consumers' planned purchases shift the demand curve. ◆

Supply

The quantity supplied of a good is the amount that producers plan to sell in a given period of time. The **quantity supplied** is not the amount a firm would like to sell but the amount it definitely plans to sell. However, the quantity supplied is not necessarily the same as the quantity actually sold. If consumers do not want to buy the quantity a firm plans to sell, the firm's sales plans will be frustrated. Like quantity demanded, the quantity supplied is expressed as an amount per unit of time.

What Determines Selling Plans?

The amount that firms plan to sell of any particular good or service depends on many factors. The main ones are:

◆ The price of the good
◆ The prices of factors of production
◆ The prices of related goods
◆ Expected future prices
◆ The number of suppliers
◆ Technology

Because the theory of demand and supply makes predictions about prices and quantities bought and sold, we focus first on the relationship between the price of a good and the quantity supplied. In order to study this relationship, we hold constant all the other influences on the quantity supplied. We ask: how does the quantity supplied of a good vary as its price varies?

The Law of Supply

The law of supply states:

Other things being equal, the higher the price of a good, the greater is the quantity supplied.

Why does a higher price lead to a greater quantity supplied of a good? It is because the cost of producing an additional unit of the good increases (at least eventually) as the quantity produced increases. To induce them to incur a higher cost and increase production, firms must be compensated with a higher price.

Supply Schedule and Supply Curve

A **supply schedule** lists the quantities supplied at each different price, when all other influences on the amount firms plan to sell are held constant. Let's construct a supply schedule. To do so, we examine how the quantity supplied of a good varies as its price varies, holding constant the prices of other goods, the prices of factors of production used to produce it, expected future prices and the state of technology.

The table in Fig. 4.4 sets out a supply schedule for tapes. It shows the quantity of tapes supplied at each possible price. For example, if the price of a tape is 40 pence, no tapes are supplied. If the price of a tape is £1.60, 5 million tapes are supplied each week.

A supply schedule can be illustrated by drawing a supply curve. A **supply curve** graphs the relationship between the quantity supplied and the price of a good, holding everything else constant. Using the numbers listed in the table, the graph in Fig. 4.4 illustrates the supply curve for tapes. For example, point d represents a quantity supplied of 5 million tapes a week at a price of £1.60 a tape.

Minimum Supply Price

Just as the demand curve has two interpretations, so too does the supply curve. So far we have thought about the supply curve and the supply schedule as showing the quantity that firms will supply at each possible price. But we can also think about the supply curve as showing the minimum price at which the last unit will be supplied. Looking at the supply schedule in this way, we ask: what is the minimum price that brings forth a supply of a given quantity? For firms to supply the 3 millionth tape each week, the price has to be at least 80 pence a tape. For firms to supply the 5 millionth tape each week, they have to get at least £1.60 a tape.

FIGURE 4.4

The Supply Curve

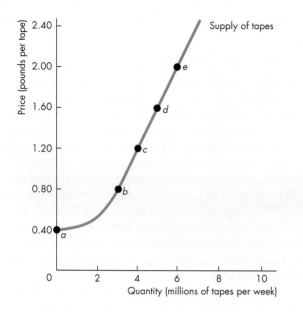

	Price (pounds per tape)	Quantity (millions of tapes per week)
a	0.40	0
b	0.80	3
c	1.20	4
d	1.60	5
e	2.00	6

The table shows the supply schedule of tapes. For example, at 80 pence a tape, 3 million tapes a week are supplied; at £2.00 a tape, 6 million tapes a week are supplied. The supply curve shows the relationship between the quantity supplied and price, holding everything else constant. The supply curve usually slopes upward: as the price of a good increases, so does the quantity supplied. A supply curve can be read in two ways. For a given price, it tells us the quantity that producers plan to sell. For example, at a price of £1.20 a tape, producers plan to sell 4 million tapes a week. The supply curve also tells us the minimum acceptable price at which a given quantity will be offered for sale. For example, the minimum acceptable price that will bring forth a supply of 5 million tapes a week is £1.60 a tape.

A Change in Supply

The term **supply** refers to the entire relationship between the quantity supplied of a good and its price. The supply of tapes is described by both the supply schedule and the supply curve in Fig. 4.4. To construct a supply schedule and supply curve, we hold constant all the other influences on suppliers' plans. Let's now consider these other influences.

1. Prices of Factors of Production   The prices of the factors of production used to produce a good influence its supply. For example, an increase in the prices of the labour and the capital equipment used to produce tapes increases the cost of producing tapes, so the supply of tapes decreases.

2. Prices of Related Goods   The supply of a good can be influenced by the prices of related goods. For example, if a motor car assembly line can produce either sports cars or saloons, the quantity of saloons produced will depend on the price of sports cars and the quantity of sports cars produced will depend on the price of saloons. These two goods are *substitutes in production*. An increase in the price of a substitute in production lowers the supply of the good. Goods can also be complements in production. *Complements in production* arise when two things are, of necessity, produced together. For example, extracting chemicals from coal produces coke, coal tar and nylon. An increase in the price of any one of these by-products of coal increases the supply of the other by-products.

Tapes have no obvious complements in production, but they do have substitutes in production: prerecorded tapes. Suppliers of tapes can produce blank tapes and prerecorded tapes. An increase in the price of prerecorded tapes encourages producers to increase the supply of pre-recorded tapes and decrease the supply of blank tapes.

3. Expected Future Prices   If the price of a good is expected to rise, it makes sense to sell less of the good today and more in the future, when its price is higher. Similarly, if its price is expected to fall, it pays to expand today's supply and sell less later, when the price is expected to be lower. Thus other things being equal, the higher the expected future price of a good, the smaller is today's supply of the good.

4. The Number of Suppliers   Other things remaining

the same, the larger the number of firms supplying a good, the larger is the supply of the good.

5. Technology New technologies that enable producers to use fewer factors of production will lower the cost of production and increase supply. For example, the development of a new technology for tape production by companies such as BASF, Sony and Minnesota Mining and Manufacturing (3M) has lowered the cost of producing tapes and increased their supply.

A summary of influences on supply and the directions of those influences is presented in Table 4.2. Over the long term, changes in technology are the most important influence on supply.

Movement Along Versus a Shift in the Supply Curve

Changes in the influences on producers cause either a movement along the supply curve or a shift in it.

TABLE 4.2

The Supply of Tapes

THE LAW OF SUPPLY

The quantity of tapes supplied

Decreases if:	*Increases if:*
◆ The price of a tape falls	◆ The price of a tape rises

CHANGES IN SUPPLY

The supply of tapes

Decreases if:	*Increases if:*
◆ The price of a factor of production used to produce tapes increases	◆ The price of a factor of production used to produce tapes decreases
◆ The price of a substitute in production rises	◆ The price of a substitute in production falls
◆ The price of a complement in production falls	◆ The price of a complement in production rises
◆ The price of a tape is expected to rise in the future	◆ The price of a tape is expected to fall in the future
◆ The number of firms supplying tapes decreases	◆ The number of firms supplying tapes increases
	◆ More efficient technologies for producing tapes are discovered

Movement Along the Supply Curve If the price of a good changes but everything else influencing suppliers' planned sales remains constant, there is a movement along the supply curve. For example, if the price of tapes increases from \$1.20 to \$2.00 a tape, there will be a movement along the supply curve from point *c* (4 million tapes a week) to point *e* (6 million tapes a week) in Fig. 4.4.

A Shift in the Supply Curve If the price of a good remains constant but another influence on suppliers' planned sales changes, then there is a change in supply and a shift in the supply curve. For example, as we have already noted, technological advances lower the cost of producing tapes and increase their supply. As a result, the supply schedule changes. The table in Fig. 4.5 provides some hypothetical numbers that illustrate such a change. The table contains two supply schedules: the original, based on 'old' technology, and one on 'new' technology. With the new technology, a given quantity of tapes will be supplied at a lower price. Equivalently, more tapes are supplied at each price. The graph in Fig. 4.5 illustrates the resulting shift in the supply curve. When tape-producing technology improves, the supply curve of tapes shifts to the right, as shown by the shift arrow and the red supply curve.

A Change in Supply versus a Change in the Quantity Supplied A point on the supply curve shows the quantity supplied at a given price. A movement along the supply curve shows a **change in the quantity supplied**. The entire supply curve shows supply. A shift in the supply curve shows a **change in supply**.

Figure 4.6 illustrates and summarizes these distinctions. If the price of a good falls but nothing else changes, then there is a decrease in the quantity supplied of that good (a movement down the supply curve S_0). If the price of a good rises but nothing else changes, there is an increase in the quantity supplied (a movement up the supply curve S_0). When any other influence on sellers changes, the supply curve shifts and there is a *change in supply*. If the supply curve is S_0 and there is, say, a technological change that reduces the amounts of the factors of production needed to produce the good, then supply increases and the supply curve shifts to the red supply curve S_2. If production costs rise, supply decreases and the supply curve shifts to the red supply curve S_1.

FIGURE 4.5

A Change in Supply

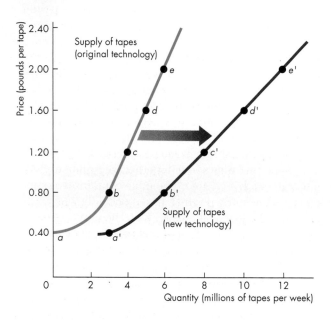

	Original technology			New technology	
	Price (pounds per tape)	Quantity (millions of tapes per week)		Price (pounds per tape)	Quantity (millions of tapes per week)
a	0.40	0	a′	0.40	3
b	0.80	3	b′	0.80	6
c	1.20	4	c′	1.20	8
d	1.60	5	d′	1.60	10
e	2.00	6	e′	2.00	12

If the price of a good remains constant but another influence on its supply changes, there will be a new supply schedule and the supply curve will shift. For example, if BASF, Sony and 3M invent a new, cost-saving technology for producing tapes, the supply schedule changes, as shown in the table. At 80 pence a tape, producers plan to sell 3 million tapes a week with the old technology and 6 million tapes a week with the new technology. Improved technology increases the supply of tapes and shifts the supply curve of tapes to the right.

REVIEW

T he quantity supplied is the amount of a good that producers plan to sell in a given period of time. Other things being equal, the quantity supplied of a good increases if its price rises. Supply can be represented by a schedule or a curve that shows the relationship between the quantity supplied of a good and its price. Supply describes the quantity that will be supplied at each possible price. Supply also describes the lowest price at which producers will supply the last unit. ◆ ◆

FIGURE 4.6

A Change in Supply versus a Change in the Quantity Supplied

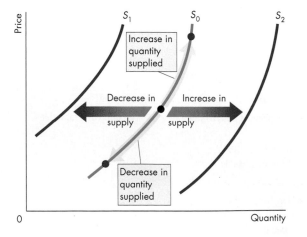

When the price of a good changes, there is a movement along the supply curve and a *change in the quantity of the good supplied*. For example, if the supply curve is S_0, a rise in the price of the good produces an increase in the quantity supplied, and a fall in the price produces a decrease in the quantity supplied. The blue arrows on curve S_0 represent these movements along the supply curve. If some other influence on supply changes, increasing the quantity that producers plan to sell, there is a shift in the supply curve to the right (from S_0 to S_2) and an *increase in supply*. If some other influence on supply changes, reducing the quantity the producers plan to sell, there is a shift to the left in the supply curve (from S_0 to S_1) and a *decrease in supply*.

Supply increases if the prices of the factors of production used to produce the good fall, the prices of substitutes in production fall, the prices of complements in production rise, the expected future price of the good falls, or when technological advances lower the cost of production. If the price of a good changes but all other influences on producers' plans are held constant, there is a change in the quantity supplied and a movement along the supply curve but *no change in supply*. ◆ ◆ A change in any other influence on producers' plans changes supply and shifts the supply curve. Changes in the prices of factors of production, prices of substitutes in production and complements in production, in expected future prices, or in technology shift the supply curve and are said to change supply. ◆

Let's now bring the two concepts of demand and supply together and see how prices are determined.

Price Determination

We have seen that when the price of a good rises, the quantity demanded decreases and the quantity supplied increases. We are now going to see how adjustments in price coordinate the choices of buyers and sellers.

Price as a Regulator

The price of a good regulates the quantities demanded and supplied. If the price is too high, the quantity supplied exceeds the quantity demanded. If the price is too low, the quantity demanded exceeds the quantity supplied. There is one price, and only one price, at which the quantity demanded equals the quantity supplied. We are going to work out what that price is. We are also going to discover that natural forces operating in a market move the price towards the level that makes the quantity demanded equal the quantity supplied.

The demand schedule shown in the table in Fig. 4.1 and the supply schedule shown in the table in Fig. 4.4 appear together in the table in Fig. 4.7. If

the price of a tape is 40 pence, the quantity demanded is 9 million tapes a week, but no tapes are supplied. The quantity demanded exceeds the quantity supplied by 9 million tapes a week. In other words, at a price of 40 pence a tape, there is a shortage of 9 million tapes a week. This shortage is shown in the final column of the table. At a price of 80 pence a tape, there is still a shortage but only of 3 million tapes a week. If the price of a tape is £1.60, the quantity supplied exceeds the quantity demanded. The quantity supplied is 5 million tapes a week, but the quantity demanded is only 3 million. There is a surplus of 2 million tapes a week. There is one price and only one price at which there is neither a shortage nor a surplus. That price is £1.20 a tape. At that price the quantity demanded is equal to the quantity supplied with 4 million tapes a week.

The market for tapes is illustrated in the graph in Fig. 4.7. The graph shows both the demand curve of Fig. 4.1 and the supply curve of Fig. 4.4. The demand curve and the supply curve intersect when the price is £1.20 a tape. At that price, the quantity demanded and supplied is 4 million tapes a week. At each price *above* £1.20 a tape, the quantity supplied exceeds the quantity demanded. There is a surplus of tapes. For example, at £1.60 a tape the surplus is 2 million tapes a week, as shown by the blue arrow in the figure. At each price *below* £1.20 a tape, the quantity demanded exceeds the quantity supplied. There is a shortage of tapes. For example, at 80 pence a tape, the shortage is 3 million tapes a week, as shown by the red arrow in the figure.

Equilibrium

We defined *equilibrium* in Chapter 1 as a situation in which opposing forces balance each other, and in which no one is able to make a better choice given the available resources and actions of others. In an equilibrium, the price is such that opposing forces exactly balance each other. The **equilibrium price** is the price at which the quantity demanded equals the quantity supplied. The **equilibrium quantity** is the quantity bought and sold at the equilibrium price. To see why equilibrium occurs where the quantity demanded equals the quantity supplied, we need to examine the behaviour of buyers and sellers a bit more closely. First, let's look at the behaviour of buyers.

Discovering the Laws of Demand and Supply

'When demand and supply are in stable equilibrium, if any accident should move the scale of production from its equilibrium position, there will be instantly brought into play forces tending to push it back to that position; just as, if a stone hanging by a string is displaced from its equilibrium position, the force of gravity will at once tend to bring it back to its equilibrium position.'

ALFRED MARSHALL
Principles of Economics

Railways in the 1850s were as close to the cutting edge of technology as airlines are today. Railway investment was profitable, but as in the airline industry today, competition was fierce.

The theory of demand and supply was being developed at the same time as railways were expanding, and it was their economic problems that gave the newly emerging theory its first practical applications.

In France, Jules Dupuit worked out how to use demand theory to calculate the value of railway bridges. His work was the forerunner of what is today called cost-benefit analysis. Working with the very same principles invented by Dupuit, economists today calculate the costs and benefits of roads, airports, dams and power stations.

In the United Kingdom, Dionysius Lardner showed railway companies how they could increase their profits by cutting rates on long-distance business, where competition was fiercest, and raising rates on short-haul business, where they had less to fear from other suppliers. The principles first worked out by Lardner in the 1850s are used by economists working for the major airline companies today to work out the freight rates and passenger fares that will give the airline the largest possible profit. And the rates that result have a lot in common with those railway rates of the nineteenth century. The airlines have local routes that feed like the spokes of a wheel into a hub on which there is little competition and on which they charge high fares (per mile), and they have long-distance routes between hubs on which they compete fiercely with other airlines and on which fares per mile are lowest.

Dupuit used the law of demand to determine whether a bridge or canal would be valued enough by its users to justify the cost of building it, and Lardner first worked out the relationship between the cost of production and supply and used demand and supply theory to explain the costs, prices and profits of railway operations and to discover ways of increasing revenue by raising rates on short-haul business and lowering them on long-distance freight.

Today, using the same principles devised by Dupuit, economists calculate whether the benefits of expanding airports and air traffic control facilities are sufficient to cover their costs, and airline companies use the principles developed by Lardner to set their prices and to decide when to offer 'seat sales'.

The Discoverers of the Laws of Demand and Supply

The law of demand was discovered by Antoine-Augustin Cournot (1801–1877), pictured right, professor of mathematics at the University of Lyon, France, and it was he who drew the first demand curve in the 1830s. The first practical application of demand theory, by Jules Dupuit (1804–1866), a French engineer/economist, was the calculation of the benefits from building a bridge – and, given that a bridge had been built, of the correct toll to charge for its use.

The laws of demand *and* supply and the connection between the costs of production and supply were first worked out by Dionysius Lardner (1793–1859), an Irish professor of philosophy at the University of London. Known satirically among scientists of the day as 'Dionysius Diddler', Lardner worked on an amazing range of problems from astronomy to railway engineering to economics. A colourful character, he would have been a regular guest of Des O'Connor and Danny Baker if their talk shows had been around in the 1850s. He visited the Ecole des Ponts et Chaussées (the School of Bridges and Roads) in Paris and must have learned a great deal from Dupuit, who was doing his major work on economics at the time.

ANTOINE-AUGUSTIN COURNOT

Many others had a hand in refining the theory of demand and supply, but the first thorough and complete statement of the theory as we know it today was that of Alfred Marshall (1842–1924), pictured left, professor of political economy at the University of Cambridge, who, in 1890, published a monumental treatise – *Principles of Economics* – a work that became *the* textbook on economics for almost half a century. Marshall was an outstanding mathematician, but he kept mathematics and even diagrams in the background. His own supply and demand diagram (reproduced here at its original size) appears only in a footnote.

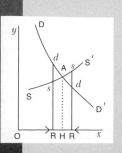

ALFRED MARSHALL

FIGURE 4.7

Equilibrium

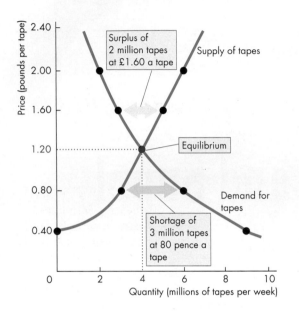

The table lists the quantities demanded and quantities supplied as well as the shortage or surplus of tapes at each price. If the price of a tape is 80 pence, 6 million tapes a week are demanded and 3 million are supplied. There is a shortage of 3 million tapes a week, and the price rises. If the price of a tape is £1.60, 3 million tapes a week are demanded but 5 million are supplied. There is a surplus of 2 million tapes a week, and the price falls. If the price of a tape is £1.20, 4 million tapes a week are demanded and 4 million are supplied. There is neither a shortage nor a surplus. Neither buyers nor sellers have any incentive to change the price. The price at which the quantity demanded equals the quantity supplied is the equilibrium price.

Price (pounds per tape)	Quantity demanded (millions of tapes per week)	Quantity supplied (millions of tapes per week)	Shortage (–) or surplus (+) (millions of tapes per week)
0.40	9	0	–9
0.80	6	3	–3
1.20	4	4	0
1.60	3	5	+2
2.00	2	6	+4

The Demand Curve and the Willingness to Pay

Suppose the price of a tape is 80 pence. In such a situation, producers plan to sell 3 million tapes a week. Consumers cannot force producers to sell more than they want to sell, so the quantity sold is also 3 million tapes a week. What is the highest price that buyers are willing to pay for the 3 millionth tape each week? The answer can be found on the demand curve in Fig. 4.7 – it is £1.60 a tape.

If the price remains at 80 pence a tape, the quantity of tapes demanded is 6 million tapes a week, 3 million tapes more than are available. In such a situation, the price of a tape does not remain at 80 pence. Because people want more tapes than are available at that price and because they are willing to pay up to £1.60 a tape, the price rises. If the quantity supplied stays at 3 million tapes a week, the price rises all the way to £1.60 a tape.

In fact, the price doesn't have to rise by such a large amount because at higher prices the quantity supplied increases. The price will rise from 80 pence a tape to £1.20 a tape. At that price, the quantity supplied is 4 million tapes a week, and £1.20 a tape is the highest price that consumers are willing to pay. At £1.20 a tape, buyers are able to make their planned purchases and producers are able to make their planned sales. Therefore no buyer has an incentive to bid the price higher.

The Supply Curve and the Minimum Supply Price

Suppose that the price of a tape is £1.60. In such a situation, the quantity demanded is 3 million tapes a week. Producers cannot force consumers to buy more than they want, so the quantity bought is 3 million tapes a week. Producers are willing to sell 3 million tapes a week for a price lower than £1.60 a tape. In fact, you can see on the supply curve in Fig. 4.7 that suppliers are willing to sell the 3 millionth tape each week at a price of 80 pence. At £1.60 a tape, they would like to sell 5 million tapes each week. Because they want to sell more than 3 million tapes a week at £1.60 a tape, and because they would be willing to sell the 3 millionth tape for as little as 80 pence, they will continuously undercut each other to get a bigger share of the market. They will cut their price all the way to 80 pence a tape if only 3 million tapes a week can be sold.

In fact, producers don't have to cut their price to 80 pence a tape because the lower price brings forth an increase in the quantity demanded. When the price falls to £1.20, the quantity demanded is 4 million tapes a week, which is exactly the quantity that producers want to sell at that price. So when the price reaches £1.20 a tape, producers have no incentive to cut the price any further.

The Best Deal Available for Buyers and Sellers Both situations we have just examined result in price changes. In the first case, the price starts out at 80 pence and is bid upward. In the second case, the price starts out at £1.60 and producers undercut each other. In both cases, prices change until they hit the price of £1.20 a tape. At that price, the quantity demanded and the quantity supplied are equal, and no one has any incentive to do business at a different price. Consumers are paying the highest acceptable price and producers are selling at the lowest acceptable price.

When people can freely make bids and offers and when they seek to buy at the lowest price and sell at the highest price, the price at which they trade is the equilibrium price – the quantity demanded equals the quantity supplied.

R E V I E W

The equilibrium price is the price at which the plans of buyers and sellers match each other – the price at which the quantity demanded equals the quantity supplied. If the price is below equilibrium, the quantity demanded exceeds the quantity supplied, buyers offer higher prices, sellers ask for higher prices, and the price rises. If the price is above equilibrium, the quantity supplied exceeds the quantity demanded, buyers offer lower prices, sellers ask for lower prices, and the price falls. Only when the price is such that the quantity demanded and the quantity supplied are equal are there no forces acting on the price to make it change. Therefore that price is the equilibrium price. At that price, the quantity actually bought and sold is also equal to the quantity demanded and the quantity supplied. ◆

The theory of demand and supply that you have just studied is now a central part of economics. But

that was not always so. Only 100 years ago, the best economists of the day were quite confused about these matters, which today even students in introductory courses find relatively easy to get right (see Our Advancing Knowledge on pp. 88–89).

As you'll discover in the rest of this chapter, the theory of demand and supply enables us to understand and make predictions about changes in prices – including the price slides, rockets and roller-coasters described in the chapter opener.

Predicting Changes in Price and Quantity

The theory we have just studied provides us with a powerful way of analysing influences on prices and the quantities bought and sold. According to the theory, a change in price stems from either a change in demand or a change in supply or a change in both – see Reading Between the Lines on pp. 96–97. Let's look first at the effects of a change in demand.

A Change in Demand

What happens to the price and quantity of tapes if demand for tapes increases? We can answer this question with a specific example. If the price of a Walkman falls from £125 to £30, the demand for tapes increases as is shown in the table in Fig. 4.8. The original demand schedule and the new one are set out in the first three columns of the table. The table also shows the supply schedule.

The original equilibrium price was £1.20 a tape. At that price, 4 million tapes a week were demanded and supplied. When demand increases, the price that makes the quantity demanded equal the quantity supplied is £2.00 a tape. At this price, 6 million tapes are bought and sold each week. When demand increases, both the price and the quantity increase.

We can illustrate these changes in the graph in Fig. 4.8. The graph shows the original demand for and supply of tapes. The original equilibrium price is £1.20 a tape and the quantity is 4 million tapes a week. When demand increases, the demand curve shifts to the right. The equilibrium price rises to £2.00 a tape and the quantity supplied increases to 6

FIGURE 4.8

FIGURE 4.8

The Effects of a Change in Demand

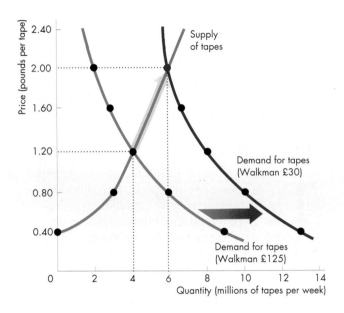

Price (pounds per tape)	Quantity demanded (millions of tapes per week)		Quantity supplied (millions of tapes per week)
	Walkman £125	Walkman £30	
0.40	9	13	0
0.80	6	10	3
1.20	4	8	4
1.60	3	7	5
2.00	2	6	6

With the price of a Walkman at £125, the demand for tapes is the blue curve. The equilibrium price is £1.20 a tape and the equilibrium quantity is 4 million tapes a week. When the price of a Walkman falls from £125 to £30, there is an increase in the demand for tapes and the demand curve shifts to the right – the red curve. At £1.20 a tape, there is now a shortage of 4 million tapes a week. The quantities of tapes demanded and supplied are equal at a price of £2.00 a tape. The price rises to this level and the quantity supplied increases. But there is no change in supply. The increase in demand increases the equilibrium price to £2.00 and increases the equilibrium quantity to 6 million tapes a week.

million tapes a week, as is highlighted in the figure. There is an increase in the quantity supplied but *no change in supply*.

The exercise that we've just conducted can easily be reversed. If we start at a price of £2.00 a tape, trading 6 million tapes a week, we can then work out what happens if demand falls back to its original level. You can see that the fall in demand decreases the equilibrium price to £1.20 a tape and decreases the equilibrium quantity to 4 million tapes a week. Such a fall in demand could arise from a decrease in the price of compact discs or of CD players.

We can now make our first two predictions. Holding everything else constant:

◆ When demand increases, both the price and the quantity increase.
◆ When demand decreases, both the price and the quantity decrease.

A Change in Supply

Suppose that Sony and 3M have just introduced a new cost-saving technology in their tape-production plants. The new technology changes the supply. The new supply schedule (the same one that was shown in Fig. 4.5) is presented in the table in Fig. 4.9. What is the new equilibrium price and quantity? The answer is highlighted in the table: the price falls to 80 pence a tape and the quantity rises to 6 million a week. You can see why by looking at the quantities demanded and supplied at the old price of £1.20 a tape. The quantity supplied at that price is 8 million tapes a week and there is a surplus of tapes. The price falls. Only when the price is 80 pence a tape does the quantity supplied equal the quantity demanded.

Figure 4.9 illustrates the effect of an increase in supply. It shows the demand curve for tapes and the original and new supply curves. The initial equilibrium price is £1.20 a tape and the original quantity is 4 million tapes a week. When the supply increases, the supply curve shifts to the right. The equilibrium price falls to 80 pence a tape and the quantity demanded increases to 6 million tapes a week, highlighted in the figure. There is an increase in the quantity demanded but *no change in demand*.

The exercise that we've just conducted can easily be reversed. If we start out at a price of 80 pence a tape with 6 million tapes a week being bought and sold, we can work out what happens if

FIGURE 4.9

The Effects of a Change in Supply

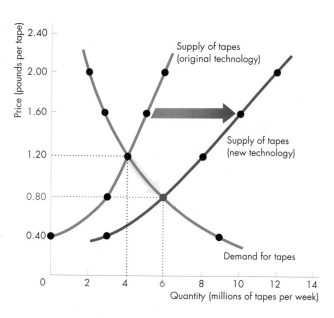

Price (pounds per tape)	Quantity demanded millions of tapes per week	Quantity supplied (millions of tapes per week)	
		Original technology	New technology
0.40	9	0	3
0.80	6	3	6
1.20	4	4	8
1.60	3	5	10
2.00	2	6	12

With the original technology, the supply of tapes is shown by the blue curve. The equilibrium price is £1.20 a tape and the equilibrium quantity is 4 million tapes a week. When the new technology is adopted, there is an increase in the supply of tapes. The supply curves shifts to the right – the red curve. At £1.20 a tape, there is now a surplus of 4 million tapes a week. The quantities of tapes demanded and supplied are equal at a price of 80 pence a tape. The price falls to this level and the quantity demanded increases. But there is no change in demand. The increase in supply lowers the price of tapes to 80 pence and increases the quantity to 6 million tapes a week.

the supply curve shifts back to its original position. You can see that the fall in supply increases the equilibrium price to £1.20 a tape and decreases the equilibrium quantity to 4 million tapes a week. Such a fall in supply could arise from an increase in the cost of labour and raw materials.

We can now make two more predictions. Holding everything else constant:

◆ When supply increases, the quantity increases and the price falls.
◆ When supply decreases, the quantity decreases and the price rises.

Changes in Both Supply and Demand

In the above exercises, either demand or supply changed, but only one at a time. If just one of these changes, we can predict the direction of change of the price and the quantity. If both demand and supply change, we cannot always say what will happen to both the price and the quantity. For example, if both demand and supply increase, we know that the quantity increases, but we cannot predict whether the price will rise or fall. To make such a prediction, we need to know the relative magnitude of the increase in demand and supply. If demand increases and supply decreases, we know that the price rises, but we cannot predict whether the quantity will increase or decrease. Again, to be able to make a prediction about the quantity, we need to know the relative magnitudes of the changes in demand and supply.

As an example of a change in both supply and demand, let's take one final look at the market for tapes. We've seen how demand and supply determine the price and quantity of tapes, how an increase in demand resulting from a fall in the price of a Walkman both raises the price of tapes and increases the quantity bought and sold, and how an increase in the supply of tapes resulting from an improved technology lowers the price of tapes and increases the quantity bought and sold. Let's now examine what happens when both of these changes – a fall in the price of a Walkman (which increases the demand for tapes) and an improved production technology (which increases the supply of tapes) – occur together.

The table in Fig. 4.10 brings together the numbers that describe the original quantities demanded and supplied and the new quantities demanded and

FIGURE 4.10

The Effects of a Change in Both Demand and Supply

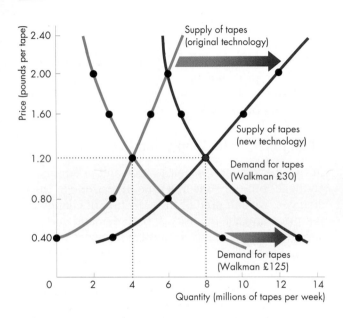

	Original quantities (millions of tapes per week)		New quantities (millions of tapes per week)	
Price (pounds per tape)	Quantity demanded (Walkman £125)	Quantity supplied (original technology)	Quantity demanded (Walkman £30)	Quantity supplied (new technology)
0.40	9	0	13	3
0.80	6	3	10	6
1.20	4	4	8	8
1.60	3	5	7	10
2.00	2	6	6	12

When a Walkman costs £125, the price of a tape is £1.20 and the equilibrium quantity is 4 million tapes a week. A fall in the price of a Walkman increases the demand for tapes, and improved technology increases the supply of tapes. The new technology supply curve intersects the higher demand curve at £1.20, the same price as before, but the quantity increases to 8 million tapes a week. The increase in both demand and supply increases the quantity but leaves the price unchanged.

supplied after the fall in the price of the Walkman and the improved tape-production technology. These same numbers are illustrated in the graph. The original demand and supply curves intersect at a price of £1.20 a tape and a quantity of 4 million tapes a week. The new supply and demand curves also intersect at a price of £1.20 a tape but at a quantity of 8 million tapes a week. In this example, the increases in demand and supply are such that the rise in price brought about by an increase in demand is offset by the fall in price brought about by an increase in supply – so the price does not change. An increase in either demand or supply increases the quantity. Therefore when both demand and supply increase, so does quantity. Note that if demand had increased slightly more than shown in the figure, the price would have risen. If supply had increased by slightly more than shown in the figure, the price would have fallen. But in both cases, the quantity would have increased. Box 4.1 provides an algebraic explanation of how to calculate the equilibrium price and quantity.

CD Players, Live Concerts and Coffee

At the beginning of this chapter, we looked at some facts about prices and quantities of CD players, live concerts and coffee. Let's use the theory of demand and supply that we have just studied to explain the movements in the prices and the quantities of those goods. Figure 4.11 illustrates the analysis.

First, let's consider the CD player, shown in part (a). In 1983, only a small number of firms were able to use the new technology to produce CD players and the supply of CD players was S_0. The 1983 demand curve is D_0. The quantities supplied and demanded in 1983 were equal at Q_0, and the price was P_0. As more and more firms learned how to use the new technologies and produce CD players, the supply increased and the supply curve shifted to the right from S_0 to S_1. At the same time, increasing incomes and an increasing variety of discs increased the demand for CD players, but not by as much as the increase in supply. The demand curve shifted from D_0 to D_1.

With the new demand curve D_1 and supply curve S_1, the equilibrium price is P_1 and the quantity is Q_1. The large increase in supply combined with a smaller increase in demand resulted in an increase in the quantity of CD players and a dramatic fall in their price.

FIGURE 4.11

More Changes in Supply and Demand

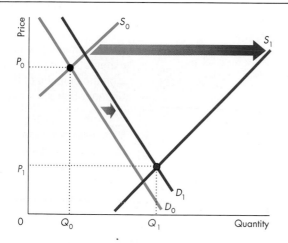

(a) CD players

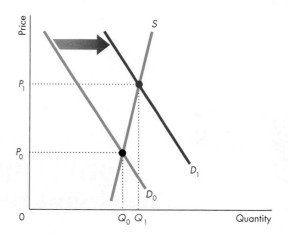

(b) Live concerts

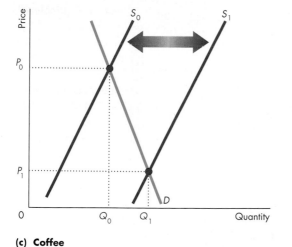

(c) Coffee

A large increase in the supply of CD players, from S_0 to S_1, combined with a small increase in demand, from D_0 to D_1, results in a fall in the price of the CD player, from P_0 to P_1, and an increase in the quantity, from Q_0 to Q_1 (part a).

An increase in the demand for live concerts produces a large increase in the price, from P_0 to P_1, but only a small increase in the quantity, from Q_0 to Q_1 (part b).

Variations in the weather and in growing conditions lead to fluctuations in the supply of coffee, between S_0 and S_1, which produce fluctuations in the price of coffee, between P_0 and P_1, and in the quantity, between Q_0 and Q_1 (part c).

Next, let's consider live concerts in Fig. 4.11(b). The supply of live performances is described by supply curve S. The supply curve is steep, reflecting the fact that there is a limited number of highly talented performers. As the incomes and the population grow, the demand for live concert seats increases. The demand curve shifts from D_0 to D_1. As a result, the price increases from P_0 to P_1 and the quantity also increases, but not as much as price.

Finally, let's consider the market for coffee, shown in Fig. 4.11(c). The demand for coffee is described by curve D. The supply of coffee fluctuates between S_0 and S_1. When growing conditions are good, the supply curve is S_1. When there are adverse growing conditions such as frost, the supply decreases and the supply curve is S_0. As a consequence of fluctuations in supply, the price of coffee fluctuates between P_0 (the maximum price) and P_1 (the minimum price). The quantity fluctuates between Q_0 and Q_1.

Demand and Supply

THE INDEPENDENT, 13 APRIL 1994

Hunt is up for weekend retreats

David Lawson

WHEN the Channel Tunnel finally opens this year, the first passengers may find themselves greeted with hugs and kisses at Calais by several hundred excited people with strangely familiar accents.

The British have already arrived in northern France. In fact, they started swarming in more than five years ago, goggling at every tumbledown farmhouse with a scrawled *'à vendre'* sign nailed to the gate.

They were so cheap! And the tunnel was *bound* to push up prices, wasn't it?

Then came disaster. Interest rates soared, redundancies proliferated and prices crashed. 'It's a buyers' market out there now around the mouth of the tunnel in Picardy and Somme,' says Alistair Williamson, a Hampshire-based agent who specialises in French property. 'Prices have come down as much as 20 per cent and there is an enormous amount of property available.'

Property is no longer cheap, however, in the popular area up to 20 miles inland, and along the Pas de Calais. 'You will need to spend £30,000 on a two-bed farmhouse and perhaps £50,000 on one close to shops and good roads,' says Mr Rutherford, another experienced Channel-hopping agent.

For the classic tumbledown cottage so beloved of the British – and shunned by the French – buyers must head west into Normandy and Brittany.

This is too far from the tunnel for quick visits, relying chiefly on more ponderous ferries for access. Buyers tend to be looking for something a bit bigger where they can spend more than the odd weekend, and perhaps rent out to help meet costs.

A more important reason than the tunnel for buying now is that the French economy is lagging behind the UK by around 18 months.

'But the banks are supporting property owners and buyers rather than "pulling the rug", says Mr Williamson. Loans are available for between 60 and 70 per cent of the purchase price at rates around 8.75 per cent spread over 20 years. He recommends Credit Agricole as a good source.

Buying from British sellers can also wipe out any disadvantage from the post-EMS devaluation, says Mr Rutherford, as they merely want to get their sterling price back. One disadvantage is that these homes are usually more expensive than those being sold by the French.

© The Independent. Reprinted with permission.

In recent years, a number of British people have bought cheap property in France along the Channel coast, in part seeing it as an investment given the expectation of price rises with the opening of the Channel Tunnel.

Recession in France then meant that the French housing market slumped, with prices falling by as much as 20 per cent.

Now is a good time to buy, because a number of the British people who bought houses then are now seeking to sell them and because the French banks are offering very good deals to people wanting to buy houses.

Background and Analysis

The Banque de France estimates that by 1989 British people had invested about £150 million in property in France.

With the opening of the Channel Tunnel, travel between the United Kingdom and France will be quicker and cheaper, so that a second home for British people in France could be used much more frequently, perhaps even lived in, with the owners commuting to the United Kingdom.

The figure shows the supply curve of housing in France and demand curves for housing in France demanded by British people. D_0 shows demand at the peak in the late 1980s and D_1 shows current demand.

Demand from British people increased during the 1980s because they expected higher future house prices in France after the Channel Tunnel opened. It was also felt that the Tunnel would make commuting from France feasible. Thus because of the lower level of house prices in France near the Channel coast there was now a lower priced substitute for expensive housing in the South East of England.

A further reason, similar to the economic relationship explored in Fig. 4.8, is that a lower travel cost between the United Kingdom and France would also be expected to increase the demand for houses in France.

The increased demand for French houses by British people had no significant impact on the price of houses in France because the number of British people in the French housing market was small. The demand from French people decreased because of the recession in France, lowering the equilibrium price by up to 20 per cent.

At the peak around 1989, about 100,000 houses were bought each year by British people. Now the figure is closer to 10,000. This lower demand from British people is also partly due to the continuing recession in the United Kingdom.

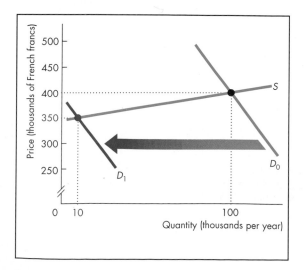

◆ ◆ ◆ ◆ By using the theory of demand and supply, you will be able to explain past fluctuations in prices and quantities and also make predictions about future fluctuations. But you will want to do more than predict whether prices are going to rise or fall. In your study of microeconomics, you will learn to predict *by how much* they will change. In your study of macroeconomics you will learn to explain fluctuations in the economy as a whole. In fact, the theory of demand and supply can help answer almost every economic question.

SUMMARY

Demand

The quantity demanded of a good or service is the amount that consumers plan to buy in a given period of time at a particular price. Demands are different from wants. Wants are unlimited, whereas demands reflect decisions to satisfy specific wants. The quantity that consumers plan to buy of any good depends on:

◆ The price of the good
◆ The prices of related goods – substitutes and complements
◆ Income
◆ Expected future prices
◆ Population
◆ Preferences

Other things being equal, the higher the price of a good, the smaller is the quantity of that good demanded. The relationship between the quantity demanded and price, holding constant all other influences on consumers' planned purchases, is illustrated by the demand schedule or demand curve. A change in the price of a good produces movement along the demand curve for that good. Such a movement is called a change in the quantity demanded.

Changes in all other influences on buying plans are said to change demand. When demand changes, there is a new demand schedule and the demand curve shifts. When there is an increase in demand, the demand curve shifts to the right; when there is a decrease in demand, the demand curve shifts to the left. (pp. 78–83)

Supply

The quantity supplied of a good or service is the amount that producers plan to sell in a given period of time. The quantity that producers plan to sell of any good or service depends on:

◆ The price of the good
◆ The prices of factors of production
◆ The prices of related goods
◆ Expected future prices
◆ The number of suppliers
◆ Technology

Other things being equal, the higher the price of a good, the larger is the quantity of that good supplied. The relationship between the quantity supplied and price, holding constant all other influences on firms' planned sales, is illustrated by the supply schedule or supply curve. A change in the price of a good produces movement along the supply curve for that good. Such a movement is called a change in the quantity supplied.

Changes in all other influences on selling plans are said to change supply. When supply changes, there is a new supply schedule and the supply curve shifts. When there is an increase in supply, the supply curve shifts to the right; when there is a decrease in supply, the supply curve shifts to the left. (pp. 83–86)

Price Determination

Price regulates the quantities supplied and demanded. The higher the price, the greater is the quantity supplied and the smaller is the quantity demanded. At high prices, there is a surplus – an excess of the quantity supplied over the quantity demanded. At low prices, there is a shortage – an excess of the quantity demanded over the quantity supplied. There is one price and only one price at which the quantity demanded equals the quantity supplied. That price is the equilibrium price. At that price, buyers have no incentive to offer a higher price and suppliers have no incentive to sell at a lower price. (pp. 87–89)

Predicting Changes in Price and Quantity

Changes in demand and supply lead to changes in price and in the quantity bought and sold. An increase in demand leads to a rise in price and to an increase in quantity. A decrease in demand leads to a fall in price and to a decrease in quantity. An increase in supply leads to an increase in quantity and to a fall in price. A decrease in supply leads to a decrease in quantity and a rise in price.

A simultaneous increase in demand and supply increases the quantity bought and sold, but can raise or lower the price. If the increase in demand is larger than the increase in supply, the price rises. If the increase in demand is smaller than the increase in supply, the price falls. (pp. 89–98)

KEY ELEMENTS

Key Terms

Key Figures and Tables

REVIEW QUESTIONS

1 Define the quantity demanded of a good or service.

2 Define the quantity supplied of a good or service.

3 List the main factors that influence the amount that consumers plan to buy and say whether an increase in each factor increases or decreases consumers' planned purchases.

4 List the main factors that influence the amount that firms' plan to sell and say whether an increase in each factor increases or decreases firms' planned sales.

5 State the law of demand and the law of supply.

6 If a fixed amount of a good is available, what does the demand curve tell us about the price that consumers are willing to pay for that fixed quantity?

7 If consumers are willing to buy only a certain fixed quantity, what does the supply curve tell us about the price at which firms will supply that quantity?

8 Distinguish between:
  a A change in demand and a change in the quantity demanded
  b A change in supply and a change in the quantity supplied

9 Why is the price at which the quantity demand-ed equals the quantity supplied the equilibrium price?

10 What happens to the price of a tape and the quantity of tapes sold if:
a The price of CDs increases.
b The price of a Walkman increases.
c The supply of live concerts increases.
d Consumers' incomes increase and firms producing tapes switch to new cost-saving technology.
e The prices of the factors of production used to make tapes increase.
f A new good comes onto the market that makes tapes obsolete.

P R O B L E M S

1 Suppose that one of the following events occurs:
a The price of petrol rises.
b The price of petrol falls.
c All speed limits on motorways are abolished.
d A new fuel-effective engine that runs on cheap alcohol is invented.
e The population doubles.
f Robotic production plants lower the cost of producing cars.
g A law banning car imports from Japan is passed.
h The rates for car insurance double.
i The minimum age for drivers is increased to 19 years.
j A massive and high-grade oil supply is dis covered in Mexico.
k The environmental lobby succeeds in closing down all nuclear power stations.
l The price of cars rises.
m The price of cars falls.
n The summer temperature is 10 degrees lower than normal and the winter tempera ture is 10 degrees higher than normal.

State which of the above events will produce:
(1) A movement along the demand curve for petrol
(2) A rightward shift of the demand curve for petrol
(3) A leftward shift of the demand curve for petrol
(4) A movement along the supply curve of petrol
(5) A rightward shift of the supply curve of petrol
(6) A leftward shift of the supply curve of petrol
(7) A movement along the demand curve for cars

(8) A movement along the supply curve of cars
(9) A rightward shift of the demand curve for cars
(10) A leftward shift of the demand curve for cars
(11) A rightward shift of the supply curve of cars
(12) A shift of the supply curve of cars left-ward
(13) An increase in the price of petrol
(14) A decrease in the quantity of oil bought and sold

2 The demand and supply schedules for bags of crisps are as follows:

Price (pence per bag)	Quantity demanded	Quantity supplied
	(millions of bags per week)	
10	200	0
20	180	30
30	160	60
40	140	90
50	120	120
60	100	140
70	80	160
80	60	180
90	40	200

a What is the equilibrium price of a bag of crisps?
b How many bags are bought and sold each week?

Suppose that a huge fire destroys one-half of the crisp-producing factories. Supply decreases to one-half of the amount shown in the above supply schedule.

c What is the new equilibrium price of a bag of crisps?

d How many bags are now bought and sold each week?

e Has there been a shift in or a movement along the supply curve of crisps?

f Has there been a shift in or a movement along the demand curve for crisps?

g As the crisp factories destroyed by fire are rebuilt and gradually resume crisp production what will happen to:

(1) The price of a bag of crisps

(2) The quantity of crisps bought

(3) The demand curve for crisps

(4) The supply curve of crisps

3 Suppose the demand and supply schedules for crisps are those in Problem 2. An increase in the teenage population increases the demand for crisps by 40 million bags a week.

a Write out the new demand schedule for crisps.

b What is the new quantity of crisps bought

and sold each week?

c What is the new equilibrium price of crisps?

d Has there been a shift in or a movement along the demand curve for crisps?

e Has there been a shift in or a movement along the supply curve of crisps?

4 Suppose the demand and supply schedules for crisps are those in Problem 2. An increase in the teenage population increases the demand for crisps by 40 million bags a week, and simultaneously the fire described in Problem 2 occurs, wiping out one-half of the crisp-producing factories.

a Draw a graph of the original and new demand and supply curves.

b What is the new quantity of crisps bought and sold each week?

c What is the new equilibrium price of crisps?

BOX 4.1: THE MATHEMATICS OF DEMAND AND SUPPLY

1. Demand and Supply Equations

The demand curve can be represented by the equation:

$$Q^d = a - b^P$$

The equation says that the quantity demanded, Q^d is equal to a constant amount a plus an amount that varies with price, P. Each unit increase in a brings b units decrease in the quantity demanded. A change in P brings a movement along the demand curve represented by the above equation. An increase in demand occurs if a increases.

The supply curve can be represented by the equation:

$$Q^s = f + g^P$$

The equation says that the quantity supplied, Q^s is equal to a constant amount f plus an amount that varies with price, P. Each unit increase in a brings g units increase in the quantity supplied. A change in P brings a movement along the supply curve represented by the above equation. An increase in supply occurs if f increases.

In equilibrium, the quantity supplied equals the quantity demanded. That is,

$$Q^s = Q^d.$$

2. Equilibrium Price

To find the equilibrium price, use the supply and demand equations above and make the quantities supplied and demanded equal. That is,

$$f + g^P = a - b^P$$

Move the P terms to the left and the constants to the right to give

$$(b + g)^P = a - f$$

and then divide both sides by $(b + g)$ to give the equilibrium price as

$$P = (a - f)/(b + g)$$

The key predictions about price can now be seen. If a increases, demand increases and so does the price. If f increases, supply increases and the price falls. And if both a and f increase, both demand and supply increase, and the effect on price is ambiguous.

3. Equilibrium Quantity

To find the equilibrium quantity, substitute the equilibrium price into either the demand or supply equation (we'll use the demand equation) to give,

$$Q = a - b(a - f)/(b + g)$$

You can simplify this solution by putting the left side of the equation on the common denominator $(b + g)$ as

$$Q = [a(b + g) - b(a - f)]/(b + g)$$

Notice that ab and ab cancel to give

$$Q = (ag + bf)/(b + g)$$

The key predictions about quantity can now be seen. If a increases, demand increases and so does the quantity. If f increases, supply increases and again, so does the quantity. If a increases and f decreases, demand increases and supply decreases, the effect on quantity is ambiguous.

CHAPTER 5

ELASTICITY

After studying this chapter you will be able to:

◆ Define and calculate the price elasticity of demand

◆ Explain what determines the elasticity of demand

◆ Use elasticity of demand for a particular good or service to determine whether a price change will increase or decrease expenditure on it

◆ Define and calculate other elasticities of demand

◆ Define and calculate the elasticity of supply

I F THE SUPPLY OF A GOOD OR SERVICE DECREASES, ITS PRICE RISES. BUT HOW MUCH will the price rise and how much will the quantity decrease? And will total spending by consumers increase or decrease? For many producers these are crucial questions. ◆ ◆ Suppose you have just been made economic adviser for OPEC – the Organization of Petroleum Exporting Countries. You want to bring more money into OPEC. Would you restrict the supply of oil to raise oil prices? Or would you produce more oil? As OPEC's economic adviser, you need to know about the demand for oil in great detail. For example, as the world economy grows, how much will the demand for oil grow? What about substitutes for oil? Will we discover inexpensive methods to convert coal and tar sands into usable fuel? Will nuclear energy become safe and cheap enough to compete with oil? ◆ ◆ A bumper grape crop is good news for

OPEC's Dilemma

wine consumers. It brings plentiful supplies at lower prices. But is it good news for grape growers? Do they make a bigger income? Or does the lower price more than wipe out their gains from larger quantities sold? ◆ ◆ Looking for greater tax revenues, the government decides to increase the tax rates on tobacco and alcohol. Do the higher tax rates bring in more tax revenue? Or do people switch to substitutes for tobacco and alcohol on such a massive scale that the higher tax rate brings in less tax revenue?

◆ ◆ ◆ ◆ In this chapter you will learn how to tackle questions such as the ones just posed. You will learn how we measure the responsiveness of the quantities bought and sold to changes in prices and other influences on buyers or sellers.

Price Elasticity of Demand

et's begin by looking a bit more closely at your task as OPEC's economic adviser. You want to decide whether to advise a cut in output to shift the supply curve to the left and raise the price of oil. To make this decision, you need to know how the quant-ity of oil demanded will respond to a change in price and you need a way of measuring that response.

Two Possible Scenarios

It is easy to show how important it is to know what the response will be. To do this let's compare two possible scenarios in the oil industry, shown in Fig. 5.1. In the two parts of the figure, the supply curves are identical, but the demand curves differ.

In each part of the figure, the supply curve labelled S_0 shows the initial supply. And in each part S_0 intersects the demand curve at a price of $10 a barrel and a quantity of 40 million barrels a day. Suppose you contemplate a cut in supply that shifts the supply curve from S_0 to S_1. In part (a), the new supply curve S_1 intersects the demand curve D_a at a price of $30 a barrel and a quantity of 23 million barrels a day. In part (b), with demand curve D_b, the same new supply curve S_1 intersects the differ-ent demand curve D_b at a price of $15 a barrel and a quantity of 15 million barrels a day.

You can see that the price rises by more in part (a) than in part (b) while the quantity decreases by more in part (b) than in part (a). What happens to the total revenue of the oil producers in these two cases? The **total revenue** from the sale of a good or service equals the price of the product multiplied by the quantity sold.

A rise in price has two opposing effects on rev-enue. First, the higher price means more revenue is received from each unit that is sold. This increase in revenue is shown by the blue areas. Second, the higher price decreases the quantity sold and this results in less revenue. This decrease in revenue is shown by the red areas. In part (a) the first effect is larger as the blue area exceeds the red area, so rev-enue increases. In part (b) the second effect is larger as the red area exceeds the blue area, so rev-enue decreases.

You can check these results by calculating and comparing the original and new total daily revenues.

FIGURE 5.1

Demand, Supply and Revenue

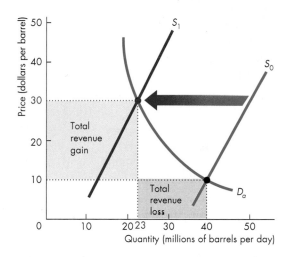

(a) More total revenue

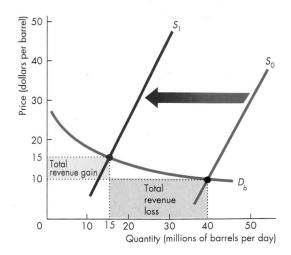

(b) Less total revenue

If supply is cut from S_0 to S_1, the price rises and the quantity traded decreases. In part (a), total revenue – that is the quantity multiplied by price – rises from $400 million to $690 million a day. Here, the increase in total revenue from a higher price (blue area) exceeds the decrease in total revenue from lower sales (red area). In part (b), total revenue falls from $400 million to $225 million a day. Here, the increase in total revenue from a higher price (blue area) is smaller than the decrease in total revenue from lower sales (red area). These two dif-ferent responses in total revenue arise from different responses of the quantity demanded to a change in price.

In each case, the original daily revenue was $400 million, that is $10 a barrel multiplied by 40 million barrels. In part (a) the daily revenue increases to $690 million, that is $30 a barrel multiplied by 23 million barrels. In part (b), the daily revenue decreases to $225 million, that is $15 a barrel multiplied by 15 million barrels.

Slope Depends on Units of Measurement

What differs in these two cases is how the quantity demanded responds to a change in the price of oil. It might seem easiest to compare the slopes of the demand curves for oil – D_a and D_b. For the same cut in supply, the steeper demand curve causes a bigger rise in price and a smaller drop in the quantity sold.

However we cannot compare two demand curves simply by measuring their slopes because the slope of a demand curve depends on the units that we put on the axes of the figure. Simply by changing these units we can make any demand curve appear steep or flat.

Also, we often need to compare the demand curves for different goods and services. For example, when deciding by how much to change tax rates, the government needs to compare the demand for oil and the demand for cigarettes. Which is more responsive to changes in price? Which can be taxed at an even higher rate without decreasing the tax revenue? Comparing the slopes of these two demand curves has no meaning since oil is measured in litres and cigarettes in packets – completely unrelated units.

To overcome these problems, we need a measure of response that is independent of the units of measurement of prices and quantities. Elasticity is such a measure. The **price elasticity of demand** for a good or service measures the responsiveness of the quantity of it that is demanded to a change in its price. It is calculated by using the following formula:

$$\frac{\text{Price elasticity}}{\text{of demand}} = \frac{\text{Percentage change in quantity demanded}}{\text{Percentage change in price}}$$

Calculating Elasticity

Let's practise using the formula for price elasticity of demand. To calculate a price elasticity, we need to know what the quantities demanded would be at different prices if nothing else that might affect consumers' buying plans changed, for only then can we be sure that we are measuring the responsiveness of the quantity demanded of a good or service to a change in its price. As an example, let's assume we have the relevant data on prices and quantities demanded for the oil industry. The calculations we will perform are shown in Table 5.1. You can use the symbols and the formulas shown in the final column of the table to perform the same calculations on any set of numbers.

In this example we are told that the original price is $9.50 a barrel, and that at that price 41 million barrels a day are sold. As the price rises to $10.50 a barrel, the quantity demanded decreases to 39 million barrels a day. So when the price rises by $1 a barrel, the quantity demanded decreases by 2 million barrels a day. To calculate the price elasticity of demand, we have to express changes in price and changes in quantity demanded as percentage changes. But there are two prices and two quantities – the original and the new. Which price and which quantity do we use for calculating the percentage changes? Should we work out the percentage change in quantity by expressing the change in quantity (2 million) as a percentage of the original quantity (41 million) or of the new quantity (39 million)? In fact we do neither.

Instead we express the change in quantity as a percentage of the average quantity (40 million in this example) and we express the change in price as a percentage of the average price. There is a good reason for this convention. It means we get the same number for price elasticity whether we consider a rise in price from $9.50 to $10.50 or a fall from $10.50 to $9.50. If economists decided, say, always to express the changes as percentages of the original values, then they would express the change in quantity of 2 million as a percentage of 41 million if prices rose from $9.50 to $10.50 and as a percentage of 39 million if prices fell back again. So they would get a different figure for the price elasticity if prices rose from the figure they would get if prices fell back. By working out the change as a percentage of the average, economists express the change in quantity as a percentage of 40 million whichever way the price is changing.

Let's now calculate the price elasticity in our example. The original price was $9.50 and the new price is $10.50, so the average price is $10 and the change in price is $1. The change of $1 is 10 per

---

TABLE 5.1

Calculating the Price Elasticity of Demand

	Symbols and formulas*	Numbers
Prices (dollars per barrel)		
Original price	P_0	$9.50
New price	P_1	$10.50
Change in price	$\Delta P = P_1 - P_0$	$1.00
Average price	$P_{ave} = (P_0 + P_1)/2$	$10.00
Percentage change in price	$(\Delta P/P_{ave}) \times 100$	10%
Quantities (millions of barrels per day)		
Original quantity demanded	Q_0	41
New quantity demanded	Q_1	39
Change in quantity demanded	$\Delta Q = Q_1 - Q_0$	-2
Average quantity demanded	$Q_{ave} = (Q_0 + Q_1)/2$	40
Percentage change in quantity demanded	$(\Delta Q/Q_{ave}) \times 100$	-5%
Price elasticity of demand	$= (\Delta Q/Q_{ave})/(DP/P_{ave})$	-0.5
Elasticity of demand	η	0.5

*The Greek letter *delta* (Δ) stands for 'change in'.

---

cent of the average price. The original quantity was 41 million barrels and the new quantity is 39 million barrels, so the average quantity demanded is 40 million barrels and the change is –2 million barrels. The change of –2 million barrels is –5 per cent of the average quantity. So the price elasticity of demand is:

$$\frac{-5\%}{10\%} = -0.5 \ .$$

Minus Sign and Elasticity

The price elasticity of demand we have just calculated was negative, as it was *minus* 0.5. Because a positive change in the price always results in a negative change in the quantity demanded, the price elasticity of demand is negative. But it is the *absolute value* of the price elasticity of demand

that tells us how responsive – how elastic – demand is. To make it easier to compare elasticities, we drop the minus sign and use the term **elasticity of demand** to mean the *absolute value* of the price elasticity of demand. So in our example, we would say that elasticity of demand was 0.5. We shall use the Greek letter η to refer to the elasticity of demand.

Percentages and Proportions

Although price elasticity is the percentage change in the quantity demanded divided by the percentage change in the price, it is also, equivalently, the *proportional* change in the quantity demanded divided by the *proportional* change in the price. In Table 5.1, notice that although the formula multiplies both the proportional change in price $(\Delta P/P_{ave})$ and the proportional change in quantity demanded $(\Delta Q/Q_{ave})$ by 100, to create the percentage changes, those hundreds cancel when we divide.

Elastic and Inelastic Demand

The elasticity that we calculated in our example is 0.5. Does this indicate a high or low responsiveness for quantity demanded in relation to a change in price? The size of the elasticity of demand can range between zero and infinity.[1] The elasticity of demand would be zero if the quantity demanded did not change at all when the price changed. You can work out by assuming that for one good a change in price had no effect on the quantity demanded. In this case, the percentage change in the quantity demanded is zero. It doesn't matter what the percentage change in the price is because if we divide zero by any number, we get zero. An example of a good that has an elasticity of demand that is close to zero (perhaps even zero) is insulin. Insulin is of such importance to many diabetics that they would buy the quantity they need for their health at almost any price.

If a price rise causes a decrease in the quantity demanded, the elasticity is greater than zero. When

---

[1] Elasticity of demand would be negative in the case of any product where the quantity demanded actually fell if price fell. Such products are called 'Giffen goods'; see the discussion in Chapter 8.

TABLE 5.2

Elastic and Inelastic Demand

Effects of a 10 per cent price change

	Original quantity demanded	New quantity demanded	Change in quantity demanded	Average quantity demanded	Percentage change in quantity demanded	Elasticity of demand
Inelastic	41	39	−2	40	−5	0.5
Unit elastic	42	38	−4	40	−10	1.0
Elastic	50	30	−20	40	−50	5.0

the percentage change in the quantity demanded is smaller than the percentage change in price, the elasticity is less than 1 (the example that we calculated in Table 5.1 is such a case). If the percentage change in the quantity demanded equals the percentage change in price, the elasticity of demand is 1. If the percentage change in the quantity demanded is larger than the percentage change in price, the elasticity is greater than 1.

In an extreme case, the quantity demanded may be infinitely sensitive to price changes. Consider the owners of one hop farm in Kent. They are in competition with many other hop farms. If they set their price at just 1 penny a tonne above the prices set by their rivals, they might sell no hops at all – the brewery companies would buy all the hops they need from this farm's rivals. A subsequent fall in the price by 1 penny a tonne, a virtually negligible amount, could be enough to stop the brewers staying away, and so could result in a great increase in sales. If a very large increase in quantity demanded is associated with a negligible fall in price, then the elasticity could be effectively infinity, for we would have a large percentage change in quantity divided by a virtually zero percentage change in price.

For elasticities between zero and 1, elasticity of demand is said to be **inelastic**. For elasticities between 1 and infinity, elasticity of demand is said to be **elastic**. The dividing line between inelastic and elastic demand is 1 which is called **unit elastic demand**. When elasticity is equal to infinity, demand is called **perfectly elastic**; when elasticity is equal

to zero, demand is called **perfectly inelastic**.

Table 5.2 shows three examples of elasticity of demand, one inelastic, one unit elastic and one elastic. In each case we suppose there is a 10 per cent rise in the price. The elasticities differ because in each example there is a different response in quantity demanded. The first row simply reproduces the calculations that you worked through in Table 5.1. Here the percentage change in quantity was −5 per cent. With a −5 per cent change in quantity demanded and a 10 per cent change in price, we get a price elasticity of demand of −0.5 and an elasticity of demand of 0.5. This is between 0 and 1, so demand is inelastic. The second row shows the case of a unit elastic demand. Here the initial quantity demanded was 42 million barrels a day and the new quantity demanded is 38 million, so the average quantity demanded is 40 million and the change in the quantity demanded is −4 million. The percentage change in the quantity demanded is −10. With a −10 per cent change in quantity demanded and a 10 per cent change in price, we get a price elasticity of demand of −1 and an elasticity of demand of 1. The final case is one where the original quantity demanded was 50 million and the new quantity demanded is 30 million. The average quantity demanded is still 40 million but the change in quantity demanded is now −20 million, which is −50 per cent. With a −50 per cent change in quantity demanded and a 10 per cent change in price, we get a price elasticity of demand of −5 and an elasticity of demand of 5. This is greater than 1, so demand here is elastic.

This table may give you the idea that elasticities are simply numbers. But elasticities are not just numbers calculated by economists. Whether demand is elastic or inelastic is of enormous importance to each of us on an individual level. In the early 1970s, when there was no oil coming in from the North Sea, OPEC did cut back on the supply of oil and the price of oil rose dramatically. UK citizens found that their demand for oil was inelastic and this meant that they spent far more on oil; the situation resembled the one shown in Fig. 5.1(a). As a result, people had to spend less on other items such as holidays and consumer durables. Also, people started to insulate their homes and buy less thirsty cars.

Arc Elasticity and Point Elasticity

We have now seen how to calculate elasticity of demand when price changes. However, the elasticity of demand generally changes as we move along a demand curve. To see this, suppose the demand curve for oil is as shown in Fig. 5.2.

Let's start with a price of $90 a barrel. What is the elasticity if the price falls to $30? The average price is $60. The change in the price is –$60 which is –100 per cent of the average price. The original quantity demanded is 20 million barrels a day and the new quantity demanded is 30 million barrels a day, so the average quantity demanded is 25 million barrels a day. The change in the quantity demanded is 10 million barrels a day which is 40 per cent of the average quantity. So the price elasticity of demand is 40/–100 which is –0.4, and the elasticity of demand is 0.4.

Next, let's start with a price of $30 a barrel. What is the elasticity if we reduce the price from $30 to $20? The average price is $25. The change in the price is –$10 which is –40 per cent of the average price. The original quantity demanded is 30 million barrels a day and the new quantity demanded is 50 million barrels a day, so the average quantity demanded is 40 million barrels a day. The change in the quantity demanded is 20 million barrels a day which is 50 per cent of the average quantity. So the price elasticity of demand is 50/–40 which is –1.25, and the elasticity of demand is 1.25.

The elasticities of demand which we have just calculated are called arc elasticities. An **arc elasticity** gives an estimate of the elasticity over a stretch, or

FIGURE 5.2

Arc Elasticity of Demand

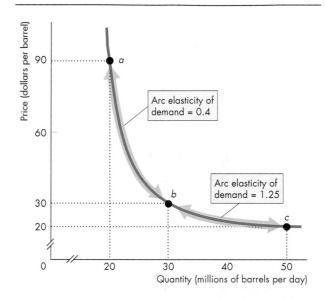

If an increase in supply reduces the price from $90 a barrel to $30 a barrel, the quantity demanded increases from 20 million barrels a day to 30 million barrels a day and there is a movement along the demand curve from *a* to *b*. The elasticity of demand along this arc of the demand curve – the arc elasticity – is 0.4. The fall in price of $60 is 100 per cent of the average price and the increase in the quantity demanded of 10 million barrels a day is 40 per cent of the average quantity, so the elasticity of demand is 40/100 = 0.4. If a further increase in supply reduces the price from $30 a barrel to $20 a barrel, the quantity demanded increases from 30 million barrels a day to 50 million barrels a day and there is a movement along the demand curve from *b* to *c*. The arc elasticity of demand from *b* to *c* is 1.25. The fall in price of $10 is 40 per cent of the average price and the increase in the quantity demanded of 20 million barrels a day is 50 per cent of the average quantity, so the elasticity of demand is 50/40 = 1.25.

arc, of a curve. Figure 5.2 shows the two arcs for which we have calculated arc elasticities. We can calculate arc elasticities for any arc simply by considering the percentage changes in price and quantity demanded along the arc concerned.

You may think the elasticity varied along the demand curve in Fig. 5.2 simply because the demand curve there was curved. But the elasticity also varies along most straight-line demand curves. You can see this by looking at the demand curve shown in Fig. 5.3. There, if the price of oil falls

FIGURE 5.3

Elasticity Along a Straight-line Demand Curve

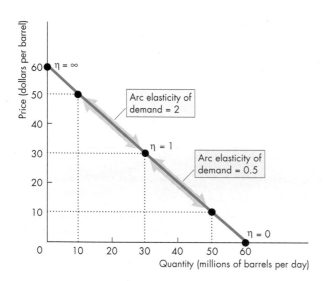

On a straight-line demand curve, elasticity decreases as the price falls and the quantity demanded increases. The arc elasticity of demand between a price of $50 and $30 a barrel is 2 while the arc elasticity of demand between a price of $30 and $10 a barrel is 0.5. Above the mid-point, demand is elastic (elasticity is between 1 and ∞). Below the mid-point, demand is inelastic (elasticity is between 0 and 1). The point elasticity of demand is 1 at the mid-point of the demand curve (unit elasticity of demand). The point elasticity of demand is ∞ where the curve cuts the price axis and 0 where it cuts the quantity axis.

from $50 a barrel to $30, the quantity demanded increases from 10 million barrels a day to 30 million. The increase in quantity is 20 million barrels and the average quantity is 20 million barrels, so the percentage change in quantity is 100. The change in price is –$20 and the average price is $40, so the percentage change in price is –50. So the arc elasticity of demand is 100/50 which is 2. If, instead, the price of oil falls from $30 a barrel to $10 a barrel, the quantity demanded increases from 30 million barrels a day to 50 million. The increase in quantity is 20 million barrels and the average quantity is 40 million barrels, so the percentage change in quantity is 50. The change in price is

–$20 and the average price is $20, so the percentage change in price is –100. So the arc elasticity of demand is 50/100 which is 0.5.

If you calculate arc elasticities on a straight-line demand curve, you will find that the elasticity of demand decreases as you move down the curve. You will also find that the elasticity along any arc above the mid-point is a number greater than 1 (like the 2 we found between $50 and $30 a barrel) while the elasticity along any arc below the mid-point is a number lower than 1 (like the 0.5 we found between $30 and $10 a barrel). This means that demand is elastic above the mid-point and inelastic below the mid-point, as shown on Fig. 5.3.

Sometimes it is useful to know the elasticity at a particular point on a curve, that is a **point elasticity**. The easiest way of doing this is shown in Box 5.1 on pp. 130–131. We shall make little use of point elasticities in this book. But it is worth noting that on a straight-line demand curve the elasticity at the mid-point is 1. Also, at the point where the demand curve cuts the price axis the elasticity is infinity, while at the point where it cuts the quantity axis it is zero. These results are also shown in Fig. 5.3.

Why Elasticity is Smaller at Lower Prices

Why is elasticity of demand smaller at lower prices along a straight-line demand curve? It is because the *levels* of price and quantity demanded affect their *percentage* changes. For a given change in price, the percentage change is small at a high price and large at a low price. Similarly, for a given change in quantity demanded, the percentage change is small at a large quantity and large at a small quantity. So for a given change in price, the lower the initial price, the larger is the percentage change in price, the smaller is the percentage change in the quantity demanded, and the smaller is the elasticity.

Constant Elasticity Demand Curves

We saw that the elasticity varies along the straight-line demand curve in Fig. 5.3. Indeed elasticity varies along most demand curves. But it is possible to draw demand curves that have a constant elasticity. Figure 5.4 illustrates three such curves. The curve in part (a) is vertical. Any vertical demand curve has a constant elasticity of zero as any price

FIGURE 5.4

Demand Curves with Constant Elasticity

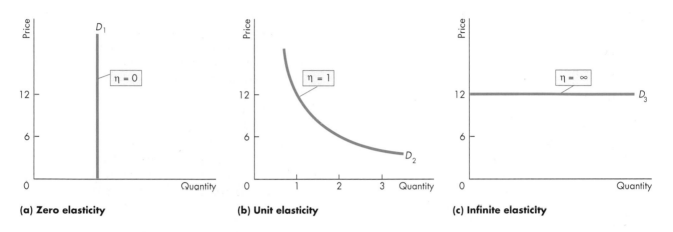

(a) Zero elasticity   **(b) Unit elasticity**   **(c) Infinite elasticity**

Each demand curve shown here has a constant elasticity. Vertical demand curves, like the demand curve in part (a), have a constant elasticity of zero. Demand curves that result in the same level of spending and revenue at each price, like the demand curve in part (b), have constant unit elasticity (elasticity equals 1); in this case spending is always 12. Demand curves that are horizontal, like the demand curve in part (c), have constant infinite elasticity (elasticity equals infinity).

change leads to a zero quantity change. Such a curve is said to be a perfectly inelastic demand curve. The curve in part (b) may not look very special, but it has been carefully drawn so that total spending is the same at each price. It is 12 at each price, as quantity is 1 at a price of 12, 2 at a price of 6 and so on. In other words, as price increases, the percentage change in quantity always offsets the percentage change in price so that total spending and revenue stay the same. On this curve, elasticity of demand is 1 throughout. The curve in part (c) is horizontal. Any horizontal demand curve has a constant elasticity of demand of infinity as the tiniest possible price change can lead to an enormous quantity change. Such a curve is said to be a perfectly elastic demand curve. It is possible – with great care – to draw curves which have a constant elasticity of any number. Box 5.2 on pp. 132 shows how to draw a demand curve with a constant elasticity of demand of 2.

The example we gave earlier of a good where the responsiveness of quantity to changes in price is very low was insulin. Insulin might even have a

demand curve like the one in Fig. 5.4(a). Regardless of the price, the quantity demanded remains constant in part (a). An example of a good whose elasticity is close to 1 is electricity. It will have a demand curve similar to the one shown in Fig. 5.4(b). As an example of a good whose elasticity of demand is infinite, we suggested the produce of one Kent hop farm. This farm will face a demand curve like the one shown in Fig. 5.4(c), which is horizontal at the price level set by its rivals. If this farm sets a price above that of its rivals, then no brewers will buy its hops. In contrast, if it sets its price below that of its rivals, then every brewer will want its hops and it will face a far bigger demand than it can possibly meet. If it sets the same price as its rivals, as it no doubt will, then there is no unique quantity demanded.

Real-world Elasticities

Actual values of elasticities of demand have been estimated from the average spending patterns of consumers and some examples are set out in Table

TABLE 5.3

Some Price Elasticities in the UK Economy

Product	Elasticity
ELASTIC DEMANDS	
Gas	2.26
Foreign travel	1.83
UNIT ELASTICITY	
Chemists' goods	1.00
INELASTIC DEMANDS	
Car travel	0.83
Meat	0.56
Books and magazines	0.52
Clothing	0.50
Fruit	0.49
Cigarettes and tobacco	0.26
Vegetables	0.26
Housing	0.23

Source: Angus Deaton, *'Models and Projections of Demand in Post-War Britain'*. (London: Chapman & Hall, 1975), 176–80.

5.3. What makes the demand for some goods and services elastic and the demand for others inelastic? The elasticity for a good or service depends on:

◆ The ease with which another good or service can be substituted for it
◆ The proportion of income spent on it
◆ The amount of time elapsed since the price change

Substitutability Substitutability depends on the nature of the good or service itself. For example, oil, a good with an inelastic demand, certainly has substitutes, but none of these is very close (imagine a steam-driven, coal-fuelled car or a nuclear-powered airliner). On the other hand gas, a good with an elastic demand, has a very good substitute in the form of electricity.

The degree of substitutability between two goods depends on how narrowly (or broadly) we define them. For example, even though oil does not have a close substitute, different types of oil substitute for each other without much difficulty. Oils from different parts of the world differ in weight and chemical composition. Let's consider a particular kind of oil – called Saudi Arabian Light. Its elasticity is relevant to Saudi Arabia. Suppose Saudi Arabia is contemplating a unilateral price rise in this type of oil, which means that the prices of other types of oil will stay the same. Although Saudi Arabian Light has some unique characteristics, other oils can easily substitute for it, and most buyers will be very sensitive to its price relative to the prices of other types of oil. The quantity in this case is highly elastic, that is, very responsive to changes in price.

This example, which distinguishes between oil in general and different types of oil, has broad applications. For example, the elasticity of demand for meat in general is inelastic while the elasticity of demand for beef, lamb or pork is very elastic. The elasticity of demand for personal computers is inelastic, but the elasticity of demand for an IBM, Amstrad, or Apple is very elastic.

It is not only the availability of substitutes which affects elasticity. The price of the substitute is also relevant. Silver-plated cutlery is a substitute for stainless-steel cutlery, but silver-plated cutlery is much more expensive than stainless-steel cutlery. So we would find that stainless-steel cutlery prices could rise a long way before many people opted for the silver-plated substitute. So the demand for stainless-steel cutlery could be inelastic even though there is a very serviceable substitute.

Proportion of Income Spent on a Good Other things being equal, elasticity is higher for goods (and services) on which people spend the largest proportions of their incomes. If only a small fraction of a consumer's income is spent on a good, then even a large change in its price will have little impact on the consumer who may continue buying almost as much as before. In contrast, if a large fraction of a consumer's income is spent on a good, then even a small rise in its price will probably force the consumer to buy substantially less.

To appreciate the importance of the proportion of income spent on a good, consider the elasticities of demand by students for textbooks and paperclips. If the price of textbooks doubles there is an enormous decrease in the quantity of textbooks bought; there is also an increase in book sharing and illegal photocopying. If the price of paperclips doubles, there is almost no change in the quantity of paperclips demanded. Why is there this difference? Textbooks take a large proportion of students' incomes while paperclips take only a tiny portion. Students don't like either price to increase, but they would hardly notice the effects of higher paperclip prices, while higher textbook prices would have a big impact.

Time For some goods and services, elasticity also depends on the amount of time elapsed since a price change. The reason is related to substitutability. The greater the passage of time, the more it becomes possible to develop substitutes for a good whose price has increased. Thus at the moment of a price increase, consumers often have little choice but to continue consuming similar quantities of a good. However, given enough time, they find alternatives and gradually buy less of the items that have become more expensive. For example, if rush-hour bus fares in Birmingham rise, then initially most of those commuters who used to travel by bus may continue to do so. But in time some may switch to using cars, some may buy bicycles, others will decide to jog to work, others will move homes (or jobs) and some may give up work altogether. So in time the quantity of bus journeys demanded may decrease appreciably – see Reading Between the Lines, pp. 122–123. This factor of time is not always important: if the price of beans rises, for example, consumers do not take long to buy more peas or sprouts as substitutes.

Two Time Frames for Demand

To take account of the importance of time on the elasticity of demand, we distinguish between two time frames for demand:

◆   Short-run demand
◆   Long-run demand

Short-run Demand The **short-run demand curve** describes the initial response of buyers to a change in the price of a good or service. The short-run response depends on whether the price change is seen as permanent (or, at least, long-lasting) or temporary. A price change that is

believed to be temporary produces a highly elastic response from consumers. Why would you pay a higher price now if you can get the same thing for a lower price a few days from now? And if the price is temporarily low, why wouldn't you take advantage of it and buy a lot before the price goes up again?

Examples of temporary price changes abound. For example, you can make telephone calls in the United Kingdom at much lower rates after 18.00 on weekdays. The drop in price in the evening produces a large increase in the quantity of private telephone calls – the demand for them is highly elastic. Other examples are off-peak rail tickets and seasonal variations in the price of fresh fruits and vegetables.

When a price change seems permanent, the quantity bought may not change much in the short run. So short-run demand is often inelastic. The reason is that people often find it hard to change their buying habits and need time to do so. We saw in an earlier example that the commuters in Birmingham might take a long time to adjust fully to a rise in bus fares.

An example of a permanent, or at least a long-lasting, price change occurred in the market for oil in the early 1970s. At the end of 1973 and the beginning of 1974, the price of oil increased fourfold, leading in turn to a sharp rise in the costs of home heating and petrol. Initially, consumers had little choice but to accept the price increases and maintain oil consumption at more or less their original levels. Their homes may not have been well insulated and their cars may not have been fuel-efficient but such things cannot be altered overnight. Drivers could reduce their average speeds and economize on petrol – but this meant that journeys took longer. Thermostats could be turned down – but that meant that people were less comfortable. As a consequence, there were severe limits to the extent to which people were willing to cut back on their consumption of the now much more costly oil products. The short-run consumer response in the face of this sharp price increase was inelastic.

Long-run Demand The **long-run demand curve** describes the response of buyers to a change in price after all possible adjustments have been made. Long-run demand is generally more elastic than short-run demand. The 1974 rise in the price of oil and petrol produced a clear demonstration of the distinction between long-run and short-run demand. Initially, buyers responded to higher oil and petrol prices by using almost as much as before. With a longer time to respond, people were able to improve the insulation of their homes with double glazing and cavity-wall insulation and they were able to buy a new generation of more fuel-efficient cars. Within a few years cars were being made that were 25 per cent more fuel efficient than cars of a similar size had been in 1970.

Two Demand Curves   The short-run and long-run demand curves for oil in 1974 looked like those in Fig. 5.1. Look back at that figure and refresh your memory about the demand curves in parts (a) and (b). The short-run demand curve is D_a and the long-run demand curve is D_b. The price of a barrel of oil in 1974 was $10 and 40 million barrels a day were bought and sold. At that price and quantity, long-run demand, D_b, is much more elastic than short-run demand, D_a.

R E V I E W

The price elasticity of demand is a unit-free measure of the response of a change in the quantity demanded to a change in price. It is calculated as the percentage change in the quantity demanded divided by the percentage change in price. Because demand curves slope downward, price elasticities of demand are negative. We usually avoid negative numbers by talking instead about the elasticity of demand which we define as the absolute value of the price elasticity of demand. The elasticity of demand ranges between zero and infinity. Goods and services that have an elasticity of demand between infinity and 1 are those that have close substitutes and on which a large proportion of income is spent. Goods and services that have an elasticity of demand between 1 and zero are those that do not have good substitutes and on which a small proportion of income is spent. Elasticity is also higher, the longer the time lapse since a price change. ◆

Elasticity, Revenue and Expenditure

The total revenue received by the producers of a good (or service) equals the price of the good multiplied by the quantity *sold*. The total expenditure made by purchasers is the price of a good multiplied by the quantity *bought*. Thus revenue and expenditure are two sides of the same coin – revenues are the receipts of sellers while expenditures are the outlays of the buyers. When the price of a good rises, the quantity sold decreases. What happens to revenue and expenditure depends on the extent to which the quantity sold decreases as the price rises. If a 1 per cent rise in the price reduces the quantity sold by less than 1 per cent, then revenue increases. If a 1 per cent rise in price lowers the quantity sold by more than 1 per cent, then revenue falls. If a 1 per cent rise in price lowers the quantity sold by 1 per cent, then the price rise and the quantity decrease just offset each other and revenue stays constant. But we now have a precise way of linking the percentage change in the quantity sold to the percentage change in price – the elasticity of demand. When the price of a good rises, the size of the elasticity of demand determines whether revenue rises or falls. Table 5.4 provides some examples based on the three cases in Table 5.2.

In case *a*, the elasticity of demand is 0.5. When the price rises from $9.50 to $10.50, the quantity sold decreases from 41 million to 39 million barrels a day. Revenue, which equals price multiplied by quantity sold, was originally $9.50 multiplied by 41 million, which is $389.50 million a day. After the price rises, revenue rises to $409.50 million a day. So the rise in price leads to an *increase in revenue* of $20 million a day.

In case *b*, the elasticity of demand is 1. The quantity sold decreases from 42 million to 38 million barrels a day as the price rises from $9.50 to $10.50. Revenue in this case is the same at each price, $399 million a day. Here, where the elasticity of demand is 1, the rise in price has *no effect on revenue*.

In case *c*, the elasticity of demand is 5. When the price rises by $1, the quantity sold decreases by 20 million barrels a day. The original revenue was $475 million a day but the new revenue is $315 million a day. So the rise in price leads to a *fall in revenue* of $160 million a day.

TABLE 5.4

Elasticity of Demand, Revenue and Expenditure

| | Elasticity | Price (dollars per barrel) | | Quantity demanded (millions of barrels per day) | | Revenue/expenditure (millions of dollars per day) | | |
		Original	New	Original	New	Original	New	Change
a	0.5	9.50	10.50	41	39	389.50	409.50	+20.00
b	1.0	9.50	10.50	42	38	399.00	399.00	0
c	5.0	9.50	10.50	50	30	475.00	315.00	−160.00

Elasticity and revenue are closely connected. When the elasticity of demand is less than 1, the percentage decrease in quantity is less than the percentage rise in price so that a rise in price causes a rise in revenue. In contrast, when the elasticity is greater than 1, the percentage decrease in quantity is greater than the percentage rise in price so that a rise in price causes a fall in revenue. When the elasticity of demand is 1, the percentage decrease in the quantity demanded equals the percentage rise in price and revenue remains constant. The increase in revenue which results from a higher price is exactly offset by the loss in revenue from the smaller quantities sold.

As we have seen, long-run demand curves are more elastic than short-run demand curves. It is possible, therefore, that an increase in price will result in an increase in revenue in the short run and yet result in a fall in revenue in the long run. Such an outcome will occur if the short-run elasticity is less than 1 while the long-run elasticity is greater than 1.

The price elasticity of demand that we have been studying is the most important of all elasticities. But there are some other elasticities which we must now consider.

More Demand Elasticities

As we noted in Chapter 4, the quantity demanded of any good or service is affected by several factors other than its price. These other factors include consumers' incomes and the prices of other relevant goods and services. We can calcu-late elasticities which measure the responsiveness of quantity demanded to changes in these other variables as well. Let's now examine these additional elasticities.

Income Elasticity of Demand

As the total income of a country grows, how will the demand for a particular good (or service) change? The answer depends on the income elasticity of demand for the good. The **income elasticity of demand** is the percentage change in the quantity of the good (or service) demanded divided by the percentage change in income. It is represented by η_y. That is:

$$\eta_y = \frac{\text{Percentage change in quantity demanded}}{\text{Percentage change in income}}$$

Income elasticities of demand can be positive or negative. There are three interesting ranges for the income elasticity of demand:

1. Greater than 1 (income elastic)
2. Between zero and 1 (income inelastic)
3. Less than zero (negative income elasticity)

These three cases are illustrated in Fig. 5.5 where quantities demanded are shown on the vertical axes and incomes on the horizontal axes.

Part (a) shows a case where income elasticity of demand is greater than 1. As income rises here, the quantity demanded increases, as shown by the curve sloping upward. Moreover, the quantity demanded increases proportionately faster than income, as shown by the fact that the curve gets progressively steeper. Goods and services that fall into this category include, clothing, works of art and ocean cruises.

FIGURE 5.5

Income Elasticity of Demand

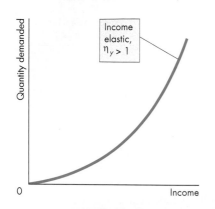

(a) Elasticity greater than 1

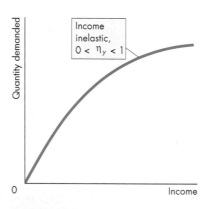

(b) Elasticity between zero and 1

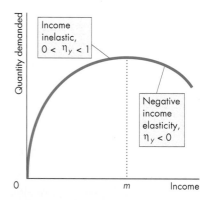

(c) Elasticity less than 1 and becomes negative

There are three ranges of values for income elasticity of demand. In part (a), income elasticity of demand is greater than 1. In this case, as income increases, the quantity demanded increases but by a bigger percentage than the increase in income. In part (b), income elasticity of demand is between 0 and 1. In this case, as income increases, the quan-tity demanded increases but by a smaller percentage than the increase in income. In part (c), the income elasticity of demand is positive at low incomes but becomes negative as income rises above level m. Maximum consumption occurs at the income level m.

Part (b) shows a case where income elasticity of demand is between zero and 1. In this case, too, the quantity demanded increases as income rises, as shown by the curve sloping upward. But here the quantity demanded increases proportionately more slowly than income, as shown by the curve becom-ing progressively flatter. Goods that fall into this category include meat, housing and beer.

Part (c) illustrates a third category of goods and services that is a bit more complicated. For these items, as income rises, the quantity demanded increases until it reaches a maximum at income m. Beyond that point, as income continues to rise, the quantity demanded declines. The elasticity of demand is positive but less than 1 up to income m. Beyond income m, the income elasticity of demand is negative because here income and quantity move in opposite directions – when income rises the quan-tity decreases. Examples of goods in this category include small motor bikes and rice. Low income con-sumers buy most of these goods. In countries where incomes are low, the demand for such goods increas-es as income rises. Eventually, income reaches a

level m where consumers replace these goods with superior alternatives. For example, a small car replaces the motor bike while more meat appears in a diet that included a lot of rice.

Goods whose income elasticities of demand are positive are called *normal goods*. Goods whose income elasticities of demand are negative are called *inferior goods*. They are 'inferior' in the sense that as income increases they are replaced with 'superior' but more expensive substitutes. So the items in parts (a) and (b) of Fig. 5.5 are normal at all income levels while the good in part (c) is nor-mal at low incomes and inferior at high incomes.

Let's calculate the income elasticity of demand for a normal good – fish. We can imagine that the relationship between consumers' incomes and the quantity of fish demanded would be similar to the line shown in Fig. 5.5(b). Suppose that if con-sumers' combined incomes were £760 million per day then the quantity of fish demanded would be 1,980 tonnes per day. And suppose that if con-sumers' incomes rose to £840 million per day the quantity of fish demanded would increase to 2,020 tonnes per day. What would the income elasticity of demand be here? The average quantity of fish demanded is 2,000 tonnes. The change in the quantity is an increase of 40 tonnes per day which is 2 per cent of the average quantity. The average level of incomes is £800 million per day. The change in incomes is £80 million per day which is 10 per cent of the average income. The result is that the income elasticity of demand is 2/10 or 0.2.

Notice that we worked out the percentage changes in quantity demanded and income as percentages of the average quantity and the average income. Strictly speaking, this means that the elasticity of 0.2 is an arc income elasticity of demand. In other words, it is a measure of the average income elasticity between income levels of £760 and £840 million per day. We could work out a point income elasticity of demand using methods similar to those outlined in Box 5.1 on pp. 130–131.

Real-world Income Elasticities of Demand Some estimates of actual income elasticities of demand in the United Kingdom are given in two groups in Table 5.5. The first group lists items with income elasticities greater than 1. These items are said to have income elastic demands. The second group lists items whose income elasticities are less than 1 and whose demands are said to be income inelastic.

By using estimates of income elasticity of demand, we can translate projections of average income growth rates into growth rates of demand for particular goods and services. For example, if average incomes grow by 4 per cent a year, the demand for car travel will grow by about 5 per cent a year (4 per cent multiplied by 1.23, the income elasticity of demand for car travel as shown in Table 5.5).

Cross Elasticity of Demand

The quantity demanded of any good (or service) depends on the prices of its substitutes and complements. The responsiveness of the quantity demanded of a particular good to changes in the price of one of its substitutes or complements is measured by **cross elasticity of demand**, which is represented by η_x. The cross elasticity of demand is calculated as the percentage change in the quantity demanded of the one good divided by the percentage change in the price of another good. This other good may be a substitute or a complement for the first good. That is:

TABLE 5.5

Some Income Elasticities of Demand in the United Kingdom

ELASTIC

Gas	5.24
Foreign travel	3.32
Chemists' goods	2.07
Clothing	1.47
Car travel	1.23

INELASTIC

Books and magazines	0.95
Meat	0.79
Cigarettes and tobacco	0.77
Housing	0.54
Fruit	0.52
Beer	0.51
Potatoes and vegetables	0.26

Source: Angus Deaton, *'Models and Projections of Demand in Post-War Britain'*. (London: Chapman & Hall, 1975) 176–80.

$$\eta_x = \frac{\text{Percentage change in quantity demanded of one good}}{\text{Percentage change in the price of another good}}$$

The cross elasticity of demand with respect to the price of a substitute is positive. The cross elasticity of demand with respect to the price of a complement is negative. The examples in Fig. 5.6 make it clear why. When the price of coal (a substitute for oil) rises, then the demand for oil increases, but when the price of cars (a complement for oil) rises, then the demand for oil declines.

The degree to which the quantity of a good demanded changes when the prices of substitutes or complements change depends on how close the substitute or complement is. So there will be a more positive cross elasticity of demand for beef with respect to pork than there will be for beef with respect to kippers. Also there will be a more negative cross elasticity of

FIGURE 5.6

Cross Elasticities: Substitutes and Complements

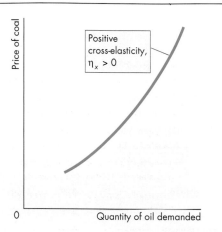

(a) Substitutes

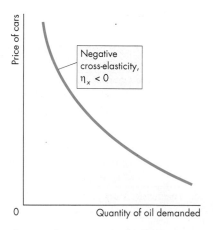

(b) Complements

Part (a) shows the cross elasticity of demand with respect to the price of a substitute. When the price of coal increases, the quantity of oil demanded also increases. Part (b) shows the cross elasticity of demand with respect to the price of a complement. When the price of cars increases, the quantity of oil demanded decreases.

demand for bread with respect to butter than there will be for bread with respect to honey.

Table 5.6 provides a compact summary of all the different kinds of demand elasticities you've just studied.

Let us now turn our attention to the supply curve and study the concept of the elasticity of supply.

Elasticity of Supply

When a change in supply alters the price of a good (or service), we measure the effect of that price change on the quantity demanded by using the elasticity of demand. But a *change in demand* – a shift in a demand curve – can also alter a good's price. When it does so, there is a movement along the supply curve. In this case, the change in the quantity depends on the responsiveness of the *quantity supplied* to a change in price. To measure this responsiveness we use the concept of the elasticity of supply. The **elasticity of supply** is the percentage change in the quantity supplied of a good (or service) divided by the percentage change in its price. It is represented by η_s. That is:

$$\eta_s = \frac{\text{Percentage change in quantity supplied}}{\text{Percentage change in price}}$$

As with elasticity of demand, we usually calculate the elasticity of supply as an arc elasticity – the elasticity along an arc or stretch of the supply curve. Let's look at an example. Figure 5.7 shows the supply curve of aluminium. Initially the price is £800 per tonne and the quantity supplied is 600 tonnes a day – at point a. Then an increase in demand occurs and the price rises to £1,200. The quantity supplied increases to 1,400 tonnes a day – at point b. We can calculate the elasticity of supply along the arc of the supply curve between a and b. Along this arc, the change in quantity is 800 tonnes (1,400 – 600). The average quantity is 1,000 tonnes a day (the average of 600 and 1,400), so the change in the quantity supplied is 80 per cent of the average quantity. The change in the price is £400 a tonne (£1,200 – £800) and the average price is £1,000 a tonne, so the change in price is 40 per cent of the average price. We can use these two percentage changes to give the elasticity of supply along the arc from a to b as 80/40 which is 2.

This elasticity is positive. The elasticity of supply is always positive so long as the supply curve slopes upward, as all the supply curves we have considered in this chapter (and in Chapter 4) did. Upward-sloping supply curves produce positive elasticities of supply because the price and quantity supplied always change in the same direction. When the price increases the quantity supplied also increases,

TABLE 5.6

A Compact Glossary of Elasticities of Demand

ELASTICITY OF DEMAND (η)

The relationship is described as	When η is	Which means that*
Perfectly elastic or completely elastic	Infinity	The smallest possible fall in price causes an infinitely large increase in the quantity demanded
Elastic	Between infinity and 1	The percentage increase in the quantity demanded exceeds the percentage fall in price
Unit elasticity	1	The percentage increase in the quantity demanded equals the percentage fall in price
Inelastic	Between 1 and zero	The percentage increase in the quantity demanded is less than the percentage fall in price
Perfectly inelastic or completely inelastic	Zero	The quantity demanded is the same at all prices

INCOME ELASTICITY OF DEMAND (η_y)

The relationship is described as	When η_y is	Which means that*
Income elastic	Greater than 1	The percentage increase in the quantity demanded is greater than the percentage rise in income
Income inelastic (normal good)	Between 1 and zero	The percentage increase in the quantity demanded is less than the percentage rise in income
Negative income elasticity (inferior good)	Less than zero	When income rises, quantity demanded decreases

CROSS ELASTICITIES OF DEMAND (η_x)

The relationship is described as	When η_x is	Which means that*
Perfect substitutes	Infinity	The smallest possible rise in the price of one product causes an infinitely large increase in the quantity demanded of the other product
Imperfect substitutes	Between infinity and zero	If the price of one product rises, the quantity demanded of the other product also increases
Independent	Zero	If the price of one product rises, the quantity demanded of the other product remains constant
Complements	Less than zero	If the price of one product rises the quantity demanded of the other product decreases

*In each case the directions of change may be reversed. For example, when price elasticity is perfectly elastic, the smallest possible decrease in price causes an infinitely large increase in quantity demanded.

FIGURE 5.7

Arc Elasticity of Supply

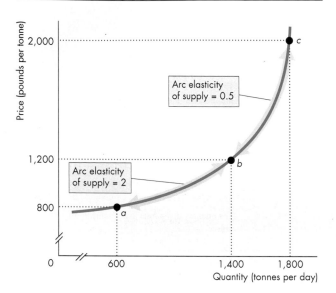

If an increase in demand raises the price from £800 a tonne to £1,200 a tonne, the quantity supplied increases from 600 tonnes a day to 1,400 tonnes a day and there is a movement along the supply curve from *a* to *b*. The elasticity of supply along this arc of the supply curve is 2 – the rise in price of £400 is 40 per cent of the average price and the increase in the quantity supplied of 800 tonnes a day is 80 per cent of the average quantity, so the elasticity of supply is 80/40 = 2.

If a further increase in demand raises the price from £1,200 a tonne to £2,000 a tonne, the quantity supplied increases from 1,400 tonnes a day to 1,800 tonnes a day and there is movement along the supply curve from *b* to *c*. The elasticity of supply along this arc of the supply curve is 0.5 – the rise in the price of £800 is 50 per cent of the average price and the increase in quantity supplied of 400 tonnes a day is 25 per cent of the average quantity, so the elasticity of supply is 25/50 = 0.5. Elasticity varies along most supply curves, as it does along this one.

and when the price falls the quantity supplied also decreases.

The elasticity of supply is seldom constant along the supply curve, even if the supply curve is a straight line. So the arc elasticity changes as we move along the supply curve. For example, suppose that the demand for aluminum increases again, taking its price to £2,000 a tonne in Fig. 5.7. The quantity supplied increases to 1,800 a day – at point *c*. We can now calculate the elasticity of supply

along the arc of the supply curve between *b* and *c*. Along this arc, the change in quantity is 400 tonnes (1,800 – 1,400). The average quantity is 1,600 tonnes a day (the average of 1,400 and 1,800), so the change in the quantity supplied is 25 per cent of the average quantity. The change in price is £800 a tonne (£2,000 – £1,200) and the average price is £1,600 a tonne, so the change in the price is 50 per cent of the average price. Combining these two percentage changes gives the elasticity of supply along the arc from *b* to *c* as 25/50 which is 0.5.

Although the elasticity of supply generally varies as we move along a supply curve, there are some supply curves along which the elasticity is constant. Three such cases are shown in Fig. 5.8. Part (a) shows a case where the quantity supplied is fixed regardless of the price, so that the supply curve is vertical. Here we have **perfectly inelastic supply**, that is an elasticity of supply equal to zero, all along the curve as an increase in price leads to no change in the quantity supplied.

Part (b) shows a case where the supply curve is a straight line through the origin. This curve has **unit elastic supply**, that is an elasticity of supply equal to 1, all along the curve. The same applies to all straight-line supply curves through the origin, irrespective of their slopes. This is because along curves like this, any increase in price is matched by an equal percentage increase in quantity. For instance, suppose the price in part (b) rises from 4 to 6 so that the quantity increases from 6 to 9. The rise in price is 2 and the average price is 5, so the rise is 40 per cent of the average price. And the increase in quantity is 3 which is 40 per cent of the average price of 7½. So the elasticity is 40/40 which is 1.

Part (c) shows a case where there is a price below which nothing will be supplied and at which suppliers are willing to sell any quantity that may be demanded, so that the supply curve is horizontal. Here we have **perfectly elastic supply**, that is an elasticity of supply equal to infinity, all along the curve. The smallest fall in price would reduce the quantity supplied from some positive amount to zero.

The magnitude of the elasticity of supply for any particular good or service depends on:

◆ The elasticity of the supply of the inputs used in its production

◆ The amount of time elapsed since the price change

FIGURE 5.8

Supply Curves with Constant Elasticity

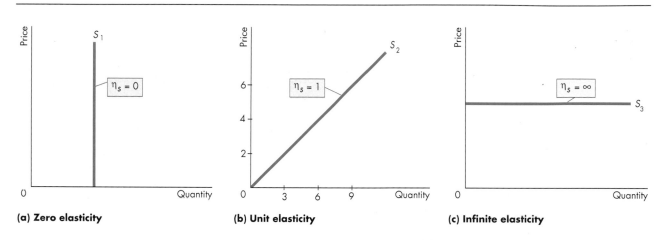

(a) Zero elasticity   **(b) Unit elasticity**   **(c) Infinite elasticity**

Each supply curve shown here has a constant elasticity. Vertical supply curves, like the supply curve in part (a), have a constant elasticity of zero. Supply curves that are straight lines through the origin, like the supply curve in part (b), have constant unit elasticity (elasticity equals 1) no matter how steep or flat they are. Supply curves that are horizontal, like the supply curve in part (c), have constant infinite elasticity (elasticity equals infinity).

The Elasticity of the Supply of the Inputs Used

The importance of the elasticity of the supply of the inputs used in production is best illustrated by considering two extreme examples. First consider emerald necklaces. These are made from emeralds which are in inelastic supply – even if the price of emeralds doubles or trebles not many more can be found. If the price of emerald necklaces rose, necklace makers would certainly like to supply more necklaces and would be willing to pay more for the extra emeralds they would want. However, they would be unable to acquire many more emeralds, even if they offered higher prices, as very few more emeralds could be found. So the necklace makers would not be able to respond to a rise in the price of necklaces by producing many more. In other words, the supply of emerald necklaces is inelastic because the supply of emeralds is inelastic.

Next consider silicon chips. These are made from silicon which comes from sand, and sand is available in almost limitless quantities at virtually constant production costs and so has a highly elastic supply. If the price of silicon chips rose, then their makers would like to supply more and they would be able to

get extra sand at about the same price they paid before. So they could supply more chips at about the same price as before. So the chip makers would be able to supply more chips at their present price. In other words, the supply of silicon chips is highly elastic because the supply of silicon is highly elastic.

Time Frame for Supply

Now let's see how the length of time that has elapsed after a price change affects the responsiveness of the quantity supplied. We know producers will want to produce more of a good when its price goes up. But there are technological reasons why they may find it easy to raise output if they are given plenty of time to do so, but may find it hard to raise output if they are given only a little time. To look at this more closely, we distinguish between three time frames of supply:

1. Long-run supply
2. Short-run supply
3. Momentary supply

Long-run Supply   The **long-run supply curve** for a good shows the quantity that producers will produce

Elasticity in Action

THE TIMES, 12 MARCH 1994

The Times pulls even further ahead

*T*HE *TIMES* is the most successful national newspaper in Britain.

Average daily sales have risen by more than 120,000 since the weekday price was reduced to 30p in September, an increase of 26 per cent in six months.

Sales in January were up by 16,000 compared with December. That success continued last month, when sales increased by another 12,500 – against a drop of 18,000 for *The Daily Telegraph*.

The Times is now 63,000 ahead of *The Guardian* and 175,000 ahead of *The Independent*, which now sells fewer copies than any other national daily and was overtaken last month by the *Financial Times*.

At 40p on Saturdays, 30p less than *The Daily Telegraph*, *The Times* is the best value, with the best writing, of any quality paper.

© The Times. Reprinted with permission.

The quantity of *The Times* newspaper sold has increased significantly since its price was cut in September 1993 from 45 pence to 30 pence on weekdays and from 50 pence to 40 pence on Saturdays.

The Times now outsells most of its rivals and is catching up with *The Daily Telegraph*, whose sales are falling.

The Times claims to be the most successful newspaper in the United Kingdom.

This claim is based on the fact that, since the price cut, average daily sales have increased proportionately more than for any other newspaper.

A fall in the price of *The Times* has resulted in an increase in the quantity demanded.

With a little more information (thanks to *The Times* for supplying this), we can calculate the price elasticity of demand (η) for *The Times*.

Even if we assume that all other factors influencing the quantity demanded of *The Times* remain the same, we still face one problem.

In the figure, a fall in price brings about an immediate increase in the quantity demanded. In reality, the quantity demanded might be slow to respond to the price change.

The table shows that the quantity sold continued to rise after the initial price fall.

To estimate η for *The Times*, we need to look over as long a period as we can for which the assumption that all other factors remain the same might still hold (if we wait too long, the price of other newspapers will change, people's incomes will change and so on).

The table shows the estimation of η using the formula:

$$\frac{\Delta Q/Q}{\Delta P/P}$$

The longer we wait, the larger is the estimated η, since the quantity sold has risen more for the initial fall in price.

	Average daily sales	η
1993		
Aug	354,280	–
Sep	442,103	0.74
Oct	444,503	0.76
Nov	445,343	0.77
Dec	439,327	0.72
1994		
Jan	455,628	0.86
Feb	468,174	0.96
Mar	470,742	0.99
Apr	478,419	1.05

The figure is similar to Fig. 5.2. It considers the demand curve in three time frames and, assuming that all other factors remain the same, shows that the demand curve becomes more elastic over time as more information comes in.

Using the elasticity formula to calculate η for September, ΔP is 15 and ΔQ is just under 88,000. By the time we calculate the figure for April, however, over a longer time frame, ΔP is still 15 (the price cut from 45 pence to 30 pence), but ΔQ has risen to over 124,000.

Our estimation for η for the last month where sales figures are available suggests that *The Times* is price elastic. This may be expected if we consider *The Times*, *The Daily Telegraph* and *The Guardian* to be reasonably close substitutes for each other.

Subsequently, *The Daily Telegraph* cut its price to 30 pence and *The Times* cut its price further, to 20 pence. This violates our assumption that all other factors remain the same (the price of a substitute has changed), so we cannot continue the analysis in the table beyond this point.

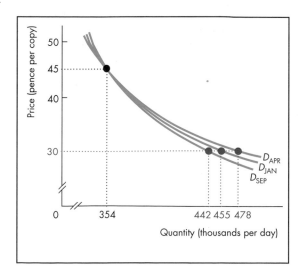

at each possible price if they are given long enough between each price change to alter the amounts they use of every input. For example, the long-run supply curve of plastic bags would show how many bags suppliers would produce – each week perhaps – at each price if the suppliers were given enough time between price rises to build more factories, to acquire new machinery and to recruit and train more workers. The long-run supply curve would even allow for wholly new firms to be set up in response to price rises. Likewise, the long-run supply curve for milk would show how much milk farmers would like to produce – each day perhaps – at each possible price if enough time was given between each price rise for new dairy farms to be established and for existing ones to acquire new cows, more pasture and extra workers.

Long-run supply curves enable us to see how responsive quantities supplied will be to changes in prices after all the technologically possible ways of adjusting output have been exploited. For some goods it may be a long time before all the possible ways of raising output can be exploited. For example, it might take ten years for a rubber producer to grow extra trees capable of producing rubber, and it might take a hundred years for a forester to grow oak trees large enough to produce large planks of oak. However, for most manufactured products the time needed is usually only the year or two it would take to build a new factory or acquire new plant, for capital like this is generally the input which takes the longest to adjust.

Short-run Supply   The **short-run supply curve** for a good shows the amounts that producers would like to produce at each possible price if they had enough time to vary the amounts of some of the inputs they used but not all. For example, the makers of plastic bags might find that while it would take some years to alter the amounts of some of their inputs, they could alter the quantity of others very quickly. In turn they could alter their weekly output to some extent very quickly. For example, they could probably persuade some workers to work overtime on any day they wanted overtime done, and they could set these workers to work with raw materials taken out of stocks. Again, farmers might not be able to acquire more pastures right away, but they might raise milk output a little in a week or two by buying cows and cattle food from abroad and having existing workers do overtime.

The short-run supply curve enables us to measure the responsiveness of quantity supplied to changes in price when some inputs can be varied while others cannot. The number of inputs which can be varied will increase as time passes, so there may not be a unique short-run supply curve. Instead there may be a sequence of short-run supply curves which become progressively more elastic.

Momentary Supply   We have suggested that the makers of plastic bags can probably raise their production almost instantaneously if they wish to produce more in response to a rise in price. The same applies to many producers of manufactured goods. However, there are some producers who

---

FIGURE 5.9

Milk Supply: Momentary, Short-run and Long-run

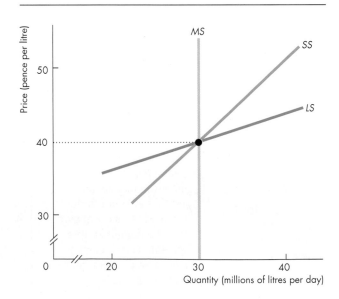

The momentary supply curve (*MS*) shows how the quantity of milk supplied responds to a price change the moment that it occurs. The very light blue momentary supply curve shown here is perfectly inelastic. The medium blue short-run supply curve (*SS*) shows how the quantity of milk supplied responds to a price change after some adjustments to production have been made. The dark blue long-run supply curve (*LS*) shows how the quantity of milk supplied responds to a price change when all the technologically possible adjustments to the production process have been made.

cannot make instantaneous increases in output because there are some critical inputs whose amounts cannot be instantly increased. For example, milk producers might not be able to produce any more milk for a week or two after an increase in demand until they can acquire more cows, while rubber producers might not be able to produce any more rubber for ten years after an increase in demand until they can grow more rubber trees. In these cases there is a vertical **momentary supply curve** which shows the fixed amount that will be produced at each possible price while the amount that can be used of some crucial input is fixed. These momentary supply curves show us how responsive the quantity supplied is to changes in price while the critical input remains fixed. There is no quantity response during this period as the supply curve is vertical and the elasticity of supply is zero. Notice that the term *momentary* can be a little misleading – the suppliers of large oak planks cannot alter their output for the next hundred years!

Three Supply Curves   Three supply curves corresponding to the three time frames are illustrated in Fig. 5.9. They are the supply curves in the UK market for milk at a time when the price is 40 pence a litre and the quantity of milk produced each day is 30 million litres. The three supply curves all pass through that point. The momentary supply curve

(MS) is perfectly inelastic at 30 million litres. The long-run supply curve (LS) is the most elastic of the three curves. The short-run supply curve (SS) lies between the other two curves. In fact, there is a series of successively more elastic short-run supply curves between the momentary and the long-run curves. As more time elapses following a price change, more changes can be made by producers to increase output. The short-run supply curve (SS) shown in Fig. 5.9 is an example of one of these short-run supply curves.

The momentary supply curve (MS) is vertical because, at a given moment, no matter what the price of milk, producers cannot change their output. They have a certain number of cows and there is a given amount of output that can be produced. But as time elapses, dairy farmers can increase their capacity. They can buy more cows, convert more fields into pasture and train more workers. In the long run, they can build more milking parlours and increase the quantity supplied even more in response to a given price rise.

◆ ◆ ◆ ◆   You have now studied the theory of demand and supply, and you have learned how to measure the responsiveness of the quantities demanded and supplied to changes in price and income. In the next chapters we are going to use what we have learned to study some real-world markets – markets in action.

SUMMARY

Price Elasticity of Demand

Price elasticity of demand measures the responsiveness of the quantity demanded of a good or service to a change in its price caused by a shift in its supply curve. It enables us to calculate the effect of such a change in price on the quantity demanded and total revenue. Price elasticity of demand equals the percentage change in the quantity demanded divided by the percentage change in price. Because demand curves slope downward, price elasticities are negative. To avoid minus

signs, we often talk instead about elasticity of demand which we define as the absolute value of the price elasticity of demand. Elasticities of demand range from zero to infinity. The larger they are, the more responsiveness quantity demanded is to a given change in price.

When the proportional change in the quantity demanded is smaller than the proportional change in price, elasticity is between zero and 1 and demand is inelastic. When the proportional change in the quantity demanded and the proportional change in price are similar, elasticity is 1 and demand is unit elastic. When the proportional change in the quantity demanded is bigger than the proportional change in price, elasticity is greater than 1 and demand is elastic. Elasticity varies along most demand curves. On a straight-line demand curve, elasticity decreases as the price falls and the quantity demanded increases.

The size of the elasticity for a good or service depends on how easily another may serve as a substitute for it, on the proportion of income spent on it, and on the time that has elapsed since the price change. We use two time frames to analyse demand: short-run and long-run. Short-run demand describes the initial response of buyers to a price change. Long-run demand describes the response of buyers to a price change after all possible adjustments have been made. Short-run demand is usually less elastic than long-run demand. (pp. 105–114)

Elasticity, Revenue and Expenditure

If the elasticity of demand is less than 1, a decrease in supply leads to an increase in revenue. This is because the percentage increase in price is greater than the percentage decrease in the quantity traded. If the elasticity of demand is greater than 1, then a decrease in supply leads to a decrease in revenue. This is because the percentage increase in price is less than the percentage decrease in the quantity bought. (pp. 114–115)

More Demand Elasticities

Income elasticity of demand measures the responsiveness of quantity demanded to a change in income. Income elasticity of demand is calculated as the percentage change in the quantity demanded divided by the percentage change in income. The larger the income elasticity of demand, the greater is the responsiveness of the quantity bought to a given change in income. When income elasticity is between zero and 1, demand is income inelastic. In this case, as income increases the quantity bought increases but the percentage of income spent on a good decreases. When income elasticity is greater than 1, demand is income elastic. In this case, as income increases the quantity bought increases and

the percentage of income spent on the good also increases. When income elasticity is less than zero, demand is negative income inelastic. In this case, as income increases the quantity bought decreases. Income elasticities are greater than 1 for items typically consumed by the rich; they are positive but less than 1 for more basic consumption items. Income elasticities are less than zero for inferior goods – goods that are consumed only at low incomes and that disappear as budgets increase.

Cross elasticity of demand measures the responsiveness of quantity demand for one good (or service) to a change in the price of another such as a substitute or a complement. Cross elasticity of demand is calculated as the percentage change in the quantity demanded of one good divided by the percentage change in the price of another. The cross elasticity of demand with respect to the price of a substitute is positive. The cross elasticity of demand with respect to the price of a complement is negative. (pp. 115–118)

Elasticity of Supply

The elasticity of supply measures the responsiveness of the quantity supplied of a good or service to a change in its price caused by a shift in its demand curve. Elasticity of supply is calculated as the percentage change in the quantity supplied of a good or service divided by the percentage change in price. On most supply curves, elasticity of supply varies as we move along the curve.

Supply elasticities are usually positive with values between zero, as with a vertical supply curve, and infinity, as with a horizontal supply curve. We classify supply according to three different time frames: long run, short run and momentary. Long-run supply refers to the response of suppliers to a price change when all the technologically feasible adjustments in production have been made. Short-run supply refers to the response of suppliers to a price change after some adjustments in production have been made. Momentary supply refers to the response of any suppliers who cannot change their output levels at all for some time after the price changes. Supply becomes more elastic as suppliers have more time to respond to price changes. (pp. 118–125)

KEY ELEMENTS

Key Terms

Arc elasticity, 109
Cross elasticity of demand, 117
Elastic demand, 108
Elasticity of demand, 107
Elasticity of supply, 118
Income elasticity of demand, 115
Inelastic demand, 108
Long-run demand curve, 113
Long-run supply curve, 124
Momentary supply curve, 124
Perfectly elastic demand, 108
Perfectly elastic supply, 121
Perfectly inelastic demand, 108
Perfectly inelastic supply, 120
Point elasticity, 110
Price elasticity of demand, 106
Short-run demand curve, 113
Short-run supply curve, 124

Total revenue, 105
Unit elastic demand, 108
Unit elastic supply, 120

Key Figures and Tables

Figure 5.2 Arc Elasticity of Demand, 109
Figure 5.3 Elasticity Along a Straight-line Demand Curve, 110
Figure 5.4 Demand Curves with Constant Elasticity, 111
Figure 5.5 Income Elasticity of Demand, 116
Figure 5.7 Arc Elasticity of Supply, 120
Figure 5.8 Supply Curves with Constant Elasticity, 121
Table 5.1 Calculating the Price Elasticity of Demand, 107
Table 5.6 A Compact Glossary of Elasticities of Demand, 119

REVIEW QUESTIONS

1   Define price elasticity of demand and elasticity of demand.

2   Why is elasticity of demand a more useful measure of responsiveness than slope?

3   Distinguish between arc elasticity of demand and point elasticity of demand.

4   Draw a graph of, or describe the shape of, a demand curve that along its whole length has an elasticity of demand of:
    a Infinity
    b Zero
    c One

5   What three factors determine the size of the elasticity of demand?

6   What do we mean by short-run demand and long-run demand?

7   Explain why the short-run demand curve is usually less elastic than the long-run demand curve.

8   What is the connection between elasticity of demand and revenue? If the elasticity of demand is 1, by how much does a 10 per cent price increase change revenue?

9   Define income elasticity of demand.

10 Give an example of a good whose income elasticity is:
    a Greater than one
    b Less than zero

11 Define cross elasticity of demand. What determines whether cross elasticity of demand is positive or negative?

12 Define elasticity of supply. Is the elasticity of supply usually positive or negative?

13 Give an example of a good whose elasticity of supply is:
   a Zero
   b Between zero and infinity
   c Infinite

14 What do we mean by momentary, short-run and long-run supply?

15 What do we mean when we say that the momentary supply curve for a good is perfectly in elastic?

16 Why is the long-run supply curve for a good more elastic than the short-run supply curve?

P R O B L E M S

1 Suppose the demand schedule for hiring video-tapes is:

Price (£)	Quantity demanded (thousands per day)
0.00	120
0.50	100
1.00	80
1.50	60
2.00	40
2.50	20
3.00	0

   a At what price is the elasticity of demand equal to
      (1) Infinity?
      (2) One?
      (3) Zero?
   b Which price would bring in the most revenue per day?
   c Calculate the arc elasticity of demand for a rise in price from 50 pence to £1.50.

2 Assume that at each price the quantity of videotapes demanded increases by 10 per cent from the figures shown in Problem 1.

   a Draw the old and new demand curves.
   b Calculate the arc elasticity of demand for a rise in the rental price from 50 pence to £1.50. Compare your answer with that of Problem 1(c).

3 Which item in each of the following pairs is likely to have the more elastic demand?

   a Daily newspapers or the *Independent*
   b Meat or beef
   c Soft drinks or lemonade

4 You have been hired as an economic consultant by OPEC and given the following schedule showing the world demand for oil:

Price (dollars per barrel)	Quantity demanded (millions of barrels per day)
15	60,000
25	40,000
35	24,000
45	16,000
55	10,000

Your advice is needed on the following questions:

   a If the supply of oil is cut back so that the price rises from $15 to $25 a barrel, will the revenue from oil sales rise or fall?
   b What will happen to the revenue if the suply of oil is cut back further and the price rises to $35 a barrel?
   c What will happen to revenue if the supply of oil is cut back further still so that the price rises to $45 a barrel?
   d What is the price that will achieve the highest revenue?
   e What quantity of oil will be sold at the price that answers Problem 4(d)?
   f What are the values of the arc elasticity of demand for price increases of $10 a barrel if the starting prices are $15, $25, $35 and $45 a barrel?
   g Over what price range is the demand for oil inelastic?

5 State the sign (positive or negative) and, where possible, the probable range (less than 1, 1, greater than 1) of the following elasticities:

   a The cross elasticity of demand for coal with respect to the price of oil b The income elasticity of demand for diamonds

c The income elasticity of demand for toothpaste

d The elasticity of supply of Loch Tay salmon

e The cross elasticity of demand for floppy disks with respect to the price of personal computers

6 The following tables give some data on the quantities of milk demanded and supplied:

Price (pence per pint)	Quantity demanded (thousands of pints per day)	
	Short-run	Long-run
20	700	1,000
30	500	500
40	200	0

Price (pence per pint)	Quantity demanded (thousands of pints per day)		
	Momentary	Short-run	Long-run
20	500	200	0
30	500	500	500
40	500	700	10,000

Using 30 pence a pint as the average price of a pint and 500,000 pints a day as the average quantity, calculate:

a The short-run elasticity of demand

b The long-run elasticity of demand

c The momentary elasticity of supply

d The short-run elasticity of supply

e The long-run elasticity of supply

BOX 5.1: CALCULATING POINT ELASTICITIES OF DEMAND

Point price elasticity of demand measures the price elasticity of demand at a given point on a demand curve. In Table 5.1, we gave the formula for the price elasticity of demand along an arc as:

$$\text{Arc price elasticity of demand} = \frac{\Delta Q/Q_{ave}}{\Delta P/P_{ave}}.$$

We will refer to this equation as calculating the arc price elasticity of demand (see also Figures 5.2 and 5.3 which illustrate arc elasticity of demand).

The formula can be arranged as:

$$\text{Arc price elasticity of demand} = \frac{\Delta Q/\Delta P}{Q_{ave}/P_{ave}}.$$

In this equation, the numerator is the ratio of the change in quantity demanded to the change in price along an arc of the demand curve. This ratio is the inverse of the slope of the demand curve. The denominator is the ratio of the average quantity demanded to the average price.

When we want to determine the price elasticity of demand at a point, we are in effect looking at an infinitely small arc. The average price and average quantity demanded on this infinitely small arc are the price and quantity demanded at that point. So we substitute P for P_{ave} and Q for Q_{ave} and the formula becomes:

$$\text{Point price elasticity of demand} = \frac{\Delta Q/\Delta P}{Q/P}.$$

Because a positive price change results in a negative change in the quantity demanded, both arc price elasticity of demand and point price elasticity of demand are negative. But sometimes we drop the minus sign and refer to arc elasticity of demand and point elasticity of demand.

The Straight-line Demand Curve Case

Figure 5.3 shows that the point elasticity of demand is infinity when the price is $60 a barrel, 1 when the price is $30 a barrel and 0 when the price is $0 a barrel. Let's use the formula to check these point elasticities.

First we need to know the slope of the demand curve at a given point (see also Box 2.1, p. 49). Because the demand curve is a straight line its slope is constant. To calculate the slope, consider what happens if the price falls from $60 per barrel to $0 while the quantity demanded increases from 0, to 60 million barrels per day. The slope is:

$$\frac{\Delta P}{\Delta Q} = \frac{-60}{60,000,000} = \frac{-1}{1,000,000}. \quad \text{(Step 1)}$$

The formula for point price elasticity of demand uses $\Delta Q/\Delta P$, so the above formula needs to be inverted to give:

$$\frac{\Delta Q}{\Delta P} = \frac{1,000,000}{-1} = -1,000,000. \quad \text{(Step 2)}$$

At a price of $60 a barrel, the quantity demanded is 0, so the point price elasticity of demand is:

$$\text{Point price elasticity of demand} = \frac{-1,000,000}{(0/60)} \quad \text{(Step 3)}$$

$$= \frac{-60,000,000}{0} = -\infty$$

The elasticity of demand at this point is the *absolute value* of the point price elasticity of demand, that is ∞.

At a price of $30 a barrel, the quantity demanded is 30 million barrels per day, so by repeating Steps 1 to 3, the point price elasticity of demand is:

$$\text{Point price elasticity of demand} = \frac{-1,000,000}{(30,000,000/30)} = -1.$$

The elasticity of demand at this point is the absolute value of the point price elasticity of demand, that is 1.

At a price of $0 a barrel, the quantity demanded is 60 million barrels per day. Again, by repeating Steps 1 to 3, the point price elasticity of demand is:

$$\text{Point price elasticity of demand} = \frac{-1,000,000}{(60,000,000/0)} = 0.$$

The General Demand Curve Case

Figure 5.2 shows a curved demand curve. In this figure, the arc elasticity of demand is 0.4 along the arc between the prices of $30 and $20 a barrel. Let's use the formula for point price elasticity of demand to find the point elasticity of demand when the price is $30 a barrel.

To calculate the point elasticity of demand, it is necessary to calculate the inverse of the slope of the demand curve at a given point, that is $\Delta Q/\Delta P$. The slope of a curved line at a given point is equal to the slope of the tangent to the line drawn at that point. If you draw the tangent to the demand curve in Fig. 5.2 at the price of $30 a barrel, you will find that it cuts the x-axis at 45 million barrels and the y-axis at $59 a barrel. So:

$$\frac{\Delta Q}{\Delta P} = \frac{-45,000,000}{59} = -760,000$$

At a price of $30 a barrel, the quantity demanded is 30 million barrels, so:

$$\text{Point price elasticity of demand} = \frac{-76,000,000}{30,000,000/30} - 0.76.$$

The point elasticity of demand is the absolute value of the point price elasticity of demand at this point and is 0.76.

Using Calculus to Calculate Point Elasticity

The formula for point price elasticity of demand when using calculus is

$$\text{Point price elasticity of demand} = \frac{dQ/dP}{Q/P}.$$

Suppose that a demand curve is described by the equation:

$$Q = 100 - P^2.$$

Let's calculate the point price elasticity of demand when the price is $5. At this price, the quantity demanded is

$$Q = 100 - (5)^2$$
$$= 75.$$

To find how the quantity demanded responds to a change in price, differentiate Q with respect to P

$$dQ/dP = -2P.$$

When P = 5, $dQ/dP = -10$.

Substituting these values into the point price elasticity of demand equation, we get

$$\text{Point price elasticity of demand} = \frac{-10}{(75/5)} = \frac{-10}{15} = -0.67.$$

The point elasticity of demand is the absolute value of the point price elasticity of demand and is 0.67 when the price is $5.

BOX 5.2: DEMAND CURVES WITH CONSTANT ELASTICITY

Sometimes the elasticity of demand is constant along the entire length of the demand curve. This is illustrated in Fig. 5.4(b) which has a constant elasticity of 1, but there are many other examples.

Constant elasticity of 1

In Fig. 5.4(b) notice that when the price is 12 the quantity demanded is 1 and when the price is 6 the quantity demanded is 2. At all points on this demand curve,

$$PQ = 12.$$

By moving the terms around in the equation, we can derive the formula $Q = 12/P$ or $Q = 12P^{-1}$, so that

$$dQ/dP = -12P^{-2}.$$

Box 5.1 showed us how to calculate the point price elasticity of demand using

$$\text{Point price elasticity of demand} = \frac{dQ/dP}{Q/P}.$$

Using $dQ/dP = -12P^{-2}$, the point price elasticity of demand is

$$\text{Point price elasticity of demand} = \frac{-(12/P^{-2})}{Q/P}. \quad \text{(Step 1)}$$

At a price of 12 and quantity of 1, the point price elasticity of demand can be found by substituting the correct values into the formula given in Step 1, which gives

$$\text{Point price elasticity of demand} = \frac{-(12/12^2)}{1/12}.$$

$$= -1.$$

So the absolute value for the point elasticity of demand when the price is 12 is 1.

At a price of 6 and quantity of 2, the point price elasticity of demand can be found by sub-stituting the correct values into the formula given in Step 1, which gives

$$\text{Point price elasticity of demand} = \frac{-(12/6^2)}{(2/6)}.$$

$$= -1$$

Hence, when the price is 6 the point elasticity of demand is 1.

Constant elasticity of *k*

Any demand curve whose equation is of the form

$$Q = kP^{-a},$$

where a and k are constants, has a point price elasticity of demand of $-a$. To show this, let's first recall the formula for point price elasticity of demand given in Box 5.1.

$$\text{Point price elasticity of demand} = \frac{dQ/dP}{Q/P}.$$

To calculate the point price elasticity of demand, first differentiate Q with respect to P,

$$dQ/dP = -akP^{-(a+1)}$$

Substituting the above formula into the point price elasticity of demand equation gives

$$\frac{dQ/dP}{Q/P} = \frac{-akP^{-(a+1)}}{Q/P}.$$

But the equation of the demand curve is $Q = kP^{-a}$. So $Q/P = kP^{-(a+1)}$. Using this expression for Q/P in the above equation gives

$$\text{Point price elasticity of demand} = \frac{-akP^{-(a+1)}}{kP^{-(a+1)}} = -a.$$

So the absolute value of the point elasticity of demand at any point on the demand curve $Q = kP^{-a}$ is equal to a.

CHAPTER 6

MARKETS
IN
ACTION

After studying this chapter you will be able to:

◆ Explain the short-run and long-run effects of a change in supply on price and the quantity bought and sold

◆ Explain the short-run and long-run effects of a change in demand on price and the quantity bought and sold

◆ Explain the effects of price controls

◆ Explain why price controls can lead to black markets

◆ Explain how taxes on expenditure and subsidies affect prices

◆ Explain why the European Union operates an agricultural policy and why its policies have led to mountains of surplus food

◆ Explain how making a product illegal affects its price and the quantity bought and sold

IN 1906, SAN FRANCISCO SUFFERED A DEVASTATING EARTHQUAKE. THE earthquake destroyed countless buildings but killed very few people, so the population had somehow to fit into a vastly smaller number of homes. How did the San Francisco housing market cope with this enormous shock? What happened to rents and to the quantity of housing units available? Did rents have to be controlled to keep housing affordable? ◆ ◆ Almost every day, new machines are invented that save labour and increase productivity. How do labour markets cope with the changing patterns in the demand for labour? Does falling demand make the wages of unskilled workers fall lower and lower? Is it necessary to have minimum wage laws to prevent wages from falling? ◆ ◆ Most of the things we buy are taxed and a few are subsidized. How do taxes and subsidies affect the prices and quantities of the

Turbulent Times

things we buy? Do the prices we pay change by the full amount of the taxes and subsidies? ◆ ◆ The EU's Common Agricultural Policy (CAP) has led to higher food prices and mountains of surplus food. Why does the European Union have such an agricultural policy? What is the European Union doing to reform the CAP? ◆ ◆ Trading in some goods, such as drugs, automatic firearms and enriched uranium, is illegal. How does the ban on trade affect the actual amounts of the goods consumed? And how does it affect the prices paid by those who trade illegally?

◆ ◆ ◆ ◆ In this chapter, we use the theory of demand and supply (of Chapter 4) and the concept of elasticity (of Chapter 5) to answer questions such as those we have just posed. Let's begin by studying how a market responds to a severe supply shock.

Housing Markets and Rent Ceilings

To see how an unregulated market copes with a massive supply shock, let's transport ourselves to San Francisco in April 1906, as the city is facing the effects of a massive earthquake and the ensuing fire. Overnight, more than half the people in a city of 400,000 lost their homes. Temporary shelters and camps alleviated some of the problem, but it was also necessary for the blocks of flats and houses left standing to accommodate 40 per cent more people than they had before the earthquake. How did San Francisco cope with such a devastating reduction in the supply of housing?

The Market Response to an Earthquake

Figure 6.1 shows the market for housing in San Francisco. Part (a) shows the situation before the earthquake and parts (b) and (c) show the situation after the earthquake. The horizontal axis of each part measures the quantity of housing units and the vertical axis measures the monthly rent of a unit of housing.

Look first at the situation before the earthquake in Fig. 6.1(a). The demand curve for housing is D. There are two supply curves: the short-run supply curve, labelled SS, and the long-run supply curve, labelled LS. The short-run supply curve shows how the quantity of housing units supplied varies as the price (rent) varies, while the number of houses and blocks of flats remains constant. This supply response arises from a variation in the intensity with which existing buildings are used. The quantity of housing units supplied increases as families rent out rooms or parts of their houses and flats to others, and the quantity supplied decreases as families occupy a larger number of the rooms under their control.

The long-run supply curve shows how the quantity supplied varies after enough time has elapsed for new blocks of flats and houses to be erected or existing buildings to be destroyed. The long-run supply curve is shown as being perfectly elastic. We do not actually know that the long-run supply curve is perfectly elastic, but it is a reasonable assumption. It implies that the cost of building a flat is pretty much the same regardless of whether there are 50,000, 100,000 or 150,000 flats in existence. It also implies that plenty of building land is available.

The equilibrium price (rent) and quantity are determined at the point of intersection of the *short-run* supply curve and the demand curve. Before the earthquake, that equilibrium rent is $110 a month and the quantity of housing units is 100,000. In addition – but only because we are assuming it to be so – the housing market is shown to be on its long-run supply curve, LS. Let's now look at the situation immediately after the earthquake.

Short-run Adjustments Figure 6.1(b) shows the short-run adjustment after the earthquake. As 56,000 units of housing are lost and this decreases supply, so the supply curve shifts to the left from SS to SS_A (A stands for after the earthquake). If people use the remaining housing units with the same intensity as before the earthquake and if the rent remains at $110 a month, only 44,000 units of housing are available. But rents do not remain at $110 a month. They rise to $120 a month and 74,000 units of housing are available. Where do the extra units come from? They arise because at $120 a month, people economize on their use of space and make spare rooms, attics and basements available to others.

Although 74,000 units are available, some 26,000 households who had homes in San Francisco before the earthquake did not have one after the earthquake. What happened to them in the new short-run equilibrium? Some of them left the city and others were accommodated in temporary camps.

The situation illustrated in Fig. 6.1(b) takes place in the short run. What happens in the long run?

Long-run Adjustments With sufficient time for new blocks of flats and houses to be built, supply will increase. The long-run supply curve tells us that in the long run, housing will be supplied at a rent of $110 a month. Since the current rent of $120 a month is higher than the long-run supply price of housing, there will be a rush to build new flats and houses. As time passes, more flats and houses are built, and the short-run supply curve starts moving back gradually to the right.

Figure 6.1(c) illustrates the long-run adjustment. As the short-run supply curve shifts back to

FIGURE 6.1

The San Francisco Housing Market in 1906

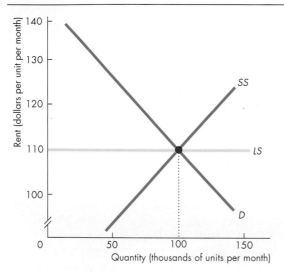

(a) Before earthquake

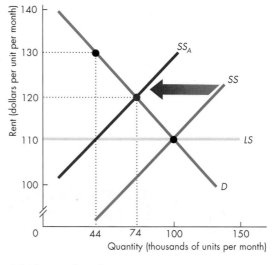

(b) After earthquake

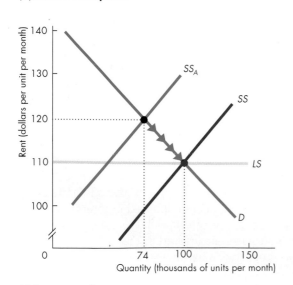

(c) Long-run adjustment

Before the earthquake, the San Francisco housing market is in equilibrium with 100,000 housing units being traded each month at an average rent of $110 a month. This equilibrium is at the intersection of demand curve *D*, short-run supply curve *SS*, and long-run supply curve *LS*. After the earthquake, the short-run supply curve shifts from *SS* to *SS*_A (part b). The equilibrium rent rises to $120 a month and the number of housing units available falls to 74,000 a month. The rent rises because at the old rent of $110 a month, 100,000 units of housing would be demanded whereas only 44,000 units will be supplied; the price that demanders are willing to pay for the 44,000th unit is $130 a month. With rents at the new level of $120 a month, there is a profit in building new flats and houses. As the building programme proceeds, the short-run supply curve shifts to the right. As it does so (part c), rents gradually fall back to $110 a month and the number of housing units available increases gradually to 100,000. Note that we use a special arrowed line to indicate such gradual movements along a curve.

the right, it intersects the demand curve at lower rents and higher quantities. The market follows the arrows down the demand curve. The process ends when there is no further profit in building new housing units. Such a situation occurs at the original rent of $110 a month and the original quantity of 100,000 units of housing.

REVIEW

The earthquake reduced the short-run supply of housing, raising rents and reducing the quantity. Higher rents immediately brought forth an increase in the quantity of housing units supplied as people economized on their own use of space and made rooms available for rent to others. High rents also led to increased building activity, which caused the short-run supply curve to shift gradually back to the right. As this process continued, the price of housing fell and the quantity rose. The original (pre-earthquake) equilibrium would eventually be restored provided nothing happened to shift the long-run supply curve or the demand curve. ◆

A Regulated Housing Market

We've just seen that a decrease in the supply of housing brings an increase in rents. Suppose that the government passes a law to stop rents from rising. In other words, it imposes a rent ceiling. A **rent ceiling** is a regulation making it illegal to charge a rent higher than a specified level. What would have happened if a rent ceiling of $110 a month – the rent before the earthquake – had been imposed? This question is answered in Fig. 6.2.

When a rent ceiling of $110 a month is imposed, the quantity of housing available remains at 44,000 units, but the quantity demanded remains constant at 100,000 units. There is an excess quantity demanded – that is a shortage – of 56,000 units. With only 44,000 units of housing being offered, people are willing to pay much more than the ceiling rent of $110 a month. The demand curve tells us how much more. People are willing to pay $130 a month if they can rent only 44,000 units of housing. Two mechanisms come into play in this situation. They are:

◆ Search activity
◆ Black markets

Search Activity

The time and effort spent searching for someone with whom to do business is called **search activity**. Even in markets where prices are allowed to fluctuate to bring equality between the quantities demanded and supplied, search activity takes place. But when the price is regulated, search activity increases. When the quantity demanded exceeds the quantity supplied, many suppliers are sold out and have nothing left to sell. Only a few

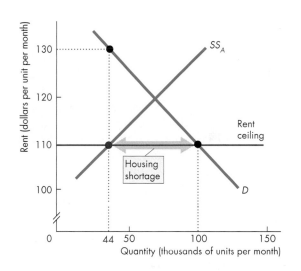

FIGURE 6.2

A Rent Ceiling

If there had been a rent ceiling of $110 a month following the earthquake, the quantity of housing supplied would have been stuck at 44,000 units. People would have willingly paid $130 a month for the 44,000th unit. The difference between the rent ceiling and the maximum price willingly paid is the value of the time used up in searching for an available flat. The individuals doing the searching are those with the lowest opportunity cost of time. Those whose value of time is high avoid search costs by renting on an illegal black market.

suppliers have products available. So buyers must spend more time searching for a supplier with whom they can do business.

The time spent searching for available supplies imposes costs on buyers. The amount of search activity that takes place is determined by the difference between the regulated price and the maximum price that buyers are willing to pay. In the present example, buyers are willing to pay $130 a month but the maximum they are permitted to pay is $110. So buyers will use up to $20 of time a month in search activity for an available unit of housing. The *opportunity cost* of housing is equal to the rent paid to the owner plus the time spent searching for the available supply. So rent ceilings increase the opportunity cost of housing.

Black Markets

A person with a high opportunity cost of time has another way of obtaining a good – buying it from someone whose opportunity cost of time is lower. A person with a low wage can devote time to searching out the available supplies and then resell to someone whose opportunity cost of searching is higher. This creates what is known as a black market. A **black market** is an illegal trading arrangement in which buyers and sellers do business at a price higher than the legally imposed price ceiling. The black market supplier, the person who has found a home, may simply sublet it to the black market buyer – the person who will actually live in it – at an illegally high price. But the black market supplier would be in trouble if this rent were to be discovered. Buyers and sellers may prefer to create the appearance of abiding by the law by actually having a rent of $110 and finding some other way for the black market supplier to get more money from the black market buyer. For example, the supplier might take a bribe or accept some absurdly high price for a few pieces of furniture. The actual price paid in a black market depends on how tightly the government polices its price regulations.

Rent Ceilings in Practice

In the United Kingdom, rent ceilings were first introduced as an emergency measure during World War I. In 1915 controls were introduced over rents for unfurnished property and tenants were given security from eviction. This emergency measure has been modified many times but never fully removed. Indeed in 1974 rent controls were extended to some furnished property. There has been some relaxation of controls since 1979. Since 1980, tenants and landlords have been allowed to agree 'short-term' lets of between one and five years with no security from eviction once the agreed period has elapsed. More importantly, for most tenancies dating from 1988, tenants can object to a rent rise only if a local Rent Assessment Committee believes the new rent to be above the market rent. The long period of widespread rent controls before 1988 made letting homes unattractive, and privately let accommodation now accounts for only about 10 per cent of dwellings.

We've now seen how a market responds, in both the short run and the long run, to a change in supply, and we've seen how a regulated market works in

the face of such a supply shock. Let's now see how a market responds, in both the short run and the long run, to a change in demand. We'll study how an unregulated market handles such a shock and we'll also look at the effects of government intervention to limit price movements.

The Labour Market and Minimum Wage Requirements

Labour-saving technology is constantly being invented and, as a result, the demand for certain types of labour, usually the least skilled types, is constantly decreasing. How does the labour market cope with this continuous decrease in the demand for unskilled labour? Does it mean that the wages of unskilled workers are constantly falling? To study this question, let's examine the market for unskilled labour.

Figure 6.3(a) represents the market for unskilled labour. The quantity of labour (millions of hours per year) is measured on the horizontal axis and the wage rate (pounds per hour) on the vertical axis. The demand curve for labour is D. There are two supply curves of labour: the short-run supply curve SS and the long-run supply curve LS. In this labour market the long-run supply curve is assumed to be perfectly elastic – a horizontal curve. In some labour markets the long-run supply curve slopes upward, but it is always more elastic than the short-run supply curve.

The short-run supply curve shows how the hours of labour supplied by a given number of workers varies as the wage rate varies. To get workers to work longer hours, firms have to pay workers more. More precisely, employers have to pay their workers to work more overtime. So employers pay for more work to be done on high overtime hourly wage rates, and the average wage per hour received by workers rises.

The long-run supply curve shows the relationship between the quantity of labour supplied and the wage rate when the number of workers in the market varies. The number of people in this unskilled labour market depends on the wage in this market compared with other opportunities. If the wage is

FIGURE 6.3

A Market for Unskilled Labour

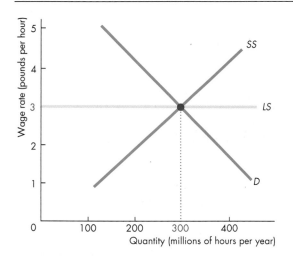

(a) Before invention

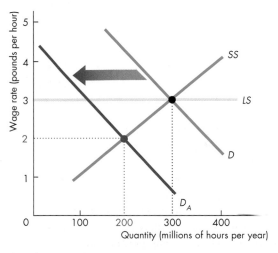

(b) After invention

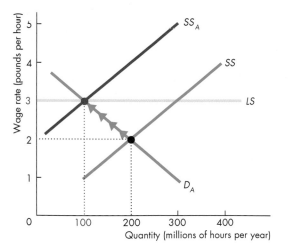

(c) Long-run adjustment

Part (a) shows a market for unskilled labour in equilibrium at a wage rate of £3 an hour with 300 million hours of labour a year being traded. The short-run supply curve (SS) slopes upward because employers have to pay a higher wage to get more hours out of a given number of workers (the wage rate can be taken to be the average of normal and overtime wage rates). The long-run supply curve (LS) is perfectly elastic because workers will eventually enter this labour market if the wage rate is above £3 an hour or leave it if the wage rate is below £3 an hour. Part (b) shows what happens in the short run if the invention of a labour-saving machine shifts the demand curve from D to D_A. The wage rate falls to £2 an hour and employment falls to 200 million hours a year. Part (c) shows what happens in the long run. With the lower wage, some workers begin to leave this market and undertake training for skilled work. As they do so, the short-run supply curve shifts to SS_A. As the supply curve shifts, the wage rate gradually increases and the employment level decreases. Ultimately, wages return to £3 an hour and employment falls to 100 million hours a year.

high enough, people will enter this market. If the wage is too low, people will leave this unskilled labour market and seek training to enter a different market – the skilled market. The long-run supply curve tells us the conditions under which workers supply labour in this unskilled market after enough time has passed for people to have acquired new skills and moved to new types of jobs.

The unskilled labour market is initially in equilibrium at a wage rate of £3 an hour and with 300

million hours of labour being supplied. We'll now analyse what happens in this labour market if the demand for unskilled labour falls as a result of the introduction of some labour-saving technology. Figure 6.3(b) shows the short-run effects. The demand curve before the new technology is introduced is D. After the new technology is introduced the demand curve shifts to the left, to D_A. The wage rate falls to £2 an hour and the quantity of labour employed falls to 200 million hours. However, this short-run effect on wages and employment is not the end of the story.

People who are now earning only £2 an hour look around for other opportunities. They see, for example, that the new labour-saving equipment doesn't always work properly and, when it breaks down, it is maintained by more highly paid, highly skilled workers. There are many other jobs in skilled labour markets that pay wages higher than £2 an hour. One by one, workers decide to leave this market for unskilled labour. Some go to colleges to learn new skills, while others take jobs that offer on-the-job training. As a result of these decisions, the short-run supply curve begins to shift to the left.

Figure 6.3(c) shows the long-run adjustment. As the short-run supply curve shifts to the left, it intersects the demand curve D_A at higher wage rates and lower levels of employment. In the long run, the short-run supply curve will have shifted all the way to SS_A. At this point, the wage rate has returned to £3 an hour, and the level of employment has fallen to 100 million hours.

In this example the long-run supply curve was taken to be perfectly elastic. If it had been slightly upward-sloping, the long-run equilibrium would have been at a lower wage rate than the original one. Nevertheless, the point remains that the effect on wages of the labour-saving machinery will be much more marked in the short run than in the long run.

Sometimes the long-run adjustment process that we have just described will take place fairly quickly. At other times it can be a very long drawn-out affair. If the adjustment process is long and drawn out and wages remain very low for a prolonged period, the government may be tempted to intervene in the market, setting a minimum wage to protect the incomes of the lowest-paid workers. What are the effects of imposing a minimum wage?

The Minimum Wage

Suppose that when the demand for labour decreases from D_A to D, as illustrated in Fig. 6.3(b), and the wage falls to £2 an hour, the government passes a minimum wage law. A **minimum wage law** is a regulation that makes it illegal for employers to pay less than a specified wage rate. To see the effects of such a law, suppose that the government declares that the minimum wage is £3 an hour. What will happen?

The answer can be found by studying Fig. 6.4. In

this figure, the minimum wage is shown as the horizontal red line labelled 'Minimum wage'. At the minimum wage, only 100 million hours of labour are demanded (point a). But there are 300 million hours of labour available at that wage (point b). As fewer hours are demanded than are supplied, 200 million hours of available labour go unemployed.

What are the workers doing with their unemployed hours? They are looking for work. It pays to spend a lot of time searching for work. With only 100 million hours of labour being employed, there are many people willing to supply their labour for wages much lower than the minimum wage. In fact, the 100-millionth hour of labour will be supplied for as little as £1.

How do we know that there are people willing to work for as little as £1 an hour? Look again at Fig. 6.4. Point c on the supply curve tells us that when there are only 100 million hours of work available, the lowest wage at which workers will supply that 100-millionth hour is £1. Someone who manages to find a job will earn £3 an hour, which is £2 an hour more than the lowest wage at which someone is willing to work. It pays the unemployed, therefore, to spend a considerable amount of time and effort looking for work. Even though workers actually find only 100 million hours of employment, each person will spend time and effort searching for one of the scarce jobs.

A minimum wage law creates gainers and losers. The people who supply the 100 million hours that are worked gain, because they earn £3 an hour instead of £2. But without the law there would have been an extra 100 million hours worked, and the people who would have worked these hours lose because they now cannot find work. There are likely to be other losers too. These will probably include employers, who make less profit now that labour costs have risen, and all the people who buy products from the firms concerned, because some of the extra costs will be reflected in higher prices.

Notice that the severity of the unemployment generated by a minimum wage depends on the demand and supply for labour. You can see that if the supply curve were further to the left, unemployment would be less. In fact, if the supply curve cut the demand curve at point a, the minimum wage would be the same as the unregulated wage and there would be no unemployment. You can also see that if the demand curve for labour were further to

FIGURE 6.4

Minimum Wages and Unemployment

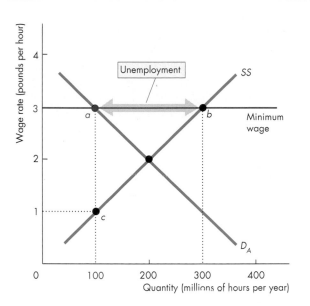

The demand curve for labour is D_A and the supply curve is SS. In an unregulated market, the wage rate is £2 an hour and 200 million hours of labour a year are employed. If a minimum wage of £3 an hour is imposed, only 100 million hours of labour are hired but 300 million hours are available. This results in unemployment – ab – of 200 million hours of labour a year. With only 100 million hours of labour being demanded, workers will willingly supply that 100-millionth hour for £1. It will pay such suppliers to spend the difference between the minimum wage and the wage for which they are willing to work – £1 an hour – in time and effort looking for a job.

the right, unemployment would be less. If the demand curve cut the supply curve at point b, then, again, the minimum wage would be the same as the unregulated wage, and there would be no unemployment.

The Minimum Wage in Reality

Several EU countries have general minimum wage laws which make it illegal to hire a worker for less than a specified hourly rate. There is no such law in the United Kingdom although it is Labour Party policy to have one. The nearest there has been to it was a series of around 35 Wages Councils for different types of workers in industries where unions had little power. These Councils were allowed to specify minimum wages for the workers in their industries, but they have been largely disbanded in recent years. Economists do not agree on the effects of a minimum wage or on how much unemployment it would cause. However, they do agree that a minimum wage would bite hardest on unskilled workers. Since there is a preponderance of unskilled workers among young people – who have had less opportunity to obtain work experience and acquire skills – we would expect a minimum wage to cause more unemployment among young workers than among older workers. However, there is currently some doubt on this point as there is not much evidence that youth unemployment is more serious in those countries where there are more general minimum wage laws. As it happens, the unemployment rate in the United Kingdom for people aged under 25 is almost double the rate for people aged between 25 and 60. In the absence of a minimum wage, it is clear that other factors must be causing this high youth unemployment.

REVIEW

G overnments which introduce minimum wages intend them to protect the incomes of the lowest paid. But a minimum wage lowers the quantity of labour demanded and hired. Some people will want to work, but they will be unemployed and will spend time searching for work. Young people and unskilled workers are hit hardest by the minimum wage. ◆

We've now seen how price ceilings and price floors affect prices and quantities. But maximum and minimum prices are not the only ways in which governments can affect markets. Let's now consider some other ways in which governments interfere. First we will look at taxes and subsidies.

Taxes on Expenditure and Subsidies

One reason why the demand and supply model was developed in the nineteenth century was to enable predictions to be made about the effects of taxes on prices and on the quantities produced and consumed (see Our Advancing Knowledge, pp.150–151). We'll look at the effects of taxes.

Taxes on Expenditure

A **tax on expenditure** is a tax on the sale of a particular commodity. The tax may be set as a fixed amount in pence per unit of the commodity, in which case it is called a **specific tax**. Alternatively, the tax may be set as a fixed percentage of the value of the commodity, in which case it is called an ***ad valorem* tax**. The United Kingdom's excise duties on alcoholic drinks, petrol and tobacco products are all examples of specific taxes. Value Added Tax (VAT) is an example of an *ad valorem* tax.

Do the prices of the goods and services you buy increase by the full amount of a tax on expenditure? The tax is added to the price of a product when you pay for it at the cash register, so isn't it obvious that *you* pay the entire tax? Isn't the price higher than it otherwise would be by an amount equal to the tax? The answer is that it can be, but usually isn't. It is even possible that you, the consumer, actually pay none of the tax, forcing the seller to pay it for you. Let's see how we can make sense of these apparently absurd statements.

Who Pays the Tax?

To study the effect of a tax on expenditure, we need to start by looking at what would happen in a market in which there is no such tax. We'll then introduce a tax and see the changes it brings.

The market for beer is shown in Fig. 6.5. The demand curve is *D* and the supply curve is *S*. With no sales tax, the equilibrium occurs at a price of 85 pence a pint and 40 million pints a day bought and sold.

A specific tax of 25 pence a pint is now imposed.

FIGURE 6.5

A Specific Tax on Expenditure

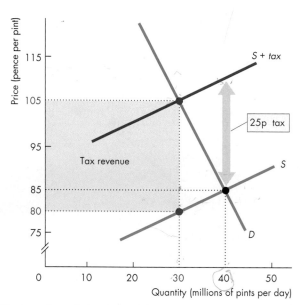

The demand curve for beer is *D* and the supply curve is *S*. In the absence of any taxes, the price of beer will be 85 pence a pint and 40 million pints a day will be bought and sold. When a tax of 25 pence a pint is imposed, the supply curve shifts upward to the curve labelled *S + tax*. The new equilibrium price is 105 pence a pint and 30 million pints a day are traded. The tax is shared between the consumers, who pay 20 pence more per pint, and the producers, who receive 5 pence less per pint.

When a pint of beer is sold, the 25 pence tax must be added to its price. Does the price increase by 25 pence, from 85 pence to 110 pence, with the quantity of beer staying at 40 million pints a day? No, because any rise in the price will reduce the quantity of beer demanded to below 40 million pints a day.

However, the introduction of the tax will increase the price of beer, although by less than 25 pence a pint. To determine the new price, we must construct a new supply curve which arises when the tax is introduced. The new supply curve is labelled *S + tax* in Fig. 6.5. It is above the old one, and the distance between the two equals the amount of the tax. To see why we have a new supply curve, consider any point on the old curve.

Let's take the point of the original equilibrium. This point tells us that, without the tax, a price of 85 pence will persuade producers to produce 40 million pints a day. If there is a 25 pence tax, it would take a price of 110 pence to persuade producers to produce 40 million pints a day. This is because they want to get the 85 pence a pint they received before, plus the additional 25 pence beer tax that they now have to pay to the government. Likewise, any other point on S tells us the price producers need to receive to produce the quantity at that point if there is no tax. Introducing the 25 pence tax means producers now want 25 pence more. So, at each quantity, the point on $S + tax$ is 25 pence higher than the corresponding point below on S. The curve $S + tax$ describes the terms on which the good is supplied.

A new equilibrium is determined where the new supply curve intersects the demand curve. This equilibrium is at a price of 105 pence a pint and a quantity of 30 million pints a day. So the 25 pence tax has increased the price paid by the consumer by only 20 pence. But if the government collects 25 pence a pint in tax, and if consumers pay only an extra 20 pence a pint for beer, who pays the other 5 pence? The answer is the producers. Originally they charged consumers 85 pence a pint. Now they charge 105 pence a pint but give 25 pence to the government, leaving themselves with only 80 pence a pint. So their net receipts are 5 pence a pint lower than before. In Fig. 6.5 we can read the 80 pence off S at the point immediately below the new equilibrium on $S + tax$. The price here is 25 pence below the price paid by consumers as the gap between the two supply curves equals the amount of the tax, that is 25 pence.

The tax brings in tax revenue to the government equal to the tax per item multiplied by the items sold after the tax is imposed. The revenue is illustrated by the blue shaded area in the figure. The 25 pence tax on beer, levied on 30 million pints a day, brings in a tax revenue of £7,500,000 a day.

In this example, part of the tax is paid by the buyer and part by the seller – the buyer pays 20 pence and the seller pays 5 pence. However, the sharing of the tax varies from product to product. Some split of the tax between the buyer and seller is usual but cases in which either the buyer or the seller pays the entire tax can occur. Let's see how the shares are determined.

Division of the Tax and Elasticity

The division of the tax between buyers and sellers depends, in part, on the elasticities of supply and demand. There are four extreme cases:

◆ Perfectly elastic supply – buyer pays
◆ Perfectly inelastic supply – seller pays
◆ Perfectly elastic demand – seller pays
◆ Perfectly inelastic demand – buyer pays

Figure 6.6(a) shows the marker for sand from which computer-chip makers extract silicon. There is a virtually unlimited quantity of this sand available, and its owners are willing to supply any quantity at a price of 10 pence a kilogram. The supply is perfectly elastic and the supply curve is S_E. The demand curve for sand is D. With no tax, the price is 10 pence a kilogram and 5,000 kilograms a week are bought.

If this sand is taxed at 1 penny a kilogram, we must add the tax to the minimum price at which the owners are willing to sell the sand to determine the terms on which this sand will be available to computer-chip makers. Since without the tax the suppliers of sand are willing to supply any quantity at 10 pence a kilogram, with the 1 penny tax they are willing to supply any quantity at 11 pence a kilogram along the curve $S_E + tax$. This new supply curve intersects the demand curve at the new equilibrium. The price increases to 11 pence a kilogram and 3,000 kilograms a week are bought and sold. The tax has increased the price paid by consumers by the entire amount of the tax – 1 penny a kilogram – and has decreased the quantity sold.

Figure 6.6(b) shows the market for water from a mineral spring that flows at a constant rate that can't be controlled. The quantity supplied is 100,000 bottles a week, regardless of the price. The supply is perfectly inelastic and the supply curve is S_I. The demand curve for the water from this spring is D. With no tax, the price is 50 pence a bottle and 100,000 bottles a week are bought.

If this mineral water is taxed at 5 pence a bottle, we must add the tax to the minimum price at which the spring owners are willing to sell the water to determine the terms on which this water will be available to consumers. But the spring owners are able to supply only one quantity – 100,000 bottles a week – at any price (greater than zero). Consumers on the other hand, are willing to buy the 100,000

FIGURE 6.6

Specific Tax and Elasticity

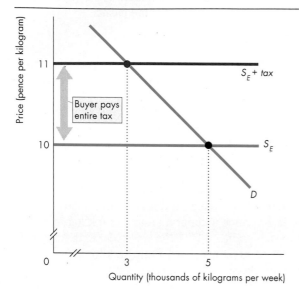

(a) Perfectly elastic supply

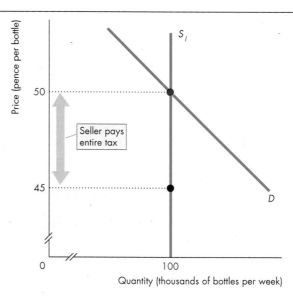

(b) Perfectly inelastic supply

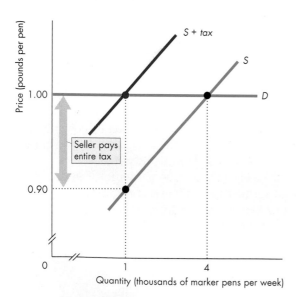

(c) Perfectly elastic demand

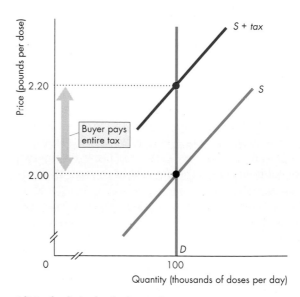

(d) Perfectly inelastic demand

In part (a), the supply of sand is perfectly elastic. With no tax, the price is 10 pence a kilogram and 5,000 kilograms a week are bought. A tax of 1 penny a kilogram shifts the supply curve to S_E + *tax*. The price increases to 11 pence a kilogram and the buyer pays the entire tax. In part (b), the supply of water is perfectly inelastic. With no tax, the price is 50 pence a bottle. A tax of 5 pence decreases the price received by sellers, but the price remains at 50 pence a bottle. The seller pays the entire tax. In part (c), the demand for pink marker pens is perfectly elastic at £1 a pen (the price of other coloured pens). With no tax, the price of a pink marker pen is £1 and 4,000 a week are bought. A tax of 10 pence a pink marker pen shifts the supply curve to S + *tax*. The price remains at £1 a pen and the seller pays the entire tax. In part (d), the demand for insulin is perfectly inelastic. With no tax, the price is £2 a dose and 100,000 doses a day are bought. A tax of 20 pence a dose shifts the supply curve to S + *tax*. The price rises to £2.20 a dose and the buyer pays the entire tax.

bottles available each week only if the price is 50 pence a bottle. So the price remains at 50 pence a bottle, and the suppliers pay the entire tax. A tax of 5 pence a bottle reduces the price received by suppliers to 45 pence a bottle.

Figure 6.6(c) shows the market for pink marker pens. Apart from a few people, no one cares whether they use a pink, blue, yellow or green marker pen. If pink markers are less expensive than the others, everyone will use pink. If pink markers are more expensive than the others, no one will use them. The demand for pink markers is perfectly elastic at the price of other coloured marker pens – £1 a pen. The demand curve for pink markers is the horizontal curve D. The supply curve is S. With no tax, the price of a pink marker is £1 and 4,000 a week are bought.

If a tax of 10 pence a pen is levied on pink, and only pink, marker pens, we must add the tax to the minimum price at which suppliers are willing to sell them to determine the terms on which pink marker pens will be available to consumers. The new supply curve is $S + tax$. The new equilibrium is at a price of £1 a pen, the same as before, and the quantity of pink marker pens sold decreases to 1,000 a week. The 10 pence tax has left the price paid by the consumer unchanged, but decreased the amount received by the supplier by the entire amount of the tax – 10 pence a pen. As a result, sellers decrease the quantity offered for sale. (In the case of pink marker pens, it is likely that once sellers have run down their stocks, supply will also be perfectly elastic. In this case, pink marker pens will disappear!)

Figure 6.6(d) shows the market for insulin, a vital daily medication for diabetics. The quantity demanded is 100,000 doses a day, regardless of the price. That is, a diabetic would sacrifice all other goods and services rather than not consume the insulin dose that provides good health and survival. The demand for insulin reflects this fact and is perfectly inelastic. It is shown by the vertical curve D. The supply curve of insulin is S. With no tax, the price is £2 a dose and 100,000 doses a day are bought.

If insulin is taxed at 20 pence a dose, we must add the tax to the minimum price at which the drug companies are willing to sell it to determine the terms on which insulin will be available to consumers. The result is a new supply curve $S + tax$. The new equilibrium occurs at a price of £2.20 a dose, but the quantity bought does not change. The buyer pays the entire tax of 20 pence a dose.

Reading Between the Lines on pp.156–157 shows how different levels of specific taxes on alcohol in Britain and France influence consumers' buying decisions.

Ad Valorem Taxes

A very similar analysis can be used for *ad valorem* taxes such as VAT. As with specific taxes, the tax falls chiefly on consumers if supply is more elastic than demand, and chiefly on producers if demand is more elastic than supply. To illustrate a situation where the tax might fall more heavily on producers, Fig. 6.7 shows what might happen to the market for mineral water if it became liable for VAT at the standard UK rate of 17.5 per cent. It is assumed that supply is less

FIGURE 6.7

An *Ad Valorem* Tax on Expenditure

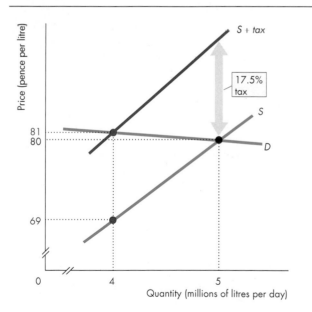

The demand curve for mineral water is *D* and the supply curve is *S*. In the absence of a tax, the price of mineral water is 80 pence a litre and 5 million litres a day are bought and sold. If a tax of 17.5 per cent were imposed, the supply curve would shift upward to the curve labelled *S + tax*. The new equilibrium price would be 81 pence a litre and 4 million litres a day would be traded. The tax is shared between the consumers, who pay 1 penny more per litre, and the producers, who receive 11 pence less per litre.

elastic than demand. The elasticity of supply may be limited by the fact that there are few places where very pure water can be found, whereas demand may be very elastic because there are many alternative soft drinks.

The quantity of mineral water (measured in millions of litres per day) is shown on the horizontal axis and the price of mineral water (measured in pence per litre) is on the vertical axis. The demand curve for mineral water is D and the supply curve is S. At present there is no VAT and the price is 80 pence a litre and 5 million litres a day are bought and sold.

Let's suppose that a 17.5 per cent VAT is imposed on mineral water. Again the supply curve moves upward to $S + tax$. The only difference from the previous case of a specific tax is that this time $S + tax$ is not parallel to S. To see how the curve shifts we can again consider any one point. We'll take the point of the original equilibrium. That point tells us that, without the tax, a price of 80 pence a litre will persuade producers to produce 5 million litres a day. If there is a 17.5 per cent tax, it would take a price of 94 pence a litre to persuade producers to produce 5 million litres a day. This is because they want to get the 80 pence a litre they received before, plus an extra 17.5 per cent – which is 14 pence – as they would have to hand over this amount to the government in VAT. Likewise any other point on S tells us the price producers would want to be persuaded to produce the quantity at that point if there were no tax. And the point moves up by 17.5 per cent of the price on S to $S + tax$ if a 17.5 per cent tax is introduced, as producers would want 17.5 per cent more to be persuaded to carry on producing that quantity.

The market would settle where the new supply curve intersects the demand curve. This is at a quantity of 4 million litres a day and at a price of 81 pence a litre. The consumers are paying only 1 penny more than before – 81 pence a litre instead of 80 pence. But producers are receiving only 69 pence a litre – 11 pence less than they received before. So the tax falls chiefly on producers.

A similar analysis to this can be used for percentage taxes imposed in the labour market – for example, personal income tax and National Insurance contributions.

Let's now leave our study of taxes and turn to an examination of subsidies.

Subsidies

A **subsidy** is a payment by a government to a firm or an industry that helps to keep prices down and maintain output. There are several different types of subsidy. One type is a **lump-sum subsidy** which involves occasional payments to a firm, often just once a year. In the United Kingdom, such subsidies are often given to opera companies, theatres and other arts concerns. Another type of subsidy is a **labour subsidy** which is paid to help firms meet their labour costs. For example, in the United Kingdom the government operates a youth training scheme, which encourages firms to take on young employees. A third type of subsidy is a **subsidy on expenditure** which is paid by the government to a firm for each unit of output supplied. This sort of subsidy is like a negative tax on expenditure. It is this final sort of subsidy that we will discuss here. We'll study subsidies by examining the market for bus rides.

Suppose that in one large city there are many bus companies which initially receive no subsidies. The bus ride market is illustrated in Fig. 6.8. The demand curve is D and the supply curve is S. One thousand million passenger miles are travelled each year at a price of 12 pence a mile. Now suppose the government offers bus companies a subsidy. It might offer a specific subsidy – say 1.5 pence a passenger mile – or an *ad valorem* subsidy – say 12 per cent. We'll assume it offers a specific subsidy of 1.5 pence a passenger mile.

• If suppliers are willing to supply 1,000 million passenger miles a year for 12 pence a mile without a subsidy, they will be willing to supply that same quantity for 10.5 pence a mile with a 1.5 pence subsidy. The supply curve for passenger miles therefore shifts *downward* by the amount of the subsidy and becomes the curve labelled $S - subsidy$. The new equilibrium is where the new supply curve intersects the demand curve at a price of 11 pence a mile and a quantity of 1,100 million miles a year. The price of passenger miles falls by 1 penny a mile so consumers pay 1 penny a mile less. Producers receive 11 pence a mile from consumers along with the subsidy of 1.5 pence a mile to make a total of 12.5 pence a mile. So they end up with 0.5 pence a mile more.

In this example supply is more elastic than demand and consumers benefit more from the subsidy than producers – consumers end up paying 1 penny a mile less while producers end up receiving

FIGURE 6.8

FIGURE 6.8

A Specific Subsidy

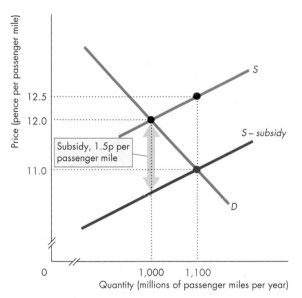

The demand curve for bus travel is *D* and the supply curve is *S*. A competitive market with no taxes or subsidies produces 1,000 million passenger miles a year at a price of 12 pence a mile. If the government subsidizes bus transport by 1.5 pence a passenger mile, the supply curve shifts downward to the curve labelled *S – subsidy*. The price of bus travel for consumers falls to 11 pence a passenger mile and the quantity produced increases to 1,100 million miles a year. Bus companies receive 1 penny a mile less from consumers, but allowing for the 1.5 pence a mile subsidy, they receive 12.5 pence a mile altogether.

0.5 pence a mile more. If demand is more elastic than supply, then the subsidy benefits producers more than consumers.

R E V I E W

T he effects of a tax on expenditure or a subsidy depend on the elasticities of supply and demand. If demand is more elastic than supply, then a tax hurts producers more than consumers and a subsidy benefits producers more than consumers. If demand is less elastic than supply, then a tax hurts consumers more than producers and a subsidy benefits consumers more than producers. ◆

We have now seen how governments can intervene in markets by setting maximum or minimum prices and by using taxes and subsidies, but other methods are sometimes used. These other methods include import duties, rationing and government purchases. All of these – along with subsidies – have been used to intervene in UK agricultural markets in the last 50 years. We will therefore look at agricultural markets to see why these different methods have been used in them and to compare their effects.

Policies on Agriculture

L et's start our look at agriculture by asking briefly why it has long enjoyed official support. Then let's look at the various ways in which that support has been given, ending with the present system which is the Common Agricultural Policy (CAP) implemented by the European Union.

The Reasons for Supporting Agriculture

Agriculture is supported in many countries for various reasons. In the United Kingdom the main aims of support have always been to preserve a reasonable degree of self-sufficiency in food and to try to stabilize food prices. If there is no government intervention, the prices of agricultural products, especially crops, may fluctuate sharply. This is because the supply curves of crops tend to move around from year to year depending upon the weather. In years of bad weather, the supply curves move to the left and prices rise, while in years of good weather the supply curves move to the right and prices fall.

UK Agricultural Policy Before 1973

UK intervention with agriculture began with the Corn Laws which were introduced in the fifteenth century. The aim of these laws was to prohibit imports except in years when there was a bad harvest. The method used was to impose taxes, called tariffs, on corn imports unless home corn prices rose above a specified level. This arrangement meant that imports were permitted only in years when corn crops were poor so that corn prices were very high.

In other years, home producers were protected from foreign competition. The Corn Laws protected home farmers and encouraged corn production, but by generally keeping out imported corn they led to higher prices for consumers. The laws were repealed in 1846 after the Irish famines made import controls unacceptable.

Later in the nineteenth century, UK farmers faced growing competition from North America and Australasia as improvements in transport made it cheaper for those countries to export products to the United Kingdom. Lacking government protection, the UK farming industry became depressed, and by 1914 about half of all food consumed in the United Kingdom was imported. This caused serious problems in World War I, but little remedy was made afterwards, partly because it was hoped that World War I was the war to end all wars. However, some subsidies were introduced to encourage home production in the 1930s when another world war seemed possible.

UK Policy During World War II More dramatic policies were adopted when World War II started. Different approaches were used for different foods, but the most common approach was rationing. The key elements of rationing are outlined in Fig. 6.9 which illustrates the butter market. Suppose that in 1939 demand by UK consumers was as shown by the curve labelled D. There was extensive international trade in butter and the United Kingdom was a relatively small part of the world, so it could effectively buy any amount of butter it wished at the world price of 10d (ten old pence) an ounce. So the supply of butter to UK consumers was as shown by the horizontal curve labelled S. The market settled with 150 million ounces sold each week at a price of 10d.

Some of this 150 million ounces was supplied by UK farmers. Their supply curve is shown by the curve labelled S_{UK}. This shows that at a price of 10d an ounce, UK farmers were willing to supply just 70 million ounces, under half of the 150 million ounces bought by UK consumers. The other 80 million ounces were supplied by farmers in other countries.

Imagine that by 1941 shipping losses caused all butter imports to cease. The only supply came from UK farmers whose supply curve is S_{UK}. Without government intervention, the equilibrium quantity would decrease to 90 million ounces a week and the price would rise to 16d an ounce. At this price, many people would scarcely be able to afford any

FIGURE 6.9

Wartime Agricultural Policy

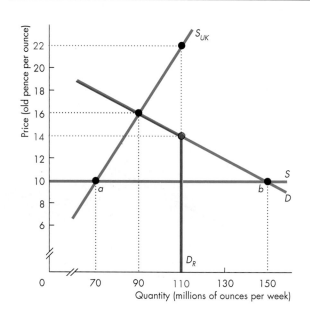

D shows the demand for butter by UK consumers. Before the war they could buy as much as they wished on world markets at 10d (ten old pence) an ounce, so they faced the horizontal supply curve S and they bought 150 million ounces a week. UK farmers had the supply curve labelled S_{UK}. At the price of 10d an ounce they supplied just 70 million ounces a week. The remaining 80 million ounces, represented by the distance between a and b, was imported. Wartime shipping losses effectively put an end to butter imports so that S_{UK} became the supply curve facing consumers. Without intervention the price would have risen to 16d an ounce and the quantity traded would have been 90 million ounces a week. But the government bought butter from farmers at 22d an ounce, so they supplied 110 million ounces. The government limited demand to this amount by ruling that people could buy butter legally only with ration tickets, and it issued ration tickets that permitted each person to purchase just 2 ounces a week. The government could have sold the 110 million ounces at any price below 14d an ounce. Typically it sold it at the pre-war price of 10d an ounce.

butter. So the government wanted a lower price for consumers plus, if possible, a higher output.

The government tackled the problem in two stages. First, it offered to buy all butter from farmers at a price of 22d, even higher than the price they would receive without government intervention. Looking at S_{UK} you can see that this price encouraged farmers to produce 110 million ounces a week. Looking at curve D you can see that the government could have just sold this quantity if it sold it at a price of 14d. However, even at that price many people could afford very little butter, while at any lower price it seemed the quantity demanded would exceed the 110 million ounces available and so cause queues for butter. No government, especially in wartime, wants people to waste time in queues.

So the government issued everyone with ration tickets for 2 ounces of butter a week. This amounted to about 110 million ounces a week for the whole country. The government allowed butter to be sold only to people who gave ration tickets to shopkeepers when they bought butter. In this way, the demand was really represented by the kinked curve D_R. This is vertical below the price of 14d since, although people would like to buy more than 110 million ounces at prices below 14d, legally no more than 110 million ounces a week could be demanded. D_R slopes at higher prices than 14d because, although people were legally allowed to buy 110 million ounces, at such high prices they would actually buy less.

Even if the government had chosen to sell the 110 million ounces of butter at a mere 1d an ounce there would have been no queues at shops as total purchases were restricted to the 110 million ounces available. So the government could set the price as low as it wished. Typically it chose the pre-war price which was 10d. This meant that consumers paid no more than before the war and consumed more than they would with a free wartime market (without trade) in butter.

UK Policy from 1945 to 1973 When World War II ended, imports resumed and rationing gradually disappeared. But governments were reluctant to allow markets to settle exactly as they had before the war because it was felt that the United Kingdom was too reliant on imports. Let's look at this in the context of butter once again as shown in Fig. 6.10. The problem of inflation has been ignored so that the curves and prices given here are readily comparable with those in Fig. 6.9.

Once shipping companies built up their fleets, butter imports resumed. So within a few years UK consumers again faced a horizontal supply curve. This curve is labelled S and it shows that consumers were able to buy as much butter as they wished at the world price of 10d an ounce. So the UK market

settled down again with a price of 10d an ounce and a quantity of 150 million ounces a week.

The government knew that if it took no action to help UK farmers, they would go back to producing only 70 million ounces. Remember that the curve labelled S_{UK} shows the supply curve for UK farmers. It shows they will produce only 70 million ounces a week at a price of 10d an ounce. If production fell to this level, the country would supply less than half its butter.

The government tackled this problem by subsidiz-

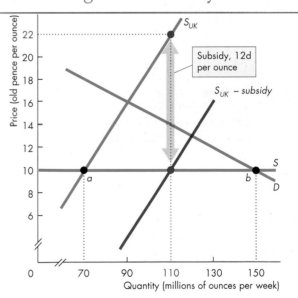

FIGURE 6.10

Post-war Agricultural Policy

Trade recovered after the war. UK consumers could again buy butter on world markets at a price taken here to be 10d an ounce, so they faced the supply curve S. UK consumers had the demand curve labelled D, so they bought 150 million ounces a week at a price of 10d an ounce. UK farmers had the supply curve S_{UK}. Without intervention by the government they would have supplied only 70 million ounces at the going price of 10d an ounce so that 80 million ounces of butter – over half the total consumed – would have been imported, as represented by the gap between a and b. To raise self-sufficiency the government subsidized butter. Suppose there was a specific subsidy of 12d an ounce. The supply curve for UK farmers would be S_{UK} – subsidy. Farmers would now receive 22d for each ounce sold – 10d from consumers and 12d from the government – so they would be willing to supply 110 million ounces a week instead of 70 million. Imports would fall to 40 million ounces and self-sufficiency would increase.

Who Pays the Taxes?

> 'Thus, although the French may tax our goods, and so inflict a loss on themselves and on us, this is no reason for our inflicting an additional loss on the two communities by taxing the import of their goods.'
>
> FLEEMING JENKIN
> *'On the Principles which Regulate the Incidence of Taxes'*

Taxes increase the price paid by the buyer and decrease the price received by the seller. As a result, they decrease the quantities bought and sold and inflict costs on both buyers and sellers. These costs must be weighed against the benefits of the things on which that government spends the taxes it collects.

In the late nineteenth century, economists worked out how to measure the costs of taxes and to determine who bears those costs. At this time, most of the taxes were those on international trade – like the taxes we impose on imported Japanese cars today. It was discovered that a critical factor determining the effects of taxes is what we now call the *elasticity of demand*. Taxing goods that have an inelastic demand has a bigger effect on the price than on the quantity and brings in a large tax revenue. The smaller the effect of a tax on the quantity bought, the less the tax decreases consumption and the lower is its cost. So it pays to tax items – sometimes luxuries such as boats and expensive cars and sometimes necessities such as petrol – that have an inelastic demand.

It was also discovered that the *elasticity of supply* plays an important role in determining the effects of taxes. Taxing goods that have an inelastic supply lowers the price received by the seller but has a small effect on the quantity sold and brings in a large tax revenue. The smaller the effect of a tax on the quantity sold, the less the tax decreases consumption and the lower is its cost. So it also pays to tax items that have an inelastic supply. This explains why land is a common item to tax.

Taxes are the revenue source that enables governments to provide a wide range of valuable public services. But taxes also impose a burden on those who pay them. When those who pay get none of the benefits, the seeds of a tax revolt are sown. Such was the situation in 1773 when the British Parliament imposed a tea tax on its American colonists. Rather than buy tea and pay this tax, the colonists held a tea party of a different kind, dumping valuable cargoes of British tea into the waters of Boston harbour.

Every time you buy a litre of petrol in Europe, the government of the particular country collects part of what you pay as tax. And these taxes are large. The average for the 12 EU states is 0.34 Ecu a litre. The lowest rate is 0.20 Ecu in Spain and the highest is 0.53 Ecu in Italy. The UK charges 0.31 Ecu a litre. Who really pays these high petrol taxes? Do the buyers pay? Does the seller pay? Or do the buyer and seller share the burden of the tax? If they share it, in what proportions?

Fleeming Jenkin: An Engineer's Contribution to Economics

FLEEMING JENKIN

Fleeming Jenkin (1833–1885) was a distinguished engineer who put his clear mind to work on a wide range of problems. Jenkin was not a famous economist in his own day, and his contributions to economic science were subsequently rediscovered by others. But he was a remarkable person who made a remarkable contribution to economics.

Jenkin worked on submarine cables, electrical standards, urban sanitation, and developing an electrical monorail transportation system. Between all these engineering projects, he was one of the first people to work out the laws of supply and demand and to put them to work on practical questions. One of these questions was: Who pays the taxes imposed on the sale of goods and services – the buyer or the seller or a combination of the two? The answer he came up with is the right one and is explained in this chapter.

ing farmers. This seemed the obvious strategy as, throughout the war, farmers had effectively been subsidized because governments had given farmers more money for butter than consumers paid. Suppose the government introduced a specific subsidy of 12d an ounce. This would shift the supply curve for UK farmers to S_{UK} – *subsidy*. These farmers would now be willing to sell 110 million ounces a week to UK consumers at 10d an ounce, because they would get another 12d an ounce from the subsidy and so get the 22d an ounce they really needed to be persuaded to produce 110 million ounces a week. With UK farmers supplying 110 million ounces, imports fell to only 40 million ounces, the gap between UK production and UK consumption.

The policy of subsidies was applied to many food products. It raised self-sufficiency in food to around 70 per cent. It also raised the income of the farming community. Without the subsidy, butter producers would have sold 70 million ounces a week at 10d an ounce, whereas with the subsidy they sold 110 million ounces a week and received 22d an ounce – 10d from consumers and 12d from the subsidy. Governments did not mind this because wages were typically low in agriculture and governments were happy to adopt a policy which raised low farm incomes. Notice that farmers' incomes were increased at the expense of other citizens who had to pay the taxes that financed the subsidies. So there was a redistribution within the United Kingdom to people in the farming sector from other people.

The policy actually had a third aim, which was to create greater stability in farm incomes. Farm incomes tend to be unstable. This problem is most acute with crops where output and prices fluctuate owing to changes in the weather. But there are also problems for producers of products like butter. Cows eat food which is grown, and fluctuations in cow food prices cause fluctuations in costs for butter producers. Fluctuations in butter costs around the world lead in turn to fluctuations in butter prices.

The subsidy policy pursued from 1945 to 1973 helped a little as it at least insured that farmers faced stable prices. In the case of butter, for instance, governments might determine a price of 22d an ounce for farmers, and they would vary the subsidy whenever world prices altered to keep the price at 22d. So if world prices fell to 8d an ounce the subsidy would rise to 14d, and if world prices rose to 12d the subsidy would fall to 10d.

Agricultural Policy in Mainland Europe

The main difference between farming on the European mainland and in the United Kingdom was that mainland farms changed less when the strip system of feudal times was abolished in the eighteenth and nineteenth centuries. When this system was abolished in the United Kingdom, large efficient farms were created, though there was much hardship for those who lost the right to farm their strips and who could not find work on the new farms. In much of mainland Europe the people who had previously had a right to farm the strips became the owners of the strips and ended up owning inefficient small farms that were divided into several separate parts.

When competition increased from North America and Australasia, many mainland European countries responded to the threat to the livelihood of their inefficient farmers by imposing tariffs on imported food. This was in contrast to the United Kingdom which, as we have seen, pursued a free trade policy for many years after 1846. The protectionism on the mainland led to much greater self-sufficiency in food production.

Choosing an Agricultural Policy for the European Union

One of the main reasons why the European Union was established was to abolish all tariffs between its member countries. This promotes trade between members and allows citizens in each country to benefit from the gains of specialization and exchange that we looked at in Chapter 3. As the EU countries abolished all internal tariffs, they had to set common tariffs on products from other countries. If, for example, France set a higher tariff than Italy on sugar imported from the West Indies, then French people could avoid paying the higher French tariff by buying sugar that was imported through Italy, knowing that Italy had a lower tariff on West Indian sugar and that there would be no tariff applied by the French on sugar imported from another EU country. So it was impossible for member countries to have different tariffs on imports from non-members.

Consequently, the EU countries agreed to have common tariffs on imports of many products, including food, from non-members. The original EU countries were reasonably self-sufficient in food, because of their history of tariffs, and the chief aim of their new CAP was to ensure that farmers did not suffer too much from outside competition. There were other aims including an attempt to stabilize food prices and farm incomes.

The European Union could have protected farmers by using subsidies instead of tariffs. However, the EU countries had no history of agricultural subsidies, and in any case they had large farming sectors so that the subsidies needed would have been very costly for taxpayers. Nevertheless, even tariffs effectively transferred income to the farming communities. Farmers gained because they could sell at high prices without losing out to foreign farms whose products were subject to tariffs. Other citizens lost because they paid higher prices to the farmers for home-produced food.

When the United Kingdom joined the European Union in 1973, it had to join in the CAP, though it was given some time to adjust. The result was the ending of most food subsidies and the imposition of tariffs on food from non-member countries. But this EU policy has fallen into disrepute because of the famous food mountains and lakes. What are these mountains and lakes, and how did they come into being? To answer these questions we must look a little more closely at the CAP.

The Common Agricultural Policy

As we have seen, the EU's **Common Agricultural Policy** (CAP) boosts farm incomes chiefly by imposing tariffs on imports. Let's look again at the case of butter. This is illustrated in Fig. 6.11. Suppose that the price of butter on world markets is now 150 pence a kilogram. This means that non-EU farmers are willing to supply any amount of butter to the European Union for 150 pence a kilogram. So if there is no EU intervention, EU consumers face the horizontal supply curve labelled S. Given the demand curve labelled D for EU citizens, the market in the European Union would settle down where D and S intersect with a price of 150 pence a kilogram and a quantity of 100 million kilograms per week. In this situation there would be little production by EU farmers whose supply curve is labelled S_1. At a price of 150 pence a kilogram they will produce just 60 million kilograms per week.

In practice the European Union does intervene and EU farmers are helped by the imposition of a tariff on butter imported from non-EU countries.

FIGURE 6.11

The EU's Common Agricultural Policy

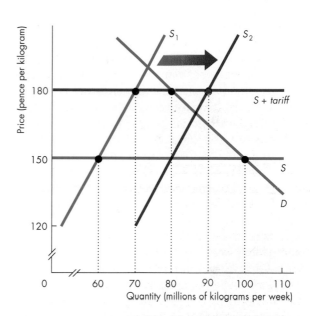

The demand curve for EU consumers is the curve labelled D. The world price of butter here is 150 pence a kilogram. Without EU intervention, consumers could buy as much butter as they liked at this price. They would face the supply curve S and would buy 100 million kilograms per week. The supply curve for EU farmers is S_1. At 150 pence a kilogram, they would supply 60 million kilograms per week. To raise farm incomes, the CAP imposes a tariff of 30 pence a kilogram on imported butter. Consumers now face the supply curve S + tariff and buy 80 million kilograms a week at a price of 180 pence a kilogram – 150 pence goes to foreign farmers and 30 pence to the European Union. At 180 pence a kilogram, EU farmers produce 70 million kilograms a week. So they sell more than they would without the CAP and they sell it at a higher price. If improvements in technology shifted the supply curve to S_2 and the CAP kept the price at 180 pence a kilogram, EU farmers would supply 90 million kilograms a week – 10 million kilograms more than consumers buy. The CAP would have to buy this surplus and so begin to build up a butter mountain.

Suppose the European Union adds a tariff of 30 pence a kilogram. This means that the price EU citizens must pay for non-EU butter is 180 pence a kilogram as consumers will pay 150p to the non-EU exporters and 30p in a tariff. The tariff paid by any individual consumer actually goes into the EU's own budget, not to that individual's own government. It should be mentioned that the CAP raises the tariff when world butter prices fall and reduces it when world butter prices rise. The result is that the total price to EU citizens is relatively stable. The CAP adopts similar procedures with its tariffs on other foods, and for this reason its food tariffs are often referred to as *variable levies*.

As a result of the tariff, the consumers face the new supply curve $S + tariff$ for non-EU butter. The market settles down where this intersects D, at a price of 180 pence a kilogram and a quantity of 80 million kilograms per week. At a price of 180 pence a kilogram, S_1 shows that EU farmers – whose butter is naturally exempt from the tariff – are willing to sell 70 million kilograms per week. So they sell more than they would without the CAP and they sell it at a higher price. It is clear that the policy of tariffs meets the chief aim of the CAP, namely protecting farmers from competition from cheap imports. The CAP also succeeds in promoting self-sufficiency in the European Union. Figure 6.11 shows that the CAP reduces the gap between consumption from 40 million kilograms – that is 100 million kilograms minus 60 million kilograms – to 10 million kilograms – that is 70 million kilograms minus 60 million kilograms.

A further aim of the CAP is to promote price stability. How does the CAP do this, given that world butter prices may fluctuate? The answer is that the European Union varies the tariff so that the combined world price plus the tariff is fairly constant. It is this combined price, which was 180 pence a kilogram in Fig. 6.11, that consumers actually pay.

So far it all looks straightforward enough, though of course the help to farmers has raised the prices everyone has to pay for food. But a big problem arises if the supply curve for EU farmers shifts. Suppose EU's farmers improve their productivity and are willing to produce more butter at each possible price. This means that their supply curve shifts to the right. Say that in time S_1 is replaced by S_2. Suppose, too, that the European Union wishes to pursue its aim of price stability by keeping the price for EU's farmers and consumers at 180 pence a kilogram. At this price, consumers want only the 80 million kilograms per week they were buying before yet EU's farmers want to produce 90 million kilograms, as shown by S_2.

It is interesting to reflect that the problem of excess supply might not arise, despite the tendency for supply to increase over time, if the EU's demand for food also increased over time. For many products,

demand does increase over time. This is because incomes increase over time and consumers demand more of most products when their incomes rise. But consumers do not demand much more food when their incomes rise – that is there is a low income elasticity of demand for food – and we reflect this by not shifting the demand curve in Fig. 6.11.

When a surplus like the one in Fig. 6.11 arises, what do the officials who run the CAP do? They buy up 10 million kilograms of butter each week! They quickly have a butter mountain on their hands. They are reluctant to reduce the price from 180 pence a kilogram, even though that would persuade consumers to buy more and farmers to produce less, because it would mean a fall in farm incomes as EU's farms produced less and sold it at a lower price. The key reason for the CAP mountains and lakes is that, in many agricultural products, improvements in farm productivity have led to EU's farmers producing more than EU's consumers want to buy at the price which the CAP wants to keep stable. To soak up the excess production, the European Union has to buy it and store it.

What happens to the food which the European Union buys and stores? This depends on what happens next to the supply curve. What the European Union hopes for is a significant fall in supply by EU's farmers. If supply falls for any reason, and if the supply curve shifts back to the left far enough, say to the original position, then EU consumption will exceed production at 180 pence a kilogram and the European Union will try to sell off its butter mountain. But if the supply curve does not shift, then the European Union must sell the mountain abroad. This means it will make a loss because it bought the butter at 180 pence a kilogram and, abroad, it must sell butter at the world price of 150 pence a kilogram. EU consumers always complain, understandably enough, if EU-produced food is sold cheaper to, say, the Russians than to people in the European Union. Sometimes people say the mountains should be sold off cheaply to pensioners and others on low incomes in the European Union. But if this happens, then the demand for newly produced butter will fall and there will be even more surpluses.

Why the CAP is Controversial

We have seen that the CAP pushes food prices for EU consumers above the levels of food prices in the rest of the world. It also tends to create food surpluses and mountains. But these are not the only controversial effects of the CAP. Another point of concern is its promotion of inefficiency. This inefficiency comes about because the CAP promotes food production in the European Union, where it is relatively costly, at the expense of food production in countries where it is relatively cheap.

The CAP redistributes income and is unpopular with those who lose out. For example, the CAP redistributes income from EU consumers to EU farmers. It hurts EU consumers by forcing them to pay higher prices than would otherwise prevail, and it helps EU farmers by raising their incomes above the levels that they would otherwise receive.

The CAP also redistributes income between EU member countries. For example, it redistributes income away from the United Kingdom. This happens for two reasons, both of which stem from the fact that the United Kingdom has a relatively small agricultural sector. First, all consumers suffer equally as all pay, say, 180 pence instead of 150 pence a kilogram for butter, but against this, the United Kingdom gets relatively less benefit as it has relatively fewer farmers. Second, the United Kingdom, being less self-sufficient, imports more food from non-EU countries and so its citizens pay more in the way of tariffs. These tariffs go to the EU budget where they are largely used to buy surplus food from non-UK farmers. So it is not surprising that the United Kingdom is more opposed to the CAP than most EU members.

The effects of the CAP go beyond the European Union. Most notably, by protecting and supporting food production within the European Union, the CAP reduces the demand for food produced elsewhere. This reduces the incomes of farmers in non-EU countries. Among those hurt by the CAP are poor farmers in many developing countries. An important consequence of hurting people in other countries is that it makes other countries reluctant to reduce their tariffs on EU products. So EU producers of these products are also affected. We look at tariffs and worldwide attempts to reduce them in Chapter 35, but we should note here that in 1993 an agreement was reached by the members of the international body called the General Agreement on Tariffs and Trade (GATT) which binds all signatories to reduce their protective policies. The European Union is a signatory and is particularly obliged to give less protection to EU farmers.

Reforming the CAP

Apart from the impetus given by the 1993 GATT agreement, the problems with the CAP have led to some attempts at reform. These attempts have focused on reducing EU production in an effort to reduce or eliminate the embarrassing food mountains. Three main methods that have been used so far to reduce EU food production.

The first method is to give farmers output quotas. **Output quotas** are upper limits on output production. The first quotas were introduced in 1984 for milk and there are now quotas for sugar as well. Farmers who exceed their quotas can be penalized in various ways, and certainly the CAP will not buy the excess. A problem with quotas is that they are hard to extend in an ordered way to those crops where output is very dependent on the weather. Farmers objected strongly to milk quotas which were based on their past production levels. They felt the quotas protected existing farmers at the expense of new, more efficient milk farmers who might enter the industry. This objection has since been softened by allowing farmers with quotas to sell them to other farmers.

Second, the CAP has tried to reduce production by the set-aside scheme. Under **set-aside**, farmers are paid to remove some of their land from agricultural production. Of course farmers tend to set aside the least productive land, but there is still a resulting fall in food output. The set-aside land may be actively converted to other uses, such as recreation, or left alone to become a haven for wild flora and fauna.

Third, the CAP is using **budget stabilizers** which means cumulative reductions in the level of tariffs. This reduces the price that farmers receive, and hence discourages them from producing so much. Some economists would favour eliminating all tariffs on food and helping any farmers who subsequently become very poor in the same ways that other poor people are helped. (We look at the relief of poverty in Chapter 18.)

Other methods of reducing food production could also be introduced. Most notably, perhaps, farmers could be encouraged to produce less food on the same amount of land. This can be achieved by using less intensive production methods. For example, egg producers could be encouraged to use free-range hens instead of battery hens, and crop farmers could be encouraged to use less fertil-

Markets in Action

THE INDEPENDENT, 13 APRIL 1994

Channel bootleggers tax the system

John Shepherd

BOOTLEGGERS are making more than £22 m a year by running vanloads of alcoholic drinks across the Channel, Whitbread, the UK brewer, claimed in a survey published yesterday.

The study, *Cross Channel Shopping – The Facts*, says that the effects from bootlegging and from legal shipments are felt throughout the UK.

Only 21 per cent of the £1bn worth of beers, wines and spirits brought across the Channel is reckoned to be destined for the Carlton and London television regions. The Meridian and Anglia TV regions each account for 14 per cent, while Yorkshire and Tyne-Tees account for a combined 9 per cent.

In total, the loss of sales for every supermarket, off-licence and licensed outlet in Britain is estimated at £20,000 a year. That equates to £359m of beer, £304m of table wine, £201 m of spirits, £161 m of sparkling wine and £11 m of fortified wine.

Whitbread's survey is the latest of several from the drinks industry in a concerted push to persuade the Government to reduce UK excise duty rates, which are among the highest in Europe.

Simon Ward, strategic affairs director of the brewer, pub operator and food retailer, said: 'We think the Government needs to reduce duty by half, equal to 15p per pint. That would be enough to deter the illegal trade and day-trippers.'…

As part of its campaign, Whitbread has produced a graph which, it said, shows that reductions in duty lead to higher consumption, and therefore, increased revenue for the Treasury.

Duty receipts fell by 50 per cent over the 12 years following a 27 per cent duty increase in 1947, it pointed out. Beer consumption in that period fell from nearly 34 million to 25 million barrels, or from 9.8 billion to 7.2 billion pints. Consumption then recovered to more than 40 million barrels by 1980 before the Government doubled duty and increased VAT from 8 to 15 per cent.

What was clear, according to Whitbread, was that the most recent increase in taxation on alcoholic drinks had tested the laws of diminishing returns. A 8.4 per cent increase in duty rates in 1992 yielded a 2.2 per cent rise in tax revenues.

Estimates of the lost revenue to the Treasury from personal and illegal imports of drinks last year extend to £470m – almost double the amount in 1992 before the relaxation of Customs quotas. Personal imports of beer are now said to exceed 1.25 million barrels, representing 3.5 per cent of the UK market.

Recent increases in the rate of duty levied by the UK government on alcoholic drinks have increased the quantity of beers, wines and spirits imported by private individuals, according to a study by Whitbread.

This problem of cheaper imports replacing domestic drinks has been exacerbated by cheap ferry fares, partly seen as a response to the threat from the Channel Tunnel.

The total cost advantage of buying alcoholic drinks in France is sufficient to attract people from all parts of the United Kingdom.

In 1992, the 8.4 per cent rise in duty resulted in only 2.2 per cent more tax revenue earned by the UK Treasury, an average loss of £20,000 a year per licensed outlet.

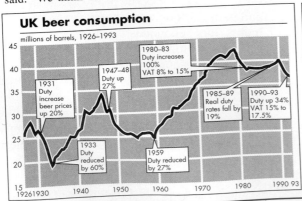

UK beer consumption

millions of barrels, 1926–1993

1931 Duty increase beer prices up 20%

1933 Duty reduced by 60%

1947–48 Duty up 27%

1959 Duty reduced by 27%

1980–83 Duty increases 100% VAT 8% to 15%

1985–89 Real duty rates fall by 19%

1990–93 Duty up 34% VAT 15% to 17.5%

Estimated turnover lost to cross-Channel shopping in 1993

Beer £359m –

Table wine £304m –

Spirits £201m –

Sparkling wine £161m –

Fortified wine £11m –

© The Independent. Reprinted with permission.

The graph in the article plots beer consumption over time, and shows the increases in duty. The graph confirms that a cut in duty increases consumption and an increase in duty decreases consumption.

Some people travelling to France are creating a black market by buying alcoholic drinks in bulk in France and then selling them illegally in the United Kingdom at a price lower than drinks in the United Kingdom.

By increasing the price of UK drinks, the government is reducing the relative price of a close substitute, drinks privately imported from France.

Whitbread claims that if the duty were halved, then the price differential would be reduced sufficiently to remove the incentive for people to buy their drinks in France.

Tax revenue from the duty would decline, but it would be partially offset by higher domestic sales of drinks.

The figure shows the price and quantity of beer consumed at the initial duty level.

The increase in duty moves the $S + duty$ curve upwards. The price rises and consumption falls.

If we assume elastic demand (that is, good transport links between the Kent coast and French ports like Calais making drinks bought in the United Kingdom and France close substitutes), the lower demand for drinks from United Kingdom outlets outweighs the rise in price and tax revenue is lost.

By reducing the duty and thereby reducing the price difference between United Kingdom and French alcoholic drinks, the price advantages for consumers gained by going to France would be removed. A reduction in the price would reduce the scope for these people to make a profit from arbitrage.

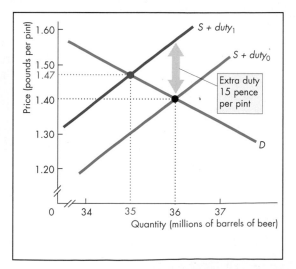

izer or even adopt organic farming methods. There is already some encouragement from consumers for farmers to use less intensive methods.

R E V I E W

There are many reasons why countries intervene with agriculture. These include promoting price stability, promoting self-sufficiency and raising farm incomes. Before it joined the European Union, the United Kingdom relied chiefly on subsidies to protect farmers from foreign imports. The EU's CAP relies chiefly on tariffs to reduce imports. This increases the price which consumers must pay. A problem arises in the European Union when EU farmers wish to produce more than EU consumers wish to buy. The CAP has typically resolved this problem by buying surplus food and storing it. The hope is that future EU production may fall below the level of EU consumption, in which case the mountains can be sold off. The mountains could be sold outside the European Union, but only at world prices that are below the EU prices the CAP paid for them. ◆

Markets for Illegal Goods

We have seen several methods in which governments can intervene in markets. We now turn to a particularly draconian method of intervention. This is **prohibition** which is making the buying and selling of some particular product illegal. The best known examples are illegal drugs.

Despite being illegal, trade in drugs does take place. In fact it is a multi-billion pound business. Such trade can be understood using the same economic models and principles that explain trading in markets for legal products. Also, economic models help us to understand the debate about drugs by answering questions such as: what would happen if drugs were legalized? Would they become cheaper? Would their consumption increase?

A Reminder About the Limits of Economics

Before we study the market for drugs, let's remind ourselves that economics is a science that tries to answer questions about how the economic world works. It neither condones nor condemns the activities it seeks to explain. It is vital that as a well-informed citizen, you have an opinion about drugs and about public policy towards them. What you learn about the economics of markets for illegal goods is one input into developing your opinion. But it is not a substitute for your moral judgements and does not help you to develop those judgements. What follows contains no moral judgements. It is a value-free analysis of how markets for illegal goods work, and not an argument about how they ought to be regulated and controlled.

To study the market for illegal goods, we're first going to examine the prices and quantities that would prevail if these goods were legal. Next we'll see how prohibition works. Then we'll see how a tax might be used to limit the consumption of these goods.

A Free Market for Drugs

The demand for drugs is determined by the same forces that determine the demand for other goods. Other things being equal, the lower the price of drugs, the larger is the quantity of drugs demanded. The demand curve for drugs, D, is shown in Fig. 6.12. The supply of drugs is also determined in a similar way to the supply of other goods and is shown as the supply curve S in the figure. If drugs were legal, the quantity bought and sold would be Q_c and the price would be P_c.

Making Drugs Illegal

When any activity such as trading in a good is made illegal, people who continue to undertake the activity run the risk of being caught and punished. In effect, they face an extra cost. You can think of this cost as reflecting the efforts of trying not to be caught plus the risk of suffering from fines or other penalties. The extent of the extra costs depends on the effectiveness with which the law is enforced and the penalties that are imposed on law-breakers. Who bears these extra costs when trading in drugs is made illegal? This depends on whether selling, or buying, or both are outlawed.

FIGURE 6.12

The Market for an Illegal Drug

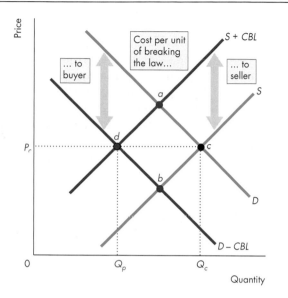

If consuming a drug is legal, the demand curve for a drug is D and the supply curve is S. So the market settles at point c where the quantity consumed is Q_c and the price is P_c. If selling the drug becomes illegal, the cost of breaking the law by selling drugs (CBL) is added to the other costs and supply decreases to $S + CBL$. The market moves to point a with a lower quantity consumed and a higher price. If buying drugs becomes illegal, the cost of breaking the law is subtracted from the maximum price that buyers are willing to pay and demand decreases to $D - CBL$. The market moves to point b with a lower quantity consumed and a lower price. If both buying and selling become illegal, both the supply and the demand curves shift. The market moves to point d with an even lower quantity consumed, but (in this example) the price remains at its unregulated level – point d.

Penalties on Sellers When sellers of illegal goods such as drugs are penalized, the costs of selling increase. Supply decreases and the supply curve shifts. In Fig. 6.12, the cost of breaking the law by selling drugs (CBL) is added to the other costs and the supply curve shifts to $S + CBL$. If penalties are imposed only on sellers, the market moves from point c to point a. The price increases and the quantity bought decreases.

Penalties on Buyers When buyers of illegal goods are penalized, the goods have less value to buyers. The cost of breaking the law must be subtracted from the value of the good to determine the maxi-

mum price buyers are willing to pay. Demand decreases and the demand curve shifts. In Fig. 6.12, the demand curve shifts to $D - CBL$. If penalties are imposed only on buyers, the market moves from point c to point b. The price falls and the quantity bought decreases.

Penalties on Both Sellers and Buyers If penalties are imposed on both sellers *and* buyers, both supply and demand decrease and both the supply curve and the demand curve shift. If the costs of breaking the law are the same for both buyers and sellers, both curves shift by the same amount. This is the case in Fig. 6.12. The market moves to point d. The price remains at the competitive market price but the quantity bought decreases to Q_p. But other distributions of penalties are possible. If sellers are policed more vigorously and punished more severely than buyers, then the supply curve shifts more than the demand curve and the price rises above the free market price. If buyers are policed more vigorously and punished more severely than sellers, then the demand curve shifts more than the supply curve and the price falls below the free market price.

With high enough penalties and effective law enforcement, it is possible to decrease demand and supply to the point at which the quantity bought is zero. But in reality, such an outcome is unusual. It does not happen in the case of illegal drugs. The key reason is the high cost of law enforcement and insufficient resources for the police to achieve effective enforcement. This is why some people suggest that drugs (and other illegal goods) should be legalized and sold openly, but should also be taxed at a high rate in the same way that legal drugs such as alcohol are taxed. How would such an arrangement work?

Legalizing and Taxing Drugs

If drugs were legalized, there would be no costs of law breaking. With no taxes on drugs, the quantity Q_c in Fig. 6.12 would be consumed. But suppose that drugs were taxed at a high rate. Figure 6.13 shows the effects of such an arrangement. Here, the tax rate has been chosen to make the quantity bought the same as with prohibition. The tax shifts the supply curve to $S + tax$. Equilibrium occurs at a quantity of Q_p. The price paid by consumers increases to P_b and the price received by

FIGURE 6.13

Legalizing and Taxing Drugs

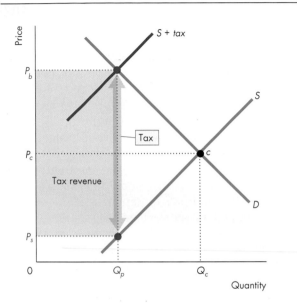

In this example, drugs are legalized but taxed at a high rate. The tax added to production costs raises the supply curve from S to $S + tax$. The quantity bought decreases to Q_p, the price paid by consumers increases to P_b, and the price received by suppliers decreases to P_s. The government collects a tax revenue equal to the blue shaded area.

suppliers decreases to P_s, that is P_b minus the tax which suppliers must hand over to the government. The government collects a tax revenue equal to the blue shaded area in the figure.

Illegal Trading to Evade the Tax It is likely that an extremely high tax rate would be needed to cut drug consumption to the level prevailing with prohibition. It is also likely that many drug dealers and consumers would try to cover up their activities to evade the tax. If they did this, they would face the cost of breaking the law, this time the tax law. If the penalty for tax law violation is as severe and as effectively policed as drug dealing laws, the analysis we've already conducted in Fig. 6.13 would still apply. The quantity of drugs consumed would

remain at Q_p. But to the extent that the tax was successfully evaded, the tax revenue would fall short of the area highlighted in Fig. 6.13.

Some Pros and Cons of Taxes versus Prohibition
Which is more effective, prohibition or taxing? The comparison we've just made suggests that the two methods can be made equivalent in terms of price and quantity traded if the taxes and penalties are set at the appropriate levels. But there are some other differences between the two policies.

An argument which favours taxes is that the tax revenue can be used to make law enforcement more effective, or to run a more effective education campaign against drugs, or indeed for any other purpose. An argument in favour of prohibition is that a prohibition sends a signal that may influence consumers' preferences and so decrease the demand for drugs. Another is that some people intensely dislike the idea of the government profiting from trade in harmful substances.

R E V I E W

P enalizing dealers for the sale of an illegal good increases the cost of selling the good and decreases the supply of it. Penalizing buyers for the consumption of an illegal good decreases the willingness to pay for the good and decreases the demand for it. The quantity bought decreases and the price increases if penalties for selling are higher than those for consuming and the price decreases if penalties for consuming are higher than those for selling. Taxing a good at a sufficiently high rate can achieve the same consumption level as prohibition. ◆

◆ ◆ ◆ ◆ We've now completed our study of demand and supply and its applications. You've seen how this powerful model enables us to make predictions about prices and quantities traded and also how it enables us to understand a wide variety of markets and situations. ◆ ◆ We're now going to start looking a bit more deeply at how people make economic choices, and in the next two chapters, we'll study the economic choices of households.

SUMMARY

Housing Markets and Rent Ceilings

A sudden decrease in the supply of housing shifts the short-run supply curve to the left. If there is a free market, rents increase. In the short run, higher rents bring forth an increase in the quantity of housing units supplied (from the existing stock) as people economize on the available space. In the long run, the higher rents stimulate building activity, resulting in a shift to the right of the short-run supply curve. Through this process, rents gradually decrease, and the quantity of housing available gradually increases.

If a rent ceiling prevents rents from increasing, the quantity of housing supplied is lower, in both the short run and the long run, than it would be in an unregulated market. There is no inducement for people to economize on space in the short run and no incentive to build new housing units in the long run. Equilibrium is achieved by people spending time searching for housing. The total cost of housing, including the value of the time spent searching, exceeds the cost in an unregulated market. (pp. 135–138)

The Labour Market and Minimum Wage Regulations

A decrease in the demand for unskilled labour lowers wages and reduces employment in the short run. Low wages in a particular market encourage people to leave that market and to acquire skills and to seek different, more highly paid work. As they do so, the short-run supply curve for unskilled labour shifts to the left. As it does so, it intersects the demand curve for unskilled labour at higher wages and lower levels of employment. Eventually, the wage returns to its previous level but at a much lower employment level.

If the government imposes a minimum wage, a decrease in the demand for labour results in an increase in unemployment and an increase in the amount of time spent searching for a job. Minimum wages bite hardest on those having the fewest skills and such workers tend to be young people. The unemployment rate among such people is about twice the average rate. (pp. 138–141)

Taxes on Expenditure and Subsidies

The imposition of a tax on a product shifts its supply curve upward. This raises the price that consumers must pay and it lowers the quantity traded. Consumers suffer as the price they pay rises, and producers suffer as the price they receive (once the tax has been paid to the government) falls. This means there is a burden on both consumers and producers. The extent to which the burden is shared between consumers and producers depends on the elasticities of demand and supply. The more elastic is supply in relation to demand, the more the burden falls on the consumer.

The imposition of a subsidy on an item shifts its supply curve downward. This means the price paid by consumers falls while the price received by producers (after allowing for receipt of the subsidy) rises. The extent to which the benefits from a subsidy are shared between consumers and producers depends on the elasticities of supply and demand. The more elastic is supply in relation to demand, the more the benefit falls on the consumer. Note that a subsidy also increases the quantity traded. (pp. 142–147)

Policies on Agriculture

Farmers in the United Kingdom have been supported by government action since before World War II. The main aim has been to raise output. Farmers in the rest of the European Union have been supported by government action since the last century. The main aim has been to protect farmers from foreign competition and to keep farm incomes at a reasonable level.

The United Kingdom relied chiefly on subsidies until it joined the European Union in 1973. Since then it has joined the Common Agricultural Policy (CAP). This sets high prices and imposes tariffs on cheap non-EU food. If EU farmers produce more food at the high prices than EU consumers want to buy, the European Union itself buys the surplus and so builds up mountains of food products. (pp. 147–158)

Markets for Illegal Goods

The effects of making a drug illegal depend on whether selling it, buying it, or both, are illegal. When selling is illegal, the risk of penalties forms an extra cost for suppliers, so the supply decreases. When buying is illegal, the risk of the penalties reduces demand. When both selling and buying are illegal, both supply and demand decrease. In all cases the quantity traded falls. The price rises if penalties for sellers are higher than penalties for buyers, and it falls if penalties for sellers are lower than penalties for buyers. Effective law enforcement and high enough penalties can decrease demand and supply to the point at which the good disappears.

A tax set at a sufficiently high rate can decrease the quantity of the drug traded to the same level that would be achieved by making it illegal. However, there will be a tendency for the tax to be evaded, so the tax law needs to be policed and backed up by penalties. Tax revenue from a drug tax could be used to pay for law enforcement and for a campaign against drugs. But making drugs illegal sends a signal that may influence preferences, decreasing the demand for drugs. (pp. 158–160)

K E Y   E L E M E N T S

Key Terms

Ad valorem tax, 142
Black market, 138
Budget stabilizers, 155
Common Agricultural Policy, 153
Labour subsidy, 146
Lump-sum subsidy, 146
Minimum wage law, 140
Output quotas, 155
Prohibition, 158
Rent ceiling, 137
Search activity, 137
Set-aside, 155
Specific tax, 142
Subsidy, 146

Subsidy on expenditure, 146
Tax on expenditure, 142

Key Figures

Figure 6.1   The San Francisco Housing Market in 1906, 136
Figure 6.2   A Rent Ceiling, 137
Figure 6.3   A Market for Unskilled Labour, 139
Figure 6.4   Minimum Wages and Unemployment, 141
Figure 6.5   A Specific Tax on Expenditure, 142
Figure 6.7   An *Ad Valorem* Tax on Expenditure, 145
Figure 6.11 The EU's Common Agricultural Policy, 153
Figure 6.12 The Market for an Illegal Drug, 159

R E V I E W   Q U E S T I O N S

1   Describe what happens to the rent and to the quantity of housing available if an earthquake suddenly and unexpectedly reduces the supply of housing. Trace the evolution of the rent and the quantity traded over time.

2   In the situation described in Question 1, how will things be different if a rent ceiling is imposed?

3   Describe what happens to the price and quantity traded in a market in which there is a sudden increase in supply. Trace the evolution of the price and quantity traded in the market over time.

4   Describe what happens to the price and quantity traded in a market in which there is a sudden increase in demand. Trace the evolution of the price and quantity traded in the market over time.

5   Describe what happens to the wage rate and quantity of labour employed when there is a sudden increase in demand for labour. Trace the evolution of the wage rate and employment over time.

6   In the situation described in Question 5, how are things different if a minimum wage is introduced?

7 When a government regulation prevents a price from changing, what forces come into operation to achieve an equilibrium?

8 What affects the extent to which the burden of a tax on expenditure is shared between consumers and producers? When would the burden fall wholly on consumers, and when would it fall chiefly but not wholly on producers?

9 What affects the extent to which the benefit of a subsidy is shared between consumers and producers? When would the benefit fall wholly on producers, and when would it be split equally between producers and consumers?

10 Why have governments in the United Kingdom and other countries operated policies that support agriculture?

11 Compare the options of supporting agriculture with tariffs and subsidies. What are the differences from the point of view of (a) consumers, (b) farmers and (c) governments?

12 Why has the operation of the CAP often led to mountains of surplus food?

13 Why does the United Kingdom's participation in the CAP lead to income being redistributed from the United Kingdom to other EU countries?

14 How does a law making it illegal to sell a good affect the demand for and supply of the good? How does it affect the price of the good and the quantity bought?

15 How does a law making it illegal to buy a good affect the demand for and supply of the good? How does it affect the price of the good and the quantity bought?

16 Explain the alternative ways in which the consumption of harmful drugs can be controlled. What are the arguments for and against each method?

PROBLEMS

You may find it easier to answer some of these problems by drawing the supply and demand curves on graph paper.

1 You have been given the following information about the market for rental housing in your town:

Rent (pounds per month)	Quantity demanded (per month)	Quantity supplied (per month)
50	20,000	0
100	15,000	5,000
150	10,000	10,000
200	5,000	15,000
250	2,500	20,000
300	1,500	25,000

a What is the equilibrium rent?
b What is the equilibrium quantity of housing traded?

2 Suppose a rent ceiling of £100 a month is imposed in the housing market described in Problem 1.
a What is the quantity of housing demanded?

b What is the quantity of housing supplied?
c What is the excess quantity of housing demanded?
d What is the maximum price that demanders are willing to pay for the last unit available?
e Suppose that the average wage rate is £5 per hour. How many hours a month will a person spend looking for housing?

3 Return to the original position in the housing market as it was in Problem 1. Suppose the government introduces a specific subsidy of £100 per month on rented accommodation.
a Which curve is affected by the subsidy? Does it shift up or down?
b What happens to the rent paid by tenants as a result of the subsidy?
c What happens to the quantity of housing demanded by tenants as a result of the subsidy?
d The landlords receive the rent paid by tenants plus the subsidy. What are their total receipts from each unit let?
e What is the total cost of the subsidy to the government?

4 Suppose the demand for and supply of teenage labour in your town are as follows:

Wage rate (pounds per hour)	Hours demanded (per month)	Hours supplied (per month)
1	3,000	1,000
2	2,500	1,500
3	2,000	2,000
4	1,500	2,500
5	1,000	3,000

a What is the equilibrium wage rate?
b What is the level of employment?
c What is the level of unemployment?
d If the government imposes a minimum wage of £2.50 an hour for teenagers, what are the employment and unemployment levels?
e If the government imposes a minimum wage of £3.50 an hour for teenagers, what are the employment and unemployment levels?
f If there is a minimum wage of £3.50 an hour and the demand increases by 500 hours, what is the level of unemployment?

5 The following table gives three supply schedules for bus travel:

Price (pence per passenger mile)	Quantity supplied (millions of passenger miles per week)		
	Momentary	Long run	Short run
2	500	300	100
4	500	350	200
6	500	400	300
8	500	450	400
10	500	500	500
12	500	550	600
14	500	600	700
16	500	650	800
18	500	700	900
20	500	750	1,000

a If the price is 10 pence per passenger mile, what is the quantity supplied:
   (1) In the long run?
   (2) In the short run?
b Suppose that the price is initially 10 pence but that it then rises to 14 pence. What will be the quantity supplied:
   (1) Immediately following the price rise?
   (2) In the short run?

(3) In the long run?

6 Suppose that the supply of bus travel is the same as in Problem 5. The following table gives two demand schedules – original and new:

Price (pence per passenger mile)	Quantity demanded (millions of passenger miles per week)	
	Original	New
2	10,000	10,300
4	5,000	5,300
6	2,000	2,300
8	1,000	1,300
10	500	800
12	400	700
14	300	600
16	200	500
18	100	400
20	0	300

a What is the original equilibrium price and quantity?
b After the increase in demand has occurred, what is:
   (1) The momentary equilibrium price and quantity?
   (2) The short-run equilibrium price and quantity?
   (3) The long-run equilibrium price and quantity?

7 The short-run and long-run demand for bus travel is as follows:

Price (pence per passenger mile)	Quantity (millions of passenger miles per week)	
	Short run	Long run
2	700	10,000
4	650	5,000
6	600	2,000
8	550	1,000
10	500	500
12	450	400
14	400	300
16	350	200
18	300	100
20	250	0

The supply of bus travel is the same as in Problem 5.

a What is the long-run equilibrium price and quantity of bus travel?

b Terrorist attacks on several major bus depots destroy one-fifth of the buses, and supply falls by 100 million passenger miles. What happens to the equilibrium price and quantity of bus travel:

(1) In the short run?

(2) In the long run?

8 The long-run supply of and demand for bus travel are as shown in Problems 5 and 7 and the market is in long-run equilibrium. Suppose the government introduces a 50 per cent *ad valorem* tax on bus travel.

a What is the new long-run equilibrium price and quantity of bus travel?

b In this equilibrium, what is the actual tax per passenger mile?

c How much of the tax is borne by consumers and how much by producers?

9 Suppose that the supply of beef by EU farmers and the demand for beef by EU consumers are as follows:

Price (pounds per tonne)	Quantity demanded (tonnes per month)	Quantity supplied (tonnes per month)
6,000	16,000	6,000
8,000	12,000	7,000
10,000	10,000	8,000
12,000	9,000	9,000
14,000	8,500	10,000

The price for beef on world markets is £6,000

per tonne. Suppose the European Union operates no policy to help its beef farmers.

a What price will EU consumers pay?

b How much will EU consumers buy?

c How much will EU producers supply?

d How much will be imported into the European Union?

10 Suppose the supply of and demand for beef in the European Union are as shown in Problem 9 and suppose the world price of beef is as given there. A CAP is introduced with the aim of raising supply by EU farmers to 8,000 tonnes per month. Suppose the CAP aims to achieve this with a tariff on imported beef.

a What tariff on imported beef would be needed?

b What would happen to the level of imports into the European Union?

c What would happen to the beef price paid by consumers?

11 Suppose the European Union operated the CAP outlined in Problem 10 for some time and then decided to raise the price received by EU farmers from £10,000 to £12,000 per tonne.

a What level of tariff would be needed?

b What price would consumers now face?

c How much would EU consumers now buy?

d How much would EU producers now produce?

e How much beef would the European Union have to buy?

f How much would the European Union have to spend on this beef?

P A R T 3

HOUSEHOLDS' & FIRMS' CHOICES

Talking with John Sutton

John Sutton graduated in physics and worked in the UK engineering industry before studying economics at Trinity College Dublin. He is Professor of Economics at the London School of Economics where he directs the Economics of Industry Group. While he has published widely in various areas of economic theory, his interests in recent years have been in developing and testing game-theoretic models of market structure. In 1990, he was awarded the Franqui medal for his contribution to the field of Industrial Organization.

What originally attracted you to the study of economics?

Like most economists, I was drawn to the subject in the first place by a concern with the big issues: development, unemployment, and so on. But what fascinated me when I began studying economics was that it did seem possible to find at least some models that 'worked', more or less. I still find this remarkable – there's no general reason why any usefully simple model should work in a social science; the world is just too complex. Yet the workings of the market mechanism constrain the pattern of outcomes in a way which, in certain definable circumstances, overrides all the accidents of personality and history. Economics isn't like physics, but it's not like history either. It's somewhere in between, and defining exactly how far we can push the scope of formal models is half the challenge.

How well do economists understand the way firms act?

Firms may have all kinds of aims and motivations which run beyond the economists' 'profit maximization' hypothesis. But there's a very old argument that says, 'firms may not maximize

'**E**conomics isn't like physics, but it's not like history either. It's somewhere in between, and defining exactly how far we can push the scope of formal models is half the challenge.'

profits at all times, but firms that seriously deviate from profit maximizing strategies won't survive – so the profit maximization model may work quite well in depicting market outcomes'. I'm very fond of that 'survivor' argument, in spite of its serious limitations, because I think something like this really is right. I'm continually struck, in looking at those bits of economics that work really well empirically, to find that the key results can often be derived by invoking quite weak assumptions as to firms' aims and actions. Two things keep appearing. One is this 'survivor principle'. The other is what financial economists call an 'arbitrage principle' – which basically says, if a profitable opportunity exists in the market, some firm will take it up. Now that's really very little to assume – but for some purposes, it may be all you need.

The profit maximizing model turns out to be just the right point of departure. Once you've understood what that leads to, you may find that some of your conclusions still hold good even if some – or many – of the firms are quite far away from 'maximizing' behaviour. The market imposes a discipline, which is why economists are much

better at analysing market outcomes than they are at modelling exactly what any individual agent will do.

Can economists determine the real factors influencing consumer choice or should we leave that to psychologists or sociologists?

This is a hard one. I'm pretty open minded on the issue, but you'll certainly find a range of different views on this among economists. There's an old tradition in the discipline which is very hostile to 'importing psychology into economics'. Hand in hand with that view goes a notion that we can say all we need to say about consumer choice by just appealing to very weak restrictions regarding consumers' preferences. The trouble with this view is that it runs into some serious difficulties, most notably in areas which involve uncertainty. There's a huge body of pretty impressive work in which experimental subjects faced with choices under uncertainty behave in ways which are hard to square with the conventional economic model, which assumes that each consumer simply chooses the action which maximizes the expected values of his or her utility. Current

research by economists and psychologists suggests a more complex story.

Would you agree that the existence of branded goods signifies a lack of competition?

No – it just indicates that there's another dimension to competition. Firms compete in both price and in non-price strategies. Product design, innovation, branding, advertising: it's a rich mix. The question does have another side, however. Why brands are so effective is, I believe, a puzzle for economists. This really is an area where we need the psychologists.

Do you believe game theory is a revolution in economic theory?

Yes I do; I think its roots go very deep. One of the most fundamental concepts in economics is that of equilibrium in a competitive system. There are two great historical traditions which offer us different ways of capturing that notion. One goes back to Edgeworth, who thought of equilibrium as a situation in which no opportunity remained for mutually advantageous trade between any group of agents. The other tradition began with Cournot.

167

He defined equilibrium by looking at a situation where each firm chooses an optimal 'strategy' ('set the level of output', say) taking as given the strategies followed by its rivals. In this setting, equilibrium is defined as a set of strategies such that no firm wants to deviate from its strategy, given the strategy of its rivals.

Now this is a very fruitful way to begin. You can use it – as Cournot did – to capture the idea of perfect competition, which we approach as the number of firms in the market becomes very large. But you can also use it when the market contains few firms – or when it's dominated by a handful of major sellers; and you can extend it to cover a wide menu of complex strategies that firms may use. The equilibrium it defines need not be 'static'; it can involve a rich description of scenarios that will evolve over time in response to any 'deviation' by a firm from its equilibrium actions. Now what game theory does is to provide us with the mathematical machinery to develop this kind of model in a manner which is flexible enough to capture the huge variety of competitive interactions we see in real markets.

The big issue now lies in putting some order on the results that emerge. Are there any assumptions which are valid across an interestingly wide range of settings, and which allow us to make any broad claims about oligopolistic markets?

Can policy intervention in product markets be justifiable on the grounds that it 'enhances competition'?

Yes – sometimes. I favour a pretty 'conservative' approach on this, in the sense that I feel the burden lies with the policy maker in justifying intervention. Only if a fairly clear case can be made that intervention will improve things should it be undertaken. At the same time, I would not accept the 'ultra-liberal' view that the market 'always knows best'. I just don't think that holds up.

For example, take 'predatory pricing'. A large firm uses its 'long purse' to underwrite loss-making prices in order to drive competitors out of the market and thereby establish a monopoly. Cases of this occur every now and then – in areas ranging from airlines to newspapers. You can certainly justify rules constraining the use of this kind of strategy – and indeed that's pretty much accepted in many countries.

What principles have guided your analysis most?

If you want models that work, don't expect to be able to do your theory on the back of an enve-

'The market imposes a discipline, which is why economists are much better at analysing market outcomes than they are at modelling exactly what any individual agent will do.'

lope. Theory takes time, and patience. Theorists should be allowed lots of rope – but in the end, a theory should be judged on one criterion: does it work?

Which economist do you admire most?

Louis Bachelier – by a wide margin. Bachelier was an extraordinary figure. In his PhD thesis submitted in 1900, he developed an entire theory of prices for financial securities, anticipating by half a century much of the work of the 1960s in the field. He then went on to derive predictions for the pricing of options, and – this is the good bit – he went out and tested his theory with some success for option prices on the Paris Bourse.

What I most like about Bachelier is his faith in the possibility of finding models that work in economics. Today, the theory of option pricing is the one that economists most often cite when asked to name an economic theory that works really well.

Unfortunately, there's a sad ending: like Cournot before him, he was ahead of his time. The mathematicians didn't think his proofs were rigorous enough and the economists of that era were so far from taking mathematical models seriously that his work struck

no chord. Bachelier made no further contribution to the field, which lay dormant until the late 1950s.

Do you have any hints or tips for students coming into economics?

Be sceptical about assumptions. When we build 'examples' we quite rightly use lots of assumptions just to keep the algebra simple. But when we build a theory, all this has to be stripped away; a theory uses just a few strong, simple assumptions.

Now it's essential to make some strong and simple assumptions in order to cut through all the irrelevant complexities, and isolate the things that matter. But you should ask at every step: What extra content does this assumption add to the predictions

of the theory? What does the theory say if you remove or reverse this assumption? Is this assumption compelling, or just 'plausible' – maybe true, maybe false? If so, can you identify circumstances where it's probably true, and where it's probably false?

The great temptation in economics is to keep adding assumptions until you have a nice model with a unique equilibrium and lots of sharp predictions. But by the time you've made enough assumptions to do that, what you may well be left with is another theory that doesn't work. These come cheap.

Good assumptions are rare in economics. When we find one, we should treasure it – and push its implications to the limit.

CHAPTER 7

UTILITY
AND
DEMAND

After studying this chapter you will be able to:

◆ Explain the connection between individual demand and market demand

◆ Define total utility and marginal utility

◆ Explain the marginal utility theory of consumer choice

◆ Use the marginal utility theory to predict the effects of a change in prices

◆ Use the marginal utility theory to predict the effects of a change in income

◆ Define and calculate consumer surplus

◆ Explain the paradox of value

WE NEED WATER TO LIVE. WE DON'T NEED DIAMONDS FOR MUCH BESIDES decoration. If the benefits of water far outweigh the benefits of diamonds, why, then, does water cost practically nothing while diamonds are terribly expensive? ◆ ◆ When OPEC restricted its sale of oil in 1973, it created a dramatic rise in price. But despite the price rise, people continued to use almost as much oil as they had before. Our demand for oil was inelastic. When Philips and Sony introduced the CD player in 1982, its price was around £500, and consumers didn't buy very many of them. Since then, the price has decreased dramatically, and people are buying them in enormous quantities. Our demand for CD players is elastic. What makes the demand for some things inelastic and the demand for others elastic?

Water, Water, Everywhere

◆ ◆ Over the past 40 years, there have been dramatic changes in the way we spend our incomes. Expenditure on cars has increased from less than 1 per cent of total spending in 1950 to 15 per cent today. Expenditure on food has fallen from 25 per cent of total expenditure in 1950 to 14 per cent today. Why, as incomes rise, does the proportion of income spent on some goods rise and on others fall?

◆ ◆ ◆ ◆ The last three chapters have shown us that demand has an important effect on the price of a good. But so far we have *assumed* the law of demand – that when the price of a good rises the quantity demanded decreases. Because demand is such a central and powerful economic force we want to probe more deeply into what shapes it, at both the individual and the market level. The marginal utility theory of demand that you'll study in this chapter provides some answers. It is also the intellectual foundation on which all attempts to influence demand by advertising and marketing are based.

Individual Demand and Market Demand

Т he relationship between the total quantity of a good demanded and its price is called **market demand**. But goods and services are de-manded by individuals. The relationship between the quantity of a good demanded by a single individ-ual and its price is called **individual demand**. Market demand is the sum of all individual demands.

The table in Fig. 7.1 illustrates the relationship between individual demand and market demand. In this example Katie and Paul are the only people. The market demand is the total demand of Katie and Paul. At £3 a bottle of wine, Katie demands 5 bottles and Paul 2, so that the total quantity demanded by the market is 7 bottles a month. Figure 7.1 illustrates the relationship between individual and market demand curves. Katie's demand curve for wine in part (a) and Paul's in part (b) sum *horizontally* to the market demand curve in part (c).

The market demand curve is the horizontal sum of the individual demand curves formed by adding the quantities demanded by each individual at each price.

Let's investigate an individual demand curve by studying how a household makes its consumption choices.

FIGURE 7.1

Individual and Market Demand Curves

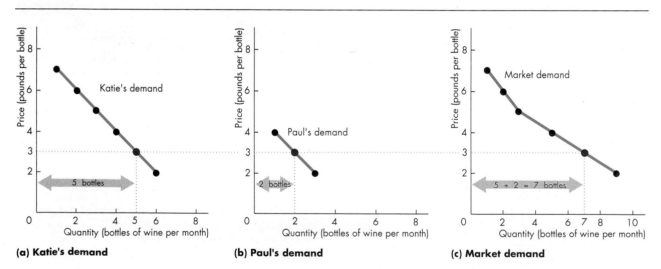

(a) Katie's demand **(b) Paul's demand** **(c) Market demand**

Price of wine (pounds)	Quantity of wine demanded		
	Katie	Paul	Market
7	1	0	1
6	2	0	2
5	3	0	3
4	4	1	5
3	5	2	7
2	6	3	9

The table and diagram illustrate how the quantity of wine demanded varies as its price varies. In the table, the market demand is the sum of the individual demands. For example, at a price of £3, Katie demands 5 bottles of wine and Paul demands 2 bottles, so that the total quantity demanded in the market is 7 bottles. In the diagram, the market demand curve is the horizontal sum of the individual demand curves. Thus when the price is £3 a bottle, the market demand curve shows that the quantity demanded is 7 bottles, the sum of the quantities demanded by Katie and Paul.

Household Consumption Choices

A household's consumption choice is determined by two factors:

◆ Constraints
◆ Preferences

Constraints

A household's choices are constrained by its income and the prices of the goods and services that it buys. Marginal utility theory assumes that the household has a given income to spend and it can't influence the prices of the goods and services that it buys.

To study marginal utility theory, we'll examine Katie's consumption choices. Katie has a monthly income of £30, and spends it on only two goods – pizzas and wine. Pizzas cost £6 each and wine costs £3 a bottle. Figure 7.2 illustrates Katie's possible consumption levels of pizzas and wine. Rows *a* to *f* in the table show six possible ways of allocating £30 to these two goods. For example, Katie can buy 2 pizzas for £12 and 6 bottles for £18 (row *c*). The same possibilities are represented by the points *a* to *f* in the figure. The line passing through those points is a boundary between what Katie can and cannot afford. Her choices must lie inside the orange area or along the line *af*.

Preferences

How does Katie divide her £30 between these two goods. The answer depends on her likes and dislikes – on her *preferences*. Marginal utility theory uses the concept of utility to describe preferences. The benefit or satisfaction that a person gets from the consumption of a good or service is called **utility**. But what exactly is utility and in what units can we measure it? Utility is an abstract concept and the units of utility are chosen arbitrarily.

Let's now see how we can use the concept of utility to describe preferences.

Total Utility and Consumption

Total utility is the total benefit or satisfaction that a person gets from the consumption of goods

FIGURE 7.2

Consumption Possibilities

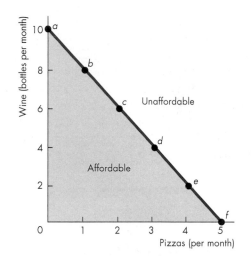

Possibility	Pizzas		Wine	
	Quantity	Expenditure (pounds)	Bottles	Expenditure (pounds)
a	0	0	10	30
b	1	6	8	24
c	2	12	6	18
d	3	18	4	12
e	4	24	2	6
f	5	30	0	0

Rows *a* to *f* in the table show six possible ways of allocating £30 to wine and pizza. For example, Katie can buy 6 bottles of wine and 2 pizzas (row *c*). Each row shows the combinations of wine and pizzas that cost £30. These possibilities are points *a* to *f* in the figure. The line through those points is a boundary between what Katie can and cannot afford. Her choices must lie inside the orange area or along the line *af*.

and services. Total utility depends on the person's level of consumption – more consumption gives more total utility. Table 7.1 shows Katie's total utility from consuming different quantities of pizzas and wine. If she buys no pizzas, she gets no utility from pizzas. If she buys 1 pizza in a month, she gets 50 units of utility. As the number of pizzas she buys in a month increases, her total utility increases

TABLE 7.1

Katie's Total Utility from Pizzas and Wine

Pizzas		Wine	
Quantity per month	Total utility	Bottles per month	Total utility
0	0	0	0
1	50	1	75
2	88	2	117
3	121	3	153
4	150	4	181
5	175	5	206
6	196	6	225
7	214	7	243
8	229	8	260
9	241	9	276
10	250	10	291

so that if she buys 10 pizzas a month, she gets 250 units of total utility. The other part of the table shows Katie's total utility from wine. If she drinks no wine, she gets no utility. As the amount of wine she drinks increases, her total utility increases.

Marginal Utility

Marginal utility is the change in total utility resulting from a one-unit increase in the quantity of a good consumed. The table in Fig. 7.3 shows the calculation of Katie's marginal utility of pizzas. When her consumption of pizzas increases from 4 to 5 pizzas a month, her total utility from pizzas increases from 150 units to 175 units. Thus for Katie, the marginal utility of buying a fifth pizza each month is 25 units. Notice that marginal utility appears midway between the quantities of consumption. It does so because it is the *change* in consumption from 4 to 5 pizzas that produces the *marginal* utility of 25 units. The table displays calculations of marginal utility for each level of pizza consumption.

Figure 7.3(a) illustrates the total utility that Katie gets from pizzas. As you can see, the more

pizzas Katie buys in a month, the more total utility she gets. Part (b) illustrates her marginal utility. This graph tells us that as Katie buys more pizzas, the marginal utility that Katie gets from pizzas decreases. For example, her marginal utility from the first pizza is 50 units, from the second, 38 units, and from the third, 33 units. We call this decrease in marginal utility as the consumption of a good increases the principle of **diminishing marginal utility**.

Marginal utility is positive but diminishes as the consumption of a good increases. Why does marginal utility have these two features? In Katie's case, she likes pizzas, and the more she buys the better. That's why marginal utility is positive. The benefit that Katie gets from the last pizza bought is its marginal utility. To see why marginal utility diminishes, think about how you'd feel in the following two situations. In one, you've just been studying for 29 evenings in a row, fuelled by coffee and potato crisps. A friend invites you to join her at a pizza restaurant and you jump at the offer. The utility you get from that pizza is the marginal utility from one pizza in a month. In the second situation, you've been on a pizza binge. For the past 29 nights, you have not even seen an essay or assignment. You are up to your eyeballs in pizzas. You are happy enough to go to the pizza restaurant once more. But the thrill that you get out of that thirtieth pizza in 30 days is not very large. It is the marginal utility of the thirtieth pizza in a month.

REVIEW

Katie divides her income of £30 a month between pizzas that cost £6 each and wine that costs £3 a bottle. Katie's preferences are described by using the concept of utility: the more pizzas Katie buys in a given month, the more total utility she gets; the more wine she drinks in a month, the more total utility she gets. The increase in total utility that results from the last unit of a good consumed is called marginal utility. As the quantity of a good consumed increases, marginal utility decreases. ◆

FIGURE 7.3

Total Utility and Marginal Utility

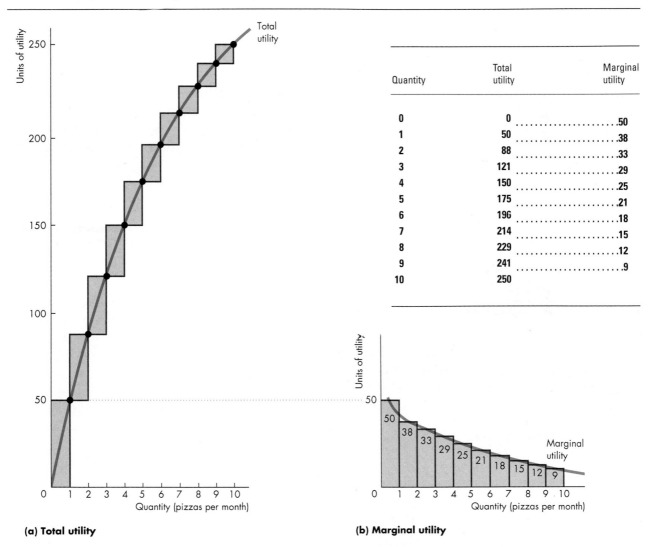

Quantity	Total utility	Marginal utility
0	0	.50
1	50	.38
2	88	.33
3	121	.29
4	150	.25
5	175	.21
6	196	.18
7	214	.15
8	229	.12
9	241	.9
10	250	

(a) Total utility

(b) Marginal utility

The table shows that as Katie's consumption of pizza increases, so does the total utility she derives from pizza. The table also shows her marginal utility. Marginal utility declines as consumption increases. Katie's total utility and marginal utility from pizzas are graphed in the figure. Part (a) shows total utility. It

also shows the extra total utility gained from each additional pizza – marginal utility – as a bar. Part (b) shows the diminishing marginal utility from pizzas by placing the bars shown in part (a) side by side as declining steps.

Utility Maximization

Utility maximization is the attainment of the greatest possible utility. A household's income and the prices it faces limit the utility that it can obtain. We assume that a household consumes in a way that

maximizes its total utility taking into consideration its income and the prices that it faces. In Katie's case, we examine how she allocates her income between pizzas and wine to maximize her total utility, assuming that pizzas cost $6 each, wine costs $3 a bottle, and Katie has only $30 a month to spend.

The Utility-maximizing Choice

Let's calculate how Katie spends her money to maximize her total utility by constructing a table. Table 7.2 considers the same affordable combinations of pizzas and wine that are shown in Fig. 7.2. It records three things: first, the number of pizzas consumed and the total utility derived from them (the left side of the table); second, the number of bottles of wine consumed and the total utility derived from them (the right side of the table); and third, the total utility derived from both pizzas and wine (the middle column of the table).

Consider, for example, the first row of Table 7.2. It shows Katie buys no pizzas, getting no utility from pizzas but getting 291 units of total utility from drinking 10 bottles of wine. Her total utility from pizzas and wine is 291 units. The rest of the table is constructed in exactly the same way.[1]

The consumption of pizzas and wine that maximizes Katie's total utility is highlighted in the table. When Katie consumes 2 pizzas and 6 bottles of wine, she gets 313 units of total utility. This is the best Katie can do given that she has only £30 to spend and given the prices of pizzas and bottles. If she buys 8 bottles of wine, she can buy only 1 pizza and gets 310 units of total utility, 3 less than the maximum attainable. If she buys 3 pizzas and drinks only 4 bottles, she gets 302 units of total utility, 11 less than the maximum attainable.

We've just described a consumer equilibrium. A **consumer equilibrium** is a situation in which a consumer has allocated his or her income in a way that maximizes total utility.

In finding Katie's consumer equilibrium, we measured her total utility from the consumption of pizzas and wine. There is a better way of determining a consumer equilibrium, which does not involve measuring total utility at all. Let's look at this alternative.

Equalizing Marginal Utility per Pound Spent

Another way to find out the allocation that maximizes a consumer's total utility is to make the marginal utility per pound spent on each good equal for all goods. The **marginal utility per pound**

TABLE 7.2

Katie's Utility-maximizing Combinations of Pizzas and Wine

Pizzas		Total utility from pizzas and wine	Wine	
Quantity	Total utility		Total utility	Bottles
0	0	291	291	10
1	50	310	260	8
2	88	313	225	6
3	121	302	181	4
4	150	267	117	2
5	175	175	0	0

spent is the marginal utility obtained from the last unit of a good consumed divided by the price of the good. For example, Katie's marginal utility from consuming the first pizza is 50 units of utility. The price of a pizza is £6, which means that the marginal utility per pound spent on pizzas is 50 units divided by £6, or 8.33 units of utility per pound.

Total utility is maximized when all the consumer's income is spent and when the marginal utility per pound spent is equal for all goods.

Katie maximizes total utility when she spends all her income and consumes pizzas and wine such that

$$\frac{\text{Marginal utility from pizzas}}{\text{Price of pizzas}} = \frac{\text{Marginal utility from wine}}{\text{Price of wine}}.$$

Call the marginal utility from pizzas MU_p, the marginal utility from wine MU_w, the price of pizzas P_p, and the price of wine P_w. Then Katie's utility is maximized when she spends all her income and when

$$\frac{MU_p}{P_p} = \frac{MU_w}{P_w}.$$

Let's use this formula to find Katie's utility-maximizing allocation of her income.

Table 7.3 sets out Katie's marginal utilities per pound spent for both pizzas and wine. For example, in row b Katie's marginal utility from pizzas is 50

---

[1] The restaurant that Katie frequents does not sell fractions of a pizza, so Katie can only change the quantity of pizzas she buys by a whole pizza.

TABLE 7.3

Maximizing Utility by Equalizing Marginal Utilities per Pound Spent

	Pizzas (£6 each)			Wine (£3 per bottle)		
	Quantity	Marginal utility	Marginal utility per pound spent	Bottles	Marginal utility	Marginal utility per pound spent
a	0	0		10	15	5.00
b	1	50	8.33	8	17	5.67
c	2	38	6.33	6	19	6.33
d	3	33	5.50	4	28	9.33
e	4	29	4.83	2	42	14.00
f	5	25	4.16	0	0	

FIGURE 7.4

Equalizing Marginal Utility per Pound Spent

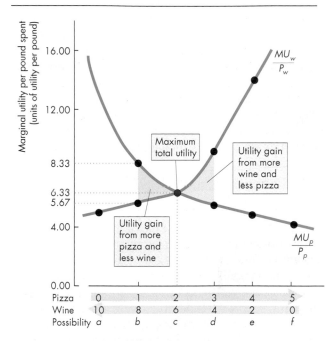

If Katie consumes 1 pizza and 8 bottles of wine (possibility *b*) she gets 8.33 units of utility from the last pound spent on pizzas and 5.67 units of utility from the last pound spent on wine. She can get more total utility by buying one more pizza. If she consumes 3 pizzas and 4 bottles of wine (possibility *d*) she gets 5.50 units of utility from the last pound spent on pizzas and 9.33 units of utility from the last pound spent on wine. She can get more total utility by buying one fewer pizza. When Katie's marginal utility per pound spent on both goods is equal her total utility is maximized.

units and, since pizzas cost £6 each, her marginal utility per pound spent on pizzas is 8.33 units per pound (50 units divided by £6). Each row contains an allocation of Katie's income that uses up her £30. You can see that Katie's marginal utility per pound spent on each good, like marginal utility itself, decreases as consumption of the good increases.

Total utility is maximized when the marginal utility per pound spent on pizzas is equal to the marginal utility per pound spent on wine – possibility *c*, where Katie consumes 2 pizzas and 6 bottles – the same allocation as we calculated in Table 7.2.

Figure 7.4 shows why the rule 'equalize marginal utility per pound spent on all goods' works. Suppose that instead of consuming 2 pizzas and 6 bottles (possibility *c*), Katie consumes 1 pizza and 8 bottles (possibility *b*). She then gets 8.33 units of utility from the last pound spent on pizzas and 5.67 units from the last pound spent on wine. In this situation, it pays Katie to spend less on wine and more on pizzas. If she spends a pound less on wine and a pound more on pizzas, her total utility from wine decreases by 5.67 units and her total utility from pizzas increases by 8.33 units. Katie's total utility increases if she spends less on wine and more on pizzas.

Or suppose that Katie consumes 3 pizzas and 4 bottles (possibility *d*). In this situation, her marginal utility per pound spent on pizzas is less than her

marginal utility per pound spent on wine. Katie can now get more total utility by cutting her spending on pizzas and increasing her spending on wine.

Units of Utility

In calculating the utility-maximizing allocation of income in Table 7.3 and Fig. 7.4 we have not used the concept of total utility at all. All the calculations have been performed using marginal utility and price. By making the marginal utility per pound spent equal for both goods, we know that Katie has maximized her total utility.

This way of viewing maximum utility is important;

it means that the units in which utility is measured do not matter. We could double or halve all the numbers measuring utility, or multiply them by any other positive number, or square them, or take their square roots. None of these transformations of the units used to measure utility make any difference to the outcome. It is in this respect that utility is analogous to temperature.

Temperature – an Analogy   Like utility, temperature is an abstract concept and the units of temperature are chosen arbitrarily. You know when you feel hot and you know when you feel cold. But you can't *observe* temperature. You can observe water turning to steam if it is hot enough or turning to ice if it is cold enough. You can construct an instrument, called a thermometer, that will predict when such changes will occur. The scale on the thermometer is what we call temperature. But the units in which we measure temperature are arbitrary. For example, we can accurately predict that when a Celsius thermometer shows a temperature of 0°C, water will turn to ice. But the units of measurement do not matter because this same event also occurs when a Fahrenheit thermometer shows a temperature of 32°F.

The concept of utility helps us make predictions about consumption choices in much the same way that the concept of temperature helps us make predictions about physical phenomena.

Just as our prediction about the freezing of water does not depend on the temperature scale, so our prediction about maximizing utility does not depend on the units of utility. It has to be admitted, though, that the marginal utility theory is not as precise as the theory that enables us to predict when water will turn to ice or steam.

REVIEW

Consumers maximize total utility. A consumer spends his or her income in order to make the marginal utility per pound spent on each good equal. Once the marginal utilities per pound spent are equal, the consumer cannot reallocate spending to get more total utility. The units in which utility is measured are irrelevant – all that matters is that the marginal utility per pound is equal for all goods. ◆

Predictions of Marginal Utility Theory

Let's now use marginal utility theory to make some predictions. What happens to Katie's consumption of pizzas and wine when their prices change and when her income changes?

A Fall in the Price of Pizzas

To determine the effect of a change in price on consumption requires three steps. First, determine the combinations of pizzas and wine that can be bought at the new prices. Second, calculate the new marginal utilities per pound spent. Third, determine the consumption of each good that makes the marginal utility per pound spent on each good equal and that just exhausts the money available for spending.

Table 7.4 shows the combinations of pizzas and wine that exactly exhaust her £30 of income when pizzas cost £3 each and wine costs £3 a bottle. Katie's preferences do not change when prices change, so her marginal utility schedule remains the same as that

---

TABLE 7.4

How a Change in the Price of a Pizza Affects Katie's Choices

Pizzas (£3 each)		Wine (£3 per bottle)	
Quantity	Marginal utility per pound spent	Bottles	Marginal utility per pound spent
0		10	5.00
1	16.67	9	5.33
2	12.67	8	5.67
3	11.00	7	6.00
4	9.67	6	6.33
5	8.33	5	8.33
6	7.00	4	9.33
7	6.00	3	12.00
8	5.00	2	14.00
9	4.00	1	25.00
10	3.00	0	

in Table 7.3. But now we divide her marginal utility from pizzas by £3, the new price of a pizza, to get the marginal utility per pound spent on pizzas.

What is the effect of the fall in the price of a pizza on Katie's consumption? You can find the answer by comparing her new utility-maximizing allocation (Table 7.4) with her original allocation (Table 7.3). Katie responds to a fall in the price of a pizza by buying more pizzas (up from 2 to 5 a month) and drinking less wine (down from 6 to 5 bottles a month). That is, Katie substitutes pizzas for wine when the price of a pizza falls. Figure 7.5 illustrates these effects. In part (a) a fall in the price of a pizza produces a movement along Katie's demand curve for pizzas and in part (b) it shifts her demand curve for wine.

A Rise in the Price of Wine

Table 7.5 shows the combinations of pizzas and wine that exactly exhaust her £30 of income when pizzas cost £3 each and wine costs £6 a bottle. Now we divide her marginal utility from wine by £6, the new price of a bottle, to get the marginal utility per pound spent on wine.

The effect of the rise in the price of wine on Katie's consumption is seen by comparing her new utility maximizing allocation (Table 7.5) with her previous allocation (Table 7.4). Katie responds to a rise in the price of wine by drinking less wine (down from 5 to 2 bottles a month) and buying more pizzas (up from 5 to 6

TABLE 7.5

How a Change in the Price of a Wine Affects Katie's Choices

Pizzas (£3 each)		Wine (£6 per bottle)	
Quantity	Marginal utility per pound spent	Bottles	Marginal utility per pound spent
0		5	4.17
2	12.67	4	4.67
4	9.67	3	6.00
6	7.00	2	7.00
8	5.00	1	12.50
10	3.00	0	

FIGURE 7.5

A Fall in the Price of Pizzas

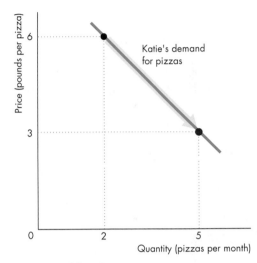

(a) Demand for pizzas

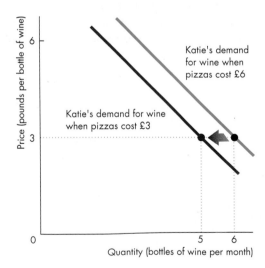

(b) Demand for wine

When the price of pizzas falls and the price of wine remains constant, the quantity of pizzas demanded by Katie increases and in part (a), Katie moves along her demand curve for bottles of wine. Also, Katie's demand for wine decreases and in part (b), her demand curve for wine shifts to the left.

FIGURE 7.6

A Rise in the Price of Wine

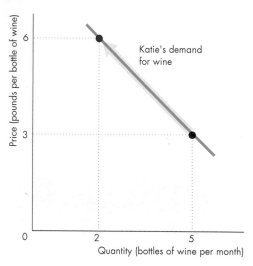

(a) Demand for wine

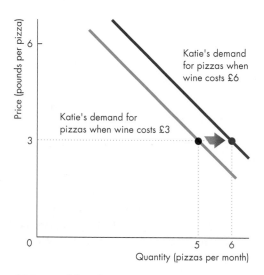

(b) Demand for pizza

When the price of wine rises and the price of pizzas remains constant, the quantity of wine demanded by Katie decreases and in part (a), Katie moves along her demand curve for bottles of wine. Also, Katie's demand for pizzas increases and in part (b), her demand curve for pizzas shifts to the right.

a month). That is, Katie substitutes pizzas for wine when the price of wine rises. Figure 7.6 illustrates these effects. In part (a) a rise in the price of wine produces a movement along Katie's demand curve for wine and in part (b) it shifts her demand curve for pizzas.

REVIEW

When the price of a pizza falls but the price of wine stays constant, Katie increases her consumption of pizzas and reduces her consumption of wine. There is a movement along her demand curve for pizzas and a shift in her demand for wine. When the price of a pizza stays constant but the price of wine increases, Katie reduces her consumption of

wine and increases her consumption of pizzas. There is a movement along her demand curve for wine and a shift in her demand for pizzas. When the price of a pizza falls or the price of wine rises and Katie does not change her consumption, her marginal utility per pound spent on pizzas exceeds that on wine. To restore the equality of the marginal utility per pound spent on each good, she increases her consumption of pizzas and decreases her consumption of wine. ◆

Marginal utility theory predicts these two results: when the price of a good rises, the quantity demanded of that good decreases; if the price of one good rises, the demand for another good that can serve as a substitute increases. Does this sound familiar? It should. These predictions of marginal utility theory correspond to the assumptions that we made about consumer demand in Chapter 4. There we *assumed* that the demand curve for a good sloped downward, and we *assumed* that a rise in the price of a substitute increased demand. Marginal utility theory predicts these responses to price changes. In doing so it makes three assumptions. First, that consumers maximize total utility. Second, that they get more utility as they consume more of a good. Third, as consumption increases, marginal utility declines.

Next let's see the effects of a change in income on consumption.

The Effects of a Rise in Income

Let's suppose that Katie's income increases to £42 a month and that a pizza costs £3 and a bottle of wine costs £3 (as in Table 7.4). We saw in Table 7.4 that with these prices and an income of £30 a month, Katie consumes 5 pizzas and 5 bottles of wine a month. We want to compare this consumption of pizzas and wine with Katie's consumption at an income of £42. Table 7.6 shows the calculations. With £42, Katie can buy 14 pizzas a month and no wine or 14 bottles of wine a month and no pizzas or any combination of the two goods as shown in the rows of the table. We calculate the marginal utility per pound spent in exactly the same way as we did before and find the quantities at which the marginal utilities per pound spent on pizzas and on wine are equal. With an income of £42, the marginal utility per pound spent on each good is equal when Katie buys 7 pizzas and drinks 7 bottles of wine a month.

By comparing this situation with that in Table 7.4, we see that with an additional £12 a month, Katie consumes 2 more bottles of wine and 2 more pizzas. This response arises from Katie's preferences, as described by her marginal utilities. Different preferences produce different quantitative responses. But for normal goods, a higher income always brings a larger consumption of all goods. For Katie, wine and pizzas are normal goods. When her income increases, Katie buys more of both goods.

Marginal Utility and the Real World

The marginal utility theory is summarized in Table 7.7. This theory can be used to answer a wide range of questions about the real world. For example, why is the demand for some goods, such as audio headsets, elastic and the demand for other

TABLE 7.6

Katie's Choices with an Income of £42 a Month

Pizzas (£3 each)		Wine (£3 per bottle)	
Quantity	Marginal utility per pound spent	Bottles	Marginal utility per pound spent
0		14	
1	16.67	13	
2	12.67	12	
3	11.00	11	
4	9.67	10	5.00
5	8.33	9	5.33
6	7.00	8	5.67
7	6.00	7	6.00
8	5.00	6	6.33
9	4.00	5	8.33
10	3.00	4	9.33
11		3	12.00
12		2	14.00
13		1	25.00
14		0	

goods, such as oil, inelastic; and why, as income increases, does the proportion of income spent on some goods, such as cars, increase while the proportion spent on other goods, such as food, decreases? These patterns in our spending result from the speed with which our marginal utility for each good diminishes as its consumption is increased. Goods whose marginal utility diminishes rapidly have inelastic demands and small income effects: goods whose marginal utility diminishes slowly have elastic demands and large income effects.

But the marginal utility theory can do much more than this. It can be used to explain *all* household choices. One of these choices, the allocation of time between work in the home, office, or factory and leisure is the theme of Our Advancing Knowledge on pp.182–183.

Understanding Human Behaviour

The economic analysis of human behaviour, in the workplace, in the markets for goods and services, in the markets for labour services, in financial markets, and in transactions with each other in social as well as economic situations, is based on the idea that our behaviour can be understood as a response to scarcity. Everything we do can be understood as a choice that maximizes utility subject to the constraints imposed by our limited resources and technology. If people's preferences are stable in the face of changing constraints, then we have a chance of predicting how they will respond to an evolving environment.

> 'Economy is the
> art of making
> the most
> of life.'
>
> GEORGE BERNARD SHAW
> *'Man and Superman'*

The incredible change that has occurred over the past 100 years in the way women allocate their time can be explained as the consequence of changing constraints. Technological advances have equipped the nation's factories with machines that have increased the productivity of both women and men, thereby raising the wages they can earn. The increasingly technological world has increased the return to education for both women and men and has led to a large increase in the number of both men and women staying in full-time school and college education. And equipped with a wide array of gadgets and machines that cut the time of household jobs, women have increasingly allocated their time to work outside the home.

This economic view might not be correct, but it is a powerful one. And if it is correct, the changing attitudes towards women are a consequence, not a cause, of their economic advancement.

Economists explain people's actions as the consequence of choices that maximize utility subject to constraints. In the 1890s, fewer than 5 per cent of women chose paid employment and most of those who did had low-paying and unattractive jobs. The other 95 per cent of women chose unpaid work in the home. What were the constraints that led to these choices?

By 1990, more than 60 per cent of women had paid work and, although many had low-paying jobs, more and more women were found in the professions and in executive positions. What brought about this dramatic change compared with 100 years earlier? Was it a change in preferences or a change in the constraints that women face?

Bentham, Jevons & Becker: Understanding People's Choices

JEREMY BENTHAM

Many economists have contributed to our understanding of human behaviour, but three stand out from the rest. They are Jeremy Bentham (1748–1832), pictured left, William Stanley Jevons (1835–1882), pictured right, and Gary Becker (1930–). Bentham, who lived in London (and whose embalmed body is preserved to this day in a glass cabinet in the University of London), was the first to use the concept of utility to explain and prescribe human choices. The distinction between explanation and prescription was not a sharp one in Bentham's day. He was a founder of social security and advocated guaranteed employment, minimum wages, and social benefits such as free education and free medical care.

WILLIAM STANLEY JEVONS

Jevons' main claim to fame in his own day was his proposal – wrong as it turned out – that economic fluctuations are caused by sun spots. He was a co-discoverer of the concept of *marginal utility*, and it was he who developed the theory explained in this chapter.

Gary Becker teaches both economics and sociology at the University of Chicago. He used the ideas of Bentham and Jevons to explain a wide range of human choices, including the choices made by women about how many children to bear and how much and what type of work to do.

TABLE 7.7

Marginal Utility Theory

ASSUMPTIONS

◆   A consumer derives utility from the goods consumed.

◆   Each additional unit of consumption yields additional utility; marginal utility is positive.

◆   As the quantity of a good consumed increases, marginal utility decreases.

IMPLICATION

◆   Utility is maximized when the marginal utility per pound spent is equal for all goods.

PREDICTIONS

◆   Other things remaining the same, the higher the price of a good, the lower is the quantity bought (the law of demand).

◆   The higher the price of a good, the higher is the consumption of substitutes for that good.

◆   The higher the consumer's income, the greater is the quantity demanded of normal goods.

Criticisms of Marginal Utility Theory

Marginal utility theory helps us to understand the choices people make, but there are some criticisms of this theory. Let's look at them.

Utility Can't be Observed or Measured

Agreed – we can't observe utility. But we do not need to observe it to use it. We can and do observe the quantities of goods and services that people consume, the prices of those goods and services, and people's incomes. Our goal is to understand the consumption choices that people make and to predict the effects of changes in prices and incomes on these choices. To make such predictions, we *assume* that people derive utility from their consumption, that more consumption yields more utility, and that marginal utility diminishes. From these assumptions, we make predictions about the directions of change in consumption when prices and incomes change. As we've already seen, the actual numbers we use to express utility do not matter. Consumers maximize utility by making the marginal utility per pound spent on each good equal. As long as we use the same scale to express utility for all goods, we'll get the same answer regardless of the units on our scale. In this regard, utility is similar to temperature – water freezes when it's cold enough, and that occurs independently of the temperature scale used.

'People Aren't that Smart'

Some critics maintain that marginal utility theory assumes that people are supercomputers. It requires people to look at the marginal utility of every good at every different quantity they might consume, divide those numbers by the prices of the goods, and then calculate the quantities so as to equalize the marginal utility of each good divided by its price.

Such criticism of marginal utility theory confuses the actions of people in the real world with those of people in a model economy. A model economy is no more an actual economy than a model railway is an actual railway. The people in the model economy perform the calculations that we have just described. People in the real world just consume. We observe their consumption choices, not their mental gymnastics. The marginal utility theory proposes that the consumption patterns we observe in the real world are similar to those implied by the model economy in which people do compute the quantities of goods that maximize utility. We test how closely the marginal utility model resembles reality by checking the predictions of the model against observed consumption choices.

Marginal utility theory also has some broader implications that provide an interesting way of testing its usefulness. Let's examine two of these.

Some Implications of Marginal Utility Theory

We all love bargains – paying less for something than its usual price. One implication of the marginal utility theory is that we almost *always* get a bargain when we buy something. That is, we place a higher total value on the things we buy than the amount that it costs us. Let's see why.

Consumer Surplus and the Gains from Trade

In Chapter 3, we saw how people can gain by specializing in the things at which they have a comparative advantage and then trading with each other. Marginal utility theory provides a precise way of measuring the gains from trade.

When Katie buys pizzas and wine, she exchanges her income for them. Does Katie profit from this exchange? Are the pounds she has to give up worth more or less than the pizzas and wine are worth to her? As we are about to discover, the principle of diminishing marginal utility guarantees that Katie, and everyone else, gets more value from the things they buy than the amount of money they give up in exchange.

Calculating Consumer Surplus

The **value** a consumer places on a good is the maximum amount that person would be willing to pay for it. The amount actually paid for a good is its price. **Consumer surplus** is the difference between the value of a good and its price. Diminishing marginal utility guarantees that a consumer always makes some consumer surplus. To understand why, let's look again at Katie's consumption choices.

As before, let's assume that Katie has £30 a month to spend, that pizzas cost £3 each, and that she buys 5 pizzas each month. Now let's look at Katie's demand curve for pizzas, shown in Fig. 7.7. We can see from Katie's demand curve that if she were able to buy only 1 pizza a month she would be willing to pay £7 for it. She would be willing to pay £6 for a second pizza, £5 for a third, and so on.

Luckily for Katie, she has to pay only £3 for each pizza she buys – the market price of a pizza. Although

she values the first pizza she buys in a month at £7, she pays only £3, which is £4 less than she would be willing to pay. The second pizza she buys in a month is worth £6 to her. The difference between the value she places on the pizza and what she has to pay is £3. The third pizza she buys in a month is worth £5 to her, which is £2 more than she has to pay for it, and the fourth pizza is worth £4, which is £1 more than she has to pay for it. You can see this progression in Fig. 7.7, which highlights the difference between the price she pays (£3) and the higher value she places on the first, second, third and fourth pizzas. These differences are a gain to Katie. Let's calculate her total gain.

The total amount that Katie is willing to pay for the 5 pizzas that she buys is £25 (the sum of £7, £6, £5, £4 and £3). She actually pays £15 (5 pizzas multiplied by £3). The extra value she receives from the pizzas is therefore £10. This amount is the value of Katie's consumer surplus. From buying 5 pizzas a month, she gets £10 worth of value in excess of what she has to spend to buy them. Reading Between the Lines on pp.186–187 considers how changes in price can affect the level of consumer surplus.

FIGURE 7.7

Consumer Surplus

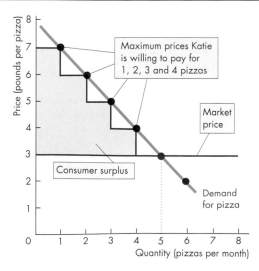

Katie is willing to pay £7 for the first pizza, £6 for the second, £5 for the third, £4 for the fourth and £3 for the fifth. She pays £3 for each pizza and has a consumer surplus on the first four pizzas equal to £10 (£4 + £3 + £2 + £1).

Anyone for Tennis?

The Essence of the Story

THE INDEPENDENT, 12 APRIL 1994

A seat on Centre Court for £19,625

John Roberts, Tennis Correspondent

THE hottest tickets in sport are about to go on offer. Stump up a mere £19,625 and a ticket for Wimbledon is yours.

This may not appear the greatest snip of all time, but the latest debenture scheme launched by the All England Club will raise £35.7m towards the cost of redeveloping Wimbledon for the 21st century. And through the club's ingenious 'white market', part of the outlay can be recouped.

Under the scheme, which will be offered to existing debenture holders first, the investment of £19,625 buys a Centre Court ticket for each day of the championships for five years, from 1996–2000, and use of a special lounge at the club.

Of the total price, Wimbledon, which is offering 2,100 new debentures, keep £15,000; £2,000 is returnable after five years and the rest goes on VAT.

The cost of a Centre Court debenture ticket would thus average £271.15 per day's play over the five years. Centre Court tickets for this year's tournament range from £19 for the opening Monday to £49 for the men's final, a total of £430 for the 13 days. Successful applicants in the public ballot are restricted to purchasing one pair of tickets per household.

For the past five years, Wimbledon has organised an 'official white market service' for debenture holders. The club acts as broker for a 10 per cent administrative charge, helping to satisfy the demand for corporate hospitality by buying and reselling debenture seat tickets at 'competitive prices'.

Last year, the 'white market' rate ranged from £200 for the first Monday to £900 for the men's final.

Plans for the club's long-term rebuilding project were announced last year, with a new No. 1 Court the priority.

Since 1922, when the first issue of five-year debentures raised £75,000 to fund the club's move from Worple Road to their current site on Church Road, the system has enabled extensive ground improvements to be carried without use of the annual profits from the championships.

These are passed onto the Lawn Tennis Association to finance the British game. Last year's sum of £16.4 m brought the pre-tax total since 1981 to more than £100m.

In order to raise money for the redevelopment of Wimbledon's tennis facilities, the All England Club is issuing debentures.

Debentures are effectively loans, with the purchasers paying £19,625 and receiving back £2,000 after five years plus guaranteed Centre Court tickets for each of the next five years.

For the remainder of the sum, the purchaser of a debenture is paying as much for a day's attendance as a person who gets tickets through the public ballot would have to pay for more than a week of tennis. They do, however, benefit from knowing this place is guaranteed.

© The Independent. Reprinted with permission.

Background and Analysis

Seats at Wimbledon are scarce. Usually the number of seats demanded exceeds the capacity of the stadium.

Because the quantity demanded exceeds the number of seats available, the market clearing price of a ticket to Wimbledon is high.

The utility gained from watching the best tennis players in the world play live is also high.

The All England Club has decided to keep the price of tickets below their market clearing level. As a result the market works by using a ballot as a rationing device.

Because of the excess demand, there is substantial consumer surplus that could be exploited. The issuing of debentures means that the All England Club obtains some of this.

Because of the high price of debentures, only those with a high willingness to pay have their consumer surplus reduced in this way.

Most tennis fans are only affected to the extent that tickets guaranteed to debenture holders reduce the number of tickets available to the public through the ballot.

In the figure, *S* shows the fixed Centre Court capacity of 13,000, and *D* illustrates the demand. The equilibrium price is £200. The average price charged to people successful in the ballot is £34.50.

The total consumer surplus is about £2.7 million, shown in the figure as area *defg*.

The number of seats allocated to debenture holders is 2,100, at a higher average ticket price of £271.15.

By charging debenture holders this higher price, the area *dhij* is the amount of the debenture holders' consumer surplus transferred to the All England Club (a value of just under £500,000 or nearly 20 per cent of the total consumer surplus).

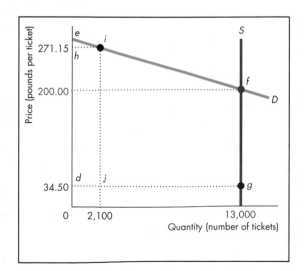

Let's now look at another implication of the marginal utility theory.

The Paradox of Value

More than 200 years ago, Adam Smith posed a paradox that we also raised at the start of this chapter. Water, which is essential to life itself, costs little, but diamonds, which are useless compared with water, are expensive. Why? Adam Smith could not solve the paradox. Not until the theory of marginal utility had been invented could anyone give a satisfactory answer.

You can solve Adam Smith's puzzle by distinguishing between total utility and marginal utility. The total utility that we get from water is enormous. But remember, the more we consume of something, the smaller is its marginal utility. We use so much water that the marginal utility – the benefit we get from one more glass of water – diminishes to a tiny value. Diamonds, on the other hand, have a small total utility relative to water, but because we buy few diamonds, they have a high marginal utility.

Our theory also tells us that consumers spend their income in a way that makes the marginal utility from each good divided by its price equal for all goods. This also holds true for their spending on diamonds and water: diamonds have a high marginal utility divided by a high price, while water has a low marginal utility divided by a low price. In each case, the marginal utility per pound spent is the same.

◆ ◆ ◆ ◆   We've now completed our study of the marginal utility theory of consumption. We've used that theory to examine how Katie allocates her income between the two goods that she consumes – pizzas and wine. We've also seen how the theory can be used to resolve the paradox of value. Furthermore, we've seen how the theory can be used to explain our real-world consumption choices.
◆ ◆   In the next chapter, we're going to study an alternative theory of household behaviour. To help you see the connection between the marginal utility theory of this chapter and the more modern theory of consumer behaviour of the next chapter, we'll continue with the same example. We'll meet Katie again and discover another way of understanding how she gets the most out of her £30 a month.

S U M M A R Y

Individual Demand and Market Demand

Individual demand represents the relationship between the price of a good and the quantity demanded by a single individual. Market demand is the sum of all individual demands. (pp. 174)

Household Consumption Choices

The marginal utility theory explains how people divide their spending between goods and services. The theory is based on a model that assumes certain characteristics about the consumer: the consumer derives utility from the goods consumed and the consumer's total utility increases as consumption of the goods increases. The change in total utility resulting from a one-unit increase in the consumption of a good is called marginal utility. Marginal utility declines as consumption increases. The consumer's goal is to maximize total utility, which occurs when the marginal utility per pound spent on each good is equal. (pp. 175–180)

Predictions of Marginal Utility Theory

Marginal utility theory predicts how prices and income affect the amounts of each good consumed. First, it predicts the law of demand. That is, other things being equal, the higher the price of a good, the lower is the quantity demanded of that good. Second, it predicts that, other things being equal, the higher the consumer's income, the greater is the consumption of all normal goods. (pp. 180–186)

Criticisms of Marginal Utility Theory

Some people criticize marginal utility theory because utility cannot be observed or measured. However, the size of the units of measurement of utility do not matter. All that matters is that the ratio of the marginal utility from each good to its price is equal for all goods. Any units of measure consistently applied will do. The concept of utility is analogous to the concept of temperature – it cannot be directly observed but it can be used to make predictions about events that are observable.

Another criticism of marginal utility theory is that consumers can't be as smart as the theory implies. In fact, the theory makes no predictions about the thought processes of consumers. It only makes predictions about their actions and assumes that people spend their income in what seems to them to be the best possible way. (pp. 186)

Some Implications of Marginal Utility Theory

Marginal utility theory implies that every time we buy goods and services we get more value for our expenditure than the money we spend. We benefit from consumer surplus, which is equal to the differ-ence between the maximum amount that we are willing to pay for a good and the price that we actu-ally pay.

Marginal utility theory resolves the paradox of value: water is extremely valuable but cheap, while diamonds are less valuable though expensive. When we talk loosely about value, we are thinking of total utility. The total utility of water is higher than the total utility of diamonds. The marginal utility of water, though, is lower than the marginal utility of diamonds. People choose the amount of water and diamonds to consume so as to maximize total utility. In maximizing total utility, they make the marginal utility per pound spent the same for water as for dia-monds. (pp. 187–190)

K E Y   E L E M E N T S

Key Terms

Key Figures and Tables

R E V I E W   Q U E S T I O N S

1 What is the relationship between individual demand and market demand?

2 How do we construct a market demand curve from individual demand curves?

3 What do we mean by utility?

4 Distinguish between total utility and marginal utility.

5 How does marginal utility change as the level of consumption of a good changes?

6 Susan is a consumer. When is Susan's utility maximized?

   a When she has spent all her income

   b When she has spent all her income and mar-ginal utility is equal for all goods

   c When she has spent all her income and the marginal utility per pound spent is equal for all goods

Explain your answers.

7 What does the marginal utility theory predict about the effect of a change in price on the quantity of a good consumed?

8 What does the marginal utility theory predict about the effect of a change in the price of one good on the consumption of another good?

9 What does the marginal utility theory predict about the effect of a change in income on the consumption of a good?

10 How would you answer someone who says that the marginal utility theory is useless because

utility cannot be observed?

11 How would you respond to someone who tells you that the marginal utility theory is useless because people are not clever enough to compute a consumer equilibrium in which the marginal utility per pound spent is equal for all goods?

12 What is consumer surplus? How is consumer surplus calculated?

13 What is the paradox of value? How does the marginal utility theory resolve it?

P R O B L E M S

1 Shirley's demand for yoghurt is given by the following:

Price (pounds per carton)	Quantity (cartons per week)
1	12
2	9
3	6
4	3
5	1

a Draw a graph of Shirley's demand for yoghurt.

Don also likes yoghurt. His demand for yoghurt is given by the following:

Price (pounds per carton)	Quantity (cartons per week)
1	6
2	5
3	4
4	3
5	2

b Draw a graph of Don's demand curve.

c If Shirley and Don are the only two individuals, construct the market demand schedule for yoghurt.

d Draw a graph of the market demand for yoghurt.

e Draw a graph to show that the market demand curve is the horizontal sum of

Shirley's demand curve and Don's demand curve.

2 Calculate Katie's marginal utility from wine from the numbers given in Table 7.1. Draw two graphs, one of her total utility and the other of her marginal utility from wine. Make your graphs look similar to those in Fig. 7.3.

3 Max enjoys windsurfing and water skiing. He obtains the following utility from each of these sports:

Half-hours per month	Utility from windsurfing	Utility from water skiing
1	60	20
2	110	38
3	150	53
4	180	64
5	200	70
6	206	75
7	211	79
8	215	82
9	218	84

a Draw graphs showing Max's utility from windsurfing and from water skiing.

b Compare the two utility graphs. Can you say anything about Max's preferences?

c Draw graphs showing Max's marginal utility from windsurfing and from water skiing.

d Compare the two marginal utility graphs. Can you say anything about Max's preferences?

4 Max has £35 to spend. Equipment for windsurf-

ing is rented for £10 a half-hour while water skiing equipment is rented for £5 a half-hour. Use this information together with that given in Problem 3 to answer the following questions:

a What is the marginal utility per pound spent on water skiing if Max water skis for

(1) Half an hour?

(2) One and a half hours?

b What is the marginal utility per pound spent on windsurfing if Max windsurfs for

(1) Half an hour?

(2) One hour?

c How long can Max afford to water ski if he windsurfs for

(1) Half an hour?

(2) One hour?

(3) One and a half hours?

d Will Max choose to water ski for one hour and windsurf for one and a half hours?

e Will he windsurf for more or less than one and a half hours?

f How long will Max choose to windsurf and to water ski?

5 Max's sister gives him £20 to spend on his leisure pursuits, so he now has £55 to spend. How long will Max now windsurf and water ski?

6 If Max has only £55 to spend and the rent on windsurfing equipment halves to £5 a half-hour, how will Max now spend his time windsurfing and water skiing?

7 Does Max's demand curve for windsurfing slope downward or upward?

8 Max takes a Club Med holiday, the cost of which includes unlimited sports activities – including windsurfing, water skiing and tennis. There is no extra charge for any equipment. Max decides to spend three hours each day on both windsurfing and water skiing. How long does he windsurf? How long does he water ski?

9 Sarah's demand for windsurfing is given by:

Price (pounds per half-hour)	Time windsurfing (half-hours per month)
12.50	8
15.00	6
17.50	4
20.00	2

a If windsurfing costs £17.50 an hour, what is Sarah's consumer surplus?

b If windsurfing costs £12.50 a half-hour, what is Sarah's consumer surplus?

CHAPTER 8

POSSIBILITIES, PREFERENCES AND CHOICES

After studying this chapter you will be able to:

◆ Calculate and graph a household's budget line

◆ Work out how the budget line changes when prices and income change

◆ Make a map of preferences by using indifference curves

◆ Calculate a household's optimal consumption plan

◆ Predict the effects of price and income changes on the pattern of consumption

◆ Explain why the average number of hours worked each week gets shorter as wages rise

◆ Explain how budget lines and indifference curves can be used to understand all household choices

LIKE THE CONTINENTS FLOATING ON THE EARTH'S MANTLE, OUR SPENDING patterns change steadily over time. On such subterranean movements, business empires rise and fall. Goods such as home videos and microwave popcorn now appear on our shopping lists while 78 rpm gramophone records and horse-drawn carriages have disappeared. Miniskirts appear, disappear and reappear in cycles of fashion. ◆ ◆ But the glittering surface of our consumption obscures deeper and slower changes in how we spend. In the last few years, we've seen a proliferation of gourmet food shops and designer clothing boutiques. Yet we spend a smaller percentage of our income today on food and clothing than we did in 1950. At the same time, the percentage of our income spent on housing, transport and recreation has grown steadily. Why does consumer spending change over the

Subterranean Movements

years? How do people react to changes in income and changes in the prices of the things they buy? ◆ ◆ Similar subterranean movements govern the way we allocate our time. For example, the average number of hours worked each week has fallen steadily from 70 in the nineteenth century to 35 today. Although we work fewer hours a week than we did before, far more people now have jobs. Why has the average number of hours worked each week declined?

◆ ◆ ◆ ◆ This chapter presents an alternative model of household choice to that of Chapter 7. The model in this chapter is based on *indifference curves*, a method of describing preferences that does not rely on the abstract notion of utility. With the methods you learn in this chapter, you will deepen your understanding of the law of demand and be able to understand how people choose what to buy, how much work to do, and how much to save, borrow and lend.

Consumption Possibilities

A household's consumption choices are limited by its income and by the prices of the goods and services it buys. A household has a given amount of income to spend and cannot influence the prices of the goods and services it buys. It takes prices as given. The limits to a household's consumption choices are described by its **budget line.**

To make the concept of the household's budget line clear, we'll consider a concrete example. Katie has an income of £30 a month to spend. She buys two goods – pizzas and wine. Pizzas cost £6 each; wine costs £3 for a bottle. If Katie spends all of her income, she will reach the limits of her consumption of pizzas and wine.

In Fig. 8.1, each row of the table shows an affordable way for Katie to consume pizzas and wine. Row *a* indicates that she can buy 10 bottles of wine and no pizza. You can see that this combination of pizza and wine exhausts her monthly income of £30. Row *f* says that Katie can buy 5 pizzas and drink no wine – another combination that exhausts the £30 available. Each of the other rows also exhausts Katie's income. (Check that each of the other rows costs exactly £30.) The numbers in the table define Katie's consumption possibilities. We can graph Katie's consumption possibilities as points *a* to *f* in Fig. 8.1.

Divisible and Indivisible Goods Some goods – called divisible goods – can be bought in any quantity desired, such as petrol and electricity. We can best understand the model of household choice we're about to study if we suppose that all goods and services are divisible. For example, Katie can consume a half a bottle of wine a month *on average* by consuming one bottle every two months. When goods are divisible, the consumption possibilities are not just the points *a* to *f* shown in Fig. 8.1, but those points plus all the intermediate points that form the line running from *a* to *f*. Such a line is a budget line.

Katie's budget line is a constraint on her choices. It marks the boundary between what is affordable and what is unaffordable. She can afford all the points on the line and inside it. She cannot afford points outside the line. The constraint on her consumption depends on prices and on her income, and the constraint changes when prices and her income change. Let's see how by studying an equation that describes her consumption possibilities.

FIGURE 8.1

The Budget Line

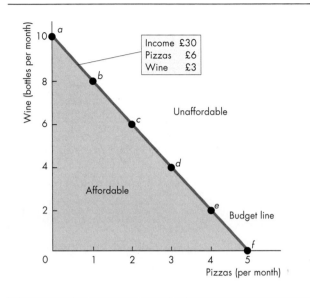

Income	£30
Pizzas	£6
Wine	£3

Consumption possibility	Pizzas (per month)	Wine (bottles per month)
a	0	10
b	1	8
c	2	6
d	3	4
e	4	2
f	5	0

Katie's budget line shows the boundary between what Katie can and cannot afford. The table lists Katie's affordable combinations of pizzas and wine when she has an income of £30 and when wine costs £3 a bottle and pizzas cost £6 each. For example, row *a* tells us that Katie can buy 10 bottles of wine and no pizzas – a combination that exhausts her £30 income. The figure graphs Katie's budget line. Points *a* to *f* on the graph represent rows of the table. For divisible goods, the budget line is the continuous line *af*.

The Budget Equation

The **budget equation** states the limits to consumption for a given income and for given prices. Such an equation and the way it is calculated is shown in Table 8.1. Part 1 of the table lists the variables – income, the prices of the goods consumed and the

TABLE 8.1

Calculating the Budget Equation

In general		In Katie's case	

1. THE VARIABLES

Income	=	y		y	=	£30
Price of pizzas	=	P_p		P_p	=	£6
Price of wine	=	P_w		P_w	=	£3
Quantity of pizzas	=	Q_p		Q_p	=	Katie's choice
Quantity of wine	=	Q_w		Q_w	=	Katie's choice

2. THE BUDGET

$$P_w Q_w + P_p Q_p = y$$ $$£3Q_w + £6Q_p = £30$$

3. CALCULATING THE BUDGET EQUATION

♦ Divide the budget equation by P_w to obtain:

$$Q_w + \frac{P_p}{P_w} Q_p = \frac{y}{P_w}$$

♦ Divide the budget equation by £3 to obtain:

$$Q_w + 2Q_p = 10$$

♦ Subtract $(P_p/P_w)Q_p$ from both sides to obtain:

$$Q_w = \frac{y}{P_w} - \frac{P_p}{P_w} Q_p$$

♦ Subtract $2Q_p$ from both sides to obtain:

$$Q_w = 10 - 2Q_p$$

---

quantities consumed – that affect a household's budget. In Katie's case, her income is £30, the prices are £6 for a pizza and £3 for a bottle of wine, and Katie will choose the quantities of pizzas and wine to consume.

Part 2 of the table says that expenditure – equal to the sum of the expenditures on each of the goods – equals income. Expenditure on any one good equals its price multiplied by the quantity consumed.

Part 3 of the table shows you how to derive the budget equation:

$$Q_w = \frac{y}{P_w} - \frac{P_p}{P_w} Q_p.$$

This equation tells us how the consumption of one good varies as consumption of the other good varies. To interpret the equation, let's go back to the budget line of Fig. 8.1 and check that the budget equation derived in Table 8.1 delivers the graph of the budget in Fig. 8.1. Begin by setting the quantity of pizzas, Q_p, equal to zero. In this case, the budget equation tells us that the quantity of wine, Q_w, will be y/P_w, which is £30/£3, or 10 bottles. This combination of Q_w and Q_p is the same as that shown in row a of the table in Fig. 8.1. Setting Q_p equal to 5 makes Q_w equal to zero (row f of the table in Fig. 8.1). Check that you can derive the other rows of the table.

The budget equation contains two variables chosen by the household (Q_p and Q_w) and two variables (y/P_w and P_p/P_w) that the household takes as given. Let's look more closely at these variables.

Real Income The variable y/P_w is the maximum number of bottles of wine that can be bought, and is called real income in terms of wine. **Real income** is income expressed in units of goods. It is money income divided by the price of a good. In Katie's case, her real income in terms of wine is 10 bottles. Real income is the point at which the budget line intersects the y-axis in Fig. 8.1.

Relative Price The variable P_p/P_w is the relative price of pizza in terms of wine. A **relative price** is the price of one good divided by the price of another good. In the equation, P_p/P_w is equal to 2. That is, to buy one more pizza, Katie must give up 2 bottles of wine. In Fig. 8.1, the relative price of pizzas to wine is the magnitude of the slope of the budget line. To calculate the slope of the budget line, recall the formula for slope that was introduced in Chapter 2: the slope of a line equals the change in the variable measured on the y-axis divided by the change in the variable measured on the x-axis as we move along the line. In this case, the variable measured on the y-axis is the quantity of wine and the variable measured on the x-axis is the quantity of pizzas. Along Katie's budget line, as wine decreases from 10 to 0, pizzas increase from 0 to 5. Therefore the slope of the budget line is –10/5, or –2. The relative price of one good in terms of another is the opportunity cost of the first good in terms of the second. In Katie's case, the opportunity cost of 1 pizza is 2 bottles of wine. Equivalently, the opportunity cost of 2 bottles of wine is 1 pizza.

A Change in Prices When prices change, so does the budget line. The lower the price of the good measured on the x-axis, other things remaining the same, the less steep is the budget line. For example, if the price of pizzas falls to £3 a pizza, the budget line shifts outward and becomes less steep as shown in Fig. 8.2(a). The higher the price of the good measured on the x-axis, other things remaining the same, the steeper is the budget line. For example, if the price of pizzas rises to £12 a pizza, the budget line shifts inward and becomes steeper as in Fig. 8.2(a).

A Change in Income A change in income changes real income but leaves the slope of the budget line unchanged. The higher a consumer's income, the further to the right is the budget line. The lower a consumer's income, the further to the left is the budget line. The effect of a change in income on Katie's budget line is shown in Fig. 8.2(b). The initial budget line is the same one that we began with in Fig. 8.1 when Katie's income is £30. A new budget line shows how much Katie is able to consume if her income falls to £15 a month. Her new line is parallel to the old one but further in. The two budget lines are parallel – have the same slope – because the relative price is the same in both cases. The new budget line is further in than the initial one because Katie's real income has decreased.

R E V I E W

The budget line describes the maximum amounts of consumption that a household can undertake given its income and the prices of the goods that it buys. A change in the price of one good changes the slope of the budget line. If the price of the good measured on the x-axis rises, the budget line gets steeper. A change in income makes the budget line shift, but its slope does not change. ◆

Let's now leave the budget line and look at the second ingredient in the model of household choice: preferences.

FIGURE 8.2

Prices, Income and the Budget Line

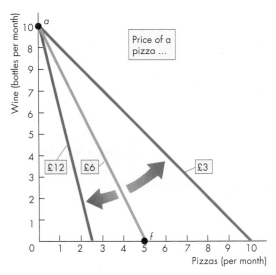

(a) A change in price

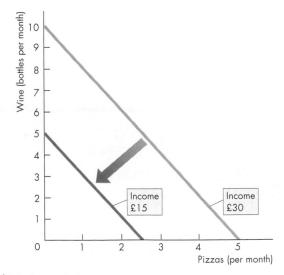

(b) A change in income

In part (a), the price of a pizza changes. A fall in the price from £6 to £3 shifts the budget line outward and makes it less steep. A rise in the price from £6 to £12 shifts the budget line inward and makes it steeper. In part (b), income falls from £30 to £15, but prices remain constant. The budget line shifts to the left but its slope does not change.

Preferences and Indifference Curves

Preferences are a person's likes and dislikes. We are going to discover a very neat device – that of drawing a map of a person's preferences. Let's see how we can draw a map of a person's preferences by making a map of Katie's preferences for pizza and wine. Figure 8.3 shows how such a map is made.

We measure the quantity of pizzas on the x-axis and the number of bottles of wine on the y-axis, just like we do for the budget line. Focus on point c, where Katie consumes 2 pizzas and 6 bottles of wine. We will use this point as a reference and ask how Katie likes other points in relation to point c.

Katie can rank all the possible combinations of pizzas and wine. She can say whether she prefers one combination to another or whether she is equally happy with one combination or another. Katie is said to be *indifferent* among combinations with which she is equally happy. These combinations lie on Katie's indifference curve. An **indifference curve** is a line that shows all the combinations of goods among which a consumer is *indifferent*. Such a curve is shown in Fig. 8.3 as the green line that passes through point c. That line defines the boundary between points that Katie prefers to point c – shown in orange – and points she regards as inferior to point c – shown in grey. Katie is indifferent between point c and the other points on the curve such as point g.

The indifference curve shown in Fig. 8.3 is just one of a whole family of such curves. This indifference curve appears again in Fig. 8.4. It is labelled I_1 and passes through points c and g. Two other indifference curves are I_0 and I_2. Katie prefers any point on indifference curve I_2 to those on indifference curve I_1, and she prefers any point on I_1 to those on I_0. We refer to I_2 as being a higher indifference curve than I_1 and I_1 as higher than I_0.

Indifference curves never intersect each other. To see why, consider indifference curves I_1 and I_2 in Fig. 8.4. We know that point j is preferred to point c. We also know that all points on indifference curve I_2 are preferred to all points on indifference curve I_1. If these indifference curves did intersect, the consumer would be indifferent between the combination of goods at the intersection point and combinations c and j. But we know

FIGURE 8.3
Mapping Preferences

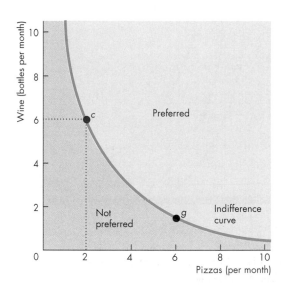

If Katie consumes 6 bottles of wine and 2 pizzas, she consumes at point c. She prefers any point at which she consumes more of both wine and pizzas to point c (all the points in the orange area). She prefers point c to any point at which fewer pizzas and bottles of wine are consumed (all the points in the grey area). Whether she prefers buying more pizzas but having less wine than at point c depends on how many more pizzas and how much less wine she has. Similarly, if she consumes more wine and buys fewer pizzas than at point c, whether she prefers that situation to c depends on how much more wine and how many fewer pizzas she has. The boundary between points that she prefers to point c and those to which c is preferred is called an indifference curve. Katie is indifferent between points such as g and c on the indifference curve. She prefers any point above the indifference curve (orange area) to any point on it, and she prefers any point on the indifference curve to any point below it (grey area).

that j is preferred to c, so such a point cannot exist. Hence the indifference curves never intersect.

A preference map consists of a series of indifference curves. The indifference curves shown in Fig. 8.4 are only a part of Katie's preference map. Her entire map consists of an infinite number of indifference curves, all of them sloping downward and none of them intersecting. They resemble the contour lines on a map measuring the height of mountains. An indifference curve joins points representing combinations of

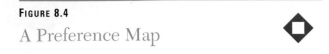

FIGURE 8.4

A Preference Map

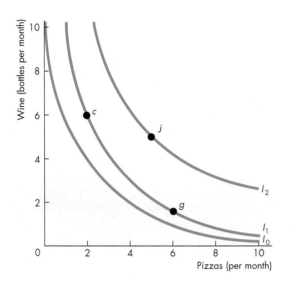

A preference map consists of an infinite number of indifference curves. Here, we show just three – I_0, I_1, and I_2 – that are part of Katie's preference map. Each indifference curve shows points among which Katie is indifferent. For example, she is indifferent between point c and point g on indifference curve I_1. But points on a higher indifference curve are preferred to points on a lower indifference curve. For example, Katie prefers all the points on indifference curve I_2 to all the points on indifference curve I_1; she prefers point j to points c or g.

goods among which a consumer is indifferent in much the same way that contour lines on a map join points of equal height above sea level. By looking at the shape of the contour lines on a map, we can draw conclusions about the terrain. In the same way, by looking at the shape of a person's indifference curves we can draw conclusions about preferences. But interpreting a preference map requires a bit of work. It also requires some way of describing the shape of the indifference curves. In the next two sections, we'll learn how to 'read' a preference map.

Marginal Rate of Substitution

The concept of the marginal rate of substitution is used to describe the shape of an indifference curve. The **marginal rate of substitution** (or *MRS*) is the

rate at which a person will give up good y (the good measured on the y-axis) in order to get more of good x (the good measured on the x-axis) and at the same time remain indifferent. The marginal rate of substitution is measured from the slope of an indifference curve. If the indifference curve is steep, the marginal rate of substitution is high. The person is willing to give up a large quantity of good y in exchange for a small quantity of good x while remaining indifferent. If the indifference curve is flat, the marginal rate of substitution is low. The person is willing to give up only a small amount of good y and must be compensated with a large amount of good x to remain indifferent.

Let's work out the marginal rate of substitution in two cases, both illustrated in Fig. 8.5. The curve labelled I_1 is one of Katie's indifference curves. Suppose that Katie drinks 6 bottles of wine and eats 2 pizzas (point c in the figure). What is her marginal rate of substitution at this point? It is calculated by measuring the magnitude of the slope of the indifference curve at that point. To measure the slope, place a straight line against, or tangential to, the indifference curve at that point. The slope of that line is the change in the number of bottles of wine divided by the change in the quantity of pizzas as we move along the line. As wine consumption decreases by 10 bottles, pizza consumption increases by 5. The slope of the line is –2. Thus when Katie is consuming 2 pizzas and 6 bottles of wine, her marginal rate of substitution is 2.

Now, suppose that Katie is consuming 6 pizzas and 1½ bottles of wine (point g in Fig. 8.5). What is her marginal rate of substitution at this point? The answer is found by calculating the slope of the indifference curve at that point. That slope is the same as the slope of the straight line drawn tangential to the indifference curve at point g. Here, as wine consumption decreases by 4½ bottles, pizza consumption increases by 9. Hence, the slope equals –½. Katie's marginal rate of substitution is ½. Thus when Katie eats 6 pizzas and consumes 1½ bottles of wine a month, she is willing to substitute pizzas for wine at the rate of half a bottle per pizza while remaining indifferent. Her marginal rate of substitution is ½.

Notice that if Katie drinks a lot of wine and does not eat many pizzas, her marginal rate of substitution is high. If she eats a lot of pizzas and does not drink much wine, her marginal rate of substitution is low. This feature of the marginal rate of substitution is the central assumption of the theory of consumer

FIGURE 8.5

The Marginal Rate of Substitution

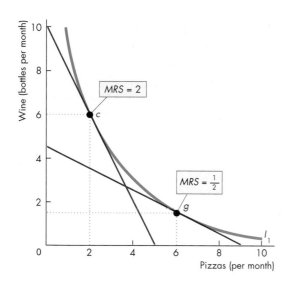

The magnitude of the slope of an indifference curve is called the marginal rate of substitution, or *MRS*. The marginal rate of substitution tells us how much of one good a person is willing to give up to gain more of another good, while remaining indifferent. The marginal rate of substitution at point *c* is 2; at point *g* it is ½.

behaviour and is referred to as the diminishing marginal rate of substitution. The assumption of **diminishing marginal rate of substitution** is a general tendency for the marginal rate of substitution to diminish as the consumer moves along an indifference curve, increasing consumption of good x and decreasing consumption of good y.

You may be able to appreciate why we assume the principle of a diminishing marginal rate of substitution by thinking about your own preferences. Imagine two situations: in one, you are eating 3 pizzas a night but have no wine. In the other, you have 6 bottles of wine and no pizzas. In the first situation, you will probably willingly give up eating 1 pizza if you can get just a small amount of wine in exchange. In the second situation, you will probably be willing to give up quite a lot of wine to eat just 1 pizza. Your preferences satisfy the principle of diminishing marginal rate of substitution.

The shape of the indifference curves incorporates

the principle of the diminishing marginal rate of substitution because the curves are bowed toward the origin. The tightness of the bend of an indifference curve tells us how willing a person is to substitute one good for another while remaining indifferent.

Degree of Substitutability

Most of us would not regard pizza and wine as being close substitutes for each other. We probably have some fairly clear ideas about how many pizzas we want to buy each month and how many bottles of wine we want to drink. Nevertheless, to some degree, we are willing to substitute between these two goods. No matter how much wine you like, there is surely some increase in the number of pizzas you can buy that will compensate you for being deprived of a bottle of wine. Similarly, no matter how addicted you are to pizzas, surely some bottles of wine will compensate you for being deprived of buying one pizza. A person's indifference curves for pizza and wine might look something like those shown in Fig. 8.6(a).

Close Substitutes Some goods substitute so easily for each other that most of us do not even notice which we are consuming. A good example concerns different brands of personal computers. Compaq, Dell and Tandy are all clones of the IBM PC – but most of us can't tell the difference among the three clones and, indeed, the IBM machine itself. The same holds true for marker pens. Most of us don't care whether we use a marker pen from the university bookshop or the local supermarket. When two goods are perfect substitutes for each other, their indifference curves are straight lines that slope downward, as illustrated in Fig. 8.6(b). The marginal rate of substitution between perfect substitutes is constant.

Complements Some goods cannot substitute for each other at all. Instead, they are complements. The complements in Fig. 8.6(c) are left and right running shoes. Indifference curves of perfect complements are L-shaped. One left running shoe and one right running shoe are as good as one left shoe and two right ones. Two of each are preferred to one of each, but two of one and one of the other are no better than one of each.

The extreme cases of perfect substitutes and perfect complements shown here don't often happen in reality. They do, however illustrate that the shape of the indifference curve shows the degree of substitutability between two goods. The more perfectly substitutable the two goods, the more nearly are their indifference curves straight lines and the less quickly does the marginal rate of substitution fall. Poor substitutes for each other have tightly curved indifference curves, approaching the shape of those shown in Fig. 8.6(c).

R E V I E W

A person's preferences can be represented by a preference map. A preference map consists of a series of indifference curves. Indifference curves slope downward, bow toward the origin and do not intersect each other. The magnitude of the slope of an indifference curve is called the marginal rate of substitution. The marginal rate of substitution falls as a person consumes less of the good measured on the y-axis and more of the good measured on the x-axis. The tightness of an indifference curve tells us how well two goods substitute for each other. Indifference curves that are almost straight lines indicate that the goods are close substitutes. Indifference curves that are tightly curved and that approach an L-shape indicate that the two goods complement each other. Reading Between the Lines on pp. 208–209 shows how mad cow disease is affecting peoples preferences for beef and other meat. ◆

The two components of the model of household choice are now in place: the budget line and the preference map. We will now use these two components to work out the consumer's choice.

FIGURE 8.6

The Degree of Substitutability

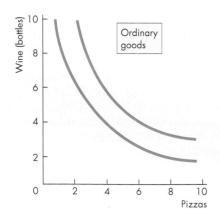

(a) Ordinary goods

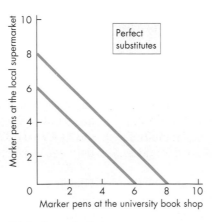

(b) Perfect substitutes

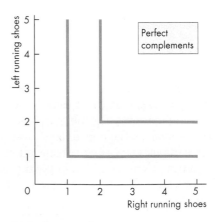

(c) Perfect complements

The shape of the indifference curves reveals the degree of substitutability between two goods. Part (a) shows the indifference curves for two ordinary goods: pizzas and bottles of wine. To remain indifferent as less wine is consumed, one must buy more pizzas. The number of pizzas that compensates for a reduction in wine increases as less wine is consumed. Part (b) shows the indifference curves for two perfect substitutes. For the consumer to remain indifferent, one fewer marker pen from the local supermarket must be replaced by one extra marker pen from the university book shop. Part (c) shows two perfect complements – goods that cannot be substituted for each other at all. Two left running shoes with one right running shoe is no better than one of each. But two of each is preferred to one of each.

Choice

Recall that Katie has £30 to spend and she buys only two goods: pizzas (at £6 each) and wine (at £3 a bottle). We've learned how to construct Katie's budget line, which summarizes what she can buy, given her income and the prices of pizzas and wine (Fig. 8.1). We've also learned how to characterize Katie's preferences in terms of her indifference curves (Fig. 8.4). We are now going to bring Katie's budget line and indifference curves together and discover her best affordable consumption of pizzas and wine.

The analysis is summarized in Fig. 8.7. You can see in that figure the budget line from Fig. 8.1 and the indifference curves from Fig. 8.4. Let's first focus on point h on indifference curve I_0. That point is on Katie's budget line, so we know that she can afford it. But does she prefer this combination of pizzas and wine over all the other affordable combinations? The answer is no, she does not. To see why not, consider point c, where she consumes 2 pizzas and 6 bottles of wine. Point c is also on Katie's budget line, so we know she can afford to consume at this point. But point c is on indifference curve I_1, a higher indifference curve than I_0. Therefore we know that Katie prefers point c to point h.

Are there any affordable points that Katie prefers to point c? The answer is that there are not. All Katie's other affordable consumption points – all the other points on or below her budget line – lie on indifference curves that are below I_1. Indifference curve I_1 is the highest indifference curve on which Katie can afford to consume.

Let's look more closely at Katie's best affordable choice.

Properties of the Best Affordable Point

The best affordable point – point c in this example – has two properties. It is *on*:

◆ The budget line
◆ The highest attainable indifference curve

On the Budget Line   The best affordable point is *on* the budget line. If Katie chooses a point inside the budget line, she will have an affordable point on the budget line at which she can consume more of both goods. Katie prefers that point to the one

FIGURE 8.7

The Best Affordable Point

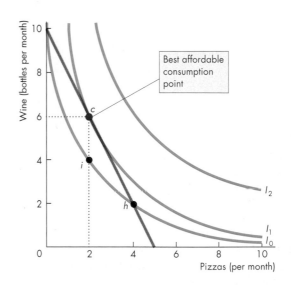

Katie's best affordable consumption point is c. At that point, she is on her budget line and so spends her entire income on the two goods. She is also on the highest attainable indifference curve. Higher indifference curves (such as I_2) do not touch her budget line and so she cannot afford any point on them. At point c, the marginal rate of substitution (the magnitude of the slope of the indifference curve) equals the relative price of pizzas (the magnitude of the slope of the budget line). A point such as h on the budget line is not Katie's best affordable consumption point because at that point she is willing to give up more pizzas in exchange for wine than she has to. She can move to a point such as i, which she regards as being just as good as point h and which allows her to have some income left over. She can spend that income and move to c, a point that she prefers to point i.

`inside the budget line. The best affordable point cannot be outside the budget line because Katie cannot afford such a point.

On the Highest Attainable Indifference Curve   The chosen point is on the highest attainable indifference curve where that curve has the same slope as the budget line. Stated another way, the marginal rate of substitution between the two goods (the magnitude of the slope of the indifference curve) equals their relative price (the magnitude of the

To see why this condition describes the best affordable point, consider point h, which Katie regards as inferior to point c. At point h, Katie's marginal rate of substitution is less than the relative price – indifference curve I_0 is flatter than Katie's budget line. As Katie gives up pizzas for wine and moves up indifference curve I_0, she moves inside her budget line and has some money left over. She can move to point i, for example, where she consumes 2 pizzas and 5 bottles of wine and has £3 to spare. She is indifferent between the combination of goods at point i and at point h. But she prefers point c to point i, since at c she has more wine than at i and buys the same number of pizzas.

By moving along her budget line from point h towards point c, Katie passes through a whole array of indifference curves (not shown in the figure) located between indifference curves I_0 and I_1. All of these indifference curves are higher than I_0 and therefore any point on them is preferred to point h. Once she gets to point c, Katie has reached the highest attainable indifference curve. If she keeps moving along the budget line, she will now start to encounter indifference curves that are lower than I_1.

R E V I E W

The consumer has a given income and faces fixed prices. The consumer's problem is to allocate that fixed income in the best possible way. Affordable combinations of goods are described by the consumer's budget line. The consumer's preferences are represented by indifference curves. The consumer's best allocation of income occurs when all income is spent (on the budget line) and when the marginal rate of substitution (the magnitude of the slope of the indifference curve) equals the relative price (the magnitude of the slope of the budget line). ◆

We will now use this model of household choice to make some predictions about changes in consumption patterns when income and prices change.

Predicting Consumer Behaviour

Let's examine how consumers respond to changes in prices and income. We'll start by looking at the effect of a change in price. By studying the effect of a change in price on a consumer's choice, holding all other effects constant, we are able to derive a consumer's demand curve.

A Change in Price

The effect of a change in price on the quantity of a good consumed is called the **price effect**. We will use Fig. 8.8(a) to work out the price effect of a fall in the price of a pizza. We start with a pizza costing £6, wine costing £3 a bottle, and with Katie's income at £30 a month. In this situation, she consumes at point c, where her budget line is tangential to her highest attainable indifference curve, I_1. She consumes 6 bottles of wine and 2 pizzas a month.

Now suppose that the price of a pizza falls to £3. We've already seen how a change in price (in Fig. 8.2a) affects the budget line. With a lower price of pizzas, the budget line rotates outward and becomes less steep. The new budget line is the dark orange one in Fig. 8.8(a). Katie's best affordable point is j, where she consumes 5 pizzas and 5 bottles of wine. As you can see, Katie drinks less wine and eats more pizzas now that pizzas cost less. She reduces her wine consumption from 6 to 5 bottles, and increases her pizza consumption from 2 to 5. Katie substitutes pizzas for wine when the price of a pizza falls, and the price of wine and her income remain constant.

The Demand Curve

This analysis of the effect of a change in the price of a pizza enables us to derive Katie's demand curve for pizzas. Recall that the demand curve graphs the relationship between the quantity demanded of a good and its price, holding constant all other influences on the quantity demanded. We can derive Katie's demand curve for pizzas by gradually lowering the price of a pizza and working out how many pizzas she buys by finding her best affordable point at each different price. Figure 8.8(b) highlights just

FIGURE 8.8

Price Effect and Demand Curve

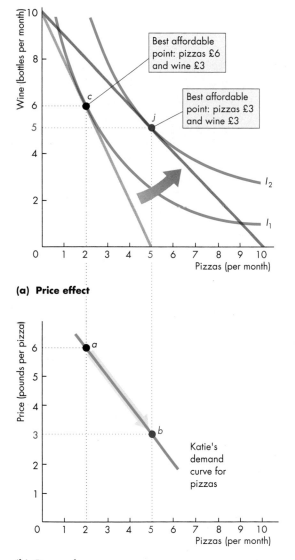

Best affordable point: pizzas £6 and wine £3

Best affordable point: pizzas £3 and wine £3

(a) Price effect

Katie's demand curve for pizzas

(b) Demand curve

Initially, Katie consumes at point *c* (part a). If the price of a pizza falls from £6 to £3, she consumes at point *j*. The increase in the consumption of pizzas from 2 to 5 per month is the price effect. When the price of a pizza falls, Katie consumes more pizzas. She also consumes less wine. Katie's demand curve for pizzas is shown in part (b). When the price of a pizza is £6, she consumes 2 a month, at point *a*. When the price of a pizza falls to £3, she consumes 5 a month, at point *b*. The demand curve is traced by varying the price of pizzas and calculating Katie's best affordable consumption of pizzas for each different price.

two prices and two points that lie on Katie's demand curve for pizzas. When the price of a pizza is £6, Katie consumes 2 pizzas a month at point *a*. When the price falls to £3, she increases her consumption to 5 pizzas a month at point *b*. The entire demand curve is made up of these two points plus all the other points that tell us Katie's best affordable consumption of pizzas at each price – more than £6, between £6 and £3, and less than £3 – given the price of wine and Katie's income. As you can see, Katie's demand curve for pizzas slopes downward – the lower the price of a pizza, the more she buys each month. This is the law of demand that we *assumed* in Chapter 4.

Next, let's examine what happens when Katie's income changes.

A Change in Income

The effect of a change in income on consumption is called the **income effect**. Let's work out the income effect by examining how consumption changes when income changes with constant prices. We've already seen, earlier in this chapter, how a change in income shifts the budget line. We worked out and illustrated (in Fig. 8.2b) that a decrease in income shifts the budget line to the left, with its slope unchanged.

It will be clear to you that, as income increases, a person can consume more of all goods. But being able to consume more of all goods does not mean that a person will do so. Goods are classified into two groups: normal goods and inferior goods. A *normal good* is a good whose income effect is positive – consumption increases as income increases. An *inferior good* is a good whose income effect is negative – consumption decreases as income increases.

As the name implies, most goods are normal goods. But a few are inferior goods. Rice and potatoes are perhaps the most obvious. People with low incomes often consume a lot of rice or potatoes. As incomes increase, people substitute chicken and fish for rice and potatoes. Thus as income increases, the consumption of chicken or fish increases but that of rice or potatoes decreases. Therefore chicken and fish are normal goods, while rice and potatoes are inferior goods. In Katie's case, as her income increases, she consumes more pizzas and more wine. For Katie, both pizzas and wine are normal goods.

FIGURE 8.9

The Income Effect

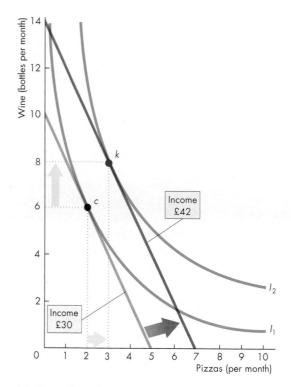

(a) Normal goods

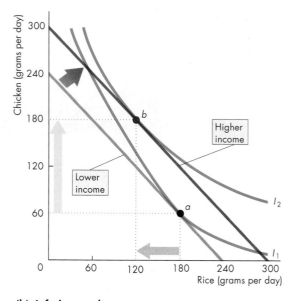

(b) Inferior goods

An increase in income increases the consumption of most goods. These goods are normal goods. In part (a), Katie consumes more of both wine and pizzas (as shown by the green arrows) as her income increases. Wine and pizzas are normal goods, but some goods are inferior goods. The consumption of inferior goods decreases as income increases. In part (b), as income increases, the consumption of rice decreases (shown by the red arrow) and more chicken is consumed (shown by the green arrow). For this consumer, rice is an inferior good.

Figure 8.9 illustrates the two types of income effect. Part (a) shows the income effect for normal goods, using Katie's consumption as an example. With an income of £30 and with pizzas costing £6 each and wine £3 a bottle, she consumes at point *c* – 2 pizzas and 6 bottles of wine. If her income goes up to £42, she consumes at point *k* – 3 pizzas and 8 bottles of wine. Thus with a higher income, Katie consumes more of both goods. These income effects are marked on the axes of Fig. 8.9(a). As you can see, both income effects are positive. Figure 8.9(b) shows the income effect for an inferior good – rice. At the initial income level, the household consumes at point *a*, 60 grams of chicken and 180 grams of rice a day. When income increases, consumption of chicken increases to 180 grams a day, but consumption of rice decreases to 120 grams a day, at point *b*. The income effect for an inferior good is negative.

A Change in Price: Income and Substitution Effects

We've now worked out the effects of a change in the price of a pizza and the effects of a change in Katie's income on the consumption of pizzas and wine. We've discovered that when her income increases, she increases her consumption of both goods. Pizzas and wine are *normal goods*. When the price of a pizza falls, Katie increases her consumption of pizzas and decreases her consumption of wine. A fall in the price of a normal good leads to an increase in the consumption of that good, as well as to a decrease in the consumption of the substitutes for that good. In this example, a fall in the price of pizzas leads to an increase in the consumption of pizzas, as well as to a decrease in the consumption of wine, a substitute for pizzas. To see why these changes in spending patterns occur when there is a change in price, we separate the effect of the change into two parts. One part is called the substitution effect; the other part is called the income effect. The price effect and its separation into a substitution effect and an income effect are illustrated in Fig. 8.10. Part (a) shows the price effect that you've already worked out in Fig. 8.8. Let's see how that price effect comes about, first by isolating the substitution effect.

The Substitution Effect The **substitution effect** is the effect of a change in price on the quantities consumed when the consumer (hypothetically) remains indifferent between the original and the new combinations of goods consumed. To work out Katie's substitution effect, we have to imagine that when the price of pizzas falls, Katie's income also decreases by an amount that is just enough to leave her on the same indifference curve as before.

The substitution effect is illustrated in Fig. 8.10(b). When the price of a pizza falls from £6 to £3, let's suppose (hypothetically) that Katie's income decreases to £21. What's special about £21? It is the income that is just enough, at the new price of a pizza, to keep Katie's best affordable point on the same indifference curve as her initial consumption point c. Katie's budget line in this situation is the light orange line shown in Fig. 8.10(b). With the new price of a pizza and the new lower income, Katie's best affordable point is l on indifference curve I_1. The move from c to l isolates the substitution effect of a price change. The substitution effect of the fall in the price of a pizza is an increase in the consumption of pizzas from 2 to 4 and a decrease in the consumption of wine. The direction of the substitution effect never varies: when the relative price of a good falls, the consumer substitutes more of that good for the other good.

Income Effect To calculate the substitution effect, we gave Katie a £9 pay cut. Now let's give Katie her money back. This means shifting Katie's budget line, as shown in Fig. 8.10(c). That move does not involve any change in prices. The budget line moves outward, but its slope does not change. This change in the budget is similar to the one that occurs in Fig. 8.9 where we study the effect of income on consumption. As Katie's budget line shifts outward, her consumption possibilities expand and her best affordable point becomes j on indifference curve I_2. The move from l to j isolates the income effect of a price change. In this example, the increase in income increases the consumption of both pizzas and wine; they are normal goods.

Price Effect As Fig. 8.10 illustrates, we have separated the effect of a change in price in part (a) into two parts: part (b) keeps the consumer indifferent between the two situations (by making a hypothetical income change at the same time) and looks at the substitution effect of the price change; part (c) keeps prices constant and (hypothetically) restores the original income. It looks at the income effect. The substitution effect always works in the same direction – the consumer slides along an indifference curve, buying more of the good whose price has fallen. The direction of the income effect depends on whether the good is normal or inferior. By definition, normal goods are ones whose consumption increases as income increases. In our example, pizzas and wine are normal goods because the income effect increases their consumption. Both the income effect and the substitution effect increase Katie's consumption of pizzas.

The substitution and income effects of a price change are marked off on the axes in parts (b) and (c) of Fig. 8.10. The move from point c to point l is the substitution effect, and the move from point l to point j is the income effect. For pizzas, the income effect reinforces the substitution effect with the result that Katie's consumption of pizzas increases. For wine, the substitution effect and the income effect work in opposite directions with the result that Katie's consumption of wine decreases.

The example that we have just studied is that of a change in the price of a normal good. The effect of a change in the price of an inferior good is different. Recall that an inferior good is one

FIGURE 8.10

Price Effect, Substitution Effect and Income Effect

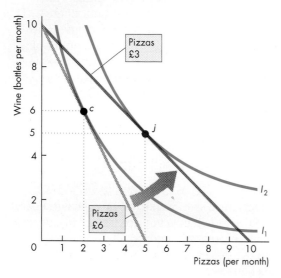

(a) Price effect

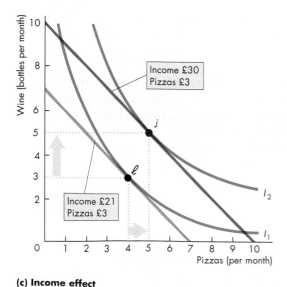

(c) Income effect

The price effect can be separated into substitution effect and income effect. The price effect is shown in part (a) and is the same as that in Fig. 8.8(a).

The substitution effect in part (b) is calculated by imagining that Katie's income decreases at the same time as the fall in the price of a pizza, so that when she chooses her best affordable point, she is indifferent between that and the original situation. The move from c to ℓ is the substitution effect. The substitution effect of a price change always results in more consumption of the good whose price has fallen. The green arrow shows the increase in consumption.

The income effect (part c) is calculated by reversing the imaginary pay cut. Income is increased by holding prices constant at their new level. The budget line moves outward and more of both goods is consumed, as shown by the green arrows. The move from ℓ to j is the income effect.

whose consumption decreases as income increases. For an inferior good, the income effect is negative. Thus for an inferior good it is not always the case that a lower price leads to an increase in the quantity

demanded of the inferior good. The lower price has a substitution effect that tends to increase the quantity demanded. But the lower price also has a negative income effect, which reduces the demand for an inferior good. Thus the income effect offsets the substitution effect to some degree.[1]

Back to the Facts

We started this chapter by observing how consumer spending has changed over the years. The theory of consumption choice studied in this chapter can be used to explain those changes. Spending patterns are interpreted as being the best choices households can make, given their preferences and incomes and given the prices of the goods they consume. Changes in prices and in income lead to changes in the best possible choice – changes in consumption patterns.

Models based on the same ideas that you've studied here are used to explain the actual changes that occur and to measure the response of consumption to changes in prices and in income – the price and income elasticities of demand. You met some measures of these elasticities in Chapter 5. Most of those elasticities were measured by using models of exactly the same type that we've studied here (but models that have more than two goods).

But the model of household choice can do much more than explain consumption choices. It can be used to explain a wide range of other household choices. Let's look at some of these.

Other Household Choices

Households make many choices other than those about how to spend their income on the various goods and services available. But we can use the model of consumer choice to understand many other household choices. Some of these are discussed in Our Advancing Knowledge on pp.182–183. Here, we'll study the two key choices that households make. They are:

◆ How many hours to work
◆ How much to save

Work Hours and Labour Supply

Every day, we have to allocate our 24 hours between leisure, working for ourselves and working for someone else. When we work for someone else, we are supplying labour.

We can understand our labour supply decisions by using the theory of household choice. Supplying more labour is exactly the same thing as consuming less leisure. Leisure is a good, just like pizzas and wine. Other things being equal, a situation that has more leisure is preferred to one that has less leisure. We have indifference curves for leisure and consumption goods similar to those that we've already studied. For example, we can relabel the axes of Fig. 8.4 so that instead of wine, we measure all consumption goods on the y-axis and instead of pizzas, we measure leisure on the x-axis.

We can't have as much leisure and consumption as we'd like. Our choices are constrained by the wages that we can earn. For a given hourly wage rate, increasing our consumption of goods and services is only possible if we decrease our leisure time and increase our supply of labour. The wage rate that we can earn determines how much extra consumption we can undertake by giving up an extra hour of leisure. The magnitude of the slope of our indifference curve tells us the marginal rate of substitution – the rate at which we will be willing to give up consumption of goods and services to get one more hour of leisure while remaining indifferent. Our best choice of consumption and leisure has exactly the same properties as our best choice of pizzas and wine. We get on to the highest possible indifference curve by making the marginal rate of substitution between consumption and leisure

---

[1]It has been suggested that the negative income effect for some goods is so large that it dominates the substitution effect. As a result, a lower price leads to a decrease in the quantity demanded for such a good. Goods of this type are called 'Giffen' goods, named after Robert Giffen, a nineteenth century English statistician. Alfred Marshall reported that Giffen had noted that when the price of bread increased, poor families consumed more bread, not less. They did so because bread made up such a large part of their diets that when the price of bread rose, consumers couldn't afford to buy meat or other bread substitutes, which were all even more expensive. Giffen goods are very uncommon. Thus even though some goods do have a negative income effect, that effect is usually not large enough to outweigh the substitution effect. So the law of demand still operates – when the price of a good falls, the quantity of that good demanded increases.

Mad Cows and Consumer Behaviour

Bovine Spongiform Encephalopathy (BSE), or mad cow disease, has affected many beef herds in the United Kingdom.

Germany threatened to ban imports of UK beef but dropped this threat following an EU deal banning trade of bone-in beef meat from any animal exposed to BSE in the last six years.

Most of the United Kingdom's beef exports to the rest of the European Union are currently bone-in from herds that could have been affected.

Trade in beef is very complex, so that while many cattle will not have been exposed to BSE, it is impossible to prove this.

As a result of the EU deal, exports could fall by up to 80 per cent.

THE GUARDIAN, 22 JULY 1994

Export threatened by mad cow 'victory'

James Erlichman, Agriculture Correspondent

MOST of Britain's £400 million a year beef export trade to Europe could be wiped out by the 'mad cow' agreement claimed as a victory by the Government this week....

The deal, agreed on Monday by Gillian Shephard, the former Agriculture Minister, appears to have averted a German threat to impose unilateral restrictions on British beef imports because of fears about Bovine Spongiform Encephalopathy (BSE), or mad cow disease.

But Britain agreed in return to accept a European Union-wide export ban on beef from any animal that had been exposed to BSE within the last six years unless all its bones and lymphatic tissue had been removed first. Exposure is defined as having been in a herd where there has been at least one case of the disease.

Colin McLean, director general of the Meat and Livestock Commission, said the ban would affect 80 per cent of current exports to the EU. Just over half of British dairy herds have had one or more BSE cases. But the ban sweeps in even more cattle, he said, because few cattle remain in the herd where they were born, but pass via markets to more than one farm. The complexity of the trade means that animals free from exposure may not be certified as such because records are inadequate to trace their history....

Britain exported 128,000 tonnes of beef to the EU last year, and this year's trade is believed to be stronger. Most of the trade – 102,000 tonnes – was in carcasses with bones in tact, and most of this was the hindquarters of old dairy cows bought by the French....

Suzi Leather, a member of the ministry's consumer panel said: 'Whatever the risk from BSE, the effect of this agreement appears to load more of these animals on the home market and the British consumer.'

A ministry spokeswoman denied the export trade faced a long-term crisis. 'There will be short-term disruption and we have told the industry that the new rules will not be easy,' she said.

The solution would be to convince EU customers, and principally the French, to accept boneless cuts butchered in Britain. 'The problem is that the French have traditionally cut meat in their own way,' said Mr Gardiner, 'and they may be reluctant to change.'

© The Guardian. Reprinted with permission.

Background and Analysis

Fears about the possible impact of BSE on human health through Creutzfeldt-Jakob Disease (CJD), the human version of BSE, has led to a fall in demand for UK beef.

Germany wished to ban UK beef, given its very tough food hygiene regulations.

The EU response to the German threat was one that was to be common to all member countries. It involved banning trade in the meat that was most likely to have been exposed to BSE.

Much of the meat thus affected would have gone to France.

France has traditionally produced its own cuts from bone-in beef imported from the United Kingdom. A key task of UK exporters is to get the French to accept bone-less beef from the United Kingdom cut in a different way.

Figure 1 shows the situation before the BSE health scare. Figure 2 shows the consequence of the concern about BSE (as well as the accompanying trade restrictions).

The lower demand for UK bone-in beef results in a fall in price. Assuming there is no change in the price of other meat, the budget line becomes steeper.

BSE causes consumers' preferences to change from UK bone-in beef to other meat. This affects the benefit consumers get from UK bone-in beef and means that the indifference map changes (see Fig. A8.1).

Where the budget line and the indifference curve are tangential in Fig. 2 is at a point where the marginal rate of substitution *(MRS)* is high. With the health concerns about BSE, consumers can be expected to give up a lot of UK bone-in beef to gain an extra unit of other meat.

The lower total consumption of meat in Fig. 2 principally reflects the high marginal rate of substitution. Also the presence of BSE may result in some people ceasing to consume meat at all.

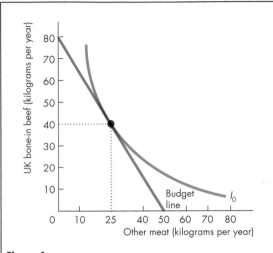

Figure 1

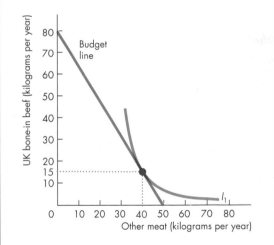

Figure 2

equal to the wage rate relative to the price of consumption goods.

Changes in wages affect our choice of consumption and leisure in a similar way to that in which a change in the price of pizzas affects our consumption of pizzas and wine. A higher wage rate makes leisure more expensive. There is a substitution effect encouraging us to take less leisure and work longer hours, thereby consuming more goods and services. But a higher wage rate also has an income effect. A higher wage leads to a higher income, and with a higher income we consume more of all normal goods. Leisure is a normal good. Other things remaining the same, the higher the income, the more leisure we take.

People who can earn only a very low hourly wage rate tend to work fewer hours, or perhaps not at all. As the wage rate increases, the substitution effect encourages less leisure and more work to be undertaken. But as the wage rate keeps on increasing, the income effect eventually comes to dominate the substitution effect. The higher wage leads to higher consumption of goods and services and to additional leisure. It is the ultimately dominant role of the income effect that has resulted in a steadily shorter work week despite the fact that wages have increased.

Saving

We don't have to spend all our income here and now. Nor are we constrained to consuming only our current income. We can consume less than our current income, saving the difference for future consumption. Or we can consume more than our current income, borrowing the difference but putting ourselves in a position where we must consume less later in order to repay our loan. Choosing when to consume, how much to save and how much to borrow

can also be understood by using the same theory of household choice that explained Katie's allocation of her income to pizzas and wine.

Other things being equal, more consumption today is preferred to less. Also, other things remaining the same, more consumption in the future is preferred to less. As a consequence, we have indifference curves for consumption now and in the future that are similar to our indifference curves for any pair of goods. Of course, we cannot consume as much as we'd like to today or in the future. Our choices are constrained. The constraint on our choices depends on our income and the interest rate that we can earn on our savings or that we have to pay on our borrowing. The interest rate is a relative price – the relative price of consumption today versus consumption in the future. We choose the timing of consumption (and the amount of saving or borrowing to undertake) by making the marginal rate of substitution between current and future consumption equal to the interest rate. Thus high interest rates will discourage borrowing and lead to lower current consumption and higher future consumption.

◆ ◆ ◆ ◆   We've now completed our study of household choices. We've seen how we can derive the law of demand from a model of household choice. We've also seen how that same model can be applied to a wide range of other choices, including the demand for leisure and the supply of labour. ◆ ◆   In Chapters 9–13, we're going to study the choices made by firms. We'll see how, in the pursuit of profit, firms make choices governing the supply of goods and services and the demand for factors of production (inputs). ◆ ◆   After completing these chapters, we'll then bring the analysis of households and firms back together again, studying their interactions in markets for good and services and factors of production.

S U M M A R Y

Consumption Possibilities

A household's budget line shows the limits to consumption given the household's income and the prices of goods. The budget line is the boundary

between what the consumer can and cannot afford.

Changes in prices and changes in income produce changes in the budget line. The magnitude of the slope of the budget line equals the relative price of the two goods. The point at which the budget line intersects each axis marks the consumer's real income in terms of the good measured on that axis. (pp. 194–196)

Preferences and Indifference Curves

A consumer's preferences can be represented by indifference curves. An indifference curve joins all the combinations of goods among which the consumer is indifferent. A consumer prefers points above an indifference curve to the points on it and points on an indifference curve to all points below it. Indifference curves bow toward the origin.

The magnitude of the slope of an indifference curve is called the marginal rate of substitution. A key assumption is that of a diminishing marginal rate of substitution. In other words, the marginal rate of substitution diminishes as consumption of the good measured on the y-axis decreases and consumption of the good measured on the x-axis increases. The better two goods substitute for each other, the straighter are the indifference curves. The less easily they substitute, the more tightly curved are the indifference curves. Goods that are always consumed together are complements and have L-shaped indifference curves. (pp. 197–200)

Choice

A household consumes at the best affordable point. Such a point is on the budget line and on the highest attainable indifference curve. At that point the indifference curve and the budget line have the same slope – the marginal rate of substitution equals the relative price. (pp. 201–202)

Predicting Consumer Behaviour

Goods are classified into two groups: normal goods and inferior goods. Most goods are normal. When income increases, a consumer buys more normal goods and fewer inferior goods. If prices are held constant, the change in consumption resulting from a change in income is called the income effect.

The change in consumption resulting from a change in the price of a good is called the price effect. The price effect can be divided into a substitution effect and an income effect. The substitution effect is calculated as the change in consumption resulting from the change in price accompanied by a (hypothetical) change in income that leaves the consumer indifferent between the initial situation and the new situation. The substitution effect of a price change always results in an increase in consumption of the good whose price has decreased. The income effect of a price change is the effect of (hypothetically) restoring the consumer's original income but keeping the price of the good constant at its new level. For a normal good, the income effect reinforces the substitution effect. For an inferior good, the income effect offsets the substitution effect. (pp. 202–207)

Other Household Choices

The model of household choice also enables us to understand household choices regarding the allocation of time between leisure and work, the allocation of consumption over time, and decisions regarding borrowing and saving. (pp. 207–210)

K E Y E L E M E N T S

Key Terms

Key Figures and Tables

R E V I E W   Q U E S T I O N S

1 What determines the limits to a household's consumption choices?

2 What is the budget line?

3 What determines the intercept of the budget line on the y-axis?

4 What determines the intercept of the budget line on the x-axis?

5 What determines the slope of the budget line?

6 What do all the points on an indifference curve have in common?

7 What is the marginal rate of substitution?

8 How can you tell how closely two goods substitute for each other according to the preferences of a consumer by looking at the consumer's indifference curves?

9 What two conditions are satisfied when a consumer makes the best possible consumption choice?

10 What is the effect of a change in income on consumption?

11 What is the effect of a change in price on consumption?

12 Define and distinguish between the income effect and the substitution effect of a price change.

P R O B L E M S

1 Sarah has an income of £9 a week. Chocolates costs £1 a box and lemonade costs £1.50 a litre.
   a What is Sarah's real income in terms of lemonade?
   b What is her real income in terms of chocolates?
   c What is the relative price of lemonade in terms of chocolates?
   d What is the opportunity cost of a litre of lemonade?
   e What is Sarah's budget equation?
   f Calculate the equation for Sarah's budget line (placing the quantity of lemonade on the left side).
   g Draw a graph of Sarah's budget line with chocolates on the x-axis.
   h In Problem (g), what is the slope of Sarah's budget line? What is it equal to?

2 Suppose that with the same income and prices as above, Sarah chooses to consume 4 litres of lemonade and 3 boxes of chocolates each week.
   a Is Sarah on her budget line?
   b What is her marginal rate of substitution of lemonade for chocolates?

3 Now suppose that the price of lemonade doubles to £3 a litre and the price of chocolates doubles to £2 a box. At the same time Sarah's income doubles to £18 a week.
   a Can Sarah still buy the same quantities of lemonade and boxes of chocolates as before if she wants to?
   b What now is Sarah's real income? What now is the real price? Describe how Sarah's budget line has changed.

4 In Problem 3, what are your answers if only:
   a The price of lemonade changed?
   b The price of chocolates changed?
   c Sarah's income changed?

5 Jerry buys beer that costs £1 a pint and comic books that cost £2 each. Each month Jerry buys 20 pints of beer and 10 comic books. He spends all of his income. Next month the price of a pint of beer will fall to 50 pence, but the price of a comic book will rise to £3.
   a Will Jerry be able to buy 20 pints of beer and 10 comic books next month?
   b Will he want to?
   c If he changes his consumption, which good will he buy more of and which less?
   d Which situation does Jerry prefer: beer at £1

a pint and comic books at £2 or beer at 50 pence a pint and comic books at £3?

e When the prices change next month will there be an income effect and a substitution effect at work or just one of them? If there is only one effect at work, which one will it be?

6 Now suppose that the prices of beer and comic books are at their original levels – £1 and £2 respectively. Jerry's income increases by £10 a month. He now buys 16 comic books and 18 pints of beer. For Jerry are beer and comic books normal goods or inferior goods?

APPENDIX

If you have studied both Chapters 7 and 8, you've seen two models of consumer choice. This appendix deals with the connection between the two models. When you have read this appendix, you will be able to reinterpret each model in terms of the other.

Utility and Indifference Curves

A key element in each theory of choice is its way of describing the consumer's preferences. The marginal utility theory of Chapter 7 describes preferences in terms of the utility derived from consumption. In the indifference curve theory of Chapter 8, indifference curves represent preferences. You can understand how the two models relate to each other by thinking of an indifference curve as connecting points of equal utility. Katie is indifferent between 3 pizzas and 4 bottles of wine and 2 pizzas and 6 bottles of wine. Another way of saying that she is indifferent is that she gets equal utility from the two.

You can see the connection between utility and

indifference curves by looking at the two parts of Fig. A8.1. Part (a) has three dimensions: the quantity of wine, the quantity of pizzas and the level of total utility. Part (b) has just two dimensions – the quantities of wine and pizzas consumed.

In part (a), the utility that Katie gets from wine alone (with no pizzas) appears as the left-hand yellow line. It shows that as Katie's consumption of wine rises, so does the total utility she gets from wine. Katie's total utility from pizzas, which appeared in Fig. 7.3, appears here as the right-hand yellow line. It shows that as Katie's consumption of pizzas increases, so does the total utility she gets from pizzas. Katie's indifference curve for pizzas and wine is also visible, and in both parts of the figure. It appears as the blue line in part (b). It can also be seen in part (a). There it appears as a contour line on a map that shows the height of the terrain. Viewed in this way, an indifference curve can be interpreted as a contour line that measures equal levels of total utility.

We can work either with total utility curves, as we did in Chapter 7, or with indifference curves, as we did in Chapter 8. They each give the same answers. There are, though, some interesting differences between the two theories.

Utility and Indifference Curves

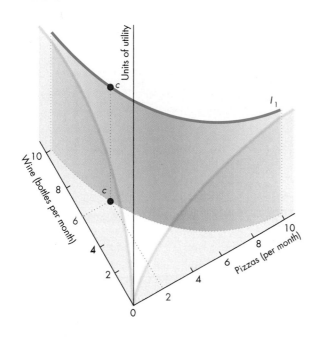

(a) Total utility from pizzas and wine

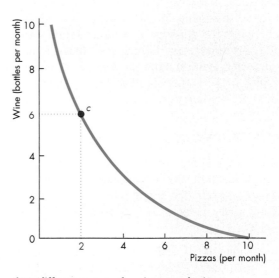

(b) Indifference curve for pizzas and wine

We can represent preferences in two ways: by using total utility curves or indifference curves. These two methods are different ways of looking at the same thing. Part (a) shows the total utility received from wine when no pizzas are consumed (the left-hand yellow curve) and the total utility received from pizzas when no wine is consumed (the right-hand yellow curve). It also shows an indifference curve that tells us the combinations of wine and pizzas that give equal (constant) total utility – the blue curve.

Part (b) shows an indifference curve for pizzas and wine. You can see that it is exactly the same as the indifference curve in part (a). Point *c* in part (a) is exactly the same as point *c* in part (b). The indifference curve in part (b) is what you would see if you looked straight down on top of the three-dimensional diagram shown in part (a).

Maximizing Utility and Choosing the Best Affordable Point

According to marginal utility theory, the consumer maximizes utility by dividing the available income among different goods and services so that the marginal utility per pound spent on each is equal. In Katie's case, she maximizes utility by making the marginal utility of a pound spent on pizzas equal to the marginal utility of a pound spent on wine. Her choice of pizzas and wine satisfies the following equation:

$$\frac{\text{Marginal utility of pizzas}}{\text{Price of pizzas}} = \frac{\text{Marginal utility of wine}}{\text{Price of wine}}$$

In the indifference curve theory, the best consumption point is chosen by making the marginal rate of substitution between the two goods equal to their relative price. In terms of our example, Katie makes her marginal rate of substitution of pizzas for wine equal to the relative price of pizzas in terms of wine.

That is, her choice of pizzas and wine satisfies the following:

$$\text{Marginal rate of substitution} = \frac{\text{Price of pizzas}}{\text{Price of wine}}$$

In Chapter 8, we learned how to calculate the marginal rate of substitution as the magnitude of the slope of the indifference curve. The marginal rate of substitution is, therefore, the absolute value of the ratio of the change in the quantity of wine to the change in the quantity of pizzas, such that Katie remains indifferent. 'Indifference' in the indifference curve theory means the same thing as 'constant total utility' in the marginal utility theory. The two situations that derive the same utility are two situations between which Katie is indifferent. The marginal rate of substitution, therefore, is the absolute value of the ratio of the change in the consumption of wine to the change in the consumption of pizzas, holding total utility constant. But, according to the utility theory, when consumption changes total utility changes. Total utility, in fact, changes in accordance with the following equation:

$$\begin{array}{ll}\text{Change in} \\ \text{total utility}\end{array} = \begin{array}{l}\text{Marginal utility of pizzas} \times \Delta Q_p \\ + \text{Marginal utility of wine} \times \Delta Q_w\end{array}$$

where Δ stands for 'change in'. If Katie is indifferent, the change in total utility must be zero, so

$$\begin{array}{l}\text{Marginal utility} \\ \text{of wine}\end{array} \times \Delta Q_w = - \begin{array}{l}\text{Marginal utility} \\ \text{of pizzas}\end{array} \times \Delta Q_p .$$

If we divide both sides of the above equation by ΔQ_p, and both sides by the marginal utility of wine, we get

$$\frac{\Delta Q_w}{\Delta Q_p} = \frac{-\text{Marginal utility of pizzas}}{-\text{Marginal utility of wine}} .$$

We've just calculated the change in wine divided by the change in pizzas, while holding total utility constant or, equivalently, while staying on an indifference curve. Therefore the absolute value of this ratio is the marginal rate of substitution. That is,

$$\begin{array}{l}\text{Marginal rate} \\ \text{of substitution}\end{array} = \frac{\text{Marginal utility of pizzas}}{\text{Marginal utility of wine}} .$$

You are now ready to see directly the connection between the two theories. The utility theory says that

Katie chooses her consumption of pizzas and wine to ensure that

$$\frac{\begin{array}{l}\text{Marginal utility} \\ \text{of pizzas}\end{array}}{\text{Price of pizzas}} = \frac{\text{Marginal utility of wine}}{\text{Marginal price of wine}} .$$

The indifference curve theory says that Katie chooses her consumption of pizzas and wine to ensure that

$$\begin{array}{l}\text{Marginal rate} \\ \text{of substitution}\end{array} = \frac{\text{Marginal utility of pizzas}}{\text{Marginal utility of wine}} .$$

Substituting for the marginal rate of substitution in terms of marginal utilities, we get

$$\frac{\text{Marginal utility of pizza}}{\text{Marginal utility of wine}} = \frac{\text{Price of pizzas}}{\text{Price of wine}} .$$

All that you now have to do is to notice that you can manipulate the marginal utility condition by dividing both sides by the marginal utility of wine and multiplying both sides by the price of pizzas. Thus you end up with exactly the same equation that the indifference curve theory uses to characterize the consumer's best affordable choice.

Equivalently, you can go the other way and start with the indifference curve equation. Multiply both sides by the marginal utility of wine and divide both sides by the price of pizzas and you arrive at the condition for maximizing utility. Thus the condition for maximizing utility, according to the marginal utility theory, and the condition for choosing the best affordable consumption point, according to the indifference curve theory, are equivalent to each other.

Differences between the Theories

The key difference between the two models of consumer choice is that the indifference curve approach does not require us to use the concept of utility. We merely have to talk about preferences between different pairs of goods. We have to say whether the consumer prefers one combination to another or is indifferent between the two combinations. We don't have to say anything about *how* the consumer makes such evaluations. Although the indifference curve theory does not require the concept of utility, as we've seen, it is not inconsistent with marginal utility theory.

CHAPTER 9

ORGANIZING
PRODUCTION

After studying this chapter you will be able to:

◆ Explain what a firm is and describe the economic problems that all firms face

◆ Describe and distinguish between different forms of business organization

◆ Describe the main ways in which firms raise the finance for their operations

◆ Calculate and distinguish between a firm's historical costs and its opportunity costs

◆ Define technological efficiency and economic efficiency and distinguish between them

◆ Explain why firms solve some economic problems while markets solve others

IN 1976, ANITA RODDICK TOOK OUT A £4,000 LOAN AND OPENED THE FIRST BODY Shop. Twelve years later she opened the 322nd Body Shop and was launching into the United States. By then she had stores in many countries and ran an empire with an annual turnover of £28.5 million. Her chain of natural cosmetics stores has created over 3,000 jobs in the United Kingdom and many more overseas. Another spectacular growth story is that of Apple Computer. Apple began its life with Steven Jobs and Stephen Wozniak, two students at Stanford University in the United States, who worked in a garage. They bought a few components and produced the world's first commercially successful personal computer, the Apple. From that modest start, Apple Computer has grown into a giant. ◆ ◆ Two-thirds of all firms are operated by their owners, as Body Shop and Apple once were. But

An Apple a Day

companies, like Body Shop and Apple today, account for about 90 per cent of all business sales. What are the different forms a firm can take? Why are most firms owner-operated, while most business is undertaken by companies? ◆ ◆ The market is an amazing mechanism for coordinating the economic actions of millions of individuals. Firms are another type of coordination mechanism. Why do firms coordinate some activities and markets others? Why don't people simply buy everything they need from each other in markets?

◆ ◆ ◆ ◆ In this chapter we are going to learn about the many different types of firms, but we'll understand better the behaviour of all firms if we focus first on the things they have in common.

The Firm and Its Economic Problem

The 2.5 million firms in the United Kingdom differ enormously in size, in what they do and in their survival power. What do they have in common? What is the distinguishing characteristic of a firm? What are the different ways in which firms are organized? Why are there different forms of organization? These are the questions that we will tackle first.

What is a Firm?

A **firm** is an institution that buys or hires inputs and *organizes* them to produce and sell its output. Its inputs include the factors of production – that is, labour, land and capital – along with intermediate products, such as raw materials, that are bought from other firms and used up in production. Its output may be goods or services. To organize production, a firm enters into a wide range of relationships with a large number of individuals and other firms.

One of these relationships is that between the firm and its owner (or owners), for a firm has a separate legal identity from the individuals who own it. For example, if you buy a share in ICI, you are one of the owners of that company and your relationship with the company will define your rights to vote for the directors and say how much of the profits will be distributed to shareholders.

Another relationship is that between a firm and its employees. For example, if you get a job at ICI as a deputy plant manager, you are an employee of the company and your relationship with the company will define your obligations to perform certain tasks and the remuneration you will receive in return.

A firm also has relationships with other firms. For example, if you run an advertising company and get a contract with ICI to advertise its paint, your relationship with ICI defines your agreement to perform a specific service for a specific price.

Principal–Agent Relationships

The relationships between a firm and its owners, employees and other firms are called **agency relationships**. In an agency relationship an *agent* undertakes an action which affects a *principal*. An

agent is person (or firm) hired by a firm (or by another person) to do a specified job. A **principal** is a firm (or a person) that hires a person (or firm) to undertake a specified job. For example, as a shareholder of ICI, you are a principal and the directors are your agents. Your profit depends on how good a job the managers do. As a deputy plant manager for ICI, your plant manager is a principal and you are an agent. Your performance determines whether the plant works efficiently, so helping the plant manager to meet the operating targets laid down for him or her by more senior managers. As the advertising expert, you are also an agent and ICI is the principal. ICI wants many people to know about its paint, but it's the quality of your work which determines how many people notice the advertisements.

The Firm's Decisions

Firms exist because of scarcity. They enable us to get more out of our scarce resources than would be possible without the relationships they use in organizing production. But each firm has to solve its own economic problem. That is, each firm has to get the most it can out of the scarce resources under its control. To do so, a firm has to decide on the following:

◆ What goods and services to produce and in what quantities
◆ Which inputs to use and in what quantities
◆ Which techniques of production to use
◆ How to organize its management structure

A firm's income from the sale of goods and services that it produces is called its *total revenue*. The total expenditure made by a firm on its inputs is called its *total cost*. The difference between a firm's total revenue and total cost is its *profit* (if revenue exceeds cost) or its *loss* (if cost exceeds revenue). A firm's total revenue, total cost and profits (or losses) are obviously affected by the choices that a firm makes to solve its economic problem.

The goal of a firm's owners is to make the largest possible profit. But running a firm is not just a matter of giving orders and getting them obeyed. In most firms, it isn't possible for the shareholders to monitor the managers or even for the managers to monitor all the other employees and all the other firms which supply it with goods and services. To achieve their goal, the firm's owners (principals) must induce its managers (agents) to pursue the maximum possible profit. And the managers (principals) must induce the other employees and other firms (agents) to work efficiently. Each principal attempts to do this by creating incentives that induce each agent to work in the interests of the firm. For example, managers often share in a firm's profits, and other employees get bonuses for meeting production targets.

But the perfect incentive scheme does not exist. Managers pursue their own goals and so do other employees. None the less, firms constantly strive to find ways of improving performance and increasing profits.

Although all firms face common problems, they do not solve their problems in the same way. In particular, the management structure and the arrangements for compensating factors of production vary from firm to firm and lead to different forms of business organization. Let's look at these different forms.

The Forms of Business Organization

There are three main forms of business organization:

◆ Sole proprietorship
◆ Partnership
◆ Company

Which form a firm takes influences its management structure, how it compensates its factors of production and how much tax the firm and its owners have to pay. It also affects who receives the firm's profits and who is liable for its debts if it has to go out of business.

Sole Proprietorship Most firms are sole proprietorships. Examples of sole proprietors are found in many farms, restaurants and shops. A **sole proprietorship** is a firm with a single owner – a sole proprietor – though it may have many employees. The owner has unlimited liability. **Unlimited liability** is the legal responsibility for all the debts of a firm up to an amount equal to the entire wealth of the owner. Suppose Mr Patel sets up a grocery shop with the help of a £10,000 loan from a bank and uses some of this money to pay one month's advance rent on a shop and the rest to buy fruit and vegetables. He takes on one assistant and together with this assistant works in the shop for one day selling produce for £500. Mr Patel deposits this sum in his bank on the way home. Then on the second day Mr Patel is taken ill and his assistant decides to resign.

When Mr Patel returns to the shop at the end·of the month the grocery produce is too old to sell. He has no ready money to pay another month's rent so he decides to wind up the business. He has to repay £10,000 to the bank, but the only money in the firm's bank account is the first day's takings of £500. So by law Mr Patel must sell personal property – maybe his furniture, car or even his house – until he has paid off the firm's debts. The only way he can pay less is if his personal wealth is too small.

The management structure of a sole proprietorship is very simple. Its owner makes all the management decisions. The sole proprietor is also the firm's only residual claimant. A firm's **residual claimant** is the agent (or agents) who receives the firm's profits and who is responsible for its losses.

The profits of a sole proprietorship are treated as the income of the proprietor. They are added to any other income that he or she has – for instance from interest on a bank deposit or shares in a company – and are taxed as personal income. The sole proprietorship does not pay taxes in its own right. Profits are taxed just once, when the owner receives them.

Partnership Partnerships are the second most common type of business organization. Most estate agents, solicitors and accountants work in businesses that are partnerships. A **partnership** is a firm with two or more owners who have unlimited liability. Generally partnerships are forbidden to have over 20 partners, but exceptions can be made. A partnership has a more complicated management structure than a sole proprietorship. The partners must agree on an appropriate management structure and on how to run the firm. They also must agree on how to divide the firm's profits between themselves.

As in a sole proprietorship, the profits of a partnership are taxed as the personal income of the owners. But each partner is legally liable for all the debts of the partnership. For example, suppose that Amanda and Neil graduate in law and decide to set up as practising solicitors in a new partnership. They borrow £10,000 from a bank to pay one month's advance rent on office space and to hire a secretary. Unfortunately they attract no customers so at the end of the month they decide to wind up the business. Amanda goes round to Neil's flat to ask him how much of the £10,000 he can repay from his personal wealth – but Neil has vanished! Unless Amanda can also vanish – or find Neil and force him to pay something – she will have to pay all the £10,000 herself (or at least as much as she can given her own wealth). Liability for the full debts of the partnership is called **joint unlimited liability**.

Companies Companies are the best known types of business organizations, though they are not the most common. Whitbread the brewers and Pilkington the glass manufacturers are examples of companies. Many companies, such as ICI, Shell and Honda, are multinational giants.

A **company** is a firm owned by two or more shareholders who have limited liability. **Limited liability** means the owners have legal liability only for the value of their financial investment; we will see shortly what that means. Shareholders in a company own ordinary shares which are each a title to the ownership of a fraction of a company. Usually ordinary shares are simply called shares. Suppose Donald and Glenda leave college as qualified engineers and decide to set up a company making cheese-flavoured ice-creams. They need £10,000 to get going. So they borrow £5,000 from a bank and raise the remaining £5,000 by selling 5,000 shares at £1 each. They may buy some shares themselves and sell the others to anyone they can persuade to buy – probably friends and relatives. Shares in small companies like theirs can usually be bought and sold only by mutual agreement between the shareholders. Such companies are called private companies. In contrast, most large companies are public companies whose shares can be bought and sold on stock markets such as the London Stock Exchange.

The management structures of companies vary enormously. Some companies are no bigger than a typical sole proprietorship and have one main owner who makes all the decisions. Large companies have elaborate management arrangements. Typically, they have a board of directors who are elected by the shareholders – with each share attracting one vote. The directors then usually elect a chairman to be in overall charge, though some companies have a chairman who is really a figurehead, in which case there is also a managing director in overall charge. Below the board there are usually senior executives responsible for areas such as production, finance, marketing and perhaps research. These senior executives are in turn served by a series of specialists and sub-specialists.

The company receives much of the money it needs to get going from its owners – the shareholders. The firm's profits belong to its owners, the shareholders.

The shareholders can decide to have some of the profits distributed between themselves as dividends and to have the rest kept by the company, either to finance expansion or to set aside so that dividends can be paid in future even if profits fall. So the shareholders get some reward from dividends. They also hope to get a reward by seeing rises in the market price – that is, the second-hand value – of their shares. Companies also raise some money by borrowing.

As long as a company makes profits, the residual claimants to those profits are its shareholders. If a company incurs losses on such a scale that it becomes bankrupt, the residual loss is absorbed by the banks and other people who have lent money to the company. The shareholders themselves, having limited liability, can lose no more than the value of their investment. For example, suppose that at the end of their first month of operation Donald and Glenda find that sales have been only £1,000 so they decide to wind the business up. The bank demands repayment of its loan of £5,000, but Donald and Glenda point out that the only money in the firm's bank account is the £1,000 from its sales. This may be augmented by, say, £500 as a result of selling off the company's ice-cream-making machine as scrap metal. That still leaves £3,500 worth of unrepaid loan, but, because the firm was a company with its liability limited to the assets of the firm, the law says that the bank will have to absorb this loss. Donald and Glenda and the other shareholders will not get any money back from the company – unless by chance the machine raises more than £4,000 so that the company has more than enough funds to repay the bank. But at least no one can force Donald, Glenda or any of the other shareholders to sell any of their private property – liability is limited to what the shareholders have invested in the company.

The government taxes the profits of a company independently of the incomes of its shareholders. In the United Kingdom, the tax on company profits is called **corporation tax** which is levied on most companies at a rate of 33 per cent. Some of the remaining profits are paid as dividends and the shareholders are, in principle, liable for personal income tax on these dividends. However, because the profits have already been taxed, the government allows shareholders to regard their dividends as having already been taxed for personal income tax, although it assumes that the profits have only been taxed at the lowest rate of personal income tax which is 20 per cent. So shareholders who pay personal income tax at higher rates have to pay more tax on their dividends.

It is important to see that the profits earned by companies really belong to their shareholders and are, typically, taxed more heavily than the profits earned by sole proprietorships and partners. For if the owners of a sole proprietorship or a partnership pay income tax at the lowest rate, they will pay tax at 20 per cent on their profits, so the government effectively receives 20 per cent of the firm's profits. But if all the shareholders of a company pay income tax at the lowest rate, the government will receive 33 per cent of the company's profits as it will take this much in corporation tax.

Other Types of Firms

Although most firms are sole proprietorships, partnerships or companies, there are three other less common types of firms – non-profit-making firms, cooperatives and nationalized industries.

A **non-profit-making** firm is an organization that is set up by a group of people on the understanding that they will not receive any profits from it. Examples include universities and colleges, independent schools, churches and some insurance companies. These firms usually seek only to raise enough revenue to cover their costs. If they raise more than enough revenue, then the excess – which is called a surplus rather than a profit – is retained to help meet costs incurred in the future. In general, these organizations do not pay corporation tax and have unlimited liability. If they defaulted on repaying on a loan, then liability would lie with those who have been appointed or elected to run them.

A **cooperative** is owned by a group of people with a common objective who collectively share in its profits. There are two main groups of cooperatives. The best known are the retail cooperative societies which were set up following a successful experiment in Rochdale in 1844. Essentially, these shops belong to any of their customers who are prepared to pay a minimum amount to become owners. The owners may be rewarded in various ways including occasional cash bonuses. The other type of cooperative is a producers' cooperative which is owned by the people who work there. Such firms are rare and usually small. It is perhaps helpful to regard all cooperatives as unusual sorts of companies that are owned by members rather than by shareholders. For, like other companies, cooperatives have limited liability and are liable for corporation tax.

A **nationalized industry** is a firm that is publicly owned and operated under government supervision. Some of the best known nationalized industries were 'privatized' during Mrs Thatcher's period as prime minister. These included British Airways, British Gas, British Telecom, the English and Welsh water boards and the electricity companies. Four examples of surviving nationalized firms are British Coal, the Post Office, the Bank of England and the companies that British Rail was divided into in 1994. As with cooperatives, it is perhaps helpful to regard nationalized industries as special sorts of companies in which all the shares are owned by the government, for, like other companies, nationalized industries have limited liability and have to pay corporation tax.

The Relative Importance of the Different Types of Firms

In the United Kingdom sole proprietorships are the most numerous form of business while companies are the least numerous. But while only about a third of firms are companies, companies account for about 90 per cent of total turnover.

Sole proprietorships are particularly important in agriculture and fishing, and they are quite important in construction and retailing. Partnerships are common in the law and other professions such as accountancy and estate agents, and, like sole proprietorships, they are also important in agriculture, fishing, construction, retailing and catering. Companies are important in all sectors and have manufacturing almost to themselves.

Why do companies dominate the business scene? And if they have some special advantages, why do other forms of organization, such as sole proprietorships and partnerships, survive? The answer to these questions lies in the pros and cons of the various different forms of business organization.

Since each of the three main types of firms exists in large numbers, each type obviously has advantages in particular situations. Each type also has its disadvantages, which explains why it has not driven out the other two. Table 9.1 summarizes the pros and cons of each type of firm.

TABLE **9.1**

The Pros and Cons of Different Types of Firms

Type of firm	Pros	Cons
Sole proprietorship	◆ Easy to set up ◆ Simple decision-making ◆ Profits taxed only once as owner's income	◆ Bad decisions not checked by need for consensus ◆ Owner's entire wealth at risk ◆ Firm dies with owner ◆ Capital is expensive ◆ Labour is expensive
Partnership	◆ Easy to set up ◆ Diversified decision-making ◆ Can survive withdrawal of partner ◆ Profits taxed only once as owners' incomes	◆ Achieving consensus may be slow and expensive ◆ Owners' entire wealth at risk ◆ Withdrawal of partner may create capital shortage ◆ Capital is expensive
Company	◆ Owners have limited liability ◆ Large-scale, low-cost capital available ◆ Professional management not restricted by abilities of owners ◆ Perpetual life ◆ Long-term labour contracts can cut labour costs	◆ Complex management structure can make decisions slow and expensive ◆ Profits bear corporation tax which is at a higher rate than the standard rate of income tax

How Firms Raise Money

In principle a firm might manage without owning any land or capital if it used only rented land, rented buildings, and hired plant, vehicles and machinery. But in practice all firms use some assets that belong to the firm. It is the responsibility of the owners of firms to see that enough money is available to purchase these assets. In essence, firms acquire some of the money they need from their owners and borrow whatever else they require. Broadly speaking, the result is that sole proprietorships and partnerships can raise far less money than companies, which means that there is a much lower limit on the size of sole proprietorships and partnerships than there is on companies.

There are two reasons why sole proprietorships and partnerships find it hard to raise the huge sums that companies can raise. First, the limited number of owners usually places a modest limit on the amount that the owners can provide themselves. Second, sole proprietorships and partnerships often have limited lifespans which tends to restrict the extent to which they can borrow, at least on a long-term basis.

Companies need not suffer from either of these problems. If they need extra money, they can often secure huge sums from their owners, of whom there may be very many. Also, their perpetual life makes it much easier for them to obtain long-term loans. Taken together, these factors enable companies such as airlines and oil companies to raise hundreds of millions of pounds to buy new jets and to build North Sea drilling rigs and oil refineries.

When companies borrow, they may borrow from banks or other financial businesses. Alternatively they may issue items which used usually to be called debentures but which are now usually called bonds. When they raise money from their owners they issue shares. Let's take a look at debentures, bonds and shares.

Selling Debentures or Bonds   A **debenture** or **bond** is a piece of paper which carries an obligation by a company to pay specified sums of money at specified future dates. Usually a company bond specifies that a certain sum of money called the redemption value of the bond will be paid at a certain future date called the redemption date. In addition, another sum will be paid each year between the date of issue of the bond and the redemption date. The sum of money paid each year is called the interest payment.

Bonds provide a company with medium- and long-term financing at a predictable and guaranteed cost. Bonds are attractive to purchasers because of the security they provide. Just as they give the company predictable interest costs, so they provide the investor with predictable interest income. But bonds are risky things to buy in the sense that if a company goes bankrupt it may not be able to pay the bondholders. Nevertheless, if a company does go bankrupt, then any money realized by selling its assets must be used to pay the bondholders – and anyone else who has lent money to the company – before anything is paid to the shareholders.

Issuing Shares   There are three main types of company shares:

◆ Ordinary shares
◆ Preference shares
◆ Convertible shares

Ordinary shares entitle their holders to vote at shareholders' meetings and to participate in the election of directors. The holders of ordinary shares are the true owners of a company and the money which a company has raised by selling ordinary shares is called its *equity capital.* The owners of ordinary shares hope to get a dividend each year, and they hope that the amount of dividend will tend to grow from year to year. However, the amount of dividend they get is generally decided by the directors and depends on how well the firm is doing. In bad years there may be no dividend at all.

Preference shares are much more like bonds than ordinary shares. Usually their holders are entitled to a fixed rate of interest – though the payments are rather unhelpfully called dividends – and have few if any voting rights. The holders of preference shares stand before holders of ordinary shares but after bondholders if the company cannot meet all its obligations.

Convertible shares are like bonds and preference shares in that their holders receive fixed interest payments. In addition, though, the holders have the right to convert their convertible shares into ordinary shares at some future specified date.

Millions of shares have been issued. Most companies are relatively small and their shares are traded privately. But the large well-known companies have thousands of shareholders and their shares are traded on stock exchanges. A **stock exchange** is an organized market for trading in securities such as shares and bonds. The United Kingdom has over 20 stock exchanges, but the London Stock Exchange is by far the biggest. With computers and advanced electronic communications, many UK citizens also trade on the major stock exchanges in New York, Tokyo and elsewhere. Share prices on these stock exchanges fluctuate daily. What causes them to rise and fall? There are two main factors.

The first factor that affects share prices is the rate of interest that investors can obtain by depositing their money with banks or lending it, perhaps by lending it to the government or by buying company bonds. If interest rates on these alternative investments rise, shares seem relatively less attractive and their prices fall. So when interest rates rise – or indeed even when they are expected to rise – you may reasonably expect to hear that share prices have fallen. Equally, share prices tend to rise when interest rates fall or are expected to fall.

To understand the second factor that affects share prices, suppose interest rates are unchanged for many months. We will not find that share prices remain constant. Some share prices will rise, some will be stable and some will fall. These fluctuations will result from changes in the expected future performance of individual companies. More precisely, the price people will pay for the shares in any particular company depends on the dividends they expect it to earn.

Suppose that on the shares of one company the dividend is zero and is expected to be zero forever. In this case, the value of the shares will be exactly zero! Nobody would pay even 1 penny for a piece of paper which they expected to entitle them to zero dividends for ever. But as soon as a company is expected to pay some dividends, its shares will attract a price on the stock exchange. Whenever investors expect a company's dividends to rise, the share price will rise, and whenever they expect its dividends to fall, the share price will tend to fall. Of course, investors do not know future dividend levels for sure, they can only estimate them, and their estimates can change. These changing expectations cause share prices to fluctuate dramatically. Because companies pay dividends out of their profits, news about a firm's profitability can change investors' expectations of its future dividends.

A firm is an institution that uses inputs to produce outputs. There are three main types of firm: sole proprietorships, partnerships and companies. Each has its advantages and disadvantages as summarized in Table 9.1. Firms raise money from their owners and by borrowing. Companies have access to more funds than sole proprietorships and partnerships. ◆

Costs and Profits

C osts are the payments made by a firm for the services of its inputs. There are two ways of measuring costs: the accountant's way and the economist's way.

Accountants measure historical cost. **Historical cost** values inputs at the prices actually paid for them. Economists measure opportunity costs. *Opportunity costs* are the best alternatives forgone. For you, the opportunity cost of a cup of tea is bar of chocolate, if that is the best alternative forgone. Likewise, a restaurant may reckon that the opportunity cost of some sprouts is the beans that it could have bought instead, if beans are the best alternative forgone.

Although an opportunity cost is something real, it is often convenient to talk about the pound equivalent of opportunity costs. So we say that for you the opportunity cost of a 25 pence cup of tea is 25 pence because 25 pence is the spending power you sacrificed to buy the tea. Likewise, the opportunity cost of £10 worth of sprouts is £10 as that is the spending power sacrificed by the restaurant to buy the sprouts. Although we often value opportunity cost in terms of pounds, we must not lose sight of the fact that such a measure is just a convenience.

This method of using pounds is especially convenient when we calculate the costs of firms. What we're really asking is: what was given up to produce this good? But we use pounds as a convenient unit of accounting.

Historical cost equals opportunity cost when a firm uses up an input soon after paying for it. Historical cost is the amount of money paid for that input. The opportunity cost (expressed in pounds) is also this amount of money. Thus for a restaurant, the opportunity cost (expressed in pounds) of £10 worth of sprouts is £10, just as for you, the opportunity cost of a 25 pence cup of tea is 25 pence. Labour is the most important input whose historical cost typically equals its opportunity cost.

Historical costs and opportunity costs may differ for two reasons:

◆ When a firm pays for an input but uses it some time later
◆ When a firm uses an input for which it has not paid

Let's look at these in turn.

Pay Now, Use Later

Inputs that are not used up in a single production period are called **durable inputs**. When a firm uses a durable input, it usually pays for it long before it finishes using it. For example, a furniture factory buys a new lathe and then uses it over a period of a few years. Similarly, it may carry stocks of timber and semifinished products that it uses over a long period. What is the opportunity cost of using capital equipment bought several years earlier? What is the opportunity cost of taking items from stocks? Let's explore these questions by looking first at buildings, plant and machinery costs and then at stock costs.

Buildings, Plant and Machinery Costs

There are two components to the cost of buildings, plant and machinery:

◆ Depreciation
◆ Interest

Let's look at these costs and see how accountants measure them. Then we'll see how economists measure them.

Depreciation   The fall in the value of a durable input over a given period of time is **depreciation**. Accountants assess this fall in value by applying a conventional depreciation rate to the original purchase price. For industrial plant, a common depreciation allowance is 10 per cent a year. So if a firm builds an assembly line for £100,000, an accountant regards 10 per cent of that amount,

£10,000, as a cost of production in the first year and in each of the following nine years. In the eleventh year, and any subsequent year, the accountant assumes that the depreciation cost is nil as it is assumed that the plant is worthless by then! The accountant uses different depreciation rates for different types of inputs. Ten per cent is common for plant, but higher rates are used for vehicles and lower rates for buildings.

Interest If a firm borrows money to buy a building, plant or machinery, the accountant counts the interest on the borrowing as a cost of production. So, in this case, if the firm borrows the entire £100,000 and if the interest rate is 10 per cent a year, the accountant treats the £10,000 interest payment as a cost of production. If the firm has not borrowed anything to build the factory but has instead used retained profits from earlier years, its own previously earned profits, the accountant regards the interest cost incurred in production as zero.

Next, let's see how economists measure depreciation and interest costs to assess the cost of buildings, plant and machinery. We will see how they use opportunity costs.

Economists and Depreciation The change in the market price of a durable input over a given period is **economic depreciation**. For example, economic depreciation over a year is calculated as the market price of the input at the beginning of the year minus its market price at the end of the year. The original cost of the equipment is not directly relevant to this calculation. The equipment could have been sold at the beginning of the year for the market price then prevailing. The opportunity cost of keeping the equipment, therefore, is the value lost by not selling it. If a firm has kept the equipment for a year and used it, the difference between its market prices at the beginning and the end of the year tells us how much of its value has been used up as a result of keeping it for use in production.

A situation sometimes arises in which a firm has bought some capital equipment and the equipment is in place and functioning well but has no resale value. An example of this situation is a railway tunnel. No one wants a railway tunnel, except the railway company, so its resale value is zero. What is the opportunity cost of using the tunnel? The answer is zero, as nothing is lost by not selling it. Accountants call the cost of buying such equipment a sunk cost. A **sunk cost** is the historical cost of buying buildings, plant and machinery that have no current resale value.

Economists and Interest Costs The other cost of using durable inputs is interest. Whether a firm borrows to buy its plant, buildings and machinery, or whether it uses previously earned profits to pay for them, makes no difference to the opportunity cost of the funds tied up in its productive assets. If the firm borrows the money, then it makes an interest payment. (That's the payment the accountant picks up using the historical cost method.) If the firm uses its own funds, then the opportunity cost is the amount that could have been earned by using those funds for something else. A firm could always sell the equipment at the beginning of the year and use the funds from the sale for some other purpose. For example, the firm could put the money in the bank and earn interest, and this interest forgone is the opportunity cost of the funds tied up in equipment that has been bought out of retained profits. So, the economist's measure of the interest cost of a durable input – its opportunity cost – is the value of the input at the beginning of the year multiplied by the current year's interest rate.

Interest Costs and Inflation Inflation complicates the calculation of opportunity cost. To avoid being misled by inflation, economists measure the opportunity costs of the inputs used in a particular year in terms of the prices prevailing in that year. Suppose that in 1988 a firm used some retained profits to buy some plant for £100,000. If interest rates then were around 12 per cent, the opportunity cost of using those profits, in terms of interest forgone, was £12,000 in 1988. Suppose that this plant was reckoned to lose half its value in five years, what was the opportunity cost of the plant in 1993 in terms of interest forgone? It might be supposed economists would reckon that the plant could be sold then for £50,000, so that they would work out how much interest could be earned on £50,000 at 1993 interest rates which were around 7 per cent. This approach would suggest an opportunity cost of £3,500 (7 per cent of £50,000). But in fact inflation took place between 1988 and 1993, so that in 1993 comparable new plant might cost £120,000. In this case, the second-hand value of the plant in 1993 is

£60,000, and the opportunity cost of the plant in terms of interest forgone is 7 per cent of that, which is £4,200. As a result of the high inflation rates of the 1970s and early 1980s, accountants, too, have begun to pay attention to the distortions that inflation can cause in measuring historical cost and in comparing costs between one year and another.

Implicit Rental Rate   To measure the opportunity cost of using plant, buildings and machinery, we calculate the sum of economic depreciation and interest costs. Another way of looking at this opportunity cost is as the income that the firm forgoes by not renting its assets out to another firm and instead renting the assets to itself. When a firm rents assets to itself, it pays an **implicit rental rate** for their use. You are familiar with the idea of renting equipment. People commonly rent homes, cars, televisions and videotapes; firms commonly rent diggers and cranes and so on. When someone rents a piece of equipment, that person pays an *explicit* rent. When an owner uses a piece of equipment rather than renting it out, the economist notes that the owner could have rented the equipment out instead. By not doing so, owners *implicitly* rent from themselves. Another term that is sometimes used to describe an implicit cost or rent is 'imputed cost'. An **imputed cost** is an opportunity cost that does not require an actual expenditure of cash.

Now let's examine the costs of stocks.

Stock Costs

Stocks are stores of raw materials, semifinished goods and finished goods held by firms. Some firms have small stocks or stocks that turn over very quickly. In such cases, the accountant's historical cost and the economist's opportunity cost are the same. But when a production process requires stocks to be held for a long time, the two measurements differ, possibly in important ways.

Historical Cost Measures of Stocks   To measure the cost of using stocks, accountants usually use a historical cost method called FIFO, which stands for 'First In, First Out'. This measure assumes, as a convenient fiction, that the first item placed into the stock – that is, the item which has been in the stock the longest – will be the first item to come out – that is, it will be the one removed when some-

one next takes an item out. An alternative accountant's measure that is occasionally used is called LIFO, which stands for 'Last In, First Out'. If prices have been constant, then the price of the 'first in' item and the 'last in' item will be the same, and each price will be the same as the price that must now be paid to replace the item taken from the stock. So each price gives the opportunity cost of taking something from the stock. But if prices have been changing, LIFO gets closer to the opportunity cost than FIFO.

Opportunity Cost Measures   The opportunity cost of using an item taken from stock is its current replacement cost. If an item is taken out of stock, it will have to be replaced by a new item. The cost of that new item is the opportunity cost of using the stock.

Inputs Not Paid For

A firm's owners often use their own inputs so that the firm doesn't directly pay for these inputs. But although they are not paid for, these inputs do have opportunity costs. Let's see what they are.

Owners' Labour   Ordinary shareholders seldom work for the companies which they partly own, and if by chance they do work for a company in which they own shares, they are paid a wage by the firm. In contrast, the owners of sole proprietorships and partnerships often put a great deal of time and effort into working for their firm but rarely take an explicit wage payment for this work. Instead, these owners withdraw money from the business to meet their living expenses. Accountants regard such withdrawals of money as part of the profits of the business and not as part of the firms' costs. But really these withdrawals are the costs incurred by firms for the time of their owners. The owners could have worked at some other activities and earned wages. The opportunity cost of the owners' time is the income forgone by the owners by not working in the best alternative jobs.

Patents, Trademarks and Names   Many firms have patents, trademarks or names that have come to be associated with quality, reliability, service or some other desirable characteristic. Sometimes firms have acquired these things by their own past efforts. In other cases, they have bought them. A firm always has the option of selling its patents, trademarks or name to other firms.

In calculating historical cost, these items are ignored unless the firm actually bought them. But they have an opportunity cost regardless of whether or not they were bought. The opportunity cost of a firm's patents, trademarks or name used in this year's production is the change in their market value – the change in the best price for which they could be sold. If their value falls over the year, there is an additional opportunity cost of production. If their value rises, there is a negative opportunity cost, or a reduction in the opportunity cost of production.

The Bottom Line

What does all this add up to? Is the historical measure of cost higher or lower than the opportunity cost measure? And what about the bottom line – the profit or loss of the firm? Does the accountant come up with the same answer as the economist or is there a difference in the measurement of profit as well?

A firm's profit is the difference between its total revenue and its total cost. There is no difference in the accountant's measure and the economist's measure of a firm's receipts or total revenue. However, their measures of cost generally differ. Opportunity cost generally includes more things than historical cost, so the historical measure of cost understates the opportunity cost of production. Thus profit, as measured by economists, is generally lower than profit as measured by accountants. **Economic profit** is total revenue minus total costs, when the opportunity costs of production are included in cost.

To see how this works out, let's look at an example. Dawson owns a shop that sells mountain bikes. His total revenue, total costs and profit appear in Table 9.2, with the historical view on the left-hand side

TABLE 9.2

Dawson's Mountain Bikes' Revenue, Cost and Profit Statement

The accountant		The economist	
Item	Amount (£)	Item	Amount (£)
Total revenue	300,000	Total revenue	300,000
Costs:		Costs:	
Wholesale cost of bikes	150,000	Wholesale cost of bikes	150,000
Rates, heating & other services	20,000	Rates, heating & other services	20,000
Wages	50,000	Wages	50,000
Bank interest	12,000	Bank interest	12,000
Depreciation	22,000	Economic depreciation[1]	10,000
		Dawson's wages (imputed)[2]	40,000
		Interest on Dawson's money invested in firm (imputed)[3]	11,500
Total costs	254,000	Total costs	293,500
Profit	46,000	Profit	6,500

Notes

1 The fall in the market value of the firm's assets. It is the opportunity cost of not selling the assets one year ago, and is part of the opportunity cost of using them for the year covered by the table.

2 Dawson worked 2,000 hours on the firm's business. He could have worked elsewhere for £20 an hour, which means that the opportunity cost of his time was £40,000.

3 Dawson has invested £115,000 in the firm. If the current rate of interest is 10 per cent a year, the opportunity cost of those funds is £11,500.

and the economic view on the right-hand side.

Dawson sold £300,000 worth of bikes during the year. This amount appears as his total revenue. He bought these bikes from a wholesaler for £150,000. He also spent £20,000 on rates, heating and other items such as electricity and invoice sheets. And he paid £50,000 in wages to his sales assistant and his mechanic. Dawson also paid £12,000 in interest to the bank. All of the items just mentioned appear in both the accountant's and the economist's statement.

The remaining items differ between the two statements and some notes at the foot of the table explain the differences. The only additional cost considered by the accountant is depreciation, which the accountant calculates as a fixed percentage of Dawson's assets. The economist also includes depreciation as a cost but measures it as economic depreciation. The economist also imputes a cost to Dawson's time and money invested in the firm. The historical cost method puts Dawson's costs at £254,000 and his profit at £46,000. In contrast, the opportunity cost of Dawson's year in business was £293,500 and his economic profit was £6,500. Reading between the Lines on pp.234–235 shows how this analysis can be used to compare two alternative activities.

REVIEW

A firm's economic profit is the difference between its total revenue and its total opportunity cost of production. Opportunity cost differs from historical cost. Historical cost measures costs as the pounds spent to buy inputs. Opportunity cost measures costs as the value of the best alternative forgone. The most important differences between the two measures arise when assessing the costs of inputs that are not used as soon as they are bought and when measuring the costs of inputs that the firm does not directly buy, such as the labour of the owner. ◆

We are interested in measuring the opportunity cost of production not for its own sake but so that we can compare the efficiency of alternative methods of production. What do we mean by efficiency?

Economic Efficiency

How does a firm choose between alternative methods of production? What is the most efficient way of producing? There are two concepts of efficiency: technological efficiency and economic efficiency.

Technological efficiency occurs when it is impossible to increase output without increasing the usage of inputs, or, equivalently, when it is impossible to reduce the usage of inputs without reducing output. Suppose that Ian and James both deliver newspapers. Each boy is responsible for a single long street. Ian walks all along one side and then back down the other, while James does the first house on the left, then the first on the right, the second on the left, the second on the right, and so on. James is not technologically efficient because he spends so long crossing the road. If he adopts Ian's method, he can increase his output and deliver more newspapers without using any more labour, or equivalently, he can reduce his input of labour without reducing his output. Ian is technologically efficient because he cannot increase his output without increasing his labour input, nor, equivalently, could he reduce his labour input without reducing his output.

For any firm, there may be several different technologically efficient methods of production, but only one of these will also be economically efficient. **Economic efficiency** occurs when the cost of producing a given level of output is as low as possible. The method with the lowest cost will also be the one with the lowest opportunity cost. This arises from the fact that the prices that must be paid for inputs reflect the values that other possible users of the inputs place on them and so, in turn, reflect the values of the outputs that those inputs could produce in other possible uses; so a firm's expenditure on inputs reflects the value of the alternative output possibilities of those inputs.

Technological efficiency is often said to be an 'engineering' matter. We can check on whether a firm is technologically efficient merely by seeing whether it could get more output from its present inputs or whether it needs fewer inputs for its present output. Economic efficiency goes further than technological efficiency. To see whether a firm is economically efficient we must first check whether it is technologically efficient. If it is, then we must list the alternative technologically efficient methods it could employ. Finally, we have to see whether its current technology produces the output in a cheaper way than the alternatives. So we have to look at the prices of inputs used in the various alternative methods. There is no need to look at input prices when checking whether a firm is technologically efficient. Notice that a firm which is technologically efficient may not be economically efficient. But a firm which is economically efficient is always technologically efficient.

Let's explore the differences and the connection between technological efficiency and economic efficiency by looking at an example.

Suppose that there are four ways of making TV sets:

a *Robot products.* One person monitors the entire computer-driven assembly process.

b *Human products.* Each person specializes in a small part of the job as the emerging TV set passes by.

c *Human products.* Each person follows a TV set along the assembly line and performs each and every task, using the appropriate piece of machinery as it is needed.

d *Hand-tooled assembly.* Each TV set is assembled completely by a single worker who uses just a few hand tools.

Table 9.3 sets out the amount of labour and capital required to make 10 TV sets a day by each of

these four methods. Are all of these alternative methods technologically efficient? By inspecting the numbers in the table you will be able to see that method *c* is not technologically efficient – in other words it is technologically inefficient. It requires 100 workers and 10 units of capital to produce 10 TV sets. But it would be possible to have this output with fewer inputs using method *b*, for although method *b* needs as much capital as method *c*, method *b* needs far less labour. The other methods are all technologically efficient. Suppose the firm is

TABLE 9.3

Four Ways of Making 10 TV Sets per Day

| | Method | Quantities of inputs | |
		Labour	Capital
a	Robot assembly line	1	1,000
b	Human assembly line	10	10
c	Human assembly line	100	10
d	Hand-tooled assembly	1,000	1

TABLE 9.4

Costs of Four Ways of Making 10 TV Sets per Day

Method	Labour cost when each worker costs £75 per day (£)		Capital cost when each unit of capital costs £250 per day (£)		Total cost (£)	Cost per TV set (£)
a	75	+	250,000	=	250,075	25,007.50
b	750	+	2,500	=	3,250	325.00
c	7,500	+	2,500	=	10,000	1,000.00
d	75,000	+	250	=	75,250	7,525.00

TABLE 9.5

Costs of Three Ways of Making 10 TV Sets: High Labour Costs

Method	Labour cost when each worker costs £150 per day (£)		Capital cost when each unitof capital costs £1 per day (£)		Total cost (£)	Cost per TV set (£)
a	150	+	1,000	=	1,150	115.00
b	1,500	+	10	=	1,510	151.00
d	150,000	+	1	=	150,001	15,000.10

using method c. Suppose it contemplates switching to method b, and then later to method a. Each time, it can maintain its output and use less labour, but each time it will also need more capital. So we cannot say it will need fewer inputs altogether, and so we cannot describe method c or method b as technologically inefficient.

What about economic efficiency? Are methods a, b and d all economically efficient? To answer that question, we need to know the labour and capital costs. Let's suppose that labour costs £75 per person-day and that capital costs £250 per machine-day. Recall that economic efficiency occurs with the least expensive production process. Table 9.4 sets out the costs of using the four different methods of production. As you can see, the least expensive method of producing a TV set is b. Method a uses less labour but more capital. The combination of labour and capital needed by

method a ends up costing much more than that of method b. Method d, the other technologically efficient method, uses much more labour and hardly any capital. Like a, it costs far more to make a TV set using method d than method b.

Method c is technologically inefficient. It uses the same amount of capital as b but 10 times as much labour. It is interesting to notice that although c is technologically inefficient, it costs less to produce a TV set using method c than it does using the technologically efficient methods a and d. But method b dominates method c. Because method c is not technologically efficient, there is always a lower-cost method available. That is, a technologically inefficient method is never economically efficient.

Although method b is the economically efficient method in this example, methods a or d could be economically efficient in other circumstances.

TABLE 9.6

Costs of Three Ways of Making 10 TV Sets: High Capital Costs

Method	Labour cost when each worker costs £1 per day (£)		Capital cost when each unit of capital costs £1,000 per day (£)		Total cost (£)	Cost per TV Set (£)
a	1	+	1,000,000	=	1,000,001	100,000.10
b	10	+	10,000	=	10,010	1,001.00
d	1,000	+	1,000	=	2,000	200.00

Let's see when.

First, suppose that labour costs £150 a person-day and capital only £1 a machine-day. Table 9.5 shows the costs of making a TV set now. In this case, method *a* is economically efficient. Capital is now sufficiently cheap relative to labour that the method using the most capital is the economically efficient method.

Next suppose that labour costs only £1 a day while capital costs £1,000 a day. Table 9.6 shows the costs in this case. As you can see, method *d*, which uses a lot of labour and little capital, is now the economically efficient method.

A firm that does not use the economically efficient method of production makes a smaller profit than it could make. Competition between firms favours those that choose the economically efficient method of production and goes against firms that do not. In extreme cases, an inefficient firm may go bankrupt or be taken over by another firm that can see the possibilities for lower cost and greater profit. Efficient firms will be stronger and better able to survive temporary adversity than inefficient ones.

Firms and Markets

At the beginning of this chapter, we defined a firm as an institution that buys or hires inputs and organizes them to produce and sell its output. In organizing production, firms coordinate the economic activities of many individuals. But a firm is not the only institution that coordinates economic activity. Coordination can also be achieved by using the market. In Chapter 1, we defined markets as mechanisms for coordinating people's buying and selling plans. By buying inputs in many individual markets, each one of us can organize the production of the goods and services that we consume. Suppose, for example, that your car is reluctant to start in the morning and you consider two ways in which you might get it repaired:

◆ *Firm coordination* You take the car to the garage and leave it to the garage to fix it. The garage owner coordinates the buying of the new parts required, the availability of the tools needed to fit them, and also the mechanic's time. You pay one bill for the entire job.

◆ *Market coordination* You hire a mechanic who diagnoses the problems and makes a list of the parts required and the tools needed to fix them. You buy the parts from the local autoshop and rent the tools from the local plant hire company. Then you hire the mechanic once more to fit the new parts. You return the tools and pay your bills – wages to the mechanic, rental to the plant hire company and purchases of parts from the autoshop.

What determines the method that you use? The answer is cost. Taking account of the opportunity cost of your own time as well as the costs of the other inputs that you'd have to buy, you will use the method that costs least. In other words, you will use the economically efficient method.

It will pay someone to set up a firm in situations where a firm can coordinate economic activity more efficiently than markets. But if markets can perform the task of coordination more efficiently than firms, people will use markets and any attempt to set up a firm to replace such market coordination will be doomed to failure.

Why Firms?

There are three key reasons why, in many instances, firms are more efficient than markets as coordinators of economic activity. Firms achieve

◆ Lower transactions costs
◆ Economies of scale
◆ Economies of team production

Transactions Costs The idea that firms exist because there are activities in which they are more efficient than markets was first suggested by Ronald Coase of the University of Chicago.[1]

---

[1] Coase R.H. (November 1977). The Nature of the Firm. *Economica*, 386–405

Cutting Costs with Old Technology

The Essence of the Story

Bracknell Forest Borough Council has replaced a worn-out tractor with two shire horses rather than a new tractor.

The attractions to the council of doing this are economic: two horses have lower running costs than a tractor.

Data from the Shire Horse Society suggests that the cost of purchasing and maintaining two horses is about a fifth lower than that for a lorry.

The working life of a horse is twice that of a tractor.

Moreover, the two horses would produce manure worth £90 a year which could be sold or used in the council's gardens.

Horse-drawn vehicles are slower than tractors and lorries, but for tasks where time and distance are not important factors, horses cost less.

THE TIMES, 13 MAY 1992

Horsepower pulls ahead of tractors

David Young

THE two newest members of Bracknell Forest Borough Council gardening department will clock on for the first time next Monday to be rewarded for an eight hour shift with a handful of carrots, a bale of hay and a bucket of oats.

The council in Berkshire has gone green. Instead of spending £20,000 or more to replace a worn-out tractor, it has bought two £4,000 Shire horses who will pull trailers around the town's gardens, and lug tankers used for watering its hanging baskets. Their working life could span 15 years, double the average tractor's. The council will save on a road fund licence and the insurance premiums will be lower.

Alan Stanton, environmental health officer, said: 'We looked at the figures very closely and, on the economics, are in favour of the horses. We have drawn on the experience of other horse users, such as the brewers, who have found them to be more economical for local work than lorries.'

Several authorities are considering heavy horses. Aberdeen has bought 14 Clydesdales for the parks department, Luton, whose fortunes owe much to the international combustion engine, has bought a Shire horse. Bradford, West Yorkshire, uses three to pull flower-watering machines, street cleaning equipment and mowers at its industrial museum.

Winning ride: research for the Shire Horse Society shows that, in most cases, horsepower can work out cheaper than motor power, with horses also earning unquantifiable amounts of goodwill for their users. The society can provide figures which show that horses win over lorries by a short neck when used for local journeys during an eight-hour day. In addition, each horse produces £45 worth of manure each year.

How the Costs Compare

Two Horses	£8,000	Lorry	£14,400
Stabling	£2,223	Garaging	£1,332
Insurance	£216	Insurance	£270
Tax	Nil	Tax	£427
Wages	£12,600	Wages	£10,800
Keep	£3,481	Fuel	£792
Depreciation	£436	Depreciation	£2,876
Maintenance	£540	Maintenance	£2,605
		Tyres	£243

All costs are based on 1981 prices supplied by The Shire Horse Society (adjusted to 1991 prices)

© The Times. Reprinted with permission.

A number of councils have identified tasks for which shire horses could be employed more cheaply than tractors and other mechanical alternatives.

The data from the Shire Horse Society indicates a number of areas where costs for two horses are lower than the cost of a lorry.

The initial purchase cost of two horses is lower than for one lorry and the depreciation of horses is also significantly lower. These differences are further amplified by the councils' prediction that two horses will have twice the operational life of a lorry.

All other figures for the annual running costs indicate that it will cost the councils about the same to operate two horses as to operate one lorry.

By changing the technology employed, the councils are able to make economic efficiency gains by lowering the costs of producing the same output.

The figure compares the costs for two horses with those for a lorry.

Costs of Horse and Lorry

Accountant's costs		
Item	Two horses	Lorry
Purchase	£8,000	£14,400
Depreciation	£436	£2,876
Housing	£2,223	£1,332
Insurance	£216	£270
Tax	£0	£427
Fuel	£3,487	£792
Maintenance	£540	£2,605
Tyres	£0	£243
Totals	£14,902	£22,945

Economist's opportunity costs			
Item	Two horses	Lorry	
Purchase price	£8,000	£14,400	
less			
Market value at year end	£7,000	£10,000	(assumed)
equals			
Economic depreciation	£1,000	£4,400	
Interest (at 5% pa)	£400	£720	
Housing	£2,223	£1,332	
Insurance	£216	£270	
Tax	£0	£427	
Fuel	£3,487	£792	
Maintenance	£540	£2,605	
Tyres	£0	£243	
Totals	£7,866	£10,789	

Coase focused on the firm's ability to reduce or eliminate transactions costs. **Transactions costs** are the costs arising from finding someone with whom to do business, of reaching an agreement about the price and other aspects of the exchange, and of ensuring that the terms of the agreement are fulfilled. *Market* transactions require the final consumer to get together and negotiate the terms and conditions of trading with many suppliers. Sometimes lawyers have to be hired to draw up contracts. A broken contract leads to still more expenses. A *firm* can lower such transactions costs by reducing the number of individual transactions undertaken.

Consider, for example, the two ways of getting your car fixed that we've just described. The first method requires that you undertake only one transaction with one firm. It's true that the firm has to undertake several transactions – hiring the labour and buying the parts and tools required to do the job. But the firm doesn't have to undertake those transactions simply to fix your car. One set of such transactions can enable the firm to fix hundreds of cars. So there is an enormous reduction in the number of individual transactions that take place if people get their cars fixed at garages rather than going through the elaborate sequence of market transactions that we described above.

Economies of Scale

Economies of scale exist when the cost of producing a unit of a product falls as the quantity produced increases. Many industries experience economies of scale – car and television manufacturing are two examples. Economies of scale can be reaped only by a large organization; so they give rise to firm coordination rather than market coordination. There are various reasons why economies of scale may exist and we will look at some of these in Chapter 10. But it is helpful to look at one here – team production.

Team production is a production process in which each member of a group of individuals specializes in mutually supportive tasks. Football provides a good example of team activity. Some team members specialize in shooting, some in passing, some in marking and some in goalkeeping. The production of goods and services also offers many examples of team activity. For example, production lines in car and TV manufacturing plants work

most efficiently when individuals work in teams, each specializing in a small task. You can also think of an entire firm as being a team. The team has buyers of raw material and other inputs, production workers and salespersons. There are even sub-specialists within these various groups. Each individual member of the team specializes, but the value of the output of the team and the profit that it earns depend on the coordinated activities of all the team's members. The idea that firms arise as a consequence of the economies of team production was first suggested by Adam Smith and developed by Armen Alchian and Harold Demsetz of the University of California at Los Angeles.[2]

Because firms can economize on transactions costs, reap economies of scale and organize efficient team production, it is firms rather than markets that coordinate most of our economic activity. There are, however, limits to the economic efficiency of firms. If firms become too big or too diversified in the things that they seek to do, the cost of management and monitoring per unit of output begins to rise and, at some point, the market becomes more efficient at coordinating the use of resources.

◆ ◆ ◆ ◆   In the next two chapters, we are going to study the choices of firms. We will study their production decisions, how they minimize costs and how they choose the amounts of the various inputs to employ.

---

[2] Smith, Adam (1776). *The Wealth of Nations* 1964 Everyman edn. London, Vol 1, p. 5. Alchian A., Demsetz H. (December 1972). Production, Information Costs and Economic Organization. *American Economic Review*, **57**(5),777–795

SUMMARY

The Firm and Its Economic Problem

A firm is an institution that enters into a wide range of agency relationships to hire and buy inputs that it organizes to produce and sell its output. In an agency relationship, an agent undertakes an action which affects a principal and the principal sets the terms of the relationship to best achieve the principal's ends. Firms decide what to produce and in what quantities, the techniques of production to use, the quantities of each input to employ, and their organization and management structure.

There are three main forms of business organization: sole proprietorship, partnership and company. Each has its advantages and disadvantages. Sole proprietorships are easy to set up and they face lower taxes than companies, but they are risky and they face higher costs of capital and of labour. Partnerships can draw on diversified expertise but they can also involve decision conflicts. Companies have limited liability so they can obtain large-scale capital from shareholders at relatively low cost, and they can hire professional management. But complex management structures can slow down decisions. Companies pay taxes on profits so that a larger share of their profits ends up with the government. Sole proprietorships are the most common form of business organization, but companies account for most of the economy's production. (pp.220–226)

Costs and Profits

Business profits are calculated as the difference between total revenue and total cost. Accountants and economists measure costs in different ways. Accountants measure historical costs, while economists measure opportunity costs. Total opportunity cost usually exceeds total historical cost because it includes imputed costs that are not counted as part of historical cost. The different measures of cost lead to different measures of profit. Economic profit equals total revenue minus opportunity cost. (pp. 226–230)

Economic Efficiency

There are two concepts of efficiency: technological efficiency and economic efficiency. A method of production is technologically efficient when, to produce a given output, it is not possible to use less of one input without at the same time using more of another. A method of production is economically efficient when the cost of producing a given output is as low as possible. Economic efficiency requires technological efficiency. Economic efficiency also takes into account the relative prices of inputs. Economically efficient firms have a better chance of surviving than inefficient ones. (pp. 230–233)

Firms and Markets

Consumers can have the economic activities they wish to consume coordinated either by themselves dealing directly with numerous markets or by employing firms who will do the coordination for them. It is profitable for firms to coordinate economic activities when they are able to achieve lower costs than consumers can manage by doing the coordination themselves through markets. It is often possible for firms to secure lower costs because they can economize on transactions costs and they can achieve the benefits of economies of scale. (p. 233–236)

KEY ELEMENTS

Key Terms

Agency relationship, 220
Agent, 220
Bond, 224
Cooperative, 223
Company, 222
Convertible share, 225
Corporation tax, 222
Debenture, 224
Depreciation, 226
Durable inputs, 226
Economic depreciation, 227
Economic efficiency, 230

Key Tables

R E V I E W   Q U E S T I O N S

1 What is a firm?

2 What are the economic problems that all firms face?

3 List the three main forms of business organization and the advantages and disadvantages of each.

4 What are the different types of shares that companies issue?

5 Distinguish between historical cost and opportunity cost.

6 What are the main items of opportunity cost that don't get counted as part of historical cost?

7 What is economic depreciation?

8 Define technological efficiency.

9 Define economic efficiency.

10 Distinguish between economic efficiency and technological efficiency.

11 Why do firms, rather than markets, coordinate such a large amount of economic activity?

P R O B L E M S

1 One year ago, Jack and Jill set up a vinegar–bottling firm called JJVB.

   ◆ Jack and Jill put $50,000 of their own money into the firm.

   ◆ They bought equipment for $30,000 and a stock of bottles and vinegar for $15,000.

   ◆ They hired one employee to help them for an annual wage of $20,000.

   ◆ JJVB's sales for the year were $100,000.

   ◆ Jack gave up his previous job, at which he earned $30,000, and spent all his time working for JJVB.

   ◆ Jill kept her old job, which pays $30 an hour, but gave up 10 hours of leisure each week (for 50 weeks) to work for JJVB.

   ◆ The cash expenses of JJVB were $10,000 for the year.

   ◆ The market value of the equipment at the end of the year was $28,000.

   ◆ JJVB's accountant depreciated the equipment by 20 per cent a year.

   a Construct JJVB's profit and loss account as recorded by its accountant.

   b Construct JJVB's profit and loss account

based on opportunity cost rather than historical cost concepts.

2 You can use three technologies for working out your tax return: a personal computer, a pocket calculator, or a pencil and paper. With a PC, you complete the job in an hour; with a pocket calculator, it takes 12 hours; and with a pencil and paper, it takes two days. The PC and its software cost $1,000, the pocket calculator costs $10, and the pencil and paper cost $1.

a Which, if any, of the above methods are technologically efficient?

b Suppose your wage rate is $5 an hour. Which of the above methods is economically efficient?

c Suppose your wage rate is $50 an hour. Which of the above methods is economically efficient?

d Suppose your wage rate is $500 an hour. Which of the above methods is economically efficient?

CHAPTER 10

OUTPUT
AND
COSTS

After studying this chapter, you will be able to:

◆ Explain the objective of a firm

◆ Explain what limits a firm's profitability

◆ Explain the relationship between a firm's output and its costs

◆ Derive a firm's short-run cost curves

◆ Explain how cost changes when a firm's plant size changes

◆ Derive a firm's long-run average cost curve

◆ Explain why some firms operate with excess capacity and others overutilize their plants

SIZE DOES NOT GUARANTEE SURVIVAL IN BUSINESS. TRUE, UNILEVER AND Shell have been around a long time and have grown pretty large. But most of the giants of fifty years ago don't even exist today. However remaining small does not guarantee survival either. Every year, millions of small businesses close down. Try phoning a random selection of restaurants and fashion boutiques from *last* year's Yellow Pages and see how many have vanished. What does a firm have to do to be a survivor? ◆ ◆ Firms differ in lots of ways – from the local bakery to multinational giants producing hi-tech goods. But regardless of their size or what they produce all firms must decide what to produce, how much to produce and how to produce it. How do firms make these decisions? ◆ ◆ Most European car makers can produce far more cars than they can sell. Why do car makers have

Survival of the Fittest

equipment that isn't fully used? In many other industries, such as electricity generation, there isn't always enough equipment on hand to meet demand. Some producers often have to buy electricity from other producers. Why don't such firms have more equipment so that they can supply the market themselves?

◆ ◆ ◆ ◆ In Chapter 9 we saw that firms exist because they enable factors of production to be organized to produce and sell goods and services at the least possible cost. This chapter studies firms' costs more closely. It explains what determines a firm's costs and how those costs change as the firm varies its output and as it grows. In subsequent chapters, we study the behaviour of firms: that is, the quantities produced and prices, costs and profits. So we begin this chapter by looking at the objectives of firms and the constraints they face.

Firms' Objectives and Constraints

To understand and predict the behaviour of firms, we will start by describing a firm's objectives – what it is trying to achieve.

The Objective: Profit Maximization

The firm that we will study in this chapter, Knitters, has a single objective: profit maximization. **Profit maximization** is striving for the highest possible profit. As you know, the fundamental problem from which all economic activity springs is scarcity. Profit maximization is a direct consequence of scarcity. Seeking to make the best possible use of scarce resources is the same thing as trying to make the highest possible profit. A firm that tries to maximize profit has the best chance of surviving in a competitive environment and of avoiding being the target of a successful takeover by another firm.

Sidney, the owner of Knitters, is constantly striving to make the highest possible profits, but there are limits to, or constraints on, the profits that a firm can make. What are they?

Constraints

There are two types of constraints that limit the profits a firm can make. They are:

◆ Market constraints
◆ Technology constraint

Market Constraints   A firm's **market constraints** are the conditions under which it can buy its inputs and sell its output. On the output side, people have a limited demand for each good or service and will buy additional quantities only at lower prices. Firms have to recognize this constraint on how much they can sell. A small firm competing with many other firms in a large market has no choice but to sell its output at the same price as everyone else. It cannot, through its own actions, influence the market price. A large firm that dominates the market for a particular good can manipulate the price to its own advantage. But in so doing, it has to accept the fact that at higher prices it will sell lower quantities at higher prices.

On the input side, people have a limited supply of the factors of production that they own and will supply additional quantities only at higher prices. Most firms, even large ones, compete with many other firms in the markets for factors of production and have no choice but to buy their inputs at the same prices as everyone else. Except in rare circumstances, firms cannot manipulate the market prices of their factors of production through their own actions.

We will study the output market constraints on firms more thoroughly in Chapters 11 to 13 and the input market constraints in Chapters 14 to 16. Knitters is small and cannot influence the prices at which it sells its sweaters or at which it buys the inputs used to make them.

Technology Constraint   Firms use inputs to produce outputs. Any feasible way in which inputs can be converted into output is called a **technique**. For example, one technique that Knitters can adopt to produce sweaters uses workers equipped with knitting needles. A second technique uses labour and hand-operated knitting machines. A third technique uses automated knitting machines that require a small amount of labour to set them going and to reset them for different sizes and styles of sweaters. A fourth technique uses robotic knitting machines controlled by computers that automatically adjust the size, type and colour of the sweaters with human intervention only at the point of programming the computer. These different techniques use different amounts of labour and capital. But they are all capable of producing the same total output.

Some techniques are capital intensive and some are labour intensive. A **capital-intensive technique** uses a relatively large amount of capital and a relatively small amount of labour. A computer-controlled automated knitting machine is an example of a capital-intensive technique. A **labour-intensive technique** uses a relatively large amount of labour and a relatively small amount of capital. Knitting sweaters by hand – where the only capital equipment used is knitting needles – is an example of a labour-intensive technique.

To maximize profit, a firm will choose a technologically efficient production method. Recall the definition of technological efficiency that you encountered in Chapter 9 – a state in which no more output can be produced without using more inputs. Technological efficiency does not necessarily require the use of up-to-date or sophisticated equipment. When knitters are working flat out, even if they are using only needles, sweaters are being produced in a technologically efficient way. To produce more sweaters will require more knitters. No resources are being wasted. Similarly, when a computerized automated knitting plant is operating flat out, sweaters are also being produced in a technologically efficient way.

A firm can do no better than use an efficient technique. But it must determine which efficient technique to employ, for not all technologically efficient methods of production are economically efficient. Furthermore, the possibilities open to the firm will depend on the length of the planning period over which the firm is making its decisions. A firm that wants to change its output rate overnight has far fewer options than one that can plan ahead and change its output rate several months in the future. In studying the way a firm's technology constrains its actions, we distinguish between two planning horizons – the short run and the long run.

The Short Run and the Long Run

The **short run** is a period of time in which the quantity of at least one input is fixed and the quantities of the other inputs can be varied. The **long run** is a period of time in which the quantities of all inputs can be varied. Inputs whose quantity can be varied in the short run are called **variable inputs**. Inputs whose quantity cannot be varied in the short run are called **fixed inputs**.

There is no fixed amount of time that can be marked on the calendar to separate the short run from the long run. The short-run and long-run distinction varies from one industry to another. For example, if an electric power company decides that it needs a bigger production plant, it will take several years to implement its decision. If British Airways decides that it needs 20 additional Airbus 300s, it will take a few years for Airbus to turn out the new planes needed to accommodate British Airways' demand. The short run for these firms is several years in length. At the other extreme, a launderette or a copying service has a short run of just a month or two. New premises can be acquired and new machines installed and made operational quickly.

Knitters has a fixed amount of capital equipment in the form of knitting machines, and to vary its output in the short run it has to vary the quantity of labour that it uses. For Knitters, labour is the variable input. The quantity of knitting machinery is fixed in the short run and this equipment is Knitters' fixed input. In the long run, Knitters can vary the quantity of both knitting machines and labour employed.

Let's look a bit more closely at short-run technology constraint.

Short-run Technology Constraint[1]

To increase output in the short run, a firm must increase the quantity of a variable input. The firm's short-run technology constraint determines how much additional variable input is needed to produce a given amount of additional output. A firm's short-run technology constraint is described using three related curves that show the relationship between the quantity of a variable input and:

◆ Total product
◆ Marginal product
◆ Average product

Total Product

The total quantity produced is called **total product**. The **total product curve** shows the maximum output attainable with a given amount of capital as the amount of labour employed is varied. Equivalently, the relationship between total product and the amount of labour employed can be described by a schedule that lists the amounts of labour required to produce given amounts of output. Knitters' total product schedule and curve are shown in Fig. 10.1. As you can see, when employment is zero, no sweaters are knitted. As employment increases, so does the number of sweaters knitted. The total product curve for Knitters, labelled *TP*, is based on

---

[1] If you are anxious to move more quickly to a study of costs you may omit this section and jump immediately to the section entitled 'Short-run Cost'.

FIGURE 10.1

Total Product

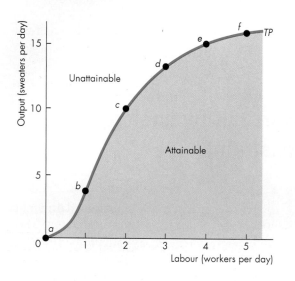

	Labour (workers per day)	Output (sweaters per day)
a	0	0
b	1	4
c	2	10
d	3	13
e	4	15
f	5	16

The numbers in the table show how, with 1 knitting machine, Knitters can vary the total output of sweaters by varying the amount of labour it employs. For example, 1 worker (row b) produces 4 sweaters a day; 2 workers (row c) produce 10 sweaters a day. The short-run production function is graphed here as the total product curve TP. Points a to f on the curve correspond to the rows of the table. The total product curve separates the attainable output from the unattainable.

the schedule in the figure. Points *a* to *f* on the curve correspond to the same rows in the table.

The total product curve has a lot in common with the *production possibility frontier* you met in Chapter 3. It separates the attainable output levels from those that are unattainable. All the points that lie above the curve are unattainable. Points that lie below the curve, in the orange area, are attainable.

But they are inefficient – they use more labour than is necessary to produce a given output. Only the points *on* the total product curve are technologically efficient.

Marginal Product

The **marginal product** of any input is the increase in total product resulting from an increase of one unit of that input. The **marginal product of labour** is the change in total product resulting from a one-unit increase in the quantity of labour employed, holding the quantity of capital constant. It is calculated as the change in output divided by the change in the quantity of labour employed. In Knitters' case, the marginal product of labour is the additional number of sweaters knitted each day that results from hiring one additional worker each day. The magnitude of that marginal product depends on how many workers Knitters is employing. Knitters' marginal product of labour is calculated in the table of Fig. 10.2. The first two columns of the table are the same as the table in Fig. 10.1. The last column shows the calculation of marginal product. For example, when the quantity of labour increases from 1 to 2 workers, total product increases from 4 to 10 sweaters. The change in total product – 6 sweaters – is the marginal product of the second worker.

Knitters' marginal product of labour is illustrated in the two parts of Fig. 10.2. Part (a) reproduces the total product curve that you met in Fig. 10.1. Part (b) shows the marginal product curve (labelled *MP*). In part (a), the marginal product of labour is illustrated by the orange bars. The height of each bar measures marginal product. Marginal product is also measured by the slope of the total product curve. Recall that the slope of a curve is the change in *y* – output – divided by the change in *x* – labour input – as we move along the curve. A one-unit increase in labour input, from 1 to 2 workers, increases output from 4 to 10 sweaters, so the slope from point *b* to point *c* is 6, exactly the same as the marginal product that we've just calculated.

Notice the relationship between the total and marginal product curves. The steeper the *slope* of the total product curve, the higher is the *level* of the marginal product curve. The total product curve in part (a) shows that an increase in employment from 1 to 2 workers increases output from 4 to 10 sweaters (an increase of 6). The increase in output of 6 sweaters appears on the vertical axis of part (b)

FIGURE 10.2

Total Product and Marginal Product

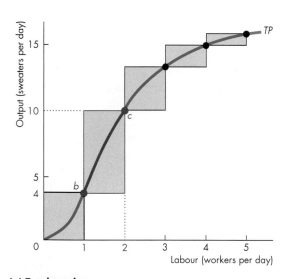

(a) Total product

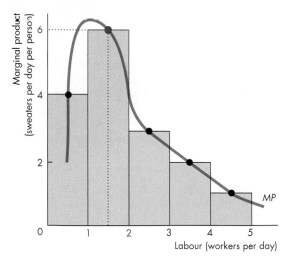

(b) Marginal product

	Labour (workers per day)	Output (sweaters per day)	Marginal product (sweaters per worker)
a	0	0	
			4
b	1	4	
			6
c	2	10	
			3
d	3	13	
			2
e	4	15	
			1
f	5	16	

The table calculates marginal product as the change in total product resulting from a one-unit increase in labour input. For example, when labour increases from 1 to 2 workers a day (row *b* to row *c*), total product increases from 4 to 10 sweaters a day. The marginal product of the second worker is 6 sweaters. (Marginal product is shown midway between the rows to emphasize that it is the result of *changing* inputs — moving from one row to the next.)

Marginal product is illustrated in both parts of the figure by the orange bars. The height of the bars indicates the size of the marginal product. For example, when labour increases from 1 to 2, marginal product is the orange bar whose height is 6 sweaters (visible in each part of the figure). The steeper the slope of the total product curve (*TP*) in part (a), the higher is marginal product (*MP*) in part (b). Marginal product increases to a maximum (when 1 worker is employed in this example) and then declines — diminishing marginal product.

as the marginal product of the second worker. We plot that marginal product at the midpoint between 1 and 2 workers per day. Notice that marginal product shown in Fig.10.2(b) reaches a peak at one unit of labour and at that point marginal product is more than 6 sweaters. The peak occurs at one unit of labour because the total product curve is steepest at one unit of labour.

Average Product

Total product per unit of variable input is called **average product**. In Knitters' case, average product is the total number of sweaters produced each day, divided by the number of workers employed each day. Knitters' average product is calculated in the table in Fig.10.3. For example, 3 workers can knit 13

FIGURE 10.3

Total Product, Marginal Product and Average Product

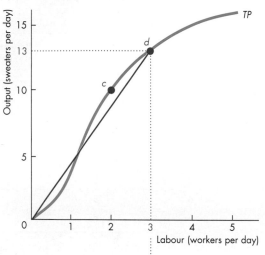

(a) Total product

(b) Marginal product and average product

	Labour (workers per day)	Output (sweaters per day)	Average product (sweaters per worker)
b	1	4	4.00
c	2	10	5.00
d	3	13	4.33
e	4	15	3.75
f	5	16	3.20

Average product – total product per unit of labour – is calculated in the table by dividing total product by the quantity of labour employed. For example, in a day, 3 workers produce 13 sweaters, so the average product of 3 workers is 4.33 sweaters per worker.

The two parts of the figure show two ways of representing average product on a graph. In part (a), average product is measured as the slope of a straight line from the origin to a point on the total product curve. The straight line to point *d* is such a line. The slope of that line is 4.33 (13 sweaters divided by 3 workers). Part (b) also graphs average product. Points *b* to *f* on the average product curve, *AP*, correspond to the rows of the table. Part (b) shows the connection between the average product and marginal product curves. When marginal product exceeds average product, average product is increasing. When marginal product is less than average product, average product is decreasing. When marginal product and average product are equal, average product is at its maximum. Part (b) also shows that marginal product increases from 0 to 1 worker and decreases thereafter and that average product increases from 0 to 2 workers and decreases thereafter.

sweaters a day, so the average product is 13 divided by 3, which is 4.33 sweaters per worker.

Average product is illustrated in the two parts of Fig.10.3. First, average product can be measured in part (a) as the slope of a line from the origin to a point on the total product curve. For example, at point *d* 3 workers knit 13 sweaters. The slope of the line from the origin to point *d* is equal to the output –13 sweaters – divided by the quantity of labour used

– workers. The result is an average product for 3 workers of 4.33 sweaters per worker. You can use this method of calculating average product to check that point *c* is the point of maximum average product. The steepest line from the origin that touches the total product curve touches only at *c*. Place a ruler on the curve and check that. Since the slope of such a line measures average product and this line is steepest when 2 workers are employed, average product is at a maximum at that point.

Part (b) graphs the average product curve, *AP*, and also shows the relationship between average product and marginal product. Points *b* to *f* on the average product curve correspond to those same rows in the table. Average product increases from 1 to 2 workers (its maximum value at point *c*), but then decreases as yet more workers are employed. Notice also that the highest average product occurs where average and marginal product are equal to each other. That is, the marginal product curve cuts the average product curve at the point of maximum average product. When marginal product exceeds average product, average product is increasing. When marginal product is less than average product, average product is decreasing.

Why does Knitters care about diminishing marginal product and diminishing average product? Because they have an important influence on the costs of producing sweaters and the way those costs vary as the production rate varies. We will examine these matters soon, but first we will take one more look at how marginal product and average product are related, for you will meet this type of relationship many times in your study of economics. You can also see it in your everyday life.

Relationship Between Marginal and Average Values

We have seen, in Fig. 10.3, that when marginal product exceeds average product, average product is increasing and when marginal product is less than average product, average product is decreasing. We have also seen that when marginal product equals average product, average product is neither increasing nor decreasing – it is at its maximum and is constant. These relationships between the average and marginal product curves are a general feature of the relationship between the average and marginal values of any variable. Let's look at a familiar example.

Sidney (the owner of Knitters) attends an introductory economics class with his friends Steve and Sam. During the first term they each receive a score of 70 per cent in the course, but they achieved this in different ways. Table 10.1 illustrates how. They took four tests, each worth a quarter of the final mark. Sidney, preoccupied with managing Knitters, started out disastrously with 55 per cent but then steadily improved. Steve started

TABLE 10.1

Average and Marginal Test Scores

Test	Test score	Aggregate score	Average score	Marginal score
Sidney				
1	55	55	55	
				65
2	65	120	60	
				75
3	75	195	65	
				85
4	85	280	70	
Steve				
1	85	85	85	
				75
2	75	160	80	
				65
3	65	225	75	
				55
4	55	280	70	
Sam				
1	70	70	70	
				70
2	70	140	70	
				70
3	70	210	70	
				70
4	70	280	70	

On the second test, Sidney scores 65 per cent. After the first two tests, he has an average score of 60 per cent. On the third test, Sidney scores 75 per cent. His marginal score is the change in his aggregate score as the result of doing one more test. The marginal score after three tests is 75 per cent. This score is located midway between the scores for the second and third tests to emphasize that it is associated with doing one more test. His marginal score now exceeds his previous average (60 per cent), so that his average after three tests is higher (65 per cent). Steve's marginal score is below his average score so his average falls. Sam's marginal score equals his average score so his average remains constant.

out brilliantly but then nosedived, while Sam scored 70 per cent on every test.

We can calculate the average and the marginal scores of these three students. The average score is simply the total marks obtained divided by the number of tests written. After two tests, Sidney has an aggregate score of 55 per cent plus 65 per cent, which is 120 per cent, so his average score is 60 per cent. A student's marginal score is the score on the last test written. After two tests, Sidney's marginal score was 65 per cent.

Over the four tests, Sidney's marginal score rises, Steve's falls and Sam's is constant. But notice what the average scores are doing. For Sidney, the average is rising. His marginal score is higher than his average score and his average rises. For Steve, the marginal score falls. So, too, does his average. Steve's marginal score is always below his average score and pulls his average down. Sam's marginal score equals his average score, so his average stays constant.

These examples of an everyday relationship between marginal and average values agree with the relationship between marginal and average product that we have just discovered. Average product rises when marginal product exceeds average product (Sidney). Average product falls when marginal product is below average product (Steve). Average product is at a maximum and constant (it neither rises nor falls) when marginal product equals average product (Sam).

The Shapes of the Product Curves

Now let's get back to studying production. The total, marginal and average product curves are different for different firms and different types of goods. Mars' production function for chocolate bars differs from that of Jim's Shoe Shine Stand, which, in turn, differs from that of Sidney's sweater factory. But the shapes of the product curves are similar, because almost every production process incorporates two features:

◆ Increasing marginal returns initially
◆ Diminishing marginal returns eventually

Increasing Marginal Returns **Increasing marginal returns** occur when the marginal product of an additional worker exceeds the marginal product of the previous worker. If Sidney employs just one worker at Knitters, that person has to learn all the different aspects of sweater production – running the knitting machines, fixing breakdowns, packaging and mailing sweaters, buying and checking the type and colour of the wool. All of these tasks have to be done by that one person. If Sidney hires a second person, the two workers can specialize in different parts of the production process. As a result, two workers produce more than twice as much as one. This is the range over which marginal returns are increasing.

Diminishing Marginal Returns *Increasing* marginal returns do not always occur, but all production

---

TABLE 10.2

A Compact Glossary on Product

Term	Symbol	Equation	Definition
Fixed input			**An input whose quantity used cannot be varied in the short run**
Variable input	*L*		**An input (labour in our examples) whose quantity used can be varied in the short run**
Total product	*TP*		**Output produced**
Marginal product	*MP*	$MP = \Delta TP \div \Delta L$	**Change in total product resulting from a unit rise in variable input (equals change in total product divided by change in variable factor)**
Average product	*AP*	$AP = TP \div L$	**Total product per unit of variable input (equals total product divided by number of units of variable factor)**

processes eventually reach a point of *diminishing* marginal returns. **Diminishing marginal returns** occur when the marginal product of an additional worker is less than the marginal product of the previous worker. If Sidney hires a third worker, output increases but not by as much as it did when he added the second worker. With a third worker, the factory produces more sweaters, but the equipment is being operated closer to its limits. Furthermore, there are times when the third worker has nothing to do because the plant is running without the need for further attention. Adding yet more workers continues to increase output but by successively smaller amounts. This is the range over which marginal returns are diminishing. This phenomenon is such a pervasive one that it is called 'the law of diminishing returns.' The **law of diminishing returns** states that:

As a firm uses more of a variable input, with the quantity of fixed inputs constant, its marginal product eventually diminishes.

Because marginal product eventually diminishes, so does average product. Recall that average product decreases when marginal product is less than average product. If marginal product is diminishing it must eventually become less than average product and, when it does so, average product begins to decline.

The product and technology concepts we've just studied are summarized in a compact glossary in Table 10.2.

R E V I E W

Three curves – total product, marginal product and average product – show how the output rate of a given plant varies as the input of labour is varied. Initially, as the amount of labour increases, average product and marginal product increase. But eventually, average product and marginal product decline. When marginal product exceeds average product, average product increases. When marginal product is below average product, average product decreases. When marginal product and average product are equal, average product is at its maximum. ◆

Short-run Cost

To produce more output in the short run, a firm must employ more labour. But if it employs more labour its costs increase. Thus to produce more output, a firm must increase its costs. We're going to examine how a firm's costs vary as it varies its output by studying Knitters' costs.

Knitters cannot influence the prices of its inputs and has to pay the market price for them. Given the prices of its inputs, Knitters' lowest attainable cost of production for each output level is determined by its technology. Let's see how.

Total Cost

A firm's **total cost** is the sum of the costs of all the inputs it uses in production. It includes the cost of renting land, buildings and equipment and the wages paid to the firm's work force. Total cost is divided into two categories: fixed cost and variable cost. A **fixed cost** is a cost that is independent of the output level. A **variable cost** is a cost that varies with the output level. **Total fixed cost** is the cost of the fixed inputs. **Total variable cost** is the cost of the variable inputs. We call total cost TC, total fixed cost TFC, and total variable cost TVC.

Knitters' total cost and its division into total fixed cost and total variable cost appears in the table of Fig. 10.4. Knitters has one knitting machine and this is its fixed input. To produce more sweaters Sidney must hire more labour, and the first two columns of the table show how many sweaters can be produced at each level of employment. This is Knitters' technology constraint.

Let's suppose that Knitters rents its knitting machine for $25 a day. This amount is its total fixed cost. Let's suppose that Knitters can hire workers at a wage rate of $25 a day. Total variable cost depends on the quantity of labour hired. For example, when Knitters employs 3 workers, total variable cost is $75 (3 multiplied by $25). Total cost is the sum of total fixed cost and total variable cost. For example, when Knitters employs 3 workers, total variable cost is $75, total fixed cost is $25 and total cost is $100.

Marginal Cost

A firm's **marginal cost** is the increase in total cost resulting from a unit increase in output. To calculate marginal cost, we find the change in total cost and divide it by the change in output. For example, when output increases from 4 to 10 sweaters, total cost increases from £50 to £75. The change in output is 6 sweaters and the change in total cost is £25. The marginal cost of one of those 6 sweaters is £4.17 (£25 divided by 6).

Notice that when Knitters hires a second worker, marginal cost decreases from £6.25 for the first worker to £4.17 for the second worker. But when a third, fourth and fifth worker is employed, marginal cost successively increases. Marginal cost increases because each additional worker produces a successively smaller addition to output – *the law of diminishing returns.*

Average Cost

Average cost is the cost per unit of output. There are three average costs:

◆ Average fixed cost
◆ Average variable cost
◆ Average total cost

Average fixed cost (*AFC*) is total fixed cost per unit of output. **Average variable cost** (*AVC*) is total variable cost per unit of output. **Average total cost** (*ATC*) is total cost per unit output. Average fixed cost plus average variable cost equals average total cost. For example, in the table in Fig. 10.4 when output is 10 sweaters, average fixed cost is £2.50 (£25 divided by 10), average variable cost is £5.00 (£50 divided by 10) and average total cost is £7.50 (£75 divided by 10 or, equivalently, £2.50 fixed cost plus £5.00 average variable cost).

Short-run Cost Curves

We can illustrate Knitters' short-run costs as short-run cost curves (Fig. 10.4a). Total fixed cost is a constant £25. It appears in the figure as the horizontal green curve labelled *TFC*. Total variable cost and total cost both increase with output. They are graphed as the purple total variable cost curve (*TVC*) and the blue total cost curve (*TC*) in the figure. The vertical distance between those two curves is equal to total fixed cost – as indicated by the arrows.

The average cost curves appear in Fig. 10.4(b). The green average fixed cost curve (*AFC*) slopes

downward. As output increases, the same constant fixed cost is spread over a larger output: when Knitters produces only 4 sweaters, average fixed cost is £6.25; when it produces 16 sweaters, average fixed cost is £1.56.

The blue average total cost curve (*ATC*) and the purple average variable cost curve (*AVC*) are U-shaped curves. The vertical distance between the average total cost and average variable cost curves is equal to average fixed cost – as indicated by the arrows. That distance shrinks as output increases since average fixed cost declines with increasing output.

Figure 10.4(b) also illustrates the marginal cost curve. It is the red curve labelled *MC*. That curve is also U-shaped. It cuts the average variable cost curve and the average total cost curve at their minimum points. That is, when marginal cost exceeds average cost, average cost is increasing and when marginal cost is less than average cost, average cost is decreasing. This relationship holds for both the *ATC* and the *AVC* curve. You may wonder why the marginal cost curve cuts both the average total cost curve and the average variable cost curve at their minimum points. It does so because the source of the change in total cost, from which we calculate marginal cost, is variable cost. For average variable cost to decrease, marginal cost must be less than average variable cost, and for average variable cost to increase, marginal cost must exceed average variable cost. Similarly, for average total cost to decrease, marginal cost must be less than average total cost, and for average total cost to increase, marginal cost must exceed average total cost. This is exactly the same relationship that we found when studying students' grades in Table 10.1.

Why the Average Total Cost Curve is U-Shaped

The U-shape of the average total cost curve arises from the influence of two opposing forces:

◆ Decreasing average fixed cost
◆ Eventually increasing average variable cost

Because total fixed cost is constant, as output increases average fixed cost decreases – the average fixed cost curve slopes downward. But at low output levels the average fixed cost curve is steep while at high output levels it is relatively flat.

FIGURE 10.4

Short-run Costs

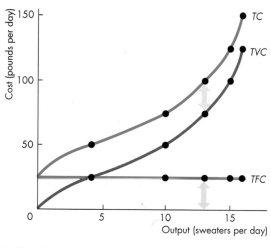

(a) Total costs

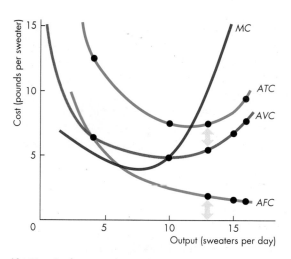

(b) Marginal cost and average costs

Labour (workers per day)	Output (sweaters per day)	Total fixed cost (TFC)	Total variable cost (TVC)	Total cost (TC)	Marginal cost (change in total cost per change in output) (MC)	Average fixed cost (AFC)	Average variable cost (AVC)	Average total cost (ATC)
		(pounds per day)				(pounds per sweater)		
0	0	25	0	25		-	-	-
					............6.25			
1	4	25	25	50		6.25	6.25	12.50
					............4.17			
2	10	25	50	75		2.50	5.00	7.50
					............8.33			
3	13	25	75	100		1.92	5.77	7.69
					............12.50			
4	15	25	100	125		1.67	6.67	8.33
					............25.00			
5	16	25	125	150		1.56	7.81	9.38

Short-run costs are calculated in the table and illustrated in the graphs. At each level of employment and output in the table, total variable cost (TVC) is added to total fixed cost (TFC) to give total cost (TC). The change in total cost per unit change in output gives marginal cost (MC). Average costs are calculated by dividing the total costs by output.

The firm's total cost curves are shown in part (a). Total cost (TC) increases as output increases. Total fixed cost (TFC) is constant – it graphs as a horizontal line – and total variable cost (TVC) increases in a similar way to total cost. The vertical distance between the TC and TVC curves equals total fixed cost (TFC).

The average and marginal cost curves are shown in part (b). Average fixed cost (AFC) decreases as the constant total fixed cost is divided by ever higher output levels. The curves showing average total cost (ATC) and average variable cost (AVC) are U-shaped. The vertical distance between them is equal to average fixed cost, which becomes smaller as output increases. The marginal cost curve (MC) is also U-shaped. It cuts the average variable cost curve and the average total cost curve at their minimum points.

TABLE 10.3

A Compact Glossary on Cost

Term	Symbol	Equation	Definition
Fixed cost			**Cost that is independent of the output level**
Variable cost			**Cost that varies with the output level**
Total fixed cost	**TFC**		**Cost of the fixed inputs (equals their number times their unit price)**
Total variable cost	**TVC**		**Cost of the variable inputs (equals their number times their unit price)**
Total cost	**TC**	**TC = TFC + TVC**	**Cost of all inputs (equals fixed costs plus variable costs)**
Output (total product)	**TP**		**Output produced**
Marginal cost	**MC**	**MC = △TC ÷ △TP**	**Change in total cost resulting from a unit rise in total product (equals the change in total cost divided by the change in total product)**
Average fixed cost	**AFC**	**AFC = TFC ÷ TP**	**Total fixed cost per unit of output (equals total fixed cost divided by total product)**
Average variable cost	**AVC**	**AVC = TVC ÷ TP**	**Total variable cost per unit of output (equals total variable cost divided by total product)**
Average total cost	**ATC**	**ATC = AFC + AVC**	**Total cost per unit of output (equals average fixed cost plus average variable cost)**

Because of diminishing returns, average variable cost eventually increases – the average variable cost curve eventually slopes upward and gets steeper.

Since average total cost is the sum of average fixed cost and average variable cost, the average total cost curve combines these two effects. At first the average total cost curve slopes downward because the effect of spreading fixed costs over larger output levels is the dominant influence on average total cost. But as output increases, diminishing returns bring ever higher average variable cost, and the average total cost curve slopes upward. At the point at which these two opposing influences on average total cost are balanced, average total cost is at its minimum.

The cost concepts we've just studied are summarized in a compact glossary in Table 10.3.

Cost Curves and the Technology Constraint

The shapes of a firm's cost curves are determined by its technology and there are some interesting relationships between its cost curves and its product curves.

First, there is a relationship between the total variable cost curve in Fig. 10.4(a) and the total product curve in Fig. 10.1. They both slope upward,

but look closely at their shapes. Initially, as more labour is employed, the total product curve gets steeper and the total variable cost curve gets less steep. This is the range over which marginal product is increasing. Once diminishing returns set in, as more labour is employed, the total variable cost curve gets steeper and the total product curve gets less steep.

Second, there is a relationship between the marginal product curve in Fig. 10.2 and the marginal cost curve in Fig. 10.4(b). The marginal cost curve is like the flip side of the marginal product curve. Marginal cost is at a minimum at the same output at which marginal product is at a maximum. The output range over which marginal cost is decreasing is the same as that over which marginal product is increasing. Similarly, the output range over which marginal cost is increasing is the same as that over which marginal product is decreasing – the range of diminishing marginal product.

Third, there is a relationship between the average product curve in Fig. 10.3(b), and the average cost curve in Fig. 10.4(b). It is similar to the relationship between the marginal curves that we've just described. The average cost curve is like the flip side of the average product curve. Average variable cost is at a minimum at the same output at which average product is at a maximum (10 sweaters). The output range over which average variable cost is decreasing is the same as that over which average product is increasing. Similarly, the output range over which average variable cost is increasing is the same as that over which average product is decreasing.

As the demand for sweaters grows, Knitters adjusts its rate of sweater production by varying the amount of labour it employs and varying the extent to which it utilizes its fixed amount of knitting machinery – its physical plant. But when does it pay Knitters to install additional knitting machines and increase its plant size? Let's now answer this question.

Plant Size, Cost and Capacity

We have studied how the cost of production varies for a given sweater plant when different quantities of labour are used. The output rate at which a plant's average total cost is at a minimum is called the **capacity** of the plant. If a plant's output is below the point of minimum average total cost – that is, if it produces a lower amount than its capacity – it is said to have **excess capacity**. If a plant's output is above the point of minimum average total cost – that is, if it produces a higher amount than its capacity – it is said to have **overutilized capacity**.

The economist's use of the word capacity differs from the everyday use. It seems more natural to talk about a plant operating at capacity when it cannot produce any more. However, when we want to refer to the maximum output that a plant can produce, we call that output the **physical limits** of the plant.

The cost curves shown in Fig. 10.4 apply to a plant size of one knitting machine that has a fixed cost of £25. There is a set of short-run cost curves like those shown in Fig. 10.4 for each different plant size. In the short run, a firm will be economically efficient if it produces at a point on the short-run cost curve for its given plant. In the long run, though, the firm can do better. It can choose

its plant size and therefore can create a different short-run cost curve on which it will operate.

The Capacity Utilization Puzzle

It is not uncommon for firms to operate their plant at levels above excess capacity and close to their physical limits. High-quality gardeners, plumbers, electricians, painters and other suppliers of services often work so hard that they produce at an average total cost that is higher than their minimum average cost. To get the work done, they have to hire extra help at overtime wage rates and work evenings and weekends, thereby incurring high marginal costs of production.

Operating with increasing average total cost looks uneconomic. Why don't such firms buy more capital equipment and increase the scale of their business to meet the obvious high demand for their output? Is there an economic reason why they don't?

In contrast, it is not uncommon in many industries to have an almost permanent excess capacity. European steel production is an example. Excess capacity also occurs in the motor car industry, in many mining operations and in a host of other industries, not only in Europe but around the world. Producers of these goods claim that they could increase their output if the demand for their product was higher and, as a result, could produce at a lower average total cost.

It sounds as if these firms have invested in too big a production plant. It seems as if the steel producers and car makers would be better off if they had smaller plants so that they could produce closer to the point of minimum average total cost. Is this in fact the case? Or is there some economic explanation for why firms in such industries persistently have excess capacity? This section provides a large part of the answers to these questions.

You have already studied how a firm's costs change when it varies its use of labour, while holding constant the size of its production plant. This cost behaviour is described by the firm's short-run cost curves. Now we are going to study how a firm's costs vary when all its inputs vary – both labour and the scale of the production plant. These variations in costs are described by the firm's long-run cost curves.

Although we want to understand the behaviour of

real firms, we will, as before, spend most of our time studying the long-run costs of our imaginary firm – Knitters. We will then use the insights that we get from Sidney's sweater factory to make sense of the behaviour of real firms.

Short-run Cost and Long-run Cost

Short-run cost is the sum of fixed cost and variable cost. Fixed cost is the cost of the fixed quantity of plant and equipment. Variable cost is the cost of the variable input, which is usually labour. The behaviour of short-run cost depends on the *short-run production function* – the relationship between the quantity of labour employed and output. **Long-run cost** is the cost of production when a firm varies its plant size and uses the least-cost or economically efficient plant size. The behaviour of long-run cost depends on the firm's production function. A firm's

production function is the relationship between the maximum output attainable and the quantities of inputs used as *all* the inputs are varied.

The Production Function

Knitters' production function is shown in Fig. 10.5. In the table, we look at four different plant sizes and five different quantities of labour input. Perhaps you will recognize the numbers in the column for a plant size of one knitting machine. This is the sweater factory whose short-run product and cost curves we have just studied. With one knitting machine, output varies as the labour input is varied, as described by the numbers in that column. The table also shows three other plants sizes – two, three and four times the size of the original one. If Sidney doubles the plant size (to two knitting machines), the various amounts of labour can pro-

---

FIGURE 10.5

The Production Function

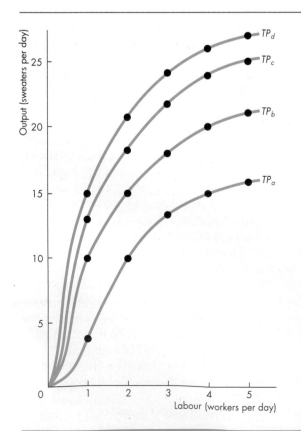

Labour	Output (sweaters per day)			
(workers per day)	Plant *a*	Plant *b*	Plant *c*	Plant *d*
1	4	10	13	15
2	10	15	18	21
3	13	18	22	24
4	15	20	24	26
5	16	21	25	27
Knitting machines (number)	1	2	3	4

The table shows four short-run production functions for four plant sizes. These production functions are plotted in the graph and are labelled TP_a (1 knitting machine), TP_b (2 knitting machines), TP_c (3 knitting machines) and TP_d (4 knitting machines). Each total product curve shows diminishing marginal product. The bigger the plant, the larger the total product for any given amount of labour employed.

The highlighted numbers in the table show what happens as the firm changes its scale of production. Doubling the scale from 1 machine and 1 worker to 2 machines and 2 workers more than doubles the output – increasing returns to scale. Increasing the scale again from 2 workers and 2 machines to 3 workers and 3 machines and to 4 workers and 4 machines increases output by a smaller percentage than the increase in inputs – decreasing returns to scale.

duce the outputs shown in the second column of the table. The other two columns show the outputs of yet larger plants. Each of the columns of the table is a short-run production function. The production function itself is just the collection of all the short-run production functions.

The total product curves for these four different plant sizes appear in Fig. 10.5. As you can see, each total product curve has the same basic shape, but the bigger the sweater plant, the larger the number of sweaters knitted each day by a given number of workers. One of the fundamental technological facts reflected in the shape of a total product curve is the law of diminishing returns.

Diminishing Returns

Diminishing returns occur in all four plants as the labour input increases. You can check that fact by doing similar calculations for the larger plants to those done in Fig. 10.2. Regardless of the size of the plant, the larger the labour input, the lower (eventually) its marginal product.

Just as we can calculate the marginal product of labour for each plant size, we can also calculate the marginal product of capital for each quantity of labour. The **marginal product of capital** is the change in total product resulting from a one-unit increase in the quantity of capital employed, holding the quantity of labour constant. It is calculated in a similar way to the marginal product of labour. Also, it behaves in a similar way to the marginal product of labour. That is, if the labour input is held constant as the capital input is increased, the marginal product of capital diminishes.

The law of diminishing returns tells us what happens to output when a firm changes one input, either labour or capital, and holds the other input constant. What happens to output if a firm changes both labour and equipment?

Returns to Scale

A change in scale occurs when there is an equal percentage change in the use of all the firm's inputs. For example, if Knitters has been employing one worker and has one knitting machine and then doubles its use of both inputs (to use two workers and two knitting machines), the scale of the firm will double. **Returns to scale** are the increases in output that result from increasing all inputs by the

same percentage. There are three possible cases:

◆ Constant returns to scale
◆ Increasing returns to scale
◆ Decreasing returns to scale

Constant Returns to Scale   **Constant returns to scale** occur when the percentage increase in a firm's output is equal to the percentage increase in its inputs. If constant returns to scale are present, when a firm doubles all its inputs, its output exactly doubles. Constant returns to scale occur if an increase in output is achieved by replicating the original production process. For example, Rover can double its production of Metros by doubling its production facility for those cars. It can build an identical production line and hire an identical number of workers. With the two identical production lines, Rover will produce exactly twice as many cars.

Increasing Returns to Scale   **Increasing returns to scale** (also called **economies of scale**) occur when the percentage increase in output exceeds the percentage increase in inputs. If economies of scale are present when a firm doubles all its inputs, its output more than doubles. Economies of scale occur in production processes where increased output enables a firm to use a more productive technology. For example, if Rover produces only 100 cars a week, it will not pay to install an automated assembly line. The cost per car will be lower if instead Rover uses skilled, but expensive, workers equipped only with inexpensive hand tools. But at an output rate of a few thousand cars a week, it will pay Rover to install an automated assembly line. Workers will each specialize in a small number of tasks at which they will become highly proficient. Rover may use 100 times more capital and labour, but the number of cars it can make will increase much more than a hundredfold. It will experience increasing returns to scale.

Decreasing Returns to Scale   **Decreasing returns to scale** (also called **diseconomies of scale**) occur when the percentage increase in output is less than the percentage change in inputs. For example, if inputs double and output increases by 50 per cent, diseconomies of scale are present. Diseconomies of scale occur in all production processes at some output rate, but perhaps at a very high one. The most common source of diseconomies of scale is the increasingly complex management and organizational structure required to control a large firm. The larger the organization, the larger the number of layers in the management pyramid and the greater the costs of monitoring and maintaining control of all the various stages in the production and marketing process.

Scale Economies at Knitters Knitters' production possibilities, set out in Fig. 10.5, display both economies of scale and diseconomies of scale. If Sidney has 1 knitting machine and employs 1 worker, his factory will produce 4 sweaters a day. If he doubles the firm's inputs to 2 knitting machines and 2 workers, the factory's output increases almost fourfold to 15 sweaters a day. If he increases his inputs another 50 per cent to 3 knitting machines and 3 workers, output increases to 22 sweaters a day – an increase of less than 50 per cent. Doubling the scale of Knitters from 1 to 2 units of each input gives rise to economies of scale, but the further increase from 2 to 3 units of each input gives rise to diseconomies of scale.

Whether a firm experiences increasing, constant or decreasing returns to scale has an important effect on its long-run costs. Let's see how.

Plant Size and Cost

Earlier in this chapter, we worked out Knitters' short-run costs when it has a fixed amount of capital – 1 knitting machine – and a variable number of workers. We can also work out the short-run costs of different plant sizes. It takes longer to change the size of the plant than to change the size of the plant's work force. That is why we speak of a short run for each different plant size. But Sidney can buy another knitting machine and put it into his existing factory. He will then have a different size of plant. He can vary the amount of labour employed in that plant and, as he does so, we can trace the short-run cost curves associated with those different levels of variable input.

Let's look at the short-run costs for different plants and see how plant size itself affects the short-run cost curves.

Four Different Plants

We've already studied the costs of a plant with 1 knitting machine. We'll call the average total cost curve for that plant ATC_1 in Fig. 10.6. The average total cost curve for larger plants (with 2, 3 and 4 knitting machines respectively) are also shown in Fig. 10.6 as ATC_2 (for 2 machines), ATC_3 (for 3 machines) and ATC_4 (for 4 machines). The average total cost curves have the same basic U-shape for all the plant sizes. And because larger plants produce larger outputs with the same amount of labour, the ATC curves for successively larger plants lie further to the right. Which of these cost curves Knitters operates on depends on its plant size. For example, if Knitters has 1 machine, then its average total cost curve is ATC_1 and it costs £7.69 per sweater to knit 13 sweaters a day. But Knitters can produce 13 sweaters a day with any of these 4 different plant sizes. If it uses 2 machines, the average total cost curve is ATC_2 and the average total cost of a sweater is £6.80. If it uses 4 machines, the average total cost curve is ATC_4, and the average total cost of a sweater is £9.50. If Knitters wants to produce 13 sweaters a day, the economically efficient plant size is 2 machines – the one with the lowest average total cost of production.

The Long-run Average Cost Curve

The **long-run average cost curve** traces the relationship between the lowest attainable average total cost and output when both capital and labour inputs can be varied. This curve is illustrated in Fig. 10.7 as $LRAC$. It is derived directly from the four short-run average total cost curves that we have just reviewed in Fig. 10.6. As you can see, ATC_1 has the lowest average total cost for all output rates up to 10 sweaters a day. ATC_2 has the lowest average total cost for output rates between 10 and 18 sweaters a day. ATC_3 has the lowest average total cost for output rates between 18 and 24 sweaters a day. And ATC_4 has the lowest average total cost for output rates above 24 sweaters a day. The segments of the four average total cost curves for which each plant has the lowest average total cost are highlighted in Fig. 10.7. The scallop-shaped curve made up of these four segments is the long-run average cost curve.

Knitters will be on its long-run average cost curve if it does the following: to produce up to 10 sweaters a day it uses 1 machine; to produce between 11 and 18 sweaters a day it uses 2 machines; to produce

FIGURE 10.6

Short-run and Long-run Costs

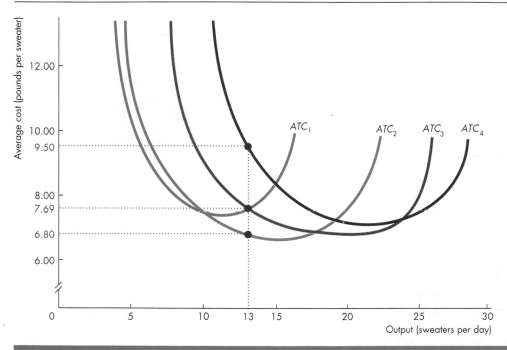

The short-run average total cost curve for a plant with 1 knitting machine is ATC_1. As the number of machines increases, the average total cost curve shifts to the right. ATC curves for 2, 3 and 4 machines are shown as ATC_2, ATC_3 and ATC_4. The least-cost way of producing 13 sweaters a day is to use a plant with 2 machines and produce on ATC_2 for £6.80 a sweater. With 1 machine (on ATC_1) or with 3 machines (on ATC_3) it costs £7.69 a sweater. With 4 machines (on ATC_4) it costs £9.50 a sweater.

FIGURE 10.7

The Long-run Average Cost Curve

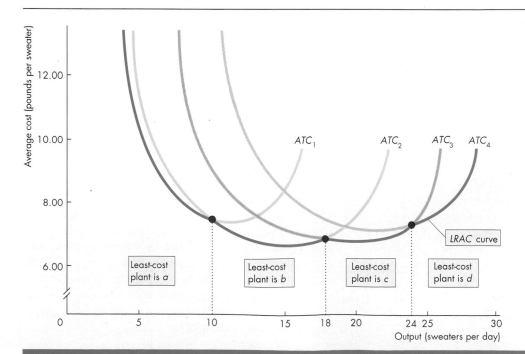

The long-run average cost curve – the blue curve – traces the lowest attainable costs of production at each output when both capital and labour inputs are varied. On the long-run average cost curve, Knitters uses 1 machine and is on ATC_1 to produce up to 10 sweaters a day; 2 machines and is on ATC_2 to produce between 11 and 18 sweaters a day; 3 machines and is on ATC_3 to produce between 19 and 24 sweaters a day; 4 machines and is on ATC_4 to produce more than 24 sweaters a day.

Firms and Costs

'Outside the firm, price movements direct production, which is coordinated through a series of exchange transactions on the market. Within a firm, these market transactions are eliminated...'

RONALD H. COASE
'The Nature of the Firm'

Why do firms exist? Ronald H. Coase was the first to ask and answer this question. Firms exist, he said, because they enable us to avoid costs arising from market transactions. Without firms, each individual would have to find the best way of selling her or his own resources in a wide range of markets. The time cost of these activities would be extremely large. With firms, each person sells her or his resources to just one firm – the one offering the highest price – and managers direct the resources hired by the firm to their highest-value uses.

How are firms' costs related to their output? Jacob Viner answered this question, showing how a firm's short-run and long-run cost curves are related to each other. But he didn't get it quite right, and his mistake can reinforce your understanding of the short-run average cost curve (*SRAC*) and the long-run average cost curve (*LRAC*). (Viner's mistake is contained in an article that has been reprinted many times. One of its most accessible sources is in Kenneth E. Boulding and George J. Stigler (eds.), *Readings in Price Theory* (Chicago: Richard D. Irwin, 1952), 198–232. The article was first published in *Zeitschrift für Nationalkonomie*, III (1931), 23–46.)

Viner asked his draftsman to draw a long-run average cost curve that satisfied two conditions:

◆ Not rise above any *SRAC* curve at any point
◆ Pass through the minimum point of each *SRAC* curve

The *SRAC* curve in Fig. 1 is never below the *LRAC* and thus satisfies Viner's first condition – that the *LRAC* not rise above any *SRAC* at any point. But it does not satisfy the second – that the *LRAC* pass through the minimum points of each *SRAC*. Viner's wrong version of a long-run average cost curve is shown in Fig. 2. That curve does pass through the minimum points of the *SRAC* curves and so satisfies the second condition but not the first.

It is not possible to draw a curve that satisfies both Viner's conditions (except when there are constant returns to scale and *LRAC* is horizontal). The curve in Fig. 1 is a long-run average cost curve, and Viner's curve in Fig. 2 is not.

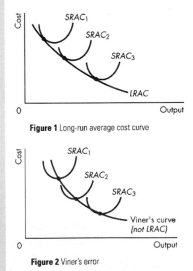

Figure 1 Long-run average cost curve

Figure 2 Viner's error

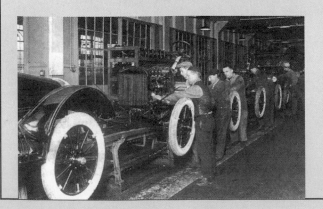

Factories employing hundreds of workers using specialized machinery became common in the industrial revolution of the eighteenth century. By organizing production on a large scale and by allocating resources directly rather than indirectly through markets, firms were able to cut the costs of production. This process saw a further advance with the development of the production line method in the car industry of the 1920s.

In the modern world, marketing costs, not production costs, are the largest for many goods. By finding ways to economize on marketing costs, a new firm can find a niche in which to set out on the road to becoming a major player. Michael Dell, owner and founder of Dell Computers, has created such a firm. Buying computers and parts at the lowest possible prices and selling directly to the consumer by direct mail, Dell has cut the costs of transacting and made big inroads into the business of previously established firms.

Ronald Coase & Jacob Viner: Understanding How Firms Work

Our understanding of the working of firms was developed in the 1930s, and many economists contributed to our advancing knowledge. Two important contributers were Ronald H. Coase (1910–), pictured right, and Jacob Viner (1892–1970), pictured left.

Coase was born in the United Kingdom but has lived in the United States since 1951, which he first visited as a 20-year-old on a travelling scholarship during the depths of the Great Depression. It was on that visit, and before he had completed his bachelor's degree, that he conceived the ideas for his paper, 'The Nature of the Firm', cited 60 years later by the Swedish Academy of Sciences as his main contribution to economics when awarding him the Nobel Prize for Economic Science.

Viner was born in Montreal, Canada, the son of a poor immigrant family from Eastern Europe. He was educated at McGill and Harvard Universities and taught at Chicago and Princeton. Viner's main contribution was to explain the nature of a firm's costs, and it was he who first described the firm's cost curves that are explained in this chapter.

JACOB VINER

RONALD COASE

between and 19 and 24 sweaters it uses 3 machines; and, finally, to produce more than 24 sweaters it uses 4 machines. Within these ranges, it varies its output by varying the amount of labour employed.

Long-run Cost and Returns to Scale   There is a connection between the long-run average cost curve and returns to scale. Figure 10.8 shows this connection. When long-run average cost is decreasing, there are increasing returns to scale (or economies of scale). When long-run average cost is increasing, there are decreasing returns to scale (or diseconomies of scale). At outputs up to 15 sweaters a day, Knitters experiences economies of scale; at 15 sweaters a day, long-run average cost is at a minimum. When output increases to more than 15 sweaters a day, Knitters experiences diseconomies of scale.

The long-run average cost curve we derived for Knitters has two special features that will not always be found in a firm's long-run cost curve. First, Knitters is able to adjust its plant size only in big jumps. In contrast, we can imagine varying the plant size in tiny increments so that there is an infinite number of plant sizes. In such a situation, there is an

infinite number of short-run average total cost curves, one for each plant. Second, Knitters' long-run average cost curve is U-shaped – it slopes either downward (economies of scale) or upward (diseconomies of scale). In contrast, many production processes have constant returns to scale over some intermediate range of output and long-run average cost is constant. The long-run average cost curve is horizontal.

The first time the long-run average cost curve appeared in print, it was drawn incorrectly. Take a look at Our Advancing Knowledge (pp. 258–259) to see why. You will understand the connection between short-run and long-run average cost curves more thoroughly after you have studied that material.

Long-run Costs Are Total Costs   When we examine short-run costs, we distinguish between fixed, variable and total cost. We make no such distinctions for long-run costs. All inputs vary in the long run, so there are no long-run fixed costs. Since there are no long-run fixed costs, long-run total cost and long-run variable cost are the same thing. The long-run average variable cost is the long-run average cost.

FIGURE 10.8

Returns to Scale

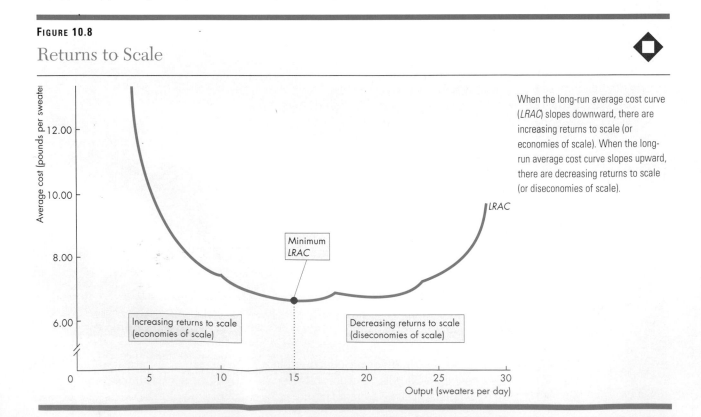

When the long-run average cost curve (*LRAC*) slopes downward, there are increasing returns to scale (or economies of scale). When the long-run average cost curve slopes upward, there are decreasing returns to scale (or diseconomies of scale).

There is a long-run marginal cost curve that goes with the long-run average cost curve. The relationship between the long-run average cost curve and the long-run marginal cost curve is similar to that between the short-run average cost curve and the short-run marginal cost curve. When long-run average cost is decreasing, long-run marginal cost is less than long-run average cost. When long-run average cost is increasing, long-run marginal cost exceeds long-run average cost, and when long-run average cost is constant, long-run marginal cost is equal to long-run average cost.

Shifts in Cost Curves

Both short-run and long-run cost curves depend on two things: the production function and input prices. A change in technology shifts the production function and thus shifts the cost curves. Technological advances increase the output that can be produced from given inputs. They also shift the total product curve as well as the average and the marginal product curves upward, and they shift the cost curves downward. For example, advances in genetic engineering are making it possible to increase the milk production of a cow without increasing the amount of food that it eats – a technological advance that lowers the cost of milk production.

Resource or input prices also affect the cost curves. If the price of an input increases, it directly increases cost and shifts the cost curves upward. The effect of a fall in input prices is shown in Reading Between the Lines on pp. 262–263.

Returns to Scale in Reality

Let's close this chapter by looking at some real-world examples and see why there is a great deal of excess capacity in some industries while in others firms are operating flat out.

Excess Capacity

It has been estimated that one vacuum cleaner factory can produce more than the entire UK market buys, and it would still be operating on the falling section of its long-run average cost. But the United Kingdom has more than one vacuum cleaner factory, so each

factory is operating at an output rate below that at which long-run average cost is at a minimum. The situation also holds for TV picture tubes and for steel, cars, oil refining, cigarettes, semiconductors and matches.

Figure 10.9 illustrates the situation that prevails in those industries that can lower their average production costs if the market is big enough to permit them to expand to their most efficient scale. Output, limited by the extent of the market, is Q_0. The firm is producing efficiently at an average total cost of ATC_0. But the firm has excess capacity. It can lower its costs to ATC_{min} even with its existing plant if output can be increased to Q_c, and it can lower its costs even more by switching to a bigger plant. But the firm can't sell more than Q_0. So, even when it is operating as efficiently as possible, the firm has excess capacity. The production of vacuum cleaners, TV picture tubes, steel, cars and the other products mentioned above are examples of industries in which the situation shown in Fig. 10.9 prevails.

FIGURE 10.9

Excess Capacity

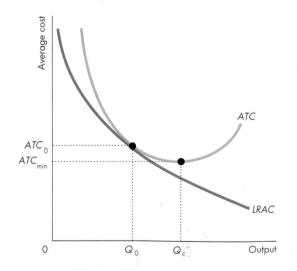

The size of the market limits a firm's output to Q_0. At output Q_0, the long-run average cost curve is downward sloping – there are economies of scale. To produce Q_c at least cost, the firm installs a plant with a capacity of Q_0 and operates the plant below capacity. This situation prevails in many industries, including those manufacturing vacuum cleaners, TV picture tubes, steel, cars, cigarettes, semiconductors and matches.

Office Cost Curves

THE TIMES, 20 APRIL 1994

Office efforts add to cuts in business costs

Derek Harris

REDUCED bills in two key areas helped to bring down office costs in the first quarter of this year. In real terms, screening out inflation, overall costs went down just over 1 per cent.

This emerges from the latest quarterly *The Times*/Procord office costs index. Procord is a leading facilities management company....

Generally, prices affecting office costs are stable. There are inflationary pressures on material prices and labour rates, but Mr Burstow, the facilities cost consultant who conducts the Procord analysis, says these are being offset by improved working practices and management techniques now being used throughout the facilities management sector.

Two developments have lowered prices. The electricity component in property – running costs has fallen by 6 per cent and the bill for communications has been shaved by 2 per cent. Electricity is the second biggest element in property running costs while communications represents by far the biggest single component in office services costs.

Electricity pricing has become far more competitive as the contract-purchasing market has been liberalised. Big users needing 1 megawatt or more have long been able to shop around for the best price but now so can more modest users down to the 100 kilowatts level....

Mr Burstow says '...For sites benefiting from the new threshold, there have been reports of reductions averaging 8 per cent to 12 per cent.'

Such sites were typically in the range of 6p and 7p a kilowatt hour before the introduction of the lower threshold electricity costs. In contrast tender rates for the largest sites have been as low as 3.95p a kilowatt hour.

Communications have benefitted from a pricing formula imposed by Oftel, the industry watchdog, which is having a continuing downward effect because of currently low inflation. The formula is based on the retail price index minus 7.5 per cent. The latest symptom of the increasing competition in this sector has been BT's scrapping of the morning peak rate, saving about 25 per cent on these calls. Total communications cost is down £17 for every person occupying premises.

In reprographics, the second greatest element service cost, there has been a marginal saving. Catering, transport and office equipment have increased largely in line with inflation but in stationery, still a highly competitive area, prices have been marginally lower.

*The index does not include location-dependent elements such as rent, rates, service charge, insurance and depreciation. Nor does it cover costs of small project work, furniture, information technology installations and VAT. It is based on information from 100 big office properties around Britain.

© The Times. Reprinted with permission.

The results of a survey of 100 large office properties have revealed that, over the space of three months, businesses reduced office costs by over 1 per cent in real terms.

The main sources of these cost reductions were lower electricity bills and lower communications costs, principally telephone bills.

In the other areas where offices face large bills, such as reprographics, equipment and stationery, costs moved either in line with inflation or slightly below it.

In the electricity market, very big users have been able to search for the best deal on electricity prices.

When the government privatized the utilities, it tried to limit the potential for abuse of monopoly power by introducing certain regulations limiting price rises or by introducing competition to the market. Price rises are limited to an amount less than the rate of inflation, given by the formula $RPI - x$, where Oftel determines the value of x.

The $RPI - x$ formula applies to all of British Telecom's charge bands on average, so some calls may effectively have price cuts imposed, especially when the inflation rate is low.

Partly in order to help stay within the very tight limit of $RPI - 7.5$ per cent imposed by Oftel, BT has abolished its peak rate, charging all calls made at the standard rate. This change has resulted in lower telephone charges and lower costs for firms.

The survey also established that, while certain costs faced by firms are rising, such as labour costs, these are being offset by savings on management costs, realized partly by the contracting out of certain managerial functions.

The cut in variable costs, such as electricity and telephone charges, will not, other things remaining the same, affect the total product curve such as that shown in Fig. 10.1, but it will reduce total cost by lowering total variable cost.

As a result, average cost and marginal cost will be reduced. Fig. 2 shows the reduction in these costs are reduced.

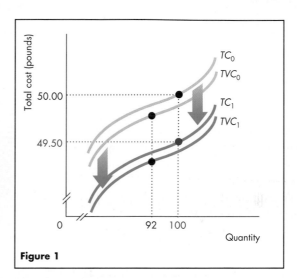

Figure 1

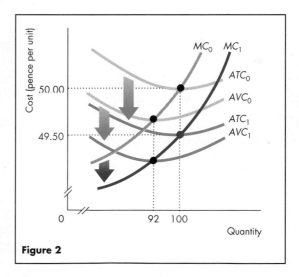

Figure 2

Operating Flat Out

Many firms operate flat out and produce an output level greater than that at which average fixed cost is a minimum. Why don't such firms build additional plants and expand their capacity and lower their average total cost? Fig. 10.10 illustrates such a firm and gives you a big clue as to why it wouldn't increase its plant size. Let's look a bit more closely at this firm.

This firm's average total cost is a minimum at an output level of Q_c and the level of minimum average total cost is ATC_{min}. But the firm produces an output of Q_1 at an average total cost of ATC_1. Why? And why doesn't the firm add more plant?

The firm produces this level of output because demand in this industry is large enough for this quantity to be bought. But the firm would be foolish to add to its capacity. Demand for output in this industry is so large that this firm is producing a quantity at which it experiences decreasing returns to scale (diseconomies of scale). As a result, even when it is minimizing its costs, it produces at an average total cost that exceeds the minimum average total cost. If the firm increased its plant size its average total cost would increase. If the quantity that this firm wants to produce is Q_1, there is *no* plant size that does this job at a lower average total cost than the one it is operating.

So, operating flat out does not imply that a bigger plant is needed. It can be a condition in which the firm is doing the best it can. Such a situation does not usually last indefinitely because other firms have an incentive to enter the industry and take some of the market, but it could prevail for some time. We'll return to this type of situation when we study competitive markets in the next chapter.

◆ ◆ ◆ ◆ We've now studied the way in which a firm's costs vary as it varies its inputs and output rate. We've seen how the fact that marginal product eventually diminishes gives rise to eventually

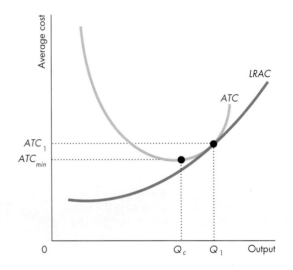

FIGURE 10.10

Overutilizing Capacity

Some firms face a steeply increasing marginal cost curve and operate on its upward-sloping portion as shown in the figure. Average total cost is a minimum at Q_c but the firm produces Q_1. It does not pay this firm to increase its plant size because it faces decreasing returns to scale (diseconomies of scale). A larger plant would increase its costs. The firm has the correct plant size to minimize the cost of producing an output of Q_1.

increasing average and marginal cost. We've also seen how long-run cost curves take their shape from economies and diseconomies of scale – long-run average cost decreasing as output increases with economies of scale and long-run average cost increasing as output increases with diseconomies of scale. ◆ ◆ Our next task is to study the interactions of firms and households in markets for goods and services and see how prices, output levels and profits are determined.

S U M M A R Y

Firms' Objectives and Constraints

Firms aim to maximize profit. Profit maximization stems directly from scarcity. Only firms that maximize profits can survive in a competitive environment.

The market and technology impose constraints on profit maximization. Some firms operate in such competitive markets that they have no choice but to sell their output at the going price. In other cases, the firm can choose the price of its output. However, at higher prices it will sell less. Most firms are unable to influence the markets for their inputs and have to buy them at the going prices. Technology limits the production process of firms. If firms are technologically efficient, then they can increase their output only by using more inputs.

In the short run, some inputs cannot be changed. In most cases, the capital input is fixed in the short run while labour can be varied. (pp. 242–243)

Short-run Technology Constraint

The short-run production function describes the limits to output as a firm changes the quantity of a variable input such as labour. The short-run production function is described by the total, marginal and average product curves. Total product is the output produced in a given period. Average product is total product per unit of variable input. Marginal output is the change in total product resulting from a one-unit increase in the variable input. As the variable input is increased, marginal product increases at first until it reaches a peak, and thereafter it declines – diminishing returns begin. When marginal product exceeds average product, average product is increasing. When marginal product is less than average product, average product is decreasing. When marginal product equals average product, average product is at its maximum. (pp. 243–249)

Short-run Cost

Total cost is divided into total fixed cost and total variable cost. As output increases, total cost increases because total variable cost increases. Marginal cost is the additional cost of producing one more unit of output. Average total cost is total cost per unit of output.

Costs depend on how much a firm produces. Average fixed cost decreases as output increases. Average variable cost and average total cost curves are U-shaped. The marginal cost curve is also U-shaped. When marginal cost is less than average cost, average cost is decreasing, and when marginal cost exceeds average cost, average cost is increasing. When average product is at a maximum, average variable cost is at a minimum. When average product is increasing, average variable cost is decreasing, and when average product is decreasing, average variable cost is increasing. (pp. 251–257)

Plant Size, Cost and Capacity

Plant capacity is the output rate with the lowest average total cost. Firms that produce a smaller amount than their capacity are said to have excess capacity; those that produce a larger amount than their capacity are said to have overutilized their capacity. Firms choose their plant size to minimize long-run cost.

Long-run cost is the cost of production when all inputs – labour as well as plant and equipment – have been adjusted to their economically efficient levels. The behaviour of long-run cost depends on the firm's production function. As a firm uses more labour while holding capital constant, it eventually experiences diminishing returns. When it uses more capital while holding labour constant, it also experiences diminishing returns. When it varies all its inputs in equal proportions, it experiences returns to scale. Returns to scale can be constant, increasing or decreasing. (pp. 253–256)

Plant Size and Cost

There is a set of short-run cost curves for each different plant size. There is one least-cost plant for each output. The higher the output, the larger the plant that will minimize average total cost.

The long-run average cost curve traces the relationship between the lowest attainable average total cost and output when both capital and labour inputs can be varied. With increasing returns to scale, the long-run average cost curve slopes downward. With decreasing returns to scale, the long-run average cost curve slopes upward.

There is no distinction between fixed cost and variable cost in the long run. Since all inputs are variable, all costs are also variable.

Cost curves shift when either input prices or technology change. An improvement in technology increases the output from a given set of inputs and shifts the cost curves downward. A rise in input prices shifts the cost curves upward. (pp. 256–261)

Returns to Scale in Reality

Some firms, including those that make vacuum cleaners, TV picture tubes and cars, have increasing returns to scale (economies of scale). Usually economies of scale exist when the total market is too small to allow the efficient scale of production. In such industries, firms operate efficiently with excess capacity.

Some firms overutilize their plants, operating them at an output rate that exceeds capacity. Electricity generating firms are good examples. Though the marginal cost of electric power increases as output increases, only rarely does an electricity generating firm produce so much power that it is operating on the upward-sloping section of its short-run average total cost curve. Only if a firm persistently operates on the upward-sloping part of its short-run average total cost curve will it be efficient for the firm to increase its plant size. (pp. 261–264)

K E Y   E L E M E N T S

Key Terms

Key Figures and Tables

R E V I E W   Q U E S T I O N S

1   Why do we assume that firms maximize profit?

2   What are the main constraints on a firm's ability to maximize profit?

3   Distinguish between the short run and the long run.

4   Define total product, average product and marginal product. Explain the relationships between a total product curve, average product curve and marginal product curve.

5   State the law of diminishing returns. What does

this law imply about the shapes of the total, marginal and average product curves?

6 Define total cost, total fixed cost, total variable cost, average total cost, average fixed cost, average variable cost and marginal cost.

7 What is the relationship between the average total cost curve, the average variable cost curve and the marginal cost curve?

8 Define the long-run average cost curve. What is the relationship between the long-run average cost curve and the short-run average total cost curve?

9 What does the long-run average cost curve tell us?

10 Define economies of scale. What effects do economies of scale have on the shape of the long-run average cost curve?

11 When does the long-run average cost curve touch the minimum point of a short-run average total cost curve?

12 When does the long-run average cost curve touch a point on the short-run average total cost curve to the left of its minimum point?

13 When does the long-run average cost curve touch a point on the short-run average total cost curve to the right of its minimum point?

14 Why might long-run average cost decline? Why might long-run average cost increase?

15 What makes the short-run cost curves shift (a) upward or (b) downward?

P R O B L E M S

1 The total product schedule of Rubber Tubs, a firm making rubber boats, is described by the following:

Labour (number of persons employed per week)	Output (rubber boats per week)
1	1
2	3
3	6
4	10
5	15
6	21
7	26
8	30
9	33
10	35

a Draw the total product curve.
b Calculate average product and draw the average product curve.
c Calculate marginal product and draw the marginal product curve.
d What is the relationship between average product and marginal product at output rates below 30 boats a week? Why?
e What is the relationship between average

and marginal product at outputs above 30 boats a week? Why?

2 Suppose that the price of labour is £400 a week, the total fixed cost is £10,000 a week, and the total product schedule is the same as in Problem 1.

a Calculate the firm's total cost, total variable cost and total fixed cost for each of the outputs given.
b Draw the total cost, total variable cost and total fixed cost curves.
c Calculate the firm's average total cost, average fixed cost, average variable cost and marginal cost at each of the outputs given.
d Draw the following cost curves: average total cost, average variable cost, average fixed cost and marginal cost.

3 Suppose that total fixed cost increases to £11,000 a week. How will this affect the firm's average total cost, average fixed cost, average variable cost and marginal cost curves in Problem 2?

4 Suppose that total fixed cost remains at £10,000 a week, but that the price of labour increases to £450 a week. Using these new costs, rework Problems 2(a) and (b) and draw the new cost curves.

APPENDIX

Input Substitution

You would be hard-pressed to think of many goods that can be produced in only one way. Just about every good and service can be produced by using a capital-intensive technique or a labour-intensive technique. For example, cars can be made with computer-controlled robotic assembly lines that use enormous amounts of capital and hardly any labour, a capital-intensive technique, or they can be built by skilled labour using only hand tools, a labour-intensive technique.

The firm's technically feasible range of production possibilities is described by its production function. For example, Knitters' production function tells us the maximum daily output of sweaters that can be produced by using different combinations of labour and capital. Figure A10.1 shows Knitters' production function. It tells us, for example, that when Sidney hires 2 workers a day and rents 2 machines, the output produced is 15 sweaters a day. The figure highlights that Knitters can use three different techniques to produce 15 sweaters a day and two different techniques to produce 10 and 21 sweaters a day.

The production function in Fig. A10.1 can be used to calculate the marginal product of labour and the marginal product of capital. The *marginal product of labour* is the change in total product per unit change of labour, holding the amount of capital constant. We've already learned how to calculate the marginal product of labour, so we will not repeat the calculations here. The marginal product of capital is the change in total product per unit change in capital, holding the amount of labour constant. Although we have not calculated the marginal product of capital, it is done in exactly the same way as the calculation of the marginal product of labour. Furthermore, the law of diminishing returns applies to capital just as it does to labour. That is, holding labour input constant, the marginal product of capital diminishes as the capital input increases.

It's easy to see why the law of diminishing returns applies to capital by imagining this scene in Knitters' factory. Suppose that there is 1 worker with 1 machine. Output (as shown in Fig. A10.1) is 4 sweaters a day. If an extra machine is installed, the 1 worker can still easily handle the 2 machines. One machine can be set to knit blue sweaters and the other, red sweaters. There's no need to stop

Knitters' Production Function

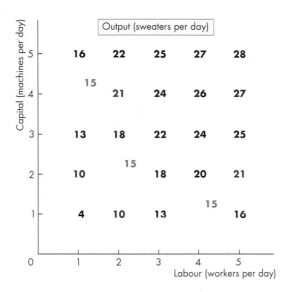

The figure shows how many sweaters cab be produced per day by various combinations of labour and capital inputs. For example, by using 1worker and two machines, Knitters can produce 10 sweaters a day; and by using 4 workers and 2 machines, Knitters can produce 21 sweaters a day.

the machines to change the wool colour. Output more than doubles to 10 sweaters a day. But if a third machine is added, a single worker finds it hard to cope with the increasingly complex factory. For example, there are now three times as many breakdowns as there were with just 1 machine. The worker has to spend an increasing amount of time fixing problems. Output increases to only 13 sweaters a day.

Although all goods and services can be produced by using a variety of alternative methods of production, the ease with which capital and labour can be substituted for each other varies from industry to industry. The production function reflects the ease with which inputs can be substituted for each other. Also, the production function can be used to calculate the degree of substitutability between inputs. Such a calculation involves a new concept – that of the marginal rate of substitution of capital for labour.

Substituting between Capital and Labour to Produce 15 Sweaters

Method	Capital (K)	Labour (L)	Fall in capital ($-\Delta K$)	Rise in labour (ΔL)	Marginal rate of substitution of labour for capital ($\Delta K/\Delta L$)
a	4	1			
			 2	1	2
b	2	2			
			 1	2	1/2
c	1	4			

Switching from method a to method b involves cutting capital ($-\Delta K$) by 2 machines and raising labour (ΔL) by 1 worker. The marginal rate of substitution of labour for capital – which is the ratio of the fall in capital ($-\Delta K$) to the rise in labour (ΔL) – is 2. Switching from method b to method c involves cutting capital by 1 machine and raising labour by 2 workers, which means that the marginal rate of substitution of labour for capital is 1/2.

The Substitutability of Capital and Labour

The **marginal rate of substitution of labour for capital** is the decrease in capital needed per unit increase in labour that keeps output constant. Table A10.1 illustrates how to calculate the marginal rate of substitution of labour for capital. As we saw in Fig. A10.1, an output of 15 sweaters a day can be produced with 4 knitting machines and 1 worker, 2 units of each input, or 1 knitting machine and 4 workers. Let's call those methods *a*, *b* and *c*.

We can calculate the marginal rate of substitution of labour for capital by changing the method of producing 15 sweaters a day, and calculating the ratio of the fall in capital to the rise in labour. Switching the method from *a* to *b* reduces the capital input by 2 machines and raises the labour input by 1 worker. The marginal rate of substitution is 2. Switching from method *b* to *c* reduces capital by 1 machine and raises labour by 2 workers. The marginal rate of substitution is ½.

The marginal rates of substitution we've just calculated obey the **law of diminishing marginal rate of substitution** which states that:

The marginal rate of substitution of labour for capital falls as the amount of capital decreases and the amount of labour increases.

You can see that the law of diminishing marginal rate of substitution makes sense by considering Knitters' sweater factory. With 1 worker racing between 4 knitting machines, desperately trying to keep them all operating, coping with breakdowns and keeping the wool from tangling, output can be held constant at 15 sweaters a day by getting rid of 1 machine and hiring only a small additional amount of labour. The marginal rate of substitution is high. At the other extreme, 4 workers are falling over each other to operate 1 machine. In this situation, output can be kept constant at 15 sweaters a day by laying off 2 workers and installing 1 additional machine. The marginal rate of substitution is low. The principle of the diminishing marginal rate of substitution applies to (almost) all production processes.

Isoquants

A graph of the different combinations of labour and capital that produce 15 sweaters a day is called an isoquant. An **isoquant** is a curve that shows the different combinations of labour and capital required to produce a given quantity of output. The word *isoquant* means 'equal quantity' – *iso* meaning equal and *quant* meaning quantity. There is an isoquant for each output level. The series of isoquants is called an **isoquant map**. Figure A10.2 shows an isoquant map. It has three isoquants: one for 10 sweaters, one for 15 sweaters and one for 21 sweaters. Each isoquant shown is based on the production function presented in Fig. A10.1. But Fig. A10.2 does not show all the isoquants. For example, Knitters' isoquant for 10 sweaters shows all the techniques of production – the combinations of workers and knitting machines – that can produce 10 sweaters a day. Isoquants for larger outputs are further from the origin. That is because for any given capital input, to produce more output Knitters needs more labour, and for any given labour input, to produce more output Knitters needs more capital. For example, if Sidney hires 1 worker and rents 2 machines (point *a*), Knitters' output is 10 sweaters a day. But if Sidney rents 2 more machines (point *b*), Knitters' output increases to 15 sweaters a day. Or if Sidney hires 4 more workers (point *c*), Knitters' output increases to 21 sweaters a day.

An Isoquant Map

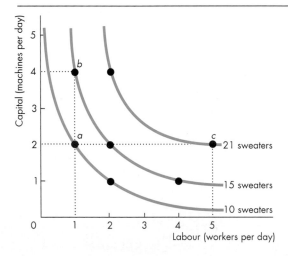

The figure illustrates an isoquant map, but one that shows only 3 isoquants – those for 10, 15 and 21 sweaters a day. These curves correspond to the production function shown in Fig. A10.1 If Knitters uses 2 machines and 1 worker (point *a*), it produces 10 sweaters. If it uses 4 machines and 1 worker (point *b*), it produces 15 sweaters. And if it uses 1 machine and 5 workers, it produces 21 sweaters (point *c*).

Marginal Rate of Substitution

The marginal rate of substitution equals the magnitude of the slope of the isoquant. Figure A10.3 illustrates this relationship. The figure shows the isoquant for 13 sweaters a day. Pick any point on this isoquant and imagine increasing labour by the smallest conceivable amount and decreasing capital by the amount necessary to keep output constant at 13 sweaters. As we lower the capital input and raise the labour input, we travel along the isoquant. If the isoquant is steep (as at point *a*), the capital input falls by a large amount relative to the rise in the labour input. The marginal rate of substitution is high. But if the isoquant has a gentle slope (as at point *b*), the fall in capital is small relative to the rise in labour, and the marginal rate of substitution is small.

The marginal rate of substitution at point *a* is the magnitude of the slope of the straight red line that is tangential to the isoquant at point *a*. The slope of the isoquant at point *a* is the same as the slope of the line. To calculate that slope, let's move along the red

FIGURE A10.3

The Marginal Rate of Substitution

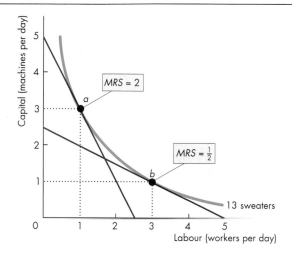

The marginal rate of substitution is measured by the magnitude of the slope of the isoquant. To calculate the marginal rate of substitution at point *a* use the red line that is tangential to the isoquant at point *a*. Calculate the slope of that line to find the slope of the isoquant at point *a*. The magnitude of the slope at point *a* is 2. Thus at point *a*, the marginal rate of substitution of labour for capital is 2. The marginal rate of substitution at point *b* is found from the slope of the line tangential to the isoquant at that point. That slope is $1/2$. Thus, the marginal rate of substitution of labour for capital at point *b* is $1/2$.

line from 5 knitting machines and no workers to 2.5 workers and no knitting machines. Capital falls by 5 knitting machines and labour rises by 2.5 workers. The magnitude of the slope is 5 divided by 2.5, which equals 2. Thus when using technique *a* to produce 13 sweaters a day, the marginal rate of substitution of labour for capital is 2.

The marginal rate of substitution at point *b* is the magnitude of the slope of the straight red line that is tangential to the isoquant at point *b*. This line has the same slope as the isoquant at point *b*. Along this red line, if capital falls by 2.5 knitting machines, labour increases by 5 workers. The magnitude of the slope is 2.5 knitting machines divided by 5 workers, which equals ½. Thus when using technique *b* to produce 13 sweaters a day, the marginal rate of substitution of labour for capital is ½.

You can now see that the law of diminishing marginal rate of substitution is embedded in the shape of the isoquant. When the capital input is large and the

labour input is small, the isoquant is steep. As the capital input decreases and the labour input increases, the slope of the isoquant diminishes. Only curves that are bowed toward the origin have this feature; hence, isoquants are always bowed toward the origin.

Isoquants are very nice, but what do we do with them? The answer is that we use them to work out a firm's least-cost technique of production. But to do so, we need to illustrate the firm's costs in the same sort of diagram that contains the isoquants.

Isocost Lines

An **isocost line** shows all the combinations of capital and labour that can be bought for a given total cost. To make the concept of the isocost line as clear as possible, we'll consider the following example. Knitters is going to spend a total of £100 a day producing sweaters. Knitting-machine operators can be hired for £25 a day, and knitting machines can be rented for £25 a day. The points *a*, *b*, *c*, *d* and *e* in Fig. A10.4 show five possible combinations of labour and capital that Knitters can employ for a total cost of £100. For example, point *b* shows that Knitters can use 3 machines (costing £75) and 1 worker (costing £25). If Knitters can employ workers and machines for fractions of a day, then any of the combinations along the line *a* to *e* can be employed for a total cost of £100. This line is Knitters' isocost line for a total cost of £100.

The Isocost Equation

The isocost line can be described by an isocost equation. An **isocost equation** states the relationship between the quantities of inputs that can be hired for a given total cost. Table A10.2 works out the isocost equation by using the symbols that apply to any situation.

The variables that affect the firm's total cost (TC) are the prices of the inputs – the price of labour (P_L) and the price of capital (P_K) – and the quantities of the inputs employed – L of labour and K of capital. In Knitters' case, we're going to look at the amount of labour and capital that can be employed when these two inputs each cost £25 a day and when total cost is £100.

Swanky's Input Possibilities

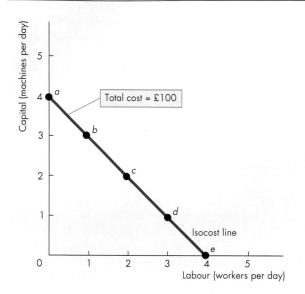

For a given cost Knitter's input possibilities depend on input prices. If labour and capital each cost £25.00 per day, for a total cost of £100 Swanky can employ combinations of capital and labour shown by points *a* to *e*. The line passing through these points is an isocost line. It shows the combinations of capital and labour when each costs £25 a day that have a cost of £100.

The cost of the labour employed $(P_L \times L)$ plus the cost of the capital employed $(P_K \times K)$ is the firm's total cost (TC). That is,

$$P_L L + P_K K = TC,$$

and, in Knitters' case,

$$25L + 25K = 100.$$

To calculate the isocost equation, divide the firm's total cost by the price of capital, and then subtract $(P_L/P_K)L$ from both sides of the resulting equation. The isocost equation is

$$K = TC/P_K - (P_L/P_K)L.$$

It tells us how the capital input varies as the labour input varies, holding total cost constant. Knitters' isocost equation is

$$K = 4 - L.$$

This equation corresponds to the isocost line in Fig. A10. 4.

Calculating an Isocost Equation

In general		In Knitters' case
1. THE VARIABLES		
Total cost	$= TC$	$TC = £100$
Price of labour	$= P_L$	$P_L = £25$
(daily wage rate)		
Price of capital (daily rental rate of machine)	$= P_K$	$P_K = £25$
Quantity of labour number of knitting machine operators)	$= L$	L = Knitters' choice
Quantity of capital (number of knitting machines)	$= K$	K = Knitters' choice
2. FIRM'S TOTAL COST		
$P_L L + P_K K = TC$		$£25 L + £25K = £100$
3. CALCULATING THE ISOCOST EQUATION		
Divide by P_K to give: $(P_L/P_K)L + K = TC/P_K$		Divide by P_K to give: $L + K = 4$
Subtract $(P_L/P_K)L$ from both sides to give: $K = TC/P_K - (P_L/P_K)L$		Subtract L from both sides to give: $K = 4 - L$

The Effect of Input Prices

Along the isocost line that we have just calculated, capital and labour each cost £25 a day. Because these input prices are the same, in order to increase labour by 1 unit, capital must be lowered by 1 unit. The magnitude of the slope of the isocost line shown in Fig. A10.4 is 1. The slope tells us that 1 unit of labour costs 1 unit of capital.

Next, let's consider some different prices, as shown in the table for Fig. A10.5. If the daily wage rate is £50 and the daily rental rate for knitting machines remains at £25, then 1 worker costs the same as 2 machines. Holding total cost constant at £100, to use 1 more worker now requires using 2 fewer machines. With the wage rate double that of

FIGURE A10.5

Input Prices and the Isocost Line

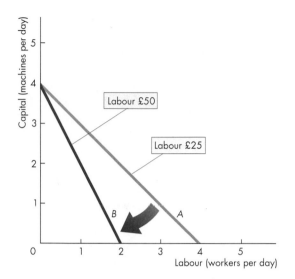

(a) An increase in the price of labour

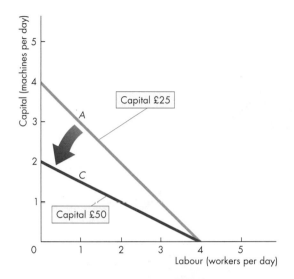

(b) An increase in the price of capital

The slope of the isocost line depends on the relative input prices. Three cases are set out in the table (each for a total cost of £100). In case *A*, both labour and capital have a price of £25 a day and the isocost line is that labelled *A*. In case *B*, the price of labour rises to £50 but the price of capital remains £25 and the isocost line becomes that labelled *B*. Its slope is twice that of *A*. In case *C*, the price of capital rises to £50 and the price of labour remains constant at £25 and the isocost line becomes that labelled *C*. Its slope is half that of *A*.

Isocost line	Price of capital (rental rate per day)	Price of labour (wage per day)	Isocost equation
A	£25	£25	$K = 4 - L$
B	£25	£50	$K = 4 - 2L$
C	£50	£25	$K = 2 - (1/2)L$

the machine rental rate, the isocost line is line *B* in Fig. A10.5(a), and the magnitude of its slope is 2. That is, in order to hire 1 more worker and keep total cost constant, Knitters must give up 2 knitting machines.

If the daily wage rate remains at £25 and the daily rental rate of a knitting machine rises to £50, then 2 workers cost the same as 1 machine. In this case, in order to hire 1 more worker and keep total cost constant, Knitters must give up only half a knitting machine. The magnitude of the slope of the isocost line is now ½, as shown by line *C* in Fig. A10.5(b).

The higher the relative price of labour, the steeper the isocost line. The magnitude of the slope of the isocost line measures the relative

price of labour in terms of capital – that is, the price of labour divided by the price of capital.

The Isocost Map

An **isocost map** shows a series of isocost lines, each for a different level of total cost. The larger the total cost, the larger the quantities of all inputs that can be employed. Figure A10.6 illustrates an isocost map. In this figure, the middle isocost line is the original one that appears in Fig. A10.4. It is the isocost line for a total cost of £100 when both capital and labour cost £25 a day each. The other two isocost lines in Fig. A10.6 are for a total cost of £125 and £75, holding the prices of the inputs constant at £25 each.

An Isocost Map

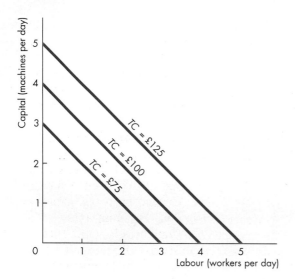

There is an isocost line for each level of cost, and the lines shown here are just a sample. This isocost map shows three isocost lines, one for a total cost of £75, one for £100, and one for £125. For each isocost line, the prices of capital and labour are £25 each. The slope of the lines in an isocost map is determined by the relative price of the two inputs – the price of labour divided by the price of capital. The higher the total cost, the further is the isocost line from the origin.

The Least-cost Technique of Production

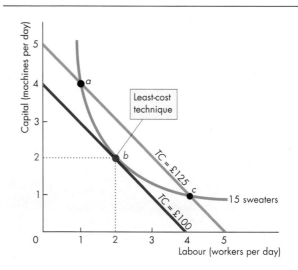

The least-cost technique of producing 15 sweaters occurs when 2 machines and 2 workers are employed at point *b*. An output of 15 sweaters can be produced with the technique illustrated by point *a* (4 machines and 1 worker) or with the technique illustrated by point *c* (1 machine and 4 workers). With either of these techniques, the total cost is £125 and exceeds the total cost at *b* of £100. At *b*, the isoquant for 15 sweaters is tangential to the isocost line for £100. The isocost line and the isoquant have the same slope. If the isoquant intersects the isocost line – for example at *a* and *c* – the least-cost technique has not been found. With the least-cost technique, the marginal rate of substitution (slope of isoquant) equals the relative price of the inputs (slope of isocost line).

The Least-cost Technique

The **least-cost technique** is the combination of inputs that minimizes the total cost of producing a given output. Let's suppose that Knitters wants to produce 15 sweaters a day. What is the least-cost way of doing this? The answer can be seen in Fig. A10.7. The isoquant for 15 sweaters is shown and the three points on that isoquant (marked *a*, *b* and *c*) illustrate the three techniques of producing 15 sweaters that were shown earlier in Fig. A10.1. The figure also contains two isocost lines – each drawn for a price of capital and a price of labour of £25. One isocost line is for a total cost of £125 and the other is for a total cost of £100.

First, consider point *a*, which is on the isoquant for 15 sweaters and also on the isocost line with a total cost of £125. Knitters can produce 15 sweaters at point *a* by using 1 worker and 4 machines. The total cost, using this technique of production, is £125. Point *c*, which uses 4 workers and 1 machine, is similar to point *a*, except that it shows another technique by which the firm can produce 15 sweaters for a cost of £125.

Next look at point *b*. At this point, Knitters uses 2 machines and 2 workers to produce 15 sweaters at a total cost of £100. Point *b* is the *least-cost technique* or the *economically efficient technique* for producing 15 sweaters, when knitting machines and workers each cost £25 a day. At those input prices, there is no way that Knitters can produce 15 sweaters for less than £100.

There is an important feature of point b, the least-cost technique. At that point, the isoquant on which Knitters is producing (the isoquant for 15 sweaters) has a slope equal to that of the isocost line. The isocost line (for a total cost of £100) is tangential to the isoquant (for 15 sweaters).

Notice that although there is only one way that Knitters can produce 15 sweaters for £100, there are several ways of producing 15 sweaters for more than £100. Techniques shown by points a and c are two examples. All the points between a and b and all the points between b and c are also ways of producing 15 sweaters for a cost that exceeds £100 but is less than £125. That is, there are isocost lines between those shown, for total costs falling between £100 and £125. Those isocost lines cut the isoquant for 15 sweaters at the points between a and b and between b and c. Knitters can also produce 15 sweaters for a cost that even exceeds £125. That is, the firm can change its technique of production by moving to a point on the isoquant higher than point a, and using a more capital-intensive technique than at point a. Or, the firm could move to a point on the isoquant lower than point c, and use a more labour-intensive technique than at point c. All of these ways of producing 15 sweaters are economically inefficient.

You can see that Knitters cannot produce 15 sweaters for less than £100 by imagining the isocost line for £99. That isocost line will not touch the isoquant for 15 sweaters. That is, the firm cannot produce 15 sweaters for £99. At £25 for a unit of each input, £99 will not buy the inputs required to produce 15 sweaters.

Marginal Rate of Substitution Equals Relative Input Price

When a firm is using the least-cost technique of production, the marginal rate of substitution between the inputs equals their relative price. Recall that the marginal rate of substitution is the magnitude of the slope of an isoquant. Relative input prices are measured by the magnitude of the slope of the isocost line. We've just seen that producing at least cost means producing at a point where the isocost line is tangential to the isoquant. Since the two curves are tangential, their slopes are equal. Hence the marginal rate of substitution (the magnitude of the slope of isoquant) equals the relative input price (the magnitude of the slope of isocost line).

You'll perhaps better appreciate the importance of relative input prices if we examine what happens to the least-cost technique when those prices change.

Changes in Input Prices

The least-cost technique of production depends in an important way on the relative prices of the inputs. The case that we've just studied is one in which capital and labour each cost £25 a day. Let's look at two other cases: one where capital costs twice as much as labour and the other where labour costs twice as much as capital.

If knitting machines cost £25 a day and a worker is paid £50 a day, the isocost line becomes twice as steep as the one in Fig. A10.8. That is, to hire 1 more worker, while holding total cost constant, Knitters has to operate 2 fewer knitting machines. Let's see how this change in input prices changes the least-cost production technique. Figure A10.8(a) illustrates this. You can see in that figure the isoquant for 15 sweaters a day and the initial inputs of 2 knitting machines and 2 workers. When wages are £50 a day and knitting machines £25 a day, the isocost line becomes steeper. Also, to continue producing 15 sweaters a day, total cost has to rise. That is, the minimum total cost for producing 15 sweaters is higher than originally. The new, steeper isocost line in the figure is that for the minimum cost at which 15 sweaters can be produced at the new input prices. Along that isocost line, Knitters is spending £140. This is the least-cost method of producing 15 sweaters a day; it is achieved by using 3 machines and 1.3 workers a day. (These inputs cost £140: 3 machines × £25 = £75 and 1.3 workers × £50 = £65.)

Next, let's see what happens if wages stay constant but the cost of a machine increases. In particular, suppose that knitting machines cost £50 a day while wages stay at £25 a day. In this case, the isocost line becomes less steep. Knitters now has to give up only half a worker-day to get one more machine. The effect of this change on the least-cost technique is illustrated in Fig. A10.8(b). Again, the initial isocost line and least-cost technique are shown in the figure. When the cost of capital increases, the isocost line flattens. The least-cost method of producing 15 sweaters a day now uses 1.3 machines and 3 workers a day. This combination again costs Knitters £140 a day, but it is the least-cost method of producing 15 sweaters a day when machines cost £50 and labour £25 a day.

Changes in Input Prices

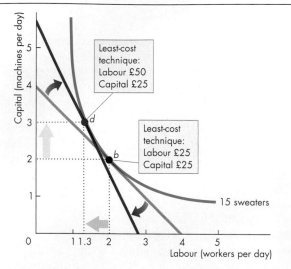

(a) An increase in wages

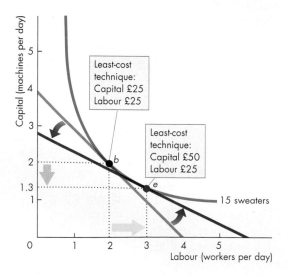

(b) An increase in the price of capital

If the price of labour doubles while the price of capital is held constant, the isocost line becomes twice as steep (part a). The least cost method of producing 15 sweaters a day changes from point *b* to point *d* (using one more machine and 0.7 fewer workers per day). If the price of capital doubles while the price of labour is held constant, the isocost line becomes half as steep (part b). The least cost method of producing 15 sweaters a day now changes from point *b* to point *e*. One additional worker is hired and 0.7 fewer machines are used.

A change in input prices leads to input substitution. Less of the input whose price has increased and more of the other input are used to produce a given output level. The size of this substitution depends on the technology itself. If the inputs are very close substitutes for each other, the isoquants will be almost straight lines and substitution will be large. If the inputs are not close substitutes for each other, the isoquants will be curved very tightly and quite large changes in input prices will lead to only small substitution effects.

Marginal Product and Marginal Cost

When we studied short-run and long-run cost in Chapter 10, we learned about the connection between the marginal product curve of a variable input and the marginal cost curve. In the output range over which marginal product increases, marginal cost decreases; in the output range over which marginal product decreases, marginal cost increases. We also learned in Chapter 10 that it pays a firm to change its plant size if a different plant can produce the firm's desired output at a lower short-run cost than the existing plant. In this appendix, we learned how to calculate the firm's cost-minimizing combination of capital (plant) and labour. Thus our discussion of product curves and cost curves in Chapter 10 and of isocost lines, isoquants and least-cost techniques of production in this appendix both deal with the same problem. But they're looking at the problem from different viewpoints. Let's examine the connection between these two approaches to the firm's cost minimization problem.

First, we're going to learn about the relationship between the marginal rate of substitution and marginal products.

Marginal Rate of Substitution and Marginal Products

The marginal rate of substitution and the marginal products are linked together in a simple formula:

The marginal rate of substitution of labour for capital equals the marginal product of labour divided by the marginal product of capital.

A few steps of reasoning are needed to establish this fact. First, we know that output changes when a firm changes the amount of labour and capital employed. Furthermore, we know that the effect on output of a change in one of the inputs is determined by the marginal product of the input. That is,

$$\text{Change in output} = MP_L \times \Delta L + MP_K \times \Delta K.$$

That is, the change in output is equal to the change in the labour input multiplied by its marginal product plus the change in the capital input multiplied by its marginal product.

Suppose now that the firm wants to remain on an isoquant – that is, Knitters wants to produce the same number of sweaters when it changes its labour and capital inputs. To remain on an isoquant, the change in output must be zero. We can make the change of output zero in the above equation, and doing so yields the equation

$$MP_L \times \Delta L = -MP_K \times \Delta K$$

This equation tells us what must happen to the capital and labour inputs for Knitters to stay on an isoquant. If the labour input rises, the capital input must fall or, equivalently, if the labour input falls, the capital input must rise. Thus we can write this equation in a slightly different way:

$$MP_L \times \Delta L = MP_K \times -\Delta K$$

If we divide both sides of the above equation by the rise in the labour input (ΔL) and also divide both sides by the marginal product of capital (MP_K), we get

$$-\Delta K/\Delta L = MP_L/MP_K$$

This equation tells us that, when Knitters remains on an isoquant, the fall in its capital input ($-\Delta K$) divided by the rise in its labour input (ΔL) is equal to the marginal product of labour (MP_L) divided by the marginal product of capital (MP_K). But we have defined the marginal rate of substitution of labour for capital as the fall in capital divided by the rise in labour when we remain on a given isoquant. What we have discovered, then, is that the marginal rate of substitution of labour for capital is the ratio of the marginal product of labour to the marginal product of capital.

Marginal Cost

We can use the fact that we have just discovered – that the marginal rate of substitution of labour for capital equals the ratio of the marginal product of labour to the marginal product of capital – to work out an important implication of cost minimization. A few steps are needed and Table A10.3 provides a guide to those steps.

Part (a) defines some symbols. Part (b) reminds us that the marginal rate of substitution of labour for capital is the slope of the isoquant, which in turn equals the ratio of the marginal product of labour (MP_L) to the marginal product of capital (MP_K). Part (b) also reminds us that the magnitude of the slope of the isocost line equals the ratio of the price of labour (P_L) to the price of capital (P_K). Part (c) of the table summarizes some propositions about a firm that is using the least-cost technique of production.

The first of these propositions is that when the least-cost technique is employed, the slope of the isoquant and the isocost line are the same. That is,

$$MP_L/MP_K = P_L/P_K.$$

The second proposition is that total cost is minimized when the marginal product per pound spent on labour equals the marginal product per pound spent on capital. To see why, just rearrange the above equation in the following way. First, multiply both sides by the marginal product of capital and then divide both sides by the price of labour. We then get

$$MP_L/P_L = MP_K/P_K.$$

This equation says that the marginal product of labour per pound spent on labour is equal to the marginal product of capital per pound spent on capital. In other words, the extra output from the last pound spent on labour equals the extra output from the last pound spent on capital. This makes sense. If the extra output from the last pound spent on labour exceeds the extra output from the last pound spent on capital, it will pay the firm to use less capital and more labour. By doing so, it can produce the same output at a lower total cost. Conversely, if the extra output from the last pound spent on capital exceeds the extra output from the last pound spent on labour it will pay the firm to use less labour and more capital. Again, by doing so, it lowers the cost of producing a given output. A firm achieves the least-cost technique of production only when the extra output from the last pound spent on all the inputs is the same.

TABLE A10.3

The Least-cost Technique

(a) SYMBOLS

Marginal rate of substitution of labour for capital	*MRS*
Marginal product of labour	MP_L
Marginal product of capital	MP_K
Price of labour	P_L
Price of capital	P_K

(b) DEFINITIONS

The magnitude of the slope of the isoquant (*MRS*)	MP_L/MP_K
The magnitude of the slope of the isocost line	P_L/P_K

(c) THE LEAST-COST TECHNIQUE

Slope of the isoquant = Slope of the isocost line

Therefore:	$MP_L/MP_K = P_L/P_K$
Equivalently:	$MP_L/P_L = MP_K/P_K$

That is,

Total cost is minimized when the marginal product per pound spent on labour equals the marginal product per pound spent on capital.

Equivalently, flipping the last equation over:

$$P_L/MP_L = P_K/MP_K$$

That is,

Marginal cost with fixed capital and a change in labour input equals marginal cost with fixed labour and a change in capital input.

The third proposition is that marginal cost with fixed capital and variable labour equals marginal cost with fixed labour and variable capital. To see this proposition, simply flip the last equation over and write it as

$$P_L/MP_L = P_K/MP_K.$$

Expressed in words, this equation says that the price of labour divided by its marginal product must equal the price of capital divided by its marginal product. But what is the price of an input divided by its marginal product? The price of labour divided by the marginal product of labour is marginal cost when the capital input is held constant. To see why this is so, first recall the definition of marginal cost. *Marginal cost* is the change in total cost resulting from a unit increase in output. If output rises because one more unit of labour is employed, total cost rises by the cost of the extra labour, and output rises by the marginal product of the labour. So marginal cost is the price of labour divided by the marginal product of labour. For example, if labour costs £25 a day and if the marginal product of labour is 2 sweaters, then the marginal cost of a sweater is £12.50 (£25 divided by 2).

The price of capital divided by the marginal product of capital has a similar interpretation. The price of capital divided by the marginal product of capital is marginal cost when the labour input is constant. As you can see from the above equation, with the least-cost technique of production, marginal cost is the same regardless of whether the capital input is constant and more labour is used, or the labour input is constant and more capital is used.

CHAPTER 11

COMPETITION

After studying this chapter you will be able to:

◆ Define perfect competition

◆ Explain why a perfectly competitive firm cannot influence the market price

◆ Explain how a competitive industry's output changes when price changes

◆ Explain why firms sometimes shut down temporarily and lay off workers

◆ Explain why firms enter and leave an industry

◆ Predict the effects on an industry and on a typical firm of a change in demand and of a technological advance

◆ Explain why perfect competition is efficient

I T IS MORNING RUSH HOUR AND A SIX-VEHICLE PILE-UP SNARLS THE TRAFFIC ON London's north circular road. Human injuries are light, but the toll in dented car bodies, buckled wheels and damaged tyres, and crushed bumpers is heavy. Competition to clean up the mess begins. Fifty towing companies compete for the initial clean-up. Several hundred body shops battle for a place in a crowded market. How does competition affect prices and profits? ◆ ◆ Whether you want your car fixed, a spectacles prescription filled, or a pizza delivered, you have lots of choice. Just look in the Yellow Pages if you're not convinced! In these fiercely competitive markets, new firms enter and try their luck while other firms are squeezed out of the business. What are the causes and the effects of new firms entering and old firms leaving an industry? ◆ ◆ Car makers, builders and computer manu-facturers sometimes shut down temporarily

Collision Course in Car Repairs

and lay off their workers. Why do firms sometimes act in this way? ◆ ◆ Over the past few years, the prices of goods such as VCRs, Walkmans and personal computers have fallen. What exactly goes on in an industry when the price of its output falls dramatically? What happens to the profits of the firms producing such goods?

◆ ◆ ◆ ◆ This chapter tackles questions like these by studying markets in which firms are locked together in such stiff competition – *perfect* competition – that the best a firm can do is to match its rivals in terms of quality and price. The chapter builds on the cost curves of the previous chapter and introduces some new revenue concepts. It explains how a firm's supply decisions and the market price are determined.

Perfect Competition

In order to study competitive markets, we are going to build a model of a market in which competition is as fierce and extreme as possible. Economists call the most extreme form of competition perfect competition. **Perfect competition** occurs in a market where:

◆ There are many firms, each selling an identical product.
◆ There are many buyers.
◆ There are no restrictions on entry into the industry.
◆ Firms in the industry have no advantage over potential new entrants.
◆ Firms and buyers are completely informed about the prices of the products of each firm in the industry.

Therefore in perfect competition no single firm can exert a significant influence on the market price of a good. Firms in such markets are said to be price takers. A **price taker** is a firm that cannot influence the price of its product.

Perfect competition rarely occurs, but in many real-world industries competition is so fierce that the model of perfect competition is of enormous help in predicting the behaviour of the firms in these industries. Vehicle towing, panel beating, tyre fitting, farming, estate agency, double glazing, plant hire, grocery retailing, roofing, plumbing and decorating are all examples of industries that are highly competitive.

When a Firm Can't Influence Price

Perfectly competitive or, equivalently, price-taking behaviour occurs in markets in which a single firm produces a small fraction of the total output of a particular good. Imagine for a moment that you are a wheat farmer in Yorkshire. You have 100 hectares under cultivation – which sounds like a lot. But then you go on a drive, first heading west. The land turns into rolling hills, but everywhere you look you see fields of wheat. Driving east to the North Sea or south towards Derbyshire reveals similar vistas. You also find fields and fields of wheat in other parts of the world – Australia, Canada, the United States, Argentina and Ukraine. Your 100 hectares is a drop in the ocean.

You are a price taker. Nothing makes your wheat any better than any other farmer's. If everybody else sells their wheat for £115 a tonne and you want £116, why would people buy from you? They can simply go to the next farmer, and the one after that, and buy all they need for £115 a tonne.

Elasticity of Industry and Firm Demand

A price-taking firm faces a demand curve that is perfectly elastic. To see why this is so, let's consider an example. Suppose that there are 1,000 firms of equal size producing a good. Even if one firm doubles its output (a big change for an individual firm), industry output will rise by only 0.1 per cent (one thousandth is 0.1 per cent). Suppose that the elasticity of industry demand for the good is 0.5, then this increase in industry output results in a 0.2 per cent fall in price. To put things in perspective, a price change of this magnitude is £1 on a £500 holiday, 10 pence on a £50 dress, or 1 penny on a £5 concert ticket. But these price changes, although small, are much larger than the ones that result from changes in output of a magnitude that a firm might actually make. Therefore when a firm changes its output rate, the effect of that change on price is tiny and the firm ignores it. The firm behaves as if its own actions have no effect on the market price.

Table 11.1 works through a real-world example – the market for fish – and shows the relationship between the elasticity of demand facing an individual competitive fishery and the fish market as a whole. The elasticity of the market demand for fish is 0.42, but the elasticity of an individual producer's demand is a little more than 40,000.

When we studied the concept of elasticity in Chapter 5, we discovered that a horizontal demand curve has an elasticity of infinity. An elasticity of 40,000 is not quite infinity, but it is very large. A firm whose demand has such an elasticity has, for all practical purposes, an infinitely elastic demand. Such a firm's demand curve is horizontal. The firm is a price taker.

Competition in Everyday Life

We have defined perfect competition as a market where a firm has no choice but to be a price taker. Even massive percentage changes in a firm's own output have only a negligible effect on the market price. In such a situation, there is little point in a firm attempting to set its own price at a level different

TABLE 11.1

Elasticity of a Fishery's Demand

(a) DATA

◆ World output of fish is 76.8 billion kilograms a year.

◆ The average fishery produces 0.8 million kilograms a year.

◆ The average price of fish is 42.5 pence a kilogram.

◆ The elasticity of demand for fish and fish products (η_m) is 0.42.

(b) EFFECT ON WORLD PRICE

◆ If an average fishery raises output by 100 per cent, world output rises by 0.8 million kilograms – 0.00104 per cent.

◆ To calculate change in world price, use the formula

$$\eta_m = \frac{\text{Percentage change in quantity}}{\text{Percentage change in price}}$$

which means that

$$\text{Percentage change in price} = \frac{\text{Percentage change in quantity}}{\eta_m}$$

◆ To find the fall in price use the formula

$$\text{Percentage change in price} = \frac{0.00104}{0.42}$$

$$= 0.00248 \text{ per cent}$$

So a price fall of 0.00248 per cent is a fall of 0.0011 pence per kilogram.

◆ When a firm doubles its output, the price falls by 0.0011 pence per kilogram.

(c) ELASTICITY OF A FISHERY'S DEMAND

◆ The elasticity of a firm's demand (η_f) is given by

$$\eta_f = \frac{\text{Percentage change in firm's output sold}}{\text{Percentage change in price}}$$

$$= \frac{100}{0.00248}$$

$$= 40,323$$

Part (a) provides some data about the market for fish. Most fish is sold frozen and the market for fish is a worldwide market. Part (b) calculates the effects on the world market price of fish if one fishery doubles its output. If one fishery doubles its output, world output will rise by 0.8 million kilograms or change by approximately 0.001 per cent. As a result of this increase in output, the world price of fish falls by 0.00248 per cent or 0.0011 pence a kilogram. Part (c) calculates the elasticity of the individual producer's demand, hf . That elasticity is

from the market. If a firm tries to charge a higher price, no one will buy its output; if it offers its goods for a lower price, it will sell them, but it can sell them for the market price so there is no point in price cutting. Reading between the Lines on pp. 304–305 considers how competition restricts firms' ability to freely determine their own price.

The inability of a perfectly competitive firm to compete by price cutting makes it seem as if a perfectly competitive market is not, in fact, very competitive at all. If firms don't compete on price, in what sense are they competing with each other?

Firms compete with each other in much the same way as athletes or football teams do. Firms try to find new tricks that will give them the edge over their competitors and enable them to win. Sometimes, though, the competition that they face is so stiff that they are left with little room to manoeuvre. This happens in sporting events, too. For example, when two wrestlers are closely matched, they compete with each other, but neither of them has much room to manoeuvre. They are locked in such fierce competition that the best they can do is to match each other's moves, try not to make a mistake, and accept the inevitable – that the outcome will be close and may even be a tie.

Like evenly matched athletes, firms in perfect competition are locked in such a fierce competitive struggle with each other that they have no choice but to mimic each other's actions and put up with an outcome analogous to a tie. They produce comparable quality goods at comparable prices.

Let's now study the behaviour of a perfectly competitive industry, beginning with an examination of the choices made by a typical firm in such an industry.

Firms' Choices in Perfect Competition

A perfectly competitive firm has to make three key decisions:

Whether to stay in the industry or to leave it
If the decision is to stay in the industry, whether to produce or shut down temporarily
If the decision is to produce, how much to produce

◆ In studying the competitive firm's choices, we will continue to look at a model firm whose single objective is to maximize its profit. We'll first consider a situation in which a firm decides to produce. We will then look at the other cases – firms that decide to shut down production temporarily or to leave the industry altogether.

Profit and Revenue

Profit is the difference between a firm's total revenue and total cost. We defined and studied the behaviour of total cost in the last two chapters. But what is total revenue? Let's begin by looking at the concepts of revenue.

Total revenue is the value of a firm's sales. It equals the price of the firm's output multiplied by the number of units of output sold (price × quantity sold). **Average revenue** is total revenue divided by the total quantity sold – revenue per unit sold. Since total revenue is price times quantity sold, average revenue (total revenue divided by quantity sold) equals price. **Marginal revenue** is the change in total revenue resulting from a one-unit increase in the quantity sold. Since, in the case of perfect competition, the price remains constant when the quantity sold changes, the change in total revenue is equal to price multiplied by the change in quantity. Therefore in perfect competition, marginal revenue equals price.

An example of these revenue concepts is set out for Linentex in Fig. 11.1. The table shows three different quantities of linen sold. For a price taker, as the quantity sold varies, the price stays

---

FIGURE 11.1

Demand, Price and Revenue in Perfect Competition

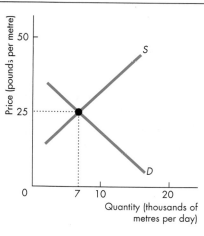

(a) Linen industry

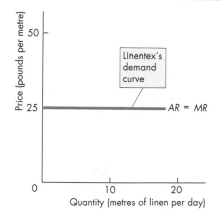

(b) Linentex's demand, average revenue and marginal revenue

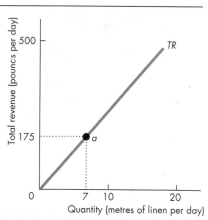

(c) Linentex's total revenue

Quantity sold (Q) (metres per day)	Price (P) (pounds per metre)	Total revenue (TR = P x Q) (pounds)	Average revenue (AR = TR/Q) (pounds per metre)	Marginal revenue (MR = ΔTR/ΔQ) (pounds per metre)
7	25	175	25	
				25
8	25	200	25	
				25
9	25	225	25	

In perfect competition, price is determined where the industry demand and supply curves intersect. Such an equilibrium is illustrated in part (a) where the price is £25 and 7,000 metres are bought and sold. Linentex, a perfectly competitive firm, faces a fixed price, £25 in this example, regardless of the quantity it produces. The table calculates Linentex's total, average and marginal revenue. For example, when 7 metres are sold, total revenue is £175, and average revenue is £25. When sales increase from 7 metres to 8 metres, marginal revenue equals £25. The demand curve faced by Linentex is perfectly elastic at the market price and is shown in part (b) of the figure. Linentex's demand curve is also its average revenue curve and marginal revenue curve (AR = MR). Linentex's total revenue curve (TR) is shown in part (c). Point a on the total revenue curve corresponds to the first row of the table.

An example of these revenue concepts is set out for Linentex in Fig. 11.1. The table shows three different quantities of linen sold. For a price taker, as the quantity sold varies, the price stays constant – in this example at ₤25 a metre. Total revenue is equal to price multiplied by quantity. For example, if Linentex sells 8 metres, total revenue is 8 times ₤25, which equals ₤200. Average revenue is total revenue divided by quantity. Again, if Linentex sells 8 metres, average revenue is total revenue (₤200) divided by quantity (8), which equals ₤25. Marginal revenue is the change in total revenue resulting from a one-unit change in quantity. For example, when the quantity sold rises from 7 to 8 metres, total revenue rises from ₤175 to ₤200, so marginal revenue is ₤25. (Notice that in the table, marginal revenue appears *between* the lines for the quantities sold. This arrangement presents a visual reminder that marginal revenue results from the *change* in the quantity sold.)

Suppose that Linentex is one of a thousand similar small producers of linen. The demand and supply curves for the entire linen industry are shown in Fig. 11.1(a). Demand curve *D* intersects supply curve *S* at a price of ₤25 and a quantity of 7,000 metres. Figure 11.1(b) shows Linentex's demand curve. Since the firm is a price taker, its demand curve is perfectly elastic – the horizontal line at ₤25. The figure also illustrates Linentex's total, average and marginal revenues, calculated in the table. The average revenue curve and marginal revenue curve are the same as the firm's demand curve. That is, the firm's demand curve tells us the revenue per metre sold and the change in total revenue that results from selling one more metre. Linentex's total revenue curve (part c) shows the total revenue for each quantity sold. For example, when Linentex sells 7 metres, total revenue is ₤175 (point *a*). Since each additional metre sold brings in a constant amount – in this case ₤25 – the total revenue curve is an upward-sloping straight line.

revenue and marginal revenue are each equal to the price, so the marginal revenue and average revenue curves are the same as the firm's demand curve. Total revenue rises as the quantity sold rises. ◆

Profit-maximizing Output

Profit is the difference between a firm's total revenue and total cost. Maximizing profit is the same thing as maximizing the difference between total revenue and total cost. Even though a perfectly competitive firm cannot influence its price, it can influence its profit by choosing its level of output. As we have just seen, a perfectly competitive firm's total revenue changes when its output changes. Also, as we discovered in Chapter 10, a firm's total cost varies as its output varies. By changing its inputs and its output, a firm can change its total cost. In the *short run*, a firm can change its output by changing its variable inputs and by changing the intensity with which it operates its fixed inputs. In the *long run*, a firm can vary all its inputs. Let's work out how a firm maximizes profit in the short run.

Total Revenue, Total Cost and Profit Figure 11.2 shows Linentex's total revenue, total cost and profit both as numbers (in the table) and as curves (in the graphs). Part (a) of the figure shows Linentex's total revenue and total cost curves. These curves are graphs of the numbers shown in the first three columns of the table. The total revenue curve (*TR*), is the same as that in Fig. 11.1(c). The total cost curve (*TC*), is similar to the one that you met in Chapter 10. Notice that Linentex's total cost is ₤25 when output is zero. This amount is Linentex's fixed cost – the cost that is incurred even if nothing is produced and sold. As output increases, so does total cost.

The difference between total revenue and total cost is profit. As you can see in Fig. 11.2(b), Linentex will make a profit at any output above 4 and below 12 metres a day. At outputs below 4 metres, Linentex makes a loss. A loss is also made if output exceeds 12 metres a day. At outputs of 4 metres and 12 metres, total cost equals total revenue. Linentex makes zero profit. An output at which total cost equals total revenue is called a **break-even point**.

Linentex's profit, calculated in the final column of the table, is graphed in Fig. 11.2(b). Notice the

---

R E V I E W

A firm in a perfectly competitive market is a price taker. The firm's demand curve is perfectly elastic at the market price. The firm's average

FIGURE 11.2

Total Revenue, Total Cost and Profit

(a) Revenue and cost

(b) Profit and loss

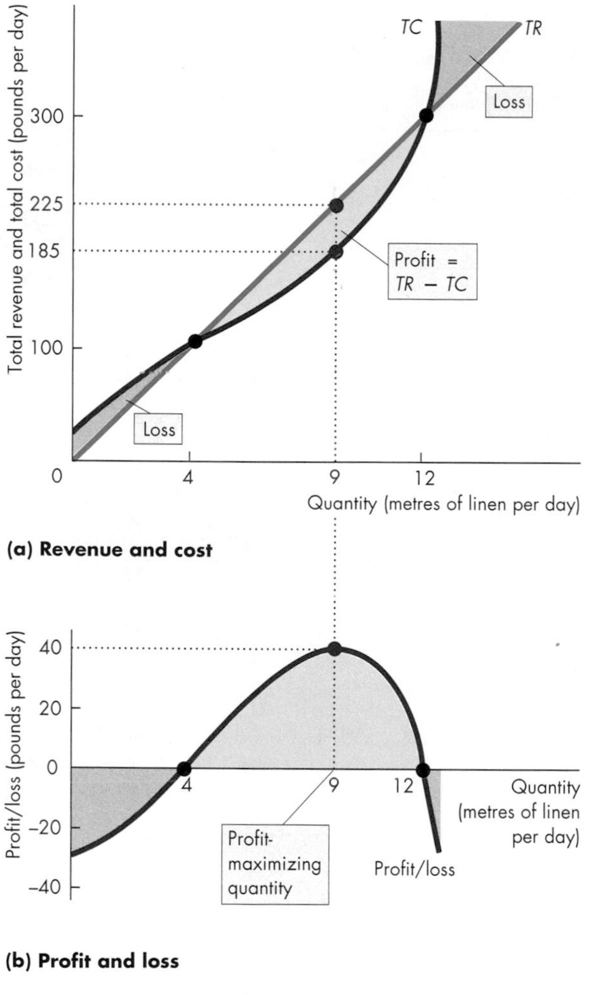

Quantity (Q) (metres per day)	Total revenue (TR) (pounds)	Total cost (TC) (pounds)	Profit (TR − TC) (pounds)
0	0	25	−25
1	25	49	−24
2	50	69	−19
3	75	86	−11
4	100	100	0
5	125	114	11
6	150	128	22
7	175	144	31
8	200	163	37
9	225	185	40
10	250	212	38
11	275	246	29
12	300	300	0
13	325	360	−35

The table lists Linentex's total revenue, total cost and profit. Part (a) graphs the total revenue and total cost curves. Profit is seen in part (a) as the blue area between the total cost and total revenue curves. The maximum profit, £40 a day, occurs when 9 metres are produced — where the vertical distance between the total revenue and total cost curves is at its largest. At outputs of 4 metres a day and 12 metres a day, Linentex makes zero profit — these are break-even points. At outputs below 4 and above 12 metres a day, Linentex makes a loss. Part (b) of the figure shows Linentex's profit curve. The profit curve is at its highest when profit is at a maximum and cuts the horizontal axis at the break-even points.

relationship between the total revenue, total cost and profit curves. Profit is measured by the vertical distance between the total revenue and total cost curves. When the total revenue curve in part (a) is above the total cost curve, between 4 and 12 metres, the firm is making a profit and the profit curve in part (b) is above the horizontal axis. At the break-even point, where the total cost and total revenue curves intersect, the profit curve cuts the horizontal axis.

When the profit curve is at its highest, the distance between TR and TC is greatest. In this example, profit maximization occurs at an output of 9 metres a day. At this output, profit is £40 a day.

Marginal Calculations In working out Linentex's profit-maximizing output, we examined its cost and revenue schedules and from all the possibilities

FIGURE 11.3

Marginal Revenue, Marginal Cost and Profit-maximizing Output

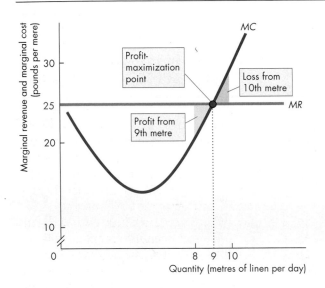

Quantity (Q) (metres per day)	Total revenue (TR) (pounds)	Marginal revenue (MR) (pounds per metre)	Total cost (TC) (pounds)	Marginal cost (MC) (pounds per metre)	Profit (TR−TC) (pounds)
0	0		25		−25
		25		24	
1	25		49		−24
		25		20	
2	50		69		−19
		25		17	
3	75		86		−11
		25		14	
4	100		100		0
		25		14	
5	125		114		11
		25		14	
6	150		128		22
		25		16	
7	175		144		31
		25		19	
8	200		163		37
		25		22	
9	225		185		40
		25		27	
10	250		212		38
		25		34	
11	275		246		29
		25		54	
12	300		300		0
		25		60	
13	325		360		−35

Another way of finding the profit-maximizing output is to determine the output at which marginal revenue equals marginal cost. The table shows that if output rises from 8 to 9 metres, marginal cost is £22, which is less than the marginal revenue of £25. If output rises from 9 to 10 metres, marginal cost is £27, which exceeds the marginal revenue of £25. The figure shows that marginal cost and marginal revenue are equal when Linentex produces 9 metres a day. If marginal revenue exceeds marginal cost, an increase in output increases profit. If marginal revenue is less than marginal cost, an increase in output lowers profit. If marginal revenue equals marginal cost, profit is maximized.

picked out the point at which profit is at a maximum. There is a quicker, neater and more powerful way of figuring out the profit-maximizing output. All Linentex has to do is to calculate its marginal cost and marginal revenue and compare the two. If marginal revenue exceeds marginal cost, it pays to produce more. If marginal revenue is less than marginal cost, it pays to produce less. When marginal revenue and marginal cost are equal, profit is maximized. Let's convince ourselves that this rule works.

Look at the table in Fig. 11.3. It records Linentex's marginal revenue and marginal cost. Recall that marginal revenue is the change in revenue per unit change in the quantity sold and is, for a perfectly competitive firm, the same as its price. In this case,

marginal revenue is £25. Marginal cost is the change in total cost per unit change in output. For example, when output rises from 8 to 9 metres, total cost rises from £163 to £185, a rise of £22, which is the marginal cost of changing the output rate from 8 to 9 metres a day. The marginal revenue and marginal cost curves corresponding to the table appear in Fig. 11.3.

Now focus on the highlighted row of the table. When output rises from 8 to 9 metres, marginal cost is £22. Since marginal revenue is £25, the rise in total revenue exceeds the rise in total cost. Profit goes up by the difference – £3. By looking at the last column of the table, you can see that profit does indeed rise by £3. Because marginal revenue exceeds marginal cost, it pays to expand output from 8 to 9 metres. At 8 metres a day, profit is £37 and at 9 metres a day it is £40 – £3 more.

Suppose that output is expanded further to 10 metres a day. Marginal revenue is still £25, but marginal cost is now £27. Marginal cost exceeds marginal revenue by £2. So the increase in output to 10 metres increases total cost by £2 more than total revenue and profit falls by £2.

So, to maximize profit, all Linentex has to do is to compare marginal cost and marginal revenue. As long as marginal revenue exceeds marginal cost, it pays to increase output. Linentex keeps increasing output until the cost of producing one more metre equals the price at which the metre can be sold. At that point it is making maximum profit. If Linentex makes one more metre, that metre will cost more to produce than the revenue it will bring in, so Linentex will not produce it.

Profit in the Short Run

We've just seen that we can calculate a firm's profit-maximizing output by comparing marginal revenue with marginal cost. But maximizing profit is not the same thing as *making* a profit. Maximizing profit can

mean minimizing loss. We cannot tell whether a firm is actually making a profit only by comparing the marginal revenue and marginal cost curves. To check whether a firm is making a profit, we need to look at total revenue and total cost, as we did before, or we need to compare average total cost with price. When a firm makes a profit, average total cost is lower than price. If average total cost exceeds price, the firm makes a loss. When average total cost equals price, the firm breaks even.

Three Possible Profit Outcomes   The three possible profit outcomes in the short run are illustrated in Fig. 11.4. In part (a), Linentex is making an economic profit. At a price of £25, marginal revenue equals marginal cost at an output of 9 metres a day. That is, the profit-maximizing output is 9 metres a day. Average total cost is £20.56, which is lower than the market price. Linentex's economic profit is represented by the blue rectangle. The height of that rectangle is the gap between price and average total cost, or economic profit per metre. Its length shows the quantity of metres produced. So the rectangle's area measures Linentex's economic profit: profit per metre (its height – £4.44 a metre) multiplied by the

---

FIGURE 11.4

Three Possible Profit Outcomes in the Short Run

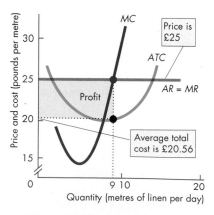

(a) Economic profit

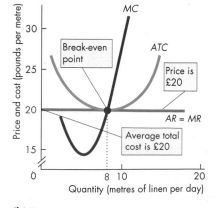

(b) Zero economic profit

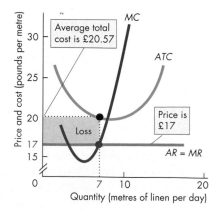

(c) Economic loss

In the short run a firm's economic profit may be positive, zero (a break-even) or negative (a loss). If the market price is greater than the average total cost of producing the profit-maximizing output, the firm makes a profit (part a). If price

equals minimum average total cost, the firm breaks even (part b). If the price is below minimum average total cost, the firm makes a loss (part c). The firm's profit is shown as the blue rectangle and the firm's loss is the red rectangle.

number of metres produced (its length – 9 metres) equals total profit (its area – £40).

In part (b), Linentex breaks even. At a price of £20, Linentex's profit-maximizing output is 8 metres a day. The average total cost of producing this output level is £20, the same as its price. It is also the minimum average total cost. The maximum profit that Linentex can make in this case is zero.

In part (c), Linentex incurs an economic loss. At a price of £17, the profit-maximizing output is 7 metres a day. At that output, average total cost is £20.57, so the firm is losing £3.57 a metre and incurring a total loss of £25.

Temporary Plant Shutdown   There are some situations in which a firm's profit-maximizing decision is to shut down temporarily, lay off its workers and produce nothing. A firm's **shutdown point** is the level of output and price where the firm is just covering its total *variable* cost. If the price is so low that total revenue is not enough to cover total variable cost, the firm shuts down.

A firm cannot escape its fixed costs. These costs are incurred even at zero output. A firm that shuts down and produces no output makes a loss equal to its total fixed cost. If the price just equals average variable cost, total revenue equals total variable cost and the firm's loss equals its total fixed cost. But if price is below average variable cost, total revenue does not cover total variable cost and if the firm produces just one unit of output, its loss exceeds total fixed cost. It is in such a situation that the firm minimizes its loss by shutting down. Its loss then equals total fixed cost.

The shutdown point is reached when the market price falls to a level equal to the minimum average variable cost. Table 11.2 illustrates what happens at the shutdown point. The table has two parts: part (a) shows a case in which it just pays the firm to keep producing, and part (b) shows a case in which it just pays the firm to shut down. The table shows Linentex's total fixed cost, total variable cost and total cost of producing 6, 7 and 8 metres a day. It also shows the average variable cost and marginal cost. The cost data are the same in parts (a) and (b) of the table.

Next let's look at the revenue. In part (a), the price of linen is £17 a metre. To find Linentex's total revenue, multiply the price by the quantity sold. We calculate the profit or loss (and they are all losses in this case) by subtracting total cost from total revenue.

For example, if Linentex sells 7 metres at £17 a metre, then total revenue is £119. Total cost is £144, so the loss equals £144 minus £119, which is £25. We calculate the loss from producing 6 metres or 8 metres in a similar way.

The minimum loss occurs when 7 metres are produced. You can see that fact directly by looking at the profit or loss column. You can also check that the loss is minimized by looking at marginal cost and marginal revenue. Increasing output from 6 to 7 metres has a marginal cost of £16 but a marginal revenue of £17, so total revenue rises by more than total cost. Increasing output still further, from 7 to 8 metres, has a marginal cost of £19, which exceeds marginal revenue, so profit falls (loss rises).

Linentex's loss when producing 7 metres exactly equals its total fixed cost – £25. Alternatively, if Linentex produces nothing, it will also lose its £25 of total fixed cost. So, at a price of £17 Linentex is indifferent between producing and shutting down – it makes a loss equal to its fixed cost.

In part (b) the price is £16.99 – a lower price but by just 1 penny. Costs are unchanged. We calculate total revenue and profit in the same way as before. The output that maximizes profit (minimizes loss) is still 7 metres but, in this case, the minimum possible loss is £25.07. Linentex loses 7 pence more than it would if it produced nothing at all. The firm will shut down. Its minimum average variable cost is £17. At £17, it just pays to produce and at £16.99 it just pays to shut down. The minimum output that it pays Linentex to produce is 7 metres.

Real-world Shutdowns   Shutdowns occur in the real world either because of a fall in price or because of a rise in costs. Shutdowns occur most frequently in raw material producing sectors as a result of fluctuating prices. For example, if the price of gold falls, gold mines temporarily stop producing. If the price of tin falls, tin mines shut down. Shutdowns also occur in many industries such as those producing cars and agricultural equipment, and in agriculture, forestry and fisheries.

A recent real-world example of a shutdown occurred at Harland and Wolff, one of the largest shipbuilders in the United Kingdom. As reported in the press, the reason for this shutdown was the lack of orders for ships. But translated into economic terms, what this shutdown means is that the price at which Harland and Wolff could sell ships did not enable it to cover its variable costs.

TABLE 11.2

The Shutdown Point

(a) LINENTEX KEEPS ON PRODUCING

Output (metres per day)	Total fixed cost (pounds)	Total variable cost (pounds)	Total cost (pounds)	Average variable cost (pounds per metre)	Marginal cost (pounds per metre)	Price (pounds per metre)	Total revenue (pounds)	Marginal revenue (pounds per day)	Profit (+) Loss (−) (pounds)
6	25	103	128	17.17		17	102		−26
					16			17	
7	25	119	144	17.00		17	119		−25
					19			17	
8	25	138	163	17.25		17	136		−27

(b) LINENTEX SHUTS DOWN

Output (metres per day)	Total fixed cost (pounds)	Total variable cost (pounds)	Total cost (pounds)	Average variable cost (pounds per metre)	Marginal cost (pounds per metre)	Price (pounds per metre)	Total revenue (pounds)	Marginal revenue (pounds per day)	Profit (+) Loss (−) (pounds)
6	25	103	128	17.17		16.99	101.94		−26.06
					16			16.99	
7	25	119	144	17.00		16.99	118.93		−25.07
					19			16.99	
8	25	138	163	17.25		16.99	135.92		−27.08

The shutdown point occurs at the point of minimum average variable cost. If price equals minimum average variable cost, Linentex is indifferent between producing at the shutdown point and producing nothing. If price falls below minimum average variable cost, Linentex will maximize its profit by producing nothing. Minimum average variable cost is £17 and occurs at 7 metres of linen a day. If the price is £17 a metre and Linentex produces 7 metres, its loss equals its total fixed cost of £25 (part a). If the price falls to £16.99, even when Linentex produces at the point of minimum average variable cost, it would make a loss that is bigger than its total fixed cost and so it would shut down (part b).

REVIEW

In perfect competition, a firm's marginal revenue equals its price. A firm maximizes profit by producing the output at which marginal cost equals marginal revenue (equals price). The smallest output a firm will produce is that at which average variable cost is at a minimum. If price falls below the minimum of average variable cost, the best a firm can do is to stop producing and make a loss equal to its total fixed cost. Maximizing profit is not the same thing as making a profit. In the short run, a firm can make a profit, break even or make a loss. The maximum loss that a firm will make is equal to its total fixed cost. ◆

The Firm's Supply Curve

A **perfectly competitive firm's supply curve** shows how a firm's profit-maximizing output varies as the market price varies, other things remaining constant. We are now going to derive Linentex's supply curve. Actually, we have already calculated three points on Linentex's supply curve. We discovered that when the price is £25, Linentex produces 9 metres a day; when the price is £20, Linentex produces 8 metres a day; and when the price is £17, Linentex is indifferent between producing 7 metres a day and shutting down. We are now going to derive Linentex's entire supply curve. Figure 11.5 illustrates the analysis.

Figure 11.5(a) shows Linentex's marginal cost and average variable cost curves and Fig. 11.5(b) shows its supply curve. There is a direct connection between the marginal cost and average variable cost curves and the supply curve. Let's see what that connection is.

The smallest quantity that Linentex will supply is at the shutdown point. When the price is equal to the minimum average variable cost, the marginal revenue curve is MR_0 and the firm produces the output at its shutdown point – point s in the figure. If the price falls below minimum average variable cost, Linentex produces nothing. As the price rises above its minimum average variable cost, Linentex's output rises. Since Linentex maximizes profit by producing the output at which marginal cost equals price, we can determine from its marginal cost curve how much the firm produces at each price. At a price of £25, the marginal revenue curve is MR_1. Linentex maximizes profit by producing 9 metres. At a price of £31, the marginal revenue curve is MR_2 and Linentex produces 10 metres. The supply curve, shown in Fig. 11.5(b), has two separate parts. First, in the range of prices that exceed the minimum average variable cost, the supply curve is the same as the marginal cost curve – above the shutdown point (s). Second, at prices below minimum average variable cost, Linentex shuts down and produces nothing and its supply curve runs along the vertical axis.

So far, we have studied a single firm in isolation. We have seen that the firm's profit–maximizing actions depend on the market price, which the firm takes as given. The higher the price, the larger is the quantity that the firm will choose to produce – the firm's supply curve is upward sloping. But how is the market price determined? To answer this question, we need to study not one firm in isolation but the market as a whole.

FIGURE 11.5

Linentex's Supply Curve

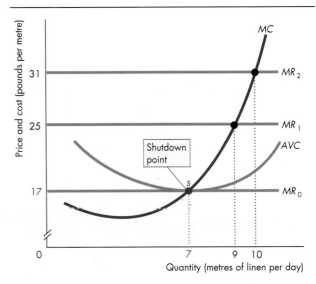

(a) Marginal cost and average variable cost

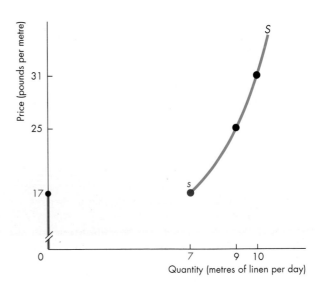

(b) Firm's supply curve

Part (a) shows Linentex's profit-maximizing output at each market price. At £25 a metre, Linentex produces 9 metres. At £17 a metre, Linentex produces 7 metres. At any price below £17 a metre, Linentex produces nothing. Linentex's shutdown point is s. Part (b) shows Linentex's supply curve – the number of metres Linentex will produce at each price. Linentex's supply curve is made up of its marginal cost curve (part a) at all points above the average variable cost curve, and the vertical axis at all prices below minimum average variable cost.

Output, Price and Profit in the Short Run

Market price is determined by industry demand and industry supply. It is the price that makes the quantity demanded equal the quantity supplied. But the quantity supplied depends on the supply decisions of all the individual firms in the industry. Those supply decisions, in turn, depend on the market price.

A short-run equilibrium prevails in a competitive market when each firm operates its plant to produce the profit-maximizing output level and when the total quantity produced by all the firms in the market equals the quantity demanded at that price. To find the short-run equilibrium, we first need to construct the short-run industry supply curve.

Short-run Industry Supply Curve

The **short-run industry supply curve** shows how the total quantity supplied in the short run by all firms in an industry varies as the market price varies. The quantity supplied in the short run by the industry at a given price is the sum of the quantities supplied in the short run by all firms in the industry at that price. To construct the industry supply curve, we sum horizontally the supply curves of the individual firms. Let's see how we do that.

Suppose that the competitive linen industry consists of 1,000 firms exactly like Linentex. The relationship between a firm's supply curve and the industry supply curve, for this case, is illustrated in Fig. 11.6. Each of the 1,000 firms in the industry has a supply schedule like Linentex's, set out in the table. At a price below £17, every firm in the industry will shut down production so that the industry will supply nothing. At £17, each firm is indifferent between shutting down and producing 7 metres. Since each firm is indifferent, some firms will produce and others will shut down. Industry supply can be anything between 0 (all firms shut down) and 7,000 (all firms producing 7 metres a day each). Thus at £17, the industry supply curve is horizontal – it is perfectly elastic. As the price rises above £17, each firm increases its quantity supplied and the industry quantity supplied also increases, but by 1,000 times that of each individual firm.

The supply schedules set out in the table form the basis of the supply curves that are graphed in Fig. 11.6. Linentex and every other firm has the supply curve S_F shown in Fig. 11.6(a); the industry supply curve S_I is shown in Fig. 11.6(b). Look carefully at the units on the horizontal axes of parts (a) and (b) and note that in part (a) the units are metres while in part (b) they are thousands of metres. There are two important differences. First, at each price, the quantity supplied by the industry is 1,000 times the quantity supplied by a single firm. Second, at a price of £17, the firm supplies either nothing or 7 metres a day. There is no individual firm supply curve between those two numbers. But for the industry, any quantity between zero and 7,000 will be produced, so the industry supply curve is perfectly elastic over that range.

Short-run Competitive Equilibrium

Price and industry output are determined by industry demand and supply. Three different possible short-run competitive equilibrium positions are shown in Fig. 11.7. The supply curve S is the same as S_I, which we derived in Fig. 11.6. If the demand curve is D_1, the equilibrium price is £25 a metre and industry output is 9,000 metres a day. If the demand curve is D_2, the price is £20 and industry output is 8,000 metres a day. If the demand curve is D_3, the price is £17 and industry output is 7,000 metres a day.

To see what is happening to each individual firm and its profit in these three situations, you need to check back to Fig. 11.4. With demand curve D_1, the price is £25 a metre, each firm produces 9 metres a day and makes a profit, as shown in Fig. 11.4(a); if the demand curve is D_2, the price is £20 a metre, each firm produces 8 metres a day and makes a zero profit, as shown in Fig. 11.4(b); and if the demand curve is D_3, the price is £17 a metre, each firm is indifferent between producing 7 metres a day and shutting down and, in either event, is making a loss equal to total fixed cost, as shown in Fig. 11.4(c). If the demand curve shifts further to the left than D_3, the price will remain constant at £17 a metre since the industry supply curve is horizontal at that price. Some firms will continue to produce 7 metres a day and others will shut down. Firms will be indifferent between these two activities and, whichever they choose, will make a loss equal to their total fixed cost. The number of firms continuing to produce will just be enough to satisfy the market demand at a price of £17.

FIGURE 11.6

Firm and Industry Supply Curves

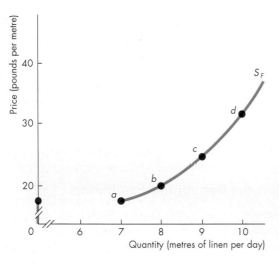

(a) Linentex

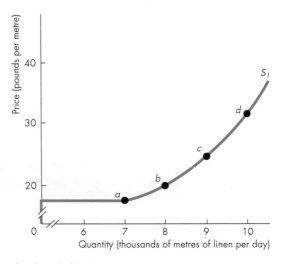

(b) Linen industry

The industry supply schedule is the sum of the supply schedules of all individual firms. An industry that consists of 1,000 identical firms has a supply schedule similar to that of the individual firm. But the quantity supplied by the industry is 1,000 times as large as that of the individual firm (see table). At the shutdown price, the firm produces either 0 or 7 metres per day. The industry supply curve is perfectly elastic at the shutdown price. Part (a) shows Linentex's supply curve, S_F, and part (b), the metre industry supply curve, S_I. Points a, b, c and d correspond to the rows of the table. Note that the unit of measurement on the horizontal axis for the industry supply curve is 1,000 times the unit for Linentex.

	Price (pounds per metre)	Quantity supplied by Linentex (metres per day)	Quantity supplied by industry (metres per day)
a	17	0 or 7	0 to 7,000
b	20	8	8,000
c	25	9	9,000
d	31	10	10,000

R E V I E W

In a competitive industry, the price and quantity sold are determined by industry supply and industry demand. Industry supply is the sum of the supplies of all the individual firms. The price determined by industry demand and supply cannot be influenced by the actions of any one individual firm. Each firm takes the market price and, given that price, maximizes profit. The firm maximizes its profit by producing the output at which marginal cost equals marginal revenue (equals price), as long as price is not lower than minimum average variable cost. If the price falls below minimum average variable cost, the firm shuts down and incurs a loss equal to its total fixed cost. ◆

FIGURE 11.7

Three Short-run Equilibrium Positions for a Competitive Industry

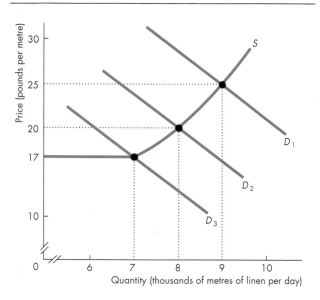

The competitive linen industry's supply curve is *S*. If demand is D_1, the price is £25 and the industry produces 9,000 metres. If demand is D_2, the price is £20 and industry output is 8,000 metres. If demand is D_3, the price is £17 and industry output is 7,000 metres. To see what is happening to the individual firms, look back at Fig.11.4. When the price is £25, the firms are making a profit; when the price is £20, they are breaking even (making zero profit); and when the price is £17 they are incurring a loss. Even when they make a loss, the firms are maximizing profit (minimizing loss).

Output, Price and Profit in the Long Run

We have seen that in short-run equilibrium a firm might make a profit, a loss or break even. Though each of these three situations is a short-run equilibrium, only one of them is a long-run equilibrium. To see why, we need to examine the dynamic forces at work in a competitive industry. An industry adjusts over time in two ways. First, the number of firms in the industry changes; second, the

existing firms change the scale of their plants, thereby shifting their short-run cost curves. Let's study the effects of these two dynamic forces in a competitive industry.

Entry and Exit

Entry is the act of setting up a new firm in an industry. **Exit** is the act of closing down a firm and leaving an industry. When will a new firm enter an industry or an existing one leave? How do entry and exit affect the market price, profit and output in an industry? Let's first look at the causes of entry and exit.

Profits and Losses as Signals   What triggers entry and exit? The prospect of profit triggers entry and the prospect of continuing losses triggers exit. Temporary profits and temporary losses that are purely random, like the winnings and losings at a casino, do not trigger entry or exit, but the prospect of profits or losses for some foreseeable future period does. An industry making economic profits attracts new entrants; one making economic losses induces exits; and an industry in which neither economic losses nor economic profits are being made stimulates neither entry nor exit. Thus profits and losses are the signals to which firms respond in making entry and exit decisions.

What are the effects of entry and exit on price and profits?

Effects of Entry and Exit on Price and Profits   The immediate effect of entry and exit is to shift the industry supply curve. If more firms enter an industry, the industry supply curve shifts to the right: supply increases. If firms exit an industry, the industry supply curve shifts to the left: supply falls. The effects of entry and exit on price and on the total quantity sold in the linen industry are shown in Fig. 11.8.

Entry   First, let's look at what happens when new firms enter an industry. Suppose that the demand curve for metres is D_1 and the industry supply curve is S_1, so linen sells for £25 a metre and 9,000 metres are being bought and sold. Now suppose that some new firms enter the industry. As they do so, the industry supply curve shifts to the right to become S_2. With the higher supply and unchanged demand, there is a fall in price from £25 to £20 a metre and

FIGURE 11.8

Entry and Exit

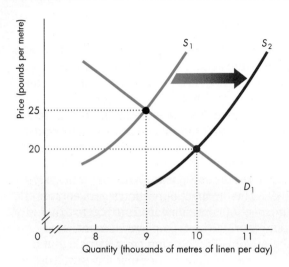

(a) Effect of entry

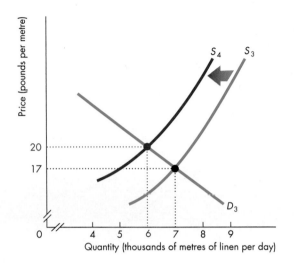

(b) Effect of exit

When new firms enter the linen industry, the industry supply curve shifts to the right, from S_1 to S_2 (part a). The equilibrium price falls from £25 to £20, and the quantity sold increases from 9,000 to 10,000 metres. When firms exit

the linen industry, the industry supply curve shifts to the left, from S_3 to S_4 (part b). The equilibrium price rises from £17 to £20, and the quantity sold decreases from 7,000 to 6,000 metres.

an increase in the quantity of metres traded from 9,000 to 10,000.

As the price falls, Linentex and the other firms in the industry will react by cutting their output. That is, for each existing firm in the industry, its profit-maximizing output falls. Since the price falls, and since each firm sells less, profit falls for each firm. You can see this reduction of profit by glancing back at Fig. 11.4. Initially, when the price is £25 a metre, each firm makes a profit and is in the situation shown in Fig. 11.4(a). When the price falls to £20 a metre, the firm's profit disappears and it is in the situation shown in Fig. 11.4(b).

You have just discovered an important result:

As new firms enter an industry, the price falls and the profit of each existing firm falls.

A good example of this process has occurred in the last few years in the personal computer industry. When IBM introduced its first personal computer in the early 1980s, the price of the machines gave IBM

a big profit. Very quickly thereafter new firms such as Compaq, Zenith, Olivetti, Amstrad and a host of others entered the industry with machines technologically identical to IBM's. In fact, they were so similar that they came to be called clones. The massive wave of entry into the personal computer industry shifted the supply curve to the right and lowered the price and the profits for all firms.

Exit   Let's see what happens when firms leave an industry. Again, the impact of a firm leaving is to shift the industry supply curve, but this time to the left as Fig. 11.8(b) illustrates. Suppose that initially the demand curve is D_3 with an industry supply curve S_3, so the market price is £17 a metre and 7,000 metres are being sold. As firms leave the industry, the supply curve shifts to the left and becomes S_4. With the fall in supply, industry output falls from 7,000 to 6,000 metres and the price rises from £17 to £20 a metre.

To see what is happening to Linentex, go back

again to Fig. 11.4. With the demand curve D_3 and a price of £17 a metre, Linentex is in a situation like that illustrated in Fig. 11.4(c). Price is lower than average total cost and Linentex is making a loss. Some firms exit and Linentex (and some others) hang on. As firms exit, the price rises from £17 to £20 a metre, so the firms that remain increase their output and their losses vanish. They are then back in a situation like that illustrated in Fig. 11.4(b).

You have just worked out the second important result:

As firms leave an industry, the price rises and so do the profits of the remaining firms.

Examples of real-world firms that have exited an industry are Laker Airways and De Lorean Cars. Laker pioneered low-cost transatlantic air travel, but when the major airlines matched its prices, Laker sustained persistent losses and exited the industry. De Lorean attempted to break into the luxury sports car market, but was not able to produce at a cost that could compete with established firms, such as Porsche and Ferrari, and so it exited.

Long-run Equilibrium   We've seen that the prospect of profit triggers entry and the prospect of continuing loss triggers exit. We have also seen that entry into an industry lowers the profits of the existing firms and that exit from an industry increases the profits of the remaining firms. Long-run equilibrium results from the interaction of profits and losses as signals to entry and exit and the effects of entry and exit on profits and losses.

Long-run equilibrium occurs in a competitive industry when economic profits are zero. If an industry makes economic profits, firms enter the industry and the supply curve shifts to the right. As a result, the market price falls and so do profits. Firms continue to enter and profits continue to fall as long as the industry is earning positive economic profits.

In an industry with economic losses, some firms will exit. As those firms leave the industry, the supply curve shifts to the left and the market price rises. As the price rises, the industry's losses shrink. As long as losses continue, some firms will leave the industry. Only when losses have been eliminated and zero economic profits are being made will firms stop exiting.

Let's now examine the second way in which the competitive industry adjusts in the long run – by existing firms changing their plant size.

Changes in Plant Size

A firm will change its plant size whenever it can increase its profit by doing so. A situation in which a firm can profitably expand its output by increasing its plant is illustrated in Fig. 11.9. In that figure the price (and marginal revenue) is £20. With its current plant, Linentex's marginal and average total cost – its short-run costs – are shown by the curves *SRMC* and *SRAC*. Linentex maximizes profit by producing 8 metres a day, but with its existing plant, Linentex makes zero economic profit.

Linentex's long-run average cost curve is *LRAC*. By installing more knitting machines – increasing its plant size – Linentex can lower its costs and operate at a positive economic profit. For example, if Linentex increases its plant size so that it operates at point *m*, the minimum of its long-run average cost, it lowers its average cost from £20 to £14 and makes a profit of £6 a metre. Since Linentex is a price taker, expanding output from 8 to 12 metres does not lower the market price and so would be a

---

FIGURE 11.9

Changes in Plant Size

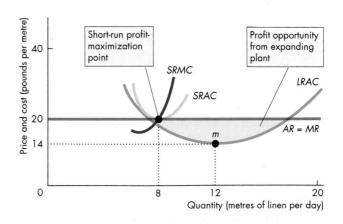

Linentex has a plant whose short-run cost curves are *SRMC* and *SRAC*. The price of a metre is £20, so average revenue and marginal revenue (*AR* = *MR*) are £20. The profit-maximizing short-run output is 8 metres a day. Linentex's long-run costs are described by the long-run average cost curve (*LRAC*). The firm will want to expand its plant to take advantage of lower average costs and make a bigger profit – it will want to move into the blue area. As firms expand, the industry supply increases and the price falls.

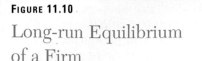

FIGURE 11.10

Long-run Equilibrium of a Firm

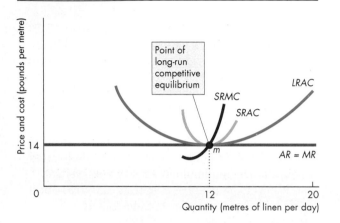

As firms expand their plant, industry supply increases and the price falls. Long-run equilibrium occurs when the price equals £14 and each firm is producing at point m, its point of minimum long-run average cost.

profitable thing for Linentex to do. Because it takes time to change the production plant, the short-run equilibrium prevails. Nevertheless, over time, the firm will gradually expand its plant.

As firms expand their plants, the short-run industry supply curve starts to shift to the right. (Recall that the industry supply curve is the sum of the supply curves of all the individual firms.) With increases in supply and a given demand, the price gradually falls. As the price falls, so do profits. Firms will continue to expand their plants as long as profits are positive. Only when economic profits become zero will firms stick with their existing plant size. There is only one possible plant size that is consistent with long-run equilibrium in a competitive industry and that is the one associated with the minimum long-run average cost (point *m*) in Fig. 11.9.

Figure 11.10 illustrates the long-run competitive equilibrium. It occurs at a price of £14 with each firm producing 12 metres a day. Each firm in the industry has the plant size such that its marginal cost and average total cost curves are *SRMC* and *SRAC*. Each firm produces the output at which its short-run marginal cost equals price. No firm can change its output in the short run and make more

profit. As each firm is producing at minimum long-run average cost (point *m* on *LRAC*) no firm has an incentive to expand or contract its production plant – a bigger plant or a smaller plant will lead to a higher long-run average cost and an economic loss. Finally, no firm has an incentive to leave the industry or to enter it.

REVIEW

Long-run competitive equilibrium is described by three conditions:

◆ Firms maximize short-run profit so that marginal cost equals marginal revenue (equals price).
◆ Economic profits are zero so that no firm has an incentive to enter or to leave the industry.
◆ Long-run average cost is at a minimum so that no firm has an incentive to expand or to contract its plant. ◆

Responding to Changing Tastes and Advancing Technology

Increased awareness of the health hazard of smoking has caused a decrease in the demand for tobacco and cigarettes. The development of inexpensive car and air transport has caused a huge decrease in the demand for long-distance trains and buses. Solid-state electronics have caused a large decrease in the demand for TV and radio repair. The demand for cars made in the European Union has decreased as a result of high-quality alternatives from Japan. What happens in a competitive industry when there is a permanent decrease in the demand for its products?

The development of the microwave oven has produced an enormous increase in demand for paper, glass and plastic cooking utensils, and for cling film. The demand for almost all products is steadily increasing as a result of population growth and increasing incomes. What happens in a competitive industry when the demand for its product increases?

Advances in technology are constantly lowering the costs of production. New biotechnologies have dramatically lowered the costs of many food and pharmaceutical products. New electronic technologies have lowered the cost of producing just about every good and service. What happens in a competitive industry when technological change lowers its production costs?

Let's use the theory of perfect competition to answer these questions.

A Permanent Decrease in Demand

Suppose that an industry starts out in long-run competitive equilibrium, as shown in Fig. 11.11(a). The demand curve labelled D_0 and the supply curve labelled S_0 represent the initial demand and supply in the market. The price initially is P_0 and the total industry output is Q_0. A single firm is shown in

Fig. 11.11(b). Initially, it produces the quantity q_0 and makes zero economic profit.

Now suppose that demand decreases to D_1, as shown in part (a). This decrease in demand causes the price to drop to P_1. At this lower price, each firm produces a smaller output (q_1), and the quantity supplied by the industry decreases from Q_0 to Q_1 as the industry slides down its short-run supply curve (S_0). The industry is now in short-run equilibrium but not long-run equilibrium. It is in short-run equilibrium because each firm is maximizing profit. But it is not in long-run equilibrium because each firm is making an economic loss – its average total cost exceeds the price.

In this situation, firms will leave the industry. As they do so, the industry supply curve starts shifting to the left, the quantity supplied shrinks and the price

FIGURE 11.11

A Decrease in Demand

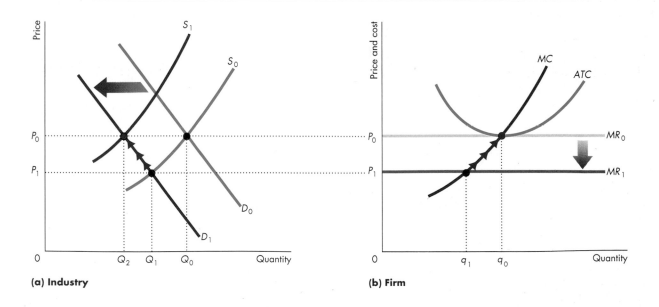

(a) Industry

(b) Firm

An industry starts out in long-run competitive equilibrium. Part (a) shows the industry demand curve D_0 and the industry supply curve S_0, the equilibrium quantity Q_0 and the market price P_0. Each firm sells at price P_0, so its marginal revenue curve is MR_0 in part (b). Each firm produces q_0 and makes a zero profit. Demand decreases from D_0 to D_1 (part a). The equilibrium price falls to P_1, each firm lowers its output to q_1 (part b) and industry output falls to Q_1. In this new situation, firms are making losses and some firms will leave the industry.

As they do so, the industry supply curve gradually shifts to the left, from S_0 to S_1. This shift gradually raises the industry price from P_1 back to P_0. While the price is below P_0, firms are making losses and some are leaving the industry. Once the price has returned to P_0, the smaller number of firms whose supply curves add up to the industry supply curve (S_1) will each be making a zero profit. There will be no further incentive for any firm to leave the industry. Each firm produces q_0 and industry output is Q_2.

gradually rises. At each higher price, the profit-maximizing output is higher, so the firms remaining in the industry raise their output as the price rises. Each slides up its marginal cost or supply curve (part b). Eventually, enough firms will have left the industry for the supply curve to have shifted to S_1 (part a). When that has happened, the price will have returned to its original level (P_0). At that price, the firms remaining in the industry will produce the same amount as they did before the fall in demand (q_0). No firms will want to leave the industry because of losses and none will want to enter. The industry supply curve settles down at S_1 and total industry output is Q_2. The industry is again in long-run equilibrium.

The difference between the initial long-run equilibrium and the final long-run equilibrium is the number

of firms in the industry. Fewer firms remain after the adjustment. Each remaining firm produces the same output in the new long-run equilibrium as it did initially. While moving from the original equilibrium to the new one, firms that remain in the industry suffer losses. But they keep their losses to a minimum because they adjust their output to keep price equal to marginal cost.

A Permanent Increase in Demand

What happens in a competitive industry when the demand for its product increases? Let's begin the story again in long-run equilibrium, as shown in Fig. 11.12(a). With demand curve D_0 and supply curve S_0, the market price is P_0 and quantity Q_0 is sold by

FIGURE 11.12

An Increase in Demand

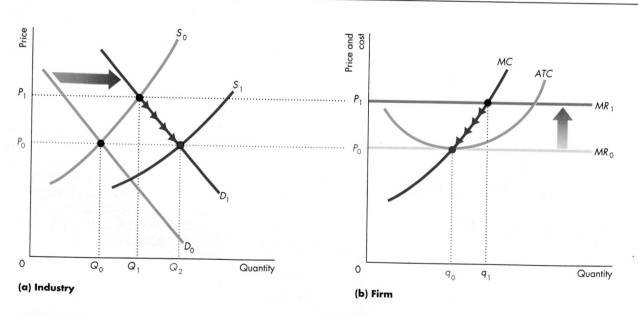

(a) Industry

(b) Firm

A competitive industry is in long-run equilibrium. The demand curve is D_0 and the supply curve S_0 (part a). The industry's output is Q_0 and the market price is P_0. Each firm faces the marginal revenue curve MR_0 and maximizes profit by producing q_0 (part b). Demand increases from D_0 to D_1. The price rises to P_1 and industry output rises to Q_1. Each firm increases its output to q_1. In this situation, firms are making a profit (price is greater than average total cost). New firms will enter the industry and as they do so, the industry supply curve shifts to the right. As the supply curve shifts to the right, the price gradually

falls and each individual firm gradually cuts its output from q_1 back to q_0. Since firms are entering the industry, total industry output rises even though each firm's output is cut back. The new equilibrium occurs when enough firms have entered the industry for the supply curve to have moved to S_1, with the price restored to its original level, P_0, and with each firm making zero profit. At this point, industry output is at Q_2. Since each firm is making a zero profit, there is no further tendency for new firms to enter the industry, so the supply curve remains stationary at S_1.

the industry. Figure 11.12(b) shows a single firm. At price P_0, the firm is making zero economic profit and producing an output of q_0. Now suppose that the demand for the industry's output increases from D_0 to D_1. The increased demand raises the price to P_1. The quantity supplied by the industry rises from Q_0 to Q_1 as each firm increases its output from q_0 to q_1 (part b). At price P_1 and quantity Q_1 the industry is in short-run equilibrium but not in long-run equilibrium. Firms in the industry are making economic profits. These economic profits will attract new firms into the industry.

As new firms enter, the industry supply curve starts shifting to the right, and as it does so it intersects the demand curve at lower and lower prices and higher and higher quantities. Firms in the industry react to the falling price by cutting their output. That is, in Fig. 11.12(b) each firm slides back down its marginal cost curve in order to maximize profit at each successively lower price. Eventually, enough new firms enter the industry to shift the industry supply curve all the way to S_1. By that time, the market price falls to P_0, the original price, and the industry output is Q_2. At a price of P_0, each firm cuts its output back to its original level, q_0. Each firm is again making zero economic profit and no firms enter or exit the industry. This new situation is a long-run equilibrium. During the adjustment process from the initial long-run equilibrium to the new one, all firms – both those firms that were in the industry originally and those that entered – make economic profits.

External Economies and Diseconomies

One feature of the predictions that we have just generated seems odd: in the long run, regardless of whether demand increases or decreases, the price returns to its original level. Is that outcome inevitable? In fact, it is not. It is possible for the long-run equilibrium price to rise, fall or stay the same. Figure 11.13 illustrates these three cases. In part (a), the long-run supply curve (LS_A) is perfectly elastic. In this case, an increase in demand from D_0 to D_1 (or a decrease in demand from D_1 to D_0) results in a change in the quantity sold but an unchanged price. This is the case that we have just analysed. In part (b), the long-run supply curve (LS_B) slopes upward. In this case, when demand increases from D_0 to D_1, the price increases, and

when demand decreases from D_1 to D_0, the price decreases. Finally, part (c) shows a case in which the long-run supply curve (LS_C) slopes downward. In this case, an increase in demand from D_0 to D_1 results in a fall in the price in the long run. A decrease in demand from D_1 to D_0 results in a higher price in the long run.

Whichever outcome occurs depends on external economies and external diseconomies. **External economies** are factors beyond the control of an individual firm that lower its costs as industry output rises. **External diseconomies** are factors outside the control of a firm that raise its costs as industry output rises. There are many examples of external economies and diseconomies. They are both well illustrated in the agricultural sector.

One of the best examples of external economies is the growth of specialist support services for an industry as it expands. As total agricultural production increased in the nineteenth and early twentieth centuries, the services available to individual farmers expanded and their costs fell. Farm machinery, fertilizers, transport networks, storage and marketing facilities all improved, lowering farm costs. Farms enjoyed the benefits of external economies. As a consequence, as the demand for farm products increased, the quantity produced increased but the price fell (as in Fig. 11.13c).

One of the best examples of external diseconomies is congestion. The airline industry provides a good illustration. With bigger airline industry output, there is greater congestion of both airports and airspace, which results in longer delays and extra waiting time for passengers and aircraft. These external diseconomies mean that as the demand for air transport continues to increase, eventually (in the absence of further technological change) prices will rise (as in Fig. 11.13b).

Technological Change

Industries are constantly discovering lower-cost techniques of production. Most cost-saving production techniques cannot be implemented, however, without investing in new plant and equipment. As a consequence, it takes time for a technological advance to spread through an industry. Some firms whose plants are on the verge of being replaced will be quick to adopt the new technology, while other firms whose plants have

FIGURE 11.13

Long-run Price and Quantity Changes

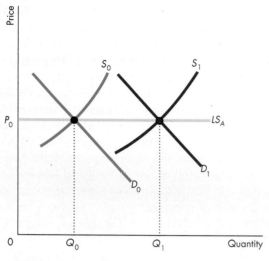

(a) Constant cost industry

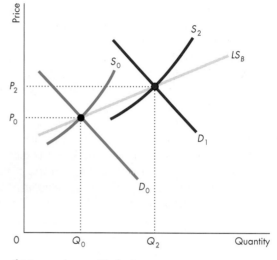

(b) Increasing cost industry

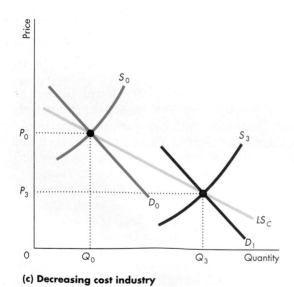

(c) Decreasing cost industry

Three possible long-run changes in price and quantity are illustrated. When demand increases from D_0 to D_1, entry occurs and the industry supply curve shifts from S_0 to S_1. In part (a), the long-run supply curve LS_A is horizontal. The quantity increases from Q_0 to Q_1 and the price remains constant at P_0. In part (b), the long-run supply curve is LS_B; the price increases to P_2 and the quantity increases to Q_2. This case occurs in industries with external diseconomies. In part (c), the long-run supply curve is LS_C; the price decreases to P_3 and the quantity increases to Q_3. This case occurs in an industry with external economies.

recently been replaced will continue to operate with older technology until they can no longer cover their average variable cost. Once average variable cost cannot be covered, it pays a firm to scrap even a relatively new plant (embodying the original technology) in favour of a plant with the new technology.

Let's work out exactly what happens to the output and profit of each firm in an industry reshaped by a new technology. Figure 11.14(a) shows the demand curve for an industry (D), and an initial supply curve (S_0). The price is P_0 and the quantity Q_0. Initially there are only original-technology firms in existence (Fig. 11.14b). Each firm has a marginal cost curve MC_O and an average total cost curve ATC_O. At the market price (P_0), each firm faces a marginal revenue curve MR_0, produces an output q_0^O and makes zero economic profit. The industry is in long-run competitive equilibrium.

New technology allows firms to produce at substantially lower cost than the existing technology. The cost curves of firms with the new technology are shown in part (c). Suppose that one firm with the new technology enters the industry. Since the indus-

try is competitive, this one firm will be a negligible part of the total industry and will hardly affect the industry supply, so that the supply curve remains at S_0. The price remains at P_0 and the new-technology firm produces a profit-maximizing output of q_0^N and makes a positive economic profit.

Gradually, more new-technology firms enter the industry and, after a period, enough have entered to shift the industry supply curve to S_1 in part (a). By this time, the market price has fallen to P_1 and the industry output has risen to Q_1. Each firm takes the price P_1 and maximizes its profit. Each new-technology firm, in part (c), maximizes profit by producing the output q_1^N and continues to make

FIGURE 11.14

Technological Change in a Competitive Industry

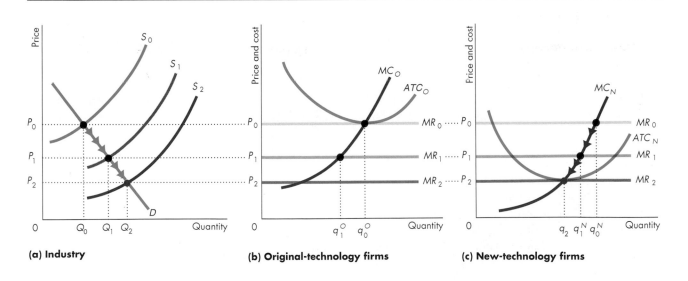

(a) Industry   **(b) Original-technology firms**   **(c) New-technology firms**

Initially the industry supply curve is S_0 and the demand curve is D, so the equilibrium price is P_0 and quantity Q_0 is bought and sold (part a). Each individual firm, shown in part (b), produces q_0^O and makes a zero profit. A new technology is developed. The costs associated with the new technology (ATC_N and MC_N) are shown in part (c) and are lower than those for the original technology. A new-technology firm, faced with the price P_0, produces a profit-maximizing output of q_0^N and makes a profit. Since the new technology is profitable, more and more firms will use it. As they do so, the industry supply curve begins to shift to the right, from S_0 to S_1. With an increase in industry supply, industry output rises to Q_1, but the price falls to P_1. As a result, new-technology firms will cut their output from q_0^N to q_1^N, but they will

still be making a profit. Original-technology firms will cut their output from q_0^O to q_1^O. They will be making losses. As firms with the original technology begin to close down and more new-technology firms enter the industry, the industry supply curve continues to shift to the right, from S_1 to S_2. At S_2, the price is P_2 and industry output is Q_2. Each new-technology firm is now producing q_2 and making a zero profit and there are no firms using the original technology.

The effect of the introduction of the new technology has been to increase output and lower price. In the process, firms that adopted the new technology early made profits while firms that stuck with the original technology for too long incurred losses.

a positive economic profit. Each original-technology firm, in part (b), minimizes its loss by producing the output q_1^O.

More new-technology firms will continue to enter since the new technology is profitable. Original-technology firms will begin to leave the industry or switch to the new technology because the original technology is unprofitable. Eventually all the firms in the industry will be new-technology firms and, by this time, the industry supply curve will have moved to S_2. The supply curve S_2 is based on the marginal cost curves of the new-technology firms. The supply curve S_0 is based on the marginal cost curves of the original-technology firms. The supply curve S_1 is based on the marginal cost curves for both original-technology and new-technology firms. With supply curve S_2, the market price is P_2 and the industry output Q_2. At price P_2, the new-technology firms produce a profit-maximizing output of q_2, making zero profits. The industry long-run equilibrium price is P_2.

The process that we have just analysed is one in which some firms experience economic profits and others economic losses. It is a period of dynamic change for an industry. Some firms do well and others do badly. Often a change of the kind that we have just examined will have a geographical dimension to it. For example, the new-technology firms may be located in a new industrial region of a country, while the original-technology firms may be located in a traditional industrial region. Alternatively, the new-technology firms might be in a foreign country, while the original-technology firms are in the domestic economy. The struggles of the UK machine tool industry to keep up with the fierce competition from Germany and Japan is a good example of this phenomenon.

R E V I E W

When the demand for a competitive industry's product declines, firms begin to incur losses and leave the industry. Exiting firms decrease supply and the price begins to increase. Eventually, enough firms exit and the remaining firms just cover their costs. When the demand for a competitive industry's product increases, firms make profits and new firms enter. Entry increases supply and the price begins to fall. Eventually, enough firms enter to compete away all the economic profit. ◆ ◆ When a new technology lowers costs, supply increases and price falls. Firms that adopt the new technology make a profit and those sticking with the old technology incur a loss. Old-technology firms either adopt the new technology or exit. Eventually, all firms remaining in the industry have adopted the new technology and are just covering their costs. ◆

You've now studied how a competitive market works and have used the model of perfect competition to interpret and explain a variety of aspects of real-world economic behaviour. The last topic that we'll study in this chapter is the efficiency of perfect competition.

Competition and Efficiency

In perfect competition, freedom of entry ensures that firms produce at the least possible cost. Also, the fact that each firm is a price taker, facing a perfectly elastic demand curve, results in firms producing a quantity such that marginal cost equals price. These features of a perfectly competitive market have important implications for the efficiency of such a market.

Allocative Efficiency

Allocative efficiency occurs when no resources are wasted – when no one can be made better off without someone else being made worse off. If someone can be made better off without making someone else worse off, a more efficient allocation of resources can be achieved. Three conditions must be satisfied to achieve allocative efficiency:

◆ Economic efficiency
◆ Consumer efficiency
◆ Equality of marginal social cost and marginal social benefit

We defined economic efficiency in Chapter 9 as a situation in which the cost of producing a given output is minimized. Economic efficiency involves technological efficiency – producing the maximum possible output from given inputs – as well as using inputs in their cost-minimizing proportions. Economic efficiency occurs whenever firms maximize profit. Since firms in perfect competition maximize profit, perfect competition is economically efficient.

Consumer efficiency occurs when consumers cannot make themselves better off by reallocating their budget. A consumer's best possible budget allocation is summarized in the consumer's demand curves. That is, a demand curve tells us the quantity demanded at a given price when the consumer has made the best possible use of a given budget. Thus when the quantity bought at a given price is a point on the demand curve, the allocation satisfies consumer efficiency.

The third condition occurs in perfect competition if there are no external costs and benefits. **External costs** are those costs not borne by the producer but borne by other members of society. Examples of such costs are the costs of pollution and congestion. **External benefits** are those benefits accruing to people other than the buyer of a good. Examples of such benefits are the pleasure we get from well-designed buildings and beautiful works of art. As long as *someone* buys these things, *everyone* can enjoy them.

Marginal social cost is the cost of producing one additional unit of output, including external costs. **Marginal social benefit** is the pound value of the benefit from one additional unit of consumption, including any external benefits. Allocative efficiency occurs when marginal social cost equals marginal social benefit. Figure 11.15 illustrates such a situation. The marginal social benefit curve is *MSB* and the marginal social cost curve is *MSC*. Allocative efficiency occurs at a quantity Q^* and price P^*. In this situation, there is no waste. No one can be made better off without someone else being made worse off. If output is above Q^*, marginal social cost will exceed marginal social benefit. The cost of producing the last unit will exceed its benefit. If output is below Q^*, marginal social benefit will exceed marginal social cost. Producing one more unit will bring more benefit than it costs.

Perfect competition is allocative efficiency when there are no external costs and benefits. That is, when all the costs are borne by the producers of the good and all the benefits accrue to the buyers of the

good. In this case, the marginal social cost curve is the industry supply curve and the marginal social benefit curve is the same as the industry demand curve. Hence, with no external costs and benefits, the perfectly competitive market shown in Fig. 11.15 produces an output Q^* at a price P^*. Perfect competition delivers allocative efficiency.

To check that in this situation no resources are being wasted – no one can be made better off without someone being made worse off – consider what will happen if output is restricted to Q_0. At that output, marginal social cost is C_0 but marginal social benefit is B_0. Everyone can be made better off by increasing output. Producers will willingly supply more of the good for a price higher than C_0. Consumers will willingly buy more of the good for a

FIGURE 11.15

Allocative Efficiency

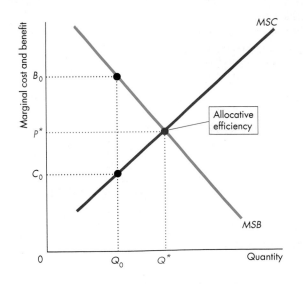

Allocative efficiency, which occurs when no resources are wasted, requires that marginal social cost (*MSC*) be equal to marginal social benefit (*MSB*). Allocative efficiency occurs at output Q^*. If output is Q_0, marginal social cost (C_0) will be less than marginal social benefit (B_0). The benefit from one additional unit of output exceeds its cost. A perfectly competitive market delivers allocative efficiency when there are no external costs and benefits. In such a situation, the marginal social cost curve is the industry supply curve and the marginal social benefit curve is the industry demand curve. The price is P^* and the quantity traded Q^*.

Competition and Costs

FINANCIAL TIMES, 12 JULY 1994

Intense competition holds manufacturer's prices steady

Gillian Tett, Economics Staff

THE recent rise in commodity prices helped push input prices for manufacturers to higher-than-expected levels last month, official figures yesterday showed.

But intense competition has so far prevented manufacturers from passing these rises on to their customers, the data suggested.

The cost of materials and fuel purchased by manufacturers rose by a seasonally adjusted 0.8 per cent in June compared with May, the Central Statistical Office said. Measured over the year as a whole, input prices rose 1.6 per cent.

However, the price of goods leaving factory gates in the manufacturing sector as a whole remained flat between June and May.

Measured without the volatile food, beverages, tobacco and petroleum sectors, output prices rose 0.1 per cent between May and June, and 1.9 per cent over the year.

The rise in input prices was higher than the City had expected, with some analysts warning that this might feed through to output price inflation later this summer.

But the fact that input prices have been rising faster than output prices for several months now, reversing the trend seen last year, suggests that the intense competitive pressures are forcing manufacturers to absorb the costs themselves, analysts said.

A rise in the price of metals and other imported commodities accounted for nearly half of the 0.8 per cent change in the input index, with the metals sector seeing the sharpest monthly rise in input prices, reflecting the recent surge in commodity prices. Metal input prices rose 1.5 per cent between May and June, and 8.3 per cent over the year.

This rise was partly offset by a fall in the cost of domestically produced commodities and fuel. The cost of home-produced food manufacturing inputs and fuel both fell 1.2 per cent last month.

Nevertheless, nearly all categories within the manufacturing sector saw input prices rise at a faster rate than output prices last month.

The wood and wood products sector saw the sharpest yearly rise in input prices, with input prices growing 5.6 per cent over the year, after edging up rapidly in recent months. Output prices, by contrast, grew just 2.6 per cent in the same period.

The price of manufactured output in the United Kingdom rose 0.1 per cent between May and June 1994.

This small output price rise occurred despite input prices rising eight times as fast over the same period.

Output price rises were limited by the level of competition between manufacturers.

Input prices have been rising faster than output prices for several months, indicating that manufacturers are absorbing higher input costs, rather than passing them on to consumers.

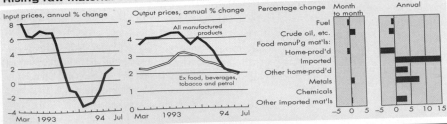

Rising raw material costs squeeze factory profit margins

© The Financial Times. Reprinted with permission.

Background and Analysis

Greater competition between manufacturers is shown to mean competition in terms of the selling price of output.

In order to be able to compete on output price in the face of rising input prices, firms are having to absorb these higher input prices by lowering profit margins or making cost savings elsewhere in production.

A large element of the higher input costs is accounted for by the higher price of imported commodities.

A lower value of the pound would, other things remaining the same, increase the price of imports and thus fuel input price inflation. There is a specific problem with commodities such as metals, however, because prices on world commodity markets are prone to greater volatility than prices on other markets.

On these commodity markets, demand and supply are typically relatively inelastic, so fluctuations in either demand or supply will produce magnified price movements.

In Fig. 1, competition is low and large profits are being earned.

In Fig. 2 rising input costs shift the marginal cost *(MC)* and average total cost *(ATC)* curves up from MC_0 to MC_1 and ATC_0 to ATC_1, but the price being charged is driven down from P_0 to P_1.

Unless cost savings are made elsewhere to slow down or halt the rise in marginal cost and average total cost, the lower price and higher input costs will result in lower profits for the firms.

The people who benefit from this competition are consumers, for whom prices of manufactured goods are rising very slowly, despite the higher price of the inputs that go into what they buy.

If some firms increase their price, consumers will switch and buy from other firms charging a lower price. To the extent that this consumer behaviour prevents firms from raising prices, each firm individually is a price taker.

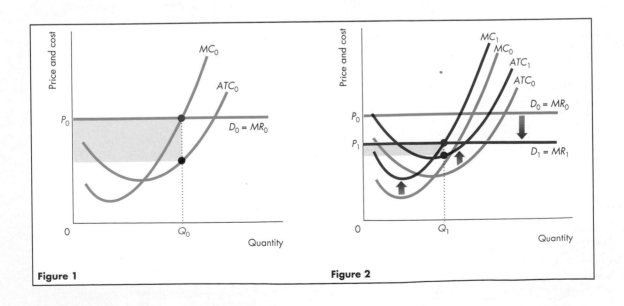

Figure 1

Figure 2

price lower than B_0. Everyone would like to trade more. But once output has increased to Q^*, there are no further available gains from increasing the output of this good. The benefit to the consumer of the last unit produced exactly equals the cost to the producer of the last unit.

The Invisible Hand

The founder of economic science, Adam Smith, suggested that a competitive market acts like an invisible hand to guide buyers and sellers to achieve the best possible social outcome. Each participant in a competitive market is, according to Smith, 'led by an invisible hand to promote an end which was no part of his intention'. You can see the invisible hand at work in the cartoon. Adam Smith was not able to work out his conclusion with the clarity and precision with which we are able to do so today. It is the work of Léon Walras, Vilfredo Pareto and, more recently, Nobel Prize-winning American economists Kenneth Arrow and Gérard Debreu that demonstrated the precise conditions under which perfect competition and maximum social welfare coincide.

Obstacles to Efficiency

The two main obstacles to allocative efficiency are:

◆ External costs and external benefits
◆ Monopoly

External costs and external benefits mean that many goods cannot be efficiently produced even in perfectly competitive markets. Such goods as national defence, the enforcement of law and order, the provision of clean drinking water, and the disposal of sewage and refuse are all examples of goods in which there are enormous external benefits. Left to competitive markets, we would have too small a production of such goods. There are also many examples of goods that impose high external costs. The production of steel and chemicals generates air and water pollution. Perfect competition will result in an overproduction of such goods. One of the key functions of government is to modify the outcome of competitive markets in cases such as these. Government institutions (which we study in Chapters 19 and 20) arise, in part, because of external costs and benefits.

Drawing by M. Twohy; © 1985 The New Yorker Magazine, Inc.

Another obstacle to allocative efficiency is the existence of monopoly. Monopoly results in the restriction of output below its competitive level in order to increase price and make a larger profit. Precisely how it achieves this outcome is the subject of the next chapter.

◆ ◆ ◆ ◆ We have now completed our study of perfect competition. We have seen how a firm in a perfectly competitive market chooses its profit-maximizing output. We have seen how the actions of all the firms in a market combine to determine the market supply curve and how the market sup-

quantity. We have seen how a competitive industry operates in the short run, and we have studied the dynamic forces that move such a market to a long-run equilibrium. We have used the model of perfect competition to understand several important features of real-world markets. Finally, we have seen that under some specific circumstances, perfect competition delivers an economically efficient allocation of resources. ◆ ◆ Although many markets approximate the model of perfect competition, many do not. Our next task, in Chapters 12 and 13, is to study markets that depart from perfect competition. When we have completed this study, we'll have a toolkit of alternative models of markets that will enable us to study all the possible situations that arise in the real world. We begin, in the next chapter, by going to the opposite extreme of perfect competition – pure monopoly. Then, in Chapter 13, we'll study the markets between perfect competition and pure monopoly – monopolistic competition and oligopoly (competition among a few producers).

S U M M A R Y

Perfect Competition

Perfect competition occurs in a market in which a large number of firms produce an identical good; there are many buyers; firms face competition from potential new entrants; and all firms and buyers are fully informed about the prices charged by each firm. In perfect competition, each firm sells its good for the same price and no single firm can influence the market price. Even if one firm doubles its output, the industry output will change by a tiny percentage and the market price will hardly be affected at all. (pp. 281–282)

Firms' Choices in Perfect Competition

A competitive firm takes the market price and has to choose how much to produce, when to shut down temporarily and when to leave an industry permanently. The firm's choices are motivated by its desire to maximize profit.

A firm's maximum profit is not necessarily a positive profit. If price is above average total cost, the firm makes a profit. If price equals average total cost, the firm breaks even. If price is below average total cost, the firm makes a loss. If price is low enough, the firm maximizes profit by temporarily shutting down and laying off its workers. It pays to shut down production if price is below minimum average variable cost. When price equals minimum average variable cost, the firm makes a loss equal to its total fixed costs whether it produces the profit-maximizing output or shuts down.

The firm's supply curve is the upward-sloping part of its marginal cost curve at all points above the point of minimum average variable cost, and runs along the vertical axis at all prices below minimum average variable cost. (pp. 282–290)

Output, Price and Profit in the Short Run

The short-run industry supply curve shows how the total quantity supplied in the short run by all the firms in an industry varies as the market price varies.

The market price occurs where the quantity supplied and the quantity demanded are equal. Each firm takes the market price as given and chooses the output that maximizes profit. In short-run equilibrium, each firm can make an economic profit, an economic loss, or it can break even. (pp. 291–292)

Output, Price and Profit in the Long Run

If the firms in an industry make positive economic profits, existing firms will expand and new firms will enter the industry. If the firms in an industry make economic losses, some firms will leave the industry and the remaining firms will produce less. Entry and exit shift the industry supply curve. As firms enter, the industry supply curve shifts to the right. As firms leave, the industry supply curve shifts to the left. Entry causes profits of existing firms to fall and exit causes profits of existing firms to rise (or losses to fall). In long-run equilibrium, firms make zero economic profit. No firm wants to enter or leave the industry and no firm wants to expand or contract its production plant. Long-run competitive equilibrium occurs when each firm maximizes its short-run profit (marginal cost equals marginal revenue equals price); economic profit is zero, so that there is no entry or exit; and each firm produces at the point of minimum long-run average cost, so it has no incentive to change its plant size. (pp. 293–296)

Responding to Changing Tastes and Advancing Technology

In a perfectly competitive market, a permanent decrease in demand leads to a lower industry output and a smaller number of firms in the industry. A permanent increase in demand leads to a rise in industry output and an increase in the number of firms in the industry. If there are no external economies or diseconomies, the market price remains constant in the long run as demand changes. If there are external economies, price falls in the long run as demand rises. If there are external diseconomies, price rises in the long run as demand rises.

New technology increases the industry supply, and in the long run the market price falls and the quantity sold rises. The number of firms in the industry falls. Firms that are slow to change to the new technology will make losses and eventually will go out of business. Firms that are quick to adopt the new technology will make economic profits initially, but in the long run they will make zero economic profit. (pp. 296–302)

Competition and Efficiency

Allocative efficiency occurs when no one can be made better off without making someone else worse off. Three conditions for allocative efficiency – economic efficiency, consumer efficiency, and equality of marginal social cost and marginal social benefit – occur in perfect competition when there are no external costs and benefits. It is this situation that Adam Smith was describing when he talked of the economy being led by an 'invisible hand'.

There are two main obstacles to the achievement of allocative efficiency – the existence of external costs and external benefits and of monopoly. (pp. 302–306)

KEY ELEMENTS

R E V I E W   Q U E S T I O N S

1 What are the main features of a perfectly competitive industry?

2 Why can't a perfectly competitive firm influence the industry price?

3 List the three key decisions that a firm in a perfectly competitive industry has to make in order to maximize profit.

4 Why is marginal revenue equal to price in a perfectly competitive industry?

5 When will a perfectly competitive firm temporarily stop producing?

6 What is the connection between the supply curve and marginal cost curve of a perfectly competitive firm?

7 What is the relationship between a firm's supply curve and the short-run industry supply curve in a perfectly competitive industry?

8 When will firms enter an industry and when will they leave it?

9 What happens to the short-run industry supply curve when firms enter a competitive industry?

10 What is the effect of entry on the price and quantity produced?

11 What is the effect of entry on profit?

12 Trace the effects of a permanent increase in demand on price, quantity sold, number of firms and profit.

13 Trace the effects of a permanent decrease in demand on price, quantity sold, number of firms and profit.

14 Under what circumstances will a perfectly competitive industry have:

  a A perfectly elastic long-run supply curve

  b An upward-sloping long-run supply curve

  c A downward-sloping long-run supply curve

15 What is allocative efficiency and under what circumstances does it arise?

P R O B L E M S

1 Suppose that a firm produces one-hundredth of an industry's output. The elasticity of the industry's demand is 4. What is the elasticity of the firm's demand?

2 Pat's Pizza Kitchen is a price taker. It has the following hourly costs:

Output (pizzas per hour)	Total cost (pounds per hour)
0	10
1	21
2	30
3	41
4	54
5	79
6	96

  a If pizzas sell for £14, what is Pat's profit-maximizing output per hour? How much profit does he make?

  b What is Pat's shutdown point?

  c Derive Pat's supply curve.

  d What price will cause Pat to leave the pizza industry?

  e What price will cause other firms with costs identical to Pat's to enter the industry?

  f What is the long-run equilibrium price?

3 Why have the prices of personal computers and VCRs fallen?

4 What has been the effect of a rise in world population on the wheat market and the individual wheat farmer?

5 How has the non-disposable nappy industry been affected by the fall in the United Kingdom birth rate and the development of disposable nappies?

6 The market demand for compact discs is as follows:

Price (pounds per CD)	Quantity demanded (CDs per week)
3.65	500,000
4.40	475,000
5.20	450,000
6.00	425,000
6.80	400,000
7.60	375,000
8.40	350,000
9.20	325,000
10.00	300,000
10.80	275,000
11.60	250,000
12.40	225,000
13.20	200,000
14.00	175,000
14.80	150,000

The market is perfectly competitive and each firm has the same cost structure described by the following table:

Output (CDs per week)	Marginal cost	Average variable cost	Average total cost
		(pounds per CD)	
150	6.00	8.80	15.47
200	6.40	7.80	12.80
250	7.00	7.00	11.00
300	7.65	7.10	10.43
350	8.40	7.20	10.06
400	10.00	7.50	10.00
450	12.40	8.00	10.22
500	17.20	9.00	11.00

There are 1,000 firms in the industry.

a What is the industry price?
b What is the industry's output?
c What is the output of each firm?
d What is the economic profit of each firm?
e What is the shutdown point?

f What is the long-run equilibrium price?
g What is the number of firms in the long run?

7 The same demand conditions as those in Problem 6 prevail and there are still 1,000 firms in the industry, but fixed costs increase by £980.

a What is the short-run profit-maximizing output for each firm?
b Do firms enter or exit the industry in the long run?
c What is the new long-run equilibrium price?
d What is the new long-run equilibrium number of firms in the industry?

8 The same cost conditions as those in Problem 6 prevail and there are 1,000 firms in the industry, but the falling price of prerecorded tapes decreases the demand for compact discs and the demand becomes as follows:

Price (pounds per CD)	Quantity demanded (CDs per week)
2.95	500,000
3.54	475,000
4.13	450,000
4.71	425,000
5.30	400,000
5.89	375,000
6.48	350,000
7.06	325,000
7.65	300,000
8.24	275,000
8.83	250,000
9.41	225,000
10.00	200,000
10.59	175,000
11.18	150,000

a What is the short-run profit-maximizing output for each firm?
b Do firms enter or exit the industry in the long run?
c What is the new long-run equilibrium price?
d What is the new long-run equilibrium number of firms in the industry?

CHAPTER 12

MONOPOLY

After studying this chapter you will be able to:

◆ Define monopoly

◆ Explain the conditions under which monopoly arises

◆ Distinguish between legal monopoly and natural monopoly

◆ Explain how a monopoly determines its price and output

◆ Define price discrimination

◆ Explain why price discrimination leads to a bigger profit

◆ Compare the performance of a competitive and a monopolistic industry

◆ Define rent seeking and explain why it arises

◆ Explain the conditions under which monopoly is more efficient than competition

YOU HAVE BEEN HEARING A LOT IN THIS BOOK ABOUT FIRMS THAT WANT TO maximize profit. But perhaps you've been looking around at some of the places where you do business and wondering if they are really so intent on profit. After all, doesn't the bank give you a special deal on your bank charges because you are a student? Don't you also get a special student fare on the coach when you go home for the weekend? And what about the airline that gives a discount for buying a ticket in advance? Are your bank, and the long-distance bus company, as well as the airline operator, simply generous people to whom the model of profit-maximizing firms does not apply? Aren't they simply throwing profit away by giving you reduced prices? ◆ ◆ When you want to travel to London by train, you have only one choice – British Rail. Regardless of where you live, you have no choice about

The Profits of Generosity

the supplier of your gas, electricity or water. If you want to post a letter, there is only one producer of letter-carrying services (apart from expensive couriers), the Post Office. These are examples of a single producer of a good or service controlling its supply. Such firms are obviously not like firms in perfectly competitive industries. How do they behave? How does their behaviour compare with firms in perfectly competitive industries? Do such firms charge prices that are too high and that damage the interests of consumers? And do such firms bring any benefits?

◆ ◆ ◆ ◆ Firms operating in perfectly competitive markets are so small that they are unable to influence price. The firms that we study in this chapter control the entire market for their product and by choosing the quantity of goods to supply exert a decisive influence on price.

How Monopoly Arises

A monopoly is an industry in which there is one supplier of a good, service or resource that has no close substitutes, and in which there is a barrier preventing the entry of new firms. The supply of water is an example of a local monopoly – monopoly restricted to a given location. The Post Office is an example of a national monopoly – a sole supplier of letter-carrying services.

Barriers to Entry

The key feature of a monopoly is the existence of barriers preventing the entry of new firms. **Barriers to entry** are legal or natural impediments protecting a firm from competition from potential new entrants.

Legal Barriers to Entry Legal barriers to entry give rise to legal monopoly. **Legal monopoly** occurs when a law, licence or patent restricts competition by preventing entry.

The first type of legal barrier to entry is an exclusive right granted to a firm to supply a good or service. An example of such a monopoly is the Post Office, which has the exclusive right to supply letter-carrying services. Another is British Rail, which has the exclusive right to supply train services.

A second legal barrier is a government licence that controls entry into particular occupations, professions and industries. Government licensing in the professions is the most important example of this type of barrier to entry. For example, a licence is required to practise medicine, law, dentistry, school-teaching, architecture and a variety of other professional services and industries. Licensing does not create monopoly, but it does restrict competition.

A third legal restriction on entry is a patent. A **patent** is an exclusive right granted by the government to the inventor of a product or service. It is valid for a limited time period that varies from country to country. In the United Kingdom, a patent is valid for 16 years. Patents protect inventors by creating a property right and thereby encourage invention by preventing others from copying an invention until sufficient time has elapsed for the inventor to have reaped some benefits. They also stimulate *innovation* – the use of new inventions – by increasing the incentives for inventors to publicize their discoveries and offer them for use under licence.

Natural Barriers to Entry Natural barriers to entry give rise to natural monopoly. **Natural monopoly** occurs when there is a unique source of supply of a raw material or when one firm can supply the entire market at a lower price than two or more firms can. As the definition of natural monopoly implies, natural barriers to entry take two forms. First, a single firm may own and control the entire supply of a mineral or natural resource. This type of monopoly occurs in the production of particular types of mineral water, for which there is just a single, unique source, and for some raw materials such as diamonds and chromium. De Beers, a South African company, for example, owns and controls four-fifths of the world's diamond mines. Also, all the sources of chromium, again concentrated in southern Africa, are controlled by a small number of producers.

Natural monopoly can also arise because of economics of scale. When a single producer can supply the entire market at a lower average total cost of production than can two or more firms, only a single firm can survive in the industry. Examples of natural monopoly arising from economies of scale are public utilities, such as the distribution of electricity, natural gas and water.

Most monopolies in the real world, whether legal or natural, are regulated in some way by government or by government agencies. We will study such regulation in Chapter 20. Here we will consider an unregulated monopoly for two important reasons. First, we can better understand why governments regulate monopolies and the effects of regulation if we also know how an unregulated monopoly would behave. Second, even in industries with more than one producer, firms often have a degree of monopoly power, arising from locational advantages or from important differences in product quality protected by patents. The theory of monopoly sheds important light on the behaviour of such firms and industries.

We will begin by studying the behaviour of a single-price monopoly. A **single-price monopoly** is a monopoly that charges the same price for each and every unit of its output. How does a single-price monopoly determine the quantity to produce and the price to charge for its output?

Single-price Monopoly

The starting point for understanding how a single-price monopoly chooses its price and output is to work out the relationship between the demand for the good produced by the monopoly and the monopoly's revenue.

Demand and Revenue

Since in a monopoly there is only one firm, the demand curve facing that firm is the industry demand curve. Let's look at an example: Jackie's hairdressing salon, the sole supplier of haircuts in Askrigg, in the Yorkshire Dales. The demand schedule that Jackie faces is set out in Table 12.1. At a price of £10, Jackie sells no haircuts. The lower the price, the more haircuts per hour Jackie is able to sell. For example, at a price of £6, consumers demand 4 haircuts per hour (row *e*) and at a price of £2, they demand 8 haircuts per hour (row *i*).

Total revenue (*TR*) is the price (*P*) multiplied by the quantity sold (*Q*). For example, in row *d*, Jackie sells 3 haircuts at £7 each, so total revenue is £21. *Marginal revenue* (*MR*) is the change in total revenue (ΔTR) resulting from a one-unit rise in the quantity sold. For example, if the price falls from £9 (row *b*) to £8 (row *c*), the quantity sold rises from 1 to 2 haircuts. Total revenue rises from £9 to £16, so the change in total revenue is £7. Since the quantity sold rises by 1 haircut, marginal revenue equals the change in total revenue and is £14. When recording marginal revenue, it is written between the two rows to emphasize that marginal revenue relates to the *change* in the quantity sold.

Figure 12.1 shows Jackie's demand curve (*D*). Each row of Table 12.1 corresponds to a point on the demand curve. For example, row *d* in the table and point *d* on the demand curve tell us that at a price of £7, Jackie sells 3 haircuts. The figure also shows Jackie's marginal revenue curve (*MR*). Notice that the marginal revenue curve is below the demand curve. That is, at each level of output marginal revenue is less than price. Why is marginal revenue less than price? Because when the price is lowered to sell one more unit, there are two opposing effects on total revenue. The lower price results in a revenue loss and the increased quantity sold results in a revenue gain. For example, at a price of £8 Jackie sells 2 haircuts (point *c*). If she reduces

TABLE 12.1

Single-price Monopoly's Revenue

Price *P* (pounds per haircut)	Quantity demanded *Q* (haircuts per hour)	Total revenue *TR* = *P* × *Q* (pounds)	Marginal revenue *MR* = $\Delta TR/\Delta Q$ (pounds per haircut)
a	10	0	0	
				9
b	9	1	9	
				7
c	8	2	16	
				5
d	7	3	21	
				3
e	6	4	24	
				1
f	5	5	25	
				............−1
g	4	6	24	
				............−3
h	3	7	21	
				............−5
i	2	8	16	
				............−7
j	1	9	9	
				............−9
k	0	10	0	

The table shows Jackie's demand schedule – the number of haircuts demanded per hour at each price. Total revenue (*TR*) is price multiplied by quantity sold. For example, row *c* shows that when the price is £8 a haircut, two haircuts are sold for a total revenue of £16. Marginal revenue (*MR*) is the change in total revenue resulting from a one-unit rise in the quantity sold. For example, when the price falls from £8 to £7 a haircut, the quantity sold increases from 2 to 3 haircuts and total revenue increases by £5. The marginal revenue of the third haircut is £5. Total revenue rises up to row *f*, where 5 haircuts are sold for £5, and it falls thereafter. In the output range over which total revenue is increasing, marginal revenue is positive; in the output range over which total revenue is decreasing, marginal revenue is negative.

the price to £7, she sells 3 haircuts and has a revenue gain of £7 on the third haircut. But she receives only £7 on the first two as well – £1 less than before – so her revenue loss on the first 2 haircuts is £2. She has to deduct this amount from the revenue gain of £7. Marginal revenue – the difference between the revenue gain and the revenue loss – is £5.

FIGURE 12.1

Demand and Marginal Revenue for a Single-price Monopoly

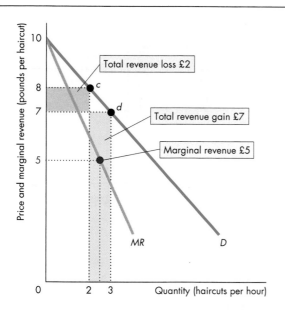

The monopoly demand curve (D) is based on the numbers in Table 12.1. At a price of £8 a haircut, Jackie sells 2 haircuts an hour. If she lowers the price to £7, she sells 3 haircuts an hour. The sale of the third haircut brings a revenue gain of £7 (the price charged for the third haircut). But there is a revenue loss of £2 (£1 per haircut) on the 2 haircuts that she could have sold for £8 each. The marginal revenue (extra total revenue) from the third haircut is the difference between the revenue gain and the revenue loss – £5. The marginal revenue curve (MR) shows the marginal revenue at each level of sales. Marginal revenue is lower than price.

Figure 12.2 shows Jackie's demand curve, marginal revenue curve (MR) and total revenue curve (TR) and illustrates the connections between them. Again, each row in Table 12.1 corresponds to a point on the curves. For example, row d in the table and point d on the graphs tell us that when 3 haircuts are sold for £7 each (part a) total revenue is £21 (part b). Notice that as the quantity sold rises, total revenue rises to a peak of £25 (point f) and then declines. To understand the behaviour of total revenue, notice what happens to marginal revenue as the quantity sold increases. Over the range 0 to 5 haircuts, marginal revenue is positive. When more than 5 haircuts are sold, marginal revenue becomes negative. The output range over which marginal rev-

enue is positive is the same as that over which total revenue is rising. The output range over which marginal revenue is negative is the same as that over which total revenue declines. When marginal revenue is zero, total revenue is at a maximum. The concept of marginal revenue was first used by Joan Robinson – see Our Advancing Knowledge pp. 320–321.

Revenue and Elasticity

When we studied elasticity in Chapter 5, we discovered a connection between the elasticity of demand and the effect of a change in price on total expenditure or total revenue. Let's refresh our memories of that connection.

Recall that the elasticity of demand is the percentage change in the quantity demanded divided by the percentage change in price. If a 1 per cent decrease in price results in a greater than 1 per cent increase in the quantity demanded, the elasticity of demand is greater than 1 and demand is *elastic*. If a 1 per cent decrease in price results in a less than 1 per cent increase in the quantity demanded, the elasticity of demand is less than 1 and demand is *inelastic*. If a 1 per cent decrease in price results in a 1 per cent increase in the quantity demanded, the elasticity of demand is 1 and demand is *unit elastic*.

The elasticity of demand influences the change in total revenue. If demand is elastic, total revenue increases when the price decreases; if demand is inelastic, total revenue decreases when the price decreases; and if demand is unit elastic, total revenue does not change when the price changes.

The output range over which total revenue increases when the price decreases is the same as that over which marginal revenue is positive, as shown in Fig. 12.2. Thus the output range over which marginal revenue is positive is also the output range over which demand is elastic – over which the elasticity of demand is greater than 1. The output range over which total revenue decreases when price decreases is the same as that over which marginal revenue is negative. Thus the output range over which marginal revenue is negative is also the output range over which demand is inelastic – over which the elasticity of demand is less than 1. The output at which total revenue remains constant when price decreases is that at which marginal revenue is zero. Thus the output at which marginal revenue is zero is also the output at which demand is

FIGURE 12.2

A Single-price Monopoly's Revenue Curves

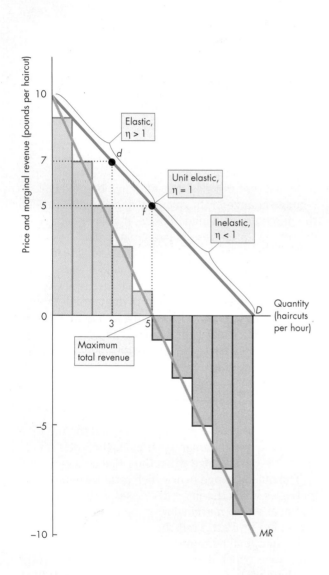

(a) Demand and marginal revenue curves

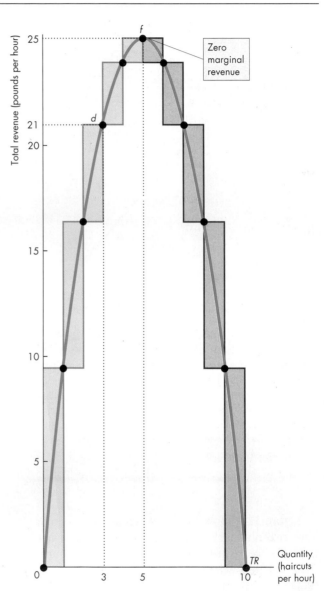

(b) Total revenue curve

Jackie's demand curve (*D*) and marginal revenue curve (*MR*), shown in part (a), and total revenue curve (*TR*), shown in part (b), are based on the numbers in Table 12.1. For example, at a price of £7, Jackie sells 3 haircuts an hour (point *d* in part a) for a total revenue of £21 (point *d* in part b). Over the range 0 to 5 haircuts an hour, total revenue is increasing and marginal revenue is positive, as shown by the blue bars. Over the range 5 to 10 haircuts an hour, total revenue declines – marginal revenue is negative, as shown by the red bars. Over the output range for which marginal revenue is positive demand is elastic. Over the output range for which marginal revenue is negative demand is inelastic. At the output at which marginal revenue is zero demand is unit elastic.

unit elastic – at which the elasticity of demand is 1.

The relationship that you have just discovered has an important implication: a profit-maximizing monopoly never produces an output in the inelastic range of its demand curve. If it did so, marginal revenue would be negative – each additional unit sold would lower total revenue. Since marginal costs are always positive, marginal revenue would not equal marginal cost. In such a situation, the monopoly would increase its profit by producing a smaller quantity and charging a higher price. But exactly what price and quantity does a profit-maximizing monopoly firm choose?

Price and Output Decision

Profit is the difference between total revenue and total cost. To determine the output level and price that maximize a monopoly's profit, we need to study the behaviour of both revenue and costs as output varies.

A monopoly faces the same types of technology and cost constraints as a competitive firm. The monopoly has a production function that is subject to diminishing returns. The monopoly buys its inputs in competition with other firms, at prices that it cannot influence. The sole difference between the monopoly that we'll study here and a perfectly competitive firm lies in the market constraint for the output that each firm faces. The competitive firm is a price taker, whereas the monopoly supplies the entire market. Because the monopoly supplies the entire market, its output decision affects the price at which that output is sold. It is this fact that gives rise to the difference between the decisions faced by these two types of firm.

We have already looked at Jackie's revenue in Table 12.1 and Figs. 12.1 and 12.2. The revenue information contained in Fig. 12.3 is extracted from Table 12.1. The figure also contains information on Jackie's costs and profit.

Total cost (TC) rises as output rises and so does total revenue (TR). Profit equals total revenue minus total cost. As you can see in the table, the maximum profit (£6) occurs when Jackie sells 3 haircuts for £7 each. If she sells 2 haircuts for £8 each or 4 haircuts for £6 each, her profit will be only £4.

You can see why 3 haircuts is the profit-maximizing output by looking at the marginal revenue and marginal cost columns. When Jackie increases output from 2 to 3 haircuts, she generates a marginal

FIGURE 12.3

The Monopoly's Output and Price

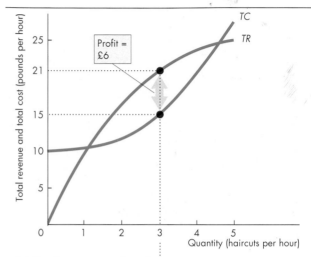

(a) Total revenue and total cost curves

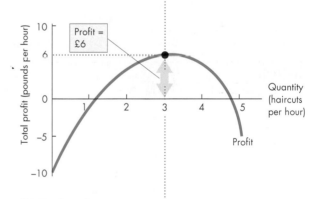

(b) Total profit curve

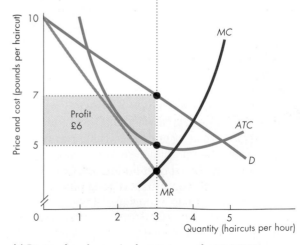

(c) Demand and marginal revenue and cost curves

FIGURE 12.3 (CONTINUED)

Price *P* (pounds per haircut)	Quantity demanded *Q* (haircuts per hour)	Total revenue *TR* = *P* × *Q* (pounds)	Marginal revenue *MR* = Δ*TR*/Δ*Q* (pounds per haircut)	Total cost *TC* (pounds)	Marginal cost *MC* = Δ*TC*/Δ*Q* (pounds per haircut)	Profit *TR* − *TC* (pounds)
10	0	0		10.00		−10.00
			9		0.50	
9	1	9		10.50		−1.50
			7		1.50	
8	2	16		12.00		+4.00
			5		3.00	
7	3	21		15.00		+6.00
			3		5.00	
6	4	24		20.00		+4.00
			1		7.50	
5	5	25		27.50		−2.50

The table adds information about total cost (*TC*), marginal cost (*MC*) and profit (*TR−TC*) to the information on demand and revenue in Table 12.1. For example, at a price of £8, 2 haircuts will be sold for a total revenue of £16. The total cost of producing 2 haircuts is £12, so profit equals £4 (£16 − £12). Profit is at a maximum in the row highlighted in red.

The numbers in the table are graphed in the three parts of the figure. The total cost and total revenue curves appear in part (a). The vertical distance between total revenue (*TR*) and total cost (*TC*) equals total profit. Maximum profit occurs at 3 haircuts an hour. Part (b) shows the total profit curve. This

curve reaches a maximum at 3 haircuts an hour. The total profit curve is at a maximum (part b) when the vertical distance between the total revenue and total cost curves is also at a maximum (part a). Where total revenue equals total cost (in part a), the total profit curve cuts the horizontal axis (in part b). Part (c) shows that at the profit-maximizing output of 3 haircuts, marginal cost (*MC*) equals marginal revenue (*MR*). The monopoly sells the output for the maximum possible price as determined by its demand curve. In this case, that price is £7. The monopoly's profit is illustrated in part (c) by the blue rectangle. That profit is £6 – the profit per haircut (£2) multiplied by 3 haircuts.

revenue of £5 and incurs a marginal cost of £3. Profit increases by the difference – £2. If Jackie increases output yet further, from 3 to 4 haircuts, she generates a marginal revenue of £3 and a marginal cost of £5. In this case, marginal cost exceeds marginal revenue by £2, so profit falls by £2. Jackie will always increase her profit by producing more if marginal revenue exceeds marginal cost and by producing less if marginal cost exceeds marginal revenue. Jackie's profit will not change by producing either more or less if marginal cost and marginal revenue are equal. Thus the profit-maximizing output occurs when marginal revenue equals marginal cost.

The information set out in the table is shown graphically in Fig. 12.3. Part (a) shows Jackie's total revenue curve (*TR*) and total cost curve (*TC*). Profit is the vertical distance between *TR* and *TC*. Jackie

maximizes her profit at 3 haircuts an hour – profit is £21 minus £15, or £6. Part (b) shows how Jackie's profit varies with the number of haircuts sold.

Figure 12.3(c) shows the demand curve (*D*) and the marginal revenue curve (*MR*) along with the marginal cost curve (*MC*) and average total cost curve (*ATC*). The profit-maximizing output is 3 haircuts, where marginal cost equals marginal revenue. The price charged is found by reading from the demand curve the highest price at which 3 haircuts will be bought. That price is £7. When Jackie produces 3 haircuts, average total cost is £5 (read from the *ATC* curve). Her profit per haircut is £2 (£7 minus £5). Jackie's total profit is indicated by the blue rectangle, which equals the profit per haircut (£2) multiplied by the number of haircuts (3), for a total profit of £6. Since price always *exceeds* marginal revenue, and at the profit-maximizing output marginal revenue equals marginal cost, price always exceeds marginal cost.

Jackie makes a positive profit. But there is nothing to guarantee that a monopoly will be able to make a profit. A monopoly can make a zero profit or even, in the short run, a loss. Figure 12.4 shows the conditions under which these other two outcomes will occur.

If Jackie's average total cost is ATC_a, as shown in Fig. 12.4(a), then the profit-maximizing output, where marginal revenue equals marginal cost, will be 3 haircuts. At this output, average cost just equals price, so both the profit per haircut and total profit are zero. If Jackie's average total cost curve is ATC_b, as shown in Fig. 12.4(b), then marginal cost equals marginal revenue at 3 haircuts and average total cost is £8. But 3 haircuts can only be sold for £7 each, so Jackie makes a loss of £1 a haircut. That loss, however, is the minimum possible loss, so

Jackie is still maximizing profit. A monopoly that makes a loss will only do so in the short run. If the situation shown in Fig. 12.3(b) were permanent, Jackie would go out of business.

When we studied a competitive firm, we checked to see whether price was higher or lower than average variable cost. With a price below average variable cost, the firm will shut down temporarily and produce nothing. It makes a loss equal to total fixed cost. Like a competitive firm, Jackie also needs to check her average variable cost to see whether her loss will be minimized by shutting down temporarily. There is no point in any firm, competitor or monopoly, making a loss that exceeds total fixed cost.

If firms in a perfectly competitive industry are making a positive economic profit, new firms enter. That does not happen in a monopoly industry. Barriers to entry prevent new firms from entering. So a firm can make a positive economic profit and

---

FIGURE 12.4

Short-run Profit, Costs and Demand

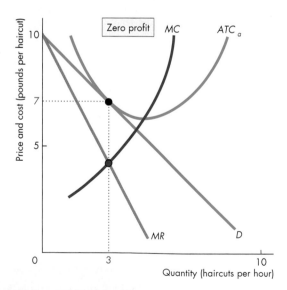

(a) Zero economic profit

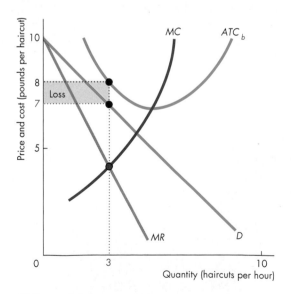

(b) Economic loss

In the short run, a monopoly can make zero profit or even a loss. Part (a) shows a monopoly making zero profit. At the profit-maximizing output – 3 haircuts an hour – average total cost and price are each £7. Part (b) shows a monopoly

making a short-run loss. In this case, at the profit-maximizing output (again 3 haircuts an hour) average total cost is £8 and price is £7, so the firm incurs a loss of £3. The loss is represented by the red rectangle.

Understanding Monopoly Power

Monopolies may well be greedy, but are they able to convert their greed into higher prices than those charged by competitive firms? If so, to what extent? And being big, are monopolies able to exploit their workers and suppliers, paying lower wages and prices than smaller firms must pay?

These questions puzzled generations of economists. Adam Smith said, 'The price of a monopoly is upon every occasion the highest which can be got.' But Smith was wrong. The questions were first answered correctly by Antoine-August Cournot, although his answer was not appreciated until almost a century later when Joan Robinson explained how monopolies behave.

> **'People in the same trade seldom meet together, even for merriment and diversion, but the conversation ends in... some contrivance to raise prices.'**
>
> ADAM SMITH
> *The Wealth of Nations*

Questions about monopoly behaviour took on an urgent and practical tone during the 1870s, a time when rapid technological change and falling transportation costs enabled huge monopolies to emerge in the United States. Monopolies dominated oil, steel, railways, tobacco and even sugar, and industrial empires grew ever larger. In Europe concern about monopoly is greater now than then. Discussion is focused on firms who have gained a technological advantage with their product which has allowed them to capture markets and practise monopoly pricing.

The success of the nineteenth-century monopolies led to the creation of our competition policy and laws – laws that limit the use of monopoly power. These laws have been used to prevent monopolies from being set up and to break up existing monopolies. Competition has been encouraged by restricting mergers or by limiting restrictive trade practices, which are those aspects of firms' activities that restrict competition and price changes. Recent examples include the deregulation of bus routes, the restructuring of the brewing and pub industry and also the introduction of competition in the telecommunications industry. But in spite of competition policy and laws, monopolies still exist. One of the most prominent is cable television. Like their notorious forerunners, the cable television companies use their monopoly power and make large profits.

Ruthless greed, exploitation of both workers and customers – these are the traditional images of monopolies and the effects of their power. And these images appeared to be an accurate description in the 1880s, when monopolies were at their peak of power and influence. One mono-polist, John D. Rockefeller, Sr, had built his giant Standard Oil Company, which, by 1879, was refining 90 per cent of the United States' oil and controlling its entire pipeline capacity.

In spite of competition policy and laws that regulate monopolies, they still exist. One of the most prominent is that in cable television. In most cities, one firm decides which channels viewers will receive and the price they will pay. During the 1980s, with the advent of satellite technology and specialist cable programme producers such as CNN and BSkyB, the cable companies expanded their offerings. At the same time, they steadily increased prices and their businesses became very profitable. Are the local cable companies exploiting their customers? What would happen to their prices if they were regulated? And what would happen to the number of channels and to the quality and variety of the programmes they offered?

Joan Robinson: Discovering the Limits to Monopoly Power

At the age of 30, Joan Robinson (1903–1983) published *The Economics of Imperfect Competition*, a book that revolutionized industrial economics, introduced *marginal revenue* into the economics vocabulary, and originated the modern diagram of monopoly price, output and profit. (Compare the figure with Figure 12.3c.)

Robinson was a formidable debater and revelled in verbal battles, a notable one of which was with the famous MIT economist Paul Samuelson. Anxious to make a point on the blackboard, Samuelson asked Robinson for the chalk. Monopolizing the chalk and board, the unyielding Robinson snapped, 'Say it in words, young man'.

This story illustrates Joan Robinson's approach to economics: work out the answers to economic problems using the most powerful methods of logic available, but then 'say it in words'. Don't be satisfied with a formal argument if you don't *understand* it.

JOAN ROBINSON

continue to do so indefinitely in a monopoly industry. Sometimes that profit is large, as in the case of the Post Office in the United Kingdom.

No Monopoly Supply Curve

Unlike a perfectly competitive firm, a monopoly does not have a supply curve. Recall that a supply curve shows the quantity supplied at each price. A change in demand in a competitive industry results in the industry moving along its supply curve and each firm moving along its marginal cost curve. A change in demand in a monopoly also produces a change in price and quantity, but the monopoly does not slide along a supply curve. Instead, given the new demand conditions, the monopoly picks the combination of output and price that maximizes profit, given its cost curves. As in competitive conditions, the monopoly chooses to sell a quantity such that marginal revenue equals marginal cost. But the relationship between price and marginal revenue, and between price and marginal cost, depends on the shape of the demand curve. For a given profit-maximizing quantity, the steeper the demand curve, the higher is the price at which that quantity is sold. This is why there is no unique relationship between the monopoly's profit-maximizing quantity and price, and therefore no such thing as a monopoly's supply curve.

R E V I E W

A single-price monopoly maximizes profit by producing an output at which marginal cost equals marginal revenue. At that output, the monopoly charges the highest price that consumers are willing to pay. Since a monopoly's price exceeds its marginal revenue, its price also exceeds its marginal cost. But there is no guarantee that a monopoly will make a profit in the short run. Depending on its cost curves and the demand for its output, the monopoly might make a positive economic profit, or a zero profit, or incur a loss. But a monopoly can make a positive economic profit even in the long run since there are barriers to the entry of new firms. There is no unique relationship between the quantity that a monopoly produces and its price – there is no monopoly supply curve. ◆

Price Discrimination

Price discrimination is the practice of charging some customers a higher price than others for an identical good or of charging an individual customer a higher price on a small purchase than on a large one. An example of price discrimination is the practice of banks giving students a special low rate for bank charges. Another example is the common practice of giving discounts to students for weekend coach and train tickets. Price discrimination can be practised in varying degrees. **Perfect price discrimination** occurs when a firm charges a different price for each unit sold and charges each consumer the maximum price that he or she is willing to pay for each unit. Though perfect price discrimination does not happen in the real world, it shows the limit to which price discrimination can be taken.

Not all price *differences* imply price *discrimination*. In many situations, goods that are similar but not identical have different costs, and sell for different prices *because* they have different costs. For example, the marginal cost of producing electricity depends on the time of day. If an electric power company charges a higher price for consumption between 7.00 and 9.00 in the morning and between 4.00 and 7.00 in the evening than it does at other times of the day, this practice is not price discrimination. Rather, it reflects the differences in the costs of production at peak and off-peak hours. In contrast, price discrimination charges varying prices to consumers, not because of differences in the cost of producing the good, but because different consumers have different demands for the good. Reading Between the Lines on pp. 334–335 looks at price discrimination in the UK milk market.

At first sight, it appears that price discrimination contradicts the assumption of profit maximization. Why would British Rail charge students less than it charges other people? Why would a bank charge students less for banking services? Aren't these producers losing profit by being nice?

Deeper investigation shows that far from losing profit, price discriminators actually make a bigger profit than they would otherwise. Thus a monopoly has an incentive to try to find ways of discriminating among groups of consumers and charging each group the highest possible price. Some people may pay less with price discrimination, but others pay more. How does price discrimination bring in more total revenue?

Price Discrimination and Total Revenue

The total revenue received by a single-price monopoly equals the quantity sold multiplied by the single price charged. That revenue is illustrated in Fig. 12.5(a). Suppose that Jackie sells 4 haircuts for a single price of £6 each. Jackie's total revenue, £24, is the area of the blue rectangle – the quantity sold, 4 haircuts, multiplied by the price, £6.

Now suppose that Jackie can sell some haircuts for one price and some for another, higher price. Figure 12.5(b) illustrates this case. The first 2 haircuts are sold for £8 each and then two more are sold for the original price, £6. In this case, Jackie has greater total revenue than when she charges a single price. The extra revenue earned on the first 2 haircuts sold has to be added to the original revenue. Total revenue, the blue area shown in part (b), is £28 (2 at £6 plus 2 at £8).

What happens if Jackie can perfectly price

discriminate? The answer is shown in Fig. 12.5(c). Each haircut is sold for the maximum possible price. The first haircut sells for £9, the next for £8, the third for £7 and the fourth for £6. Total revenue, the blue area in part (c), is £30.

Price Discrimination and Consumer Surplus

Demand curves slope down because the value that an individual places on a good falls as the quantity consumed of that good increases. When all the units consumed can be bought for a single price, consumers benefit. We call this benefit *consumer surplus*. (If you need to refresh your understanding of consumer surplus, look back to Chapter 7.) Price discrimination can be seen as an attempt by a monopoly to capture the consumer surplus (or as much of the surplus as possible) for itself.

Discriminating among Units of a Good One form of price discrimination charges each single buyer a different price on each unit of a good bought. An example of this type of discrimination is a discount

FIGURE 12.5

Total Revenue and Price Discrimination

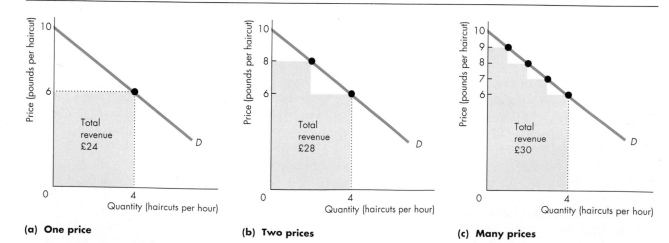

(a) One price

(b) Two prices

(c) Many prices

If Jackie sells 4 haircuts for the same price – £6 each – her total revenue is £24, as shown by the blue rectangle in part (a). If she charges two prices – £8 each for the first 2 haircuts and £6 each for the next 2 – her total revenue will be £28, as shown by the blue area in part (b). If Jackie charges four different

prices – £9 for the first haircut, £8 for the second haircut, £7 for the third haircut and £6 for the fourth haircut – her total revenue will be £30, as shown by the blue area in part (c). The more finely a monopoly can discriminate, the larger the total revenue from a given level of sales.

for bulk buying. The larger the order, the larger is the discount – and the lower is the price. This type of price discrimination works because each individual's demand curve slopes downward. For example, suppose that Katie is willing to pay £7 for the first pizza each month, £6 for the second pizza and £5 for the third pizza. If the price of a pizza is £5, she buys 3 pizzas and pays £5 for each. But the value to her of the first pizza is £7 – £2 more than she pays for it. The value to her of the second pizza is £6 – £1 more than she pays for it. Katie's consumer surplus is £3.

Now imagine that a pizza parlour makes a special offer: 1 pizza a month for £7, 2 pizzas a month for £13, or 3 pizzas a month for £18. If Katie opts for the three-pizza package, the pizza parlour extracts Katie's entire consumer surplus. But to extract every pound of consumer surplus from *every* buyer, the monopolist has to offer each individual customer a separate contract based on that customer's own demand curve. Clearly such price discrimination cannot be carried out in practice, because a firm does not have sufficient information about each individual consumer's demand curve to be able to do the necessary calculations. But by making arrangements of the type just described that extract most of the consumer surplus of a typical customer, firms can move towards perfect price discrimination.

Discriminating among Individuals   Even when it is not possible to charge each individual a different price for each unit bought, it may still be possible to discriminate among individuals. This possibility arises from the fact that some people place a higher value on consuming one more unit of a good than do others. By charging such people a higher price, the producer can obtain some of the consumer surplus that would otherwise accrue to its customers.

Let's look a bit more closely at the price and output decisions of a monopoly that practises price discrimination.

Price and Output Decisions with Price Discrimination

Price discrimination often takes the form of discriminating between different groups of consumers on the basis of age, employment status, or other easily distinguished characteristics. Price discrimination works only if each group has a different price elasticity of demand for the product. If one group has a high elasticity and the other a low elasticity, then a firm can increase profit by charging a lower price to the group with the high elasticity and a higher price to the group with a low elasticity.

Jackie suspects that the students of Askrigg have a higher elasticity of demand for haircuts than do other people – they do not seem to care as much about getting a bit shaggy as other clients. Let's see how Jackie exploits these differences in demand and increases her profit by price discriminating. Until now, Jackie has sold 3 haircuts an hour at £7 a haircut, for a total revenue of £21. With a total cost of £15 an hour, Jackie makes an hourly profit of £6. Jackie's costs, revenues and profit were shown in the table in Fig. 12.3.

Jackie has noticed that students come in less frequently than other clients. In fact, of the 3 haircuts she does each hour, only one is for a student and two are for other clients. Jackie knows that to get students to have a haircut more often, she has to lower the price she charges them. She suspects that her other clients will still turn up for haircuts at the rate of 2 an hour, even if she charges them a higher price. Jackie decides to price discriminate between the two groups, but she has to work out what price to charge each group to maximize her profit.

Table 12.2 sets out the calculations that Jackie performs. It shows Jackie's estimates of the demand schedules for her two groups of customers. It also shows the total revenue and marginal revenue calculations for the two separate groups. Jackie's marginal costs are the same for both groups – hair is hair, whether it belongs to a student or another client. But marginal revenue differs between the two groups of customers. For example, when the price falls from £9 to £8, the marginal revenue from students is zero, while that from others is £7. When the price falls from £8 to £7, the marginal revenue from students is £7, while that from others is *minus* £2.

Jackie calculates her profit-maximizing prices and output in the following way. She knows that the marginal cost of the third haircut is £3. (To see this, look back at the table for Fig. 12.3.) If her output increases, the marginal cost of the fourth haircut is £5. She looks at her marginal revenues and compares them with this £5 marginal cost. She notices that by charging her other clients £8, this group buys 2 haircuts an hour for a marginal revenue of £7. If she charges students £6, that group buys 2 haircuts an hour and brings in a marginal revenue of £5. Thus when she sells a total of 4 haircuts (2 to

TABLE 12.2

Profiting from Price Discrimination

Price P (pounds per haircut)	Students			Other clients		
	Quantity demanded Q (haircuts per hour)	Total revenue TR (pounds)	Marginal revenue MR (pounds per haircut)	Quantity demanded Q (haircuts per hour)	Total revenue TR (pounds)	Marginal revenue MR (pounds per haircut)
10	0	0		0	0	
			············· 0			··············· 9
9	0	0		1	9	
			············· 0			··· ············· 7
8	0	0		2	16	
			············· 7			·············· −2
7	1	7		2	14	
			············· 5			·············· −2
6	2	12		2	12	
			············· 3			·············· −2
5	3	15		2	10	

Profit calculation:

Profit = TR − TC = (£6 × 2) + (£8 × 2) − £20 = £8

As a single-price monopoly, Jackie sells 3 haircuts an hour for £7 each and makes a maximum profit of £6, as was shown in Fig. 12.3. By discriminating between two groups of customers – the first group consisting of students and the second group consisting of all other customers – Jackie is able to make a bigger profit. She raises the price of regular haircuts to £8 and lowers the price for students to £6. Her sales rise to 4 haircuts an hour and her profit rises to £8.

students and 2 to other customers) the marginal revenue from the students, $5, just equals the marginal cost of the fourth haircut.

But she can see that if she lowers the price to either group, marginal revenue will fall short of marginal cost. Marginal cost will climb to $7.50 for a fifth haircut and marginal revenue will fall to $3 if an extra haircut is sold to students. Other customers have an inelastic demand curve and will not buy any more than 2 haircuts, so that marginal revenue from lowering the price to that group is negative. Thus Jackie can make no more profit than that arising from charging students $6 and other customers $8 and producing 4 haircuts an hour. The profit from such price discrimination is $8. (The calculation is set out at the foot of Table 12.2.)

Perfect Price Discrimination

Suppose that Jackie is able to devise a means of being a perfect price discriminator. How much profit can she make in this case? Jackie's demand and cost curves are shown in Fig. 12.6. As a single-price monopoly, she produces 3 haircuts, sells them for $7 each and makes a profit of $6 – the light blue rectangle. (Refresh your memory if necessary by referring back to Fig. 12.3c.) If Jackie can get each of her customers to pay the maximum price that each is willing to pay for a haircut, then she can sell the first haircut for $9. She makes an extra profit of $2 ($9 minus $7) from that first haircut sold. She can sell the second haircut for $8, $1 more than before. She will still sell the third for $7, since that is the maximum price that the third customer is willing to pay

FIGURE 12.6

Output and Profit with Perfect Price Discrimination

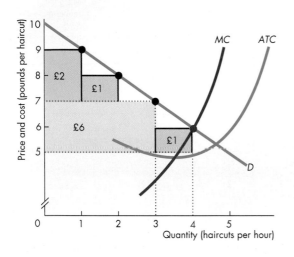

Maximum profit with single price:	£6	Quantity: 3 haircuts
add extra profit from 1st haircut	+ £2	
add extra profit from 2nd haircut	+ £1	
add extra profit from 4th haircut (extra revenue from 4th haircut is £6 and marginal cost is £5)	+ £1	
equals maximum profit with price discrimination	£10	Quantity: 4 haircuts

Jackie's profit as a single-price monopoly, shown by the light blue area, is £6. With perfect price discrimination, Jackie charges £9 for the first haircut, £8 for the second, £7 for the third and £6 for the fourth. Marginal revenue equals price in each case because, with perfect price discrimination, the marginal revenue curve is the same as the demand curve. Profit is maximized when the demand curve intersects the marginal cost curve. It does not pay Jackie to sell a fifth haircut because its marginal revenue (price) is less than its marginal cost. Jackie's additional profit as a perfect price discriminator, shown by the dark blue areas, is £4. Her maximum total profit with perfect price discrimination is £10.

for a haircut. If Jackie continues to produce 3 haircuts, her profit rises to £9, an increase of £3.

But Jackie will not stop at 3 haircuts an hour. To see why, consider the marginal revenue from selling a fourth haircut and the marginal cost of producing it.

The fourth haircut can be sold for £6. The marginal cost of the fourth haircut, from the table in Fig. 12.3, is only £5. So by producing a fourth haircut and selling it for £6, Jackie makes a further £1 profit. The maximum profit with perfect price discrimination occurs when Jackie sells 4 haircuts, each for the maximum price that the consumers are willing to pay. That profit is £10. It is illustrated in the figure as the sum of the light blue and the three dark blue rectangles. The table in Fig. 12.6 summarizes this calculation.

When a firm practices perfect price discrimination, its output exceeds that of a single-price monopoly. It produces up to the point at which the marginal cost curve cuts the demand curve. The less perfect the price discrimination, the smaller is the additional output produced.

REVIEW

Price discrimination increases a monopoly's profit by increasing its total revenue. By charging the highest price for each unit of the good that each person is willing to pay, a monopoly perfectly price discriminates and captures all of the consumer surplus. Much price discrimination takes the form of discriminating among different groups of customers, charging a higher price to some and a lower price to others. Such price discrimination increases total revenue and profit, but it is possible only if the two groups have different elasticities of demand. A price-discriminating monopoly produces a larger output than a single-price monopoly. ◆

Discrimination among Groups

You can now see why it pays to price discriminate. The sign in Jackie's window – 'Haircuts £8: special for students, only £6' – is no generous gesture. It is profit-maximizing behaviour. The model of price discrimination that you have just studied explains a wide variety of familiar pricing practices, even by firms that are not pure monopolies. For example, airlines offer lower fares for advance-purchase tickets than for last-minute travel. Last-minute travellers usually have a low elasticity of demand, while vacation travellers who can plan ahead have a higher elasticity of demand. Retail stores of all kinds hold seasonal 'sales' when they reduce their prices, often by substantial amounts. These 'sales' are a form of price discrimination. Each season, the newest fashions carry a high price tag but retailers do not expect to sell all their stock at such high prices. At the end of the season, they sell off what is left at a discount. Thus such stores discriminate between buyers who have an inelastic demand (for example, those who want to be instantly fashionable) and buyers who have an elastic demand (for example, those who pay less attention to up-to-the-minute fashion and more attention to price).

Limits to Price Discrimination

Since price discrimination is profitable, why don't more firms do it? What are the limits to price discrimination?

Profitable price discrimination can take place only under certain conditions. First, it is possible to price discriminate only if the good cannot be resold. If a good can be resold, then customers who get the good for the low price can resell it to someone willing to pay a higher price. Price discrimination breaks down. It is for this reason that price discrimination usually occurs in markets for services rather than in markets for storable goods. One major exception, price discrimination in the sale of fashion clothes, works because at the end of the season when the clothes go on sale, the fashion-conscious people are looking for next season's fashions. People buying at a sale have no one to whom they can resell the clothes at a higher price.

Second, a price-discriminating monopoly must be able to identify groups with different elasticities of demand. The characteristics used for discrimination must also be within the law. These requirements usually limit price discrimination to cases based on either age or employment status, or on the timing of the purchase.

Despite these limitations, there are some ingenious criteria used for discriminating. For example, British Airways discriminates between six different passenger groups on many of its international flights. The economy class alternatives between London and Miami in April 1994 were:

- ◆ £1,772 – no restrictions
- ◆ £738 – direct to destination
- ◆ £534 – 7 days in advance, maximum stay 6 months
- ◆ £470 – 7 days in advance, maximum stay 1 month
- ◆ £418 – 21 days in advance, maximum stay 7 nights
- ◆ £345 – 14 days in advance, no refund

These different prices discriminate between different groups of customers with different elasticities of demand.

Comparing Monopoly and Competition

We have now studied a variety of ways in which firms and households interact in markets for goods and services. In Chapter 11, we saw how perfectly competitive firms behave and discovered the price and output at which they operate. In this chapter, we have studied the price and output of a single-price monopoly and a monopoly that price discriminates. How do the quantities produced, prices and profits of these different types of firms compare with each other?

To answer this question, let's imagine an industry made up of a large number of identical competitive firms. We will work out what the price charged and quantity traded will be in that industry. Then we will imagine that a single firm buys out all the individual firms and creates a monopoly. We will then work out the price charged and quantity produced by the monopoly, first when it charges a single price, and second when it price discriminates.

Price and Output

We will conduct the analysis by using Fig. 12.7. The industry demand curve is D and the industry supply curve is S. In perfect competition, the market equilibrium occurs where the supply curve and the demand curve intersect. The quantity produced by the industry is Q_C and the price is P_C.

Each firm takes the price P_C and maximizes its

profit by producing the output at which its own marginal cost equals the price. Since each firm is a small part of the total industry, there is no incentive for any firm to try to manipulate the price by varying its output.

Now suppose that this industry is taken over by a single firm. No changes in production techniques occur, so the new combined firm has identical costs to the original separate firms. The new single firm recognizes that by varying output it can influence price. It also recognizes that its marginal revenue curve is MR. To maximize profit, the firm chooses an output at which marginal revenue equals marginal cost. But what is the monopoly's marginal cost curve? To answer this question, you need to recall the relationship between the marginal cost curve and the supply curve of a competitive firm. The supply curve of an individual competitive firm is its marginal cost curve. The supply curve of a competitive industry is the sum of the supply curves of individual firms. The industry supply curve tells us how the sum of the quantities supplied by each firm varies as the price varies. Thus the industry supply curve is also the industry's marginal cost curve. (The supply curve has also been labelled MC to remind you of this fact.) Therefore, when the industry is taken over by a single firm, that firm's marginal cost curve is the same as what used to be the competitive industry's supply curve.

We have seen that a competitive industry always operates at the point of intersection of its supply and demand curves. In Fig. 12.7, this is the point at which price is P_C and the industry produces the quantity Q_C. In contrast, the single-price monopoly maximizes profit by restricting output to Q_M, where marginal revenue equals marginal cost. Since the marginal revenue curve is below the demand curve, output Q_M will always be smaller than output Q_C. The monopoly charges the highest price for which output Q_M can be sold, and that price is P_M.

If the monopoly can perfectly price discriminate, it will charge a different price for each unit sold and increase output to Q_C. The highest price charged is P_A and the lowest price charged is P_C, the price in a competitive market. The price P_A is the highest that is charged because at yet higher prices nothing can be sold. The price P_C is the lowest charged because when a monopoly perfectly price discriminates, its marginal revenue curve is the same as the demand curve and at prices below

FIGURE 12.7

Monopoly and Competition Compared

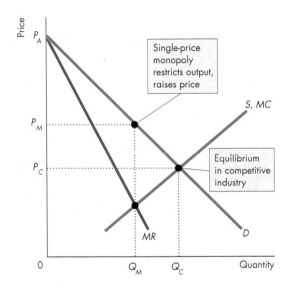

A competitive industry has a demand curve D and a supply curve S. Equilibrium occurs where the quantity demanded equals the quantity supplied at quantity Q_C and price P_C. If all the firms in the industry are taken over by a single producer who sells the profit-maximizing output for a single price, marginal revenue is MR and the supply curve of the competitive industry, S, becomes the monopoly's marginal cost curve, MC. The monopoly produces the output at which marginal revenue equals marginal cost. A single-price monopoly produces Q_M and sells that output for the price P_M. A perfectly price-discriminating monopoly produces Q_C and charges a different price for each unit sold. The prices charged range from P_A to P_C.

Monopoly restricts output and raises the price. But the more perfectly a monopoly can price discriminate, the closer its output gets to the competitive output.

P_C marginal cost exceeds marginal revenue.

The key price and output differences between competition and monopoly are the following:

◆ Monopoly price exceeds the competitive price.
◆ Monopoly output is less than competitive output.
◆ The more perfectly the monopoly can price discriminate, the closer its output gets to the competitive output.

Allocative Efficiency

Monopoly is usually less efficient than competition. It prevents some of the gains from trade from being achieved. To see why, look at Fig. 12.8. The maximum price that consumers are willing to pay for each unit is shown by the demand curve. The difference between the maximum price that they are willing to pay for each unit bought and the price they do pay is *consumer surplus*. Under perfect competition (part a), consumers have to pay only P_C for each unit bought and obtain a consumer surplus represented by the green triangle.[1]

A single-price monopoly (part b) restricts output to Q_M and sells that output for P_M. Consumer surplus is reduced to the smaller green triangle. Consumers lose partly by having to pay more for what is available and partly by getting less of the good. But is the consumers' loss equal to the monopoly's gain? Is there simply a redistribution of the gains from trade? A closer look at Fig. 12.8(b) will convince you that there is a reduction in the gains from trade. It is true that some of the loss in consumer surplus does accrue to the monopoly – the monopoly gets the difference between the higher price (P_M) and P_C on the quantity sold (Q_M). So the monopoly has taken the blue rectangle part of the consumer surplus.

What though has become of the rest of the consumer surplus? The answer is that because output has been restricted, it is lost. But more than that has been lost. The total loss resulting from the lower monopoly output (Q_M) is the grey triangle in Fig. 12.8(b). The part of the grey triangle above P_C is the loss of consumer surplus and that part of the triangle below P_C is a loss to the producer – a loss of producer surplus. **Producer surplus** is the difference between a producer's revenue and the opportunity cost of production. It is calculated as the sum of the differences between price and the marginal cost of producing each unit of output. Under competitive conditions, the producer sells the output between Q_M and Q_C for a price of P_C.

FIGURE 12.8

The Allocative Inefficiency of Monopoly

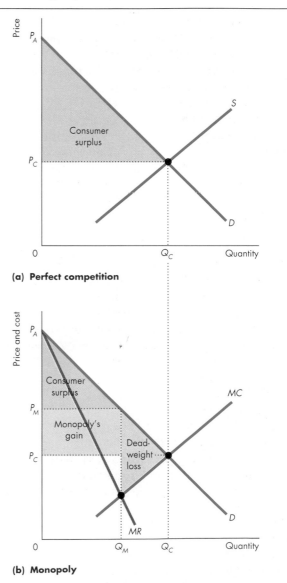

(a) Perfect competition

(b) Monopoly

In perfect competition (part a), demand curve *D* intersects supply curve *S* at quantity Q_C and price P_C. Consumer surplus is represented by the green triangle. With free entry, firms' profits in long-run equilibrium are zero. Consumer surplus is maximized. Under a single-price monopoly (part b), output is restricted to Q_M and the price increases to P_M. Consumer surplus is reduced to the smaller green triangle. The monopoly takes the blue rectangle for itself, but the grey triangle is a deadweight loss. Part of the deadweight loss (above P_C) is a loss of consumer surplus, and part (below P_C) is a loss of producer surplus.

---

[1] In Fig 7.7, Katie's consumer surplus is less than the entire area between her demand curve for pizzas and the price paid because pizzas can be bought only in whole units. For a good that is divisible into arbitrarily small units, consumer surplus is the entire area between the demand curve and the price paid, as shown in Fig. 12.8(b).

The marginal cost of producing each extra unit of output through that range is shown by the marginal cost (supply) curve. Thus the vertical distance between the marginal cost curve and price represents a producer surplus. Part of the producer surplus is lost when a monopoly restricts output below its competitive level.

The grey triangle, which measures the total loss of both consumer and producer surplus, is called the deadweight loss. **Deadweight loss** measures allocative inefficiency as the reduction in consumer and producer surplus resulting from a restriction of output below its efficient level. A monopoly's reduced output and higher price results in the monopoly capturing some of the consumer surplus. It also results in the elimination of the producer surplus and consumer surplus on the output that a competitive industry would have produced but that the monopoly does not.

We have seen that a single-price monopoly creates a deadweight loss by restricting output. What is the deadweight loss if the monopoly practises perfect price discrimination? The answer is zero. A perfect price discriminator produces the same output as the competitive industry. The last item sold costs P_C, the same as its marginal cost. Thus from the point of view of allocative efficiency, a perfect price-discriminating monopoly achieves the same result as perfect competition.

Redistribution

Under perfect competition, the consumer surplus is the green triangle in Fig. 12.8(a). With free entry, the long-run equilibrium economic profit of each perfectly competitive firm is zero. We've just seen that the creation of monopoly reduces consumer surplus. Further, in the case of a single-price monopoly, a deadweight loss arises. But what happens to the distribution of surpluses between producers and consumers? The answer is that the monopoly always wins. In the case of a single-price monopoly (Fig. 12.8b), the monopoly gains the blue rectangle at the expense of the consumer. It has to offset against that gain its loss of producer surplus – its share of the deadweight loss. But there is always a net positive gain for the monopoly and a net loss for the consumer. We also know that because there is a deadweight loss, the

consumer loses more than the monopoly gains.

In the case of a perfect price-discriminating monopoly, there is no deadweight loss but there is an even larger redistribution away from consumers to the monopoly. In this case, the monopoly captures the entire consumer surplus, the green triangle in Fig. 12.8(a).

REVIEW

T he creation of a monopoly results in a redistribution of economic gains away from consumers and to the monopoly producer. If the monopoly can perfectly price discriminate, it produces the same output as a competitive industry and achieves allocative efficiency, but it captures the entire consumer surplus. If the monopoly cannot perfectly price discriminate, it restricts output below the level that a competitive industry would produce and creates a deadweight loss. The monopoly gains and the consumer loses, but the loss of the consumer exceeds the gain of the monopoly. In this case, monopoly creates allocative inefficiency. ◆

Rent Seeking

Operating a monopoly is more profitable than operating a firm in a perfectly competitive industry. Economic profit can be made in a competitive industry in the short run but not in the long run. Freedom of entry brings new firms into a profitable industry and results in economic profit being competed away. Barriers to entry prevent this process in a monopoly industry, so a monopoly can enjoy economic profit even in the long run. Because monopoly is more profitable than perfect competition, there is an incentive to attempt to create monopoly. The activity of creating monopoly is called **rent seeking**. The term *rent seeking* arises from the fact that another name for consumer surplus and producer surplus is rent. We've just seen that a monopoly makes its profit by diverting part of the consumer surplus to itself.

Thus pursuing maximum monopoly profit is the same thing as diverting consumer surplus, or rent seeking.

Rent seeking is not a costless activity. To obtain a monopoly right, resources have to be used. Furthermore, everyone has an incentive to seek monopoly power, so there will be competition for monopoly rights. There are two ways in which people compete for monopoly rights: they buy an existing right or they create a new one. But existing monopoly rights had to be created at some time so, ultimately, competition for monopoly rights is a process that uses productive resources in order to establish a monopoly right. What is the value of the resources that a person will use to obtain a monopoly right? The answer is any amount up to the monopoly's profit. If the value of resources spent trying to acquire a monopoly exceeds the monopoly's profit, the net result is an economic loss. But as long as the value of the resources used to acquire a monopoly falls short of the monopoly's profit, there is a profit to be earned. If there is no barrier to entry, the value of the resources used up in rent seeking will, in equilibrium, equal the monopoly's profit.

Because of rent seeking, monopoly imposes costs that exceed the deadweight loss that we calculated earlier. To calculate that cost, we must add to the deadweight loss the value of resources used in rent seeking. That amount equals the entire monopoly profit since that is the value of the resources that it pays to use in rent seeking. Thus the cost of monopoly is the deadweight loss plus monopoly profit.

What exactly are the resources used in rent seeking? What do rent seekers do? One form of rent seeking is the searching out of existing monopoly rights that can be bought for a lower price than the monopoly's economic profit – that is, seeking to acquire existing monopoly rights. This form of rent seeking results in a market price for monopoly rights that is close to the economic profit. There are many real-world examples of this type of rent-seeking activity. One that is well known is the purchase of taxi licences. Most cities regulate taxis, restricting both the fares and the number of taxis that are permitted to operate. Operating a taxi is profitable – resulting in economic profit or rent being earned by the operator.

A person who wants to operate a taxi has to buy the right to do so from someone who already has that right. Competition for that right leads to a price sufficiently high to eliminate long-run economic profit. For example, in some UK cities, the price of a taxi licence is £10,000.

Rent seeking is also big business among the airlines. An example is the purchase of British Caledonian by British Airways. In buying British Caledonian, British Airways also bought the rights to compete on international air routes that it was previously prevented from entering because of restrictions imposed by an international air transport agreement. To acquire those routes, British Airways had to pay British Caledonian a price that provided as much profit as it would have earned had it kept those rights and operated the routes itself. The price paid by British Airways was determined by competition between potential buyers. The routes (and some equipment) went to the airline willing to pay the highest price. That airline was the one which believed it could operate the routes and earn the largest profit.

Although a great deal of rent-seeking activity involves searching out existing monopoly rights that can be profitably bought, much of it is devoted to the creation of monopoly. This type of rent-seeking activity takes the form of lobbying and seeking to influence the political process. Sometimes firms make contributions to political parties in order to gain legislative support, or they seek to influence political outcomes indirectly through contacts with politicians and bureaucrats. (This type of rent seeking is discussed and explained more fully in Chapters 19 and 20.)

R E V I E W

When rent seeking is taken into account, there are no guaranteed long-run profits, even from monopoly. Competition for monopoly rights results in the use of resources to acquire those rights equal in value to the potential monopoly profit. As a consequence, monopoly imposes costs equal to the deadweight loss plus the monopoly's economic profit. ◆

Gains from Monopoly

In our comparison of monopoly and competition, monopoly comes out in a pretty bad light. If monopoly is so bad, why do we put up with it? Why don't we have laws that crack down on monopoly so hard that it never rears its head? As we'll see in Chapter 20, we do indeed have laws that limit monopoly power. We also have laws that regulate those monopolies that exist. But monopoly is not all bad. Let's look at its potential advantages and some of the reasons for its existence.

The main reasons for the existence of monopoly are:

◆ Economies of scale and economies of scope
◆ Incentive to innovate

Economies of Scale and Scope   You met economies of scale in Chapters 9 and 10. There, we defined *economies of scale* as decreases in average total cost resulting from increasing a firm's scale. The scale of a firm increases when it increases all its inputs – capital, labour and materials – in the same proportions. For example, if all inputs double, total cost also doubles. If output more than doubles, average total cost declines or, equivalently, the firm has economies of scale.

Economies of scope are decreases in average total cost made possible by increasing the number of different goods produced. Economies of scope are important when highly specialized (and expensive) technical inputs can be shared by different goods. For example, Burger King can produce both hamburgers and chips at an average total cost that is lower than what it would cost two separate firms to produce the same goods because hamburgers and chips share the use of specialized food storage and preparation facilities. Firms producing a wide range of goods can hire specialist computer programmers, designers and marketing experts whose skills can be used across the product range, thereby spreading their costs and lowering the cost of production of each of the goods.

Large-scale firms that have control over supply and can influence price – and therefore behave like the monopoly firm that we've been studying in this chapter – can reap these economies of scale and scope. Small, competitive firms cannot. As a consequence, there are situations in which the comparison of monopoly and competition that we made earlier in this chapter is not a valid one. Recall that we imagined the takeover of a large number of competitive firms by a single monopoly firm. We also assumed that the monopoly would use exactly the same technology as the small firms and have the same costs. But if one large firm can reap economies of scale and scope, its marginal cost curve will lie below the supply curve of a competitive industry made up of thousands of small firms. It is possible for such economies of scale and scope to be so large as to result in a higher output and lower price under monopoly than a competitive industry would achieve.

Figure 12.9 illustrates such a situation. Here, the demand curve and the marginal revenue curve are the same regardless of whether the industry is a competitive one or a monopoly. With a competitive industry, the supply curve is S, the quantity produced is Q_C and the price is P_C. With a monopoly that can exploit economies of scale and scope, the marginal cost curve is MC_M. The monopoly maximizes profit by producing the output (Q_M) at which marginal revenue equals marginal cost. The price that maximizes profit is P_M. By exploiting a superior technology not available to each of the large number of small firms, the monopoly is able to achieve a higher output and lower price than the competitive industry.

There are many industries in which economies of scale are so important that they lead to an outcome similar to that shown in Fig. 12.9. Examples of these are public utilities such as those providing gas, electricity, water, telephone services and refuse collection. There are also many examples where a combination of economies of scale and economies of scope are important, such as the brewing of beer, the manufacture of refrigerators, other household appliances and pharmaceuticals, and the refining of petroleum.

Innovation   Innovation is the first-time application of new knowledge in the production process. *Innovation* is the development of a new good or the act of putting in place a lower-cost way of making

FIGURE 12.9

When Economies of Scale and Scope Make Monopoly More Efficient

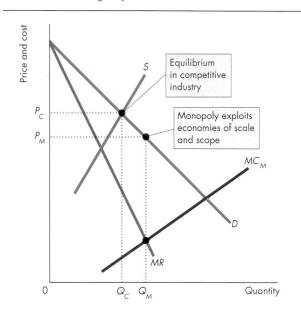

In some industries, economies of scale and economies of scope result in the monopoly's marginal cost curve (MC_M) lying below the competitive industry supply curve (S). In such a case, it is possible that the single-price monopoly output (Q_M) exceeds the competitive output (Q_C) and that the monopoly price (P_M) is below the competitive price (P_C).

Competitive firms must strive to innovate and cut costs even though they know that they cannot hang on to the benefits of their innovation for long. But that knowledge spurs them on to greater and faster innovation.

A matter such as this one cannot be resolved by listing arguments and counterarguments. It requires a careful empirical investigation. Many such investigations have been conducted. But the evidence that they bring to bear on this question is mixed. They show that large firms do much more research and development than small firms. They also show that large firms are significantly more prominent at the development end of the research and development process. But measuring research and development is measuring the volume of inputs into the process of innovation. What matters is not input but output. Two measures of the output of research and development are the number of patents and the rate of productivity growth. On these measures, there is no clear evidence that big is best.

But there is a clear is pattern of diffusion of technological knowledge. After innovation, a new process or good spreads gradually through the industry. Whether an innovator is a small firm or a large firm, large firms jump on the bandwagon more quickly than small firms. Thus large firms are important in speeding up the process of diffusion of technological advances.

In determining public policy towards monopoly (discussed in Chapter 20), laws and regulations are designed that balance these positive aspects of monopoly against the deadweight loss and redistribution that they also generate.

◆ ◆ ◆ ◆ We've now studied two models of market structure – perfect competition and monopoly. We've used these two models to make predictions about the effects on prices and quantities of changing cost and demand conditions. ◆ ◆ Although some markets in the EU economy are highly competitive or highly monopolistic, the markets for most goods and services lie somewhere between these extremes. In the next chapter, we're going to study the middle ground between monopoly and competition. We're going to discover that many of the lessons that we learned from these two extreme models are still relevant and useful in understanding behaviour in real-world markets.

an existing good. Controversy has raged among economists over whether large firms with monopoly power or small competitive firms are the most innovative. It is clear that some temporary monopoly power arises from innovation. A firm that develops a new good or process and patents it obtains exclusive right to that good or process for the term of the patent.

But does the granting of a monopoly, even a temporary one, to an innovator increase the pace of innovation? One line of reasoning suggests that it does. With no protection, an innovator is not able to enjoy the profits from innovation for very long. Thus the incentive to innovate is weakened. A contrary argument is that monopolies can afford to be lazy while competitive firms cannot.

Churning up the Milk Market

FINANCIAL TIMES, 27 JULY 1993

Pretty penny on the price of a pinta

Deborah Hargreaves and Maggie Ury

As 300 dairy farmers converge on London's Queen Elizabeth conference centre today, for the last annual general meeting of the Milk Marketing Board, they fear that the milk market is about to turn sour. The meeting coincides with the final passage of the Agriculture Bill, which will abolish the board and its statutory monopoly over milk purchasing in the UK.

The end of the monopoly under which farmers must sell their milk to the milk board, which then sells it to dairies, will unleash free-market forces on an industry which has been strictly controlled for 60 years....

The changes in the milk industry bear the hallmarks of the government's privatisation of the energy industry, particularly British Gas, which has faced years of regulatory struggle and investigation by competition authorities because it was privatised as a monopoly.

The milk board system – the sole milk outlet for the UK's 29,000 dairy farmers of England and Wales.

The board system brought order to the market. Farmers sold their milk to the board, which pays them the same 'pool' price, regardless of the quantity of milk sold or the distance the tanker must travel to their farm. Farmers have come to rely on the daily tanker collections and monthly milk cheque.

'The milk board system is strong in the farmer's culture, and farmers are conservative people,' said one dairy executive....

Milk Marque hopes to sign up most of the farmers selling to the board and so retain more than 80 per cent of milk production in England and Wales. If it achieves that aim, it will give farmers the security of price and collection many seek. But it could be open to accusations of abusing its dominant market position if it forces up prices to dairy company buyers, which in turn may pass them to consumers.

Several dairy companies and food processors – such as Northern Foods, Nestlé and MD Foods – plan to challenge Milk Marque by buying their milk direct from farmers or setting up their own co-operatives.

© The Financial Times. Reprinted with permission.

The Milk Marketing Board for England and Wales (MMB) is to be abolished.

The MMB has acted as the monopoly buyer of milk since 1933.

The plan is to replace it with Milk Marque, a voluntary producer co-operative.

This new organization will face competition from other companies seeking to buy milk direct from farmers or from other cooperatives farmers may now establish.

The MMB is, however, trying to persuade dairy farmers to remain with it after it has become Milk Marque.

The MMB was created to give farmers some bargaining power in negotiations with the large dairy companies.

The MMB was the sole buyer of milk from farmers. The dairy companies then negotiated with the MMB for their milk supplies.

Given its monopoly position, the MMB was able effectively to practise price discrimination. The figure shows two standard monopolies, representing the sale of milk to the liquid milk sector (the doorstep pinta) and the manufacturing sector (the use of milk for butter, cheese and so on).

The MMB was able to obtain a higher price for milk going to the liquid milk sector than for milk going to the manufacturing sector.

The MMB has said that when it becomes Milk Marque, the price differentials will be removed.

Some dairy companies are establishing their own cooperatives. For example, Northern Foods has recently established the Northern Milk Partnership and is promising to pay a price higher than that paid by Milk Marque.

The trend of co-operatives and dairies promising producers higher prices in order to get farmers to sell their milk to them could result in higher prices for consumers.

Recent trends in dairy production and processing indicate that economies of scale are present. The introduction of competition could raise prices, with processors needing to guarantee a high volume of milk throughput in order to exploit these economies.

The Dairy Trade Federation believes that with Milk Marque still likely to be controlling over two-thirds of milk supplies, its dominant position will allow it to charge high prices much like the MMB.

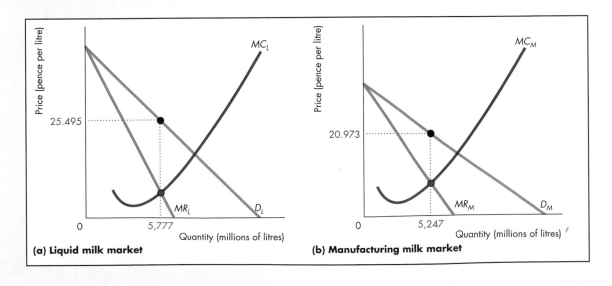

(a) Liquid milk market

(b) Manufacturing milk market

SUMMARY

How Monopoly Arises

Monopoly arises because of barriers to entry that prevent competition. Barriers to the entry of new firms may be legal or natural. Legal barriers take the form of state monopolies, government licence or patent. Natural barriers exist when economies of scale are so large that a single firm can supply an entire market at a lower average total cost than can several firms. (p. 313)

Single-price Monopoly

A monopoly is an industry in which there is a single supplier of a good, service, or resource. A single-price monopoly is a firm that charges the same price for each unit of output. The monopoly's demand curve is the market demand curve for the good. For a single-price monopoly, marginal revenue is less than price. Total revenue rises at first, but above some output level it begins to decline. When total revenue is rising, marginal revenue is positive. When total revenue is falling, marginal revenue is negative. When marginal revenue is positive (total revenue rising), the elasticity of demand is greater than 1. The elasticity of demand equals 1 when total revenue is at a maximum.

A monopoly's technology and costs behave in a way similar to those of any other type of firm. The monopoly maximizes profit by producing the output that makes marginal revenue equal to marginal cost and by charging the maximum price that consumers are willing to pay for that output. The price charged always exceeds marginal cost. A monopoly has no supply curve. (pp. 314–322)

Price Discrimination

Price discrimination is the practice of charging some consumers a higher price than others for an identical item or charging an individual customer a higher price on a small purchase than on a large one. Price discrimination is an attempt by the monopoly to convert consumer surplus into profit. Perfect price discrimination extracts all the consumer surplus. Such a monopoly charges a different price for each unit sold and obtains the maximum price that each consumer is willing to pay for each unit bought.

With perfect price discrimination, the monopoly's marginal revenue curve is the same as its demand curve and the monopoly produces the same output as would a perfectly competitive industry.

A monopoly can discriminate between different groups of customers on the basis of age, employment status, or other distinguishable characteristics. Such price discrimination increases the monopoly's profit if each group has a different elasticity of demand for the product. To maximize profit with price discrimination, the monopoly produces an output such that marginal cost equals marginal revenue, but then charges each group the maximum price that it is willing to pay.

Price discrimination can be practised only when it is impossible for a buyer to resell the good and when consumers with different elasticities can be identified. (pp. 322–327)

Comparing Monopoly and Competition

If a monopoly takes over all the firms in a perfectly competitive industry and if the technology and input prices in the industry remain unchanged, the monopoly charges a higher price and produces a lower quantity than would prevail in a perfectly competitive industry. If the monopoly can perfectly price discriminate, it produces the competitive quantity and sells the last unit for the competitive price.

Monopoly is less efficient than competition because it prevents some of the gains from trade from being achieved. A monopoly captures some part of the consumer surplus, but to do so it has to restrict output so that when it maximizes profit it creates a deadweight loss. The more a monopoly is able to price discriminate, the smaller the deadweight loss but the larger the monopoly profit and the smaller the consumer surplus.

Monopoly always redistributes the gains from trade away from consumers towards the producer. The more perfectly a monopoly can price discriminate, the smaller the deadweight loss but the larger the reallocation of surpluses from consumers to the producer.

Monopoly imposes costs that equal its deadweight loss plus the cost of the resources devoted to rent seeking – searching out profitable monopoly opportunities. It pays to use resources equal in value to the entire monopoly profit that might be attained. As a result, the cost of monopoly equals its deadweight loss plus the entire monopoly profit.

There are some industries in which a monopoly is more efficient than a large number of perfectly competitive firms. Such industries are those in which economies of scale and scope are so large that the monopoly's output is higher and price lower than those that would arise if the industry had a large number of firms. There are also situations in which monopoly may be more innovative than competition, resulting in a faster pace of technological change. (pp. 327–333)

KEY ELEMENTS

Key Terms

Barriers to entry, 313
Deadweight loss, 330
Economies of scope, 332
Legal monopoly, 313
Monopoly, 313
Natural monopoly, 313
Patent, 313
Perfect price discrimination, 322
Price discrimination, 322
Producer surplus, 329
Rent seeking, 330
Single-price monopoly, 313

Key Figures

Figure 12.1   Demand and Marginal Revenue for a Single-price Monopoly, 315
Figure 12.2   A Single-price Monopoly's Revenue Curves, 316
Figure 12.3   The Monopoly's Output and Price, 317–318
Figure 12.7   Monopoly and Competition Compared, 328
Figure 12.8   The Allocative Inefficiency of Monopoly, 329

REVIEW QUESTIONS

1 What is a monopoly? What are some examples of monopoly in your town?

2 How does monopoly arise?

3 Distinguish between a legal monopoly and a natural monopoly. Give examples of each type.

4 Explain why marginal revenue is always less than average revenue for a single-price monopoly.

5 Why does a monopoly's profit increase as output rises initially but eventually decrease when output gets too big?

6 Explain how a monopoly chooses its output and price.

7 Does a monopoly operate on the inelastic part of its demand curve? Explain your answer.

8 Explain why a monopoly produces a smaller output than an equivalent competitive industry.

9 Is monopoly as efficient as competition?

10 What is deadweight loss?

11 Can any monopoly price discriminate? If yes, why? If no, why not?

12 Show graphically the deadweight loss under perfect price discrimination.

13 As far as allocative efficiency is concerned, is single-price monopoly better or worse than perfect price discrimination? Why?

14 Explain why people indulge in rent-seeking activities.

15 When taking account of the cost of rent seeking, what is the social cost of monopoly?

16 What are economies of scale and economies of scope? What effects, if any, do they have on allocative efficiency of monopoly?

17 Monopoly redistributes consumer surplus. Compare what the consumer loses under perfect price discrimination and single-price monopoly.

PROBLEMS

1 Minnie's Mineral Springs, a single-price monopoly, faces the following demand schedule and total cost for bottled mineral water:

Quantity (bottles)	Price (pounds per bottle)	Total cost (pounds)
0	5.0	0.5
1	4.0	1.5
2	3.0	3.5
3	2.0	6.5
4	1.0	10.5
5	0.5	15.5

a Calculate Minnie's total revenue schedule.
b Calculate Minnie's marginal revenue schedule.
c At what price is the elasticity of demand equal to one?

2 Calculate the profit-maximizing levels of
a Output.
b Price.
c Marginal cost.
d Marginal revenue.
e Profit.

3 Suppose that Minnie's can perfectly price discriminate. What is its profit-maximizing
a Output?
b Total revenue?
c Profit?

4 How much would someone be willing to pay Minnie's for a licence to operate its mineral spring?

5 Two demand schedules for round-trip flights between Manchester and Sydney are set out below. The schedule for weekday travellers is for those making round-trips on weekdays and returning within the same week. The schedule for weekend travellers is for those who stay through the weekend. (The former tend to be business travellers and the latter vacation and pleasure travellers.)

Weekday travellers		Weekend travellers	
Price (pounds per trip)	Quantity demanded (thousands of trips)	Price (pounds per trips)	Quantity demanded (thousands of trips)
1,500	0	500	0
1,000	10	250	10
500	20	125	20
250	30	0	30
125	40		
0	50		

The marginal cost of a round-trip is $125. If a single-price monopoly airline controls the Manchester–Sydney route, use a graph to find:
a What price is charged?
b How many passengers travel?
c What is the consumer surplus?

6 If the airline in Problem 5 discriminates between round-trips within a week and round-trips through the weekend:
a What is the price for the round-trip within the week?
b What is the price of the airline ticket with a weekend stay?
c What is the consumer surplus?

7 Helen runs a snack bar on a lonely stretch of the road from Edinburgh to Inverness. She has a monopoly and faces the following demand schedule for meals:

Price (pounds per meal)	Quantity demanded (meals per week)
1.00	160
1.50	140
2.00	120
2.50	100
3.00	80
3.50	60
4.00	40
4.50	20
5.00	10

Helen's marginal cost and average total cost are a constant $2 per meal.

a If Helen charges all customers the same price for a meal, what price is it?

b What is the consumer surplus of all the customers who buy a meal from Helen?

c What is the producer surplus?

d What is the deadweight loss?

CHAPTER 13

MONOPOLISTIC COMPETITION AND OLIGOPOLY

After studying this chapter you will be able to:

- ◆ Describe and distinguish among market structures that lie between perfect competition and monopoly

- ◆ Define monopolistic competition and oligopoly

- ◆ Explain how price and output are determined in a monopolistically competitive industry

- ◆ Explain why the price may be sticky in an oligopolistic industry

- ◆ Explain how price and output are determined when there is one dominant firm and several small firms in an industry

- ◆ Explain what game theory is

- ◆ Explain the prisoners' dilemma game

- ◆ Explain duopoly and oligopoly as games that firms play

- ◆ Predict the price and output behaviour of duopolists

- ◆ Make predictions about price wars and competition among small numbers of firms

HAVE YOU NOTICED THAT EVERY FIRM SELLS THE BEST PRODUCT, AND JUST the one you are looking for? From cat food to cosmetics, from air fresheners to no-brand detergent: every firm has the best deal available! One claims the lowest price, another the best brands, yet another the best value for money even if its prices are not the lowest. How do firms that are locked in fierce competition with other firms set their prices and choose the quantities to produce? How are their profits affected by the actions of other firms? ◆ ◆ Suddenly, in 1973, the prices that people paid for petrol depended on the actions of the Organization of Petroleum Exporting Countries (OPEC). In that year, OPEC raised the price of oil from $3 to $12 a barrel. And it kept on increasing prices to $35 a barrel by 1982. Then, equally suddenly and to the surprise of millions of people,

We're the Best

OPEC fell apart. By 1986 the price of oil had collapsed to half of its 1982 level. Headlines screamed, 'The Price War Is Here', and 'Frenzied Petrol Wars Push Down Pump Prices'. How did OPEC increase the price of oil in the 1970s? And why did OPEC's stranglehold on oil prices disappear?

◆ ◆ ◆ ◆ The theories of monopoly and perfect competition do not predict the kind of behaviour that we've just described. There are no best prices, best brands, or price wars in perfect competition because each firm produces an identical product and is a price taker. And there are none in monopoly because each firm has the entire market to itself. The models presented in this chapter will help us to understand the behaviour we've just described.

Varieties of Market Structure

We have studied two types of market structure – perfect competition and monopoly. In perfect competition, a large number of firms produce identical goods and there are no barriers to the entry of new firms into the industry. In this situation, each firm is a price taker and, in the long run, there is no economic profit. The opposite extreme, monopoly, is an industry in which there is one firm. That firm is protected by barriers preventing the entry of new firms. The firm sets its price to maximize profit and enjoys economic profit even in the long run.

Many real-world industries are not well described by the models of perfect competition and monopoly. They lie somewhere between these two cases. There are many situations in which firms are in fierce competition with a large number of other firms but they do have some power to set prices. There are other cases in which the industry consists of very few firms and each firm has considerable power in price determination.

Measures of Concentration

In order to tell how close to the competitive or monopolistic extreme an industry comes, economists have developed measures of industrial concentration. These measures are designed to indicate the degree of control that a small number of firms have over a market.

The most commonly used measure of concentration is called the five-firm concentration ratio. The **five-firm concentration ratio** is the percentage of the value of sales accounted for by the largest five firms in an industry. (Concentration ratios are also defined and measured for the largest three firms in an industry.) Table 13.1 sets out two hypothetical concentration ratio calculations, one for tyres and one for printing. In this example, there are 15 firms in the tyre industry. The biggest five have 80 per cent of the sales of the industry, so the five-firm concentration ratio for that industry is 80 per cent. In the printing industry, with 1,005 firms, the biggest five firms account for only 0.5 per cent of total industry sales. In this case, the five-firm concentration ratio is 0.5 per cent.

TABLE 13.1

Concentration Ratio Calculations (hypothetical)

Tyremakers		Printers	
Firm	Sales (millions of pounds)	Firm	Sales (millions of pounds)
Top, plc	200	Fran's	2.2
ABC, plc	180	Yoshi's	2.0
Big, plc	160	Ted's	1.6
PQR, plc	150	Triona's	1.2
XYZ, plc	<u>110</u>	Jill's	<u>1.0</u>
Top 5 sales	800	Top 5 sales	8.0
Other 10 firms	<u>200</u>	Other 1,000 firms	<u>1,592.0</u>
Industry sales	<u>1,000</u>	Industry sales	<u>1,600.0</u>

Five-firm concentration ratios:

Tyremakers: 800/1,000 = 80%   Printers: 8/1,600 = 0.5%

Concentration in the United Kingdom

Concentration ratios in the United Kingdom are calculated using data on individual firms' sales for a large number of industry groups. A selection of such calculations are shown in Fig. 13.1. As you can see, some industries – from printing and publishing to clothing, hats and gloves, leather goods and saw-milling and planing of wood – have low concentration ratios. These industries are highly competitive. At the other extreme are industries with a high concentration ratio such as tobacco, iron and steel, manmade fibres, and motor vehicles and their engines. These are industries in which there is competition but among a small number of firms, each of which has considerable control over its price. Industries that have medium concentration

ratios are those producing pharmaceutical products, bread, biscuits and flour confectionery and footwear.

Limitations of Measures of Concentration

The idea behind calculating concentration ratios is to provide information about the degree of competitiveness of a market: a low concentration ratio indicates a high degree of competition, and a high concentration ratio indicates an absence of competition. In the extreme case of monopoly, the concentration ratio is 100 – the largest (and only) firm makes the entire industry sales. But there are problems with concentration ratios as measures of competitiveness. Although the ratios themselves are useful, they have to be supplemented by other information. There are three key problems:

FIGURE 13.1

Some Concentration Measures in the United Kingdom

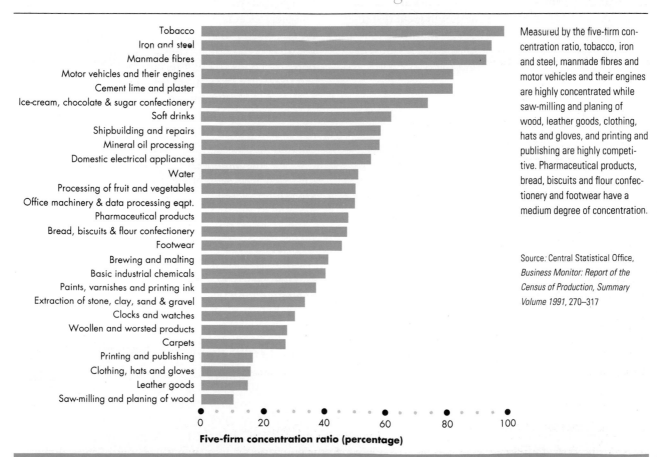

Measured by the five-firm concentration ratio, tobacco, iron and steel, manmade fibres and motor vehicles and their engines are highly concentrated while saw-milling and planing of wood, leather goods, clothing, hats and gloves, and printing and publishing are highly competitive. Pharmaceutical products, bread, biscuits and flour confectionery and footwear have a medium degree of concentration.

Source: Central Statistical Office, *Business Monitor: Report of the Census of Production, Summary Volume 1991*, 270–317

1. Geographical Scope of the Market Concentration ratio data are based on a national view of the market. Many goods are indeed sold on a national market but some are sold on a regional market and some on a global one. The beer industry is a good example of one in which the local market is more important than the national market. Thus although the concentration ratio for beer is not high, there is nevertheless a high degree of concentration in the beer industry in most regions. The car industry is an example of one for which there is a global market. Thus although the biggest five UK car producers account for almost 90 per cent of all cars sold by UK producers, they account for a much smaller percentage of the total UK car market (including imports) and an even smaller percentage of the European market for cars.

2. Barriers to Entry and Turnover Measures of concentration do not tell us how severe are the barriers to entry in an industry. Some industries, for example, are highly concentrated but have virtually free entry and experience an enormous amount of turnover of firms. A good example is the market in local restaurants. Many small towns have few restaurants. But there are no restrictions on entering the restaurant industry and indeed firms do enter and exit with great regularity.

3. Market and Industry The classifications used to calculate concentration ratios allocate every firm in the UK economy to a particular industry. But markets for particular goods do not always correspond exactly to particular industries. For example, Pearson International produces textbooks, crystal and news media, among many other goods. Thus this one firm operates in three quite separate markets. Furthermore, the market or markets in which a firm operates depend on the profit opportunities that exist. There are many examples of firms that have built their initial organization on one good but then diversified into a wide variety of others. For example, Virgin began by producing records. They have since developed into an airline (Virgin Atlantic), radio station (Virgin 1215) and stores (Virgin Megastores). They no longer produce records.

Nevertheless, concentration ratios combined with information about the geographical scope of the market, barriers to entry and the extent to which large, multi-product firms straddle a variety of markets do provide the basis for classifying industries. The less

concentrated an industry and the lower the barriers to entry, the more closely it approximates the perfect competition case. The more concentrated an industry and the higher the barriers to entry, the more it approximates the monopoly case.

But there is a great deal of space between perfect competition and monopoly. That space is occupied by two other market types. The first of these is monopolistic competition. **Monopolistic competition** is a market type in which a large number of firms compete with each other by making similar but slightly different goods. Making a good slightly different from the good of a competing firm is called **product differentiation**. Because of product differentiation, a monopolistically competitive firm has an element of monopoly power. The firm is the sole producer of the particular version of the good in question. For example, in the breakfast cereal market, only Cereal Partners makes Shredded Wheat. Only the Kellogg Company makes Frosties. And only Weetabix Ltd makes Weetabix. Each of these firms has a monopoly on a particular type of cereal. Differentiated goods are not necessarily different in an objective sense. For example, Aspro and other brands of aspirin are different ways of packaging an identical commodity. What matters is that consumers perceive goods to be differentiated.

Oligopoly is a market type in which a small number of producers compete with each other. There are hundreds of examples of oligopolistic industries. Oil and petrol production, the manufacture of electrical equipment and international air transport are but a few. In some oligopolistic industries, each firm produces an almost identical good while in others goods are differentiated. For example, oil and petrol are essentially the same whether they are made by Shell or Esso. But a Ford Fiesta is a differentiated commodity from a Rover Metro and a Vauxhall Astra.

Table 13.2 summarizes the characteristics of the two market types that we're going to study in this chapter, monopolistic competition and oligopoly, along with those of perfect competition and monopoly.

Market Types in the United Kingdom

Three-quarters of the value of goods and services bought and sold in the United Kingdom are traded in markets that are essentially competitive – markets that have almost perfect competition or monopolistic competition. Monopoly is rare – accounting for less than 3 per cent of the value of

TABLE 13.2

Market Structure

Characteristics	Perfect competition	Monopolistic competition	Oligopoly	Monopoly
Number of firms in industry	**Many**	**Many**	**Few**	**One**
Product	**Identical**	**Differentiated**	**Either identical or differentiated**	**No close substitutes**
Barriers to entry	**None**	**Some**	**Scale and scope economies**	**Scale and scope economies or legal barriers**
Firm's control over price	**None**	**Some**	**Considerable**	**Considerable or regulated**
Concentration ratio (0 to 100)	**0**	**Low**	**High**	**100**
Examples	**Wheat, corn**	**Food, clothing**	**Cars, breakfast cereals**	**Telephone service, electric and gas utilities**

goods and services in the United Kingdom – and is found mainly in public utilities and public transport. A similarly small number of markets – accounting for less than 3 per cent of the value of sales – are dominated by one or two firms, but are not monopolies. These, too, are in the public utilities and transport sectors. Oligopoly, found mainly in manufacturing, accounts for about 18 per cent of sales.

Monopolistic Competition

Three conditions define a monopolistically competitive industry:

◆ Each firm faces a downward-sloping demand curve.
◆ There is free entry.
◆ There are a large number of firms in the industry.

Because each firm faces a downward-sloping demand curve, it has to choose its price as well as its output. Also the firm's marginal revenue curve is different from its demand curve. These features of monopolistic competition are also present in monopoly. The important difference between monopoly and monopolistic competition lies in free entry.

In monopoly, there is no entry. In monopolistic competition, there is free entry. As a consequence, though monopolistic competition enables economic profits to occur in the short run, they cannot persist forever. When profits are available, new firms will enter the industry. Such entry will result in lower prices and lower profits. When losses are being incurred, firms will leave the industry. Such exit will increase prices and increase profits. In long-run equilibrium, firms will neither enter nor leave the industry, and firms will be making a zero economic profit.

Because the industry consists of a large number of firms, no one firm can effectively influence what other firms will do. That is, if one firm changes its price, that firm is such a small part of the total industry that it will have no effect on the actions of the other firms in the industry.

Price and Output in Monopolistic Competition

To see how price and output are determined by a firm in a monopolistically competitive industry, let's look at Fig. 13.2. Part (a) deals with the short run and part (b) the long run. To keep things simple, we will suppose that the industry consists of a large number of firms with a differentiated product and that all firms in the industry have identical demand and cost curves. Let's concentrate initially on the short run. The demand curve D is the demand curve for the firm's own variety of the good. For example, it is the demand for Dispirin rather than for painkillers in general; or for McDonald's hamburgers

rather than for hamburgers in general. The curve MR is the marginal revenue curve associated with the demand curve. The firm's average total cost (ATC) and marginal cost (MC) are also shown in the figure. A firm maximizes profit in the short run by producing output Q_S, where marginal revenue equals marginal cost, and charging the price P_S. The firm's average total cost is C_S and the firm makes a short-run profit, as measured by the blue rectangle.

So far, the monopolistically competitive firm looks just like a monopoly. It produces the quantity at which marginal revenue equals marginal cost and then charges the highest possible price for that quantity. The key difference between monopoly and monopolistic competition lies in what happens next.

There is no restriction on entry in monopolistic competition so, with economic profit being earned, new firms enter the industry and take some of the

---

FIGURE 13.2

Monopolistic Competition

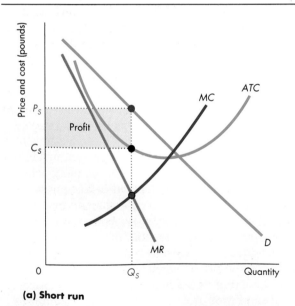

(a) Short run

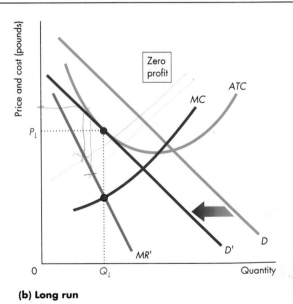

(b) Long run

Under monopolistic competition, a firm faces a downward-sloping demand curve and so has to choose its price and the quantity to produce. Profit is maximized where marginal revenue equals marginal cost. Part (a) of the figure shows a short-run profit-maximizing situation. The quantity produced is Q_S, the price is P_S, average total cost is C_S, and profit is represented by the blue rectangle.

Profit encourages new entrants and so the firm's demand curve begins to shift to the left, as shown in part (b). As the demand curve shifts to the left, so too does the firm's marginal revenue curve. When the demand curve has shifted all the way from D to D', the marginal revenue curve is MR' and the firm is in a long-run equilibrium. The output that maximizes profit is Q_L and the price is P_L. Profit, in long-run equilibrium, is zero. There is no further entry into the industry.

market away from the existing firms. As they do so, the firm's demand curve starts to shift to the left. The marginal revenue curve also starts to shift to the left. At each point in time, the firm will seek to maximize its short-run profit. That is, it chooses its output so that marginal revenue equals marginal cost, and it charges the highest possible price for the good. But as the demand curve shifts to the left, the profit-maximizing quantity and price fall. In long-run equilibrium, shown in Fig. 13.2(b), the firm produces Q_L and sells it at a price of P_L. In this situation, the firm is making a zero economic profit. Average total cost exactly equals price. There is no incentive for firms to enter or exit.

Excess Capacity

Recall that a firm's capacity output is the output produced when average total cost is at its minimum point – the output at the bottom of the U-shaped *ATC* curve. In monopolistic competition, in the long run, firms always have excess capacity. That is, they produce a lower output than that which minimizes average total cost. As a consequence, the consumer pays more than the minimum average total cost. This result arises from the fact that the firm faces a downward-sloping demand curve. Only if the demand curve facing the firm is perfectly elastic is the long-run equilibrium at the point of minimum average total cost. The demand curve slopes down because of product differentiation. If each firm produces an identical good, each firm's output will be a perfect substitute for the outputs of all other firms and so the demand curve will be perfectly elastic. Thus product differentiation produces excess capacity.

Efficiency of Monopolistic Competition

When we studied a perfectly competitive industry, we discovered that in some circumstances such an industry achieves allocative efficiency. A key feature of allocative efficiency is that price equals marginal cost. Recall that price measures the value placed on the last unit bought by the consumer and marginal cost measures the opportunity cost of producing the last unit. We also discovered that monopoly is allocatively inefficient because it restricts output below the level at which price equals marginal cost. As we have just discovered, monopolistic competition shares this feature with monopoly. Even though there is zero profit in long-run equilibrium, the

monopolistically competitive industry produces an output at which price equals average total cost and exceeds marginal cost.

Does this feature of monopolistic competition mean that this market structure, like monopoly, is allocatively inefficient? It does not. It is true that if the firms in a monopolistically competitive industry all produce identical goods – goods that are perfect substitutes – then each firm will face a perfectly elastic demand curve. In the long run, such firms will produce at the point of minimum average total cost and charge a price equal to marginal cost. But achieving that outcome will itself have a cost. The cost is the absence of product differentiation. Variety is valued by consumers, but variety is only achievable if firms make differentiated goods. The loss in allocative efficiency that occurs in monopolistic competition has to be weighed against the gain of greater good variety.

Product Innovation

Another source of gain from monopolistically competitive industries is product innovation. Monopolistically competitive firms are constantly seeking out new goods that will provide them with a competitive edge, even if only temporarily. A firm that manages to introduce a new and differentiated variety will temporarily face a steeper demand curve than before and will be able to increase its price temporarily. Entry of new firms will, eventually, compete away the profit arising from this initial advantage.

Advertising

Monopolistically competitive firms seek to differentiate their goods partly by designing and introducing goods that actually are different from those of the other firms in the industry. But they also attempt to differentiate the consumer's perception of the good. Advertising is the principal means whereby firms seek to achieve this end. But advertising increases the monopolistically competitive firm's costs above those of a competitive firm or a monopoly that does not advertise.

To the extent that advertising provides consumers with information about the precise nature of the differentiation of goods, it serves a valuable purpose to the consumer, enabling a better choice of good to be made. But the opportunity cost of the additional information through advertising has to be offset against the gain to the consumer from making a better choice.

The bottom line on the question of allocative efficiency of monopolistic competition is ambiguous. In some cases, the gains from extra product variety unquestionably offset the costs in the form of advertising and excess capacity. The tremendous varieties of books and magazines, of clothing, food and drink are examples of such gains. It is less easy to see the gains from being able to buy brand-name drugs that have an identical chemical composition to a generic alternative. But some people do willingly pay more for the brand-name alternative.

REVIEW

A firm in a monopolistically competitive industry faces a downward-sloping demand curve and so has to choose its price as well as the quantity to produce. Such firms also compete on product variety and by advertising. A lack of barriers to entry into such an industry ensures that economic profit is competed away. In long-run equilibrium, firms make zero economic profit, charging a price equal to average total cost. But price exceeds marginal cost and the quantity produced is below that which minimizes average total cost. The cost of monopolistic competition is excess capacity and high advertising expenditure; the gain is a wide product variety. ◆

Oligopoly

We have defined oligopoly as a market in which a small number of producers compete with each other. In such a market, each producer is interdependent. The sales of any one producer depend upon that producer's price and the prices charged by the other producers. To see this interplay between prices and sales, suppose you run one of the three petrol stations in a small town. If you lower your price and your two competitors don't lower theirs, your sales increase, but the

sales of the other two firms decrease. In such a situation, the other firms will, most likely, lower their prices too. If they do cut their prices your sales and profits will take a tumble. So, before deciding to cut your price, you try to predict how the other firms will react and you attempt to calculate the effects of those reactions on your own profit.

A variety of models have been developed to explain the determination of price and quantity in oligopoly markets and no one theory has been found that can explain all the different types of behaviour that we observe in such markets. The models fall into two broad groups: traditional models and game theory models. We'll look at examples of both types, starting with the traditional models.

Traditional Models of Oligopoly

Economists have studied oligopoly and duopoly since the time of Cournot in the 1830s. The earliest models were based on assumptions about the beliefs of each firm concerning the reactions of another firm (or firms) to its own actions. A particularly influential model was proposed in the 1930s by Paul M. Sweezy (editor of the *Monthly Review* for the past 40 years). It is known as the kinked demand curve model.

The Kinked Demand Curve Model

Sweezy's concern was to explain why prices did not fall more quickly during the years of the Great Depression. He proposed a theory based on the following propositions about the beliefs held by firms:

◆ If I increase my price, I will be on my own – others will not follow me.
◆ If I decrease my price, so will everyone else.

If these beliefs are correct, a firm faces a demand curve for its product that has a kink occurring at the current price, P, as shown in Fig. 13.3. At prices above P, the demand curve is relatively elastic. It reflects the belief that if the firm increases its price, it will be out of line with all other firms and so will experience a large fall in the quantity demanded. At prices below P, the demand curve is less elastic. It reflects the belief that if the firm decreases its price, all other firms will match the price cut and so it will experience a small increase in the quantity demanded. This increase in the quantity demanded will not be as large as the decrease in the quantity demanded resulting from a price rise.

The kink in demand curve D creates a break in the marginal revenue curve (MR). To maximize profit, the firm produces the quantity that makes marginal cost and marginal revenue equal. But that output, Q, is where the marginal cost curve passes through the discontinuity in the marginal revenue curve – the gap ab. If marginal cost fluctuates between a and b, an example of which is shown in the figure with the marginal cost curves, MC_0 and MC_1, the firm will change neither its price nor its quantity of output. Only if marginal cost fluctuates outside the range ab will the firm change its price and quantity produced. The price is sticky.

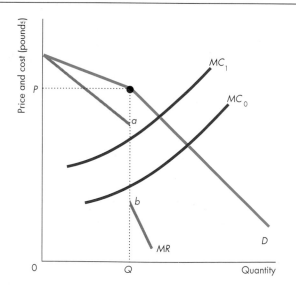

FIGURE 13.3

The Kinked Demand Curve Model

The price in an oligopoly market is P. Each firm believes it faces the demand curve D. At prices above P, demand is highly elastic because the firm believes that its price increases will not be matched by other firms. At prices below P, demand is less elastic because the firm believes its price cuts will be matched. Because the demand curve is kinked, the marginal revenue curve, MR, has a break ab. Profit is maximized by producing Q. The marginal cost curve passes through the break in the marginal revenue curve. Marginal cost changes inside the range ab leave the price and quantity unchanged.

Thus the kinked demand curve model predicts that price and quantity will be insensitive to small cost changes, but will respond if cost changes are large enough. But there are two problems with the kinked demand curve model:

◆ It does not tell us how the price, P, is determined.
◆ It does not tell us what happens if firms discover that their belief about the demand curve is incorrect.

Suppose, for example, that marginal cost increases by enough to cause the firm to increase its price and that all firms experience the same increase in marginal cost so they all increase their prices together. Each firm bases its action on the belief that other firms will not match its price increase, but that belief is incorrect. The firm's beliefs are inconsistent with reality, and the demand and marginal revenue curves which summarize those beliefs are not the correct ones for the purpose of calculating the new profit-maximizing price and output. A firm that bases its actions on beliefs that are wrong does not maximize profit and might well end up incurring a loss leading to its eventual exit from the industry.

The kinked demand curve model is an attempt to understand price and output determination in an oligopoly in which the firms are of similar size. Another traditional model deals with the case in which firms differ in size and one firm dominates the industry.

Dominant Firm Oligopoly

Suppose there are 11 firms operating petrol stations in a city. Big-G is huge and controls 50 per cent of all the city's petrol sales. The others are small, accounting for only 5 per cent of the city's petrol sales each. The market for petrol in this city is a type of oligopoly, but one with a dominant firm.

To see how the price and quantity of petrol sales are determined, look at Fig. 13.4. Here, in part (a), the demand curve D tells us how the total quantity of petrol demanded in the city is influenced by its price. The supply curve S_{10} is the supply curves of the 10 small price-taking suppliers added together.

Part (b) shows the situation facing Big-G, the dominant firm. Big-G's marginal cost curve is MC. The demand curve for petrol facing Big-G is XD. This curve is found by working out the amount of excess demand arising from the rest of the market. It graphs the difference between the quantity demanded and the quantity supplied in the rest of

FIGURE 13.4

A Dominant Firm Oligopoly

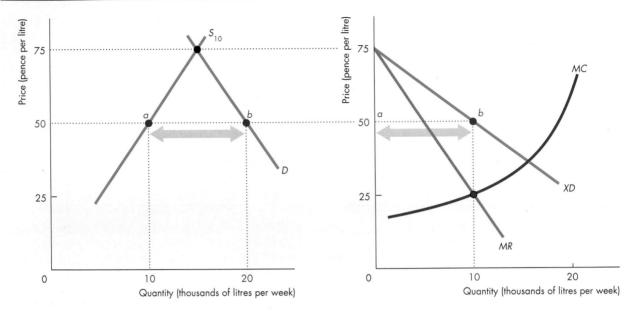

(a) Ten small firms and market demand

(b) Big-G's price and output decision

The demand curve for petrol in a city is *D* in part (a). There are 10 small firms who (taking all 10 together) have a supply curve of S_{10} in part (a). In addition there is one large firm, Big-G, shown in part (b). Big-G faces the demand curve, *XD*, determined as market demand *D* minus the supply of the other firms S_{10} –

the excess demand not satisfied by the small firms. Big-G's marginal revenue is *MR* and marginal cost is *MC*. Big-G sets the price to maximize profit by equating marginal cost, *MC*, and marginal revenue, *MR*. The price is 50 pence a litre. Big-G sells 10,000 litres and the other 10 firms sell 1,000 litres each.

the market at each price. Thus, for example, at a price of 50 pence a litre, there is an excess demand in the rest of the market measured by the distance *ab* in part (a). That same distance *ab* at the price 50 pence a litre, in part (b), provides us with one point, point *b*, on Big-G's demand curve, *XD*.

If Big-G sold petrol in a perfectly competitive city petrol market, it would be willing to supply it at the prices indicated by its marginal cost curve. The city market would operate at the point of intersection of Big-G's marginal cost curve and its demand curve. But Big-G can do better for itself than that. Because it controls 50 per cent of the city's petrol market it can restrict its sales, decreasing the amount of petrol available and increasing its price.

To maximize its profit, Big-G operates like a monopoly. It calculates the extra revenue obtained from selling one more litre of petrol – its marginal

revenue curve. It then sells the quantity that makes its marginal revenue equal to its marginal cost. Thus it sells 10,000 litres of petrol for 50 pence a litre. This price and quantity of sales gives Big-G the biggest possible profit. The quantity of petrol demanded in the entire city at 50 pence a litre is 20,000 litres, as shown in part (a). The additional 10,000 litres are sold by 10 small firms which sell 1,000 litres each.

R E V I E W

I n oligopoly, the profit of any one producer depends on the prices charged by that producer and all the other producers. So any theory of oligopoly must contain an account of how firms react to each other's price changes. One traditional model, the kinked demand curve model, assumes that if a firm increases its price no other firm will follow, but if a firm decreases its price, so will all the other firms. Each firm faces a kinked demand curve for its product, and the kink occurs at the current price and quantity. The kink creates a break in the marginal revenue curve and a range over which marginal cost can vary without causing a change in the profit-maximizing price. Hence prices are sticky. Another traditional model, the dominant firm model, assumes that the dominant firm acts like a monopoly and sets its profit-maximizing price. The other firms take this price as given and act like competitive firms. ◆

The dominant firm model of oligopoly works for some markets in which there really is a dominant producer. But even in such markets, it does not explain why sometimes the dominant firm tries to drive the smaller firms out of business rather than just putting up with their competition. Also it is of no help in predicting prices and quantities in markets in which firms are of similar size. The kinked demand curve model is an attempt to deal with this alternative case. But, as we've seen, that model has some weaknesses.

The weaknesses of traditional theories and a widespread dissatisfaction with them is one of the main forces leading to the development of new oligopoly models based on game theory.

The situation faced by firms in an oligopolistic industry is not unlike that faced by military planners. For example, in deciding whether to launch an attack on Iraq in the summer of 1990, Allied military planners had to take into account the effects of their actions on the behaviour of Iraq. Would Iraq counter by firing chemical-laden SCUD missiles at Israel? Similarly, in making its plans, Iraq had to take into account the reactions of the Allies, as well as Israel. Neither side can assume that its rival's behaviour will be independent of its own actions.

Whether we're studying price wars or real wars, we need a method of analysing choices that takes into account the interactions between agents. Such a method has been developed and is called game theory.

Oligopoly and Game Theory

Acting in a way that takes into account the expected behaviour of others and the mutual recognition of interdependence is called **strategic behaviour**. **Game theory** is a method of analysing strategic behaviour. Game theory was invented by John von Neumann in 1937 and extended by von Neumann and Oskar Morgenstern in 1944 and is the topic of a massive amount of current research in economics.

Game theory seeks to understand oligopoly as well as political and social rivalries by using a method of analysis specifically designed to understand games of all types, including the familiar games of everyday life. We will begin our study of game theory, and its application to the behaviour of firms, by considering those familiar games.

Familiar Games: What They Have in Common

What is a game? At first, the question seems silly. After all, there are many different games. There are ball games and parlour games, games of chance and games of skill. What do games of such diversity and variety have in common? In answering this question, we will focus on those features of games that are relevant and important for game theory and for analysing oligopoly as a game. All games have three things in common:

◆ Rules
◆ Strategies
◆ Payoffs

Let's see how these common features of ordinary games apply to oligopoly.

Rules of the Oligopoly Game

The rules of the oligopoly game have not been written down by the 'Oligopoly League'. They arise from the economic, social and political environment in which the oligopolists operate.

One rule of the oligopoly game is the number of players – the number of firms in the market. Another rule is the method of calculating the score. This rule states that the score of each player is the player's economic profit or loss. The goal of each player of the oligopoly game is to make the largest possible profit. The remaining rules of the oligopoly game are determined by the framework of laws within which the oligopolists are operating. Oligopolists' actions are restricted only by the legal code.

Strategies in the Oligopoly Game

In game theory as in ordinary games, **strategies** are all the possible actions of each player. A comprehensive list of strategies in the oligopoly game would be very long, but it would include, for each player, such actions as:

◆ Raise price, lower price, hold price constant
◆ Raise output, lower output, hold output constant
◆ Increase advertising, cut advertising, hold advertising constant
◆ Enhance features of good, simplify good, leave good unchanged

Payoffs in the Oligopoly Game

In game theory, the score of each player is called the **payoff**. In the oligopoly game, the payoffs are the profits and losses of the players. These payoffs are determined by the oligopolists' strategies and by the constraints that they face. Constraints come from customers who determine the demand curve for the good of the oligopoly industry, from the technology available, and from the prices of the resources used by the oligopolists.

To understand how an oligopoly game works, it is revealing to study a special case of oligopoly called duopoly. **Duopoly** is a market structure in which there are two producers of a commodity competing with each other. There are few cases of duopoly on a national and international scale, but many cases of local duopolies. For example, in some communities, there are two suppliers of milk, two local newspapers, two taxi companies, or two car rental firms. But the main reason for studying duopoly is not its 'realism' but the fact that it captures all the essential features of oligopoly and yet is more manageable to analyse and understand. Furthermore, there is a well-known game called 'the prisoners' dilemma' that captures some of the essential features of duopoly. It provides a good illustration of how game theory works and how it leads to predictions about the behaviour of the players. Let's now turn our attention to studying a duopoly game, beginning with the prisoners' dilemma.

The Prisoners' Dilemma

Alf and Bob have been caught red-handed stealing a car and have been remanded in custody. Facing watertight cases, they will receive a sentence of 2 years each for their crime. During his interviews with the two prisoners, the police officer begins to suspect that he has stumbled on the two people who were responsible for a multimillion-pound bank robbery some months earlier. The police officer also knows, however, that this is just a suspicion. He has no evidence on which he can convict them of the greater crime unless he can get each of them to confess. He comes up with the following idea.

He places the prisoners in separate rooms so that they cannot communicate with each other. Each prisoner is told that he is suspected of having carried out the bank robbery and that if he and his accomplice both confess to that crime, each will receive sentences of 3 years. Each is also told that if he alone confesses and his accomplice does not, he will receive an even shorter sentence of 1 year while his accomplice will receive a 10 year sentence. The prisoners know that if neither of them confesses, then they will only be tried for and convicted of the lesser offence of car theft, which carries a 2 year prison term. How do the prisoners respond to the police officer?

First, notice that the prisoners' dilemma is a game with two players. Each player has two strategies: to confess to the multimillion-pound bank robbery or to deny the charge. Because there are two players, each with two strategies, there are four possible outcomes:

◆ Neither player confesses.
◆ Both players confess.
◆ Alf confesses but Bob does not.
◆ Bob confesses but Alf does not.

Each prisoner can work out exactly what will happen to him – his payoff – in each of these four situations. We can tabulate the four possible payoffs for each of the prisoners in what is called a payoff matrix for the game.

The Payoff Matrix A **payoff matrix** is a table that shows the payoffs for every possible action by each player for every possible action by each other player.

Table 13.3 shows a payoff matrix for Alf and Bob. The squares show the payoffs for each prisoner – the red triangle in each square shows Alf's and the

TABLE 13.3

Prisoners' Dilemma Payoff Matrix

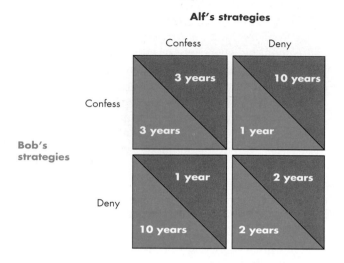

Each square shows the payoffs for the two players, Alf and Bob, for each possible pair of actions. In each square, Alf's payoff is shown in the red triangle and Bob's in the blue triangle. For example, if both confess, the payoffs are in the top left square. Alf reasons as follows: if Bob confesses, it pays me to confess because then I get 3 years rather than 10. If Bob denies, it pays me to confess because then I get 1 year rather than 2. Regardless of what Bob does, it pays me to confess. Alf's dominant strategy is to confess. Bob reasons similarly: if Alf confesses, it pays me to confess and get 3 years rather than 10. If Alf denies, it pays me to confess and get 1 year rather than 2. Bob's dominant strategy is to confess. Since each player's dominant strategy is to confess, the equilibrium of the game is for both players to confess and to each get 3 years.

blue triangle Bob's. If both prisoners confess (top left), they each get a prison term of 3 years. If Bob confesses but Alf denies (top right), Alf gets a 10 year sentence and Bob gets a 1 year sentence. If Alf confesses and Bob denies (bottom left), Alf gets a 1 year sentence and Bob gets a 10 year sentence. Finally, if both of them deny (bottom right), neither can be convicted of the bank robbery charge but both are sentenced for the car theft – a 2 year sentence.

The Dilemma The dilemma is seen by considering the consequences of confessing and not confessing. Each prisoner knows that if he and his accomplice remain silent about the bank robbery, they will be sentenced to only 2 years for stealing the car.

Neither prisoner, however, has any way of knowing that his accomplice will remain silent and refuse to confess. Each knows that if the other confesses and he denies, the other will receive only a 1 year sentence while the one denying will receive a 10 year sentence. Each poses the following questions. Should I deny and rely on my accomplice to deny so that we may both get only 2 years? Or should I confess in the hope of getting just 1 year (providing my accomplice denies), but knowing that if my accomplice does confess we will both get 3 years in prison? Resolving the dilemma involves finding the equilibrium for the game.

Equilibrium The equilibrium of a game is called a Nash equilibrium, so named because it was first proposed by John Nash. A **Nash equilibrium** occurs when player *A* takes the best possible action given the action of player *B*, and player *B* takes the best possible action given the action of player *A*. In the case of the prisoners' dilemma, the equilibrium occurs when Alf makes his best choice given Bob's choice, and when Bob makes his best choice given Alf's choice.

The prisoners' dilemma is a game that has a special kind of Nash equilibrium called a dominant strategy equilibrium. A **dominant strategy** is a strategy that is the same regardless of the action taken by the other player. In other words, there is a unique best action regardless of what the other player does. A **dominant strategy equilibrium** occurs when there is a dominant strategy for each player. In the prisoners' dilemma, Alf's best strategy is always to confess regardless of Bob's strategy – Alf has a dominant strategy; and Bob's best strategy is always to confess regardless of Alf's strategy – Bob has a dominant strategy. Thus the equilibrium of the prisoners' dilemma is a dominant strategy equilibrium – each player confesses.

If each prisoner plays the prisoners' dilemma game in his own individual best interest, the outcome of the game will be that each confesses. To see why each player confesses, let's consider again their strategies and the payoffs from the alternative courses of action.

Strategies and Payoffs Look at the situation from Alf's point of view. Alf realizes that his outcome depends on the action Bob takes. If Bob confesses, it pays Alf to confess also, for in that case, he will be sentenced to 3 years rather than 10 years. But if Bob does not confess, it still pays Alf to confess for in that case he will receive 1 year rather than 2 years. Alf reasons that regardless of Bob's action, his own best action is to confess.

The dilemma from Bob's point of view is identical to Alf's. Bob knows that if Alf confesses, he will receive 10 years if he does not confess or 3 years if he does. Therefore if Alf confesses, it pays Bob to confess. Similarly, if Alf does not confess, Bob will receive 2 years for not confessing and 1 year if he confesses. Again, it pays Bob to confess. Bob's best action, regardless of Alf's action, is to confess.

Each prisoner sees that regardless of what the other prisoner does, his own best action is to confess. Since each player's best action is to confess, each will confess, each will get a 3 year prison term, and the district attorney has solved the bank robbery. This is the equilibrium of the game.

A Bad Outcome For the prisoners, the equilibrium of the game, with each confessing, is not the best outcome. If neither of them confesses, each will get only 2 years for the lesser crime. Isn't there some way in which this better outcome can be achieved? It seems that there is not, because the players cannot communicate with each other. Each player can put himself in the other player's place, and so each player can figure out that there is a dominant strategy for each of them. The prisoners are indeed in a dilemma. Each knows that he can serve 2 years only if he can trust the other not to confess. Each prisoner also knows, however, that it is not in the best interest of the other to not confess. Thus each prisoner knows that he has to confess, thereby delivering a bad outcome for both.

Let's now see how we can use the ideas we've just developed to understand price fixing, price wars and the behaviour of duopolists.

A Duopoly Game

To study a duopoly game, we're going to build a model of a duopoly industry[1]. Suppose that only two firms, Trick and Gear, make a particular kind of electric switchgear. Our goal is to make predictions about the prices charged and the outputs produced by each of the two firms. We are going to pursue that goal by constructing a duopoly game that the two

firms will play. To set out the game, we need to specify the strategies of the players and the payoff matrix. Another game based on real-world events, that of price wars between supermarkets, is considered in Reading Between the Lines on pp. 362–363.

We will suppose that the two firms enter into a collusive agreement. A **collusive agreement** is an agreement between two (or more) producers to restrict output in order to raise prices and profits. Such an agreement is illegal and is undertaken in secret. A group of firms that has entered into a collusive agreement to restrict output and increase prices and profits is called a **cartel**. The strategies that firms in a cartel can pursue are:

◆ To comply
◆ To cheat

Complying simply means sticking to the agreement. Cheating means breaking the agreement in a manner designed to benefit the cheating firm and harm the other firm.

Since each firm has two strategies, there are four possible combinations of actions for the two firms:

◆ Both firms comply.
◆ Both firms cheat.
◆ Trick complies and Gear cheats.
◆ Gear complies and Trick cheats.

We need to work out the payoffs to each firm from each of these four possible sets of actions. To do that we need to explore the costs and demand conditions in the industry.

Cost and Demand Conditions

The cost of producing switchgear is the same for both Trick and Gear. The average total cost curve (*ATC*) and the marginal cost curve (*MC*) for each firm are shown in Fig. 13.5(a). The market demand curve for switchgears (*D*) is shown in Fig. 13.5(b). Each firm produces an identical switchgear product, so one firm's switchgear is a perfect substitute for the other's. The market price of each firm's product, therefore, is identical. The quantity demanded depends on that price – the higher the price, the lower is the quantity demanded.

---

[1] The model is inspired by a real-world case known as 'the incredible electrical conspiracy', which we examine below. But don't lose sight of the fact that what follows is a *model*. It is not a description of a real historical episode.

FIGURE 13.5

Costs and Demand

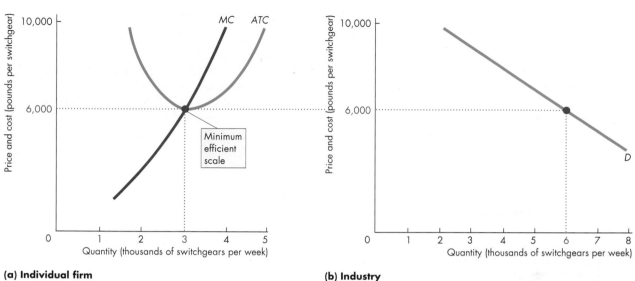

(a) Individual firm

(b) Industry

Part (a) shows the costs facing Trick and Gear, two duopolists which make switchgear. Each firm faces identical costs. The average total cost curve for each firm is *ATC* and the marginal cost curve is *MC*. For each firm the minimum efficient scale of product is 3,000 units per week and the average total

cost of producing that output is £6,000 a unit. Part (b) shows the industry demand curve. At a price of £6,000, the quantity demanded is 6,000 units per week. There is room for only two firms in this industry.

Notice that in this industry there is room for only two firms. For each firm the *minimum efficient scale* of production is 3,000 switchgear units a week. When the price equals the average total cost of production at the minimum efficient scale, total industry demand is 6,000 switchgear units a week. Thus there is no room for three firms in this industry. If there were only one firm in the industry, it would make an enormous profit and invite competition. If there were three firms, at least one of them would make a loss. Thus the number of firms that an industry can sustain depends on the relationship between cost and the industry's demand conditions.

In the model industry that we're studying here, the particular cost and demand conditions assumed are designed to generate an industry in which two firms can survive in the long run. In real-world oligopoly and duopoly, barriers to entry may arise from economies of scale of the type featured in our model

industry but there are other possible barriers as well (as discussed in Chapter 12).

Colluding to Maximize Profits

Let's begin by working out the payoffs to the two firms if they collude to make the maximum industry profit – the profit that would be made by a single monopoly. The calculations that the two firms will perform are exactly the same calculations that a monopoly performs. (You have already studied such calculations in the previous chapter.) The only additional thing that the duopolists have to do is to agree on how much of the total output each of them will produce.

The price and quantity that maximizes industry profit for the duopolists is shown in Fig. 13.6. Part (a) shows the situation for each firm and part (b) for the industry as a whole. The curve labelled *MR* is the industry marginal revenue curve. The curve labelled MC_I is the industry marginal cost curve if each firm produces the same level of output. That curve is constructed by adding together the outputs of the two firms at each level of marginal cost. That is, at each level of marginal cost, industry output is twice as much as the output of each individual firm. Thus the curve MC_I in part (b) is twice as far to the right as the curve *MC* in part (a).

To maximize industry profit, the duopolists agree to restrict output to the rate that makes the industry marginal cost and marginal revenue equal. That output rate, as shown in part (b), is 4,000 switchgear units a week. The highest price for which the 4,000 units can be sold is £9,000 each. Let's suppose that

Trick and Gear agree to split the market equally so that each firm produces 2,000 switchgear units a week. The average total cost (*ATC*) of producing 2,000 units a week is £8,000, so the profit per unit is £1,000 and the total profit is £2 million (2,000 units × £1,000 per unit). The profit of each firm is represented by the blue rectangle in Fig. 13.6(a).

We have just described one possible outcome for the duopoly game: the two firms collude to produce the monopoly profit-maximizing output and divide that output equally between themselves. From the industry point of view, this solution is identical to a monopoly. A duopoly that operates in this way is indistinguishable from a monopoly. The profit that is made by a monopoly is the maximum profit that can be made by colluding duopolists.

FIGURE 13.6

Colluding to Make Monopoly Profits

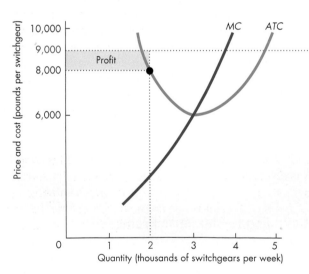

(a) Individual firm

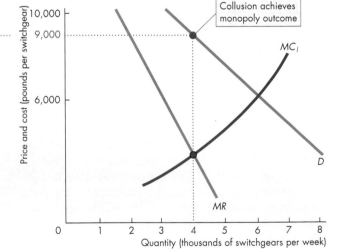

(b) Industry

If Trick and Gear come to a collusive agreement, they can act as a single monopolist and maximize profit. Part (a) shows the consequences of reaching such an agreement for each firm and part (b) shows the situation in the industry as a whole.

To maximize profit, the firms first calculate the industry marginal cost curve (*MC*$_I$) shown in part (b) – the horizontal sum of the two firms' marginal cost curves (*MC*) in part (a). Next they calculate the industry marginal revenue, *MR* in part (b). They then choose the output rate that makes marginal

revenue equal to marginal cost (4,000 units per week). They agree to sell that output for a price of £9,000, the price at which 4,000 switchgear units are demanded.

The costs and profit of each firm are seen in part (a). Each firm produces half the total output – 2,000 units per week. Average total cost is £8,000 per unit, so each firm makes a profit of £2 million (blue rectangle) – 2,000 units multiplied by £1,000 profit per unit.

Cheating on a Collusive Agreement

Under a collusive agreement, the colluding firms restrict output to make their joint marginal revenue equal to their joint marginal cost. They set the highest price for which the quantity produced can be sold – a price higher than marginal cost. In such a situation, each firm recognizes that if it cheats on the agreement and raises its output, even though the price will fall below that agreed to, more will be added to revenue than to cost, so its profit will increase. Since each firm recognizes this fact, there is a temptation for each firm to cheat. There are two possible cheating situations:

◆ One firm cheats.
◆ Both firms cheat.

One Firm Cheats What is the effect of one firm cheating on a collusive agreement? How much extra profit does the cheating firm make? What happens to the profit of the firm that sticks to the agreement in the face of cheating by the other firm? Let's work out the answers to these questions.

There are many different ways for a firm to cheat. We will work out just one possibility. Suppose that Trick convinces Gear that there has been a fall in industry demand and that it cannot sell its share of the output at the agreed price. It tells Gear that it plans to cut its price in order to sell the agreed 2,000 switchgear units each week. Since the two firms produce a virtually identical product, Gear has no alternative but to match the price cut of Trick.

In fact, there has been no fall in demand and the lower price has been calculated by Trick to be exactly the price needed to sell the additional output that it plans to produce. Gear, though lowering its price in line with that of Trick, restricts its output to the previously agreed level.

Figure 13.7 illustrates the consequences of Trick cheating in this way: part (a) shows what happens to Gear (the complier); part (b) shows what happens to Trick (the cheat); and part (c) shows what is happening in the industry as a whole.

Suppose that Trick decides to raise output from 2,000 to 3,000 units a week. It recognizes that if Gear sticks to the agreement to produce only 2,000 units a week, total output will be 5,000 a week, and given demand in part (c), the price will have to be cut to £7,500 a unit.

Gear continues to produce 2,000 units a week at a cost of £8,000 a unit, and incurs a loss of £500 a

unit or £1 million a week. This loss is represented by the red rectangle in part (a). Trick produces 3,000 units a week at an average total cost of £6,000 each. With a price of £7,500, Trick makes a profit of £1,500 a unit and therefore a total profit of £4.5 million. This profit is the blue rectangle in part (b).

We have now described a second possible outcome for the duopoly game – one of the firms cheats on the collusive agreement. In this case, the industry output is larger than the monopoly output and the industry price is lower than the monopoly price. The total profit made by the industry is also smaller than the monopoly's profit. Trick (the cheat) makes a profit of £4.5 million and Gear (the complier) incurs a loss of £1 million. The industry makes a profit of £3.5 million. Thus the industry profit is £0.5 million less than the maximum profit would be with a monopoly outcome. But that profit is distributed unevenly. Trick makes an even bigger profit than it would under the collusive agreement, while Gear makes a loss.

We have just worked out what happens if Trick cheats and Gear complies with the collusive agreement. There is another similar outcome that would arise if Gear cheated and Trick complied with the agreement. The industry profit and price would be the same but in this case Gear (the cheat) would make a profit of £4.5 million and Trick (the complier) would incur a loss of £1 million.

There is yet another possible outcome: both firms cheat on the agreement.

Both Firms Cheat Suppose that instead of just one firm cheating on the collusive agreement, both firms cheat. In particular, suppose that each firm behaves in exactly the same way as the cheating firm that we have just analysed. Each firm tells the other that it is unable to sell its output at the going price and that it plans to cut its price. But since both firms cheat, each will propose a successively lower price. They will only stop proposing lower prices when the price has reached £6,000. That is the price that equals minimum average cost. At a price of less than £6,000, each firm will make a loss. At a price of £6,000, each firm will cover all its costs and make zero economic profit. Also, at a price of £6,000, each firm will want to produce 3,000 units a week, so that the industry output will be 6,000 units a week. Given the demand conditions, 6,000 units can be sold at a price of £6,000 each.

The situation just described is illustrated in Fig. 13.8.

FIGURE 13.7

Cheating on a Collusive Agreement

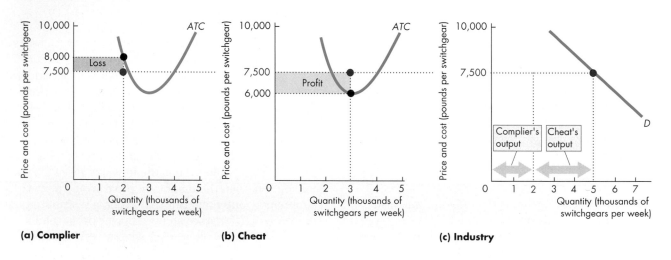

(a) Complier **(b) Cheat** **(c) Industry**

In part (a), one firm complies with the agreement. In part (b), the other firm cheats by raising output above the agreed limit to 3,000 switchgears per week. Either firm can be the complier and the other the cheat. In part (c), the effect on the industry price of the actions of the cheat are shown. As a result of cheating, industry output rises to 5,000 units a week and the market price falls to £7,500 – the price at which 5,000 switchgear units can be sold.

Part (a) describes the complier's situation. Output remains at 2,000 units and average total cost remains at £8,000 per unit. The firm loses £500 per switchgear and makes a total loss of £1 million (red rectangle). Part (b) describes the cheat's situation. Average total cost is £6,000 per unit and profit per switchgear is £1,500, so the cheat's total profit is £4.5 million (blue rectangle).

Each firm, shown in part (a) of the figure, is producing 3,000 units a week, and this output level occurs at the point of minimum average total cost (£6,000 per unit). The market as a whole, shown in part (b), operates at the point at which the demand curve (D) intersects the industry marginal cost curve (MC_I). This marginal cost curve is constructed as the horizontal sum of the marginal cost curves of the two firms. Each firm has lowered its price and increased its output in order to try to gain an advantage over the other firm. They have each pushed this process as far as they can without incurring losses.

We have now described a third possible outcome of this duopoly game – both firms cheat. If both firms cheat on the collusive agreement, the output of each firm is 3,000 units a week and the price is £6,000. Each firm makes zero profit. Notice that this outcome is the same as that in a perfectly competitive market in the long run.

The Payoff Matrix and Equilibrium

Now that we have described the strategies and payoffs in the duopoly game, let's summarize the strategies and the payoffs in the form of the game's payoff matrix and then calculate the equilibrium.

Table 13.4 sets out the payoff matrix for this game. It is constructed in exactly the same way as the payoff matrix for the prisoners' dilemma in Table 13.3. The squares show the payoffs for the two firms – Gear and Trick. In this case, the payoffs are profits. (In the case of the prisoners' dilemma, the payoffs were losses.)

The table shows that if both firms cheat (top left), they achieve the perfectly competitive outcome – each firm makes zero economic profit. If both firms comply (bottom right), the industry makes the monopoly profit and each firm earns a profit of £2 million. The top-right and bottom-left squares show what happens if one firm cheats while the other complies. The firm that cheats collects a

FIGURE 13.8

Both Firms Cheat

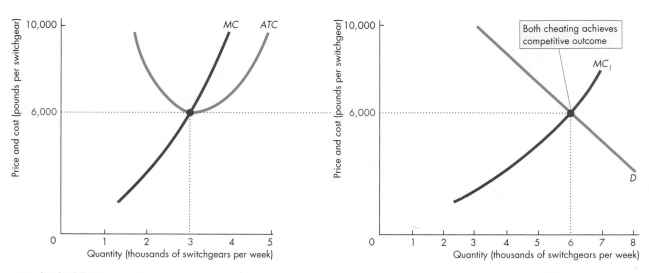

(a) Individual firm

(b) Industry

If both firms cheat by raising their output and lowering the price, the collusive agreement completely breaks down. The limit to the breakdown of the agreement is the competitive equilibrium. Neither firm will want to cut the price below £6,000 (minimum average total cost), for to do so will result in losses. Part (a) shows the situation facing each firm. At a price of £6,000, the firm's profit-maximizing output is 3,000 units per week. At that output rate, price

equals marginal cost, and it also equals average total cost. Economic profit is zero. Part (b) describes the situation in the industry as a whole. The industry marginal cost curve (MC_I) – the horizontal sum of the individual firms' marginal cost curves (MC) – intersects the demand curve at 6,000 switchgear units per week and at a price of £6,000. This output and price is the one that would prevail in a competitive industry.

profit of £4.5 million and the one that complies makes a loss of £1 million.

This duopoly game is, in fact, the same as the prisoners' dilemma that we examined earlier in this chapter; it is a duopolist's dilemma. You will see this once you have determined what the equilibrium of this game is.

Equilibrium To find the equilibrium, let's look at things from the point of view of Gear. Gear reasons as follows: suppose that Trick cheats. If we comply with the agreement, we make a loss of £1 million. If we also cheat, we make a zero profit. Zero profit is better than a £1 million loss, so it will pay us to cheat. But suppose Trick complies with the agreement. If we cheat, we will make a profit of £4.5 million, and if we comply, we will make a profit of £2 million. A £4.5 million profit is better than a £2

million profit so it would again pay us to cheat. Thus regardless of whether Trick cheats or complies, it pays us to cheat. Gear's dominant strategy is to cheat.

Trick comes to the same conclusion as Gear. Therefore both firms will cheat. The equilibrium of this game then is that both firms cheat on the agreement. Although there are only two firms in the industry, the price and quantity are the same as in a competitive industry. Each firm makes zero profit.

Although we have done this analysis for only two firms, it would not make any difference (other than to increase the amount of arithmetic) if we were to play the game with three, four or more firms. In other words, though we have analysed duopoly, the game theory approach can also be used to analyse oligopoly. The analysis of oligopoly is much harder, but the essential ideas that we have learned apply to oligopoly.

TABLE 13.4

Duopoly Payoff Matrix

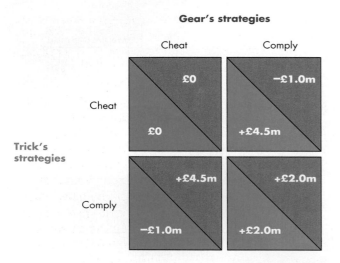

Each square shows the payoffs from a pair of actions. For example, if both firms comply with the collusive agreement, the payoffs are recorded in the square at the bottom right corner of the table. Gear's payoff is shown in the red triangle and Trick's in the blue triangle. Gear reasons as follows: if Trick cheats, it pays me to cheat and make a zero economic profit rather than a £1 million loss. If Trick complies, it pays me to cheat and make a £4.5 million profit rather than a £2 million profit. Cheating is Gear's dominant strategy. Trick reasons similarly: if Gear cheats it pays me to cheat and make a zero profit rather than a £1 million loss. If Gear complies, it pays me to cheat and make a £4.5 million profit rather than a £2 million profit. The equilibrium is a Nash equilibrium in which both firms cheat.

Repeated Games

The first game that we studied, the prisoners' dilemma, was played just once. The prisoners did not have an opportunity to observe the outcome of the game and then play it again. The duopolist game just described was also played only once. But real-world duopolists do get opportunities to play repeatedly against each other. This fact suggests that real-world duopolists might find some way of learning to cooperate so that their efforts to collude are more effective.

If a game is played repeatedly, one player always has the opportunity to penalize the other player for previous 'bad' behaviour. If Trick refuses to cooperate this week, then Gear can refuse to cooperate next week (and vice versa). If Gear cheats this week, won't Trick cheat next week? Before Gear cheats this week, shouldn't it take account of the possibility of Trick cheating next week?

What is the equilibrium of this more complicated prisoners' dilemma game when it is repeated indefinitely? Actually there is more than one possibility. One is the Nash equilibrium that we have just analysed. Both players cheat with each making zero profit forever. In such a situation, it will never pay one of the players to start complying unilaterally, for to do so would result in a loss for that player and a profit for the other. The price and quantity will remain at the competitive levels forever.

But another equilibrium is possible – one in which the players make and share the monopoly profit. How might this equilibrium come about? Why wouldn't it always pay each firm to try to get away with cheating? The key to answering this question is the fact that when a prisoners' dilemma game is played repeatedly, the players have an increased array of strategies. Each player can punish the other player for previous actions.

There are two extremes of punishment. The smallest penalty that one player can impose on the other is what is called 'tit-for-tat'. A **tit-for-tat strategy** is one in which a player cooperates in the current period if the other player cooperated in the previous period, but cheats in the current period if the other player cheated in the previous period. The most severe form of punishment that one player can impose on the other arises in what is called a trigger strategy. A **trigger strategy** is one in which a player cooperates if the other player cooperates, but plays the Nash equilibrium strategy forever thereafter if the other player cheats. Since a tit-for-tat strategy and a trigger strategy are the extremes of punishment – the most mild and most severe – there are evidently other intermediate degrees of punishment. For example, if one player cheats on the agreement, the other player could punish by refusing to cooperate for a certain number of periods. In the duopoly game between Gear and Trick, it turns out that a tit-for-tat strategy keeps both players cooperating and earning monopoly profits. Let's see why.

Table 13.5 sets out the profits that each firm will make in each period of play under two sets of

TABLE 13.5

Repeated Duopoly Game

Period of play	Collude		Cheat with tit-for-tat strategy	
	Trick's profit	Gear's profit	Trick's profit	Gear's profit
	(millions of pounds)			
1	2	2	2.0	2.0
2	2	2	4.5	−1.0
3	2	2	−1.0	4.5
4	2	2	2.0	2.0
·	·	·	·	·
·	·	·	·	·
·	·	·	·	·

If duopolists repeatedly play the 'cooperate' strategy, they each make £2 million in each period. If one player cheats in one period, the other player cheats in the following period – tit-for-tat. The profit from cheating can be made only for a single period. In the following period, the other player cheats and the first player must cooperate if the cooperative agreement is to be restored in period 4. The profit from cheating, calculated over 4 periods of play, is lower than that from colluding. Under collusion, each player makes £8 million; with a single cheat responded to with a tit-for-tat, each makes a profit of £7.5 million. It pays each player to cooperate, so cooperation is an equilibrium.

conditions: first, if they cooperate, and second, if cheating is responded to with a tit-for-tat strategy. As you can see, as long as both firms stick to the collusive agreement, they make the monopoly profit (£2 million per period each). Suppose that Trick contemplates cheating in period 2. The cheating produces a quick £4.5 million profit and inflicts a £1 million loss on Gear. In the next period Gear will hit Trick with its tit-for-tat response and cheat. If Trick reverts to cooperating (to induce Gear to cooperate in period 4), Gear now makes a profit of £4.5 million and Trick makes a loss of £1 million. Adding up the profits over two periods of play, Trick comes out ahead by cheating (£6.5 million compared with £4 million). But if we run the game forward for four periods, Trick would be better off having cooperated. In that case, it would have made £8 million in profit compared with £7.5

million from cheating and generating Gear's tit-for-tat response.[2]

Though we have just worked out what happens if Trick cheats, we can turn the tables and perform the same thought experiment for Gear cheating. We will come up with the same conclusion – it pays Gear to collude. Since it pays both firms to stick to the collusive agreement, both firms will do so and the monopoly price, quantity and profit will prevail in the industry. This equilibrium is called a **co-operative equilibrium** – an equilibrium resulting from each player responding rationally to the credible threat of the other player to inflict heavy damage if the agreement is broken. But in order for this strategy to work, the threat must be credible; that is, each player must recognize that it is in the interest of the other player to respond with a tit-for tat. The tit-for-tat strategy is credible because if one player cheats, it clearly does not pay the other player to continue complying. So the threat of cheating in the next period is credible and sufficient to support the monopoly equilibrium outcome.

REVIEW

G ame theory is a tool that can be used to explain the behaviour of oligopolists. A classic game, the prisoners' dilemma, explains the behaviour of duopolists. Two firms form a cartel to charge the same price as a monopoly would charge and share the monopoly profit. Each firm may either comply with the agreement or break it. If the game is played just once, both firms break the agreement. The price is competed down to the competitive level and profits are competed away. If the game is played repeatedly, cheating can be punished and this threat enables the duopolists to make the monopoly price stick and share the monopoly profit. ◆

---

[2] In calculating Trick's profits from colluding compared with cheating, we've ignored the fact that future profits have a smaller present value than current profits (see Chapter 9). However, provided that the interest rate at which future profits are discounted is not too high, it will still pay Trick to cooperate rather than cheat.

Supermarket Price Wars

The Essence of the Story

Competition between supermarkets has increased.

Tesco's profits fell sharply.

There is the prospect of even greater price pressures in the coming year.

Tesco expects to face still greater competition over the coming years.

Tesco plans to become more price competitive by introducing 'Value Lines' which already represent 3 per cent of total sales.

THE TIMES, 13 APRIL 1994

Supermarket price wars put the brake on Tesco

Susan Gilchrist

THE supermarket price wars have hit Tesco, keeping the underlying profits of Britain's second biggest food retailer static last year and leading the company to give warning of further price pressures in the coming 12 months.

David Malpas, managing director, said that the need to cut prices on basic commodities to meet consumers' demand for value and to counteract competition from discounters had hit gross margins. He predicted further, smaller falls in the current year in spite of a slight recovery since the year end. 'There was a sharp downwards adjustment in margins last year,' he said. 'For the next year or so, we are going to see some aftershocks from that adjustment but we don't think we are on a downwards spiral.'

Mr Malpas said that Kwik Save's recent cutting of prices on leading brands by up to 15 per cent was one 'aftershock', although Tesco did not plan to respond immediately. 'We think the market is likely to become more competitive, not less competitive, during the year and we therefore think it is wise to be cautious,' he said.

Pre-tax profits tumbled from £558 million to £435.5 million for the year to February 26....

Sales from Tesco's British supermarkets moved ahead strongly, rising by 10.3 per cent, from £8.13 billion to £8.97. Its 26 new stores contributed 7 per cent, with like-for-like sales from existing outlets adding 3.3 per cent.

Mr Malpas said that Tesco's increased price competitiveness had driven the rise in sales, with higher volumes being sold to more customers, albeit at lower prices. The economy Value Lines range, launched last August, had proved successful and now accounted for 3 per cent of turnover.

© The Times. Reprinted with permission.

Background and Analysis

During the 1980s, the supermarket sector was oligopolistic, with the few players (for example, Tesco, Sainsbury's and Safeway) all making profits.

They undertook substantial expansion, principally into large out-of-town stores. The growth in concentration was due in large part to economies of scale in distribution.

In the late 1980s competition from discount retailers increased. The result was intensified price competition and greater non-price competition, such as selling non-food items like petrol, clothes and newspapers.

With the onset of recession, consumers started demanding value for money. The response of the major players was the proliferation of own brand products.

Recently, two distinct types of discounter have entered the supermarket grocery sector.

High Street discounters such as Aldi, Netto and the established Kwik Save sell only branded products very cheaply in High Street outlets.

Warehouse clubs, however, which originated in the United States, set up in out-of-town stores.

This can be simplified as an economic game. Consider the figure, where retailers can either cut prices or hold prices. For simplicity, we will assume that there are two players, Tesco and Kwik Save (the established discounter).

The figures in the boxes represent profits resulting from each of four possible outcomes from the game. The figures in the blue areas represent Tesco's profits and the figures in the red areas represent Kwik Save's profits. (All figures are hypothetical.)

If Kwik Save cuts its prices, Tesco maximizes its profits by also cutting prices. If Kwik Save decides to hold its prices, it will still pay Tesco to cut its prices. If the analysis is reversed, whatever Tesco does, Kwik Save will maximize its profits by cutting prices.

The figure therefore represents the special case of Nash equilibrium known as a dominant strategy equilibrium.

This analysis is limited as it only represents a game played once. Repeated games may yield different outcomes, since further price cuts will affect the various profit outcomes. This would explain why retailers do not continually cut prices down below certain levels.

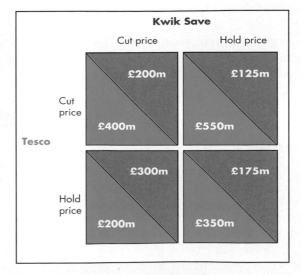

	Kwik Save	
	Cut price	Hold price
Tesco Cut price	£200m / £400m	£125m / £550m
Hold price	£300m / £200m	£175m / £350m

Uncertainty

In reality, there are random fluctuations in demand and in costs that make it impossible for one firm to detect whether the other firm is cheating. For example, a fall in demand can lower the industry price. One firm increasing its output can also lower the industry price. If a firm observes only that the industry price has fallen, it cannot tell which of these forces caused it. If it knows that the price has fallen because of a fall in demand, its profit-maximizing action will be to continue cooperating with the other firm to maintain the monopoly agreement. But if the price fall resulted from the other firm cheating and increasing its output, the profit-maximizing response will be to hit the other firm with a tit-for-tat in the next period. Yet by observing only the price fall, neither firm can tell whether the other firm has cheated. What can the firms do in a situation such as this one?

If they each always *assume* that whenever the price falls it is because the other firm has cheated, the monopoly agreement will repeatedly break down and the firms will fail to realize the potentially available monopoly profits. If, on the other hand, one firm assumes that the other firm is always cooperating and that any price falls have resulted from market forces beyond the control of either firm, then that other firm will have an incentive to cheat. (Recall that with one firm cheating and the other cooperating, the cheat makes even bigger profits than when they both cooperate.) To remove that incentive to cheat, each firm will assume that the other is cooperating, provided the price does not fall by more than a certain amount. If the price does fall below that predetermined amount, each firm will react as if the other firm had cheated. When market forces take the price back up above the critical level, the firms will cooperate again.

Games and Price Wars

Let's see whether the theory of price and output determination under duopoly can help us to understand real-world behaviour and, in particular, price wars. Suppose that two (or more) producers reach a collusive agreement and set their prices at the monopoly profit-maximizing level. Each firm adopts the strategy of cooperating and sticking to the agreement unless the price falls below a certain critical level. If the price falls below the critical level, each firm breaks the agreement and increases output. Fluctuations in demand lead to fluctuations in the industry price and output. Most of the time these fluctuations are small, and the price does not fall far enough to make either firm depart from the agreement. But a large decrease in demand makes the price fall below the critical level. Each firm responds by abandoning the agreement.

The events that follow look exactly like a price war. It is unlikely that each firm will abandon the agreement and increase production at exactly the same moment. When one firm breaks the agreement, the price falls by more than the fall that triggered its decision. When the second firm abandons the agreement, its behaviour looks like retaliation. But what is actually happening is that each firm is reacting to the large price fall in a manner that maintains the credibility of the threat to the other firm and that preserves the monopoly cooperative equilibrium in normal demand conditions. When demand increases again and market forces increase the price, the firms revert to their cooperative behaviour and reap the monopoly profit.

Thus there will be cycles of price wars and the restoration of collusive agreements. The behaviour of prices and outputs in the oil industry can be explained by the type of game that you have just studied. The market for crude oil is dominated by the OPEC cartel and, from time to time, to increase the price of oil, the cartel has agreed to production limits for each member. But also, from time to time, the agreements have broken down. Members of the cartel have exceeded their agreed production levels and oil prices have fallen.

Other Strategic Variables

We have focused here on firms that play a simple game and consider only two possible strategies (complying and cheating) concerning two variables (price and quantity produced). However, the approach that we have used can be extended to deal with a much wider range of choices facing firms. For example, a firm has to decide whether to enter or leave an industry; whether to mount an expensive advertising campaign; whether to modify its good; how reliable to make its good (the more reliable a good, usually, the more expensive it is to produce); whether to price discriminate and if so among which groups of customers and to what degree; whether to undertake a large research and development (R&D) effort aimed at lowering production costs. All of these choices that firms make can be analysed by using game theory. The basic method of analysis that you have studied can be applied to these problems by working out the payoff for each of the alternative strategies and then finding the equilibrium of the game. Let's look at an example – based on an important, real-world case – of an R&D game.

An R&D Game in the Disposable Nappy Industry

Since the 1980s, the two market leaders in the disposable nappy industry have been Procter & Gamble (makers of Pampers) and Peaudouce. Procter & Gamble has 34 per cent of the total market while Peaudouce has 16 per cent. When the product was first introduced in 1970s, it had to be cost-effective in competition against reusable, cloth nappies. A massive research and development effort resulted in the development of machines that could make disposable nappies at a low enough cost to achieve that initial competitive edge. The nappy industry is fiercely competitive. As it has matured, a large number of firms have tried to get into the business and take market share away from the two leaders and the leaders themselves have fought each other to maintain or increase their own market share.

The disposable nappy industry is one in which technological advances that result in small decreases in the average total cost of production can provide an individual firm with an enormous competitive advantage. The current machines can produce disposable nappies at 10 times the output rate just a decade earlier. The firm that develops and uses the least-cost technology gains a competitive edge, undercutting the rest of the market, increasing its market share and increasing its profit. But R&D effort that has to be undertaken to achieve even small cost reductions is itself very costly. Its cost has to be deducted from the profit resulting from the increased market share that lower costs

achieve. If no firm does R&D, every firm can be better off, but if one firm initiates the R&D activity, all must.

Each firm in the disposable nappy industry is in an R&D dilemma. Table 13.6 illustrates the dilemma (with hypothetical numbers) for the R&D game that Peaudouce and Procter & Gamble are playing. Each firm has two strategies: to spend £25 million a year on R&D or to spend nothing on R&D. If neither firm spends on R&D, they make a joint profit of £100 million, £30 million for Peaudouce and £70 million for Procter & Gamble (bottom right square in payoff matrix). If each firm conducts R&D, market shares are maintained but each firm's profit is lower, by the amount spent on R&D (top left square of payoff matrix). If Peaudouce pays for R&D but Procter & Gamble does not, Peaudouce gains a large part of Procter & Gamble's market.

TABLE 13.6

An R&D Game Payoff Matrix

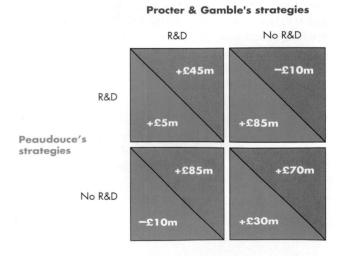

If both firms undertake R&D, their payoffs are those shown in the top left square. If neither firm undertakes R&D, their payoffs are in the bottom right square. When one firm undertakes R&D and the other one does not, their payoffs are in the top right and bottom left squares. The dominant strategy equilibrium for this game is for both firms to undertake R&D. The structure of this game is the same as that of the prisoners' dilemma.

Peaudouce profits and Procter & Gamble loses (top right square of payoff matrix). Finally, if Procter & Gamble invests in R&D, and Peaudouce does not, Procter & Gamble gains market share from Peaudouce, increasing its profit while Peaudouce makes a loss.

Confronted with the payoff matrix in Table 13.6, the two firms calculate their best strategies. Peaudouce reasons as follows: if Procter & Gamble does not undertake R&D, we make £85 million if we do and £30 million if we do not; therefore it pays to conduct R&D. If Procter & Gamble conducts R&D, we lose £10 million if we do not and make £5 million if we do. Again, R&D pays off. Thus conducting R&D is a dominant strategy for Peaudouce. Doing it pays regardless of Procter & Gamble's decision.

Procter & Gamble reasons similarly: if Peaudouce does not undertake R&D, we make £70 million if we follow suit and £85 million if we conduct R&D. It therefore pays to conduct R&D. If Peaudouce does undertake R&D, we make £45 million by doing the same and lose £10 million by not doing R&D. Again, it pays to conduct R&D. So, for Procter & Gamble, R&D is also a dominant strategy.

Since R&D is a dominant strategy for both players, it is the Nash equilibrium. The outcome of this game is that both firms conduct R&D. They make lower profits than they would if they could collude to achieve the cooperative outcome of no R&D.

The real-world situation has more players than Peaudouce and Procter & Gamble. There are a large number of other firms sharing a small portion of the market, all of them ready to eat into the market share of Procter & Gamble and Peaudouce. So the R&D effort by these two firms not only serves the purpose of maintaining shares in their own battle, but also helps to keep the barriers to entry high enough to preserve their joint market share.

Marketing Games

The producers of Coke and Pepsi are examples of firms that are locked in fierce competition with each other in a prisoners' dilemma. But they don't compete on price, or at least not primarily on price. Nor do they compete by outperforming each other on R&D. Their main weapons are advertising and marketing on which they spend millions of pounds each year. Each firm must contemplate the outcome if it spends millions of pounds on advertising and if it does not. If neither Pepsi nor Coke advertises, neither loses market share to the other and both keep the funds that would otherwise be paid to the advertising company. If one advertises and the other does not, the advertiser takes market share and its profits increase. The one that does not advertise loses. If both advertise, neither loses market share to the other, but both earn a smaller profit than with no advertising by either.

The payoff matrix for this game looks just like that for the R&D game that we've already studied. Advertising is a dominant strategy, so Coke and Pepsi advertise.

◆ ◆ ◆ ◆ We have now studied the four main market types – perfect competition, monopolistic competition, oligopoly and monopoly – and discovered how prices and outputs, revenue, cost and profit are determined in these industries. We have used the various models to make predictions about behaviour and to assess the efficiency of alternative market structures. ◆ ◆ A key element in our analysis of the markets for goods and services is the behaviour of costs. Costs are determined partly by technology and partly by the prices of factors of production. We have treated those factor prices as given. We are now going to see how factor prices are themselves determined.

S U M M A R Y

Varieties of Market Structure

Most real-world industries lie between the extremes of perfect competition and monopoly. The degree of competition is sometimes measured by the five-firm concentration ratio – the percentage of the value of the sales of an industry accounted for by its five largest firms. High concentration ratios indicate a relatively low degree of competition and vice versa, with some important qualifications. Three problems with concentration ratios are: (1) they refer to the national market but some industries are local while others are international; (2) they do not tell us about the degree of turnover of firms and the ease of entry; and (3) some firms classified in one particular industry operate in several others. In the United Kingdom, most industries are effectively competitive, but there are important non-competitive elements.

Two models of industries that lie between monopoly and perfect competition are monopolistic competition and oligopoly. Monopolistic competition is a market type where a large number of firms compete, each making a slightly differentiated good from the others by competing on price, quality and advertising. Oligopoly is a market type in which a small number of firms compete with each other and in which the actions of any one firm have an important impact on the profit of the others. (pp. 342–345)

Monopolistic Competition

Monopolistic competition occurs when a large number of firms compete with each other by making slightly different products. Under monopolistic competition, each firm faces a downward-sloping demand curve and so has to choose its price as well as its output level. Because there is free entry, in long-run equilibrium zero economic profit is earned. When profit is maximized, with marginal cost equal to marginal revenue, average cost also equals price in the long run. But average cost is not at its minimum point. That is, in monopolistic competition firms operate with excess capacity. (pp. 345–348)

Oligopoly

Oligopoly is a situation in which a small number of producers compete with each other. The key feature of oligopoly is that the firms strategically interact. Each firm has to take into account the effects of its own actions on the behaviour of other firms and the effects of the actions of other firms on its own profit. (p. 348)

Traditional Models of Oligopoly

The kinked demand curve model of oligopoly is based on the assumption that each firm believes its price cuts will be matched by its rivals but its price increases will not be matched. If these beliefs are correct, each firm faces a kinked demand curve for its product, the kink occurring at the current price, and has a break in its marginal revenue curve. To maximize profit, the firm produces the quantity that makes marginal cost and marginal revenue equal, an output level such that the marginal cost curve passes through the break in the marginal revenue curve. Fluctuations in marginal cost inside the range of the break in marginal revenue have no effect on either price or output.

The dominant firm model of oligopoly assumes that an industry consists of one large firm and a large number of small firms. The large firm acts like a monopoly and sets a profit-maximizing price. The small firms take this price as given and act like perfectly competitive firms. (pp. 348–351)

Oligopoly and Game Theory

Game theory is a method of analysing strategic behaviour. Game theory focuses on three aspects of a game:

◆ Rules
◆ Strategies
◆ Payoffs

The rules of the oligopoly game specify the permissible actions by the players. These actions are limited only by the legal code and involve such things as raising or lowering prices; raising or lowering output; raising or lowering advertising effort; and enhancing or not enhancing the product. The strategies in the oligopoly game are all the possible actions that each player can take given the action of the other player. The payoff of the oligopoly game is the player's profit or loss. It depends on the actions of both the players and on the constraints imposed by the market, technology and input costs.

Duopoly is a market structure in which there are two producers of a good competing against each other. Duopoly is a special case of oligopoly. The duopoly game is similar to the prisoners' dilemma game. Two prisoners are faced with the problem of deciding whether or not to confess to a crime. If neither confesses, they are tried for a lesser crime and receive a light penalty. If both confess, they receive a higher penalty. If one confesses and the other does not confess, the one confessing receives the lightest of all penalties and the one not confessing receives a very heavy penalty.

The prisoners' dilemma has a dominant strategy Nash equilibrium. That is, regardless of the action of the other player there is a unique best action for each player – to confess. (pp. 351–354)

A Duopoly Game

A duopoly game can be constructed in which two firms contemplate the consequences of colluding to achieve a monopoly profit or of cheating on the collusive agreement to make a bigger profit at the expense of the other firm. Such a game is identical to the prisoners' dilemma. The equilibrium of the game will be one in which both firms cheat on the agreement. The industry output will be the same in this case as it would be if the industry was perfectly competitive. The industry price will also be the competitive price and firms will make zero economic profit. If the firms are able to enforce the collusive agreement, the industry will look exactly like a monopoly industry. Price, output and profit will be the same as in a monopoly.

If a game is repeated indefinitely, there is an opportunity for one player to punish another player for previous 'bad' behaviour. In such a situation, a tit-for-tat strategy can produce an equilibrium in which both firms stick to the agreement. A tit-for-tat strategy is one in which the players begin by colluding. If one player cheats, the other player responds at the next play by also cheating. Since each knows that it pays the other to respond in this manner, no one cheats. This equilibrium is a cooperative equilibrium – one in which each player cooperates because such behaviour is a rational response to the credible threat of the other to inflict damage if the agreement is broken. Uncertainty makes it possible for such an equilibrium to break down from time to time. (pp. 354–364)

Games and Price Wars

Price wars can be interpreted as the outcome of a repeated duopoly game. The competing firms comply with the agreement unless market forces bring about a sufficiently large fall in price. A large fall in price is responded to as if it had resulted from the other firm cheating. Only by responding in this manner can each firm maintain the credible threat that it will punish a cheat and thereby ensure that the ever-present temptation to cheat is held in check and the monopoly agreement maintained. When market conditions bring about an increase in price, the firms revert to their cooperative behaviour. Industries will go through cycles, starting with a monopoly price and output and occasionally, when demand falls by enough, temporarily pursuing non-cooperative actions. At these times, the industry price and output will be the competitive ones. (p. 364)

Other Strategic Variables

Firms in oligopolistic industries have to make a large range of decisions: whether to enter or leave an industry; how much to spend on advertising; whether to modify their products; whether to price discriminate; whether to undertake research and development. All these choices result in payoffs for the firm and the other firms in the industry and a game can be constructed to predict the outcome of such choices.

An interesting real-world example is the R&D game played by producers of disposable nappies. The equilibrium of this game results in a large amount of R&D being undertaken and lower profits than would emerge if the firms could collude somehow to keep out new entrants and undertake less R&D. Thus this game is similar to the prisoners' dilemma. (pp. 364–366)

K E Y   E L E M E N T S

Key Terms

R E V I E W   Q U E S T I O N S

1   What are the main varieties of market structure? What are the main characteristics of each of these market structures?

2   What is a five-firm concentration ratio? If the five-firm concentration ratio is 90 per cent, what does it mean?

3   Give some examples of industries in the United Kingdom that have a high concentration ratio and industries in the United Kingdom that have a low concentration ratio.

4   What are barriers to entry? Give some examples of barriers in your country's economy.

5   Explain how a firm can differentiate its good.

6   What is the difference between monopolistic competition and perfect competition?

7   Is monopolistic competition more efficient or less efficient than perfect competition?

8   What is the difference between duopoly and oligopoly?

9   Why might the demand curve facing an oligopolist be kinked, and what happens to a firm's marginal revenue curve if its demand curve is kinked?

10 In what circumstances might the dominant firm model of oligopoly be relevant?

11 What is the essential feature of both duopoly and oligopoly?

12 List the key features that all games have in common with each other.

13 What are the features of duopoly that make it reasonable to treat duopoly as a game ?

14 What is the prisoners' dilemma?

15 What is a dominant strategy equilibrium?

16 What is meant by a repeated game?

17 Explain what a tit-for-tat strategy is.

18 What is a price war? What is the effect of a price war on the profit of the firms in the industry and on the profitability of the industry itself?

P R O B L E M S

1   A monopolistically competitive industry is in long-run equilibrium as illustrated in Fig. 13.2(b). Demand for the industry's product increases, increasing the demand for each firm's output. Using figures similar to those in Fig. 13.2, analyse the short-run and long-run effects on price, output and profit of this increase in demand.

2   Another monopolistically competitive industry is in long-run equilibrium, as illustrated in Fig. 13.2(b), when it experiences a large increase in wages. Using figures similar to those in Fig. 13.2, analyse the short-run and long-run effects on price, output and profit of this increase in wages.

3   A firm with a kinked demand curve experi-

ences an increase in its fixed cost. Explain the effects on the firm's price, output and profit/loss.

4 An industry with one very large firm and 100 very small firms experiences an increase in the demand for its product. Explain the effects on:

   a The price, output and profit of the large firm

   b The price, output and profit of a typical small firm

5 Describe the game known as the prisoners' dilemma. In describing the game:

   a Make up a story that motivates the game.

   b Work out a payoff matrix.

   c Describe how the equilibrium of the game is arrived at.

6 Consider the following game. There are two players and they are each asked a question. They can answer the question honestly or they can lie. If they both answer honestly, they each receive a payoff of £100. If one answers honestly and the other lies, the liar gains at the expense of the honest player. In this event, the liar receives a profit of £500 and the honest player gets nothing. If they both lie then they each receive a payoff of £50.

   a Describe this game in terms of its players, strategies and payoffs.

   b Construct the payoff matrix.

   c What is the equilibrium for this game?

7 Explain the behaviour of oil prices by using a

repeated prisoners' dilemma game.

8 Two firms, Soapy and Suddies, are the only two producers of soap powder. They collude and agree to share the market equally. If neither firm cheats on the agreement, they can each make £1 million profit. If either firm cheats, the cheater can increase its profit to £1.5 million, while the firm that abides by the agreement makes a loss of £0.5 million. Neither firm has any way of policing the actions of the other.

   a Describe the best strategy for each firm in a game that is played once.

   b What is the payoff matrix and equilibrium of a game that is played just once?

   c If the buyers of washing powder lobby successfully for government regulation of the washing powder industry, explain what happens to the price and the profits made by the washing powder industry.

   d If this duopolist game can be played many times, describe some of the strategies that each firm may adopt.

9 Explain the behaviour of world oil prices since 1973 by using a repeated prisoners' dilemma game. Describe the types of strategy that individual countries that belong to OPEC have adopted.

10 Use the model of oligopoly to explain why, in the disposable nappy industry, Procter & Gamble and Peaudouce spend so much on R&D.

PART 4
MARKETS, UNCERTAINTY, AND DISTRIBUTION

Talking

with

Tony

Atkinson

Tony Atkinson was born in Caerleon, Wales. He studied economics at Cambridge University, has been a professor at the University of Essex, the London School of Economics, and has recently become Warden of Nuffield College Oxford. Professor Atkinson's major contributions have been in the area of taxation and the distribution of income.

How did you get interested in economics?

Like many other economists, I began as a mathematics student and then became interested in social problems. In the 1960s, we believed that we could change the world for the better – and I am not sure that we were wrong.

What are the key principles of economics that you have repeatedly found useful in your work?

I should say that I am suspicious of 'general principles' in economics. When I hear people say 'economic theory tells us x', I am immediately on my guard. Increasingly, I have become impressed with the importance of blending economic theory with the institutional realities of particular countries and particular time periods. Historical, cultural and social factors mean that an economic model that is applicable to Europe might not be equally relevant to the United States or Japan. Too often, economic theory is applied without regard to such institutional features. The standard economic treatment of unemployment insurance, for example, ignores important features of real-world unemployment insurance schemes, which may change its economic impact.

Why is a background in economics useful today?

What I believe economics can teach is not a set of universally applicable tools, like a wrench that will always undo a nut, but an *approach*. After receiving an economics degree, a student should not expect to have the answers but to be able to ask the right questions. When considering a particular policy change, for example, an economist will ask how the new policy might affect the behaviour of different groups and will ask who gains and who loses from its introduction.

One particular question that I have found useful to ask is 'What is the quantitative importance of different phenomena? Is the effect under discussion large or small?' One major contribution that economists can make is in evaluating and providing statistical information. I was once a member of a multidisciplinary group investigating the transmission of deprivation from generation to generation. It turned out that there was, at the time, no information at all about the proportion of children from poor families who went on to create poor families themselves. This led to a fascinating piece of research in which we traced the children of families who had been poor when studied a generation earlier. From this detective work, we were able to quantify the extent to which these children faced a greater risk of poverty.

Of course, everyone knows that statistics can be misused, and one should certainly not treat numbers in statistical yearbooks

'**W**hat I believe economics can teach is not a set of universally applicable tools, like a wrench that will always undo a nut, but an *approach*.'

with undue reverence. At the same time, one cannot discuss applied economic problems without a view of their quantitative importance. A first reaction of the good economist should be to reach for the numbers.

What drew you to work on problems of poverty and the distribution of income?

There were two important influences that affected the direction of my first research. The first was the lectures and writing of James Meade, who later won the Nobel Prize. From him, I learned both that economic analysis could contribute to understanding issues of inequality and that explaining the distribution of income was an intellectual challenge. The second was reading *The Poor and the Poorest* by Brian Abel-Smith and Peter Townsend, two British experts on social policy. Published in 1965, the book described the poverty in the United Kingdom despite the welfare state and despite – at that time – full employment. It demonstrated the potential impact of careful empirical research.

How does the study of income distribution relate to the main body of economics?

For classical economists, such as Adam Smith or David Ricardo, the

distribution of income was central to the study of economics. Today, on the other hand, the distribution of income is often treated as a special subject – one that sits uneasily between macroeconomics and microeconomics.

This seems to me a great pity, since distributional issues are at the heart of economics. Aggregate objectives, such as the growth of GDP, are only a means of achieving the more fundamental goal of improving the welfare of individuals. The welfare of individuals in turn depends on how total GDP is distributed. By this, I do not just mean the distribution of money income, but also the provision of public goods and the quality of the environment. It is paradoxical that Western democratic societies, with their emphasis on individual liberty, should be so preoccupied with macroeconomic aggregates and show much less interest in measuring individual welfare.

Which economic systems stand out as having achieved the greatest measure of equality and which as having determined the greatest inequality?

In the case of the former Soviet union, it used to be very difficult to obtain firm evidence about income inequality, which appeared on the list of censored subjects along with alcoholism and drug addiction. With *glasnost*, however, much infor-mation has been made available. It now appears that under Khrushchev, wage dispersion was indeed reduced below that in the United Kingdom, particularly because of the minimum wage. But in the 1980s there was little difference, and Gorbachev's wage reform actually widened differentials. On the other hand, the distribution of *income*, taking into account transfer payments and capital income and including those not in the labour force, did appear to be significantly less unequal in the USSR than in the United Kingdom in the mid-1980s. This conclusion might be modified if a value could be placed on the non-monetary advantages of the elite, but, on the other hand, fringe benefits for executives add to inequality in Western countries.

However, these conclusions cannot be attributed simply to the differences in economic systems, since the situation in the Central European communist countries appears to be distinctly different from that in the former Soviet Union. In particular, former Czechoslovakia has a much lower recorded degree of earnings dispersion and income inequality than Western countries. From our research, I conclude that the degree of inequality is influenced by the particular traditions and history of the country and that it can be affected by government policy.

A grand solution to the redistribution problem is the negative income tax. What are its major attractions to economists? And what are the major impediments in the political arena to its introduction?

A negative income tax means different things to different people. In its least radical form, it would involve the Inland Revenue paying to people below the tax threshold a proportion of the extent to which their income falls below that amount. As such, it appears to some economists as a better targeted form of redistribution, being directly related to income, rather than paid on the basis of unemployment, sickness, family size or other criteria. The effectiveness of such a proposal depends on the level of the tax threshold and on the proportion of the gap filled, but it does not seem realistic to suppose that it would allow existing social security programmes to be dismantled.

A more radical proposal, which has attracted more support in Europe, is for a *basic income policy*. In its pure form, this would replace all income tax exemptions and social security and welfare benefits by a basic income payable at so many pounds a week to every citizen. This would provide a comprehensive guaranteed minimum income and would greatly simplify the benefit system. The problem is that the abolition of tax exemptions means that income tax would be due on every pound of income. Moreover, to finance an adequate basic income, the tax rate would have to be set at a level that frightens politicians. The electorate has not been asked whether it would support such a plan, but politically it might be easier to redistribute by other means.

If you could start from scratch to write the tax code for a country like the United Kingdom or an emerging political grouping such as the European Union, what would the code contain?

I have difficulty answering this question, since I do not believe in immutable principles of economic policy. Economists have, for example, strongly advocated an expenditure tax in place of the income tax, and I can see the attractions. However, I do not believe that an expenditure tax is necessarily better in all circumstances. Similarly, economists have objected to the use of earmarked taxes, but again there may be occasions when they are desirable.

My conception of the proper role of the public finance economist is that of illuminating the choices open to governments and to the voters who elect them. To this end, I would be happy to draw up a menu of choices – to draft two or three alternative tax codes – as the basis for political discussion and to advise on their possible implications.

This gives the central role to the political authority, which is where it belongs in a democratic country. But one has to recognize that governments change, and one general principle that I will accept is that any tax code should ideally be sustainable in the face of changes in public opinion. No doubt rates of tax will be different with different governments, but a hallmark of a successful tax code is one that can accommodate different political preferences.

CHAPTER 14

PRICING
AND
ALLOCATING
FACTORS
OF
PRODUCTION

After studying this chapter you will be able to:

◆ Explain how firms choose the quantities of labour, capital and land to employ in their production activities

◆ Explain how households choose the quantities of labour, capital and land to supply

◆ Explain how wages, interest and rent are determined in competitive factor markets

◆ Explain the concept of economic rent

◆ Distinguish between economic rent and transfer earnings

I T MAY NOT BE YOUR BIRTHDAY, AND EVEN IF IT IS THE CHANCES ARE THAT YOU ARE spending most of it working. But at the end of the week or month (or, if you're devoting all your time to being a student, when you graduate), you will receive the *returns* from your labour. Those returns vary a lot. Brian Jones, who spends his days in a small container suspended from the top of a tall London office block cleaning windows, makes a happy return of £6.30 an hour. Roberto Baggio, who plays football for the Italian club Juventus, makes a very happy return of £2 million a year plus bonuses. Students working at McDonald's and Turkish immigrant workers in Germany are paid just a few pounds an hour. What determines the wages we are paid?

◆ ◆ Most of us have little trouble spending our income. But most of us do manage to save some of what we earn. What determines the amount people save and the

Many Happy Returns

interest they make on that saving? How do the returns on saving influence the allocation of savings across the many industries and activities that use our capital resources? ◆ ◆ Some people receive income from renting land, but the amount earned varies enormously with its location and quality. For example, a hectare of farmland in Scotland rents for about £300 a year while a block in London's West End rents for several million pounds a year. What determines the rent that people are willing to pay for different blocks of land? Why are rents so high in big cities and so relatively low in the farming regions of the country?

◆ ◆ ◆ ◆ In the previous five chapters, we've studied the decisions firms make in output markets. In this chapter, we study markets for factors of production. We learn how factor prices and people's incomes are determined.

Factor Prices and Incomes

Factors of production are the inputs into production. They are divided into three broad categories:

◆ Labour
◆ Capital
◆ Land

The owners of factors of production receive an income from the firms that use those factors as inputs into their production activities. These incomes are:

◆ Wages paid for labour
◆ Interest paid for capital
◆ Rent paid for land

Wages include all labour income including salaries, commissions, bonuses and any other supplementary forms of income paid in compensation for labour. *Interest* includes all forms of capital income including dividends paid by firms. *Rent* is the income paid for the use of land and natural resources. Rent for a flat includes an element of rent and also an element of interest – a payment for the use of capital.

Labour is by far the most important factor of production and generates 70 per cent of all income and that percentage has been steadily increasing over the years.

In this chapter, we're going to build a model of a factor market, a model that determines factor prices, the quantities of factors used, and the incomes that factors of production earn.

An Overview

Factor prices are determined in factor markets, and we can understand those prices by using the model of demand and supply. The quantity of a factor of production demanded depends upon the factor's price. That is, the quantity of labour demanded depends on the wage rate, the quantity of capital demanded depends on the interest rate, and the quantity of land demanded depends on the rent. The law of demand applies to factors of production just as it applies to all other economic entities. Thus as the price of a factor of production decreases, the quantity of the factor demanded increases. The demand curve for a factor of production is shown in

Fig. 14.1 as the curve labelled *D*.

The quantity supplied of a factor of production depends on its price. With some exceptions that we'll identify later in this chapter, the law of supply applies to factors of production: as the price of a factor of production increases, the quantity of the factor supplied increases. The supply of a factor of production is shown in Fig. 14.1 as the curve labelled *S*.

The equilibrium factor price is determined at the point of intersection of the factor demand and factor supply curves. Figure 14.1 shows such an equilibrium – *QF* is the quantity of the factor of production used and *PF* is the factor price.

The income earned by a factor of production is its price multiplied by the quantity used. In Fig. 14.1, the price is measured by the distance from the origin to *PF*, and the quantity used is measured by the distance from the origin to *QF*. The factor income is

FIGURE 14.1

Demand and Supply in a Factor Market

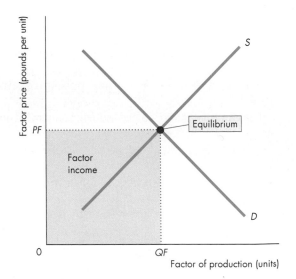

The demand curve for a factor of production (*D*) slopes downward and the supply curve (*S*) slopes upward. Where the demand and supply curves intersect, the factor price (*PF*) and the quantity of the factor used (*QF*) are determined. The factor income is the product of the factor price and the quantity of the factor, as represented by the blue rectangle.

the product of these two distances and it is equivalent to the blue area in the figure.

All the influences on the quantity of a factor bought other than its price result in a shift in the factor demand curve. We'll study what those influences are in the next section. For now, let's simply work out the effects of a change in the demand for a factor of production. An increase in demand for a factor of production, as illustrated in Fig. 14.2(a), shifts the demand curve to the right, leading to an increase in the quantity of the factor used and an increase in its price. Thus when the demand curve shifts from D_0 to D_1, the quantity used increases from QF_0 to QF_1 and the price increases from PF_0 to PF_1. An increase in the demand for a factor of production increases that factor's income. The dark blue area in Fig. 14.2(a) illustrates the increase in income.

When the demand for a factor of production decreases, its demand curve shifts to the left. Figure 14.2(b) illustrates the effects of a decrease in demand. The demand curve shifts to the left from D_0 to D_2, the quantity used decreases from QF_0 to QF_2, and the price decreases from PF_0 to PF_2. When the demand for a factor of production decreases, the income of that factor also decreases. The light blue area in Fig. 14.2(b) illustrates the decrease in income.

The extent to which a change in the demand for a factor of production changes the factor price and the quantity used depends on the elasticity of supply. If the supply curve is very flat (supply is elastic), the change in the quantity used is large and the change in the price is small. If the supply curve is very steep (supply is inelastic), the change in the price is large and the change in the quantity used is small.

A change in the supply of a factor of production also changes the price and quantity used as well as the income earned by those supplying the factor. An increase in supply results in an increase in the quantity used and a decrease in the factor price. A decrease in supply results in a decrease in the quantity used and an increase in the factor price. But whether a change in supply increases or decreases income depends on the elasticity of demand for the factor.

Suppose that the quantity used of the factor of production illustrated in Fig. 14.3 decreases from 3 units to 2 units. Initially, the price is £10 a unit. If the demand curve is D_0, the decrease in supply results in an increase in the price of the factor but a decrease in the income of those supplying this factor

FIGURE 14.2

Changes in Demand

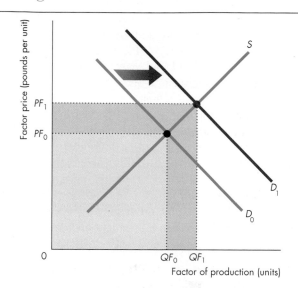

(a) An increase in demand

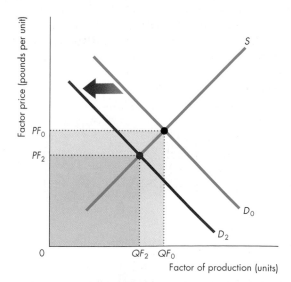

(b) A decrease in demand

An increase in the demand for a factor of production (part a) shifts its demand curve to the right – from D_0 to D_1. The quantity used increases from QF_0 to QF_1 and the price increases from PF_0 to PF_1. The factor income increases, and that income increase is shown by the dark blue area. A decrease in the demand for a factor of production from D_0 to D_2 results in a decrease in the quantity used, from QF_0 to QF_2, and a decrease in the factor price, from PF_0 to PF_2. The decrease in demand results in a decrease in the factor income. That decrease in income is illustrated by the light blue area.

of production. You can see that income decreases by multiplying the factor price by the quantity used. Initially, when the quantity is 3 units and the price is £10, the income earned by the suppliers of this factor of production is £30 (the £20 light blue area plus the £10 red area). When the quantity decreases to 2 units and the price increases to £14, income decreases by £10 (the red area) but increases by £8 (the dark blue area) for a net decrease to £28. Over the range of the price change that we've just considered, the demand curve D_0 is elastic – its elasticity is greater than 1.

Conversely, suppose that the demand curve is D_1. In this case, when the quantity decreases to 2 units, the price increases to £20 a unit. Income increases to £40. The smaller quantity lowers income by £10 (red area), but the higher factor price increases income by £20 (dark blue area plus green area). Over the range of the price change that we've just considered, the demand curve D_1 is inelastic – its elasticity is less than 1.

The markets for factors of production determine factor prices in much the same way as goods and services markets determine the prices of goods and services. Factor markets also determine factor incomes. Factor income is the factor price multiplied by the quantity of the factor used. Thus to work out the influences on factor incomes we have to pay attention simultaneously to the determination of the prices and the quantities used of the factors of production.

We're going to spend the rest of this chapter exploring more closely the influences on the demand for and supply of factors of production. We're also going to discover what determines the elasticities of supply and demand for factors. These elasticities are important because of their effects on factor prices and the incomes earned. Let's begin by studying the demand for inputs.

FIGURE 14.3

Factor Income and Demand Elasticity

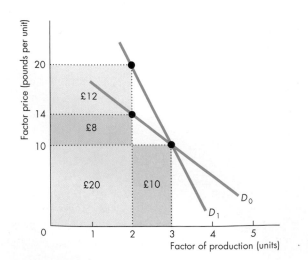

A decrease in the quantity used of a factor of production may result in a decrease or an increase in the factor's income. If the demand curve is D_0 (an elastic demand curve over the relevant range), a decrease in the quantity from 3 to 2 results in a decrease in the factor income of £30 to £28. If the demand curve is D_1 (an inelastic demand curve over the relevant range), a decrease in the quantity from 3 to 2 results in an increase in the factor's income from £30 to £40.

Demand for Factors

The demand for any factor of production is a derived demand. A **derived demand** is a demand for an input not for its own sake but in order to use it in the production of goods and services. A firm's derived demand for inputs depends on the constraints the firm faces – its technology constraint and its market constraint. It also depends on the firm's objective. The objective of the model firms that we have studied is to maximize profit. We'll continue to study the behaviour of such firms.

A firm's demand for factors stems from its profit-maximization decision. *What* to produce and *how* to produce it are the questions that the firm must answer in order to make maximum profit. These choices have implications for the firm's demand for inputs, which we'll now investigate.

Profit Maximization

In the short run, a firm's inputs fall into two categories: fixed and variable. In most industries, the fixed inputs are capital (that is, plant, machinery and buildings) and land; and the variable input is labour. A firm meets permanent changes in output by changing the scale of all of its inputs – capital, land and labour. It meets short-run variations in output by varying its input of labour.

Profit-maximizing firms produce the output at which marginal cost equals marginal revenue. This principle holds true whether the firm is in a perfectly competitive industry, in monopolistic competition, in oligopoly, or a monopoly. If one more unit of output adds less to total cost than it adds to total revenue, the firm can increase its profit by producing more. A firm maximizes profit by producing the output at which the additional cost of producing one more unit of output equals the additional revenue from selling it. If we shift our perspective slightly, we can also state the condition for maximum profit in terms of the marginal cost of an input and the marginal revenue that input generates. Let's see how.

Marginal Revenue Product and Factor Price

The change in total revenue resulting from employing one more unit of any factor is called the factor's **marginal revenue product**. The concept of marginal revenue product sounds a bit like the concept of marginal revenue that you have met before. These concepts are indeed related but there is an important distinction between the two. *Marginal revenue product* is the extra revenue generated as a result of employing one extra unit of a factor; *marginal revenue* is the extra revenue generated as a result of selling one additional unit of output.

A profit-maximizing firm hires the quantity of a factor that makes the marginal revenue product of the factor equal to the marginal cost of the factor. For a firm that buys its factors of production in competitive factor markets, the marginal cost of a factor is the factor's price. That is, in a competitive factor market, each firm is such a small demander of the factor that it has no influence on its price. The firm simply has to pay the going factor price – market wage rate for labour, interest rate for capital and rent for land.

Factor Price as Opportunity Cost   You may be wondering why the interest rate is the factor price for capital. It looks different from the other two factor prices. Why isn't the factor price for capital the price of a piece of machinery – the price of a knitting machine for Knitters' sweater factory, the price of a computer for a tax consultant, or the price of a car assembly line for Rover? The answer is that these

prices do not represent the opportunity cost of *using* capital equipment. They are the prices at which a piece of capital can be bought. A firm can buy or sell a piece of capital equipment at its going market price. The opportunity cost of *using* the equipment is the interest rate that has to be paid on the funds tied up in its purchase. These funds may be borrowed, in which case there is an explicit payment of interest to the bank or other lender. Or the funds may be owned by the firm, in which case there is an implicit interest cost – the interest that could have been earned by using those funds in some other way.

Quantity of Factor Demanded   We have defined the additional revenue resulting from employing one more unit of a factor as the factor's marginal revenue product. We have seen that in competitive factor markets, the marginal cost of a factor equals its price. Therefore a profit-maximizing firm – a firm that makes the marginal revenue product equal to the marginal cost of each input – hires each factor up to the point at which its marginal revenue product equals the factor's price. As the price of a factor varies, the quantity demanded of it also varies. The lower the price of a factor, the larger is the quantity demanded of that factor. Let's illustrate this proposition by working through an example – that of labour.[1]

The Firm's Demand for Labour

Labour is a variable input. A firm can change the quantity of labour it employs in both the short run and the long run. Let's focus first on a firm's short-run demand for labour.

A firm's short-run technology constraint is described by its *total product schedule*. Table 14.1 sets out the total product schedule for a car wash operated by Wendy's Wash 'n' Wax. (This total product schedule is similar to the one we studied in Chapter 10, Fig. 10.1.) The numbers in the first two columns of the table tell us how the maximum number

---

[1] The principles governing the demand for factors of production are the same for all factors – labour, capital and land. There are some interesting special features concerning the demand for capital, however, that are explained in greater detail in Chapter 16. This part of Chapter 16 is relatively self-contained and may be studied at the same time as the material that you are now studying in this chapter.

of car washes each hour varies as the amount of labour employed varies. The third column shows the *marginal product of labour* – the change in output resulting from a one-unit increase in labour input.

Wendy's market constraint is the demand curve for her good. If, in the goods market, a firm is a monopoly or engaged in monopolistic competition or oligopoly, it faces a downward-sloping demand curve for its good. If a firm is perfectly competitive, it faces a fixed price for its good regardless of its output level and therefore faces a horizontal demand curve for its good. We will assume that Wendy operates the car wash in a perfectly competitive market and can sell as many washes as she chooses at a constant price of £4 a wash. Given this information, we can calculate Wendy's total revenue (fourth column) by multiplying the number of cars washed per hour by £4. For example, if 9 cars are washed each hour (row *c*), total revenue is £36.

The fifth column shows the calculation of marginal revenue product of labour – the change in total revenue per unit change in labour input. For example, if Wendy hires a second worker (row *c*), total revenue increases from £20 to £36, so marginal revenue product is £16. There is an alternative way of calculating the marginal revenue product of labour – multiply marginal product by marginal revenue. To see that this method gives the same answer, multiply the marginal product of hiring a second worker – 4 cars an hour – by marginal revenue – £4 a car – and notice that the answer is the same (£16).

Total revenue divided by the quantity of the factor hired is called the **average revenue product** of the factor. Thus average revenue product is the average contribution of each unit of an input to the firm's total revenue. The last column of Table 14.1 shows the average revenue product of labour. For example, when Wendy employs 3 workers (row *d*), total revenue is £48. Thus the average revenue product of labour is £48 divided by 3 workers, which

TABLE 14.1

Marginal Revenue Product and Average Revenue Product at Wendy's Wash 'n' Wax

Quantity of labour (L) (workers)	Output (Q) (cars washed per hour)	Marginal product (MP = ΔQ/ΔL) (washes per worker)	Total revenue (TR = P × Q) (pounds)	Marginal revenue product (MR = ΔTR/ΔL) (pounds per worker)	Average revenue product (ARP = TR/L) (pounds per worker)
a 0	0		0		
		 5		 20	
b 1	5		20		20
		 4		 16	
c 2	9		36		18
		 3		 12	
d 3	12		48		16
		 2		 8	
e 4	14		56		14
		 1		 4	
f 5	15		60		12

The marginal revenue product of labour is the change in total revenue that results from a one-unit increase in labour input. To calculate marginal revenue product, first work out total revenue. If Wendy hires 1 worker (row *b*), output is 5 washes an hour, and total revenue, at £4 a wash, is £20. If she hires 2 workers (row *c*), output is 9 washes an hour, and total revenue is £36.

By hiring the second worker, total revenue rises by £16 – the marginal revenue product of labour is £16. The average revenue product of labour is total revenue per unit of labour employed. For example, when Wendy employs 2 workers, total revenue is £36, and average revenue product is £18 (£36 divided by 2).

is £16 per worker.

Notice that as the quantity of labour rises, the marginal revenue product of labour falls. When Wendy hires the first worker, the marginal revenue product of labour is £20. If Wendy hires a second worker, the marginal revenue product of labour is £16. Marginal revenue product of labour continues to decline as Wendy hires more workers.

Marginal revenue product diminishes as Wendy hires more workers because of the principle of diminishing returns that we first studied in Chapter 10. With each additional worker hired, the marginal product of labour falls and so brings in a smaller marginal revenue product. Because Wendy's Wash 'n' Wax is a perfectly competitive firm, the price of each additional car wash is the same and brings in the same marginal revenue. If instead Wendy had a monopoly, she would have to lower her price to sell more washes. In such a case, the marginal revenue product of labour diminishes even more quickly than in perfectly competitive conditions. Marginal revenue product diminishes because of diminishing marginal product of labour and also because of diminishing marginal revenue. Table 14.2 provides a compact glossary of factor market terms.

We can illustrate the average revenue product and marginal revenue product of labour as curves. The **average revenue product curve** shows the average revenue product of a factor at each quantity of the factor hired. The **marginal revenue product curve** shows the marginal revenue product of a factor at each quantity of the factor hired.

Figure 14.4(a) shows the marginal revenue product and average revenue product curves for workers employed by Wendy. The horizontal axis measures the number of workers that Wendy hires and the vertical axis measures the average and marginal revenue product of labour. The curve *ARP* is the average revenue product curve and is based on the numbers in Table 14.1. For example, point *d* on the *ARP* curve represents row *d* in the table. Wendy employs 3 workers and the average revenue product of labour is £16 a worker. The blue bars show the marginal revenue product of labour as Wendy employs more workers. These bars correspond to the numbers in Table 14.1. The curve *MRP* is the marginal revenue product curve.

The firm's demand for labour curve is based on its marginal revenue product curve. You can see Wendy's demand for labour curve (*D*) in Fig. 14.4(b). The horizontal axis measures the number of workers

TABLE 14.2

A Compact Glossary of Factor Market Terms

Factors of production	Labour, capital and land (including raw materials)
Factor prices	Wages – price of labour; interest – price of capital; rent – price of land
Marginal product	Output produced by last unit of input hired; for example, the marginal product of labour is additional output produced by employing one more person
Average product	Output per unit of input; for example, average product of labour is output divided by labour input
Marginal revenue	Revenue resulting from selling one additional unit of output
Marginal revenue product	Revenue resulting from hiring one additional unit of factor of production; for example, marginal revenue product of labour is the additional revenue resulting from selling the output produced by employing one more person
Average revenue product	Total revenue per unit of input; calculated as total revenue divided by labour input

hired – the same as part (a). The vertical axis measures the wage rate in pounds per hour. The demand for labour curve is exactly the same as the firm's marginal revenue product curve. For example, when Wendy employs 3 workers an hour, her marginal revenue product is £10 an hour, as in Fig. 14.4(a); and at a wage rate of £10 an hour, Wendy hires 3 workers an hour, as in Fig. 14.4(b).

But why is the demand for labour curve identical to the marginal revenue product curve? Because the firm hires the profit-maximizing quantity of labour. If the cost of hiring one more worker – the wage rate – is less than the additional revenue that worker will bring in – the marginal revenue product of labour – then it pays the firm to employ one more worker. Conversely, if the cost of hiring one more worker is greater than the additional revenue

FIGURE 14.4

Marginal Revenue Product and the Demand for Labour at Wendy's Wash 'n' Wax

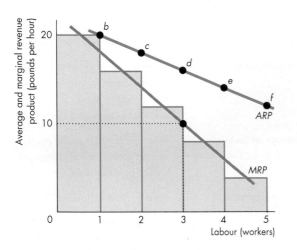

(a) Average and marginal revenue product

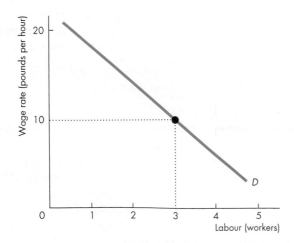

Part (a) shows the average and marginal revenue product curves for Wendy's Wash 'n' Wax. Points *b* to *f* on the average revenue curve correspond to the rows of Table 14.1. The blue bars representing marginal revenue product are also based on the numbers in that table. (Each point is plotted midway between the labour points used in its calculation.) Average revenue product and marginal revenue product decline and the marginal revenue product curve is always below the average revenue product curve. Part (b) shows Wendy's demand for labour curve. It is identical to her marginal revenue product curve. Wendy demands labour up to the point at which the wage rate (the worker's marginal cost) equals marginal revenue product.

that worker will bring in – the wage rate exceeds the marginal revenue product – then it does not pay the firm to employ one more worker. When the cost of the last worker hired equals the revenue brought in by that worker, the firm is making the maximum possible profit. Such a situation occurs when the wage rate equals the marginal revenue product. Thus the quantity of labour demanded by the firm is such that the wage rate equals the marginal revenue product of labour.

REVIEW

A firm chooses the quantity of labour to hire so that its profit is maximized. The additional total revenue generated by hiring one additional worker is called the marginal revenue product of labour. It is the change in total revenue generated by a one-unit change in labour input. In a competitive industry, the marginal cost of labour is the wage rate. Profit is maximized when the marginal revenue product of labour equals the wage rate. The marginal revenue product of labour curve is the firm's demand for labour curve. The lower the wage rate, the higher is the quantity of labour demanded. ◆

Two Conditions for Profit Maximization When we studied firms' output decisions, we discovered that a condition for maximum profit is that marginal revenue equals marginal cost. We've now discovered another condition for maximum profit – marginal revenue product of a factor equals the factor's price. How can there be two conditions for a maximum profit? It is because they are equivalent to each other. When marginal revenue equals marginal cost, the marginal revenue product of a factor equals the factor's price. The equivalence of these two conditions is set out in Table 14.3.

We have just derived the law of demand as it applies to the labour market. And we've discovered that the same principles that apply to the demand for goods and services apply here as well. The demand for labour curve slopes downward. Other things remaining the same, the lower the wage rate

TABLE 14.3

Two Conditions for
Maximum Profit

SYMBOLS

Marginal product	**MP**
Marginal revenue	**MR**
Marginal cost	**MC**
Marginal revenue product	**MRP**
Factor price	**PF**

TWO CONDITIONS FOR MAXIMUM PROFIT

1.   **MR = MC**   2.   **MRP = PF**

EQUIVALENCE OF CONDITIONS

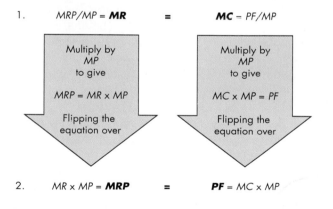

1.   MRP/MP = **MR**   =   **MC** – PF/MP

Multiply by MP to give

MRP = MR × MP   MC × MP = PF

Flipping the equation over

2.   MR × MP = **MRP**   =   **PF** = MC × MP

Marginal revenue product (*MR*) equals marginal cost (*MC*), and marginal revenue product (*MRP*) equals the price of the factor (*PF*). The two conditions for maximum profit are equivalent because marginal revenue product (*MRP*) equals marginal revenue (*MR*) multiplied by marginal product (*MP*), and the factor price (*PF*) equals marginal cost (*MC*) multiplied by marginal product (*MP*).

(the price of labour) the greater is the quantity of labour demanded. Let's now study the influences that result in a change in the demand for labour and, therefore, in a shift in the demand for labour curve.

Shifts in the Firm's Demand for Labour Curve   The position of the demand for labour curve depends on three factors:

◆ The price of the firm's output
◆ The prices of other inputs
◆ Technology

The higher the price of a firm's output, the greater is the quantity of labour demanded by the firm, other things remaining the same. The price of output affects the demand for labour through its influence on marginal revenue product. A higher price for the firm's output increases marginal revenue which, in turn, increases the marginal revenue product of labour. A change in the price of a firm's output leads to a shift in the firm's demand for labour curve. If the output price increases, the demand for labour increases – the demand for labour curve shifts to the right.

The other two influences on the demand for labour have their main effects not in the short run but in the long run. The **short-run demand for labour** is the relationship between the wage rate and the quantity of labour demanded when the firm's capital is fixed and labour is the only variable input. The **long-run demand for labour** is the relationship between the wage rate and the quantity of labour demanded when all inputs can be varied. A change in the relative price of inputs – such as the relative price of labour and capital – leads to a substitution away from the input whose relative price has increased and towards the input whose relative price has decreased. Thus if the price of using capital decreases relative to that of using labour, the firm substitutes capital for labour, increasing the quantity of capital demanded and decreasing its demand for labour.

Finally, a technological change that influences the marginal product of labour also affects the demand for labour. For example, the development of electronic telephones with memories and a host of clever features decreased the marginal product of and the demand for telephone operators. At the same time, it increased the marginal product of and the demand for telephone engineers trained in the installation and maintenance of the new telephones. Again, these effects are felt in the long run when the firm adjusts all its inputs and incorporates new technologies into its production process. Table 14.4 summarizes the influences on a firm's demand for labour.

As we saw earlier, Fig. 14.2 illustrates the effects

TABLE 14.4

A Firm's Demand for Labour

THE LAW OF DEMAND

The quantity of labour demanded by a firm

Decreases if: | *Increases if:*

◆ **The wage rate increases** | ◆ **The wage rate decreases**

CHANGES IN DEMAND

A firm's demand for labour

Decreases if: | *Increases if:*

◆ **The firm's output price decreases** | ◆ **The firm's output price increases**

◆ **The prices of other inputs decrease** | ◆ **The prices of other inputs increase**

◆ **A technological change decreases the marginal product of labour** | ◆ **A technological change increases the marginal product of labour**

of a change in the demand for a factor. If that factor is labour, then Fig. 14.2 shows the effects of a change in the demand for labour on the wage rate and the quantity of labour hired. But we can now say why the demand for labour curve shifts. For example, an increase in the price of the firm's output, an increase in the price of capital, or a technological change that increases the marginal product of labour shifts the demand for labour curve from D_0 to D_1 in Fig. 14.2. Conversely, a decrease in the price of the firm's output, a decrease in the price of capital, or a technological change that lowers the marginal product of labour shifts the demand curve for labour from D_0 to D_2 in Fig. 14.2(b).

Market Demand

So far, we've studied only the demand for labour by an individual firm. Let's now look at the market demand. The market demand for a factor of production is the total demand for that factor by all firms. The market demand curve for a given factor is

obtained by adding up the quantities demanded of that factor by each firm at each given factor price. Thus the concept of the market demand for labour curve is exactly like the concept of the market demand curve for a good or service. The market demand curve for a good or service is obtained by adding together the quantities demanded of that good or service by all households at each price. The market demand curve for labour is obtained by adding together the quantities of labour demanded by all firms at each wage rate.

Elasticity of Demand for Labour

The elasticity of demand for labour measures the responsiveness of the quantity of labour demanded to the wage rate. We calculate this elasticity in the same way that we calculate a price elasticity: the elasticity of demand for labour equals the percentage change in the quantity of labour demanded divided by the percentage change in the wage rate. The elasticity of demand for labour depends on the elasticity of demand for the good that the firm is producing and on the properties of the firm's total product curve – on how rapidly the marginal product of labour diminishes. There is, however, a slight difference in the things that affect the elasticity of demand for labour in the short run and in the long run.

Short-Run Elasticity The **short-run elasticity of demand for labour** is the magnitude of the percentage change in the quantity of labour demanded divided by the percentage change in the wage rate when labour is the only variable input. The short-run elasticity of demand for labour depends on three things:

1. *Labour intensity.* The larger the labour component total cost – the more labour intensive the production process – the more elastic is the demand for labour. Compare a barber with an airline pilot. A barber's wages are about 80 per cent of the cost of producing a haircut. So a 10 per cent change in a barber's wages generates an 8 per cent change in the cost of a haircut. But airline pilots' wages are about 5 per cent of the cost of producing an aeroplane trip. So a 10 per cent change in the wage of a pilot generates only an 0.5 per cent change in the cost of a trip. If the price of a haircut increases by 9 per cent, other

things remaining the same, people economize on haircuts and the number of barbers demanded falls. If airfares increase by 0.5 per cent, there is almost no change in the quantity of trips demanded and the number of airline pilots demanded barely changes. So, other things being equal, the greater the degree of labour intensity, the more elastic is the demand for labour.

2. *The slope of the marginal product of labour curve.* The slope of the marginal product of labour curve depends on the production technology. In some activities marginal product diminishes quickly. For example, the marginal product of one bus driver is high, but the marginal product of a second driver on the same bus is close to zero. In other activities marginal product is fairly constant. For example, hiring a second window cleaner on a team almost doubles the amount of glass that can be cleaned in an hour – the marginal product of the second window cleaner is almost the same as the first. The steeper the slope of the marginal product curve, the more responsive is marginal revenue product to a change in labour input and the less responsive is the quantity of labour demanded to a change in the wage rate – the less elastic is the firm's demand for labour.

3. *The short-run elasticity of demand for the good.* This effect is a more complicated one. If a wage rate changes, so does the marginal cost and supply of the good produced by the labour whose wage has changed. A change in supply changes the price of the good and changes the quantity of the good demanded. The greater the elasticity of demand for the good, the larger is the change in the quantity demanded of both the good and the labour used to produce it.

Long-run Elasticity The **long-run elasticity of demand for labour** is the magnitude of the percentage change in the quantity of labour demanded divided by the percentage change in the wage rate when all inputs are varied. The long-run elasticity of demand for labour depends on *labour intensity* and on the long-run elasticity of demand for the product. In addition, it depends on the *substitutability of capital for labour*. The more easily capital can be substituted for labour in production, the more elastic is the long-run demand for labour. For example, it is fairly easy to substitute robots for assembly-line workers in car factories and automatic picking machines for labour in vineyards and orchards. At the other extreme, it is difficult (though not impossible) to substitute robots for newspaper reporters, bank loan officers and stockbrokers. The more readily capital can be substituted for labour, the more elastic is the firm's demand for labour in the long run.

REVIEW

The short-run elasticity of demand for labour depends on three factors:

- Labour intensity of the production process
- The slope of the marginal product of labour curve
- The short-run elasticity of demand for the product

The long-run elasticity of demand for labour also depends on three factors:

- Labour intensity of the production process
- Substitutability of capital for labour
- The long-run elasticity of demand for the product ◆

Supply of Factors

The supply of factors is determined by the decisions of households. Households allocate the factors of production that they own to their most rewarding uses. The quantity supplied of any factor of production depends on its price. Usually, the higher the price of a factor of production, the larger is the quantity supplied. There is an important possible exception to this general law of supply concerning the supply of labour. It arises from the fact that labour is the single most important factor of production and the source of the largest portion of household income.

Let's examine household factor supply decisions, beginning with the supply of labour.

Supply of Labour

A household chooses how much labour to supply as part of its time allocation decision. Time is allocated between two broad activities:

◆ Market activity
◆ Non-market activity

Market activity is the same thing as supplying labour. **Non-market activity** consists of leisure and non-market production activities including education and training. The household obtains an immediate return from market activities in the form of an income. Non-market activities generate a return in the form of goods and services produced in the home, in the form of a higher future income, or in the form of leisure, which is valued for its own sake and which is classified as a good.

In deciding how to allocate its time between market activity and non-market activity, a household weighs the returns that it can get from the different activities. We are interested in the effects of the wage rate on the household's allocation of its time and on how much labour it supplies.

Wages and Quantity of Labour Supplied   To induce a household to supply labour, it must be offered a high enough wage rate. Non-market activities are valued by households either because the time is used in some productive activity or because of the value they attach to leisure. In order for it to be worthwhile to supply labour, a household has to be offered a wage rate that is at least equal to the value it places on the last hour it spends in non-market activities. This wage rate – the lowest one for which a household will supply labour to the market – is called its **reservation wage**. At wage rates below the reservation wage, the household supplies no labour. Once the wage rate reaches the reservation wage, the household begins to supply labour. As the wage rate rises above the reservation wage, the household varies the quantity of labour that it supplies. But a higher wage rate has two offsetting effects on the quantity of labour supplied – a *substitution effect* and an *income effect*.

Substitution Effect   Other things remaining the same, the higher the wage rate, the more will people economize on their non-market activities and increase the time they spend working. As the wage rate rises, the household will discontinue any non-market

activity that yields a return that is less than the wage rate; instead, the household will switch to market activity. For example, a household might use some of its time to cook meals and do laundry – non-market activities – that can, alternatively, be bought for £5 an hour. If the wage rate available to the household is less than £5 an hour, the household will cook and wash for itself. If the household's wage rate rises above £5 an hour, it will be worthwhile for the household to work more hours and use part of its income (£10) to buy laundry services and to eat out. The higher wage rate induces a switch of time from non-market activities to market activities.

Income Effect   The higher the household's wage rate, the higher is its income. A higher income, other things remaining the same, induces a rise in demand for most goods. Leisure, a component of non-market activity, is one of those goods. Since an increase in income creates an increase in the demand for leisure, it also creates a decrease in the amount of time allocated to market activities and, therefore, to a fall in the quantity of labour supplied.

Backward-bending Household Supply of Labour Curve
The substitution effect and the income effect work in opposite directions. The higher the wage rate, the higher is the quantity of labour supplied via the substitution effect, but the lower is the quantity of labour supplied via the income effect. At low wage rates, the substitution effect is larger than the income effect. As the wage rate rises, the household supplies more labour. But as the wage rate continues to rise, there comes a point at which the substitution effect and the income effect just offset each other. At that point, a change in the wage rate has no effect on the quantity of labour supplied. If the wage rate continues to rise, the income effect begins to dominate the substitution effect and the quantity of labour supplied declines. The household's supply of labour curve does not slope upward throughout its entire length but begins to bend back on itself. It is called a backward-bending supply curve.

Three individual household labour supply curves are shown in Fig. 14.5(a). Each household has a different reservation wage. Household *A* has a reservation wage of £1 an hour, household *B* of £4 an hour, and household *C* of £7 an hour. Each household's labour supply curve is backward bending.

FIGURE 14.5

The Supply of Labour

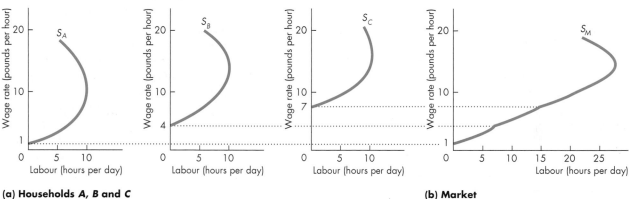

(a) Households A, B and C

(b) Market

Part (a) shows the labour supply curves of three households (S_A, S_B, and S_C). Each household has a reservation wage below which it will supply no labour. As the wage rises above the reservation wage, the quantity of labour supplied rises to a maximum. If the wage continues to rise, the quantity of labour supplied begins to decline. Each household's supply curve eventually bends backward. When the quantity of labour supplied increases as the wage increases, the substitution effect dominates the income effect. When the quantity of labour supplied begins to fall as the wage rate increases, the income effect (which leads people to demand more leisure) dominates the

substitution effect.

Part (b) shows how, by adding together the quantities of labour supplied by the individual households at each wage rate, we derive the market supply curve of labour (S_M). The market supply curve also eventually bends backward, but in the real world at a higher wage rate than that currently experienced. The upward-sloping part of the labour supply curve before it bends backward is the part along which the market operates.

Market Supply The quantity of labour supplied to the entire market is the total quantity supplied by all households. The market supply of labour curve is the sum of the supply curves of all the individual households. Figure 14.5(b) shows the market supply curve (S_M) derived from the supply curves of the three households (S_A, S_B, and S_C) in Fig. 14.5(a). At wage rates of less than $1 an hour, the three households do laundry and cook, but they do not supply any market labour. The household most eager to supply market labour has a reservation wage of $1 an hour. As the wage rate rises to $4 an hour, household A increases the quantity of labour that it supplies to the market. The reservation wage of household B is $4 an hour, so as the wage rate rises above $4 an hour, the quantity of labour supplied in the market is the sum of the labour supplied by households A and B. When the wage rate reaches $7 an hour, household C begins to supply some labour to the market. At wage rates above $7 an hour, the quantity supplied in the market is equal to the sum of the quantities supplied by the three households.

Notice that the market supply curve S_M, like the individual household supply curves, eventually bends backward. But the market supply curve has a long upward-sloping section. The reason why the market supply curve slopes up for such a long stretch is that the reservation wages of individual households are not equal and at higher wage rates additional households are confronted with their reservation wage and so begin to supply labour.

Although the market supply curve eventually bends backward, no real-world wage rate is so high that the economy operates on the backward-bending portion of its labour supply curve. But many individual households are on the backward-bending portion of their own labour supply curve. Thus as wage rates rise, some people work fewer hours. But higher wage rates induce those workers who are on the upward-sloping part of their labour supply curve to supply more hours and induce additional workers to enter the work force. The response of these workers to higher wage rates dominates that of those whose work hours decline as wage rates rise.

Therefore, for the economy as a whole, the labour supply curve slopes upward. For this reason, we will restrict our attention to the upward-sloping part of the labour supply curve in Fig. 14.5.

Supply to Individual Firms   We've studied the labour supply decisions of individual households and seen how those decisions add up to the total market supply. But how is the supply of labour to each individual firm determined? The answer to this question depends on the degree of competitiveness in the labour market. In a perfectly competitive labour market, each firm faces a perfectly elastic supply of labour curve. This situation arises because the individual firm is such a small part of the total labour market that it has no influence on the wage rate.

Some labour markets are non-competitive in the sense that firms can and do influence the price of the labour that they hire. In these cases, firms face an upward-sloping supply of labour curve. The more labour they wish to employ, the higher is the wage rate they have to offer. We examine how this type of labour market operates in Chapter 15. Here, we deal only with the case of perfectly competitive input markets.

REVIEW

At real wage rates above the household's reservation wage, the household supplies labour to the market. An increase in the wage has two opposing effects on the quantity of labour supplied: a substitution effect (higher wage, more work) and an income effect (higher wage, less work). At low real wages, the substitution effect is the more powerful and the labour supply curve slopes upward. At high real wages, the income effect is the more powerful and the labour supply curve bends backward. The market supply of labour curve is the sum of the supply curves of individual households. Actual economies operate on the upward-sloping part of the market supply of labour curve. The supply of labour curve faced by each individual firm depends on the degree of competitiveness of the labour market. In a perfectly competitive labour market, each firm faces a perfectly elastic supply curve.

Supply of Capital

Capital – the physical plant, buildings and equipment used in production – is purchased by firms using funds borrowed from households. These funds are channelled through a complex network of financial institutions (banks, insurance companies and others) and financial markets (bond and stock markets). But the amount of capital that firms can buy depends on the amount of saving that households undertake. For, ultimately, households supply capital to firms by consuming less than their income. Thus the scale on which a household supplies capital depends on how much of its income it saves.

The most important factors determining a household's saving are:

◆ Its current income in relation to its expected future income
◆ The interest rate

Current and Future Income   A household with a current income that is low compared with its expected future income saves little and might even have negative saving. A household with a current income that is high compared with its expected future income saves a great deal in the present in order to be able to consume more in the future. The stage in the household's life cycle is the main factor influencing whether current income is high or low compared with expected future income. Young households typically have a low current income compared with their expected future income, while older households have a high current income relative to their expected future income. The consequence of this pattern in income over the life cycle is that young people have negative saving and older people have positive saving. Thus young people incur debts (such as mortgages and consumer credit) to acquire durable goods and to consume more than their income, while older people save and accumulate assets (often in the form of pension and life insurance arrangements) to provide for their later retirement years.

Interest Rate and Capital Supply Curve   A household's supply of capital is the stock of capital that it has accumulated as a result of its past saving. The household's supply curve of capital shows the relationship between the quantity of capital supplied and the interest rate. Other things being equal, a higher interest rate encourages people to economize on current consumption in order to take advantage of the higher return available from saving. Thus the higher the interest rate, the greater is the quantity of capital supplied.

Market Supply The market supply of capital is the sum of the supplies of all the individual households. The market supply curve of capital shows how the quantity of capital supplied varies as the interest rate varies. In the short run, the supply of capital is inelastic and might even be perfectly inelastic. Such a case is illustrated in Fig. 14.6 as the vertical supply curve *SS*. The long-run supply of capital is elastic. Such a case is illustrated in Fig. 14.6 by the supply curve *LS*.

Supply to Individual Firms In the short run a firm can vary its labour input but not its capital. Thus in the short run, the firm's supply of capital is fixed. It has a specific set of capital assets. For example, a car producer has a production assembly line; a launderette operator has a number of washing machines and dryers; the High Street print shop has a number of photocopying and other printing machines. These pieces of capital cannot be quickly disposed of or added to.

In the long run a firm can vary all its inputs – capital as well as labour. A firm operating in a competitive capital market can obtain any amount of capital it chooses at the going market interest rate. Thus it faces a perfectly elastic supply of capital.

The fact that the short-run supply of capital is inelastic and the long-run supply is elastic has important implications for the returns obtained from different types of capital. We'll explore those implications later in this chapter when we study equilibrium in the capital market. But before that, let's complete our analysis of the supply of factors of production by examining the supply of land.

Supply of Land

Land is the stock of natural resources and its aggregate quantity supplied cannot be changed by any individual decisions. Individual households can vary the amount of land they own, but whatever land is acquired by one household is sold by another so that the aggregate quantity of land supplied of any particular type and in any particular location is fixed regardless of the decisions of any individual household. This fact means that the supply of each particular piece of land is perfectly inelastic. Figure 14.7 illustrates such a supply. Regardless of

FIGURE 14.6

Short-run and Long-run Supply of Capital

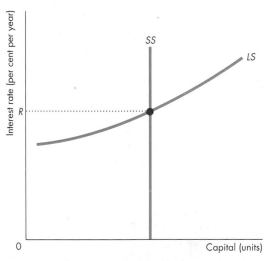

The long-run supply of capital (*LS*) is highly elastic. If the interest rate is above *R*, households increase their saving and increase the total amount of capital supplied. If the interest rate is below *R*, households decrease their saving and reduce the amount of capital supplied. The short-run supply of capital (*SS*) is highly inelastic (perfectly inelastic in the figure). For the economy as a whole and for individual firms in the short run, once capital is put in place, it is difficult to vary its quantity easily and quickly. Thus no matter what the interest rate, at a given point in time there is a given amount of capital supplied.

the rent available, the quantity of land supplied in London's West End is a fixed number of square metres.

Expensive land can be, and is, used more intensively than inexpensive land. For example, high-rise buildings enable land to be used more intensively. However, to use land more intensively, it has to be combined with another factor of production – capital. Increasing the amount of capital per block of land does nothing to change the supply of land itself.

Although the supply of each type of land is fixed and its supply is inelastic, each individual firm, operating in competitive land markets, faces an elastic supply of land. That is, each firm can acquire the land that it demands at the going rent, as determined in the marketplace. Thus provided land markets are highly competitive, firms are price takers in these

FIGURE 14.7

The Supply of Land

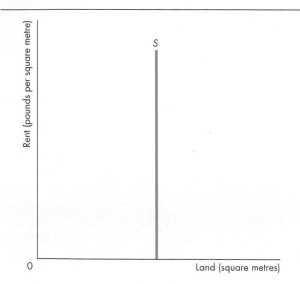

The supply of a given piece of land is perfectly inelastic. No matter what the rent, no more land than exists can be supplied.

markets, just as they are in the markets for other factors of production.

REVIEW

The supply of capital is determined by households' saving decisions. Other things remaining the same, the higher the interest rate, the greater is the amount of capital supplied. The supply of capital to individual firms is highly inelastic in the short run but elastic in the long run. ◆◆ Individual households can vary the amount of land that they supply but the aggregate supply of land is determined by the fact that there is a given, fixed quantity of it available. Thus the supply of each particular piece of land is perfectly inelastic. In a competitive land market, each firm faces an elastic supply of land at the going rent. ◆

Let's now see how factor prices and quantities are determined.

Competitive Equilibrium

The price of a factor of production and the quantity of it used are determined by the interaction of the demand for the factor and its supply. We'll illustrate competitive equilibrium by looking at the markets for labour, capital and land and by looking at two examples of each.

Labour Market Equilibrium

Figure 14.8 shows two labour markets. That in part (a) is the labour market for footballers. Such people have a very high marginal revenue product and this is reflected in the demand curve for their services, curve D_F. The supply of individuals with the required talents for this kind of job is low, and this fact is reflected in the supply curve S_F. Equilibrium occurs at a high wage rate (£4,000 per game in this example) and a low quantity employed, Q_F.

Figure 14.8(b) shows another market, that for fast-food servers. Although people value the output of fast-food servers, the marginal revenue product of their services is low, a fact reflected in demand curve D_S. There are many households, typically those with school and college students, willing to supply these services and the supply curve is S_S. This market achieves an equilibrium at a low wage rate (£2 an hour in this example) and at a relatively high quantity employed, Q_S.

If there is an increase in the demand for footballers, the demand curve D_F in Fig. 14.8(a) shifts to the right, increasing their wage rate and increasing the quantity employed. The higher wage rate will induce more people to offer their services in this activity. If there is an increase in demand for fast-food servers, the demand curve D_S in Fig. 14.8(b) shifts to the right, increasing their wage rate and increasing the quantity employed. Again, a higher wage rate will induce an increase in the quantity supplied. Movements in wage rates occur to achieve a balance between the quantities demanded and supplied in each individual labour market. Changes in demand result in changes in the wage rate that achieve a reallocation of the labour force.

Capital Market Equilibrium

Figure 14.9 shows capital market equilibrium. In Fig. 14.9(a), we illustrate the part of the capital market in

FIGURE 14.8

Labour Market Equilibrium

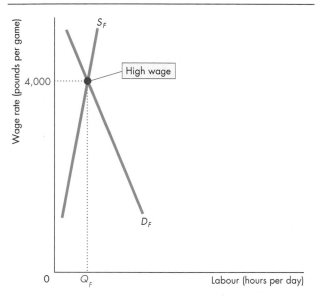

(a) Footballers

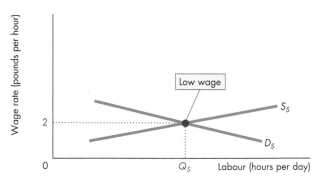

(b) Fast-food servers

Footballers (part a) have a high marginal revenue product, which is reflected in the high demand for their services – curve D_F. The number of people with the talents required for this job is few and the supply curve is S_F. Equilibrium occurs at a high wage rate of £4,000 per game and a low quantity employed, Q_F. The marginal revenue product of fast-food servers (part b) is low, so the demand curve is D_S. There is a huge supply of fast-food servers and the supply curve is S_S. Equilibrium occurs in this market at a low wage rate of £2 an hour and a high quantity employed, Q_S.

the steel industry – the market for steel mills. The long-run supply of capital to the steel industry is shown as the perfectly elastic supply curve LS. But the actual quantity of steel mills in place is Q_1, and the short-run supply curve is SS_1. The demand curve for steel mills, determined by their marginal revenue product, is D_1. The interest rate earned by the owners of steel mills – the shareholders in British Steel and similar firms – is R_1.

Figure 14.9(b) shows the part of the capital market in the computer industry. Again, the long-run supply curve is LS, the same curve as in the steel industry. That is, in the long run, capital is supplied to each of these industries at an interest rate R. But the amount of computer-producing capital in place is Q_3, and the short-run supply curve is SS_3 in part (b). The demand curve for computer-producing capital, determined by its marginal revenue product, is D_2. The interest rate earned by the owners of computer-producing equipment – the shareholders of Acorn, Amstrad, Apple and similar firms – is R_2.

You can see that the interest rate paid to owners of capital in the steel industry is less than that paid to owners of capital in the computer industry. This inequality of interest rates sets up a dynamic adjustment process that gradually lowers the stock of capital in the steel industry and increases the stock of capital in the computer industry. With a low interest rate on capital in the steel industry and a high interest rate on capital in the computer industry, people will reduce their investment in the steel industry and increase their investment in the computer industry. But physical plant and equipment have been built for the steel industry and cannot be readily transformed into computer-making equipment. An individual steel producer could sell off its unwanted capital or operate it until it has worn out. Even if it does sell off the equipment, the firm that buys it will pay only a low price for it and then will not replace it when it is worn out. Whether the capital is operated by its present owner or a new owner that buys it for a low price, the equipment continues to be operated. But it gradually wears out and is not replaced, so the capital stock in the steel industry declines. The short-run supply curve shifts to the left, to SS_2. Conversely, as capital is freed up and additional saving is made, it is directed towards the computer industry, so that its short-run supply curve shifts to the right, to SS_4. During this process, interest rates adjust in the two industries, increasing in the steel industry and decreasing in the computer industry.

FIGURE 14.9

Capital Market Equilibrium

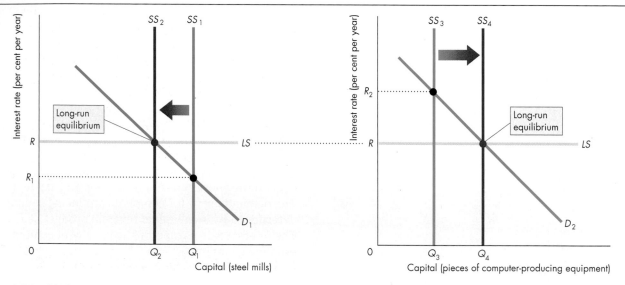

(a) Steel industry

(b) Computer industry

The long-run supply curve of capital (*LS*) in the steel industry (part a) and the computer industry (part b) is perfectly inelastic. The number of steel mills in place is fixed at Q_1, so the short-run supply curve in the steel industry is SS_1. The demand curve for steel mills is D_1. The interest rate on capital invested in steel is R_1. The amount of computer-producing equipment is fixed at Q_3, so the short-run supply curve in the computer industry is SS_3. The demand curve for computer-producing equipment is D_2. The interest rate in the computer industry

is R_2. With a higher interest rate in the computer industry, capital leaves the steel industry and goes into the computer industry. The short-run supply curves shift. In the steel industry, the short-run supply curve shifts to the left, to SS_2, and the interest rate rises. In the computer industry, the short-run supply curve shifts to the right, to SS_4, and the interest rate falls. In long-run equilibrium, interest rates are the same in both industries.

Eventually, in long-run equilibrium, the interest rate on capital in the two industries will have equalized at R.

The Stock Market In the story of a contracting steel industry and expanding computer industry that we have just worked through, you may be wondering why people are willing to own shares in the steel industry when the rate of return on steel mills is below that on computer-producing equipment. The answer is that the stock market reacts by lowering the value of steel shares relative to computer shares. The fall in the price of steel shares increases the expected interest rate that can be earned on steel shares to equal that on computer shares. That is, during the period in which the steel industry is declining and its capital stock is decreasing, the stock market lowers the value of the steel industry to equalize the expected return on shares in that industry and in all other industries.

Reading Between the Lines on pp. 398–399 looks at how government policy can affect the stock market.

Next, let's see how rents are determined in the market for land.

Land Market Equilibrium

Equilibrium in the land market occurs at rents that allocate the fixed amounts of land available to their highest value uses. Figure 14.10 illustrates two land markets. Part (a) shows the market for land in London's West End. Its marginal revenue product gives rise to the demand curve D_L. There are a fixed number of square metres of land, Q_L, so the supply of land is inelastic, as shown by the curve S_L. Equilibrium occurs at a rent of £2,000 a square metre a year.

Figure 14.10(b) illustrates the market for farmland in Scotland. Here, the marginal revenue

FIGURE 14.10

Land Market Equilibrium

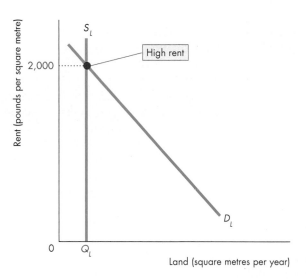

(a) London's West End

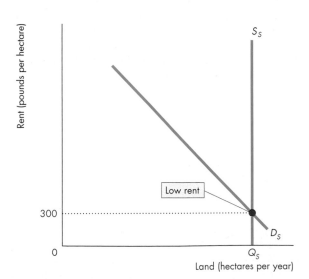

(b) Scottish farmland

The marginal revenue product of land in London's West End gives rise to the demand curve D_L (part a). The quantity of land in the West End is fixed at Q_L so the supply curve is S_L. Equilibrium occurs at an annual rent of £2,000 a square metre. The marginal revenue product of farmland in Scotland (part b) gives rise to a demand curve D_S. The quantity of farmland in Scotland is fixed at Q_S and the supply curve is S_S. Equilibrium occurs at an annual rent of £300 a hectare.

product produces the demand curve D_S. There is a lot of land available but again, only a fixed quantity – in this case, Q_S. Thus the supply curve lies a long way to the right but is vertical – perfectly inelastic – at S_S. Here the equilibrium rent occurs at £300 a hectare a year. The explanation of land rents given here can be extended to the rents and prices of all natural resources, and a discussion of some of these broader issues can be found in Our Advancing Knowledge on pp. 394–395.

We've now studied the markets for the three factors of production and seen how wages, interest and rent are determined. Our final task in this chapter is to define and distinguish between economic rent and transfer earnings.

Economic Rent and Transfer Earnings

The total income of a factor of production is made up of its economic rent and its transfer earnings. **Economic rent** is an income received by the owner of a factor over and above the amount required to induce that owner to offer the factor for use. The income required to induce the supply of a factor of production is called **transfer earnings**.

Figure 14.11 illustrates the concepts of economic rent and transfer earnings. The figure shows the market for a factor of production. It could be *any* factor of production – labour, capital or land. The demand curve for the factor of production is D and its supply curve is S. The factor price is PF and the quantity of the factor used is QF. The income of the factor is the sum of the yellow and green areas. The yellow area below the supply curve measures transfer earnings and the green area below the factor price but above the supply curve measures economic rent.

To see why the area below the supply curve measures transfer earnings, recall that a supply curve can be interpreted in two different ways. The standard interpretation is that a supply curve indicates the quantity supplied at a given price. But the alternative interpretation of a supply curve is that it shows the minimum price at which a given quantity is willingly supplied. If suppliers receive only the minimum

Running Out of Space?

Is there a limit to economic growth, or can we expand production and population without effective limit? One of the most influential answers to these questions was given by Thomas Malthus in 1798. He reasoned that population, unchecked, would grow at a geometric rate – 1, 2, 4, 8, 16 ... – while the food supply would grow at an arithmetic rate – 1, 2, 3, 4, 5 .... To prevent the population from outstripping the available food supply, there would be periodic wars, famines and plagues. In Malthus's view, only 'moral restraint' could prevent such periodic disasters.

> 'Men, like all animals, naturally multiply in proportion to the means of their subsistence.'
>
> ADAM SMITH
> *The Wealth of Nations*

As industrialization proceeded through the nineteenth century, Malthus's idea came to be applied to all natural resources, especially those that are exhaustible. A modern day Malthusian, ecologist Paul Ehrlich, believes that we are sitting on a 'population bomb' and that the government must limit both population growth and the resources that may be used each year.

In 1931, Harold Hotelling developed a theory of natural resources with different predictions from those of Malthus. The Hotelling Principle is that the relative price of an exhaustible natural resource will rise steadily, bringing a decline in the quantity used and an increase in the use of substitute resources.

Julian Simon, a contemporary economist, has challenged both the Malthusian gloom and the Hotelling Principle. He believes that *people* are the 'ultimate resource' and predicts that a rising population *lessens* the pressure on natural resources. A bigger population provides a larger number of resourceful people who can work out more efficient ways of using scarce resources. As these solutions are found, the prices of exhaustible resources actually fall. To demonstrate his point, in 1980 Simon bet Ehrlich that the prices of five metals – copper, chrome, nickel, tin and tungsten – would fall during the 1980s. Simon won the bet!

No matter whether it is agricultural land, an exhaustible natural resource, or the space in the centre of Manchester and no matter whether it is 1992 or, as shown here, 1914, there is a limit to what is available, and we persistently push against that limit. Economists see urban congestion as a consequence of the value of doing business in the city centre relative to the cost. They see the price mechanism, bringing ever higher rents and prices of raw materials, as the means of allocating and rationing scarce natural resources. Malthusians, in contrast, explain congestion as the consequence of population pressure, and they see the solution as population control.

In Tokyo, the pressure on space is so great that in some residential neighbourhoods, a parking space costs £1,000 a month. To economize on this expensive space – and to lower the cost of car ownership and hence boost the sale of cars – Honda, Nissan and Toyota, three of Japan's big car producers, have developed a parking machine that enables two cars to occupy the space of one. The most basic of these machines costs a mere £7,500 – less than 6 months' worth of parking fees.

HUNT.

HAROLD HOTELLING

A Parson and a Mathematician Probe the Pressure on Resources

Thomas Robert Malthus (1766–1834), pictured right, a British parson and a professor, was an extremely influential social scientist. In his best-selling *Essay on the Principle of Population*, published in 1798, he argued that population growth would outstrip food production. Modern-day Malthusians believe that his basic idea was right and that it applies to all natural resources.

The most profound work on the economics of natural resources is that of Harold Hotelling (1895–1973), pictured above. Hotelling worked as a journalist, schoolteacher and mathematical consultant before becoming an economics professor at Columbia University. He explained how the price mechanism allocated exhaustible resources, making them progressively more expensive. Their higher price encourages the development of new technologies, the discovery of new sources of supply and the development of substitutes.

THOMAS ROBERT MALTHUS

amount required to induce them to supply each unit of the factor of production, they will be paid a different price for each unit. The prices will trace the supply curve and the income received is entirely transfer earnings – the yellow area in Fig. 14.11.

The concept of economic rent is similar to the concept of consumer surplus that you met in Chapter 7. Consumer surplus is the difference between the price the household pays for a good and the maximum price it would be willing to pay, as indicated by the demand curve. In a parallel sense, economic rent is the difference between the factor price a household actually receives and the minimum factor price at which it would be willing to supply a given amount of a factor of production.

It is important to distinguish between *economic rent* and *rent*. Rent is the price paid to the factor of production, land. Economic rent is a component of the income received by every factor of production.

The portion of the income of a factor of production that consists of economic rent depends on the

elasticity of the supply of the factor of production. When the supply of a factor of production is inelastic, its entire income is economic rent. Most of Roberto Baggio's income is economic rent. When the supply of a factor of production is perfectly elastic, none of its income is economic rent. Most of the income of a fast-food server is transfer earning. In general, when the supply curve is neither perfectly elastic nor perfectly inelastic (like that illustrated in Fig. 14.11), some part of the factor income is economic rent and the other part transfer earnings.

Figure 14.12 illustrates the three possibilities. Part (a) shows the market for a particular parcel of land in Glasgow. The land is fixed in size at L square metres. Therefore the supply curve of the land is vertical – perfectly inelastic. No matter what the rent on the land is, there is no way of increasing the quantity that can be supplied.

The demand for that block of land is determined by its marginal revenue product. The marginal revenue product in turn depends on the uses to which the land can be put. In a central business district of Glasgow, the marginal revenue product is high because a large number of people are concentrated in that area, making it a prime place for conducting valuable business. Suppose that the marginal revenue product of this block of land is shown by the demand curve in Fig. 14.12(a). Then it commands a rent of R. The entire income accruing to the owner of the land is the green area in the figure. This income is *economic rent*. The rent charged for this piece of land depends entirely on its marginal revenue product – on the demand curve. If the demand curve shifts to the right, the rent rises. If the demand curve shifts to the left, the rent falls. The quantity of land supplied remains constant at L.

Is coffee expensive in Glasgow because rents are high or are rents high because people in Glasgow are willing to pay a high price for coffee? The conclusion we've just reached answers this question. We've seen that the rent of a Glasgow block is determined entirely by the demand for it and that the demand, in turn, is determined by its marginal revenue product. Land has a high marginal revenue product only if people are willing to pay a high price to use the land. Of course, from the point of view of restaurateurs, they feel that they have to charge a high price for coffee in the business district of Glasgow because of the high rent they pay there. But the rent wouldn't be high if they (and other potential users) did not have a high marginal revenue product 'attached' to that land,

---

FIGURE 14.11

Economic Rent and Transfer Earnings

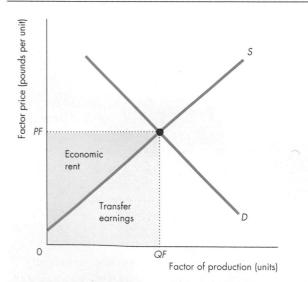

The total income of a factor of production is made up of its economic rent and its transfer earnings. Transfer earnings are measured by the yellow area under the supply curve, and economic rent by the green area above the supply curve and below the factor price.

FIGURE 14.12

Economic Rent and Supply Elasticity

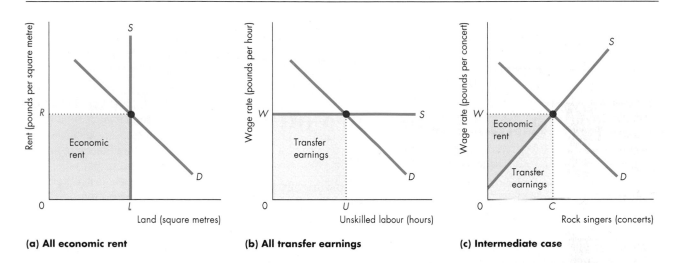

(a) All economic rent **(b) All transfer earnings** **(c) Intermediate case**

When the supply of the factor of production is perfectly inelastic (the supply curve is vertical) as in part (a), the entire factor income is economic rent. When the supply of the factor of production is perfectly elastic, as in part (b), the factor's entire income is transfer earnings. When a factor supply curve slopes upward, as in part (c), part of the factor income is economic rent and part is transfer earnings. Land is the example shown in part (a); unskilled labour in poor countries such as India and China in part (b); and rock singers in part (c).

making them willing to pay those high rents.

Figure 14.12(b) shows the market for a factor of production that is in perfectly elastic supply. An example of such a market might be that for unskilled labour in a poor country such as India or China. In those countries, large amounts of labour flock to the cities and are available for work at the going wage rate (in this case, W). Thus in these situations, the supply of labour is almost perfectly elastic. The entire income earned by this labour is transfer earnings. They receive no economic rent.

Figure 14.12(c) shows the market for rock singers. To induce a rock singer to sing at a larger number of concerts, a higher income has to be offered – the rock singer's supply curve is upward-sloping. The demand curve – measuring the marginal revenue product of the rock singer – is labelled D. Equilibrium occurs where the rock singer receives a wage of W and sings in C concerts. The green area above the rock singer's supply curve is economic rent and the yellow area below the supply curve is the rock singer's transfer earnings. If the rock singer is not offered at least the amount of the transfer earnings, then the singer will withdraw from the rock concert market and perform an alternative activity.

◆ ◆ ◆ ◆ We've now studied the market for the three factors of production – labour, capital and land – and we've seen how the returns to these factors of production – wages, interest and rent – are determined. We've seen the crucial role played in determining the demand for a factor of production by the factor's marginal revenue product. We've seen how the interaction of demand and supply determines factor prices and factor incomes. We've also seen how changes in these prices and incomes come about from changes in demand and supply. Finally, we've distinguished between economic rent and transfer earnings. ◆ ◆   In the next chapter, we're going to examine some detailed features of the labour market more closely, explaining differences in wage rates between skilled and unskilled workers and between males and females.

The Ups and Downs of Shares

THE TIMES, 8 FEBRUARY 1994

More than £14 bn wiped off shares

Michael Clark and Philip Pangalos

SHARE prices and government bonds on the London stock market fell sharply in response to Friday's decision by the Federal Reserve Board to raise short-term interest rates in America.

More than £14 billion was wiped from Britain's publicly quoted companies in a day of nervous and volatile trading as London followed other markets lower. The FT-SE 100 index ended the session 56.3 points down at 3,419.1, a fall of 1.6 per cent, having been almost 100 points lower at one stage as market-makers anxiously awaited the start of trading in New York.

In the face of stock market jitters, Kenneth Clarke, the Chancellor, has, if anything, become more upbeat on prospects for the economy. In an interview in *Le Figaro,* the French newspaper, today, Mr Clarke says tax increases will not hold back recovery and growth could be higher than he predicted at the time of the Budget. 'My forecast, made last November, of growth at 2.5 per cent this year seems to be more and more modest.'

He says tax increases may hold back household consumption, but not the economy as a whole. His comments suggest that he would favour a recovery in which exports and investment played a larger part, rather than one dependent on consumption, and .is prepared to see consumption reined back....

At the low-point of the day, £22 billion had been wiped off share values, the biggest cash write-off, in cash terms, since the 1987 crash....

Robert Buckland, equity strategist at NatWest Securities, said: 'The message we gave to our clients was 'don't panic'. The more the market fell, the better... We view this as an opportunity to buy.'

In the wake of interest rate increases by the Federal Reserve Board in the United States, there were significant falls on stock markets all over the world.

There were fears that such a movement in interest rates in the United States could have repercussions on interest rate levels in other countries too.

The impact of this was for traders to sell, pushing down the price of shares.

Despite this shock, the Chancellor of the Exchequer was confident that tax increases in the United Kingdom would not seriously impede economic recovery. Firms would still export and invest.

STOCK MARKETS TAKE FRIGHT ACROSS THE WORLD

LONDON
FT-SE 100
Monday open: 3,475.4
close: 3,419.1

PARIS
CAC-10
Monday open: 2,329.17
close: 2,264.03
Down 65.14

NEW YORK
Wall Street Dow Jones Industrial Average
Friday close: 3,871.24
Down 96.24
Monday
open: 3,877.42
Midday price: 3,871.05
Up: 5.63

FRANKFURT
Dax
Monday open: 3,043.9
close: 2,978.25
Down 65.65

HONG KONG
Hang Seng
Monday open: 12,157.57
close: 11,414.27
Down 743.30

TOKYO
Nikkei 225
Monday open: 20,301.43
close: 20,014.40
Down 287.03

SYDNEY
All Ordinaries
Monday open: 2,332.8
close: 2,281.1
Down 51.7

Figure refers to zone times kept on land and sea compared with 12:00 (noon) Greenwich Mean Time

1:00 2:00 3:00 4:00 5:00 6:00 7:00 8:00 9:00 10:00 11:00 12:00 13:00 14:00 15:00 16:00 17:00 18:00 19:00 20:00 21:00 22:00 23:00 24:00

MONDAY

TUESDAY

© The Times. Reprinted with permission.

Background and Analysis

If capital is highly mobile internationally, an increase in the rate of interest in the United States may mean that interest rates in other countries have to rise, in order to prevent capital moving out of other countries to the United States to take advantage of these higher rates of interest.

If UK interest rates were to rise, the level of new investments undertaken by firms could be affected.

Higher interest rates would also attract new capital inflows, pushing up the exchange rate and reducing firms' exports.

Fears about firms reducing investment plans and losing export sales affect traders' perceptions about the ability of firms to survive and develop. If they sell shares, share prices would fall and lower the value of firms (measured by their total share value), restricting further firms' ability to raise funds to make new investments.

This reaction may create a self-fulfilling prophecy, in that the fears about lower investment by traders result in firms not being able to undertake new investments.

Experts, however, suggest that shares have been overvalued, meaning a fall would simply return them to a level that more accurately reflects a firm's true value.

Experts also suggest that there is no reason why interest rates in the United Kingdom actually need to increase in response to US interest rates.

Most of the falls in the total value of shares came in foreign markets. Total trading on the London market was actually lower than the level of the previous few weeks. The value of UK companies should therefore not be badly affected.

Lower share prices could lead to more shares being bought. This raises the level of household savings, making more funds available to firms to invest.

READING BETWEEN THE LINES

SUMMARY

Factor Prices and Incomes

The factors of production – labour, capital and land – earn a return – wages, interest and rent. Labour is the most important source of income. Factor prices are determined by the demand for and supply of factors of production. Incomes are determined by the prices of factors of production and the quantities used. An increase in the demand for a factor of production increases the factor's price and income; a decrease in the demand for a factor of production decreases its price and income. An increase in supply increases the quantity used of a factor of production but decreases its price. A decrease in supply decreases the quantity used and increases the factor's price. Whether an increase in supply leads to an increase or decrease in the income of a factor of production depends on the elasticity of demand of the factor. When elasticity of demand is greater than 1, an increase in supply leads to an increase in the factor's income. When the elasticity of demand for a factor is less than 1, an increase in supply leads to a decrease in the factor's income. (pp. 376–378)

Demand for Factors

A firm's demand for a factor stems from its desire to maximize profit. The extra revenue generated by hiring one more unit of a factor is called the marginal revenue product of the factor. A firm's demand curve for a factor is derived from that factor's marginal revenue product curve. A firm demands an input up to the point at which the marginal revenue product of the factor equals the factor's price.

A firm's labour input is variable in both the short run and the long run. The firm's capital input may be varied only in the long run. The elasticity of the demand for labour in the short run depends on the short-run elasticity of demand for the firm's good, on the labour intensity of the production process, and on the slope of the marginal product of labour curve. The long-run elasticity of a firm's demand for labour depends on the long-run elasticity of demand for the good, on labour intensity and on the ease with which

capital can be substituted for labour.

The market demand for labour is the sum of the demands by each individual firm. (pp. 378–385)

Supply of Factors

The supply of factors is determined by households' decisions on the allocation of their time and the division of their income between consumption and saving. In choosing how much time to allocate to market activities, each household compares the wage rate that can be earned with the value of its time in other non-market activities. The household will supply no market labour at wage rates below its reservation wage. At wage rates above the household's reservation wage, the quantity of labour supplied rises as long as the substitution effect of the higher wage rate is larger than the income effect. As the wage rate continues to rise, the income effect, which leads to more time taken for leisure, becomes larger than the substitution effect, and the quantity of labour supplied by the household falls.

The market supply curve of labour is the sum of the supply curves of all households. Like the household's labour supply curve, the market supply of labour curve eventually bends backward. However, the response to higher wage rates of those on the upward-sloping part of the labour supply curve dominates the response of those on the backward-bending part and the market supply curve slopes upward over the range of wage rates that we experience.

Households supply capital by saving. Saving increases as the interest rate increases. The supply of capital to an individual firm is highly inelastic in the short run but highly elastic in the long run.

The supply of land is fixed and independent of its rent. (pp. 385–390)

Competitive Equilibrium

In a competitive factor market, the factor price and quantity used are determined at the point of intersection of the demand and supply curves. High factor prices occur for factors of production that have a high marginal revenue product and a low supply. Low factor prices occur for factors of production with a low marginal revenue product and a high supply. (pp. 390–393)

Economic Rent and Transfer Earnings

Economic rent is that part of the income received by a factor owner over and above the amount needed to induce the owner to supply the factor of production for use. The rest of a factor's income is transfer earnings. When the supply of a factor is perfectly inelastic, its entire income is made up of economic rent. Factors that have a perfectly elastic supply receive only transfer earnings. In general the supply curve of a factor is upward-sloping and part of its income received is transfer earnings (below the supply curve) and part is economic rent (above the supply curve but below the factor price). (pp. 393–397)

KEY ELEMENTS

Key Terms

Average revenue product, 380
Average revenue product curve, 381
Derived demand, 378
Economic rent, 393
Long-run demand for labour, 383
Long-run elasticity of demand for labour, 385
Marginal revenue product, 379
Marginal revenue product curve, 381
Market activity, 386
Non-market activity, 386
Reservation wage, 386
Short-run demand for labour, 383
Short-run elasticity of demand for labour, 384
Transfer earnings, 393

Key Figures and Tables

REVIEW QUESTIONS

1   Explain what happens to the price of a factor of production and its income if the following occurs:
    a   There is an increase in demand for the factor.
    b   There is an increase in supply of the factor.
    c   There is a decrease in demand for the factor.
    d   There is a decrease in supply of the factor.

2   Explain why the effect of a change in supply of a factor on a factor's income depends on the elasticity of demand for the factor.

3   Define marginal revenue product and distinguish between marginal revenue product and marginal revenue.

4   Why does marginal revenue product decline as the quantity of a factor employed increases?

5   What is the relationship between the demand curve for a factor of production and its marginal revenue product curve? Why?

6   Show that the condition for maximum profit in the product market – marginal cost equals marginal revenue – is equivalent to the condition for maximum profit in the factor market – marginal revenue product equals marginal cost of factor (equals factor price in a competitive factor market).

7   Review the main influences on the demand for

a factor of production – the influences that shift the demand curve for a factor.

8 What determines the short-run and the long-run elasticity of demand for labour?

9 What determines the supply of labour?

10 Why might the supply of labour curve bend backward at a high enough wage rate?

11 What determines the supply of capital?

12 Define economic rent and transfer earnings and distinguish between these two components of income.

13 Suppose that a factor of production is in perfectly inelastic supply. If the marginal revenue product of the factor decreases, what happens to the price, quantity used, income, transfer earnings and rent of the factor?

P R O B L E M S

1 Wanda owns a fish shop. She employs students to sort and pack the fish. Students can pack the following amounts of fish in an hour:

Number of students	Quantity of fish (kilograms)
1	20
2	50
3	90
4	120
5	145
6	165
7	180
8	190

a Draw the average and marginal product curves of these students.

b If Wanda can sell her fish for 50 pence a kilogram, draw the average and marginal revenue product curves.

c Draw Wanda's demand for labour curve.

d If all fish packers in Wanda's area pay their packers £7.50 an hour, how many students will Wanda hire?

2 The price of fish falls to 33.33 pence a kilogram, and fish packers' wages remain at £7.50 an hour.

a What happens to Wanda's average and marginal product curves?

b What happens to her average and marginal revenue product curves?

c What happens to her demand for labour curve?

d What happens to the number of students that she hires?

3 Fish packers' wages increase to £10 an hour but the price of fish remains at 50 pence a kilogram.

a What happens to the average and marginal revenue product curves?

b What happens to Wanda's demand curve?

c How many packers does Wanda hire?

4 Using the information provided in Problem 1, calculate Wanda's marginal revenue and marginal cost, marginal revenue product and marginal cost of labour. Show that when Wanda is making maximum profit, marginal cost equals marginal revenue and marginal revenue product equals the marginal cost of labour.

5 You are given the following information about the labour market in an isolated town in the Amazon rainforest. Everyone works for logging companies, but there are many logging companies in the town. The market for logging workers is perfectly competitive. The town's labour supply is given as follows:

Wage rate (cruzados per hour)	Quantity of labour supplied (hours)
200	120
300	160
400	200
500	240
600	280
700	320
800	360

The market demand for labour from all the logging firms in the town is as follows:

Wage rate (cruzados per hour)	Quantity of labour demanded (hours)
200	400
300	360
400	320
500	280
600	240
700	200
800	160

a What is the competitive equilibrium wage rate and the quantity of labour employed?

b What is total labour income?

c How much of that labour income is economic rent and how much is transfer earnings? (You may find it easier to answer this question by drawing graphs of the demand and supply curves and then finding the economic rent and transfer earnings as areas on the graph, as in Fig. 14.11.)

6 British Steel experiences a *permanent* decrease in the demand for its product. Explain what happens to the following:

a The price of a share of its stock

b The dividends it pays to its shareholders

c The amount of capital that it employs

  (1) in the short run

  (2) in the long run

d The quantity of labour that it employs

  (1) in the short run

  (2) in the long run

7 Suppose that the decrease in the demand for British Steel in Problem 6 is *temporary*. Demand decreases for a few months and then returns to its previous level. Explain what happens to the following:

a The price of a share of its stock

b The dividends it pays to its shareholders

c The amount of capital that it employs

  (1) in the short run

  (2) in the long run

d The quantity of labour that it employs

  (1) in the short run

  (2) in the long run

8 Suppose there is a hugh increase in the demand for Big Macs and McDonald's is able to double its prices with no decrease in sales. What happens to the rents that McDonald's is willing to pay for the land on which its restaurants are located?

CHAPTER 15

LABOUR MARKETS

After studying this chapter you will be able to:

◆ Explain why skilled workers earn more, on average, than unskilled workers

◆ Explain why people who have undertaken higher education generally earn more, on average, than people who have not

◆ Explain why union workers earn higher wages, on average, than non-union workers

◆ Explain why men, on average, earn more than women

◆ Predict the effects of pay equity legislation

A S YOU WELL KNOW, THERE IS MORE TO STUDENT LIFE THAN A BUSY social scene. Coursework, tests, dissertations and exams require a lot of hard work. Are they worth the effort that goes into them? What is the payoff? Does it compensate for the costs of being a student and the earnings that were sacrificed during the years at college? ◆ ◆ Many workers belong to trade unions. Usually, union workers earn a higher wage than non-union workers in comparable jobs. Why? How are unions able to secure higher wages for their members than the wages paid to non-union workers? ◆ ◆ Among the most visible and persistent differences in earnings are those between men and women. Looking at full-time workers, we find that, on average, women receive about 71 per cent of the earnings received by men. Certainly, many individuals defy the aver-

The Sweat of Our Brows

ages, but why do women generally earn less than men? Is it because of discrimination and exploitation? Or is it because of economic factors? Or is it a combination of the two? ◆ ◆ Some people advocate pay equity legislation to try and ensure that jobs of equivalent value receive the same pay regardless of the pay set by the market. Can pay equity laws bring economic help to women?

◆ ◆ ◆ ◆ In this chapter, we study the way labour markets work and answer questions such as these. We begin by using the competitive labour market model developed in Chapter 14 to analyse the effects on wages of differences in education and training. We then extend the model to explain differences in union and non-union wages, in pay among men and women and to analyse the effects of pay equity laws.

Skill Differentials

Differences in earnings among workers with varying levels of education and training can be explained using a model of competitive labour markets. There are many levels and varieties of education and training in the real world. To keep our analysis as clear as possible, we'll study a model economy in which there are just two levels of education and training that result in two types of labour, which we will call skilled labour and unskilled labour. We'll study the demand for and supply of these two types of workers and see why there is a difference in their wages and what determines that difference. Let's begin by looking at the demand for the two types of labour.

The Demand for Skilled and Unskilled Labour

Skilled workers can perform a wide variety of tasks that unskilled workers would perform badly or perhaps could not even perform at all. Imagine an untrained, inexperienced person performing surgery or piloting an aeroplane. Because skilled workers perform complex tasks, they generally have a higher marginal revenue product than unskilled workers. As we learned in Chapter 14, the demand for labour curve is derived from the marginal revenue product curve. The larger the marginal revenue product of labour, the greater is the demand for labour.

Figure 15.1(a) shows the demand curves for skilled and unskilled labour. At the same level of employment of skilled and unskilled workers, firms are willing to pay a higher wage to a skilled worker than to an unskilled worker. The gap between these two wages is the difference between the marginal revenue products of a given number of skilled and unskilled workers. This difference is the marginal revenue product (*MRP*) of skill. For example, at an employment level of 2,000 hours a day, firms are willing to pay $12.50 an hour for a skilled worker and only $5.00 an hour for an unskilled worker. The difference in the two marginal revenue products is $7.50 an hour. So the marginal revenue product of skill is $7.50 an hour.

The Supply of Skilled and Unskilled Labour

Skills are costly to acquire. Furthermore, a worker pays the cost of acquiring a skill before benefiting

from a higher wage. For example, attending college or university usually leads to a higher income, but that income is not earned until after graduation. These facts make the acquisition of skills similar to investment. To emphasize the investment nature of acquiring a skill, we call that activity an investment in human capital. **Human capital** is the accumulated skill and knowledge of human beings. The value of a person's human capital is the present value of the extra earnings that will be received in the future as a result of acquiring skill and knowledge in the past.[1]

The cost of acquiring a skill includes the actual costs of items such as tuition fees and books and also costs in the form of lost or reduced earnings while the skill is being acquired. Many people acquire skills through full-time education. For them there is a cost equal to earnings forgone less any student grants or gifts from parents. Other people acquire skills through on-the-job training. Usually a worker undergoing on-the-job training is paid a lower wage than one doing a comparable job but not undergoing training. For these people there is a cost equal to the difference between the wage paid to a person not being trained and that paid to a person being trained.

Supply Curves of Skilled and Unskilled Labour Figure 15.1(b) shows two supply curves, one for skilled workers, S_S, and one for unskilled workers, S_U. The position of the supply curve of skilled workers reflects the cost of acquiring the skill, so this supply curve lies above the unskilled worker's supply curve.

The vertical gap between the two supply curves is the compensation for the cost of acquiring the skill. For example, suppose that the quantity of unskilled labour supplied is 2,000 hours a day at a wage rate of $5 an hour. This wage rate compensates the unskilled workers purely for their time on the job. To induce 2,000 hours of skilled labour to be supplied, firms have to pay a wage rate of $8.50 an hour. This wage rate for skilled labour is higher than that for unskilled labour since skilled workers must be compensated not only for the time on the job but also for the time and other costs of acquiring the skill.

---

[1] The concept of present value is explained in Chapter 16. It is equivalent to a sum of money that, if invested today at the average current interest rate, will yield a stream of income equivalent to the extra earnings resulting from a person's acquired knowledge and skills.

FIGURE 15.1

Skill Differentials

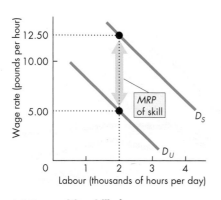

**(a) Demand for skilled
and unskilled labour**

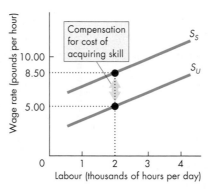

**(b) Supply of skilled
and unskilled labour**

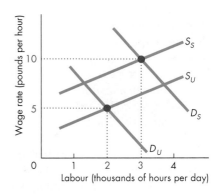

**(c) Markets for skilled
and unskilled labour**

Part (a) illustrates the marginal revenue product of skill. Unskilled workers have a marginal revenue product that gives rise to the demand curve marked D_U. Skilled workers have a higher marginal revenue product; therefore the demand curve for skilled workers, D_S, lies above D_U. The vertical gap between these two curves is the marginal revenue product of the skill. Part (b) shows the effects of the cost of acquiring skills on the supply curves of labour. The supply curve for unskilled workers is S_U. Skilled workers have to incur costs in order to acquire their skills; so they will supply labour services only at a wage rate that exceeds that of unskilled labour. The supply curve for skilled workers is S_S. The vertical gap between these two curves is the compensation required for the cost of acquiring a skill.

Part (c) shows the determination of the equilibrium levels of employment and the wage differential between skilled and unskilled labour. In equilibrium, for each type of labour the quantities demanded and supplied are equal. Unskilled workers earn £5 an hour and are hired for 2,000 hours a day. Skilled workers earn £10 an hour and are hired for 3,000 hours a day.

Wage Rates of Skilled and Unskilled Labour

To work out the wage rates of skilled and unskilled labour, we bring together the effects of skill on the demand and supply of labour. Figure 15.1(c) shows the demand and supply curves for skilled and unskilled labour, exactly as they were plotted in parts (a) and (b). Equilibrium occurs in the market for unskilled labour where the supply and demand curves for unskilled labour intersect. The equilibrium wage rate is £5 an hour and the quantity of unskilled labour employed is 2,000 hours a day. Equilibrium in the market for skilled workers occurs where the supply and demand curves for skilled workers intersect. The equilibrium wage rate is £10 an hour and the quantity of skilled labour employed is 3,000 hours a day.

As you can see in Fig. 15.1(c), the equilibrium wage rate of skilled labour is higher than that of unskilled labour. This difference occurs for two reasons: first, skilled labour has a higher marginal

revenue product than unskilled labour; second, skills are costly to acquire. The wage differential, which is £5 an hour in this example, depends on both the marginal revenue product of the skill and the cost of acquiring it. The higher the marginal revenue product of the skill, the larger is the vertical gap between the demand curves for skilled and unskilled labour. The more costly it is to acquire a skill, the larger is the vertical gap between the supplies of skilled and unskilled labour. The higher the marginal revenue product of the skill and the more costly it is to acquire, the larger is the wage differential between skilled and unskilled workers.

In our example there were just two types of labour. In the real world there are thousands – perhaps millions – of different types of labour. Sometimes you will find examples of skilled workers who receive low pay. For instance, many church ministers and school-teachers are paid little. These workers have high knowledge and skills but find that they can sell their labour for only a low price – they have a low marginal revenue product. Why does anyone train for jobs like these if the pecuniary rewards are low? The answer is that these people feel their jobs bring rewards other than money and they invest in acquiring skills to enjoy these non-pecuniary rewards.

In contrast, there are some workers who spend little time acquiring skills and yet find they have a high marginal product and can earn high wages. Examples include coal miners and long-distance lorry drivers. Why, you may ask, don't millions of other unskilled workers flock to these jobs – pushing the supply curves for these sorts of labour to the right and so forcing the wage rates down? The answer is that these jobs have unpleasant features, such as dirty cramped conditions or long periods spent away from home, and these non-pecuniary factors discourage many people from working in these jobs despite the high wages and the low costs of training.

Do Education and Training Pay?

Although some highly skilled people earn little while some relatively unskilled people earn a lot, the overall picture is one of large differences in earnings based on the level of education and training. An indication of those differences can be seen in Fig. 15.2, which is based on figures for male employees. This figure highlights two important sources of earnings differences. The first is the level of education itself: the higher the level of education, the higher are a person's earnings, other things being equal. The second is age: age is strongly correlated with experience and the degree of on-the-job training a person has had, so as a person gets older, up to middle age, earnings increase. If we compare graduates with people of similar age but no qualifications, we find the graduate earns about 50 per cent more when aged around 22 and well over twice as much when aged around 60. Notice that Fig. 15.2 reflects earnings by men. Too few figures are published for women to enable us to plot a similar graph for women or for both sexes combined. The figures for women that are available suggest that, for them, earnings differences are rather more sensitive to qualifications and slightly less sensitive to age than applies to men.

We can see from Fig. 15.2 that each extra level of qualification – from GCSE up to degree level – leads to a higher income. But do qualifications which require people to stay on at school beyond the compulsory school leaving age of 16 pay in the sense of

FIGURE 15.2

Education and Earnings

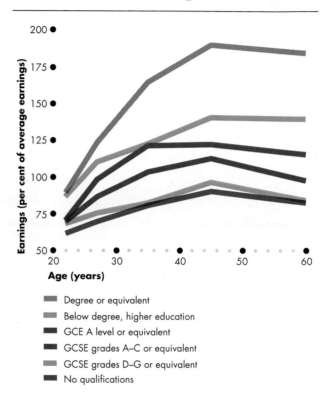

The figure shows the average earnings in 1991 of male employees at various ages and with varying levels of education. Earnings increase with the level of educational qualification. They also increase with age but only up to around 50. Beyond that age earnings decrease. These differences show the importance of education and experience in influencing skill differentials.

Source: Office of Population Censuses and Surveys, *General Household Survey, 1991*, London, HMSO, 1993, Table 10.12.

yielding enough income to compensate for the cost of education and for the delay in the start of earnings? For most people, post-16 education does indeed pay. Rates of return have been calculated suggesting that a post-secondary degree is a better investment than almost any other a person can undertake. Rates of return as high as 15 per cent, after allowing for inflation, are not uncommon.

Differences in education and training are an important source of differences in earnings. But they are not the only source. Another is the activities of trade unions. Let's see how unions affect wages and why, on average, union wages exceed non-union wages.

Union–Non-union Wage Differentials

A **trade union** is a group of workers organized principally for the purpose of increasing wages and influencing other job conditions. A union acts in the labour market like a monopolist in the product market. The union seeks to restrict competition and, as a result, raise the price at which labour is traded. A compact glossary of labour terms can be found in Table 15.1.

There are two main types of union: closed unions and open unions. A **closed union** is a group of workers who have a similar range of skills but who may work for many different employers. The National Union of Mineworkers is a closed union whose members work for a single employer, while the Fire Brigades Union is a closed union whose members work for various employers. An **open union** is a group of workers who have a variety of skills and job types. Examples include the Transport and General Workers Union and the Amalgamated Engineering and Electrical Union.

There are some 275 unions in the United Kingdom. About a fifth of these are affiliated to the

Trades Union Congress (TUC). However, most of the big unions are affiliated and the TUC covers about 80 per cent of all union members. The TUC often acts as the national voice of organized labour in the media and in politics.

Unions vary enormously in size. Many of the smallest closed unions have under 100 members. At the other extreme is Unison, formed in 1993 by a merger of three older unions, with 1.4 million members. The total number of union members was over 13 million in 1979 but has fallen by over 25 per cent since. There are several reasons for this. One is the growth in unemployment while another is the decline of several industries that were highly unionized – for instance mining and shipbuilding. Today union membership accounts for less than half of the number of employees.

In some firms or plants where a union operates, there is a closed shop. A **closed shop** is a plant or firm in which all the employees are required to belong to the trade union. Some people oppose closed shops on the grounds that people who want to work in a particular plant or firm should be free to decide whether to join a union. Others support the requirement that union membership is compulsory, for otherwise non-members can try to enjoy the benefits secured by the union without having to

TABLE 15.1

A Compact Glossary on Unions

Trade union	A group of workers organized principally for the purpose of increasing wages and improving other conditions of employment.
TUC	A federation of unions. Only a fifth of unions are affiliated, but these include most of the big unions and almost 80 per cent of all union members. The TUC acts as the voice of organized labour in the media and in the political arena.
Closed union	A union with membership limited to a particular type of worker. The workers may be employed by one employer – as applies to members of the National Union of Mineworkers – or by many employers – as applies to members of the National Union of Teachers.
Open union	A union in which workers have a variety of skills and job types – for instance the Transport and General Workers Union.
Closed shop	A plant or firm in which all the employees are required to join a specified union.
Collective bargaining	The process of negotiation between employers (or their representatives) and a union on wages and other employment conditions.
Strike	A group decision to refuse to work under prevailing conditions.
Lockout	A firm's refusal to allow its labour force to work.
Binding arbitration	Determination of wages and other employment conditions by a third party (an arbitrator) acceptable to both parties.

contribute to the costs of running the union. The government has made it hard for unions to operate closed shops and the number of people in closed shops is now no more than 500,000.

Unions negotiate with employers (or their representatives) in a process called **collective bargaining**. The main weapons available to the union and the employer in collective bargaining are the strike and the lockout. A **strike** is a group decision to refuse to work under prevailing conditions. Legislation passed in the United Kingdom since 1979 has restricted the ability of union leaders to call strikes, which are now illegal unless a ballot of members has taken place. It is also harder to sustain a strike because mass picketing by strikers to discourage strike breaking has been outlawed, and so have 'sympathy' strikes by unions not directly involved in a dispute.

A **lockout** – which is extremely rare – is a firm's refusal to operate its plant and employ its workers. Each party uses the threat of a strike or a lockout to try to get an agreement in its own favour. Sometimes when the two parties in the collective bargaining process cannot agree on wages and other conditions of employment, they agree to put their disagreement to binding arbitration. **Binding arbitration** is a process in which a third party – an arbitrator – determines wages and other employment conditions on behalf of the negotiating parties. The most common third party in the United Kingdom for such agreements is the Arbitration and Conciliation Service (ACAS).

Though not trade unions in a legal sense, professional associations act, in many ways, like unions. A **professional association** is an organized group of professional workers, such as lawyers, dentists or doctors, that seeks to influence the compensation and other labour market conditions affecting its members. An example of a professional association is the Association of University Teachers.

Unions' Objectives and Constraints

Unions have three broad objectives:

◆ Improving compensation
◆ Improving working conditions
◆ Expanding job opportunities

Each of these objectives contains a series of more detailed goals. For example, in seeking to improve members' compensation, a union negotiates on a variety of issues such as the wage rate, fringe benefits and the standard working week, that is the number of hours which must be worked before high overtime wage rates are paid. In seeking to improve working conditions, a union is concerned with occupational health and safety as well as the environmental quality of the workplace. In seeking to expand job opportunities, a union tries to obtain greater job security for existing members and to find ways of creating additional jobs for existing and new members.

A union's ability to pursue its objectives is restricted by two sets of constraints: one on the supply side and the other on the demand side of the labour market. On the supply side, the union's activities are limited by how well it can restrict non-union workers from offering their labour. The larger the fraction of the work force controlled by the union, the more effective the union can be. The groups best able to restrict supply are the professional associations for people such as lawyers and accountants. These associations control the number of qualified workers by controlling the examinations that new entrants must pass. At the other extreme, there are severe limits on the effectiveness of unions in markets such as that for waiters and waitresses. The abundant supply of casual labour for this type of work makes it very difficult for a union to restrict the supply of employees.

The constraint facing a union on the demand side of the labour market arises because the union cannot force firms to hire more labour than the quantity they demand at the current wage. Actions that raise wages or other employment costs can be expected to lower the quantity of labour demanded. Unless the union can take actions that increase the demand for the kind of labour that it represents, it has to accept the fact that higher wages can generally be secured only at the cost of lower employment. Recognizing the importance of the demand for labour, unions would like the demand for their labour to rise and to become more inelastic. It is not easy for them to affect the demand for their labour, but here are some of the methods they occasionally use:

◆ Encouraging import restrictions
◆ Supporting minimum wage laws
◆ Increasing product demand
◆ Increasing the marginal product of union members

One of the best examples of the encouragement of import restrictions is the National Union of Mineworkers' advocacy of limitations on the import of foreign coal.

Unions of skilled workers often support minimum wage laws which will raise the wages of unskilled workers. The members of the skilled workers' unions may well have a genuine sympathy for unskilled workers on low pay, but a minimum wage law would also benefit skilled workers. This is because such a law would increase the cost of unskilled labour and so reduce the quantity demanded. In turn, it would increase the demand for skilled labour which is, to some extent at least, a substitute for unskilled labour.

Increasing product demand increases the price of products and so increases the marginal revenue product of the workers who make it. This in turn increases the demand for those workers and so makes a wage increase likely. Good examples of this sort of union activity occur in the car industry, where workers themselves are encouraged to buy cars produced by the firms for which they work.

To increase the marginal product of union members, unions support devices such as apprenticeships and training. The rise in marginal product leads directly to a rise in the demand for this type of labour.

Unions in a Competitive Labour Market

When a union starts to operate in a labour market, it seeks chiefly to raise wages. It may try to do this by restricting the supply of labour. Alternatively, it may try to do it by simply demanding a pay rise from the employers, threatening a strike if they don't agree. With either method, it would like, if possible, to limit the employment reductions that would follow from a rise in the wage rate by increasing the demand for the labour of its members. Let's see what happens when a union starts to operate in a labour market that was previously competitive – that is a labour market that was characterized by many hirers of labour and many workers all acting independently.

Figure 15.3 illustrates a competitive labour market. The demand curve is D_C and the supply curve is S_C. Here, the equilibrium wage rate is £5 an hour and 1,000 hours of labour are employed each day. Suppose now that a union is formed to organize the workers in this market, and suppose it tries to raise

wages by restricting the supply of labour. Perhaps it negotiates with employers, or with representatives of the employers, and agrees with them that in future new recruits must have extra qualifications. In time this will shift the supply curve to the left, to S_U, because old workers will retire while fewer new workers will want to come into the market now that the entry qualifications are tougher. If this is all the union does, employment will fall to 700 hours of labour a day and the wage rate will rise to £8 an hour. But if the union can also take steps that increase the demand for labour to D_U, it can achieve a bigger rise in the wage rate with a smaller fall in employment.

FIGURE 15.3

A Union Restricting Supply in a Competitive Labour Market

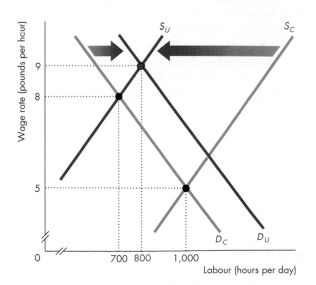

In a competitive labour market, the demand curve is D_C and the supply curve S_C. Competitive equilibrium occurs at a wage rate of £5 an hour with 1,000 hours of labour employed each day. By restricting employment below its competitive level, the union shifts the supply of labour to S_U. If the union can do no more than that, the wage rate will rise to £8 an hour but employment will fall to 700 hours a day. If the union can also increase the demand for labour (for instance by increasing the demand for the product produced by the union members or by raising the price of substitute labour) and shift the demand curve to D_U, then it can raise the wage rate still higher, to £9 an hour, and achieve employment of 800 hours a day.

By maintaining the labour supply at S_U, the union raises the wage rate to £9 an hour and achieves an employment level of 800 hours of labour a day.

In practice, the union may find it hard to insist on higher entry qualifications, so it may try to affect the supply side of the market in a different way. It could simply demand from employers that they agree to raise the wage rate to £8 and threaten a strike if employers refuse. The effects of this strategy are shown in Fig. 15.4. As in Fig. 15.3, S_C and D_C show the supply and demand curves before the union takes any action and equilibrium occurs with the wage rate at £5 and employment at 1,000 hours a day. The union's demand for a wage rate of £8 effectively shifts the supply curve to the kinked line S_U, for it is saying that no labour will be supplied at a wage lower than £8. (The new supply curve follows the old one at high employment levels, because there is a limit to how many hours will be supplied at a wage of £8.)

Figure 15.4 suggests that the market settles with a new equilibrium where the wage rate is £8 and where fewer hours a day, 700, are employed. This will be the new equilibrium position if the union's demands are met. But the employers might opt to reject the demand and prepare to sit out a long strike. In that case the members might eventually give up, and return to work on £5 an hour as before, or their union might negotiate a compromise with the wage rate at, say, £7, in which case the new supply curve would resemble S_U except that its horizontal part would be at the £7 level. The union's chances of success depend greatly on how many workers are members, for this affects the concern employers will feel at the prospect of a strike. If the union is successful in raising the wage rate to £8 an hour, it may be worried by the fall in hours employed. It may try to reduce the fall in hours by raising the demand for labour, say to D_U. This will raise the hours to 900 a day. Notice, though, that whether demand stays at D_C or rises to D_U, more hours will be offered than employers want to employ at a wage rate of £8 an hour.

In both Fig. 15.3 and Fig. 15.4, we saw that union activity restricted the hours worked in the markets in which they operate. This means they reduce the number of people employed in those markets. In turn, it means that unions increase the supply of labour in non-union markets. Those who can't get union jobs must look elsewhere for work. This increase in supply in non-union markets lowers the

wage rate in those markets and further widens the union–non-union differential. But low non-union wages decrease the demand for union labour and limit the increase in wages that unions can achieve.

We next consider the case in which employers have considerable influence in the labour market.

Monopsony

A **monopsony** is a market structure in which there is just a single buyer. With the growth of large-scale production over the past century, large plants, such as car plants, steelworks and shipyards, became the major employers of labour in some regions, and in

---

FIGURE 15.4

A Union Demanding a Wage Increase in a Competitive Labour Market

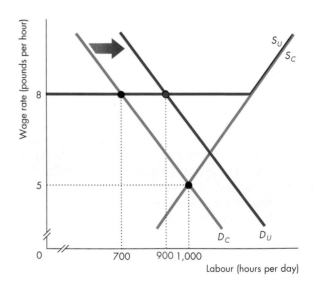

In a competitive labour market, the demand curve is D_C and the supply curve is S_C. Competitive equilibrium occurs at a wage rate of £5 an hour with 1,000 hours of labour employed each day. By demanding a wage rise to £8 an hour, and threatening a strike if the demand is not met, the union is offering the supply curve S_U. If the employers give in to this threat, the market settles down with a new wage of £8 an hour and 700 hours a day. If the union also manages to raise demand to D_U, employment rises to 900 hours while wages stay at £8 an hour.

some places a single firm employed almost all the labour. Such a firm is a monopsonist in the local labour market. Monopsony also arises when there is only one employer of a particular kind of labour in a town or region. Thus an airport is usually a monopsonist in the local market for airport security staff.

You will be able to think of many monopsonistic employers in the public sector. A local authority will be the only employer of firemen in a local market, just as the central government is the only employer of income-tax collectors and the Royal Mint is the only employer of coin makers. But as these employers are not generally concerned with maximizing profits, the analysis given below may not explain the wages they pay or their employment levels.

A monopsonist can make a bigger profit than a group of firms that have to compete with each other for labour. Figure 15.5 illustrates how a monopsonist operates. The monopsonist's marginal revenue product curve, labelled *MRP*, tells us how much total revenue increases from selling the output produced by the last hour of labour hired. The curve labelled *S* is the supply curve of labour, which tells us how many hours are supplied at each possible wage rate and, conversely, the wage that is needed to secure each possible quantity of labour.

The monopsonist recognizes that to hire more labour it must pay a higher wage. This situation arises because it is the only employer of its type of labour, at least in its area, and to acquire more labour it must raise the wage to attract workers from other labour markets. Equivalently, if it hires less labour it can get away with paying a lower wage. The monopsonist takes account of this fact when calculating its marginal cost of labour, which is shown in Fig. 15.5 by the curve *MCL*.

The relationship between the marginal cost of labour curve and the supply curve is similar to the relationship between the marginal cost and average total cost curves that you studied in Chapter 10. The supply curve is like the average total cost of labour curve. For example, the firm in Fig. 15.5 can hire 50 hours of labour at £5 an hour with a total labour cost of £250 (£5 an hour × 50 hours). But suppose that the firm hires slightly less than 50 hours of labour, say 49 hours. The wage rate at which 49 hours of labour can be hired is £4.90 an hour. The firm's total labour cost is now £240.10 (49 × £4.90). Hiring the fiftieth hour of labour raises the total cost of labour from £240.10 to £250, which is

about £10. The curve *MCL* shows the £10 marginal cost of hiring the fiftieth hour of labour.

To calculate the profit-maximizing quantity of labour to hire, the firm chooses the quantity where the marginal cost of labour is equal to the marginal revenue product of labour. In Fig. 15.5, this outcome occurs when the monopsony employs 50 hours of labour. If employment is below this level, it pays the firm to hire more labour because each extra hour of labour adds more to revenue, as shown by *MRP*, than it adds to costs, as shown by *MCL*. Conversely, if employment is above 50 hours, it pays the firm to hire less labour because each hour saved reduces revenue, as shown by *MRP*, by less than it reduces costs, as shown by *MCL*. To hire 50 hours of labour, the firm has to pay £5 an hour, as shown by *S*. The marginal revenue product of labour, however, is £10 an hour, which means that the firm makes an economic profit of £5 on the

---

FIGURE 15.5

A Monopsony Labour Market

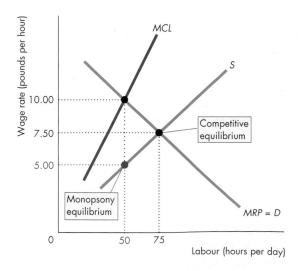

A monopsony is a market structure in which there is a single buyer. A monopsonist whose marginal revenue product curve is *MRP* faces a labour curve *S* and has a marginal cost of labour curve *MCL*. Profit is maximized by making the marginal cost of labour equal to marginal revenue product. The monopsonist hires 50 hours of labour per day and pays the lowest wage for which that amount of labour can be hired, £5 an hour.

last hour of labour that it hires. Each worker gets paid £5, and marginal revenue product is £10. So the firm gets an extra £5 economic profit out of the last hour of labour hired.

The ability of a monopsonist to make an economic profit depends on the elasticity of labour supply. The more elastic the supply of labour, the less opportunity a monopsonist has to make an economic profit. If the labour market in Fig. 15.5 were competitive, the wage rate would be £7.50 and the level of employment 75 hours. Employment and the wage rate are lower under monopsony than in a competitive labour market.

Monopsony Tendencies With today's low costs of transport, it is unlikely that many pure monopsonists remain. Workers can easily commute long distances to a job, so most people do not have just one potential employer. Nevertheless, many firms still face an upward-sloping supply of labour curve. Though they are not pure monopsonists, there is a monopsony tendency in their market in the sense that they have to offer higher wages to attract more workers. A firm's monopsony element may come from its location if it is more conveniently reached by some workers than others. Firms compete with each other for labour by offering wages that compensate their workers not only for time on the job but also for commuting time. The more workers a firm hires, the longer the commute for the marginal worker and, therefore, the higher the wage the firm has to pay to attract that worker.

Next, let's see the effects of minimum wage laws and unions in a monopsonistic labour market.

Monopsony, Minimum Wage and Unions

In Chapter 6, we saw that a minimum wage usually decreases employment. In a situation where a firm is a monopsonist, however, minimum wage regulations can actually raise both the wage rate and employment. A union can also raise both the wage rate and employment. Let's see how.

Minimum Wages and Monopsony Suppose the situation starts as shown in Fig. 15.6(a) with the firm having the marginal revenue product curve *MRP* and facing the supply curve of labour *S* with the associated marginal cost of labour curve *MCL*. The firm employs 50 hours of labour a day – as that level equates the marginal revenue product of

labour with the marginal cost of labour – and it pays a wage rate of £5 an hour as the supply curve shows this is the rate needed to secure 50 hours of labour. The government now passes a minimum wage law that prohibits anyone from hiring labour for less than £7 an hour. Firms can hire labour for more than £7 an hour but not for less. The monopsonist in Fig. 15.6(a) now faces a perfectly elastic supply of labour at £7 an hour up to 70 hours a day. To raise the quantity of hours supplied above 70 hours a day, a higher wage than £7 an hour would have to be offered. So the supply curve faced by the monopsonist becomes the kinked curve *S'*. As the wage rate is a fixed £7 an hour up to 70 hours a day, the marginal cost of labour is also constant at £7 up to 70 hours – each extra hour costs the firm £7. But beyond 70 hours, the marginal cost of labour rises above £7 an hour. Indeed, beyond 70 hours the marginal cost is exactly what it was before, as the firm faces the same supply conditions as before. So the firm ends up with the curious new marginal cost curve *MCL'*. This has two separate parts – it follows *S'* below 70 hours and it follows *MCL* above 70 hours.

To maximize profit, the monopsonist raises the quantity of labour so long as the marginal cost of labour is less than its marginal revenue product. It therefore employs 70 hours of labour, since with less labour the marginal cost is less than the marginal revenue product, while with more labour the marginal cost is higher than the marginal revenue product. To secure 70 hours, *S'* shows that the firm must pay a wage of £7 an hour. The minimum wage law has raised the wage rate by £2 an hour *and* raised the amount of labour employed by 20 hours a day.

Would further increases in the minimum wage continue indefinitely to raise employment? No it would not! The original supply curve *S* cuts *MRP* at a wage of £7.50. If the minimum wage is raised successively from the original £5 to £7.50, then each rise will raise employment too – the equilibrium moves north-eastward along *S*. But once the minimum wage is raised above £7.50, each rise brings about a fall in employment.

To see this, look at Fig. 15.6(b) which shows the results if the minimum wage is raised to £9. As in Fig. 15.6(a) there is a new kinked supply curve, *S'*, which is horizontal at the minimum wage until it meets *S*. There is also a new two-part marginal cost of labour curve, *MCL'*, which follows *S'* to the left of

FIGURE 15.6

Minimum Wage in Monopsony

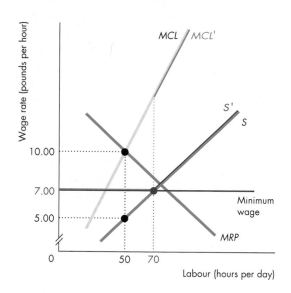

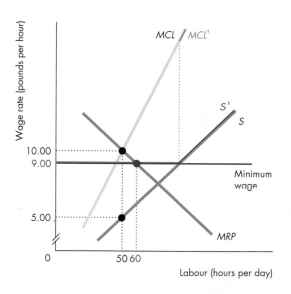

(a) Minimum wage below competitive equilibrium

(b) Minimum wage above competitive equilibrium

Without a minimum wage rule the monopsonist employs 50 hours of labour a day – the level where the marginal revenue product of labour equals its marginal cost, as shown by the intersection of *MRP* and *MCL*. The labour supply curve, *S*, shows the monopsonist must pay £5 an hour to secure 50 hours a day. If a minimum wage rule is introduced, there is a new kinked supply curve, *S'*. In part (a) the minimum wage is £7 an hour and in part (b) it is £9. Associated with each new supply curve there is a new marginal cost of labour curve, *MCL'*. This follows *S'* until the kink in *S'* and then follows the old *MCL*. The firm employs more labour so long as *MRP* exceeds *MCL'*, that is, so long as each extra hour yields more extra revenue than it costs to hire. In part (a) the firm chooses 70 hours

and in part (b) it chooses 60. As the minimum wage rises, employment also rises provided the minimum wage does not exceed £7.50 (where *MRP* cuts the original *S*). If a union enters the market, it may try to increase the wage rate above £5 an hour by threatening a strike unless the firm agrees to some new wage level above £5. How far the union can raise the wage depends on how powerful it is *vis-à-vis* the firm. If the wage ends up at £7, 70 hours will be employed, as in part (a). If the wage ends up at £9, 60 hours will be employed, as in part (b). Rising wages raise employment also until the wage reaches £7.50. Thereafter rising wages cut employment. The wage could rise to £10 an hour without employment falling below the original 50 hours a day.

the kink in *S'* and which follows the original *MCL* to the right of the kink in *S'*.

As before, the firm takes on more labour so long as its marginal cost is less than its marginal revenue product. In Fig. 15.6(b) this means employing just 60 hours of labour a day, for until labour reaches 60 hours, its marginal revenue product, shown by *MRP*, exceeds its marginal cost, shown by *MCL'*. *S'* shows that to secure 60 hours the firm must pay a wage of £9. So here the wage has risen to £9 an hour, but fewer hours are employed than in Fig. 15.6(a) when the wage was £7 an hour. You can no doubt work out that if the minimum wage rose above £10

an hour, the level of employment would fall below the original level of 50 hours.

Monopsony and Unions When we studied monopoly in Chapter 12, we discovered that a single seller in a market is able to determine the price in that market. We have just studied monopsony – a market with a single buyer – and discovered that in such a market the buyer is able to determine the price. Suppose that a union starts to operate in a monopsony labour market. A union is like a monopoly. It controls the supply of labour and acts like a single seller of labour. If the union (monopoly seller) faces a monopsony buyer, the situation is one of **bilateral monopoly**. In bilateral monopoly, the wage rate is determined by bargaining between the two traders. Let's study the bargaining process.

Recall that if the monopsony in Fig. 15.5 is free to determine the wage rate without negotiating with a union, it will hire 50 hours of labour a day for a wage rate of £5 an hour. Now suppose the workers form a union and negotiate a wage rate of £7 an hour. The firm will actually be in the situation shown in Fig. 15.6(a) since the agreed wage rate of £7 is now the lowest it can pay. The wage rate will rise to £7 an hour and employment will rise to 70 hours a day. If the union negotiates a yet higher wage rate, say £9 an hour, the firm will be in the position shown in Fig. 15.6(b), since the agreed wage rate of £9 an hour is the lowest it can now pay. The wage will rise to £9 an hour and employment will be 60 hours a day. By inspecting the two figures, you will be able to see that the highest employment level the union can secure is 75 hours a day which it could have if it agreed the wage rate of £7.50 an hour which applies at the point where *MRP* cuts *S*. The highest wage the union can have with employment no less than the original 50 hours a day is £10 an hour. So long as the wage ends up between £5 and £10 an hour, the quantity of labour will be more than 50 hours.

The actual outcome of the bargaining depends on the costs that each party can inflict on the other as a result of a failure to agree on the wage rate. The firm can shut down the plant and lock out its workers, and the workers can shut down the plant by striking. Each party knows the strength of the other. It also knows what it itself stands to lose if it does not agree to the demands of the other. The stronger the employer is relative to the union, the nearer the wage will be to the original £5 an hour. The stronger the union is relative to the employer, the higher the wage will be, perhaps reaching £10 an hour or conceivably more. Usually, an agreement is reached without a strike or a lockout. The threat – the knowledge that such an event can occur – is usually enough to bring the bargaining parties to an agreement. When strikes or lockouts do occur, it is because one party has misjudged the situation.

The Scale of Union–Non-union Wage Differentials

We have seen that unions can influence the wages of their members, partly by restricting the supply of labour or by threatening a strike if wages are not raised, and partly by manipulating the demand for labour. How much of a difference to wage rates do unions make in practice?

The answer to this question is not known with certainty. Assessing the effects of unions is difficult because so many different factors can cause a differential in earnings. For example, in some industries, union wages are higher than non-union wages because union members do jobs that involve greater skill. Even without a union, those who perform such tasks receive a higher wage. To calculate the effects of unions, the analyst has to examine the wages of unionized and non-unionized workers who do nearly identical work.

Many studies have been made and they have given different results. No doubt this is partly because the union mark-up varies between industries and over time. However, the studies suggest that the mark-up usually lies in a range between 2 per cent and 30 per cent, probably averaging around 8 per cent.

Differences in earnings based on skill or education level arise because skilled labour has a higher marginal revenue product than unskilled labour and because skills are costly to acquire. Union workers have higher wages than non-union workers because unions are able to control the supply of labour and may be able, indirectly, to influence the marginal revenue product of their members. ◆

Wage Differentials between the Sexes

There are substantial differences between the average earnings of men and women. On average, full-time working women have earnings that are just 71 per cent those of full-time working men. This difference does not necessarily mean that women get less pay for similar jobs. It arises substantially because women are generally dominant in low-paid jobs – such as shop assistants – while men are generally dominant in well-paid jobs – such as office managers. Even if female shop assistants and female office managers were paid just as well as their male counterparts, women on average would earn less than men because most office managers are men while most shop assistants are women.

However, even within categories such as shop assistants and office managers, females on average receive less than males. Figure 15.7 provides a snapshot of the differences in 1993 for a number of occupations. We chose these particular occupations because they are performed by substantial numbers of both men and women – it is much harder to make meaningful comparisons in occupations such as garage mechanics or typists where one sex is dominant.

Why do these differentials exist, and why do they persist? Do they arise because there is discrimination against women or is there some other explanation? This controversial question generates an enormous amount of passion. It is not our intention to make you angry, though that may happen as an unintended consequence of this discussion. The objective of this section is to show you how to use economic analysis to address controversial and emotionally charged issues.

We are going to examine three possible explanations for these earnings differences:

◆ Discrimination
◆ Differences in human capital
◆ Differences in degree of specialization

Discrimination

At first it might be wondered if women clerks or assemblers receive less than men because employers pay men more than women for doing identical jobs. However, the 1970 Equal Pay Act makes such discrimination illegal. This may not mean that such discrimination never occurs, but it suggests that it is unlikely to be a major cause of the differences in pay between the sexes.

Instead, the major reason is that within each of the categories shown in Fig. 15.7 – and indeed within other categories of work as well – the better-paid jobs are held disproportionately by men. For example, a disproportionate number of secondary school heads are male, just as a disproportionate number of shop managers are male. Thus the question of why women are paid less than men is substantially a

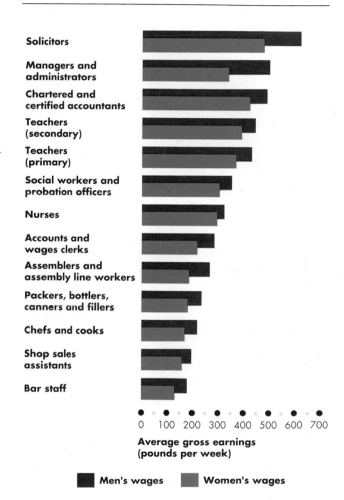

FIGURE 15.7

Sex Differentials in Earnings for Selected Occupations

For full-time employees, women, on average, earn about 71 per cent of the amount earned by men. Much of this difference is accounted for by the fact that women predominate in lower-paid jobs. The figure compares the average gross weekly wages of full-time adults in selected occupations. Here females' earnings as a percentage of males' range from 68 per cent (managers and administrators) to 92 per cent (nurses).

Source: Department of Employment, *New Earnings Survey 1993: Part D*, 1993, Tables 86 and 87.

question of why the better-paid jobs in each occupation tend to be dominated by men.

Part of the answer may be one of prejudice among those who appoint people to the better-paid jobs.

Because many firms are currently managed predominantly by men, it follows that appointments to better-paid jobs are typically made by men. Some men may be prejudiced against women and this may help account for the difficulty women have in securing better job positions.

Unfortunately for women, there are yet other prejudices that could affect their chances of being well paid. To see how another prejudice can affect earnings, let's look at an example – the market for life insurance salespeople. These people are employed by finance companies and advise members of the public on suitable life insurance policies for their particular needs. Whenever someone takes out a policy on their advice, some of the premiums paid on the policy are given to the finance company employing the salesperson concerned.

Suppose that there are two groups of insurance salespeople – women and men – who are identical in terms of giving good advice about suitable policies.

Figure 15.8 shows the supply curve of women, S_W, in part (a) and the supply curve of men, S_M, in part (b). These supply curves are identical.

Suppose that everyone in this society is free from prejudice about sex. Then the marginal revenue product curves for insurance salespeople are identical irrespective of whether they are women or men. These curves are shown by the two curves labelled MRP in parts (a) and (b). The market for saleswomen determines a wage rate of £40,000 a year and there are 2,000 saleswomen. The market for salesmen also determines a wage rate of £40,000 a year, and there are 2,000 salesmen.

In contrast to the previous situation, now suppose that people who take out life insurance policies are prejudiced against women. As before, the two types of advisers are equally able, but the prejudice is so strong that people are more reluctant to take out a policy advised by a woman than one advised by a man. Because of the differences in the numbers of

FIGURE 15.8

Discrimination

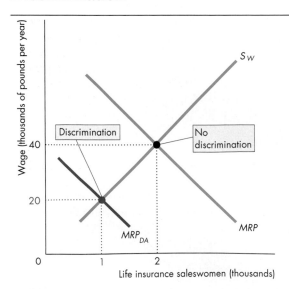

(a) Women

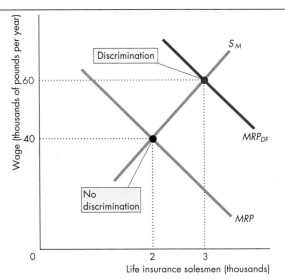

(b) Men

The supply curve for insurance saleswomen is S_W (in part a) and the supply curve for insurance salesmen is S_M (in part b). If the marginal revenue product of both groups of salespeople is MRP (the same curve in each part), the equilibrium wage rate for each group is £40,000 a year and 2,000 of each sex are employed. If there is discrimination against women, the marginal revenue product curve of the saleswomen is to the left of the original curve. It is the

curve labelled MRP_{DA} – DA standing for 'discriminated against'. There is discrimination in favour of salesmen, so their marginal revenue product curve is MRP_{DF} – DF standing for 'discriminated in favour of'. The wage rate for women falls to £20,000 a year and only 1,000 are employed. The wage rate for men rises to £60,000 a year and 3,000 are employed.

policies that each sex can sell, based purely on the prejudices of people taking out life insurance policies, the marginal revenue products of the two groups are different. The abilities of the two groups are the same, but the values that prejudiced citizens place on their output are not the same. Suppose that the marginal revenue product of the women, when discriminated against, is the line labelled $MRP_{DA} - DA$ standing for 'discriminated against'. Suppose that the marginal revenue product for men, the group discriminated in favour of, is $MRP_{DF} - DF$ standing for 'discriminated in favour of'. Given these marginal revenue product curves, the markets for the two groups of salespeople now determine very different wages and employment levels. The women earn £20,000 a year and only 1,000 will be employed. The men earn £60,000 a year and 3,000 of them will be employed. Thus purely on the basis of the prejudice of the people taking out life insurance policies, women in this lucrative field will earn one-third the wages of men, and three-quarters of all salespeople will be men.

This example of how prejudice by the general public can produce differences in earnings is purely hypothetical, just as the earlier suggestion of prejudice among some of those responsible for appointing people for better-paid jobs was hypothetical. Does prejudice actually cause wage differentials? Economists disagree for a simple reason, but one that is difficult to overcome: you can recognize prejudice when you see it, but you cannot easily measure it. Our model shows how sex differentials might come from prejudice. But without a way of measuring prejudice in the real world, we cannot easily test that model to see if it is true.

We need to make another point. Our model of prejudice shows an equilibrium, albeit an unhappy one. But simply because a model is in equilibrium does not mean that the equilibrium is either desirable or inevitable. Economic theory makes predictions about the way things will be, not moral statements about the way things ought to be. Policies designed to bring equal wages and employment prospects to women can be devised. But to be successful, such policies must be based on careful economic analysis. Good intentions are not enough to bring about equality.

Human Capital Differences

As we saw earlier in this chapter, wages compensate people partly for time spent on the job and partly for the cost incurred in acquiring skill and knowledge –

in acquiring human capital. The more human capital a person supplies, the more that person earns, other things being equal. It is possible that men, on average, have more human capital than women. If so, they might well find it easier to get better-paid jobs. Measuring human capital with any precision is difficult, but there are some indicators which suggest that, on average, men do have more.

One indicator of human capital is the amount of education a person has had. Here the gap between men and women is narrowing or even reversing. The gap has narrowed markedly at the graduate level in the United Kingdom. Thus among 50 and 60 year olds, there are more than 3 male graduates for every female graduate, but among 20 and 30 year olds, there are under 1½ male graduates for every female graduate. The attainment gap has actually reversed at sixth form level. In 1969-1970, for example, 14 per cent of boys left school with two or more 'A' levels (or three or more 'Highers') compared with 12 per cent of girls, but 20 years later the figures were 20 per cent for boys and 21.5 per cent for girls.

A second possible indicator of human capital is experience, which is affected by time out of employment. Traditionally, women's careers have been interrupted more frequently than men's, usually for bearing and rearing children. On average, the earnings of men and women rise by 3 per cent each year when they are in work and fall by 3 per cent for each year when they are out of work – a fact which suggests that human capital depreciates when not in use. Suppose that Samuel and Samantha work for a few years after leaving college and then have some children. Samantha takes seven years out to look after the children. If she was paid as much as Samuel when she left the work force, she can expect to be paid only two-thirds as much when she returns. However, career interruptions for women are becoming less severe. Maternity leave and day-care facilities are providing an increasing number of women with uninterrupted employment that makes their human capital accumulation indistinguishable from that of men.

There are, however, other aspects of experience which may count against women. For example, women are more often absent, partly because they usually end up looking after sick children and partly because they are more prone than men to long-term illness. Also, women can retire on state pensions at 60 whereas men must wait until they are 65. As a result, many women retire earlier than men so there are more old male employees around to apply for jobs where experience is important. This factor should disappear between 2010 and 2020 when the state pension age for women will gradually be raised to 65.

We can conclude that human capital differences help account for earnings differentials between the sexes. The gap is closing but is not wholly disappearing. Reading Between the Lines on pp. 422–423 looks at the factors causing a rising number of women to train as airline pilots.

Degrees of Specialization

People undertake two kinds of production activities: they supply labour services to the market (market activity) and they undertake household production (non-market activity). **Household production** creates goods and services to be consumed within the household, rather than to be supplied to the market. Such activities include cooking, cleaning, minor repair work, education, and organizational services such as arranging holidays and other leisure activities. Bearing and rearing children is another important non-market activity.

In Chapter 3, we saw that people can gain from specializing in activities and trading their output with each other. Specialization and the gains from trade do not operate exclusively in the marketplace. They also occur within the household. It is not uncommon for one member of a household to specialize in shopping, another in cleaning, another in gardening and so on. Specialization in bearing children is a biological necessity, although rearing them is not.

Consider a household that has two members – Bob and Sue. They must decide how to allocate their time between market activity and various non-market household production activities. One solution is for Bob to specialize in market activity and for Sue to specialize in non-market activity. Another solution is to reverse the roles and for Sue to specialize in market activity and Bob in non-market activity. Alternatively, one or both of them can become diversified, doing some market and some non-market activity. An egalitarian allocation will have them share the non-market tasks equally and devote the same amount of time and energy to market activity.

In deciding which of the allocations to choose, Bob and Sue will consider their future plans for having children. The allocation chosen by Bob and Sue will depend on their preferences and also on their market earning potential. An increasing number of households are choosing the egalitarian allocation

with each person diversified between non-market household production and market activity. Many households, however, still choose an allocation that would have Bob almost fully specialized in market activity and Sue covering a diversity of tasks in both the job market and the household. What are the effects of this more common assignment of market and non-market tasks? Does it result in men earning more per hour than women? We have already seen one reason for believing that it does, because it results in men having more experience than women. But it has been argued that there is another reason why it could result in men earning more than women. The argument is that if Sue devotes a great deal of productive effort to ensuring Bob's mental and physical well-being, the quality of Bob's market labour will be higher than if he were undertaking half the household production tasks. If the roles were reversed, Sue would have a higher earning potential in the marketplace than Bob.

Economists have attempted to test whether the degree of specialization can account for earnings differentials between the sexes by examining the wages of men and women where, as far as possible, the degree of specialization is held constant. For example, if the degree of specialization is an important factor influencing a person's wage, then men and women of identical ages and educational backgrounds in identical occupations will be paid different wages depending on whether they are single, married to a spouse who specializes in household production, or married to a spouse who works. Single men and women who live alone and who are equally specialized in household and market production and who have the same amounts of human capital and who do similar jobs will be paid the same wage. To make non-market factors as similar as possible, two groups have been chosen for analysis. They are 'never married' men and 'never married' women. The available evidence suggests that, on average, when they have the same amount of human capital – measured by years of schooling, work experience and career interruptions – the wages of these two groups are still not identical but they are much closer than the difference between *average* wages for men and women. When allowance is made for degree of specialization and human capital, the wage differential comes down to between 5 and 10 per cent, by some estimates. Some economists suspect the remaining discrepancy stems from discrimination against women, although the difficulty of measuring such discrimination makes this hypothesis hard to test.

Most of the difference in men's and women's wages arises from the fact that men and women do different jobs and, for the most part, men's jobs are better paid than women's jobs. There are, however, an increasing number of women entering areas that were traditionally the preserve of men. The narrowing of the attainment gap in education, which we mentioned earlier, should greatly help this trend.

Pay Equity Laws

The 1970 Equal Pay Act requires equal pay for equal work without discrimination on the basis of sex. Increasingly, attempts are being made to find ways of comparing jobs that are essentially different but require, on some criteria, similar degrees of skill.

Such comparisons lead to a broader concept than 'equal pay for equal work'; they call for equal pay for comparable work. Paying the same wage for different jobs that are judged to be comparable is called **equal pay for work of equal value**.

Advocates of pay equity laws argue that wages should be determined by analysing the characteristics of jobs and determining their worth on objective grounds. Such a method of determining wage rates might be capable of achieving greater equity in situations in which discrimination is at work. But when earnings differences result from differences in productivity, they will not achieve the objectives sought by supporters of wage equality. Let's see why.

Figure 15.9 shows two markets: that for oil rig operators in part (a) and that for shepherds in part (b). The marginal revenue product curves (MRP_R and MRP_S) and the supply curves (S_R and S_S) are shown for each type of labour. Competitive equilibrium generates a wage rate W_R for oil rig operators and W_S for shepherds.

FIGURE 15.9

A Problem with Equal Pay for Work of Equal Value

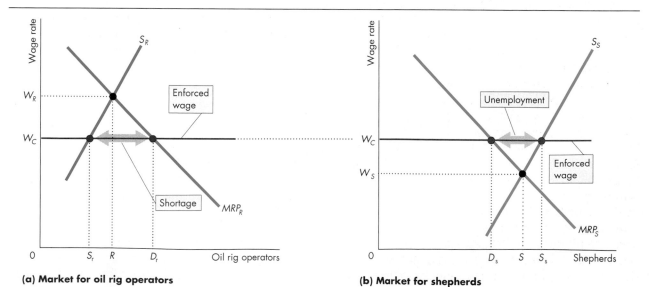

(a) Market for oil rig operators

(b) Market for shepherds

The demand for and supply of oil rig operators, MRP_R and S_R, are shown in part (a), and those for shepherds, MRP_S and S_S, in part (b). The competitive equilibrium wage rate for oil rig operators is W_R, and that for shepherds is W_S. If an evaluation of the two jobs finds that they are of equal value and rules that the wage rate W_C be paid to both types of workers, there is an excess of demand for oil rig operators and an excess supply of shepherds. There are $S_s - D_s$ shepherds unemployed and a shortage of $D_r - S_r$ oil rig operators. Oil producers have to find other labour-saving ways of producing oil, that are more expensive, and shepherds have to find other jobs, that are less desirable to them.

Female Pilots

Men outnumber women as civil commercial pilots by more than 60 to 1.

The airlines say that there is no discrimination and highlight a number of reasons why such a male bias should have come about.

The cost of training a pilot is £60,000.

This cost is very high and, if not sponsored by an airline, an individual may well have to take out a very large loan, something women have traditionally been less inclined to do than men.

The number of women pilots is predicted to increase in the future.

THE TIMES, 4 FEBRUARY 1992

Sky is no limit as women take wing

Beryl Dixon

THERE are more women commercial pilots than a decade ago: 95 of the 5,880 British Airline Pilots' Association members are female, but that is still a small minority.

Captain Yvonne Sintes, Britain's first female commercial pilot, flew on the De Havilland Comet, the BAC 1-11 and the IIS 748 for Dan-Air from 1969 until she retired in 1980. Dan-Air now employs seven more women pilots, including one captain of a Boeing 727, who has been flying for 20 years. The others are first officers based at Manchester, Aberdeen and Gatwick flying Boeing 727, 737s, BAC-111 and IIS 748 aircraft.

Monarch has three, Air UK 14, two of whom are captains, while British Midland has one, who qualified last March. British Airways has 30, none yet at captain level, but that, says the airline, is only a matter of time.

There is no prejudice, the airlines hasten to stress. Women simply do not apply in the same numbers as men. There are, however, two hurdles for anybody who hopes to become a pilot. The first is the competition for sponsored training places. Airlines willing to pay all, or even part, of the cost of a pilot's training can take their pick from 10,000 applicants whenever they advertise. Of those, 100 might make it to an air training college.

The second is the cost of training. In order to fly a British-registered aircraft for hire and reward, it is essential to hold a commercial pilot's licence (CPL), awarded by the Civil Aviation Authority. Some achieve this by first gaining a private pilot's licence. This is not cheap, since it requires 35 hours' tuition. Then there is the further expense of logging the 700 hours of flying experience required before sitting practical and written tests for the commercial licence.

The alternative is to take a course at a flying school. Several exist though not all take students up to full CPL standard. A student hoping to enter either the Oxford or Prestwick schools, the two which offer the full training, will need to find more than £60,000. In general, women are less willing than men to take out such large bank loans. However, this did not deter Sally Griffiths, another British Airways pilot and former stewardess, who made the headlines two years ago by giving up her job and selling her house to finance her training.

© The Times. Reprinted with permission.

The main reason for the lack of women pilots is the traditionally lower level of human capital in women.

In order to be able to qualify for a commercial pilot's licence (CPL), candidates must have a minimum number of public examinations – GCSEs or, if requiring sponsorship from a major airline, A levels.

These qualifications include a maths and science/physics bias which previously would have affected women more than men.

More girls in school are now studying for science qualifications. In addition, there are now more girls than boys leaving school with two or more A levels.

In both absolute and relative terms, therefore, the level of human capital appropriate for pilot training embodied in women has been rising in recent years.

There is also a physical reason why women may be excluded from becoming a pilot, in that there can be a minimum height specified for applicants.

British Airways says the height requirement is necessary in order for pilots to reach all of the controls, though there may be an element of discrimination in the way cockpits are constructed.

In the figure, as the human capital in women increases with more appropriate qualifications and more women being willing to invest in their own future skills, so the supply curve of women in the market for pilot training places will shift to the right.

The supply of women increases and, if there is no discrimination in the selection of candidates, there will be more women being taken on for training and eventually more women pilots.

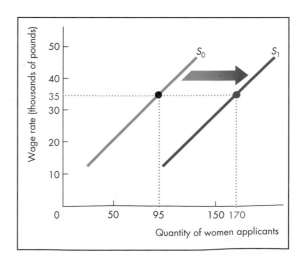

Suppose that the knowledge and skills required in those two occupations – the mental and physical demands, the responsibilities and the working conditions – result in a judgement that these two jobs are of comparable worth. The wage rate that is judged to apply to each of them is W_C, and the courts enforce this wage rate. What happens? First, there is a shortage of oil rig operators. Oil rig companies are able to hire only S_r workers at the wage rate W_C. They cut back their production or build more expensive labour-saving oil rigs. There is also a fall in the number of shepherds employed. But this fall occurs because farmers demand fewer shepherds. At the higher wage W_C, farmers demand only D_s shepherds. The quantity of shepherds supplied is S_s and the difference between S_s and D_s is the number of unemployed shepherds looking for jobs. These shepherds eventually accept other types of jobs. Their new jobs will be ones they like less than looking after sheep, either in terms of pay or job satisfaction, since otherwise they would not have been shepherds in the first place. Thus legislated equal pay for work of equal value may have serious and costly unintended consequences.

REVIEW

Wage differences between the sexes may arise partly from discrimination and from differences in human capital. They may also arise from differences in the degree of specialization between women and men. To reduce differentials, it is necessary to reduce discrimination and to reduce differences in marginal revenue product. The process of equalization of human capital and of the degree of specialization will lead to lower differentials and may possibly eliminate them. ◆

◆ ◆ ◆ ◆   In this chapter, we have extended the factor markets model and applied it to an understanding of a wide variety of phenomena in labour markets, especially phenomena concerning wage differentials. In the next chapter, we apply and extend the factor markets model to deal with markets for capital and for natural resources.

SUMMARY

Skill Differentials

Skill differentials in wage rates arise partly because skilled labour has a higher marginal product than unskilled labour and partly because skills are costly to acquire. The higher marginal product of skilled workers results in a higher marginal revenue product. Since the demand for labour curve is derived from the marginal revenue product curve, the higher the marginal revenue product of skilled labour, the greater is the demand for skilled labour.

Skills are costly to acquire because households have to invest in human capital to become skilled. Investment sometimes means making direct payments, such as tuition and other training fees, and it sometimes means living on a low grant or a low wage during on-the-job training. Because skills are costly to acquire, households supply skilled labour on terms that compensate them for both the time spent on the job and the costs of acquiring the skills. Thus the supply curve of skilled labour lies above the supply curve of unskilled labour.

The wage rates of skilled and unskilled labour are determined by demand and supply in the two labour markets. The equilibrium wage rate for skilled labour exceeds that for unskilled labour. The wage differential reflects the higher marginal product of skill and the cost of acquiring skill. (pp. 406–409)

Union–Non-union Wage Differentials

Trade unions seek to raise wages in various ways. They may try to affect the supply side of the labour market, perhaps by threatening strikes or reducing the supply of labour, for instance by negotiating higher entry qualifications for new workers. Unions may also try to affect the demand side of the labour market, perhaps by trying to reduce competitive imports, or raising the demand for their members' outputs, or raising productivity. Each of these steps should increase the demand for their members' labour.

In competitive labour markets, action by unions

on the supply side results in higher wages only at the expense of lower employment. In a monopsony – a market in which there is a single buyer – unions can increase wages to a certain extent without sacrificing employment. For wage increases will raise the quantity of labour demanded until it reaches the level that would be employed in a competitive labour market. Thereafter, further wage rises will reduce employment.

A situation where the union is a monopoly seller of labour, the firm is a monopsony buyer of labour and the wage rate is determined by bargaining between the two parties is called bilateral monopoly.

In practice, union workers in the United Kingdom earn an estimated 8 per cent more than comparable non-union workers. (pp. 409–416)

Wage Differentials between the Sexes

There are persistent differentials in earnings between women and men. Three possible explanations are discrimination, differences in human capital and differences in the degree of specialization.

Discrimination results in lower wage rates and lower employment for those discriminated against, and higher wage rates and higher employment levels for those discriminated in favour of. Human capital differences result from differences in education and work experience. Differentials based on education have been falling. Differentials based on work experience have kept women's pay below men's because women's careers have traditionally been interrupted more frequently than those of men, resulting, on average, in a smaller accumulation of human capital. This difference is less important today than in the past. Differentials arising from different degrees of specialization are probably important and may persist. Men have traditionally been more specialized in market activity than women. Women have traditionally undertaken both non-market (household production) activities and market activities. Attempts to test for the importance of the degree of specialization suggest that it is an important source of the earnings difference between men and women. (pp. 416–421)

Pay Equity Laws

Pay equity laws would determine wages by assessing the value of different types of jobs on objective characteristics rather than on what the market will pay. Determining wages through the principle of equal pay for work of equal value would reduce the number of workers willing to work in occupations where the market places a higher value than the law, and it would reduce the number of jobs available in occupations where the market places a lower value than the law. So an attempt to achieve equal pay for work of equal value will have costly, unintended consequences. (pp. 421–424)

K E Y   E L E M E N T S

Key Terms

Key Figures and Tables

R E V I E W Q U E S T I O N S

1 Explain why skilled workers are paid more than unskilled workers.

2 What are the main types of trade union?

3 Describe two ways in which a union can try to influence the supply side of the market for its members' labour.

4 How might a trade union increase the demand for its members' labour?

5 Under what circumstances would a minimum wage increase employment?

6 How big are the union–non-union wage differentials in the United Kingdom today?

7 What are the three main reasons why earnings differentials exist between men and women?

8 How would pay equity laws work? What would be their predicted effects?

P R O B L E M S

1 Wendy owns an apple orchard. She employs students to pick the apples. In an hour, they can pick the following quantities of apples:

Number of students	Quantity of apples (kilograms)
1	20
2	50
3	90
4	120
5	145
6	165
7	180
8	190

a Draw the average and marginal product curves of these students.

b If Wendy can sell her apples for 40 pence a kilogram, draw Wendy's average and marginal revenue product curves.

c Draw Wendy's demand for labour curve.

d If all apple growers in Wendy's neighbourhood pay their pickers £6 an hour, how many students will Wendy hire?

2 Assume that fruit pickers become unionized and student pickers are outlawed. If the union gets the wage increased to £8 an hour, how many unionized pickers will Wendy hire?

3 In a small isolated town in Scotland, the only firm hiring workers is a whisky distillery. The marginal revenue product of labour for the firm is as follows:

Quantity of labour (hours per day)	Marginal revenue product (pounds from an extra hour)
100	10
150	9
200	8
250	7
300	6
350	5
400	4

The supply of labour by the townspeople is given by:

Wage rate (pounds per hour)	Quantity supplied (hours per day)
3	150
4	200
5	250
6	300
7	350
8	400

a Draw a graph showing the marginal revenue product curve of labour for this firm.

b On the same graph show the supply curve of labour to the firm.

c Suppose the firm was hiring 50 hours a day and wanted to hire 51. Assuming that a wage of £3.02 would be needed to secure 51 hours per day, how much would the firm's labour costs rise if it hired the extra hour? (Give your answer to the nearest pound.)

d Suppose the firm was hiring 300 hours a day and wanted to hire 301. Assuming that a wage of £6.02 would be needed to secure 301 hours per day, how much would the firm's labour costs rise if it hired the extra hour? (Give your answer to the nearest pound.)

e Using your answers to (c) and (d), plot the firm's marginal cost of labour curve on your graph.

f How many hours will the firm wish to employ?

g What wage rate will the firm have to pay to secure this number of hours?

4 Suppose the workers in the town referred to in Problem 3 form a union whose representatives negotiate a higher wage with the distillery management.

a How many hours will be hired by the firm if the new wage is £6?

b How many hours will be hired by the firm if the new wage is £9?

CHAPTER 16

CAPITAL AND NATURAL RESOURCE MARKETS

After studying this chapter you will be able to:

◆ Define and distinguish between financial and physical assets, capital and investment

◆ Define and distinguish between saving and portfolio choice

◆ Describe the structure of capital markets in the United Kingdom today

◆ Explain how interest rates and stock prices are determined and why the stock market fluctuates

◆ Define natural resources and explain how their prices are determined

◆ Explain how markets regulate the pace at which we use exhaustible resources such as oil

A N AIR OF PANIC FILLED THE WORLD'S STOCK EXCHANGES ON MONDAY, 19 October, 1987. For several years, share prices around the world had followed a rising trend. But on that single day, share prices in New York fell by 23 per cent, and this spectacular fall sparked off falls in other stock markets later the same day – 4.6 per cent in Paris, 7.0 per cent in Frankfurt and 10.8 per cent in London. Why does the stock market boom for several years and then crash suddenly and spectacularly? ◆ ◆ Every year, billions of pounds are saved and flow into the world's capital markets. The money people save flows through banks, insurance companies and stock exchanges and ends up financing the pur-chases of machinery, factory and office buildings, cars and homes. How does a pound saved and placed on deposit in a bank enable Schweppes to open a new bottling plant? ◆ ◆ Many of our natural resources are exhaustible and yet we are using them up at a rapid rate. Every year we use billions of litres of petrol and millions of tonnes of coal. Aren't we one day going to run out of these and other natural resources? How are their prices determined? And do their prices adjust to encourage conservation, or does the market need help to ensure that we do not pillage nature's exhaustible endowments?

Boom and Bust

◆ ◆ ◆ ◆ In this chapter, we study capital and natural resource markets. We'll find out what determines the amount of saving and purchases of new capital equip-ment, and how interest rates and stock values are determined. In our study of natural resource markets, we'll discover how market forces encourage conserva-tion.

Capital, Investment and Saving

Let's begin with some capital market vocabulary and define three key terms:

◆ Asset
◆ Liability
◆ Balance sheet

An **asset** is anything of value that a household, firm, or government *owns*. A **liability** is a debt – something that a household, firm, or government *owes*. A **balance sheet** is a list of assets and liabilities.

Table 16.1 shows a very simple example of a balance sheet for a firm – that for Dawson's Mountain Bikes which is a sole proprietorship. It lists three assets, a deposit in the bank, a stock of bikes, and fixtures and fittings, that add up to £243,000. The balance sheet contains two liabilities, a bank loan of £120,000 and the amount the firm owes to Dawson – Dawson's contribution to the firm – £123,000. To see why the two sides balance, you might find it helpful to consider how the firm acquired the money to purchase its £243,000 worth of assets. It acquired £120,000 from the bank and the rest from Dawson. Dawson probably found most of this money over the years from the profits of his bike shop, but he may also have used money from other sources such as interest on a building society deposit.

Financial Assets and Real Assets

Assets can be divided into two broad groups: financial and physical. A **financial asset** is a claim against another household, firm or government. It is a type of IOU. When you hold an IOU, it means that somebody else owes you money. Similarly, if you own a financial asset, someone else has a financial liability and owes you money. For example, your bank deposit is an asset to you but a liability of your bank. The difference in value between financial assets and financial liabilities is called **net financial assets**. Net financial assets are the net value of the claims that one household, firm or government has against everyone else.

Physical assets are physical things such as plant, buildings, vehicles, machinery and stocks. Physical assets are also called capital. The **capital**

TABLE 16.1

Balance Sheet of Dawson's Mountain Bikes on 1 January 1994

Assets	£	Liabilities	£
Deposit in bank	18,000	Bank loan	120,000
Stock of bikes	15,000	Dawson's contribution	123,000
Fixtures and fittings	210,000		
Total assets	243,000	Total liabilities	243,000

of a household, firm or government is the value of its physical assets.

Table 16.2 illustrates the distinction between financial assets and physical assets by presenting the information contained in the balance sheet of Dawson's Mountain Bikes in a different way. This time the information is sorted into financial and physical items. The financial items include the bank deposit (an asset) and the bank loan (a liability). To calculate net financial assets, we must

TABLE 16.2

Financial Assets and Physical Assets of Dawson's Mountain Bikes on 1 January 1994

FINANCIAL ASSETS (+) AND FINANCIAL LIABILITIES (–)	£
Cash in bank	18,000
Bank loan	–120,000
Dawson's contribution	–123,000
Net financial assets	–225,000

PHYSICAL ASSETS	
Stock of bikes	15,000
Fixtures and fittings	210,000
Capital	225,000

subtract financial liabilities from financial assets, so the bank loan and Dawson's contribution appear with negative signs. The net financial assets of Dawson's Mountain Bikes are –£225,000. The real assets are the stock of bikes and the fixtures and fittings – the firm's capital – which add up to £225,000.

Capital and Investment

All the assets and liabilities recorded in a balance sheet are stocks. A **stock** is a quantity measured at a point in time. An example of a stock is the amount of water in Lough Neagh, the largest lake in the British Isles, at a given moment. Capital is a stock because it is the quantity of plant, buildings, vehicles, machinery and stocks in existence at a given point in time.

A concept related to the stock of capital is the flow of investment. A **flow** measures a quantity per unit of time. An example of a flow is the volume of water an hour passing from various streams into Lough Neagh. This flow adds to the stock of water in Lough Neagh. **Investment** by a firm is the amount of new capital purchased in a given time period. There is another flow that reduces the stock of capital, like the water flowing out of Lough Neagh through the River Bann. That flow is **depreciation** which is the fall in the value of capital resulting from its use and from the passage of time.

Investment increases the capital stock while depreciation reduces it. The net change in the capital stock is the difference between investment and depreciation. To emphasize this fact, we distinguish between **gross investment**, the value of all the new capital purchased in a given time period, and **net investment**, which equals gross investment minus depreciation.

Saving and Portfolio Choice

The quantity of capital supplied in the economy results from households' saving decisions. **Saving** is income minus consumption. Households use their saving to acquire assets. They also acquire assets by using any bequests or gifts they have received and by borrowing. We can see this by looking at Table 16.3 which shows the balance sheet for Dawson's household. This is quite separate from the balance sheet for Dawson's Mountain

TABLE 16.3

Balance Sheet of Dawson Household on 1 January 1994

Assets	£	Liabilities	£
Deposit in bank	10,000	Mortgage	140,000
House and contents	210,000	Loan for buying car	10,000
Car	15,000	Gifts and bequests	50,000
Contribution to Dawson's		Dawson household's	
Mountain Bikes	123,000	contribution	158,000
Total assets	358,000	Total liabilities	358,000

Bikes. The Dawson household's assets comprise a bank deposit, the house itself together with its contents, and the car. The liabilities include a mortgage, that is a loan taken out to help pay for the home, a loan to help pay for the car, some bequests and gifts, and the household's own contribution. This contribution comes chiefly from past saving. But if the value of the home rose at any time, then the value of the household's own contribution would be written down as a higher amount to make the two sides balance. Effectively the household would be credited with having secured the increased value of the house.

A household's choice regarding how much to hold in various assets and how much to owe in various liabilities is called its **portfolio choice**. For example, if a household decides to borrow £100,000 from a bank and to use that £100,000 to buy shares in a company, the household is making a portfolio choice. It is choosing the amount of an asset (the shares) and the amount of a liability (the loan).

In everyday language, we often refer to the purchase of securities such as shares as investment. That everyday use of the word 'investment' can cause confusion in economic analysis, and it is to avoid that confusion that we use the term 'portfolio choice' to refer to the choices that households make in deciding what liabilities and assets to have. What do economists mean by the word 'investment'? There would be much to be said for economists using the word investment to cover *all* purchases of physical assets by households or firms – or, indeed, governments. In practice, though, the word usually has a slightly narrower coverage, for while in the case of firms and governments it is taken to cover all purchases of physical assets, in the case of households it is taken to cover only purchases of buildings. When the households in an economy spend money on physical assets other than buildings, such expenditure is generally regarded as forming part of the consumers' expenditure in that economy rather than part of the investment expenditure in that economy.

Let's look at an example of a household balance sheet to illustrate the concept of portfolio choice. For our example we'll take the Dawson household's situation. Table 16.4 shows the same information that we saw in Table 16.3, but it distinguishes between financial assets and physical assets, and it shows financial liabilities with a minus sign. You can see that the Dawson household's net financial assets amount to –£17,000. What is the household's wealth? **Wealth** is the sum of a household's capital stock and net financial assets. Since this household's net financial assets are negative - on balance it owes £17,000 - its wealth is its £225,000 capital stock minus the £17,000 that is owed, which is £208,000.

TABLE 16.4

Financial Assets and Physical Assets for Dawson's Household

FINANCIAL ASSETS (+) AND FINANCIAL LIABILITIES (–)	£
Contribution to Dawson's Mountain Bikes	123,000
Deposit in bank	10,000
Mortgage	–140,000
Loan for buying car	–10,000
Net financial assets	–17,000
PHYSICAL ASSETS	
House and contents	210,000
Car	15,000
Capital	225,000
Wealth	208,000

REVIEW

There are two kinds of assets, financial and physical. Financial assets are the claims that lenders have on borrowers. One person's financial asset is another person's financial liability. Physical assets are plant, buildings, vehicles, machinery and stocks. Capital is the stock of physical assets in existence at a point in time. Capital wears out over time in a process called depreciation. A household's wealth is its stock of physical assets plus its net financial assets. The allocation of wealth among different assets is called portfolio choice. ◆

Capital Markets in the United Kingdom Today

We have seen that investment is generally defined as all purchases of capital by firms and governments, along with purchases of homes by households. Let's consider how firms, governments and households get the money they need to finance their investment. Figure 16.1 illustrates the financing of investment. It shows that households ultimately finance all investment.

Households can finance investment in three ways. They can:

1. Purchase capital, especially new homes and new assets for the sole proprietorships and partnerships that they own.

2. Buy securities which are issued by firms and by governments. Securities issued by firms are usually called shares whereas those issued by central governments and local authorities are usually called bonds.

3. Deposit or lend money to financial intermediaries.

Financial intermediaries are firms that take money from households which are saving and use it to help anyone who needs money to finance investment. They include banks and building societies, where households generally place money in the form of short-term deposits, and they include pension

FIGURE 16.1

Capital Market Flows

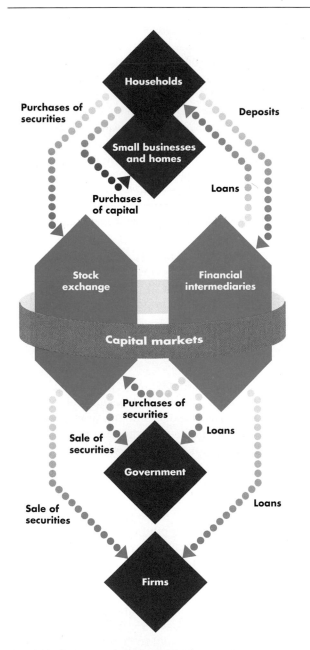

Households, firms, governments and financial intermediaries have extensive interactions in capital markets. Households purchase homes, they purchase assets for sole proprietorships and partnerships, they place money with financial intermediaries and they purchase securities on the stock exchange. Financial intermediaries lend money to households, firms and governments, and they also buy securities on the stock exchange.

funds and life insurance companies, which households entrust with money they wish to save for longer periods. People save with pension funds until they retire when they receive a pension in return. People save with life insurance companies by buying life insurance policies. These policies come in many forms, but typically people who save in this way agree to make a series of payments over many years in return for a guaranteed sum to be repaid either at a specified future date or on death. Figure 16.1 shows that financial intermediaries lend some money to households, who need it to finance their purchases of homes or assets in small businesses such as sole proprietorships and partnerships, and they also lend money to companies and governments. In addition, financial intermediaries buy securities.

The Nation's Balance Sheet

How large are the capital markets? How big a role do the various elements play? To give some idea of this, let's recall from Fig. 16.1 that households can allocate their saving in three main ways: purchasing capital, especially new homes and new assets for sole proprietorships and partnerships; buying securities issued by firms and governments; and entrusting their money to financial intermediaries. Households also have small amounts of other assets, notably cash, which are not shown on the figure. Every year extra household saving is channelled into aquiring more assets. Table 16.5 shows the total values of the different types of assets held by households on 31 December 1993. On that day, total household assets were worth £3,087 billion. Against this, households had financial liabilities of some £506 billion and hence a total wealth of £2,581 billion (this figure excludes assets in the form of consumer durables such as cars, radios and carpets). The huge size of this wealth can perhaps be best appreciated by saying it was four times the total output of the country in 1993.

The numbers in Table 16.5 give you an idea of the scale of the operations of the various elements in the capital markets. But they do not provide a flavour of the huge volume of transactions that take place – the flow of activity each day – or of the dynamic change over time in the scale of capital market transactions. The daily turnover in the ownership of securities is enormous. On a quiet day on the London Stock Exchange some 20,000 deals may be struck between buyers and sellers, but on 20 October 1987 some 79,000 deals were made.

TABLE 16.5

The Balance Sheet for the United Kingdom's Personal Sector on 31 December 1993 (billions of pounds)

PHYSICAL ASSETS	
Housing	**1,304**
Physical assets used by sole proprietorships and partnerships	**119**
FINANCIAL ASSETS	
Securities	**325**
Funds with financial intermediaries	**1,214**
Other	**125**
Total assets	**3,087**
FINANCIAL LIABILITIES	
Loans for house purchase	**353**
Loans from banks	**77**
Other	**76**
Total financial liabilities	**506**
Wealth (excluding consumer durables)	**2,581**

Source: Central Statistical Office *United Kingdom National Accounts the CSO Blue Book 1994 Edition*, p.104.

Demand for Capital

The demand by firms for capital, like the demand for any other input, stems from firms' profit-maximizing choices. As a firm increases the quantity of capital employed, other things being equal, the marginal revenue product of its capital diminishes. To maximize profit, a firm uses additional amounts of capital until the marginal revenue product of capital equals the opportunity cost of a unit of capital. That is, the firm increases its capital stock until the additional total revenue generated by one extra unit of capital equals the opportunity cost of using one unit of capital.

Sometimes a firm rents capital equipment and sometimes it buys it. When a firm rents capital equipment, its calculations are identical to those it makes in choosing its labour input. The firm faces an hourly rate for renting a machine. This is the machine's opportunity cost. To decide whether or not to rent a unit of capital for one more hour the firm calculates the marginal revenue product of the machine per hour and compares that number with the hourly rental rate. So long as the marginal revenue product per hour exceeds the rental rate per hour, the firm increases the number of units of capital hired each hour. Many machines are, in fact, rented – for example diggers, cars and cranes – so these calculations are relevant in such cases.

But most capital is not rented. Firms buy buildings, plant and equipment and operate them for several years. To decide how much capital equipment to buy, the firm has to compare the price of the equipment to be paid now with the return – the marginal revenue product – that the equipment will generate over its entire life. So the firm needs to compare an expenditure today with income in the future.

You may think that comparing amounts of money at different times presents no special problem. Isn't a pound today the same as a pound next year or a pound in five years' time? Certainly a pound coin will look the same, and, if there were no inflation, it would buy as much in the future as it would buy now.

Nevertheless, if you are given the choice between a pound today and a pound a year from today, you will choose a pound today. A pound in 1995 is worth more than a pound in 1996 and even more than a pound in 1999. The reason is simple. A pound today is worth more than a pound in the future because today's pound can be invested to earn interest. If you have a pound today and lend it at 5 per cent, you will have £1.05 in a year's time. We would say that a pound today has a value next year of £1.05, or, equivalently, that £1.05 in a year's time has a present value of one pound.

To see how a firm decides how much capital to buy, we need to convert the future stream of marginal revenue products into its present value so that it can be compared directly with the price of buying a new piece of capital equipment.

Discounting and Present Value

The next few paragraphs contain several calculations, but they are well worth persevering with. An understanding of this material will often help you to make the right decisions in your own life, decisions about whether to rent or to buy a videotape or a VCR, whether to buy something for cash or on credit, or whether to buy in bulk or buy more frequently in smaller quantities. Any calculation that involves comparing a sum of money today with a sum of money at a later date involves calculating a present value. Let's learn how to do such a calculation.

Calculating a Present Value Suppose that the interest rate is 10 per cent a year. If you have a sum of money today and lend it out for interest, then you will have a bigger sum next year. For example, if you lend £100 this year at 10 per cent, it will be worth £110 one year from now. We can turn the tables and say that £110 a year from now is worth £100 today. The **present value** of a future sum of money is the amount which, if lent today, will grow as large as that future sum, taking into account the interest that it will earn. Let's express this idea with an equation:

Future sum = Present value × $(1 + i)$

In this equation i is the rate of interest. Suppose the rate of interest is 10 per cent. Then the rate of interest is ten 100ths, or 10/100, that is 0.1. If you have £100 today and the interest rate is 10 per cent a year (0.1), one year from today you will have £110. The above formula gives this answer as £100 multiplied by 1.1 (that is $1 + 0.1$) equals £110.

We have just used the formula to calculate a future sum from the present value and an interest rate. We can calculate the present value of a future sum of money by working backwards. Instead of multiplying the present value by $(1 + i)$, we divide the future sum by $(1 + i)$. That is,

$$\text{Present value} = \frac{\text{Future sum}}{(1 + i)}$$

We can use this formula to calculate present values. Calculating a present value is called discounting. **Discounting** is the conversion of a future sum of money to its present value. Let's check that we can use the present value formula by calculating the present value of £110 one year from now when the interest rate is 10 per cent a year. You already know that the answer is £100 because we just calculated

that £100 invested today at 10 per cent a year becomes £110 in one year. But let's use the formula. Putting the numbers into the above formula we have:

$$\text{Present value} = \frac{£110}{(1 + 0.1)}$$

$$= \frac{£110}{100}$$

$$= £100$$

Calculating the present value of a sum of money one year from now is the easiest case. But we can also calculate the present value of a sum any number of years in the future. As an example, let's see how we calculate the present value of a sum of money available two years from now.

Suppose that you lend £100 today for two years at an interest rate of 10 per cent a year. The money will earn £10 in the first year, which means that by the end of the first year you will have £110. Suppose you lend the whole of this sum for the second year. Then the interest earned in the second year will be 10 per cent of £110 which is £11. So at the end of the second year you will have £121. From the definition of present value, you can see that, at 10 per cent, £121 two years hence has a present value of £100. That is, £100 is the present sum which, if invested at 10 per cent interest, will grow to £121 two years from now.

To calculate the present value of a sum of money two years in the future we use the formula

$$\text{Present value} = \frac{\text{Sum of money two years in future}}{(1 + i)^2}$$

To check that the formula works, let's calculate the present value of £121 two years in the future when the interest rate is 10 per cent a year. Putting these numbers into the above formula gives

$$\text{Present value} = \frac{£121}{(1 + i)^2}$$

$$= \frac{£121}{(1.1)^2}$$

$$= \frac{£121}{1.21}$$

$$= £100$$

We can calculate the present value of a sum of money any number of years in the future by using a formula based on the two that we've already used. The general formula is:

$$\text{Present value} = \frac{\text{Money available } n \text{ years in future}}{(1 + i)^n}$$

For example, if the interest rate is 10 per cent a year, £100 received 10 years from now will have a present value of £38.55. That is, if £38.55 is lent today at an interest rate of 10 per cent, it will increase to £100 in 10 years. (You may want to check that calculation on your pocket calculator. The easiest way to do this is to work out that $(1 + i)$ is 1.1, and then to work out that 1.1^{10} is 2.594. The present value is £100/2.594 which is £38.55.)

Sometimes we need to calculate the total present value of a series of future sums of money. Generally this is straightforward. All we need to do is to find the present value of each of those future sums and then add the results together. But what happens if the series goes on for ever?

For instance, suppose the government issues a security and offers to pay its owner £3 a year for ever. The government did indeed issue some securities like this about a century ago. If you are offered one today, you might ask what is the present value of £3 next year plus £3 the year after plus £3 the year after that, and so on to infinity. It seems you will have a lot of calculating and adding up to do! Fortunately, there is a simple formula in this case. If the interest rate is i, the present value of a series of annual payments of £3 a year for ever is £3/i. So if i is 10 per cent, that is 0.1, then the total present value of that infinite number of payments is £3/0.1 which is £30. You may like to look at the proof of this result which is shown in Box 16.1.

Net Present Value of Investment

Let's use our understanding of present values to consider decisions by firms about buying capital. We'll calculate the present value of the marginal revenue product of a capital input and see how a firm can use the result to make an investment decision. Table 16.6 summarizes the data that we'll use.

Anne runs a firm called Taxsave. The firm sells advice to taxpayers to help minimize the taxes that they have to pay. One June Anne considers buying a new computer that will cost £10,000. The computer has a life of two years, after which it will be worthless. Although Anne works hard all year studying tax law and writing complex computer programs that will help her to get a good share of the market, she

generates an income only once each year – in May and June when people complete their tax returns. If she buys the computer, Anne expects to be able to sell tax advice in each of the next two years that will bring in £5,900 each June. The interest rate that she will receive if she lends money is 4 per cent a year.

We can calculate the present value of the marginal revenue products of Taxsave's computer by using a formula similar to the one we have just met. The formula is set out in Table 16.6(b). The present value (PV) of £5,900 one year in the future is £5,900 divided by $(1 + i)$. The present value of £5,900 two years in the future is £5,900 divided by $(1 + i)^2$. In each case, i is the interest rate expressed as a decimal. As the interest rate is 4 per cent, that is 4/100, i is 0.04. We can work out these present values as £5,673 and £5,455. These figures tell us that Anne would have to lend £5,673 at 4 per cent if she wanted to have £5,900 in one year's time, and she would

---

TABLE 16.6

Net Present Value of an Investment by Taxsave

(a) DATA

Price of computer	**£10,000**
Life of computer	**2 years**
Marginal revenue product	**£5,900 at end of each year**
Interest rate	**4% a year**

(b) PRESENT VALUE OF THE FLOW OF MARGINAL REVENUE PRODUCT

$$PV = \frac{MRP}{1 + i} + \frac{MRP}{(1 + i)^2}$$

$$= \frac{£5,900}{1.04} + \frac{£5,900}{(1.04)^2}$$

$$= £5,673 + £5,455$$

$$= £11,128$$

(c) NET PRESENT VALUE OF INVESTMENT

$$NPV = PV \text{ of Marginal revenue product} - \text{Cost of computer}$$

$$= £11,128 - £10,000$$

$$= £1,128$$

have to lend a further £5,455 at 4 per cent if she wanted to have a further £5,900 in two years' time. Altogether, then, she would have to lend £5,673 plus £5,455, that is £11,128, if she wanted to earn from her loans as much as she will earn from the computer. So £11,128 is the present value of the flow of the marginal revenue product from the machine.

To decide whether or not to buy the computer, Anne compares the present value of its stream of marginal revenue product with its price. She makes this comparison by calculating the net present value (*NPV*) of the investment. The **net present value of an investment** is the present value of the stream of marginal revenue products generated by the investment minus the cost of the investment. If the net present value of an investment is positive, it pays to buy the item. If the net present value of an investment is negative, it does not pay to buy this item. Part (c) of Table 16.6 shows the calculation of the net present value of Anne's investment in a computer. It is £1,128 – a positive number – so the investment is worth undertaking.

To see why Anne buys the computer, notice that the machine produces a stream of income equal to what could be obtained by lending £11,128, yet it costs only £10,000. If, for example, Anne already has £10,000, she would be better off using it to buy the machine than lending it. This is because the machine has a stream of income that could be obtained only by lending £11,128, so it has a stream of income that is greater than that which could be obtained by lending £10,000. If, instead, Anne has to borrow at 4 per cent, the machine is still worth buying. She is borrowing £10,000, so the present value of her loan is £10,000, yet the present value of the income she will get from the machine is £11,128.

Like all other inputs, capital is subject to diminishing marginal returns. The more capital is added, the lower is its marginal product and the lower is its marginal revenue product. We saw in the above example that it pays the firm to buy one machine because that investment yields a positive net present value. Should Anne invest in two computers or three? To answer this question, she must do more calculations similar to those shown in Table 16.6.

Suppose, in particular, that Taxsave's investment opportunities are as set out in Table 16.7. Anne can buy any number of computers. They each cost £10,000 and have a life of two years. The marginal revenue product generated each year by each computer depends on how many Taxsave operates. If it operates just one computer, it has a marginal revenue product of £5,900 a year (the case just reviewed). If Taxsave uses a second computer, marginal revenue product falls to £5,600 a year, and in the case of a third computer, to £5,300 a year. Table 16.7(b) calculates the present value of the marginal revenue product of each of these three levels of investment in computers.

We have seen that if the interest rate is 4 per cent, it pays to invest in the first computer – the net present value of that computer is positive. You can see from Table 16.6 that it also pays to invest in a

---

TABLE 16.7

Taxsave's Investment Decision

(a) DATA

Price of computer	**£10,000**
Life of computer	**2 years**
Marginal revenue product:	
Using 1 computer	**£5,900 a year**
Using 2 computers	**£5,600 a year**
Using 3 computers	**£5,300 a year**

(b) PRESENT VALUE OF THE STREAM OF MARGINAL REVENUE PRODUCT

If $i = 0.04$ (4% a year):

Using 1 computer $\quad PV = \dfrac{£5,900}{1.04} + \dfrac{£5,900}{(1.04)^2} = £11,128$

Using 2 computers $\quad PV = \dfrac{£5,600}{1.04} + \dfrac{£5,600}{(1.04)^2} = £10,562$

Using 3 computers $\quad PV = \dfrac{£5,300}{1.04} + \dfrac{£5,300}{(1.04)^2} = £9,996$

If $i = 0.08$ (8% a year):

Using 1 computer $\quad PV = \dfrac{£5,900}{1.08} + \dfrac{£5,900}{(1.08)^2} = £10,521$

Using 2 computers $\quad PV = \dfrac{£5,600}{1.08} + \dfrac{£5,600}{(1.08)^2} = £9,986$

If $i = 0.12$ (12% a year):

Using 1 computer $\quad PV = \dfrac{£5,900}{1.12} + \dfrac{£5,900}{(1.12)^2} = £9,971$

second computer. The present value of the marginal revenue product resulting from a second computer is £10,562 which exceeds the £10,000 cost of the second machine by £562. However, it does not pay to invest in a third computer. The present value of the marginal revenue product resulting from a third computer is £9,996. But the computer costs £10,000, so the net present value of a third computer is −£4. Anne buys a second computer but not a third one.

We have just discovered that at an interest rate of 4 per cent a year it pays Anne to buy two computers but not three. Suppose that the interest rate is higher – say 8 per cent a year. In this case, the present value of one machine (see the calculations in Table 16.7b) is £10,521. Therefore it still pays to buy the first machine. But its net present value is smaller when the interest rate is 8 per cent than at the lower 4 per cent interest rate. At an 8 per cent interest rate, the net present value of a second machine is negative. The present value of the marginal revenue product, £9,986, is less than the £10,000 that the second computer costs. Therefore at an interest rate of 8 per cent it pays Anne to buy one computer but not two. Why does Anne buy fewer machines when the interest rate rises? If she has the money already, it is because lending money has become more attractive. If she has to borrow the money, it is because borrowing has become more expensive.

Suppose that the interest rate is even higher – say, 12 per cent a year. In this case the present value of the marginal revenue product of the first computer is £9,971 (see Table 16.7b). At this interest rate, it does not pay to buy even one computer.

The calculations that you have just reviewed trace out Taxsave's demand schedule for capital. It shows the number of computers demanded by Taxsave at each interest rate. As the interest rate falls, the quantity of capital demanded increases. At an interest rate of 12 per cent a year, the firm demands no computers; at 8 per cent a year, one computer is demanded; at 4 per cent a year, two computers are demanded; and, although we have stopped our calculations at 4 per cent and three computers, Anne would demand even more computers if the interest rate continued falling below 4 per cent a year.

Demand Curve for Capital

A firm's demand curve for capital relates the quantity of capital demanded to the interest rate. Figure 16.2 illustrates the demand for computers (D_F) by Anne's firm. The horizontal axis measures the value of the computers that Taxsave owns and the vertical axis measures the interest rate. Points a, b and c correspond to the example that we have just worked through. At an interest rate of 12 per cent a year, it does not pay Anne to buy any computers – point a. At an interest rate of 8 per cent, it pays to buy 1 computer worth £10,000 – point b. At an interest rate of 4 per cent, it pays to buy 2 computers worth £20,000 – point c.

In our example, we've considered only a single type of computer – one that costs exactly £10,000. Consequently Taxsave's demand is represented by the points a, b and c but not by a continuous demand curve. This is because Taxsave cannot, for instance, buy one and a half computers if the inter-

---

FIGURE 16.2

Taxsave's Demand Curve for Computers

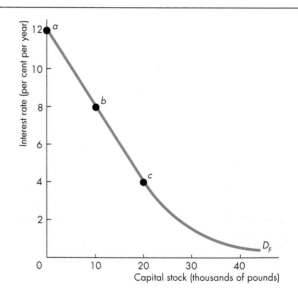

Taxsave will demand more capital (taken here to be computers) so long as the present value of the stream of marginal revenue product earned by the last computer exceeds its price. The present value depends on the interest rate. The lower the interest rate, the higher is the number of computers demanded. At an interest rate of 12 per cent a year, Taxsave demands no computers (point *a*). At an interest rate of 8 per cent, the firm demands 1 computer worth £10,000 (point *b*). At an interest rate of 4 per cent, the firm demands 2 computers worth £20,000 (point *c*). If computers of different types (fractions of a £10,000 computer) can be bought, a demand curve that passes through points *a*, *b* and *c* is generated.

est rate is 6 per cent. In practice, though, Anne could consider buying different types of computer whose powers could be expressed as a multiple or fraction of one of the £10,000 computers that we've been considering here. For example, there may be a £5,000 computer that has half the power of a £10,000 machine, and a bigger machine costing £12,500 that has one and a quarter times the power of a £10,000 machine. If we consider all the different types of computer that Anne can buy, we will generate not just points *a*, *b* and *c* but an entire demand curve, such as the one shown in the figure. This shows the value of the computers Anne will want Taxsave to own at each possible interest rate.

The market demand curve for any particular type of capital, such as cash dispensers, is obtained by adding together all the demand curves for that type of capital for all the individual firms that want to buy it. For some types of capital, such as office blocks, it is necessary to add in the demands by governments as well as the demands by firms to get the market demand. Note, though, that as governments do not set out to maximize profit, their demand curves cannot be derived in quite the same way that we used to derive Anne's demand curve. For homes, the market demand for capital is the sum of the demands by all owner-occupied households as well as the demand by all firms that own homes for letting out.

Sometimes it is helpful to go beyond thinking about the market demand curve for any particular type of capital and to think about the market demand curve for all types of capital taken together. How can we do that when there are many different types of capital? What we do is to use a common unit of measurement for the quantity of each different type of capital. The pound value is a convenient unit. The market demand curve is shown in Fig. 16.3. It measures possible interest rates on the vertical axis and the total quantity of capital demanded in billions of pounds on the horizontal axis. On that curve, at an interest rate of 6 per cent a year, the quantity of capital demanded is £120 billion. Like the firm's demand curve, the market demand curve slopes downward.

Changes in the Demand for Capital

The demand for capital is constantly changing, so the demand curve for capital is constantly shifting. Also, the composition of the demand for

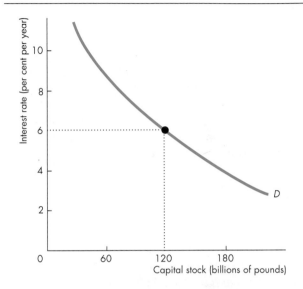

FIGURE 16.3

The Market Demand for Capital

The market demand curve for capital is obtained by adding together the demand curves for all different types of capital by all the firms and governments in the economy, and it also includes the demand curves for homes by owner-occupiers. An example of a market demand curve is *D*. On this curve, the quantity of capital demanded is £120 billion when the interest rate is 6 per cent per year, and the quantity of capital demanded falls as the interest rate rises, other things being equal.

capital is constantly changing because the demand for some types of capital increases while the demand for other types decreases. Technological change is the main force generating these changes in the demand for capital. For example, developments since World War II in road and air transport technology have led to a massive increase in the demand for roads, lorries, airports and aircraft; and they have led to some decline in the demand for railway transport equipment. In recent years, the development of desktop computers has led to a large increase in demand for office and research computing equipment and to a decline in the demand for typewriters.

The general trend resulting from the development of new technology and its exploitation through innovation is for the demand for capital to increase steadily over time with a shift to the right of the demand curve for capital.

he demand for capital by firms is determined by their profit-maximizing choices. The marginal product of capital declines as the amount of capital used rises. As a consequence, the marginal revenue product of capital declines as more capital is used. Capital is demanded up to the point at which the present value of its stream of marginal revenue products equals its price. The interest rate is an important factor in the present value calculation. The higher the interest rate, the lower is the present value of the stream of marginal revenue products.

◆ ◆ A demand curve for capital is the relationship between the quantity of capital demanded and the interest rate. We have considered the demand curve by one firm for a particular type of capital, the market demand curve for a particular type of capital, and the overall market demand curve for all types of capital. The higher the interest rate, the lower is the present value of the stream of marginal products and the smaller is the quantity of capital demanded. Demand curves for capital slope downward. The demand for capital changes as a result of technological change. There is a general tendency for the demand for capital to increase over time with the demand curve for capital shifting to the right. ◆

The Supply of Capital

e saw in Fig. 16.3 a demand curve showing the total value of all the capital goods demanded at each possible interest rate. But how much money will be made available for purchasing capital goods at each interest rate? In other words, how much capital will be supplied at each interest rate?

To answer this we need to ask how much money will be made available by households, for Fig. 16.1 showed that households ultimately supply the money needed for purchasing capital. The money that households supply is that part of their income

which they save rather than spend on consumer goods and services. They channel their saving into purchases of capital either by investing in homes, or by buying capital for sole proprietorships and partnerships, or by buying securities on the stock exchange, or by channelling their saving through financial intermediaries.

As the quantity of capital supplied results from the saving decisions of households, we need to consider what factors affect the level of household saving. The most important factors affecting the saving by an individual household are:

◆ The household's current income in relation to its expected future income
◆ The interest rate

The major factor influencing whether a household's current income is high or low compared with its expected future income is the household's stage in its life cycle. Households smooth their consumption over the life cycle. As we saw in Chapter 14, young households typically have low current income compared with their expected future income, so they incur debts. Conversely, older households have high income relative to expected future income, so they accumulate assets. A household's savings depend on how much it smooths its consumption over the life cycle.

Interest Rate

The interest rate has two distinct effects on the level of savings:

◆ A substitution effect
◆ An income effect

Substitution Effect   A higher interest rate increases the future payoff from saving today. In turn, it increases the opportunity cost of current consumption. So a higher interest rate encourages people to economize on current consumption and take advantage of the higher return available on savings. As the interest rate rises, people substitute higher future consumption for current consumption and so saving rises.

Income Effect   Changes in interest rates change people's incomes. In turn they change the level of saving. This is because, other things being equal, the higher a person's income, the more that person saves.

How do changes in interest rates affect incomes? The effect of a change in the interest rate on income, and therefore on saving, depends on whether a person is a borrower or a lender. For a lender – a person with positive net financial assets – an increase in interest rates increases income, so the income effect is positive. The income effect reinforces the substitution effect, and a higher interest rate results in higher saving.

For a borrower – a person with negative net financial assets – an increase in interest rates decreases the income available for consumption. In this case, the income effect is negative – higher interest rates lower consumption and saving. The income effect works in the opposite direction to the substitution effect, so a higher interest rate may result in lower savings.

Supply Curve of Capital

The quantity of capital supplied is the total stock of accumulated savings. The supply curve of capital shows the relationship between the quantity of capital supplied and the interest rate. We've seen that this relationship depends on the relative strength of the income effect and the substitution effect. For an individual household, the relationship may be either positive or negative. For the economy as a whole, however, the substitution effect is stronger than the income effect, so a higher interest rate encourages saving and the supply curve of capital is upward sloping. Figure 16.4 illustrates the supply curve of capital. On that curve, at an interest rate of 6 per cent per year, the quantity of capital supplied is £120 billion.

Changes in the Supply of Capital

The supply of capital changes constantly. The main influences on the supply of capital are demographic. As the size and the age distribution of the population change, so does the supply of capital. The age distribution of the population affects the supply of capital as a result of the life cycle consumption smoothing described above. A population with a larger proportion of young people has a smaller supply of capital than a population with a larger proportion of middle-aged people.

Another influence on the supply of capital is the average income level. The higher the level of income, the larger is the supply of capital. A steadily rising income results in a gradual shift to the right of the supply of capital curve.

FIGURE 16.4

The Supply of Capital

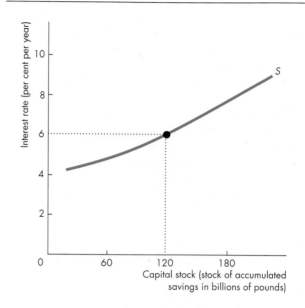

The higher the interest rate, the greater is the quantity of capital that households supply, so the supply curve of capital slopes upward. At an interest rate of 6 per cent a year, the quantity of capital supplied is £120 billion.

R E V I E W

The quantity of capital supplied is determined by households' saving decisions. The supply curve of capital shows the relationship between the interest rate and the quantity of capital supplied. The supply curve slopes upward because, other things being equal, a rise in the interest rate encourages households to save more. ◆ ◆ The level of saving also depends on the size and the age distribution of the population. If the population increases in size or in average age, the supply curve of capital will shift to the right. The age distribution affects the level of saving because households smooth consumption over their life cycles. The more smoothing households do, the more a tendency for the population to get older will shift the supply curve of capital to the right as old people save more than young people. ◆

Now that we have studied the demand for and supply of capital, we can bring them together and study the determination of interest rates and asset prices. We'll then be able to answer some of the questions posed at the beginning of this chapter about the stock market and understand the forces that produce stock market booms and crashes.

Interest Rates and Asset Prices

Plans made by households over their total level of savings have to be coordinated with the plans made by people who want to own capital goods. These people are those who run firms and governments – and also those in households who want to own their own homes. These plans for savings and capital goods are coordinated through capital markets. The prices of financial assets and their returns – or interest rates – adjust to make these plans compatible. We are now going to see how these market forces work. We are also going to discover what determines the stock market value of a firm.

Two Sides of the Same Coin

The returns and prices of financial assets can be viewed as two sides of the same coin. But there are some differences between different types of financial assets. To illustrate these, let's suppose that on 1 January 1995 you placed £100 in three different financial assets. You placed £100 in a bank deposit offering an interest rate of 4 per cent a year. You also spent £100 on a new local authority bond that offers a fixed annual rate of 6 per cent a year. A fixed annual rate is sometimes called a coupon. In addition, you spent £100 on second-hand shares in Taxsave plc. Let's also suppose that Taxsave's shares currently have a second-hand value of 50 pence – so you buy 200 – and that in recent years Taxsave has paid a dividend of 4 pence a share.

With the bank deposit, the sum you have on deposit is constant unless you personally raise or lower your deposit. So you can always get your £100 back if you wish. In contrast, your annual interest income is likely to change as time passes because banks alter their rates from time to time. So if you keep your deposit at £100 you may earn £4 in 1995, but you might earn more or less in 1996 if the bank changed its rates meanwhile.

With your bond, the amount of interest you get each year is guaranteed. The price paid to the local authority for the new bond was £100 and the coupon is 6 per cent, so the holder of this bond will always receive £6 interest each year as £6 is 6 per cent of the original value. But if you sell the bond at any time it might not fetch £100. Maybe you will sell it in 1997 and perhaps then interest rates turn out to be generally higher than they were in 1995. In that case you might find that you can sell it for only £60. The new owner will still get £6 each year, but this is 10 per cent of the current price, so the new owner gets a return of 10 per cent on the money spent buying the bond from you. The term **interest yield** expresses the annual income as a percentage of the current second-hand price. Notice that the interest yield rises when the second-hand price falls and vice versa – they are the opposite sides of a coin.

Ordinary shares in a company resemble the bank deposit in that the annual income can rise or fall, for a company's dividends tend to rise and fall in line with changes in its profit. So Taxsave's dividend in 1996 could be greater or less than the recent 4 pence a share. Moreover, the price of Taxsave's shares will rise and fall over time. At the time of buying, the annual dividend was 4 pence a share and the price was 50 pence a share. The **dividend yield** is the current dividend as a percentage of the current second-hand price, so when you bought the shares the dividend yield was 8 per cent, that is, 4 pence as a percentage of 50 pence. Suppose the dividend stays put at 4 pence while the price falls to 40 pence. Then the dividend yield rises to 10 per cent, that is, 4 pence as a percentage of 40 pence. So, for a given level of dividend, the price and the yield are again closely related.

This connection between the price of financial assets issued by companies and the yields of those assets means that in capital markets the market forces of supply and demand simultaneously determine asset prices and asset yields. We regard asset yields as the rate of interest which people who hold assets receive, expressed as a percentage of their current value. We will first look at capital market equilibrium in terms of interest rate (or yield) determination and then in terms of the stock market value of a particular firm.

Equilibrium Interest Rate

Figure 16.5 brings together the relevant parts of the previous analysis of the demand for and supply of capital. The diagram shows the entire capital market. The horizontal axis measures the total quantity of capital. The vertical axis measures the interest rate. The demand curve D is the market demand for capital that you met in Fig. 16.3. The supply curve S is the market supply of capital shown in Fig. 16.4.

For the capital market to be in equilibrium, the quantity of capital supplied must equal the quantity of capital demanded. In Fig. 16.5, this equilibrium occurs at an interest rate of 6 per cent a year with £120 billion of capital supplied and demanded. Will market forces bring this equilibrium about? In other words, if interest rates are currently 8 per cent, so that there is an excess supply of capital, will this excess supply cause interest rates to drop to 6 per cent?

On the basis of the supply and demand analysis that we looked at in earlier chapters, it is tempting to think that the answer to these questions is a simple 'yes'. In fact the situation is rather more complex here. The reason is that at any point in time the interest rate is actually fixed in a quite different market – the money market – as we explain in Chapter 28. It is possible that the interest rate which is established in the money market is different from the one needed to give equilibrium in the capital market. However, if this occurs, various forces come into play which will shift the supply and demand curves for both money and capital, and eventually the money market will settle down with an equilibrium interest rate that also gives equilibrium in the capital market. Reading Between the Lines on pp. 452–453 shows how equilibrium is also attained between markets in different countries.

To give an example of this, suppose that initially the money market does produce an interest rate of 6 per cent so that the capital market is in equilibrium with a capital stock of £120 billion. Then suppose the government reduces the supply of money, causing the money market to create a new higher interest rate of 8 per cent. In that case, firms will want less capital than before. To achieve a lower capital stock they may simply stop replacing equipment when it wears out. Such a move reduces investment which

FIGURE 16.5

Capital Market Equilibrium

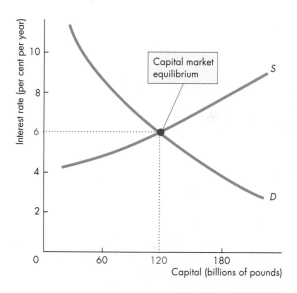

For the capital market to be in equilibrium, the interest rate must be such that the quantity of capital demanded equals the quantity of capital supplied. Here the demand curve is D and the supply curve is S. These curves intersect at an interest rate of 6 per cent a year and a capital stock of £120 billion. The capital market will eventually settle at the point where the two curves intersect.

reduces the incomes of people who make capital goods. This fall in income will reduce saving and so cut the supply of capital. It will also affect the demand for money. So both the capital and money markets will be affected, and the economy will not settle down again until there is an interest rate which gives equilibrium in the capital market.

Let's return to Fig. 16.5 and suppose the market has settled with an interest rate of 6 per cent and a capital stock of £120 billion. The interest rate of 6 per cent is really the *average* interest rate in this economy. Interest rates on individual assets are distributed around that average, based on their relative degree of risk. An asset with a high degree of risk earns an interest rate that exceeds the average, and a very safe asset earns an interest rate that is less than the average. For example, with the average interest rate at 6 per cent a year, as shown in Fig. 16.5, the interest rate on a bank deposit, which is a safe asset, might be 4 per cent a year, while the rate on an ordinary share in Taxsave plc, which is riskier than a bank deposit, might be 8 per cent a year.

We've now seen how asset yields or interest rates are determined. Let's look at the other side of the coin – asset prices. To determine asset prices, we will change our focus and look not at the capital market in aggregate but at the stock market value of an individual firm.

Stock Market Value of a Firm

We've seen that there is a connection between the price of an asset and its yield (or interest rate). The yield is the earnings on the asset expressed as a percentage of the asset's current price. Let's use this fact to work out the stock market value of a firm. Suppose that a firm finances its purchases of capital by selling ordinary shares. What determines the price of its shares? What determines the total current value of all the shares sold?

The value of a share depends on the value of the firm and the number of shares sold. The value of one share is equal to the value of the firm divided by the number of shares sold; equivalently, the value of the firm is equal to the value of one share multiplied by the number of shares sold. So for a firm with a given number of shares, asking what determines the price of a share is the same as asking what determines the value of the firm.

When a person buys a share in a firm, that person becomes entitled to receive a dividend each year. The price that people are willing to pay for a share depends on the expected future dividends to be paid out by the firm and also on how much interest people could get by investing their money elsewhere. If a firm is expected to pay out no dividends at all in the future, no one will buy its shares so they are worthless. If it is expected to pay out 10 pence every year on each share and the interest rate is 10 per cent a year, its shares are worth 100 pence each. If it is expected to pay out 10 pence every year on each share and the interest rate is 5 per cent, its shares are worth 200 pence each.

Price–Earnings Ratio

A commonly used measure to describe the performance of a firm's shares is its price–earnings ratio. A **price-earnings ratio** is the current price of a share divided by the most recent year's profit per share. The price–earnings ratios of shares in different companies often vary greatly. In November 1993, for instance, the price–earnings ratio for Marley plc, the supplier of building materials, was 52.8, while the price–earnings ratio of Tottenham Hotspur, the football club, was 5.4. Why do price–earnings ratios vary so much?

We have seen that the price of a share depends on the expected future profit of the company. The higher the *expected future* profit, the higher is *today's* price. Thus the price–earnings ratio of a company depends on its current profit in relation to its expected future profit. When expected future profit is high relative to current profit, the price–earnings ratio is high. When expected future profit is low relative to current profit, the price–earnings ratio is low. Fluctuations in the price–earnings ratio arise from fluctuations in expected future profit relative to current profit.

Stock Market Volume and Prices

Sometimes the prices quoted on the stock exchange rise or fall with little trading taking place. At other times, stock market prices rise or fall with a huge volume of trading. On yet other occasions, there is little change in the prices but there is a huge volume of trading. Why do share prices rise or fall and what determines the volume of trading on the stock exchange?

Share prices rise and fall because of changes in expectations of future profits. Consider a company whose profit per share last year was 24 pence and which pays all its profit out in dividends. Suppose that the interest rate on assets that are as risky as a share in this company stock is 8 per cent a year. Suppose further that the company's profit in this year and each future year is expected to be exactly the same as last year's. The price of the firm's shares will adjust until a share can be bought for the price that makes the dividend yield equal to 8 per cent a year. That price is £3. People will buy shares in this company for £3 and expect to earn 24 pence a share each year, that is, to have a dividend yield of 8 per cent (24 pence is 8 per cent of £3). The price–earnings ratio will be 12.5 as this is today's price of 300 pence divided by the most recent year's profit – or earnings – per share of 24 pence.

Suppose that market conditions change and people now expect the firm's profit to rise by one-third to 32 pence a share starting this year. With an expected profit of 32 pence a share the stock market price jumps by one-third to £4. This price jump to £4 occurs entirely because people observe some event today that leads them to expect higher profits in the future. Suppose that the change in market conditions leading to expected higher future profits is so obvious that everyone can see it and everyone agrees that this firm's earnings are indeed going to rise by one-third. In such a situation, the market value of the firm's shares rises to £4 but no one actually buys or sells any shares. This is because existing shareholders are happy with the shares they already hold. If the price does not rise to £4, everyone will want to buy some shares. If the price rises to more than £4, all existing shareholders will want to sell some shares. If the price rises to exactly £4, everyone will be indifferent between hanging on to those shares or buying some other shares that are currently yielding 8 per cent a year.

On the other hand, suppose that the event that changed expectations about this firm's profitability is difficult to interpret. Some people think it will lead to profit rising by one-third to 32 pence a share while others think it will lead to profit falling by one-third to 16 pence a share. Let's call the first group optimists and the second group pessimists. The optimists will want to buy shares in this company and will be willing to do so as long as the price does not exceed £4. Any existing shareholders who are pessimists will sell their shares as long as the price is over £2 – for so long as the price is over £2 they expect the future yield to be below 8 per cent. In such a situation, the pessimists will sell and the optimists will buy. The price may change very little, or even not change at all, from the original £3, but there will be a large volume of trading activity. What causes the trading activity is the disagreement, not the event that triggered the change in expected profitability.

We can see from this discussion that a high volume of trading on the stock exchange implies a large amount of disagreement. A large volume of trading with hardly any price change means that the underlying changes are difficult to interpret: some people predict that things will move in one direction while others predict the opposite. In contrast, a low volume of trading combined with large price changes implies a great deal of agreement over some fundamental change.

Takeovers and Mergers

The theory of capital markets that you've now studied can be used to explain why takeovers and mergers occur. A **takeover** is the purchase by one

firm of another firm. When the firms are companies, the buying company purchases the shares of the company that is being taken over. Suppose that a company called Taxavoid wishes to take over Taxsave. Then Taxavoid must offer shareholders in Taxsave a price that induces at least half the shares to be sold to Taxavoid. Assuming that most of Taxsave's shareholders have no interest in selling their shares at the current market price, Taxavoid must offer a significantly higher price than the market price to persuade enough Taxsave shareholders to sell. Why might Taxavoid be willing to offer more than the current market price for Taxsave's shares?

To answer this, suppose Taxsave's annual profit is £100,000 and is expected to stay that way. And suppose that for firms as risky as Taxsave people want a yield of 10 per cent. Then the total value of Taxsave's shares will be £1 million – as £100,000 is 10 per cent of £1 million. If Taxsave has issued 250,000 shares, the price of each share will currently be £4. Why would Taxavoid be willing to offer more than £4 a share to encourage Taxsave shareholders to sell their shares? The most probable reason is that Taxavoid believes it has superior management which, once applied to Taxsave, will raise Taxsave's profit above £100,000 a year and so give Taxavoid a reasonable return on the money spent buying Taxsave.

A **merger** is the combining of two (or more) firms to form a single new firm. Mergers take place when two firms believe that by combining, they can increase their combined profit. For example, the merger of British Midland and Scandinavian Airlines System in 1989 enabled these two firms to form a more effective company to compete in the European air travel market against such giants as British Airways and Lufthansa.

REVIEW

Saving plans and investment plans are coordinated through capital markets. Adjustments in asset prices and interest rates make the saving plans and investment plans compatible. Interest rates and asset prices are two sides of the same coin. The interest rate on an asset is the income from the asset divided by its price. The average interest rate makes the quantity of capital demanded equal to the quantity of savings supplied. ◆ ◆ The value of a share of a firm's stock is determined by the firm's current and expected future profit. Expected future profit is based on expectations of the future prices, costs and technologies that the firm will face. The stock market value of a firm is often expressed as a ratio of the firm's current profit per share – the price–earnings ratio – which depends on expected profit growth. ◆ ◆ Stock exchange prices sometimes move dramatically, and the volume of trading on the stock exchange is sometimes high and sometimes low. Prices change quickly when there are changes in expectations of future profitability. The volume of stock exchange trading rises when people disagree strongly about what the future holds. ◆ ◆ Mergers and takeovers occur when the stock exchange value of a firm is lower than the present value of the future profit stream that another firm believes it could generate with the first firm's assets. ◆

The lessons that we've just learned about capital markets have a wider application than explaining fluctuations in the stock market. They also enable us to understand how natural resource markets operate. Let's now turn to this important range of issues.

Natural Resource Markets

Natural resources are the non-produced factors of production with which we are endowed. They fall into two categories: renewable and non-renewable. **Renewable natural resources** are natural resources that can be used repeatedly without depleting what's available for future use. Examples of renewable natural resources are soil, the sea, rivers, rain and sunshine. Timber and fish are also examples of renewable natural resources. If timber felling and fishing are carried out in moderation, nature will see to it that the felled trees and caught fish are replaced by new trees and fish. But if felling and catching are excessive, then the stocks of timber and fish will gradually diminish. **Non-renewable natural resources** are natural resources that can be used only once and cannot be replaced once used. Examples of non-renewable natural resources are coal, natural gas and oil – the hydrocarbon fuels.

Natural resources have two important economic dimensions – a stock dimension and a flow dimension. The stock of a natural resource is determined by nature and by the previous rate of use. The flow of a natural resource is the rate at which it is being used. Human choices determine this flow, which in turn determines whether a given stock of natural resources is used up quickly, slowly or not at all. In studying the operation of natural resource markets, we'll begin by considering the stock dimension of a natural resource. Here we are talking about the ownership of the world's stock of resources such as oil, gas and coal under the ground. How much of these resources is supplied and how much stock is demanded – that is, how much stock do people wish to own?

Supply and Demand in a Natural Resource Market

The stock of a natural resource supplied is the amount of the resource in existence. For example, the stock of oil supplied is the total volume beneath the earth's surface. This amount is not influenced by the resource's price. So the supply curve of the stock of the natural resource is perfectly inelastic. Its position depends on the amount of the resource available initially and on the rate at which it has been used up in the past. The smaller the initial stock and the faster the rate of use, the smaller is the stock available.

It is helpful to distinguish between the stock of the resource in existence and the amount actually known about. The known quantity does depend on the price because a higher price encourages people to look for more. For example, in 1973, when the price of oil was $3 a barrel, known reserves were 580 billion barrels. By 1990, after some 350 billion barrels had been consumed, the price had risen to $30 a barrel, and known remaining reserves exceeded 1,000 billion barrels. However, we are concerned here with the total stock in existence.

What determines the demand for this stock? The demand for a stock of a natural resource is determined in the same way as the demand for any asset, that is by what it is expected to earn, expressed as a percentage, or interest rate. But what is the interest rate on a natural resource? It is the rate of increase in the price of the resource. If you buy a stock of a natural resource, you buy it at today's price. If you sell your natural resource stock a year later, you sell it at the price prevailing at that time. The percentage change in the price of the resource over the year is the interest rate you make from holding the stock of the natural resource over the year. So, other things being equal, the more rapid the increase in the price of a natural resource, the larger is the interest rate on that natural resource.

If the expected interest rate on a stock of a natural resource exceeds that on other assets (with comparable risk), people allocate more of their net worth to owning the natural resource and less to other assets. Conversely, if the expected interest rate on a natural resource falls short of that on other assets (with comparable risk), people reallocate their net worth by selling the stock of a natural resource and buying other assets.

Stock Equilibrium Equilibrium in the market for a stock of a natural resource occurs when the interest rate on that resource equals the interest rate on other comparably risky assets. In such a situation, there is no tendency for people either to buy or sell stocks of natural resources or other assets. They are satisfied with their existing portfolio allocation and with the quantity of the stock of the natural resource that they are holding.

Since the interest rate on a natural resource stock is the rate at which the price of the resource rises, the expected interest rate on the resource stock is the rate at which the price of the resource is *expected* to rise over time. That rate equals the expected interest rate on other assets. This proposition is known as the **Hotelling Principle**.[1]

Why is the price of a natural resource expected to grow at a rate equal to the interest rate on other assets? It is to make the expected interest rate on the natural resource equal to the expected interest rate on other comparably risky assets.

The supply of and demand for the stock of a natural resource determine the interest rate from owning that stock. In other words, they determine

how rapidly people expect the price of the resource to increase. But the supply of and demand for the stock of the resource do not determine the current *level* of the price of the resource. For instance, if interest rates are around 10 per cent, the supply of and demand for stocks of oil will result in people expecting oil prices to rise by about 10 per cent a year. But will the price be $30 a barrel this year, $33 a barrel next year and $36.30 a barrel the year after that? Or will the price be $40 this year, $44 a barrel next year and $48.40 a barrel the following year? Or will the prices follow some other sequence rising at 10 per cent a year? To determine the level of the price of a natural resource, we have to consider not only the supply of and demand for the stock of the resource but also the demand for its flow.

Price of a Natural Resource

To determine the price of a natural resource, we first consider the influences on the demand for the flow of the natural resource, and then we study the equilibrium that emerges from the interaction of the demand for the flow and the available stock.

Demand for a Flow The flow of a natural resource demanded is the quantity demanded in a period of time, such as a year. The quantity demanded for the flow of a natural resource which is used only as an input for firms – such as copper, lead and zinc – is determined in the same way as the demand for any other input. It arises from firms' profit-maximizing decisions. A firm maximizes profit when the marginal revenue product of an input equals the marginal cost of the input. In a perfectly competitive input market, the marginal cost of an input equals its price. The quantity demanded of a flow of a natural resource is the quantity used in a period of time that makes the marginal revenue product of the resource equal to the price of the resource. As is the case for all other inputs, the marginal revenue product of a natural resource diminishes as the quantity used in a period of time increases. Thus the lower the price of a resource, the greater is the quantity demanded of the flow of the natural resource.

When a resource is demanded by households as well as by firms – as with coal, gas and oil – the demands by households for the flow of the resource must be added to the demands of firms to obtain the

[1] The Hotelling Principle, discovered by Harold Hotelling, first appeared in 'Economics of Exhaustible Resources', *Journal of Political Economy*, 39 (April 1931): 137–75.

market demand curve, but again the demand curve will slope downward. Figure 16.6 illustrates the demand for a flow of oil.

The demand for a flow of any natural resource has one special feature. For any resource, there is a high price at which no one will buy the resource. The price at which no one will buy a natural resource is called the **choke price**. Figure 16.6 shows the choke price of a barrel of oil, P_C. Everything has substitutes, and at a high enough price, a substitute is used. For example, we do not have to use oil as fuel for cars; we could use alcohol or gas. We do not have to use oil in power stations; we could use more natural gas or coal instead. The same applies to other resources. For instance, we do not have to use aluminum to make cans for soft drinks; we could use plastic instead. The natural resources that we *do* use are the least expensive resources available. They cost us less than the next best alternative would.

Equilibrium Stock and Flow The price and the flow of a natural resource depend on three things:

◆ The interest rate
◆ The demand for the flow
◆ The stock of the resource remaining

Figure 16.7 shows how these three factors combine to determine the current price of a barrel of oil, the expected future path of the price of oil, the rate at which oil is used up and the stock of oil remaining. Let's take one part of the figure at a time.

Part (a) shows the expected path of the price of oil. This path is determined by the interest rate r. The red line with a slope of $1 + r$ shows the relationship between the price in the current year and the price next year if the price rises at a rate equal to the interest rate. If the rate of interest is 10 per cent, so that r is 0.1 (that is 10/100), $1 + r = 1.1$ and the slope of the red line is 1.1.

Suppose that initially the price is P_0. Next year, the price will rise to P_1, the price that is r per cent higher than P_0. You can see the future rises in price by following the steps between the 45° line and the line with a slope of $1 + r$. Each step represents a price increase. The height of each step is a constant percentage of the previous year's price, so the steps themselves become progressively larger. Since the price keeps rising, it eventually reaches the choke price, identified as P_C in the figure.

Next, consider Fig. 16.7(b). This shows the rate at which the resource is used up. The demand for the flow is illustrated by the curve D; for simplicity this curve has been assumed to stay constant. In the initial year, at a price of P_0, the quantity Q_0 is used. In the following year, we know from part (a) that the price increases to P_1. At this price, the quantity used up is Q_1. Each year, as the price increases, the quantity used decreases.

Figure 16.7(c) shows the initial stock and the stock remaining after each year. For example, the stock after one year is the initial stock minus Q_0, the amount used up in the first year. In this example, there is no stock left after six years. The price increases from P_0 to the choke price P_C, and the quantity used in each year declines until, in the final year, it equals the quantity of the flow of oil demanded at the choke price, that is zero.

How do we know that P_0 is the current price? Because it is this price that achieves an equilibrium between the remaining stock and the current year's flow and the future years' expected flows. That is,

FIGURE 16.6

Demand for a Flow of Natural Resources

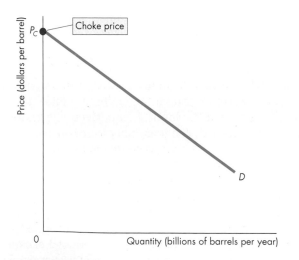

Natural resources have substitutes. If the price of a natural resource is too high, a substitute will be used. The figure shows the market for oil. At a price below P_C, the quantity of oil demanded is positive. The lower the price, the larger is the quantity of oil demanded. The price P_C is called the choke price. At P_C, no oil is demanded and substitutes will be used.

FIGURE 16.7

A Non-renewable Natural Resource Market

The expected rate of increase in the price of a natural resource equals the interest rate. The figure illustrates the oil market. Starting at P_0, in part (a), the price of oil increases at first to P_1 and eventually to P_C. The price path follows the steps shown, with each step bigger than the previous one. Part (b) shows the rate at which oil is used up. Its demand curve, D, determines the quantity demanded for use (a flow) at each price. Initially, when the price is P_0, that flow is Q_0. As the price increases, the flow decreases. When the price reaches the choke price, P_C, the flow is zero. For simplicity, the demand curve has been assumed to stay constant throughout. Part (c) illustrates the stock that remains after each year. The initial stock is used up in decreasing amounts until, after six years, all the stock is exhausted. The price P_0 is the initial equilibrium price of oil because it achieves equality between the initial stock and the sum of the flows in each year.

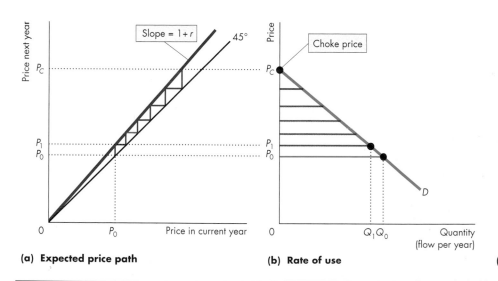

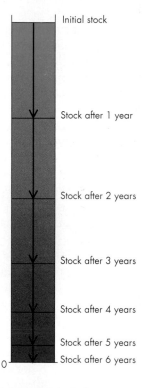

(a) Expected price path   **(b) Rate of use**   **(c) Remaining stock**

it is the only current price that leads to a sequence of future prices (growing at the interest rate) that generate a sequence of flows such that the stock is exhausted in the same year that the choke price is reached. If the current price is more than P_0 and future prices are expected to rise at the interest rate, the choke price will be reached before the stock is exhausted – and resource owners would never set prices which produced this result. If the current price is less than P_0 and future prices are expected to rise at the interest rate, the stock will be exhausted before the choke price is reached – and resource owners would never set prices which produced this result.

We can now see how the current price is determined by the three factors identified above. First,

the higher the interest rate, the lower is the current price of a natural resource. A higher interest rate means that the price is going to increase more quickly. This means that if we start from the same initial price, the choke price will be reached sooner. But if the choke price is reached sooner, the stock available will not be used up at that point in time. So the initial price has to be lower when the interest rate is higher to ensure that by the time the price does reach the choke price, the total stock available has been used.

Second, the higher the marginal revenue product of the natural resource – and hence the higher the demand for the flow – the higher is the current price. You can see why this relationship exists by looking again at Fig. 16.7(b). If the demand for the flow of oil were higher than that shown in this fig-ure, the demand curve would lie to the right of the one shown. If the prices in each year were the same as those shown in part (b), more oil would be used in each of the early years, and the stock would be exhausted before the choke price was reached. To prevent this happening, higher prices are needed in each year. So the initial price must exceed P_0.

Third, the larger the initial stock of the natural resource, the lower the current price. You can see why this relationship holds by considering Fig. 16.7(c). If the initial stock is larger than that shown in the figure, P_0 cannot be the equilibrium price. This is because an initial price of P_0 will lead to a sequence of future prices that will generate a sequence of quan-tities demanded that will not exhaust the stock by the time the choke price is reached. So the initial price will have to be less than P_0 to ensure that the larger stock is exhausted by the time the choke price is reached.

Equilibrium in the market for a natural resource determines the current price of the natural resource and the expected path of future prices. But the price path actually followed is rarely the same as its expected path. For example, in 1984, expectations about the future price of oil were that it would rise at a rate equal to the interest rate. Opinions differed about the long-term average interest rate, so projections ranged from a low growth rate of 1.8 per cent a year to a high growth rate of 7.1 per cent a year. As events have turned out, the price of oil fell after 1984 (see Fig. 16.8).

Why do natural resource prices change unex-pectedly, sometimes even falling rather than following their expected path?

Unexpected Price Changes

The price of a natural resource depends on expecta-tions about future events. So it depends on expectations about the future interest rate, the future demand for the flow of the resource and the size of the remaining stock. Natural resource markets are constantly being bombarded by new information that leads to new expectations. For example, new information about the stock of a resource or the technologies available for its use can lead to sudden and perhaps quite large changes in its price.

FIGURE 16.8

Unfulfilled Expectations

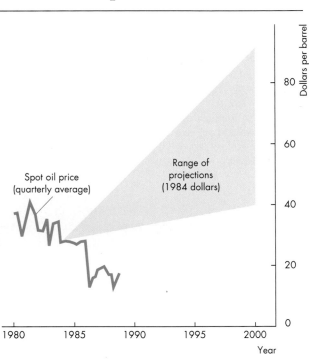

In 1984, the price of oil was expected to increase at a rate equal to the inter-est rate. There were different views of the future interest rate, so there was a range of expected price increases. Then the events of the later 1980s unfold-ed in a way that was different from what had been expected in 1984. Higher interest rates, the discovery of new reserves and new energy-saving technolo-gies all contributed to a falling price of oil. The weakening of the OPEC cartel also had significant effect.

Source: 'Future Imperfect', *The Economist*, 4 February, 1989, 67. © 1989 The Economist Newspaper Limited. Reprinted with permission.

All these forces have been at work in many of the markets for non-renewable natural resources in recent years. The market for oil illustrates these effects very well. The discovery of new reserves and the development of new extraction technologies has led to unexpected increases in the supply of oil. The development of more efficient car engines and improving insulation of buildings have decreased the demand for oil. And the combination of these fac-tors has depressed the price of oil.

An additional force leading to price changes in

natural resource markets in general, and in the oil market in particular, is the degree of competitiveness in the market. The model of the oil market that we have been studying is a perfectly competitive one. But the real-world market for oil has oligopolistic elements (some of which we analysed in Chapter 13). Oligopolistic influences on price can produce price fluctuations over and above those arising from the forces at work in a competitive market. The weakening of OPEC contributed significantly to the fall in the price of oil in the 1980s.

You can see that to forecast the future price of a natural resource correctly, it is necessary to forecast future changes in market structure. Adding this complication to an already complex forecasting problem makes it clear that the fluctuations in prices of natural resources such as oil cannot, for the most part, be forecast accurately.

Conservation and Doomsday

The analysis that you have just reviewed has important implications for the popular debate about natural resources and their use. Many people fear that we are using the earth's non-renewable natural resources at such a rapid pace that we shall eventually (perhaps in the not very distant future) run out of important sources of energy and of other crucial raw materials. Such people urge slowing the rate of use of non-renewable natural resources so that the limited stocks available will last longer.

This topic is an emotional one and generates passionate debate. It is also a matter that involves economic issues that can be understood using the economic model of a non-renewable natural resource that you have just studied.

The economic analysis of a non-renewable natural resource market predicts that doomsday – the using up of the entire stock of a natural resource – will eventually arise if our use of natural resources is organized in competitive markets. But it also implies that a competitive market will provide an automatic conservation programme, arising from a steadily rising price. As a natural resource gets closer and closer to being depleted, its price will get closer to the choke price – the price at which no one wants to use that resource any more. Each year, as the price rises, the quantity demanded of the flow declines.

What happens if the resource is completely used up? Won't we have a real problem then? What we will have is the problem of scarcity in a slightly more acute form than we had it before. The market economy handles the depleting stocks of natural resources by persistently forcing up their prices. Higher prices cause people to ration their use and eventually drive the flow quantity demanded to zero when the stock quantity supplied disappears.

An important economic question arises here. Does a competitive market lead us to use our scarce non-renewable natural resources at an efficient rate? Recall that we studied the allocative efficiency of a perfectly competitive market in Chapter 11. There we discovered that perfectly competitive markets achieve allocative efficiency if there are no external costs and benefits. The same conclusion applies to markets for natural resources. If no external costs or benefits impinge on these markets, then the rate of use determined in a perfectly competitive market is the allocatively efficient one. But if there are external costs associated with the use of the natural resource, allocative efficiency will result from a slowdown in the rate of use of the resource compared with that arising in the competitive market. For example, if burning hydrocarbon fuels increases the carbon dioxide in the atmosphere and so warms the earth's atmosphere – this is known as the the greenhouse effect – then the costs associated with this atmospheric change have to be added to the costs of using oil and coal as fuels. When these costs are taken into account, the allocatively efficient rate of using these fuels is lower than that resulting from a perfectly competitive market. We will examine ways in which government intervention can achieve allocative efficiency in such a situation in Chapter 19.

◆ ◆ ◆ ◆ We have now studied the way in which factor markets allocate scarce productive resources – labour, capital and land – and the determination of factor prices and factor incomes. The outcome of the operation of the factor markets is the determination of the distribution of income among individuals and families – the determination of for whom goods and services are produced. We are now going to examine that distribution and discover the main features and sources of income and wealth inequality in our economy.

The Global Capital Market

THE ECONOMIST, 16 NOVEMBER 1991

The surprising emergence of distant shares

'EMERGING markets' once seemed an optimistic term. Now it is really happening. The stock markets of Asia and Latin America, plus a handful of others classified as 'emerging' by the International Finance Corporation (IFC, the private-sector arm of the World Bank), have collectively grown fourfold since 1985. Last year they provided $22 billion of fresh money for companies.... The IFC reckons that foreigners' stake in the young markets has grown from nothing a decade ago to around $17 billion.

By the end of the decade, this sum may seem paltry. For reasons unconnected with the individual charms of these markets, the world's biggest savings institutions – pension and mutual funds, insurance companies – are keener to spread their assets internationally; Salomon Brothers, an American investment bank, reckons that the value of cross-border equity flows increased 20 times during the 1980s. As they diversify, fund managers establish benchmarks to guide their asset allocation. A popular solution is to allocate money in proportion to the capitalisation of each market. If this were applied to the developing world, the result would be a deluge of foreign capital.

Each year the rich world's savers invest something like $1 trillion of new money in equities. Together the emerging markets represent 5% of world stockmarket capitalisation, so the benchmark would imply an annual transfer of $50 billion. If the savings institutions also began to shift existing funds to reflect that proportion, the transfers could be even bigger – perhaps amounting to $100 billion a year....

Next consider the scope for issuing international equity. The new rival to the growth of cross-border equity flows is 'cross-exchange' trading.... Salomon Brothers calculates that the volume of cross-exchange equity trading jumped from $583 billion in 1989 to $874 billion last year.

Developing countries have recently begun to exploit investors' appetite for international listings. The most noted example is Telmex, Mexico's telephone company, whose listing on the New York Stock Exchange in May [1991] raised $2.2 billion; on October 28th [1991] Telmex was the exchange's most actively traded stock. South Korean, Indonesian and Thai companies issued $1.6 billion of international equity and convertible bonds between them during the 18 months from January 1990. Indian and Brazilian rivals are tipped to join in next.

© The Economist. Reprinted with permission.

The stock markets of Asia and Latin American (plus a few others) have grown four-fold since 1985. In 1990, $22 billion of savings were channelled through these markets, $17 billion of which were foreign savings.

The world's pension and mutual funds and insurance companies have spread their assets internationally, resulting in a twenty-fold increase in the value of cross-border equity flows during the 1980s.

If these institutions also shift existing funds in proportion to market size, the transfers will be $100 billion a year.

An alternative to allocating funds to foreign stock markets is for investors to buy foreign shares in their own countries – cross-exchange trading – which increased from $583 billion in 1989 to $874 billion in 1990.

Background and Analysis

The world capital market is made up of thousands of local markets, but it is a single integrated market. People with funds to lend supply them where they can get the highest interest rate. People borrowing funds to buy capital demand them where they can get the lowest interest rate. As a result, each local capital market has the same interest rate.

The figure shows how the world capital market for equity capital – shares in companies – works. Part (a) illustrates the Asian and Latin American 'emerging' markets, and part (b) illustrates the New York market. Initially, the demand and supply curves are D_0 and S_0. The interest rate is r_N and the quantities of equity capital are K_N in New York and zero in the emerging markets.

Then the demand for equity capital increases in Asia and Latin America, and the demand curve for capital shifts to the right, to D_1. (Such an increase occurred in Asia and Latin American during the 1980s partly because the number of profitable business opportunities increased and partly because banks stopped lending to companies in these regions.)

Other things remaining equal, the interest rate rises in the emerging markets to r_E and the quantity of equity capital increases to K_E.

But other things do not remain equal. With the interest rate in the emerging markets higher than that in New York, US institutions with funds to lend move them from the New York market to the emerging markets. The supply curves shift to S_2 (in both markets). These are the 'cross-border equity flows' in the story.

Also, borrowers in Asia and Latin America switch their borrowing from their local market to the New York market. The demand curves shift to D_2 in both markets. This is the 'cross-exchange trading' in the story.

As a consequence of these changes in supply and demand, the interest rate rises in the New York market and falls in the emerging markets. When the two rates are equal at r_W, the demand and supply curves stop shifting and a single interest rate prevails in both markets.

The capital markets of Asia and Latin American are 'emerging' and 'cross-exchange' trading is expanding because, if they did not, interest rates in the two markets would diverge and profits could be made simply by borrowing in the market that has the low interest rate and lending in the other market.

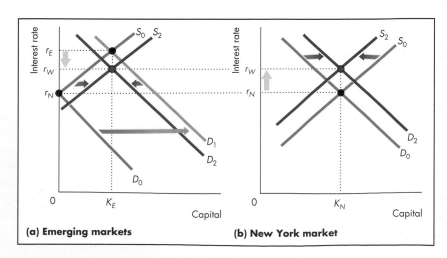

(a) Emerging markets

(b) New York market

SUMMARY

Capital, Investment and Saving

There are two kinds of assets: financial and physical. Financial assets are all the claims of one economic agent against others. Physical assets, or capital, are the stock of all the productive assets owned by households, firms and governments. Investment is the flow of additions to the stock of capital. Depreciation is the flow reduction in the stock of capital through use or the passage of time.

People's saving decisions determine the quantity of capital supplied. Saving equals income minus consumption. People allocate their savings to a variety of alternative financial and real assets. (pp. 430–432)

Capital Markets in the United Kingdom Today

Capital markets provide the link between the saving decisions of households and the investment decisions of households, firms and governments. Households buy homes for themselves, they finance firms' investment partly by buying capital goods for sole proprietorships and partnerships, and they finance company and government investment partly by buying securities and partly by placing funds with financial intermediaries that, in turn, buy securities in or make loans to companies and governments. (pp. 432–434)

Demand for Capital

The demand for capital by firms is determined – like the demand for all other inputs – by firms' profit-maximizing choices. The quantity of capital demanded by a firm is such that the marginal revenue product of capital equals its opportunity cost. A firm can make the comparison between marginal revenue product and cost by calculating the total present value of all the future marginal revenue products and comparing that total present value with the price of new capital.

The quantity of capital demanded by a firm depends on the interest rate. The higher the interest rate, the lower is the present value of the future stream of marginal revenue products, and the smaller is the quantity of capital equipment a firm buys. The lower the interest rate, the greater is the quantity of

capital demanded – the demand curve for capital is downward sloping. The demand curve for capital shifts steadily to the right as a result of technological change and the general tendency to exploit innovations over time. (pp. 434–440)

The Supply of Capital

The quantity of capital supplied results chiefly from the saving decisions of households. Savings depend on how much households smooth their consumption over the life cycle and on the interest rate. The supply curve for capital is upward sloping, so that the quantity of capital supplied increases as interest rates rise. The supply curve of capital shifts over time as a result of changes in the population and its age composition, and in the level of income. (pp. 440–442)

Interest Rates and Asset Prices

Interest rates and asset prices can be viewed as two sides of the same coin. In the long run they settle so that there is equality between the quantity of capital demanded and the quantity supplied. Interest rates on particular assets are distributed around the average rate according to the degree of risk of different types of assets.

The stock market value of a company depends on its current profit and on expectations of its future profit. The higher the expected growth rate of a company's profit, the higher is the price of its shares. The price–earnings ratio is the ratio of the current price of a company's shares to its current profit per share. That ratio depends on the price of the shares which depends on the expected growth rate of profit.

The volume of trading on the stock exchange is determined by the extent of the divergence of expectations of the future. When everyone agrees about the future, the volume of trading is low. When there is widespread disagreement, the volume of trading is high. There can be large changes in prices with a low or high volume of trading. Price changes occur when there is a change in expectations about profit growth.

Mergers and takeovers occur as part of the process of maximizing profit. If a firm's stock market value is lower than the value of its assets when used by another firm, it will benefit that other firm to take over the first one. Mergers occur when there is a mutually agreed benefit from combining the assets of two (or more) firms. (pp. 442–446)

Natural Resource Markets

Natural resources are the non-produced factors of production with which we are endowed. The price of a non-renewable natural resource is determined by the interest rate, the demand for its flow (which in the case of demands by firms depends on the resource's marginal revenue product) and the stock of the natural resource remaining. The price of a natural resource is such that its future price is expected to rise at a rate equal to the interest rate and to reach the choke price at the time at which the resource is exhausted. The actual price changes constantly to take account of new information. Even though the future price is expected to increase, the actual price often decreases as a result of new information leading to an increase in the estimate of the remaining stock or to a decrease in the demand for the flow of the resource. (pp. 446–451)

KEY ELEMENTS

Key Terms

Key Figures and Tables

REVIEW QUESTIONS

1   Why does the quantity of capital demanded by a firm rise as the interest rate falls?

2   Set out the key reasons for differences in interest rates on different types of assets.

3   What is the relationship between interest rates and asset prices?

4   Explain how the stock market value of a firm is determined.

5 Define the price-earnings ratio and explain how it is determined.

6 Why are there some occasions on which stock market prices change a lot but with little trading and others when prices are stable but trading volumes are high?

7 Why do mergers and takeovers occur?

8 Distinguish between the stock and the flow of a non-renewable natural resource.

9 Explain why the price of a non-renewable natural resource is expected to rise at a rate equal to the interest rate.

10 What determines the price of a natural resource?

11 Why is it impossible to forecast most of the fluctuations in the price of a natural resource?

P R O B L E M S

1 At the end of 1993, a firm had a production plant worth £1,000,000. During 1994, its plant depreciated by 10 per cent. During the same year, the firm bought new capital equipment for £250,000. What was the value of the firm's stock of capital at the end of 1994? What was the firm's gross investment during 1994? What was the firm's net investment during 1994?

2 You earn £10,000 (after tax) per year for three years, and you spend £8,000 each year. How much do you save each year? What happens to your wealth during this three year period?

3 What are the ways in which a holder of wealth can channel capital into firms?

4 Why is a deposit in a financial intermediary less risky than buying company shares or government bonds?

5 A firm is considering buying a new machine. It is estimated that the marginal revenue product of the machine will be £10,000 per year for five years. The machine will have a scrap value at the end of five years of £10,000. The interest rate is 10 per cent a year.

   a What is the maximum price that the firm will pay for the machine?

   b If the machine costs £40,000, would the firm buy the machine if the interest rate is 10 per cent? What is the highest interest rate at which the firm would buy the machine?

BOX 16.1:CALCULATION OF PRESENT VALUE

The present value of $A a year for ever when the interest rate is i per year is A/i. Let's consider the present value of $3 next year, plus $3 the following year, plus $3 in every subsequent year. To work this out, first write out the formula for the present value (PV) of $A a year forever at an interest rate of i per year:

$$PV = \frac{\$A}{(1+i)} + \frac{\$A}{(1+i)^2} + \ldots + \frac{\$A}{(1+i)^n} + \ldots$$

The dots stand for the years between year 2 and year n and the years beyond n. Next, divide this equation by $(1+i)$ to give:

$$\frac{PV}{(1+i)} = \frac{\$A}{(1+i)^2} + \frac{\$A}{(1+i)^3} + \ldots + \frac{\$A}{(1+i)^{n+1}} + .$$

Now subtract the second equation from the first to give:

$$PV - \frac{PV}{(1+i)} = \frac{\$A}{(1+i)} .$$

Multiply both sides of this equation by $(1+i)$ to give:

$$(1+i)\,PV - PV = \$A$$

and simplify the left-hand side to give:

$$iPV = \$A$$

Finally, divide both sides of the previous equation by i to give:

$$PV = \frac{\$A}{i}$$

For example, if $A = $3, and $i = 0.1$ (the interest rate is 10 per cent a year),

$$PV = \frac{\$A}{i} = \$30.$$

That is the present value of $3 a year forever when the interest rate of 10 per cent a year is $30.

CHAPTER 17

UNCERTAINTY
AND
INFORMATION

After studying this chapter you will be able to:

◆ Explain how people make decisions when they are uncertain about the consequences

◆ Explain why people buy insurance and how insurance companies make a profit

◆ Explain why buyers search and sellers advertise

◆ Explain how markets cope with incomplete information

◆ Explain how people use financial markets to lower risk

L IFE IS LIKE A LOTTERY. YOU WORK HARD AT UNIVERSITY, BUT WHAT WILL THE payoff be? Will you get an interesting, well-paying job or a miserable, low-paying one? You set up a small summer business and work hard at it. But will you make enough profit to keep you at university next year or will you get wiped out? How do people make a decision when they don't know its consequences? ◆ ◆ As you cross an intersection on a green light, you see a car on your left that's still moving. Will it stop or will it run the red light? You buy insurance against such a risk, and insurance companies profit from your business. Why are we willing to buy insurance at prices that leave insurance companies

with a profit? ◆ ◆ Buying a new car – or a used car – is fun, but it's also scary. You could get stuck with a lemon. And cars are not unique. Just about every complicated product you buy could be defective.

Lotteries and Lemons

How do car dealers and retailers induce us to buy what may turn out to be a lemon? ◆ ◆ People keep some of their wealth in the bank, some in bonds and some in shares; and they hold a diversity of shares. Some of these ways of holding wealth have a high return and some a low return. Why don't people put all their wealth in the place that has the highest return? Why does it pay to diversify?

◆ ◆ ◆ ◆ In this chapter we answer questions such as these. We'll begin by explaining how people make decisions when they're uncertain about the consequences. We'll see how it pays to buy insurance, even if its price leaves the insurance company with a profit. We'll explain why we use scarce resources to generate and disseminate information. And we'll look at transactions in a wide variety of markets in which uncertainty and the cost of acquiring information play important roles.

Uncertainty and Risk

Although we live in an uncertain world, we rarely ask what uncertainty is. Yet to explain how we make decisions and do business with each other in an uncertain world, we need to think more deeply about uncertainty. What exactly is uncertainty? We also live in a risky world. Is risk the same as uncertainty? Let's begin by defining uncertainty and risk and distinguishing between them.

Uncertainty is a state in which more than one event may occur, but we don't know which one. Usually, the event that does occur affects our economic well-being. For example, when farmers plant their crops, they are uncertain about the weather during the growing season, but their profits depend on the weather.

To describe uncertainty we use the concepts of probability and risk. A *probability* is a number between zero and one that measures the chance of some possible event occurring. A zero probability means the event will not happen. A probability of one means the event will occur for sure – with certainty. A probability of 0.5 means that half the time the event will occur and half the time it will not. An example is the probability of a tossed coin coming down heads. In a large number of tosses, half of them are most likely to be heads and the other half tails.

In ordinary speech, risk is the probability of incurring a loss (or some other misfortune). In economics, **risk** is a state in which more than one outcome may occur, and the *probability* of each possible outcome can be estimated. Sometimes probabilities can be measured. For example, the probability that a tossed coin will come down heads is based on the fact that, in a large number of tosses, half are heads and half are tails; the probability of a car in Manchester in 1996 being involved in an accident is based on police and insurance records of previous accidents.

Some situations cannot be described using probabilities based on observed events. These situations may be unique events, such as the introduction of a new product. How much will sell and at what price? This question cannot be answered by looking at the previous occasions on which *this particular* new product was introduced. But it can be answered by looking at past experience with *similar* new products, supported by some judgements. Such judgements are called *subjective probabilities*.

Regardless of whether the probability of some event occurring is based on actual data or judgements – or even guesses – we can use probability to study the way in which people make decisions in the face of uncertainty. The first step in doing this is to describe how people assess the cost of risk.

Measuring the Cost of Risk

Some people are more willing to take chances than others, but everyone prefers less risk to more, other things being equal. We measure people's attitudes towards risk by using their utility of wealth schedules and curves. The **utility of wealth** is the amount of utility a person attaches to a given amount of wealth. The greater a person's wealth, other things being equal, the higher is the person's utility. Not only does greater wealth bring higher utility, but as wealth increases, each additional unit of wealth increases utility by a smaller amount. That is, the *marginal utility of wealth diminishes*.

Figure 17.1 sets out Tania's utility of wealth schedule and curve. Each point *a* to *e* on Tania's utility of wealth curve corresponds to the row of the table identified by the same letter. You can see that as her wealth increases, so her utility of wealth also increases. You can also see that her marginal utility of wealth diminishes. When wealth increases from £1,500 to £3,000, utility increases by 20 units, but when wealth increases by a further £1,500 to £4,500, utility increases by only 10 units.

We can use Tania's utility of wealth curve to measure her cost of risk. The bigger the risk Tania faces, the worse off she is and the less she likes it. To measure Tania's cost of risk, let's see how she evaluates two alternative summer jobs that involve different amounts of risk.

One job, working as a painter, pays enough for her to save £2,500 by the end of the summer. There is no uncertainty about the income from this job. If Tania takes this job, by the end of the summer her wealth will be £2,500. The other job, selling cosmetics door-to-door, is risky. If she takes this job, her wealth at the end of the summer depends entirely on her success at selling. She might be a good salesperson or a poor one. A good salesperson makes £4,500 in a summer and a poor one makes £1,500. Tania has never tried this line of business before, so she doesn't know how successful she'll be. She assumes that there is an equal chance – a probability of 0.5 – of making either £1,500 or £4,500. Which

FIGURE 17.1

The Utility of Wealth

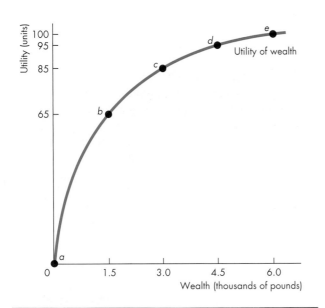

Wealth (thousands of pounds)	Utility (units)	Marginal utility (units)
a 0	0	
		 65
b 1.5	65	
		 20
c 3.0	85	
		 10
d 4.5	95	
		 5
e 6.0	100	

The table shows Tania's utility of wealth schedule, and the figure shows her utility of wealth curve. Utility increases as wealth increases, but the marginal utility of wealth diminishes.

outcome does Tania prefer, £2,500 for sure from the painting job or a 50 per cent chance of either £1,500 or £4,500 from the sales job?

When there is uncertainty, people do not know the *actual* utility they will get from taking a particular action. But it is possible to calculate the utility

FIGURE 17.2

Choice under Uncertainty

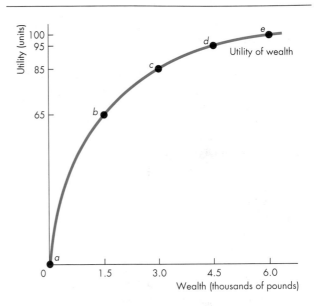

If Tania's wealth is £2,500 and she faces no risk, her utility is 80 units. If she faces an equal probability of having £4,500 or £1,500, her expected wealth is £3,000. But her expected utility is 80 units – the same as with £2,500 and no uncertainty. Tania is indifferent between these two alternatives. Tania's extra £500 of expected wealth is just enough to offset her extra risk.

they *expect* to get. **Expected utility** is the average utility arising from all the possible outcomes. Equivalently, it is the average utility the person would get if the action could be repeated a large number of times. So, to choose her summer job, Tania calculates the expected utility arising from painting and sales. Figure 17.2 shows how she does this.

If Tania takes the painting job, she has £2,500 of wealth and 80 units of utility. There is no uncertainty in this case, so her expected utility equals her actual utility – 80 units. But suppose she takes the job selling cosmetics. If she makes £4,500, her utility is 95 units, and if she makes £1,500, her utility is 65 units. Her *expected utility* is the average of these two possible outcomes and is 80 units – calculated as $(95 \times 0.5) + (65 \times 0.5)$.

Tania chooses the job that maximizes her expected utility. In this case, the two alternatives give the same expected utility – 80 units – so she is indifferent between them. She is equally likely to take either job. The difference between Tania's expected wealth of £3,000 from the risky job and £2,500 from the no-risk job – £500 – is just large enough to offset the additional risk that Tania faces.

The calculation that we've just done enables us to measure Tania's cost of risk. The cost of risk is the amount by which expected wealth must be increased to give the same expected utility as a no-risk situation. In Tania's case, the cost of the risk arising from an uncertain income of £1,500 or £4,500 is £500.

If the amount Tania can make from painting falls to £1,500, the extra income from the risky job will be more than enough to cover her cost of the risk and she will take the risky alternative of selling cosmetics. An income of £1,500 for certain gives only 65 units of utility, an amount less than the 80 units expected from the sales job.

If the amount Tania can make from painting remains at £2,500 and the expected income from sales also remains constant while its range of uncertainty increases, Tania will take the painting job. To see this conclusion, suppose that good salespeople make £6,000, and poor ones makes nothing. The average income from sales is unchanged at £3,000, but the range of uncertainty has increased. Looking at the table in Fig. 17.1 you can see that Tania gets 100 units of utility from a wealth of £6,000 and zero units of utility from a wealth of zero. Thus in this case, Tania's expected utility from selling cosmetics is 50 units – calculated as $(100 \times 0.5) + (0 \times 0.5)$. Since the expected utility from sales is now less than that from painting, she chooses painting.

Risk Aversion and Risk Neutrality

There is an enormous difference between George Graham, manager of Arsenal, who favours a cautious game and Johann Cruyff, of Barcelona, who favours a risky game. They have different attitudes towards risk. Graham is much more *risk averse* than is Cruyff. Tania is also *risk averse* – other things being equal, she prefers situations with less risk. The shape of a person's utility of wealth curve tells us about their attitude towards risk – about the person's degree of *risk aversion*. The more rapidly a person's marginal utility of wealth diminishes, the more the person dislikes risk – the more risk averse they are. You can see this fact best by considering an extreme case, that of *risk neutrali-*

ty. A risk-neutral person is one for whom risk is costless. Such a person cares only about *expected wealth* and does not mind how much uncertainty there is.

Figure 17.3 shows the utility of wealth curve of a risk-neutral person. It is a straight line and the marginal utility of wealth is constant. If this person has an expected wealth of £3,000, expected utility is 50 units regardless of the range of uncertainty around that average. An equal probability of having £1,500 or £4,500 gives the same expected utility as an equal probability of having £0 or £6,000, which is also the expected utility of a certain £3,000. Real people are risk averse and their utility of wealth curves look like Tania's. But the extreme case of risk neutrality illustrates the importance and the consequences of the shape of the utility of wealth curve for a person's degree of risk aversion.

FIGURE 17.3

Risk Neutrality

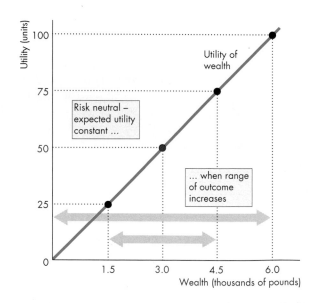

People dislike risk because they have diminishing marginal utility of wealth. A (hypothetical) risk-neutral person has a linear utility of wealth curve. Expected utility is constant, regardless of the range of uncertainty. The cost of risk is zero.

Insurance

One way of reducing the risk we face is to buy insurance. How does insurance reduce risk? Why do people buy insurance? And how much do we spend on insurance? Let's answer this last question first, and take a look at the insurance industry in the United Kingdom today.

Insurance Industry in the United Kingdom

On average UK households spend over 5 per cent of their income on insurance. That's as much as they spend on clothes and more than they spend on domestic fuels, such as gas, electricity and oil. When we buy insurance, we enter into an agreement with an insurance company to pay an agreed price – called a *premium* – in exchange for benefits to be paid to us if some specified event occurs. There are two main types of insurance:

◆ Life insurance
◆ Property and casualty insurance

Life Insurance   Life insurance reduces the risk of financial loss in the event of death. About two-thirds of UK households have life insurance. More than 250 companies supply life insurance and the total premiums paid in a year are around $9 billion.

Property and Casualty Insurance   Property and casualty insurance reduces the risk of financial loss in the event of an accident involving damage to persons or property. It includes car insurance – its biggest component – and the insurance of homes and their contents.

How Insurance Works

Insurance works by pooling risks. It is possible and profitable because people are risk averse. The probability of any one person having a serious car accident is small, but the cost to that person of an accident is enormous. For a large population, the probability of one person having an accident is the proportion of the population that does have an accident. Since this probability is known, the total cost of accidents can be predicted. An insurance company can pool the risks of a large population and share the costs. It does so by collecting premiums from everyone

and paying out benefits to those who suffer a loss. If the insurance company does its calculations right, it collects at least as much in premiums as it pays out in benefits and operating costs.

To see why people buy insurance and why it is profitable, let's consider an example. Dan has the utility of wealth curve shown in Fig. 17.4. He owns a car worth $5,000 and that is his only wealth. If there is no risk of his having an accident, his utility will be 100 units. But there is a 10 per cent chance (a probability of 0.1) that he will have an accident within a year. Suppose Dan does not buy insurance. If he does have an accident his car is worthless, and with no insurance, he has no wealth and no utility. Because the probability of an accident is 0.1, the probability of *not* having an

FIGURE 17.4

Insurance

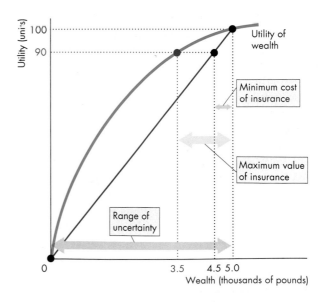

Dan has a car valued at £5,000 which gives him a utility of 100 units, but there is a 0.1 probability that he will have an accident making his car worthless (wealth and utility equal to zero). With no insurance, his expected utility is 90 units and he is willing to pay up to £1,500 for insurance. An insurance company (with no operating expenses) can offer insurance to Dan and the rest of the community for £500. Hence, there is a potential gain from insurance for both Dan and the insurance company.

TABLE 17.1

Risk Taking versus Insurance

(a) POSSIBLE OUTCOMES

	No accident			Accident	
Probability		0.9			0.1	
	Wealth	Utility		Wealth	Utility
No insurance	£5,000	100		£0	0
Insurance	£4,000	95		£4,000	95

With no insurance, Dan's expected wealth is £4,500 and his expected utility is 90 units. By buying insurance for £1,000, Dan's expected wealth falls to £4,000, but he has no uncertainty and his expected utility increases to 95 units.

(b) EXPECTED OUTCOMES

	Expected wealth	Expected utility
No insurance	(£5,000 × 0.9) + (£0 × 0.1) = £4,500	(100 × 0.9) + (0 × 0.1) = 90
Insurance	(£4,000 × 0.9) + (£4,000 × 0.1) = £4,000	(95 × 0.9) + (95 × 0.1) = 95

accident is 0.9. Dan's expected wealth, therefore, is £4,500 (£5,000 × 0.9), and his expected utility is 90 units (100 × 0.9).

Given his utility of wealth curve, Dan has 90 units of utility if his wealth is £3,500 and he faces no uncertainty. That is, Dan's utility is the same if he has a guaranteed wealth of £3,500 or a 90 per cent chance of having wealth of £5,000 and a 10 per cent chance of having nothing. If Dan can buy, for less than £1,500 (£5,000 minus £3,500), insurance that pays out in the event of an accident he will do so. Thus Dan has a demand for insurance at premiums less than £1,500.

Suppose there are lots of people like Dan, each with a £5,000 car and each with a 10 per cent chance of having an accident within the year. If an insurance company agrees to pay each person who has an accident £5,000, the company will pay out £5,000 to one-tenth of the population, or an average of £500 per person. This amount is the insurance company's minimum premium for such insurance. It is less than the value of insurance to Dan because Dan is risk averse. He is willing to pay something to reduce the risk he faces.

Suppose the insurance company's operating expenses are a further £500 and that it offers insurance for £1,000. The company now covers all its costs – the amounts paid out to policyholders for

their losses plus the company's operating expenses. But Dan – and all the other people like him – will maximize their utility by buying this insurance. The calculations in Table 17.1 summarize the gain each makes. With no insurance, expected utility is 90 units. But with insurance costing £1,000, utility is 95 units, a gain of 5 units. Equivalently, Dan's maximum value from insurance is £1,500. The insurance premium is £1,000, so Dan has £500 of wealth more than that needed to give him the same utility with no insurance – £3,500. And with wealth of £4,000, he has 95 units of utility – a gain of 5 units over his utility with no insurance.

REVIEW

Households in the United Kingdom spend 5 per cent of their income, on average, on insurance, chiefly life insurance and property and casualty insurance. Insurance works by pooling risks. Every insured person pays in but only those who suffer a loss are compensated. Insurance is worth buying and insurance is profitable because people are risk averse and are willing to pay for lower risk. ◆

Much of the uncertainty we face arises from ignorance. We just don't know all the things we could benefit from knowing. But knowledge or information is not free. We must make decisions about how much information to acquire. Let's now study the choices we make about obtaining information and see how incomplete information affects some of our economic transactions.

Information

We spend a huge quantity of our scarce resources on economic information. **Economic information** includes data on the prices, quantities and qualities of goods and services and factors of production.

In the models of perfect competition, monopoly and monopolistic competition, information is free. Everyone has all the information they need. Households are completely informed about the prices of the goods and services they buy and the factors of production they sell. Similarly, firms are completely informed.

In contrast, information is scarce in the real world. If it were not, we wouldn't need The *Financial Times* and the BBC. And we wouldn't need to shop around for bargains or spend time looking for a job. The opportunity cost of economic information – the cost of acquiring information on prices, quantities and qualities of goods and services and factors of production – is called **information cost**. Let's look at some of the consequences of information cost.

Searching for Price Information

When many firms sell the same good or service, there is a range of prices and buyers want to find the lowest price. But searching takes time and is costly. So buyers must balance the expected gain from further search against the cost of further search. To perform this balancing act, they use a decision rule called the *optimal-search rule* – or *optimal-stopping rule*. The optimal-search rule is:

◆ Search for a lower price until the expected marginal benefit of search equals the marginal cost of search.
◆ When the expected marginal benefit is less than or equal to the marginal cost, stop searching and buy.

To implement the optimal-search rule, buyers set a reservation price. The buyer's **reservation price** is the highest price that the buyer is willing to pay for a good. The buyer will continue to search for a lower price if the lowest price found exceeds the reservation price, but will stop searching and buy if the lowest price found is less than or equal to the reservation price. At the buyer's reservation price, the expected marginal benefit of search equals the marginal cost of search.

Figure 17.5 illustrates the optimal-search rule. You've decided to buy a used Rover Metro. Your marginal cost of search is $£C$ per dealer visited and is shown by the horizontal orange line in the figure. Your expected marginal benefit of visiting one more dealer depends on the lowest price that you've found. The lower the price you've already found, the lower is your expected marginal benefit of visiting one more dealer, as shown by the blue curve in the figure.

The price at which expected marginal benefits equals marginal cost is your reservation price – $£4,000$ in the figure. If you find a price below your reservation price, you stop searching and buy. If you find a price that exceeds your reservation price, you continue to search for a lower price. Individual shoppers differ in their marginal cost of search and so have different reservation prices. As a result, identical items can be found selling for a range of prices.

Buyers are not alone in creating information. Sellers do a lot of it too – in the form of advertising. Let's see what the effects of advertising are.

Advertising

Advertising constantly surrounds us – on television, radio or billboards, and in newspapers or magazines – and costs billions of pounds. How do firms decide how much to spend on advertising? Does advertising create information, or does it just persuade us to buy things we don't really want? What does it do to prices?

FIGURE 17.5

Optimal-search Rule

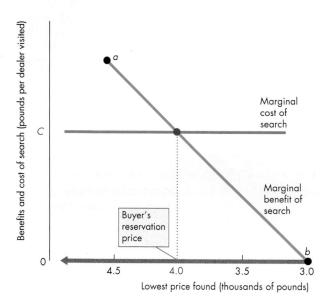

The marginal cost of search is constant at £C. As the lowest price found (measured from right to left on the horizontal axis) declines, the expected marginal utility of further search diminishes. The lowest price found at which the marginal cost equals the expected marginal benefit is the reservation price. The optimal-search rule is to search until the reservation price (or lower) is found and then buy at that lowest found price.

Advertising for Profit Maximization   A firm's advertising decision is part of its overall profit-maximization strategy. Firms in perfect competition don't advertise because everyone has all the information there is. But firms selling differentiated products in monopolistic competition and firms locked in the struggle of survival in oligopoly advertise a lot.

The amount of advertising undertaken by firms in monopolistic competition is such that the marginal revenue from advertising equals the marginal cost of advertising. The amount of advertising undertaken by firms in oligopoly is determined by the game they are playing. If that game is a *prisoners' dilemma*, they might spend amounts that lower their combined profits but they must advertise to avoid being wiped out by other firms in the industry.

Persuasion or Information   Much advertising is designed to persuade us that the product being advertised is the best in its class. For example, the Pepsi advertisement tells us that Pepsi is really better than Coke. The Coca-Cola advertisement tells us that Coke is really better than Pepsi. But advertising also informs. It provides information about the quality and price of a good or service.

Does advertising mainly persuade or mainly inform? The answer varies for different goods and different types of markets. Goods whose quality can be assessed *before* they are bought are called *search goods*. Typically, the advertising of search goods mainly informs – gives information about price, quality and location of suppliers. Examples of such goods are petrol, basic foods and household goods. Goods whose quality can be assessed only *after* they are bought are called *experience goods*. Typically, the advertising of experience goods mainly persuades – it is designed to encourage the consumer to buy now and make a judgement later about quality, based on experience with the good. Cigarettes and alcoholic beverages are in this category.

Because most advertising involves experience goods, it is likely that advertising is more often persuasive rather than merely informative. But persuasive advertising doesn't necessarily harm the consumer. It might result in lower prices.

Advertising and Prices   Advertising is costly, but does it increase the price of the good advertised? Since firms advertise to increase their profits, it only makes sense for them to do so if the consumer is willing to pay the advertising cost.

But two lines of reasoning tell us that advertising can actually lower prices. The first is that if advertising is informative, it *increases* competition. By informing potential buyers about alternative sources of supply, advertising forces firms to keep their prices low. There is evidence of such effects, especially in retailing. The second is that if advertising enables firms to increase their output and reap economies of scale, it is possible that the price of the good will be lower with advertising than without it, provided competition prevents monopoly pricing. So, provided the firm does not become so large that it is able to extract monopoly profits, consumers will benefit from advertising.

The final cost-benefit calculation on advertising is not yet available and whether these pro-consumer aspects of advertising are the largest ones is not known.

REVIEW

Data on the prices, quantities and qualities of goods and services and factors of production – economic information – is scarce and people economize on its use. Buyers searching for price information stop when they find their reservation price, the price that makes the expected marginal benefit of search equal the marginal cost of search. Sellers advertise to inform potential buyers of the good or to persuade them to buy it. Advertising can increase competition and may raise or lower the price of the advertised good. ◆

Private Information

So far we have looked at situations in which information is available to everyone and can be obtained with an expenditure of resources. But not all situations are like this. For example, someone might have private information. **Private information** is information available to one person, but too costly for anyone else to obtain.

Private information affects many economic transactions. One is your knowledge about your driving. You know much more than your car insurance company does about how carefully and defensively you drive. Another is your knowledge about your work effort. You know far more than your employer about how hard you work. Yet another is your knowledge about the quality of your car. You know whether it's a lemon. But the person to whom you are about to sell it does not and can't find out until after he or she has purchased it from you, and then it's too late.

Private information creates two problems:

◆ Moral hazard
◆ Adverse selection

Moral hazard exists when one of the parties to an agreement has an incentive, *after the agreement is made*, to act in a manner that brings additional benefits to himself or herself at the expense of the other party. It arises because it is too costly for the injured party to monitor the actions of the advantaged party. For example, Jackie hires David as a salesperson and pays him a fixed wage regardless of his sales. David faces a moral hazard. He has an incentive to put in the least possible effort, benefiting himself and reducing Jackie's profits. For this reason, salespeople are not paid a fixed wage. Instead they receive an income that depends in some way on the volume (or value) of their sales.

Adverse selection is the tendency for the people who accept contracts to be those with private information that they plan to use to their own advantage and to the disadvantage of the less informed party. For example, if Jackie really offers the type of contract we've just described, it will attract lazy salespeople. Hardworking salespeople will prefer *not* to work for Jackie because they can earn more by working for someone who pays by results. The fixed wage contract adversely selects those with private information (knowledge about their work habits) who can use that knowledge to their own advantage and to the disadvantage of the other party.

A variety of devices have evolved that enable markets to function in the face of moral hazard and adverse selection. We've just seen one, the use of incentive payments for salespeople. Let's look at some more and also see how moral hazard and adverse selection influence three real-world markets:

◆ The market for used cars
◆ The market for loans
◆ The market for insurance

The Market for Used Cars

When a person buys a new car it may turn out to be a lemon. If the car is a lemon it is worth less to the person who bought it and to everyone else than if it has no defects. Does the used car market have two prices reflecting these two values – a low price for lemons and a higher price for cars without defects? It does not. To see why, let's look at a used car market, first with no dealer warranties and second with warranties.

Used Cars without Warranties   To make the points as clearly as possible, we'll make some extreme assumptions. There are just two kinds of cars, lemons and those without defects. A lemon is worth £1,000 both to its current owner and to anyone who buys it. A car without defects is worth £5,000 to its current and potential future owners. Whether a car is a lemon is private information to the person who owns it and has spent enough time driving it to discover its quality. Buyers of used cars can't tell whether they are buying a lemon until *after* they have bought the car and learned as much about it as its current owner knows. There are no dealer warranties.

The first thing to notice is that because buyers can't tell the difference between a lemon and a good car, they are willing to pay only one price for a used car. What is that price? Are they willing to pay £5,000, the value of a good car? They are not, because there is at least some probability that they are buying a lemon worth only £1,000. If buyers are not willing to pay £5,000 for a used car, are the owners of good cars willing to sell? They are not because a good car is worth £5,000 to them, so they hang on to their cars. Only the owners of lemons are willing to sell – as long as the price is £1,000 or higher. But, reason the buyers, if only the owners of lemons are selling, all the used cars available are lemons so the maximum price worth paying is £1,000. Thus the market for used cars is a market for lemons and the price is £1,000.

Moral hazard exists in the car market because sellers have an incentive to claim that lemons are good cars. But, given the assumptions in the above description of the car market, no one believes such claims. Adverse selection exists resulting in only lemons actually being traded.

The market for used cars is not working well. Good used cars just don't get bought and sold, but people want to be able to exchange good used cars. How can they do so? The answer is by introducing warranties into the market.

Used Cars with Warranties Car dealers perform two economic functions: they are intermediaries between buyers and sellers and they do car maintenance work (usually on the cars they have sold). The information they get from their car maintenance business is useful in helping them make the market for used cars operate more efficiently than the market for lemons that we've just described.

Buyers of used cars can't tell a lemon from a good car but car dealers can. From their maintenance records, they have as much information about a car's quality as its owner has. They know, therefore, whether they are buying a lemon or a good car and

can offer £1,000 for lemons and £5,000 for good cars.[1] But how can they convince buyers that it is worth paying £5,000 for what may be a lemon? The answer is by giving a guarantee in the form of a warranty. The dealer *signals* which cars are good ones and which are lemons. A **signal** is an action taken outside a market that conveys information that can be used by that market. In this case, the dealer takes an action in the market for car repairs that can be used by the market for cars. For each good car sold, the dealer agrees to pay the costs of repairing the car if it turns out to have a defect. Cars with a warranty are good; cars without a warranty are lemons.

Why do buyers believe the signal? It is because the cost of sending a false signal is high. A dealer who gives a warranty on a lemon ends up paying the high cost of repairs – and risks gaining a bad reputation. A dealer who gives a warranty only on good cars has no repair costs and a reputation that gets better and better. It pays to send an accurate signal. It is rational, therefore, for buyers to believe the signal. Warranties break the lemon problem and enable the used car market to function with two prices, one for lemons and one for good cars.

The Markets for Loans

When a bank makes a loan, it is uncertain about whether the loan will be repaid. Low-risk borrowers default on their debts only for reasons beyond their control. For example, a firm might borrow to finance a project that fails and be unable to repay the bank. High-risk borrowers take excessive risks with the money they borrow and frequently default on their loans. But banks have no sure way of knowing whether they are lending to a low-risk or a high-risk borrower.

If the loans market was like the market for wheat, the interest rate would make the quantity of loans demanded equal the quantity supplied and the banks would lend to anyone willing to commit to paying the market determined interest rate. But there would be both moral hazard and adverse selection. High-risk borrowers would face a moral hazard and try to pass themselves off as low-risk

---

[1] In this example, to keep the numbers simple, we'll ignore dealers' profit margins and other costs of doing business and suppose that dealers buy cars for the same price as they sell them. The principles are the same with dealers' profit margins.

borrowers. The interest rate would be high, reflecting the high cost of lending to high-risk borrowers. Adverse selection would result in a large number of loans being made to high-risk borrowers and a small number to low-risk borrowers.

The market for loans does not work like this. Faced with moral hazard and adverse selection, banks use *signals* to discriminate between borrowers and they *ration* or limit loans to amounts below those demanded. Using signals such as length of time in a job, ownership of a home, marital status and age, banks restrict the amounts they are willing to lend to each type of borrower.

Figure 17.6 shows how the market for loans works in the face of moral hazard and adverse selection. The demand for loans is D and the supply is S. Loan limits based on signals restrict total loans made to L. At the interest rate charged, there is an excess demand for loans. A bank cannot increase its profit by making more loans because it can't identify the type of borrower taking the loans. And because the signals used mean that more high-risk borrowers are unsatisfied than low-risk borrowers, it is unlikely that any additional lending will be biased towards high-risk (and high-cost) borrowers.

The Market for Insurance

People who buy insurance face a moral hazard problem and insurance companies face an adverse selection problem. The moral hazard problem is that a person with insurance coverage for a loss has less incentive than an uninsured person to avoid such a loss. For example, a business with fire insurance has less incentive to take precautions against fire than a business with no fire insurance. The adverse selection problem is that only the people who expect to benefit from the insurance choose to buy it. For example, a business that is doing badly has an incentive to buy fire insurance and then be careless about fire prevention.

Insurance companies have an incentive to find ways around the moral hazard and adverse selection problems. By doing so, they can lower premiums and increase the amount of business they do. Real-world insurance markets have developed a variety of devices for overcoming or at least moderating these private information problems. One device is that of using signals.

One of the clearest signals a person can give a car insurance company is her or his driving record.

FIGURE 17.6

The Market for Loans

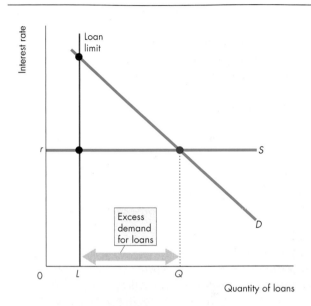

If a bank supplied loans on demand at the going interest rate, the quantity of loans would be Q, but most of the loans would be taken by high-risk borrowers. Banks use signals to distinguish between low-risk and high-risk borrowers and they ration loans. Banks have no incentive to increase interest rates and increase the quantity of loans because the additional loans would be to high-risk borrowers.

Suppose that Dan is a good driver and rarely has an accident. If he can demonstrate to the insurance company that his driving record is impeccable over a long enough period, then the insurance company will recognize him as a good driver. Dan will work hard at establishing a reputation as a good driver because he will be able to get his insurance at a lower price.

If all drivers, good and bad alike, can establish good records, then simply having a good record will not convey any information. For the signal to be informative, it must be difficult for bad drivers to fake low risk by having a good record. The signal used in car insurance are the 'no-claim' bonuses that drivers accumulate when they do not make an insurance claim.

Another device used by insurance companies is an excess. An excess is the amount of a loss that the insured agrees to bear. For example, most car insurance policies have the insurer paying the first few hundred pounds' worth of damage. The premium varies with the excess and in a significant way. That is, the decrease in the premium is more than proportionate to the increase in the excess. By offering insurance with full coverage on terms attractive only to the highest-risk people and then by offering coverage with an excess on more favourable terms, insurance companies can do profitable business with everyone. High-risk people fully cover but at the full cost of their risk, and lower-risk people partially cover and at a cost commensurate with their risk.

REVIEW

Private information creates moral hazard and adverse selection. In the markets for used cars, loans and insurance, methods such as warranties, loan limits, and no-claim bonuses and excesses have been devised to limit the problems caused by private information. ◆

Managing Risks in Financial Markets

Risk is a dominant feature of markets for shares and bonds – indeed for any asset whose price fluctuates and is determined by demand and supply in a market. One thing people do to cope with risky asset prices is diversify their asset holdings. Reading Between the Lines on pp.472–473 shows how a company facing risk in production can also reduce this risk by diversification.

Diversification to Lower Risk

The idea that diversification lowers risk is very natural. It is just an application of not putting all one's eggs into the same basket. How exactly does diversification reduce risk? The best way to answer this question is to consider an example.

Suppose there are two risky projects that you can undertake. Each involves investing £100,000. They are each independent of the other, but they each promise the same degree of risk and return.

Project 1 will either lose £25,000 or make £50,000, and the chance that either of these things will happen is 50 per cent. The expected return is $-(£25,000 \times 0.5) + (£50,000 \times 0.5)$, which is £12,500.

Project 2 also holds out the same promise of return – a 50 per cent chance of losing £25,000 and a 50 per cent chance of making £50,000. But the two projects are completely independent. The outcome of one project in no way influences or is related to the outcome of the other.

Undiversified Suppose you put all your eggs in one basket – investing the £100,000 in either Project 1 or Project 2. You will either lose £25,000, or make £50,000 and the probability of each of these outcomes is 50 per cent. Your expected return is the average of these two outcomes – an expected return of £12,500. But there is no chance that you will actually make a return of £12,500.

Diversified Suppose instead that you diversify by putting 50 per cent of your money into Project 1 and 50 per cent into Project 2. (Someone else is putting up the other money in these two projects.) What now are your possible returns? If both projects lose, your loss is £12,500 on each project or a total loss of £25,000. If Project 1 turns out be a winner and Project 2 a loser, you lose £12,500 on Project 1 and make £25,000 on Project 2, or in total you make £12,500. Also if Project 1 turns out to be a loser and Project 2 a winner, you make £12,500. If both projects turn out to be winners, you make £50,000. There are now four possible outcomes and each is equally probable. Each outcome has a 25 per cent chance of occurring. You have lowered the chance that you will earn £50,000, but you have also lowered the chance that you will lose £25,000. And you have increased the chance that you will actually make your expected return of £12,500. By diversifying your portfolio of assets you have reduced its riskiness while maintaining an expected return of £12,500.

If you are risk averse – that is, if your utility of wealth curve looks like Tania's which you studied earlier in this chapter – you'll prefer the diversified portfolio to the one that is not diversified. That is, your *expected utility* with a diversified set of assets is greater.

A further consequence of risk is the development of market that enable people to avoid risk – forward and futures markets.

Forward and Futures Markets

Producers are especially concerned about two uncertainties: the price at which they will be able to sell their product and the conditions affecting how much of their product will be produced. Farmers provide a clear illustration of the importance of these two uncertainties. First, when farmers decide how many acres of corn to plant, they do not know the price at which the corn will be sold. Knowing the price of corn today does not help them make decisions about how much seed to sow today. Today's planting becomes tomorrow's crop, and so tomorrow's price determines how much revenue farmers get from today's sowing. Second, when farmers plant corn, they do not know what the growing conditions will be. Conditions may be excellent, producing a high yield and a bumper crop, or conditions such as drought and inadequate sunshine may lead to a low crop yield and disaster.

Uncertainty about the future price of a good can arise from uncertainty about its future demand or its future supply. We have just considered some uncertainties about supply. There are also many uncertainties about demand. We know that demand for a good depends on the prices of its substitutes and complements, income, population and preferences. Demand varies as a result of fluctuations in all these influences on buyers' plans. Since these influences *do* fluctuate and are impossible to predict exactly, the level of future demand is always uncertain.

Forward Markets   Uncertainties about future supply and demand make future prices uncertain. But producers must make decisions today even though they do not know the price at which their output will be sold. In making such decisions, farmers are able to take advantage of special types of markets – forward markets. A **forward market** is a market in which a commitment is made at a price agreed here and now to exchange a specified quantity of a particular commodity at a specified future date.

Forward markets are useful for farmers and others whose production decisions yield an output with a time lag. By engaging in a forward transaction it is possible to know the price at which the output will be sold even though the output is not yet available.

Futures Market   Forward contracts enable farmers and others engaging in transactions for the future to reduce their risk arising from price variations. But they don't eliminate risk altogether. The person holding the contract has to stand ready to deliver or make delivery at the agreed price. In some situations it might not be convenient actually to deliver goods. In such a case the person holding a promise to deliver might want to sell that promise. To facilitate such exchanges, futures markets have been developed. A **futures market** is an organized market in which large-scale contracts for the future delivery of goods can be exchanged. Rarely do futures contracts result in an actual delivery taking place. All futures contracts are liquidated through subsequent resale of the future promise before the delivery date becomes due. The existence of futures markets enables people to diversify risk in much the same way as holding a range of assets in a portfolio enables risks to be diversified.

Rational Expectations

To decide whether to engage in a forward or futures transaction, traders and producers must make forecasts of future prices. How do they do that?

Forecasting Prices   To forecast prices, people use all the relevant information available to them. And they use this information to make a forecast that they believe will be right on average and have the smallest possible range of error. If any information is available that can improve a forecast, that information will be used. The forecast that uses all of the relevant information available and that has the least possible error is called a **rational expectation**.

We calculate the rational expectation of a price by using demand and supply. We know that next year's demand and next year's supply determine next year's price. So we forecast the factors that influence demand and supply. Let's work out a rational expectation of the future price of corn.

To forecast the future price of corn, we must forecast next year's demand and supply of corn. The demand for a good depends on the prices of its substitutes and complements, income, population and preferences. The expected demand, therefore, depends on the expected values of these variables. So to form an expectation of the future demand curve for corn, it is necessary to forecast the future prices of corn's substitutes and complements, income, population and current trends that might

Burberrys Planning for a Rainy Day

THE TIMES, 17 JANUARY 1994

Fashion

Iain R Webb

AT the end of 1993, *I.D.*, the alternative style magazine, featured a fashion story entitled 'New Looks for '94'. Written by the fashion editor, Edward Enninful, the article looked forward not only to new fashion horizons, but also picked over the trends of 1993.

'As the underground elements disappeared from deconstruction, so did all the good ideas.' Enninful wrote, with the kind of certainty enjoyed only by the youthful.

However, it was not Enninful's post-mortem of 1993 which aroused interest, but his predictions for 1994. 'I predict a hybrid of Rock and Classics', he wrote. 'Names like Burberrys, Scotch House, and Pringle will be worn with old denim, mesh, silver jewellery, pop socks, and other rock'n'roll essentials.'

Burberrys are well known the world over. So well known, in fact, that their name is included in the Oxford English Dictionary: 'Burberry, n. A kind of waterproof cloth, coat, etc. of this, made by a company of that name.' Even though the rainwear represents less than 35 per cent of their total production, it is this which is synonymous with the name. Not, however, as instantly recognisable as Burberrys' house check.

The red, black and white plaid set against a beige background was introduced in 1924, and was originally used to line raincoats.

In 1967 it was used for an umbrella in a fashion show in Paris. It was an instant hit, and became a *de rigueur* accessory for the Parisian chic. Five years ago the French, again, took to wearing the Burberrys' house-check scarf, and last year in Japan, teenagers became enamoured with the Burberrys' sock. The fad swept the country, and the company sold more than 1.5 million pairs. 'The plaid has regularly been a cult item for as long as I can remember', Mr Peacock, the company's managing director, says.

Sadly, there is a downside to the story. For, as quickly as style spotters find themselves a new label to show off, or a new item of clothing or accessory to shout about, they can just as quickly tire of it.

It is unlikely that this will worry Burberrys. During the 1980s the company added several new lines alongside their men's and women's ranges: children and babywear, a selection of foodstuffs, and the Thomas' Burberry Collection aimed at a younger clientele. They already sell 350,000 traditional checked cashmere scarves (a year), and use approximately two million metres of check lining, each year.

© The Times. Reprinted with permission.

Burberrys produces a range of well known, high quality clothing and accessory items, many of which are in the red, black and white Burberrys plaid colours.

Burberrys is a long established company with established sales markets at home and abroad (the company is the United Kingdom's largest clothing exporter).

On occasion, Burberrys has enjoyed brief periods when its products have achieved cult status in different countries.

In 1993, one fashion writer identified Burberrys' items as likely to be part of a fashion style for 1994.

It is noted that many fashions and trends are short lived.

In planning production, firms need to take account of the expected consumption levels of their products.

Long established firms with established products and non-fickle customers will generally have a good idea about what their future sales are likely to be and can plan accordingly.

Even they, however, face an element of uncertainty, in that there is always the potential for unforeseen events to affect demand. In the case of Burberrys, occasionally one or more of its product lines becomes the target of the fashion conscious.

Such an event cannot be predicted, and cannot have a probability of occurrence assigned. Nor can the end of a fad (and the fall in sales) be predicted.

Burberrys also exports much of its product. Demand for exports will partly depend on the exchange rate and how it affects the selling price in the importing country, but in this case Burberrys could be said to face risk, as economists could assign a probability to different exchange rates occurring in the future.

Such problems with risk and uncertainty can be reduced by diversification. As the article indicates, this has been a policy of Burberrys, with the extension of the product range into different sectors of the clothing market and also into non-clothing sectors including watches and pens.

This means that even if Burberrys faces an increase or decrease in demand for one of its product lines, it is in a position to cope with such a change.

In the figure, assuming sales levels are known, the cost curves MC and ATC are drawn. The demand curve, D, represents the expected average and the marginal revenue curve is MR.

In the face of uncertain demand, however, the actual demand (D_U) and marginal revenue (MR_U) curves shift to the left of the average D and MR curves.

The firm produces one million coats less than it would do under certainty and at a lower price of £360, thus generating lower profits. The more the firm can reduce the uncertainty, for example by diversification, the closer price and quantity will be to their certainty values (1.2 million coats sold at £385 each).

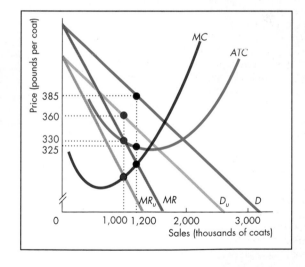

influence tastes. By taking into account every conceivable piece of available information that helps forecast such variables, farmers – or the specialists from whom farmers buy forecasts – can form a rational expectation of next year's demand for corn.

The supply of a good depends on the prices of its substitutes and complements in production, the prices of the resources used to produce the good, and the weather. Expected supply depends on the expected values of these variables. So to form an expectation of the future supply of corn, it is necessary to forecast the future prices of corn's substitutes and complements in production, the prices of the resources used to produce corn (the wages of farm workers and the prices of seed and fertilizers) as well as any current trends in weather patterns that might influence growing conditions. By taking into account every available piece of information that helps forecast such variables, farmers can form a rational expectation of the next year's corn supply.

Figure 17.7 illustrates how to calculate a rational expectation of next year's price of corn. The horizontal axis measures the quantity expected next year. The vertical axis measures the price expected next year. The curve *ED* is the best forecast available of next year's demand for corn. The curve *ES* is the best forecast available of next year's supply of corn. The rational expectation of the price of corn next year is £3,000 a tonne – the price at which the expected quantity demanded equals the expected quantity supplied. It is a rational expectation because the forecast is based on all the available relevant information. Farmers use the forecast of next year's price to decide how many acres of corn to plant today.

What are the implications of rational expectations for the way in which competitive asset markets work? Let's answer this question by looking at the stock market.

The Stock Market   The stock market – the market in which the stocks of companies are traded – works like the market we've just examined. If the price of a share of stock was higher than its expected price, people would sell the stock. If the price of a share of stock was less than its expected price, people would buy the stock. As a result of such trading, the *current period supply* is perfectly elastic at the expected price. Since the actual price of a share of stock is equal to its expected price, the price embodies all the relevant information that is avail-

FIGURE 17.7

A Rational Expectation of Price

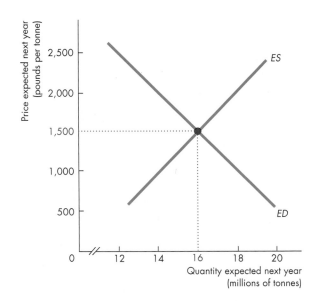

Expected price is determined by expected supply and expected demand. The point where expected demand, *ED*, cuts expected supply, *ES*, determines the rational expectation of the price, (£3,000 a tonne) and quantity (16 million tonnes).

able about the stock. A market in which the actual price embodies all currently available relevant information is called an **efficient market**. In an efficient market, it is impossible to forecast changes in price. Why? If your forecast is that the price is going to rise in the next period you will buy now (since the price is low today compared with what you predicted it is going to be in the future). Your action of buying today acts like an increase in demand today and increases today's price. It's true that your action – the action of a single trader – is not going to make much difference to a huge market like the London Stock Exchange. But if traders in general expect a higher price in the next period and they all act today on the basis of that expectation, then today's price will rise. It will keep on rising until it reaches the expected future price. For only at that price do traders see no profit in buying more stock today.

There is an apparent paradox about efficient markets. Markets are efficient because people try to make a profit. They seek a profit by buying at a low price and selling at a high price. But the very act of buying and selling to make a profit means that the market price moves to its expected future value. Having done that, no one, not even those who are seeking to profit, can *predictably* make a profit. Every profit opportunity seen by a trader leads to an action that produces a price change that removes the profit opportunity for others. Even the possibility of an intergalactic attack on New York City is taken into account in determining stock market prices – see the cartoon.

Thus an efficient market has two features:

◆ Its price equals the expected future price and embodies all the available information.
◆ There are no forecastable profit opportunities available.

The key thing to understand about an efficient market such as the stock market is that if something can be anticipated it will be, and the anticipation will be acted upon.

Volatility in Stock Prices   If the price of a stock is always equal to its expected future price, why is the stock market so volatile? The answer must be that expectations themselves are subject to fluctuation. Expectations depend on the information available. As new information becomes available, stock traders form new expectations about the future state of the economy and in turn new expectations of future stock prices. Expectations about the economy are of crucial importance. Is the economy going to enjoy sustained rapid expansion? Or is it going to suffer a recession? Macroeconomic events, such as expansion and recession, influence stock prices. Individual stock prices are influenced by technological change, which in turn influences the supply of and demand for particular goods and services. Since new information is being accumulated daily about all these matters, expectations about the future price of a

"Drat! I suppose the market has already discounted this, too."

Drawing by Lorenz: © 1986 The New Yorker Magazine, Inc.

share of stock are constantly being re-evaluated. It is this process of re-evaluation that leads to high volatility in the stock market. As expectations change from being optimistic to being pessimistic, the stock market can plunge many percentage points – as it did dramatically on 19 October, 1987. On the other hand, a sustained period of increasing optimism can produce a long upswing in stock prices. The five-year run from mid-1982 to mid-1987 is an example of such stock market behaviour.

◆ ◆ ◆ ◆   We've studied the way people cope with uncertainty and how markets work when there are important information problems. In the next chapter we're going to see how the market economy solves one of its biggest problems – determining the distribution of the gains from economic activity. We'll also see how government programmes modify the outcome of a pure market economy.

S U M M A R Y

Uncertainty and Risk

Uncertainty is a state in which more than one event may occur, but we don't know which one. To describe uncertainty we use the concepts of probability and risk. A probability is a number between zero and one that measures the chance of some possible event occurring. Risk is uncertainty with probabilities attached to each possible outcome. Sometimes the probabilities can be measured and sometimes they cannot. When they cannot be measured, they are subjective probabilities.

People's attitudes towards risk are described by their utility of wealth schedules and curves. Greater wealth brings higher utility, but as wealth increases, the marginal utility of wealth diminishes. The cost of risk is measured as the pound change in expected wealth necessary to keep expected utility constant in the face of a given increase in risk. Faced with uncertainty, people choose the action that maximizes expected utility. (pp. 460–462)

Insurance

UK households spend 5 per cent of their income on insurance, one of the most important ways in which they reduce risk. The two main types of insurance are life insurance and property and casualty insurance. Insurance works by pooling risks, and it pays people to insure because they are risk averse – they value risk reduction. By pooling risks, insurance companies can eliminate the risks people face (from insured activities) at a low cost in terms of reduced expected wealth. The lower risk is valued much more highly than the lower expected wealth. (pp. 463–465)

Information

Economic information is data on the prices, quantities and qualities of goods and services and factors of production. Information is scarce and people economize on their use of information just like they economize on their use of other productive resources.

Buyers search for price information – looking for the least-cost source of supply. In doing so, they use the optimal-search rule of searching for a lower price until the expected marginal benefit of search equals the marginal cost of search. When the expected marginal benefit equals the marginal cost, stop searching and buy. There is a reservation price at which the expected marginal benefit of search equals the marginal cost of search. When a price equal to (or less than) the reservation price is found, the search ends and the item is bought.

Sellers advertise, sometimes to persuade and sometimes to inform. Advertising is part of a firm's profit-maximization strategy. The general presumption is that advertising increases prices. But advertising can increase competition and enable economies of scale to be experienced in which case it is possible that some prices are lower because of advertising. (pp. 465–467)

Private Information

Private information is knowledge of one person that is just too costly for anyone else to discover. Private information creates the problems of moral hazard – the use of private information to the advantage of the informed and the disadvantage of the uninformed; and adverse selection – the tendency for the people who accept contracts to be those with private information that can be used to their own advantage and to the disadvantage of the uninformed person or firm. Devices that enable markets to function in the face of moral hazard and adverse selection are incentive payments, guarantees and warranties, and signals. (pp. 467–470)

Managing Risk in Financial Markets

Risk can be lowered by diversifying asset holdings thereby combining the returns on projects that are independent of each other and whose returns are uncorrelated. Risk can also be lowered by trading in forward markets which enables producers to know the future price at which their output will be sold. Futures markets provide yet further opportunities for risk reduction, enabling people to take positions in forward markets without necessarily taking delivery of goods. Decisions to engage in a forward or futures transaction are based on rational expectation of future prices. A rational expectation is one that uses all the available and relevant information. It is correct on average and has the smallest possible range of forecast error. Asset markets determine a price that embodies a rational expectation of the future price and are efficient. The stock market is an example of such a market. In such markets there are no forecastable price changes or profit opportunities. (pp. 470–475)

KEY ELEMENTS

Key Terms

Adverse selection, 467
Economic information, 465
Efficient market, 474
Expected utility, 461
Forward market, 471
Futures market, 471
Information cost, 465
Moral hazard, 467
Private information, 467
Rational expectation, 471
Reservation price, 465

Risk, 460
Signal, 468
Uncertainty, 460
Utility of wealth, 460

Key Figures

Figure 17.1   Utility of Wealth, 461
Figure 17.2   Choice under Uncertainty, 461
Figure 17.4   Insurance, 463
Figure 17.5   Optimal-search Rule, 466
Figure 17.7   A Rational Expectation of Price, 474

REVIEW QUESTIONS

1 What is the difference between uncertainty and risk?

2 How do we measure a person's attitude towards risk? How do these attitudes vary from one person to another?

3 Why is information valuable?

4 Why do people buy insurance and why do insurance companies make a profit?

5 What determines the amount of searching you do for a bargain?

6 Why do firms advertise?

7 What are moral hazard and and adverse selection and how do they influence the way markets for loans and insurance work?

8 Explain how the used car market works.

9 Why do firms give warranties and guarantees?

10 How do excesses make insurance more efficient and enable insurance companies to discriminate between high-risk and low-risk customers?

11 How does diversification lower risk?

12 What is the difference between a forward market and a futures market?

13 What is a rational expectation? How is such an expectation arrived at?

14 What is an efficient market? What types of markets are efficient?

PROBLEMS

1 Jimmy and Zenda have the following utility of wealth schedules:

Wealth	Jimmy's utility	Zenda's utility
0	0	0
100	200	512
200	300	640
300	350	672
400	375	678
500	387	681
600	393	683
700	396	684

Who is more risk averse, Jimmy or Zenda?

2 Suppose that Jimmy and Zenda each have $400 and that each sees a business project that involves committing their entire $400 to the project. They reckon that the project could return $600 (a profit of $200) with a probability of 0.85, or $200 (a loss of $200) with a probability of 0.15. Who goes for the project and who hangs on to the initial $400?

3 Who is more likely to buy insurance, Jimmy or Zenda, and why?

4 There are two independent investment projects: Project 1 is expected to give the investor a wealth of £200 with a probability of 0.5 and a wealth of zero with a probability of 0.5. Project 2 is expected to give a wealth of £300 with a probability of 0.5 and a wealth of zero with a probability of 0.5.

a Which project would a risk-neutral person invest in?

b How much would Jimmy (from Problem 1) be willing to invest in Project 1? In Project 2?

c How much would Zenda (from Problem 1) be willing to invest in Project 1? In Project 2?

5 Explain how the rational expectation of next year's wheat price is arrived at.

CHAPTER 18

THE DISTRIBUTION OF INCOME AND WEALTH

After studying this chapter you will be able to:

◆ Describe the distribution of income and wealth in the United Kingdom today

◆ Explain the effects of income redistribution policies

◆ Explain why the wealth distribution shows greater inequality than the income distribution

◆ Explain how the distribution of income arises from the prices of productive resources and the distribution of endowments

◆ Explain how the distribution of income and wealth is affected by individual choices

◆ Explain the different views about fairness in the distribution of income and wealth

O N 4 APRIL 1993 THE *SUNDAY TIMES* ESTIMATED THE WEALTH OF WHAT it believed to be the 400 wealthiest people in the United Kingdom. Leading this group was the Queen with an estimated wealth of £5,000 million, though most of this was accounted for by property where she was more of a custodian than an owner. Most of the wealthiest twenty people own wealth that has been recently created. They include David Sainsbury (and family) with £3,400 million, which has been acquired from the supermarket chain that began in 1955; and Richard Branson, with £475 million, whose fortune was built on the Virgin Music label. ◆ ◆ At the other end of the wealth distribution are the homeless people who sleep in hostels when they can, or otherwise in derelict buildings, doorways and parks. Compared with them, families with a home of their own seem very com-

Riches and Rags

fortable, but many households are very poor. Official statistics show that one-fifth of households have less than £80 a week to spend. ◆ ◆ Why are some people exceedingly rich while others earn very little and own almost nothing? Is the distribution becoming more equal or more unequal? How much effect do government policies have on the distribution of income? Is it fair that some people should be so incredibly rich while others live in miserable poverty? And what do we mean by fairness?

◆ ◆ ◆ ◆ In this chapter, we will study the degree of income and wealth inequality. We'll see how inequality arises and how it is affected by the choices that people make.

The UK Distribution of Income and Wealth Today

In any discussion of income distributions, we must distinguish carefully between several types of income. For the moment we will concentrate on original incomes. The **original income** of a household is the income that is received before allowing for any adjustments by the central government or local authorities. Original incomes can be thought of as indicating the purchasing power for goods and services that people would have if governments did not interfere. We will see later that governments do interfere and we will see what effects they have on those whose original incomes are low and on those whose original incomes are high.

Original incomes are earned by the factors of production. They comprise the wages (including salaries and other forms of compensation) paid to labour, the profits earned by the owners of sole proprietorships and partnerships, the interest and dividend income paid to the other owners of capital, and the rental incomes received by the owners of land, a term which is used to cover all natural resources. Labour earns the largest share of total income. Its share has been around two-thirds of the total for many years.

The distribution of original incomes among individuals and households depends on the amount of labour, capital and land that they supply, and on the wage rates, profit levels, and the interest, dividend and rental rates they receive. We all have an identical amount of time in which we can work, but the price at which each person can sell his or her time, the wage rate, depends on that person's marginal product. That marginal product, in turn, depends partly on natural ability, partly on luck or chance, and partly on the amount of human capital that the individual has built up. The income from working is a mixture of a return on human capital as well as a compensation for forgoing leisure. Ownership of the other factors of production – capital and land – is distributed with a great deal of inequality. And the profit levels, interest rates and rental rates earned per unit of capital and land supplied also vary enormously.

So original incomes are distributed unequally because of unequal wage rates, unequal ownership of capital and land, and unequal profit levels, interest rates and rental rates. Let's look at some facts about the distribution of original household incomes in the United Kingdom in 1992. In that year, the mean original income for households was £15,750. But the income levels varied greatly between households. For example, the poorest one-fifth of households had a mean original income of £1,650 while the richest one-fifth had a mean original income of £39,375. Indeed, the poorest one-fifth of households received only about 2 per cent of the total while the richest one-fifth received about 50 per cent of the total.

Wealth and income are linked in a way that we will examine shortly, but it's important to remember the distinction between them. Your income is the money that is paid to you, and is measured in pounds per period of time (such as pounds per year) while your wealth is what you own, and is measured in pounds at a particular point in time (such as pounds on 3 March 1995).

In the United Kingdom it is not easy to make a precise comparison between the distribution of income and the distribution of wealth. This is because the best figures for incomes are figures for households, whereas the best figures for wealth relate to adults. The data on the distribution of wealth measures the value of holdings of physical assets, such as land, buildings and consumer durables, and financial assets, such as cash, bank deposits and shares. In 1991, the richest 1 per cent of adults owned 18 per cent of the total wealth of all adults while the poorest 50 per cent owned merely 8 per cent.

Lorenz Curves

One way of illustrating the distributions of income and wealth is presented in Fig. 18.1. The tables there record the cumulative percentages of original income for households and of wealth for adults. For example, row *a* of the first table shows the percentage of the country's total original income that is received by the poorest 20 per cent of households, row *b* shows the percentage for the lowest 40 per cent of households, and so on. These cumulative percentages can be illustrated with what is called a Lorenz curve. A **Lorenz curve** based on these percentages shows the cumulative percentage of original income of any given cumulative percentage of tax units. The Lorenz curve is named after its founder, Konrad Lorenz, who devised this type of figure in 1905.

There are two curves plotted on the figure. One

FIGURE 18.1

Lorenz Curves for Original
Income and Wealth

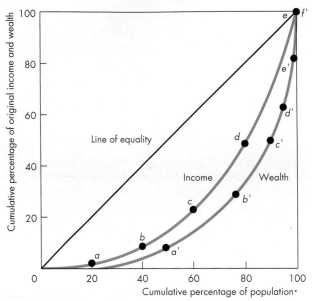

*The relevant populations are households for income and adults for wealth.

Cumulative percentage of households	Cumulative percentage of original income, 1992		Cumulative percentage of adults	Cumulative percentage of wealth, 1991
a 20	2.1	*a'*	50	8
b 40	8	*b'*	75	29
c 60	23	*c'*	90	50
d 80	49	*d'*	95	63
e 100	100	*e'*	99	82
		f'	100	100

The cumulative percentage of original income is graphed against the cumulative percentage of households while the cumulative percentage of wealth is plotted against the cumulative percentage of adults. Points *a* to *e* correspond to lines *a* to *e* on the income table while points a to *f* correspond to lines *a* to *f* on the wealth table. If both income and wealth were distributed equally, the two Lorenz curves would follow the straight 'line of equality'.

Sources: Central Statistical Office, *Economic Trends*, January 1994, 123, and Inland Revenue, *Inland Revenue Statistics 1993*, 1993, Table 13.5.

relates to income and the other to wealth. For the income distribution curve, the horizontal axis measures the cumulative percentage of households, with the poorest on the left, while the vertical axis measures the cumulative percentage of original income. For the wealth distribution curve, the horizontal axis measures the cumulative percentage of adults, with the poorest on the left, while the vertical axis measures the cumulative percentage of wealth. Points *a* to *e* on the income curve correspond to lines *a* to *e* in the first table while points *a'* to *f'* on the wealth curve correspond to lines *a'* to *f'* in the second table.

If both income and wealth were distributed equally, then the Lorenz curves would follow the straight 'line of equality'. In this situation we could take, say, any 20 per cent of the population and regard them as the poorest, and we would find that they had 20 per cent of the total income. Likewise the poorest 40 per cent would have 40 per cent of total income and 40 per cent of total wealth. All the points we would plot would fall on the line of equality.

Lorenz curves provide a graphic illustration of the degree of inequality. The closer a Lorenz curve is to the line of equality, the more equal is the distribution. You can see in Fig. 18.1 that the Lorenz curve for the income distribution is closer to the line of equality than the curve for wealth distribution, so the distribution of original income is less unequal than the distribution of wealth, though this comparison would be a little sharper if both curves related to adults. The numbers in the tables tell the same story. The 20 per cent of households with the highest original incomes had 51 per cent of total original income while the 10 per cent of adults with the most wealth had 50 per cent of the total wealth.

Qualifications to the Data   The curves in Fig. 18.1 reveal a great inequality of original incomes and wealth. But we need to be very careful when interpreting data on income and wealth distributions. Let's look at some of the reasons for this.

The income data show that the poor have very little original income. We will see later that the poorest households rely greatly on government benefits. The income data show that the poor have very little original income. We will see later that the poorest households rely on government benefits. In particular, many of the poorest households are lived in by retired people who rely on the government's state pensions. If these people had not expected to receive state pensions, they would have made other pension arrangements when they were in employment and would thus receive non-government income when they retired. So the existence of a state pension scheme makes the distribution of original incomes more equal than it would otherwise have been.

The wealth data suffer from four limitations:

1. They relate to individuals when it would be more appropriate to consider households. A man who marries a millionairess and lives in a mansion full of works of art may have negligible wealth of his own, but he is not in the same position as a man who sleeps in a cardboard box.

2. They ignore the fact that individuals have pension rights, that is, they may be enjoying or looking forward to pensions which are equivalent to substantial amounts of wealth even though they cannot be sold like shares or houses. If pension rights are allowed for, the share of the wealthiest 1 per cent falls from 18 per cent to 11 per cent while the share of the poorest 50 per cent rises from 8 per cent to 20 per cent.

3. They ignore the wealth that people hold in the form of human capital.

4. They ignore the fact that most people have far more wealth when they are old than when they are young.

We look at the significance of the last two points later in the chapter.

Inequality over Time

Lorenz curves and the data from which they are drawn are useful not only for comparing two different distributions, such as those of income and of wealth, but also for comparing distributions at different points in time. Such comparisons can reveal whether the distribution of income has become more or less equal over time.

Let's take a look at the income distribution in the United Kingdom 13 years earlier than the time that we have just been studying. Table 18.1 provides a comparison. It shows the cumulative percentage of original income shares for households in 1979 as well as those in 1992. As you can see from Table 18.1, the distribution of original income has become more unequal since the Conservatives came to power in 1979. We have not given a comparable

TABLE 18.1

A Comparison of the Distribution of Original Income in 1979 and in 1992

Cumulative percentage of households	Cumulative percentage of original income	
	1979	1992
Lowest 20	2.4	2.1
40	12	8
60	30	23
80	57	49
100	100	100

The distribution of original income has became more unequal since the 1979 election since when there has been a succession of Conservative governments. The rise in unemployment over this period has been one major factor reducing the original income of those with the lowest incomes.

Source: Central Statistical Office, *Economic Trends*, January 1994, 122–3

table showing changes in the distribution of wealth since 1979 as this distribution has scarcely changed.

R E V I E W

There is considerable inequality of both original incomes and wealth. The degree of inequality can be illustrated by Lorenz curves. The closer a Lorenz curve is to the line of equality, the more equal is the distribution concerned. From 1979 to 1992, the distribution of original incomes became more unequal. ◆

So far, our study of the distribution of income has considered only original incomes. What effect does the government's activities have? And which people are the poorest and the richest after the government has intervened?

Income Redistribution

Because poverty is so dreadful for those experiencing it and so fearful for everyone else, there is almost universal agreement that the government should be a sort of institutionalized Robin Hood, taking from the rich and giving to the poor. Governments in the United Kingdom today use two main ways of redistributing income:

◆ Transfer payments
◆ Income tax

Transfer Payments

The UK central government operates a wide range of transfer payment (or benefit) programmes. These benefit various groups of people. Some of the programmes target help more directly than others on those with low original incomes. The major programmes are:

1. State retirement pensions
2. Widows' pensions
3. Incapacity benefit
4. Job-seeker's allowance
5. Child benefit
6. Income support
7. Family credit

In addition, local authorities operate two programmes

1. Housing benefit
2. Student maintenance grants

Local authorities really act as agents of the central government when they operate their two programmes, for the rules are laid down by the central government, and virtually all the money local authorities pay out is reimbursed to them by the central government.

The detailed rules for these various programmes are very complex, but the general ideas behind them will now be outlined.

Some benefits are part of the National Insurance scheme. People who work must pay National Insurance contributions to the government. The amount of contributions that working people pay depends on their income level – for most people the contributions amount to almost 10 per cent of earnings, but the percentage is reduced for those with low earnings. These contributions are rather like insurance premiums which working people pay so that if, for any reason, they stop working, then they will be entitled to National Insurance benefits. These benefits include state pensions, which are paid to people who have stopped work to retire, widows' pensions, which are paid to widows who no longer have a working husband (or a husband entitled to a pension) to support them, incapacity benefits, which are paid to people who cannot work because they are ill or disabled, and job-seekers' allowances[1], which are paid to people who are looking for a new job. For many people, these National Insurance benefits form their main source of income, so clearly they have a marked redistributive impact. However, the National Insurance benefits that people receive take little notice of any other income they might have, so a retired company director may receive as much state pension – in addition to a company pension – as a retired manual worker who may have no pension other than the state one.

Let's now look at the programmes that are not part of National Insurance. Child benefit is paid at a rate of £10.20 for each family's first child and £8.25 a week for each subsequent child. Benefit ceases when a child leaves school. The redistributive impact is limited because the same amount is paid to high-income families as is paid to low-income families, but child benefit has a bigger proportional impact on the poor than the rich.

It is the remaining benefits that are targeted most closely on those with low incomes. Income support is designed to help people who are not working. Most people in this category are entitled to one or other National Insurance benefit, but some, such as young unmarried mothers, are not. The purposes of income support are to give modest top-ups to the incomes of those who receive National Insurance benefits and to provide adequate incomes for those who do not. Before paying income support to any individual, a check is made to see what other income they have, such as dividends, and to see how much savings they have,

---

[1] Job-seeker's allowance is due to be introduced early in 1996. It will be a slightly revised version of unemployment benefit which it will replace.

such as bank deposits. Income support is very selective and is concentrated on people with modest savings and little or no income other than National Insurance benefits.

Family credit is paid to families with at least one child and with at least one parent in work. It is paid only when earnings are low, so it is generally paid to families which have just one working parent doing a job with a low wage. The lower the earnings, the more family credit a family will receive. If the working parent in a family entitled to family credit earns more money by working overtime or by struggling to get a better paid job, then the family's entitlement to family credit will fall. So the family may end up little better off despite the extra effort.

Housing benefit has two aims, only one of which is related to housing! First, it helps low-income people who rent accommodation to pay their rents. Second, it helps low-income people pay their council tax bills. The amount of housing benefit which people receive depends on their incomes, and roughly three-quarters of the adult population have an income too high to qualify. So housing benefit gives no help to the rich but considerable help to the poor. For instance, people who are poor enough to qualify for income support automatically qualify for housing benefit at a level which covers their entire rent bills and council tax bills.

Student maintenance grants are paid to help students in full-time education, but the amounts they receive depend on their parents' income level, and may be reduced if students have any income of their own, perhaps as a result of bequests from grandparents.

Income Taxes

We have seen that the government gives a wide variety of transfer payments to households in different situations. These payments clearly increase the **disposable incomes** of the recipients, that is the amount of income that they can spend or save as they choose. However, the government also reduces the disposable incomes of most people by levying income tax.

The amount and nature of the redistribution achieved through income taxes depend on the form that those taxes take. Income taxes can be progressive, regressive or proportional. A **progressive income tax** is one where the fraction of income paid in tax is higher for people on high incomes than it is

for people on low incomes. A **regressive income tax** is one where the fraction of income paid in tax is lower for people on high incomes than it is for people on low incomes. A **proportional income tax** is one where the fraction of income paid in tax is the same regardless of the level of income.

The income tax in the United Kingdom is progressive. It is easiest to see this by looking at the rules for single people. The first step is to work out their income for tax purposes. Broadly speaking this is found by adding their original income and transfer payments (though some benefits are excluded – notably child benefit). The second step is to work out their taxable income, that is, the amount of income on which they have to pay tax. For single people in 1994, the taxable income was the income for tax purposes less £3,445. In other words, the first £3,445 of their income for tax purposes was exempt from tax. People must then pay income tax equal to 20 per cent of the first £3,000 of taxable income, plus 25 per cent of the next £23,700, plus 40 per cent of any more taxable income.

To see that income tax is progressive, consider Angela whose income for tax purposes is £7,445, and Zoe whose income for tax purposes is £16,445. Angela will be let off tax on the first £3,445 of her income and she will be taxed on her taxable income of £4,000. She will pay at a rate of 20 per cent on the first £3,000 of this taxable income, making the tax there £600, and she will pay at a rate of 25 per cent on the last £1,000, making the tax there £250. So she pays £850 in all, just over 11 per cent of her total income.

Zoe will also be let off tax on £3,445 of her income and she will be taxed on her taxable income of £13,000. She will pay at a rate of 20 per cent on the first £3,000 of this taxable income, making the tax there £600, and she will pay at a rate of 25 per cent on the last £10,000, making the tax there £2,500. So she pays £3,100 in all, just under 19 per cent of her total income. So rich Zoe pays a larger fraction of her income in tax than poor Angela.

The Poverty Trap

The combination of transfer payment programmes and a progressive income tax makes the distribution of disposable incomes much less unequal than the distribution of original incomes. However, the government's actions have an unfortunate and unintentional side-effect on people who work in low-wage jobs. The problem is that people in low-income house-holds who try to increase their income, perhaps by working overtime, may find that their efforts to improve their living standards by working harder have negligible effect, a situation which is called the **poverty trap**.

How does the poverty trap arise? Suppose Sally is a single parent entitled to housing benefit and family credit. And suppose she works as a shop assistant and decides to start working overtime in an effort to have more money to spend. As her earnings rise, she must pay more National Insurance contributions and more income tax. Also, she loses some entitlement to family credit and some of her housing benefit. So she may end up scarcely any better off after all. You can see why she may feel trapped in poverty

The Scale of Income Redistribution

How much impact do progressive income taxes and transfer payments have on the distribution of incomes? To answer this question, we need to compare the distribution of original incomes with the distribution of disposable incomes. A household's disposable income is calculated by starting with its original income, adding in any transfer payments received, and then deducting any income tax (and National Insurance contributions) paid.

Figure 18.2 illustrates the effect of redistribution in the United Kingdom in two different ways. The table repeats the information given in Fig. 18.1 to show the percentage of original income going to each 20 per cent of households with the poorest households at the top. Alongside this information it shows the percentage of disposable income which goes to the five groups. We would expect to find that the poorest groups received larger shares of dispos-able income than they received of original income, with the opposite happening to the richest groups. This is, indeed, what happens. See how the poorest 20 per cent received only 2.1 per cent of original income but received 7.4 per cent of disposable income, and the poorest 40 per cent received only 8 per cent of original income but received 18 per cent of final income. In contrast, the richest 20 per cent group received saw their share falling from 51 per cent to 42 per cent.

The effects of redistribution policies can also be seen by comparing the Lorenz curves for the distrib-ution of original income and the distribution of final income. The graph of Fig. 18.2 shows these Lorenz

FIGURE 18.2

The Effect of Taxes and Transfers on the Distribution of Income, 1992

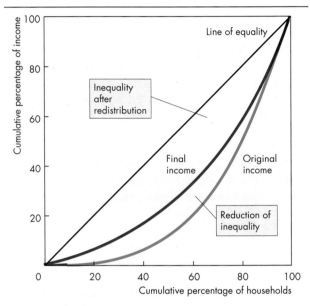

	Cumulative percentage of households	Cumulative percentage of original income	Cumulative percentage of disposable income
Lowest	20	2.1	7.4
	40	8	18
	60	23	34
	80	49	58
	100	100	100

Government policies mean that disposable incomes are less unequal than original incomes. The table shows that the redistribution occurs chiefly from the top 20 per cent to the bottom 40 per cent of households. The graph shows the effects of redistribution using Lorenz curves.

Source: Central Statistical Office, *Economic Trends*, January 1994, 123.

curves. As you can see, there is a considerable amount of redistribution, especially to boost the incomes of the very poor, but a great deal of inequality remains after redistribution. So let us now ask *who* are rich and *who* are poor, and what are the key characteristics of rich and poor households?

Who Are Rich and Who Are Poor?

The most useful statistics to shed light on these questions concern **gross incomes**, that is original incomes plus transfer payments. In 1992 the median gross income for households was £343 per week – that is to say half UK households had higher weekly incomes than this and half had lower weekly incomes. Figure 18.3 indicates four factors which help determine how far an individual household's gross income will tend to vary from the median level.

One key factor which tends to affect household incomes is the composition of households. Figure 18.3 shows how household incomes varied for one-adult and two-adult households. Households with two adults tended to have much higher incomes than households with one adult, though within each group retired households had much lower incomes. The importance of retirement also comes out when household incomes are related to the economic status of the heads of the households and to the age of the heads of the households: the

poorest households are those with the retired and oldest heads, followed by those with unemployed and young heads. Another factor is region. Households in the South East are typically the richest, followed by those in East Anglia. The regions with the lowest incomes are Northern Ireland, the North and Wales.

We noted earlier in this chapter that household incomes are greatly dependent on earnings, and earnings tend to be greatly influenced by education. This relationship is shown clearly in Fig. 18.4. This shows that in 1991 the average earnings for men and women with degrees (or equivalent qualifications) were about double the average earnings for men and women with no qualifications. The figure also reminds us that men tend to be paid more than women, an issue we have already examined in Chapter 15.

Policies to Reduce Poverty Further

Despite the government's efforts at redistribution, it is clear from Fig. 18.2 that many households live on low incomes. Why doesn't the government do more

---

FIGURE 18.3

Distribution of Income by Selected Household Characteristics, 1992

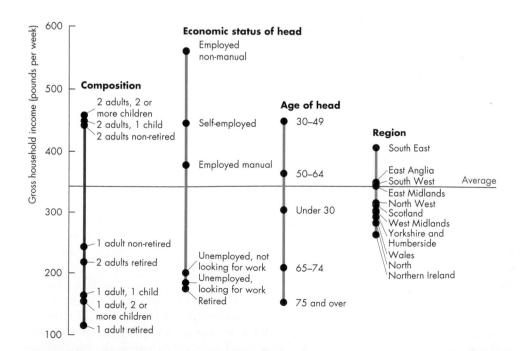

This figure shows that the poorest households are likely to have one adult who is a retired person over 75 years old, living in Northern Ireland, northern England or Wales.

Source: Central Statistical Office, *Family Spending: a Report on the Family Expenditure Survey, 1992*, 1992, pp. 56–8 and 96.

FIGURE 18.4

The Relationship Between Earnings and Education, 1991

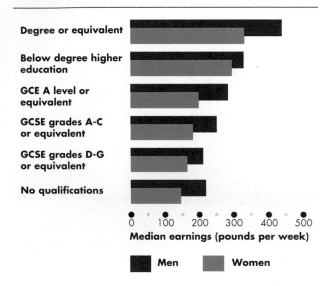

This shows how individual incomes are highest for those with the highest qualifications. Every extra rung people climb on the education ladder tends, on average, to increase their earnings.

Source: Office of Population Censuses and Surveys, *General Household Survey 1991*, 1993, Table 10.12.

to help? The main problem is that any increase in transfer payments to the poor has to be financed by higher taxes on the rich, and there is a limit to how much tax revenue governments can raise without losing large numbers of votes. For this reason, a favourite buzz-word with politicians is targeting. **Targeting** means concentrating transfer payments on the poorest households. Politicians feel that if they can alter their transfer payment programmes in a way that targets more help on the poorest households, then they may be able to alleviate poverty without raising taxes. Unfortunately, more targeting tends to make the poverty trap problem even worse.

To illustrate this, suppose the government decided to amend the child benefit programme. As we have seen, at present this programme gives money each week to the parents of every child. The payments do not depend on parents' incomes. The government could give less money to the rich on this programme by means-testing parents, so that rich parents received little or no benefit. The money saved could be used to raise payments to poor parents. Unfortunately, the result is that poor households would find that efforts to raise their incomes would be even more fruitless than they are already. For any increase in their earnings would result in lower child benefit, as well as lower family credit, lower housing benefit, and higher income tax and higher National Insurance contributions.

Alternatively, the government could make child benefit liable to income tax. In this way, most parents might lose some benefit in tax, but parents paying high income tax rates would lose more. The extra income tax revenue could be used to raise the level of child benefit payments which would especially help parents paying little or no income tax. But again the poverty trap would tend to worsen. For child benefit would form part of taxable income, so people would become liable to income tax at the initial rate of 20 per cent and the next rate of 25 per cent on lower levels of earnings than before.

REVIEW

Government policies redistribute income chiefly by means of a progressive income tax and by a variety of transfer payments to those who would otherwise have little or no means of support. The distribution of final incomes is much less unequal than the distribution of original incomes, but considerable inequality remains. In general, the poorest households are those with an old, single adult. The highest income families are middle-aged married couples, both of whom have jobs. Transfer payments could be targeted more on poor people, but this would worsen the poverty trap whereby people in low income households find that efforts to raise their household income by working harder have very little effect. ◆

We've now examined some facts about the distribution of income and wealth in the United Kingdom. But what is the reason for the enormous inequality that exists? And why do the data on wealth indicate more inequality than the data on income? Which of these two distributions paints the more accurate picture concerning the degree of inequality? In the next section, we will examine the reasons for the *differences* in the degree of inequality as measured by wealth and by income. After that, we will study some of the reasons for inequality itself.

Comparing Like with Like

To determine just how much inequality there is, it is necessary to make the correct comparisons. But what are the correct comparisons? Should we look at income or at wealth? And if we look at income, then should we be looking, as we have been, at annual income, or should we be looking at income over some other time period, such as over a person's lifetime?

Wealth and Income: Stock and Flow

Income and wealth can be considered as different ways of looking at precisely the same thing. A person's *wealth* is the *stock* of assets which he or she owns. A person's *income* is the *flow of earnings* which he or she receives. *Income* is the *flow of earnings* that results from the *stock of wealth*. So we should expect data on wealth and income distributions to give similar impressions of inequality. Why do data on wealth distributions show more inequality than data on income distributions?

The main reason is that the wealth data refer only to the ownership of *non-human capital* – physical assets and financial assets. In contrast, the income data refer to income from all sources, not only from non-human capital but also from human capital. Let's explore the sources of these differences a bit more closely by looking at an example with just two people, Peter and Paul.

Suppose Peter and Paul have the wealth and income shown in Table 18.2. Peter owns non-human capital worth £300,000. If the rate of return on assets is 5 per cent a year, Peter will receive an income of £15,000 a year (5 per cent of £300,000) from his non-human capital. Paul has non-human assets of £100,000. We assume that he can invest his wealth in a way which secures the same rate of

TABLE 18.2

Capital, Wealth and Income

	Peter		Paul	
	Wealth	Income	Wealth	Income
Non-human capital	£300,000	£15,000	£100,000	£5,000
Human capital	500,000	25,000	300,000	15,000
Total	£800,000	£40,000	£400,000	£20,000

When measures of wealth include the value of human capital as well as non-human capital, then the distribution of income and the distribution of wealth display the same degree of inequality.

return enjoyed by Peter, that is 5 per cent a year. So Paul has an income of £5,000 (5 per cent of £100,000) from his non-human capital.

Peter and Paul also have wealth only in the form of *human capital*, that is the skill and knowledge arising from training and education. Earnings received from work are partly a return on *human capital* and partly a compensation for giving up leisure time. Although human capital represents such intangible things as skills and knowledge, we can value it. We can value human capital by comparing the earnings of a person with education and training with the earnings of a person without education or training. The extra earnings of the first person are the income from human capital. The value of human capital is the amount of money that a person would have to be given today so that, if invested today, it would generate an interest income equal to the income from that person's human capital.

Suppose for simplicity that someone with no education or training would be unable to earn any income at all. Peter earns £25,000 a year. So if the interest rate is 5 per cent a year, Peter has £500,000 of human capital. (£500,000 invested at an interest rate of 5 per cent a year will earn £25,000 a year.) Paul earns £15,000 a year, so if the interest rate is 5 per cent a year, he has human capital of £300,000. These figures for their non-human capital and the income they derive from it are also shown in Table 18.2.

Table 18.2 shows that Peter's total wealth is £800,000 while Paul's total wealth is £400,000. So if the statisticians computed the total wealth of each person, they would tell us that Peter had twice the wealth of Paul. The table also shows that Peter's total income is $40,000 while Paul's total income is $20,000. So if the statisticians computed the total income of each person, they would tell us that Peter had twice the income of Paul. It does not matter whether we compare income or wealth, Peter is twice as rich as Paul. Likewise, if the statisticians in the United Kingdom measured the total income and the total wealth of all citizens, the distribution of income would turn out to be the same as the distribution of wealth.

In practice, when statisticians measure people's incomes, they try to cover their total incomes. But when they measure people's wealth, they never include the value of human capital in their estimates of wealth. So in our example, the statisticians would tell us that Peter's wealth was $300,000, and that Paul's wealth was $100,000. Because these figures cover only part of Peter's and Paul's true wealth, we cannot compare them to get a true comparison of how rich Peter is in relation to Paul. The figures of $300,000 and $100,000 suggest Peter is three times as wealthy as Paul when in truth Peter is only twice as wealthy as Paul.

You can now see that published wealth statistics give misleading results because they ignore human capital. The income statistics do take human capital into account, so it is they which give the correct measure of the distribution of economic resources. Measured wealth distributions that ignore human capital tend to overstate the inequality among individuals.

Annual or Lifetime Income and Wealth?

The income distributions that we examined earlier in this chapter were based on annual incomes, and the wealth distributions were based on wealth in a given year. But it is rather misleading to compare individuals or families in this way by looking at them in a single year.

For example, young people earn less, on average, than middle-aged people. Thus in a given year a typical young married couple has a lower income than a middle-aged couple. But when the young couple itself becomes middle-aged, its income will not differ, on average, from the income which the current middle-aged couple receives now. Thus the inequality in current incomes does not reflect an inequality between the couples over their entire lifetimes.

The case of wealth is more extreme. Most young couples have few assets and often have debts that exceed those assets. Couples between middle-age and retirement age are at a stage in life when they're building up their assets to provide for a retirement income. Again, the middle-aged couple looks wealthier than the younger couple, but by the time the younger couple reaches that later stage in the life cycle, it will have accumulated assets similar in scale to those of the current older couple.

You can see that to compare the income and wealth situation of one couple with another, we must take into account the couple's stage in the life cycle in order to avoid being misled by differences arising purely from that factor. Let's consider an example. We'll take two married couples, the Easts and the Wests, who each set up home when they are aged 25 and who each start earning equal but low incomes at that age. We'll also suppose that as they grow older, both the Easts and the Wests earn progressively more, but that at any particular age the Easts earn the same as the Wests. We'll assume, too, that at age 25 each couple borrows an equal mortgage to buy a home, that each pays off the mortgage at age 40 at which age their only asset is their home and its contents, and that each then saves the same amount at each age between 40 and 65 to have some financial assets by the time they retire. In retirement, each couple will have an income equal to the one they had at 25 and so lower than what they had at any age between 25 and 65.

You can see that we have tried hard to make the Easts and the Wests as equal as we can. But there is one difference. Today, the Easts are aged 35 while the Wests are 70. If all we look at is income, we will conclude that the 35-year-old Easts are much better off than the 70-year-old Wests. If all we look at is non-human wealth, we will conclude that the 70-year-old Wests are much better off than the Easts. The Easts are still in debt to their building society whereas the Wests own their house outright and have some financial assets as well.

Suppose we have an imaginary economy full of people like the Easts and Wests who, over their entire lifetimes, are equally well off. And suppose the people in this economy have wages that increase at an annual rate equal to the average we observe in the world we live in, and suppose these people borrow and save the same average amounts as the people in the world we live in. If the entire population of this imaginary economy is made up of couples that are identical except for their stage of the life cycle, and if there are an equal number of couples of each age, then we can discover some startling facts about the distributions of wealth and annual income.

First, let's look at the distribution of non-human wealth between adults, which is illustrated in Fig. 18.5. For comparison, the wealth distribution for adults in the United Kingdom is also shown. As you can see, the Lorenz curve for the imaginary economy's wealth distribution shows considerable inequality. However, it does mostly lie inside that for the UK economy. So wealth in the United Kingdom is more unequally distributed than wealth in the imaginary economy. This means that although the wealth inequality arising from measuring different families at different points in the life cycle accounts for much of the wealth inequality in the real world, it does not account for it all.

Second, let's consider the distribution of annual income between households. Figure 18.5 also shows the Lorenz curves for the imaginary economy and for the UK economy. As you can see, there is more income inequality in the United Kingdom than in the imaginary economy, but the inequality in the United Kingdom is smaller than it appears when we do not take account of the differences in the stage of the life cycle.

REVIEW

Income and wealth are different aspects of the same thing. Wealth is the stock of assets owned by an individual and income is the flow of earnings that results from that stock of wealth. Properly measured, the degree of inequality in wealth is identical to that in income. But the measured distribution of wealth is more unequal than that of income because it ignores human capital. ◆ ◆ Measures of inequality focus on inequality of annual income and wealth at a point in time. Much of this inequality arises from variations in income and wealth over individual people's lifetimes. Inequality in lifetime income and wealth is much less than that in annual income and wealth, though important inequalities still persist even when measured on a lifetime basis. ◆

FIGURE 18.5

Lorenz Curves for Imaginary and Actual Economies

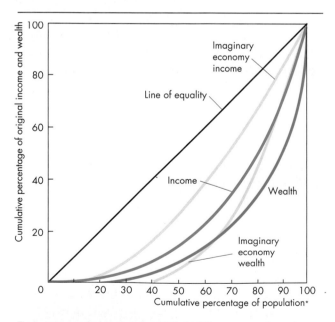

The Lorenz curves for income and wealth in the UK economy are shown alongside those for an imaginary economy in which everyone has the same lifetime income and consumption. The inequality in the imaginary economy arises partly because the curves look at the distributions in a given year rather than over people's lifetimes, and partly because the wealth curve looks only at non-human wealth. There is even more inequality in the United Kingdom.

The Sources of Inequality

Each individual owns factors of production and sells the services of those factors to provide an income. A person's income is the total of the prices paid for the use of each factor multiplied by the quantities supplied. Factor prices are determined by the forces that we analysed in Chapters 14 to 16. The amount of each factor service that an individual supplies depends partly on his or her endowment of that factor and partly on the choices that he or she makes. Let's now examine the extent to which differences in income arise from differences in factor prices and from differences in the quantities of factors that people supply.

Labour Market and Wages

We've seen that the biggest single source of income is labour. To what extent do variations in wage rates account for the unequal distribution of income? Table 18.3 helps answer this question. It shows the average hourly earnings of manual and non-manual males in a number of different occupations. Each occupation includes people on a variety of pay levels – thus merchant seamen range from lowly paid deckhands to the captain of the QE2. Nevertheless, the table brings out clearly the differences in pay levels between different occupational groups. The average rate of pay in the highest group covered –

TABLE 18.3

Average Hourly Male Earnings, 1993

Industry	Pounds per hour
MANUAL WORKERS	
Farm workers	**4.21**
Bus and coach drivers	**4.97**
Painters and decorators	**5.48**
Postal workers	**5.98**
Merchant seamen	**7.51**
Electricians	**6.61**
Average for males (all manual occupations)	**6.05**
NON-MANUAL WORKERS	
Sales assistants	**4.63**
Nurses	**8.37**
Computer programmers	**11.10**
University and polytechnic lecturers	**14.65**
Solicitors	**18.58**
Medical practitioners	**16.93**
Average for males (all non-manual occupations)	**10.69**

Average hourly earnings show considerable inequality across occupations, though the range of inequality is much lower than the inequality of income. Note that the average hourly pay for all manual workers is not much over half the average for all non-manual workers.

Source: Department of Employment, *New Earnings Survey 1993*, Part D, Table 86.

medical practitioners – is over four times the average for the lowest group covered – farm workers.

One of the factors reflected in these wage differentials is the difference in the training, or human capital, of the various workers. This helps explain why manual workers tend to earn less than non-manual workers, for generally manual workers have had the least training. It also explains why medical practitioners earn more than nurses.

The distribution of income is generated not only by differences in human capital but also by differences in the endowments or abilities of individuals. Let us now consider this source of difference.

Distribution of Endowments

Although people are endowed with equal amounts of time, they are not endowed with equal abilities. People inherit and acquire physical and mental differences which produce differences in earnings and, therefore, differences in income and wealth.

It is impossible to know for sure how such an intangible as 'earnings potential based on ability' is distributed among the population. People do, however, have many measurable characteristics that probably influence their earnings. For example, physical attributes such as height, weight, strength and endurance can all be measured objectively, as can mental attributes such as memory, vocabulary and logic.

All these measurable attributes appear to have what is called a 'normal distribution' in the population. For example, Fig. 18.6 shows the distribution of heights of male students. The horizontal axis measures those heights: the average height is 180 centimetres. The vertical axis measures the number of students of each height. The curve that traces the percentage of students at each height is bell-shaped. The curve is highest at the average, which tells us that there are more people clustered around the average than there are at the two extremes. The curve is also symmetrical, which tells us that for each person above the average height, there is another person who is below the average by the same amount.

The range of individual ability is a major source of differences in income. But it is not the only source. If it were, the distribution of earnings would look like the bell-shaped curve that describes the distribution of height in Fig. 18.6. In fact, the distribution of earnings always has an asymmetric shape like the

FIGURE 18.6

A Normal Distribution

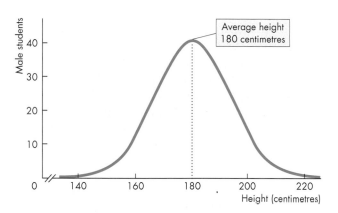

A normal distribution is bell-shaped and is symmetric around the average. The distribution shown here is the height of a group of male students. The average is 180 centimetres. For every person whose height falls above 180 centimetres, there is another person whose height falls an equal distance below 180 centimetres. A symmetric bell-shaped distribution describes a large number of human characteristics.

curve in Fig. 18.7. This particular figure is based on a survey of full-time adult male workers in 1993. The figure shows different levels of weekly earnings on the horizontal axis and the percentage of workers on the vertical axis. By definition, the median earning is the earning level that separates the population into two equal groups. Fifty per cent of workers have earnings above the median, and 50 per cent have earnings below the median. That median earning level is £305 a week. Earnings below the median range between zero and £305 a week. But earnings above the median range upward from £305 to more than £700 a week. As a consequence, the average earning is higher than the median earning and is about £330 a week. But the most common earning is below the median – at about £240 a week.

The distribution of earnings is skewed. A skewed distribution is one where there are a larger number of people on one side of the average than the other. In the case of the distribution of earnings, more people have below-average earnings than have above-average earnings. The asymmetric shape of the distribution of earnings has to be explained by

something more than the distribution of individual abilities.

Choices and the Distribution of Income and Wealth

A person's income and wealth depend in part on the choices that he or she makes. Households are paid for supplying factors of production – labour services, capital and land. The income received depends partly on the price of those factors of production and partly on the quantities that the household chooses to supply. In most cases, people can't influence factor prices. They can't go to a bank and demand that it pay a higher interest rate, or write to the companies in which they hold shares and demand that the companies increases their profits. Nor can they demand higher wages than the equilibrium wage rate for their work as baby-sitters, lorry drivers, shoe repairers or bank clerks. A bank clerk earns more than a baby-sitter because of differences in human capital, but the market still determines the wages at which labour is traded.

In contrast, people can and do choose how much of each factor to supply. They also choose whether to baby-sit or to work in a bank, whether to put their savings in the bank or in shares. So the distribution of income depends not only on factor prices but also on people's choices about supplying factors. We are going to discover that the choices that people make cause the distribution of earnings to be more unequal than the distribution of abilities. They also cause the distribution of earnings to be skewed.

Wages and the Supply of Labour

Suppose we have a small economy with five workers, Alex, Chris, Hilary, Jo and Pat. Chris, Hilary and Jo have average ability and can earn wage rates of £6 per hour. But Alex has an ability of just half the average and can earn only £3 an hour, while Pat has an ability half as high again as the average and can earn £9 an hour.

If these people all work, say, 40 hours a week, Alex will earn £120 a week, Chris, Hilary and Jo will earn £240 a week, and Pat will earn £360 a week. Their total earnings will be £1,200 (one person on £120, three on £240 and one on £360). Their average earnings will be £240 (that is £1,200 divided by five). There will be only one person below the average, that is Alex, and there be only one person above,

FIGURE 18.7

The Distribution of Earnings

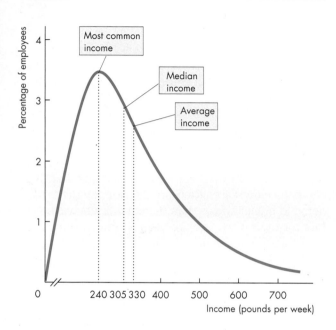

The distribution of earnings is unequal and is not symmetric around the average. There are many more people with incomes below the average than above the average. Also, the distribution has a thin upper tail representing a small proportion of people earning very large incomes. The figures in this table relate to full-time adult male workers in the United Kingdom in 1993, but similar characteristics apply in other years and for other groups of workers.

Source: Department of Employment, *New Earnings Survey 1993: Part A*, Table 14.

that is Pat. Since there will be as many people with earnings above the average as below, the distribution of earnings will be bell-shaped.

But suppose people with low abilities are discouraged by their low wage rates and work few hours. They feel little desire to work long hours for little reward. And suppose people with high abilities are tempted by their high wage rates to work long hours. So imagine that Alex decides to work only 30 hours a week and earn £90 while Pat decides to work 50 hours a week and earn £450. Meanwhile, Chris, Hilary and Jo continue to work 40 hours a week and earn £240. In this case, the total earnings will be £1,260 (one person on £90, three on £240, and one on £450). The average earnings will be £252

(that is £1,260 divided by five). So everyone except Pat will have below-average earnings and only Pat will have above-average earnings. This time, then, the distribution of earnings will be skewed.

This example is, of course, very simple and artificial. But the point it illustrates applies in the real world. Other things being equal, the higher the wage rate a person receives, the more hours that person works. The result is that the distribution of earnings is more unequal than the underlying distribution of abilities. Even if the distribution of abilities is symmetric, the distribution of earnings will be skewed. More people will have below-average earnings than above-average earnings. Reading Between the Lines on pp. 500–501 considers pay inequalities between orchestral conductors and the musicians they direct.

Savings and Bequests

Another choice that makes for unequal distributions of income and wealth is savings and bequests. A **bequest** is a gift from one generation to the next. The wealthier the family, the more it tends to save and bequeath to later generations. By making a bequest, a family can spread good and bad luck across the generations.

Savings and bequests are not inevitably a source of increased inequality. For example, savings that merely redistribute uneven income over the life cycle to enable consumption to be constant have no effect on inequality. Also, a generation that is lucky may make a bequest to a generation that is unlucky, in which case the bequest promotes equality, not inequality. But there are two features of bequests that do make intergenerational transfers of wealth a source of increased inequality:

◆ Debts cannot be bequeathed.
◆ Mating is assortative.

Debts Cannot be Bequeathed   Suppose you have an elderly friend whose will states that you may inherit all the wealth your friend has at the time of death. The smallest inheritance you can receive is nil. This is true even if your friend ended up with a negative wealth by having debts in excess of assets. For the law says that debts cannot be bequeathed. So your friend's assets would be sold and used to meet a fraction of the debts. You would receive nothing, but at least you would not receive a negative amount. Because a zero inheritance is the smallest inheritance that anyone can receive, savings and bequests can only add to future generations' wealth and income potential.

The vast majority of people inherit nothing or a very small amount from the previous generation. A tiny number of people inherit enormous fortunes. As a result of bequests, the distribution of income and wealth is not only more unequal than the distribution of ability and job skills but also more persistent. A family that is poor in one generation is more likely to be poor in the next. A family that is enormously wealthy in one generation is more likely to be enormously wealthy in the next. Yet there is a tendency for income and wealth to converge, across the generations, to the average. Although there can be long runs of good luck or bad luck or good judgement or bad judgement, they are rare across the generations. An additional feature of human behaviour does, however, slow convergence to the average and make wealth and income inequalities persist. It is called assortative mating.

Assortative Mating   **Assortative mating** means that people tend to marry within their own socio-economic class. So marriage partners tend to have similar socio-economic characteristics. Wealthy individuals seek wealthy partners. The consequence of assortative mating is that inherited wealth becomes more unequally distributed. (A further, and in some ways deeper, look at the evolution of the distribution of wealth across generations is found in Our Advancing Knowledge on pp. 496–497.)

R E V I E W

The unequal distribution of income and wealth arises from unequal wage rates, unequal endowments of factors of production, and the choices that people make. Unequal wage rates chiefly reflect differences in skills and human capital. Endowments are unequal for various environmental and biological reasons and are likely to be distributed 'normally'. The distribution of earnings is skewed so that more people have below-average earnings than above-average earnings. This skew arises from the choices that people make. People with greater ability and higher wages tend to work longer hours and earn

a disproportionately higher income. With higher incomes they save more and bequeath more to the next generation. Marriages among groups with similar wealth reinforce these effects. ◆

We've now completed our positive analysis of inequality in the distributions of income and wealth. We've described the extent of inequality and have identified some of the reasons why it exists. But we have not attempted to make any assessment about fairness or justice. Is it fair that some people can be so very rich and others so very poor? In the final section of this chapter, we will examine the way in which economists and philosophers have tried to wrestle with this type of question.

Ideas about Fairness

We all have views about what constitutes a 'fair' distribution of income and wealth. These views are diverse, and they are a source of political and philosophical debate. Throughout the ages, moral philosophers have tried to find a satisfactory theory of distributive justice. A **theory of distributive justice** is a set of principles against which people can test whether a particular distribution of economic well-being is fair.

The theories of distributive justice fall into two broad classes: end-state theories and process theories. An **end-state theory of distributive justice** focuses on the justice or fairness of the *outcomes* or *ends* of economic activity. A **process theory of distributive justice** focuses on the justice or fairness of the *mechanisms* or *means* whereby the ends are achieved. For example, the belief that each person should have exactly the same income and wealth is an end-state theory. Equality of income and wealth requires an equality of outcomes or ends. That is, when the process is over, everyone has to have the same income and wealth. In contrast, the belief that everyone should have the same opportunity to earn and accumulate wealth is a process theory. Requiring that people have equal opportunities does not imply that they will have equal incomes and wealth because people will use their opportunities in different ways. Depending on how they use their opportunities

Uncertainty and the Distribution of Income and Wealth

> 'If the children of Noah had been able and willing to pool risks... among themselves and their descendants, then the vast inequality we see today...would not exist.'
>
> ROBERT E. LUCAS, JR
> 'On Efficiency and Distribution'

Why is there such vast inequality in income and wealth? The apparently obvious answer is that there is vast inequality in luck. As Simon Kuznets saw it, a major source of good and bad luck is economic growth and the technological change that accompanies it. As technology advances, people who can move to the advancing sectors experience rising incomes, while those who remain in traditional sectors experience low income growth.

But there are many examples of bad luck that do *not* translate into poverty. We *insure* against such misfortunes as fire, earthquake, flood and sickness. So why don't companies with names like Safety Net plc spring up and do profitable business selling insurance against misfortunes such as an advance in mining technology that wipes out hundreds of jobs in the coalfields of Yorkshire?

The main reason is that most poor people are poor for their entire lives and can't afford such insurance. When an advance in mining technology destroys a job, an already poor family becomes even poorer. For poverty insurance to work, the mining family's relatively lucky ancestors – say in seventeenth-century Europe – would have had to have bought insurance for their less fortunate heirs. With no knowledge of future technological changes and with no guarantee that insurance companies would pay up, those ancestors made no demand for such insurance.

Social insurance, welfare programmes, progressive income taxes and subsidizing of health care, education and declining industries are some ways in which we pool the risks of poverty. Despite these programmes designed to lessen the severity of poverty and bring everyone's living standard up to some minimum level, people fall through the net. The so-called 'poverty trap' occurs when income rises to a point where benefits are withdrawn and taxation begins, thus discouraging work and disadvantaging the poorer members of society. Such anomalies show that despite a great deal of experience and knowledge, we have not yet been able to devise programmes that help the needy, maintain strong incentives to work and are politically acceptable.

In West European cities such as Frankfurt, Germany, poverty is virtually invisible. There is a smaller degree of economic inequality in Germany and in other West European countries than in the United States. Top income tax rates of more than 50 per cent pay for generous benefits to the sick and unemployed. Questions still arise as to the outcome of the operation of such a system both in countries that use it and in those which may wish to do so in the future. What would be the effect on employment, productivity and average incomes? Although we have learned a great deal about the effects of alternative tax redistribution arrangements, we have not yet discovered the answers to questions such as these with sufficient certainty to allow general agreement.

Because we can't buy insurance against poverty, we make other arrangements that act as substitutes. One substitute is redistribution through political institutions. Another substitute is wealth. According to Robert E. Lucas, Jr, the absence of poverty insurance is the key reason why there is so much inequality. By accumulating and bequeathing assets, people spread the effects of good and bad luck across the generations. This response to the risk of poverty decreases inequality within a family but increases inequality across families.

Understanding The Sources of Inequality

SIMON KUZNETS

Born in Kharkov, Russia, in 1901, Simon Kuznets had his first taste of the subjects that were to dominate the rest of his life when he was the teenaged head of the Ukrainian government's economic statistics department. Kuznets arrived in the United States in 1922 and immediately enrolled in economics and statistics courses at Columbia University. He went on to a life of relentless work carefully collecting, organizing and interpreting facts about economic growth and the distribution of income. For this work, in 1971, he became the third recipient of the Nobel Prize in Economic Science.

From his measurements of income distribution, Kuznets discovered that the ravages of the Great Depression of the 1930s took the largest toll, surprisingly, on the richest 5 per cent of the population, whose share in the income pie fell. Arguing the case for better economic data, Kuznets once said that the data available during the 1930s 'were neither fish nor flesh nor even red herring'.

and on a variety of good and bad luck, unequal incomes and wealth will emerge.

End-state Theories

The two leading end-state theories of distributive justice are the utilitarian theory and the Rawlsian theory. The **utilitarian theory** is that the fairest outcome is the one that makes the sum of the utilities of all the individuals in a society as large as possible. If Liz gets less utility from the last pound she spends than Nicola gets from the last pound she spends, fairness, in this theory, requires that a pound be taken from Liz and given to Nicola. The reduction in Liz's utility is less than the gain in Nicola's utility, so society is better off. Redistribution should take place until the marginal utility of the last pound spent by each individual is the same. Utilitarian theories of fairness were developed in the eighteenth and nineteenth centuries by such economists as David Hume, Adam Smith, Jeremy Bentham and John Stuart Mill.

The **Rawlsian theory of fairness** is that the fairest distribution is the one that gives the least well-off member of society the biggest income possible. In the Rawlsian view, if the poorest person can be made better off by taking income from any other person, justice requires that such redistribution take place. The Rawlsian theory of fairness was developed in the 1960s by John Rawls, a philosopher at Harvard University in the United States, and published by him in 1971.[2]

As you can see, the two end-state theories of justice differ in what they regard as the desirable end-state or outcome. For the utilitarian, it is the sum of all the individuals that counts. For Rawls, it is the least well-off individual or individuals that count.

How Much Inequality is Consistent with End-state Theories?

It used to be thought that both end-state theories of justice implied that complete equality in the distribution of income was the best outcome. This conclusion was reached by reasoning along the following lines.

First, people are much alike in their capacity for enjoyment. Using economic language, we'd say people

have identical marginal utility of income schedules. This means that if two people happened to have equal incomes, and if we gave them each an extra pound, we'd expect the marginal utility of that extra pound to be the same for each of them. Second, marginal utility declines with income. So if Liz has a higher income than Nicola, we'd expect the last pound that Liz has to give her less extra utility than an extra pound would give Nicola. Therefore, if we take a pound from a rich person like Liz and give it to a poor person like Nicola, we will increase total utility.

It follows that maximum utility, as required by the utilitarian theory, occurs when each individual has the same marginal utility. This point is reached only when incomes – after redistribution – are equal. Equality of incomes after redistribution is also required by the Rawlsian theory. This is because taking from the rich and giving to the poor increases the utility of the poor. So it is possible to carry on making the poorest people better off by redistributing money from the rich until the rich and poor are left with equal amounts of money.

The Big Tradeoff

Although it used to be thought that justice implied complete equality, it is now recognized that there exists what has been called the 'big tradeoff' between fairness and economic efficiency. (The term comes from the title of a 1975 book by Arthur Okun,[3] an American economist.)

The big tradeoff is based on the following idea. Greater equality can be achieved only by extra taxes on the rich. These extra taxes will fall on the income that rich people receive from their work and savings, so the extra taxes will reduce the after-tax income they receive. This lower after-tax income makes them work and save less, so in due course the amount of pre-tax income available to be taxed will be reduced. In turn, the amount of income available for redistribution to the poor will become smaller. It is possible that if the proportion of the income of the rich that is lost in tax goes beyond a certain level, then the actual sums transferred to the poor will diminish. Consequently, the poor will become worse off as well as the rich. On

---

[2] John Rawles, *A Theory of Justice*, Cambridge, MA : Harvard University Press, 1971.

[3] Arthur Okun, *Equality and Efficiency: The Big Tradeoff*, Washington, DC: Brookings Institution, 1975.

this line of reasoning, deciding how much redistribution to undertake requires balancing greater equality against lower average consumption.

It also must be recognized that when money is taken from the rich and given to the poor, resources are used to administer the redistribution. Tax-collecting agencies, such as the Inland Revenue, as well as all the tax accountants, auditors and tax lawyers use massive quantities of skilled labour and capital equipment, such as computers, to do their work. Likewise, much labour and capital is used by the government agencies which hand out transfer payments to the poor. Thus a pound collected from a rich person does not translate into a pound received by a poor person. The bigger the scale of redistribution, the greater are the costs of administering the process.

When these aspects of redistribution are taken into account, it is not obvious that taking a pound from a rich person to give to a poor person increases the welfare of the poor person. The wealth available for redistribution could be reduced to the point at which everyone was worse off. Taking account of the disincentive effects of redistribution and the resource costs of administering the redistribution is what produces the 'big tradeoff'. A more equally shared pie results in a smaller pie.

The Process View of Justice

The process view of distributive justice was given its most recent statement by Harvard philosopher Robert Nozick in 1974.[4] Nozick argues that no end-state theory of justice can be valid and that a theory of justice must be based on the justice of the mechanisms through which the distribution of income and wealth arises. Nozick argues for a system based on private property rights, in which private property can be acquired and transferred only through voluntary exchange.

Nozick's reasoning can be illustrated with the following story. Start out with an income distribution that you personally regard as the best possible. Now suppose that your favourite rock singer enters into a contract with a recording company and a rock concert organizer. The deal is that she will get 5 pence

for every record sold and 50 pence for every ticket sold to her rock concerts. In a given year, she sells 5 million records and 500,000 people attend her concerts. Her total income is £500,000. This income is much larger than the average and much larger than she had under the original distribution.

Is she entitled to this income? Is the new distribution fair? Nozick believes that she is entitled to the income and that the new distribution is fair. These conclusions follow from Nozick's process view of justice. It is legitimate for you and your friends to attend rock concerts and to buy records. If the consequence of the choices that you and your friends make is that someone becomes extremely wealthy, that outcome is legitimate and the new distribution of income and wealth is fair.

Those who subscribe to an end-state theory of justice disagree. If the original distribution of income was fair then the new one cannot be fair. The rock singer must be taxed and the proceeds of the tax redistributed to those who buy records and attend concerts, in order to restore a fair distribution.

The philosophical debate continues and may never be settled. This state of affairs is no deterrent to those in the practical world of politics. While moral philosophers still disagree about fairness, politicians are creating and implementing policies designed to chop off the extremes of the distribution of income and achieve a greater measure of equality.

◆ ◆ ◆ ◆   We've examined the distribution of income and wealth in the United Kingdom and seen that there is a large amount of inequality across households and individuals. Some of that inequality arises from comparing people at different stages in the life cycle. Yet even if one takes a lifetime view, a great deal of inequality remains. Some of that inequality arises from differences in rates of pay, but economic choices accentuate those differences. Also, savings and bequests result in the growth of large wealth concentrations over the generations.

◆ ◆   The topic we have examined in this chapter is highly political, and, as we've seen, governments attempt to redistribute income to alleviate the worst aspects of poverty. In the next three chapters, we're going to undertake a systematic study of a broad range of political economic issues and of the economic behaviour of government. We'll return to questions concerning the distribution of income and wealth as part of that broader study.

---

[4] Robert Nozick, *Anarchy, State and Utopia*, New York: Basic Books, 1974.

Pay Inequality in Classical Music

The Essence of the Story

In the classical music world, some conductors command huge fees for individual concerts, as well as large salaries for contracts with particular orchestras or recording studios.

This is in stark contrast to the amount most of the players in the orchestra receive.

There are many good conductors but few compare with Arturo Toscanini, Herbert von Karajan or Sir Thomas Beecham.

Most conductors today work under very different conditions compared with those of previous generations.

The concert platform was the main medium for conductors. Nowadays, more time is spent in the recording studio.

THE TIMES, 22 NOVEMBER 1993

Millionaire maestros

Julia Llewellyn Smith

EVERY exhibitionist dreams of conducting an orchestra. After all, as the writer and Nobel Laureate Elias Canetti said: 'During the performance, nothing is supposed to exist except this work, the conductor for so long is ruler of the world.'

But, for the best known conductors, supreme power is not the only reward. They earn, by any standards, enormous sums of money. They may be more moved by Mahler than Mammon. But it would be difficult to say that they suffer for their art. American tax records show that Lorin Maazel, the musical director of the Pittsburgh Symphony Orchestra, earnt $981,602 in 1990 – in addition to fees for guest conducting and a £2.1 million deal with Bavarian radio.

Maazel's position is not unusual. Conductors are in a sellers' market, where orchestras seem resigned to paying astronomical fees for guest performances. Leonard Slatkin, the chief conductor of the St Louis Symphony Orchestra, who works often with the Philharmonia in London, admits to commanding $6,000 to $10,000 a night. Compare this with Musicians' Union minimum rates for rank and file players – £45 to £62.75 for a three hour rehearsal followed by a three hour concert.

Hugh Bean, veteran leader of the Philharmonia, says: 'Conducting is a lost art. The giants like von Karajan, Beecham and Toscanini are gone. The only great conductor left is Carlos Kleiber. The rest are technically good, but they don't have the magic of making time vanish.'

The problem, he feels, is that music is dominated by CD producers. 'In the past there was a more leisurely way of working. Today time is money. The conductor is constantly on the intercom to the producer, most of whom have no classical training. There is little room for inspiration.'

The producer may rule behind the scenes, but front of house the conductor is all. Audiences need a figure to focus on and if that figure is dark, intense and sways dreamily to the music, so much the better.

© The Times. Reprinted with permission.

Background and Analysis

The factors that influence the amount conductors get paid are both economic and non-economic.

One economic factor is that there are considerably fewer conductors supplied than instrumentalists. The Royal College of Music, for example, typically trains two or three student conductors each year, out of an intake of about 180. The supply curves of conductors in Fig. 1 reflect the low quantity of conductors supplied.

This is because one orchestra, possibly consisting of 100 or more instrumentalists, needs only one conductor.

Another economic factor is the conductor's human capital. Most conducting places are postgraduate, so the total amount of musical training embodied in a conductor may be greater than that embodied in an instrumentalist who has studied only at the undergraduate level. This would affect the demand for conductors.

For the people demanding conductors, there are also important considerations. The conductor's name will often appear prominently in publicity and that name can attract (or fail to attract) a large audience – the first bassoonist, however competent, will not normally have the same effect. This factor will also increase demand for conductors.

A great conductor can inspire a great performance and, given the limited number of such conductors, they can command very high fees.

If a conductor has established a good reputation for recording, since that is an important source of income for an orchestra. This factor will also increase the demand for conductors.

Figure 1 shows the market for conductors and Figure 2 shows the market for rank and file orchestral instrumentalists for an average concert. The cost of the conductor can often be about the same as for the whole orchestra.

Thus the reference to conductors being in a seller's market reflects both the high level of demand for and the low level of supply of conductors.

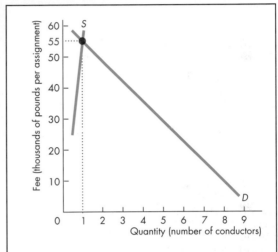

Figure 1

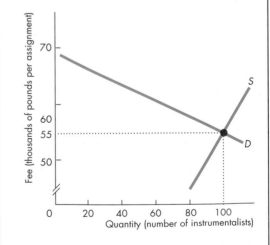

Figure 2

SUMMARY

The UK Distribution of Income and Wealth Today

Labour is the factor of production with the largest share of income – it earns about two-thirds of total income. The distributions of wealth and income among individuals are uneven. The richest 1 per cent of adults own almost one-fifth of the total wealth in the country (if pension rights are excluded). The poorest 50 per cent own just 8 per cent of the total wealth. Income is distributed less unevenly than wealth. The richest families are likely to have at least two adults with the head of household being employed and aged between 30 and 50, and they are most likely to live in the South East. (pp.481–483)

Income Redistribution

Income tax and transfer payment programmes result in a redistribution of income, transferring some income from the rich to the poor and, to some degree, alleviating poverty. The main problems with increasing the relief of poverty is that transfer payments programmes that help everybody including the poor are hugely expensive. It is therefore tempting to try to target help on the poor. But if the poor get less help when they earn more, they get trapped in poverty, finding that efforts to raise their incomes are virtually useless. (pp. 484–488)

Comparing Like with Like

To judge the extent of inequality, it is important to make valid comparisons. The measured distribution of wealth exaggerates the degree of inequality because it ignores human capital. The distributions of income and wealth exaggerate the degree of lifetime inequality because they ignore people's stages in the life cycle. (pp. 489–491)

The Sources of Inequality

Differences in income and wealth arise partly from differences in individual endowments and partly from differences in factor prices. Wage rates vary considerably with skills and other factors. But these differences, on their own, are not enough to account for differences in the distribution of income and wealth. Those differences are exaggerated by the economic choices that people make.

The economic choices that people make have an important influence on income and wealth. Attitudes towards work vary. As a result, some people take a larger amount of leisure than others and earn a smaller income. Also, savings and bequests affect wealth across the generations. Because of assortative mating – the tendency for people to marry within their own socio-economic group and thus for wealthy individuals to seek wealthy partners – bequests accentuate inequality. (pp. 491–495)

Ideas about Fairness

People disagree about what constitutes a fair distribution of income. Moral philosophers have tried to resolve the issue by finding principles on which we can all agree, but agreement still has not been reached. They have developed two broad groups of theories: end-state theories, which assert that it is the outcome that matters, and process theories, which assert that it is equality of opportunity that matters. (pp. 495–499)

KEY ELEMENTS

Key Terms

Assortative mating, 495
Bequest, 494
Disposable income, 485

End-state theory of distributive justice, 495
Gross incomes, 487
Lorenz curve, 481
Original income, 481

R E V I E W   Q U E S T I O N S

1   Which is more unequally distributed, income or wealth? In answering this question, pay careful attention both to the way in which 'income' and 'wealth' are measured by official statistics and to the fundamental concepts of the terms.

2   What is a Lorenz curve? How does a Lorenz curve illustrate inequality? How do the Lorenz curves for the distributions of income and wealth in the UK economy differ from each other?

3   What is wrong with the way in which official surveys measure the distribution of wealth?

4   Explain why the work/leisure choices made by individuals can result in a distribution of earnings that is more unequal than the distribution of ability. If ability is distributed normally (a bell-shaped curve), will the resulting distribution of income also be a bell-shaped curve?

5   Which of the following is true of the distribution of personal income in the United Kingdom today?

   a Original incomes have become less equally distributed since 1979.

   b Government policies make the distribution of disposable incomes more equal than the distribution of final incomes.

   c The distribution of earnings can be represented by a normal or bell-shaped curve.

   d More than 50 per cent of the population has an income below the average.

6   Explain how the distribution of income and wealth is influenced by bequests and assortative mating.

P R O B L E M S

1   Imagine an economy in which there are five people who are identical in all respects. To keep the arithmetic simple, suppose the interest rate in this economy is zero. For their first 14 years, each person borrows £10,000 a year to finance consumption of £10,000 a year. For the next 14 years (from age 15 to 28) each person earns £20,000 a year, using £10,000 each year to pay off past loans and £10,000 for consumption. For the next 21 years (from 29 to 49) each person earns £10,000 a year, consuming £10,000 each year and saving £10,000 each year. On their 50th birthday, each person retires with total savings of £210,000. For their last 21 years (from 50 to 70) each person consumes £10,000, financing this by using £10,000 from savings. What are the distributions of income and wealth in this economy if the individuals have the following ages:

   a 45, 45, 45, 45 and 45.

   b 25, 35, 45, 55 and 65.

Is the inequality in case (a) greater than in than case (b)?

2   You are given the following information about income and wealth shares:

	Income shares (per cent)	Wealth shares (per cent)
Lowest 20%	5	0
Second 20%	11	1
Third 20%	17	3
Fourth 20%	24	11
Highest 20%	43	85

Draw the Lorenz curves for income and wealth for this economy. Explain which of the two variables – income or wealth – is more unequally distributed.

3   An economy consists of 10 people, each of whom has the following labour supply schedule:

Wage rate (pounds per hour)	Hours worked per day
1	0
2	1
3	2
4	3
5	4

The people differ in ability and earn different wage rates. The distribution of wage rates is:

Wage rate (pounds per hour)	Number of people
1	1
2	2
3	4
4	2
5	1

a   Calculate the average wage rate.

b   Calculate the ratio of the highest wage rate to the lowest.

c   Calculate the average daily income.

d   Calculate the ratio of the highest daily income to the lowest.

e   Graph the distribution of hourly wage rates.

f   Graph the distribution of daily incomes.

g   What important lesson is illustrated by this problem?

PART 5

GOVERNMENT AND THE ECONOMY

John Kay is Chairman of London Economics, a consulting group and Professor of Economics at the London Business School. He was educated at Edinburgh University and Nuffield College, Oxford and elected to a fellowship in economics at St Johns College, Oxford. After teaching economics at Oxford University, he became Director of the Institute for Fiscal Studies, and subsequently of the Centre for Business Strategy. He is the author of *The British Tax System*, now in its fifth edition, and his most recent book, *Foundations of Corporate Success* is concerned with the application of economics to issues of business strategy.

What originally attracted you to the study of economics?

I was interested in politics and good at mathematics, and I thought that economics was where the two subjects came together. That was why, when at university in Scotland and required to do a subject outside my own course, I chose to do a term in economics. Half way through that term, I was convinced that economics was the subject I wanted to study. I have never regretted that choice.

I signed up for the course because I thought that economics was going to tell me how governments could achieve steady growth, full employment and low inflation. I learnt that economists did not know the answers to these questions. But they did know how markets worked, and they did have powerful tools for analysing the behaviour of individuals, industries and firms. So I became far more interested in microeconomics. I have never regretted that choice either.

Which economist has had the greatest influence on you?

I don't think there is one single economist whose influence I

505

would single out. But those I most admire, and those who have set traditions I hope to follow and styles I try to emulate, are those who have emphasised most that economics demands a combination of analytic rigour, flair for exposition, and an invariable sense that economics is an applied subject. George Stigler, James Meade, John Maynard Keynes and James Mirrlees have all made a deep impression on me in that way, although all of them have different perspectives on the subject. Their economics is not just technique – although technique is important to them. They see economics as a way of thinking about the world.

How important do you think the role of taxation in fiscal policy will be in the 1990s?

Until the 1980s, most people considered the main concerns of fiscal policy to be macroeconomic – the way in which government influenced the business cycle. We are now far more sceptical about the capacity of governments to do that effectively, and rightly so. The study of fiscal policy today attaches at least as much significance to the ways in which taxation, and expenditure, affect microeconomic performance – how fiscal measures change the behaviour of firms, industries and households. I think that shift in emphasis will continue.

How do fiscal measures change the behaviour of firms, industries and households?

They are concerned with how the tax system influences the amounts people save, and the ways in which they save. They determine the volume and type of

'**H**istorically, almost the only way in which budget deficits have been eliminated is by increasing taxes.'

investment undertaken by firms, and how they bear on company dividend policy or individual decisions about when to retire.

What role can direct taxes play in tackling budget deficits?

Historically, almost the only way in which budget deficits have been eliminated is by increasing taxes. Governments derive most of their revenue from three main sources: income tax, payroll tax and general sales taxes. In the United Kingdom, about two-thirds of the tax-take comes from VAT, national insurance and income tax. When a government has the political courage to do it, eliminating deficits has rarely proved difficult.

Do you see an era of integrated benefits and taxes?

Yes. The tax and benefit systems grew up separately because there was a time when each dealt with entirely different groups of people. Today, most people both receive benefits and pay taxes. There is no reason, except history, for preserving different departments, different rules, and different mechanisms of administration and payments. The logic of integrated benefits and taxes

is overwhelming, and logic mostly wins in the long run, even if the long run is slow to come.

What effects do you think direct and indirect taxes can have on European economies?

The international dimension of taxation is far more important than it was, and has not yet been much studied. It is now the most important issue in thinking about corporation tax, because most of that tax is levied on multinational companies with multinational operations. As people become more mobile, not just taking foreign holidays but increasingly living and working abroad, these questions will become more important in framing personal taxes as well.

Can government and private sector work as a cohesive partnership or is this simply political rhetoric?

They can work together, but that must be based on an appreciation of their respective roles. There are two principal models. One – which has become the Anglo-Saxon model – sees the government as referee. Government makes the regulatory rules, and imposes anti-trust policies, and the private sector works within that. That is one kind of relationship. Another model – which we see in Japan, Austria or France, and some of the newly industrialized countries – sees the government as a coach. It is a structure which has worked well, as a partnership, in some of these countries. But to be a good coach, you need the respect of the players. Our government does not have that respect and if you look at the history of industrial policy in the United Kingdom, you can see that there are good reasons why.

Is it incorrect to stress fiscal over monetary policy or vice versa?

The public, and many people beginning to learn economics, are led to believe that the economic world is divided into two camps of fiscalists and monetarists, each at each other's throats. Almost all sensible economists, and most economists are sensible, know that there is a role for both.

What advice would you give anyone starting to study economics?

First, you need numeric and mathematical competence. If economics is not a technical subject, and at root a scientific one, it is nothing. But also learn that if you do not have an intuition for what the mathematics is telling you, it may harm you more than it helps. Finally, understand that economics is most of all a style of thought. Most of the powerful ideas in economics are ones you encounter right at the beginning of your studies.

What have been the main principles that have governed your study of economics?

I hope that I have always emphasized that anything I say has to be capable of a careful and rigorous theoretical defence. But also that economics is an applied subject and a practical subject. You do not have to put over that theoretical justification in explaining your answers. But if it does not exist, your answers are without value. A doctor does not necessarily have to explain to his patient why the treatment will work – although it may work better if he does – but he is not a good or even a competent doctor if he does not know himself why it will work.

It is the combination of a clear understanding of the underlying structure of argument – and rigorous integrity in the interpretation of that – with a readiness to explain clearly and precisely what that implies in everyday life, which is the measure of the successful economist. But there are too many economists who tell their patients whatever they want to hear – and even more who never meet any patients at all.

Would you describe the United Kingdom's tax system as progressive? If not, where does the main burden of taxation fall?

There is a lot of confusion about the definition of progressivity, and different people use the term in different ways. I interpret it as meaning that the proportion of

your income taken by taxes increases with income, and the UK tax structure, measured this way, is progressive. Most of that progressivity comes from the structure of income tax.

What challenges lie ahead for microeconomists?

The greatest challenge is to become more relevant to business decisions. When I talk to business people, they think economics is macroeconomic forecasting, and since they do not think very much of macroeconomic forecasting – rightly – they do not think very much of economists. Economists also study industries and markets, prices and costs, and yet their analysis of these questions has hardly any impact on what practical people do.

CHAPTER 19

MARKET
FAILURE
AND
PUBLIC
CHOICES

After studying this chapter you will be able to:

◆ Outline the structure and scale of the government sector of the United Kingdom economy

◆ Describe the political marketplace

◆ Explain how the main political parties choose their economic policy platforms

◆ Define market failure and explain how it might be overcome by government action

◆ Describe public goods and the free-rider problem

◆ Explain how bureaucrats and politicians interact to determine the scale of public goods provision

◆ Explain how property rights and taxes and subsidies may be used to achieve a more efficient allocation of resources when externalities are present

◆ Explain why governments tax some products at much higher rates than others

◆ Explain why taxing different products at different rates can cause an inefficient allocation of resources

G OVERNMENT IS BIG BUSINESS. IN 1992, THE CENTRAL GOVERNMENT AND the local authorities in the United Kingdom employed over 5 million people and spent almost 44 pence for every pound earned by the country's citizens. What do all the public sector employees and all the public sector pounds do for us? ◆ ◆ Almost everyone grumbles about government bureaucrats. The European Commission – comprising the Eurocrats of the European Union – is also regularly criticized. Why are bureaucrats the target of so much scorn? ◆ ◆ Governments provide an enormous array of goods and services, such as roads and defence. Why do governments supply some goods and services and not others, such as clothes and car repairs? ◆ ◆ We hear a lot about our endangered planet. For instance, we burn so much coal and oil that there are serious results. What might governments do to help us to protect our environment? ◆ ◆

Government – the Solution or the Problem?

The government levies taxes on almost everything we buy. Some of these taxes are very high – for instance those on petrol, alcohol and tobacco products. These different tax rates affect the choices made by consumers and hence cause resources to be reallocated. Will the resulting allocation be efficient?

◆ ◆ ◆ ◆ Our main concern in this chapter is to describe the government sector and study the economic interactions of voters, politicians and bureaucrats to see how the scale of government activity is determined. We explain how the market economy, in the absence of a government, would fail to achieve an efficient allocation of resources. We also consider whether the government's taxes on goods and services themselves cause an inefficient allocation of resources.

The Government Sector

The government sector of the United Kingdom comprises about 10,000 organizations. Some are tiny parish or community councils while others are enormous, such as the central government and the larger local authorities. In addition, the United Kingdom is part of the European Union with its parliament in Strasbourg and its bureaucrats in Brussels. As the United Kingdom is a member of the European Union it is subject to laws made by the European Parliament and its government must pay some of the taxes it collects to the European Union. If we include the European Union, then most UK citizens find themselves concerned with five tiers of government:

◆ European Union
◆ Central
◆ County or region
◆ District
◆ Parish or community

However, in seven big conurbations – Birmingham, Leeds, Liverpool, London, Manchester, Newcastle and Sheffield – there is only one tier of local government. The authorities in this tier are called metropolitan districts (or, in London, boroughs). Elsewhere the government plans to replace the counties and districts with a single tier of intermediate size authorities.

The central government is by far the largest government. It accounts for over 70 per cent of government sector spending. Local authorities account for almost all the rest, as the European Union accounts for little more than 2 per cent.

The Scale and Growth of Government

The scale of government in relation to the economy has changed dramatically over the years. In 1890, for example, government sector expenditure accounted for under 10 per cent of the economy's total expenditure. By 1992, it exceeded 40 per cent. The government has also grown in importance by making laws and regulations that affect the economic actions of households and firms. We'll look at this aspect of government in Chapter 20, where we study the government's regulation of industry.

Our main task in this chapter is not to describe the government and its growth but to analyse the failure of markets to achieve *allocative efficiency* and to explore the role of government in coping with market failure. Before we embark on that task, we take an overview of the alternative approaches that economists use to study the economic behaviour of government.

Economic Theory of Government

We all have opinions on political matters. As students of economics, our task is to understand, explain and predict the economic choices that the government sector makes. Although we cannot suppress our political views, it is important, if we are to make progress in studying political behaviour, to remind ourselves of the distinction between positive and normative analysis. We first explored that distinction in Chapter 1. But the distinction is so important for the economic study of political behaviour that we'll recall it here.

Positive and Normative Analysis In essence, a positive statement states what *is*, or *was*, or *will be*, while a normative statement states what *ought* to be. A positive analysis of government seeks to explain the reasons for and the effects of actual or proposed government policies. A normative analysis seeks to evaluate the desirability of actual or proposed government policies. In this chapter we make a positive study of government action. So, while we seek to understand the reasons for and the effects of the actions undertaken by governments in the United Kingdom, we do not seek to establish the desirability of any particular policy.

Government economic actions stem from two aspects of economic life:

◆ Market failure
◆ Redistribution of income and wealth

Let's examine each in turn.

Market Failure

One explanation for government intervention in the economy is market failure. **Market failure** is the inability of an unregulated market to achieve allocative efficiency in certain circumstances. We discussed allocative efficiency in Chapter 11, but let's quickly remind ourselves what it means.

Allocative efficiency occurs when the country's productive resources – that is, its labour, land and capital – are used efficiently so that none of them are wasted. More precisely, allocative efficiency occurs if resources are used in such a way that it would not be possible to use them in a different way to make one person better off without making another person worse off. There are various reasons why an unregulated market economy might not achieve allocative efficiency. Let's see what these reasons are.

Inefficient Producers   We saw in Chapter 11 that allocative efficiency would not occur if firms failed to produce their output at the minimum possible cost – that is, if they were economically inefficient. If a firm does not produce at the minimum possible cost, it uses more resources than it needs, so some resources are wasted. However, this problem may be of limited importance as all profit-maximizing firms will seek to be economically efficient.

Inefficient Consumers   Another source of allocative inefficiency would be consumer inefficiency. For instance, if you buy plain chocolate by mistake when you prefer milk chocolate, it would be possible for the allocation of the country's resources to be switched fractionally from making plain chocolate towards making milk chocolate, and this could make you better off while no one else would be worse off. However, any consumers who are utility maximizers will seek to be efficient in consumption.

Imperfect Information   Unfortunately, consumers who seek to maximize their utility may fail to do so if they are not fully informed about the nature and effects of the products available to them. If they have incomplete or imperfect information, their purchasing decisions may not take them to the highest level of utility that they could reach if they had perfect or full information. Some of the problems of imperfect information can be reduced with consumer magazines which compare different products. But there is also a role for government action. Thus governments can have laws that ban misleading advertising and dangerous products, and that require cigarette packets to carry health warnings. Also, governments can put marks – such as the British Standards Kite Mark – on products which meet approved standards for quality.

Monopolies and Cartels   We discussed this cause of allocative inefficiency in Chapter 12. We shall not say much more about it in this chapter, but in Chapter 20 we will see what action the UK government and European Union take to tackle it.

Public Goods   Typically, if you consume a good, such as a grape, or a service, such as having your hair cut, other people cannot consume the same service. Only one person can eat a given grape, and only one person can be attended to by a hairdresser at a given moment in time. But there are some products which, if they are consumed by one person in a group, must also necessarily be consumed by everyone else in that group. For example, if police patrols in your street keep burglars from your house, they simultaneously keep them from other houses in your street. We call such products public goods and we look at the resource allocation problems they cause later in the chapter.

Products which Create External Benefits or External Costs   Usually when a product is produced and consumed no one is affected except the producer and consumer. This applies, perhaps, to the tomato sandwich you ate last night and to the services provided by an electrician who fixes your vacuum cleaner. But sometimes other people are affected. For example, production of petrol by an oil refinery may disturb nearby people with smells, while consumption of the services of a radio may disturb other people with noise. We look at the resource allocation problems of externalities later in this chapter.

In all cases of market failure, the unregulated market is wasteful in that a different allocation of resources could make some people better off without anyone else being worse off. It is important not to take this statement as being normative. The presence or absence of waste is a positive matter. It is a statement about what *is*. A prediction that government action *will* (or will not) occur to eliminate waste is also a positive statement. The proposition that government *ought* (or ought not) to act to eliminate waste is normative. In dealing with market failure, it is its positive aspects that are our concern.

Redistribution

Another explanation for government intervention in the economy is that it seeks to redistribute income and wealth. Such redistribution is usually justified on the basis of notions of equity or distributive justice, which we discussed in Chapter 18. Again, it is important to distinguish between positive and normative aspects of redistribution. The proposition that government intervention can redistribute income from the rich to the poor is positive. The proposition that the government *ought* to redistribute income and wealth is normative. We described the scale of income redistribution in Chapter 18, and we return to it later in this chapter. When we do so, our focus will be entirely on its positive aspect.

The Political Marketplace

The government sector is not a huge computer producing solutions to resource allocation problems that are caused by market failure. Rather, it is a complex organization made up of thousands of individuals. Government policy choices are the outcome of the choices made by these individuals.

There are three types of actors in the political marketplace:

◆ Voters
◆ Politicians
◆ Bureaucrats

Voters are the consumers of the outcome of the political process. In ordinary markets for goods and services, people express their demands by their willingness to pay. In the political marketplace, voters express their demands in three principal ways: by voting, by making contributions to the funds of political parties and by lobbying. **Lobbying** is the activity of bringing pressure to bear on government agencies or institutions through a variety of informal mechanisms. The Campaign for Nuclear Disarmament and Greenpeace are two of the most prominent examples of lobbying organizations in the United Kingdom today.

Politicians are the elected representatives at all levels of government. They include the members of the European Parliament, members of parliament and local councillors. Politicians are chosen by voters.

Bureaucrats (or civil servants) are the appointed officials who work in the many government departments, at all levels. The most senior bureaucrats are appointed by politicians while junior bureaucrats are appointed by senior ones.

Public Interest and Public Choice

There are two broad classes of economic theories of government behaviour:

◆ Public interest theories
◆ Public choice theories

A **public interest theory** of government behaviour predicts that government action will take place to eliminate waste and achieve an efficient allocation of resources. A **public choice theory** predicts that the government action is the outcome of individual choices made by voters, politicians and bureaucrats interacting with each other in a political marketplace.

According to the public interest theory of government, whenever there is market failure, government action can be designed to eliminate the consequences of that failure and to achieve allocative efficiency. According to the public choice theory, matters are not that simple. Just as market failure is possible, so too is 'government failure'. That is, it is possible that when voters, politicians and bureaucrats each pursue their own best interests and interact in the political 'marketplace', then the resulting 'public choice' may not achieve the elimination of waste and the attainment of allocative efficiency any more than an unregulated market would.

We'll see why government failure may arise in our later discussion of public goods. But before looking at public goods, let's see how political parties decide on their policies. To understand this, it helps to understand the principle of minimum differentiation.

The Principle of Minimum Differentiation

The **principle of minimum differentiation** is the tendency for competitors to make themselves almost identical in order to appeal to the maximum number of clients or voters. Let's study this principle by looking at a problem that is more familiar and concrete than that faced by political parties.

There are two ice-cream sellers on a beach. The beach is one mile long and is illustrated in Fig. 19.1 as the distance between A and B. Sunbathers lie at equal intervals over the entire mile. One ice-cream seller comes along and sets up a stand. Where will she locate? The answer is at point C – exactly halfway between A and B. By locating at C, the furthest anyone has to walk to buy an ice-cream is a

FIGURE 19.1

The Principle of Minimum Differentiation

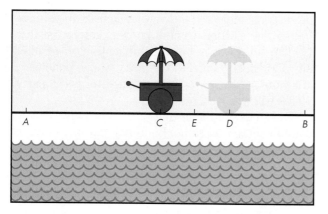

A beach stretches one mile from *A* to *B* and sunbathers are distributed at even intervals along it. The first ice-cream seller will set up her stand at point *C*. This spot keeps everyone within half a mile of the seller. If a second ice-cream seller sets up a stand, then he will decide to place it exactly next to *C* in the middle of the beach. If the second stand is placed elsewhere, say at *D*, then only the customers on the beach between *E* and *B* will buy ice-cream there. Those between *A* and *E* will go to *C*. By moving as close to *C* as possible, the second ice-cream seller picks up half the customers.

mile (half a mile to the ice-cream stand and half a mile back to the beach towel). If the ice-cream seller locates elsewhere, say at *E*, then some people near *A* may not bother to buy ice-creams at all.

Suppose a second ice-cream seller comes along. Where will he place his stand? The answer is next to the first one at *C*. To understand why, imagine the second seller locates his stand at point *D* – halfway between *C* and *B*. How many customers will he attract and how many will go to the stand at *C*? The stand at *D* will pick up all the customers on the beach between *D* and *B* because it is closer for them. It will also pick up all the customers between *D* and *E* (the point halfway between *C* and *D*), because they too will have a shorter trip by going to *D* than by going to *C*. But all the people between *A* and *C* and all those between *C* and *E* will go to the ice-cream stand at *C*. So it will get all the people on the beach between *A* and *E* while the stand at *D* will only get the people located between *E* and *B*.

Now suppose that the second seller with his stand

at *D* moves to *C*. There are now two stands at *C*. Half the customers will go to the first seller and the other half to the second. Only by each locating right in the centre of the beach can each draw half the customers. If either seller moves slightly from the centre, that seller will get less than half the customers and the one remaining at the centre will attract a majority of them. This example illustrates the principle of minimum differentiation. By having no differentiation in location, both sellers do as well as they can and share the market evenly.

The principle of minimum differentiation has been used to explain many choices. It explains how supermarkets choose their location, how the makers of cars and cassette players design their products, and how political parties choose their platforms.

The principle of minimum differentiation predicts that political parties will favour similar policies, but it does not tell us which policies they will favour. In the case of the ice-cream sellers, the best location is determined by technological considerations – minimizing the distance that the sunbathers have to walk. What determines a political party's choice of platform? Let's now address this question.

The Median Voter Theorem

An interesting proposition about a political party's choice of platform is provided by the median voter theorem. The **median voter theorem** states that political parties will pursue policies that maximize the net benefit of the median voter. What does 'median' mean?

To see what it means, let's first consider heights. Suppose you line up a group of students with the shortest at one end and the tallest at the other end. Then the median student is the one in the middle and the median height is the height of the median student. One-half of the students are taller than the median height while the other half are shorter. Of course we do not need to put the students in a line to talk about the median height! And we can talk about many other medians. For instance, we can talk about the median amount of time that Londoners spend having baths. Half Londoners spend longer in the bath than the median amount of time and half spend less time in the bath.

Let's see how the median voter theorem applies to political parties. Consider the question of how many soldiers voters want. Imagine arranging all the voters in a line according to how many soldiers

FIGURE 19.2

The Median Voter Theorem

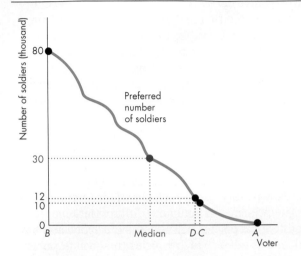

Imagine all voters placed in a line with those wanting the fewest soldiers at one end, *A*, and those wanting the most, at the other end, *B*, and the median voter in the middle. There are two political parties. If one proposes the number of soldiers desired by the voter at *C* and the other proposes the number desired by the next voter at *D*, then the second party will win. The first party will pick up all the voters between *A* and *C* while the second will pick up all the voters between *C* and *B*. The first party will have an incentive to propose slightly more soldiers than the second, and then the second party will have an incentive to respond by proposing more than the first party's revised number. Eventually each party will move towards the number desired by the median voter. When they both propose that number, each will secure half the votes and neither can improve its share.

they want the government to employ. This line is represented by the horizontal line *AB* in Fig. 19.2. The voter who wants the fewest soldiers is at one end, *A*, and the voter who wants the most soldiers is at the other end, *B*. The median voter is in the middle of the line. You can see that *A* wants no soldiers and B wants 80,000 and the median voter wants 30,000.

Suppose that two political parties propose similar but not quite identical numbers of soldiers. One party proposes 10,000 as favoured by the voter at *C* and one proposes 12,000, as favoured by the next voter at *D*. All the voters lying between *A* and *C* prefer 10,000. All the voters lying between *C* and *B* prefer 12,000. The party proposing 12,000 will win the election.

However, the party that stands to lose the elec-

tion will see that it can win by moving closer to the army size of 30,000 preferred by the median voter. But once both parties offer that army size, neither will be able to increase its share of the vote by changing its proposal. For a move by one party to a smaller or a larger army will immediately make the other party more attractive to a majority of voters. In practice, parties may not know exactly what the median voter wants, but the implication of the median voter theorem is that the party whose policies are more attractive to the median voter is the party which will win.

This does not mean that parties will always sound exactly the same. Each party wants only just over half the votes. So each party may adopt a different rhetoric, one to appeal to voters wanting more soldiers than the median voter and one appealing to voters wanting fewer soldiers than the median voter. But the median voter theorem predicts that, behind the rhetoric, they will each try to promise the number of soldiers required by the median voter.

REVIEW

Politicians seek to obtain enough votes to be elected. They do this by appealing to slightly more than half of the electorate. The key vote is that of the median voter. Each party tries to outdo the other by appealing to the median voter. ◆

Public Goods

Why do governments rather than firms provide certain goods and services such as a legal system, defence, schools, roads and health services? How much defence would the United Kingdom have if a private firm, perhaps called Britannia Protection plc, had to compete for money in the marketplace in the same way that ICI does? To answer these questions we must distinguish between what are always called *private goods* and *public goods*. But you should think of these two terms as referring to services as well as goods. Indeed, almost all so-called public goods are actually services.

Private Goods and Public Goods

A **private good** is a good (or service) each unit of which is consumed by only one individual. An example is an apple. A private good has two important features. The first feature is *rivalry*. One person's consumption can take place only at the expense of another person's. If you consume one more apple, then, other things being equal, someone else has to consume one less. The second feature is *excludability*. The owner of the orchard owns the apple initially and can exclude a greengrocer from having it by refusing to pass it over, just as the greengrocer can exclude you from having it. Excludability is important to orchard owners and greengrocers, and indeed to all firms, for they take care to exclude any customers who refuse to pay them.

A **pure public good** is a good (or service) each unit of which is consumed by everyone and from which no one can be excluded. An example is security provided by the defence system. A public good also has two important features. The first feature is *non-rivalry*. One person's consumption of a public good does not reduce the amount available for someone else. Thus your consumption of the security provided by the defence system does not decrease the security consumed by anyone else. The second feature is *non-excludability*. No one can be excluded from the security that is provided by the defence system.

Many goods (and services) called **mixed goods** lie in between a public good and a private good. An example is the space on a road which people use when they travel. When a road is little used, the space on it is non-rival because one more vehicle on the road does not reduce anyone else's consumption of space on the road. But once the road becomes congested, the addition of one more user lowers the value of space on the road for everyone else, so space on the road becomes rival.

A more interesting question is whether road space is excludable. On a road with few entry points, such as a motorway, it is possible to have a tollbooth at each entry point and so exclude people unless they pay. This occurs on some roads in several European countries, and in 1993 the UK government said it would like to introduce motorway charges as soon as it is technically feasible, perhaps at a rate of 1.5 pence a mile. With most minor roads, the number of entry points is so large that tollbooths would be prohibitively expensive to operate. But even here, electronic devices could be devised to detect which vehicles used the roads so that their owners could be billed.

Public goods and mixed goods which are close to public goods give rise to what is called the free-rider problem.

Free Riding

A **free rider** is someone who consumes a good or service without paying for it. The **free-rider problem** is the tendency for the scale of provision of a public good to be too small if it is produced and sold privately. The free-rider problem arises with public goods because people have no incentive to pay for them. This lack of an incentive arises because the amount people pay makes no difference to the quantity of the public good that they are able to consume. To see why, let's look at an example.

Suppose an effective method of reducing sulphur dioxide emissions by factories has been developed. The more widely the method is adopted, the less acid rain there will be. However, the method is costly so firms will not voluntarily adopt it. Consequently, laws are passed making adoption compulsory. But there is still a risk of violations. In an effort to enforce adoption, the government decrees that violators will be fined. Even this will not deter violators unless they think they will be detected. To aid detection, the government considers monitoring sulphur dioxide emissions by means of special satellites. We'll call one of these satellites an 'acid-rain check'.

We suppose that one satellite can observe only about one-fifth of the country. Each additional satellite put in place will deter another group of potential violators and so reduce the amount of acid rain that actually takes place. But acid-rain checks are expensive. We'll assume that the larger the number of acid-rain checks installed, the greater is their marginal cost. Our task is to work out the number of acid-rain checks to achieve allocative efficiency. We'll then examine whether private provision could achieve allocative efficiency. We'll discover that it could not because of the free-rider problem.

Benefits and Costs

The benefits provided by the acid-rain control system are based on the preferences of the consumers of the services of that system. When studying private goods, we observed that the value of a good or service to an individual is the maximum amount which that person is willing to pay for one more unit of it. We worked out this value from the individual's demand curve. The demand curve tells us the quantity demanded at a given price or, for a given quantity, the maximum price that is willingly paid for the last unit bought. We can work out the value a person places on a public good in a similar manner because the value that a person places on a public good is the maximum amount he or she is willing to pay for one additional unit of the good.

To calculate that amount, we first need to establish that person's total benefit schedule. **Total benefit** is the total value in pounds that a person places on a given level of provision of a public good. The greater the scale of provision, the larger is the total benefit. The table in Fig. 19.3 sets out the total benefits to two individuals – Nicola and Robert – of different numbers of acid-rain checks. The more acid-rain checks in place – at least until there are five covering the whole country – the greater is the reduction in acid rain.

Nicola and Robert may reckon that the total benefit to them rises by smaller amounts each time a new satellite is put in place, perhaps because the early satellites are placed over the most industrial parts of the country. The change in the total benefit from a public good that results from a unit change in the scale of its provision is called its **marginal benefit**. The marginal benefits to Nicola and Robert are calculated in the table in Fig. 19.3. As you can see, the greater the scale of provision, the smaller is the marginal benefit. If the number of satellites changes from 4 to 5, Nicola perceives no additional benefits while Robert perceives only £10 worth. Nicola's and Robert's marginal benefits are graphed as MB_N and MB_R respectively in parts (a) and (b) of the figure. The marginal benefit of a public good is the maximum amount that a person is willing to pay for one more unit of the good. As with all goods and services, this amount varies with the quantity consumed. The greater the quantity, the smaller is the maximum amount that will be paid for one more unit.

Part (c) of the figure shows the marginal benefit curve (*MB*) of the whole economy, assuming that this comprises only two people, Nicola and Robert. The marginal benefit curve of a public good for an individual is similar to the demand curve for a private good. But there is an important difference between the economy's marginal benefit curve for a public good and the market demand curve for a private good. To obtain the market demand curve for a private good, we add up the quantities demanded by each individual at each price. So we sum the individual demand curves *horizontally* (see Fig. 7.1, p.172). In contrast, to find the economy's marginal benefit curve of a public good, we add up the marginal benefits to each individual at each quantity of provision. So we sum the individual marginal benefit curves *vertically*. The resulting marginal benefit for the economy comprised of just Nicola and Robert is calculated in the table, and the economy's marginal benefit curve (*MB*) is graphed in Fig. 19.3(c).

To see why we add vertically, consider one point on *MB*. Because each extra unit brings extra benefits to all citizens, we need to add all the benefits to all the citizens together to find how much benefit the extra unit brings to society as a whole. Suppose there are two acid-rain checks in place. If a third is installed, the total benefit enjoyed by Nicola will rise by £40 while the total benefit enjoyed by Robert will rise by £30, as shown by the relevant points on MB_N and MB_R. So the total value of this third check to the two-person society is £70, and hence the relevant point on *MB* is plotted at £70. In a similar way, it follows that each point on *MB* could be plotted by adding the values of the relevant points on MB_N and MB_R. We show this clearly in Fig. 19.3(c) by plotting Robert's marginal benefit values there and plotting Nicola's values above Robert's. Each time the point at the top of the combined values gives us the relevant point on *MB*.

An economy with just two people would buy no acid-rain check satellites as total benefits would certainly fall far short of their cost. But an economy with 50 million people might buy some. To find the efficient scale of provision, consider the example set out in the table in Fig. 19.4. The second and third columns of the table show the total and marginal benefits to the entire economy. The next two columns show the total cost and marginal cost of producing acid-rain check satellites. The final column of the table shows net benefit. **Net benefit** is total benefit minus total cost. The efficient scale of provision is the one that maximizes net benefit.

FIGURE 19.3

Benefits of a Public Good

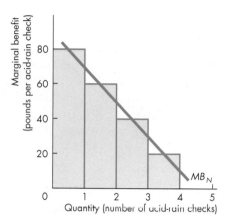

(a) Nicola's marginal benefit curve

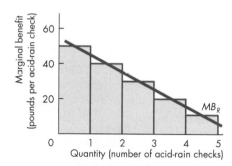

(b) Robert's marginal benefit curve

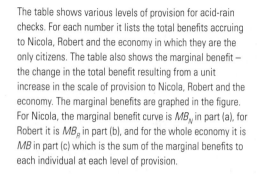

The table shows various levels of provision for acid-rain checks. For each number it lists the total benefits accruing to Nicola, Robert and the economy in which they are the only citizens. The table also shows the marginal benefit – the change in the total benefit resulting from a unit increase in the scale of provision to Nicola, Robert and the economy. The marginal benefits are graphed in the figure. For Nicola, the marginal benefit curve is MB_N in part (a), for Robert it is MB_R in part (b), and for the whole economy it is MB in part (c) which is the sum of the marginal benefits to each individual at each level of provision.

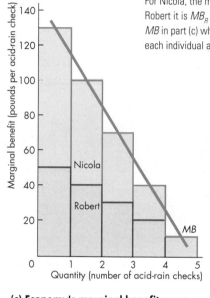

(c) Economy's marginal benefit curve

Quantity (number of acid-rain checks)	Nicola		Robert		Economy	
	Total benefit (pounds)	Marginal benefit (pounds per unit)	Total benefit (pounds)	Marginal benefit (pounds per unit)	Total benefit (pounds)	Marginal benefit (pounds per unit)
0	0		0		0	
		80		50		130
1	80		50		130	
		60		40		100
2	140		90		230	
		40		30		70
3	180		120		300	
		20		20		40
4	200		140		340	
		0		10		10
5	200		150		350	

FIGURE 19.4

The Efficient Scale of Provision of a Public Good

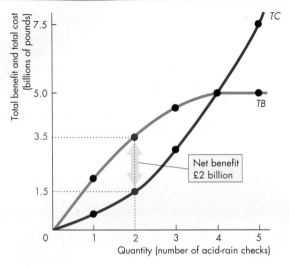

(a) Total benefit and total cost curves

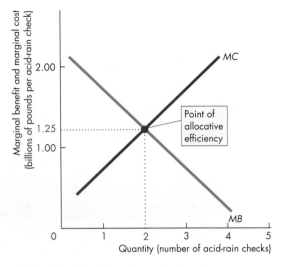

(b) Marginal benefit and marginal cost curves

Quantity (number of acid-rain checks)	Total benefit (billions of pounds)	Marginal benefit (billions of pounds)	Total cost (billions of pounds)	Marginal cost (billions of pounds)	Net benefit (billions of pounds)
0	0		0		0
		.... 2.0		.... 0.5	
1	2.0		0.5		1.5
		.... 1.5		.... 1.0	
2	. 3.5		1.5		2.0
		.... 1.0		.... 1.5	
3	4.5		3.0		1.5
		.... 0.5		.... 2.0	
4	5.0		5.0		0
		 0		.... 2.5	
5	5.0		7.5		−2.5

The table shows the total and marginal benefit to the entire economy of various levels of provision of acid-rain checks. It also shows the total and marginal cost of the various levels of provision. Part (a) shows the total benefit curve, *TB*, and the total cost curve, *TC*. The net benefit is the vertical distance between these two curves and is maximized if 2 satellites are installed. Part (b) shows the marginal benefit curve, *MB*, and marginal cost curve, *MC*. When marginal cost equals marginal benefit, net benefit is maximized and allocative efficiency is achieved.

Net benefit is illustrated in Fig. 19.4(a) as the vertical distance between the total benefit curve (*TB*) and the total cost curve (*TC*). Net benefit is maximized when that distance is at its largest, a situation that occurs with 2 satellites. This is the efficient scale of provision.

Another way of describing the efficient scale of provision is in terms of marginal benefit and marginal cost. The marginal benefit and marginal cost of acid-rain checks are graphed as the marginal benefit curve (*MB*) and marginal cost curve (*MC*) in Fig. 19.4(b). When marginal benefit exceeds marginal cost, net benefit increases if the quantity produced increases. When marginal cost exceeds marginal benefit, net benefit increases if the quantity produced decreases. When marginal benefit equals marginal cost, net benefit cannot be increased by changing the quantity of provision so provision is at its maximum possible level. So when marginal benefit equals marginal cost, net benefit is maximized and allocative efficiency is achieved.

Now that we have worked out the efficient scale of provision of a public good, let's see whether this scale would be provided by a private producer.

Private Provision

Suppose you considered establishing a private firm – Acid-Rain Detector plc – to provide acid-rain checks that would report any violators of the regulations to the police. Could you provide two checks and so maximize net benefit? Unfortunately you could not. To provide two checks, you would need to collect £1.5 billion from the 50 million people in the economy, that is £30 each. But no one would have any incentive to pay you anything. Each person would reason as follows. 'The number of acid-rain check satellites provided by Acid-Rain Detector plc won't be affected by my £30 and Acid-Rain Detector plc cannot exclude me from the benefits of any service which it manages to provide. So if I pay £30, I will have no more benefit from the satellites but I will have £30 less to spend on other products. Therefore it pays me to keep my £30 and spend it on other goods and services. In other words, it pays me to free ride on the public good and use all my money to buy private goods.' In essence, because you cannot exclude non-payers from the benefits of your service, you are asking for voluntary contributions, and all people feel their individual contributions will make no difference to the service but will make a difference to their consumption levels.

Of course each person knows that if everyone pays you nothing, then there will be no satellites at all. So some people may give you something. Certainly some goods and services in our society are provided by voluntary contributions. For example, in the United Kingdom the maintenance of historic cathedrals and the provision of the life-boat service are mostly financed in this way. But it is likely that most public goods would be produced at levels far below the efficient ones if provision were left to private firms.

Public Provision

Suppose you give up trying to produce acid-rain checks. But suppose, too, that the government in this economy makes the following proposition: it will collect £30 from each person and spend the resulting £1.5 billion to provide 2 acid-rain check satellites. The people will vote for this proposition. If there is no acid-rain control system, then the marginal benefit of installing one satellite greatly exceeds its marginal cost. By proposing to provide 2 satellites, the government is offering each voter a level of protection that maximizes net benefit. The voters obtain a benefit of £3.5 billion – £70 each – for a total cost of £1.5 billion – £30 each. Since the voters recognize this as an improvement over zero provision, they will vote for it.

Let's be clear what we have just established. First, we have established that a private producer is unlikely to provide an efficient level of public goods provision – and may produce no public goods at all – because of the free-rider problem. Second, we have established that the government can overcome the free-rider problem by making everyone pay taxes and hence is likely to produce more public goods than the private producer. Third, we have established that if the government proposed to provide the efficient level of public goods, people would accept the proposal. But will the government actually propose to provide the efficient level? Or might it provide some other level and so display government failure? Let's see what public choice theory predicts that it will do.

Public Choice Provision: The Behaviour of Politicians and Voters

People go into politics for different reasons, some perhaps interested chiefly in improving the conditions of their fellow citizens and others in their own glory. Public choice theory ignores the varying reasons and merely assumes that, in a democratic political system, the main aim of politicians is to get enough votes to be elected. Votes to politicians are like pounds of profit to private firms. One tactic politicians use to secure enough votes is to form political parties. A political party is a collection of politicians who band together to try to get elected. Political parties attempt to develop policies that appeal to a majority of the voters.

Public choice theory assumes that voters support policies which they believe will make them better off, oppose policies which they believe will make them worse off, and are indifferent towards policies which they believe will have no effect on them. Notice that voters' choices are guided by *perceptions* rather than by reality.

To obtain the support of voters, a political party must offer a package of policies – or platform – which voters believe will make them better off than the platforms proposed by the opposing political parties. All platforms include some policies that will make *everyone* better off. Providing national defence and protecting the environment are examples of such policies, though the parties must try not to promise a level of service so high that voters would prefer lower service levels and lower taxes. All platforms also include some policies which will make some voters worse off but which will also make at least 50 per cent of the voters better off. Examples of these policies include redistribution and controls on trade unions.

Let's see how politicians and voters interact and how the policy platforms of political parties emerge. To do this, we'll examine how the political process handles the provision of public goods.

Public Choice and Public Goods

Let's see how many acid-rain checks the parties will propose when the costs and benefits are as shown in Fig. 19.5. You will recognize that the curves are the same as those in Fig. 19.4 and that the efficient number of acid-rain checks is 2.

For the moment, we'll ignore different preferences between individual voters and suppose that people have identical views about the benefits of public goods. We'll consider shortly what happens when people disagree and have different preferences.

Suppose also that there are only two political parties – the Greens and the Smokes. Suppose the Greens and the Smokes propose policy platforms that are exactly the same in all respects except for acid-rain control. The Greens offer 4 acid-rain check satellites at a cost of £5 billion, with benefits of £5 billion and a net benefit of zero (£5 billion – £5 billion). The Smokes propose 1 satellite at a cost of £0.5 billion, with a benefit of £2 billion and a net benefit of £1.5 billion (£2 billion – £0.5 billion).

If there is an election, the Smokes will win. Remember that we assumed that both parties are offering programmes identical in every respect except for acid-rain control. The acid-rain control programme of the Smokes promises voters a net

FIGURE 19.5

Provision of a Public Good in a Political System

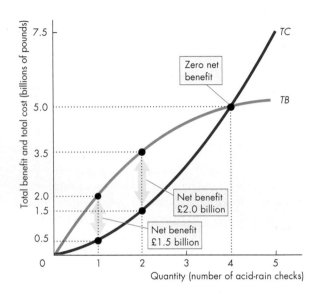

The total benefit curve for an acid-rain check system is *TB* and the total cost curve is *TC*. Net benefit is maximized if 2 acid-rain check units are installed, with a total benefit of £3.5 billion and a total cost of £1.5 billion. There are two political parties: the Smokes and the Greens. Their platforms are identical on all matters except the environment. The Smokes propose to have 1 acid-rain check unit and the Greens propose 4. In an election, the Smokes would win as their proposal generates a larger net benefit than the Greens' proposal. But if the Greens made a revised proposal for 2 units, they would beat the Smokes as the net benefit resulting from 2 units exceeds that from 1 unit. To get even, the Smokes would have to match the Greens. If voters are well informed and in general agreement about the value of a public good, competition between political parties for their votes can achieve an efficient scale of provision.

benefit of £1.5 billion over and above the taxes that they are asked to pay, while the Greens offer no net benefit, so the Smokes will get all the votes.

Now suppose that the Greens realize that their present platform will lose the election because their party is offering too high a level of acid-rain control. They calculate that to beat the Smokes they must offer net benefits in excess of £1.5 billion. So they reduce their plans and propose building 2 acid-rain check units. At this level of provision, the total cost is £1.5 billion and total benefit is £3.5 billion, so the net benefit is £2 billion (£3.5 billion – £1.5 billion).

The Greens are now offering a package that the voters prefer to the one offered by the Smokes. So in an election, the Greens will win.

The Smokes, contemplating this outcome, realize that the best they can do is to match the Greens. So they too propose providing 2 acid-rain check satellites. The voters are now indifferent between the proposals of the two parties and are indifferent about which one they vote for.

Notice two things about this result. First, the two parties will have identical platforms – a situation we predicted when we discussed the principle of minimum differentiation. Second, the platforms both include a promise to provide the number of acid-rain checks that maximizes net benefit. So both platforms promise an efficient allocation of resources to acid-rain checks. So it seems there will not be government failure.

Unfortunately, however, government failure can occur. To see how, we need to look beyond voters and politicians and introduce the third group of players – the bureaucrats.

The Behaviour of Bureaucrats

An interesting model of the behaviour of bureaucrats has been suggested by William Niskanen. In this model, each bureaucrat aims to maximize the budget of the agency – or department – in which he or she works. The chief bureaucrat in each agency likes a big budget because it enhances the chief's prestige. Other bureaucrats like big budgets because they increase the opportunities for promotion. Thus all the members of an agency have an interest in maximizing its budget. So each agency tries to find arguments that will help it squeeze more money out of the politicians. The net result is upward pressure for expenditure on all publicly provided goods and services.

The constraints on maximizing the budget of an agency are the taxes that the politicians have to levy and the implications of those taxes for the politicians' ability to win votes. Bureaucrats appreciate the interplay between their objectives and the politicians' objectives, so one of the bureaucrats' tactics is to persuade politicians that a larger budget for their agency will secure more votes. Thus budget maximization translates to some degree into political campaigns designed to explain to voters why they need more health services, more environmental protection and so on.

Let's examine the consequences of bureaucratic budget maximization for the provision of public goods by looking again at the example of acid-rain control. When we last looked at this example, in Fig. 19.5, there was an efficient level of government provision. But in that example, no bureaucrats intervened in the process. In practice, the operation of acid-rain control systems requires a large government agency. How does this Department of Clean Air influence the scale and cost of the anti-acid-rain programme? We will see the answer in Fig. 19.6 where the total cost and total benefit curves are the same as in Fig. 19.5.

We have already seen that the level of provision that maximizes net benefit is 2 units. This level of provision costs £1.5 billion and it yields a total benefit of £3.5 billion, so the net benefit is £2 billion. A political party that proposes installing 2 units will win an election because no higher net benefit is possible. But will the Department of Clean Air press parliament to vote

---

FIGURE 19.6

Bureaucratic Overprovision

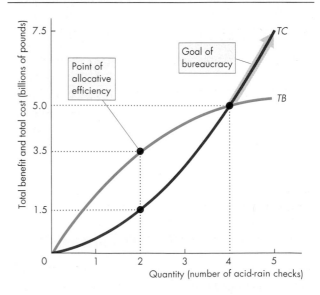

A government agency that maximizes its budget will seek to move as far up the total cost curve as possible, as shown in the figure. For example, the Department of Clean Air prefers 4 acid-rain checks at a cost of £5 billion to the allocatively efficient number 2 which cost £1.5 billion. If voters are well informed, politicians will be unable to deliver the taxes that allow the agency to get beyond the point of allocative efficiency. But if some voters are rationally ignorant while others are well informed, the agency may be able to raise its budget above the allocatively efficient level. In general, the agency will produce a higher quantity than the one that maximizes net benefit.

for just 2 acid-rain check satellites? According to Niskanen's model of bureaucracy, it will not. The bureaucracy will want to expand the scale of provision, and hence its own budget, to the largest possible level. If it can increase the number of acid-rain checks to 4, for example, it can increase its budget to £5 billion. In this situation, total benefit will equal total cost and net benefit will be zero. If the bureaucracy can increase its budget yet further, net benefit will be negative.

Could the Department of Clean Air press the politicians to approve more spending than the £1.5 billion that will maximize net benefit? Won't it pay the politicians to keep spending at £1.5 billion? For we've already seen that when two political parties compete for votes, the party that gets closest to maximizing net benefit is the one that picks up the most votes. Don't these forces of competition for votes ensure that the budget is the one that maximizes net benefit?

One reason why these forces may not work well would arise if the Department of Clean Air was an EU bureau run by Eurocrats. At present there are no Europe-wide political parties fighting for power in the European Parliament, and political control of Eurocrats is fairly loose. Euro-politicians belong to national political parties and are elected by voters on the basis of their normal party allegiances.

But suppose the Department of Clean Air is a national agency. In that case, if voters are well informed and if their perception of their self-interest is correct, then the political party that will win the election is the one that will hold the Department of Clean Air budget to the efficient level of protection. But there is another possible equilibrium. It is one based on the principles of voter ignorance and well-informed interest groups.

Voter Ignorance and Well-informed Interest Groups

One of the major propositions of public choice theory is that it does not pay voters to be well-informed about the issues on which they are voting unless those issues have an immediate and direct consequence for their own income. In other words, being rationally ignorant pays voters. **Rational ignorance** is the decision *not* to acquire information because the cost of doing so is greater than the expected benefit to be derived from having it. This principle may be expected to apply to all aspects of

government economic activity, but we'll illustrate it with our example of environmental protection.

Suppose, for example, that each voter knows that he or she can make virtually no difference to the environment policy actually pursued by the government. Each voter also knows that it takes an enormous amount of time and effort to become even moderately well-informed about alternative technologies and the most effective ways of achieving various levels of protection from acid rain. As a result, voters see it as being in their best interests to remain relatively uninformed about the technicalities of environmental protection issues and about the costs and benefits of extra acid-rain checks.

While all voters will consume a cleaner environment, few voters are involved in producing one. Those voters who do help to produce a clean environment, whether they work for firms that produce pollution control and monitoring equipment or for government agencies charged with developing an environment policy, have a direct personal interest in the environment because it affects their incomes. These voters, in collaboration with the agencies that deliver environmental protection, will exert a larger influence on this issue through the voting process than the relatively uninformed general voters who only consume this public good.

If the rationality of uninformed voters and the rationality of the informed special interest groups are taken into account, then a political equilibrium emerges in which the scale of provision of public goods exceeds the one that maximizes net benefit. This prediction of the economic model of bureaucracy applies to all items provided by governments, including national defence and public health, as well as environmental protection.

Before we leave this issue, you may wonder why, if it is predicted that the government tends to overproduce, we have so much acid rain and other atmosphere pollutants. There are two types of answer. First, many environmental pollution problems transcend national boundaries. To deal effectively with acid rain requires agreement between governments throughout the industrialized world. Just as each individual stands to gain by being a free rider, so countries can also gain by being free riders where global public goods are concerned. It is politically unpopular to propose policies to UK voters that impose costs on them that exceed the benefits accruing to them. Most of the benefits from controlling sulphur dioxide emission in the United Kingdom accrue to voters on the mainland of Europe.

A second reason why acid rain remains such a problem is a technological one. In the example that we worked with above, we imagined a technology that is not currently available. If such a technology becomes available, the predictions of the economic model of bureaucracy will become relevant and will imply a huge Department of Clean Air budget.

REVIEW

If people make their own decisions about the provision of public goods and buy them in private markets, there is a free-rider problem. It is in everyone's individual interest to free ride, so the scale of provision of the goods is smaller than that required for allocative efficiency. A government is likely to provide public goods on a much larger scale. If the government manages to balance marginal cost and marginal benefit, it will provide the public good on a scale that achieves allocative efficiency. ◆ ◆ However, politicians implement their policies through agencies – or departments – that are staffed by bureaucrats. The economic model of bureaucracy argues that bureaucrats are budget-maximizers who try to persuade politicians to increase their agency's budget. Politicians have to balance the gains from a bigger agency budget against the cost of losing votes through higher taxes. If voters are well-informed about the costs and benefits of the activities of a bureau, then the budget selected will be the one that maximizes net benefit. But if voters are rationally ignorant, the best-informed voters will be those who both produce and consume government goods and services. Voters who only consume them will be relatively uninformed. The well-informed voters, in collaboration with the relevant bureaucracies, will exert a larger influence than the uninformed voters, and so the scale of provision will exceed the one that maximizes net benefit. ◆

Let's now turn to another source of market failure, externalities.

Externalities

We have spent a lot of time in this book discussing the economic activities of production and consumption. We have seen that producers are concerned about the costs of making their goods and services and the revenues they receive from selling them. Consumers are concerned about the costs of buying goods and services and the utility – or benefit – they receive from consuming them. An **externality** arises when economic activity of either production or consumption has an effect – which is not taken into account by the producer or the consumer who is undertaking the activity – on either the costs of a producer who is not concerned with the activity or the utility of a consumer who is not concerned with the activity.

Suppose, for example, that a chemical factory produces waste products which it dumps into a river that flows into the North Sea. The waste may kill some of the fish in the river and the North Sea. Riverside anglers make fewer catches and so their utility is reduced, and North Sea fishermen work longer hours to catch the same number of fish and so their costs rise. The chemical factory is imposing an externality because it affects the utility of consumers and the costs of producers who are not concerned with the production of the chemical, and the chemical factory is not taking these effects into account. The externalities here are external costs because they affect other people adversely. The external costs are costs which arise from the production of chemicals but that the chemical factory does not have to pay and hence does not take into account when deciding how much if any waste it dumps into the river.

Production can create external benefits. For instance, when the citizens of York spend time outside, they occasionally get wafts of chocolate-scented air as a result of production by the Rowntree and Terry factories in the city. This effect of chocolate production raises the utility of consumers who like the smell of chocolate, and the effect is an externality because Rowntree and Terry do not take it into account when they decide how much chocolate to make. When an external effect raises the utility of a consumer – or when it reduces the costs of a producer – it is an external benefit.

Externalities can be created by consumption as

well as by production. When a homeowner fills a front garden with beautiful spring bulbs, an external benefit is created for all the joggers and pedestrians who pass by. Conversely, when someone drives a car without a catalytic converter, an external cost is imposed on everyone who breathes the polluted air. But, in deciding how much to spend on a springtime display and how much to drive, gardeners and private motorists ignore all the benefits except those that accrue to themselves.

Two particularly dramatic external costs have received much attention in recent years. The first arises from the use of chlorofluorocarbons (CFCs). These chemicals have been used in many products including refrigerators and aerosols. Many physicists believe that CFCs damage the atmosphere's protective ozone layer. Some scientists have estimated that a 1 per cent drop in ozone levels might cause a 2 per cent rise in the incidence of skin cancer. Diminished ozone is also believed to be a possible cause of cataracts.

The second externality arises from burning fossil fuels that add carbon dioxide and other gases to the atmosphere. These gases collect and prevent infra-red radiation from escaping, resulting in what has been called the 'greenhouse effect'. If the greenhouse scenario is correct, then the level of the world's oceans may rise. So low-lying parts of the world, such as London, the Netherlands and Bangladesh, could be submerged.

When you take a cold drink from the fridge in the summer or when you spray an oven cleaner into your oven, you compare the private benefits to yourself of the cold drink or the clean oven with the costs that *you* incur. You do not count the costs of an increase in the incidence of skin cancer as part of the price that has to be paid for cold lemonade or a shiny cooker.

Some activities have particularly important external benefits. Education is a good example. Not only do more highly educated people derive benefits for themselves in the form of higher incomes and the enjoyment of a wider range of artistic and cultural activities, they also bring benefits to others through social interaction. But in deciding how much education to undertake beyond the compulsory level, people make their calculations on the basis of the costs they themselves bear and the benefits that accrue to them as individuals. They ignore the extra benefits that they would be creating for others.

Health services also create external benefits. The pursuit of good health and personal hygiene reduces the risk that people will be infected by transmitted diseases. Yet in making economic choices about the scale of resources that they personally devote to health and hygiene, people take account only of the costs and benefits to themselves, not the greater benefits that their actions bring to others.

Government Action in the Face of Externalities

It is not surprising that external costs such as pollution receive a bad press. But if you listen to some people who are concerned about the environment, you could easily be led to assume that the aim of government policy should be to eliminate all external costs. A moment's thought will help you realize that this would be a dubious policy. For example, no one would be allowed to utter a sound in public places, no matter how much they wished to speak, just in case they in any way affected others. How can we decide what level of reduction of pollution will result in allocative efficiency?

To answer this, let's return to waste discharged into a river in the production of chemicals. But this time let's suppose that some way upstream on the river concerned there are many factories making the same chemical – perhaps there is a nearby source for an important raw material which makes this location desirable. So the industry can be taken to be in perfect competition. We illustrate the situation for this industry in Fig. 19.7. The curve labelled D is the demand curve for the chemical it produces, and this curve also shows the marginal benefit (MB) of the chemical to consumers ($D = MB$). The curve labelled S is the supply curve of the chemical. We may readily imagine that the industry will settle with an output of Q_0 which will be sold at a price of P_0, that is at the point where the two curves intersect. Remember that the supply curve for an industry is derived from the marginal cost curves of the firms in that industry. These marginal cost curves cover only the marginal costs that are met by the producers. To stress this point, we have also labelled the supply curve with the letters MPC which stand for marginal private cost ($S = MPC$). **Marginal private cost** is the marginal cost directly incurred by the producers of a good or service. So the MPC

FIGURE **19.7**

The Efficient Scale of Production when External Costs Occur

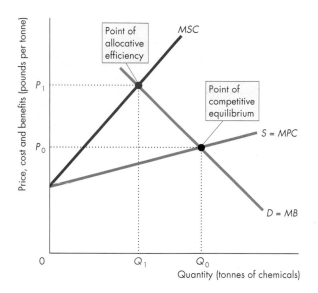

The supply and demand curves apply to a perfectly competitive chemical industry whose firms lie by a river. The demand curve, D, is also the marginal benefit curve for consumers of the chemical, MB. If production had no external costs, the efficient output would be Q_0 where the supply and demand curves intersect, and where the marginal benefit to consumers for the last unit equalled the marginal cost of producing it. But there are external costs, so the full marginal cost – the marginal social cost – of producing each unit is shown by a curve, MSC, that is above the supply or marginal private cost curve, MPC. The efficient output is Q_1 where the marginal benefit to consumers of the last tonne equals the marginal social cost of producing it. If output starts at zero and anglers are entitled to pure water, producers might bribe anglers to accept an increase in output up to Q_1, for the extra profits for each 1 tonne rise in output, shown by the gap between D and MPC, exceed the extra external costs, shown by the gap between MSC and MPC. If output starts at Q_0 and firms are allowed to pollute, anglers might bribe factories to cut output to Q_1, for the loss in profits for firms, shown by the gap between D and MPC, would be less than the gains to anglers, shown by the gap between MSC and MPC, and so less than the anglers should be prepared to offer in bribes.

curve shows the marginal cost incurred by the producers of the chemical.

We know that if there were no external effects the competitive industry would create allocative

efficiency, so that Q_0 would be the efficient output. At this output the marginal benefit to consumers of the last tonne of chemical equals the marginal cost of producing that last tonne. However, these factories discharge waste into the river thereby killing fish. Let's suppose that the only people concerned about this are anglers who like to fish downstream. There could be thousands of anglers who fish from private grounds or from angling clubs. To find the total costs of chemical production, we need to add in these external costs. This is done in the curve labelled with the letters MSC which stand for marginal social cost. **Marginal social cost** is the marginal cost incurred by the producer of a good or service together with the marginal cost imposed as an externality on others. The gap between MPC and MSC shows the extra external cost created each time the output of the chemical is raised by 1 tonne.

The efficient output of the chemical is Q_1. At this point, the marginal benefit to consumers of the last tonne of chemical equals the marginal social cost of producing it, that is, the total marginal cost of producing it taking account of both private costs and external costs. Another way of seeing that Q_1 is the efficient output is to see what would happen if output were reduced from Q_0 to Q_1. Each time output was reduced by 1 tonne between Q_0 and Q_1, the loss in benefit to consumers, as measured by the height of the demand curve D, is less than the fall in total costs, as measured by the height of the curve MSC. Notice that as Q_1 is the efficient output level for the chemical, then the waste or pollution associated with that level is the efficient – or optimal – level of waste or pollution.

How could the government try to ensure that output was cut to the efficient level? There are three main types of action that governments can take to achieve an efficient allocation of resources in the face of externalities:

◆ Establish and enforce private property rights
◆ Tax activities that produce external costs and subsidize those that bring external benefits
◆ Implement pollution controls

The evolution of our understanding of externalities and of the alternative ways of dealing with them is dealt with in Our Advancing Knowledge on pp. 528–529. Let's first consider the use of private property rights for dealing with externalities.

Private Property Rights and Externalities

In some cases, externalities can be reduced if private property rights are clearly established and enforced.[1] A **private property right** is a legal title to the ownership of a scarce resource. In the case of our chemical factories, for example, the government could make either of two decisions. First, it could decree that anyone occupying a waterside site had the right to expect the water to be pure – in which case the anglers could sue the factories for damages if they polluted the water. Second, it could decree that anyone occupying a riverside site had the right to do as they pleased with any water that passed by, in which case the factories would be entitled to discharge waste into it. Surprisingly, perhaps, either arrangement could result in the output of the chemical falling to the efficient level, that is Q_1 in Fig. 19.7.

Property Rights with Consumers To see this, suppose first that the angling clubs have the right to pure water outside their premises. The factory owners might sit back and produce nothing, but instead they might try to bribe the angling clubs to allow them to produce some chemicals and so produce some waste. Remember that each time output rises by one unit from zero, the external cost to anglers can be measured as the gap between MPC and MSC. And each time output rises by 1 tonne, the extra profit for producers is the gap between D and MPC – that is, the gap between the price or revenue they would receive from the extra tonne and the private cost they would incur in producing it.

In principle at least, the factories could bribe the anglers to allow output to rise to Q_1, because until output rises to that level, the gains to producers, which represent the amount they should be willing to offer in bribes, exceed the costs to anglers, which represent the amount they should be willing to accept in return for having fewer fish to catch. The factories would not bribe the anglers to accept an output above the efficient level of Q_1 because at higher outputs the gains to producers would be less than the costs felt by the anglers.

The result of the bribes envisaged here could come about in a different way. The factories could simply start producing and wait for the anglers to sue them for damages in the courts. So long as the factories did not raise output beyond Q_1, the actual damages caused by each extra tonne would be less than the extra profits to be gained. So if the courts set the damages appropriately, the factories will be prepared to accept paying them to produce Q_1.

Property Rights with Producers Suppose next that the factories have the right to pollute the water as much as they please. The anglers might do nothing, but they might instead try to bribe the factories to produce less output and so produce less waste. We have seen that each time output falls by 1 tonne from Q_1, the benefit to anglers can be measured by the gap between MPC and MSC. And we have seen that each time output falls by 1 tonne, the loss of profit to producers can be measured by the gap between D and MPC. So, in principle at least, the anglers could bribe the factories to cut output to Q_1 because until output falls to that level, the gains to them, which represent the amount they should be willing to offer in bribes, exceed the fall in profits of the producers, which represent the amount they should be willing to accept in return for cutting output. The anglers would not bribe the factories to reduce output below the efficient level of Q_1 because at lower outputs the gains to anglers would be less than the loss in profits felt by the factories.

Problems with the Property Rights Solution It seems that a system of bribes could result in output settling at the efficient level. To make the system work, the government would have to make clear precisely what the property rights were so that the factories and the anglers knew who would have to take what action. While the same output might result whichever property right option was selected, the government might have distributional reasons for preferring one option to the other. For in one case the factories have to bribe the anglers while in the other case the anglers have to bribe the factories.

If the government makes it crystal clear where property rights lie, then it may help to promote an efficient allocation of resources by stimulating bribes of the sort just described. But this approach is unlikely to be very successful. If the factories have to bribe or pay damages to thousands of different anglers, the administration costs could be so huge that they decide to give up. If, instead, the anglers

---

[1]This approach was first proposed by Ronald Coase, 'The Problem of Social Cost', *Journal of Law and Economics*, 1960, and is often referred to as the Coase theorem.

have to bribe the factories, the anglers would face huge costs trying to organize collective activity, and some anglers might try to become free riders and offer to contribute nothing towards the bribes, knowing that their individual contributions would have a negligible effect.

So this method is unlikely to result in an efficient level of output, that is, in an efficient allocation of society's resources, when it is relied on to handle external costs generated by production. And it is seldom likely to be successful if it is relied on to handle any other sort of externality.

Taxes and Subsidies

Because establishing and enforcing property rights is unlikely to be successful, economists have examined alternative approaches to dealing with externalities. One of these alternatives is to impose taxes on activities which generate external costs and to subsidize activities which generate external benefits.

Taxes and External Costs We noted earlier that every time you burn fossil fuel, you generate external costs. For example, every time you use a vehicle with a petrol engine, you pollute the atmosphere by creating carbon dioxide. Your vehicle has further external effects which include noise and the congestion costs it imposes on other road users whom it delays. Let's see how the government might modify your choices and encourage you to take account of the external costs that you're imposing on others.

To do so, we'll look at the market for the services supplied by petrol-driven vehicles. Figure 19.8 illustrates this market. The demand curve for these services is also the marginal benefit curve ($D = MB$). It tells us how much consumers value each different level of output. Curve MPC measures the marginal private cost of producing petrol-driven transport, that is, the marginal cost directly incurred by all those who operate petrol-driven vehicles. However, using these vehicles generates external costs. Adding all the external costs to the private cost yields the marginal social cost of the services provided by petrol-driven vehicles. Marginal social cost is illustrated by the curve MSC in Fig. 19.8. The figure supposes that the amount of external cost rises the more miles that are travelled.

Suppose this market is competitive and unregulated. People balance the marginal private cost against

FIGURE 19.8

Taxing an External Cost

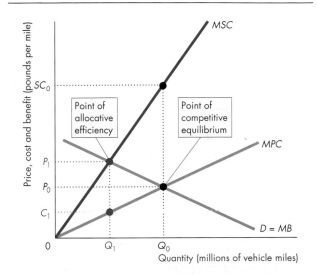

The demand curve for petrol-driven transport services, D, is also the marginal benefit curve, MB. The marginal private cost curve is MPC. Because of congestion and pollution, the marginal cost of the transport services exceeds the marginal private cost. The marginal social cost is shown by MSC. If the market is competitive, output is Q_0, price is P_0, and marginal social cost is SC_0. If a tax is imposed to confront producers of transport services with its full marginal social cost, then the MSC curve becomes the relevant marginal cost curve for suppliers' decisions. The price rises to P_1 and the quantity decreases to Q_1 to secure allocative efficiency.

the marginal benefit and travel Q_0 million miles per year at a price of P_0 per mile. This scale of travel generates a large amount of external cost. The marginal social cost is SC_0. The difference between P_0 and SC_0 represents the marginal cost imposed on others – the external marginal cost.

Now suppose that the government taxes this form of transport with a tax equal to the external marginal cost. As the external marginal cost increases when more miles are travelled, the government must have a tax whose rate rises the more miles that are travelled and falls the fewer miles that are travelled. Such a tax shifts the supply curve upward to become the MSC curve. By imposing such a tax, the government makes the marginal private cost – the original marginal private cost *plus* the tax – equal the marginal social cost. The MSC curve is now the relevant marginal cost curve for each person's decision, since

Understanding Externalities

> 'The question to be decided is: is the value of the fish lost greater than the value of the product which contamination of the stream makes possible?'
>
> R. H. COASE
> *The Problem of Social Cost*

Whether it's dead fish caused by DDT, acid rain caused by power stations, or global warming caused by burning carbon fuels, externalities are easy to see. But solutions have been slow to evolve. Fifty years ago, none of these problems was high on anyone's agenda. Why?

There are two main reasons: as incomes grow, people value the environment more highly; and as technology advances, we discover external effects that were previously unknown. In combination, these two factors have increased the demand (and willingness to pay) for a cleaner and safer environment. And as demand has grown, so has our understanding of alternative economic solutions.

One solution is regulation. For example, DDT was banned and farmers had to substitute more expensive insecticides that were easier on the environment. Were the additional costs of such insecticides lower or higher than the value of reduced toxicity of our rivers and lakes? When regulation is used to control externalities, it is regulators and law makers who make judgements about value.

Another solution is taxation. For example, electric power companies could be charged a tax proportional to the volume of pollution they create. Again, law makers and bureaucrats make the decisions about comparative values. But given those decisions, firms decide how much pollution to create.

A third solution is establishing property rights over the resources being damaged by external factors. For example, the fishermen along the Thames could be assigned property rights over the river. They would decide the value of avoiding pollution and charge polluters a price sufficiently high to compensate for lost or lowered incomes resulting from pollution.

Finally, an externality can simply be endured. This is our current 'solution' to the problem of global warming. In this case, no one has been able to implement an arrangement at a cost that is sufficiently low to result in a net social gain.

The River Thames had a reputation in early Victorian times for sustaining many aspects of commercial trade, including fishing. However, as the nineteenth century progressed, the number of factories sited near the river and using it as a dumping ground for waste products increased greatly. The result was a decline in fish stocks, particularly in salmon, until the 1940s when the Thames became incapable of sustaining a viable fish stock.

Today, the Thames supports a very diverse fish stock including the occasional salmon just as it did many years ago. The river is no longer viewed as a conduit for rubbish, industrial waste and chemicals and the result is a burgeoning ecosystem including many nesting birds. Pollutants are recognized as having potential externalities and the Department for the Environment is enforcing much more stringent laws regarding dumping. The imposition of penalties has shown how the River Thames' externality problem has been reduced by government regulation.

From Pigou to Buchanan
The Public Interest and
Public Choices

JAMES BUCHANAN

Externalities are solved by *public choices*. But for a time, economists lost sight of this fact. During the 1920s, Arthur Cecil Pigou (1877–1959), pictured left, of Cambridge, United Kingdom, pioneered a branch of economics designed to guide public choices – *welfare economics*. Pigou devised rules which, if followed, ensured that decisions about externalities were in the *public interest*. But the rules were not followed.

Not until the 1950s did economists develop *public choice theory* and explain the choices *actually* made by politicians and bureaucrats. Among the leaders in this field was the 1986 Nobel laureate James Buchanan (1919–), pictured above, of George Mason University. Because of the work of Buchanan and others, we now understand that the solutions adopted for externalities depend not on the public interest, but on private interests – on private costs and benefits. We also now appreciate, as a result of the work of Ronald H. Coase, that the transactions costs of organizing alternative solutions are crucial in determining which, if any, of these solutions is pursued.

ARTHUR CECIL PIGOU

each person now faces a marginal cost of transport equal to its marginal social cost. The price rises to P_1 and the amount of travel falls to Q_1. The marginal cost of the resources used in producing Q_1 million miles of travel is C_1, but the marginal external cost generated is P_1 minus C_1. That external marginal cost is paid by the consumer through the tax.

The situation at the price P_1 and the quantity Q_1 is allocatively efficient. At an output above Q_1, marginal social cost exceeds the marginal benefit, while at an output below Q_1, marginal social cost is less than the marginal benefit. In the first situation, producing less increases the net benefit because it reduces costs by more than it reduces benefits. In the second situation, producing more increases the net benefit because it increases benefits by more than it increases costs. Only at Q_1 is it impossible to increase net benefit. The possible use of taxes to control the greenhouse effect is considered in Reading Between the Lines on pp. 538–539.

Subsidies and External Benefits We know that the production or consumption of some goods and services brings external benefits. The government can induce additional production and consumption of such goods and services by subsidizing them. Figure 19.9 shows how subsidizing education increases the amount consumed and can achieve allocative efficiency. Suppose that there is no difference between marginal private cost and marginal social cost and that the marginal cost of producing education is shown by the curve MC. The demand curve for education, D, tells us the quantity of education demanded at each price when people are free to choose the amount of education that they undertake and have to pay for it themselves. It measures the marginal private benefit – the benefit perceived by the individuals undertaking education – so it is labelled $D = MPB$. A private competitive market for education will produce an output of Q_0 at a price of P_0.

Suppose that the external benefit – the benefit derived by people other than those undertaking education – results in marginal social benefits described by the curve MSB. Allocative efficiency occurs at output Q_1 where marginal social benefit equals marginal cost which is C_1. The government could ensure that the allocatively efficient output level Q_1 was produced by subsidizing private educational establishments as this would encourage them to supply Q_1 at a price of P_1. Alternatively, the government could set up its own schools and colleges and subsidize

FIGURE 19.9

Subsidizing an External Benefit

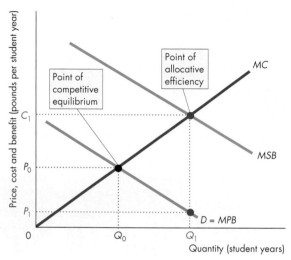

The demand curve for education, D, also measures the marginal private benefit of education, MPB. The marginal cost of education is shown by the curve MC. If education is provided in a competitive market with no government intervention, then the price of education is P_0 and the quantity bought is Q_0. But education produces an external benefit, and the marginal social benefit is shown by the curve MSB. Allocative efficiency would be achieved if the quantity were Q_1 where marginal social cost equals marginal social benefit. This quantity will be achieved if the government subsidizes education and makes it available for a price of P_1 so that the quantity demanded is Q_1.

them. In other words, by subsidizing education, the government can encourage people to undertake the amount of education that makes its marginal social benefit equal to its marginal cost.

Taxes and Subsidies in Practice Although taxes can help to tackle the inefficiencies of the market system that arise when there are externalities, they are rarely used. The most obvious example of a pollution tax in the United Kingdom is the additional fuel tax levied on leaded as opposed to lead-free fuel. In contrast, the provision of largely free education and health services can be seen as a very generous subsidy for external benefits, though free provision is also provided as part of a redistribution policy to ensure that rich and poor alike have access to education and health services. Also, free education up to the age of 16 might seem reasonable on the grounds that education up to that age is compulsory.

Regulations and Externalities

In practice, external costs are more frequently tackled by regulations than by taxes. For example, UK governments have imposed progressively more stringent requirements on water boards in the years since World War II over the quality of the water they discharge into rivers and the sea. Moreover, since 1986, the European Union has also had the power to make laws over matters such as air and water pollution and noise. How does the use of regulations compare with the use of taxes

Comparing Taxes and Regulations

To compare taxes and regulations, we'll first see that regulations might often have the advantage of being easier to operate. Then we'll see that taxes might have the advantage of securing a given reduction in pollution at a lower cost.

Operating Taxes and Regulations Suppose the government is concerned about the pollution of a river. If it taxes firms which discharge waste into the river, then it must constantly measure the amount of waste discharged by each producer. If, instead, it lays down a regulation about how much each firm can discharge, then it need only do occasional spot checks to see that the regulations are being obeyed.

The Costs to Producers of Reducing Pollution It is often much cheaper for some firms to cut their waste discharges than it is for others, for some firms have more flexible technology than others. The government will not know which firms come in which category, so its regulations may demand similar cuts from them all. Let's see why this is unsatisfactory.

Suppose there are two firms, Flexi-Tec and Rigid-Tec. Suppose that cutting discharges by 1 tonne per year would cost Flexi-Tec £1,000 and Rigid-Tec £2,000. If the government wants a cut in discharges of 10 tonnes, it may demand a fall of 5 tonnes by each firm. This will raise Flexi-Tec's production costs by £5,000 and Rigid-Tec's by £10,000, so that production costs rise by £15,000 in total.

Suppose, instead, that the government levied a tax on waste of, say, £1,500 per tonne. Then Flexi-Tec might have cut its discharge by 10 tonnes, as such a cut saves £15,000 in taxes and adds only £10,000 to its production costs. Rigid-Tec would not have cut its discharge at all, as such a cut would

raise its production costs by more than it would save in tax. So here the total fall of 10 tonnes could be achieved by adding only £10,000 to total production costs. In short, the use of taxes should ensure that a total desired fall in discharge is brought about by falls from those firms for whom cutting discharges is cheapest.

Further Problems with Securing Optimal Pollution

Whichever method is used, there remains the problem of working out what the optimal level of pollution is. To ascertain this in any particular case, as Fig. 19.7 showed, the government needs to know the shape of the marginal social cost curve. This means it needs to know the external cost of each increase in the amount of pollution that occurs. In other words, to secure the efficient amount of lead emissions from cars, it needs to know the value of the damage that such pollution creates. This is an almost impossible task. Doctors will find it hard to agree on the damage done to people's health, and even if they agreed on that it would still be difficult to place a money value on that damage.

Nevertheless, the growing concern about the environment makes it likely that there will be increased efforts to work out the optimal levels of pollution of different sorts. And the government seems to be looking with favour at adopting pollution taxes where these are feasible.

R E V I E W

When externalities are present, the market allocation of resources is not efficient. Occasionally an efficient allocation might be achieved by clearly establishing private property rights and leaving people to settle up with bribes. But in many cases, private property rights cannot be established and enforced. In these cases, if the government confronts people with a tax equivalent to the external marginal cost or a subsidy equivalent to the external marginal benefit, it induces people to produce goods on a scale that achieves allocative efficiency, even in the face of externalities. However, the use of taxes and subsidies requires constant monitoring of anyone who generates externalities. To avoid the costs of monitoring, governments are apt to rely instead on regulations to control external costs. ◆

Why Tax Rates Vary

T he UK government levies value added tax at the standard rate of 17.5 per cent on many products. But some goods – such as petrol, tobacco and alcoholic drinks – are taxed more heavily, while other goods – such as children's clothes and most food – are not taxed at all. Why is there this variety? An important reason is that taxes create *deadweight losses*, and the total deadweight loss arising from raising a given amount of revenue can be minimized by taxing different products at different rates. Minimizing deadweight loss is consistent with maximizing the number of voters to whom the range of tax rates will appeal. So let's now look at the deadweight losses that arise from taxes and see how they can be minimized.

Minimizing the Deadweight Loss of Taxes

We studied taxes on expenditure in Chapter 6. You may like to look at Fig. 6.5 to refresh your memory. It is easy to extend the analysis we used there to see how taxes create deadweight losses. Figure 19.10 considers the deadweight loss that arises from the tax on petrol. The curve labelled *S* is the supply curve that would apply if there were no tax on petrol. The equilibrium would be where this curve cuts the demand curve *D*, that is a quantity of 80 million litres being sold each day for a price of 20 pence a litre. With a tax of 40 pence a litre, the supply curve shifts upward to *S + tax* and the equilibrium price rises to 55 pence a litre while the quantity falls to 60 million litres a day. The price paid by consumers rises by 35 pence from 20 pence to 55 pence while the price received by producers falls by 5 pence from 20 pence to 15 pence; it is true that producers will receive 55 pence a litre from consumers, but 40 pence is at once paid to the government in tax which leaves producers with just 15 pence.

FIGURE 19.10

The Deadweight Loss from a Tax on Expenditure

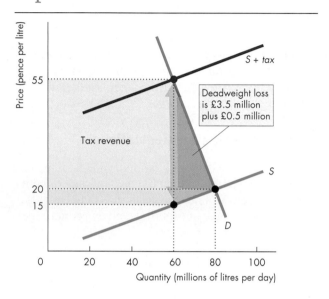

An excise tax creates a loss of both consumer surplus and producer surplus. The two green areas show the loss of consumer surplus and the two blue areas show the loss of producer surplus. Against these losses there must be set the tax revenue which can be used to benefit citizens. The value of this revenue is shown by the combined area of the two shaded rectangles. So the final net loss, or deadweight loss, is the combined area of the two triangles. The tax revenue is £24 million a day (there are 60 million litres taxed at 40 pence). The deadweight loss from the tax is £4 million a day. So in this example, raising a tax revenue of £24 million a day creates a deadweight loss of £4 million a day.

We can use Fig. 19.10 to work out the deadweight loss caused by this tax. To do so, we first work out how much worse off both consumers and producers are as a result of the tax. We do this by looking at the loss of consumer surplus for consumers and the loss of producer surplus for producers.

Let's take the loss in consumer surplus first. This loss is represented by the two green areas. The light green rectangle concerns the loss of consumer surplus on the 60 million litres which consumers continue to consume. This loss arises because they have to pay 55 pence for each of these litres instead of the old 20 pence. The money value of this rectangle is 35 pence (or £0.35) times 60 million, that is

£21 million. The dark green triangle shows the loss of consumer surplus which arises because consumers now buy only 60 million litres a day instead of 80 million – in other words it shows the consumer surplus which consumers used to enjoy on the 20 million litres they no longer buy. The money value of this triangle is £3.5 million.[2]

Next let's work out the loss in producer surplus. This loss is represented by the two blue areas. The light blue rectangle concerns the loss of producer surplus on the 60 million litres which producers continue to sell. This loss arises from the fact that they now receive only 15 pence for each of these litres instead of the old 20 pence. The money value of this rectangle is 5 pence (or £0.05) times 60 million, that is £3 million. The dark blue triangle shows the loss which results from the fact that producers now sell only 60 million litres a day instead of 80 million – in other words it shows the producer surplus which producers used to enjoy on the 20 million litres they no longer sell. The money value of this triangle is £0.5 million.[3]

We can see that the total loss of consumer surplus is £21 million plus £3.5 million, which makes £24.5 million, while the total loss for producers is £3 million plus £0.5 million, which makes £3.5 million. So the combined loss is £24.5 million plus £3.5 million which is £28 million. This tells us how much consumers and producers lose as a result of the tax. However, they have a gain to offset against this loss. The government has collected some tax revenue from the tax. It can use this revenue to provide more goods and services to benefit the country's citizens, or instead use it to reduce other taxes. Either way,

citizens should benefit from the fact that the government has collected the extra tax revenue. How much has the government collected from the petrol tax? It has collected 40 pence tax on 60 million litres which makes a tax yield of £24 million. This is actually represented in Fig. 19.10 by the combined areas of the light blue and light green rectangles, for these two rectangles form a larger rectangle whose area is 60 million litres times 40 pence (or £0.40).

We have seen that the total loss is represented by the light green rectangle plus the dark green triangle together with the light blue rectangle and the dark blue triangle. Against this there is a gain from the tax revenue which we represent by the light blue rectangle plus the light green rectangle. So the final net loss is represented by the combined area of the two triangles. The value of this net loss, or deadweight loss, is £3.5 million for the dark green triangle plus £0.5 million for the dark blue triangle, or £4 million in all. So raising a tax revenue of £24 million a day by using the petrol tax creates a deadweight loss of £4 million a day, an amount equal to one-sixth of the tax revenue.

One of the main influences on the deadweight loss arising from a tax is the elasticity of demand for the good. To see the importance of the elasticity of demand, let's consider a different commodity with a less inelastic demand – lemonade. So that we can make a direct comparison, let's assume that the lemonade market is exactly as big as the market for petrol. Figure 19.11 illustrates this market. The demand curve for lemonade is D and the supply curve is S. Lemonade is not taxed, so the price is 20 pence a litre – where the supply curve and the demand curve intersect – and the quantity of lemonade traded is 80 million litres a day.

Now suppose that the government contemplates abolishing the petrol tax and taxing lemonade instead. The demand for lemonade is less inelastic than the demand for petrol because lemonade has substitutes in the form of other drinks. The government wants to raise £24 million a day so that its total revenue is not affected by this tax change. The government's economists, armed with their statistical estimates of the demand and supply curves for lemonade that appear in Fig. 19.11, calculate that a tax of 60 pence a litre will do the job. With such a tax, the supply curve will shift upward to the curve labelled $S + tax$. This new supply curve intersects the demand curve at a price of 70 pence a litre and a quantity of 40 million litres a day. The price suppliers

---

[2] You can calculate the area of that triangle by using the following formula: area of a triangle = $\dfrac{\text{base} \times \text{height}}{2}$

The base of the triangle is 20 million and the height is 35 pence, so the area of the light green triangle is:

$\dfrac{20 \text{ million} \times £0.35}{2}$ = £3.5 million.

[3] You can also calculate the area of that triangle by using the formula: area of triangle = $\dfrac{\text{base} \times \text{height}}{2}$

The base of the triangle is 20 million and the height is 5 pence, so the area of the light blue triangle is:

$\dfrac{40 \text{ million} \times £0.05}{2}$ = £1 million.

FIGURE 19.11

Why We Don't Tax Lemonade

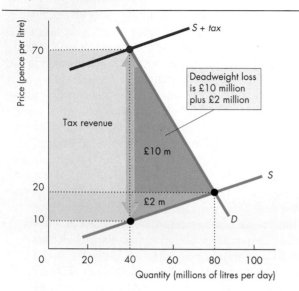

The demand curve for lemonade is D and the supply curve is S. The equilibrium price is 20 pence a litre and 80 million litres of lemonade are traded a day. To raise £24 million in tax revenue, a tax of 60 pence a litre will have to be imposed. The introduction of this tax shifts the supply curve to the one labelled S + tax. The price rises to 70 pence a litre and the quantity traded falls to 40 million litres a day. The deadweight loss is represented by the combined area of the dark green triangle and the dark blue triangle and equals £12 million a day. The deadweight loss from taxing lemonade is much larger than that from taxing petrol (Fig. 19.10) because the demand for lemonade is less inelastic than the demand for petrol. Accordingly, items that have a relatively inelastic demand are sometimes taxed more heavily than other items.

will receive after paying the tax to the government is 10 pence a litre. The government collects a tax of 60 pence a litre on 40 million litres a day, so it collects a total revenue of £24 million a day – exactly the amount that it requires.

But what is the deadweight loss in this case? The answer is the combined area of the dark green and dark blue triangles. The magnitude of the deadweight loss is £12 million.[4] Compare this case with the combined area of the dark green and dark blue triangles in Fig. 19.10. Notice how much bigger the deadweight loss is from taxing lemonade than from taxing petrol. For lemonade, the deadweight loss has a value equal to one-half of the revenue raised, while for petrol it has a value equal to only one-sixth. Yet the two supply curves are identical, and

the examples were set up to ensure that the initial no-tax prices and quantities were identical. The difference between the two cases is the elasticity of demand. With lemonade, a price rise of 50 pence caused the quantity demanded to fall by one-half, so we can deduce that a price rise of only 25 pence would have caused the quantity demanded to fall by one-quarter. With petrol, it took a price rise of 55 pence to cause the quantity demanded to fall by a quarter. So the demand for petrol is much less responsive to changes in price. (If you look back to the discussion of elasticity of demand in Chapter 5, you will be able to calculate that the arc elasticity of demand for petrol is about –0.3 while for lemonade it is –0.6).

You can now see why taxing lemonade is not on the political agenda of any of the major parties. Vote-seeking politicians seek out taxes that benefit the median voter. So, other things being equal, they try to minimize the deadweight loss of raising a given amount of revenue. Equivalently, they tend to impose heavy taxes on items such as petrol, alcohol and tobacco where demand is inelastic.

Taxes and the Allocation of Resources

We discovered in Chapter 11 that we will have an efficient allocation of resources in a market economy if all industries are perfectly competitive and if there are no special problems such as

---

[4]This deadweight loss is calculated in exactly the same way as the deadweight loss from the petrol tax (notes 2 and 3 on p. 533). The dark green triangle has a base of 40 million and a height of 50 pence, so its area is:

$$\frac{40 \text{ million} \times \pounds 0.50}{2} = \pounds 10 \text{ million}.$$

The dark blue triangle has a base of 40 million and a height of 10 pence, so its area is:

$$\frac{40 \text{ million} \times \pounds 0.10}{2} = \pounds 2 \text{ million}.$$

So the total deadweight loss is £12 million, that is £10 million plus £2 million.

imperfect information, public goods and externalities. But will we have an efficient allocation when the government starts imposing taxes on goods and services often at different rates.

To answer this question we will first look a little more fully at how a perfectly competitive economy secures an efficient allocation of resources. Then we will see that the allocation is no longer efficient if a tax is imposed on just one good or service. Finally, we will see what would happen if the government taxed all goods and services.

Perfect Competition and Allocative Efficiency

We have defined allocative efficiency as a situation where it is impossible to make one person better off without making someone else worse off. Let's see how this state of affairs occurs in a perfectly competitive economy. To simplify things, we will assume the economy produces only two commodities: apple juice and blackcurrant juice. Thus there are no public goods, and we will assume there are no other problems such as imperfect information or externalities. We will also concentrate on one consumer, Cindy.

Suppose the economy's production possibility frontier is as shown in Fig. 19.12. Resources certainly won't be allocated efficiently if production takes place at any point inside this frontier such as A where 40 million litres of blackcurrant juice and 20 million litres of apple juice are produced each day. If production were at a point like A, it would be possible to move to a point such as B and produce more of each good. In turn, all consumers – Cindy included – could be given more apple juice and more blackcurrant juice. So everyone could be made better off.

Two things must happen for a country to be on its production possibility frontier. First, there must be full employment. Let's suppose that in this economy there is always full employment. Second, industries must use resources efficiently – that is to say there must be economic efficiency. We saw in Chapter 11 that economic efficiency occurs whenever firms maximize profit. As both apple juice and blackcurrant juice are produced by perfectly competitive firms – which maximize profits – there will always be economic efficiency here.

So the economy is somewhere on the production possibility frontier. Whereabouts it is depends on the

FIGURE 19.12

A Tax and the Marginal Rate of Transformation

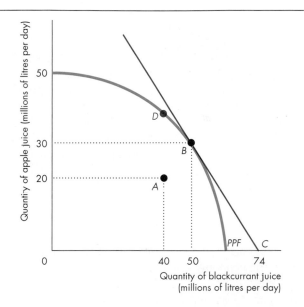

To achieve allocative efficiency, production must be on the production possibility frontier. Inside the frontier, at a point such as A, it is possible to make everyone better off simply by producing more products. The economy here starts at B. The slope of the frontier at B can be found from the tangent BC as −1.25. This means the marginal rate of transformation is 1.25 – it is possible to give up 1 litre of blackcurrant juice and produce 1.25 litres more apple juice. Thus the marginal cost of blackcurrant juice is 1.25 times that of apple juice. With perfectly competitive industries, the price of blackcurrant juice will be 1.25 times that of apple juice and consumers will adjust their purchases so that their marginal rate of substitution equals 1.25 and so equals the marginal rate of transformation. In these circumstances, it can be shown that resource allocation will be efficient. A tax on blackcurrant juice shifts production to D. The allocation of resources is disturbed and is no longer efficient. The marginal rate of transformation here is 1 and so is the relative price set by the two industries. But the tax on blackcurrant juice means that consumers face a different price ratio. They adjust their purchases so that their marginal rates of substitution equal the tax-inclusive price ratio, but these marginal rates of substitution no longer equal the marginal rate of transformation and resource allocation is no longer efficient.

demand for each juice. If consumers decide to buy more apple juice and less blackcurrant juice, then the demand for one will rise – causing economic profits in that industry and attracting new firms – while the demand for the other will fall – causing losses in that industry so driving some firms out.

Suppose that at present the economy is at B, producing 50 million litres of blackcurrant juice each day and 30 million litres of apple juice. At B the slope of the production possibility frontier is –1.25. We can find this as we saw in Figure 2.13 by drawing a tangent to the curve at B. There is a tangent drawn at B in the figure. You can find its slope by looking at BC. As we move along that tangent we move 30 million litres (of apple juice) down and 24 million litres (of blackcurrant juice) to the right, and –30/24 is –1.25.

This slope tells us that if we reduced the output of blackcurrant juice at B by 1 litre, then the resources we would release would be able to produce 1.25 litres of apple juice. We use the term the **marginal rate of transformation** to say how much more of one good we can get if we sacrifice a little of the other. In our example, the marginal rate of transformation between blackcurrant juice and apple juice is 1.25.

We must now ask if we have allocative efficiency at point B. To have allocative efficiency it is necessary for each consumer's marginal rate of substitution to equal the economy's marginal rate of transformation, that is 1.25. Why is this? Let's see by considering Cindy. Suppose that Cindy's marginal rate of substitution is 1.1. This means that if she were asked to give up 1 litre of blackcurrant juice, she would need 1.1 litres of apple juice to make her indifferent to the swap. If this is the case for Cindy, B is not allocatively efficient. For at B society could give up 1 litre of blackcurrant juice and produce 1.25 litres more apple juice. So society could make 1 less litre of blackcurrant juice, giving 1 litre less to Cindy, and produce 1.25 more litres of apple juice to give her in return. As she needs only 1.1 litres to make up for the lost blackcurrant juice, she will be better off. And no one else will be worse off.

But suppose Cindy's marginal rate of substitution is indeed 1.25. This means that if she is asked to give up 1 litre of blackcurrant juice, she would need 1.25 litres of apple juice to make her indifferent to the swap. If this is the case for Cindy, and all other customers, B is allocatively efficient. For at B, society could give up 1 litre of blackcurrant juice and produce 1.25 litres more apple juice. So society could make 1 litre less blackcurrant juice, giving 1 litre less to Cindy, and give her 1.25 litres of apple juice in return. As she needs 1.25 litres to make up for the lost blackcurrant juice, she will be no better off. So this time we cannot make Cindy better off by reallocating resources. The same applies to everyone else provided their marginal rates of substitution all equal 1.25. So if everyone's marginal

rate of substitution is 1.25, resources are allocated efficiently. The only way we could make someone like Cindy better off is to take juice from someone else and make them worse off.

Will everyone have a marginal rate of substitution of 1.25? This might seem highly unlikely, but it will happen in a perfectly competitive economy. Let's see why. Look again at point B. We saw that if the economy released resources from making 1 litre of blackcurrant juice, it could produce 1.25 litres of apple juice. This means that it takes rather more resources of land, labour and capital to produce an extra litre of blackcurrant juice than to produce an extra litre of apple juice. So it must also cost rather more to produce an extra litre of blackcurrant juice than it costs to produce an extra litre of apple juice. Suppose that it costs 100 pence to buy the resources needed to produce an extra litre of apple juice, then it would cost 125 pence to buy the resources needed to produce an extra 1.25 litres of apple juice. As these same resources could instead produce just 1 litre of blackcurrant juice, so it must cost 125 pence to produce an extra litre of blackcurrant juice.

You can see that we are establishing that if the marginal cost of apple juice is 100 pence, then the marginal cost of blackcurrant juice is 125 pence. Of course, if the marginal cost of a litre of apple juice is, say, 40 pence, then the marginal cost of a litre of blackcurrant juice will be 50 pence. We do not know what the actual marginal costs are, but we can see that the marginal cost of blackcurrant juice divided by the marginal cost of apple juice must be 1.25.

So we have established a ratio for the marginal costs at B. Now as both the industries are in perfect competition, so each has its price equal to its marginal cost. It follows that the ratio of the price of blackcurrant juice to the price of apple juice will be 1.25 : 1. So Cindy, and all other consumers, will face a price ratio of 1.25 : 1. We know that Cindy – and all other consumers – will adjust her consumption of the two goods until her marginal rate of substitution equals the price ratio that she faces (see Fig. 8.7 for an explanation of this result). So she will end up with a marginal rate of substitution equal to 1.25. So will all other consumers. Consequently, we will have an efficient allocation of resources.

How Taxes Destroy Allocative Efficiency

This result of an efficient allocation of resources holds if there are no taxes on either good. What happens if the government imposes a tax on, say, blackcurrant juice? This will force up the price that Cindy and others have to pay, so they will tend to buy less blackcurrant juice, and they will tend to buy more apple juice instead. So production will move along the production possibility frontier from point B on Fig. 19.12. Let's assume production settles down at point D. The production possibility curve is flatter here and actually has a slope of –1. So the marginal rate of transformation has fallen and is now equal to 1. This means that the ratio of the marginal cost of blackcurrant juice to the marginal cost of apple juice is now 1 : 1. So the relative prices set by producers are now 1 : 1. In other words, the two juices now have equal prices set by producers.

But, of course, there is a tax on blackcurrant juice. So Cindy – like other consumers – finds that the two prices she faces are not equal. Cindy and other consumers will settle down consuming the two juices in such a way that their marginal rates of substitution equal the relative prices they face. As these are not equal to the relative prices set by producers, so they are not equal to the marginal rate of transformation. As Cindy and other consumers have marginal rates of substitution that are not equal to the marginal rate of transformation, so resources are no longer allocated efficiently.

Let's clarify this with an example. Suppose that at D the marginal cost of each juice is 50 pence a litre, and suppose each industry has that price for producers. And suppose the tax on blackcurrant juice is 50 pence a litre. Then Cindy faces a price of 50 pence a litre for apple juice and 100 pence a litre for blackcurrant juice. She adjusts her consumption so that the last 100 pence spent on each juice brings the same satisfaction. So her last 2 litres of apple juice bring her the same satisfaction as her last 1 litre of blackcurrant juice. But notice that, at D, society could give up 1 litre of apple juice and produce 1 litre more blackcurrant juice. Indeed it could give up two 2 litres of apple juice and produce 2 litres more blackcurrant juice. If it did so, it could make Cindy better off, for it could cut apple juice production by 2 litres – giving her 2 litres less apple juice – and it could give her 2 litres of blackcurrant juice in return. She will be better off, as she needs only 1 litre of blackcurrant juice to make up for the loss of 2 litres of apple juice, and no one else will be worse off. So the situation is not allocatively efficient.

What has happened is that we started with an efficient allocation. The allocation has now been distorted by the tax on blackcurrant juice. In the eyes of Cindy – and all other consumers – things would improve if the economy reverted to producing less apple juice and more blackcurrant juice. So consumers lose out when resources are reallocated following the tax on one good. But what happens if the government taxes all goods by an equal percentage?

Taxing all Goods and Services

To see what happens when all goods and services are taxed at the same rate, remember that we want the marginal rate of transformation to equal the marginal rate of substitution. The marginal rate of transformation equals the marginal cost of blackcurrant juice divided by the marginal cost of apple juice, so it also equals the price of blackcurrant juice set by the blackcurrant juice industry divided by the price of apple juice set by the apple juice industry. In our starting position, the marginal rate of transformation was 1.25. Cindy and other consumers adjusted their consumption patterns so that their marginal rates of substitution equalled the price of blackcurrant juice faced by them divided by the price of apple juice faced by them. With no taxes, the prices faced by consumers equalled the prices set by producers, so the price to consumers of blackcurrant juice was 1.25 times the price to consumers of apple juice, and each consumer settled with a marginal rate of substitution of 1.25.

When one good was taxed, the ratio of prices set by producers – which equals the marginal rate of transformation – became different from the ratio of prices faced by consumers – which equals each consumer's marginal rate of substitution. So the marginal rate of transformation no longer equalled consumers' marginal rates of substitution. But suppose the government taxed each good by the same percentage, say 100 per cent for simplicity. Then the prices faced by consumers for each item would be double the prices set by producers for each good, but the ratio of the prices faced by consumers – which will equal their marginal rates of substitution – will be same as the ratio of the prices set by producers – which equals the marginal rate of transformation. So the marginal rate of transformation will still equal everyone's marginal rate of substitution. So it seems that we will still have allocative efficiency. This is not wholly surprising. If the government taxes everything, resource

A Global Externality

TIME, 2 JANUARY 1989

Feeling the heat

Michael D Lemonick

FOR more than a decade, many scientists have warned that cars and factories are spewing enough gases into the atmosphere to heat up the earth in a greenhouse effect that could eventually produce disastrous climatic changes.

Carbon dioxide is released in large quantities when wood and such fossil fuels as coal, oil and natural gas are burned. As society industrialized, coal-burning factories began releasing CO_2 faster than plants and oceans, which absorb the gas, could handle it. In the early 1900s, people began burning oil and gas at prodigious rates. And increasing population led to the widespread cutting of trees in less developed countries. These trees are no longer available to soak up excess CO_2, and whether they are burned or left to rot, they instead release the gas. By the late 1800s atmospheric CO_2 had risen to between 280 and 290 parts per million. Today it stands at 350 p.p.m., and by 2050 it could reach 500 to 700 p.p.m., higher than it has been in millions of years.

By far the most efficient and effective way to spur conservation is to raise the cost of fossil fuels. Current prices fail to reflect the very real environmental costs of pumping carbon dioxide into the air. The answer is a tax on CO_2 emissions – or a CO_2 user fee, if that is a more palatable term. The fee need not raise a country's overall tax burden; it could be offset by reductions in income taxes or other levies.

Imposing a CO_2 fee would not be as difficult as it sounds. It is easy to quantify how much CO_2 comes from burning a gallon of [petrol], a ton of coal or a cubic yard of natural gas. Most countries already have [petrol] taxes; similar fees, set according to the amount of CO_2 produced, could be put on all fossil-fuel sources. At the same time, companies could be given credits against their CO_2 taxes if they planted trees to take some of the CO_2 out of the air.

A user fee would have benefits beyond forcing a cutback in CO_2 emissions. The fuels that generate carbon dioxide also generate other pollutants, like soot, along with nitrogen oxides and sulphur dioxide, the primary causes of acid rain. The CO_2 tax would be a powerful incentive for consumers to switch from high-CO_2 fuels, such as coal and oil, to power sources that produce less CO_2, notably natural gas. When burned, methane generates only half as much CO_2 as coal, for example, in producing the same amount of energy....

© 1989 Time Inc. Magazine Company. Reprinted with permission.

The amount of carbon dioxide (CO_2) in the earth's atmosphere has been increasing and continues to do so.

In the late nineteenth century, atmospheric carbon dioxide was between 280 and 290 p.p.m.; in the late 1980s, it was 350 p.p.m.; by 2050, it could reach 500 to 700 p.p.m.

The most effective method for controlling the greenhouse effect is to impose a tax on carbon dioxide emissions.

The marginal private cost of generating electricity by using fossil fuels is the curve *MPC* in Figs. 1(a) and 2(a). The marginal cost of generating electricity using solar power is the curve *MC* in Figs. 1(b) and 2(b). The supply curve of electricity is *S* and the demand curve is *D* in Figs 1(c) and 2(c).

The power generated by solar energy has no externalities.

Generating power by using fossil fuel creates a carbon dioxide buildup with a possible greenhouse effect that imposes potentially large social costs. The marginal social cost of generating electricity using fossil fuels, including the external costs of the greenhouse effect, is the curve *MSC* in Figs. 1(a) and 2(a).

With no intervention (Fig. 1), equilibrium occurs at price P_0 and the quantity Q_0; only fossil fuels are used; the marginal social cost is MSC_0, which exceeds the price P_0; there is allocative inefficiency – too much electricity is generated.

If a CO_2 tax is imposed equal to the external costs (Fig. 2), fossil fuel producers of electricity face costs shown by the curve labelled $MPC + tax = MSC$.

The market supply curve becomes the curve labelled $S + tax$.

Equilibrium occurs at price P_1 and quantity Q_1; Q_F is produced by fossil fuels and Q_S by solar energy; marginal social cost is MSC_1, which equals the price P_1; allocative efficiency is achieved.

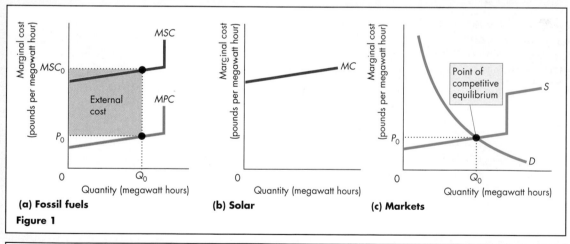

(a) Fossil fuels   **(b) Solar**   **(c) Markets**

Figure 1

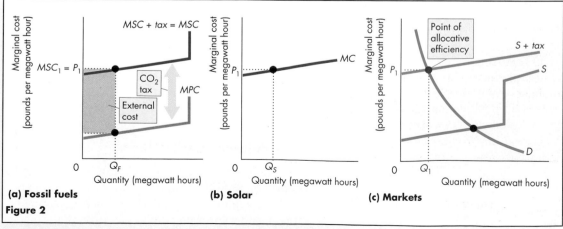

(a) Fossil fuels   **(b) Solar**   **(c) Markets**

Figure 2

allocation may not be drastically affected and could still be efficient.

This approach to the problem seems to suggest that the best way for the government to raise money with taxes on expenditure is through a tax rather like value added tax (VAT) which applies to a wide variety of goods and services. But we would want no exemptions and no specially high taxes on particular goods. So why don't governments follow the analysis outlined here and tax everything at the same rate? Why do they persist with zero taxes on some goods and services and very high rates on others? We will give five reasons.

1. Externalities – we know that governments may want high taxes on goods whose production or consumption generates external costs. This explains the high tax on petrol.

2. Equity – governments may be willing to accept allocative inefficiency if they feel it is helpful to the poor to have low tax rates on essentials such as food.

3. In reality not all industries are perfectly competitive. Accordingly, we would not have an efficient allocation with no taxes and so we would not have one if everything was taxed at exactly equal percentages.

4. One item we all consume is leisure, which we pay for by working fewer hours than we might and so having less money to spend on consumption than we might. It is not practicable to measure everyone's leisure time and tax it, so we don't tax leisure. But it is most unlikely that we would secure an efficient allocation of resources if all goods and services except leisure were taxed at one rate while leisure was tax-free. A possible strategy in this situation would be to tax heavily those goods and services which are complementary to leisure – such as sports goods, garden tools and entertainment.

5. The government may tax alcohol and tobacco at high rates partly because it feels they are bad for people who have become addicted to them and need high taxes to deter high consumption. Admittedly these goods may also generate some external costs – such as drunken and disorderly behaviour and passive smoking – which would be an additional argument for high taxes.

◆ ◆ ◆ ◆ We have now reviewed many aspects of the government sector. In the next chapter, we're going to study a further range of government actions – interventions in markets for goods and services in which there are monopoly and cartel elements.

SUMMARY

The Government Sector

The government sector of the UK economy consists of some 10,000 separate organizations employing over 5 million people and spending almost 44 per cent of all the income generated in the country. The government share of the economy has grown sharply in the twentieth century.

When economists study political behaviour, their main focus is on positive matters – on what *is* and how the political system works – not on what *ought* to be and how the political system *ought* to function. Government economic actions stem from market failure or the redistribution of income and wealth. Market failure arises chiefly with public goods, externalities, imperfect information, and monopolies and cartels.

There are two broad approaches to the economic analysis of government. Public interest theories regard government as an agent that operates in the public interest to achieve allocative efficiency. Public choice theories regard the government as operating in a political marketplace in which politicians, bureaucrats and voters interact. The public choice view believes that government failure to achieve allocative efficiency is as real a possibility as market failure. (pp. 510–512)

The Political Marketplace

The political marketplace has three types of actor – voters, politicians and bureaucrats. Voters are the consumers of the political process, paying taxes and expressing demands through voting, party contributions and lobbying. Public choices are made by politicians. Politicians seek election, and to be elected they need the support of a majority of voters which they can secure by appealing to the median voter. As parties seek to appeal to the median voter, their policies resemble each other. (pp. 512–514)

Public Goods

Pure public goods, such as defence, display non-rivalry and non-excludability. Non-rivalry means one person's consumption does not reduce the amount available for others to consume. Non-excludability means no one can be kept from sharing the consumption of such a good even if they refuse to help towards its cost.

If public goods were provided privately, there would be a free-rider problem. Individuals have little incentive to pay for a good or service if their payment has little or no effect on the quantity of the product they consume. As it pays everyone to free ride, a private producer of a public good might get little or no revenue from consumers. So few units of the public good will be produced. In contrast, the government can provide a public good, paying for it out of taxation. People will vote for the necessary taxes if the net benefit is positive. Although the government can provide more of a public good than a private producer, it does not necessarily produce an allocatively efficient amount. Government services are provided by agencies run by bureaucrats who, it is argued, seek to maximize their budgets. If voters are well-informed, politicians will not be elected if they levy taxes in excess of the amount needed to maximize net benefit. But if voters are rationally ignorant,

they may approve excessive budgets sought by bureaucrats. (pp. 514–523)

Externalities

An externality arises when the activity of production or consumption has an effect on the costs or utility of a producer or consumer who is not directly concerned with the activity. An externality may take the form of a cost or a benefit. When external costs are present, allocative efficiency requires a fall in output, and when external benefits are present, allocative efficiency requires an increase in output. Governments can attempt to deal with externalities by establishing clear private property rights and encouraging bargaining negotiations between the parties concerned, by using taxes and subsidies, or by regulations. (pp. 523–531)

Why Tax Rates Vary

Taxes on expenditure create deadweight losses whose size depends on the elasticity of demand and supply. If there is a choice between taxing two goods whose elasticities of supply are equal, then taxing the one with the more inelastic demand will minimize the deadweight loss from taxation.(pp. 532–534)

Taxes and the Allocation of Resources

In an economy with no market failure, there will be an efficient allocation of resources. But if taxes are levied on some goods and services and not others, there will be an inefficient allocation of resources. Taxing all goods and services at the same rate could restore allocative efficiency. But it could do so only if leisure were also taxed, and taxing leisure is not feasible. (pp.534–540)

KEY ELEMENTS

Key Terms

REVIEW QUESTIONS

1 What is market failure?

2 What are the sources of market failure that result in government action?

3 What is a pure public good? Give an example.

4 What is the free-rider problem? How does government action help to overcome it?

5 Who are the three groups of actors in the political marketplace?

6 What is the principle of minimum differentiation?

7 Explain the median voter theorem.

8 Why might bureaucrats be budget-maximizers?

9 Why might the level of public goods provision exceed the efficient level?

10 What is an externality? Why does it cause market failure?

11 Give three examples of externalities.

12 Describe the main methods used by governments to tackle the problem of externalities.

13 Why does the government tax some goods and not others?

14 Why would a tax on just some goods cause an inefficient allocation?

PROBLEMS

1 A community of nine people, identified by the letters A to I, have strong but differing views about a local factory that is polluting the atmosphere. Some of them work at the factory and don't want the government to take any action against it, while others want to see the imposition of a huge tax based on the scale of the pollution. The preferences of each person concerning the scale of the tax that should be imposed are as follows:

Person	Tax rate (per cent of firm's profit)
A	100
B	90
C	80
C	70
D	60
E	0
F	0
G	0
H	0
I	0

Suppose there are two political parties competing for office in this community. What tax rate will the parties propose?

2   The table below gives information about a sewage disposal system that a city of 1 million people is considering installing. Assume that all citizens value the marginal benefits in accordance with the figures that are shown in the table for one person:

Capacity (thousands of litres a day)	Marginal private benefit to one person (pounds)	Total cost (millions of pounds a day)
0		0
	 50	
1		5
	 40	
2		15
	 30	
3		30
	 20	
4		50
	 10	
5		75

a   What is the capacity that achieves maximum net benefit?

b   How much will each person have to pay in taxes in order to pay for the efficient capacity level?

c   What are the total and net benefits at the efficient level?

3   Your local authority is contemplating improvements to its system of traffic lights. By installing a computer linked to sensors at all the major intersections, the council believes it can change the timing of the signal changes to improve the flow of traffic. The bigger the computer it buys, the better the job it can do, and the more sensors it installs, the more intersections it can monitor and the faster the overall traffic flow that will result. The councillors who are working on the proposal want to determine the scale of the system that will win them the most votes. The bureaucrats in the city traffic department want to maximize the budget. Suppose you are an economist observing this public choice. Your job is to calculate the scale of provision of this public good that maximizes net benefit – that achieves allocative efficiency.

a   What data would you need to reach your own conclusions?

b   What does the public choice theory predict about the scale of provision that will be chosen?

c   How could you, as an informed voter, attempt to influence the choice?

4   A chemical factory dumps waste in a river. Damage is done to the local fish stock and membership fees at a nearby fishing club are lowered by the following amounts:

Output of chemical plant (tonnes per day)	Lost fees to fishing club (pounds per day)
0	0
100	10
200	30
300	70
400	210

Each tonne of chemical earns the factory a profit of 50 pence. At present the factory is producing 400 tonnes per day.

a   What would be the efficient output level of the firm?

b   How might private property rights be used in this situation?

4   Two countries, Greenhaven and Smokehole, have identical marginal private benefit and marginal private cost schedules for electric power generated by burning coal. These schedules are as follows:

Quantity (millions of megawatts a day)	Marginal private benefit (pounds)	Marginal private cost (pounds)
0	14	1
1	12	1
2	10	1
3	8	2
4	6	3
5	5	5
6	4	6
7	3	7
8	2	8
9	1	9
10	0	10

The people of Greenhaven believe that each megawatt generated has a marginal social cost equal to twice its marginal private cost and the government of Greenhaven imposes an electricity tax that achieves allocative efficiency. The people of Smokehole believe there are no social costs of producing electric power and there is no government intervention in the market for electricity.

a How much electricity is generated in Greenhaven?

b What is the price of electricity in Greenhaven?

c How much tax revenue does the government of Greenhaven collect on the generation of electricity?

d How much electricity is generated in Smokehole?

e What is the price of electricity in Smokehole?

5 Explain why the government subsidizes colleges and universities, permitting students to attend for tuition fees below the full cost of the education provided.

CHAPTER 20

INDUSTRY
POLICY

After studying this chapter you will be able to:

◆ Explain how governments intervene in the market

◆ Distinguish between the public interest and capture theories of government intervention in the marketplace

◆ Explain how regulation affects prices, outputs, profits and the distribution of the gains from trade

◆ Explain how public ownership affects outputs, costs and prices and the distribution of the gains from trade

◆ Describe the main elements of competition policies in the United Kingdom and the European Union

◆ Explain why both the United Kingdom and the European Union have regional policies

SOME VERY IMPORTANT GOODS AND SERVICES ARE PROVIDED BY NATURAL monopolies. Water, gas and electricity are examples. Each of these industries is regulated by government agencies. There are other government agencies which regulate industries where there is no natural monopoly. For example, the Securities and Investment Board supervises all firms engaging in financial investment. Why do we regulate some industries and not other? Whose interest is served by regulation – the consumer or the producer?

◆ ◆ From the 1940s to the 1980s, many industries were publicly owned – the nationalized industries. In the 1980s many nationalized industries such as British Gas, British Telecom and the electricity boards were sold to private owners. Why did governments nationalize some industries and not others? Why have so many nationalized industries been privatized?

Public Interest or Special Interests?

◆ ◆ In the United Kingdom and European Union there is a commission to look at monopolies and oligopolies. Whose interests does it serve? ◆ ◆ There are UK and EU laws to control restrictive practices. Do these laws always serve consumer interests, or do they sometimes serve the interest of producer groups – special interests? ◆ ◆ The UK government and the European Union also operate regional policies which try to alter the location of industry. Why do we need regional policies? And whose interests do they serve?

◆ ◆ ◆ ◆ This chapter considers how governments regulate, control and influence trading in markets for goods and services. We describe the ways in which governments intervene and identify who stands to gain and lose from their intervention. As this intervention is supplied by politicians and bureaucrats, we look at the economic behaviour of these groups.

Market Intervention

There are three main ways in which the government intervenes with producers in the marketplace to influence *what, how* and *for whom* various goods and services are produced:

◆ Nationalization
◆ Regulation of individual industries
◆ Monopoly, merger and restrictive practice policy

Nationalization

Nationalization is the act of taking a company into public – that is government – ownership. In the United Kingdom, a nationalized company owned by the central government is called a **public corporation**. The government which undertook most nationalization was the Labour government of 1945–1950 when nationalization was a major part of Labour Party policy. Generally the government set up a public corporation by acquiring most – if not all – of the companies in an industry to create a national monopoly where there had been none before. So public corporations were often referred to as **nationalized industries**. The main industries that were substantially nationalized in the 1940s were the railways, road freight, coal, electricity and gas. In 1967, a later Labour government nationalized the steel industry. Some publicly owned businesses are owned by local authorities. The main examples have been water boards and some public transport companies.

In recent years there has been a tendency to privatize public corporations. **Privatization** is the process of selling a public corporation to private shareholders. This policy has been associated with the Conservatives. It was started under Edward Heath's 1970–1974 government, which sold off the travel agent Thomas Cook and state-owned public houses around Carlisle. It gathered pace in the 1980s when many industries were sold, notably British Airways, British Telecom, the National Bus Company (which was split into many firms), British Steel, and the gas, electricity and (except in Scotland) water industries. The most important nationalized industries which survived in spring 1995 were parts of British Coal along with British Rail and the Post Office.

Regulation of Individual Industries

A principal reason why many industries were nationalized was so that the government could influence their prices and products. But governments can influence an industry without nationalizing it by means of regulation. **Regulation** consists of rules administered by an agency that is set up by the government – or the European Union – to regulate some particular industry. The agency is empowered to restrict economic activity in various ways. The most usual methods are determining prices, product standards and types, and the conditions under which new firms may enter an industry. Occasionally the regulation over new entrants is very severe.

One UK instance of strict entry controls occurs with independent broadcasting. In this industry the regulatory body issues franchises to selected firms, and without these franchises or permits no firm may enter the industry. Another instance has occurred with scheduled air services in the European Union – though the European Union itself is trying to stop this. The practice has been for pairs of governments to reach agreement on services between their countries. Typically governments have permitted only one airline from each country to operate on each route.

Regulation in the United Kingdom has a long history and gathered pace in the nineteenth century. After 1873, for example, all proposals to amalgamate railway companies had to be approved by the Railway and Canal Commission which refused many applications. Railway fares were also regulated after 1893.

Regulation was applied to other industries where local monopolies are always likely – water, gas, electricity and tramways. In the early decades of the twentieth century regulation was extended to banking – notably in 1918 in the wake of widespread amalgamations – and also to buses – notably with the introduction in 1930 of a rule regulating which companies could operate which routes. Since that time, regulation has spread to such industries as financial services, airlines and broadcasting.

Regulation has also been extended to cover some of the monopolies that have resulted from the recent privatization programme. For example, the Office of Gas Supply (OFGAS) regulates British Gas while the Office of Telecommunications (OFTEL) regulates British Telecom. These agencies are chiefly concerned with prices. In most cases, the privatized firms are allowed to increase their prices by less than the rate of inflation. In effect, they are told their prices must rise by no more each year than $RPI - X$ where RPI is the retail prices index which indicates how rapidly prices are rising and X is a figure deemed reasonable by the regulatory body. The fact that these companies must raise their prices by less than the rate of inflation indicates a belief that they should enjoy above-average increases in productivity. Each agency can alter X when it feels it is reasonable to do so. Apart from regulating prices, the agencies also seek to ensure that the companies do not exploit their monopoly position in any other ways.

There has lately been a tendency towards deregulation in the United Kingdom, the European Union and elsewhere. **Deregulation** is the process of removing restrictions on prices, product standards and types, and entry conditions. In the United Kingdom, restrictions on entry into most inter-city bus routes were lifted in 1980 while restrictions on entry for most other bus routes were lifted in 1986. Also, British Telecom's monopoly powers in telecommunications have been reduced as Mercury has been authorized to enter this industry.

Within the European Union there have been important moves to deregulate scheduled air services. The traditional agreements not only limited most routes to two carriers but also regulated the fares and encouraged the two operators to share the traffic and the route revenues equally. The result was high fares. Existing operators had little or no incentive to lower the fares and new entrants were kept away. But the European Union has been trying to reduce the regulation. It has persuaded governments to end all regulations on traffic and revenue shares, so that the two airlines on any route now have some incentive to compete with each other. They are also allowed to reduce their fares on a route unless both the governments object. In addition, the European Union is encouraging governments to allow more than two airlines to compete on each route.

Monopoly, Merger and Restrictive Practice Policy

By creating public corporations and by using agencies, governments can exert influence in particular industries. But governments like to have additional powers that enable them to interfere with any industry from time to time. So the UK government has devised some quite different intervention techniques.

One of these was the establishment in 1948 of a commission – now called the Monopolies and Mergers Commission – with the power to investigate any monopolies, and many oligopolies, as well as proposed mergers that would result in monopolies or oligopolies. The commission cannot itself control existing firms or prevent mergers, but it can recommend that the government takes action such as requiring monopolists to set lower prices, or forbidding proposed mergers.

Another way of intervening in industry is the use of legislation. Legislation to influence market behaviour takes the form of laws that define illegal conduct. These laws are then enforced through the courts. The main use of this approach in the United Kingdom concerns restrictive practices. A **restrictive practice** is an agreement between two firms not to compete in some respect such as price, output levels, or quality. Such practices are illegal unless they are found by the Restrictive Practices Court to be in the public interest, perhaps because they prevent unemployment or help exports.

Legislation affecting UK firms is not the sole prerogative of the UK government. The European Union also has laws governing industrial behaviour and these are backed up by the European Court of Justice. The laws chiefly concern businesses which use monopoly power or restrictive practices to affect the flow of trade between EU countries. The European Court can impose fines on firms that amount to 10 per cent of their annual turnover.

We have now seen that there are various ways in which governments can intervene in and so regulate the activities of firms. Let us next consider why governments intervene.

The Economic Theory of Regulation

In this section we will develop a theory that will help us understand why the government and the European Union intervene in and so regulate the market economy and that will help us work out the effects of their actions. Before we develop that model, though, we need to identify the gains and losses that government intervention can create. These gains and losses are the changes in the consumer surplus and producer surplus that arise when there is a change in the price of a good or a service, or a change in the quantity demanded. Consumer surplus and producer surplus were explained in some detail in Chapters 7 and 12, so we will now just give a brief overview of them.

Surplus and Their Distribution

Consumer surplus is the difference between the maximum amount that consumers are willing to pay and the amount that they actually do pay for a given quantity of a good or service. It is the gain from trade accruing to consumers. It can be represented on diagrams as the area below the demand curve and above the price line. *Producer surplus* is the difference between the producer's revenue and the opportunity cost of production. It is the gain from trade accruing to producers. It can be represented on diagrams as the area above the marginal cost curve and below the price line. **Total surplus** is the sum of consumer surplus and producer surplus. Allocative efficiency is achieved when total surplus is at a maximum because then it is not possible to make anyone better off without making someone else worse off.

We saw in Fig. 12.8 that total surplus is at a maximum under perfect competition. Compared with a perfectly competitive industry, a profit-maximizing monopoly will produce less output and sell it at a higher price. The increase in price and lower output result in a substantial fall in consumer surplus. To offset against this there will be an increase in producer surplus, but the increase in producer surplus will be less than the fall in consumer surplus. The net loss is the deadweight loss of monopoly.

Two important points emerge from this discussion which are central to a discussion of regulation. First, the public interest requires that industries should set the price that would be set if they were in a state of perfect competition. You will recall from Chapter 11 that perfectly competitive firms adjust their output to the level where their marginal cost equals the price they face. Equivalently, in a perfectly competitive industry, the price equals the marginal cost of production. Second, there is a tension between the public interest, which requires a maximizing of total surplus, and the monopolist's interest of maximizing monopoly profit and producer surplus.

The Basis of the Theory of Regulation

We can now develop the economic theory of regulation. The economic theory of regulation is part of the broader theory of public choice. You have already met that theory in Chapter 19 and seen the main components of a public choice model. We're going to re-examine the main features of such a model but with an emphasis on the regulatory aspects of government behaviour. We'll examine the demand for government actions, the supply of those actions, and the political equilibrium – the balancing of demands and supplies.

Demand for Regulation

The demand for regulation is expressed through political institutions. Both consumers and producers vote, lobby and campaign for regulations that best further their own interests. None of these activities is costless. Voters incur costs when they acquire information to use in deciding how to vote. Lobbying and campaigning cost time and effort, and they also cost money in the form of contributions to political parties.

Individual consumers and producers demand political action only if the benefit that they receive individually from such action exceeds the costs they incur in obtaining it. This implies that there are four main factors which affect the demand for regulation:

◆ Consumer surplus per buyer
◆ Number of buyers
◆ Producer surplus per firm
◆ Number of firms

The larger the consumer surplus per buyer resulting from regulation, the greater is the demand for regulation by buyers. Also, as the number of buyers increases, so does the demand for regulation. But numbers alone do not necessarily translate into an effective political force. The larger the number of buyers, the greater is the cost of organizing them, so the demand for regulation does not increase proportionately with the number of buyers. So for a given total consumer surplus, the fewer consumers who share it the larger is the demand for the regulation that creates it.

The larger the producer surplus per firm arising from a particular regulation, the larger is the demand for that regulation by firms. Also, as the number of firms that might benefit from some regulation increases, so does the demand for that regulation. But as in the case of consumers, large numbers do not necessarily mean an effective political force. The larger the number of firms, the greater is the cost of organizing them. So for a given total producer surplus, the fewer the firms that share it, the larger is the demand for the regulation that creates it.

The Supply of Regulation

Regulation is supplied by politicians. As we saw in the last chapter, politicians choose policies that appeal to a majority of voters so that they themselves can achieve and maintain office. Given this objective, we can show that the supply of regulation depends on:

◆ Consumer surplus per buyer
◆ Producer surplus per firm
◆ The number of persons affected

Politicians will supply regulations only if they create consumer surpluses or producer surpluses that are large enough to be noticed and only if the recipients know who is the source of the benefits. Supplying regulations that meet these conditions should secure support for the politicians from the beneficiaries. Also, politicians favour regulations that affect many people, for such regulations have the potential to secure a large number of votes. However, politicians may supply regulations that create large benefits for only a few people if they think the beneficiaries may make donations to their party funds.

Equilibrium Regulation

In equilibrium, the regulations that exist are such that no interest group feels it worth while to use extra resources to press for changes and no group of politicians feels it worth while to offer different regulations. A political equilibrium is not the same as a situation where everyone is in agreement. It is a situation where some lobby groups devote resources to trying to change the regulations that are already in place while other groups devote resources to trying to maintain the existing regulations. But no one feels it is worth while *increasing* the resources devoted to such activities. Another feature of a political equilibrium is that the political parties may not agree with each other. Probably some parties support the existing regulations while others support different regulations. But, in equilibrium, each party gives consistent support for some particular regulations.

What does a political equilibrium look like? There are two theories of political equilibrium: one is called the public interest theory and the other the capture theory. Let's look at these two theories.

Public Interest Theory The **public interest theory of intervention** states that intervention is supplied to satisfy the demand of consumers and producers for the maximization of total surplus – or the attainment of allocative efficiency. Public interest theory predicts that the political process will relentlessly look for deadweight losses and introduce regulations that eliminate them. For example, where monopolies or restrictive practices exist, the political process will introduce price regulation to ensure that output and price are close to their competitive levels.

Capture Theory The **capture theory of intervention** states that the intervention that exists is that which maximizes producer surplus. The key idea behind capture theory is that the cost of intervention is high. So the only intervention that will be supplied by the political process is intervention which increases the surpluses of small groups that are easily identified and have low organization costs. Such intervention will be supplied even if it imposes costs on others, provided those costs are spread so thinly and widely that they do not have negative effects on votes.

Whichever theory of intervention is correct, the political system tends to deliver an amount and type of intervention that best furthers the electoral success of politicians. Since we have seen that producer-oriented and consumer-oriented intervention are in direct conflict with each other, it is clear that the political process cannot satisfy both groups in any particular industry. Only one group can win. This makes the intervention of government a bit like a unique product such as a painting by Rembrandt. There is only one original, and it will be sold to just one buyer. Normally, a unique commodity is sold through an auction to the highest bidder. Equilibrium in government intervention can be thought of in much the same way: the politicians who supply intervention will satisfy the demands of the higher bidder. If the producers' demands concerning regulation offer a bigger return to the politicians, either through votes or party contributions, the producers' interests will be served. If the consumers' demands concerning regulation offer a higher return through numerous votes, the consumers' interests will be served.

R E V I E W

The demand for intervention is expressed by both consumers and producers who spend scarce resources voting, lobbying and campaigning for interventions that best further their own interests. Intervention is supplied by politicians and bureaucrats. Politicians choose actions that appeal to a majority of voters. The intervention that exists is the equilibrium that balances the opposing demand and supply forces. One possible political equilibrium is intervention that achieves allocative efficiency – the public interest theory of intervention. Another possible equilibrium is intervention that maximizes producer surplus – the capture theory of intervention. ◆

We have now completed our study of the economic theory of regulation. Let's next examine the regulation that exists today.

Regulation and Deregulation

To understand regulation, we'll start by looking at the scope of regulation. Then we'll turn to the regulatory process itself and examine how regulators control prices and other aspects of market behaviour. Finally, we'll tackle the more difficult and controversial questions. Why do we regulate some things but not others? Who benefits from the regulation that we have?

The Scope of Regulation

Regulation touches a wide range of economic activity in the United Kingdom. The major regulatory agencies and their responsibilities are noted in Table 20.1. As you can see from the table, the predominant sectors subject to regulation are finance, energy, water and telecommunications.

Local authorities also establish regulations covering a wide range of economic activity. Some of these – for example, regulations of the taxi industry and regulations on land development – have important direct effects on the marketplace. Our analysis of regulation applies with equal force to regulation at the local authority level.

Regulatory agencies have many responsibilities and carry out a variety of tasks. No two agencies have precisely the same range of responsibilities. We will focus here on only one aspect of agency work – which applies to many agencies – namely the regulation of prices.

TABLE 20.1

Regulatory Agencies Operating in the United Kingdom

Agency	Responsibility
Bank of England	**Licenses and regulates all deposit-taking institutions, notably banks and building societies, and has particular responsibility for controlling banks.**
Building Societies Commission	**Exerts general controls over building societies.**
Civil Aviation Authority (CAA)	**Regulates UK airlines, airports and air traffic control.**
Common Agricultural Policy (CAP)	**Set up by the European Union, the CAP dictates the price of many food products.**
Office of Electricity Regulation (OFFER)	**Monitors the electricity companies.**
Office of Electricity Regulation Northern Ireland (OFFER NI)	**Monitors the electricity companies in Northern Ireland.**
Office of Gas Supply (OFGAS)	**Monitors British Gas and authorizes other suppliers.**
Office of Telecommunications (OFTEL)	**Monitors British Telecom and authorizes other suppliers.**
Office of Water Supplies (OFWAT)	**Monitors the water companies of England and Wales.**
Securities and Investment Board (SIB)	**Supervises all firms engaged in financial investment (it has delegated some of its powers to a number of subsidary bodies).**

The Regulatory Process

Although regulatory agencies vary in size and scope and in the detailed aspects of economic life that they control, they have two common features that are relevant to their activities.

First, each agency has bureaucrats. The senior bureaucrats, who are the agencies' key decision makers, are appointed by the government or by the European Union. Other bureaucrats include experts in the industry being regulated. These experts are often recruited from the regulated firms. The salaries of these bureaucrats, and the agencies' other costs, are approved and paid for by the relevant parliament.

Second, each agency adopts a set of operating rules for its controls. When these controls affect prices or other aspects of economic performance, they can be based on well-defined physical and financial accounting procedures that are relatively easy to administer and to monitor.

In a regulated industry, individual firms are free to choose the technology they use in production. But they are not necessarily free to determine the prices at which they will sell their output, the quantities that they will sell, or the markets that they will serve. These matters may be under the control of the regulating agency.

To analyse the way in which regulation works, it is convenient to distinguish between the regulation of natural monopoly and the regulation of cartels. Let's begin with natural monopoly. We'll consider for an example an electricity distribution company which buys electricity from a generating company and then distributes and sells the electricity to homes and businesses.

Natural Monopoly

Natural monopoly is defined in Chapter 12 as an industry in which one large firm can supply the entire market at a lower price than two or more smaller firms can. This large firm is a natural monopoly that enjoys economies of scale. As you know, such a firm operates on the downward-sloping part of its long-run average cost curve. But natural monopolies often find that their short-run average cost curves also slope downward for all likely output levels. We make this assumption for the firm we are now discussing and show its short-run average total cost curve, *ATC*, in Fig. 20.1. The reason *ATC* slopes downward for so

long arises from the fact that the company has a heavy investment in pylons, cables and transformers and so has high total fixed costs. This high total fixed cost means that average fixed cost is very high when output is low. Average fixed cost falls as output rises, and this helps average total cost to fall as output rises.

In Fig 20.1 we also show the company's marginal cost curve, *MC*. We take this to be a horizontal line at 4 pence a unit. This is because we suppose that the company can buy any quantity of electricity it wishes and can deliver it through its cables for 4 pence a unit. In reality it may find that it must pay higher prices for electricity at times of peak

---

FIGURE 20.1

Natural Monopoly: Marginal Cost Pricing

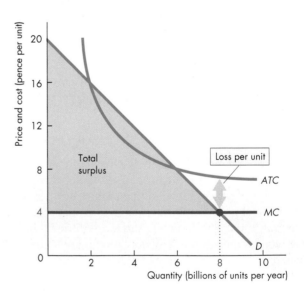

A natural monopoly occurs in an industry where one firm can supply an entire market at a lower price than two or more smaller firms can. The natural monopoly in electricity supply shown here has a demand curve *D*. Marginal costs are constant at 4 pence a unit, as shown by the curve *MC*. Fixed costs are heavy, and the average total cost curve, which includes average fixed cost, is shown as *ATC*. If the supplier followed a marginal cost pricing rule, it would settle where *MC* cuts *D* with a price of 4 pence a unit, with 8 billion units a year being sold. This rule results in the maximum possible total surplus. In the case shown here the surplus is all consumer surplus and is indicated by the green area. The producer makes a loss on each unit indicated by the red arrow. To remain in business, the producer must either use a two-part tariff or receive a subsidy.

demand, and it may eventually reach a stage when its cables are fully loaded so that no more electricity can be handled, but we ignore these possible complications here as they don't affect the main points we wish to make. Finally, Fig. 20.1 marks the demand curve, D, of the company's customers.

Regulation in the Public Interest

How will this electricity monopoly be regulated according to the public interest theory? Recall that in that theory, regulation maximizes total surplus and so achieves allocative efficiency. Allocative efficiency occurs when marginal cost equals price. In the example shown in Fig. 20.1, that outcome occurs if the price is regulated at 4 pence a unit so that 8 billion units a year are sold. Such a regulation is called a marginal cost pricing rule. A **marginal cost pricing rule** makes price equal marginal cost. It maximizes the total surplus in the regulated industry.

In the example shown in Fig. 20.1, the surplus is all consumer surplus and is shown by the area shaded green. Consumer surplus is always shown by the area below the demand curve and above the price, which here is 4 pence a unit. Any producer surplus would be shown by the area above the marginal cost curve and below the price of 4 pence a unit, but there is no producer surplus here because the marginal cost curve is horizontal at the price level of 4 pence a unit.

A natural monopoly that is regulated to charge only a price equal to marginal cost makes an economic loss if its average total cost curve is always falling. This applies to the firm in Fig. 20.1 whose ATC curve is always falling. Why must this firm make a loss if it sets a price of 4 pence a unit equal to marginal cost? To see why, remember that whenever the ATC curve slopes down, the MC curve is below the ATC curve; equivalently, when each extra unit costs less than the average, so that marginal cost is below the average total cost, the average total cost falls whenever extra units are supplied. Because the marginal cost is below the average total cost, the price too must be below the average total cost if price is equal to marginal cost. And if the price – or average revenue – is below the average total cost, the firm makes an economic loss. The difference between price and average total cost is the loss per unit produced.

A privately owned electricity company that was required to use a marginal cost pricing rule would not stay in business for long if the result was a loss. So the situation in Fig. 20.1 cannot be the end of the marginal cost pricing story. How can the company cover its costs and also obey a marginal cost pricing rule?

One possibility is to use a two-part tariff. A **two-part tariff** is a pricing arrangement that results in consumers facing a bill with two parts. For instance, an electricity company may charge all consumers a fixed amount per quarter simply for the privilege of being wired up to its network, and then also charge a certain amount per unit. Thus the company in Fig. 20.1 might charge all consumers a fixed charge of £15 a quarter in addition to the marginal cost price of 4 pence a unit. Some natural monopolies, such as telephone, electricity, gas and water companies, can use a two-part tariff fairly easily. But these companies must take care not to set the first part of the tariff too high, for with a high tariff some customers might not get connected so that the demand for the company's output would fall.

Operating a two-part tariff is much less feasible for companies such as railway companies. When a firm with a falling average total cost curve cannot, or does not, operate a two-part tariff, it can follow a marginal cost pricing rule and cover its total cost only if it receives a subsidy from the government.

How would a two-part tariff or a subsidy affect the total surplus situation as it is depicted in Fig. 20.1? If the company makes good its loss by means of a two-part tariff, it will get extra revenue and so move from having no producer surplus to having a surplus equal to this extra revenue. But this gain to the company will be precisely offset by the loss to consumers, who have to pay the extra tariff, so the total benefits from marginal cost pricing can still be represented by the green triangle.

You might think that a similar story can be told if the loss is made good by a subsidy. Surely this time the electricity company will gain a producer surplus which is offset by the losses felt by those who pay the tax needed to finance the subsidy. But we saw in Chapter 12 that taxes generate a deadweight loss – that is, they reduce consumer and producer surpluses by *more* than the amount of the revenue collected. So the total surplus arising from the electricity company operating marginal cost pricing would now equal the area of the green triangle minus the amount of the deadweight loss associated with the tax used to finance the subsidy.

This analysis suggests that if any loss is to be made good by a subsidy, then it might be better for the monopoly to follow some other pricing rule which resulted in a higher price and hence a lower subsidy. Admittedly a higher price would reduce the total surplus for the electricity industry from the maximum level shown in Fig. 20.1, but a lower subsidy would reduce the tax revenue needed to finance the subsidy and so cut the deadweight loss from the tax used to finance the subsidy. The fall in the deadweight loss on that tax might more than offset the fall in the total surplus in the electricity industry.

The industry could be regulated to set any price above 4 pence a unit. But the most obvious alternative price to consider making it adopt is one which will eliminate the electricity company's loss altogether. Such a regulation is called an average cost pricing rule. An **average cost pricing rule** sets price equal to average total cost. The average cost pricing solution is shown in Fig. 20.2 as the point where the demand curve is cut by the average total cost curve. At this point the electricity company charges 8 pence for each unit sold and sells 6 billion units a year. Notice that the average total cost is also 8 pence a unit here so that the company's price or average revenue of 8 pence a unit equals its average total cost and hence it just breaks even.

With average cost pricing, the consumer surplus is the area shaded green in Fig. 20.2, that is the area between the demand curve and the price of 8 pence a unit. This surplus is much less than in Fig. 20.1 partly because the price is higher and partly because the amount sold is lower. However, there is now some producer surplus as shown by the area shaded blue, that is the area between the marginal cost curve and the price. The producer surplus represents the gains to producers from selling units at a price higher than their marginal – or opportunity – cost. The total surplus is less than it was in the Fig. 20.1 case by the amount represented by the triangle shaded grey. This is the deadweight loss. This loss is the shortfall in total surplus compared with the situation shown in Fig. 20.1. Remember, though, that the Fig. 20.2 situation may be preferable despite this deadweight loss. This is because the electricity company makes a loss in Fig. 20.1 where it is using marginal cost pricing. If the subsidy needed to cover this loss results in a tax that has a deadweight loss larger than the one shown in Fig. 20.2, then the average cost pricing rule is better than the marginal cost pricing rule.

Capturing the Regulator What does the capture theory predict about the regulation of this electricity

FIGURE 20.2

Natural Monopoly: Average Cost Pricing

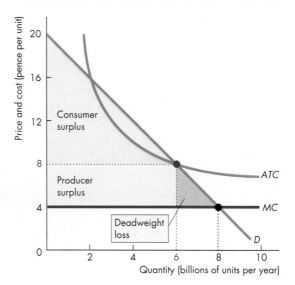

If the natural monopoly followed an average cost pricing rule, it would settle where *ATC* cuts *D* with a price of 8 pence a unit, with 6 billion units a year being sold. In this situation, the company will break even as average total cost equals price. Compared with marginal cost pricing (shown in Fig. 20.1) consumer surplus, indicated by the green area, is much lower, but the company will now have some producer surplus, indicated by the blue area, as its price is now above its marginal cost. However, the total surplus is less than with marginal cost pricing. The difference, or deadweight loss, is shown by the grey triangle.

company? Recall that the capture theory says that regulation serves the interests of the producer. The producer 'captures' – or takes control of – the regulator and sets the regulatory process to work in a way that leads to the maximum possible profit. To find the price that achieves profit maximization, we need to look at the marginal revenue and marginal cost. As you know, a monopoly maximizes profit by producing the output level where marginal revenue equals marginal cost. The monopoly's marginal revenue curve in Fig. 20.3 is the curve *MR*. Marginal revenue equals marginal cost when output is 4 billion units a year and the price is 12 pence a unit. Thus a regulation that best serves the interest of the producer will set the price at 12 pence a unit.

Look carefully at Fig. 20.3. With a price of 12 pence

a unit, the consumer surplus – shown in green – is less than before, while the producer surplus – shown in blue – is greater. The total surplus is smaller than it was in Fig. 20.2 and much smaller than it was in Fig. 20.1. The large grey triangle shows the deadweight loss, that is, the fall in total surplus from the maximum amount that arose in Fig. 20.1. Notice that producer surplus arises because the price exceeds marginal cost. The profit is less than the producer surplus by the amount of fixed costs. The profit is not marked in Fig. 20.3. It is the top part of the blue area, the part between the price of 12 pence a unit and the average total cost of 10 pence a unit.

But how can a producer go about obtaining regulation that results in this monopoly profit-maximizing outcome? To answer this question, we need to look at the way in which agencies determine the level at

FIGURE 20.3

Natural Monopoly: Profit Maximization

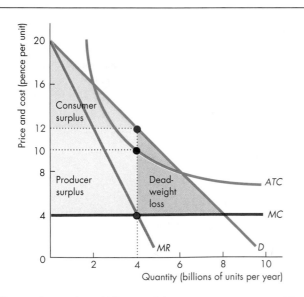

The natural monopoly would like to maximize profit by setting output at 4 billion units a year where marginal revenue (*MR*) equals marginal cost. Selling this output requires a price of 12 pence a unit. Consumer surplus is reduced to the green triangle. The deadweight loss increases to the grey triangle. The monopoly has a producer surplus shown by the blue area. Its profit is only part of the blue area – it is the top part between the average total cost of 10 pence a unit and the price of 12 pence a unit. If the producer can capture the regulator, the outcome will be as shown here.

which to set a regulated price. The key method used is called rate of return regulation.

Rate of Return Regulation **Rate of return regulation** determines a regulated price by setting the price at a level that enables the regulated firm to earn a specified target percentage return on its capital. The target rate of return is determined with reference to the normal rate in competitive industries. This rate of return is part of the opportunity cost of the natural monopolist and is included in the firm's average total cost. By examining the firm's total cost, including the normal rate of return on capital, the regulator attempts to determine the price at which average total cost is covered. Thus rate of return regulation is equivalent to average cost pricing.

In the example that we have just been examining – in Fig. 20.2 – average cost pricing results at a regulated price of 8 pence a unit with 6 billion units a year being sold. Thus rate of return regulation, based on a correct assessment of the producer's average total cost curve, results in a price and quantity that favours the consumer and does not enable the producer to maximize monopoly profit. The special interest group of the producer has failed to capture the regulator, and the outcome will be closer to that predicted by the public interest theory of regulation.

But there is an important feature of many real-world situations that the above analysis does not take into account. This is the ability of the monopoly firm to mislead the regulator about its true costs.

Padding Costs The senior managers of the electricity company may be able to pad the firm's costs by spending part of the firm's revenue on inputs that are not strictly required for the production of the good. By this device, the firm's apparent cost curves exceed the true cost curves. There are various ways in which managers can pad costs. For instance, they can provide themselves with on-the-job luxury in the form of sumptuous office suites, limousines, free tickets for sports events (disguised as public relations expenses), company jets and lavish international travel. Also, they can have lax cost control systems and allow other costs to rise, perhaps by hiring more workers than are strictly needed.

If the electricity company manages to pad its costs and persuade the regulatory agency that its true cost curve is that shown as *ATC (padded)* in Fig. 20.4, then the regulator, applying the normal rate of return principle, will set the price at 12 pence a unit. In this example, the price and quantity will be the same as those under profit-maximizing monopoly. Although it may be impossible for a real-world firm to pad its costs as much as shown in the figure, to the extent that costs can be padded, the apparent average total cost curve will lie somewhere between the true *ATC* curve and *ATC (padded)*. The more a firm can pad its costs, the closer its profit (measured in economic terms) approaches the maximum possible. The economic profit is shaded blue in the figure. But the shareholders of this firm don't receive this economic profit. Instead, it gets used up on the activities used to pad the company's costs.

Public Interest or Capture?

It is not clear whether actual regulation produces prices and quantities that correspond more closely with the predictions of capture theory or with those of public interest theory. One thing is clear, however: price regulation does not usually require natural monopolies to use the marginal cost pricing rule. If it did, most natural monopolies would either need hefty government subsidies to enable them to remain in business, or they would adopt a two-part tariff. Admittedly some natural monopolies do operate a two-part tariff and make a profit. For instance the electricity distribution companies usually levy a fixed 'basic charge' each quarter and then a fixed amount per unit supplied, and British Telecom charges a fixed fee each quarter for connection to its telephone system and then also charges for each call. But in each case the charges per unit supplied are way above the marginal cost.

A test of whether natural monopoly regulation is in the public interest or in the interest of the producer is to examine the rates of return earned by regulated natural monopolies. If, over a period of years, those rates of return are significantly higher than the rates of return in the rest of the economy, then, to some degree, the regulators may have been captured by the producers. If the rates of return in the regulated monopoly industries are similar to those in the rest of the economy, then we cannot be sure whether the regulators have been captured, for we cannot know how far the managers of the regulated firms have padded costs. Most of the UK's regulated monopolies have been in the private sector for too short a time for this test to yield any definitive conclusions.

We've now examined the regulation of natural monopoly. Let's next turn to regulation in oligopolistic industries – to the regulation of cartels.

FIGURE 20.4

Natural Monopoly: Padding Costs

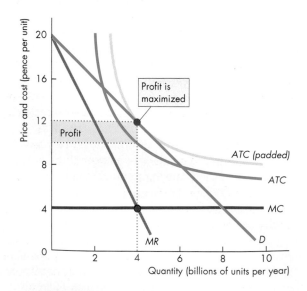

If the electricity company can inflate its costs to *ATC (padded)* and persuade the regulator that these are genuine minimum costs of production, rate of return regulation will result in a price of 12 pence a unit – the profit-maximizing price. To the extent that the producer can pad costs, price will rise, output will fall and deadweight loss will increase.

Cartel Regulation

A *cartel* is a collusive agreement between a number of firms designed to restrict output and achieve a higher profit for the members of the cartel. Formal cartels, with binding agreements between producers, are illegal in the United Kingdom. But it is possible that informal arrangements are made from time to time. Such agreements are most likely to emerge in oligopolistic industries. An *oligopoly* is an industry in which a small number of firms compete with each other. We studied oligopoly in Chapter 13. There we saw that if firms can collude and behave like a monopoly, they can set the same price and sell the same total quantity as a monopoly firm would. But we also discovered that in such a situation, each firm will be tempted to 'cheat', increasing its own output and profit at the expense of the other firms. The result of such cheating on the collusive agreement is the unravelling of the monopoly equilibrium and the emergence of a competitive outcome with zero profit for producers. Such an outcome will benefit consumers at the expense of producers.

How is oligopoly regulated? Does regulation prevent or encourage monopoly practices?

According to the public interest theory, oligopoly is regulated to ensure a competitive outcome. Consider, for example, the market for transporting raspberries from the fields of the Tay valley in the east of Scotland to Glasgow in the west, as illus-

trated in Fig. 20.5. The demand curve for trips is D. The industry marginal cost curve – and the supply curve that would apply if the industry were competitive – is MC. Public interest regulation would set the price of a trip at £40. There would be 150 trips a week.

How would this industry be regulated according to the capture theory? Regulation that is in the producer's interest will set the price at £60 a trip and, to ensure that that price is maintained, will restrict the number of trips to 100 a week. At this output level, the industry marginal revenue will equal the industry marginal cost. So the output level is the one which would be set if all the transport were in the hands of a monopolist. Moreover, the total profit for the industry will equal the profit that a monopolist would secure, and this is the maximum possible level for this industry. How can the monopoly output and price level be achieved if there are, say, 10 transport firms? They can be achieved by issuing a production quota to each firm restricting it to 10 trips a week, so that the total number of trips in a week is 100. Penalties can be imposed to ensure that no single producer violates its quota.

What does regulation of oligopoly do in practice? It is often held that regulation tends to favour the producer but it is hard to demonstrate this. The most useful analysis to undertake is to examine an industry before and after deregulation and see what happens to prices when competition is stimulated by deregulation. But the results are contentious since any fall in prices, or indeed any rise, may be partly attributable to other coincidental factors. For instance, when inter-city bus transport was deregulated in 1980, there was initially a dramatic fall in prices as new firms entered the industry, but then prices rose when some firms were driven out by fierce competition; but the evidence suggests that costs were reduced.[1] It is even harder to draw firm conclusions from the later deregulation of local bus services since many local authority subsidies were reduced at the same time. But it does seem that the subsequent competition caused costs to fall by 14 per cent in real terms between 1985–1986 and 1990–1991.[2]

FIGURE 20.5

Collusive Oligopoly

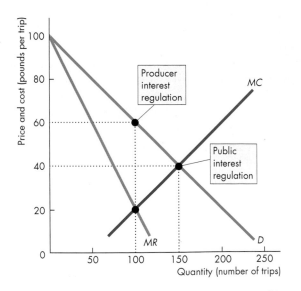

Suppose 10 transport firms use lorries to take raspberries from the Tay valley to Glasgow. The demand curve for transport is *D*, and the industry's marginal cost curve is *MC*. If the industry were to become competitive, *MC* would be the industry supply curve. 150 trips would be made each week at a price of £40. To maximize their combined profits, the 10 producers will demand regulation that restricts entry and holds output to 100 trips a week, so causing the price to be £60 a trip. At this output level the industry marginal revenue will equal industry marginal cost. So the industry's profits are just the same as would apply if all the transport were done by a single monopolist.

---

[1] S. A. Jaffer and D. J. Thompson, 'Deregulating Express Coaches: A Reassessment', *Fiscal Studies*, Vol. 9, 1988.

[2] A. Griffiths and S. Wall, *Applied Economics*, 1993, pp. 249–50.

Regulating Competitive Industries

We have looked at why there is a case for regulating monopolies and oligopolies where cartels may emerge. Curiously, perhaps, one of the most important forms of regulation in Europe today concerns agriculture, which is a highly competitive industry. We looked at agriculture in Chapter 6 and saw that there were arguments in favour of self-sufficiency that originally helped justify regulation at prices above those which would apply in a competitive market with no controls over international trade. Yet the degree of regulation is now of such immense benefit to producers that it must be asked whether, numerous as they are, they have managed to capture the regulator.

As an example of the benefits to producers, consider the period from 1980 to 1988. During those few years, the price of food on world markets outside the European Union fell slightly, yet in this same period the Common Agriculture Policy (CAP) raised food prices inside the European Union by 70 per cent![3]

Making Predictions

Most industries have many consumers and relatively few producers. Even in agriculture the number of producers is trivial compared with the number of consumers. In these cases, public choice theory predicts that regulation will protect producer interests as a small number of people stand to gain a large amount, a situation that makes them fairly easy to organize as a cohesive lobby. Under such circumstances, politicians may be rewarded with party contributions rather than, or as well as, votes. But there are cases where the consumer interest is strong and well organized and so able to prevail.

Deregulation raises one of the hardest questions for economists seeking to understand and make predictions about regulation. Why, for instance, is the European Union trying to reduce the support given to the agriculture industry? Given that the producers gain from regulation and were apparently strong enough to have favourable regulation maintained for so long, what happened in the 1980s to

change the equilibrium to one in which more attention is being given to consumer interests?

One possibility is that regulation has become so costly to consumers and the potential benefits to them from deregulation are so great that the cost of organizing the consumer voice has become one worth paying. Another possibility is the growing environmental concern over intensive farming. Why keep prices so high that they encourage intensive farming? Also, it has become increasingly clear that by maintaining high food production in the European Union, the CAP has reduced imports from other countries. Many of the countries that have lost out on exporting food to the European Union are developing countries which are very poor. As voters in the European Union become more aware of the impact of the CAP on the world's poor, so more votes may be lost by persisting with the policy.

REVIEW

Natural monopolies are regulated in the United Kingdom by various government agencies. Regulation in the public interest would look favourably at marginal cost pricing, perhaps allowing firms with falling average costs to make good their losses with two-part tariffs. Regulation in the interest of the producer would result in output being restricted to the level at which marginal revenue equals marginal cost so that the price of the good or service was equal to that charged by an unregulated monopoly. In practice, regulation often uses rate of return regulation which, if producers can pad their costs, results in the situation intermediate between unregulated profit maximization and public interest regulation. ◆ ◆ Regulation sometimes extends to industries where there are a few firms operating cartels, and sometimes to industries where there are many firms, notably agriculture. Regulation in these industries has tended to favour producers. In recent years, a change in the political equilibrium has led to some deregulation that appears to be in the interests of consumers. ◆

---

[3] M. J. Artis (ed.), *Prest and Coppock's the UK Economy: a Manual of Applied Economics* (12th edn), London, Weidenfeld & Nicolson, 1989, p. 204

Let's now turn to another major method of intervention in markets – public ownership.

Public Ownership

At the beginning of the 1980s there were many public corporations in the United Kingdom. It is perhaps appropriate to divide these into three groups. First, there were industries which were nationalized by Labour governments purely as part of an attempt to get the so-called 'commanding heights' of the economy – that is, key strategic industries – into public ownership. These industries included British Coal, British Steel, the National Bus Company and the National Freight Corporation, of which only part of the first was still publicly owned by 1995. The reasons for nationalizing industries like these are largely political, reflecting a desire to control and plan the economy in detail and a belief in the 'rightness' of public ownership as an ideal.

Second, there were public corporations which arose when private firms were taken into public ownership to rescue them from bankruptcy. These included British Waterways, British Leyland cars (now Rover cars), Rolls-Royce aero engines and British Shipbuilders. Only the first was still in private hands by 1995. It is reasonable for a government to buy a company that would otherwise go bankrupt if the government believes it can in time make that company profitable and sell it off once again. Taxpayers will want to ensure that the price at which the company is sold off will give them a fair return on any public money that has been used to put the company back on its feet. But it should be realized that there may be other gains to the taxpayer. For example, by not allowing British Leyland to go bankrupt the government saved thousands of jobs in that firm, and in the firms which supplied it with components, so the taxpayer was saved from paying out large sums to unemployed people.

Third, and most importantly, there were natural monopolies – the Post Office, the electricity, gas and (except in Scotland) water supply industries, British Telecom, the British Airports Authority and, arguably, British Rail. The reason why it is less clear whether British Rail is a natural monopoly is that while it might be wasteful to have more than one railway track between two towns, different companies could be allowed to operate competing services on the same track. Thus there is a natural monopoly in track ownership but not in operating trains. By 1995, the only industries in this group left in public ownership were the Post Office and British Rail. It should be stressed that in many other European countries most, if not all, of the analogous natural monopolies have long been in public ownership and seem likely to remain so.

Since nationalization has been used as a form of regulating natural monopolies, we must ask what the effects of such a form of control are. We must also ask how a public corporation operates. Let's begin our discussion by considering some alternative patterns of behaviour for such corporations.

An Efficient Public Corporation

One possibility is that a public corporation is operated in a manner that results in economic efficiency – maximization of total surplus. Figure 20.6(a) illustrates this. This figure continues with the example of the electricity company that we analysed in Figs. 20.1 to 20.4. To be efficient, a public corporation must produce an output where price equals marginal cost. In this example, that output level is 8 billion units a year at a price – and marginal cost – of 4 pence a unit. Yet the corporation is facing an average total cost of well over 4 pence a unit. So if the corporation adopts marginal cost pricing it will make a loss.

If it is to set a price of 4 pence a unit, a nationalized industry must either operate a two-part tariff or it must be given a subsidy financed from taxation, just like the privately owned monopolist considered in Fig. 20.1. If the subsidy option is used, there will be a deadweight loss from the tax which is raised to finance the subsidy, and this deadweight loss must be set against the consumer surplus that arises with marginal cost pricing. It is possible that it would be better to require electricity prices to be based on an average cost pricing rule of the sort illustrated in Fig. 20.2.

Let's suppose that the corporation manages to make good its loss by means of a two-part tariff. In that case the situation depicted in Fig. 20.6(a) is the one that maximizes total surplus, so it achieves economic efficiency. But it is not an outcome that is necessarily compatible with the interests of the managers of the public corporation. One model of the behaviour of these managers is suggested by the economic theory of bureaucracy, which we looked at in Chapter 19. What does that model predict about public corporation behaviour?

FIGURE 20.6

Public Enterprise

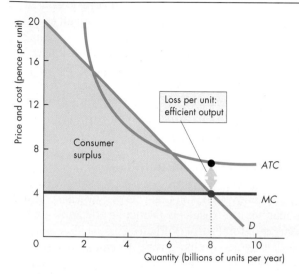

(a) Allocative efficiency

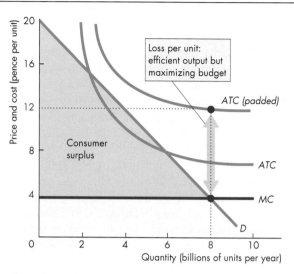

(b) Budget maximization

Part (a) illustrates a public corporation that achieves allocative efficiency in the supply of electricity. Output is at the level where price equals marginal cost, that is 8 billion units a year. At this output, price and marginal cost both equal 4 pence a unit. At this price the enterprise will make a loss and so require a subsidy unless it uses a two-part tariff.

If the managers of the corporation pursue their own interest, maximizing their budget, costs are padded and the maximum possible cost rises to *ATC (padded)* in part (b). If the corporation is constrained to keep price equal to marginal cost, it continues to produce an output that achieves allocative efficiency, but the managers use the first part of a two-part tariff to divert the entire consumer surplus to the firm.

A Bureaucracy Model of Public Enterprise

The basic assumption of the economic theory of bureaucracy is that bureaucrats aim to maximize the budget of their bureau. The equivalent assumption for the managers of a public corporation is that they seek to maximize the budget of their corporation. To work out what the pursuit of this objective implies for the behaviour of a public corporation, we need to know the constraints under which its managers are operating. We will suppose that the managers are required to set their price equal to marginal cost and to avoid a loss by means of a two-part tariff.

Budget Maximization with Marginal Cost Pricing If the bureau maximizes its budget but adopts marginal cost pricing, it will operate in a manner illustrated in Fig. 20.6(b). Its output will remain at the economically efficient level – 8 billion units a year – and it

will sell the output for 4 pence a unit. But the corporation will operate in a manner that does not minimize production cost. It will become inefficient in the sense that its costs will be padded. Its managers will enjoy on-the-job luxury and they will hire more workers than the number strictly required to produce the output. As a result, the average total cost of the corporation will rise to *ATC (padded)*. Will this inefficiency raise marginal cost also? This depends on the actual situation. If the corporation always requires more workers than a profit-maximizing firm would hire, marginal cost would rise. But if it simply employs extra workers who stand idle much of the time, marginal cost could fall as they could be brought into action when output rose. For simplicity, we have assumed that marginal cost is not affected.

To what extent can the corporation pad its costs? The answer can be taken as the maximum amount that the buyers of electricity can be made to pay in the first part of the two-part tariff it needs to break even. This amount is the total consumer surplus. That consumer surplus is the area beneath the demand curve and above the marginal cost curve. You can work out how big it is by using the usual formula for the area of the triangle – half base times height. The base of this triangle is 8 billion units a year and its height is 16 pence, so the consumer surplus is £640 million. This is the surplus people get by consuming electricity at 4 pence a unit. But if they have to pay more than £640 million in connection fees to consume electricity at all, they will not connect and the corporation will lose all its custom. Spread over 8 billion units, £640 million gives a loss of 8 pence a unit, the amount shown in the figure. But this loss will be covered with a two-part tariff.

Incidentally, if the corporation's loss is made good by a tax-financed subsidy rather than a two-part tariff, padded costs will have to be a shade lower. The upper limit to the tax burden that a democratic government could extract from its taxpayers – who also consume the corporation's product – would be £640 million. But we know that the total burden of a tax on taxpayers is larger than the sum raised because of the additional deadweight loss. So if the total burden is £640 million, the amount raised will be rather less. This smaller amount must be spread over 8 billion units and the subsidy per unit will be rather less than 8 pence a unit.

Compromise Outcomes

Each of the two situations that we have just examined – Fig. 20.6(a) and (b) – results in an efficient output level of 8 billion units. These are efficient outcomes because in each case total surplus is maximized. But the positions are extreme ones because in one much of the surplus accrues to consumers while in the other the whole surplus accrues to producers.

Consider Fig. 20.6(a). This figure shows a consumer surplus of £640 million and no producer surplus. In reality the picture for consumers is rather worse than this since, in addition to the price of 4 pence shown, they have to pay the first part of a two-part tariff. However, the amount they lose by paying this tariff is precisely offset by an equal value gain to the producer. The producer now receives a producer surplus because the corporation receives that amount in excess of marginal cost (the reasoning here is exactly the same as that outlined for Fig. 20.1).

Next consider Fig. 20.6(b). Here the consumer surplus of £640 million is precisely offset by the first-part tariff of £640 million. But producers receive that £640 million in addition to their revenue from the price of 4 pence a unit. The producer surplus would be zero if the only revenue came from the price of 4 pence a unit, so the producer surplus is £640 million with the two-part tariff.

In general, to achieve any particular distribution – or redistribution – of the gains from trade, agents must incur costs. To achieve the outcome of Fig. 20.6(a), political parties and voters must incur costs of organization in order to press for and secure the highest possible consumer benefits which result if the corporation keeps its costs to the lowest possible. To achieve the outcome of Fig. 20.6(b) producers must organize and influence the political process in order to achieve their best interests – which means not having their padded costs controlled.

When the costs of political organization and the efficient degree of voter ignorance are taken into account, the actual outcome for the behaviour of a public enterprise is likely to lie somewhere between the extremes that we've considered. There will be tendency for the corporation to pad its budget, but not to the extent shown in Fig. 20.6(b). There will be a tendency for consumer interest to have some effect, but not to the degree shown in Fig. 20.6(a). The basic prediction concerning a public corporation, then, is that to the extent that its costs are padded, it will be less efficient than the profit-maximizing private firm.

Public Corporations in Reality

So far, we've considered only model public corporations that pursue either the consumer or the producer interest or some compromise of the two. How do actual public corporations behave? Several studies have been directed to answering this question. One of the most fruitful ways of approaching the question is to compare public and private enterprises in which, as far as possible, other things are equal. There are two well-known and well-studied cases for which other things do seem to be fairly equal. One is Canada's public and private railways – Canadian National and Canadian Pacific. The other is from Australia, which has two domestic airlines, one private and the other public, that fly almost identical routes at almost identical times every day. Economists have studied the costs of these similar enterprises and concluded that each of the publicly owned enterprises operates with a cost structure that is significantly higher than that of the corresponding private firm. In the case of the Canadian railways the estimated difference was 14 per cent.[4]

Some related evidence for the United Kingdom comes from a study of refuse collection. Until the 1980s, local authorities generally employed their own workers to collect rubbish, so that rubbish collection could be seen as handled by public sector producers. But from 1980 many local authorities started to allow private firms collect rubbish if they could do it cheaper. In many cases private firms took the job away from local authorities, while in others local authorities managed to cut their costs radically. Overall, in local authorities where private firms were allowed to compete, costs fell by about 20 per cent between 1984 and 1988.[5]

Privatization

Largely because of an increasing understanding of how bureaucracies work and of the inefficiency of publicly operated enterprises, there has been a worldwide move to sell off public corporations. This move gathered pace in the 1980s. It was particularly strong in the United Kingdom where Margaret Thatcher's enthusiasm for reducing the size of the public sector seemed as strong as the Labour government's opposite policies were in the 1940s.

In the 1980s, the government often privatized public corporations by selling shares in them to the public. This method was used for Associated British Ports, British Aerospace, British Gas, British Steel, British Telecom, the electricity industry, the water companies of England and Wales, Jaguar Cars and Rolls-Royce aero engines. Other methods of sale have also been used. The Rover Group (formerly British Leyland) was sold to

British Aerospace, Sealink was sold to British Ferries, National Freight was sold to a consortium of managers, employees and company pensioners, and the National Bus Company was sold as 72 separate companies.

The three main nationalized industries that have not yet been sold off are British Coal, the various companies into which British Rail was divided in 1994, and the Post Office. A major problem with the coal and rail industries is that they have a record of unprofitability. However, the government has closed many loss-making coal pits and was selling many of the survivors by the end of 1994. It also proposes to try to privatize the various new railway companies before the end of the century. The government is considering options for privatizing the Post Office, or at least the mail side of its activities. There is concern about privatizing the Post Office's branches for fear that many would be found unprofitable and closed under private ownership, thus causing difficulties in rural areas for people who go to these branches to claim their state pensions and some other transfer payments.

As privatization takes place, we witness a gradual change in the political equilibrium. Economists are only beginning their study of this kind of process, and at this stage they cannot predict whether recent privatization moves constitute a fundamental change or a temporary departure from the previous trend towards greater government involvement and ownership in industry. To some extent, of course, future policy will depend on how well the privatized industries perform. It is too early to come to a firm conclusion on this, but it seems possible that those firms which face competition – for example British Aerospace and British Steel – may make more effort to control costs than those which are natural monopolies. Indeed, many of the former nationalized industries are still monopolies and have price ceilings set by their regulatory bodies (such as OFGAS and OFTEL). The extent to which these companies reduce costs may chiefly depend on how accurately their regulatory bodies predict and enforce potential cost savings. Reading Between the Lines on pp. 568–569 shows how regulation in the UK gas market is being eased as competition increases.

Let's now turn to the third method of intervention in markets.

---

[4] W. S. W. Caves and L. Christensen, 'The Relative Efficiency of Public v. Private Firms in a Competitive Environment: the Case of Canada's Railroads', *Journal of Political Economy*, 88, 5 (September–October 1980): 958–76.

[5] S. Szymanski and S. Wilkins, 'Cheap rubbish? competitive tendering and contracting out in refuse collection, 1981–88', *Fiscal Studies*, Vol. 14, 1993.

Monopoly, Merger and Restrictive Practice Policy

Monopoly, merger and restrictive practice policy provides an alternative method for the government to influence the marketplace. Unlike regulation and public ownership, this method enables the government to interfere in almost any industry. But, like regulation and public ownership, it can operate in the public interest to maximize total surplus, or in private interests to maximize the surpluses of particular special interest groups, such as producers.

The UK's Monopoly and Merger Policies

The UK's current monopoly and merger policies derive from those implemented in the Monopolies and Restrictive Practices Act of 1948. Table 20.2 lists the main subsequent acts.

As its name suggests, the 1948 Act was concerned with monopolies and restrictive practices

TABLE 20.2

The Main UK Acts Promoting Competition

Year	Act
1948	Monopolies and Restrictive Practices Act
1956	Restrictive Trade Practices Act (minor amendments in the 1976 and 1977 Restrictive Trade Practices Acts)
1964	Resale Prices Act (minor amendments in the 1976 Resale Prices Act)
1965	Monopolies and Mergers Act
1973	Fair Trading Act
1980	Competition Act

(but not mergers). It set up a Monopolies and Restrictive Practices Commission. This was allowed to look at any industry referred to it by the government where there was a monopoly or restrictive practice. It then prepared a report to say whether action was needed in the public interest. The definition of a monopoly used was any industry where one producer had a market share in excess of 30 per cent – so economists would have argued that, strictly, the commission should have been called the Monopolies, Oligopolies and Restrictive Practices Commission. If the commission found some monopoly action or a restrictive practice that was not in the public interest, the government could take regulatory action in the industry concerned. But the firms involved usually took action voluntarily.

The 1956 Restrictive Trades Practices Act removed consideration of restrictive practices from the commission which was renamed the Monopolies Commission. The commission continued looking at monopolies – and oligopolies – when asked, as before. But its role was widened following the 1965 Monopolies and Mergers Act. This Act allowed the government to refer to the commission any proposed merger that would create a new monopoly, extend an existing monopoly, or simply result in a firm with assets above a certain level: the level was originally £5 million but by 1990 had been raised to £30 million. The Act also empowered the government to forbid any merger found by the commission to be contrary to the public interest. Finally, the Act gave the commission its present name – the Monopolies and Mergers Commission (MMC).

The 1973 Fair Trading Act widened the official definition of a monopoly to cover firms with a market share as low as 25 per cent, and it allowed 'local monopolies' to be examined – so a firm which supplies just 25 per cent of a local market can be examined. The 1973 Act also created a new office, the Office of Fair Trading, whose director-general (DGFT) can refer monopolies for examination, though the government can still do so as well, and it allowed the DGFT to recommend to the government which mergers should be referred to the MMC. Finally, the 1980 Competition Act widened the MMC's powers a little, chiefly by enabling public corporations to be investigated.

The Monopolies and Mergers Commission in Practice

Let's look at some typical MMC investigations. In 1966 the MMC found that Kodak supplied more than 75 per cent of the film sold in the United Kingdom and felt that Kodak's profit margin was too high. Kodak subsequently cut its prices. In 1966 the MMC also recommended that Unilever and Procter & Gamble cut their advertising outlays by 40 per cent and their prices by 20 per cent. The two firms subsequently cut their prices and their advertising, though in 1981 the government withdrew the controls on advertising expenditure which subsequently grew dramatically. In 1973 the MMC recommended price cuts for two pharmaceutics made by Hoffman LaRoche.

The MMC can recommend action other than price controls. In 1976 it recommended that London Brick should not subsidize the cost of transporting bricks to distant users since this was an unfair form of competition. The MMC has rarely recommended that a monopoly be split up, but in 1981 it recommended the disbanding of a company called British Posters which had a large share of the advertisement hoarding market. And in 1989 it recommended that no brewer should own more than 2,000 public houses – to the consternation of several brewers who owned far more, over 7,000 in the case of Bass.

Despite its promotion of the public interest, the MMC's record on investigating monopolies has often been accused of being inadequate. One problem is that with limited resources it can look at only a few monopolies every year. Another is that it is perceived as being soft. For example, it concluded that Pedigree Petfoods, which had a 50 per cent market share, achieved a 46 per cent rate of return on its capital simply by being efficient. And it was hardly concerned at Rank Xerox's 40 per cent rate of return on capital at a time when it had a market share of 96 per cent for plain paper photocopiers, feeling this was a reward for risk.

The MMC is also concerned with mergers. Again it has limited resources and about 97 per cent of proposed mergers take place without referral. However, the majority of the mergers which are referred are either abandoned or rejected. A complacent view might be that the DGFT and government are very astute in their selections for referral. A less complacent view would be that

many non-referred mergers may actually be against the public interest.

Mergers come in three forms. One group is **horizontal mergers** which involve firms with similar products. These clearly reduce competition and may enable the merged firms to exploit their oligopolistic or monopolistic power, but they may still be in the public interest if costs fall substantially as a result of economies of scale. The MMC has opposed several of these, including Barclays Bank and Lloyds Bank in 1966, Beechams and Glaxo in 1972, Initial and Johnson Group Cleaners in 1982, and GEC and Plessey in 1986. But the MMC did approve the merger of Europcar and Godfrey Davis in 1980, Nabisco Brands and Huntley and Palmer in 1982, and P&O and European Ferries in 1986.

There are also **vertical mergers** where a firm merges with a supplier or customer. It might be thought that, as the merged firms have different products, these would be of less concern to the MMC. Certainly it approved the 1965 merger of Pressed Steel (which made car bodies) with the British Motor Corporation (later British Leyland and then Rover Group) and the 1968 merger of Thorn (electronics) with Radio Rentals. But it did oppose the merger of Pilkington (the glass maker) with UK Optics, one of its customers, in 1976.

Finally, there are **conglomerate mergers** which are between two firms with products that are little related. These mergers often occur when firms wish to diversify in order to reduce the risk of a large drop in profits should one of their interests hit hard times. Such mergers may do little to reduce competition, so it is not surprising that some are approved, such as Allied Lyons (the food group) with Elders IXL (the brewers) in 1985, but others seem less innocuous and have been opposed, such as Berisford and Tate & Lyle (two rather different food companies) in 1986.

Monopoly and Merger Policy in the European Union

The European Union is also concerned about monopolies, oligopolies and mergers, though its policies are less clearly stated than those of the United Kingdom. The European Union prohibits any abuse of a dominant market position within the single market. There is no legal definition of market dominance although shares of 40 per cent have been cited as indicating dominance. In practice, the abuses which have been investigated are more akin to restrictive practices – discussed below – than to the mere fact that a dominant firm might enjoy high returns by charging very high prices.

Since 1990 the European Union has been empowered to look at proposed mergers which meet various detailed criteria. It focuses on mergers where at least one firm does at least a third of its business outside its own country and where the total sales of the combined firm would exceed about £3 billion. It has so far banned only one proposed merger, in 1991. It was to be between three aircraft manufacturers – Aérospatiale of France, Alenia of Italy and De Havilland of Canada – and would have created a firm with a 67 per cent share of the EU market for short-haul aircraft with 20–70 seats. If the European Union does block a merger, the firms concerned can appeal to the European Court.

Restrictive Practices Policy in the United Kingdom

As we have seen, the 1948 Act established a commission to investigate restrictive practices as well as monopolies. But the 1956 Restrictive Trade Practices Act removed restrictive practices from this commission. The new procedure that it established for restrictive practices has survived little altered since 1956 and is much firmer than the procedure for monopolies.

The first part of the policy for restrictive practices is that firms wishing to operate them must register them. Initially it was only suppliers of goods that had to register them with a Registrar of Restrictive Practices, but following the 1973 Fair Trading Act suppliers of services also had to register restrictive practices, and the register became the responsibility of the DGFT. The acts define restrictive practices in legal terms, but broadly speaking a restrictive practice occurs when trade between two firms is conducted on a particularly favourable basis in respect of matters such as price, terms, conditions and geographical area. Thus a supplier is operating a restrictive practice if it agrees with a particular buyer to sell at a special price not available to other buyers, or if it agrees to supply more promptly than it supplies to other buyers, or if it agrees not to sell to other firms competing with the buyer.

Registered agreements must then be taken

TABLE 20.3

Gateways Which Can Be Used to Defend a Restrictive Practice

1 The practice is reasonably necessary to protect the public against injury.

2 Removing the practice would cause consumers to lose specific and substantial benefits.

3 The practice is reasonably necessary to counteract measures taken by other producers to restrict competition.

4 The practice is reasonably necessary to enable fair terms to be negotiated with an important supplier or buyer.

5 Removing the practice would be likely to have a serious and persistent effect on unemployment in some particular area.

6 Removing the practice would be likely to cause a substantial fall in exports.

7 The practice is reasonably necessary to maintain another practice which the RPC has found to be not contrary to the public interest.

8* The practice does not restrict or discourage competition to any material degree and is unlikely to do so.

* This gateway was added in 1968.

before the Restrictive Practices Court (RPC) to see if they are in the public interest. When they appear before the RPC the parties to the agreement are allowed to use only eight reasons or 'gateways' in its defence. These gateways are listed in Table 20.3. To defend their practice the parties must show that it passes one of these gateways and that the benefits that result outweigh any drawbacks. If the parties fail to convince the RPC that their practice is, on balance, justifiable, then that practice is at once illegal and must cease. Thus the RPC has a much more emphatic and powerful role than the MMC which merely recommends action to the government.

Several thousand restrictive practices have been registered since the register was opened, but fewer than 100 have been brought before the RPC. This doesn't mean that the process has had little effect. On the contrary, the RPC has found against the

TABLE 20.4

Gateways Which Can Be Used to Defend Resale Price Maintenance

1   **Ending the practice would substantially reduce the quality and variety of goods available for sale.**

2   **Ending the practice would substantially reduce the number of retail outlets where the goods were sold.**

3   **Ending the practice would cause the retail prices of the goods to rise.**

4   **Ending the practice would mean that goods would be sold in conditions likely to cause danger to health.**

5   **Ending the practice would mean that necessary services provided in connection with the sale of the goods would be substantially reduced.**

majority of practices brought before it, and as a result most of the others that were registered were voluntarily abandoned. There is no point in firms spending money on defending their practices in court if they are almost certain to lose. Of course, some practices may have continued without being registered, although this is illegal.

One type of restrictive practice was excluded from the 1948 and 1956 Acts – resale price maintenance. **Resale price maintenance** (RPM) is a situation where a manufacturer supplies goods to retailers on condition that the goods are sold to consumers at a specified price. Such a practice restricts competition between shops. RPM made life hard for firms wishing to establish chain stores or self-service supermarkets as they could not pass on their cost savings to customers. The 1964 Resale Prices Act effectively made RPM a restrictive practice and firms operating it had to register the fact. The RPC then started hearing selected cases. Firms were given only five gateways to use when trying to justify RPM. These gateways are listed in Table 20.4. The RPC found against almost all the practices it heard so that most firms stopped using RPM. The only important cases where the RPC allowed RPM were books, maps and some medications.

Restrictive Practices Policy in the European Union

Quite apart from UK policy, firms wishing to operate restrictive practices risk breaking EU law. The Treaty of Rome declares that agreements between firms, or groups of firms, which may affect trade between member states and which have the aim of preventing, restricting or distorting competition within the European Union are incompatible with a common market. Such restrictive practices are illegal unless the European Commission or the European Court grant exemption. The Commission or Court may permit restrictive practices which pass through certain gateways, though these are more severe than the UK gateways.

Firms can register their restrictive practices with the European Commission. Technically speaking they do not have to do so, but if they do not then the practice is at once illegal. If they do register, then the practice can be continued, at least until it has been investigated. The Commission has the power to fine companies which breach the regulations. Fines can be up to 10 per cent of a firm's total turnover in the last year. An example of a modest fine was one of £200,000 imposed on British Leyland (later Rover Group) for trying to stop UK importers buying Austin Metros on the continent.

Public or Special Interest?

It is clear from the historical contexts in which competition policies have evolved that their aim has been to protect the public interest and restrain the profit-seeking and anti-competitive actions of producers. Even so, the interests of producers may have sometimes influenced the way in which the policies have been applied. Nevertheless, the overall thrust of competition policies appears to have been directed towards achieving allocative efficiency and, therefore, to serving the public interest.

It is interesting to note that there is an important difference in the way the MMC works compared with the RPC and the European Union. The MMC is a bureaucracy that gives advice to the Secretary of State for Trade and Industry – which means the advice is considered by officials at the Department for Trade and Industry which is another bureaucracy. In contrast, the RPC and the European Union use legal procedures that are interpreted and enforced by the legal process. Economists are now beginning to extend theories of public choice to include an economic analysis of the law and the way the courts interpret the law. It is interesting to speculate that the legal institutions such as the RPC and the European Court may be more sensitive to the public interest than the political and bureaucratic institutions that lie behind the work of the MMC.

It will be difficult to reach a firm conclusion on how the two processes compare. What can be said is that most monopolies and mergers are never examined to see whether they are in the public interest. In contrast, the fact that the law is against restrictive practices means that most firms do not indulge in them – or at least if they do they keep very quiet about it.

Regional Policy

We now turn our attention away from industry policies aimed at individual firms and industries to policies that affect whole regions.

The Case for a Regional Policy

A **regional policy** is a policy that seeks to reduce disparities between different regions. The most usual disparity tackled has been different unemployment rates. If unemployment soars in one particular area, people there naturally feel the government should intervene on their behalf. But we may ask whether market forces could solve the problem. Surely wage rates would fall in the region with excess labour? If so, either new investment will be attracted by cheap labour or some workers will leave for areas where wages are higher. Either way, it seems, the unemployment problem should soon disappear.

Unfortunately, market forces may not always work very well. For instance, nationwide bargaining between employers and employees in a particular industry may preclude falls in wages in the region where they are needed. Also, people who live in council homes may be reluctant to

leave an area of high unemployment since they could be placed in a long queue for a council home at their new location.

A further problem with relying on market forces in the United Kingdom has been that the regions traditionally most affected – Scotland, Northern Ireland, Wales and northern England – have seen employment fall as industries such as coal mining, cotton textiles and shipbuilding have declined. These industries were located in those areas for special reasons, such as the availability of coal and suitable locations for shipyards. In contrast, most of the expanding industries of the post-World War II era, such as vehicles and consumer durables manufacturing, have been able to locate anywhere. And while low wages in depressed areas might attract them, they also have an incentive to locate near the big markets of south-east England and the continent to cut the costs of delivering products to retail outlets. So wages would have to fall quite appreciably in the depressed areas to offset their locational disadvantages.

A final problem with relying on market forces is that they could take a long time, especially if emigration from the depressed area is relied on. Suppose an area has 500,000 unemployed and that 100,000 of these find jobs in other regions and emigrate, leaving 400,000 unemployed workers. Suppose, too, that 400,000 employed workers leave in search of higher wages so that the remaining 400,000 can take their places. Will the unemployment problem be solved? Sadly no, because 500,000 people have left, along with their dependants, and this reduces demand in local shops and other businesses. So unemployment reappears. In turn, another wave of emigration may occur causing more local people to lose their jobs. Eventually this local multiplier process may work itself out, but the level of emigration needed to solve the problem may be very high.

There's a further reason for not relying wholly on market forces. Firms that locate their new plants in response to market forces look only at factors which affect their revenues and costs. They don't look at the external costs they impose on others. Consequently, they may all want to expand in south-east England without taking into account that their expansion will aggravate congestion and impose congestion costs on other firms there. For example, firms that expand in the south-east may

British Gas, Price Capping and Competition

THE TIMES, 28 JANUARY 1994

Regulator relaxes British Gas price cap

Ross Teiman, Industrial Correspondent

HOUSEHOLD gas users must pay more to compensate British Gas for losing sales to more profitable business customers, Clare Spottiswoode, the head of Ofgas has decided.

In her first key ruling since taking office in November, the Director-General yesterday replaced the formula capping British Gas household prices from inflation-minus-five per cent to inflation-minus-four per cent. The change will enable the company to charge households some £30 million more in a full year, City analysts said....

British Gas welcomed the change, insisting it was overdue. However, Ian Powe, director of the Gas Consumers Council, said: 'If the price of competition is bigger bills, consumers may prefer it had not been invented.' He added: 'British Gas deserves no favours after admitting it can shed 20,000 jobs and save £370 million in annual salary costs.'

In making the adjustment, Ms Spottiswoode, a former Treasury mandarin and self-made business woman, has followed the recommendations of an 18-month enquiry by the Monopolies and Mergers Commission.

The adjustment, she said was 'intended to strike a broad balance between the need of British Gas to attract capital, which has been affected by the introduction of competition, and the interest of consumers in maintaining low prices'.

However, at the same time she has reduced the scope of the formula to cover only the tariff market below 2,500 therms. This includes almost all supplies to Britain's 18$\frac{1}{4}$ million household gas users in addition to many small businesses.

However, it indicates a fundamental shift in the attitude of Ofgas to British Gas's role in industrial and commercial markets where the company has faced rapidly accelerating competition. In effect, Ms Spottiswoode has signalled a belief that competition will henceforth be effective in restraining prices in commercial and industrial markets and price controls are therefore no longer needed.

© The Times. Reprinted with permission.

When British Gas (BG) was privatized, the independent watchdog, Ofgas, was established to oversee the operations of the company.

At this time, BG faced very little competition so Ofgas introduced direct price control.

Greater competition in the market to supply gas to commercial and industrial enterprises has meant that Ofgas now finds direct price control unnecessary.

Large companies have had the price cap totally removed.

Small companies and domestic users face a more relaxed price ceiling and the likelihood of higher prices, given the lack of competition in that sector.

This change follows the recommendation of a recent Monopolies and Mergers Commission (MMC) report on the gas industry.

In privatizing the public utilities, the UK government faced two issues regarding pricing policy. Either prices should be restrained through competition or, where such competition did not exist, should be controlled directly.

While BG still has a large market share, this is being eroded and with it BG's ability to charge monopoly prices.

Ofgas loosened the price constraint in accordance with the MMC recommendation to offset the lower profits from reducing the number of industrial consumers whose bills are subject to the 'monopoly threshold' (down from 25,000 therms to 2,500 therms). Gas consumption measured in therms defines the size of customer buying gas from BG.

The gain from allowing profit levels to be restored is primarily to facilitate investment in new projects.

The figure shows the market for industrial sales for 1988, 1990 and 1992, following Fig. 20.5. Initially, in 1988 regulation kept the price charged to industrial users below the profit-maximizing level. As more gas suppliers entered the market, in 1990 and 1992 regulation was eased, with prices moving towards profit-maximizing levels.

Over time, however, the increase in competition also results in the demand curve getting less steep as more gas suppliers enter the market. Overall, the unregulated price is seen to fall as a result of competition.

The introduction of competition is one of the functions of Ofgas, and it will decide on granting new firms permission to supply gas subject to criteria such as safety and security of supply, not just on the need to introduce competition to a monopoly market sector.

The long-term plan, however, is to introduce competition into the whole of the gas market at the start of the next decade. In the mean time, the plan is to reduce the monopoly threshold from 2,500 to 1,500 therms in 1997.

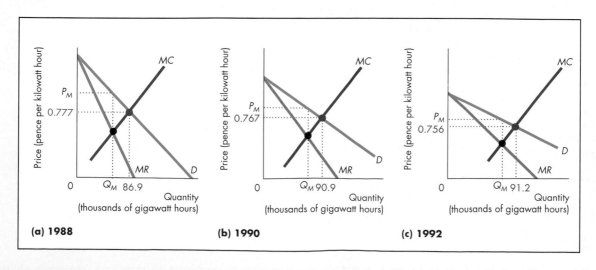

(a) 1988   (b) 1990   (c) 1992

raise labour costs there and so raise the costs of other firms, and they may add to the traffic on the roads, so causing extra traffic jams and raising transport costs for other firms.

The European Union is particularly concerned with regional problems. Before the formation of the European Union, a country with high unemployment could reduce the value of its currency in an attempt to stimulate the demand for its goods. But the European Union is anxious to have exchange rate stability within its area to stop individual members depreciating their currencies in an effort to help their producers at the expense of producers elsewhere in the European Union. If it wants currency stability, it has to be concerned with areas where unemployment is especially high.

UK Regional Policy in Practice

Regional policies in the United Kingdom date back to the 1930s and became a permanent feature after World War II. Some policies were designed to help people move from selected areas, perhaps by helping them retrain or by helping them finance a move. But most of the effort has been devoted to trying to encourage as much new investment as possible to take place in the areas most needing help. If the capital stock in these areas rises, so the number of employees required should rise. The precise areas concerned have been redefined periodically as the situation and funds available have changed.

One way of trying to divert investment to the selected areas has been to make it hard for firms to get permission to expand elsewhere. This policy was used extensively until the 1970s and was abandoned after 1982. The trouble with it was a fear of what would happen to firms that wanted to expand in a prosperous area but failed to get permission. Some might indeed go instead to an area of high unemployment, but others might decide not to expand at all.

Another method was to try to simulate market forces by reducing labour costs in the areas needing help. This policy was pursued through a device known as the Regional Employment Premium between 1967 and 1976. This was a subsidy paid on all employees in selected areas. It was eventually abolished at the request of the European Union on the grounds that such a subsidy infringed its rules of fair competition. It should be added that the policy was not without its critics. Some argued that the policy was wasteful since it subsidized all workers including those who would have been employed anyway. Others argued that it would not succeed in persuading firms to relocate unless they thought the premium would last for many years and so make a substantial saving in costs, yet no one could guarantee that all future governments would keep it in place.

A third option has been to subsidize new plant in the areas needing help. From 1972 to 1988 there were two forms of assistance. These were Regional Development Grants, which were paid automatically to meet up to 22 per cent of the cost of new investments by manufacturing firms in the most needy areas, and Regional Selective Assistance Grants, which were paid on a discretionary basis. These discretionary grants could be paid as an extra inducement to investment in the most needy areas or as the sole inducement in less needy areas where Regional Development Grants were not paid. After 1988 the automatic Regional Development Grants were abolished while Regional Selective Assistance Grants were increased. The assisted areas where discretionary grants may be given include Northern Ireland, much of northern and central Scotland, parts of north and south Wales, much of northern England and the Midlands along with most of Cornwall.

The reason for ending automatic grants and having more discretionary grants was a hope that, by giving more discretion to the Department of Trade and Industry, regional policy funds could be used more cost effectively. Certainly cost effectiveness is now especially important because the level of assistance is much lower than it was for most of the 1960s and 1970s. The policies used then seem to have been very effective, for estimates suggest that they created 780,000 jobs between 1960 and 1981, of which 600,000 were still in existence in 1981.

The government is not alone in trying to entice investment to the assisted areas. In Scotland and Wales there are Development Areas which assist firms to relocate or expand there. Many local authorities also try to help in any way they can.

EU Regional Policy

The main thrust of the EU's regional policy lies with what are termed structural funds. These funds have the following six broad aims:

◆ To promote the development of less developed areas

◆ To promote the development of rural areas

◆ To help restructure areas affected by industrial decline

◆ To help develop areas suffering from long-term unemployment

◆ To help areas where young people are in particular need of training to find jobs

◆ To help areas where the agricultural and forestry industries need to adjust their production

The first three objectives are the most important in financial terms. Assistance with the first objective is paid to the whole of the Republic of Ireland, Greece and Portugal, and to most of Spain, southern Italy and Northern Ireland. Assistance with objectives 2 and 3 is much more widely spread. The European Union has agreed to raise spending on structural funds to some 27,400 million ECUs – that is about £21,000 million – by 1999. This is a tiny share of total GDP in the European Union, but the funds are welcomed by those who receive them. The main thrust of structural

fund payments is to support a share, which rarely exceeds 65 per cent, of approved projects undertaken by central governments, local authorities or private firms. Many of the projects involve improvements to roads and energy supplies and labour training programmes in the hope that this will make the areas concerned more attractive places for firms to invest in.

◆◆◆◆ In this chapter, we've seen how the government intervenes in markets where there is monopoly or oligopoly to affect prices, quantities, the gains from trade and the division of those gains between consumers and producers. We've seen that there is a conflict between the pursuit of the public interest – achieving allocative efficiency – and the pursuit of the special interests of producers – maximizing monopoly profit. The political and legal arenas are the places in which these conflicts are resolved. We've reviewed the two theories – public interest and capture – concerning the type and scope of government intervention. We've also looked at competition policies and regional development policies.

S U M M A R Y

Market Intervention

The government can intervene to regulate monopolistic and oligopolistic markets in three ways: regulation of particular industries, nationalization, and monopoly, merger and restrictive practice policy. All of these methods are used in the United Kingdom.

Government action can influence consumer surplus, producer surplus and total surplus. Consumer surplus is the difference between what consumers are willing to pay for a given consumption level and what they actually pay. Producer surplus is the difference between a producer's revenue from its sales and the opportunity cost of production. Total surplus is the sum of consumer surplus and producer surplus. Total surplus is maximized under competition. Under monopoly, producer surplus is increased and consumer surplus decreased, and a deadweight loss is created. (pp. 547–548)

The Economic Theory of Regulation

Consumers and producers express their demand for the intervention that influences their surpluses by voting, lobbying and making campaign contributions. The larger the surplus that can be generated by a particular regulation and the smaller the number of people affected, the larger is the demand for the intervention. A small number of people are easier than a large number to organize into an effective political lobby. Intervention is supplied by politicians who pursue their own best interests. The larger the surplus per head generated and the larger the number of people affected by it, the larger is the supply of intervention. In equilibrium, the intervention that exists is such that no interest group feels it worth while to employ scarce resources to press for further changes. There are two theories of political equilibrium: public interest theory and capture theory. Public interest theory predicts that total surplus will be maximized; capture theory predicts that producer surplus will be maximized. (pp. 548–551)

Regulation and Deregulation

Regulation of particular industries goes back to the railway industry in the nineteenth century. In the twentieth century it has been extended to cover several more industries including agriculture and finance. New bodies were established in the 1980s to regulate some of the recently privatized industries. On the other hand, some industries – such as buses – have been deregulated.

Regulation is conducted by regulatory agencies that are controlled by politically appointed bureaucrats and staffed by a permanent bureaucracy of experts. Regulated firms are required to comply with various rules which often cover price, product quality and output levels. Two kinds of industries that are often regulated are natural monopolies and cartels. Regulation has often enabled firms in the industries affected to achieve profit levels equal to or greater than those attained on average in the rest of the economy. This outcome is closer to the predictions of the capture theory of regulation than to the predictions of the public interest theory. (pp. 551–558)

Public Ownership

There used to be many public corporations in the United Kingdom, but following a substantial programme of privatization in the 1980s the main ones left are the Post Office, parts of British Coal and British Rail. There are rather more public corporations in many other European countries.

The economic model of public enterprise is the same as that of bureaucracy. The managers of a public enterprise are assumed to maximize their budget. The political process places constraints on that aim. The outcome is a tendency for public enterprises to be inefficient in that their costs are higher than the minimum possible ones. Australian and Canadian studies of public and private enterprises operating in similar circumstances indicate that public enterprises are significantly less efficient than their private enterprise counterparts. The privatization process has gathered pace around the world as there has been a tendency for the consumer interest to be more assertive. (pp. 559–562)

Monopoly, Merger and Restrictive Practice Policy

Monopoly, merger and restrictive practice policies enable government to exert some control in almost any industry. The United Kingdom's first major attempt at such a policy started in 1948. Control of monopolies, with a definition that also includes oligopolies, and control of mergers is made by the government on the recommendation of the Monopolies and Mergers Commission. Restrictive practices are the responsibility of the Restrictive Practices Court. The European Union also has legal powers which have been chiefly directed against monopolists and oligopolists that indulge in restrictive practices. The policies all claim to favour the consumer. It is possible, though, that some attention is paid to producer interests, particularly when intervention is in the hands of politicians and bureaucrats rather than the courts. (pp. 563–567)

Regional Policy

Regional policies have usually concentrated on helping areas with relatively high rates of unemployment. Market forces should also help these areas, but the forces may work very slowly. Also, relying wholly on market forces means that firms are likely to ignore external costs of congestion when they invest in prosperous areas. The main thrust of UK regional policy has been to try to stimulate investment in the areas with the highest unemployment – the assisted areas. The main policy now is one of discretionary grants to help finance investment costs in those areas. The European Union also has a regional policy. It has chiefly attempted to improve the infrastructure in selected areas to make them more attractive to investors. (pp. 567–571)

KEY ELEMENTS

Key Terms

Average cost pricing rule, 554
Capture theory of intervention, 550
Conglomerate merger, 564
Deregulation, 548
Horizontal merger, 564
Marginal cost pricing rule, 553
Nationalization, 547
Nationalized industry, 547
Privatization, 547
Public corporation, 547
Public interest theory of intervention, 550
Rate of return regulation, 555
Regional policy, 567
Regulation, 547
Resale price maintenance, 566
Restrictive practice, 548
Total surplus, 549

Two-part tariff, 553
Vertical merger, 564

Key Figures and Tables

REVIEW QUESTIONS

1 What are the three main ways in which the government can intervene with producers in the marketplace?

2 What is consumer surplus? How is it calculated? How is it represented in a diagram?

3 What is producer surplus? How is it calculated? How is it represented in a diagram?

4 What is total surplus? How is it calculated? How is it represented in a diagram?

5 Why do consumers demand regulation? In what kinds of industries would you most expect them to demand regulation?

6 Why do producers demand regulation? In what kinds of industries would you most expect them to demand regulation?

7 Explain the public interest and capture theories of the supply of intervention. What does each theory imply about the behaviour of politicians?

8 How do publicly owned corporations behave according to the economic theory of bureaucracy?

9 How are mergers regulated in the United Kingdom?

10 How are restrictive practices regulated in the United Kingdom?

11 How does the European Union help to promote competition?

12 Why is a regional policy needed?

13 How are firms encouraged to invest in areas of high unemployment?

PROBLEMS

1 Mountain Water plc is a natural monopoly that bottles water from a spring high in the Grampian mountains of Scotland. The total fixed cost it incurs is £80,000 and its marginal cost is 10 pence a bottle. The demand schedule for bottled water from Mountain Water is:

Price (pence per bottle)	Quantity demanded (thousands of bottles per year)
100	0
90	100
80	200
70	300
60	400
50	500
40	600
30	700
20	800
10	900
0	1000

Assuming Mountain Water is unregulated and wishes to maximize its profit:

a What price does it set for a bottle of water?

b How many bottles does it sell?

c Does Mountain Water maximize total surplus or producer surplus?

2 The government decides to regulate Mountain Water by imposing a marginal cost pricing rule.

a What is the price of a bottle of water?

b How many bottles does Mountain Water sell?

c What is Mountain Water's producer surplus?

d What is the consumer surplus?

e Is the regulation in the public interest or in the private interest?

3 The government decides to change its regulation and now requires Mountain Water to adopt an average cost pricing rule.

a What is the price of a bottle of water?

b How many bottles does Mountain Water sell?

c What is Mountain Water's producer surplus?

d What is the consumer surplus?

e Is the regulation in the public interest or in the private interest?

4 The value of the capital invested in Mountain Water is £2 million. The government introduces a new regulation requiring the firm to sell its water for a price that gives it a rate of return of 5 per cent on its capital.

a What is the price of a bottle of water?

b How many bottles does Mountain Water sell?

c What is Mountain Water's producer surplus?

d What is the consumer surplus?

e Is the regulation in the public interest or in the private interest?

PART 6
MACROECONOMIC PROBLEMS AND POLICIES

Talking with Patrick Minford

Professor Patrick Minford has been Edward Gonner Professor of Applied Economics, University of Liverpool since 1976, and a visiting Professor at the Cardiff Business School since 1993. He has been a member of the Monopolies and Mergers Commission since March 1990 and one of H.M. Treasury's Panel of Forecasters ('Six Wise Men') since its inception in January 1993. He is the author of books and articles on exchange rates, unemployment, housing and macroeconomics. In 1979 he started the Liverpool Research Group in Macroeconomics with the aim of developing new methods of macroeconomic forecasting and policy analysis.

What originally attracted you to the study of economics?

I had the usual young person's concern with social deprivation; I was especially interested in developing countries, where I travelled to visit my father, who was in the United Kingdom diplomatic corps. He was the one to suggest that economics had the intellectual tools for dealing with these problems. As I studied it and tried to apply it I increasingly agreed with him.

Which economist has had the greatest influence on you?

Milton Friedman – in many ways. His methodological approach: use the simplest possible assumptions to generate far-reaching testable predictions. His vision of the free market society. His monetary economics and theory of the natural rate. These ideas made macroeconomics once again a matter of (aggregate) supply and demand, fully integrated with the rest of economics, and paved the way for rational expectations and modern thinking. Finally his no-nonsense ability to explain his ideas to ordinary thinking people. Since economics affects them so vitally, they must understand the basis of it if they are to accept new policies.

> '
> The continental obsession with the "social dimension" has fixed labour costs at a greatly excessive level, just as we did in the United Kingdom in the 1960s and 1970s.'

Why have the problems of the labour market been a focus of your work?

My interest began early in the 1980s when it became apparent that rigorous UK monetary policy was bringing inflation down without any return to full employment. This failure threatened the whole basis of Margaret Thatcher's programme of free market reform. I concluded that the natural rate of unemployment had shifted quite substantially and was forced to develop a model of this, in order to propose relevant policy measures and get some idea of their quantitative effects and so their order of priority. The result of this work was to identify unemployment benefits, available indefinitely, as the basic mechanism preventing wages adjusting to create jobs; but given this mechanism was in place, other factors, especially trade union power, taxes and housing restrictions, could seriously worsen unemployment. I urged the Thatcher government to tackle union power and the benefit regime as soon as possible. It got off to a rather slow start, seriously tackling union power from 1982 but not really getting to grips with benefits until 1986.

Why did unemployment refuse to decline as much as hoped in the 1980s boom?

In fact unemployment did decline sharply from 1986, reaching 5.6% in 1990. 1986 was the year in which finally action was taken to reform benefits – the 'Restart' programme (which made benefits conditional again on serious job search) came in and shortly afterwards benefit rates were cut for single people and adjusted across the board to reduce the 'poverty trap'. The boom of 1987–1988 created overheating in the goods market. Demand was allowed to grow too fast, mainly because we cut interest rates in order to hold down the exchange rate within the 'shadow ERM'. But the labour market showed no signs of overheating; indeed real wages decelerated. The 1980s reforms therefore had an effect as our equations suggest they should have. It was unfortunate that errors of monetary policy undermined progress. After a relaxation in 1988, policy was excessively tightened, culminating in official entry to the ERM at a revalued exchange rate that required ever higher real interest rates to defend it.

> '**E**conomists should be stubborn in setting out their preferred prescriptions because in the end these can become "politically possible" as the climate of opinion changes.'

Can the United Kingdom ever have 2–3% unemployment again?

Yes, the United Kingdom can. According to my estimates the natural rate is now down to around this level. Allowing for lags in the installation of physical capital, and assuming no further upsets in monetary policy, it could be reached within 3–5 years. But for Europe generally the outlook is poor. The continental obsession with the 'social dimension' has fixed labour costs at a greatly excessive level, just as we did in the United Kingdom in the 1960s and 1970s. Europe has caught the 'British disease', just as we are convalescing from our cure.

As a proponent of rational expectations can you stress its importance to macroeconomic theory?

Rational expectations is a good example of Friedman's methodology: a simple assumption, which is obviously not strictly realistic, but generates powerful testable predictions. Economics is founded on the model of *homo economicus* who efficiently maximizes his utility subject to constraints of prices and resources. Rational expectations extends this model to information – he now uses information efficiently

as well, in forming expectations about these constraints. Previously all sorts of arbitrary assumptions were made about how these expec-tations might be formed. Since this extended model is being applied to average behaviour, its lack of individual realism need not matter. We can imagine ways in which institutions (such as the forecasting industry) could generate informational efficiency in market behaviour. With the rational expectations hypothesis it is possible to formulate 'Computable General Equilibrium' (CGE) models in which all agents' optimizing strategies over time can be precisely defined (because they are calculated rationally) and we can solve for the path of the economy that accommodates them. These CGE models – once we can properly estimate them – offer the prospect of a macroeconomics that is securely based on rational behaviour.

Is it frustrating advising a government if political expediency overrides economic principles?

Yes it is. But it has to be accepted and immediate advice has to take it into account. Economic advice is like economic behaviour: it has to maximize subject to restraints

– in this case, the constraints are political! Having said this, I believe that economists should be stubborn in setting out their preferred prescriptions because in the end these can become 'politically possible' as the climate of opinion changes. Primarily as economists we should address ourselves to shaping and leading this climate of opinion.

Do you feel the role of economists is important enough in UK policy determination?

Economists have, as a profession, a considerable influence in UK policy, much more than is realized. This is assisted by a government economic service extending to all departments, a fairly sophisticated body of economic journalists, and an increasingly open public debate to which the panel of 'Six Wise Men' started by the Treasury in 1993 has probably contributed. It is important for our profession that economists debate in public according to the coherent body of economic principles. As UK politics becomes more dominated by a free market consensus, that is increasingly happening and will add to the influence of economics.

In Europe generally, the problem is much harder because of the dominance on the continent of the Social/Christian Democrat philosophy, which favours interventionism and 'social justice'. However, since this philosophy is the cause of Europe's current unemployment and stagnation it will eventually give way to market capitalism. As economists we must not compromise in setting out the proper route for Europe to follow and so speed this process.

As a former adviser to developing nations, are there any lessons from developed nations' performance that can be used fruitfully to shape developing nations' policies?

The emerging economies – such as the Little Dragons – and the dreadful plight of many African states have clear lessons: that free markets and secure property rights are the key ingredients of development. When they are trampled on, as in Africa, the economy goes backwards.

If you were made prime minister tomorrow, how would you structure your economic policy and what would be the main instruments of the policy?

I would set out the goal of a free market society underpinned by a social safety net. To that end the key remaining UK reforms are to the welfare system whose rules have created a dependent class exploiting their provisions. The system has to be decentralized to local bodies capable of monitoring household needs and giving welfare assistance selectively. In fiscal policy tax rates should be moved over time to a flat proportional income tax, set so as to generate a stable debt/GNP ratio over the long term. Government spending should be cut back by progressive privatization. In monetary policy I can see no alternative at present to setting interest rates in relation to a (forecast) inflation target and the state of the business cycle. While monetary indicators continue to be destabilized by technological change and financial liberalization, they can only be used as adjunct indicators, with heavy adjustment for these factors.

What advice would you give anyone starting to study economics?

First, don't be discouraged by its difficulty: it is hard to understand until you have got a picture of the subject as a whole. Second, get stuck into the mathematics: it greatly simplifies the study of economics.

CHAPTER 21

UNEMPLOYMENT, INFLATION, CYCLES AND DEFICITS

After studying this chapter you will be able to:

◆ Define unemployment and explain its costs

◆ Distinguish between the various types of unemployment

◆ Define inflation and explain its effects

◆ Define gross domestic product (GDP)

◆ Distinguish between nominal GDP and real GDP

◆ Explain the importance of changes in real GDP

◆ Define the business cycle

◆ Describe how unemployment and inflation fluctuate over the business cycle

◆ Define the government budget deficit and the country's international deficit

In 1993, for every nine people with jobs, one other person was looking for work and unable to find any. Many more people were so discouraged about their chances of finding jobs that they had stopped looking. Why are jobs so hard to find? ◆ ◆ People who do find jobs worry about what their wages will buy, and for good reason. A trolley-load of groceries that cost £17 in 1973 costs over £100 today, and prices continue to rise. Does this matter? What are the effects of persistently rising prices and wages? ◆ ◆ While prices rise, so too does the value of the goods and services we produce. Between 1973 and 1993, the value of the goods and services produced in the United Kingdom rose eight-fold. How much of the growth in the value of our output is real and how much of it is an illusion created by inflation? ◆ ◆ The UK economy does not follow a smooth and predictable course. Sometimes, such as from 1986 to 1990, output rises steadily and unemployment falls. At other times, such as from 1990 to 1993, output sags and unemployment rises. Why do we have waves of expansion and contraction? ◆ ◆ We hear a lot these days about two deficits. One is the government's deficit. The other is the UK's international deficit. What are these deficits? Why are they so big? Why have they grown in recent years?

Jobs, Prices and Incomes

◆ ◆ ◆ ◆ These questions are the subject matter of macroeconomics. With what you learn in this chapter and those that follow, you'll be better able to understand the macroeconomic problems that face us today. But before we turn to these problems, let's pause for a moment to contrast macroeconomics with the microeconomics that we have been studying so far.

Microeconomics and Macroeconomics

You have already seen how microeconomics studies the choices made by individual households and firms, and you have seen that it studies individual markets – such as the markets for tapes, pizzas, wine, unskilled labour, life insurance salespeople, computers and oilfields. In contrast, macroeconomics, as we explained in Chapter 1, is the branch of economics that studies the economy as a whole. This means that our studies now have a very different flavour from what has gone before.

For example, instead of looking at the output of individual goods and services, we will look at the overall level of output. Instead of looking at the prices of individual goods and services, we will look at the overall level of prices. Instead of looking at the employment levels and wages for different types of labour, we will look at the total level of employment and the overall level of wages. Instead of looking at the provision of particular public goods and the effects of individual taxes, we will look at the total levels of government spending and taxing. Instead of asking why individuals trade with each other, we will ask why countries trade with each other, and we will ask why there may be a large gap between the values of a country's exports and imports.

You can see that there is a big difference in the sorts of questions that are discussed in macroeconomics and microeconomics. There is a corresponding difference in the sorts of government policies we need to consider. In microeconomics we considered why governments might interfere in individual markets – such as those where supply is in the hands of a monopolist or those where there are externalities. In macroeconomics, we consider how the government might tackle broad macroeconomic problems such as unemployment or inflation or the international deficit.

The macroeconomic events through which we are now living are as exciting and tumultuous as any in history. Governments all around the world face a daily challenge to find policies that will give all of us a smoother macroeconomic ride. With what you learn in these chapters, you will be better able to understand these macroeconomic policy challenges and the political debate that surrounds them. We begin our study of macroeconomics by looking at unemployment.

Unemployment

At many times in the UK's history, unemployment has been a severe problem. For example, in 1985 and 1986 over 3 million people were seeking jobs, and the figure nearly reached 3 million again in 1993. What exactly is unemployment? How is it measured? Why has its rate fluctuated? What are its costs?

What is Unemployment?

Unemployment is a state in which there are qualified workers who are available for work at the current wage rate and who do not have jobs. The total number of people who do have jobs – the employed – plus the number of people who do not have jobs – the unemployed – is the **labour force**. A country's **unemployment rate** is its unemployment expressed as a percentage of the labour force. However, the official statistics of unemployment in different countries are calculated in varying ways and may not fully square with the true definitions. Let's see how both employment and unemployment are measured in the United Kingdom.

Measuring Employment and Unemployment

Both employment and unemployment are measured in the United Kingdom every month by the Department of Employment. The figures are used as the basis for the employment and unemployment figures reported monthly in the news media. The official figures for employment show the number of adult workers (people aged 16 and over) who have jobs, along with workers in work-related government training schemes. Although there is sometimes debate about whether some people on training schemes have 'proper' jobs, this measure of employment is a reasonable one.

The official figures for unemployment show the number of adult workers who are not employed and who are claiming job-seeker's allowance.[1] There are five reasons why these official figures do not give an accurate estimate of true unemployment in the United Kingdom. Let's examine these five reasons. The first four concern situations where some true unemployment may not be recorded by the official figures. The fifth concerns a situation where the official figures may include some people who should not be regarded as unemployed.

Part-time Workers We have said that the official unemployment figures count only those people who are claiming job-seeker's allowance. We saw in Chapter 18 that working people pay National Insurance contributions and can then claim job-seeker's allowance if they become unemployed. But some people who lose their jobs are unable to find a full-time job and instead take a part-time job. To economists, these people are partially unemployed as they work for fewer hours than they wish. However, they will almost certainly lose their entitlement to job-seeker's allowance – unless they work very few hours – so the official figures for unemployment will ignore them. This is potentially a serious deficiency in the official figures.

Unemployed People Aged Over 59 Are Not Eligible for Job-seeker's Allowance Our description of job-seeker's allowance implies that all unemployed people are entitled to claim it, but this is not so. For example, people aged 60 or more who become unemployed cannot claim it. Such people who want to work and who have no jobs are excluded from the official figures for the unemployed simply because their age disqualifies them from job-seeker's allowance. Incidentally, although these people are not entitled to job-seeker's benefit, they are often entitled to other state benefits.

Unemployed People Aged Under 18 Are Not Eligible for Job-seeker's Allowance Adults aged 16 and 17 are not entitled to job-seeker's allowance and so people in this age range who are not working are not included in the official figures for the unemployed. Such people may be entitled to other state benefits, but most of them go on one of several training schemes initiated

by the government. In many cases they do some work for an employer who offers some training in return and who is given some money by the government. People on training schemes do not count as unemployed even though they may not regard themselves as having the proper jobs they would like.

Many Unemployed People Between 18 and 59 Are Not Entitled to Job-seeker's Allowance We have seen that to claim job-seeker's allowance you must be in the 18–59 age range. But even in this age range there are many people who want jobs and who do not have them and yet who are not entitled to job-seeker's allowance and so do not get included in official figures for the unemployed. Some people are in this position because they have never had jobs, or at least not for long enough to qualify for job-seeker's allowance if they lose their jobs. The most important group of people in this position are mothers who have spent some years looking after young children but who have done little or no paid work. The time may come when they feel their family commitments enable them to seek employment, but while they are looking for jobs they are not eligible for job-seeker's allowance.

Another reason why people in the 18–59 age range may not be eligible for job-seeker's allowance arises from a rule that claimants must be actively seeking jobs. But many people who fail to find a suitable job after a prolonged and extensive search effort come to believe that there is no work available for them. They become discouraged and stop looking for work. Such people are called discouraged workers. **Discouraged workers** are people who do not have jobs and would like to work, but have stopped seeking employment. Discouraged workers are not officially counted as unemployed because they are not actively looking for jobs and so are not eligible for job-seeker's allowance.

Unrealistic Wage Expectations If someone is willing to do a job, but only for a much higher wage than the prevailing one, then it does not make sense to count that person as unemployed. For example, suppose that a jobless school leaver has applied for work as a check-out operator in a local supermarket. He is offered such a job at a wage rate of £3 an hour. He doesn't like the pay, so he rejects the offer and keeps looking for a job that pays more. Such a person could have a job but is not prepared to work at the wage rate offered. Nevertheless, he is counted

---

[1] Job-seeker's allowance is due to be introduced early in 1996. It will be a slightly revised form of unemployment benefit which it will replace.

as unemployed. Correcting the unemployment data to take account of unrealistic wage expectations would result in a lower measured unemployment rate. But how much lower we do not know.

The Unemployment Record

The UK unemployment record from 1900 to 1993 is set out in Fig. 21.1. It should be stressed that the unemployment figures recorded in this table are not all precisely comparable owing to changes made to the way in which unemployment has been recorded. The figures after the mid-1980s would probably be about 2 per cent higher if the earlier methods had continued in use.

The worst period was the Great Depression of the early 1930s when over 22 per cent of the labour force was unemployed. Although nothing as devastating as the Great Depression has been experienced in recent years, there have been some high unemployment rates. Two such periods are highlighted in

Fig. 21.1 – the years after the 1980–1981 recession and the 1991–1992 recession. There have also been periods of stable and low unemployment. The most notable example – also highlighted in the figure – was from World War II until the mid-1970s. The average unemployment rate over the whole 93-year period was 6.4 per cent.

The rates of unemployment in different countries tend to rise and fall roughly in line. You can see something of this from Fig. 21.2 which looks at the unemployment rates over the last 25 years in a number of European countries. Figure 21.2 also highlights the fact that some countries – such as Germany and Sweden – have typically had much lower unemployment rates than others – such as Ireland and the United Kingdom.

Three Types of Unemployment

Unemployment is a highly charged topic. People tend to regard the course of the unemployment rate as a

---

FIGURE 21.1

UK Unemployment, 1900–1993

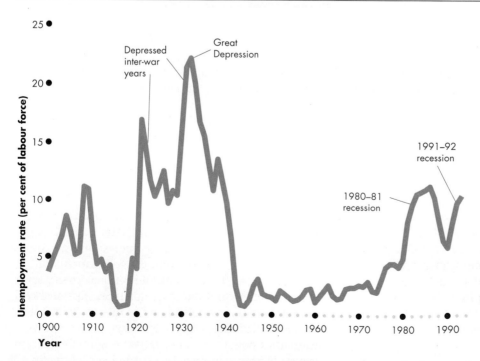

Unemployment is a persistent feature of economic life, but its rate varies considerably. The rate was very low in the two World Wars but peaked in between them during the Great Depression, when over 22 per cent of the labour force was unemployed. The level was very low between 1945 and 1975 but has been much higher since with a peak in 1986 of over 11 per cent.

Sources: For 1900–1964, B. R. Mitchell, *British Historical Statistics*, Cambridge, Cambridge University Press, 1988, p. 124 (the data for 1900–1912 are based on Feinstein's estimate but rescaled by the average ratio of his estimates to the National Insurance measure for the years of overlap (1913–1965) while the 1913–1964 figures are based on National Insurance records). For 1965–1993, Central Statistical Office, *Economic Trends Annual Supplement, 1994 Edition*, pp. 164–7, and *Economic Trends*, November 1994, T32.

FIGURE 21.2

Unemployment in Selected European Countries, 1968–1992

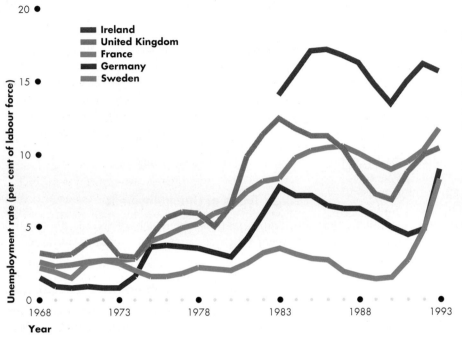

Over the last two decades, some countries – such as Ireland – have had much worse unemployment problems than others – such as Sweden. But unemployment tends to rise and fall at roughly the same time in different countries whose economies are closely linked, like those in Western Europe.

Sources: OECD, *Economic Outlook 35*, July 1984, Table R 12, and *Economic Outlook 55*, June 1994, Annex Table 20 (These OECD figures are based on figures supplied by individual countries, but the OECD adjusts the figures supplied by the countries to make them as comparable as possible. Consequently the UK figures are not necessarily the same as those in Fig. 21.1. The OECD prepared no comparable figures for Ireland before 1983.)

measure of the country's economic health, just as a doctor keeps track of a patient's temperature. What does the unemployment rate tell us about the economic health of the nation? Does all unemployment have the same origin, or are there different types of unemployment with different origins? In fact there are three different sources of unemployment and they give rise to three different types of unemployment. The three types of unemployment are:

◆ Frictional
◆ Structural
◆ Cyclical

Frictional Unemployment Unemployment that arises from the normal turnover of people in the labour market is called **frictional unemployment**. Normal labour market turnover arises from two sources. First, people are constantly changing their economic activities. Thus young people leave school and join the labour force, old people retire and leave it, and some people leave it temporarily, often to raise children,

and then rejoin it. Second, the fortunes of individual businesses are constantly changing, so some are closing down and laying off their workers while others are starting up and hiring new workers.

These persistent changes result in frictional unemployment. There are always some firms with unfilled vacancies and some people looking for work. Unemployed people don't usually take the first job that comes their way. Instead, they spend time searching out what they believe will be the best job available to them. By doing so, they hope to match their own skills and interests with the available jobs, finding a satisfying job and income.

It is unlikely that frictional unemployment will ever disappear. The amount of frictional unemployment depends on the rate at which people enter and leave the labour force and on the rate at which jobs are created and destroyed. For example, the post-war baby boom of the late 1940s brought a bulge in the number of people entering the labour force in the 1960s and an increase in the amount of frictional unemployment. When a major new shopping centre is built, jobs become available in the centre and a similar number of jobs are lost in the older part of town where shops are struggling to survive. The people who lose jobs aren't always the first to get the new jobs, and while they are between jobs, they are frictionally unemployed.

The length of time that people take to find a job is influenced by the level of state benefits they can claim. The more generous the benefits, the longer is the average time taken in job search and the higher is the rate of frictional unemployment.

Structural Unemployment Unemployment that arises when the number of jobs available in a particular region or industry falls is called **structural unemployment**. Such a decline can occur because of permanent technological change, for example, the automation of a car plant. It can also occur because of a permanent change in international competition, for example the decline in the number of jobs in the UK coalmining industry caused by a surge of cheaper imports from other countries.

The distinction between structural and frictional unemployment is not always sharp but some cases are clear. A person who loses a job in a high street shop and gets a job a few weeks later in a new out-of-town shopping centre has experienced frictional unemployment. A car worker who loses his job and, after a period of retraining and prolonged search, perhaps lasting more than a year, eventually gets a job as an insurance salesperson has experienced structural unemployment.

At some times, the amount of structural unemployment is modest, and at other times it is large. It was very large during the 1980s when employment in UK manufacturing industry fell by over a quarter.

Cyclical Unemployment Unemployment that arises from a slowdown in the pace of economic expansion is called **cyclical unemployment**. The pace of economic expansion is sometimes rapid, sometimes slow, and occasionally even negative, as in 1991–1992. When the economy expands rapidly, cyclical unemployment disappears, and when the economy expands slowly or contracts, cyclical unemployment can become extremely high. For example, a bricklayer who is laid off because the economy is going through a slow period and who gets rehired some months later when economic activity speeds up has experienced cyclical unemployment.

Full Employment

Because unemployment is so painful for those experiencing it, the government is often pressed to pursue policies which will secure 'full employment'. But this does not mean zero unemployment. You can see from Fig. 21.1 that there never has been zero unemployment. **Full employment** means a state in which the quantity of labour demanded equals the quantity of labour supplied. So full employment occurs when there is no cyclical unemployment and the only unemployment is frictional and structural. As there is *always* some frictional and structural unemployment, so there is always some unemployment, even at full employment.

The unemployment rate at full employment is called the **natural rate of unemployment**. The natural unemployment rate fluctuates because the number of people who are frictionally or structurally unemployed fluctuates. Some economists believe that the natural rate of unemployment in the United Kingdom tends to vary relatively little and is around 5–6 per cent of the labour force. Other economists believe that the natural rate of unemployment varies appreciably and is especially high when demographic or technological changes lead to high frictional and structural unemployment.

The Costs of Unemployment

There are four main costs of unemployment. They are:

◆ Loss of output and income
◆ Loss of human capital
◆ Increase in crime
◆ Loss of human dignity

Loss of Output and Income The most obvious costs of people being unemployed are the loss of output that they would have produced and the loss of income that they would have earned if they had had jobs. If the actual rate of unemployment in an economy is much in excess of the natural rate – that is, if the level of employment is below the full employment level – then the lost output from unemployment may be enormous. In fact, it appears that if actual employment is 1 per cent below the full employment level, then output may be below the level it would be with full employment by 2 per cent or more.

To see the main reason for this, consider an imaginary small economy with a workforce of 100,000, and suppose it initially has unemployment at the natural level of, say, 5 per cent. So unemployment is 5,000 while 95,000 people have jobs. Next, suppose output falls so that firms need less labour, and suppose unemployment rises to 6,000, that is 6 per cent. As 1,000 of the 95,000 workers have lost their jobs, that is about 1 per cent of the workers, it might be thought that output must have fallen by about 1 per cent, but it is probable that output will have fallen by 2 per cent. The point is that if output fell by 2 per cent, then certainly firms might want to cut the number of hours of work done for them by 2 per cent, but they would probably arrange for about half of this reduction to be handled through less use of overtime and about half through employing fewer people. So a rise in unemployment of 1 per cent might indicate a drop in output of 2 per cent.

Let's translate this discovery to the United Kingdom in 1993. In that year, unemployment was around 10 per cent, that is about 5 per cent above what some economists would believe to be the country's natural rate of unemployment. This suggests that output might have been 10 per cent below the level that it would have been had unemployment been at the natural level. The value of this loss in output is about £1,000 for every person in the country.

Those economists who believe that the natural rate of unemployment itself varies think that the lost output cost of unemployment is small. They regard the fluctuations in the unemployment rate as arising from fluctuations in structural unemployment. With rapid structural change, people need to retrain and find their most productive new jobs. A period of high unemployment is like an investment in the future. It is the price paid today for a larger future income.

Loss of Human Capital   A second cost of unemployment is the permanent damage that can be done to an unemployed worker by hindering his or her career development and acquisition of human capital. **Human capital** is the value of a person's education and acquired skills. For example, Judy finishes law school at a time when unemployment is high, and she just can't find a job in a law office. Desperately short of income, she becomes a taxi driver. After a year in this work, she discovers it is impossible to compete with the new crop of law graduates and is stuck with taxi driving. Her human capital as a lawyer has been wiped out by high unemployment.

Increase in Crime   A high unemployment rate may lead to a high crime rate. It is hard to be sure about this. In the United Kingdom, for instance, crime was low in the 1930s when unemployment was high. Nevertheless, it is notable that there was an unusual drop in crime around 1988 when there had recently been a sharp fall in unemployment.

There are two reasons why a rise in unemployment might lead to a rise in crime. First, when people cannot earn an income from legal work, they sometimes turn to illegal work so the amount of theft may increase sharply. Second, with low incomes and increased frustration, family life begins to suffer and there may be increases in crimes such as child beating, wife assault and suicide.

Loss of Human Dignity   The final cost of unemployment is difficult to quantify, but it is large and very important. It is the loss of self-esteem that afflicts many who suffer prolonged periods of unemployment. It is probably this aspect of unemployment that makes it so highly charged with political and social significance.

REVIEW

There have been large fluctuations in the unemployment rate, but no matter how low its rate, unemployment never disappears. Some unemployment is frictional, arising from labour market turnover. Some is structural, arising from the decline in certain industries and regions. And some is cyclical, arising from a slowdown in the pace of economic expansion. Full employment occurs when the only unemployment is frictional and structural. The natural rate of unemployment is that unemployment rate at which there is no cyclical unemployment. This rate fluctuates with changes in the frictional and structural unemployment rate. The costs of unemployment include lost output and income, loss of human capital, an increase in crime and a loss of human dignity.   ◆

Unemployment is not the only indicator of the state of the nation's economic health. Another is inflation. Let's now examine that.

Inflation

Inflation is a sustained upward movement in the average level of prices (see also Chapter 30). The word 'sustained' is an important part of this definition. If prices rise on a once-off basis, as might happen if the government raised value added tax, then that once-off rise would not be regarded as an inflation. The term **deflation** is sometimes used for a sustained downward move in prices, a phenomenon that is the opposite of inflation. Deflation has been very rare since the 1930s. The boundary between inflation and deflation is price stability. **Price stability** occurs when the average level of prices is moving neither up nor down. The average level of prices is called the **price level**. It is measured by a price index. A **price index** measures the average level of prices in one period as a percentage of their average level in another period called the base period.

Price indexes have been produced in the United Kingdom for many years. Figure 21.3 shows what happened to prices between 1900 and 1993. You will see that prices were very stable between 1900 and World War I. In fact prices had also been pretty stable throughout the preceding century. And although prices rose sharply during World War I, they then fell back significantly afterwards. But since the mid-1930s prices have risen inexorably. They are now more than 35 times higher than they were in 1934. Indeed, the average rate of inflation since 1934 has been just over 6 per cent. But prices have not moved upward at a constant and steady pace. During some periods, such as the years of World War I and between 1973 and 1982, the increase was exceptionally high – at times exceeding 20 per cent a year. These were the most sustained bursts of high inflation for the United Kingdom in the twentieth century. At the opposite extreme there are some years in which prices have fallen. The last occasion on which this occurred in a sustained way

---

FIGURE 21.3

The UK Price Level, 1900–1993

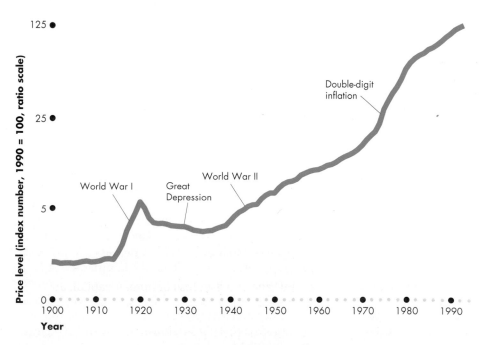

Before 1914 the general level of prices fluctuated a little, but falls were as common as rises. Prices rose sharply during World War I and then fell back in the aftermath of the war and in the Great Depression. Since 1934 prices have risen continuously; the general level of prices is 35 times higher than it was then. Inflation was particularly rapid in the late 1970s and early 1990s.

Sources: For 1900–1948, B. R. Mitchell, *British Historical Statistics*, Cambridge, Cambridge University Press, 1988 (the deflator for GDP at factor cost was calculated from data for nominal GDP, pp. 833–5, and for real GDP, pp. 839–41, and separate series were spliced together with 1980 taken as the base year). For 1948–1993, Central Statistical Office, *Economic Trends Annual Supplement, 1994 Edition*, p. 8, and *Economic Trends*, November 1994, T2.

was during the Great Depression years of 1927–1933.

Inflation Rate and the Price Level

The **inflation rate** is the percentage change in the price level. The formula for the annual inflation rate is:

$$\text{Inflation rate} = \frac{\begin{array}{c}\text{Current year's}\\\text{price level}\end{array} - \begin{array}{c}\text{Last year's}\\\text{price level}\end{array}}{\text{Last year's price level}} \times 100.$$

A common way of measuring the price level is to use the Retail Prices Index or RPI. (We'll learn more about the RPI in Chapter 22.) We can illustrate the calculation of the annual inflation rate by using this index. In August 1993, the RPI was 141.3 and in August 1992 it was 138.9. The base period for these figures was January 1987. Substituting these values into the above formula gives the rate of inflation from August 1992 to August 1993 as:

$$\text{Inflation rate} = \frac{141.3 - 138.9}{138.9} \times 100$$

$$= 1.7 \text{ per cent}$$

The Recent Inflation Record

There have been some dramatic changes in the inflation rate in the United Kingdom in the last 25 years. Fig. 21.4 shows the inflation rate in each of these years both in the United Kingdom and in some other West European countries. Inflation rates had typically been low in the 1950s and early 1960s, but began to accelerate towards 1970. You can see in the figure how inflation rates rose dramatically between 1968 and the mid-1970s. There was some tendency for the rates to fall between the mid-1970s and the early 1980s, and there were much greater falls later. The figure also shows that inflation rates have typically been higher in some countries – such as Ireland and the United Kingdom – than in others – such as France and Germany.

Although the inflation rate has gone up and down over the years, the price level rarely falls. The last time UK prices fell over a year as a whole was in 1933, but recently they have occasionally fallen for a month or two. For instance, prices fell during September 1992 and during January 1993. In such months the inflation rate was negative. Reading Between the Lines on pp. 590–591 considers how prices have risen in recent years for a specific set of goods, namely those bought to celebrate Christmas.

Inflation and the Value of Money When inflation is present, money loses value. The **value of money** is the amount of goods and services that can be bought with a given amount of money. If there is inflation, you cannot buy as many groceries with £50 this year as you could last year. The rate at which the value of money falls depends on the inflation rate. When the inflation rate is high, as it was in 1975, money loses its value rapidly. When inflation is low, as it was in 1993, the value of money falls slowly.

We saw in Fig. 21.4 that inflation rates in different countries can differ by a lot over a prolonged period of time. When this happens, there is a change in the foreign exchange value of different currencies. A **foreign exchange rate** is the rate at which one country's currency – or money – can be exchanged for another's. For example, in March 1993 1 pound sterling exchanged for 2.41 Deutschmarks or for 2,328 Italian lire. A decade earlier, in 1983, 1 pound exchanged for 3.59 Deutschmarks or for 2,128 Italian lire. Thus in the decade after 1983, the value of the pound fell sharply in terms of the mark but rose a little in terms of the lire. This performance reflects the fact that the value of money in the United Kingdom has fallen much more quickly than the value of money in Germany but slightly slower than the value of money in Italy. We'll learn more about exchange rates and how they are influenced by inflation in Chapter 35.

Is Inflation a Problem?

Is it a problem if money loses its value and at a rate that varies from one year to another? It is, indeed, a problem, but to understand why, we need to distinguish between anticipated and unanticipated inflation. When prices are moving upward, most people are aware of that fact. They also have some notion about the rate at which they are rising. The rate at which people (on average) believe that the price level will rise is called the **expected inflation rate**. But expectations may be right or wrong. If they turn out to be right, the actual inflation rate equals the expected inflation rate and inflation is said to be anticipated. That is, an **anticipated inflation** is an inflation rate that has been correctly forecast (on average). To the extent that the inflation rate is wrongly forecast, it is said to be unanticipated. That is, **unanticipated inflation** is the part of the inflation rate that has caught people by surprise.

FIGURE 21.4

Inflation in Selected European Countries, 1968–1992

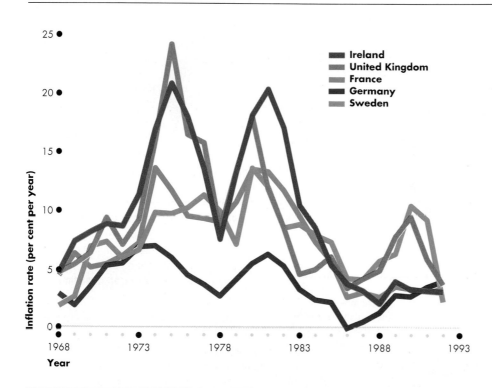

Inflation is a persistent feature of modern economic life in all countries. But some countries, such as Germany, have persistently had lower inflation than other countries, such as Ireland. European countries tended to have low inflation in the 1950s and 1960s, and then more rapid inflation until a decline set in during the early 1980s.

Sources: OECD, *Economic Outlook 41*, June 1987, Table R 10, *Economic Outlook 47*, June 1990, Table 49, and *Economic Outlook 55*, June 1994, Annex Table 15.

The problems arising from inflation differ depending on whether its rate is anticipated or unanticipated. Let's begin by looking at the problems arising from unanticipated inflation.

The Problem of Unanticipated Inflation

Unanticipated inflation is a problem because it produces unanticipated changes in the value of money. Money is used as a measuring rod of value in the transactions that we undertake. Borrowers and lenders and workers and their employers all make contracts in terms of money. If the value of money varies unexpectedly over time, then the amounts *really* paid and received differ from those that people intended to pay and receive when they signed the contracts. Measuring value with a rod whose units vary is a bit like trying to measure a piece of cloth with an elastic ruler. The size of the cloth depends on how tightly the ruler is stretched.

Let's take a look at the effects of unanticipated inflation by considering what happens to agreements between borrowers and lenders and between workers and employers.

Borrowers and Lenders People often say that inflation is good for borrowers and bad for lenders. To see how they reach that conclusion – and why it's not always correct – consider the following situation.

Sue borrows $5,000 from the bank to buy a car and agrees to repay the loan with interest one year later. The agreed interest rate is 10 per cent a year. After one year Sue repays the loan of $5,000 and also pays interest of $500. So altogether she gives the bank $5,500. Suppose there is no inflation. The goods and services that can be bought with $5,000 are the same after one year as they are when Sue borrows the money. In this situation, to pay the bank $500 in interest, Sue has to forgo the consumption of $500 worth of goods and services. In contrast, the

Inflation and the Cost of Christmas

The Times compiles an index each year of the cost of celebrating Christmas.

The index is based on a basket of goods first examined in 1973 and shows that in the subsequent 20 years, the cost of celebrating Christmas increased five and a half times.

There are a number of complications in this calculation because the nature of some of the goods in the basket has changed over time.

Changes like better quality Christmas trees with non-dropping needles and the spread of metric measurements could affect the calculations made.

THE TIMES, 24 DECEMBER 1993

Tree and treats add pounds to price of family Christmas

Robin Young

CELEBRATING Christmas will cost the average family more than five and half times as much this year as it did 20 years ago. The increased expense since last year alone amounts to £11.64 (plus a notional $^1/_2$p), bringing the total bill for festivities for two adults and two children to an estimated £193.93$^1/_2$. In 1973, the total was said to be just £34.89$^1/_2$.

The figures are calculated according to an index devised by Baroness Oppenheim-Barnes, a former consumer affairs minister and National Consumer Council chairman. As the conservative MP Sally Oppenheim, she claimed in 1977 that under a Labour Government the cost of Christmas had doubled since 1973, and produced a costed shopping list to prove it. *The Times* has recosted the same items regularly since 1978, revisiting the same north London supermarket to compare prices.

Many things have happened to complicate the calculations in the intervening years – not least the abolition of the half-penny, which still features in the sums because of unit pricing. Manufacturers no longer favour 40 oz Christmas cakes, or even 1$^1/_2$ lb puddings. Our 1$^1/_2$ lb pudding is therefore as notional as the halfpenny, based on the price per pound of 2 lb puddings. Buying one weight [at] 1 lb and another weighing 8 oz would have put the bill up by an extra 52p.

The bottles of spirits – now the supermarket's own brand – are 5 cl smaller than in 1973, when the standard size was still 75 cl. The single pint of beer, always rather an anomaly when compared with the average family's supposed consumption of three bottles of spirits, is based on the supermarket's unit price for cans of traditional bitter.

The Christmas tree is specially expensive this year, because our shop, which stopped selling them for a number of years, has resumed with some particularly fine, ready-mounted, non-needle dropping specimens. At market stalls nearby it is still possible to buy more traditionally scraggy affairs at £1 a foot.

None of the toys priced by *The Times* when we first took over the calculation in 1978 is still sold, so we have priced what we hope is a similarly typical selection designed to please today's youngsters.

COST OF CHRISTMAS

	1973	1993
Turkey, 14 lb fresh	£ 7.06	£13.96
Mince pies, 6	12p	59p
Christmas pudding, 1$^1/_2$ lb	34p	£ 2.82
Christmas cake, 40 oz	90p	£ 4.50
Brussels sprouts	12p	52$^1/_2$p
Potatoes, 3 lb	7$^1/_2$p	30p
$^1/_2$ lb of chocolates	40p	£ 1.49
Assorted nuts, $^1/_2$ lb	17p	49$^1/_2$p
Christmas tree, 5 ft	60p	£25.00
Tree lights	99p	£ 6.99
Tinsel	60p	£ 1.45
Christmas crackers	49p	£ 4.49
Bottle of gin	£ 2.45	£ 8.95
Bottle of whisky	£ 2.39	£ 8.95
Bottle of brandy	£ 4.44	£ 9.59
Pint of beer	19p	69$^1/_2$p
24 Christmas cards	60p	£ 2.49
5 sheets wrapping paper	15p	59p
Postage, first class × 24	84p	£ 6.00
Toys and games	£10.95	£81.16
Parcel post, 4 × 2 kg	£ 1.08	£13.00
Total	**£34.89$^1/_2$**	**£193.93$^1/_2$**

© The Times. Reprinted with permission.

Background and Analysis

When the inflation rate is calculated, it is based on the rise in prices of a basket of commodities bought by an average household. The basket of commodities here relates to Christmas, but the principle is just the same.

Inflation is normally expressed as an annual percentage increase, but the calculation also allows us to express price rises in other terms, for example the extent to which prices rise over a given period of time (20 years in this article):

$$\frac{£193.935 - £34.895}{£34.895} \times 100$$

By considering the same basket of goods over the last 20 years a direct comparison is easy to make, but it assumes that people buy the same commodities now as they did 20 years ago.

In taking the same basket each year and looking only at the change in prices, it is hard to account for quality changes over time. The price of a Christmas tree has risen dramatically, but so has the quality (we may be paying more, but we are getting more for our money).

In expressing how much more people have to pay to celebrate Christmas, the article does not consider the extent of wage increases over the same period.

The figure compares the cost of Christmas, the general price level and personal disposable income between 1973 and 1993. It shows that the cost of Christmas has risen by just over five and a half times, the general price level has risen by nearly six times whereas personal disposable income has risen by over eight and a half times.

Thus it can be seen that the cost of Christmas has risen but by less than the general price level. Both have risen less than people's personal disposable income.

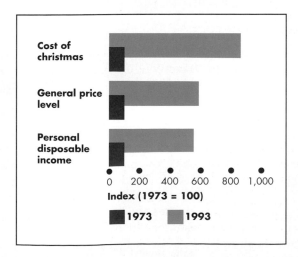

bank ends up with £500 more than it started with and could – if it chose – buy more goods and services than it could have done at the start.

Next, suppose that Sue and the bank made the same agreement but the economy is experiencing inflation at a rate of 10 per cent a year. Once again Sue gives the bank £5,500 at the end of the year – £5,000 as repayment and £500 in interest. In this case, when the bank receives £5,500, the quantity of goods and services that it can buy with that money is exactly what it could have bought with £5,000 a year earlier. (With a 10 per cent inflation rate, the price of a car like the one Sue bought, for example, will have risen from £5,000 to £5,500.) As far as Sue is concerned, although she pays the bank £500 in interest, that payment imposes no opportunity cost on her. Over the year, the value of money has fallen. The £5,000 that she borrowed is now worth less in terms of goods and services. It now costs £5,500 to buy what cost £5,000 at the start, but Sue is repaying only £5,000. This fall in the value of the loan cancels out the £500 interest payment and leaves her having *really* paid no interest at all. Sue, the borrower, gains at the expense of the bank, the lender.

But the borrower does not always necessarily gain and the lender lose when there is inflation. Suppose that both Sue and the bank anticipate a 10 per cent inflation rate. They can act to offset the decreasing value of money by adjusting the interest rate they agree upon. If they agree that 10 per cent is the appropriate interest rate with no inflation, they may agree to a 20 per cent interest rate. Let's see what happens in this case.

Sue pays the bank £6,000 at the end of the year. Of this, £5,000 is the amount borrowed and £1,000 is the interest payment (20 per cent of £5,000). Although this £1,000 is all called interest, only £500 is *really* interest – the other £500 is compensation for the loss in the value of money. Sue *really* pays a 10 per cent interest rate and that's what the bank *really* receives. To see this, notice that when Sue repays the bank, the bank would need £5,500 to buy as much as it could have bought for £5,000 at the beginning of the year. So lending the money to Sue enables the bank to buy only £500 more goods and services than it could have initially bought with £5,000 if it had spent the £5,000 itself.

If borrowers and lenders correctly anticipate the inflation rate, interest rates will be adjusted to cancel

out inflation's effect on the interest *really* paid and *really* received. It is only when borrowers and lenders make errors in forecasting the future inflation rate that one of them gains and the other loses. But those gains and losses can go either way. If the inflation rate turns out to be higher than is generally expected, then the borrower gains and the lender loses. Conversely, if the inflation rate turns out to be lower than is generally expected, then the borrower loses and the lender gains.

Thus it is not inflation itself that produces gains and losses for borrowers and lenders. It is an *unanticipated increase* in the inflation rate that benefits borrowers and hurts lenders and an *unanticipated decrease* in the inflation rate that benefits lenders and hurts borrowers.

In the United Kingdom, in the late 1960s and 1970s, the inflation rate kept rising and to some degree the rise was unanticipated, so borrowers tended to gain. In the mid-1980s, the inflation rate fell more quickly than was anticipated so lenders gained. On the international scene, many developing countries, such as Mexico and Brazil, borrowed large amounts of money from abroad in the late 1970s and early 1980s at high interest rates, anticipating that an inflation rate of more than 10 per cent a year would persist. These countries are now stuck with paying the interest on these loans without the extra revenue that they expected to receive from the higher prices for their exports.

Workers and Employers Another common belief is that inflation redistributes income between workers and their employers. Some people believe that workers gain at the expense of employers, and others believe the contrary.

The previous discussion concerning borrowers and lenders applies to workers and their employers as well. If inflation turns out to be higher than was anticipated, then wages will have been set too low. Profits will be higher than expected and wages will buy fewer goods and services than expected. So employers will gain at the expense of workers. Conversely, if inflation turns out to be lower than was anticipated, then wages will have been set too high and profits will be squeezed. Workers will be able to buy more goods and services than was originally anticipated. In this case workers will gain at the expense of employers.

In recent years, unanticipated changes in the inflation rate have produced fluctuations in the buying power of earnings – the value of pay cheques in terms of the goods and services they buy. For example, in 1980, when the inflation rate climbed to more than 18 per cent a year, the buying power of earnings continued to increase but at a substantially slower pace than normal. When the inflation rate came down sharply in 1992, wage growth outpaced inflation and real wages grew unusually quickly.

We've seen the problems that unanticipated inflation can bring. Let's now turn to anticipated inflation.

The Problem of Anticipated Inflation

Anticipated inflation is hardly a problem at all if the inflation rate is low. But anticipated inflation becomes a problem for four reasons when the inflation rate is high. It imposes an opportunity cost on holding money in the form of cash or a bank balance on which little or no interest is paid. It encourages a wasteful increase in the volume and frequency of transactions that people undertake. It requires producers to update frequently their information on prices – the resulting costs being known as menu costs. And it causes resources to be switched from productive activities into forecasting inflation. Let's look at these points more closely.

Opportunity Cost of Holding Money When you hold money in the form of cash or a bank balance on which no interest is paid, your money loses value if there is inflation. Even if you correctly anticipate the rate of inflation, your money still loses value. You can minimize this loss by minimizing the amount of money you hold in this way, but doing so is not easy. You may be able to switch your bank balance into an account which earns interest, but it is hard to economize on holding cash. Suppose you have an interest-earning bank deposit and suppose you spend £300 cash each month. You could go to the bank once a month and withdraw £300, or once every 10 days and withdraw £100, or once each day and withdraw £10. You can see that to have, on average, less cash and more money in your deposit, you will need to make more frequent trips to the bank to withdraw cash when you need it. Such trips incur costs, often known as shoe-leather costs, though in fact it is the time and effort involved rather than the wear on your shoes that will most affect you. Another way of reducing

the amount of cash you hold is to make more of your purchases by cheque. But this is also time consuming, and hence not often used for small day-to-day purchases.

Volume and Frequency of Transactions There is another way of holding less cash or money in non-interest earning deposits. This is to spend your money as soon as you are paid. However, transacting at a high frequency is much less convenient and more costly than transacting at a lower frequency. But the higher the anticipated inflation, the higher is the frequency with which transactions are undertaken. This aspect of the problem of anticipated inflation can be serious if the inflation rate is sufficiently high. For example, during *hyperinflations* – situations in which prices are rising faster than 50 per cent per month – the opportunity cost of holding money is enormous.

There have been some severe hyperinflations in Europe in this century. Hyperinflation occurred in several countries during the 1920s, notably in Germany. If a price index there had been given a value of 100 in 1920, then the index for 1923 would have been 1,119,000,000,000! This hyperinflation has often been blamed for sowing the seeds of the fascists' rise to power. More recent, and even more dramatic, was the hyperinflation in Hungary after World War II. This helped bring communists to power there. Table 21.1 shows price indexes for Hungary in this period. The need to transact quickly was highlighted by the fact that people could join a bread queue when the price was 10,000 pengös a kilogram, only to find when they reached the head of the queue half an hour later that the price had risen to 50,000 pengös. Wages were usually spent within the day, if not the hour, when they were received.

Menu Costs Inflation imposes on producers the task of revising the information they publish about their prices. Among the producers concerned are restaurants and cafes which have to produce revised menus from time to time. Consequently these costs have become known as 'menu costs'. But all producers with published price lists and all retailers with price labels will be affected. Perhaps the retailers most affected are those which use slot machines. For them inflation may mean making adjustments to the machines, or the goods sold in them, as well as changes to the prices displayed on the machines.

Table 21.1

The Hungarian Inflation of 1945–1946

Date	Price index
15 July 1945	100
30 September 1945	423
30 November 1945	16,801
31 January 1946	77,054
31 March 1946	2,228,900
31 May 1946	11,700,000,000
31 July 1946	136,650,000,000,000,000

The currency in Hungary at the start of its inflation was known as the pengö. Before long there was a 'new' pengö defined as 1 million old ones. Then came the milpengö – defined as 1 million new pengös – and the bilpengö – defined as 1 million milpengös. At one stage notes were issued for 100,000,000 bilpengös. In July 1946 such a note would buy two shirts on the black market.

Source: Index derived from P. Falush 'The Hungarian Hyper-Inflation of 1945–46', *National Westminster Bank Quarterly Review,* August 1976.

High and Variable Inflation   There are costs with anticipated inflation if the rate of inflation is variable, for then people must constantly make new and revised forecasts about the future rate. The resources, chiefly labour, that are used in making these forecasts must be diverted from productive activities. It may become more profitable to forecast the inflation rate correctly than to invent a new product. Doctors, lawyers, accountants, farmers – just about everyone – can make themselves better off, not by practising the profession for which they have been trained, but by becoming amateur economists and inflation forecasters. From a social perspective, this diversion of talent resulting from inflation is like throwing our scarce resources on to the rubbish heap. This waste of resources is a cost of inflation.

Indexing

It is sometimes suggested that the costs of inflation can be avoided by indexing. **Indexing** is a technique that links payments made under a contract to the price level. With indexing, Sue in our example above would not agree to pay back the loan in terms of a set number of pounds; instead, she might have agreed to pay a rate of interest equal to 3 per cent a year plus the annual inflation rate. Similarly, an indexed employment contract does not specify the number of pounds that will be paid to workers; instead, the wage rate might be specified to be £10 an hour for the first year increasing by the same percentage amount as the annual inflation rate in subsequent years. The amount of interest to be paid on bank deposits can also be linked to the inflation rate in order to avoid the opportunity cost of holding such deposits. Indexing is actually used for some pensions and some government transfer payments.

However, adopting indexing to cope with changes in the value of money is not a simple matter. One problem is that there are actually many different indexes that could be used, and people will spend much time resolving disputes over which index should be selected for a given contract.

So, though indexing can be helpful in some situations, it is not a universal solution to the problem of inflation. Only by somehow holding the price level constant can the costs of inflation be avoided.

REVIEW

I nflation is a process in which the average level of prices rises and the value of money falls. The inflation rate is measured as the percentage change in a price index. The inflation rate rises and falls but, since the 1930s, the *price level* has risen every year. The effects of inflation depend on whether it is unanticipated or anticipated. Unanticipated inflation brings unpredictable gains and losses to borrowers and lenders, workers and employers. Anticipated inflation becomes a serious problem when its rate is high. It imposes losses on people who hold cash or bank balances that pay no interest, and so it encourages people to spend their money as soon as they receive it; it also requires regular revisions to price information, and – if the inflation rate is variable – it diverts resources from productive uses into forecasting inflation.   ◆

A third indicator of a nation's economic health is its gross domestic product. Let's now examine that.

Gross Domestic Product

The value of all the final goods and services produced in the economy in a year is called **gross domestic product** or GDP. **Final goods and services** are goods and services that are not used as inputs in the production of other goods and services, but are bought by their final user. Examples of final goods are cans of beer and cars. Examples of final services are car insurance and haircuts.

Not all goods and services are final. Some are intermediate goods and services. **Intermediate goods and services** are those used as inputs into the production process of another good or service. Examples of intermediate goods are the windscreens, batteries and gearboxes used by car producers and the paper and ink used by newspaper printers. Examples of intermediate services are the banking and insurance services bought by car producers and newspaper printers. Whether a good or service is intermediate or final depends on who buys it for what purpose. For example, electric power purchased by a car producer or a printer is an intermediate good, but electric power bought by a household is a final good.

When we measure gross domestic product, we do not include the value of intermediate goods and services produced. If we did, then we would be counting the same thing more than once. When someone buys a new car from the local Rover dealer, that is a final transaction and the full value of the car is counted as part of GDP. So we must not also count as part of GDP the amount the dealer paid to Rover for the car or the amounts that Rover paid to all its suppliers for the car's various parts.

When we measure GDP, we want to include all the final goods and services produced. Obviously, we cannot get a useful measure by adding up the numbers of all products – such as cars, newspapers, kilowatts of electric power, haircuts and car insurance policies. Instead, to calculate GDP we add up the *value* in pounds of the output of each final good or service. Thus GDP includes the value of each final good and service. Each of these values is measured in the common unit of pounds and equals the quantity produced of each final good or service multiplied by its price.

We measure GDP in pounds, but it is really a mixture of real quantities – the numbers of final goods and services produced – and pound quantities – the prices of the goods and services. So

measured GDP would change if there were a change in quantities alone or if there were a change in prices alone. In practice, however, quantities and prices are continually changing, so each change in measured GDP contains a mixture of the effects of changes in prices and changes in the quantities of final goods and services. For many purposes, it is important to distinguish price changes from quantity changes. To do so, we use the concepts of nominal GDP and real GDP. Let's examine these two concepts.

Nominal GDP and Real GDP

Nominal GDP measures the value of the output of final goods and services using *current* prices. Nominal GDP for the United Kingdom in 1993 was £627 billion. This means that the quantities of final goods and services produced in 1993 were worth £627 billion when valued at 1993 prices. **Real GDP** measures the value of the output of final goods and services using the prices that prevailed in some base period. Real GDP for the United Kingdom in 1993, with 1990 as the base year, was £546 billion. This means that the quantities of final goods and services produced in 1993 were worth £546 billion when valued at 1990 prices. An alternative name for real GDP is *GDP at constant prices*. The UK examples quoted here each referred to a time period of a year, but it is possible to measure GDP for shorter periods such as quarters. For example, the nominal GDP for the United Kingdom in the last quarter of 1993 was £161 billion.

Comparing real GDP from one year to another enables us to say whether the economy has produced more or fewer goods and services. Comparing nominal GDP from one year to another does not permit us to compare the quantities of goods and services produced in those two years. Nominal GDP may be higher next year than this year, but that might reflect only higher prices, not more production.

The importance of the distinction between real GDP and nominal GDP is illustrated in Fig. 21.5. Real GDP is shown by the height of the red area and nominal GDP is shown by the height of the red and the green areas together. The height of the green area shows the inflation component of nominal GDP. In 1968, nominal GDP was £44 billion. By 1993, it had grown to £627 billion, so it was over 14 times higher than it was in 1968. But only part of that increase represents an increase in the quantity of goods and services produced – that is, an increase in

FIGURE 21.5

Gross Domestic Product, 1968–1993

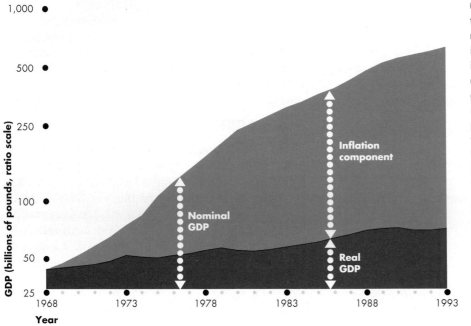

Gross domestic product increased more than 14-fold between 1968 and 1993. But much of that increase was the result of inflation. The increase in real GDP, which is that part of the increase in nominal GDP caused by an increase in the volume of goods and services produced, also increased but at a much more modest pace. The figure shows how the real and the inflation components of nominal GDP have evolved. Nominal GDP increased in every year, but real GDP fell in 1974, 1975, 1980, 1981, 1991 and 1992.

Sources: Central Statistical Office, *Economic Trends Annual Supplement 1994*, p. 12, and *Economic Trends*, April 1994, T4. (Real GDP at market prices has been rescaled to a 1968 base.)

FIGURE 21.6

UK Real GDP, 1900–1993

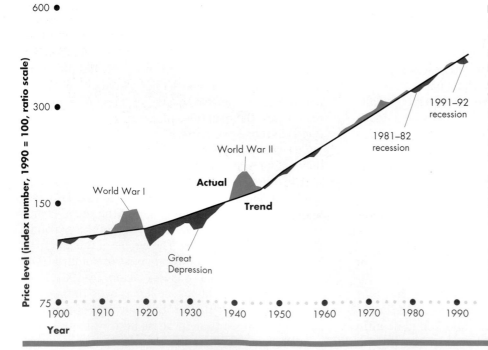

Real GDP grew at an average rate of about 1.8 per cent per year between 1900 and 1993. This general tendency of real GDP to increase is illustrated by trend real GDP. But GDP has not grown at the same rate each year. In some periods, such as World War II, real GDP expanded quickly and moved above trend. In other periods, such as the 1980–1981 and 1991–1992 recessions, real GDP declined and fell below trend.

Sources: For real GDP 1900–1948, B. R. Mitchell, *British Historical Statistics*, Cambridge, Cambridge University Press, 1988, data for real GDP (at factor cost), pp. 837–41. For real GDP 1948–1993, Central Statistical Office, *Economic Trends Annual Supplement, 1994 Edition*, p. 12, and *Economic Trends*, April 1994, T4. (Trend GDP was calculated as a fifth-order polynomial fitted to the logarithm of real GDP.)

real GDP. Real GDP in 1993 was less than double the level of 1968. Notice that nominal GDP increased every year, but real GDP declined in six different years.

Real GDP – the Record

Figure 21.6 shows the record of real GDP in the United Kingdom between 1900 and 1993. Two facts stand out. First, there has been a general tendency for real GDP to increase. Second, the rate of upward movement has not been uniform, and sometimes real GDP has actually fallen. The biggest fall occurred in the aftermath of World War I. More recently, falls occurred in the aftermath of World War II, in 1980–1981 and in 1991–1992. There have also been periods in which real GDP grew extremely quickly – for example, shortly before and during World War II.

To obtain a clearer picture of the changes in real GDP, we'll consider separately the two general tendencies we identified above. The first of these features is the general upward movement of real GDP. This feature of real GDP is called trend real GDP. Trend real GDP rises for four reasons:

◆ Growing population
◆ Population acquires more human capital
◆ Growing stock of capital equipment
◆ Advances in technology

These forces have produced the general upward tendency that you can see in Fig. 21.6. Trend real GDP is illustrated in Fig. 21.6 as a thin black line passing through the middle of the path actually followed by real GDP in its meanderings above trend and below trend.

The second feature of real GDP is its periodic fluctuation around its trend. Real GDP fluctuations are measured as percentage deviations of real GDP from trend. They are illustrated in Fig. 21.7. As you can see, real GDP fluctuations show distinct cycles in economic activity. At times such as the Great Depression and in the mid-1970s, early 1980s and early 1990s, real GDP fluctuates below trend, and during the war years it fluctuates above trend.

FIGURE 21.7

Deviations of Real GDP from Trend, 1900–1993

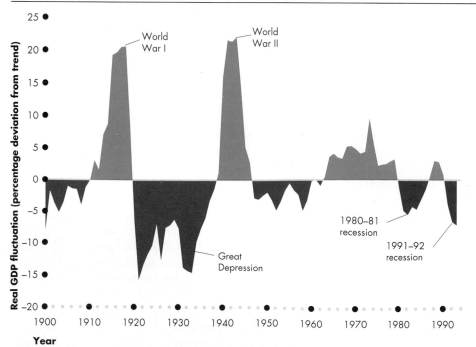

Real GDP does not grow steadily. Instead it oscillates above and below the trend line. This figure highlights the oscillations. There had been several pronounced peaks and troughs in the nineteenth century, but nothing to compare with the two World War peaks or the inter-war depression. There were important troughs in the early 1980s and early 1990s.

Source: Derived from Fig. 21.6.

The Benefits and Costs of Growth in Real GDP

The upward trend in real GDP is the major source of improvements in living standards. The pace of this upward movement has a powerful effect on the standard of living of one generation compared with its predecessor. For example, if real GDP trends upward at 1 per cent a year, then it takes 70 years for real GDP to double. But if real GDP trends upward at 10 per cent a year, then real GDP doubles in just seven years. Over the 163-year period between 1830 and 1993, the United Kingdom achieved an average growth rate of real GDP of almost exactly 2 per cent a year, which means real GDP doubled approximately every 35 years.

Rapid growth in real GDP brings enormous benefits. It enables us to consume more goods and services of all kinds. It enables us to spend more on housing and health services, more on research and exploration, more on roads and holidays. It even enables us to spend more on the environment, for instance cleaning lakes and protecting our air.

But an upward trend in real GDP has its costs. The more quickly real GDP increases, the faster exhaustible resources such as oil and natural gas are depleted, and the more severe environmental and atmospheric pollution problems become. Although people have more to spend on these problems, they become bigger problems requiring higher expenditures. Furthermore, the more quickly real GDP increases, the more people have to accept change, both in what they consume and in the jobs that they do.

The benefits of more rapid growth in real GDP have to be balanced against the costs. The choices that people make to balance these benefits and costs, acting individually and through government institutions, determine the actual pace at which real GDP increases.

As we have seen, real GDP does not increase at an even pace. In some years the economy booms and in other years it busts. Are the fluctuations in real GDP important? This question is a hard one to answer and one on which economists disagree. Some economists believe that fluctuations are costly: when real GDP is below trend GDP, output is lost, and when real GDP is above trend GDP, bottlenecks and shortages arise so that there is upward pressure on prices. With output below trend, unemployment is above its natural rate and the economy's stock of capital equipment is underused. If a downturn in real GDP can be avoided,

average income and consumption levels can be increased. If large fluctuations above trend GDP can be controlled, shortages and bottlenecks can be avoided and inflation better kept in check.

Other economists believe that the fluctuations in real GDP represent the best possible response to the uneven pace of technological change. When technological progress is rapid, capital accumulation is also rapid, so total production increases as more new-technology capital is produced. Once a boom driven by the exploitation of new technologies has run its course, the economy temporarily drops into low gear, ready to accelerate with the next burst of technological progress and innovation. We cannot smooth the rate at which new technologies are developed, so the only way we could smooth the pace of rises in real GDP would be to control the rate at which new technologies were implemented. From time to time we would have to delay their implementation, and such delays would result in never-to-be-recovered waste.

Regardless of which position economists take, they all agree that depressions as deep and long as that of the early 1930s result in extraordinary waste and human suffering. The disagreements concern the more common and gentler ebbs and flows of economic activity that have occurred in the years since World War II.

R E V I E W

Gross domestic product (GDP) is the value in pounds of all the final goods and services produced in the economy. Nominal GDP measures the value of the output of final goods and services using current prices. Real GDP measures the value of the output using the prices that prevailed in some base period. Nominal GDP increases more quickly than real GDP because of inflation. The general tendency for real GDP to increase is called trend real GDP. Economic fluctuations can be measured by examining departures from trend real GDP. The upward trend in real GDP is the major source of improvements in living standards. However, the upward trend has costs in terms of depletion of exhaustible resources and environmental pollution. ◆

Let's now take a more systematic look at the ebbs and flows of economic activity.

Business Cycles

Business cycles are the periodic but irregular up and down movements in economic activity, measured by fluctuations in real GDP and other macroeconomic variables. As we've just seen, real GDP can be divided into two components:

◆ Trend real GDP
◆ Fluctuations in real GDP

To identify business cycles, we focus our attention on the deviations of real GDP from trend because this variable gives a direct measure of the uneven pace of economic activity, separate from its underlying trend growth path. Business cycles are not a regular, predictable, or repeating phenomenon like the swings of the pendulum of a clock. Their timing is irregular and, to a large degree, unpredictable. Each business cycle is identified as a sequence of four phases:

◆ Contraction
◆ Trough
◆ Expansion
◆ Peak

These four phases are shown in Fig. 21.8. This figure, which is an enlargement of part of Fig. 21.7, shows the output gap for 1978 to 1993. Notice the four phases of the cycle. A **contraction** is a slowdown in the pace of economic activity, such as occurred between 1979 and 1981 and between 1988 and 1992. An **expansion** is a speeding up in the pace of economic activity, such as occurred between 1982 and 1988. A **trough** is the lower turning point of a business cycle, where a contraction turns into an expansion. Troughs occurred in 1981–1982 and 1992–1993. A **peak** is the upper turning point of a business cycle, where an expansion turns into a contraction. Peaks occurred in 1979 and 1988.

FIGURE 21.8

The Business Cycle

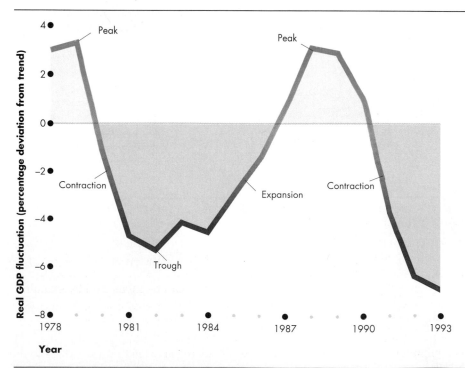

The business cycle, 1978-1993 has four phases: contraction, trough, expansion and peak. The United Kingdom's most recent experience is used to illustrate these phases. There was a trough in 1981–1982 and an expansion from 1982 until a peak was reached in 1988. After 1988 there was another contraction to a trough in 1992–1993.

Source: Derived from Fig. 21.7.

If the level of economic activity slows down sufficiently for real GDP to fall for two successive quarters, the economy is said to be experiencing a **recession**. A deep trough is called a slump or a **depression**.

Unemployment and Business Cycles

Real GDP is not the only variable that fluctuates over the course of business cycles. Its fluctuations are matched by related fluctuations in a wide range of other economic variables. One of the most important of these is unemployment. In the contraction phase of a business cycle, unemployment increases; in the expansion phase, unemployment decreases; at the peak, unemployment is at its lowest; at the trough, unemployment is at its highest. This relationship between unemployment and the phases of business cycles is illustrated in Fig. 21.9.

That figure relates to the United Kingdom from 1900 to 1993. It shows deviations of real GDP from trend – with a blue line. It also shows unemployment –

with an orange line. To help us see clearly how unemployment moves in line with deviations of real GDP from its trend, the unemployment rate has been measured with its scale inverted. That is, as we move down the vertical axis on the right-hand side, the unemployment rate increases. The inter-war depression, the 1980–81 recession and the 1991–1992 recession are highlighted in the figure. As you can see, fluctuations in unemployment closely follow those in the deviation of real GDP from trend.

Inflation and Business Cycles

We've looked at fluctuations in real variables: real GDP and the unemployment rate. We've seen that there is a systematic relationship between fluctuations in real GDP and in the unemployment rate. How does inflation behave over business cycles? Are fluctuations in its rate closely connected with business cycles, or does the inflation rate vary independently of business cycles?

FIGURE 21.9

Unemployment and the Business Cycle, 1900–1993

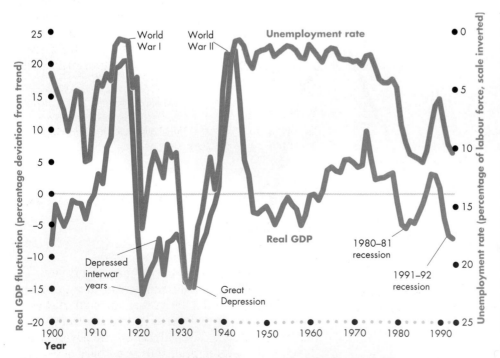

The figure shows the relationship between unemployment and the phases of the business cycle. The deviation of real GDP from trend – shown by the blue line – tells us when the economy is at a peak or trough or in a contraction or expansion phase of the business cycle. Unemployment is plotted in the same figure – with an orange line. Notice that the scale for unemployment is inverted – so the orange line is near the bottom of the graph when unemployment was at its highest in the inter-war depression, and the orange line is consistently high when unemployment was consistently low after World War II. If you look carefully, you will see that unemployment tends to fall – so the orange line goes up – when GDP moves above trend, and vice versa.

Source: Derived from Figs. 21.1 and 21.7.

To answer these questions, look at Fig. 21.10. That figure contains a scatter diagram of the inflation rate plotted against the deviation of real GDP from trend. Each point in the figure represents a year. There is a point for each year from 1900 to 1993. The pattern made by the points tells us how the inflation rate relates to the deviation of real GDP from trend – a measure of business cycles. Two clear features of this relationship are visible in the figure.

First, there is some general tendency for the inflation rate to be higher when real GDP is above the trend and lower when real GDP is below the trend.

FIGURE 21.10

Inflation and Business Cycles

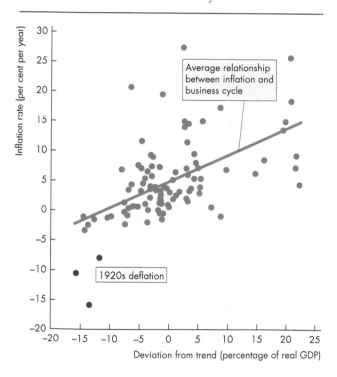

There is a loose positive relationship between the inflation rate and business cycles. On average, the larger the deviation of real GDP above trend, the higher is the inflation rate, and the larger the deviation of real GDP below trend, the lower is the inflation rate, The average relationship between inflation and business cycles is shown by the upward-sloping green line. But there are large fluctuations in the inflation rate that are independent of fluctuations in real GDP from trend. Indeed, some of the worst years for inflation coincided with times when GDP was actually below trend.

Sources: Figs. 21.3 and 21.7.

This is brought out by the green line which plots the average relationship. On average, inflation is a little higher when GDP is well above trend – on the right – and lower when GDP is below trend – on the left. The slope of the green line tells us the degree to which the inflation rate responds to the state of a business cycle, on average. That response is a small one.

Second, there is a considerable amount of independence between the inflation rate and the deviation of real GDP from trend. You might expect the years with the highest rates of inflation to be those where GDP was most above the trend, but this was not always the case.

We'll get some insights into explanations for these two features as we progress through later macroeconomic chapters.

T he business cycle is the periodic but irregular up and down movement in economic activity. It has four phases: contraction, trough, expansion and peak. A recession is a contraction in which real GDP declines for at least two quarters. Over the business cycle, real GDP and unemployment fluctuate together. During a contraction, the unemployment rate rises, and during an expansion it falls. Inflation can also move in sympathy with the business cycle but there are important fluctuations in the inflation rate that are not related to the business cycle. ◆

We've studied unemployment, inflation, real GDP fluctuations and business cycles. Let's now turn to our final topic, deficits.

Government and International Deficits

I f you spend more than you earn, you have a deficit. To cover your deficit, you have to borrow or sell off some of the things that you own. Just as individuals can have deficits, so can governments and entire nations. These deficits – the government deficit and the international deficit – have attracted a lot of attention recently.

Government Deficit

The **government deficit** – more strictly known as the **general government financial deficit** – is the difference between the amount that the government sector spends itself and the amount that the government sector receives in revenue. The government sector of the economy comprises the central government and all local governments. These governments spend money on a variety of public and social programmes and obtain most of their revenue from taxes. They also get a small amount of additional revenue from the profits of the businesses that they own and from the interest on any loans that they make. Sometimes the government sector is in surplus, and at other times it is in deficit. However, the government sector has had a deficit every year since 1972 except for the three-year period 1988–1990. The biggest deficit was in 1993 when it was almost 8 per cent of GDP.

To some degree, the balance of the government budget is related to business cycles. When the economy is in the expansion phase of a business cycle, tax receipts rise quickly and the government's spending on job-seeker's allowances decreases. Through this phase of a business cycle, the government usually runs a surplus. When the economy is in a contraction phase, tax receipts decline and job-seeker's allowances increase and the government budget goes into deficit. So it is not surprising that the government sector in the United Kingdom moved from a deficit to a surplus in 1988 when unemployment had been falling for a long time, nor that a deficit reappeared in 1990 when unemployment rose again sharply.

We'll study the government deficit more closely and at greater length in Chapter 33. In that chapter, we'll discuss its sources and consequences.

International Deficit

The difference between the value of all the goods and services that UK citizens sell to other countries (exports) and the value of all the goods and services that UK citizens buy from foreigners (imports) is called the **balance of trade**. If they sell more to the rest of the world than they buy from it, then the United Kingdom has a balance of trade surplus. If they buy more from the rest of the world than they sell to it, then the United Kingdom has a balance of trade deficit. In most years the United Kingdom runs a deficit as far as trade in goods – or visible exports and imports – is concerned. But there is usually also a surplus as far as trade in services – or invisible exports and imports – is concerned. Taking the two together, there tends to be an overall balance of trade deficit more often than a balance of trade surplus.

As it happens, the flows of money relating to exports and imports are not the only flows between the United Kingdom and the rest of the world. There are also flows of **property income** which is a term used to cover payments of interest, profits and dividends between people in different countries. And there are smaller current transfers which cover items such as aid to developing countries and payments between the United Kingdom and the European Union. As far as the United Kingdom is concerned, there is usually a surplus on these other items. If we add the surplus (or deficit) for these other items to the deficit (or surplus) for the balance of trade, then we get what is called the **current account balance**. The United Kingdom has had large current account deficits since around 1988.

When a country has a current account deficit, it is paying more money to foreign countries than it is receiving from them. It is in the same position that you or the government sector are in if you or the government sector have spending in excess of revenue. So, like you or the government sector, the country has to borrow to make up the difference. When one country needs to borrow, it has to borrow from the rest of the world. Notice that one country's current account deficit and borrowing from the rest of the world is mirrored by a current account surplus and lending to the rest of the world by some other countries. One country which has long had a current account surplus – and in recent years an increasing one – is Japan.

The causes of these international surpluses and deficits and their consequences will be discussed at greater length in Chapter 35.

◆ ◆ ◆ ◆   In our study of macroeconomics, we're going to find out what we currently know about the causes of unemployment, inflation and business cycles. We're also going to discover why there are times when the stock market is a good predictor of the state of the economy and others when it is not. And we'll discover why inflation and business cycles sometimes move in sympathy with each other and sometimes follow separate courses.

Finally, we're going to learn more about deficits – the government deficit and the international trade deficit – and their causes, their importance and their consequences. ◆ ◆ The next step in our study of macroeconomics is to learn more about macroeconomic measurement - about how we measure gross domestic product, the price level and inflation.

S U M M A R Y

Microeconomics and Macroeconomics

The microeconomics we studied before this chapter concerns choices made by individual households and firms, and concerns individual markets. In this chapter we begin our study of macroeconomics which is about the economy as a whole. (p. 581)

Unemployment

Unemployment is measured as the number of workers who are not employed and who are claiming job-seeker's allowances. Employment is the number of adult workers holding jobs. The labour force is measured as the sum of those unemployed and those employed. The unemployment rate is the percentage of the labour force unemployed. Owing to the way it is defined, the measured rate of unemployment understates the true level of unemployment.

Unemployment was a major problem in the United Kingdom during the Great Depression years of the 1930s and became an important problem again in the early 1980s and early 1990s when it reached the 10 per cent level. The unemployment rate has increased, on average, since the end of World War II.

There are three types of unemployment: frictional, structural and cyclical. Frictional unemployment arises from normal turnover of people in the labour market and the fact that people take time to find the jobs that best matches their skills. Structural unemployment arises when technological change causes a decline in jobs that are concentrated in particular industries or regions. Cyclical unemployment arises when the pace of economic expansion slows down. Full employment is a state in which all unemployment is frictional. The natural rate of unemployment is the sum of the frictional and structural unemployment rates.

The major costs of unemployment are the lost output and earnings that could have been generated if the unemployed people had been working. Other major costs include the deterioration of human capital, possible increases in crime, and, when unemployment is prolonged, severe social and psychological problems for unemployed workers and their families. (pp. 581–586)

Inflation

Inflation is a sustained upward movement in the average level of prices. To measure the average level of prices, we calculate a price index. The inflation rate is the percentage change in the value of a price index.

Inflation is a persistent feature of economic life in the United Kingdom – and other countries – but the rate of inflation fluctuates. In the early 1960s, inflation was under 5 per cent a year, and occasionally under 3 per cent a year. By 1975, it was around 25 per cent. Inflation remained high until the early 1980s and then began to fall, albeit unsteadily. In 1993 it was under 2 per cent.

Inflation is a problem because it brings a fall in the value of money at an unpredictable rate. The more unpredictable the inflation rate, the less useful is money as a measuring rod for conducting transactions. Inflation makes money especially unsuitable for transactions that are spread out over time, such as borrowing and lending or working for an agreed wage rate. A rapid unanticipated inflation rate is a problem because it makes people get rid of money as soon as possible, disrupting economic life. (pp. 587–594)

Gross Domestic Product

A country's total output is measured by its gross domestic product (GDP). Gross domestic product in the United Kingdom is the value in pounds of all final goods and services produced in the country in a given time period. Changes in gross domestic product reflect both changes in prices and changes in the quantity of goods and services produced. To separate the effects of prices from real quantities, we distinguish between nominal GDP and real GDP. The nominal GDP in any year is measured using the prices that were current in that year. Real GDP is measured using the prices for some base year.

Real GDP grows in almost every year, so the trend of real GDP is upward. But real GDP does not increase at a constant rate. Its rate of expansion fluctuates so that real GDP fluctuates around trend GDP. Increases in real GDP bring rising living standards but not without costs. The main costs of fast economic growth are resource depletion, the risk of more environmental pollution, and the need to face rapid and often costly changes in job type and location. The benefits of higher consumption levels have to be balanced against such costs. (pp. 595–598)

Business Cycles

The term business cycles refers to the periodic but irregular up-and-down movements in economic activity. Each cycle has four phases: contraction, trough, expansion and peak. When output falls for two consecutive quarters, the economy is said to be in a recession.

Unemployment fluctuates closely with business cycles. When real GDP is above trend, the unemployment rate is low; when real GDP is below trend, the unemployment rate is high.

There is no simple relationship between the inflation rate and business cycles. On average, the inflation rate is high when real GDP is above trend and low when real GDP is below trend. But there are times when the inflation rate moves independently of business cycles. Thus there are two types of forces at work generating inflation – those that are related to business cycles and those that are not. (pp. 599–601)

Government and International Deficits

The government deficit is the total expenditure of the government sector less the total revenue of that sector. Since 1972 the UK government sector has had a deficit almost every year. To some degree the government deficit fluctuates over the course of a business cycle.

A country's current account balance is the difference between the income that it receives from other countries and the money that it pays to other countries. Most of the income it receives is the result of selling exports of goods and services and most of the money it spends is the result of buying imports of goods and services. The United Kingdom has had a particularly large current account deficit since 1988. Countries with current account deficits have to borrow from abroad to make up the difference between their income and their spending. Mirroring the United Kingdom's current account deficit will be current account surpluses in some other countries. Japan is one of the countries that has had a large surplus in recent years. (pp. 601–602)

KEY ELEMENTS

Key Terms

Key Figures

R E V I E W   Q U E S T I O N S

1 Define unemployment.

2 How is the unemployment rate measured in the United Kingdom?

3 Why may the measured unemployment rate understate or overstate the true unemployment rate?

4 What are the different types of unemployment?

5 What are the main costs of unemployment?

6 What is inflation?

7 What are the main costs of inflation?

8 What, if any, are the benefits from inflation? If there are none, explain why.

9 Why doesn't inflation always benefit borrowers at the expense of lenders?

10 Why may anticipated inflation be a problem?

11 What makes GDP grow?

12 What are the costs and benefits of a high average increase in real GDP?

13 What are the costs and benefits of fluctuations in real GDP?

14 What is a business cycle? Describe the four phases of a business cycle. What was the phase of the UK business cycle in 1982, in 1985, in 1988 and in 1992?

15 When the economy is in a recovery phase, what happens to the unemployment rate?

16 How does the inflation rate fluctuate over the business cycle?

17 What is the government budget deficit?

18 What is the current account balance?

P R O B L E M S

1 At the end of 1991 the price index was 136. At the end of 1992 the price index was 139. Calculate the inflation rate in 1992.

2 In a non-inflationary world, Robert and Mary are willing to borrow and lend at 2 per cent a year. Robert expects that inflation next year will be 4 per cent and Mary expects that it will be 8 per cent. Would Robert and Mary be will-

ing to sign a contract in which one of them borrows from the other? Explain why or why not.

3 Mr and Mrs Jones run a seasonal hotel in the Welsh mountains and employ students as waiters and waitresses in the summer vacation. The Joneses expect that inflation next year will be 10 per cent. The students who want to work there expect inflation to be only 8 per cent. Will the Joneses

and the students be able to agree now on a wage rate for next summer? Explain your answer.

4   You are given the following information about the economy of Macrominor.

Year/quarter	Real GDP (billions of 1995 pounds)	Price level (index, 1995 = 100)	Unemployment rate (percentage of labour force)
1996/1	101	104	5
1996/2	102	105	5
1996/3	103	108	5
1996/4	104	110	5
1997/1	103	111	6
1997/2	102	112	7
1997/3	106	115	5
1997/4	108	119	4

a   In which period does Macrominor have a recession?

b   When the recession hit Macrominor, did the unemployment rate increase or decrease?

c   When the recession hit Macrominor, did the inflation rate increase or decrease?

d   When did Macrominor begin its recovery from recession?

e   When the recovery began in Macrominor, did the unemployment rate decrease right away?

f   When the recovery began in Macrominor, did the inflation rate increase or decrease?

CHAPTER 22

MEASURING
OUTPUT
AND THE
PRICE
LEVEL

After studying this chapter you will be able to:

◆ Describe the flows of expenditure and income

◆ Explain why aggregate expenditure and income are equal to each other

◆ Explain how gross domestic product (GDP) is measured

◆ Describe two common measures of the price level – the Retail Prices Index (RPI) and the GDP deflator

◆ Explain how real GDP is measured

◆ Distinguish between inflation and changes in relative prices

◆ Explain why real GDP is not a good measure of economic well-being

EVERY THREE MONTHS, THE CENTRAL STATISTICAL OFFICE PUBLISHES THE latest quarterly estimates of gross domestic product, or GDP – a barometer of the nation's economy. As soon as it is published, analysts pore over the data. But how do government statisticians add up all the economic activity of the country to calculate GDP? And what exactly *is* GDP? ◆ ◆ From economists to homemakers, inflation watchers of all types pay close attention to another economic barometer, the Retail Prices Index, or RPI. The Central Statistical Office publishes new figures each month. How do statisticians determine the RPI? ◆ ◆ The economy grows but to reveal the rate of growth, we must remove the effects of inflation on GDP and assess how GDP has changed because of changing production. How do we remove the inflation component of GDP? ◆ ◆ Some people

Economic Barometers

make a living from crime. Others, although doing work that is legal, try to hide the payments they receive to evade taxes or other regulations. Most people undertake some economic activity inside their homes. Cooking meals and mowing the lawn are examples. Are any of these activities taken into account when we measure GDP? If they are not taken into account, does it matter?

◆ ◆ ◆ ◆ In this chapter, we're going to learn more about the macroeconomic concepts of GDP and the price level. But we'll begin by describing the flows of expenditure and income.

The Circular Flow of Expenditure and Income

The circular flow of expenditure and income provides the conceptual basis for measuring gross domestic product. We'll see some of the key ideas and relationships more clearly if we begin with a model economy that is simpler than the one in which we live. We'll then add some features to make our simplified economy correspond with that of the real economy.

Circular Flows in a Simplified Economy

Our simplified economy has just two kinds of economic decision makers: households and firms.

Households

◆ Receive incomes in exchange for the supply of factors of production to firms
◆ Make expenditures on consumer goods and services bought from firms
◆ Save some of their incomes

Firms

◆ Pay incomes to households in exchange for the factors of production hired (these payments include wages paid for labour, interest paid for capital, rent paid for land and profits)
◆ Make investment expenditures – purchases of capital goods from other firms and changes in their stocks
◆ Receive revenue from the sale of consumer goods and services to households
◆ Receive revenue from other firms' investment expenditures
◆ Borrow to finance investment expenditures

The economy has three types of markets:

◆ Goods (and services) markets
◆ Factor markets
◆ Financial markets

Transactions between households and firms take place in these markets. In factor markets, households sell the services of labour, capital and land to firms. In exchange, firms make income payments to households. These payments are wages for labour services, interest for the use of capital, rent for the use of land and profits to the owners of firms. These

payments for factor services are households' incomes. **Aggregate income** is the amount received by households in payment for the services of factors of production.

In the markets for goods and services, firms sell consumer goods and services – such as pizzas and wine, hairdressing and chocolate bars, microwave ovens and dry cleaning services – to households. In exchange, households make payments to firms. The total payment made by households for consumer goods and services is called **consumers' expenditure**.

Firms do not sell all their output to households. Some of what they produce is new capital equipment, and it is sold to other firms. For example, General Electric sells some robots to Rover. Also, some of what firms produce might not be sold at all, but added to stocks. For example, if Rolls-Royce produces 1,000 cars and sells 950 of them to households, 50 cars remain unsold and Rolls-Royce's stock of cars increases by 50. When a firm adds unsold output to stocks, we can think of the firm as buying goods from itself. Note that unsold output includes not only finished but unsold products – such as cars – but also unfinished work in progress – such as work on a new bridge. Purchases of new plant, buildings, vehicles and machinery, along with additions to stocks, are called **investment.** To finance investment, firms borrow from households in financial markets.

These transactions between households and firms result in flows of income and expenditure as shown in Fig. 22.1. To help you keep track of the different types of flows, they have been colour-coded. The blue flow represents aggregate income which we denote by Y. The red flows represent expenditures on goods and services. Consumers' expenditure is denoted by C. Investment is denoted by I. Notice that investment is illustrated in the figure as a flow from firms through the goods markets and back to firms. It is illustrated in this way because some firms produce capital goods and other firms buy them (and firms 'buy' stocks from themselves).

There are two additional flows in the figure, shown in green. These flows do not represent payments for the services of factors of production or for the purchases of goods and services. They are saving and borrowing. Households do not spend all their income – they save some of it. In this simplified economy, saving is the difference between aggregate income and consumers' expenditure and is denoted

FIGURE 22.1

The Circular Flow of Expenditure and Income between Households and Firms

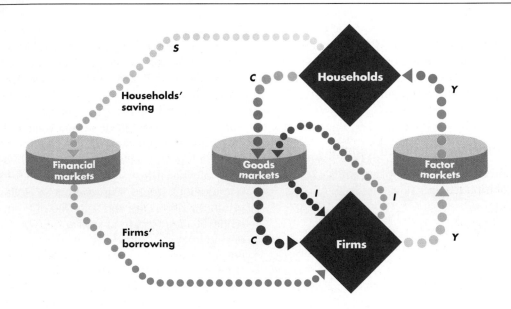

Transactions between households and firms in goods markets and factor markets generate the circular flow of expenditure and income. Households receive factor incomes (*Y*) from firms in exchange for factor services they supply (blue flow). Households purchase consumer goods and services (*C*) from firms; and firms purchase capital goods from other firms and stocks from themselves – investment (*I*) – (red flows). Outside the circular flow, households save part of their income (*S*) and firms borrow to finance their investment expenditures (green flows). Firms' receipts from the sale of goods and services are paid to households as wages, interest, rent, or profit. Aggregate expenditure (consumers' expenditure plus investment) equals aggregate income, which equals GDP.

by *S*. Saving gets channelled through financial markets, in which firms borrow the funds needed to finance their investment.

The most important of the flows illustrated in Fig. 22.1 are aggregate income (the blue flow) and expenditures (the red flows). We're going to discover that the blue flow and the two red flows in aggregate are equal. Let's see why.

Equality of Aggregate Income and Aggregate Expenditure

The sum of consumers' expenditure (*C*) and investment (*I*) is aggregate expenditure on final goods and services (more briefly, aggregate expenditure). To see the equality of aggregate income and aggregate expenditure, look again at Fig. 22.1 and focus on firms. Notice that there are two red arrows indicating flows of revenue to firms. They are consumers' expenditure (*C*) and investment (*I*), or aggregate expenditure. Everything that a firm receives from the sale of its output it also pays out for the services of the factors of production that it hires. To see why, recall that payments for factors of production include not only wages, interest and rent paid for the services of labour, capital and land, but also profits. Any difference between the amount received by a firm for the sale of its output and the amount paid to its suppliers of labour, capital and land is a profit (or loss) for the owner of the firm. The owner of the firm is a household, and the owner receives the firm's profit (or makes good the firm's loss). Thus the total income that each firm pays out to households equals its revenue from the sale of final goods and services. Since this reasoning applies to every firm in the economy, then

Aggregate expenditure = Aggregate income.

Gross Domestic Product in the Simplified Economy

Gross domestic product (GDP) is the value of all the final goods and services produced in the economy. In the simplified economy that we are studying, the final goods and services produced are the consumers' goods and services and the capital goods produced by firms. There are two ways in which we can value that production. One is to value it on the basis of what buyers have paid. This amount is aggregate expenditure. The other is to value it on the basis of the cost of the factors of production used to produce it. This amount is aggregate income. But we've just discovered that aggregate expenditure equals aggregate income. That is, the total amount spent on the goods and services produced equals the total amount paid for the factors of production used to produce them. Thus GDP equals aggregate expenditure, which in turn equals aggregate income. That is,

GDP = Aggregate expenditure = Aggregate income.

Government and Foreign Sectors   In the simplified economy that we've just examined, we focused exclusively on the behaviour of households and firms. In real-world economies, there are two other important sectors that add additional flows to the circular flow of expenditure and income: the government and the rest of the world. These sectors do not change the fundamental results that we've just obtained. GDP equals aggregate expenditure or aggregate income, no matter how many sectors we consider and how complicated a range of flows we consider between them. Nevertheless, it is important to add the government and the rest of the world to our model so that we can see the additional expenditure and income flows that they generate.

The government

◆ Makes expenditures on goods and services bought from firms
◆ Receives tax revenue from households and firms and makes transfer payments to households
◆ Borrows to finance the difference between its revenue and its spending

The rest of the world

◆ Makes expenditures on goods and services bought from domestic firms and receives revenue from the sale of goods and services to domestic firms
◆ Lends to (or borrows from) households and firms in the domestic economy

The additional flows arising from the transactions between the government, the rest of the world, and households and firms, along with the original flows that we've already considered, are illustrated in Fig. 22.2.

Let's first focus on the flows involving the government. Government purchases of goods and services from firms are shown as the flow G. This flow is shown in red (like consumers' expenditure and investment) to indicate that it is an expenditure on goods and services.

Net taxes are the net flow from households to the government.[1] These net flows are the difference between the taxes paid and transfer payments received. **Transfer payments** are flows of money from the government such as national insurance benefits. It is important not to confuse transfer payments with government purchases of goods and services. The term 'transfer payments' is designed to remind us that these items are transfers of money and, as such, are similar to taxes except that they flow in the opposite direction – they flow from government to households. Net taxes (T) are illustrated in the figure as a green flow to remind you that this flow does not represent a payment in exchange for goods and services or a factor income. It is simply a transfer of financial resources from households to the government.

The difference between the net taxes received by government and government expenditure on goods and services is the government's budget deficit. The government covers its deficit by borrowing in financial markets. Such borrowing is illustrated by the green flow in the figure.

---

[1] The figure does not show firms paying any taxes. You can think of taxes paid by firms as being paid on behalf of the households that own the firms. For example, a tax on a firm's profits means that the households owning the firm receive less income. It is as if the households receive all the profit and then pay the tax on it. This way of looking at taxes simplifies Fig. 22.2 but does not change any of the conclusions.

FIGURE 22.2

The Circular Flow Including Governments and the Rest of the World

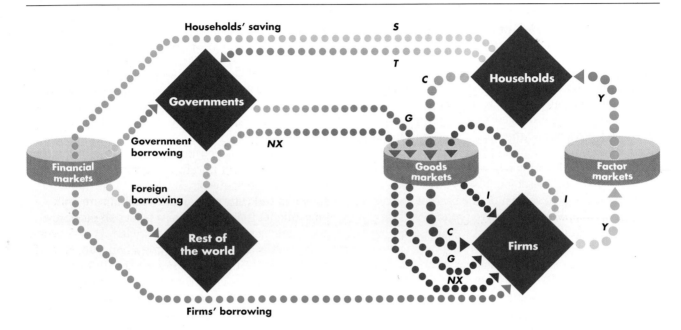

Transactions between households, firms, governments and the rest of the world in goods markets and factor markets generate the circular flow of expenditure and income. Households receive factor incomes (Y) from firms in exchange for the factor services they supply (blue flow). Households purchase consumer goods and services (C) from firms; firms purchase capital goods from other firms and stocks from themselves (I); governments purchase goods and services (G); the rest of the world purchases goods and services from firms, and firms purchase goods and services from the rest of the world (NX) – (red flows).

Outside the circular flow, households save part of their income (S) and pay net taxes (T) to governments; firms borrow to finance their investment expenditures; governments borrow to finance their deficits; and the rest of the world borrows (or lends) – (green flows).

Firms' receipts from the sale of goods and services are paid to households as wages, interest, rent, or profit. Aggregate expenditure (consumers' expenditure plus investment plus government purchases plus net exports) equals aggregate income, which equals GDP.

Next, look at transactions with the rest of the world. The red flow in Fig. 22.2 labelled NX is net exports. **Net exports** equals exports of goods and services to the rest of the world minus imports of goods and services from the rest of the world. This flow represents the expenditure by the rest of the world on goods and services produced by domestic firms (exports) minus the expenditure of domestic firms on goods and services produced in the rest of the world (imports).

If exports exceed imports, net exports are positive. There is a net flow into the domestic economy. To finance that net inflow, the rest of the world borrows from the domestic economy in financial markets. This flow is illustrated by the green flow

labelled 'Foreign borrowing'. If imports exceed exports, net exports are negative and there is a flow from domestic firms to the rest of the world. In this case, the domestic economy borrows from the rest of the world in financial markets. To illustrate this case in the figure, we would reverse the directions of the flows of net exports and foreign borrowing.

Now that we have introduced more elements of the real world into our model economy, let's check that aggregate expenditure still equals aggregate income.

Expenditure Equals Income Again   Aggregate expenditure equals aggregate income in this more complicated economy just as it does in the economy that has only households and firms. To see this equality, focus on the expenditures on goods and services (the red flows) received by firms and on firms' payments for factor services (the blue flow). We now have four flows representing firms' revenues from the sale of goods and services – consumers' expenditure (C), investment (I), government purchases of goods and services (G) and net exports (NX). The sum of these four flows is equal to aggregate expenditure on final goods and services. As before, everything that a firm receives from the sale of its output is paid out as income to the owners of the factors of production that it employs and to the households that have a claim on its profits. The blue factor income flow therefore equals the sum of the red expenditure flows. That is,

$$Y = C + I + G + NX.$$

Thus, as we discovered in the case of the simpler model economy, aggregate income equals aggregate expenditure.

GDP also equals aggregate expenditure, or aggregate income. This equality occurs because we can measure the value of output either as the sum of the incomes paid to the factors of production or as the expenditure on that output.

GDP, Consumers' Expenditure, Saving and Taxes

There is an important relationship between GDP, consumers' expenditure, saving and taxes. To see this relationship, look at households in Fig. 22.2. There is one flow into households and three flows out. The flow in is aggregate income (Y), which we've seen is equal to GDP. The flows out are consumers' expenditure (C), saving (S) and net taxes (T). Aggregate income minus net taxes (equivalently GDP minus net taxes) is called **disposable income**. Disposable income is either spent on consumer goods and services or saved. Thus **saving** equals disposable income minus consumers' expenditure. Equivalently, everything received by households is either spent on consumer goods and services, saved, or paid in taxes. That is,

$$Y = C + S + T.$$

Income and Expenditure Accounts

We can record the transactions shown in the circular flow diagram in a set of accounts, one for firms and one for households. Table 22.1(a) shows the firms' revenue and expenditure account. The first two sources of revenue are the sale of consumer goods and services to households (C) and the sale of capital goods to other firms (I). In addition, firms now receive revenue from the sale of goods and services to governments (G) and from their sale of goods and services (net of purchases) to the rest of the world (NX). The sum of all their sources of revenue ($C + I + G + NX$) equals the payments made to the owners of factors of production (Y).

The households' income and expenditure account is shown in Table 22.1(b). Households receive income (Y) in payment for the factors of production supplied and spend that income on consumer goods and services (C). They also pay net taxes (T), and, as before, the balancing item is household saving (S).

Injections and Leakages The flow of income from firms to households and of consumers' expenditure from households to firms is the circular flow of income and expenditure. **Injections** into the circular flow of income and expenditure are expenditures that do not originate with households. Investment, government purchases of goods and services, and exports are injections into the circular flow of expenditure and income. **Leakages** from the circular flow of income and expenditure are income that is not spent on domestically produced goods and services. Net taxes, saving and imports are leakages from the circular flow of expenditure and income. Let's take a closer look at these injections and leakages.

We have seen from the firms' accounts that

$$Y = C + I + G + NX.$$

Let's break net exports into its two components, exports of goods and services (EX) and imports of goods and services (IM). That is,

$$NX = EX - IM.$$

Substituting this equation into the previous one, you can see that

$$Y = C + I + G + EX - IM.$$

We have also seen from the households' accounts that
$$Y = C + S + T.$$

Since the left side of these two equations is the same, it follows that

$$I + G + EX - IM = S + T.$$

If we add IM to both sides of this equation, we get

$$I + G + EX = S + T + IM.$$

TABLE 22.1

Firms' and Households' Accounts

(a) FIRMS

Revenue		Expenditure	
Sale of consumer goods and services	C	Payments to factors of production	Y
Sale of capital goods and changes in stocks	I		
Sale of goods and services to governments	G		
Sale of goods and services to rest of world (EX)			
minus Purchases of goods and services from rest of world (IM)	NX		
Total	Y		Y

(b) HOUSEHOLDS

Income		Expenditure	
Payments for supplies of factors of production	Y	Purchases of consumer goods and services	C
		Taxes paid (*TAX*)	
		minus Transfer payments received (*TR*)	T
		Saving	S
Total	Y		Y

Firms, shown in part (a), receive revenue from consumers' expenditure (C), investment (I), government purchases of goods and services (G) and net exports (NX). Firms make payments for the services of factors of production (Y). The total income firms pay equals their total revenue: $Y = C + I + G + NX$. Households, shown in part (b), receive an income for the factors of production supplied (Y). They buy consumer goods and services from firms (C) and pay taxes (taxes minus transfer payments) to governments (T). The part of the households' income that is not spent on consumer goods or paid in net taxes is saved (S). Consumers' expenditure plus net taxes plus saving is equal to income: $Y = C + T + S$.

The left side shows the injections into the circular flow of expenditure and income, and the right side shows the leakages from the circular flow. *The injections into the circular flow equal the leakages from the circular flow.*

REVIEW

Aggregate expenditure is the sum of consumers' expenditure (C), investment (I), government purchases of goods and services (G), and exports of goods and services (EX) minus imports of goods and services (IM). Aggregate expenditure equals the value of the final goods and services produced. It also equals the aggregate income (Y) of the factors of production used to produce these goods and services. That is,

$$Y = C + I + G + EX - IM.$$

Households allocate aggregate income to three activities: consumers' expenditure (C), taxes (net of transfer payments) (T) and saving (S). That is,

$$Y = C + S + T.$$

Investment, government purchases and exports are *injections* into the circular flow of expenditure and income. Saving, net taxes (taxes minus transfer payments) and imports are *leakages* from the circular flow. Injections equal leakages. That is,

$$I + G + EX = S + T + IM. \quad \blacklozenge$$

The circular flow of income and expenditure and the income and expenditure accounts of firms and households are our tools for measuring GDP. Let's now see how the statisticians at the Central Statistical Office use these concepts to measure the UK's GDP.

The UK's National Income and Expenditure Accounts

T he Central Statistical Office collects data to measure GDP and publishes its findings in numerous publications. The data are collected by using three approaches:

◆ Expenditure approach
◆ Factor incomes approach
◆ Output approach

Let's look at what is involved in using these three alternative ways of measuring GDP.

The Expenditure Approach

The **expenditure approach** measures GDP by collecting data on consumers' expenditure (C), investment (I), government purchases of goods and services (G) and net exports (NX). This approach is illustrated in Table 22.2. The numbers refer to 1993 and are in billions of pounds. To measure GDP using the expenditure approach, we add together consumers' expenditure (C), investment (I), government purchases of goods and services (G) and net exports of goods and services (NX). There is a statistical discrepancy that we'll explain shortly.

Consumers' expenditure is the expenditure on goods and services produced by firms and sold to households. It includes goods such as pizzas, compact discs, books and magazines as well as services such as insurance, banking and legal advice. It does not include the purchase of new homes, which is counted as part of investment.

Investment is expenditure on capital equipment by firms and expenditure on new homes by households. It also includes changes in firms' stocks. **Stocks** include stocks of raw materials and stocks of unsold finished goods as well as work in progress on semi-finished goods. Stocks are an essential input

---

TABLE 22.2

GDP: The Expenditure Approach

Item	Symbol	Amount in 1993 (billions of pounds)	Percentage of GDP
Consumers' expenditure	C	405.6	64.7
Gross private domestic investment	I	82.3	13.1
Government purchases of goods and services	G	148.2	23.6
Net exports of goods and services	NX	– 8.3	– 1.3
Statistical discrepancy	–	– 0.7	– 0.1
Gross domestic product	Y	627.1	100.0

The expenditure approach measures GDP by adding together consumers' expenditure, gross private domestic investment, government purchases of goods and services, and net exports. GDP measured by the expenditure approach was £627.1 billion in 1993. The largest component of aggregate expenditure was expenditure on consumers' goods and services – almost 65 per cent of GDP.

Source: Central Statistical Office, *UK Economic Accounts*, The fourth quarter 1993, 23 and 48.

---

into the production process. For instance, if a firm does not hold stocks of raw materials, its production process can operate only as quickly as the rate at which new raw materials can be delivered. Also, if a firm does not hold stocks of finished goods, it cannot respond to fluctuations in sales, standing ready to meet an exceptional surge in demand.

The country's **capital stock** is its total amount of plant, buildings, vehicles and machinery along with its stocks of raw materials and finished goods and work in progress. Additions to the capital stock are investment.

Government purchases of goods and services are the purchases of goods and services by all levels of UK government – from Westminster to the local council. This item of expenditure includes the cost of providing national defence, health services, law and order, street lighting and roads. It does not include *transfer payments*. As we have seen, such payments do not represent purchases of goods and services but rather transfers of money from governments to households.

Net exports of goods and services are the difference between the value of exports and the value of imports. When Rover sells a car to Germany, the value of that car is part of the UK's exports. When you buy a new Sony Walkman, your expenditure is part of the UK's imports. The difference between what the country earns by selling goods and services to the rest of the world and what it pays for goods and services bought from the rest of the world is the value of net exports.

Table 22.2 shows the relative importance of the four items of aggregate expenditure. As you can see, consumers' expenditure is by far the largest component of the expenditures that add up to GDP.

Statistical discrepancy is the difference between GDP as measured by the expenditure approach and the value which the statisticians believe is correct – a value which they derive by looking at the figures for GDP that they get on the expenditure approach and on the income approach (described below). Although these two approaches rarely give the same numerical estimate of GDP, the discrepancy is usually tiny in relation to the aggregates being measured. The discrepancy shown in Table 22.2 is $0.7 billion which is about a thousandth of GDP.

The Factor Incomes Approach

The **factor incomes approach** measures GDP by adding together all the incomes paid by firms to households for the services of the factors of production they hire – wages for labour, interest for capital, rent for land and profits. The Central Statistical Office actually lumps together all payments of interest, rent and profits and simply calls them all profits. But its published tables divide these broadly defined profits into three different groups for different types of firm. So the published accounts show five components of GDP on the income approach:

◆ Income from employment
◆ Income from self-employment
◆ Gross trading profits of companies
◆ Gross trading surplus of public corporations and general government enterprises
◆ Other income

Income from employment is the total payment made by firms for labour services. This item includes the take-home wages and salaries that workers receive each week or month, plus income taxes deducted from their earnings and paid direct to the government, plus all fringe benefits such as national insurance and pension fund contributions.

Income from self-employment is the total profit made by sole proprietorships and partnerships – except for the profits of sole proprietorships and partnerships whose main line of business is letting out land and buildings which are included in 'other income' below. Sole proprietorships and partnerships supply labour and capital, and perhaps land, to their businesses. The statisticians find it difficult to split up the income earned by sole proprietorships and partnerships into its component parts – compensation for labour, capital and land, and profit. So the accounts lump all these separate factor incomes earned by sole proprietorships and partnerships into a single category.

Gross trading profits of companies are the total profits made by companies – except for the profits of companies whose main line of business is letting out land and buildings which are included in 'other income' below. Some of these profits are paid out to households in the form of interest and dividends, and some are retained by the corporations as undistributed profits.

Gross trading surplus of public corporations and general government enterprises is the total profit of all nationalized industries owned by the government – such as the Post Office and British Rail – along with the profits of other businesses owned by local authorities – such as some bus companies and cemeteries. Some of these profits are paid out as interest to households while the rest belong to the central or local government which owns the business concerned.

Other income is the total profit of businesses of all types – whether sole proprietorships, partnerships or companies – whose main line of business is letting out land and buildings. As with the other groups of firms, some of these profits are paid out as interest to households. Notice also that owner-occupiers of homes are regarded as sole proprietorships or – where there are joint owners – partnerships that let their homes to themselves, and the statisticians regard these people as paying rent to themselves; they estimate an 'imputed' rent which they think these people might reasonably pay themselves, and they include this payment in this category of income. By including this item in the accounts, the statisticians measure the total value of housing services, whether they are owned or rented.

Gross domestic product at factor cost is the sum of all factor incomes. Thus if we add together the items that we have just reviewed, we arrive at this measure of GDP. To get an estimate of GDP comparable with the figure we obtained on the expenditure approach, we have to make an adjustment. Let's see what this adjustment is.

Market Prices and Factor Cost To calculate GDP using the expenditure approach, we add together expenditures on *final goods and services*. These expenditures are valued at the prices people pay for the various goods and services. The prices that people pay for goods and services are called **market prices**.

Another way of valuing goods and services is factor cost. The **factor cost** of a good or service is its value measured by adding together the costs of all the factors of production used to produce it. If the only economic transactions were between households and firms, the market price and factor cost methods of measuring value would be identical. But the presence of indirect taxes and subsidies makes these two methods of valuation diverge.

An **indirect tax** is a tax paid by consumers when they purchase goods and services. (In contrast, a *direct* tax is a tax on income.) Examples of indirect taxes are value added tax (VAT) and taxes on alcohol, petrol and tobacco products. Indirect taxes result in the consumer paying more than the producer receives for a good. For example, suppose you buy a pair of shoes for £47. This is the market price value of the pair of shoes. But £7 of your £47 is paid to the government as VAT so that only £40 is left to divide between the shoe shop, the shoe maker and the raw materials suppliers to cover the costs of the inputs. So the factor cost value of the pair of shoes is £40. (Note that VAT in the United Kingdom is levied at 17.5 per cent of the sum received by producers which is £40 in this case; 17.5 per cent of £40 is £7.)

A **subsidy** is a payment made by the government to producers. Examples include subsidies paid to farmers. A subsidy also drives a wedge between the market price value and the factor cost value but in the opposite direction to indirect taxes. A subsidy reduces the market price below factor cost – consumers pay less for the good or service than it costs the producer to make it.

To use the factor incomes approach to measure gross domestic product, we need to add indirect taxes to total factor incomes and to subtract subsidies. Table 22.3 summarizes these calculations and shows how the factor incomes approach leads to the same estimate of GDP as the expenditure approach. The table also shows the relative importance of the various factor incomes. As you can see, income from employment is by far the most important factor income.

The Output Approach

The **output approach** measures GDP by summing the value of output in each sector of the economy. This approach breaks real GDP down into broad product categories such as agriculture, construction, manufacturing and services. In constructing the output measure for each sector, we must be careful to count only the value added by that sector. **Value added** is the value of a firm's output minus the value of *intermediate goods* bought from other firms.

TABLE 22.3

GDP: The Factor Incomes Approach

Item	Amount in 1993 (billions of pounds)	Percentage of GDP
Income from employment	350.4	55.9
Income from self-employment	59.3	9.5
Gross trading profits of companies	76.7	12.2
Gross trading surplus of public corporations and general government enterprises	3.3	0.5
Other income	54.4	8.7
Statistical discrepancy	–0.4	–0.1
Indirect taxes *minus* subsidies	83.4	13.3
Gross domestic product	627.1	100.0

The sum of all factor incomes equals GDP at factor cost. To get GDP we add in indirect taxes minus subsidies. Income from employment – wages and other labour renumeration – accounted for the largest share of GDP.

Source: Derived from Central Statistical Office, Economic Trends, April 1994, T6, and UK Economic Accounts, The fourth quarter 1993, 23 and 25.

Equivalently, it is the sum of the incomes (including profits) paid to the factors of production used by a firm to produce its output. Let's illustrate value added by looking at the production of a loaf of bread.

Figure 22.3 takes you through the brief life of a loaf of bread. It starts with the farmer, who grows the wheat. To do so, the farmer hires labour, capital equipment and land, paying wages, interest and rent. The farmer also receives a profit. The entire value of the wheat produced is the farmer's value added. The miller buys wheat from the farmer and turns it into flour. To do so, the miller hires labour and uses capital equipment, paying wages and interest, and receives a profit. The miller has now added some value to the wheat bought from the farmer. The baker buys flour from the miller. The flour includes value added by the farmer and by the miller. The baker adds more value by turning the flour into bread. Wages are paid to bakery workers, interest is paid on the capital used by the baker, and the baker makes a profit. The bread is bought from the baker by the grocer. The bread now has value added by the farmer, the miller and the baker. At this stage, the value of the loaf is its *wholesale* value. The grocer adds further value by making the loaf available in a convenient place at a convenient time. The consumer buys the bread for a price – its *retail price* – that includes the value added by the farmer, the miller, the baker and the grocer.

Final Goods and Intermediate Goods In valuing output, we count only *value added*. The sum of the value added at each stage of production equals expenditure on the *final good*. In the above example, the only thing that has been produced and consumed is one loaf of bread. But many transactions occurred in the process of producing the loaf of bread. The miller bought grain from the farmer, the baker bought flour from the miller and the grocer bought bread from the baker. These transactions were the purchase and sale of *intermediate goods*. To count the expenditure on intermediate goods and services as well as the expenditure on the final good involves counting the same thing twice, or more than twice when there are several intermediate stages, as there are in this example. Counting both expenditure on final goods and intermediate goods is known as **double counting**. Wheat, flour and even the finished loaf bought by the grocery store are all intermediate goods in the production of a loaf of bread bought by a final consumer.

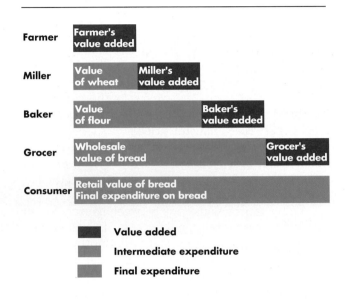

FIGURE 22.3

Value Added in the Life of a Loaf of Bread

A consumer's expenditure on a loaf of bread is equal to the sum of the value added at each stage in its production. Intermediate expenditure – for example, the purchase of flour by the baker from the miller – already includes the value added by the farmer and the miller. Including intermediate expenditure double counts the value added.

Many goods are sometimes intermediate goods and sometimes final goods. For example, the electric power used by Rover to produce cars is an intermediate good, but the electric power that you buy to use in your home is a final good. Whether a good is intermediate or final depends not on what it is, but on what it is used for.

Table 22.4 shows the output approach to measuring GDP in the United Kingdom. This approach adds together the values added in all sectors of the economy. This sum is gross domestic product at factor cost. To calculate GDP we add indirect taxes less subsidies to gross domestic product at factor cost.

Aggregate Expenditure, Income and GDP

The equality of the three concepts, aggregate expenditure, aggregate income and GDP (which is

TABLE 22.4

GDP: The Output Approach

Sector	Value added in 1993 (billions of pounds)
Agriculture, forestry and fishing	10.4
Mining and quarrying, oil and gas extraction	12.1
Manufacturing industry	118.3
Electricity, gas and water supply	14.0
Construction	29.2
Distribution, repairs, hotels and restaurants	78.3
Transport, storage and communication	46.3
Finance, land and building renting	110.2
Public administration and defence	38.2
Education, health and social work	57.5
Other services	29.6
Gross domestic product (income-based)	544.1
Statistical discrepancy	−0.4
Gross Domestic Product at factor cost	543.7
Indirect taxes *minus* subsidies	83.4
Gross domestic product at market prices	627.1

The output approach adds together the value added in each sector of the economy which is gross domestic product at factor cost. To measure GDP, indirect taxes minus subsidies is added to gross domestic product at factor cost.

Source: Derived from Table 22.3 and Central Statistical Office, *The CSO Blue Book: United Kingdom National Accounts*, 1994 edition (24–5).

FIGURE 22.4

Aggregate Expenditure, GDP and Income

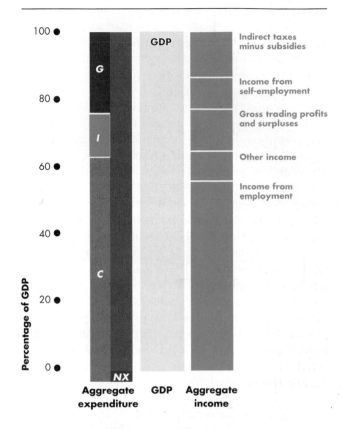

This figure illustrates the relative magnitudes of the main components of aggregate expenditure and aggregate income and also illustrates the equality between aggregate expenditure, aggregate income and GDP.

aggregate product) are illustrated in Fig. 22.4. Aggregate expenditure (left column) equals the sum of consumers' expenditure, investment, government purchases and net exports. Net exports are negative so they are subtracted from the other three items to obtain aggregate expenditure (the red column), which equals GDP and aggregate income.

Gross National Product and Gross National Disposable Income

We have now looked at GDP. But we often read about GNP, and increasingly we read about GNDI. Let's look at these two terms.

We have seen that output is produced by firms and that the income generated by their activities (Y) equals GDP. In Fig. 22.2 we show all this income flowing to the household sector. However, the income available to the household sector should really be modified in two ways.

The first modification concerns international flows of property income. Households will not receive the whole of the income generated in the United Kingdom (Y) as some of it will flow as interest, profits and dividends to foreigners who have lent money to the economy or who have bought firms or shares of firms in it. We call the money that leaves the country in this way property income paid abroad. Against this, households will receive some interest, profits and dividends from loans, businesses and shares that they own abroad, that is, property income from abroad. So really the income available to households will differ from Y (or GDP) by the amount of net property income from abroad. If we add net property income from abroad to GDP we get **gross national product** (GNP).

The second modification concerns international current transfers or gifts. Households may have more money available than GNP if the country receives gifts from other countries – either gifts from foreign private citizens or from bodies such as the European Union. Receipts of gifts from abroad are called current transfers from abroad. Against these should be deducted gifts paid to foreigners, whether to private citizens, bodies such as the European Union or payments of aid. Payments of gifts abroad are called current transfers paid abroad. If we modify GNP to allow for net payments of current transfers we get **gross national disposable income** (GNDI).

The calculations needed in the United Kingdom to go from GDP to GNP and GNDI in 1993 are shown in Table 22.5. As it happens, net payments of property income and net current transfers are very small so that GDP, GNP and GNDI have very similar values. We kept Fig. 22.2 reasonably simple by ignoring these net flows. In effect we assumed that the net flows were zero. We also assumed that these net flows were zero when we said that the income available to be allocated between C, S and T was Y. In turn we assumed that they were zero when we went on to show that injections equalled leakages. And we shall continue to assume that these net flows are zero for most of the remainder of this book.

Capital Consumption

We have looked so far at gross domestic product (GDP), gross national product (GNP) and gross national disposable income (GNDI). But sometimes people talk about net domestic product (NDP), net national product (NNP) and net national disposable income (NNDI). What do the words *gross* and *net* mean? What is the distinction between GDP and NDP, or between GNP and NNP, or between GNDI and NNDI?

For each of these three pairs of terms, the difference is accounted for by the depreciation of capital.

TABLE 22.5

GNP and GNDI

Item	Value in 1993 (billions of pounds)
GDP	627.1
Net property income from abroad	2.7
GNP	629.9
minus Net current transfers paid abroad	–5.1
GNDI	624.8

To calculate the total income available to UK citizens it is necessary to modify the factor income generated by firms. There is some additional income because receipts of property income from abroad – that is, income in the form of interest, profits and dividends – exceed payments of property income paid abroad. There is also a loss of income as current transfers – or gifts – paid abroad exceed gifts received from abroad.

Source: Central Statistical Office, *UK Economic Accounts*, The fourth quarter 1993, 21 and 59.

Depreciation is the reduction in the value of the capital stock that results from wear and tear and the passage of time. We've seen that investment is the purchase of new capital equipment. Depreciation is the opposite – the wearing out or destruction of capital equipment. Part of investment represents the purchase of capital equipment to replace equipment that has worn out. That investment does not add to the stock of capital; it simply maintains the capital stock. The other part of investment represents additions to the capital stock – the purchase of new plant, equipment and stocks. Total investment is called gross investment. **Gross investment** is the amount spent on replacing depreciated capital and on making net additions to the capital stock. The difference between gross investment and depreciation is called net investment. **Net investment** is the net addition to the capital stock. Let's illustrate these ideas with an example.

On 1 January, 1993, Knitters plc had a capital stock consisting of three knitting machines that had a market value of £7,500. In 1993, Knitters bought a new machine for £3,000. But during the year the machines owned by Knitters depreciated by a total of £1,000. By 31 December, 1993, Knitters' stock of knitting machines was worth £9,500. Knitters' purchase of a new machine for £3,000 is the firm's gross investment. The firm's net investment – the difference between gross investment (£3,000) and depreciation (£1,000) – is £2,000. These transactions and the relationship between gross investment, net investment and depreciation are summarized in Table 22.6.

The total depreciation in 1993 for all firms in the United Kingdom was £65 billion. The statisticians call this **capital consumption**. They can deduct £65 billion from any of the gross figures we have met so far to get the corresponding net figure. Thus **net domestic product** (NDP) is gross domestic product minus capital consumption, **net national product** (NNP) is gross national product minus capital consumption, and **net national disposable income** (NNDI) is gross national disposable income minus capital consumption. Let's do an example and work out NNDI for 1993. We have seen that GNDI was £625 billion and that capital consumption was £65 billion. So NNDI at market prices was £625 billion minus £65 billion which is £560 billion.

Why do we want gross figures and net figures? In producing the GDP, the value of capital stock fell by £65 billion. Suppose that GDP was also £65 billion. Then really everybody's productive efforts would have been useless. The amount produced would have been no more than the fall in value of the capital that was used to help produce it. As it happens the GDP exceeded capital consumption by £562 billion, or NDP. This gives a better view of the real worth of everyone's productive efforts.

Much the same applies to the reasons for wanting NNP and NNDI. GNP is the income after allowing for net receipts of property income, while GNDI also allows for net current transfers paid abroad. But during 1993, producers set aside £65 billion of income to help replace their capital when it finally wears out altogether. It is only the remaining income – NNP or NNDI – that can really be regarded as income to spend at will. Rather confusingly, NNP is often called national income instead.

TABLE 22.6

Capital Stock, Investment and Depreciation for Knitters plc

Capital stock on 1 January, 1993 (value of knitting machines owned at beginning of year)		£7,500
Gross investment (value of new knitting machine bought in 1993)	+3,000	
minus **Depreciation** (fall in value of knitting machines during 1993)	–1,000	
equals **Net investment**		2,000
Capital stock on 31 December, 1993 (value of knitting machines owned at end of year)		9,500

Knitters plc capital stock at the end of 1993 equals its capital stock at the beginning of the year plus net investment. Net investment equals gross investment minus depreciation. Gross investment is the value of new machines bought during the year, and depreciation is the fall in value of Knitters' machines during the year.

REVIEW

GDP can be measured by three methods: the *expenditure approach* (the sum of consumers' expenditure, investment, government purchases of goods and services, and exports minus imports), the *factor incomes approach* (the sum of wages, interest, rent and profit with the adjustment for indirect taxes and subsidies), and the *output approach* (the sum of the value added in each sector of the economy). ◆ ◆ GNP equals GDP plus net property income from abroad. GNDI equals GNP minus net current transfers (or gifts) paid abroad. We can deduct capital consumption from GDP, GNP and GNDI respectively to obtain NDP, NNP (or national income) and NNDI. ◆

So far, in our study of GDP and its measurement, we've been concerned with the pound value of GDP and its components. But GDP can change either because prices change or because there is a change in the volume of goods and services produced – a change in *real* GDP. Let's now see how we measure the price level and distinguish between price changes and changes in real GDP.

The Price Level and Inflation

The *price level* is the average level of prices measured by a *price index*. To construct a price index, we take a basket of goods and services and calculate its value in the current period and in a base period. The price index is the ratio of its value in the current period to its value in the base period. The price index tells us how much more expensive the basket is in the current period than it was in the base period, expressed as a percentage.

Table 22.7 shows you how to calculate a price index for the basket of goods that Tom buys. His basket is a simple one. It contains 2 cassettes and 6 pints of beer. The value of Tom's basket, shown in the table, in 1990, was £16.00. The same basket in 1992 cost £20.00. Tom's price index is £20.00 expressed as a percentage of £16.00. That is,

$$\frac{£20.00}{£16.00} \times 100 = 125.$$

Notice that if the current period is also the base period, the price index is 100.

There are two main price indexes used to measure the price level in the United Kingdom today: the Retail Prices Index and the GDP deflator. The **Retail Prices Index** (RPI) measures the average level of prices of the goods and services bought by typical UK households. The **GDP deflator** mea-sures the average level of prices of all the goods and services that are included in GDP. We are now going to study the method used for determining these price indexes. In calculating the actual indexes, the Central Statistical Office processes many thousands of pieces of information. But we can learn the principles involved in those calculations by working through some simple examples.

Retail Prices Index

Every month, the Central Statistical Office calculates and publishes the *Retail Prices Index*. To construct the RPI, the Central Statistical Office first selects a base period. Currently, the base period is 1987. Then, on the basis of a survey of the spending patterns of some 7,000 households, it selects a basket of goods and services – the quantities of around 500 different goods and services that were consumed by typical households in the base period.

Every month, the Central Statistical Office sends a team of observers to about 200 different areas across the United Kingdom to record the prices for these 500 or so goods and services. When all the data are collected, the RPI is calculated by valuing the base-period basket of goods and services at the current month's prices. That value is expressed as a percentage of the value of the same basket in the base period.

To see more precisely how the RPI is calculated, let's work through an example. Table 22.8 summa-

---

TABLE 22.7

Calculating a Price Index

Items in the basket	Base period (1990)			Current period (1992)	
	Quantity	Price	Expenditure	Price	Expenditure on base-period quantities
Cassettes	2	£5	£10	£6.10	£12.20
Pints of beer	6	£1	£6	£1.30	£7.80
			£16		£20.00

Price index for 1992 = $\frac{£20.00}{£16.00}$ × 100 = 125

A price for 1992 is calculated in two steps. The first step is to value the basket of goods at the prices prevailing in both 1990 and 1992. The second step is to divide the value of those goods in 1992 by their value in the base period 1990 and to multiply the result by 100.

rizes the calculations. Let's suppose that there are only three products in the typical consumer's basket: packets of biscuits, shirts and bus rides. The quantities bought and the prices prevailing in the base period are shown in the table. Total expenditure in the base period is also shown: the typical consumer buys 10 packets of biscuits at £0.80 each and so spends £8 on biscuits. Expenditure on shirts and bus rides is worked out in the same way. Total expenditure is the sum of the three expenditures which is £170.

To calculate the price index for the current period, we need only discover the prices of the products in the current period. We do not need to know the quantities bought in the current period. Let's suppose that the prices are those set out in the table under 'current period'. To calculate the current period's value of the basket of goods and services, we use the current period's prices. For example, the current price of the same type of biscuits is £1.20 per packet, so the current period's value of the base-period quantity (10 packets) is 10 multiplied by £1.20, which is £12. The base-period quantities of shirts and bus rides are valued at this period's prices in a similar way. In the current period, the total value of the base-period basket is £187.

We can now calculate the RPI – the ratio of the current-period value of the basket to the base period's value, multiplied by 100. In this example, the RPI for the current period is 110. The RPI for the base period is, by definition, 100.

GDP Deflator

The *GDP deflator* measures the average level of prices of all the goods and services that make up GDP. You can think of GDP as being like a balloon that is being blown up by growing production of goods and services and rising prices. Figure 22.5 illustrates this idea. The purpose of the GDP deflator is to let some air out of the GDP balloon – the contribution of rising prices – so that we can see what has happened to *real* GDP. Real GDP is a measure of the physical volume of output arrived at by valuing the current period output at prices that prevailed in a *base period*. Currently, the base period for calculating real GDP is 1990. We refer to the units in which real GDP is measured as '1990 pounds'. The red balloon for 1990 shows real GDP in that year. The green balloon shows *nominal* GDP in 1993. (We use the term nominal GDP because it measures the money value of output.) The red balloon for 1993 shows real GDP for that year. To see real GDP in 1993, we *deflate* nominal GDP using the GDP deflator. Let's

---

TABLE 22.8

The Retail Prices Index – A Simplified Calculation

Items in the basket	Base period (1990)			Current period (1992)	
	Quantity	Price	Expenditure	Price	Expenditure on base-period quantities
Packets of biscuits	10	£0.80	£8	£1.20	£12
Shirts	2	£11.00	£22	£12.50	£25
Bus rides	200	£0.70	£140	£0.75	£150
Total expenditure			£170		£1.87

$$\text{RPI} = \frac{170}{170} \times 100 = 100 \qquad \text{RPI} = \frac{187}{170} \times 100 = 110$$

A fixed basket of goods – 10 packets of biscuits, 2 shirts and 200 bus rides – is valued in the base period at £170. Prices change and that same basket is valued at £187 in the current period. The RPI equals the current-period value of the basket divided by the base-period value of the basket multiplied by 100. In the base period the RPI is 100, and in the current period the RPI is 110.

FIGURE 22.5

The GDP Balloon

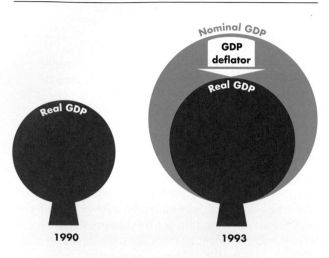

GDP is like a balloon that gets bigger because of growing output and rising prices. The GDP deflator is used to let the air resulting from higher prices out of the balloon so that we can see the extent to which production has grown.

see how we calculate real GDP and the GDP deflator.

We are going to learn how to calculate the GDP deflator by studying an imaginary economy. We will calculate nominal GDP and real GDP as well as the GDP deflator.

To make our calculations simple, let's imagine an economy that has just three final goods: the consumer good is apples; the capital good is computers; and the government good is packets of chalk bought for school use. (Net exports are zero in this example.) Table 22.9 summarizes the calculations of nominal GDP, real GDP and the GDP deflator in this economy.

First we calculate nominal GDP using the expenditure approach. The table shows the quantities of the final goods produced and their prices in the current period. To calculate nominal GDP, we work out the expenditure on each good in the current period and then add the three expenditures. Consumers' expenditure (apples) is £4,452, investment (computers) is £10,500 and government purchases (chalk packets) are £1,060, so nominal GDP is £16,012.

Next, let's calculate real GDP. To do this we value the current-period quantities at the base-period

prices. The table shows the prices for the base period. Real expenditure on apples for the current period is 4,240 bags valued at £1 per bag, which is £4,240. If we perform the same types of calculations for computers and chalk and add up the real expenditures, we arrive at a real GDP of £15,300.

To calculate the GDP deflator for the current period, we need to express nominal GDP as a percentage of real GDP. We do this by dividing nominal GDP (£16,012) by real GDP (£15,300) and multiplying the result by 100. The GDP deflator that we obtain is 104.7. If the current period is also the base period, nominal GDP equals real GDP. Thus the GDP deflator in the base period is 100, just as for the RPI.

The Retail Prices Index and the Cost of Living

Does the Retail Prices Index measure the cost of living? Does a 5 per cent increase in the RPI mean that the cost of living has increased by 5 per cent? It does not, and for three reasons. They are:

◆ Substitution effects
◆ Arrival of new goods and disappearance of old ones
◆ Quality changes

Substitution Effects   A change in the RPI measures the percentage change in the price of a *fixed* basket of goods and services. The actual basket of goods and services bought depends on relative prices and on consumers' tastes. Changes in relative prices will lead consumers to economize on goods that have become relatively expensive and to buy more of those goods whose relative prices have fallen. If chicken doubles in price but the price of beef increases by only 5 per cent, people will substitute the now relatively less expensive beef for the relatively more expensive chicken. Because consumers make such substitutions, a price index based on a fixed basket will overstate the effects of a given price change on the consumer's cost of living.

Arrival and Disappearance of Goods   Discrepancies between the RPI and the cost of living also arise from the disappearance of some commodities and the emergence of new ones. For example, suppose that you want to compare the cost of living in 1994 with that in 1894. Using a price index that has horse food in it will not work. Though that price featured in people's transport costs in 1894, it plays no role

TABLE 22.9

Nominal GDP, Real GDP and the GDP Deflator: Simplified Calculation

Item	Current period			Base period	
	Quantity	Price	Expenditure	Price	Expenditure
Bags of apples	4,240	£1.05	£4,452	£1	£4,240
Computers	5	£2,100	£10,500	£2,000	£10,000
Packets of chalk	1,060	£1	£1,060	£1	£1,060
		Nominal GDP	£16,012	Real GDP	£15,300

GDP deflator in current period $= \dfrac{£16,012}{£15,300} \times 100 = 125$

An imaginary economy produces only apples, computers and chalk packets. In the current period, nominal GDP is £16,012. If the current period quantities are valued at base-period prices, we obtain a measure of real GDP, which is £15,300. The GDP deflator in the current period – which is calculated by dividing nominal GDP by real GDP in the period and multiplying by 100 – is 104.7.

today. Similarly, a price index with petrol in it will be of little use, since petrol, while relevant today, did not feature in people's spending in 1894. Even comparisons between 1994 and 1980 suffer from this same problem. Compact discs and portable telephones that featured in our budgets in 1994 were not available in 1980.

Quality Changes The consumer price index can overstate a true rise in prices by ignoring quality improvements. Most goods undergo constant quality improvement. Cars, computers, CD players, even textbooks, get better year after year. Part of the increase in price of these items reflects the improvement in the quality of the product. Yet the RPI regards such a price change as inflation.

Substitution effects, the arrival of new goods and the departure of old ones, and quality changes make the connection between the RPI and the cost of living imprecise. To reduce the problems that arise from this source, the Central Statistical Office updates the weights used for calculating the RPI every year. Even so, the RPI is of limited value for making comparisons of the cost of living over long periods of time. But for the purpose for which it

was devised – calculating month-to-month and year-to-year rates of inflation – the RPI does a pretty good job.

R E V I E W

The Retail Prices Index is a price index based on the consumption expenditures of typical households. It is calculated as the ratio of the value of a base-period basket in the current period to its value in the base period (multiplied by 100). The GDP deflator is a price index calculated as the ratio of nominal GDP to real GDP (multiplied by 100). Real GDP values the current period's output at base-period prices. ◆ ◆ The RPI has limitations as a means of comparing the cost of living over long periods but does a good job of measuring year-to-year changes in the inflation rate ◆

Now that we've studied the measurement of GDP and the price level and know how *real* GDP is

The Development of Economic Accounting

> 'To express my self in
> Terms of Number,
> Weight, or Measure;
> to use only Arguments
> of Sense and to con-
> sider only such
> Causes as have
> visible Foundations in
> Nature'
>
> SIR WILLIAM PETTY
> *Political Arithmetick*

National income was first measured in England by William Petty in 1665. But it was not until the 1930s, when it was needed to test and use the new Keynesian theory of economic fluctuations, that national income measurement became a routine part of the operation of The Treasury.

With one exception, the national income accounts measure only *market transactions*. The exception is owner-occupied housing. National income includes an estimate of the amount that homeowners would have received (and paid) in rent if they had rented their homes rather than owned them. The idea is that regardless of whether a home is rented or owned, it provides a service, and the rent (actual or implicit) measures the value of that service.

But owner-occupied housing is not really so exceptional. We produce lots of services at home that are missed by the national accounts. Watching a video is an example. If you go to the cinema, the price you pay for the ticket includes the cost of the film, the rent of the seat, the cost of heating or cooling the cinema, the wages of the cinema workers and the profit (or loss) of the cinema owner – the full cost of your entertainment. The price of your ticket is measured as part of national income. But if you watch a home video, only the video rental is counted as part of national income. The rental cost of the television, VCR, armchair and sitting room (you rent them from yourself so there's no market transaction) is not counted.

The amount of home production has increased over the years. Kitchens equipped with microwaves and dishwashers, automatic washing machines, and living rooms containing more audio and video equipment than a 1970s TV studio have turned the home into a capital-intensive production centre.

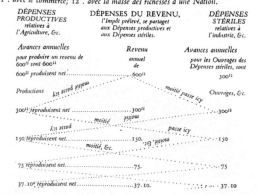

One of the earliest national economic accounts was François Quesnay's *Tableau Economique* used to measure economic activity in France in 1758. One of Quesnay's 'disciples' was so impressed with this work that he described it as being worthy of being ranked, along with writing and money, as one of the three greatest inventions of the human race. Quesnay's *Tableau* was praised by Karl Marx, the founder of socialism, and is regarded as the forerunner of the types of input-output tables used in the former Soviet Union to construct annual economic plans. Modern national accounts are less like Quesnay's *Tableau* and more like the income and expenditure accounts of large corporations. They record the incomes of factors of production and the expenditures on final goods and services.

Regardless of the method used to wash a car, the output is a clean car. And regardless of whether the factors of production are teenagers, rags, a hose, a bucket or an automated machine, these factors of production have created a good that is valued. Yet the teenagers' efforts are not measured in the national accounts, while that of the automatic car wash is. As do-it-yourself is replaced by purchasing from specialized producers, part of the apparent increase in the value of national production is just an illusion due to the way the books are kept. To avoid this illusion, it is necessary to develop methods of national income accounting that estimate the value of home production by using a method similar to that used to estimate the rental value of owner-occupied homes.

Partly because of all this capital equipment, women spend more time outside the home earning a wage and what they earn does get counted as part of national income. But both women and men are more productive in the home than ever before, and the value of this production does not get counted as part of national income.

Sir William Petty: A Pioneer of Economic Statistics

William Petty was born in England in 1623. He was a cabin boy on a merchant ship at 13, a student at a Jesuit college in France at 14, a successful doctor of medicine in his early 20s, a professor of anatomy at Oxford University at 27, and a professor of music at 28. As chief medical officer of the British army in Ireland at age 29, he managed a topographical survey of that country, from which he emerged as a substantial owner of Irish land! Petty was also an economic thinker and writer of considerable repute. He was the first person to measure national income and one of the first to propose that a government department be established for the collection of reliable and timely economic statistics. He believed that economic policy could only improve economic performance if it was based on an understanding of cause-and-effect relations discovered by the systematic measurement of economic activity – a process he called 'Political Arithmetick'.

SIR WILLIAM PETTY

measured, let's take a look at what real GDP tells us about the aggregate value of economic activity, the standard of living and economic well-being.

Real GDP, Aggregate Economic Activity and Economic Welfare

What does real GDP really measure? What does it tell us about aggregate economic activity? What does it tell us about our welfare? Some of these questions are discussed further in Our Advancing Knowledge on pp. 626–627.

Welfare is the overall well-being of a nation's citizens. Their welfare depends on many factors. For example, welfare rises if the threat of war recedes or if there is an improvement in the legal system, and it falls if diseases like AIDS spread or the crime rate rises. Most of the factors that affect welfare are outside the scope of any economic statistics, but one factor which affects welfare is related to economic statistics. This is economic welfare. Reading Between the Lines on pp. 630–631 considers additional problems when levels of economic activity and welfare in different countries are compared.

Economic welfare is that part of people's well-being which derives from their being able to enjoy goods, services and leisure. The level of the nation's economic welfare depends on the following factors:

◆ The quantity and quality of the goods and services that people can obtain
◆ The amount of leisure time available
◆ The degree of equality among individuals

We have said that GDP measures the value of goods and services produced, and that changes in real GDP measure changes in the quantity of goods and services produced. So how well do changes in real GDP indicate changes in economic welfare? The answer is that changes in real GDP have some important limitations as indicators of changes in economic welfare.

One of the problems with real GDP is that it incorrectly measures the extent to which citizens can obtain goods and services. We saw earlier in this chapter that gross national disposable income – which allows for net receipts of property income from abroad and net current transfers paid abroad – is a better indicator of people's total income. So we would be wiser to use changes in real GNDI than changes in real GDP to indicate changes in economic welfare. But we would be wiser still to use changes in real net national disposable income – real NNDI – as this allows for capital consumption which is a cost of production in the form of wear and tear of capital. This capital will eventually need to be replaced and some income must be set aside for that purpose.

So do changes in real NNDI measure changes in economic welfare? Unfortunately, even changes in real NNDI have many limitations. We will mention six:

◆ Real NNDI ignores a huge quantity of goods and services produced by households
◆ Real NNDI may ignore some goods and services obtained from the 'hidden economy'
◆ Real NNDI provides no information on leisure time
◆ Real NNDI ignores population changes
◆ Real NNDI provides no information on the distribution of income
◆ Environmental damage

Household Production Every day an enormous amount of production is done by households. Households produce goods such as home-grown vegetables and home-made clothes, and services such as shopping, cooking, cleaning, driving to work and teaching children how to talk. None of these goods and services is measured and allowed for in GDP, so none gets incorporated in other measures such as GNP, GNDI or NNDI. The only services produced by households that are included in official statistics are the accommodation services provided by owner-occupiers.

It is hard to say whether household production has risen or fallen over time. More people have joined the labour force, so they have less time for household production, but working hours have fallen, so people who do work have more time for household production than they used to have. Moreover, household production has become more capital intensive over the years. For example, a microwave meal that takes just a few minutes to prepare uses a great deal of capital and almost no labour. So household production can rise even if people spend less time on it.

Household production is almost certainly cyclical. When the economy is in recession, household production increases as households whose members are unemployed buy fewer goods and services in the marketplace and produce more for themselves. When the economy is booming, employment outside the home increases and household production decreases.

The Hidden Economy   The **hidden economy** is all economic activity that should be reported and is not. Most people who conceal their economic activity do so to evade taxes or regulations. The biggest problem for the Central Statistical Office statisticians occurs on the income approach as people have an incentive to under-record their income to evade income taxes. Indeed, you may wonder why the income-approach estimate of GDP is not much lower than the estimates on the other approaches. The reason is that the statisticians adjust their initial income approach estimates – which are always too low – by an amount which they think allows for the level of under-recording.

But how can the statisticians gauge the level of under-recording? They place great reliance on the expenditure approach. This is based largely on surveys of households and businesses to see how much consumption and investment they are doing, and the participants in these surveys have little reason to hide any of their spending. But they might hide spending on items such as illegal drugs, and they might hide their consumption of items such as private telephone calls made at their employers' expense on their employers' phones. The extent of this under-recording is not known but is probably modest. The statisticians make a guess at it which they allow for in the published figures, but they may be some way out in their guess.

Leisure Time   You might wonder why we include leisure in economic welfare. The reason is that leisure is similar to goods and services in that it can effectively be purchased. Workers can purchase leisure by working fewer hours and so having less money to spend on other goods and services. Other things remaining the same, the more leisure we have, the better off we are. Each week, every hour of our leisure time must be at least as valuable to us as the wage that we earn on the last hour we worked. If it was not, we would do more work and take less leisure.

Population Changes   Suppose that one year real NNDI rises by only 1 per cent and that the population also

rises by 1 per cent. It would be wrong to claim that, on average, people's well-being from the goods and services their income can buy has risen. To see whether people are, on average, getting better off, it is important to see whether real NNDI is rising more quickly or more slowly than population. This can be done by looking at changes in real NNDI per person.

The Distribution of Income   Suppose that NNDI per person in a country rises over a period of years. This means that the average level of incomes is rising. But suppose the average level rises only because the very rich are getting vastly richer while the poor are actually getting rather poorer. The modest loss of income to the poor may still bring a large fall in their well-being. In contrast because of diminishing marginal utility the gain of income to the rich may bring very little increase in their well-being. So a rise in NNDI associated with a rise in inequality may cause only a small rise, or even a fall, in economic welfare.

The Costs of Rises in Economic Welfare   Despite the problems of measuring economic welfare, there is little doubt that it has grown greatly since the industrial revolution. Output has risen leading to a rise in factor incomes and an increase in the goods and services we can obtain. Moreover, improving technology has reduced the length of the average working day so that most workers enjoy more leisure time than they used to.

But rises in economic welfare may not bring comparable rises in welfare as a whole. For rises in economic welfare may lead to falls in other aspects of welfare. This can happen in many different ways. For instance, higher technology may mean that more people have boring jobs on assembly lines rather than interesting ones in hand-crafted workshops. Also, some people may devote part of their rising incomes to excessive alcohol consumption which leads to domestic violence. And rising incomes may lead to some people becoming excessively materialistic.

But perhaps the most discussed cost of rising output and incomes is environmental damage. The environment can be harmed by economic activity. Important examples are the damage done to the environment by the burning of hydrocarbon fuels, the depletion of exhaustible resources, the noise from traffic, and the pollution of rivers and the sea.

Of course, as a country becomes richer, its citizens can devote more resources to cleaning up the

Exchange Rates vs Purchasing Power Parity

THE TIMES, 21 MAY 1993

IMF frees its assessments of world economies from shackles of dollar

Ian Brodie

THE International Monetary Fund's new way of assessing the world's economies could change the way politicians distribute aid.

Under the revised statistics, Britain drops from the world's sixth largest economy to eighth while India jumps into sixth place from eleventh. China moves up to become the third largest, after the United States and Japan. Its previous ranking was tenth. Other developing countries which jumped up the list include Indonesia, Mexico and Brazil....

Under the new measure, a country's economic strength will be judged by what its own currency can buy at home. In other words, the statistics will focus on how much, say, 100 yuan will buy in China regardless of the yuan's standing against the dollar in world currency markets. The new gauge is known as purchasing power parity, or PPP.

IMF officials in Washington explained that the change was considered necessary because the old system was giving a skewed view of the pattern of world growth. For example, if a country's currency depreciated by 10 per cent against the dollar its economy was shown to have shrunk by 10 per cent, which was seldom the case. Because of the use of international exchange rates, the economy of Asia (excluding Japan) was shown to have dropped over the last decade from 7.5 to 7.2 per cent of world output. Yet China has been the fastest growing region in the world. 'Obviously something was very wrong,' said one IMF official.

With PPP, a country's prosperity is measured in non-traded goods, such as housing and the costs of transport and construction. Under the old measure based on exchange rates, per-capita income for China's 1.1 billion people last year was $370 (£235), but under PPP the figure was $1,600. In Britain, per-capita purchasing power was less under the new system, $15,720 versus $17,596 under the old measure, which reflected the strengthening of sterling against the dollar. Using PPP, output of the world's industrial countries drops to 54.41 per cent, instead of 76 per cent under the old measure, while the share of developing countries increases from 20 per cent to 34.4 per cent.

© The Times. Reprinted with permission.

The International Monetary Fund (IMF) has changed the exchange rate it uses to convert the value of total economic output in each country into a common currency.

It has replaced international market exchange rates with purchasing power parity (PPP) rates, which reflect more closely the domestic value of output and less the vagaries of international currency markets.

Given that the common currency is the dollar, under the old system a movement in the dollar against another exchange rate would affect the value of that country's output (when measured in dollars) regardless of whether or not that output had actually changed.

The concept of PPP exchange rates allows a more accurate comparison of economic value to be made between countries, because strictly it is the exchange rate that equates the prices of an identical bundle of goods and services sold in different countries, when expressed in a common currency such as the dollar.

This means that any differences in the value of output so measured reflect differences in the bundle of goods and services rather than movements in currencies, which are subject to numerous external influences.

Such a change would be more likely to affect poor countries than rich countries, so comparing the two rankings in the IMF table, it can be seen that the relative positions of the developed countries remain the same (with, for example, Italy above Britain but below France), but the positions of the developing countries changes dramatically.

Within total economic activity, there are some commodities that can be traded and some that cannot. Market exchange rates will apply to tradeables, but not to non-tradeables, and will therefore undervalue the total output if non-tradeables are important in an economy.

In the IMF table, the two developing countries that move dramatically up the ranking (China and India) both have considerable non-tradeable sectors within their economies.

Other factors causing such a difference include lower labour productivity in developing countries' tradeables sectors, lower wages in developing countries leading to generally relatively lower prices and often also a lower quality of otherwise similar commodities.

The figures show the ratio of PPP to exchange rate for all the countries also featured in the IMF table. It can clearly be seen that all developed Western economies have ratios over 100 (except for the USA of course) and all developing and newly industrializing countries have values quite considerably below 100.

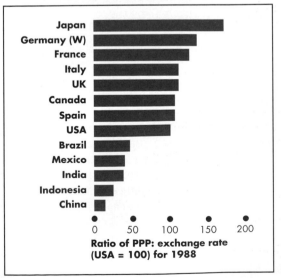

Ratio of PPP: exchange rate (USA = 100) for 1988

Source: *Penn World Table* – see Summers, R. and A. Heston (1991) *Quarterly Journal of Economics* , volume 106, pp. 327–368.

environment. But this means that not all of the rising NNDI can be devoted to purchasing things that could not be purchased before. Part of the rise in NNDI is used to sort out some of the damage done in creating it. So this is another reason why rises in NNDI do not accurately reflect increases in well-being.

Are the Shortcomings of NNDI a Problem?

We have seen that changes in real NNDI give very poor indications of changes in economic welfare. How important are the shortcomings of NNDI? The answer depends on the questions being asked. There are two main types of question:

◆ Business cycle questions
◆ Economic welfare and standard of living questions

Business Cycle Questions The business cycle fluctuations in economic activity measured by real GDP probably overstate the fluctuations in total production and economic welfare. When there is an economic downturn, household production increases and so does leisure time, but real GDP and real NNDI do not record these changes. When real GDP grows quickly, leisure time and household production probably fall. Again, this change is not recorded as part of real GDP or real NNDI. But the directions of change of real GDP and economic welfare are likely to be the same.

Economic Welfare Comparisons For comparing economic welfare in one year with a much earlier year, or for comparing economic welfare in one country with another, the various shortcomings in real NNDI are probably very important. For example, the amount of household production is a much higher fraction of economic activity in developing countries than in developed countries, so that GDP and, in turn, NNDI understate people's true economic welfare by a greater percentage. Also, in developing countries the hidden economy may be very large so that estimates of GDP and NNDI are very poor. These points alone make comparisons of GDP per person and NNDI per person between countries such as the United Kingdom and Nigeria very unreliable measures of economic welfare. A further point to note is that in some developing countries, population estimates are very poor which casts further doubt on the value of the figures for NNDI per person. Also, there may be very different amounts of leisure in different countries or in one country in different years.

Living Standards

People often talk about their standard of living. Is this the same as their economic welfare? The answer is no. But in saying this we must also say that there is no unanimity about exactly what people do mean by the standard of living.

Perhaps the best way of seeing why living standards and economic welfare are not the same is to show that living standards could actually fall over a period of years in which economic welfare rose. Remember that economic welfare depends chiefly on our ability to obtain goods and services and hence on our real incomes. Our living standards might fall when our incomes rise if we devote a much larger slice of our rising incomes to investment and actually devote less to consumption. They might also fall if, perhaps because of the threat of war, we devote a much larger slice of our rising incomes to armaments and less to consumption.

These examples show that changes in real NNDI can be very misleading as indicators of changes in living standards. We could try to improve our ability to measure improvements in living standards by replacing real NNDI with a narrower measure that omitted spending on investment and defence. But there is no agreement on what else might be omitted. If we omit defence, should we also omit spending on the police? If we omit investment in physical capital, should we also omit education which is investment in human capital?

We have preferred to avoid these debating points. There is much to be said for focusing on economic welfare because all our spending affects our well-being. For instance, investment and defence give us the promise of higher incomes in future and increased security, so they should not be dismissed as worthless.

◆ ◆ ◆ ◆ In Chapter 21, we examined the macroeconomic performance of the United Kingdom in recent years and over a longer sweep of history. In this chapter, we studied in some detail the methods used for measuring the macroeconomy and in particular the average level of prices and the overall level of real economic activity. In the following chapters, we're going to study some macroeconomic models – models designed to explain and predict the behaviour of real GDP, the price level, employment and unemployment, and other related phenomena. We start this process in the next chapter by examining a macroeconomic model of demand and supply – a model of *aggregate* demand and *aggregate* supply.

SUMMARY

The Circular Flow of Expenditure and Income

All economic agents – households, firms, government and the rest of the world – interact in the circular flow of income and expenditure. Households sell factors of production to firms and buy consumer goods and services from firms. Firms hire factors of production from households and pay incomes to households in exchange for factor services. Firms sell consumer goods and services to households and capital goods to other firms. Government collects taxes from households and firms, makes transfer payments under various social programmes to households, and buys goods and services from firms. Foreigners buy goods from domestic firms and sell goods to them.

The flow of expenditure on final goods and services ends up as somebody's income. Therefore

Aggregate income = Aggregate expenditure.

Furthermore, expenditure on final goods and services is a method of valuing the output of the economy. Therefore

GDP = Aggregate expenditure = Aggregate income.

From the firms' accounts we know that

$$Y = C + I + G + EX - IM,$$

and from the households' accounts we know that

$$Y = C + S + T.$$

Combining these two equations we obtain

$$I + G + EX = S + T + IM.$$

This equation tells us that injections into the circular flow (left side) equal the leakages from the circular flow (right side). (pp. 609–615)

The UK's National Income and Expenditure Accounts

Because aggregate expenditure, aggregate income and the value of output are equal, national income accountants can measure GDP using one of three approaches: the expenditure approach, the factor incomes approach and the output approach.

The expenditure approach adds together consumers' expenditure, investment, government purchases of goods and services, and net exports to arrive at an estimate of GDP.

The factor incomes approach adds together the incomes paid to the various factors of production plus profits paid to the owners of firms. To use the factor incomes approach, it is necessary to make an adjustment from the factor cost value of GDP to the market prices value by adding indirect taxes and subtracting subsidies.

The output approach adds together the value of output of each firm or sector in the economy. To measure the value of output, we measure the value added. The use of value added avoids double counting.

Although GDP measures all the income paid out by UK producers, it does not measure the total income of UK citizens. To measure this we add in net property income from abroad to get GNP, and then deduct net current transfers paid abroad to get GNDI. We can deduct capital consumption (depreciation) from GDP, GNP and GNDI to arrive at NDP, NNP (or national income) and NNDI. (pp. 615–621)

The Price Level and Inflation

There are two major price indexes that measure the price level and inflation: the Retail Prices Index and the GDP deflator.

The RPI measures the average level of prices of goods and services consumed by typical households in the United Kingdom. The RPI is the ratio of the value of a base-period basket of commodities at current-period prices to the same basket valued at base-period prices, multiplied by 100.

The GDP deflator is nominal GDP divided by real GDP, multiplied by 100. Nominal GDP is calculated by valuing current-period quantities produced at current-period prices. Real GDP is calculated by valuing the quantities produced in the current period at the prices that prevailed in the base period.

Because relative prices are constantly changing and causing consumers to substitute less expensive items for more expensive items, because of the disappearance of some goods and the arrival of new goods and because of quality changes, the RPI is an imperfect measure of the cost of living, especially when comparisons are made across a long time span. (pp.622–625)

Real GDP, Real NNDI and Economic Welfare

Economic welfare is the well-being we derive from being able to obtain goods and services and from leisure. Our ability to obtain goods and services depends in part on our income, and changes in our income are indicated more accurately by changes in real NNDI than by changes in real GDP. But real

NNDI is a very imperfect indicator of changes in economic welfare. It ignores virtually all household production, it incorporates uncertain estimates of concealed purchases, it ignores leisure, the distribution of income and changes in population. Changes in real NNDI also ignore the impact on non-economic aspects of welfare of increasing output and incomes. (pp. 628–632)

KEY ELEMENTS

Key Terms

Key Figures and Tables

REVIEW QUESTIONS

1   List the components of aggregate expenditure.

2   What are the components of aggregate income?

3   Why does aggregate income equal aggregate expenditure?

4 Why does the value of output (or GDP) equal aggregate income?

5 Distinguish between government purchases of goods and services and transfer payments.

6 What are injections into the circular flow of expenditure and income? What are leakages?

7 Explain why injections into the circular flow of income and expenditure equal leakages from it.

8 How does the Central Statistical Office measure GDP?

9 Explain the expenditure approach to measuring GDP.

10 Explain the factor incomes approach to measuring GDP.

11 What is the distinction between expenditure on final goods and expenditure on intermediate goods?

12 What is value added? How is it calculated? What does the sum of value added by all firms equal?

13 How does GNP differ from GDP? How does GNDI differ from GNP?

14 What are the two main price indexes used to measure the price level and inflation?

15 How is the Retail Prices Index calculated?

16 How is the basket of goods and services used in constructing the RPI chosen? Is it the same basket in 1994 as it was in 1954? If not, how is it different?

17 How is the GDP deflator calculated?

18 Is the RPI a good measure to use to compare the cost of living today with that in the 1930s? If not, why not?

19 Is GDP a good measure of economic welfare? If not, why not?

P R O B L E M S

1 The following transactions took place in Ecoland last year:

Item	Billions of pounds
Wages paid to labour	800,000
Consumers' expenditure	600,000
Taxes paid on wages	200,000
Government transfer payments	50,000
Firm's profits	200,000
Investment	250,000
Taxes paid on profits	50,000
government purchases of goods and services	£200,000
Export earnings	300,000
Saving	250,000
Import payments	250,000

a Calculate Ecoland's GDP

b Did you use the expenditure approach or the factor income approach to make this calculation?

c Does your answer to part (a) value output in terms of market prices or factor cost. Why?

d What extra information do you need in order to calculate net domestic product?

2 Judith, the owner of Judith's Cakeshop, spends £100 on eggs, £50 on flour, £45 on milk, £10 on electricity and £60 on wages to produce 200 cakes. Judith sells her cakes for £1.50 each. Calculate the value added per cake at Judith's Cakeshop.

3 A typical family living on Sandy Island consumes only apple juice, bananas and cloth. Prices in the base year are £4 a litre for apple juice, £3 a kilogram for bananas and £5 a square metre for cloth. The typical family spends £40 on apple juice, £45 on bananas and £25 on cloth. In the current year, apple juice costs £3 a litre, bananas cost £4 a kilogram, and cloth costs £7 a square metre. Calculate the Retail Prices Index on Sandy Island in the current year and inflation rate between the base year and the current year.

4 The newspaper on Sandy Island, commenting on the inflation figures that you have just calculated, runs the headline 'Inflation Results from Increase in Cloth Prices'. Write a letter to the editor pointing out the weakness in the economic reasoning of that paper's business reporter.

5 An economy has the following real GDP and nominal GDP in 1990, 1991 and 1992:

Year	Real GDP	Nominal GDP
1990	£1,000 billion	£1,000 billion
1991	£1,050 billion	£1,200 billion
1992	£1,200 billion	£1,500 billion

a What was the GDP deflator in 1991?

b What was the GDP deflator in 1992?

c What is the inflation rate as measured by the GDP deflator between 1991 and 1992?

d What is the percentage increase in the price level between 1990 and 1992 as measured by the GDP deflator?

CHAPTER 23

AGGREGATE
DEMAND
AND
AGGREGATE
SUPPLY

After studying this chapter you will be able to:

◆ Define aggregate demand and explain what determines it

◆ Explain why aggregate demand grows and fluctuates

◆ Define aggregate supply and explain what determines it

◆ Explain why aggregate supply grows and fluctuates

◆ Define macroeconomic equilibrium

◆ Predict the effects of changes in aggregate demand and aggregate supply on real GDP and the price level

◆ Explain why real GDP grows

◆ Explain why inflation rises and falls

◆ Explain why we sometimes have severe recessions

I N THE 32 YEARS FROM 1961 TO 1993, REAL GDP IN THE UNITED KINGDOM doubled. In fact, a doubling of the United Kingdom's real GDP every generation has been routine. What forces drive the economy to grow? ◆ ◆ At the same time as GDP has been growing, the UK has experienced persistent inflation. Today, you need nearly £1,200 to buy what £100 would have bought in 1960. Most of this inflation occurred during the 1970s. What causes inflation? Why did inflation explode in the 1970s and recede in the 1990s? ◆ ◆ Output in the UK economy does not increase at a constant pace. Instead, the rate of growth fluctuates over the business cycle. For example, in 1987, real GDP grew by 4.6 per cent while in 1992 a recession brought a fall in real GDP. What makes real GDP grow unevenly, sometimes speeding up and sometimes slowing down or even shrinking? ◆ ◆ Sometimes the economy

What Makes Our Garden Grow?

is influenced by events in other parts of the world such as the 1991–1992 recessions in the United States and Japan. The economy is also influenced by government policies such as cuts in defence spending or the rate of income tax. And the economy is influenced by changes in interest rates and the exchange rate brought about by the actions of the Bank of England at the request of the government. How do the world economy, the government and the Bank of England affect prices and production?

◆ ◆ ◆ ◆ To answer questions like these, we need a model – a macroeconomic model. Our first task in this chapter is to build such a model – the *aggregate demand–aggregate supply model*. We'll use this model to explain real GDP growth, inflation and fluctuations in the UK economy.

Aggregate Demand

Our model will show what factors determine the aggregate quantity of goods and services produced and the average level of prices for which they are sold. We will measure the aggregate quantity of goods and services produced by using real GDP – that is GDP valued at the prices in a base year. We will measure their average price by using the GDP deflator. The model uses the concepts of demand and supply that we met in Chapter 4. But here we use aggregate demand and aggregate supply – not the demand and supply for tapes – and the product is real GDP – not tapes – while the price is the GDP deflator – not the price of tapes.

The aggregate quantity of goods and services demanded is the quantity of real GDP demanded. That is, it is the sum of the quantities of consumer goods and services that households plan to buy, of investment goods that firms plan to buy, of goods and services that governments plan to buy, and of net exports that foreigners plan to buy. So the quantity of real GDP demanded depends on decisions made by households, firms, governments and foreigners. To study the forces influencing aggregate buying plans, we summarize the decisions of households, firms, governments and foreigners by using an aggregate demand schedule and an aggregate demand curve.

An aggregate demand schedule lists the quantity of real GDP demanded at each price level – that is at each level of the GDP deflator – holding all other influences on buying plans constant. The **aggregate demand curve** plots the quantity of real GDP demanded against the price level. **Aggregate demand** is the relationship between the quantity of real GDP demanded and the price level.

Figure 23.1 shows an aggregate demand schedule and aggregate demand curve. Each row of the table corresponds to a point in the figure. For example, row *c* of the aggregate demand schedule tells us that if the price level (the GDP deflator) is 130, the level of real GDP demanded is 600 billion 1990 pounds. This row is plotted as point *c* on the aggregate demand curve.

In constructing the aggregate demand schedule and aggregate demand curve, we hold constant all the influences on the quantity of real GDP

FIGURE 23.1

The Aggregate Demand Curve and Aggregate Demand Schedule

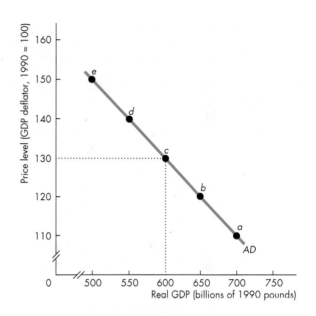

	Price level (GDP deflator)	Real GDP (billions of 1990 pounds)
a	110	700
b	120	650
c	130	600
d	140	550
e	150	500

The aggregate demand curve (*AD*) traces the quantity of real GDP demanded as the price level varies, everything else remaining the same. The aggregate demand curve is derived from the schedule in the table. Each point *a* to *e* on the curve corresponds to the row in the table identified by the same letter. Thus when the price level is 130, the quantity of real GDP demanded is £600 billion, point *c*.

demanded other than the price level. The effect of a change in the price level is shown as a movement along the aggregate demand curve. A change in any of the other influences on the quantity of real GDP demanded results in a new aggregate demand schedule and a shift in the aggregate demand curve.

Let's look at the effects of a change in the price level on the quantity of real GDP demanded. In particular, let's examine the reasons why the aggregate demand curve slopes downward – why an increase in the price level, other things remaining the same, decreases the quantity of real GDP demanded.

Changes in the Quantity of Real GDP Demanded

When the price level rises, other things remaining the same, the quantity of real GDP demanded decreases. When the price level falls, other things remaining the same, the quantity of real GDP demanded increases. These changes result in a movement along the aggregate demand curve and are illustrated in Fig. 23.2.

Figure 23.2 also summarizes why the aggregate demand curve slopes downward. Let's look at those reasons.

Why the Aggregate Demand Curve Slopes Downward

It's easy to understand why the demand curve for a single product slopes downward. If the price of Reebok running shoes rises, the quantity of Reeboks demanded falls because people switch to Nikes and other substitutes. The demand curve for Reeboks slopes downward because of a substitution effect. If the prices of Reeboks, Nikes and all other running shoes rise, the quantity of running shoes demanded falls because some people economize on their use or switch to substitute footwear and other goods. The demand curve for running shoes slopes downward because of a substitution effect.

But it's less easy to see why the demand curve for *all* goods and services slopes downward. If the prices of all goods and services increase – the price level increases – people demand less of *all* goods and services. But what do they demand more of? What do people substitute for real GDP?

Real GDP has three main substitutes: money, future real GDP and foreign real GDP. These three substitutes give rise to three effects on the demand for real GDP.

They are:

FIGURE 23.2

Changes in the Quantity of Real GDP Demanded

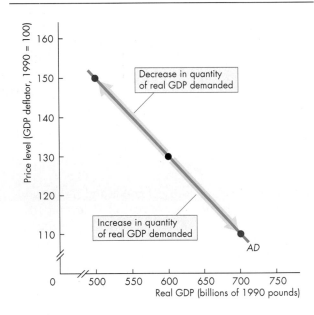

THE QUANTITY OF REAL GDP DEMANDED

Decreases if the price level *increases*	*Increases* if the price level *decreases*

because of the:

Real money balances effect

◆ An increase in the price level decreases the real money supply	◆ A decrease in the price level increases the real money supply

Intertemporal substitution effect

◆ An increase in the price level increases the cost of current goods and services relative to future goods and services	◆ A decrease in the price level decreases the cost of current goods and services relative to future goods and services

International substitution effect

◆ An increase in the price level increases the cost of domestic goods and services relative to foreign goods goods and services	◆ A decrease in the price level decreases the cost of domestic goods and services relative to foreign goods and services

◆ Real money balances effect
◆ Intertemporal substitution effect
◆ International substitution effect

Real Money Balances Effect The **real money balances effect** is the change in the quantity of real GDP demanded resulting from a change in the quantity of real money. What is real money?

Money is cash – that is notes and coins – along with deposits at banks and building societies. In other words, money includes the things you use to buy goods and services. **Real money** is the quantity of goods and services that money will buy. The higher the price level, the lower is the quantity of *real* money – the less money you *really* have. With a smaller amount of real money, you plan to spend less on goods and services and to keep more money in the bank.

Intertemporal Substitution Effect The **intertemporal substitution effect** is the change in the quantity of real GDP demanded resulting from a change in the *relative price* of goods and services now and goods in the future.

If you can buy something next year for less than the sum of today's price and the interest you earn by delaying your purchase, you might think it is worth waiting. The higher the price level, other things remaining the same, the more likely you are to wait and buy later.

International Substitution Effect The **international substitution effect** is the change in the quantity of real GDP demanded resulting from a change in the *relative price* of domestic goods and services and foreign goods and services.

If you can buy a foreign-made good for less than an equivalent domestic-made good, you will probably buy the foreign good. The higher the price level, other things remaining the same, the more foreign goods and services and the fewer domestic goods and services you will buy.

For the three reasons we've just reviewed, the higher the price level in the United Kingdom, the less is the quantity demanded of UK-made goods and services – UK real GDP. And the lower the price level in the United Kingdom, the greater is the quantity demanded of UK-made goods and services – UK real GDP.

REVIEW

T he aggregate demand curve traces the effects of a change in the price level – GDP deflator – on the aggregate quantity of goods and services demanded – real GDP demanded. A change in the price level results in a movement along the aggregate demand curve. Other things remaining the same, the higher the price level, the smaller is the quantity of real GDP demanded – the aggregate demand curve slopes downward. ◆ ◆ The aggregate demand curve slopes downward for three reasons: money and goods are substitutes (*real money balances effect*); goods today and goods in the future are substitutes (*intertemporal substitution effect*); domestic goods and foreign goods are substitutes (*international substitution effect*). ◆

Changes in Aggregate Demand

The aggregate demand schedule and aggregate demand curve describe aggregate demand at a point in time. But aggregate demand does not remain constant. It frequently changes. As a consequence, the aggregate demand curve frequently shifts. The main influences on aggregate demand that shift the aggregate demand curve are:

◆ Fiscal policy
◆ Monetary policy
◆ International factors
◆ Expectations

Let's examine each of these factors.

Fiscal Policy

The government's decisions about its purchases of goods and services, taxes and transfer payments have important effects on aggregate demand. The government's attempt to influence the economy using its spending and taxes is called **fiscal policy.** We'll study the effects of fiscal policy by looking at two actions the government can take. They are:

◆ Changes in government purchases of goods and services
◆ Changes in taxes and transfer payments

Changes in Government Purchases of Goods and Services The scale of government purchases of goods and services has a direct effect on aggregate demand. If taxes are held constant, the more roads, schools, doctors and teachers the government demands, the larger are government purchases of goods and services and so the larger is aggregate demand. Changes in the state of international tension and conflict can cause dramatic changes in government purchases of goods and services. Thus government purchases increased sharply during World War I and World War II and then declined after each. Now that the Cold War is over and the Warsaw Pact is abandoned, government defence spending is decreasing. But government purchases can also be significantly affected by other factors. For instance, rising car ownership has led to large increases in road spending, rising numbers of children staying on at school after 16 and then going on to college has led to large increases in education spending, rising crime has led to sharp increases in spending on the police and prisons, and new medical treatments have helped cause massive increases in health spending.

Changes in Taxes and Transfer Payments A decrease in taxes increases aggregate demand. An increase in transfer payments – government pensions, child benefits, job seekers' allowances and other welfare payments – also increases aggregate demand. Both of these influences operate by increasing households' *disposable* income. The higher the level of disposable income, the greater is the demand for goods and services. As lower taxes and higher transfer payments increase disposable income, they also increase aggregate demand.

This source of changes in aggregate demand has been an important one in recent years. After World War II, there was a large increase in government payments under various social programmes and these led to a sustained increase in aggregate demand. Looking ahead, the number of people aged over 65 is set to increase sharply in the next century, and this will result in a huge increase in government pensions – unless the government reduces the level of these pensions.

Monetary Policy

Decisions made by the Bank of England in consultation with the government about the money supply and interest rates have important effects on aggregate demand. The Bank of England's attempt to influence the economy by varying the money supply and interest rates is called **monetary policy.**

Money Supply The money supply is determined by the Bank of England and the banks (in a process described in Chapters 26 and 27). The greater the *quantity of money* the greater is the level of aggregate demand. An easy way to see why money affects aggregate demand is to imagine what would happen if the Bank of England borrowed the army's helicopters, loaded them with 1 million new £10 notes, and sprinkled the notes like confetti across the nation. We would all stop whatever we were doing and rush out to pick up some of the newly available money. But we wouldn't just put the money we picked up in the bank. We would spend some of it, so our demand for goods and services would increase. Although this story is pretty extreme, it does illustrate that an increase in the quantity of money increases aggregate demand.

In practice, changes in the quantity of money change interest rates and so have an additional influence on aggregate demand by affecting investment and the demand for consumer durables. When the Bank of England speeds up the rate at which new money is being injected into the economy, there's a tendency for interest rates to fall. When the Bank of England slows down the pace at which it is creating money, there's a tendency for interest rates to rise. Thus a change in the quantity of money has a second effect on aggregate demand, operating through its effects on interest rates.

Interest Rates If the Bank of England increases interest rates, households and firms change their borrowing, lending and spending plans. They try to borrow less, lend more and cut back their spending on new consumer durables and new business capital. The cut in spending on consumer durables and the fall in investment cause a decrease in aggregate demand.

Fluctuations in the quantity of money and interest rates have been important sources of changes in aggregate demand. Sustained increases in the quantity of money through the 1970s increased aggregate demand, contributing to the inflation of those years; decreases in the growth rate of the quantity of money slowed aggregate demand growth, contributing to the recessions of 1980–1981 and 1991–1992.

International Factors

There are two main international factors that influence aggregate demand. They are:

◆ The foreign exchange rate
◆ The state of the world economy

The Foreign Exchange Rate A change in the UK price level, other things remaining the same, changes the prices of goods and services produced in the United Kingdom *relative* to the prices of goods and services produced in other countries. Another influence on the price of goods and services produced in the United Kingdom relative to those produced abroad is the *foreign exchange rate*. The foreign exchange rate affects aggregate demand because it affects the prices that foreigners have to pay for goods and services produced in the United Kingdom and the prices that UK citizens have to pay for foreign-produced goods and services.

Suppose the pound is worth 8 French francs. You can buy a Renault that costs FFr120,000 for £15,000. Suppose that for £14,000 you can buy a Rover that is just as good as the more expensive Renault. In this case, you will buy the Rover.

But which car will you buy if the value of the pound rises to 10 francs and everything else remains the same? Let's work out the answer. At 10 francs per pound, you pay only £12,000 to buy the FFr120,000 needed to buy the Renault. As the Rover costs £14,000, the Renault is now cheaper and you will substitute the Renault for the Rover. The demand for cars made in the United Kingdom falls as the foreign exchange value of the pound rises. So as the foreign exchange value of the pound rises, everything else remaining the same, aggregate demand decreases.

There have been huge swings in the foreign exchange value of the pound in the last 10 years, leading to large swings in aggregate demand.

The State of the World Economy The main feature of the world economy that affects the United Kingdom is the level of income in the rest of the world. The income of foreigners affects the aggregate demand for domestically produced goods and services. For example, an increase in income in the United States, Japan, France and Germany increases the demand by US, Japanese, French and German consumers and producers for goods and services made

in the United Kingdom. These sources of change in aggregate demand have been important ones since World War II. The rapid economic growth of Western Europe, Japan and some of the newly industrializing countries of the Pacific Rim, such as South Korea and Singapore, has led to a sustained increase in demand for goods and services made in the United Kingdom.

Expectations

Expectations about all aspects of future economic conditions play a crucial role in determining current decisions. But three expectations are especially important. They are:

◆ Expected inflation
◆ Expected future incomes
◆ Expected future profits

Expected Inflation An increase in the expected inflation rate, other things remaining the same, leads to an increase in aggregate demand. The higher the expected inflation rate, the higher is the expected price of goods and services in the future and the lower is the expected real value of money and other assets in the future. As a consequence, when people expect a higher inflation rate, they plan to buy more goods and services now and hold smaller quantities of money and other financial assets.

Inflation expectations changed during the 1980s. At the beginning of the decade, people expected inflation to persist at 10 per cent a year or more. But a severe recession in 1980–1981 and a government which was willing to tolerate very high unemployment in its efforts to control inflation reduced those inflation expectations. Other things remaining the same, the effect of this decrease in inflation expectations was to decrease aggregate demand.

Expected Future Incomes An increase in expected future income, other things remaining the same, increases the amount that households plan to spend on consumer goods and services durables. When households expect slow future income growth, or even a decline in income, they scale back their spending plans.

Expectations about future income growth were pessimistic during 1991 and this factor contributed to the decrease in spending that brought on a recession in that year.

Expected Future Profits A change in expected future profit changes firms' demands for new capital equipment. For example, suppose that there has been a recent wave of technological change that has increased productivity. Firms will expect that by installing new equipment that uses the latest technology, their future profit will rise. This expectation leads to an increase in demand for new plant and equipment and so to an increase in aggregate demand.

Profit expectations were optimistic in the mid-1980s, helping to lead to sustained increases in aggregate demand. But expectations became pessimistic during 1990 and this contributed to a decrease in aggregate demand.

Time Lags in Influences on Aggregate Demand

The effects of the influences on aggregate demand that we've considered do not occur instantly. They occur with time lags. A *time lag* is a delay in the response to a stimulus. For example, when you take a tablet to cure a headache, the headache doesn't go away immediately – the medication works with a time lag. In a similar way, monetary policy influences aggregate demand with a time lag – one that spreads out over many months. For example, if the Bank of England increases the money supply, then at first there is no change in aggregate demand. A little later, as people reallocate their wealth, there is an increase in the supply of loans and interest rates fall. Later yet, confronted with lower interest rates, households and firms increase their purchases of goods and services. The total effect of the initial change in the quantity of money is spread out over many months. The next time the Bank of England takes exactly the same action, there is no guarantee that its effects will take place with exactly the same timing as before. The time lags in the effects of monetary policy on aggregate demand are both spread out and variable and, to a degree, unpredictable.

Now that we've reviewed the factors that influence aggregate demand, let's summarize their effects on the aggregate demand curve.

Shifts of the Aggregate Demand Curve

We illustrate a change in aggregate demand as a shift in the aggregate demand curve. Figure 23.3 illustrates two changes in aggregate demand, and summarizes the factors bringing about such changes. Aggregate demand is initially AD_0, the same as in Fig. 23.1.

FIGURE 23.3

Changes in Aggregate Demand

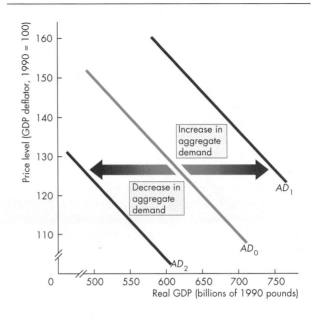

AGGREGATE DEMAND

Decreases if

◆ Fiscal policy decreases government spending or increases taxes

◆ Monetary policy decreases the money supply or increases interest rates

◆ The exchange rate increases or foreign income decreases

◆ Expected inflation, expected income or expected profits decrease

Increases if

◆ Fiscal policy increases government spending or decreases taxes

◆ Monetary policy increases the money supply or decreases interest rates

◆ The exchange rate decreases or foreign income increases

◆ Expected inflation, expected income or expected profits increase

The aggregate demand curve shifts to the right, from AD_0 to AD_1, when government purchases of goods and services increase, taxes are cut, transfer payments increase, the money supply increases and interest rates fall, the foreign exchange rate falls, income in the rest of the world increases, expected future profits increase,expected future incomes increase or the expected inflation rate increases.

The aggregate demand curve shifts to the left, from AD_0 to AD_2, when government purchases of goods and services decrease, taxes are increased, transfer payments decrease, the money supply decreases and interest rates rise, the foreign exchange rate rises, income in the rest of the world decreases, expected future profits decrease, expected future incomes decrease or the expected inflation rate decreases.

REVIEW

A change in the price level leads to a change in the aggregate quantity of goods and services demanded. That change is shown as a movement along the aggregate demand curve. A change in any other influence on aggregate demand shifts the aggregate demand curve. These other influences include:

◆ Fiscal policy
◆ Monetary policy
◆ International factors
◆ Expectations ◆

Aggregate Supply

The aggregate quantity of goods and services supplied is the sum of the quantities of all final goods and services that all the firms and government departments in the economy plan to produce. It is measured as real gross domestic product supplied. In studying aggregate supply, we distinguish between two macroeconomic time frames: the short run and the long run.

Two Macroeconomic Time Frames

The **macroeconomic short-run** is a period during which the prices of goods and services change in response to changes in demand and supply but

the prices of factors of production – wage rates and the prices of raw materials – do not change. The short run is an important time frame for two reasons. First, wage rates are determined by labour contracts that run for up to three years. As a result, wages rates change more slowly than prices. Second, the prices of some raw materials, especially oil, are strongly influenced by the actions of a small number of producers who keep the price steady in some periods but change it by a large amount in others.

The **macroeconomic long-run** is a period that is sufficiently long for the prices of all the factors of production – wage rates and other factor prices – to have adjusted to any disturbance so that the aggregate quantities demanded and supplied are equal in all markets – goods and services markets, labour markets and the markets for other factors of production. In the macroeconomic long-run, with wage rates having adjusted to bring equality between the quantities of labour demanded and supplied, there is *full employment*. Equivalently, unemployment is at its *natural rate*.

Short-run Aggregate Supply

Short-run aggregate supply is the relationship between the aggregate quantity of final goods and services (real GDP) supplied and the price level (the GDP deflator), holding everything else constant. We can represent short-run aggregate supply either as a short-run aggregate supply schedule or a short-run aggregate supply curve. The short-run aggregate supply schedule lists quantities of real GDP supplied at each price level, holding everything else constant. The **short-run aggregate supply curve** plots the relationship between the quantity of real GDP supplied and the price level, holding everything else constant.

Figure 23.4 shows a short-run aggregate supply schedule and the corresponding short-run aggregate supply curve (*SAS*). Part (a) shows the entire curve, and part (b) zooms in on the range of the curve where the economy normally operates. Each row of the aggregate supply schedule in the table corresponds to a point in the figure. For example, row a' of the short-run aggregate supply schedule and point a' on the curve tell us that if the price level is 120 (GDP deflator is 120), the quantity of real GDP supplied is 500 billion 1990 pounds.

Focus first on the entire short-run aggregate supply curve in Fig. 23.4(a). This curve has three ranges.

FIGURE 23.4

The Aggregate Supply Curves and Aggregate Supply Schedule

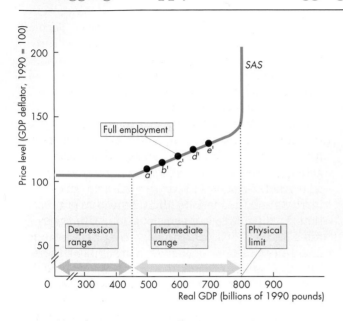

(a) The short-run aggregate supply curve

(b) The short-run and long-run aggregate supply curves

The short-run aggregate supply curve (*SAS*) traces the quantity of real GDP supplied as the price level varies, holding everything else constant. The short-run aggregate supply curves in this figure are derived from the schedule in the table. Part (a) shows the *SAS* curve over its entire range and part (b) zooms in on the intermediate range. In a depression, firms are willing to increase the quantity sold with no increase in price and the *SAS* curve is horizontal. At its physical limit, the economy can squeeze out no more production and the *SAS* curve becomes vertical. Normally the economy operates in the upward-sloping intermediate range. In that range, full employment occurs at *c'* where real GDP is £600 billion.

The long-run aggregate supply curve (*LAS*) shows the relationship between full-employment real GDP and the price level. This level of real GDP is independent of the price level so the *LAS* curve is vertical as shown in part (b). At levels of real GDP below the long-run level, unemployment is above the natural rate, and at levels of real GDP above the long-run level unemployment is below the natural rate.

	Price level (GDP deflator)	Real GDP (billions of 1990 pounds)
a'	120	500
b'	125	550
c'	130	600
d'	135	650
e'	140	700

It is horizontal over the depression range, upward sloping over the intermediate range, and vertical at the physical limit of the economy's ability to produce goods and services. Why is the short-run aggregate curve horizontal in the depression range? Why does it slope upward over the intermediate range? And why does it eventually become vertical?

Depression Range When the economy is severely depressed, firms have lots of excess capacity and are anxious to sell whatever they can at the going price. They would like to sell more and would be willing to offer more for sale with no inducement from a higher price. So each firm has a horizontal supply curve. As each firm has a horizontal supply curve, the aggregate supply curve is also horizontal. The last time the economy was on the depression range of its *SAS* curve was in the 1930s.

Intermediate Range   Normally, the economy operates in the upward-sloping intermediate range of its *SAS* curve. That's why we've zoomed in on this range in Fig. 23.4(b), and it is this part of the *SAS* curve that we'll use in the rest of the book.

Why does the *SAS* curve slope upward? To answer this question, think about the supply curve of tapes. If wage rates are constant, tape producers can make bigger profits by increasing output when the price of a tape rises. So, the higher the price of tapes, other things remaining the same, the greater is the quantity of tapes supplied. What's true for tape producers is also true for jam producers, furniture makers and firms producing every other good and service. Thus when prices rise but wage rates remain constant, the aggregate quantity of goods and services supplied – real GDP supplied – increases.

To increase their output in the short run, firms hire additional labour and work their existing labour force for longer hours. So a change in the price level, with wage rates held constant, leads to a change in the aggregate quantity of goods and services supplied and to a change in the level of employment and unemployment. The higher the price level, the greater is the aggregate quantity of goods and services supplied, the higher is the level of employment, and the lower is the level of unemployment.

The Physical Limit to Real GDP

At some level of real GDP, the short-run aggregate supply becomes vertical because there is a physical limit to the output that the economy can produce. If prices increase while wage rates remain constant, each firm increases its output. It does so by working its labour overtime, hiring more labour, and working its plant and equipment at a faster pace. But there is a limit to the amount of overtime workers are willing to accept. There is also a limit below which the unemployment rate cannot be pushed. And there is a limit beyond which firms are not willing to operate their plant and equipment because of the high cost of wear and tear and breakdowns. Once these limits are reached, no more output is produced, no matter how high prices rise relative to wage rates. At that output, the short-run aggregate supply curve

becomes vertical. In the example in Fig. 23.4, when the economy is operating at its physical limit real GDP is £800 billion.

Long-run Aggregate Supply

Long-run aggregate supply is the relationship between the aggregate quantity of final goods and services (real GDP) supplied and the price level (GDP deflator) when there is full employment.

The Long-run Aggregate Supply Curve   Long-run aggregate supply is represented by the long-run aggregate supply curve. The **long-run aggregate supply curve** plots the relationship between the quantity of real GDP supplied and the price level when there is full employment. The long-run aggregate supply curve is vertical and is illustrated in Fig. 23.4(b) as *LAS*. In this example, full employment occurs when real GDP is £600 billion. If real GDP is below this amount, a smaller quantity of labour is required and unemployment rises above its natural rate. The economy operates in the unemployment range shown in the figure. If real GDP is greater than £600 billion, a larger quantity of labour is required and unemployment falls below its natural rate. The economy operates in the above full-employment range shown in the figure.

Pay special attention to the *position* of the *LAS* curve. It is a vertical line that intersects the short-run aggregate supply curve at point *c'* on its upward-sloping intermediate range. It does not coincide with the vertical part of the *SAS* curve where the economy is operating at its physical production limit.

Why is the long-run aggregate supply curve vertical? And why is long-run aggregate supply less than the physical limits to production?

Why the Long-run Aggregate Supply Curve is Vertical
The long-run aggregate supply curve is vertical because there is only one level of real GDP that can be produced at full employment no matter how high the price level is. As we move along the long-run aggregate supply curve *two* sets of prices vary: the prices of goods and services and the prices of factors of production. And they vary by the same percentage. You can see why the level of output doesn't vary in these circumstances by thinking about the tape factory again. If the price of tapes increases and the cost of producing them also increases by the same

percentage, there is no incentive for tape makers to change their output level. What's true for tape producers is true for the producers of all goods and services, so the aggregate quantity supplied does not change.

Why Long-run Aggregate Supply Is Less than the Physical Limit of Production Real GDP cannot be increased above its physical limit. But it can be increased above its long-run level by driving unemployment below its natural rate. When this occurs, there are more unfilled job vacancies than there are people looking for work. Firms compete with each other for labour, wages rise faster than prices, and output eventually falls to its long-run level.

R E V I E W

The short-run aggregate supply curve shows the relationship between real GDP supplied and the price level, everything else remaining the same. With no change in wage rates or other factor prices, an increase in the price level results in an increase in real GDP supplied. The short-run aggregate supply curve is horizontal in a severe depression, upward-sloping in the intermediate range, and vertical when the economy is at the physical limit of its productive capacity ◆ ◆ The long-run aggregate supply curve shows the relationship between real GDP supplied and the price level when there is full employment. This level of real GDP is independent of the price level and the long-run aggregate supply curve is vertical. Its position tells us the level of real GDP supplied when the economy is at full employment, which is a lower level of real GDP than the physical production limit. ◆

A change in the price level, with everything else held constant, results in a movement along the short-run aggregate supply curve. A change in the price level, with an accompanying change in wage rates that keeps unemployment at its natural rate, results in a movement along the long-run aggregate supply curve. But there are many other influences on real GDP supplied. These influences result in a change in aggregate supply and shifts in the aggregate supply curves.

Some factors change both short-run aggregate supply and long-run aggregate supply; others affect short-run aggregate supply but leave long-run aggregate supply unchanged. Let's examine these influences on aggregate supply starting with those that affect only short-run aggregate supply.

Changes in Short-run Aggregate Supply

The only influences on short-run aggregate supply that do not change long-run aggregate supply are wage rates and the prices of other factors of production. Factor prices affect short-run aggregate supply through their influence on firms' costs. The higher the level of wage rates and other factor prices, the higher are firms' costs and the lower the quantity of output firms want to supply at each price level. Thus an increase in wage rates and other factor prices decreases short-run aggregate supply.

Why do factor prices affect short-run aggregate supply but not long-run aggregate supply? The answer lies in the definition of long-run aggregate supply. Recall that long-run aggregate supply refers to the quantity of real GDP supplied when wages and other factor prices have adjusted by the same percentage amount as the price level has changed. Faced with the same percentage increase in factor prices and the price of its output, a firm has no incentive to change its output. Thus aggregate output – real GDP – remains constant.

Shifts in the Short-run Aggregate Supply Curve A change in factor prices changes short-run aggregate supply and shifts the short-run aggregate supply curve. Figure 23.5 shows such a shift. Long-run aggregate supply is *LAS* and initially the short-run aggregate supply curve is SAS_0. These curves intersect at the price level 130. Now suppose that labour is the only factor of production and that wage rates increase from $13 an hour to $14 an hour. At the original level of wage rates, firms are willing to supply, in total, $600 billion worth of output at a price level of 130. They will supply that same level of output at the higher wage rate only if prices increase in the same proportion as wages have increased. With wages up from $13 an hour to $14 an hour, the price level that will keep the quantity supplied constant is 140. Thus the short-run aggregate supply curve shifts to SAS_1. There is a *decrease* in short-run aggregate supply.

FIGURE 23.5

A Decrease in Short-run Aggregate Supply

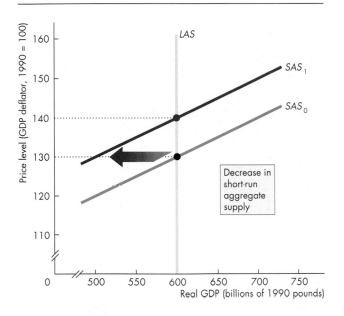

An increase in wage rates or in the prices of other factors of production decreases short-run aggregate supply but does not change long-run aggregate supply. It shifts the short-run aggregate supply curve to the left and leaves the long-run aggregate supply curve unaffected. Such a change is shown here. The original short-run aggregate supply curve is SAS_0 and after the wage rate has increased, the new short-run aggregate supply curve is SAS_1.

Changes in Both Long-run and Short-run Aggregate Supply

Three main factors influence both long-run and short-run aggregate supply and shift the aggregate supply curves (as shown in Fig. 23.6). They are:

◆ The labour force
◆ The capital stock
◆ Technology

The Labour Force The larger the labour force, the larger is the quantity of goods and services produced. Other things remaining the same, a coal pit with 500 workers produces more coal than a pit with 100 workers. The same is true for the economy as a whole. With its labour force of more than 28 million people,

FIGURE 23.6

Long-run Growth in Aggregate Supply

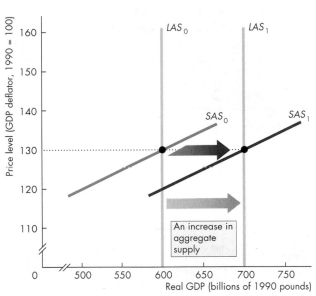

AGGREGATE SUPPLY

Increases in the long run if:

◆ The labour force increases
◆ The capital stock increases
◆ Technological change increases the productivity of labour and capital
◆ Incentives are strengthened, the climate improves, or structural change diminishes

Both the long-run and short-run aggregate supply curves shift to the right and by the same amount.

the United Kingdom produces a much larger quantity of goods and services than it would if, everything else remaining the same, it had Ireland's labour force.

The Capital Stock The larger the stock of plant and equipment, the more productive is the labour force and the greater is the output that it can produce. Also, the larger the stock of *human capital* – the skills that people have acquired in school and through on-the-job training – the greater is the level of output. The capital-rich UK economy produces a vastly greater quantity of goods and services than it would if, everything else remaining the same, it had Ukraine's stock of capital equipment.

Technology Inventing new and better ways of doing things enables firms to produce more from any given amount of inputs. So, even with a constant population and constant capital stock, improvements in technology increase production and increase aggregate supply. Technological advances are by far the most important source of increased production over the past two centuries. As a result of technological advances, in Europe today, one farmer can feed 100 people, and one worker can produce more than 10 cars in a year.

Aside from these three main factors, there are other influences on aggregate supply which include incentives, the climate and the pace of structural change.

Incentives Aggregate supply is influenced by the incentives that people face. Two examples are job-seekers' allowances and investment tax allowances. In the United Kingdom, transfer payments for the unemployed are much more generous, relative to wages, than those in the United States. So there is a greater incentive to find a job in the United States than in the United Kingdom. As a result, the UK's natural unemployment rate is higher and its long-run aggregate supply is lower than they would be if the United Kingdom had US unemployment compensation arrangements. Investment tax allowances are allowances which cut the taxes that must be paid on a firm's profits if it invests in new plant and equipment. Such allowances provide an incentive to purchase new capital and, other things remaining the same, raise aggregate supply.

Climate The climate has an obvious effect on output, especially in the agricultural sector. Ideal amounts of rainfall and sunshine and ideal temperatures can produce an increase in output while extreme climatic conditions restrict output, as happened with the Brazilian coffee harvest in 1994.

Pace of Structural Change If some sectors or regions expand rapidly while others decline, the economy undergoes structural change. An example of structural change was the explosive growth of banking and financial services and the relative decline of coal mining during the 1980s. Other things remaining the

same, the more rapid the pace of structural change, the larger is the amount of structural unemployment, and the lower is the level of aggregate supply.

Shifts in the Short-run and Long-run Aggregate Supply Curves If any of the events that change long-run aggregate supply occur, then *both* the long-run aggregate supply curve *and* the short-run aggregate supply curve shift. Most of the factors that influence both short-run and long-run aggregate supply bring an *increase* in aggregate supply. This case is summarized in Fig. 23.6.

Initially, the long-run aggregate supply curve is LAS_0 and the short-run aggregate supply curve is SAS_0. These curves intersect at a price level of 130 and a real GDP of 600 billion 1990 pounds. An increase in productive capacity that increases full-employment real GDP to 700 billion 1990 pounds shifts the long-run aggregate supply curve to LAS_1 and the short-run aggregate supply curve to SAS_1. Long-run aggregate supply is now 700 billion 1990 pounds.

REVIEW

A change in wage rates or in other factor prices changes short-run aggregate supply but leaves long-run aggregate supply unchanged. It shifts the short-run aggregate supply curve, but it does not shift the long-run aggregate supply curve. ◆ ◆ Changes in the size of the labour force, the capital stock and the state of technology, or changes in incentives, the climate and the pace of structural change, change both short-run and long-run aggregate supply. Such changes shift both the short-run and long-run aggregate supply curves in the same direction. ◆

Macroeconomic Equilibrium

The purpose of the aggregate demand– aggregate supply model is to predict changes in real GDP and the price level. To make predictions about real GDP and the price level, we need to combine aggregate demand and aggregate supply and determine macroeconomic equilibrium. **Macroeconomic equilibrium** occurs when the quantity of real GDP demanded equals the quantity of real GDP supplied. Let's see how macroeconomic equilibrium is determined.

Determination of Real GDP and the Price Level

The aggregate demand curve tells us the quantity of real GDP demanded at each price level, and the short-run aggregate supply curve tells us the quantity of real GDP supplied at each price level. There is one and only one price level at which the quantity demanded equals the quantity supplied. Macroeconomic equilibrium occurs at that price level. Figure 23.7 illustrates such an equilibrium at a price level of 130 and real GDP of 600 billion 1990 pounds (point c and c').

To see why this position is an equilibrium, let's work out what happens if the price level is something other than 130. Suppose, for example, that the price level is 140. In that case, the quantity of real GDP demanded is £550 billion (point d), but the quantity of real GDP supplied is £700 billion (point e'). There is an excess of the quantity supplied over the quantity demanded, or a surplus of goods and services. Unable to sell all their output and with stocks piling up, firms cut prices. Prices will be cut until the surplus is eliminated – at a price level of 130.

Next consider what happens if the price level is 120. In this case, the quantity of real GDP that firms supply is £500 billion worth of goods and services (point a') and the quantity of real GDP demanded is £650 billion worth (point b). The quantity demanded exceeds the quantity supplied. With stocks running out, firms raise their prices, and continue to do so until the quantities demanded and supplied are in balance – again at a price level of 130.

Macroeconomic Equilibrium and Full Employment

Macroeconomic equilibrium does not necessarily occur at full employment. At full employment, the economy is on its *long-run* aggregate supply curve. But macroeconomic equilibrium occurs at the intersection of the *short-run* aggregate supply curve and the aggregate demand curve and can occur at, below, or above full employment. We can see this fact most clearly by considering the three possible cases shown in Fig. 23.8.

FIGURE 23.7

Macroeconomic Equilibrium

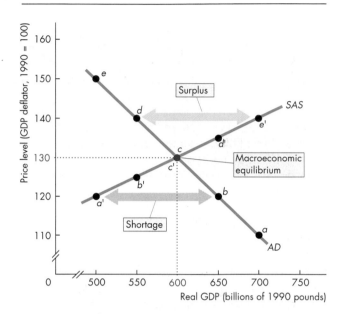

Macroeconomic equilibrium occurs when real GDP demanded equals real GDP supplied. Such an equilibrium is at the intersection of the aggregate demand curve (*AD*) and the short-run aggregate supply curve (*SAS*) – points c and c' – where the price level is 130 and real GDP is £600 billion. At price levels above 130, for example 140, there is an excess of the quantity of real GDP supplied over the quantity demanded – a surplus – and the price level falls. At price levels below 130, for example 120, there is an excess of the quantity of real GDP demanded over the quantity supplied – a shortage – and the price level rises. Only when the price level is 130 is the quantity of real GDP demanded equal to the quantity supplied. This is the equilibrium price level.

Figure 23.8(a) shows the fluctuations of real GDP for an imaginary economy over a five-year period. In year 2, real GDP falls below its long-run level and there is a recessionary gap. A **recessionary gap** is long-run real GDP minus actual real GDP when actual real GDP is below long-run real GDP. In year 4, real GDP rises above its long-run level and there is an inflationary gap. An **inflationary gap** is actual real GDP minus long-run real GDP when actual real GDP is above long-run real GDP. In year 3, actual real GDP and long-run real GDP are equal and the economy is at full employment.

These situations are illustrated in parts (b), (c), and (d) of Fig. 23.8 as the three types of macroeconomic equilibrium. In part (b) there is an

FIGURE 23.8

Three Types of Macroeconomic Equilibrium

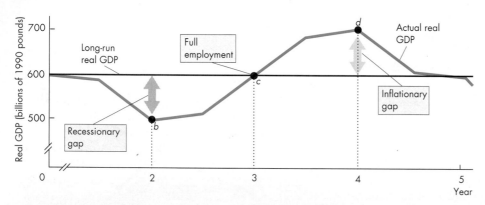

(a) Fluctuations in real GDP

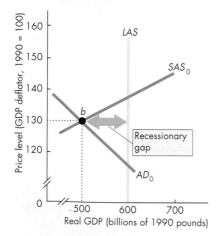

(b) Unemployment equilibrium

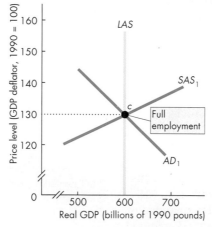

(c) Full-employment equilibrium

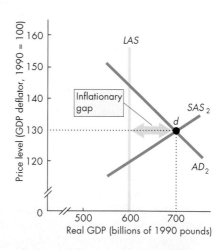

(d) Above full-employment equilibrium

In part (a) real GDP fluctuates around its long-run level. When actual real GDP is below long-run real GDP, there is a recessionary gap (as in year 2). When actual real GDP is above long-run real GDP, there is an inflationary gap (as in year 4). When actual real GDP is equal to long-run real GDP, there is full employment (as in year 3).

In year 2 there is an unemployment equilibrium as illustrated in part (b). In year 3 there is a full-employment equilibrium as illustrated in part (c). And in year 4 there is an above full-employment equilibrium as illustrated in part (d).

unemployment equilibrium. An **unemployment equilibrium** is a situation in which macroeconomic equilibrium occurs at a level of real GDP below long-run GDP. In such an equilibrium, there is a recessionary gap. The unemployment equilibrium illustrated in Fig. 23.8(b) occurs where the aggregate demand curve AD_0 intersects the short-run aggregate supply curve SAS_0 at a real GDP of 500

billion 1990 pounds and a price level of 130. There is a recessionary gap of 100 billion 1990 pounds.

Figure 23.8(c) is an example of full-employment equilibrium. **Full-employment equilibrium** is a macroeconomic equilibrium in which actual real GDP equals long-run real GDP. In this example, the equilibrium occurs where the aggregate demand curve AD_1 intersects the short-run aggregate supply curve SAS_1 at an actual and long-run real GDP of 600 billion 1990 pounds.

Finally, Fig. 23.8(d) illustrates an above full-employment equilibrium. **Above full-employment equilibrium** is a situation in which macroeconomic equilibrium occurs at a level of real GDP above long-run real GDP. In such an equilibrium, there is an inflationary gap. The above full-employment equilibrium illustrated in Fig. 23.8(d) occurs where the aggregate demand curve AD_2 intersects the short-run aggregate supply curve SAS_2 at a real GDP of 700 billion 1990 pounds and a price level of 130. There is an inflationary gap of 100 billion 1990 pounds.

The economy moves from one type of equilibrium to another as a result of fluctuations in aggregate demand and in short-run aggregate supply. These fluctuations produce fluctuations in real GDP and the price level. In 1994, the UK economy was in the type of situation shown in Fig. 23.8(b) with real GDP substantially below its long-run level.

Next, we're going to put the model to work generating macroeconomic fluctuations.

Aggregate Fluctuations and Changes in Aggregate Demand

We're going to work out what happens to real GDP and the price level following a change in aggregate demand. Let's suppose that the economy starts out at full employment and, as illustrated in Fig. 23.9, is producing 600 billion 1990 pounds, worth of goods and services at a price level of 130. The economy is on the aggregate demand curve AD_0, and it is also on both the short-run aggregate supply curve SAS_0 and the long-run aggregate supply curve LAS.

Now suppose that the Bank of England takes steps to increase the quantity of money. With more money in the economy, people increase their demand for goods and services – the aggregate demand curve shifts to the right. Suppose that the aggregate demand curve shifts from AD_0 to AD_1 in Fig. 23.9. A new equilibrium occurs, where the aggregate demand curve AD_1 intersects the short-run aggregate supply curve SAS_0. Output rises to £650 billion (1990 pounds) and the price level rises to 135. The economy is now at an above full-employment equilibrium. Real GDP is above its long-run level, and there is an inflationary gap.

The increase in aggregate demand has increased the prices of all goods and services. Faced with

higher prices, firms have increased their output rates. At this stage, prices of goods and services have increased but wage rates have not changed. (Recall that as we move along a short-run aggregate supply curve, wage rates are constant.)

The economy cannot stay above its long-run aggregate supply and full-employment levels for ever. Why not? What are the forces at work bringing real GDP back to its long-run level and restoring full employment?

If the price level has increased but wage rates have remained constant, workers have experienced a fall in the purchasing power of their wages. Furthermore, firms have experienced a fall in the real cost of labour. In these circumstances, workers demand higher wages, and firms, anxious to maintain

---

FIGURE 23.9

The Effects of an Increase in Aggregate Demand

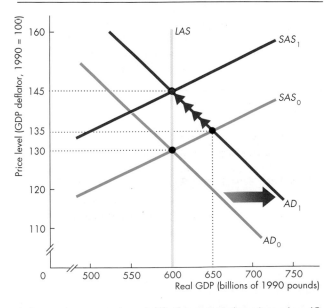

An increase in aggregate demand shifts the aggregate demand curve from AD_0 to AD_1. Real GDP increases from £600 billion to £650 billion and the price level increases from 130 to 135. There is an inflationary gap. A higher price level induces higher wage rates, which in turn cause the short-run aggregate supply curve to shift to the left. As the SAS curve shifts to the left from SAS_0 to SAS_1, it intersects the aggregate demand curve AD_1 at higher price levels and lower real GDP levels. Eventually, the price level increases to 145 and real GDP falls back to £600 billion – its full-employment level.

their employment and output levels, meet these demands. If firms do not raise wage rates, then they either lose workers or have to hire less productive ones.

As wage rates rise, short-run aggregate supply begins to decrease – the short-run aggregate supply curve shifts to the left. It moves from SAS_0 towards SAS_1. The rise in wages and the shift in the SAS curve produce a sequence of new equilibrium positions. At each point on the adjustment path, output falls and the price level rises. Eventually, wages will have risen by so much that the SAS curve is SAS_1. At this time, the aggregate demand curve AD_1 intersects SAS_1 at a full-employment equilibrium. The price level has risen to 145, and output is back where it started, at its long-run level. Unemployment is again at its natural rate.

Throughout the adjustment process, higher wage rates raise firms' costs and, with rising costs, firms offer a smaller quantity of goods and services for sale at any given price level. By the time the adjustment is over, firms are producing exactly the same amount as they initially produced, but at higher prices and higher costs. The level of costs relative to prices will be the same as it was initially.

We've just worked out the effects of an increase in aggregate demand. A decrease in aggregate demand has similar but opposite effects to those that we've just studied. That is, when aggregate demand falls, real GDP falls below its long-run level and unemployment rises above its natural rate. There is a recessionary gap. The lower price level increases the purchasing power of wages, and it increases firms' costs relative to their output prices. Eventually, as the slack economy leads to falling wage rates, the short-run aggregate supply curve shifts to the right. Real GDP gradually returns to its long-run level and full employment is restored.

Aggregate Fluctuations and Changes in Aggregate Supply

Let's now work out the effects of a change in aggregate supply on real GDP and the price level. Figure 23.10 illustrates the analysis. Suppose, as shown in part (a), that the economy is initially at full-employment equilibrium. The aggregate demand curve is AD_0, the short-run aggregate supply curve is SAS_0, and the long-run aggregate supply curve is LAS. Output is 600 billion 1990 pounds and the price level is 130.

Now suppose that the price of oil increases sharply,

as it did when OPEC used its market power in 1973–1974. With a higher price of oil, firms are faced with higher costs and they reduce their output. Short-run aggregate supply decreases and the short-run aggregate supply curve shifts to the left to SAS_1.

As a result of this decrease in short-run aggregate supply, the economy moves to a new equilibrium where SAS_1 intersects the aggregate demand curve AD_0. The price level rises to 140 and real GDP falls to 550 billion 1990 pounds. Because real GDP falls, the economy experiences recession. Because the price level increases, the economy experiences inflation. Such a combination of recession and inflation – called *stagflation* – actually occurred in the 1970s at the time of the OPEC oil price hikes.

What happens next depends on the policy response of the government and the Bank of England. If the policy is to do nothing, the economy remains stuck in an unemployment equilibrium. If the government and the Bank of England respond with a fiscal and monetary policy package that increases aggregate demand, the aggregate demand curve shifts to the right as shown in Fig. 23.10(b) and the economy returns to full employment, but at an even higher price level.

R E V I E W

M acroeconomic equilibrium occurs when the quantity of real GDP demanded equals the quantity of real GDP supplied. There are three types of macroeconomic equilibrium. These are unemployment equilibrium – a situation in which real GDP is below long-run GDP and there is a recessionary gap, full-employment equilibrium – a situation in which actual real GDP equals long-run real GDP, and above full-employment equilibrium – a situation in which real GDP is above long-run real GDP and there is an inflationary gap. As aggregate demand and aggregate supply fluctuate, the economy moves from one type of macroeconomic equilibrium to another and both real GDP and the price level fluctuate. ◆

We've now seen how changes in aggregate demand and aggregate supply influence real GDP and the price level. Let's put our new knowledge to work and see how it helps us understand recent UK macroeconomic performance.

FIGURE 23.10

The Effects of an Increase in the Price of Oil

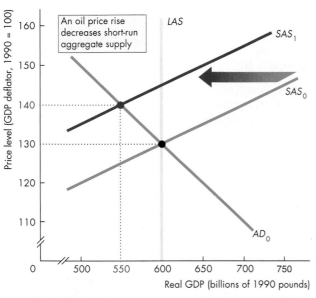

(a) In the short run

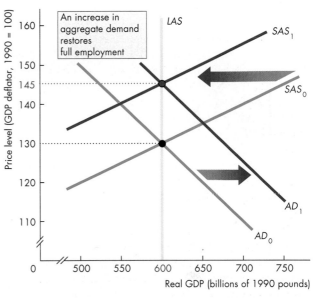

(b) In the long run

An increase in the price of oil decreases short-run aggregate supply and shifts the short-run aggregate supply curve to the left from SAS_0 to SAS_1, as shown in part (a). Real GDP decreases from £600 billion to £550 billion and the price level increases from 130 to 140. The economy experiences both recession and

inflation – *stagflation*. To counteract this, the government undertakes fiscal and monetary policy to stimulate aggregate demand and shifts the aggregate demand curve to the right from AD_0 to AD_1, as shown in part (b). Real GDP returns to its original level but the price level rises still further from 140 to 145.

Recent Trends and Cycles in the UK Economy

We're now going to use our new tools of aggregate demand and aggregate supply to interpret some recent trends and cycles in the UK economy. We'll begin by looking at the state of the UK economy in 1993.

The Economy in 1993

In 1993, the UK economy was in recession. Measured in 1990 pounds, real GDP was £546 billion. The price level was 115. We can illustrate this

state of the UK economy by using the aggregate demand and aggregate supply model. In Fig. 23.11 the aggregate demand curve in 1993 is AD_{93} and the short-run aggregate supply curve in 1993 is SAS_{93}. The point at which these curves intersect determines the price level (115) and real GDP (£546 billion) in 1993. We do not know for certain what the long-run level of real GDP was, but we will assume it was £600 billion. So we show the long-run aggregate supply curve in 1993 as LAS_{93} at a real GDP of £600 billion. We also show a recessionary gap as actual real GDP is below long-run real GDP.

The 1991–1992 recession from which the economy was still recovering in 1993 resulted from two main influences. The first influence was the monetary policy adopted by the Bank of England to reduce inflation and maintain the foreign exchange

FIGURE 23.11

The UK Economy in 1993

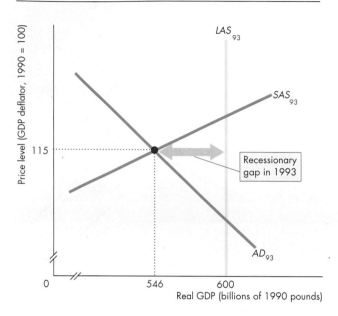

In 1993, the UK economy was on the aggregate demand curve AD_{93} and the aggregate supply curve SAS_{93}. The price level was 115 and real GDP was £546 billion. The long-run aggregate supply curve, LAS_{93}, is assumed to be at £600 billion. There was a recessionary gap of £54 billion.

value of the pound – at the time the pound was linked to other EU currencies through a mechanism known as the Exchange Rate Mechanism (ERM) which is discussed further in Chapters 27 and 35. To reduce the inflation rate and maintain the foreign exchange value of the pound, the Bank of England slowed the growth rate of the money supply. This influence decreased aggregate demand and produced a shift to the left in the AD curve. The second influence was a slowdown in the world economy. This slowdown brought slower growth in UK exports, which in turn reduced aggregate demand. Like monetary policy, this influence also shifted the AD curve to the left.

The combined effects of these influences led to the recession in 1991–1992. In September 1992, the United Kingdom left the ERM and the Bank of England at once eased its monetary policy so that there were successive decreases in interest rates that led to a gradual increase in aggregate demand. But

confidence – business confidence about profit prospects and consumer confidence about income growth – remained fairly weak, so aggregate demand did not grow quickly. Reading Between the Lines on pp. 658–659 looks at the Japanese economy and considers the paradox of economic problems cause by falling prices.

Growth, Inflation and Cycles

The economy is continually changing. If you imagine the economy as a video, then Fig. 23.11 is a freeze-frame. We'll run the video again – an instant replay – but we'll keep our finger on the freeze-frame button, looking at some important parts of the previous action. Let's run the video from 1970.

Figure 23.12 shows the state of the economy in 1970 at the point of intersection of its aggregate demand curve AD_{70} and short-run aggregate supply curve SAS_{70}. Real GDP was £350 billion and the GDP deflator was 15 – little over an eighth of its 1993 level.

By 1993, the economy had reached the point marked by the intersection of aggregate demand curve AD_{93} and short-run aggregate supply curve SAS_{93}. Real GDP was £546 billion and the GDP deflator was 115.

There are three important features of the economy's path traced by the blue and red points:

◆ Growth
◆ Inflation
◆ Cycles

Growth Over the years, real GDP grows – shown in Fig. 23.12 by the movement to the right of the points. The main force generating this growth is an increase in long-run aggregate supply. Long-run aggregate supply increases because of population growth, the accumulation of capital – both physical plant and equipment and human capital – the discovery of new resources, and the advance of technology.

Inflation The price level rises over the years – shown in Fig. 23.12 by the upward movement of the points. The main force generating this persistent increase in the price level is a tendency for aggregate demand to increase at a faster pace than the increase in long-run aggregate supply. All of the factors that increase aggregate demand and shift the aggregate demand curve influence the pace of inflation. But one factor – the quantity of money – is the

FIGURE 23.12

Aggregate Demand and Aggregate Supply: 1970–1993

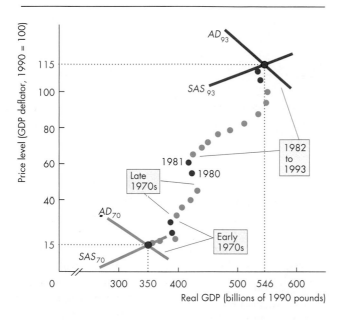

Each point indicates the value of the GDP deflator and real GDP in a given year. In 1970, these variables were determined by the intersection of the aggregate demand curve AD_{70} and the short-run aggregate supply curve SAS_{70}. Each point is generated by the gradual shifting of the AD and SAS curves. By 1993, the curves were AD_{93} and SAS_{93}. Real GDP grew and the price level increased. But growth and inflation did not proceed smoothly. Real GDP grew steadily and inflation was modest in the early 1970s; real GDP growth sagged in 1974–1975 and again, more strongly, in 1980–1981. The 1974–1975 slowdown was caused by an unusually sharp increase in oil prices. The 1980–1981 recession was caused by a slowdown in the growth of aggregate demand, which resulted mainly from the Bank of England's monetary policy. The period from 1983 to 1988 was one of strong, persistent recovery. Inflation was rapid during the 1970s but slowed after the 1981 recession. Inflation began to increase again in the late 1980s. The economy went into recession again in 1991–1992. This recession was caused by another slowdown in aggregate demand that stemmed partly from a slowdown in the world economy and partly from a tight monetary policy.

Source: Central Statistical Office, *Economic Trends Annual Supplement 1994 Edition*, 8 and 12, and *Economic Trends*, April 1994, T2 and T4.

like pattern made by the points, with recessions highlighted in red. The cycles arise because both the expansion of short-run aggregate supply and the growth of aggregate demand do not proceed at a fixed, steady pace.

The Evolving Economy: 1970–1993

During the early 1970s, real GDP growth was steady and inflation was modest. In 1974 and 1975, the United Kingdom experienced rapid inflation and recession – stagflation. The major source of these developments was a series of massive oil price increases that shifted the short-run aggregate supply curve to the left combined with rapid increases in the money supply that shifted the aggregate demand curve to the right. Recession occurred because the aggregate supply curve shifted to the left at a faster pace than the aggregate demand curve shifted to the right.

The rest of the 1970s saw high inflation – the price level increased quickly – and only moderate growth. Inflation remained high. But in 1979 the Bank of England adopted a tighter monetary policy in an effort to keep aggregate demand in check and lower inflation. During this period, most people expected high inflation to persist and wages grew at a rate consistent with those expectations. The short-run aggregate supply curve shifted to the left. Aggregate demand increased, but not fast enough to create the inflation that most people expected. As a consequence, by 1980, the shift to the left of the aggregate supply curve was so strong relative to the shift to the right of the aggregate demand curve that the economy went into a deep recession.

From 1982 to 1988, capital accumulation and steady technological advance resulted in a sustained shift to the right of the long-run aggregate supply curve. Wage growth was moderate and the short-run aggregate supply curve also shifted to the right. Aggregate demand growth kept pace with the growth of aggregate supply, which kept real GDP growing and inflation steady.

In 1989 and 1990, the growth in aggregate demand began to exceed the growth in aggregate supply and inflation began to increase. In 1991, the Bank of England cut the growth rate of the money supply and aggregate demand grew at a slower pace than did aggregate supply. Inflation fell and the economy went into recession.

most important source of *persistent* increases in aggregate demand and persistent inflation.

Over the years, the economy grows and shrinks in cycles – shown in Fig. 23.12 by the wave-

Deflation in Japan

THE ECONOMIST, 27 NOVEMBER 1993

The pain of deflation

Can too little inflation be as harmful for an economy as too much?

Back in June, the average forecast of Japan's GDP growth in 1994... was a cheery 2.8%. By November, this had been shaved to 1.6%....

Japan's industrial production has already tumbled by more than 10% since 1991; and there could be worse to come. One particular worry is that Japan could find itself with outright deflation – falling consumer prices – next year...

Negative thoughts

If high inflation is bad news, then surely falling prices – or a negative inflation rate – is good news? Only up to a point. A fall in the price of a few products, such as computers or video-cassette recorders, is certainly good news for consumers. A fall in the overall price level, however, can prove troublesome. Indeed, in some cases, such as the 1930s, deflation can be even nastier than hyperinflation.

Traditional economic theory used to stress the positive impact of falling prices – the 'real balance effect'. Falling prices, it was argued, boosted the real value of savings. Households that felt wealthier would then spend more.

However, falling prices can have the opposite effect. In particular, they swell the real value of debts. Indebted consumers and firms are likely to reduce, not increase, spending.... Japan has the highest ratio of household debt to disposable income and the highest corporate debt burden of any big industrial country.

Falling consumer prices may also encourage households to defer purchases in the hope that products will soon be cheaper. The consequent drop in demand could force prices even lower. Meanwhile, Japan's wage flexibility, usually one of its strengths, could also work against economic recovery.... In Japan, by contrast, wages respond quickly even to reductions in prices, through smaller bonuses and reduced overtime.

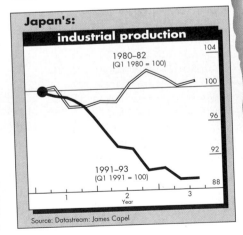

Japan's: industrial production

1980–82 (Q1 1980 = 100)

1991–93 (Q1 1991 = 100)

Source: Datastream: James Capel

© The Economist. Reprinted with permission.

- **J**apanese economic growth in 1994 will be lower than initially forecast and the economy will continue to be stagnant.

- **J**apanese industrial production has fallen by a tenth since 1991.

- **C**onsumer prices could actually fall in 1994.

- **L**ower prices might be beneficial to consumers, but they would lead to a higher real value of debts.

- **J**apan's real wage flexibility would result in nominal wages falling in response to lower prices.

- **F**or the economy as a whole, falling prices could result in lower spending or delayed spending, delaying recovery from recession.

- **I**f nominal interest rates cannot become negative, falling prices mean very high real interest rates, affecting consumers' and firms' spending decisions.

The real money balances effect measures the effect of a change in the real quantity of money held (as cash or savings) on the demand for real GDP.

Real money measures the quantity of goods and services that can be bought with a given number of yen. It is calculated as the nominal number of yen held, divided by the price level.

Real GDP is calculated as the value of all goods and services produced, adjusted to exclude the effect of inflation on this valuation.

If prices fall, the value of the real quantity of money rises. According to the real money balances effect, this would lead to a rise in real GDP demanded and the position of the economy would improve.

The real money balances effect is not leading to an improvement in the Japanese economy because any possible gains from it are being outweighed by the effect of falling prices on debt via the real interest rate.

The real interest rate is equal to the nominal interest rate minus the expected inflation rate. As expected inflation falls, so the real interest rate rises. If prices actually fall (if inflation becomes negative), real interest rates are higher than nominal interest rates.

As prices fall and real interest rates rise, so the real value of debt increases. This will lead to debt-holders reducing present consumption in order to cover the additional cost of servicing their debt holdings.

A rising debt burden is a significant problem in Japan because it has the highest household and corporate debt burdens of any major industrial country.

The problem of lower current consumption expenditure is compounded by the possibility that consumers will delay purchases, given that they expect prices to fall.

The figure shows full-employment equilibrium with AD_0. AD_0 shifts to AD_1 because of lower inflationary expectations, lower aggregate wealth (a higher value of real debt) and higher real interest rates. This creates a recessionary gap.

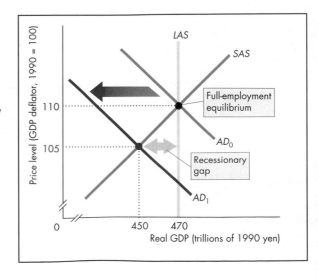

◆ ◆ ◆ ◆ This chapter has provided a model of real GDP and the GDP deflator that can be used to understand the growth, inflation and cycles that the economy follows. The model is a useful one because it enables us to keep our eye on the big picture – on the broad trends and cycles in inflation and output. But the model lacks detail. It does not tell us as much as we need to know about the components of aggregate demand – consumption, investment, government purchases of goods and services, and exports and imports. It doesn't tell us what determines interest rates or wage rates or even, directly,

what determines employment and unemployment. In the following chapters, we're going to start to fill in that detail. ◆ ◆ In some ways, the study of macroeconomics is like doing a large jigsaw puzzle. The aggregate demand and aggregate supply model provides the entire edge of the jigsaw. We know its general shape and size but we haven't filled in the middle. One block of the jigsaw contains the story of aggregate demand. Another, the story of aggregate supply. And when we place the two together, we place them in the frame of the model developed in this chapter, and the picture is completed.

S U M M A R Y

Aggregate Demand

Aggregate demand is the relationship between the quantity of real GDP demanded and the price level holding all other influences constant. Other things held constant, the higher the price level, the smaller is the quantity of real GDP demanded – the aggregate demand curve slopes downward. The aggregate demand curve slopes downward for three reasons: money and goods are substitutes (*real money balances effect*); goods today and goods in the future are substitutes (*intertemporal substitution effect*); domestic goods and foreign goods are substitutes (*international substitution effect*).

The main factors that change aggregate demand – and shift the aggregate demand curve – are fiscal policy (government purchases of goods and services and taxes), monetary policy (the money supply and interest rates), international factors (economic conditions in the rest of the world and the foreign exchange rate), and expectations (especially expectations about future inflation and profits). (pp. 639–645)

Aggregate Supply

Short-run aggregate supply is the relationship between the quantity of real GDP supplied and the price level when wage rates and other factor prices are constant. The short-run aggregate supply curve is horizontal in a deep depression, vertical at the

economy's physical production limit, but generally upward sloping. With factor prices and all other influences on supply held constant, the higher the price level, the more output firms plan to sell. Long-run aggregate supply is the relationship between the quantity of real GDP supplied and the price level when there is full employment. The long-run aggregate supply curve is vertical – long-run aggregate supply is independent of the price level.

The factors that change short-run aggregate supply shift the short-run aggregate supply curve. Factors that change long-run aggregate supply also change short-run aggregate supply. Thus anything that shifts the long-run aggregate supply curve also shifts the short-run aggregate supply curve and they shift in the same direction. The most important of these are the size of the labour force, the capital stock, the state of technology and incentives. (pp. 645–650)

Macroeconomic Equilibrium

Macroeconomic equilibrium occurs when the quantity of real GDP demanded equals the quantity of real GDP supplied. Macroeconomic equilibrium occurs at the intersection of the aggregate demand curve and the short-run aggregate supply curve. The price level that achieves this equality is the equilibrium price level and the output level is equilibrium real GDP.

Macroeconomic equilibrium does not always

occur at long-run real GDP and full employment – that is, at a point on the long-run aggregate supply curve. Unemployment equilibrium occurs when equilibrium real GDP is less than its long-run level. There is a recessionary gap and unemployment exceeds its natural rate. When equilibrium real GDP is above its long-run level, there is an inflationary gap and unemployment is below its natural rate. An increase in aggregate demand shifts the aggregate demand curve to the right and increases both real GDP and the price level. If real GDP is above its long-run level, wage rates begin to increase and, as they do so, the short-run aggregate supply curve shifts to the left. The leftward shift of the short-run aggregate supply curve results in a yet higher price level and lower real GDP. Eventually, real GDP returns to its long-run level.

An increase in factor prices decreases short-run aggregate supply and shifts the short-run aggregate supply curve to the left. Real GDP decreases and the price level rises – stagflation. (pp. 650–-654)

Recent Trends and Cycles in the UK Economy

Growth in the UK economy results from labour force growth, capital accumulation and technological change. Inflation persists in the UK economy because of steady increases in aggregate demand brought about by increases in the quantity of money. The UK economy experiences cycles because the short-run aggregate supply and aggregate demand curves shift at an uneven pace.

Large oil price hikes in 1973 and 1974 resulted in stagflation. High inflation persisted throughout the rest of the 1970s. Restraint in aggregate demand growth from 1979 resulted in a severe recession in 1980–1981. This recession resulted in slower real GDP growth and a lower inflation rate. Moderate increases in wage rates and steady technological advance and capital accumulation resulted in a sustained expansion from 1982 to 1988. But a slowdown in aggregate demand growth brought recession in 1991–1992. (pp. 655–660)

KEY ELEMENTS

Key Terms

Key Figures

REVIEW QUESTIONS

1 What is aggregate demand?

2 What is the difference between aggregate demand and the aggregate quantity of goods and services demanded?

3 List the main factors that affect aggregate demand. Separate them into those that increase aggregate demand and those that decrease it.

4 Which of the following do not affect aggregate demand?

a The quantity of money.
b Interest rates.
c Technological change.
d Human capital.

5 Distinguish between macroeconomic short-run and long-run.

6 What is short-run aggregate supply?

7 What is the difference between short-run aggregate supply and the aggregate quantity of goods and services supplied?

8 Distinguish between short-run aggregate supply and long-run aggregate supply.

9 Consider the following events:

a The labour force increases.
b Technology improves.
c The wage rate increases.
d The quantity of money increases.
e Foreign incomes increase.
f The foreign exchange value of the pound increases.

Sort these events into the following four categories:

Category A: Those that affect the long-run aggregate supply curve but not the short-run aggregate supply curve.

Category B: Those that affect the short-run aggregate supply curve but not the long-run aggregate supply curve.

Category C: Those that affect both the short-run aggregate supply curve and the long-run aggregate supply curve.

Category D: Those that have no effect on the short-run aggregate supply curve or on the long-run aggregate supply curve.

10 Define macroeconomic equilibrium.

11 Distinguish between an unemployment equilibrium and full-employment equilibrium.

12 Work out the effect of an increase in the quantity of money on the price level and real GDP.

13 Work out the effect of an increase in the price of oil on the price level and real GDP.

14 What are the main factors generating growth of real GDP in the UK economy?

15 What are the main factors generating persistent inflation in the UK economy?

16 Why does the UK economy experience cycles in aggregate economic activity?

PROBLEMS

1 The economy of Mainland has the following aggregate demand and supply schedules:

Price level	Real GDP demanded	Real GDP supplied in the short run
	(billions of 1990 pounds)	
90	450	350
100	400	400
110	350	450
120	300	500
130	250	550
140	200	550

a Plot the aggregate demand curve and short-run aggregate supply curve in a figure.

b What are the equilibrium values for real GDP and the price level in Mainland?

c Mainland's long-run real GDP is 500 billion 1990 pounds. Plot the long-run aggregate supply curve in the same figure in which you answered part (a).

d Is Mainland at, above, or below its natural rate of unemployment?

e What is the physical limit of the economy of Mainland?

2 In Problem 1, aggregate demand is increased by 100 billion 1990 pounds. What is the change in real GDP and the price level?

3 In Problem 1, aggregate supply decreases by 100 billion 1990 pounds. What is the new macroeconomic equilibrium?

4 You are the prime minister's economic advisor and you are trying to work out where the UK economy is likely to go next year. You have the following forecasts for the *AD*, *SAS* and *LAS* curves:

Price Level	Real GDP demanded	Short-run real GDP supplied	Long-run aggregate supply
	(billions of 1990 pounds)		
115	650	350	520
120	600	350	520
125	550	450	520
130	500	650	520

This year, real GDP is 500 billion 1990 pounds and the price level is 120. The prime minister wants answers to the following questions:

a What is your forecast of next year's real GDP?

b What is your forecast of next year's price level?

c What is your forecast of the inflation rate?

d Will unemployment be above or below its natural rate?

e Will there be a recessionary gap or an inflationary gap? By how much?

5 Carefully draw some figures similar to those in this chapter and use the information in Problem 4 to explain:

a What has to be done to aggregate demand to achieve full employment

b What is the inflation rate if aggregate demand is manipulated to achieve full employment

CHAPTER 24

EXPENDITURE DECISIONS AND GDP

After studying this chapter you will be able to:

◆ Describe the sizes of and the fluctuations in the components of aggregate expenditure

◆ Explain how households make consumption and saving decisions

◆ Explain how firms make investment decisions

◆ Describe how governments make decisions about the purchases of goods and services

◆ Explain what determines exports, imports and net exports

◆ Derive the aggregate expenditure curve

◆ Explain how aggregate expenditure is determined

◆ Explain the relationship between aggregate expenditure and aggregate demand

THE NEWSPAPERS SOMETIMES SEEM OBSESSED WITH SPENDING BY consumers. One day in January 1994, *The Times* had large adjacent headlines revealing 'Plummeting games sales shake Dixons' and 'Recovery in car market starts to accelerate'. Why is there so much fear and trembling over sales? Besides some retailers and manufacturers, who cares how many computer games and new cars people buy? How does consumer spending affect the rest of us? What makes consumers decide to spend less and save more? ◆ ◆ It's not only consumer spending that stirs up hopes and fears in the economy. Sometimes, orders by firms for new plant and equipment come in a flood, and sometimes they come in a trickle. Government purchases of goods and services fluctuate, and our exports to the rest of the world ebb and flow with the changing economic

Fear and Trembling Among Shoppers

fortunes of Western Europe, the United States and Japan. How do business investment, government purchases and exports affect us? How much of the country's spending do they make up when compared with consumer spending? Are fluctuations in these components of aggregate expenditure sources of fluctuations in our job prospects and living standards?

◆ ◆ ◆ ◆ The spending that people do spreads out in waves across the economy, affecting millions of people. In this chapter, we study the composition of those waves and see why consumption has a big effect outside the shops. We also study the other components of aggregate expenditure – investment, government purchases of goods and services, and net exports. Then we'll see how all the components of spending combine to determine aggregate expenditure and, in turn, GDP.

The Components of Aggregate Expenditure

T he components of aggregate expenditure are:

◆ Consumption expenditure
◆ Investment
◆ Government purchases of goods and services
◆ Net exports (exports minus imports)

Relative Sizes

Figure 24.1 shows the relative sizes of the components of aggregate expenditure between 1968 and 1993. By far the biggest portion of aggregate expenditure is consumption expenditure, which ranges

between 60 and 65 per cent and averages 62 per cent of total expenditure. The smallest component of spending is net exports, which ranges between minus 5 per cent and plus 3 per cent. Of course net exports is the gap between exports and imports which are themselves very large, ranging between 20 and 30 per cent of GDP. Investment ranges between 13 and 19 per cent of GDP and averages 16 per cent. Government purchases of goods and services is larger than investment, ranging between 21 and 26 per cent of GDP and averaging 23 per cent.

Fluctuations

Figure 24.2 shows the fluctuations in the components of aggregate expenditure. The biggest fluctuations occur in the smallest component, net exports, while the smallest fluctuations occur in the largest compo-

---

FIGURE 24.1

The Components of Aggregate Expenditure: 1968–1993

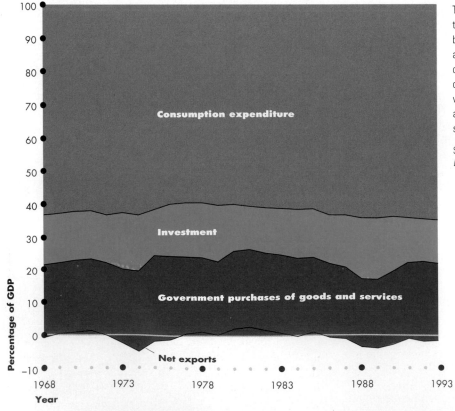

The biggest component of aggregate expenditure is consumption expenditure. It ranges between 60 and 65 per cent of GDP and averages 62 per cent. Investment averages 16 per cent of GDP, fluctuating between 13 and 19 per cent. Government expenditure on goods and services ranges between 21 and 26 per cent of GDP and averages 23 per cent. Net exports is the smallest item and averages −1 per cent.

Source: Central Statistical Office, *National Income and Expenditure Accounts*, HMSO (various years).

FIGURE 24.2

Fluctuations in the Components of Aggregate Expenditure 1970–1993

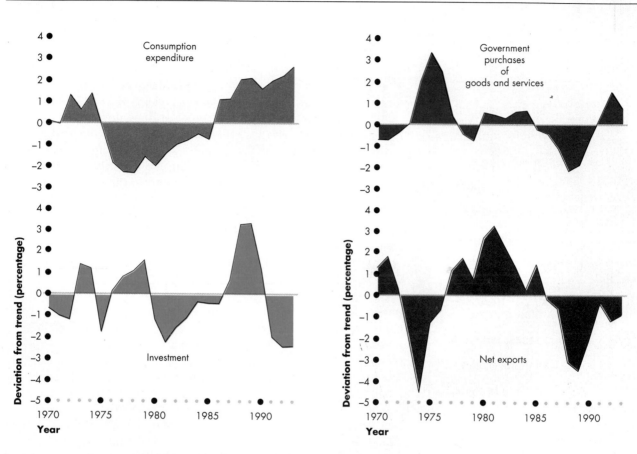

For each component of aggregate expenditure, the fluctuations in its share are shown as percentages of GDP. The fluctuation for each year is the difference between the actual value that year and the average or trend value. Although net exports is the smallest component of aggregate expenditure, it is the one that fluctuates most. And although consumption expenditure is the largest component of aggregate spending, it is the one that fluctuates the least. Investment and government purchases are much smaller components than consumption expenditure but they fluctuate a little more.

Source: See Table 24.1.

nent, consumption expenditure. Investment spending and government purchases fluctuate by roughly similar amounts, but investment is more volatile in the sense that it can be high one year and low shortly afterwards, whereas government spending tends to fluctuate more slowly.

In studying this figure, notice that the vertical axis measures the extent to which the four components of aggregate expenditure deviate from their own average percentages of GDP. The scales on which each of the four variables are measured are identical, so the

up and down movements in the lines give a precise indication of the relative volatility of the four components. Note that there is a slight tendency for the fluctuations in consumption expenditure to move up and down in sympathy with the fluctuations in investment. Note also that the biggest declines in investment – in 1981 and 1992 – occurred at precisely the time that the economy was at the trough of its most severe post-war recessions (recessions that we saw in Chapters 21 and 23). Government purchases were below trend between 1985 and 1990 but then

Discovering the Consumption Function

> 'The fundamental psychological law, upon which we are entitled to depend with confidence... is that [people] are disposed... to increase their consumption as their income increases, but not by as much as the increase in their income.'
>
> JOHN MAYNARD KEYNES
> *General Theory*

The theory that consumption is determined by disposable income was proposed by John Maynard Keynes in 1936. With newly available national income data compiled by Simon Kuznets supporting Keynes's theory, it was instantly accepted.

During the 1940s and 1950s, a lot of additional data were collected, some of which revealed shortcomings in Keynes's theory. By the late 1940s, the Keynesian consumption function began to make forecasting errors. The propensity to consume – what Keynes called a 'fundamental psychological law' – was revealed to be increasing and to depend on whether a person was young or old, black or white, or from an urban or rural area.

These failings brought forth two new theories – Franco Modigliani's life-cycle hypothesis and Milton Friedman's permanent income hypothesis – based on the proposition that consumption is determined by wealth and wealth depends on current and future income. Other things remaining the same, the wealthier a person is, the more he or she consumes. But only permanent and previously unexpected changes in income bring changes in wealth and consumption. Temporary changes in income or changes that have been foreseen change wealth by little and bring only small changes in consumption.

The revolution in macroeconomics of the 1970s brought the next reappraisal of consumption and a rational expectations theory of consumption proposed by Robert Hall of Stanford University. Hall started from the same point as Modigliani and Friedman: consumption depends on wealth and wealth depends on future income. But to make consumption decisions, people must form expectations of future income using whatever information is available. Expectations

A family whose income is permanently low has a low consumption level. But such a family doesn't always spend all its income every week. Instead, it saves a small amount to smooth its consumption between one year and the next. The amount that such a family saves is influenced by its stage in the life cycle. A young family saves a larger fraction of its income than an older family that has exactly the same level of permanent income. For most low-income families, saving does not mean putting money in the bank or in stocks and bonds. It means buying a home, buying life insurance and paying social security taxes.

College students usually have low incomes. But they consume at a much higher level than most people whose incomes are similar to theirs. They enjoy a higher standard of housing and consume a much wider range of goods and services – from books and compact discs to sports facilities and live concerts – than other people with similar incomes. The reason: college students have a high expected future income and, therefore, a high *permanent* income. They sustain a high consumption level by consuming all their income and by taking student loans that enable them to consume beyond their current income level.

change only as a result of new information, which arrives at random. Therefore people's estimates of how wealthy they are, together with their consumption, change at random. No variable other than current consumption is of any value for predicting future consumption. Consumption and income are correlated, but changes in income do not cause changes in consumption.

John Maynard Keynes: A Macroeconomic Revolutionary

When John Maynard Keynes (1883–1946) of Cambridge, United Kingdom, published his *General Theory of Employment, Interest, and Money* in 1936, he set off a revolution. The centrepieces of Keynes's theory of employment and income were the consumption function and the multiplier. Like all intellectual revolutions, this one was rejected by the older generation and embraced eagerly by the young. Many of Keynes's young adherents were in Cambridge, United Kingdom (among them Joan Robinson), but many were in Cambridge, Massachusetts.

Keynes was one of the chief architects of the International Monetary Fund and visited the United States to finalize arrangements for the world's new monetary order as World War II was ending. He used the occasion to drop in on the Keynesians of Cambridge, Massachusetts. Asked on his return to the United Kingdom what he thought of his American disciples, he reported that they were far more Keynesian than he!

JOHN MAYNARD KEYNES

rose above trend. Net exports are especially volatile and, to some degree, represent a mirror image of investment and consumption expenditure.

Let's study the choices that determine the size and volatility of the components of aggregate expenditure, beginning with the largest component, consumption expenditure.

Consumption Expenditure and Saving

Consumption expenditure is the value of the consumption goods and services bought by households. Many factors influence a household's consumption expenditure, but the most important is disposable income. **Disposable income** is the aggregate income that households receive in exchange for supplying the services of factors of production plus transfers from the government minus taxes. A household can do only two things with its disposable income: spend it on consumption goods and services or save it.

As a household's disposable income increases, so does its expenditure on food, clothing, housing, transport and most other goods and services. That is, a household's consumption expenditure increases as its income increases.

The Consumption Function and the Saving Function

The relationship between consumption expenditure and disposable income, other things remaining the same, is called the **consumption function**. The consumption function has played an important role in macroeconomics over the past 50 years and the story of its discovery is told in Our Advancing Knowledge on pp. 668–669. The relationship between saving and disposable income, other things remaining the same, is called the **saving function**. The consumption function and saving function for a typical household – the Paterson household – are shown in Fig. 24.3.

The Consumption Function   The Paterson household's consumption function is plotted in Fig. 24.3(a). The horizontal axis measures disposable income and the vertical axis measures consumption expendi-

ture (both in thousands of pounds). The points a to f in the figure correspond to the rows a to f in the table. For example, point d indicates a disposable income of £30,000 and consumption of £24,000.

The 45° Line   Figure 24.3(a) also contains a line labelled '45° line'. This line connects the points at which consumption, measured on the vertical axis, equals disposable income, measured on the horizontal axis. When the consumption function is above the 45° line, consumption exceeds disposable income; when the consumption function is below the 45° line, consumption is less than disposable income; and at the point where the consumption function intersects the 45° line, consumption and disposable income are equal.

The Saving Function   The saving function is graphed in Fig. 24.3(b). The horizontal axis is exactly the same as that in part (a). The vertical axis measures saving. Again, the points marked a to f correspond to the rows of the table.

There are two important things to note about the Paterson household's consumption and saving functions. First, even if the Paterson household has no disposable income, it still consumes. It does so by having a negative level of saving. Negative saving is called **dissaving**. Households that consume more than their disposable income do so either by living off assets or by borrowing, a situation that cannot, of course, last for ever.

Second, as the Paterson household's disposable income increases, so does the amount that it plans to spend on consumption and the amount that it plans to save. Since a household can only consume or save its disposable income, these two items always add up to its disposable income. That is, consumption and saving plans are consistent with disposable income.

This relationship between the consumption function and the saving function can be seen by looking at the two parts of the figure. When the saving function is below the horizontal axis, saving is negative (there is dissaving) and the consumption function is above the 45° line. When the saving function is above the horizontal axis, saving is positive and the consumption function is below the 45° line. When the saving function intersects the horizontal axis, saving is zero, and the consumption function intersects the 45° line.

FIGURE 24.3

The Paterson Household's Consumption Function and Saving Function

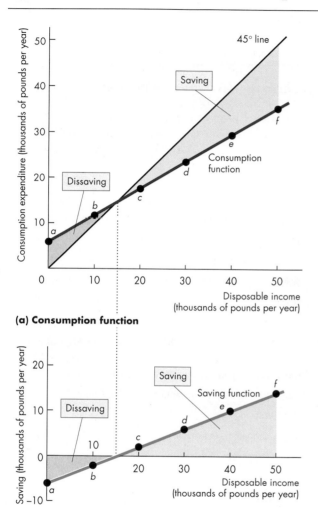

(a) Consumption function

(b) Saving function

	Disposable income	Consumption expenditure	Saving
	(thousands of pounds per year)		
a	0	6	−6
b	10	12	−2
c	20	18	2
d	30	24	6
e	40	30	10
f	50	36	14

The table sets out the consumption expenditure and saving plans of the Paterson household at various possible levels of disposable income. At each level the consumption expenditure plus the saving of the Paterson household equal its disposable income. Part (a) of the figure shows the relationship between consumption expenditure and disposable income (the consumption function). Part (b) shows the relationship between saving and disposable income (the saving function). Points *a* to *f* on the consumption and saving functions correspond to the rows in the table.

The 45° line in part (a) is the line of equality between consumption expenditure and disposable income. At the income level where the Patersons' consumption function intersects the 45° line, all their disposable income is consumed, saving is zero, and their saving function intersects the horizontal axis. At lower income levels, when the consumption function is above the 45° line, saving is negative (dissaving occurs) and the saving function is below the horizontal axis. At higher income levels, when the consumption function is below the 45° line, saving is positive and the saving function is above the horizontal axis.

Other Influences on Consumption Expenditure and Saving   Of the many other factors that influence consumption expenditure and saving, the most important is expected future income. A household's expected future income depends on the level of its income-earning assets such as shares, on its past saving, its debts, and the security and income growth prospects of the jobs that its members do. Other things remaining the same, the higher a household's expected future income, the greater is its current consumption expenditure. That is, if

there are two households that each have the same disposable income in the current year, the household with the larger expected future income will spend a larger portion of current disposable income on consumption goods and services. Consider, for example, two households whose principal income earner is a senior executive in a large company. One executive has just been told of an important promotion that will increase the household's income by 50 per cent in the following years. The other has just been told that the firm has been taken over and that there will be no further employment beyond the end of the year. The first household buys a new car and takes an expensive foreign holiday, thereby increasing its current consumption expenditure. The second household sells the family's second car and cancels its planned winter holiday, thereby cutting back on its current consumption expenditure.

Changes in factors other than disposable income that influence consumption expenditure shift both the consumption function and the saving function. For example, a fall in expected future income shifts the consumption function downward and the saving function upward, while an increase in expected future income shifts the consumption function upward and the saving function downward. It is common for such shifts to occur when the economy begins to move into a recession or begins to recover from a recession. Going into the recession people expect lower future incomes, but when the recovery begins they expect higher future incomes.

The Average Propensities to Consume and to Save

The **average propensity to consume** (*APC*) is consumption expenditure divided by disposable income. Table 24.1(a) shows you how to calculate the average propensity to consume. Let's do a sample calculation. At a disposable income of £30,000, the Paterson household consumes £24,000. Its average propensity to consume is £24,000 divided by £30,000, which equals 0.8.

As you can see from the numbers in the table, the average propensity to consume falls as disposable income rises. At a disposable income of £10,000, the household consumes £12,000, an amount greater than its income. So its average propensity to consume is £12,000 divided by £10,000 which equals 1.2. But at a disposable income of £50,000 the household consumes only £36,000, so its average propensity to consume is £36,000 divided by £50,000, which equals 0.72.

The **average propensity to save** (*APS*) is saving divided by disposable income. Table 24.1(a) shows you how to calculate the average propensity to save. For example, when disposable income is £30,000 the Paterson household saves £6,000, so that the average propensity to save is £6,000 divided by £30,000, which equals 0.2. When saving is negative, the average propensity to save is negative. As disposable income increases, the average propensity to save increases.

TABLE 24.1

Average and Marginal Propensities to Consume and to Save

(a) CALCULATING AVERAGE PROPENSITIES TO CONSUME AND TO SAVE

Disposable income (YD) (pounds per year)	Consumption expenditure (C) (pounds per year)	Saving (S) (pounds per year)	APC (C/YD)	APS (S/YD)
0	6,000	–6,000	–	–
10,000	12,000	–2,000	1.20	–0.20
20,000	18,000	2,000	0.90	0.10
30,000	24,000	6,000	0.80	0.20
40,000	30,000	10,000	0.75	0.25
50,000	36,000	14,000	0.72	0.28

(a) CALCULATING MARGINAL PROPENSITIES TO CONSUME AND TO SAVE

Change in disposable income	ΔYD	= 10,000
Change in consumption expenditure	ΔC	= 6,000
Change in saving	ΔS	= 4,000
Marginal propensity to consume	*MPC*	= $\Delta C/\Delta YD = 0.6$
Marginal propensity to save	*MPS*	= $\Delta S/\Delta YD = 0.4$

Consumption expenditure and saving depend on disposable income. At zero disposable income, some consumption is undertaken and saving is negative (dissaving occurs). As disposable income increases, so do both consumption and saving. The average propensities to consume and to save are calculated in part (a). The average propensity to consume – the ratio of consumption to disposable income – falls as disposable income increases; the average propensity to save – the ratio of saving to disposable income – increases as disposable income increases. These two average propensities sum to 1. Each additional – or *marginal* – pound of disposable income is either consumed or saved.

Part (b) calculates the marginal propensities to consume and to save. The marginal propensity to consume is the change in consumption that results from a £1 change in disposable income. The marginal propensity to save is the change in saving that results from a £1 change in disposable income. The marginal propensities to consume and to save sum to 1.

As disposable income increases, the average propensity to consume falls and the average propensity to save rises. Equivalently, as disposable income increases, the fraction of income saved increases and the fraction of income consumed decreases. These patterns in the average propensities to consume and save reflect the fact that people with very low disposable incomes are so poor that their income is not even sufficient to meet their consumption expenditure. Consumption expenditure exceeds disposable income. As people's incomes increase, they are able to meet their consumption requirements with a lower and lower fraction of their disposable income.

The sum of the average propensity to consume and the average propensity to save is equal to one. These two average propensities add up to one because consumption and saving exhaust disposable income. Each pound of disposable income is either consumed or saved.

You can see that the two average propensities add up to one by using the following equation:

$$C + S = YD.$$

Divide both sides of the equation by disposable income to obtain

$$C/YD + S/YD = 1.$$

C/YD is the *average propensity to consume* and S/YD is the *average propensity to save*. Thus

$$APC + APS = 1.$$

The Marginal Propensities to Consume and to Save

The last pound of disposable income received is called the marginal pound. Part of that marginal pound is consumed and part of it is saved. The allocation of the marginal pound between consumption expenditure and saving is determined by the marginal propensities to consume and to save.

The **marginal propensity to consume** (*MPC*) is the fraction of the last pound of disposable income that is spent on consumption goods and services. It is calculated as the change in consumption expenditure divided by the change in disposable income. The **marginal propensity to save** (*MPS*) is the fraction of the last pound of disposable income that is saved. The marginal propensity to save is calculated as the change in saving divided by the change in disposable income.

Table 24.1(b) shows the calculation of the Paterson household's marginal propensities to consume and to save. Looking at part (a) of the table, you can see that disposable income increases by £10,000 as we move from one row to the next – £10,000 is the change in disposable income. You can also see from part (a) that when disposable income increases by £10,000, consumption increases by £6,000. The marginal propensity to consume – the change in consumption divided by the change in disposable income – is therefore £6,000 divided by £10,000, which equals 0.6. The Paterson household's marginal propensity to consume is constant. It is the same at each level of disposable income. Out of a marginal pound of disposable income, 60 pence is spent on consumption goods and services.

Part (b) of the table also shows the calculation of the marginal propensity to save. You can see from that part of the table that when disposable income increases by £10,000, saving increases by £4,000. The marginal propensity to save – the change in saving divided by the change in disposable income – is therefore £4,000 divided by £10,000, which equals 0.4. The Paterson household's marginal propensity to save is constant. It is the same at each level of disposable income. Out of the last pound of disposable income, 40 pence is saved.

The marginal propensity to consume plus the marginal propensity to save equals one. Each additional pound must either be consumed or spent. In this example, when disposable income increases by £1, 60 pence more is spent and 40 pence more is saved. That is,

$$MPC + MPS = 1.$$

Marginal Propensities and Slopes The marginal propensity to consume is equal to the slope of the consumption function. You can see this equality by looking back at Fig. 24.3. In that figure, the consumption function has a constant slope that can be measured as the change in consumption divided by the change in income. For example, when income increases from £20,000 to £30,000 – an increase of £10,000 – consumption increases from £18,000 to £24,000 – an increase of £6,000. The slope of the consumption function is £6,000 divided by £10,000, which equals 0.6 – the same value as the marginal propensity to consume that we've calculated in Table 24.1.

The marginal propensity to save is equal to the slope of the saving function. You can see this equality by again looking back at Fig. 24.3. In this case, when income increases by £10,000, saving increases by £4,000. The slope of the saving function is £4,000 divided by £10,000, which equals 0.4 – the same value as the marginal propensity to save that we calculated in Table 24.1.

REVIEW

Consumption expenditure is influenced by many factors, but the most important is disposable income. Households allocate their disposable income to either consumption expenditure or saving. The relationship between consumption expenditure and disposable income, other things remaining the same, is the *consumption function* and the relationship between saving and disposable income, other things remaining the same, is the *saving function.* Changes in factors other than disposable income that influence consumption expenditure, the most important of which is expected future income, shift the consumption and saving functions. ◆ ◆ The change in consumption expenditure divided by the change in disposable income, other things remaining the same, is the *marginal propensity to consume (MPC)*, and the change in saving divided by the change in disposable income, other things remaining the same, is the *marginal propensity to save (MPS)*. Because consumption expenditure plus saving equals disposable income, $MPC + MPS = 1$. ◆

We've studied the consumption function of a household. Let's now look at the consumption function in the United Kingdom.

The Consumption Function in the United Kingdom

Data for consumption expenditure and disposable income in the United Kingdom for the years 1968 to 1993 are shown in Fig. 24.4(a). The vertical axis measures consumption expenditure (in 1990 pounds), and the horizontal axis measures disposable income (also in 1990 pounds). Each point identified by a blue dot represents consumption expenditure and disposable income for a particular year.

The orange line highlights the average relationship between consumption expenditure and disposable income and is an estimate of the consumption function in the United Kingdom. It tells us that on average, consumption expenditure has been about 90 per cent of disposable income. The slope of this consumption function – which is also the marginal propensity to consume – is 0.9. The relationship between consumption expenditure and disposable income in any given year does not fall exactly on the orange line. The reason is that the position of the consumption function depends on the other factors that influence consumption expenditure.

Consumption as a Function of GDP Our purpose in developing a theory of the consumption function is to explain the determination of aggregate expenditure and real GDP. To achieve this purpose, we need to establish the relationship between consumption expenditure and real GDP – consumption expenditure as a function of real GDP.

The blue dots in Fig. 24.4(b) show consumption expenditure and real GDP in the United Kingdom for each year between 1968 and 1993. The orange line shows consumption expenditure as a function of real GDP. Consumption expenditure is a function of real GDP because disposable income depends on real GDP. Disposable income is real GDP minus net taxes (net taxes are taxes minus transfer payments). But net taxes increase as real GDP increases. Almost all the taxes that we pay – income taxes, VAT and National Insurance contributions – increase as incomes increase. Transfer payments, such as job-seekers' allowances and housing benefits, decrease as incomes increase. Since taxes increase and transfers decrease, net taxes increase as incomes increase.

It turns out that there is a tendency for net taxes to be a fairly stable percentage of real GDP, so consumption expenditure is a fairly stable function of real GDP. The change in consumption expenditure divided by the change in real GDP is the **marginal propensity to consume out of real GDP**. It is measured by the slope of the orange line in Fig. 24.4(b).

FIGURE 24.4

The Consumption Function in the United Kingdom

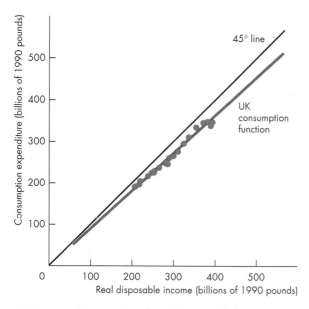

(a) Consumption as a function of disposable income

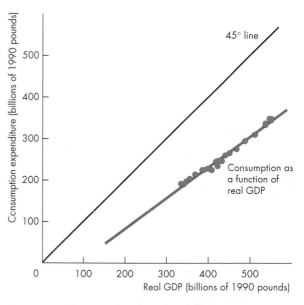

(b) Consumption as a function of real GDP

Part (a) shows the consumption function – the relationship between real consumption expenditure and real disposable income – in the United Kingdom for each year between 1968 and 1993. Each blue point represents real consumption expenditure and real disposable income for a particular year. The orange line shows the average relationship between consumption expenditure and disposable income – an estimate of the consumption function in the United Kingdom. This consumption function has a slope and a marginal propensity to consume of approximately 0.9.

Part (b) shows the relationship between consumption expenditure and real GDP. This relationship takes into account the fact that as real GDP increases, so do net taxes. Because net taxes are a fairly stable percentage of real GDP, consumption is a fairly stable function of real GDP – shown by the orange line.

Source: For 1970–1991, Central Statistical Office, *Economic Trends Annual Supplement 1993*, pp. 10 and 93. For 1992, *Economic Trends*, March 1993, pp. 10 and 12.

REVIEW

Of all the influences on consumption expenditure, disposable income is the most important. Consumption expenditure in the United Kingdom is a function of disposable income. Disposable income is, in turn, related to GDP. Therefore consumption expenditure is a function of GDP. ◆

The theory of the consumption function has an important implication. Because consumption expenditure is determined mainly by disposable income, most changes in consumption expenditure result from changes in income, and are not causes of those income changes. It is fluctuations in other components of aggregate expenditure that are the most important sources of fluctuations in income. And the most important of these is investment.

Investment

Gross investment is the purchase of new buildings, new plant, new vehicles, new machinery and additions to stocks. It has two components: *net investment* – additions to existing capital – and *replacement investment* – purchases to replace worn out or depreciated capital. As we saw in Fig. 24.2, gross investment is a volatile element of aggregate expenditure. What determines gross investment and why does it fluctuate so much? The answer lies in the investment decisions of firms – in the answers to such questions as: how does British Airways decide how much to spend on new aircraft? What determines ICI's outlays on new chemicals plants? How does British Telecom choose what it will spend on fibre optic communications systems? Let's answer questions such as these.

Firms' Investment Decisions

The main influences on firms' investment decisions are:

◆ Real interest rates
◆ Profit expectations

Real Interest Rates The **real interest rate** is the interest rate paid by a borrower and received by a lender after taking into account changes in the value of money resulting from inflation. It is approximately equal to the agreed interest rate – that is the *nominal interest rate* – minus the rate of inflation. To see why, let's take an example.

Suppose the nominal rate of interest is 8 per cent and suppose Jackie lends £100 today for one year. She will receive £108 in a year's time when the loan is repaid and the interest is due. If prices are constant – so that the rate of inflation is zero – Jackie will be 8 per cent better off in real terms in a year's time as she will be able to buy 8 per cent more with £108 then than she could buy with £100 today. Next, suppose that the rate of inflation is 3 per cent. In that case, the items Jackie could buy for £100 today will cost £103 in a year's time. But Jackie will have £108, which is about 5 per cent more than £103, so she will be about 5 per cent better off in real terms.

This example also illustrates another important point. When Jackie lends her £100 today, she knows what the agreed nominal rate of interest will be, but she does not know what the real rate of interest will be. She will discover that only after the year has passed and she finds out exactly how much prices have risen. Likewise, the borrower will not know what the real rate of interest will be until after the year has passed. Yet it is the real interest that is Jackie's reward for lending and that is the borrower's cost of borrowing. In deciding how much to lend or to borrow, lenders and borrowers

have to form expectations about the rate of inflation and hence expectations about the real rate of interest. The *expected real rate of interest* is the nominal rate of interest minus the expected rate of inflation. If two people differ over how much inflation they expect, they will also differ over the expected real rate of interest on a loan with a given nominal rate of interest.

Firms sometimes pay for capital goods with money they have borrowed, and sometimes they use their own funds – called retained earnings. But regardless of the method of financing an investment project, the real interest rate is part of its *opportunity cost*. The real interest paid on borrowed funds is a direct cost. The real interest cost of using retained earnings arises because these funds could be lent to another firm at the going real interest rate, generating income. The real interest income forgone is the opportunity cost of using retained earnings to finance an investment project.

The lower the real rate of interest, the lower is the opportunity cost of any given investment project. Some investment projects are not profitable at high real interest rates but are profitable at low real interest rates. The lower the real rate of interest, the greater the number of projects firms expect to be profitable and, therefore, the greater the amount of investment.

Let's consider an example. Suppose that the Rover Group is contemplating building a new car assembly line at a cost of £100 million. The assembly line is expected to produce cars for three years, and then it will be scrapped completely and replaced with a new line that produces an entirely new range of cars. Rover's expected net revenue in each of the first two years is £20 million and in the third year is £100 million. Net revenue is the difference between the total revenue from car sales and the costs of producing those cars. In calculating net revenue, we do not take into account the initial cost of the assembly line or the interest that has to be paid on it. We take separate account of these costs. In reality it is unlikely that net revenue would rise fivefold in the last year, but we make this assumption to keep the arithmetic in our example neat.

To build the assembly line, Rover plans to borrow the initial £100 million, and at the end of each year to use its expected net revenue to pay the interest on the loan outstanding along with as much of the loan as it can. Does it pay Rover to invest £100 million in this car assembly line? The answer depends on the real interest rate.

Case 1 in Fig. 24.5 shows what happens if the interest rate is 20 per cent a year. We'll assume the expected inflation rate is zero so the expected real interest rate is also 20 per cent a year. This is an unlikely high rate but it makes the numbers work out easily. Rover borrows £100 million and at the end of the first year has to pay £20 million in interest. It has a net revenue of £20 million and so can just meet this interest payment, but cannot reduce the size of its outstanding loan. At the end of the second year, it is in exactly the same situation as at the end of the first. It owes another £20 million on its outstanding loan. Again its revenue just covers the interest payment. At the end of the third year, Rover owes another £20 million in interest payments plus the £100 million outstanding loan. Therefore it has to pay £120 million. But net revenue in the third year is only £100 million,

FIGURE 24.5

Investment in a Car Assembly Line

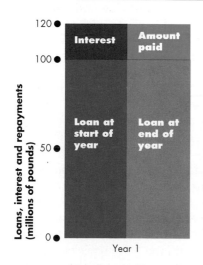

Case 1: Real interest rate is 20 per cent a year

A car assembly line costs £100 million to build. It is expected to generate the following revenue:

Year 1	£20 million
Year 2	£20 million
Year 3	£100 million

The line will then be scrapped and replaced by a new one. In Case 1 the interest rate is 20 per cent a year. The revenue stream is too low to cover the total expense, and the project is not worth undertaking. In Case 2, the interest rate is 10 per cent a year, and the project is profitable. The lower the interest rate the larger is the number of projects that are profitable and that are undertaken.

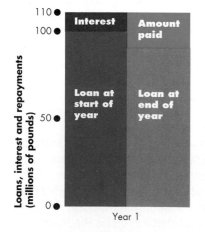

Case 2: Real interest rate is 10 per cent a year

so Rover has a £20 million loss on this project.

Case 2 in Fig. 24.5 shows what happens if the real interest rate is 10 per cent per year. Again, we'll assume the expected inflation rate is zero so the expected real interest rate is also 10 per cent a year. In this case, Rover owes £10 million interest at the end of the first year. Since it has £20 million of revenue, it can make this interest payment and reduce its outstanding loan to £90 million. In the second year, the interest owing on the loan is £9 million (10 per cent of £90 million). Again, with revenue of £20 million, Rover pays the interest and reduces its outstanding loan by £11 million to £79 million. In the third and final year of the project, the interest on the loan is £7.9 million (10 per cent of £79 million), so the total amount owing – the outstanding loan plus the interest – is £86.9 million. Rover's revenue in year 3 is £100 million, so it repays the loan, pays the interest and keeps the balance, a profit of £13.1 million. If Rover builds the assembly line it expects to make a profit of £13.1 million.

You can see that at a real interest rate of 20 per cent a year, it does not pay Rover to invest in this car assembly plant. At a 10 per cent real interest rate, it does pay. The lower the real interest rate, the larger is the number of projects, such as the one considered here, that yield a positive net profit. Thus the lower the real interest rate, the larger is the amount of investment.

Profit Expectations The higher the expected profitability of new capital equipment, the greater is the amount of investment. Rover's assembly line investment decision illustrates this effect. To decide whether or not to build the assembly line, Rover has to work out its net revenue. To perform that calculation, it has to work out the total revenue from car sales that, in turn, are affected by its expectations of car prices and the share of the market that it can attain. Rover also has to estimate its operating costs, which include the wages of its assembly workers and the costs of the products that it buys from other producers. The larger the net revenue that it expects, the more profitable it will expect the investment project that generates those net revenues to be, and the more likely it is that the project will be undertaken. This issue is also considered in Reading Between the Lines on pp. 684–685.

Many factors influence profit expectations. Among the main ones are taxes on company profits, the degree to which existing capital is being utilized,

and the state of global relations and tensions. For example, the collapse of the Soviet Union and the emergence of the new republics of Eastern Europe is likely to have a large impact on profit expectations in the 1990s – positive in some industries and negative in others.

Investment Demand

Investment demand is the relationship between the level of planned investment and the real interest rate, holding all other influences on investment constant. The investment demand schedule is a list of the quantities of planned investment at each real interest rate, holding all other influences on investment constant. The **investment demand curve** graphs the relationship between the real interest rate and the level of planned investment, everything else remaining the same. Some examples of investment demand schedules and investment demand curves appear in Fig. 24.6. The investment demand schedule and the position of the investment demand curve depend on the other influences on investment, chiefly expected profits.

Sometimes firms are pessimistic about future profits, sometimes they are optimistic and sometimes their expectations are average. Fluctuations in profit expectations are the main source of fluctuations in investment demand. The three investment demand schedules in the table in Fig. 24.6 give examples of investment demand under the three types of expectations. In the case of average profit expectations, if the real interest rate is 4 per cent a year, investment is £100 billion. If the real interest rate falls to 3 per cent a year, investment increases to £150 billion. If the real interest rate rises to 5 per cent a year, investment decreases to £50 billion. In the case of optimistic profit expectations, investment is higher at each real interest rate than it is when expectations are average. In the case of pessimistic profit expectations, investment is lower at each real interest rate than with average expectations.

The investment demand curve is shown in the figure. In part (a), the investment demand curve (*ID*) is that for average expected profit. Each point (*a*, *b* and *c*) corresponds to a row in the table. A change in the real interest rate causes a movement along the investment demand curve. Thus if the real interest rate is 4 per cent a year, planned investment is £100 billion. If the real interest rate rises to 5 per cent a year, there is a movement up the investment

FIGURE 24.6

Investment Demand Curves and Investment Demand Schedules

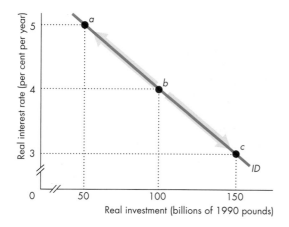

(a) The effect of a change in real interest rate

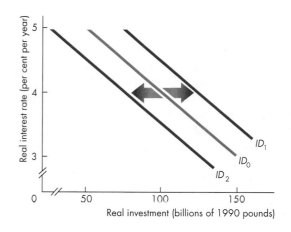

(b) The effect of a change in profit expectation

Real interest rate (per cent per year)	Investment (billions of 1990 pounds)		
	Optimistic	Average	Pessimistic
a	5	75	50	25
b	4	125	100	75
c	3	175	150	125

The table shows three investment demand schedules – for average, optimistic and pessimistic expectations. Part (a) shows the investment demand curve for average profit expectations. Along that investment demand curve, as the real interest rate rises from 4 per cent to 5 per cent, planned investment decreases – there is a movement along the investment demand curve from b to a. Part (b) shows how the investment demand curve changes when expected future profits change. With average profit expectations, the investment demand curve is ID_0 – the same curve as in part (a). With optimistic expectations about future profits, planned investment increases at each expected real interest rate and the investment demand curve shifts to the right to ID_1. With pessimistic expectations about future profits, planned investment decreases at each expected real interest rate and the investment demand curve shifts to the left to ID_2.

demand curve (see blue arrow), and planned investment decreases to $50 billion. If the real interest rate falls to 3 per cent a year, there is a movement down the investment demand curve, and planned investment increases to $150 billion.

The effects of profit expectations are shown in part (b). A change in profit expectations shifts the investment demand curve. The demand curve ID_0 is that for average expected profit. When profit expectations become optimistic, the investment demand curve shifts to the right, from ID_0 to ID_1. When profit expectations become pessimistic, the investment demand curve shifts to the left from ID_0 to ID_1.

REVIEW

Investment depends on the real interest rate and profit expectations. Other things remaining the same, the lower the real interest rate, the larger is the amount of investment. When profit expectations become optimistic, the investment demand curve shifts to the right; when profit expectations become pessimistic, it shifts to the left. Profit expectations are influenced by taxes, the degree of capacity utilization, and the global environment. ◆

We've just studied the *theory* of investment demand. Let's now see how that theory helps us to understand the fluctuations in investment that occur in the UK economy.

Investment Demand in the United Kingdom

As we saw in Fig. 24.2, investment is a volatile component of aggregate expenditure. In some years, investment is as much as 19 per cent of GDP and in others as little as 13 per cent. Let's see how we can interpret these fluctuations in investment with the theory of investment demand we've just been studying.

We'll begin by looking at Fig. 24.7. It shows investment (in billions of 1990 pounds) between 1968 and 1993. It also shows the way in which investment – gross investment – is broken down between net investment and the replacement of depreciated capital – depreciation. As you can see, both depreciation and gross investment increase over time. Depreciation follows a very smooth path. It reflects the fact that the capital stock wears out fairly steadily. Net investment

is the component of investment that fluctuates. You can see that fluctuation as the blue area between gross investment and depreciation.

The theory of investment demand predicts that fluctuations in investment result from fluctuations in the real interest rate and in future profit expectations. What is the relative importance of these two factors? Figure 24.8 shows some recent investment demand curves for the United Kingdom. Notice that in this figure we relate investment to the expected real rate of interest rather than using our normal practice of relating it to the actual real rate of interest. To see why we made this change, remember that along most investment demand curves we hold everything constant except the real rate of interest. Among the things we hold constant is the expected rate of inflation. However, when we look at UK investment over the last decade, we have a period when the expected rate of inflation varied considerably. We can overcome this problem and still plot some investment demand curves if we use the expected real rate of interest, because this takes into account variations in the expected rate of inflation.

FIGURE 24.7

Gross and Net Investment in the United Kingdom: 1968–1993

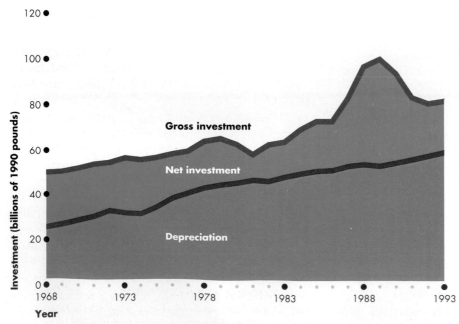

Gross investment is separated into two parts: the replacement of depreciated capital (green area) and net investment (blue area). Gross investment has fluctuated quite substantially during the last decade. It is clear from the figure that this fluctuation has been caused almost entirely by sharp fluctuations in net investment, for depreciation has risen quite steadily.

Sources: Derived from Central Statistical Office, *United Kingdom National Accounts 1993 Edition*, Tables 13.1, 13.3 and 14.6.

The points in Fig. 24.8 represent the gross investment and the expected real interest rate in the United Kingdom each year from 1983 to 1993. The figure also shows three investment demand curves, ID_0, ID_1 and ID_2. The curve ID_0 was the investment demand curve in 1983 when profit expectations were pessimistic. In the next few years expectations gradually became more optimistic, and by 1988 the investment demand curve had shifted to the right as far as the curve ID_1. Expectations remained high for the next two years but then slipped back, and by 1993 the investment demand curve had moved to the left to ID_2.

Why was investment demand so strong during the late 1980s? One reason is that the economy was moving out of the 1980–1981 recession. Another reason

probably lies in the dramatic technological advances that occurred in the electronics sector. The development of the low-cost microchip opened up an amazing array of applications for computer technology in manufacturing, transport and communications, and in consumer goods which were developed and marketed during the second half of the 1980s resulting in a prolonged investment boom comparable to that of 200 years earlier when steam power was first harnessed. The optimistic profit expectations of the 1980s turned pessimistic in 1991 as the economy went into recession, and the investment demand curve made a large shift to the left. The fluctuations in investment resulting from changes in expected profits that shift the investment curve are much larger than those resulting from changes in interest rates.

Regardless of whether the fluctuations in investment are generated by shifts in the investment demand curve or movements along it, they have important effects on the economy. We'll learn about some of these effects in Chapter 25.

Let's now turn to the third component of aggregate expenditure, government purchases of goods and services.

FIGURE 24.8

The Investment Demand Curve in the United Kingdom

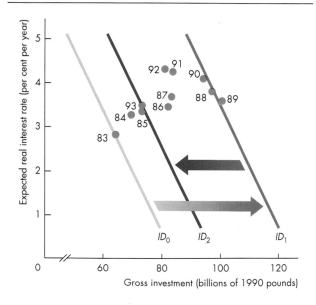

The blue points show the gross investment and the expected real interest rate in the United Kingdom for each year between 1983 and 1993. When expected profits were low in 1983, the investment demand curve was ID_0. Then expected profits gradually rose, so the demand curve moved to the right, arriving at the position shown by ID_1 in 1988. After 1990 expected profits began to fall and by 1993 the curve moved to the left to the position shown by ID_2.

Sources: Bank of England, *Statistical Abstract 1992*, Table 15.1, Fig. 24.7, and our calculations and assumptions.

Government Purchases of Goods and Services

Government purchases of goods and services cover two types of expenditure. First, they cover the goods and services which central and local governments buy on everyone's behalf from government departments. So they include the money given to the National Health Service to provide health services, money which is used to pay for doctors, nurses and drugs. They include the money given to the Ministry of Defence to provide defence services, money which is used to pay for sailors, soldiers and pilots and for the fuel and maintenance of their vehicles. And they include the money given to local education authorities to provide education, money which is used to pay for teachers and school heating. Second, government purchases include the new capital equipment which governments buy for their departments to use. So they include new hospitals, new tanks, and new classrooms and computers. Government purchases are concerned with a wide range of services aside from health, defence and education. Other activities include foreign representation, roads, the police, fire services, and refuse collection and disposal.

These expenditures are determined by political institutions. They are influenced by votes in national and local elections, the views of elected members of parliament and councillors, the actions of lobbyists, the political state of the world and the state of the UK and world economies.

Although some components of government purchases do vary with the state of the economy, most do not. We will assume, therefore, that government purchases do not vary in a systematic way with the level of GDP. They influence GDP but are not directly influenced by it.

The final component of aggregate expenditure is net exports. Let's now see how they are determined.

Net Exports

Net exports are the expenditure by foreigners on goods and services produced in the United Kingdom minus the expenditure by UK residents on goods and services produced abroad. That is, net exports is the value of the UK's exports minus the value of its imports. *Exports* are the sale of goods and services produced in the United Kingdom to the rest of the world. *Imports* are the purchase of goods and services produced in the rest of the world by firms, households and government departments in the United Kingdom.

Exports

Exports are determined by decisions made in the rest of the world and are influenced by three main factors:

◆ Real GDP in the rest of the world
◆ Prices of goods and services made in the United Kingdom relative to the prices of similar goods and services made in other countries
◆ Foreign exchange rates

Other things remaining the same, the greater the real GDP in the rest of the world, the greater is the demand by foreigners for goods and services made in the United Kingdom. For example, an economic boom in the United States increases the US

demand for goods and services made in the United Kingdom, such as chemicals, Jaguar cars and Scotch whisky. A recession in the United States cuts the US demand for goods and services made in the United Kingdom and decreases exports from the United Kingdom.

Also, other things remaining the same, the lower the price of goods and services made in the United Kingdom relative to the prices of similar goods and services made in other countries, the greater is the quantity of exports from the United Kingdom.

Finally, and again other things remaining the same, the lower the value of the pound against other currencies, the larger is the quantity of exports from the United Kingdom. For example, as the pound fell by 12 per cent against the average value of other currencies between August 1992 and August 1993, the demand by foreigners for goods and services made in the United Kingdom increased by more than 7 per cent.

Imports

Imports are determined by three main factors:

◆ Real GDP in the United Kingdom
◆ Prices of foreign-made goods and services relative to the prices of similar goods and services made in the United Kingdom
◆ Foreign exchange rates

Other things remaining the same, the greater the real GDP in the United Kingdom, the larger is the quantity of imports into the United Kingdom. For example, real income in the United Kingdom grew by 9 per cent between 1986 and 1988 and during this period the quantity of imports into the United Kingdom increased by 21 per cent.

Also, and again other things remaining the same, the higher the prices of goods and services made in the United Kingdom relative to the prices of similar goods and services made in the rest of the world, the larger is the quantity of imports into the United Kingdom.

Finally, and again other things remaining the same, the lower the value of the pound against other currencies, the smaller is the quantity of imports into the United Kingdom. For example, when the pound fell by 12 per cent against the average value of other currencies between August 1992 and August 1993, the quantity of imports fell by 2 per cent.

Net Export Function

The **net export function** is the relationship between net exports and domestic real GDP, holding constant real GDP in the rest of the world, prices and the exchange rate. The net export function can also be described by a net export schedule, which lists the net exports at each level of real GDP, with everything else held constant. The table in Fig. 24.9 gives an example of a net export schedule.

In the table, exports are a constant £120 billion – they do not depend on real GDP in the United Kingdom. Imports increase by 25 pence for each £1 increase in real GDP in the United Kingdom. Net exports, the difference between exports and imports, are shown in the final column of the table. When real GDP is £200 billion, net exports are £70 billion. Net exports decline as real GDP rises. At a real GDP of £480 billion, net exports are zero; and at real GDP levels higher than that, net exports become increasingly negative (imports exceed exports).

Exports and imports are graphed in Fig. 24.9(a) and the net export function is graphed in Fig. 24.9(b). By comparing part (a) and part (b), you can see that when exports exceed imports, net exports are above zero (there is a surplus) and when imports exceed exports, net exports are below zero

FIGURE 24.9

Net Export Function

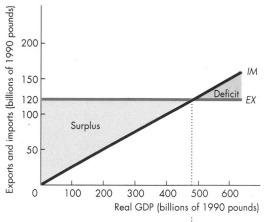

(a) Exports and imports

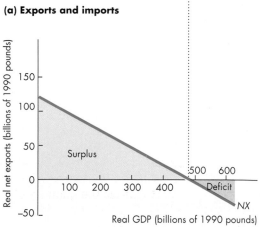

(b) Net exports

Real GDP (Y)	Exports (EX)	Imports (IM)	Net exports (EX – IM)
		(Billions of 1990 pounds)	
0	120	0	120
200	120	50	70
400	120	100	20
600	120	150	−30
800	120	200	−80
1,000	120	250	−130

The table shows the net export schedule – the relationship between net exports and real GDP. Net exports equal exports (EX) minus imports (IM). Exports are independent of real GDP, but imports rise as real GDP increases. In the table, imports are 25 per cent of real GDP. Net exports decrease as GDP increases.

Part (a) graphs the export and import schedules. As exports are independent of domestic real GDP, they are graphed as a horizontal line. As imports increase as real GDP increases, the import curve is an upward-sloping line. The distance between the export curve and the import curve represents net exports. Net exports are graphed in part (b). The net export function is downward sloping because the import curve is upward sloping. The real GDP at which the net export function intersects the horizontal axis in part (b) is the same as that at which the imports curve intersects the exports curve in part (a). That real GDP is £480 billion. Below that level of real GDP there is a surplus and above it there is a deficit.

Investment Decisions by Firms

The Essence of the Story

Investment levels by firms are lower than they could be.

Firms are not changing the way they appraise potential investments.

Firms are not taking account of the fall in inflation in their appraisal.

Firms say their investment decisions look at long-term factors.

For firms to change their appraisal techniques, a longer period of monetary stability is needed.

By continuing to require high rates of return on investment, however, firms are rejecting profitable investment opportunities.

FINANCIAL TIMES, 1 AUGUST 1994

Demands on returns 'undermines investment'

Gillian Tett, Economics Staff

Investment could be undermined by the high rates of return that companies are demanding on projects, the Bank of England has warned.

The warning follows a report from the Confederation of British Industry last week which found that most companies had not adjusted their investment assessments to take account of the recent trend of low inflation.

The warning, contained in an article in its quarterly bulletin, is based on an informal survey of 250 companies conducted in March and adds further weight to the CBI's findings. It notes that more than 70 per cent of businesses questioned had not reduced their target rates of return, while just 25 per cent had revised their investment appraisal techniques to take account of low inflation.

The main reason, it says, is that most companies argued that investment decisions were affected by longer-term considerations, and saw 'little reason yet to adjust their longer-term expectations of inflation rates and the cost of capital'.

These findings have prompted Mr Eddie George, Bank governor, to warn that companies are missing profitable investment opportunities by continuing to demand high rates of return. This view is disputed by many companies and analysts who argue that high rates of return are not the only factor holding back investment.

However Mr Andrew Wardlow, head of the Bank's conjectural assessment and projections division, and author of the report, takes a more cautious line.

Although companies' slowness to adjust their investment criterion may undermine investment in the future, it may not have been critical to investment when the survey was conducted in March, Mr Wardlow says.

He adds: 'A further period of monetary stability may be needed before a more fundamental adjustment in behaviour becomes widespread.'

The nominal rate of return on projects that companies are demanding – about 20 per cent according to the Bank's survey – was not previously unreasonable given that producer price inflation was running at an average of 9.5 per cent between 1970 and 1990, the report notes.

The Bank of England Quarterly Bulletin, August 1994.

© Financial Times. Reprinted with permission.

READING BETWEEN THE LINES

Background and Analysis

Low and stable inflation raises the chances of lower nominal interest rates. These monetary conditions also make more certain the relationship between real and nominal rates of return.

In the recent past, high and unstable inflation rates have increased the degree of uncertainty in making investment decisions.

Also in the recent past, periods of low inflation have generally been short lived. Firm will want to see the period of monetary stability sustained before reacting positively to it.

Savers too will be affected by uncertainty over inflation.

Uncertainty through high and unstable inflation will increase the real returns savers will require. This will, in turn, increase the real cost of borrowing funds for investment.

A rise in future investment levels, however, may not just require firms to adjust investment appraisal procedures to lower inflation.

Firms also consider other factors in making investment decisions. A high degree of excess capacity is seen as holding up new investments in some industries, as is a slow recovery in demand.

In the figure, the fall in real interest rates from 8 per cent to 6 per cent leads to a rise in the level of investment from £100 billion to £120 billion.

Over time, stronger demands may result in firms raising their profit expectations. This would shift ID_0 to ID_1, raising the level of investment still further to £150 billion.

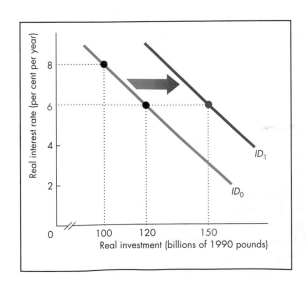

(there is a deficit). When real GDP is £480 billion, there is a balance between exports and imports.

The position of the net export function depends on real GDP in the rest of the world and on prices of goods and services made in the United Kingdom compared with the prices of those goods and services made in the rest of the world. If real GDP in the rest of the world increases, the net export function shifts to the right. If goods and services made in the United Kingdom become cheaper relative to goods and services made in the rest of the world, the net export function also shifts to the right.

We've now studied the main influences on consumption expenditure, investment and net exports. Our next task is to see how these components of aggregate expenditure interact with each other and with government purchases of goods and services to determine aggregate expenditure. Our starting point is to establish a relationship between aggregate planned expenditure and real GDP.

Aggregate Expenditure and Real GDP

There is a relationship between aggregate planned expenditure and real GDP. **Aggregate planned expenditure** is the expenditure that economic agents (households, firms, governments and foreigners) plan to undertake in given circumstances. Aggregate planned expenditure is not necessarily equal to actual aggregate expenditure. We'll see how these two expenditure concepts – planned and actual – differ from each other later in this chapter.

The relationship between aggregate planned expenditure and real GDP may be described by either an aggregate expenditure schedule or an aggregate expenditure curve. The aggregate expenditure schedule lists the level of aggregate planned expenditure generated at each level of real GDP. The **aggregate expenditure curve** is a graph of the level of aggregate planned expenditure generated at each level of real GDP.

Aggregate Expenditure Schedule

An example of an aggregate expenditure schedule is set out in Fig. 24.10. The numbers there are all in

1990 pounds. They are chosen for simplicity and are not based on real-world data. The table shows aggregate planned expenditure as well as its components. To work out the level of aggregate planned expenditure at a given real GDP, we add the various components together. The first column of the table shows real GDP and the second column shows the consumption expenditure generated by each level of real GDP. When real GDP is £200 billion, consumption expenditure is £170 billion. A £1 increase in real GDP generates a 65 pence increase in consumption expenditure. So, when real GDP increases by £200 to £400 billion, consumption expenditure increases by £130 billion to £300 billion.

The next two columns show investment and government purchases of goods and services. Recall that investment depends on the real interest rate and the state of profit expectations. Suppose that those factors are constant and, at a given point in time, generate a level of investment of £100 billion. This investment level is independent of real GDP. Government purchases of goods and services are also fixed. Their value is also £100 billion.

The next three columns show exports, imports and net exports. Exports are influenced by events in the rest of the world, by UK prices compared with prices in other countries, and by the foreign exchange value of the UK pound. They are not directly affected by the level of real GDP. In the table, exports appear as a constant £120 billion. In contrast, imports do increase as real GDP increases. In the table, a £1 increase in real GDP generates a 25 pence increase in imports. Net exports – the difference between exports and imports – also varies as real GDP varies. It decreases by 25 pence for each £1 increase in real GDP.

The final column of the table shows aggregate planned expenditure. This amount is the sum of planned consumption expenditure, investment, government purchases of goods and services, and net exports.

Aggregate Expenditure Curve

The aggregate expenditure curve appears in the diagram in Fig. 24.10. Real GDP is shown on the horizontal axis and aggregate planned expenditure on the vertical axis. The aggregate expenditure curve is the red line *AE*. Points *a* to *f* on that curve correspond to the rows in the table in Fig. 24.10. The *AE* curve is a graph of the last column,

'Aggregate planned expenditure', plotted against real GDP.

The figure also shows the components of aggregate expenditure. The constant components – investment, government purchases of goods and services, and exports – are indicated by the horizontal lines in the figure. Consumption is the vertical gap between the line $I + G + EX + C$ and the line $I + G + EX$.

To calculate the AE curve, we subtract imports from the line $I + G + EX + C$. Imports are subtracted because they are not expenditure on real GDP in the United Kingdom. The purchase of a new car is part of consumption expenditure. But suppose that car is a Toyota made in Japan. Then expenditure on it has to be subtracted from consumption expenditure to find out how much is spent on goods and services produced in the United Kingdom – on real GDP in

FIGURE 24.10

Aggregate Expenditure Curve and Aggregate Expenditure Schedule

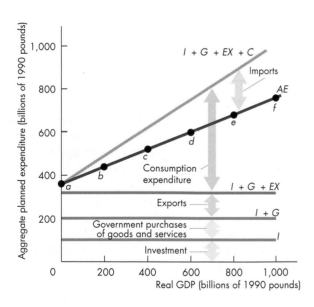

The relationship between aggregate planned expenditure and real GDP may be described by an aggregate expenditure schedule (as shown in the table) or an aggregate expenditure curve (as shown in the diagram). Aggregate planned expenditure is calculated as the sum of planned consumption expenditure, investment, government purchases of goods and services, and net exports. For example, in row b of the table, if real GDP is £200 billion, aggregate planned consumption is £170 billion, planned investment is £100 billion, planned government purchases of goods and services are £100 billion, and planned net exports are £70 billion. Thus when real GDP is £200 billion, aggregate planned expenditure is £440 billion (£170 + £100 + £100 + £70). The expenditure plans are graphed in the figure as the aggregate expenditure curve AE, the line af.

	Real GDP (Y)	Planned expenditure						Aggregate planned expenditure ($AE = C + I + G + NX$)
		Consumption expenditure (C)	Investment (I)	Government purchases (G)	Exports (EX)	Imports (IM)	Net exports (NX = EX − IM)	
				(Billions of 1990 pounds)				
a	0	40	100	100	120	0	120	360
b	200	170	100	100	120	50	70	440
c	400	300	100	100	120	100	20	520
d	600	430	100	100	120	150	−30	600
e	800	560	100	100	120	200	−80	680
f	1,000	690	100	100	120	250	−130	760

the United Kingdom. Money paid to Toyota for car imports from Japan does not add to aggregate expenditure in the United Kingdom.

We've now seen how to calculate the aggregate expenditure schedule and aggregate expenditure curve and seen that aggregate planned expenditure increases as real GDP increases. This relationship is summarized in the aggregate expenditure curve. But what determines the point on the aggregate expenditure curve at which the economy operates?

Equilibrium Expenditure

Equilibrium expenditure occurs when aggregate planned expenditure equals real GDP. At levels of real GDP below equilibrium, planned expenditure exceeds real GDP; at levels of real GDP above equilibrium, planned expenditure falls short of real GDP.

To see how equilibrium expenditure is determined, we need to distinguish between actual expenditure and planned expenditure and understand how actual expenditure, planned expenditure and real GDP are related.

Actual Expenditure, Planned Expenditure, and Real GDP

Actual aggregate expenditure is always equal to real GDP. (We established this fact in Chapter 22, pp. 611). But *planned* expenditure is not necessarily equal to actual expenditure and so it is not necessarily equal to actual real GDP. How can actual expenditure and planned expenditure differ from each other? Why don't people implement their plans? Certainly most people do have actual expenditures equal to their planned expenditures. For example, households carry out their consumption expenditure plans, the government implements its planned purchases of goods and services, and net exports are as planned.

However, there may be a difference between planned investment and actual investment. Remember that investment comprises firms' purchases of capital – that is plant, buildings, machinery and vehicles – plus any increases in stocks (or minus any

falls in stocks). Firms make plans about their purchases of capital and about their stock levels. Let's assume they plan to keep their stocks constant. In this case, their planned investment simply equals their planned purchases of capital. Their actual purchases of capital will correspond to their planned purchases. But if their stocks happen to rise, then their actual investment will include this increase and will be larger than their planned investment. If, instead, their stocks fall, then their actual investment will allow for the fall and will be less than their planned investment. It is easy for stocks to rise or fall even when firms plan that they should stay fixed. If firms want their stock to stay fixed, they will produce as many goods as they expect people to buy. If people buy more than firms expect, then stocks will fall, and if people buy less than firms expect, then stocks will rise.

It is because stocks may change even when firms plan to hold them constant that actual investment may not equal planned investment. In turn, therefore, actual expenditure may not equal planned expenditure. We have seen that stocks change when people buy different amounts from the amounts that firms produce. We can put this another way and say that stocks change when aggregate planned expenditure - that is the total amount people want to spend – is different from real GDP – that is the amount that is being produced. If real GDP exceeds planned expenditure, stocks rise, and if real GDP is less than planned expenditure, stocks fall.

When aggregate planned expenditure is equal to aggregate actual expenditure and so equal to real GDP, the economy is in an expenditure equilibrium. When aggregate planned expenditure is not equal to aggregate actual expenditure and so not equal to real GDP, changes in the economy will take place until it does. In other words, a process of convergence towards an equilibrium expenditure occurs. Let's examine equilibrium expenditure and the process that brings it about.

When Planned Expenditure Equals Real GDP

The table in Fig. 24.11 shows different levels of real GDP. Against each level of real GDP, the second column shows aggregate planned expenditure. Only when real GDP equals £600 billion is aggregate planned expenditure equal to real GDP. This level of expenditure is the equilibrium expenditure.

The equilibrium is illustrated in Fig. 24.11(a). The

aggregate expenditure curve is *AE*. As aggregate planned expenditure on the vertical axis and real GDP on the horizontal axis are both measured in the same units and on the same scale, a 45° line drawn in Fig. 24.11(a) shows all the points at which aggregate planned expenditure equals real GDP. Where the aggregate expenditure curve intersects the 45° line, at point *d*, equilibrium expenditure is determined.

Convergence to Equilibrium You will get a better idea of why point *d* is the equilibrium if you consider what would happen if the economy was not at point *d*. Suppose that real GDP is £200 billion. You can see from Fig. 24.11(a) that in this situation aggregate planned expenditure is £440 billion (point *b*). So aggregate planned expenditure is larger than real GDP. If aggregate expenditure actually equalled the

FIGURE 24.11

Equilibrium Expenditure and Real GDP

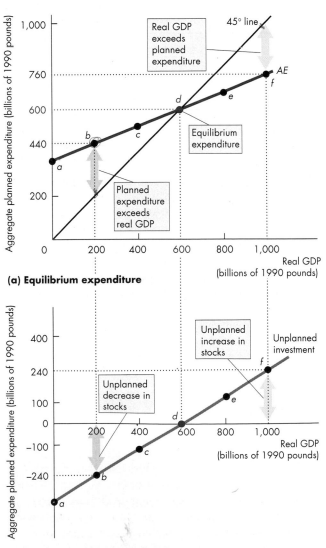

(a) Equilibrium expenditure

(b) Unplanned investment changes

	Real GDP (*Y*)	Aggregate planned expenditure (*AE*)	Unplanned stock changes (*Y − AE*)
		(billions of 1990 pounds)	
a	0	360	−360
b	200	440	−240
c	400	520	−120
d	600	600	0
e	800	680	120
f	1,000	760	240

The table shows the aggregate expenditure schedule. When real GDP is £600 billion, aggregate planned expenditure equals real GDP. At real GDP levels below £600 billion, aggregate planned expenditure exceeds real GDP. At real GDP levels above £600 billion, aggregate planned expenditure is less than real GDP.

Part (a) illustrates equilibrium expenditure. The 45° line shows those points at which aggregate planned expenditure equals real GDP. The aggregate expenditure curve is *AE*. Actual aggregate expenditure equals real GDP. Equilibrium expenditure and real GDP are £600 billion. That real GDP level generates aggregate planned expenditure that equals real GDP, shown at point *d* in part (a).

The forces bringing the equilibrium about are illustrated in parts (a) and (b). At real GDP levels below £600 billion, aggregate planned expenditure exceeds real GDP and stocks fall – for example, point *b* in both parts of the figure. In such cases, firms increase output to restore their stocks and real GDP increases. At real GDP levels higher than £600 billion, aggregate planned expenditure is less than real GDP and stocks rise – for example, point *f* in both parts of the figure. In such a situation, firms decrease output to work off excess stocks and real GDP decreases. Only where the aggregate planned expenditure curve cuts the 45° line is planned expenditure equal to real GDP. This position is the equilibrium. There are no unplanned stock changes and real GDP remains constant.

planned £440 billion, then real GDP would also be £440 billion, since every pound spent by one person is a pound of income for someone else. But real GDP is £200 billion. How can real GDP be £200 billion if people *plan* to spend £440 billion? The answer is that *actual* spending is less than *planned* spending. If real GDP is £200 billion, the value of production is also £200 billion. The only way that people can buy goods and services worth £440 billion, when the value of production is £200 billion, is if firms' stocks fall by £240 billion (point *b* in Fig. 24.11b). Since changes in stocks are part of investment, actual investment is less than planned investment.

But this is not the end of the story. Firms have target levels for stocks, and when stocks fall below those targets, they increase production to restore stocks to their target levels. To restore their stocks, firms hire additional labour and increase production. Suppose that they increase production in the next period by £200 billion. Real GDP rises by £200 billion to £400 billion. But again, aggregate planned expenditure exceeds real GDP. When real GDP is £400 billion, aggregate planned expenditure is £520 billion (point *c* in Fig. 24.11a). Again, stocks fall but this time by less than before. With real GDP of £400 billion and planned expenditure of £520 billion, stocks fall by only £120 billion (point *c* in Fig. 24.11b). Again, firms hire additional labour, and production increases; real GDP increases yet further.

The process that we have just described – where planned expenditure exceeds income, stocks fall, and production rises to restore the unplanned fall in stocks – ends when real GDP has reached £600 billion. At this level of real GDP, there is an equilibrium. There are no unplanned stock changes and firms do not change their production.

Next, let's perform a similar experiment, but one starting with a level of real GDP greater than the equilibrium. Suppose that real GDP is £1,000 billion. At this level aggregate planned expenditure is £760 billion (point *f* in Fig. 24.11a), £240 billion less than real GDP. With aggregate planned expenditure less than real GDP, stocks rise by £240 billion (point *f* in Fig. 24.11b) so there is unplanned investment. With unsold stocks on their hands, firms cut back on production. They lay off workers and reduce the amount they pay out in wages; real GDP falls. If they cut back production by £200 billion, real GDP falls by this amount to £800 billion. At that level of real GDP, aggregate planned expenditure is £680 billion (point *e* in Fig. 24.11a). Again, there is an unplanned increase

in stocks, but it is only £120 billion (point *e* in Fig. 24.11b). Again, firms will cut back production and lay off yet more workers, reducing real GDP still further. Real GDP continues to fall whenever unplanned stocks increase. As before, real GDP keeps on changing until it reaches its equilibrium level of £600 billion.

You can see, then, that if real GDP is below equilibrium, aggregate planned expenditure exceeds real GDP, stocks fall, firms increase production to restore their stocks and real GDP rises. If real GDP is above equilibrium, aggregate planned expenditure is less than real GDP, unsold stocks prompt firms to cut back on production and real GDP falls.

Only if real GDP equals aggregate planned expenditure are there no unplanned stock changes and no changes in firms' output plans. In this situation, real GDP remains constant.

REVIEW

E quilibrium expenditure occurs when aggregate planned expenditure equals real GDP. If aggregate planned expenditure exceeds real GDP, stocks fall and firms increase output to replenish their stocks. Real GDP increases and so does planned expenditure. If aggregate planned expenditure is below real GDP, stocks mount up and firms cut output to reduce their stock levels. Real GDP and aggregate planned expenditure fall. Only when aggregate planned expenditure equals real GDP are there no unplanned changes in stocks and no changes in output. Real GDP remains constant. ◆

Real GDP and the Price Level

W hen firms find unwanted stocks piling up, they cut back on orders and decrease production. They also usually cut prices. Similarly, when firms are having trouble keeping up with sales and their stocks are falling, they increase their orders and step up production. But they also usually increase their prices. So far, we've not looked at the effects of price changes. When firms change their prices, the price level changes for the economy as a whole.

To study the price level, we need to use the *aggregate demand–aggregate supply model*. We also need to work out the relationship between the aggregate demand–aggregate supply model and the aggregate expenditure model that we've used in this chapter. The key to the relationship between these two models is the distinction between the aggregate *expenditure* curve and the aggregate *demand* curve.

Aggregate Expenditure and Aggregate Demand

The aggregate expenditure curve is the relationship between aggregate planned expenditure and real GDP, holding all other influences constant. The aggregate demand curve is the relationship between the aggregate quantity of goods and services demanded and the price level, holding all other influences constant. Let's explore the links between these two relationships.

At a given price level, there is a given amount of autonomous expenditure, that is a given level of expenditure that would occur even if GDP were zero. In the case we have just studied in Fig. 24.11, autonomous expenditure was £360 billion, as shown by point *a* in part (a). At a given price level there is also a given amount of aggregate planned expenditure. This amount depends on the level of GDP, and it is shown in Fig. 24.11 by the line *AE* which starts at point *a*.

If the price level changes, so too does autonomous expenditure. So, in turn, does the amount of aggregate planned expenditure. Why does the amount of autonomous expenditure change? There are three main reasons which are explained more fully in Chapter 23. They are:

◆ Real money balances effect
◆ Intertemporal substitution effect
◆ International substitution effect

A rise in the price level, other things remaining the same, decreases the quantity of real money. A smaller quantity of real money decreases aggregate planned expenditure – the *real money balances effect*. A rise in the price level, other things remaining the same, makes current goods and services more costly relative to future goods and services, resulting in a delay in purchases – the *intertemporal substitution effect*. A rise in the price level, other things remaining the same, makes goods and services produced in the United Kingdom less competitive, increasing imports and decreasing exports

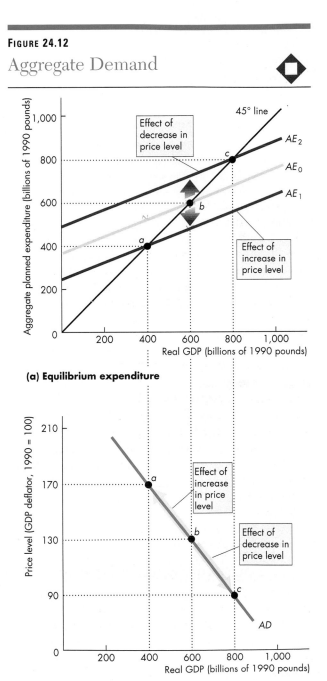

FIGURE 24.12

Aggregate Demand

(a) Equilibrium expenditure

(b) Aggregate demand

The position of the *AE* curve depends on the price level. When the price level is 130 the *AE* curve is AE_0. Equilibrium expenditure is at point *b*, and real GDP demanded is £600 billion. When the price level is 170, the *AE* curve is AE_1, and equilibrium is at point *a*. Real GDP demanded is £400 billion. When the price level is 90, the *AE* curve is AE_2, and the equilibrium is at point *c*. Real GDP demanded is £800 billion. Points *a*, *b* and *c* on the aggregate demand curve correspond to the equilibrium points *a*, *b* and *c* in part (a).

– the *international substitution effect*.

All these effects of a rise in the price level reduce aggregate planned expenditure at each level of real GDP. As a result, when the price level rises, the aggregate expenditure curve shifts downward. A decrease in the price level has the opposite effect. When the price level falls, the aggregate expenditure curve shifts upward.

Figure 24.12(a) illustrates these effects. When the price level is 130, the aggregate expenditure curve is AE_0, which intersects the 45° line at point b. Equilibrium expenditure and real GDP are £600 billion. If the price level increases to 170, the aggregate expenditure curve shifts downward to AE_1, which intersects the 45° line at point a. Equilibrium expenditure and real GDP are £400 billion. If the price level decreases to 90, the aggregate expenditure curve shifts upward to AE_2, which intersects the 45° line at point c. Equilibrium expenditure and real GDP are £800 billion.

We've just seen that when the price level changes, other things remaining the same, the aggregate expenditure curve shifts and a new expenditure equilibrium arises. But when the price level changes, other things remaining the same, there is a movement along the aggregate demand curve. Figure 24.12(b) illustrates these movements. At a price level of 130, the aggregate quantity of goods and services demanded is £600 billion – point b on the aggregate demand curve AD. If the price level increases to 170, the aggregate quantity of goods and services demanded decreases to £400 billion. There is a movement along the aggregate demand curve to point a. If the price level decreases to 90, the aggregate quantity of goods and services demanded increases to £800 billion. There is a movement along the aggregate demand curve to point c.

Each point on the aggregate demand curve corresponds to an expenditure equilibrium. The expenditure equilibrium points a, b and c in Fig. 24.12(a) correspond to the points a, b and c on the aggregate demand curve in Fig. 24.12(b).

◆ ◆ ◆ ◆   In this chapter, we've studied the factors that influence private expenditure decisions, looking at each item of aggregate expenditure – consumption expenditure, investment and net exports – in isolation from the others. We've also seen how these private components of expenditure interact with each other and with government purchases of goods and services to determine equilibrium aggregate expenditure and the position of the aggregate demand curve. In the next chapter, we'll study the sources of *changes* in the equilibrium. In particular, we'll see how changes in investment, exports and government fiscal policy actions can change equilibrium aggregate expenditure and shift the aggregate demand curve.

S U M M A R Y

The Components of Aggregate Expenditure

The components of aggregate expenditure are:

◆ Consumption expenditure
◆ Investment
◆ Government purchases of goods and services
◆ Net exports

The main component of aggregate expenditure is consumption expenditure. On average, 62 per cent of total expenditure comes from consumption expenditure. Investment accounts for 16 per cent and government purchases of goods and services accounts for 23 per cent of the total. Net exports average –1 per cent of total expenditure.

The components of aggregate expenditure that are most volatile are net exports and investment. (pp. 666–670)

Consumption Expenditure and Saving

Consumption expenditure is influenced by many factors, but the most important is disposable income. As disposable income increases so do both consumption expenditure and saving. The relationship between consumption expenditure and disposable income is the *consumption function*. The relationship between saving and disposable income is the *saving function*. At low levels of disposable income, consumption expenditure exceeds disposable income, which means that saving is negative (dissaving occurs). As disposable income increases, consumption expenditure increases but by less than the increase in disposable income.

The fraction of each additional pound of disposable income consumed is the marginal propensity to consume. The fraction of each additional pound of disposable income saved is the marginal propensity to save. All influences on consumption and saving, other than disposable income, shift the consumption and saving functions. The most important of these other influences is expected future income.

Consumption expenditure is a function of real GDP because disposable income and GDP vary together. (pp. 670–671)

Investment

The amount of investment depends on:

◆ Real interest rates
◆ Profit expectations

The lower the real interest rate, the greater is the amount of investment. And the higher the expected profit, the greater is the amount of investment.

The main influence on investment demand is fluctuations in profit expectations. Swings in the degree of optimism and pessimism about future profits lead to shifts in the investment demand curve. Swings in profit expectations are associated with business cycle fluctuations and the degree of capacity utilization. When the economy is in an expansion phase and capacity utilization is rising, profit expectations are optimistic and investment is high. When the economy is in a contraction phase and capacity utilization is falling, profit expectations are pessimistic and investment is low. (pp. 671–681)

Government Purchases of Goods and Services

Government purchases are determined by political processes and the amount of government purchases is determined largely independently of the current level of real GDP. (pp. 681–682)

Net Exports

Net exports are the difference between exports and imports. Exports are determined by decisions made in the rest of the world and are influenced by real GDP in the rest of the world, the prices of goods and services made in the United Kingdom relative to the prices of similar goods and services made in other countries, and the foreign exchange rate. Imports are determined by real GDP in the United Kingdom, the prices of foreign-made goods and services relative to the prices of goods and services produced in the United Kingdom, and the foreign exchange rate.

The net export function shows the relationship between net exports and real GDP in the United Kingdom, holding constant all the other influences on exports and imports. (pp. 682–686)

Aggregate Expenditure and Real GDP

Aggregate planned expenditure is the sum of planned consumption expenditure, planned investment, planned government purchases of goods and services, and planned net exports. The relationship between aggregate planned expenditure and real GDP can be represented by the aggregate expenditure schedule and the aggregate expenditure curve. (pp. 686–688)

Equilibrium Expenditure

Equilibrium expenditure occurs when aggregate planned expenditure equals real GDP. At real GDP levels above the equilibrium, aggregate planned expenditure is below real GDP and, in such a situation, real GDP falls. At levels of real GDP below the equilibrium, aggregate planned expenditure exceeds real GDP and real GDP rises. Only when real GDP equals aggregate planned expenditure is real GDP constant and in equilibrium. The main influence bringing real GDP and aggregate planned expenditure into equality is the behaviour of stocks. When aggregate planned expenditure exceeds real GDP, stocks decrease. To restore their stocks, firms increase output and this action increases real GDP. When planned expenditure is below real GDP, stocks accumulate and firms cut back their output. This action reduces the level of real GDP. Only when there are no unplanned stock changes do firms keep output constant so that real GDP remains constant. (pp. 688–690)

Real GDP and the Price Level

The aggregate demand curve is the relationship between the quantity of real GDP demanded and the price level, other things remaining the same. A change in the price level brings a movement along the aggregate demand curve. The aggregate expenditure curve is the relationship between aggregate planned expenditure and real GDP, other things remaining the same. At a given price level and a given level of real

GDP, there is a given aggregate expenditure curve. A change in the price level changes autonomous expenditure and shifts the aggregate expenditure curve.

Thus a movement along the aggregate demand curve is associated with a shift in the aggregate expenditure curve. (pp. 690–692)

K E Y   E L E M E N T S

Key Terms

Aggregate expenditure curve, 686
Aggregate planned expenditure, 686
Average propensity to consume, 672
Average propensity to save, 672
Consumption function, 670
Dissaving, 670
Disposable income, 670
Equilibrium expenditure, 688
Investment demand, 678
Investment demand curve, 678
Marginal propensity to consume, 673
Marginal propensity to consume out of real GDP, 674
Marginal propensity to save, 673
Net export function, 683
Real interest rate, 676

Saving function, 670

Key Figures and Table

R E V I E W   Q U E S T I O N S

1   What are the components of aggregate expenditure?

2   Which component of aggregate expenditure is the largest?

3   Which components of aggregate expenditure fluctuate the most?

4   What is the consumption function?

5   What is the chief determinant of consumption?

6   Distinguish between disposable income and GDP.

7   What is the saving function? What is the relationship between the saving function and the consumption function?

8   What is the marginal propensity to consume? Why is it less than one?

9   What is the marginal propensity to consume out of GDP? Why is it less than one?

10 Explain the relationship between the average propensity to consume and the marginal propensity to consume.

11 Explain the relationship between the marginal propensity to consume and the marginal propensity to save.

12 What determines investment? Why does investment increase as the real interest rate falls?

13 What is the effect of the following on net exports of the United Kingdom:
    a An increase in real GDP in the United Kingdom?
    b An increase in real GDP in Germany?
    c A rise in the price of Japanese-made cars with no change in the price of cars made in the United Kingdom?

14 What is the aggregate expenditure curve?

15 How is equilibrium expenditure determined? What would happen if aggregate planned expenditure exceeded real GDP?

16 What is the relationship between the aggregate expenditure curve and the aggregate demand curve?

17 The price level changes and everything else is held constant. What happens to the aggregate demand curve and the aggregate expenditure curve?

P R O B L E M S

1 You are given the following information about the Jenkin family:

Disposable income (pounds per year)	Consumption expenditure (pounds per year)
0	5,000
10,000	10,000
20,000	15,000
30,000	20,000
40,000	25,000

a Calculate the Jenkin family's marginal propensity to consume.
b Calculate the average propensity to consume at each level of disposable income.
c Calculate how much the Jenkin family saves at each level of disposable income.
d Calculate their marginal propensity to save.
e Calculate their average propensity to save at each level of disposable income.
f Draw a diagram of the consumption function. Calculate its slope.
g Over what range of income does the Jenkin family dissave?

2 A car assembly plant can be built for £10 million and it will have a life of three years. At the end of three years, the plant will have a scrap value of £1 million. The firm will have to hire labour at a cost of £1.5 million a year and will have to buy parts and fuel costing another £1.5 million. If the firm builds the plant, it will be able to produce cars that will sell for £7.5 million each year. Will it pay the firm to invest in this new production line at the following interest rates:
a 2 per cent a year?
b 5 per cent a year?
c 10 per cent a year?

3 You are given the following information about the economy of Ruritania. The marginal propensity to consume is 0.75, and taxes net of transfer payments are a quarter of real GDP. What is the marginal propensity to consume out of real GDP in this economy?

4 You are given the following information about the economy of Arthuria. When disposable income is zero, consumption is £80 billion. The marginal propensity to consume is 0.75. Investment is £400 billion; government purchases of goods and services are £600 billion; taxes are a constant £500 billion and do not vary as income varies.
    At the expenditure equilibrium, calculate:
a Real GDP
b Consumption
c Saving
d The average and marginal propensities to consume
e The average and marginal propensities to save

5 You are given the following information about the economy of Zeeland. Autonomous consumption expenditure is £100 billion and the marginal propensity to consume is 0.9. Investment is £460 billion, government purchases of goods and services are £400 billion, taxes are a constant £400 billion – they do not vary with income. Exports are £350 billion and imports are 10 per cent of income. Suppose that the price level in the economy of Zeeland is 100. Find one point on Zeeland's aggregate demand curve.

CHAPTER 25

EXPENDITURE
FLUCTUATIONS
AND
FISCAL POLICY

After studying this chapter you will be able to:

◆ Explain why changes in investment and exports change consumption expenditure and have multiplier effects on aggregate expenditure

◆ Define and calculate the multiplier

◆ Explain why changes in government purchases of goods and services have multiplier effects on aggregate expenditure

◆ Explain why changes in taxes and transfer payments have multiplier effects on aggregate expenditure

◆ Explain how the government may use fiscal policy in an attempt to stabilize aggregate expenditure

I N WEMBLEY STADIUM, MICK JAGGER BREATHES INTO A MICROPHONE AT A BARELY audible whisper. Moving to a louder passage, he increases the volume of his voice and now, through the magic of electronic amplification, booms across the stadium drowning out every other sound. ◆ ◆   Ian Saunders, the mayor of Sheffield, is being driven along the city streets inspecting the construction of Sheffield's Supertram. As the city's streets are being torn up to make way for the Supertram and temporarily patched over, the streets are rough and very uneven. The car's wheels are bouncing and vibrating but its passengers are completely undisturbed, and the mayor's notes are being written without a ripple, thanks to the car's efficient shock absorbers. ◆ ◆   Investment and exports fluctuate like the volume of Mick Jagger's voice and the uneven surface of a Sheffield street. How does the economy

Economic Amplifier or Shock Absorber?

react to those fluctuations? Does it react like Ian Saunders' car, absorbing the shocks and providing a smooth ride for the economy's passengers? Or does it behave like Mick Jagger's amplifier, blowing up the fluctuations and spreading them out to affect the many millions of participants in an economic rock concert? ◆ ◆   Is the economic machine built to a design that we simply have to live with, or can we modify it, changing its amplification and shock-absorbing powers? And can the government operate the economic machine in a way that gives us all a smoother ride?

◆ ◆ ◆   We are now going to explore these questions. We are also going to discover how the government can try to smooth out the economy by varying its purchases of goods and services and by varying tax rates.

Expenditure Multipliers

In Chapter 24, we used the aggregate expenditure model to discover what determines equilibrium expenditure. We're now going use that model again to see what happens to equilibrium expenditure when there is a *change* in investment, exports, or government purchases of goods and services. To study the effects of such changes, we classify the components of aggregate expenditure into two groups:

◆ Autonomous expenditure
◆ Induced expenditure

Autonomous Expenditure

Autonomous expenditure is the part of aggregate planned expenditure that is not influenced by real GDP. It is the amount of aggregate planned expenditure if real GDP is zero, and it is shown in row *a* of the table in Fig. 25.1. The components of autonomous expenditure are autonomous consumption expenditure, investment, government purchases of goods and services, and exports. In the table, autonomous consumption expenditure is £40 billion, investment is £100 billion, government purchases are £100 billion, and exports are £120 billion.

Autonomous expenditure is illustrated in both parts of Fig. 25.1 as the point at which the *AE* curve touches the vertical axis – the level of aggregate planned expenditure when real GDP is zero. In part (b), autonomous expenditure is highlighted by the blue arrow.

Induced Expenditure

Induced expenditure is the part of aggregate planned expenditure that varies as real GDP varies. Induced expenditure equals induced consumption expenditure minus imports. For example, in the table in Fig. 25.1, when real GDP increases from zero (row *a*) to £800 billion (row *e*), an increase of £800 billion, consumption expenditure increases from £40 billion to £560 billion, an increase of £520 billion. This is induced consumption expenditure. The £800 billion increase in real GDP increases imports by £200 billion. So induced expenditure is £320 billion – £520 billion of induced consumption expenditure minus £200 billion of induced imports.

Induced expenditure is illustrated in both parts of Fig. 25.1. In part (a), induced consumption expenditure is shown by the red arrow and imports are shown by the purple arrow. In part (b), induced expenditure is illustrated by the orange arrow.

The Marginal Propensity to Buy Domestic Goods and Services

The **marginal propensity to buy domestic goods and services** is the marginal propensity to consume out of real GDP minus the marginal propensity to import. The *marginal propensity to consume out of real GDP* (defined in Chapter 24) is the fraction of the last pound of real GDP consumed and is equal to the change in consumption expenditure divided by the change in real GDP. The **marginal propensity to import** is the fraction of the last pound of real GDP spent on imports and is equal to the change in imports divided by the change in real GDP.

In Fig. 25.1, when real GDP increases from zero (row *a*) to £200 billion (row *b*), consumption expenditure increases from £40 billion to £170 billion, an increase of £130 billion. So the marginal propensity to consume out of real GDP is £130 billion divided by £200 billion and is 0.65. The same increase in real GDP induces an increase in imports from zero to £50 billion, so the marginal propensity to import is £50 billion divided by £200 billion – that is, 0.25. The marginal propensity to buy domestic goods and services is 0.65 minus 0.25, which equals 0.4.

The marginal propensity to buy domestic goods and services is also equal to the slope of the aggregate expenditure curve. You can check this by noticing that when real GDP increases from zero to £200 billion, aggregate planned expenditure increases from £360 billion to £440 billion, an increase of £80 billion. The slope of the aggregate expenditure curve equals the increase in aggregate planned expenditure divided by the increase in real GDP – £80 billion divided by £200 billion, which equals 0.4. This value is the same as the marginal propensity to consume out of real GDP minus the marginal propensity to import that you have just calculated.

A Change in Autonomous Expenditure

There are many possible sources of a change in autonomous expenditure. A fall in the real interest rate might induce firms to increase their planned

FIGURE 25.1

Aggregate Expenditure

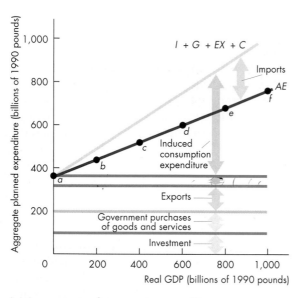

(a) Components of aggregate expenditure

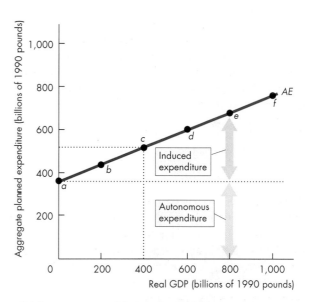

(b) Autonomous and induced expenditure

	Real GDP (Y)	Consumption expenditure (C)	Investment (I)	Government purchases (G)	Exports (EX)	Imports (IM)	Net exports (NX = EX − IM)	Aggregate planned expenditure (AE = C + I + G + NX)
				(billions of 1990 pounds)				
a	0	40	100	100	120	0	120	360
b	200	170	100	100	120	50	70	440
c	400	300	100	100	120	100	20	520
d	600	430	100	100	120	150	−30	600
e	800	560	100	100	100	200	−80	680
f	1,000	690	100	100	120	250	−130	760

(Column header group: **Planned expenditure**)

In the table, autonomous expenditure, the amount of aggregate planned expenditure when real GDP is zero, is £360 billion. Autonomous expenditure is the sum of investment, government purchases of goods and services, exports and autonomous consumption in the figure. It is the point at which the AE curve touches the vertical axis. Autonomous expenditure is shown by the blue line in part (a), and its magnitude is highlighted by the blue arrow in part (b).

Induced expenditure is equal to induced consumption expenditure minus imports. It increases as real GDP increases. In part (a), induced consumption expenditure is shown by the red arrow and imports by the purple arrow. In part (b), induced expenditure is highlighted by the orange arrow.

investment. A major wave of innovation, such as occurred with the spread of computers in the 1980s, might increase expected future profits and lead firms to increase their planned investment. Stiff competition in the car industry from Japanese imports might force Rover, Ford and Vauxhall to increase their investment in robotic assembly lines. An economic boom in North America and Japan might lead to a large increase in their expenditure on goods and services produced in the United Kingdom – on UK exports. A worsening of international relations might lead the UK government to increase its expenditure on armaments – an increase in government purchases of goods and services. These are all examples of increases in autonomous expenditure. What are the effects of such increases on aggregate planned expenditure? And do increases in autonomous expenditure affect consumers? Will they plan to increase their consumption expenditure? Let's answer these questions.

Aggregate planned expenditure is set out in the table in Fig. 25.2. Autonomous expenditure initially is £360 billion. Each £1 billion increase in real GDP induces an increase in aggregate expenditure of £0.4 billion. Adding induced expenditure and autono-mous expenditure together gives aggregate planned expenditure. This aggregate expenditure schedule is shown in the figure as the aggregate expenditure curve AE_0. Initially, equilibrium occurs when real GDP is £600 billion. You can see this equilibrium in row d of the table, and in the figure where the curve AE_0 intersects the 45° line at point d.

Now suppose that autonomous expenditure increases by £120 billion to £480 billion. What is the new equilibrium? The answer is worked out in the final two columns of the table in Fig. 25.2. When the new level of autonomous expenditure is added to induced expenditure, aggregate planned expenditure increases by £120 billion at each level of real GDP. The new aggregate expenditure curve is AE_1. The new equilibrium, highlighted in the table (row e'), occurs where AE_1 intersects the 45° line and is at £800 billion (point e'). At this level of real GDP, aggregate planned expenditure is equal to real GDP. Autonomous expenditure is £480 billion and induced expenditure is £320 billion.

The Multiplier Effect

Notice in Fig. 25.2 that an increase in autonomous expenditure of £120 billion increases real GDP by

£200 billion. That is, the change in autonomous expenditure leads, like Mick Jagger's music-making equipment, to an amplified change in real GDP. This is the *multiplier effect* – real GDP increases by *more than* the increase in autonomous expenditure. An increase in autonomous expenditure of £120 billion initially increases aggregate expenditure and real GDP by £120 billion. But the increase in real GDP *induces* a further increase in aggregate expenditure – an increase in consumption expenditure minus imports. Aggregate expenditure and real GDP increase by the sum of the initial increase in autonomous expenditure and the increase in induced expenditure. In this example, induced expenditure increases by £80 billion, so real GDP increases by £200 billion.

Although we have just analysed the effects of an *increase* in autonomous expenditure, the same analysis applies to a decrease in autonomous expenditure. If autonomous expenditure is initially £480 billion, the initial equilibrium real GDP is £800 billion. If, in that situation, there is a cut in government purchases, exports, or investment of £120 billion, then the aggregate expenditure curve shifts downward by £120 billion to AE_0. Equilibrium real GDP decreases from £800 billion to £600 billion. The decrease in real GDP is larger than the decrease in autonomous expenditure.

We have seen that a change in autonomous expenditure has a multiplier effect on real GDP. But how big is the multiplier effect?

The Size of the Multiplier

Suppose that the economy is in a recession. Profit prospects start to look better and firms are making plans for large increases in investment. The world economy is also heading towards recovery, and exports are increasing. The question on everyone's lips is: how strong will the recovery be? This is a hard question to answer. But an important ingredient in the answer is working out the size of the multiplier.

The **autonomous expenditure multiplier** (often abbreviated to simply the **multiplier**) is the amount by which a change in autonomous expenditure is multiplied to determine the change in equilibrium expenditure that it generates. To calculate the multiplier, we divide the change in equilibrium real GDP by the change in autonomous expenditure. Let's calculate the multiplier for the

FIGURE 25.2

An Increase in Autonomous Expenditure

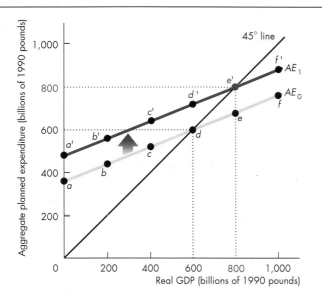

An increase in autonomous expenditure from £360 billion to £480 billion increases aggregate planned expenditure at each level of real GDP by £120 billion. As shown in the table, the initial equilibrium expenditure of £600 billion is no longer the equilibrium. At a real GDP of £600 billion, aggregate planned expenditure is now £720 billion. The new expenditure equilibrium is £800 billion, where aggregate planned expenditure equals real GDP. The increase in real GDP is larger than the increase in autonomous expenditure.

The figure illustrates the effect of the increase in autonomous expenditure. At each level of real GDP, aggregate planned expenditure is £120 billion higher than before. The aggregate planned expenditure curve shifts upward from AE_0 to AE_1 – a parallel shift. The new AE curve intersects the 45^0 line at e' where real GDP is £800 billion – the new equilibrium.

Real GDP (Y)	Induced expenditure (N)		Original			New	
			Autonomous expenditure (A_0)	Aggregate planned expenditure (AE_0)		Autonomous expenditure (A_1)	Aggregate planned expenditure (AE_1)
				(billions of 1990 pounds)			
0	0	a	360	360	a'	480	480
200	80	b	360	440	b'	480	560
400	160	c	360	520	c'	480	640
600	240	d	360	600	d'	480	720
800	320	e	360	680	e'	480	800
1,000	400	f	360	760	f'	480	880

example in Fig. 25.3(a). The economy in recession has a real GDP of £600 billion. Autonomous expenditure increases from £360 to £480 billion, and equilibrium real GDP increases from £600 billion to £800 billion, an increase of £200 billion. That is:

◆ Autonomous expenditure increases by £120 billion.
◆ Real GDP increases by £200 billion.

The multiplier is:

$$\text{Multiplier} = \frac{\text{Change in equilibrium real GDP}}{\text{Change in autonomous expenditure}}$$

$$= \frac{\text{£200 billion}}{\text{£120 billion}}$$

$$= 1.67.$$

FIGURE 25.3

The Multiplier and the Slope of the *AE* Curve

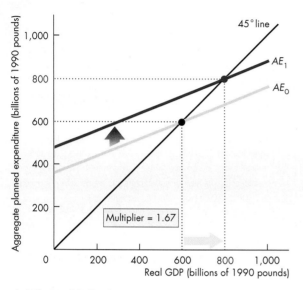

(a) The multiplier is 1.67

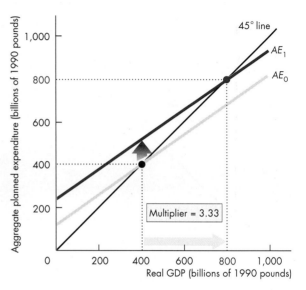

(b) The multiplier is 3.33

The size of the multiplier depends on the marginal propensity to buy domestic goods and services, g, which is also the slope of the *AE* curve. The multiplier formula, $1/(1-g)$, tells us the relationship. If the slope of the *AE* curve (g) is 0.4, the multiplier is 1.67. In this case, an increase of autonomous expenditure of £120 billion shifts the *AE* curve upward from AE_0 to AE_1 in part (a). Real GDP increases from £600 billion to £800 billion, 1.67 times the increase in

autonomous expenditure. If g equals 0.7, the multiplier is 3.33. In this case, a £120 billion increase in autonomous expenditure shifts the aggregate expenditure curve upward from AE_0 to AE_1 in part (b). Real GDP increases from £400 billion to £800 billion, 3.33 times the increase in autonomous expenditure.

Thus a change in autonomous expenditure of £120 billion produces a change in equilibrium real GDP of £200 billion, a change that is nearly double the initial change in autonomous expenditure.

Next look at Fig. 25.3(b). The economy in recession has a real GDP of £400 billion. But now, autonomous expenditure increases from £120 to £240 billion, and equilibrium real GDP increases from £400 billion to £800 billion, an increase of £400 billion. That is,

◆ Autonomous expenditure increases by £120 billion.
◆ Real GDP increases by £400 billion.

The multiplier is:

$$\text{Multiplier} = \frac{\text{Change in equilibrium real GDP}}{\text{Change in autonomous expenditure}}$$

$$= \frac{£400 \text{ billion}}{£120 \text{ billion}}$$

$$= 3.33.$$

Thus a change in autonomous expenditure of £1 billion produces a change in equilibrium real GDP of £3.33 billion.

TABLE 25.1

Calculating the Multiplier

	Symbols and Formulas*	Numbers
(a) DEFINITIONS		
Change in real GDP	ΔY	
Change in autonomous expenditure	ΔA	120
Slope of the *AE* curve	g	0.4
Change in induced expenditure	$\Delta N = g \Delta Y$	$\Delta N = (0.4)\Delta Y$
Change in aggregate planned expenditure	$\Delta E = \Delta A + \Delta N$	
The multiplier (autonomous expenditure multiplier)	$\Delta Y / \Delta A$	
(b) CALCULATIONS		
Aggregate planned expenditure	$E = A + gY$	
Change in *AE* curve	$\Delta E = \Delta A + g\Delta Y$	$\Delta E = 120 + (0.4)\Delta Y$
Change in equilibrium expenditure	$\Delta E = \Delta Y$	
Replacing ΔE with ΔY	$\Delta Y = \Delta A + g\Delta Y$	$\Delta Y = 120 + (0.4)\Delta Y$
Subtracting $g\Delta Y$ or $(0.4)\Delta Y$ from both sides and factoring ΔY	$\Delta Y(1 - g) = \Delta A$	$\Delta Y(1 - 0.4) = 120$
Dividing both sides by $(1 - g)$ or $(1 - 0.4)$	$\Delta Y = \dfrac{1}{1 - g} \Delta A$	$\Delta Y = \dfrac{1}{1 - 0.4}\, 120$
		or $\Delta Y = \dfrac{1}{(0.6)}\, 120$
		or $\Delta Y = 200$
Dividing both sides by ΔA or 120 gives the multiplier	$\dfrac{\Delta Y}{\Delta A} = \dfrac{1}{1 - g}$	$\dfrac{\Delta Y}{\Delta A} = \dfrac{200}{120} = 1.67$

*The Greek letter delta (Δ) stands for 'change in'.

The Multiplier and the Marginal Propensity to Buy Domestic Goods and Services

Why is the multiplier in Fig. 25.3(b) bigger than the multiplier in Fig. 25.3(a)? The reason is that the aggregate expenditure curve in part (b) is steeper than that in part (a). Equivalently, the marginal propensity to buy domestic goods and services is larger in part (b) than in part (a). The steeper the *AE* curve, the larger is the multiplier. In part (a), the slope of the *AE* curve is 0.4 and the multiplier is 1.67. In part (b), the slope of the *AE* curve is 0.7 and the multiplier is 3.33.

Multiplier Calculations Table 25.1 shows how to calculate the value of the multiplier. Part (a) introduces some definitions. It starts with the change in real GDP, ΔY. Our objective is to calculate the size of this change when there is a given change in autonomous expenditure, ΔA. In the example in Table 25.1, the change in autonomous expenditure is $120 billion. The slope of the aggregate expenditure curve is the marginal propensity to consume minus the marginal propensity to import. Let's call this slope g. In Table 25.1, g is equal to 0.4, the same as in Fig. 25.3(b). The change in aggregate planned expenditure (ΔE) is the sum of the change in

FIGURE 25.4

The Multiplier Process

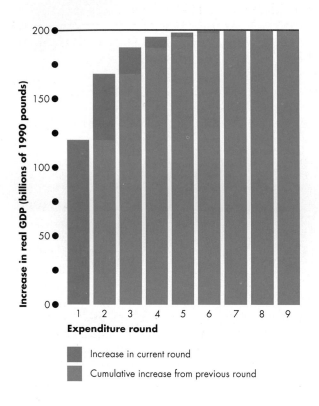

Expenditure round	Increase in aggregate expenditure	Cumulative increase in real GDP
	(billions of 1990 pounds)	
1	120.0	120.0
2	48.0	168.0
3	19.2	187.2
4	7.7	194.9
5	3.1	198.0
6	1.2	199.2
7	0.5	199.7
8	0.2	199.9
9	0.1	200.0

Autonomous expenditure increases in round 1 by £120 billion. Real GDP also increases by the same amount. Each additional pound of real GDP induces an additional 0.4 of a pound of aggregate expenditure – the slope of the aggregate expenditure curve is 0.4. In round 2, the round 1 increase in real GDP induces an increase in expenditure of £48 billion. At the end of round 2, real GDP has increased by £168 billion. The extra £48 billion of real GDP in round 2 induces a further increase in expenditure of £19.2 billion in round 3. Real GDP increases yet further to £187.2 billion. This process continues until real GDP has eventually increased by £200 billion.

autonomous expenditure (ΔA) and the change in induced expenditure (ΔN). Finally, the multiplier is defined as

$$\frac{\Delta Y}{\Delta A}.$$

Part (b) of the table sets out the calculations of the change in real GDP and the multiplier. The change in aggregate planned expenditure (ΔE) is equal to the sum of the change in autonomous expenditure (ΔA) and the change in induced expenditure ($g\Delta Y$). In the example, the change in aggregate planned expenditure is equal to £120 billion plus 0.4 of the change in real GDP. Since in equilibrium the change in aggregate planned

expenditure is equal to the change in real GDP, the change in real GDP is

$$\Delta Y = \Delta A + g\Delta Y.$$

Using our numbers,

$$\Delta Y = 120 + (0.4)\Delta Y.$$

This equation has just one unknown, ΔY, and we can find its value as shown in the next two rows of the table. Finally, dividing ΔY by ΔA gives the value of the multiplier, which is

$$\text{Multiplier} = \frac{1}{10\,(1-g)}.$$

Because g is a fraction – a number lying between 0

and 1 – so $(1 - g)$ is also a fraction and the multiplier is greater than 1. In the example, g is 0.4, $(1 - g)$ is 0.6, and the multiplier is $1 \div 0.6$, which is 1.67.

You can see that this formula works for the multiplier shown in Fig. 25.3(a). In this case, the marginal propensity to buy domestic goods and services is 0.7, g is 0.7, $(1 - g)$ is 0.3, and the multiplier is 3.33.

Why is the Multiplier Greater than 1?

The multiplier is greater than 1 because of induced expenditure – an increase in autonomous expenditure *induces* further increases in expenditure. If Vauxhall spends £10 million on a new car assembly line, aggregate expenditure and real GDP immediately increase by £10 million. But that is not the end of the story. Engineers and construction workers now have more income, and they spend part of the extra income on cars, microwaves, holidays and a host of other goods and services. Real GDP now rises by the initial £10 million plus the extra expenditure induced by the £10 million increase in income. The producers of cars, microwaves, holidays and other goods now have increased incomes, and they, in turn, also spend part of their increase in income on consumption goods and services. Additional income induces additional expenditure, which creates additional income.

This multiplier process is illustrated in Fig. 25.4. In this example, the marginal propensity to buy domestic goods and services (and the slope of the *AE* curve) is 0.4 as in Fig. 25.3(b). In round 1, there is an increase in autonomous expenditure of £120 billion. At that stage, there is no change in induced expenditure, so aggregate expenditure and real GDP increase by £120 billion. In round 2, the higher real GDP induces higher consumption expenditure. Since induced expenditure increases by 0.4 times the increase in real GDP, the increase in real GDP of £120 billion induces a further increase in expenditure of £48 billion. This change in induced expenditure, when added to the initial change in autonomous expenditure, results in an increase in aggregate expenditure and real GDP of £168 billion.

The round 2 increase in real GDP induces a round 3 increase in expenditure. The process repeats through successive rounds recorded in the table. Each increase in real GDP is 0.4 times the previous increase. The cumulative increase in real GDP gradually approaches £200 billion. After 9 rounds, it is within £0.1 billion of that level.

It appears, then, that the economy does not operate like the shock absorbers on Saunders' car. The economy's potholes and bumps are changes in autonomous expenditure – mainly brought about by changes in investment and exports. These economic potholes and bumps are not smoothed out, but instead are amplified.

REVIEW

Autonomous expenditure is the part of aggre gate expenditure that does not respond to changes in real GDP. Induced expenditure is the part of aggregate expenditure that does respond to changes in real GDP. A change in autonomous expenditure changes equilibrium expenditure and real GDP. The magnitude of the change in real GDP is determined by the multiplier. The multiplier, in turn, is determined by the marginal propensity to buy domestic goods and services (the slope of the aggregate expenditure curve), which equals the marginal propensity to consume out of real GDP minus the marginal propensity to import. The larger the marginal propensity to buy domestic goods and services, the larger is the multiplier. The multiplier acts like an amplifier. ◆

One component of autonomous expenditure that the multiplier amplifies is government purchases of goods and services. The government can take advantage of this fact and try to smooth out fluctuations in aggregate expenditure. It can also vary transfer payments and taxes. Let's now look at multipliers associated with the government's policy.

Fiscal Policy Multipliers

Fiscal policy is the government's attempt to smooth the fluctuations in aggregate expenditure by varying its purchases of goods and services, transfer payments and taxes. If the government foresees a decline in investment or exports, it may attempt to offset the effects of the decline by increasing its own purchases of goods and services, increasing transfer payments, or cutting taxes. But the government must work out the size of the increase in purchases or transfers or the size of the tax cut needed to achieve its goal. To make this calculation, the government needs to know the multiplier effects of its own actions. Let's study the multiplier effects of changes in government purchases, transfer payments and taxes.

Government Purchases Multiplier

The **government purchases multiplier** is the amount by which a change in government purchases of goods and services is multiplied to determine the change in equilibrium expenditure that it generates. Government purchases of goods and services are one component of autonomous expenditure. A change in government purchases has the same effect on aggregate expenditure as a change in any other component of autonomous expenditure. It sets up a multiplier effect exactly like the multiplier effect of a change in investment or exports. That is,

$$\text{Government purchases multiplier} = \frac{1}{(1-g)}.$$

By varying government purchases to offset a change in investment or exports the government can attempt to keep total autonomous expenditure constant (or growing at a steady rate). Because the government purchases multiplier is the same size as the investment and exports multipliers, stabilization of autonomous expenditure can be achieved by increasing government purchases by £1 for each £1 decrease in the other items of autonomous expenditure.

In practice, using variations in government purchases to stabilize aggregate expenditure is not easy because the political decision process operates with a long time lag. As a consequence, it is not possible to forecast changes in private expenditure far enough ahead to make this macroeconomic stabilization instrument as effective as it might otherwise be. This issue is also considered in Reading Between the Lines on pp 714–715.

A second way in which the government might seek to stabilize aggregate expenditure is by varying transfer payments – the flows of money from the government to households and firms such as pensions, unemployment benefits and subsidies. Let's see how this type of policy works.

Transfer Payments Multiplier

The **transfer payments multiplier** is the amount by which a change in transfer payments is multiplied to determine the change in equilibrium expenditure that it generates. A change in transfer payments influences aggregate expenditure by changing disposable income, which leads to a change in consumption expenditure. This change in consumption expenditure is a change in autonomous expenditure, and it has a multiplier effect exactly like that of any other change in autono-mous expenditure. But how large is the initial change in consumption expenditure? It is equal to the change in transfer payments multiplied by the marginal propensity to buy domestic goods and services. Let's see why.

An additional pound of transfer payments leads to an increase in consumption expenditure of an amount determined by the marginal propensity to consume out of real GDP. But part of that additional consumption expenditure is on imported goods and services. The amount of the additional imports is determined by the marginal propensity to import. So the additional autonomous expenditure is determined by the marginal propensity to buy domestic goods and services, g.

The increase in autonomous expenditure that results from an increase in transfer payments is equal to g times the autonomous expenditure multiplier. That is,

$$\text{Transfer payments multiplier} = \frac{g}{(1-g)}.$$

In our example, the marginal propensity to buy domestic goods and services is 0.4, so the transfer payments multiplier is 0.67 (0.4/0.6 = 0.67).

The use of variations in transfer payments to stabilize the economy has the same problems as the use of variations in government purchases of goods and services. Time lags in the political decision process make it difficult to adjust transfer payments quickly enough to offset fluctuations in other components of autonomous expenditure.

Tax Multipliers

A third type of fiscal stabilization policy is to vary taxes. The **tax multiplier** is the amount by which a change in taxes is multiplied to determine the change in equilibrium expenditure that it generates. An *increase* in taxes leads to a *decrease* in disposable income and a decrease in consumption expenditure. The amount by which consumption expenditure decreases initially is determined by the marginal propensity to consume. This initial response of consumption expenditure to a tax increase is exactly the same as the response of consumption expenditure to a decrease in transfer payments. Thus a change in taxes works like a change in transfer payments but in the opposite direction, and the tax multiplier equals the negative of the transfer payments multiplier. Because a tax *increase* leads to a *decrease* in equilibrium expenditure, the tax multiplier is *negative*. It is:

$$\text{Tax multiplier} = \frac{-g}{(1-g)}.$$

Figure 25.5 illustrates the multiplier effect of an increase in taxes (or a decrease in transfer payments). Initially, the aggregate expenditure curve is AE_0 and equilibrium expenditure is £600 billion. The slope of the aggregate expenditure curve AE_0 is 0.4. Taxes increase by £120 billion and disposable income falls by that amount. With a marginal propensity to buy domestic goods and services of 0.4, consumption expenditure decreases initially by £48 billion and the aggregate expenditure curve shifts downward by that amount to AE_1. Equilibrium expenditure and real GDP fall by £80 billion to £520 billion. The tax multiplier is –0.67.

The use of variations in taxes to stabilize the economy has the same problems as the use of variations in government purchases of goods and services – time lags in the political decision process. Despite this, the UK government introduced major tax reforms during the 1980s with the goal of stimulating the economy in the long run.

Balanced Budget Multiplier

A balanced budget fiscal policy action is one that keeps the government budget deficit or surplus unchanged – both government purchases and taxes change by the same amount. The **balanced budget multiplier** is the amount by which a change in government purchases of goods and services is multiplied to determine the change in expenditure equilibrium when taxes are changed by the same amount as the change in government purchases. What is the multiplier effect of this fiscal policy action?

To find out, we must combine the two multipliers that we have just worked out. We've seen that those two separate multipliers are:

FIGURE 25.5

The Tax Multiplier

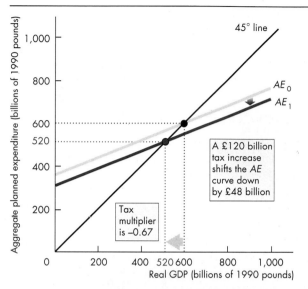

Initially, the aggregate expenditure curve is AE_0, and equilibrium expenditure is £600 billion. The marginal propensity to buy domestic goods and services is 0.4. Taxes are increased by £120 billion, so autonomous expenditure decreases by £48 billion and the aggregate expenditure curve shifts downward by this amount to AE_1. Equilibrium expenditure and real GDP decrease by £80 billion to £520 billion. The tax multiplier is –0.67.

$$\text{Government purchases multiplier} = \frac{1}{(1-g)}$$

$$\text{Tax multiplier} = \frac{-g}{(1-g)}.$$

Adding these two multipliers together gives the balanced budget multiplier, which is:

$$\text{Balanced budget multiplier} = \frac{(1-g)}{(1-g)}$$
$$= 1.$$

Figure 25.6 illustrates the balanced budget multiplier. Initially, the aggregate expenditure curve is AE_0 and real GDP is £600 billion. A £120 billion increase in taxes decreases aggregate planned expenditure by £48 billion and shifts the aggregate expenditure curve downward to AE_0'. A £120 billion increase in government purchases increases aggregate planned expenditure by the entire £120 billion and shifts the aggregate expenditure curve upward to AE_1. The net

FIGURE 25.6

The Balanced Budget Multiplier

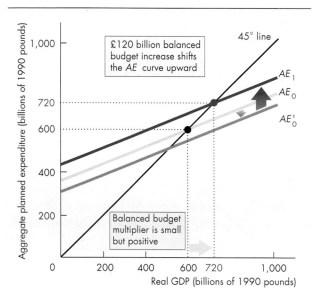

Initially, the aggregate expenditure curve is AE_0. The government increases both taxes and purchases of goods and services by £120 billion. The £120 billion tax increase shifts the aggregate expenditure curve downward by £48 billion to AE_0'. The £120 billion increase in government purchases shifts the aggregate expenditure curve upward by the entire £120 billion to AE_1. Real GDP increases by £120 billion – the balanced budget multiplier is 1.

shift in the aggregate expenditure curve is upward by £72 billion. The new equilibrium occurs at the intersection of AE_1 and the 45° line. Real GDP increases by £72 billion times the autonomous expenditure multiplier of 1.67, or £120 billion. But this amount is the same as the increase in government purchases and taxes. So the balanced budget multiplier is 1.

The balanced budget multiplier is important because it means that the government does not have to unbalance its budget and run a deficit in order to stimulate aggregate demand.

R E V I E W

The government purchases multiplier is equal to the autonomous expenditure multiplier. By varying its purchases of goods and services, the government can try to balance out the fluctuations in

investment and exports so as to keep aggregate expenditure steady. The transfer payments multiplier is equal to the marginal propensity to buy domestic goods and services multiplied by the government purchases multiplier. A change in transfer payments works through a change in disposable income. Part of the change in disposable income is spent on domestic goods and services, part is saved, and part is spent on imports. Only the part that is spent on domestic goods and services, determined by the marginal propensity to buy domestic goods and services, has a multiplier effect. ◆ ◆ The tax multiplier has the same magnitude as the transfer payments multiplier but it is negative – a tax *increase* leads to a *decrease* in equilibrium expenditure. An equal change in both purchases of goods and services and taxes has a balanced budget multiplier effect on real GDP. The balanced budget multiplier is 1. This means that the government can stimulate aggregate demand without unbalancing the budget. In practice, fiscal actions are difficult to use to stabilize the economy because of time lags in the legislative process. ◆

Automatic Stabilizers

Income taxes and transfer payments act as automatic stabilizers. An **automatic stabilizer** is a mechanism that decreases the fluctuations in *aggregate* expenditure resulting from fluctuations in a *component* of aggregate expenditure. The automatic stabilizing effects of income taxes and transfer payments means that they act like an economic shock absorber, making the effects of fluctuations in investment and exports smaller than they otherwise would be.

The scale of income taxes minus transfer payments is determined by the marginal tax rate. The **marginal tax rate** is the fraction of the last pound of income paid to the government in net taxes (taxes minus transfer payments).

The higher the marginal tax rate, the larger is the proportion of the last pound of real GDP that is paid to the government. And the larger the proportion of the last pound of real GDP paid to the government, the smaller is the marginal propensity to buy domestic goods and services.

To see how income taxes and transfer payments act as an economic shock absorber, let's see how a change in investment or exports affects equilibrium expenditure in two economies: in the first economy there are no income taxes and transfer payments, and in the second there are income taxes and transfer payments similar to those in the United Kingdom today.

No Income Taxes and Transfer Payments   An economy with no income taxes and transfer payments has a high marginal propensity to buy domestic goods and services. Suppose that the marginal propensity to buy domestic goods and services is 0.9. What is the size of the multiplier in this case? You can answer by using the formula

$$\text{Multiplier} = \frac{1}{(1-g)}.$$

The value of g is 0.9, so the multiplier is 10. In this economy, a £1 billion change in autonomous expenditure produces a £10 billion change in equilibrium expenditure. This economy has a very strong amplifier.

Income Taxes and Transfer Payments   Contrast the economy that we have just described with one that has income taxes and transfer payments and, therefore, a low marginal propensity to buy domestic goods and services, g. Suppose that g is 0.4. Then the multiplier is 1.67. The economy still amplifies shocks from changes in exports and investment, but on a much smaller scale than the economy with no income taxes and transfer payments. Thus to some degree, income taxes and transfer payments absorb the shocks of the fluctuations in autonomous expenditure. The higher the marginal tax rate, the greater is the extent to which autonomous expenditure shocks are absorbed.

The existence of taxes and transfer payments helps the shock-absorbing capacities of the economy. They don't produce the economic equivalent of the suspension of a Rolls-Royce, but they do produce the economic equivalent of something better than the springs of a stagecoach. As the economy fluctuates, the government's budget fluctuates, absorbing some of the shocks, changing taxes and transfer payments and smoothing the fluctuations in disposable income and aggregate expenditure.

Let's look at the effects of automatic stabilizers on the government's budget and its deficit or surplus.

Automatic Stabilizers and the Government Budget

Because taxes and transfer payments fluctuate with real GDP, so does the government's budget deficit or

surplus. Figure 25.7 shows how. Government purchases are independent of real GDP. In the figure, they are fixed at £100 billion – shown by the horizontal red line. Taxes net of transfer payments increase as real GDP increases. In the figure, they are shown by the upward-sloping blue line. There is a particular level of real GDP at which the government's budget is balanced – the deficit is zero. In the figure, that real GDP is £600 billion. When real GDP is less than £600 billion, there is a deficit. When real GDP exceeds £600 billion, there is a surplus.

As investment and exports fluctuate, bringing fluctuations in real GDP, taxes and the deficit also fluctuate. For example, a large increase in investment increases real GDP, increases taxes and reduces the deficit (or creates a surplus). The higher taxes act as an automatic stabilizer. They decrease disposable income and induce a decrease in consumption expenditure. This decrease dampens the effects of the initial

FIGURE 25.7

The Government Deficit

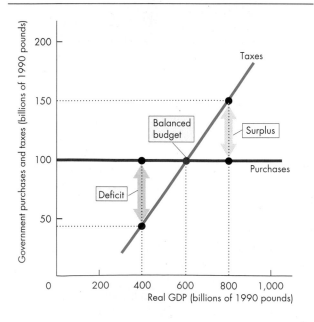

Government purchases (the red line) are independent of the level of real GDP but income taxes (the blue line) increase as real GDP increases. When real GDP is £600 billion, the government's budget is balanced. When real GDP is below £600 billion, there is a deficit, and when real GDP is above £600 billion, there is a surplus. Fluctuations in taxes act as an automatic stabilizer when the economy is hit by changes in autonomous expenditure.

increase in investment and moderates the increase in aggregate expenditure and real GDP.

Conversely, when a large decrease in investment is pushing the economy into recession, taxes decrease and the deficit increases (or the surplus decreases). The lower taxes act as an automatic stabilizer. They limit the fall in disposable income and moderate the extent of the decline in aggregate expenditure and real GDP.

R E V I E W

The presence of income taxes and transfer payments that vary with real GDP reduces the value of the multiplier and acts as an automatic stabilizer. The higher the marginal tax rate, the smaller are the fluctuations in real GDP resulting from fluctuations in autonomous expenditure. ◆

We have studied the effects of changes in autonomous expenditure and fiscal policy on real GDP, *at a given price level*. We're now going to see how the price level itself responds to changes in autonomous expenditure and fiscal policy. We're also going to see that the autonomous expenditure and fiscal policy multiplier effects on real GDP are smaller when price level changes are taken into account.

Multipliers and the Price Level

To see how big the multiplier is when we take changes in the price level into account, we use the aggregate demand–aggregate supply model. You learned about the relationship between the aggregate demand curve, the aggregate expenditure curve and the equilibrium level of aggregate expenditure in Chapter 24. You are now going to use what you learned there to work out what happens to aggregate demand, the price level and real GDP when fiscal policy changes. We'll start by looking at the effects of a change in fiscal policy on aggregate demand.

Fiscal Policy and Aggregate Demand

When the price level changes, other things remaining the same, the aggregate expenditure curve shifts and there is a movement along the aggregate demand curve. When any other influence on aggregate expenditure changes, both the aggregate expenditure curve and the aggregate demand curve shift. It is these other influences on aggregate expenditure (and sources of shifts in the aggregate expenditure curve) that you've been studying earlier in this chapter – for example, a change in investment, exports and fiscal policy. Figure 25.8 illustrates these shifts.

Initially the aggregate expenditure curve is AE_0 in part (a) and the aggregate demand curve is AD_0 in part (b). The price level is 130, real GDP is £600 billion and the economy is at point a in both parts of the figure. Now suppose that autonomous expenditure increases by £120 billion. (This increase could result from an increase in investment, exports, or government purchases of goods and services or a tax cut.) At a constant price level of 130, the aggregate expenditure curve shifts upward to AE_1. This curve intersects the 45° line at an equilibrium expenditure of £800 billion (point b). This amount is the aggregate quantity of goods and services demanded at a price level of 130, as shown by point b in part (b). Point b lies on a new aggregate demand curve. The aggregate demand curve has shifted to the right to AD_1.

The distance by which the aggregate demand curve shifts to the right is determined by the multiplier. The larger the multiplier, the larger is the shift in the aggregate demand curve resulting from a given change in autonomous expenditure. In this example, a £120 billion increase in autonomous expenditure produces a £200 billion increase in the aggregate quantity of goods and services demanded at each price level. The multiplier is 1.67. That is, a £1 billion increase in autonomous expenditure shifts the aggregate demand curve to the right by £1.67 billion.

A decrease in autonomous expenditure shifts the aggregate expenditure curve downward and shifts the aggregate demand curve to the left. You can see these effects by reversing the change that we've just studied. Suppose that the economy initially is on aggregate expenditure curve AE_1 and aggregate demand curve AD_1. There is then a decrease in autonomous expenditure and the aggregate planned expenditure curve shifts downward to AE_0. The aggregate quantity of goods and services demanded falls to £600 billion and the

FIGURE 25.8

Autonomous Expenditure and Aggregate Demand

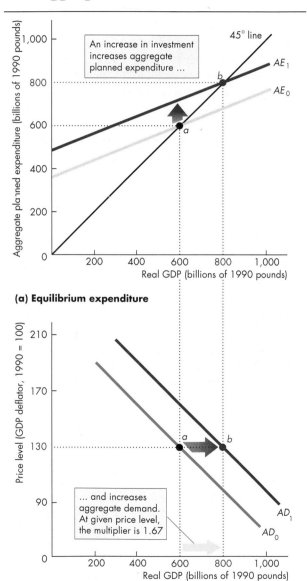

(a) Equilibrium expenditure

(b) Aggregate demand

The price level is 130. When the aggregate expenditure curve is AE_0 (part a), the aggregate demand curve is AD_0 (part b). An increase in autonomous expenditure shifts the aggregate expenditure upward to AE_1. In the new equilibrium (at b) real GDP is £800 billion. Since the quantity of real GDP demanded at a price level of 130 increases to £800 billion, the aggregate demand curve shifts to the right to AD_1.

aggregate demand curve shifts to the left to AD_0.

We can summarize what we have just discovered in the following way: an increase in autonomous expenditure arising from some source other than a change in the price level shifts the AE curve upward and shifts the AD curve to the right. The magnitude of the shift of the AD curve is determined by the change in autonomous expenditure and the autonomous expenditure multiplier.

Equilibrium GDP and the Price Level

In Chapter 23, we learned how to determine the equilibrium levels of real GDP and the price level as the intersection point of the aggregate demand and short-run aggregate supply curves. We've now put aggregate demand under a more powerful microscope and discovered that changes in autonomous expenditure and fiscal policy shift the aggregate demand curve and that the magnitude of the shift depends on the multiplier. But whether a change in autonomous expenditure results ultimately in a change in real GDP or a change in the price level or some combination of the two depends on aggregate supply. We'll look at two cases. First we'll see what happens in the short run. Then we'll look at the long run.

An Increase in Aggregate Demand in the Short Run   The economy is described in Fig. 25.9. In part (a), the aggregate expenditure curve is AE_0, and equilibrium expenditure and real GDP are £600 billion – point a. In part (b), aggregate demand is AD_0, and the short-run aggregate supply curve is SAS. (Check back to Chapter 23 if you need to refresh your understanding of this curve.) Equilibrium is at point a, where the aggregate demand and short-run aggregate supply curves intersect. The price level is 130 and real GDP is £600 billion.

Now suppose there is a tax cut that increases autonomous expenditure by £120 billion. With the price level held constant at 130, the aggregate expenditure curve shifts upward to AE_1. Equilibrium expenditure and real GDP increase to £800 billion – point b in part (a). In part (b), the aggregate demand curve shifts to the right by £200 billion, from AD_0 to AD_1. But with this new aggregate demand curve, the price level does not remain constant. It increases to 143, as determined by the point of intersection of the short-run aggregate supply curve and the new aggregate demand curve – point c. And real GDP does not increase to £800 billion, but to £733 billion.

FIGURE 25.9

Fiscal Policy, Real GDP and the Price Level

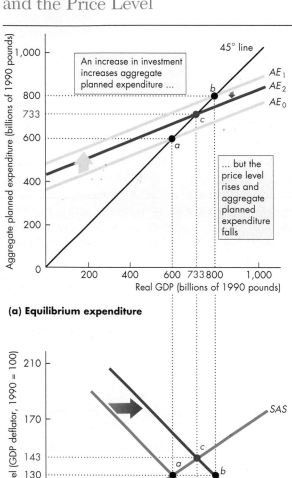

(a) Equilibrium expenditure

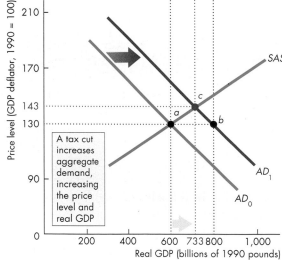

(b) Aggregate demand

A tax cut shifts the AE curve upward from AE_0 to AE_1 (part a). The AD curve shifts from AD_0 to AD_1 (part b). The economy moves from point a to point b (parts a and b), and there is excess demand. The price level rises, and the higher price level shifts the AE curve downward to AE_2. The economy moves to point c in both parts. The steeper the SAS curve, the larger is the effect on the price level change and the smaller is the change in real GDP.

At a price level of 143, the aggregate expenditure curve does not remain at AE_1 in part (a). It shifts downward to AE_2, which intersects the 45° line at a level of aggregate expenditure and real GDP of £733 billion (point c).

Taking price level effects into account, the tax cut still has a multiplier effect on real GDP, but the effect is smaller than it would be if the price level remained constant. The steeper the slope of the short-run aggregate supply curve, the larger is the increase in the price level and the smaller is the multiplier effect on real GDP.

An Increase in Aggregate Demand in the Long Run In the long run, the economy is at full-employment equilibrium and on its long-run aggregate supply curve. When the economy is at full employment, an increase in aggregate demand has the same initial effect (short-run effect) as we've just worked out, but its long-run effect is different.

To see the long-run effect, suppose that in Fig. 25.9 long-run aggregate supply is £600 billion. When aggregate demand increases, shifting the aggregate demand curve from AD_0 to AD_1, the equilibrium at point c is an above full-employment equilibrium. When the labour force is more than fully employed, there are shortages of labour and wages increase. Higher wages bring higher costs and a decrease in aggregate supply. The result is a further increase in the price level and a decrease in real GDP. Eventually, when wage rates and the price level have increased by the same percentage, real GDP is again at its full-employment level. The multiplier in the long run is zero.

We've now seen how fiscal policy multipliers can be used by the government to influence real GDP and the price level. But so far we have studied model economies. Let's now turn to the real world. How big is the multiplier in the United Kingdom?

The Multiplier in the United Kingdom

I n the model economy that we studied earlier in this chapter each additional pound of income induces 40 pence of expenditure. Its multiplier is 1.67. Let's look at some estimates of the multiplier in the United Kingdom.

The Multiplier in 1993

In 1993, the marginal propensity to consume out of disposable income in the United Kingdom was approximately 0.89 and disposable income was 0.73 GDP (since 27 per cent of income was paid in net taxes). Putting these two pieces of information together, we can calculate that the marginal propensity to consume out of GDP is 0.65 (0.89 × 0.73 = 0.65). Imports were 28 per cent of GDP. Using this percentage as an estimate of the marginal propensity to import gives a value of 0.28; each additional pound of GDP induces 28 pence of imports. Subtracting the marginal propensity to import from the marginal propensity to consume out of GDP gives the slope of the *AE* curve, which is 0.37 (that is 0.65 minus 0.28). The multiplier is 1.59. That is,

$$\text{The multiplier} = \frac{1}{1-0.37} = \frac{1}{0.63} = 1.59.$$

This multiplier formula tells us how far the *AD* curve shifts when autonomous expenditure changes. But it does not tell us about the effect on real GDP when induced price level changes are taken into account. To calculate such a multiplier, we must use the estimates made by large-scale models of the UK economy.

Econometric Models and the Multiplier

An **econometric model** is a model economy with numerical values for the marginal propensities to consume and import, and for other economic parameters, which are estimated from the data for an actual economy. Today, many such models are in use. Most of them are commercial tools that produce forecasts used by businesses and governments. But the prototypes from which the commercial models were developed were created by research economists working in the universities, the Bank of England, the Treasury and the National Institute for Economic and Social Research. The six main models, together with their estimates of the UK multiplier, are set out in Table 25.2.

The six models tell divergent stories about the UK multiplier. The largest estimate is that of the Oxford Economic Forecasting model at 1.60 and the smallest is that of the Bank of England model at 0.74. The estimate that we obtained in the previous section is similar to that of the Oxford Economic Forecasting model. The reason for different estimates of the

TABLE 25.2

Six Econometric Models, Estimates of the UK Multiplier

Model	Multiplier
LBS: London Business School	1.14
NIESR: National Institute for Economic and Social Research	1.40
HMT: Her Majesty's Treasury	0.98
BE: Bank of England	0.74
OEF: Oxford Economic Forecasting	1.60
STR: Strathclyde University	1.48

Six econometric models estimate that the UK multiplier lies between 0.74 and 1.60. Different estimates arise mainly because the models contain different assumptions about the structure of the economy.

Source: K. B. Church, P. R. Mitchell, P. N. Smith and K. F. Wallis 'Comparative Properties of Models of the UK Economy', *National Institute Economic Review*, Number 145, August 1993, pp. 87–107.

multiplier is that the models incorporate different assumptions about the influences on the components of aggregate expenditure. What one model assumes is a movement along the consumption function, another model assumes a shift of the consumption function. As a consequence, estimates of the marginal propensity to consume and therefore of the multiplier differ.

The Multiplier in Recession and Recovery

The multiplier tends to be smaller when the economy goes into recession than it is in recovery. The reason is that there are cycles in the marginal propensity to consume. Consumption expenditure depends on both current disposable income and expected future disposable income. Therefore the effect of a change in current disposable income on consumption expenditure depends on whether the change is expected to be permanent or temporary. The effects of a change in current disposable income that is expected to be permanent is larger

Tax Rises and the End of the Recession

THE TIMES, 25 JANUARY 1994

CBI says tax rises will curb recovery

Philip Bassett, Industrial Editor

BUSINESS leaders warned yesterday that the Government's planned tax rises would dampen economic recovery as the latest industrial survey suggested that the economy is now growing steadily....

Calculations published by the CBI yesterday suggested that tax rises and the Government's cuts in spending would remove 2.1 and 2.6 per cent respectively of gross domestic product from the economy in 1994–95 and 1995–96. The CBI acknowledged that the reduction of purchasing power could mean consumer demand might falter. But the confederation said that brighter job prospects and a more stable housing market may help to counteract the effects of higher tax bills.

The CBI gave warning, too, that if sterling continued to strengthen it could erode some of the competitive advantages gained since Britain withdrew from the ERM in 1992.

The confederation's industrial trends survey showed that manufacturing orders and output grew over the past four months, accompanied by a rise in export orders and deliveries: The outlook is stronger, too, and unit costs fell at the sharpest rate since the survey began in 1958.

...Leaders of the Building Employers Confederation said that the increase in new business enquiries indicated clearly that the trading climate was at last beginning to improve. But they said they remained cautious.

The upbeat note of the CBI and the building industry contrasted with a survey last week from the British Chambers of Commerce, which suggested that the recovery was in doubt. Principal findings of the CBI's survey of 1,180 manufacturing companies covering two million employees included:

☐ Output. Over the past four months, output rose at the highest rate since July 1989, with a balance of 9 per cent of companies recording a rise in output volumes.

☐ Orders. Orders rose more quickly than expected, to a balance of 11 per cent.

☐ Investment. Companies are planning to invest for the first time since July 1989. A balance of 7 per cent expect to invest in plant and machinery over the next 12 months.

☐ Employment. The fall in jobs was the slowest since jobs started to be cut in October 1989. A balance of 16 per cent of companies still expect to cut jobs, which the CBI said would lead to 27,000 lost jobs in manufacturing in the first quarter of this year.

© The Times. Reprinted with permission.

The Confederation of British Industry (CBI) has estimated that the government's planned tax increases and public expenditure cuts will restrict growth by nearly 5 per cent of GDP over the next two years, thus limiting the economic recovery now under way.

In addition, if the pound continues to appreciate, the gains in international competitiveness made following the withdrawal of the pound from the ERM in 1992 would be reduced.

The CBI suggests that a more stable job market, where people's fears of redundancy are reduced, will help to increase consumer confidence and offset the negative impact on spending of the tax rises.

The CBI survey of over 1,100 companies suggested that output and orders were rising strongly, investment was again being planned by firms, the fall in employment was slowing, unit costs were falling and confidence was up.

In order to cut its deficit, the government has planned a series of tax increases, as well as cuts in its own spending.

A cut in government expenditure will shift the aggregate expenditure *(AE)* curve downward. A tax increase will also shift the *AE* curve downward. Both policy changes will work together to cut equilibrium expenditure.

Higher producer confidence will increase investment expenditure and higher consumer confidence will increase induced consumption expenditure. As a result, the *AE* curve will shift upward.

The net effect of these various pressures will be magnified through the economy via the multiplier.

In perceiving the economy to be coming out of recession, the CBI sees the net effect on aggregate expenditure to be positive, that is the *AE* curve will shift upward, increasing equilibrium expenditure and the level of real GDP.

The CBI is concerned about lower government expenditures, higher taxes and a rise in the pound. The combined effect of these factors is to restrict the upward movement in aggregate expenditure, and to lower the value of the multiplier in the economy.

In the figure, the higher potential increase in real GDP (AE_2) over the initial position AE_0 is compared with the lower figure (AE_1), realized as a consequence of the tax rises and expenditure cuts. The multiplier, k, is

$$k = \frac{\Delta Y}{\Delta A} = 1 - \varepsilon$$

where ΔY is the change in real GDP, ΔA is the change in autonomous expenditure and ε is the marginal propensity to buy domestic goods and services.

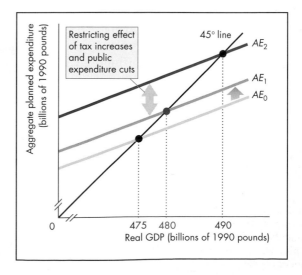

than the effect of a change that is expected to be temporary. That is, the marginal propensity to consume is larger when there is a permanent change in income than when income changes temporarily. For this reason, the marginal propensity to consume varies and in a way that is connected with the business cycle.

At the start of a recovery, income gains are expected to be permanent and the marginal propensity to consume is high. When a business cycle peak is approached, and during recessions, income changes are expected to be temporary and the marginal propensity to consume falls.

◆ ◆ ◆ ◆ We have now studied the forces that influence the components of aggregate expenditure and analysed the way the components interact with each other to determine aggregate expenditure and the position of the aggregate demand curve. We've seen that fluctuations in equilibrium expenditure and shifts in the aggregate demand curve are caused by fluctuations in autonomous expenditure. An important element of autonomous expenditure is investment, which in turn is determined by, among other things, interest rates. But what determines interest rates? That is the question to which we turn in the next two chapters.

S U M M A R Y

Expenditure Multipliers

Aggregate expenditure is divided into two components: autonomous expenditure and induced expenditure. Autonomous expenditure is the sum of investment, government purchases, exports and the part of consumption expenditure that does not vary with income. Induced expenditure is the part of consumption expenditure that does vary with income minus imports.

An increase in autonomous expenditure increases aggregate planned expenditure and shifts the aggregate expenditure curve upward. Equilibrium expenditure and real GDP increase by more than the increase in autonomous expenditure. They do so because the increased autonomous expenditure induces an increase in consumption expenditure. Aggregate expenditure increases by the sum of the initial increase in autonomous expenditure and the increase in induced expenditure.

The autonomous expenditure multiplier (or simply the multiplier) is the change in equilibrium real GDP divided by the change in autonomous expenditure that brought it about. The size of the multiplier depends on the slope of the AE curve (g), and its value is given by the formula

$$\text{Multiplier} = \frac{1}{(1-g)}.$$

Because g is a number between 0 and 1, the multiplier is greater than 1. The larger the value of g,

the larger is the multiplier. The multiplier is greater than 1 because of induced expenditure – because an increase in autonomous expenditure induces an increase in consumption expenditure. (pp. 698–705)

Fiscal Policy Multipliers

There are three main fiscal policy multipliers:

◆ Government purchases multiplier
◆ Transfer payments multiplier
◆ Tax multiplier

The government purchases multiplier is the amount by which a change in government purchases of goods and services is multiplied to determine the change in equilibrium expenditure that it generates. Because government purchases of goods and services are one of the components of autonomous expenditure, this multiplier is equal to the autonomous expenditure multiplier. That is,

$$\text{Government purchases multiplier} = \frac{1}{(1-g)}.$$

The transfer payments multiplier is the amount by which a change in transfer payments is multiplied to determine the change in equilibrium expenditure that it generates. Because a change in transfer payments influences aggregate expenditure by changing disposable income, this multiplier is equal to the marginal propensity to buy domestic goods and services (g) multiplied by the autonomous expenditure multiplier. That is,

$$\text{Transfer payments multiplier} = \frac{g}{(1-g)}.$$

The tax multiplier is the amount by which a change in taxes is multiplied to determine the change in equilibrium expenditure that it generates. A tax increase brings a decrease in equilibrium expenditure. The initial response of consumption expenditure to a tax increase is exactly the same as its response to a decrease in transfer payments. Thus a tax change works like a change in transfer payments but its multiplier is negative. That is,

$$\text{Tax multiplier} = \frac{-g}{(1-g)}.$$

If both government purchases of goods and services and taxes are changed together and by the same amount, there is a balanced budget multiplier that combines the two separate multipliers. The balanced budget multiplier is:

$$\text{Balanced budget multiplier} = \frac{(1-g)}{(1-g)}$$

which equals 1.

The tax and transfer payments system acts as an automatic stabilizer – a mechanism that decreases the fluctuations in aggregate expenditure. (pp. 705–710)

Multipliers and the Price Level

A change in autonomous expenditure not caused by a change in the price level shifts the aggregate expenditure curve and also shifts the aggregate demand curve. The magnitude of the shift in the aggregate demand curve depends on the size of the multiplier and on the change in autonomous expenditure.

Real GDP and the price level are determined by both aggregate demand and aggregate supply. If an increase in aggregate demand occurs at an unemployment equilibrium, both the price level and real GDP increase. But the increase in real GDP is smaller than the increase in aggregate demand. The steeper the short-run aggregate supply curve, the larger is the change in the price level and the smaller is the change in real GDP. If an increase in aggregate demand occurs at full employment, its long-run effect is entirely on the price level. (pp. 710–712)

The Multiplier in the United Kingdom

The multiplier in the United Kingdom ranges between 1.60 and 0.74. The multiplier fluctuates over the business cycle, rising during a recovery and falling during a recession. (pp. 712–716)

K E Y   E L E M E N T S

Key Terms

Key Figures and Table

REVIEW QUESTIONS

1 The autonomous expenditure multiplier applies to changes in which components of aggregate expenditure?

2 What is the connection between the autonomous expenditure multiplier and the slope of the *AE* curve?

3 Why is the autonomous expenditure multiplier greater than 1?

4 What is the government purchases multiplier? Is its value greater than 1?

5 What is the transfer payments multiplier?

6 What is the tax multiplier? How does it compare with the autonomous expenditure multiplier?

7 How does the transfer payments multiplier compare with the tax multiplier?

8 What is the balanced budget multiplier? Is its value greater than 1?

9 Explain how income taxes and transfer payments act as automatic stabilizers.

10 What was the size of the multiplier in the United Kingdom in 1993?

11 A change in autonomous expenditure occurs that is not produced by a change in the price level. What happens to the aggregate expenditure curve and the aggregate demand curve?

PROBLEMS

1 You are given the following information about the economy of Zeeland. Autonomous consumption expenditure is £100 billion and the marginal propensity to consume is 0.9. Investment is £460 billion, government purchases of goods and services are £400 billion, taxes are a constant £400 billion – they do not vary with income. Exports are £350 billion and imports are 10 per cent of income.

  a Calculate the slope of the *AE* curve

  b The government cuts its purchases of goods and services to £300 billion. What is the change in real GDP and the government purchases multiplier?

  c The government continues to purchase £400 billion worth of goods and services and cuts taxes to £300 billion. What is the change in real GDP and the tax multiplier?

  d The government simultaneously cuts both its purchases of goods and services and taxes to £300 billion. What is the change in real GDP? What is the name of the multiplier now at work and what is its value?

2 Everything in Zeeland remains the same as in Problem 1 except that the tax laws are changed. Instead of taxes being a constant £400 billion they become 10 per cent of real GDP

  a Calculate the slope of the *AE* curve.

  b Government purchases are cut to £300 billion. What is the change in real GDP and the government purchases multiplier?

  c What is the change in consumption expenditure? Explain why the change in consumption expenditure exceeds the change in real GDP.

  d The government introduces transfer payments of £50 billion. What is the transfer payments multiplier and the change in real GDP?

3 You are given three pieces of information about the multiplier in the economy of Alphabeta. Its average value is 2, in year A it is $3^1/2$, and in year B it is $^1/2$.

  a Was year A a recovery year or a recession year? Why?

  b Was year B a recovery year or a recession year? Why?

4 Suppose that the price level in the economy of Zeeland as described in Problem 1, is 100.

a If the government of Zeeland increases its purchases of goods and services by £100 billion, what happens to the quantity of real GDP demanded?

b In the short run, does equilibrium real GDP increase by more than, less than, or the same amount as the increase in the quantity of real GDP demanded?

c In the long run, does equilibrium real GDP increase by more than, less than, or the same amount as the increase in the quantity of real GDP demanded?

d In the short run, does the price level in Zeeland rise, fall, or remain unchanged?

e In the long run, does the price level in Zeeland rise, fall, or remain unchanged?

CHAPTER 26

MONEY, BANKS AND INTEREST RATES

After studying this chapter you will be able to:

◆ Define money and explain its functions

◆ Explain what money is today

◆ Describe the balance sheets of the main financial intermediaries

◆ Explain the economic functions of banks and other financial intermediaries

◆ Explain how banks create money

◆ Explain what determines the demand for money

◆ Explain how interest rates are determined

M ONEY HAS BEEN AROUND FOR A VERY LONG TIME. MANY ITEMS HAVE served as money including cattle, goats, cowrie shells, whales' teeth and parrots' feathers. Today, when we want to buy something, we can use coins or notes, or we can write a cheque or present a credit card. Are all these things money? ◆ ◆ When we deposit some notes into a bank or building society, are those notes still money? And what happens when the bank or the building society lends the money in our deposit to someone else? How can we get our money back if it's been lent out? Does lending by banks and building societies create money out of thin air? ◆ ◆ In the 1970s, there were two distinct types of bank deposit – current accounts that did not pay interest and other accounts that did. Today, almost all accounts earn interest. Why have bank accounts changed? ◆ ◆

Money Makes the World Go Round

There are enough bank notes and coins circulating for everyone to have a wallet stuffed with £350. There are enough deposits in banks and building societies for everyone to have more than £9,000 in these accounts. What determines the amount of money that people hold? ◆ ◆ In recent years, interest rates have tumbled. In the 1980s, a mortgage might have cost 20 per cent a year. In 1994, a mortgage cost only 8 per cent a year. Why?

◆ ◆ ◆ ◆ We use money every day, but what exactly is money? Where does it come from? And what role do banks play in creating it? These are the central questions for this chapter. But our ultimate goal is to understand how money influences the economy – the levels of real GDP, employment, interest rates and inflation. This chapter takes the first steps toward this goal.

What is Money?

What have cattle, goats, cowrie shells, whales' teeth, parrots' feathers and pound coins had in common to make them examples of money? To answer this, we need a definition of money.

The Definition of Money

Money is any commodity or token that is generally acceptable as the means of payment. The **means of payment** is the method of settling a debt. When a payment has been made there is no remaining obligation between the parties to a transaction. The particular commodities and tokens that have served this purpose have varied enormously. We're going to study money and the institutions of monetary exchange that have evolved in the UK economy. But first, let's look at the functions of money.

The Functions of Money

Money has four functions:

◆ Medium of exchange
◆ Unit of account
◆ Store of value
◆ Standard of deferred payment

Medium of Exchange   A **medium of exchange** is a commodity or token that is generally accepted in exchange for goods and services. Money acts as such a medium. Without money, it would be necessary to exchange goods and services directly for other goods and services – an exchange known as *barter*. For example, if you wanted to buy a hamburger, you might offer the paperback novel you've just finished reading, or half an hour of your labour in the kitchen in exchange for it. Barter can take place only when there is a *double coincidence of wants*. A double coincidence of wants is a situation that occurs when person A wants to buy what person B is selling, and person B wants to buy what person A is selling. That is, to get your hamburger, you'd have to find someone who's selling hamburgers and who wants your paperback novel or your work in the kitchen. The occurrence of a double coincidence of wants is sufficiently rare that barter exchange would leave most potential gains from specialization and exchange unrealized.

Money guarantees that there is always a double coincidence of wants. People with something to sell will always accept money in exchange for it, and people who want to buy will always offer money. Money acts as a lubricant that smooths the mechanism of exchange. It lowers the costs of doing transactions. The evolution of monetary exchange is a consequence of our economizing activity – of getting the most possible out of limited resources.

Unit of Account   A **unit of account** is an agreed measure for stating the prices of goods and services. To get the most out of your budget you have to calculate, among other things, whether seeing one more film is worth the cost you have to pay. But what really matters is not the cost in pounds and pence, but the opportunity cost in terms of the number of bars of chocolate, cups of coffee or pints of beer that you have to give up. It is not hard to do the calculations when all these goods have prices in terms of pounds and pence (see Table 26.1). If a cinema ticket costs £2.40 and a pint of beer costs £1.20, then you know right away that seeing one more film costs you 2 pints of beer. If a cup of coffee costs 60p, then one more cinema ticket costs 4 cups of coffee. You need do only one calculation to work out the opportunity cost of any pair of goods and services.

TABLE 26.1

A Unit of Account Simplifies Price Comparisons

Good	Price in money units	Price in units of another good
Film	£2.40 each	2 pints of beer
Pint of beer	£1.20 each	2 cups of coffee
Coffee	£0.60 a cup	3 bars of chocolate

Money as a unit of account: One cinema ticket costs £2.40 and a bar of chocolate costs 20p, so 1 ticket costs 12 bars of chocolate (£2.40 ÷ 20p = 12).
No unit of account: You go to a cinema and learn that the price of a ticket is 2 pints of beer. You go to a cafe and learn that a cup of coffee costs 3 bars of chocolate. But how many bars of chocolate does seeing a film cost you? To answer that question, you go to a pub and find that a pint of beer costs 2 cups of coffee. Now you get out your pocket calculator: 1 cinema ticket costs 2 pints of beer or 4 cups of coffee or 12 bars of chocolate!

But imagine how troublesome it would be if your local cinema advertised its price as 2 pints of beer, and if the pub listed the price of a pint of beer as 2 cups of coffee, and if the cafe said the price of a cup of coffee was 3 bars of chocolate! How much running around and calculating would you have to do to work out how much seeing a film is going to cost you in terms of the beer, coffee or chocolate that you must give up to see it? You'd get the answer for beer right away from the cinema, but for all the other goods you'd have to visit many different places to establish the price of each commodity in terms of another and calculate prices in units that are relevant for your own decision. Cover up the column labelled *Price in money units* in Table 26.1 and see how hard it is to work out the number of chocolate bars it costs to see one film. How much simpler it is for everyone to express their prices in terms of pounds and pence.

Because the prices of goods and services are measured in money, money can also be used for measuring incomes and expenditures. In turn it can be used for drawing up accounts and balance sheets.

Store of Value   Any commodity or token that can be held and exchanged later for goods and services is called a **store of value**. Money acts as a store of value. If it did not, it would not be acceptable in exchange for goods and services. The more stable the value of a commodity or token, the better it can act as a store of value, and the more useful it is as money. There are no stores of value that are completely safe. The value of a physical object, such as a house, a car, or a work of art, fluctuates over time. The values of commodities and tokens used as money also fluctuate and, when there is inflation, they persistently fall in value.

Standard of Deferred Payment   An agreed measure that enables contracts to be written for future receipts and payments is called a **standard of deferred payment**. If you borrow money to buy a house or if you save money to provide for retirement, your future commitment or future receipt will be agreed to in pounds and pence. Money is used as the standard for a deferred payment.

Using money as a standard for deferred payment is not entirely without risk because inflation leads to unpredictable changes in the value of money. But, to the extent that borrowers and lenders anticipate inflation, its rate is reflected in the interest rates

paid and received. Lenders in effect protect themselves by charging a higher interest rate and borrowers, anticipating inflation, willingly pay the higher rate.

Different Forms of Money

Money can take five different forms:

◆ Commodity money
◆ Convertible paper money
◆ Fiat money
◆ Private debt money
◆ Composite currencies

Commodity Money   *Commodity money* is a physical commodity valued in its own right and also used as a medium of exchange. An amazing array of items has served as commodity money at different times and places, several of which were described at the start of the chapter. But the most common commodity monies have been coins made from metals such as gold, silver, bronze and copper. The earliest coins date from before 1000 BC in China, and from the eighth century BC in Europe.

When William the Conqueror arrived in England in 1066, the most common coins were silver pennies, 240 of which contained one pound weight of silver. William established the Royal Mint and defined a standard purity for silver coins – the *sterling silver standard* – in which every 1,000 parts of metal used in the coins were to contain 925 parts of silver. Gold coins were introduced by King Edward III in the fourteenth century, but they were of very high value because gold was rare. Low value copper coins were introduced in the seventeenth century by King James I.

Gold coins became common in the eighteenth century following the introduction of gold from South America. The main gold coin was the guinea. As gold and silver prices fluctuated, so the price of guineas in terms of silver coins was not always stable. In 1719, the Master of the Mint – the famous scientist Sir Isaac Newton – decreed that a guinea was to be worth 21 silver shillings (a shilling was worth 12 pennies). Later the guinea coins were replaced by slightly smaller sovereign coins worth 20 shillings.

Commodity money has considerable advantages but some drawbacks. Let's look at these.

Advantages of Commodity Money   The main advantage of commodity money is that its value as money is readily known because the commodity is valued for its own sake. This fact provides a guarantee of the value of money. For example, gold may be used to fill teeth and make jewellery; its value in these uses determines its value as money. Historically, gold and silver were ideal for use as money because they were in limited supply and in constant demand (by those wealthy enough to use them) for ornaments and jewellery. Further, their quality was easily verified in the mints where they were made into coins, and coins could be made in small enough values to facilitate exchange.

Disadvantages of Commodity Money   Commodity money has two main disadvantages. First, there is a constant temptation to cheat on the value of the money. Two methods of cheating have been commonly used – clipping and debasement. *Clipping* is reducing the size of coins by an imperceptible amount, thereby lowering their metallic content. To discourage clipping, the Royal Mint put milled edges on its coins after 1663, and people became reluctant to accept coins whose milling was worn. *Debasement* is creating a coin having a lower silver or gold content, the balance being made up of some cheaper metal.

The temptation to lower the value of money led to a phenomenon known as Gresham's Law, after the sixteenth-century English financial expert Sir Thomas Gresham. *Gresham's Law* is the tendency for bad money to drive good money out of circulation. Bad money is debased money; good money is money that has not been debased. It's easy to see why Gresham's Law works. Suppose that a person is paid with two coins, one debased and the other not. Each coin has the same value if used as money in exchange for goods. But one of the coins – the one that's not debased – is more valuable as a commodity than it is as a coin. It will not, therefore, be used as money. Only the debased coin will be used as money. It is in this way that bad money drives good money out of circulation. The issue was particularly relevant in Gresham's day because successive debasements by Henry VIII and Edward VI had resulted in coins having only 250 parts of silver per 1,000 instead of 925. It was possible to make far more of the new debased coins than the old, and prices soared as the money supply rose. It was left to Elizabeth I to replace the debased coins with sterling silver ones once again.

A second major disadvantage of commodity money is that the commodity, valued for its own sake, could be used in ways other than as money – it has an opportunity cost. For example, silver used as money cannot be used to make cutlery or ornaments. This opportunity cost creates incentives to find alternatives to the commodity itself for use in the exchange process. One such alternative is a paper claim to commodity money.

Convertible Paper Money   *Convertible paper money* is a paper claim to a commodity that circulates as a medium of exchange. The first known paper money occurred in China during the Ming dynasty (AD 1368–1399). Paper money was also sometimes used in Europe in the Middle Ages.

It was the inventiveness of seventeenth century London goldsmiths and their clients that led to the widespread use of convertible paper money. Because gold was valuable, goldsmiths – people who make gold objects – had well-guarded vaults where they kept their own gold. They also rented space in their vaults to people who wanted to put their gold and other valuables, such as coins, in safekeeping. The goldsmiths issued a receipt or IOU – meaning 'I owe you' – to anyone depositing coins with them entitling the owner of the coins to reclaim their 'deposit' on demand. These IOUs were rather like the coat tokens that you get at a theatre or museum.

Suppose that Isabella has an IOU indicating that she has 1,000 silver coins deposited with Thomas Goldsmith. She wants to buy some land valued at 1,000 silver coins from Henry. There are two ways that Isabella might pay for the land. One way is to go to Thomas, hand over her IOU, collect her coins and take them to Henry. Henry now goes back to Thomas with the coins and deposits them there for safekeeping, leaving with his own IOU. The other way is for Isabella simply to hand over her IOU to Henry, completing the transaction by using the IOU as money. Obviously, it is much more convenient to complete the transaction using the IOU, provided Henry can trust Thomas. The IOU circulating as a medium of exchange is money. The paper money is *backed* by the precious-metal coins held by Thomas Goldsmith. Also the paper money is *convertible* into precious-metal coins.

You may wonder why people would take their coins to Thomas Goldsmith for safekeeping if he gave them an IOU which could itself be used in transactions. Wouldn't a thief have been just as interested in stealing the IOU as the coins? In fact thieves would have been much less willing to steal the IOUs. This was partly because they were initially issued only for very high values – over £1,000 in 1994 prices – so they would readily attract attention, and partly because they had numbers printed on them so that people would look out for ones reported as stolen.

Fractional Backing   Once the convertible paper money system is operating and people are using IOUs rather than precious-metal coins as the medium of exchange, goldsmiths notice that their vaults are storing a large number of coins that are never withdrawn. This gives them a brilliant idea. Why not lend people IOUs? The goldsmiths can charge interest on the loans and the loans are created just by writing out IOUs on pieces of paper. As long as the number of such IOUs created is not too large in relation to the stocks of coins in the goldsmiths' vaults, the goldsmiths are in no danger of being unable to honour their promise to convert IOUs into coins on demand. By this device, *fractionally backed* convertible paper money was invented.

England played a pioneering part in the evolution of fractionally backed convertible paper money in the seventeenth century and it was the London goldsmiths who became the first issuers of fractionally backed IOUs. Fractional backing frees up real resources from the exchange process, but there remains an incentive to find a yet more efficient way of facilitating exchange. This alternative is fiat money.

Fiat Money   *Fiat money* is an intrinsically worthless (or almost worthless) commodity that serves the functions of money. The term 'fiat' means 'by government order'. Some of the earliest fiat monies were issued in countries where there were revolutions. For example, so-called continental currency was issued in the United States during the Wars of Independence and so-called *assignats* were issued during the French Revolution. These early experiments with fiat money ended in rapid inflation because the amount of fiat money created was allowed to increase at a rapid pace, causing the money to lose value.

Provided the quantity of fiat money is not allowed to grow too rapidly, it has a reasonably steady value in terms of the goods and services that it will buy. People are willing to accept fiat money in exchange for the goods and services they sell only because they know it will be accepted when they go to buy goods and services.

Fiat Money in the United Kingdom   The Bank of England, which was established in 1694 with special links

with the government, soon acquired a virtual monopoly in England over issuing IOUs or bank notes. Initially these notes were convertible into coins or precious metals, but since 1931 they have not been convertible into anything, so they are now examples of fiat money. When people use fiat money, they are willing to accept pieces of paper with special watermarks, printed in coloured inks, and intrinsically worth not more than 1 or 2 pence, as a commodity, in exchange for £5, £10, £20 or £50 worth of goods and services.

Even coins are now really fiat money as they contain no precious metals. Gold coins were called in during World War I and replaced by notes. Sterling silver was used for silver coins until 1920 when the silver content was reduced from 925 parts per 1,000 to 500 parts, and since 1947 no silver at all has been used. The small seven-sided alloy disc that today forms a 20 pence piece is 84 per cent copper and 16 per cent nickel and is worth almost nothing as metal, but it pays for a local phone call and many other small commodities. The replacement of commodity money by fiat money enables the commodities themselves to be used productively.

Private Debt Money   In the modern world, there is a fourth important type of money – private debt money. *Private debt money* is a loan that the borrower promises to repay on demand. By transferring the entitlement to be repaid from one person to another, such a loan can be used as money. For example, suppose you give Mary an IOU for £10 and that Mary gives the IOU to John to buy a second-hand book. John then comes to you to demand £10 in cash. You pay John as he is now the holder of the IOU that you issued.

The most important example of private debt money is the chequable deposit at banks and building societies. A **chequable deposit** is a loan by a depositor to a bank or building society, the ownership of which can be transferred from one person to another by writing an instruction – a cheque – asking the bank or building society to alter its records. We'll say more about this type of money shortly. Before doing so, let's look at the final form of money and at money in the United Kingdom today.

Composite Currency   One interesting example of an unusual type of money is the European Currency Unit (or ECU) that is used for limited purposes in the European Union. An **ECU** is defined as a 'basket' of the currencies of all 12 EU member countries. The relative importance of each currency in the basket depends on the relative importance of that country's economy and is redefined every few years.

If you actually had a basket and put in it the appropriate number of pence and the appropriate coins from the other 11 countries, you could say that the basket contained 1 ECU. The total value of these coins in 1994 would have been around 75 pence. Moreover, if you deposited appropriate amounts of each of the 12 currencies in your bank you could claim to have, say, 1,000 ECUs. Notice that if the value of one of the currencies in your basket or bank deposit altered, then so would the value of your ECU. For example, if the value of the krone fell, your ECUs would buy you fewer dollars, or fewer pounds, if you wished to convert them all to dollars or pounds. So the value of the dollar and the pound in terms of the ECU would rise. But the value of the krone in terms of the ECU would fall as more krone would be needed to buy the appropriate amount of currencies to make up an ECU.

It is possible to measure things in ECUs and so use the ECU as a unit of account, and indeed the ECU is used by the European Union for measuring various items. For example, it was used to measure the gains of creating the single European market from 1 January, 1993 when all remaining barriers to trade within the European Union were removed. The gain was measured as between 70 and 90 billion ECUs. Some bank deposits are also measured in ECUs. These deposits can be used as a medium of exchange provided that both parties to the exchange agree. So far, payments in ECUs have been confined largely to some transactions between banks.

Money in the United Kingdom Today

Various measures of the money stock in the United Kingdom have been adopted in recent years with names like M1, M2, M3, M4 and so on[1]. At present, the official measure of money in the United Kingdom is M4. **M4** consists of cash and all deposits in banks and building societies – see Table 26.2 and Fig. 26.1. Although M4 is the official definition of money in the

---

[1] There is also a measure called M0, but this measure is not really money at all. Rather it is a measure of the base of reserves on which the banking system operates. We describe M0 and its place in the financial system in Chapter 27, pp. 749–777.

TABLE 26.2

The Official Definition of Money

M4 has three components:

1 **Cash (notes and coin) held by the public**
2 **Sterling deposits at banks**
3 **Sterling deposits at building societies**

CASH has two components:

1 **Notes, which are issued by the Bank of England, the Scottish banks and the Northern Irish banks**
2 **Coins, which are made at the Royal Mint and issued by the Bank of England**

United Kingdom, it includes some items that cannot be used as a medium of exchange. M4 includes all deposits at banks and building societies, yet not all these deposits can be used as a medium of exchange.

To illustrate this simply, let's divide bank and building society deposits into three groups. First, there are chequable deposits which can be spent instantly and which are thus clearly a medium of exchange. Second, there are some non-chequable deposits whose owners may have to give the bank or building society a week or so's notice before making payments. These deposits are so close to being a medium of exchange that economists are happy to regard them as money. Third, there are deposits where much longer notice is needed. For example, there are some deposits, known as *Certificates of Deposit* (CDs), which the owners may be unable to spend unless they give notice of up to two years. CDs earn high interest, but they cannot be used as a medium of exchange. Because M4 includes them, it is a broader aggregate than the economic concept of money.

While CDs are not usable as means of payment and are not money, they do have a very high degree of liquidity. **Liquidity** is the degree to which an asset is instantly convertible into money – into a means of payment – at a known price. CDs are liquid because their owners can, in fact, sell them, that is they can find someone who will swap them for chequable deposits. Assets vary in their degree of liquidity. Money is fully liquid while other assets range from highly liquid to far from liquid.

FIGURE 26.1

The Official Measure of Money

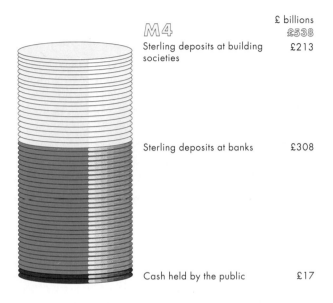

	£ billions
M4	£538
Sterling deposits at building societies	£213
Sterling deposits at banks	£308
Cash held by the public	£17

M4 consists of cash held by the public plus all deposits at banks and building societies. Bank deposits exceed building society deposits and cash is a small part of M4.

Source: *Bank of England Quarterly Bulletin*, November 1993, Tables 2 and 6.4.

Money is the means of payment, and we often pay our bills by writing cheques. So are cheques money?

Cheques Are not Money Cheques are not money, but chequable deposits are money. To see why, consider what happens when someone pays for goods by writing a cheque. Let's suppose that Sharon buys a Muddy Fox mountain bike for £500 from a shop called Cyclestore. When Sharon goes to Cyclestore she has £800 in her deposit at the Midland Bank. Cyclestore has £1,200 in its deposit which happens to be at the same bank. The total deposit of these two people is £2,000. On 11 June, Sharon writes a cheque for £500. Cyclestore takes the cheque to the Midland Bank right away. Cyclestore's deposit rises from £1,200 to £1,700. But the bank not only credits Cyclestore's deposit with £500, it also debits Sharon's deposit by £500 so that her deposit falls from £800 to £300. The total deposit of Sharon and Cyclestore is still the

same as before, £2,000. Cyclestore now has £500 more and Sharon £500 less than before. These transactions are summarized in Table 26.3.

This transaction has not changed the quantity of money in existence. It has simply transferred money from one person to another. The cheque itself was never money. That is, there wasn't an extra £500 worth of money while the cheque was in circulation. The cheque simply served as a written instruction to the bank to transfer the money from Sharon to Cyclestore.

In our example, Sharon and Cyclestore use the same bank. Essentially, the same story, though with additional steps, describes what happens if Sharon and Cyclestore use different banks. Cyclestore's bank will credit £500 to Cyclestore's deposit and then take the cheque to Sharon's bank. Sharon's bank will pay Cyclestore's bank £500 and then debit Sharon's deposit £500. This process can take a few days but the principles are the same as when two people use the same bank.

So, cheques are not money. But what about credit cards? Isn't having a credit card in your pocket and presenting the card to pay for a bike the same thing as using money? Why aren't credit cards somehow valued and counted as part of the quantity of money in M4?

Credit Cards Are not Money When you pay by cheque you are frequently asked to prove your identity by showing your cheque guarantee card. It

TABLE 26.3

Paying by Cheque

SHARON'S DEPOSIT

Date	Item	Debit	Credit	Balance
June 1	**Opening balance**			**£800.00CR***
June 11	**Cyclestore**	**£500.00**		**£300.00CR**

CYCLESTORE'S DEPOSIT

Date	Item	Debit	Credit	Balance
June 1	**Opening balance**			**£1,200.00CR**
June 11	**Sharon**		**£500.00**	**£1,700.00CR**

*CR means credit: the bank owes the depositor.

would never occur to you to think of your cheque guarantee card as money. Your cheque guarantee card is really an identity card, though it has one special feature. This feature is that it guarantees that your bank will pay at least £100 – or some other specified amount – to the person to whom you are making out the cheque, irrespective of how much money you have in your bank deposit.

A credit card is also an identity card with one special feature. This feature is that it allows you to borrow money at the instant a purchase is made on the promise of repaying later. When you make a purchase, you sign a credit card sales slip that creates a debt in your name. You are saying: I agree to pay for these products when the credit card company sends me my statement. Once you get your statement from the credit card company, you have to make the minimum payment due. To make that payment you need money – you need to have funds in your deposit so that you can write a cheque to pay the credit card company.

R E V I E W

Money has four functions: medium of exchange, unit of account, standard of deferred payment and a store of value. Any durable commodity can serve as money, but modern economies use fiat money and private debt money rather than commodity money. The most important components of money in the United Kingdom today are deposits at banks and building societies. Neither cheques nor credit cards are money. A cheque is an instruction to a bank to transfer money from one deposit to another. A credit card is an identity card that enables a person to borrow when a purchase is made on the promise of repaying later. When repayment is made, a deposit is used for the payment. ◆

We've seen that the most important components of money in the United Kingdom are deposits at banks and building societies. We need to take a look at the banks and building societies and the financial system in which they operate. But first let's take a quick look at securities as banks and building societies hold many of these.

Types of Security

There are three main types of security: fixed interest securities, bills and equities.

Fixed Interest Securities   Fixed interest securities – many of which are simply called bonds – may be issued by central or local governments or by companies. In each case the basic principles are the same. For example, the government may issue some bonds with a name such as Treasury 10% 2004. It sells each bond for £100 (the normal purchase price for new bonds) and pays its holders £10 interest – that is, 10 per cent of the purchase price – each year until 2004 when it buys the bond back. We say that the bonds mature in 2004. A few fixed interest securities have no maturity date, so their issuers must pay interest every year for ever.

Bills   Bills represent short-term loans, usually lasting just three months. Bills may be issued by central government, local governments and companies; these three types are respectively known as Treasury bills, local authority bills and commercial bills. Again the principles are very similar. A company may today issue some three-month £1,000 bills which means that anyone buying them, and so lending the company some money, will be repaid £1,000 when the bill matures in three months' time. But the buyer will not be paid any interest. Instead, buyers get a return because new bills are always sold for a discount, that is, for less than their maturity value. So maybe you would buy a new £1,000 commercial bill for £980. In three months you will be repaid £1,000.

Equities   Equities are issued only by companies and are often called ordinary shares. If you buy shares in a company such as Shell, then you are one of the owners of Shell. You will not be paid any interest, but you should receive a dividend each year. Dividends are paid out of profits, and tend to be higher in good years than bad years, though companies usually save some profits in good years to enable them to pay reasonable dividends in bad years.

All securities can be bought and sold second-hand on the Stock Exchange. The second-hand price of any given security fluctuates constantly, so people never know exactly how much they will get for them until they actually sell them.

Financial Intermediaries

We are going to study the banking and financial system by describing the main financial intermediaries that operate in the United Kingdom today, explaining their functions, and highlighting the economic role they play and the sources of their profits.

A *financial intermediary* is a firm that borrows money from households and firms and makes loans to other households and firms. There are many types of financial intermediary, but there are only two types we need to study in depth. These are the two types of financial intermediary that give deposits to the people who lend them money, and whose deposits form part of the money supply. These financial intermediaries are:

♦ Banks
♦ Building societies

Let's examine the banks.

Banks

A **bank** is a firm which has been licensed by the Bank of England to take deposits and is authorized under the Banking Act of 1987 to operate in the United Kingdom. Banks can be divided into two main groups, retail banks and wholesale banks.

Retail banks are those which operate extensive branch networks and take small deposits from small depositors. They include all the well-known High Street banks including the 'big four' in England – Barclays, Lloyds, Midland and National Westminster – the three big Scottish banks – Bank of Scotland, Clydesdale and Royal Bank of Scotland – and the Northern Irish banks. They also include the Trustee Savings Bank and the National Girobank.

Wholesale banks have few branches and accept only large deposits, often setting a minimum of £100,000. These banks can be subdivided into two groups, British banks and overseas banks, according to the country to which their owners belong. The overseas banks are subsidiaries of banks in other countries. A large proportion of their deposits are denominated in currencies other than sterling, though British banks also accept non-sterling deposits.

The scale and scope of the operations of the banks can be seen by examining the balance sheet of all the banks added together. A *balance sheet* is a statement that lists a firm's assets and liabilities. *Assets* are the things of value that a firm owns. *Liabilities* are the things that a firm owes to households and other firms. Such a balance sheet – that for all the banks in September 1993 – is set out in Table 26.4. The left side – the assets – lists the items *owned* by the banks. The right side – the liabilities – lists the items that the banks *owe* to others.

Notice first that the banks' assets and liabilities are divided into two broad groups: those denominated in sterling and those denominated in other currencies. Partly because the United Kingdom does a great deal of trade with other countries and partly because London – along with New York and Tokyo – is one of the world's three largest financial centres, a large amount of banking business is done in US dollars, Japanese yen and other foreign currencies. Table 26.4 shows that well over half of the assets and the liabilities of the banks operating in the United Kingdom are in foreign currencies. Foreign currency assets are loans or securities denominated in such currencies. Foreign currency liabilities are deposits made and repayable in foreign currencies. The level of foreign currency assets and liabilities has grown rapidly following the abolition in 1979 of all controls on the movement of money into and out of the United Kingdom.

Important though the banks' foreign currency business is, it is their business conducted in sterling that is of most concern to us, principally because this covers the sterling deposits which are included in M4. Let's look at this aspect of the banks' activities, starting on the liabilities side.

Total sterling liabilities of the banks in September 1993 were £613.7 billion. By far the most important liabilities are deposits. Your deposit at a bank is an asset to you but a liability for your bank. The bank has to repay you your deposit (and sometimes interest on it too) whenever you decide to take your money out of the bank. Why does a bank offer to pay you your money back with interest? It does so because it wants to use your deposit to make a profit for itself. The asset side of the balance sheet tells us what the banks did with their borrowed resources in September 1993.

First, the banks kept some of their assets in the

TABLE 26.4

The Balance Sheet of All Banks in the United Kingdom, September 1993

Assets (billions of pounds)		Liabilities (billions of pounds)	
Sterling assets		*Sterling liabilities*	
Notes and coin	2.9	Notes issued	1.9
Balances at the Bank of England	1.6	Deposits (other than CDs)	476.7
Loans to the discount houses	7.8	CDs	51.7
Loans to other financial intermediaries	139.9	Other liabilities	83.5
Bills	10.3		
Other securities	44.0		
Advances	383.4		
Other assets	27.6		
Total sterling assets	617.6	**Total sterling liabilities**	613.7
Other currency assets		*Other currency liabilities*	
Loans to financial intermediaries	481.4	Deposits (other than CDs)	698.7
Bills	12.6	CDs	59.7
Other securities	106.9	Other liabilities	46.9
Advances	172.3		
Other assets	28.2		
Total other currency assets	801.4	**Total other currency liabilities**	805.2
Total assets	1419.0	**Total liabilities**	1419.0

Source: *Bank of England Quarterly Bulletin*, November 1993, Table 3.

form of cash in their vaults – notice that these assets are always called 'notes and coin' rather than 'notes and coins'. They also kept some assets in the form of deposits at the Bank of England (we'll study the Bank of England in Chapter 27). The cash in a bank's vault plus its deposit at the Bank of England are called its **reserves**. You can think of a bank's deposit at the Bank of England as being similar to your deposit at your own bank. Banks use these deposits in the same way that you use your bank account. A bank deposits cash into or draws cash out of its account at the Bank of England and writes cheques on that account to settle debts with other banks.

If the banks kept all their assets in the form of deposits at the Bank of England and cash, they wouldn't make any profit. But if they didn't keep *some* of their assets as deposits at the Bank of

England and cash, they wouldn't be able to meet the demands for cash that their customers place on them. Nor could they replenish their cash dispensers every time you and their other customers empty them. So banks have a difficult choice to make. If they keep too few assets in the form of reserves, they could be in trouble if a large number of depositors want cash. But if they hold too many assets in this form, then they will make very little profit for their shareholders.

The banks use some of their borrowed resources to make interest-earning loans to other financial intermediaries. The table divides these loans into two groups – loans to financial intermediaries known as the discount houses and loans to other financial intermediaries. The discount houses are a small group of financial intermediaries that borrow from the banks on a short-term basis and use most of their loans to buy bills. We look at the discount houses again in Chapter 27.

Loans by banks to financial intermediaries include conventional loans as well as deposits and CDs in other banks and building societies. Most of these loans are very *liquid assets*, that is they can be converted quickly into a medium of exchange for a very predictable amount. This is obvious in the case of deposits but is equally true of CDs which can always be sold. It is also true of many loans. For example, loans to the discount houses are often repayable at 24 hours' notice.

Some of the banks' borrowed resources are used to buy securities. The table splits these into bills and other securities. Securities are useful assets for the banks, partly because they earn interest and dividends and partly because a bank which finds its reserves getting a little low can replenish them by selling securities. Securities are generally fairly liquid assets as they can be sold and converted fairly quickly into a fairly certain amount of a medium of exchange. As banks regard securities as a sort of back-up for reserves, they like to hold those securities which are most liquid, that is, those whose second-hand values are most predictable and least likely to shoot up or down. So they tend to hold relatively few company securities, whose prices are sensitive to the fluctuating profit performances of the companies concerned. Instead, banks prefer securities that have been issued by the government. Banks particularly like Treasury bills, especially ones near maturity, for their value is very stable. It is easy to see why. If a bill is to mature next week with a guaranteed repayment equal to its face value, then its second-hand price over the next few days is likely to stay very near to that face value.

The bulk of the banks' borrowed resources are put to work making advances to depositors. *Advances* include bank loans and overdrafts. If Richard is today given a one-year £1,000 loan, his deposit will be credited with £1,000 and he will be required to repay the loan with interest in one year's time. If Judith is today given a six-month £1,000 overdraft, she will be lent a variable amount over those six months subject to an upper limit of £1,000. The amount will vary from day to day in accordance with whatever is needed to help her meet her spending. In six months she will have to repay any outstanding borrowing and pay interest on however much has been borrowed. Most bank advances are used by businesses to make purchases of capital equipment and stocks. But banks also make advances to households. These advances are usually used to buy consumer durable goods such as cars or computers. But they may also be used for daily living expenses by people like students who have little income today and expect a high income in the future. The outstanding balances on credit card accounts are also bank advances.

Banks make a profit by earning interest and dividends on their loans, advances and securities in excess of the interest they pay on their deposits and other liabilities. Banks also receive revenue by charging fees for managing accounts.

We have seen that M4 includes all the sterling deposits held at banks. But bank deposits are not the only deposits included in M4. Building societies also take deposits that form part – and an increasing part – of the money supply. Let's now examine the building societies.

Building Societies

The building societies are established and regulated by the Building Societies Act of 1986. Although there is a legal distinction between banks and building societies, the functional distinction has become blurred. Indeed, in 1989 one of the best known building societies, the Abbey National, was reclassified as a bank. However, the differences can be seen in the balance sheet for the building societies shown in Table 26.5.

The liabilities of building societies resemble those of banks. They are deposits and CDs. And, like bank deposits, many building society deposits are chequable and so may be spent or withdrawn in cash on demand.

The assets of building societies include cash reserves but, unlike the banks, they are not required to hold deposits at the Bank of England. Instead, they hold deposits and CDs at banks and other building societies. The societies also hold securities. But what distinguishes building societies from banks is that most of their assets are mortgages – loans to finance home purchases and home improvements. These loans are often made for long terms, perhaps 25 years or more, although on average they are repaid after about seven years. Despite being long-term, these loans are very safe. When a home-buyer takes out a mortgage, the deeds of the home are given to the society. Should the borrower default, the society can sell the home to recover the debt.

TABLE 26.5

The Balance Sheet of All Building Societies in the United Kingdom, September 1993

Assets (billions of pounds)		Liabilities (billions of pounds)	
Notes and coin	0.4	Deposits (other than CDs)	219.9
Bank deposits and CDs	28.5	CDs	6.5
Building society CDs	1.7	Other liabilities	48.9
Securities	5.8		
Loans	234.8		
Other assets	4.3		
Total assets	275.3	Total liabilities	275.3

Source: *Bank of England Quarterly Bulletin*, November 1993, Table 5.2.

The Economic Functions of Financial Intermediaries

Financial intermediaries exist to make a profit from a gap or spread between the interest rates they pay on deposits and the interest rates at which they lend. Why can banks and building societies borrow at low interest rates and lend at higher ones? What services do they perform that make their depositors willing to put up with low interest rates and their borrowers willing to pay high ones? Financial intermediaries provide four main services:

◆ Minimizing the cost of obtaining funds
◆ Minimizing the cost of monitoring borrowers
◆ Pooling risk
◆ Creating liquidity

Minimizing the Cost of Obtaining Funds Finding someone from whom to borrow can be a costly business. Imagine how troublesome it would be if there were no financial intermediaries. A firm that was looking for £1 million to buy a new production plant would probably have to hunt around for several hundred people from whom to borrow in order to acquire enough funds for its capital project. Financial intermediaries lower those costs. The firm needing £1 million can go to a single financial intermediary to obtain those funds. The financial intermediary has to borrow from a large number of people, but it's not doing that just for this one firm and the £1 million it wants to borrow. The

intermediary can establish an organization that spreads the cost of raising money from a large number of depositors.

Minimizing the Cost of Monitoring Borrowers Lending money is a risky business. There's always a danger that the borrower may not repay. Most of the money lent gets used by firms to invest in projects that they hope will return a profit. But sometimes those hopes are not fulfilled. Checking up on the activities of borrowers and ensuring that they are likely to make a profit is a costly and specialized activity. Imagine how costly it would be if each household that lent money to a firm had to incur the costs of monitoring that firm directly. By depositing funds with a financial intermediary, households avoid these costs. The intermediary performs the monitoring activity by using specialized resources that have a much lower cost than each household would incur if it had to undertake the activity individually.

Pooling Risk As we noted above, lending money is risky. There is always a chance of not being repaid – of default. The risk of default can be reduced by lending to a large number of different individuals. In this case, if one person defaults on a loan, it is a nuisance but not a disaster. In contrast, if only one person borrows and that person defaults on the loan, the entire loan is a write-off. Financial intermediaries enable people to pool risk in an efficient way. Thousands of people lend money to any one financial intermediary and, in turn, the intermediary re-lends the money to hundreds, and perhaps thousands, of individual firms. If any one firm defaults on its loan, that default is spread across all the depositors with the intermediary so no individual depositor faces a high degree of risk.

Creating Liquidity   Financial intermediaries create liquidity. We defined liquidity earlier as the ease and certainty with which an asset can be converted into a medium of exchange – that is to say money. Suppose there were no financial intermediaries. Then households wishing to lend would lend money to firms wishing to borrow. The households would find that their funds were not liquid since they would have had to agree to make the loans for a specified period of time, possibly several years.

But with the existence of financial intermediaries, notably banks and building societies, households can make deposits that count as money in M4. And in the case of chequable deposits, the deposits are clearly usable as a medium of exchange. So the existence of financial intermediaries results in far more liquidity than would otherwise occur.

In essence, financial intermediaries create liquidity by borrowing short and lending long. Borrowing short means taking deposits but standing ready to repay them at short notice – and even at no notice in the case of chequable deposits. Lending long means making loan commitments for a prearranged, and often quite long, period of time. For example, when a person makes a deposit with a building society, that deposit may often be withdrawn without any notice at all. But the building society makes a lending commitment for perhaps 25 years to someone buying a new house.

R E V I E W

Most of the UK's money is made up of deposits at two types of financial intermediary – banks and building societies. The main economic functions of financial intermediaries are to minimize the cost of obtaining funds, minimize the cost of monitoring borrowers, pool risk and create liquidity.

How Banks Create Money

Money is created by the activities of banks and building societies – that is, by all those institutions whose deposits circulate as a medium of exchange. In this section, we'll use the term 'banks' to refer to both types of institution.

As we saw in Table 26.4, banks don't have £100 in cash for every £100 that people have deposited with them. In fact, a typical bank today has less than £1 in cash or on deposit at the Bank of England for every £100 deposited in it. There is no need for depositors to panic. Banks have learned, from experience, that these reserve levels are adequate for ordinary business needs. The fraction of a bank's total deposits that are held in reserves is called the **reserve ratio**. The value of a bank's reserve ratio is influenced by the actions of the bank's depositors. If a depositor withdraws cash from a bank, the reserve ratio falls. If a depositor puts cash into a bank, the reserve ratio increases. Again, if a depositor makes a cheque out in favour of a depositor at another bank, the reserve ratio falls, and if a depositor receives a cheque from a depositor at another bank the reserve ratio rises, for whenever cheques are made out by people at one bank in favour of people at another, reserves are exchanged between the banks.

All banks have a desired reserve ratio. The **desired reserve ratio** is the ratio of reserves to deposits that banks regard as necessary in order to be able to conduct their business. The desired reserve ratio is determined partly by regulation (discussed in Chapter 27) and partly by what the banks regard as the minimum prudent level for their reserve holdings. The difference between actual reserves and desired reserves are **excess reserves**.

Whenever banks have excess reserves, they are able to create money. When we say that banks create money, we don't mean that they have secret back rooms in which counterfeiters are busily working producing forged Bank of England notes or forged coins. Remember, most money is in the form of deposits, not cash. What banks create is deposits, and the main way they do this is by making loans to depositors. When a bank makes a loan to a depositor it simply writes a larger number against the deposit of the person concerned. Another way in which banks can raise deposits and so create money is by buying securities and increasing the size of the deposits of the people who sell securities to them. To see more clearly how banks create money with loans we are going to look at a model of the banking system.

Creating Deposits by Making Loans

Let's suppose that there are many banks in this system and that all the banks have a desired reserve ratio of 25 per cent. That is, for each pound deposited, they want to keep 25 pence in the form of reserves. And let's suppose that they all start with this ratio. Alan, a customer of the Argent Bank, decides to reduce the amount of cash he keeps at home and put £100 in his deposit at the bank. Suddenly, then, the Argent Bank has £100 of new deposits and £100 of additional reserves. But with £100 of new deposits the Argent Bank doesn't want to hold on to £100 of additional reserves. It has excess reserves. Its desired reserve ratio is 25 per cent and with £100 extra deposits it only wants £25 more reserves. What can it do with the £75 excess reserves?

The answer is simple. Argent can lend £75 to a depositor who wants to borrow. Say Amy is such a depositor. At the moment of making the loan, the bank simply writes an extra £75 against Amy's deposit. Notice that by the stroke of a pen – or the impact of a computer printer – total deposits in the country have risen by £75 and Argent has raised the money supply. As far as its own balance sheet is concerned, the rise in liabilities which occurs when Amy's deposit is increased will be matched by a rise in assets of £75 because the bank's advances have risen by that amount.

At this point in time Argent still has excess reserves. Since the start of our story its deposits have risen by £175 – £100 for Alan and £75 for Amy – while its reserves have risen by £100. But its excess reserves will soon disappear. Like all borrowers, Amy has borrowed in order to spend the loan. Suppose she buys a jacket for £75 from Brenda. When she buys it, her deposit will fall by £75, and what's more Argent will doubtless find its reserves falling by £75. For Amy will either withdraw the £75 in cash – in which case reserves definitely fall – or she will make out a cheque. Let's suppose for simplicity that all payments are made by cheque. As there are many banks in the system, the odds are that Brenda keeps her deposit at another bank, say the Bounty Bank. So as a result of Amy's cheque the Argent Bank will have to give £75 of reserves to the Bounty Bank. Thus the Argent Bank will now find that only Alan's deposit is higher than it was at the

beginning – by £100 – and it will find that this rise in its liabilities has been matched by a rise of £25 in reserves and £75 in advances. Of course the money supply is £75 higher than it was because Brenda has now got an extra £75 in her deposit at the Bounty Bank. As far as Argent is concerned, that is the end of the matter. But it is not the end of the story for the entire banking system. What happens next?

To understand the next stage we must turn our attention to the Bounty Bank. As a result of Brenda paying in her cheque, the Bounty Bank finds that its deposits have risen by £75. At the same time it has acquired £75 more reserves from the Argent Bank. The Bounty Bank doesn't need to hold on to the entire £75 that it has just received in reserves; it needs only a quarter of that amount – £18.75 – so it has excess reserves of £56.25. The Bounty Bank can make a loan equal to the value of its excess reserves to one of its depositors, say Bob. So it lends £56.25 to Bob by writing an extra £56.25 against his deposit. At this point Bounty Bank's deposits rise by a further £56.25, a rise matched by a rise of £56.25 in its advances. Moreover, the money supply has risen by £56.25 as Bob's deposit has risen by that amount and no one else's deposit has fallen.

Of course Bob rapidly spends his loan. Say he buys some used audio equipment from Charles. Bob writes a cheque on his account at the Bounty Bank, which Charles pays into in his account at the Commerce Bank. Consequently deposits at the Bounty Bank fall by £56.25, and the bank gives reserves of £56.25 to the Commerce Bank. Thus at the end of this stage the situation for the Bounty Bank is that the only deposit that is higher than it was to start with is Brenda's whose deposit rose by £75. Against this rise in liabilities the Bounty Bank has an increase in reserves of £18.75 – that is, the initial increase of £75 minus the loss of £56.25 to the Commerce Bank – and a rise of £56.25 in advances. And at this stage of the story the Bounty Bank has created £56.25 worth of new deposits, though the extra deposits are now in Charles's account at the Commerce Bank. Notice that the money supply at this stage has risen by £131.25. It rose by £75 when the Argent Bank lent £75 to Amy and by £56.25 when the Bounty Bank lent £56.25 to Bob.

The transactions that we've just described are summarized in Table 26.6. But the story is still incomplete. The process that we're describing continues through the remaining banks and their depositors and borrowers, all the way down the list in that table.

TABLE 26.6

Creating Money by Making Loans: Many Banks

Bank	Depositor	Borrower	New deposits (pounds)	New loans (pounds)	New reserves (pounds)	Increase in money (pounds)	Cumulative increase in money (pounds)
Argent	Alan	Amy	100.00	75.00	25.00	75.00	75.00
Bounty	Brenda	Bob	75.00	56.25	18.75	56.25	131.25
Commerce	Charles	Carol	56.25	42.19	14.06	42.19	173.44
Dependable	Diana	Duncan	42.19	31.64	10.55	31.64	205.08
Emerald	Eddie	Emily	31.64	23.73	7.91	23.73	228.81
All others			94.92	71.19	23.73	71.19	
Total banking system			400.00	300.00	100.00	300.00	300.00

By the time we get down to the Emerald Bank, Duncan has paid Eddie £31.64 for a some boxes of computer disks and so the Emerald Bank has new deposits of £31.64 and additional reserves of that same amount. As it needs only £7.91 of additional reserves, it makes a loan of £23.73 to Emily, who in turn spends the money. By this time, the total amount of money has already increased by £228.81. The new deposits at each stage of the process are listed in the first column of numbers in the table.

This process continues but with amounts that are now getting so tiny that we will not bother to keep track of them. All the remaining stages in the process taken together add up to the numbers in the second to last row of the table. The final totals appear as the totals row at the bottom of the table. Deposits have increased by £400, loans by £300 and reserves by £100. The banks have created money by making loans. The quantity of money created is £300 – the same amount as the additional loans made. It's true that deposits have risen by £400, but £100 of that increase is Alan's original deposit. The increase in his deposit did not increase the quantity of money. The cash that Alan deposited was already money. It is only the new deposits created by the lending activity of the banks that have increased the quantity of money in existence.

The ability of banks to create money does not mean that they can create an indefinite amount of money. The amount that they can create depends on the size of their reserves and on the desired reserve ratio. In this example where the desired reserve ratio is 25 per cent, bank deposits have increased by four times the amount by which the level of reserves rose. There's an important relationship between the change in reserves and the change in deposits.

The Deposits Multiplier

The deposits multiplier is the amount by which an increase in bank reserves is multiplied to calculate the effect of the increase in reserves on total bank deposits. That is:

$$\text{Deposits multiplier} = \frac{\text{Change in deposits}}{\text{Change in reserves}}.$$

In the example that we've just worked through, the deposits multiplier is 4 – a £100 increase in reserves led to a the £400 increase in deposits.

The deposits multiplier is related to the desired reserve ratio. In our example, that ratio is 25 per cent. That is:

$$\text{Desired reserves} = (\tfrac{1}{4}) \text{ Deposits.}$$

Whenever desired reserves exceed actual reserves (a situation of negative excess reserves), the banks decrease their loans. When desired reserves are below actual reserves (a situation of positive excess reserves), the banks make additional loans. By adjusting their loans, the banks bring their actual reserves into line with their desired reserves, eliminating excess reserves. Thus when banks have changed their loans and reserves to make actual reserves equal desired reserves,

$$\text{Actual reserves} = (1/4) \text{ Deposits.}$$

If we divide both sides of this equation by $1/4$ we obtain

$$\text{Deposits} = 1/(1/4) \text{ Actual reserves.}$$

If actual reserves are initially equal to desired reserves, and then actual reserves change, the banks will change their deposits in order to satisfy the above equation. So,

$$\text{Change in deposits} = 1/(1/4) \text{ Change in reserves.}$$

But $1/(1/4)$ is the deposits multiplier. It is the amount by which the change in reserves is multiplied to calculate the change in deposits. In our example, this multiplier equals 4. The relationship between the deposits multiplier and the desired reserve ratio is:

$$\text{Deposits multiplier} = \frac{1}{\text{Desired reserve ratio}}$$

UK Deposits Multiplier

The deposits multiplier in the United Kingdom differs from the one that we have just calculated for two reasons. First, the desired reserve ratio of real-world banks is much smaller than the 25 per cent that we have used here. Second, in the real world, when banks take the sort of actions outlined in Table 26.6, some reserves start leaving the banking system. For example, Brenda and Charles both ended up with more money in their bank deposits, and as a result might decide to withdraw some of this in cash. So the excess reserves of the Bounty and Commerce banks would not be quite as large as we implied. These two differences between the real-world money multiplier and the deposits multiplier that we have just calculated work in opposing directions. The smaller desired reserve ratio of real-world banks makes the real-world multiplier larger than the above numerical example. The tendency for some loans to remain outside the banks makes the real-world multiplier smaller. We study the actual values of real-world money multipliers in the Chapter 27.

REVIEW

Banks create money by making loans to depositors (and by buying securities from them). The amount of money they can create depends on their reserves and their reserve ratios. Each time they make a loan (or buy a security), deposits rise and so does the money supply. Banks stop creating money when their actual reserves equal their desired reserves. An initial change in the level of reserves held by the banks leads eventually to a much greater change in deposits. The change in deposits equals the change in reserves multiplied by the deposits multiplier. ◆

The amount of money created by the banking system has a powerful influence on the economy. Reading Between the Lines on pp. 740–741 looks at this influence in the case of Russia. This influence begins with the determination of interest rates. To understand how the quantity of money influences interest rates, we must first study the demand for money.

The Demand for Money

The amount of money we *receive* each week or month or term is income – that is a flow. The amount of money that we *hold* in our wallet or in a deposit at the bank or building society is a *stock*. There is no limit to how much income – or flow – we would like to receive each week. But there is a limit to how big a stock of money each of us would like to hold, on average.

The Motives for Holding Money

Why do people hold a stock of money? Why do you hold a store of coins in your purse and notes in your wallet, and why do you hold money in a deposit at your local bank? John Maynard Keynes pondered this question and concluded that there are three main motives for holding money:

◆ Transactions motive
◆ Precautionary motive
◆ Speculative motive

Transactions Motive   The main motive for holding money is to be able to undertake transactions and to minimize the cost of transactions. By carrying a stock of cash, you are able to undertake small transactions such as buying your lunch at the college cafeteria. If you didn't carry cash as a matter of course, you'd have to go to the bank every lunchtime to withdraw enough cash. The opportunity cost of these transactions, in terms of your own lost studying or leisure time, would be considerable. You avoid those transactions costs by keeping a stock of cash large enough to make your normal purchases over a period of perhaps a week.

You also keep a stock of money in the form of deposits at the bank to make transactions such as paying the rent on your flat or paying for books. Instead of having a stock of money in a bank deposit for these purposes, you might put all your wealth into securities – buying ICI shares or government bonds. But if you did that, you would have to telephone your stockbroker and sell some securities each time you needed to pay the rent or the bookshop. Again, you'd have to pay the opportunity cost of such transactions which would include your time, your telephone bill and your stockbroker's charges. Instead, by holding a stock of money in a bank deposit, these costs can be avoided.

Individual holdings of money for transactions purposes fluctuate during any week or month. But aggregate money balances held for transactions purposes do not fluctuate much because what one person is spending, someone else is receiving. Firms' money holdings are at their peak just before they pay their employees' wages. Households' money holdings are at a peak just after wages have been paid. As households spend their incomes, their money holdings decline and firms' holdings of money increase. Firms' holdings of money are large and this makes average money holdings seem so large. Average money holdings of households are much lower than the economy-wide averages given in the chapter opener.

Precautionary Motive   Money is held as a precaution against unforeseen events that require unplanned purchases to be made. For example, you may carry more cash with you than you think you are likely to need in case you miss the last bus home and have to take a taxi. And you may hold more money in your bank deposit than you expect to use before you next receive some income in case you suddenly find you have to buy another book to help you with your studies or in case you see some clothes in a sale that you just can't resist buying at a bargain price.

Speculative Motive   The final motive for holding money is to avoid losses from holding securities. This motive applies only to people who buy securities from time to time. Suppose, for example, a week before the stock market crash of October 1987, you had predicted the crash. On the Friday afternoon before the markets closed, you would have sold all your shares and put the proceeds into your bank deposit for the weekend. This temporary holding of money would persist until security prices had fallen to the lowest level you expected them to reach. Only then would you reduce your bank deposit and buy shares again.

The Influences on Money Holding

What determines the quantity of money that households and firms choose to hold? There are three important influences on this quantity:

◆ Prices
◆ Real expenditure
◆ The opportunity cost of holding money

The higher the level of prices, other things remaining the same, the larger is the quantity of money that people will want to hold. The higher the level of real expenditure, other things remaining the same, the larger is the quantity of money that people plan to hold. The higher the opportunity cost of holding money, the smaller is the quantity of money that people plan to hold.

These influences on individual decisions about money holding translate into three macroeconomic variables that influence the aggregate quantity of money demanded:

◆ The price level
◆ Real GDP
◆ The interest rate

Price Level and the Quantity of Money   The quantity of money measured in current pounds is called the quantity of *nominal* money. The quantity of nominal money demanded is proportional to the price level. That is, other things remaining the same, if the price level (GDP deflator) increases by 10 per cent, people will want to hold 10 per cent more nominal money than before. What matters to people is not the number of pounds that they hold but the buying power of these pounds. Suppose, for example, that to undertake your weekly expenditure on beer and rent you need an average of £35. If your income, the price of beer and rents increased by 10 per cent you would increase your average holding to cover these items by 10 per cent to £38.50.

This example shows that the quantity of nominal money people want to hold rises when prices rise. But a rise in prices does not in itself cause people to want to hold a larger stock of real money. To find out if the amount of *real* money which people holds has changed, we work out what nominal amounts they would have held in each year if prices had been constant (at, say, 1990 levels). The quantity of real money demanded is independent of the price level. In the example above, you held £35, on average, at the original price level. When prices increased by 10 per cent, the quantity of nominal money you held increased by 10 per cent. But the amount of real money you held remained constant. Your £38.50 at the new price level is the same quantity of real money as your £35 at the old price level.

Real GDP and the Quantity of Real Money   An important determinant of the quantity of real money demanded is the level of real aggregate income in the economy. We saw in Chapter 22 that aggregate income equals aggregate spending and GDP. If real GDP rises, firms are producing more final goods and services. This means they receive more real expenditure from the people who buy those goods, and it means they pay more real income to the households that own the factors of production that firms use to make those goods. The amount of real money that households and firms demand depends on the amount of real spending that they want to do. The higher this expenditure – and in turn the higher the level of income – the larger is the quantity of money demanded.

Suppose you hold an average of £50 to finance all your weekly purchases. Now imagine that all prices remain constant but that your income increases. As a consequence you now spend more and you also hold a larger amount of money to finance your higher volume of expenditure.

The Interest Rate and the Quantity of Money   You already know the fundamental principle that as the opportunity cost of something rises, people try to find substitutes for it. Money is no exception to this principle. The opportunity cost of holding money is the interest that could be earned on other assets. The higher the interest rates on these other assets, the higher is the opportunity cost of holding money and the more people will try to find substitutes for money and economize on their holdings of money.

Most of the deposits that comprise the money supply bear interest. This fact modifies the opportunity cost of holding money, but it does not change the conclusion we've just reached. The opportunity cost of holding an interest-bearing bank or building society deposit is the interest rate on a bond or other security *minus* the interest rate on the deposit. Deposit interest rates fluctuate much less than rates on securities, so when interest rates are high, the opportunity cost of holding money in all forms is high, and the quantity of money demanded declines.

The Demand for Real Money   The *demand for real money* is the relationship between the quantity of real money demanded and the level of interest rates, holding constant all other influences on the amount of money that people wish to hold. To make the demand for real money more concrete, let's consider an example. A household's demand for real money can be represented as a demand curve for real money. Such a curve sets out the quantity of real money that a household wants to hold at different levels of interest rates assuming real income is constant.

Figure 26.2 sets out some numbers for the McGregor household. All the numbers in this example will be given in 1990 prices, so any figures for income or money demanded represent real income and real money demanded. The household's real income is £20,000 a year. The table shows the quantity of real money demanded by the McGregor household at different levels of interest rates. You can think of the interest rate figures as representing the average rate of interest on all interest-earning assets. So when the average is, say, 7 per cent, rather risky assets may have interest rates of 8 per cent while very safe ones may have interest rates of 6 per cent.

Look at row *a*. When the interest rate level is 7 per cent a year, the McGregor household holds £2,400 of money, on average. When the interest rate is 5 per cent a year, real money holdings increase to £3,000, and when the interest rate falls to 3 per cent a year,

FIGURE 26.2

The McGregor Household's Demand for Real Money

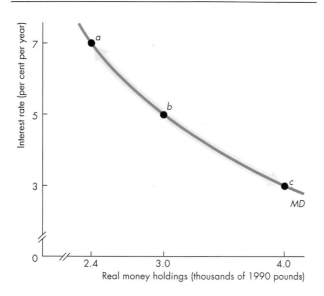

The McGregor household's real income is £20,000 in 1990 prices.

	Interest rate (per cent per year)	Real money holdings (thousands of 1990 pounds)
a	7	2.4
b	5	3.0
c	3	4.0

The table shows the McGregor household's demand schedule for real money. The lower the interest rate, the larger is the quantity of real money that the household plans to hold. The graph shows the household's demand curve for real money (*MD*). Points *a*, *b* and *c* on the curve correspond to the rows in the table. A change in the interest rate leads to a movement along the demand curve. The demand curve for real money slopes downward because the interest rate is the opportunity cost of holding money. The higher the interest rate, the larger is the interest forgone on holding another asset.

real money holdings increase to £4,000. The figure also graphs the McGregor household's demand curve for real money (*MD*). The demand curve for real money slopes downward. The reason for this is that the opportunity cost of holding money falls as the rate of interest falls. If the interest rate rises from 5 per cent to 7 per cent, the opportunity cost of holding

money rises and the McGregor household holds a smaller average amount of real money, so there is an upward movement along the curve. But if the interest rate falls from 5 per cent to 3 per cent, the opportunity cost of holding money falls and the McGregor household holds a larger average amount of real money and there is a downward movement along the curve.

Shifts in the Demand Curve for Real Money

The demand curve for real money shifts when:

◆ Real income changes
◆ Financial innovation occurs

Changes in Real Income An increase in real income shifts the demand curve for real money to the right and a decrease shifts it to the left. The effect of real income on the demand curve for real money is shown in Fig. 26.3. The table shows the effects of a change in real income on the quantity of real money demanded when the interest rate is constant at 5 per cent. Look first at row *b* of the table. It tells us that when the interest rate is 5 per cent and real income is £20,000, the quantity of real money demanded by the McGregor household is £3,000. This row corresponds to point *b* on the demand curve for real money MD_0. Continuing to hold the interest rate constant, if real income falls to £12,000, the quantity of real money held falls to £2,400. So the demand curve for real money shifts from MD_0 to MD_1 in Fig. 26.3. If the McGregor household's real income increases to £28,000, the quantity of real money held by the household increases to £3,600 and the demand curve shifts to the right from MD_0 to MD_2.

Financial Innovation

Financial innovation also results in a change in the demand for real money and a shift in the demand curve for real money. One of the most notable innovations in recent years has been the widespread use of credit cards. Computers have played an important part in the growth of credit cards. Each cardholder's account has to be checked daily to see how much interest is due on it, and each cardholder has to be sent a fully itemized statement once a month. Keeping the records and calculating the interest and outstanding debt required to operate a credit card system is feasible by using people with calculators instead of computers, but it is too costly to undertake. No one

Crisis in the Russian Economy

FINANCIAL TIMES, 17 MARCH 1994

IMF chief steps into Russia's gathering economic storm

John Lloyd, Moscow

THESE are hard times in Russia, and fears are growing that the country is becoming ungovernable, or governable only with an iron hand....

The credit squeeze of last year has worked. Inflation came down last month to 10 per cent, half of January's figure. But industrial production was also down, by 24 per cent against February 1993 as a result of the squeeze.

This may continue. Russian officials say Mr Victor Gerashchenko, the central bank chairman, has massively undershot the credit targets recommended by the government's Credit Committee, advancing only 40 per cent of the total agreed....

The budget agreed by the government – but not yet passed by parliament – is similarly tough. It proposes expenditure of around Rbs180,000bn, and an income of Rbs120,000bn – the deficit is as much as 10 per cent of gross national product (on IMF calculations, more like 16–17 per cent)....

Budgeted revenues of Rbs120,000bn now look impossible to attain – since government income is now running at Rbs70,000bn – Rbs80,000bn a year and, in the words of one western financial expert, 'there is no reason why it should get any better'.

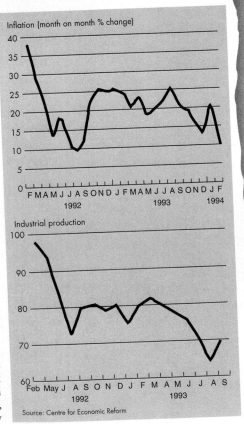

Inflation (month on month % change)
1992 1993 1994

Industrial production
1992 1993

Source: Centre for Economic Reform

© The Financial Times. Reprinted with permission.

The Russian economy is facing a severe crisis.

Inflation has been cut by means of a squeeze on credit.

A further consequence of the credit squeeze is that industrial output has fallen sharply.

The declining trend in inflation and output is likely to continue, as the central bank is lending considerably less than the amount recommended by the government.

Background and Analysis

Following the introduction of economic reforms in Russia, inflation rose to very high levels. In early 1992, inflation was running at over 35 per cent a month.

The Russian central bank has the ability to affect the supply of money in the economy by creating money. It can do this by making loans to individuals or companies.

The way in which this affects inflation can be seen by looking at the quantity theory of money – see Chapter 27. This says that the quantity of money times the velocity of circulation equals the price level times the value of real GDP.

If we assume that the velocity of circulation of money remains the same and real GDP is not affected by the quantity of money, a higher quantity of money in circulation will result in higher prices.

By sticking to, or even undershooting, the government's target for credit creation, the central bank has ensured that inflation has been reduced.

By reducing the amount of money lent to firms, however, the central bank and the government have also contributed to the industrial collapse being experienced.

Firms that are unable to borrow money from banks find it much harder to cover debts and to invest in new factories and equipment.

Firms therefore find it harder to cut costs and become profitable. Most need to do this because under the old planning system, many firms made losses but were continually subsidized by the government.

In the figure, the increase in the money supply shifts the aggregate demand curve (AD) to the right from AD_0 to AD_1. A declining real exchange rate also helps to shift the AD curve to the right. These effects together stimulate real net material product (NMP) but increase the price level.

The increase in the price level means that firms face higher costs for their inputs. A number of firms will go bankrupt as their losses become unsustainable. These effects move the SAS curve to the left from SAS_0 to SAS_1.

Real NMP has fallen and there is a recessionary gap reflecting the unemployment existing in the Russian economy. Note that NMP is the variable East European countries used instead of GDP.

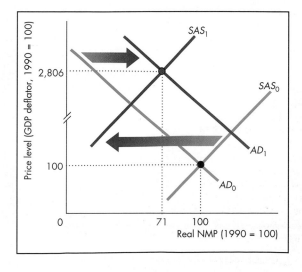

FIGURE 26.3

Changes in the McGregor Household's Demand for Real Money

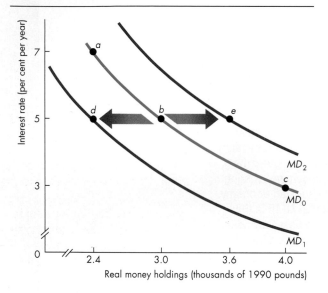

The interest rate is 5 per cent.

	Real income (thousands of 1990 pounds)	Real money holdings (thousands of 1990 pounds)
d	12	2.4
b	20	3.0
e	28	3.6

A change in real income leads to a change in the demand for real money. The table shows the quantity of real money held by the McGregor household at three different levels of real income when the interest rate is constant at 5 per cent. The graph shows the effects of a change in real income on the demand curve for real money. When real income is £20,000 and the interest rate is 5 per cent, the household is at point *b* on the demand curve for real money MD_0. When real income falls to £12,000, the demand curve is MD_1 and, at a 5 per cent interest rate, the household is at point *d*. When real income rises to £28,000, the demand curve shifts to MD_2. With an interest rate of 5 per cent, the household is at point *e*.

would find it worth while to operate a credit card company unless the calculations could be done by computer.

This innovation of credit cards has also lowered the demand for money. By using a credit card to

make purchases, it is possible for people to manage with a much lower quantity of money, especially people who receive monthly incomes. Instead of holding money for transactions purposes through the month, it is possible to charge purchases to a credit card and pay the credit card bill on, or a day or two after, payday. As a result, the average holding of money throughout the month is much lower.

Computer technology has not only led to a fall in the amount of money that people need to hold; it has also led to a change in the composition of the money that people hold. To see this, recall that M4 comprises cash, bank deposits and building society deposits.

People can manage with less money in cash form partly because they often use credit cards for transactions which used usually to be handled by cash. Purchases of petrol and long-distance rail tickets are examples. It was always possible to use cheques, but the paperwork for credit card purchases can usually be handled more quickly so that people who were reluctant to use cheques are now happy to use credit cards. Another factor reducing average cash holdings is the widespread introduction of cash dispensers. These mean that people can get cash at any time, usually with little if any wait, so people are tempted to make more frequent but smaller withdrawals than they did, so reducing their average cash holdings.

Turning to bank deposits, the tendency now is for people to hold much less in non-interest-bearing deposits and much more in interest-bearing deposits than they used to. This is because many interest-bearing deposits can now be used for cash withdrawals and cheque payments. These interest-bearing chequable accounts have to have balances and interest payments calculated on a daily basis and this has become possible at a reasonable cost only as a result of the use of computers.

Finally, people now make much more use of building society deposits for everyday transactions than they used to. This is partly because the building societies are more in competition with the banks than they used to be. And, again, it is partly because the availability of low-cost computing power has enabled the building societies to do the daily interest calculations needed on deposits which now often fluctuate on a daily basis.

Now that we have studied the theory of the demand for money, let's see how much money has been held in the United Kingdom in recent years.

And let's see how the amount has been related to real income and interest rates.

The Demand for Money in the United Kingdom

Figure 26.4 plots the quantity of M4 held against the interest rate between 1968 and 1993. M4 is measured as a percentage of GDP to remove the effects of changes in GDP on the demand for money and to isolate the effects of interest rates and financial innovation. Each dot shows the interest rate and the amount of M4 held (as a percentage of GDP) in the indicated year. For example, the dot labelled 90 is for 1990.

The predicted relationship between the interest rate and the amount of money held is present only if we allow for factors that shift the demand curve. During the late 1960s and early 1970s, the demand for M4 was MD_0. When the interest rate increased between 1968 and 1973, there was a movement along that demand curve. In 1974, the demand curve shifted to the right to MD_1, possibly because uncertainty increased when the world oil market went into turmoil. Gradually, between 1974 and 1980, the demand curve shifted to the left back to MD_0. It then shifted steadily to the right and by 1990 had reached MD_2. The reason for this shift is financial innovation. The banks and building societies offered better deals on their deposits and the opportunity cost of holding money declined, at any given interest rate. By the early 1990s, this process of financial innovation appeared to have ended and the demand function appeared to become stable (for a few years at least) at MD_2.

Interestingly, although financial innovations such as credit cards and cash dispensers enable people to manage with smaller and smaller amounts of cash, the competition between banks and building societies for deposits has led to higher interest rates on deposits, a decrease in the opportunity cost of holding money, and an increase, not a decrease, in the amount of money held, relative to income.

The demand curve shown in Fig. 26.4 removes the influence of real GDP on the demand for money from the picture. If we graphed the pound quantity of real money held against the interest rate, the demand for money curve would be even less visible than in Fig. 26.4 because rising income would be shifting the curve to the right over time.

FIGURE 26.4

The Demand for Money in the United Kingdom

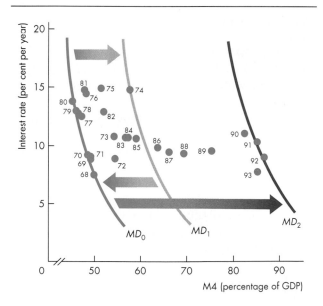

The relationship between the quantity of M4 held (expressed as a percentage of real GDP) and the interest rate is shown by the dots (one for each year indicated). The relationship shown is similar to that predicted by the theory of the demand for money. Other things remaining the same, the lower the interest rate, the greater is the quantity of money demanded. The relationship is less than exact, partly because of financial innovation.

Sources: Central Statistical Office, *Economic Trends Annual Supplement 1993 Edition*, pp. 14, 161–2 and 224, later issues of *Economic Trends*, and our calculations.

REVIEW

The quantity of money demanded depends on the price level, real GDP and the interest rate. The quantity of nominal money demanded is proportional to the price level. Real money is the quantity of nominal money divided by the price level. The quantity of real money demanded increases as real GDP increases. The opportunity cost of holding money is the interest rate. The benefit from holding money is the avoidance of frequent transactions. The higher the interest rate, the smaller is the quantity of real money demanded. ◆ ◆ The demand curve for real money shows how the quantity of real money demanded varies as the interest rate varies. When the interest rate changes, there is a movement along the demand curve for real money. Other influences on the quantity of real money demanded shift the demand curve for real money. An increase in real income shifts the demand curve to the right; financial innovations that decrease the demand for money shift the demand curve to the left. ◆

We have now studied the factors that determine the demand for money and discovered that one determinant of the quantity of real money demanded is the opportunity cost of holding it – the interest rate. We're now going to see how the interest rate is determined.

Interest Rate Determination

The interest rate on a security is its percentage yield. There is a relationship between the interest rate and the price of a security. Let's spend a moment studying that relationship before analysing the forces that determine interest rates.

Interest Rates and Asset Prices

Among the many different types of security, the most convenient one to consider for our purposes is the one known as a perpetuity. A *perpetuity* is a security – typically a bond – that promises to pay a certain fixed amount of money each year for ever. The issuer of such a bond will never buy the bond back, that is redeem it; instead, the bond will remain outstanding for ever, and it will earn a fixed payment each year. This payment is called a *coupon payment*. It is paid at a fixed percentage, known as the coupon rate, of the *original* price of the bond. Since the income payment each year is fixed, and since the current market price of the bond varies from day to day, so the fixed annual payment varies as a percentage of the marketprice. In other words, the interest rate on the bond varies. Table 26.7 illustrates this fact.

First, the table shows the formula for calculating the interest rate on a perpetuity. The interest rate (r) is the coupon payment (c) divided by the market price (p) all multiplied by 100 to convert it into a percentage. The table gives some examples for a

TABLE 26.7

The Interest Rate and Market Price of a Perpetuity

FORMULA FOR INTEREST RATE:

r = interest rate, c = coupon payment, p = current market price of perpetuity,

$$r = \frac{c}{p} 100$$

EXAMPLES

	Coupon payment (per cent)	Market price (pounds)	Interest rate (per cent per year)
a	3.50	35	10.0
b	3.50	70	5.0
c	3.50	100	3.5

perpetuity whose coupon payment is £3.50. If the perpetuity currently has a market price of £35 (row *a* in Table 26.7), then its interest rate is 10 per cent a year. That is because the holder of the perpetuity, which is worth £35, currently receives £3.50 a year.

Rows *b* and *c* of the table show two other cases. In row *b*, the current market price of the perpetuity is £70 which results in an interest rate of 5 per cent – the holder of this perpetuity which is worth £70 receives an annual income of 5 per cent of that amount, that is £3.50. In row *c*, the current market price of the perpetuity is £100 which results in an interest rate of 3.5 per cent – the holder of this perpetuity which is worth £100 receives an annual income of 3.5 per cent of that amount.

There is an inverse relationship between the price of a perpetuity and the interest rate earned on it. As a perpetuity's price rises, its interest rate declines. The same applies to all other securities, though the exact relationship between price and interest rate is more complex with most securities than it is with perpetuities.

Understanding that a security's interest rate declines when its price rises will make it easier for you to understand the process whereby the interest rate is determined. Let's now study how interest rates are determined.

Money Market Equilibrium

The interest rate is determined at each point in time by equilibrium in the markets for financial assets. We study that equilibrium in the market for money.

The Supply of Money The quantity of money supplied is determined by the actions of the banking system and the Bank of England. We'll assume that the amount of money in existence is fixed, so the supply of money is a fixed quantity. (Chapter 27 explains how the quantity of money is determined and how it can be changed.) The *real* quantity of money supplied is equal to the nominal quantity supplied divided by the price level. At a given moment in time, there is a particular price level and so the quantity of real money supplied is also a fixed amount. The supply curve of real money is shown in Fig. 26.5 as the vertical line labelled *MS*. The quantity of real money supplied is £500 billion.

The Demand for Money The demand for real money depends on the level of real GDP and on the interest rate. The table in Fig. 26.5 sets out the quantity of real money demanded at three different interest rates when real GDP and the price level are constant. These quantities are graphed as the demand curve for real money, *MD*, in the figure.

Equilibrium When the quantity of money supplied equals the quantity of money demanded, the money market is in equilibrium. This equilibrium is brought about by an adjustment in the interest rate. If the interest rate is too high, people will try to hold less money than is available. If the interest rate is too low, people will try to hold more than the amount available. When the interest rate is such that people want to hold exactly the amount of money that is available, then equilibrium prevails.

Figure 26.5 illustrates an equilibrium in the money market. The equilibrium interest rate is 5 per cent, the rate at which the quantity of money demanded equals the quantity supplied. If the interest rate is above 5 per cent, people will want to hold less money than is available. At an interest rate below 5 per cent, people will want to hold more money than is available. At a 5 per cent interest rate, the amount of money available is willingly held.

Converging to Equilibrium How does money market equilibrium come about? To answer this question

FIGURE 26.5

Money Market Equilibrium

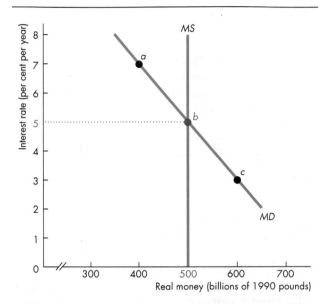

The demand for real money is given by the schedule in the table and the curve *MD*. The lower the interest rate, the greater the quantity of money demanded. The supply of real money is £500 billion (at 1990 prices) as shown in the table and by the curve *MS*. The interest rate adjusts until there is equilibrium in the money market. If real GDP is £600 billion, the demand for real money is given by curve *MD*. If the supply of real money is £500 billion – as shown by curve *MS* – the equilibrium interest rate level is 5 per cent. At interest rates above 5 per cent, the quantity of real money demanded is less than the quantity supplied, so interest rates will fall. At interest rates below 5 per cent, the quantity of real money demanded exceeds the quantity supplied, so interest rates will rise. Only at 5 per cent is the quantity of real money in existence willingly held.

let's perform a thought experiment. First, imagine that the interest rate is temporarily at 7 per cent. In this situation, people will want to hold only £400 billion in real money even though £500 billion exists. But since £500 billion exists, people must be holding it. That is, people are holding more money than they want to. In such a situation, they will try to get rid of some of their money. Each individual will try to reorganize his or her affairs in order to lower the amount of money held and take advantage of the 7 per cent interest rate by buying more securities. But everybody will be trying to buy securities, and nobody will be trying to sell them at a 7 per cent interest rate. There is an excess demand for securities such as bonds. When there is an excess demand for any-thing, its price rises. So with an excess demand for securities, the prices of securities will rise. We saw earlier that there is an inverse relationship between the price of a security and its interest rate. As the price of a security rises, its interest rate falls.

As long as anyone is holding money in excess of the quantity demanded, that person will try to lower his or her money holdings by buying additional securities. Security prices will continue to rise and interest rates will continue to fall. Only when the interest rate has moved down to 5 per cent will the amount of money in existence be held willingly. That is, people's attempts to get rid of unwanted excess money do not result in reducing the amount of money held in aggre-gate. Instead, those efforts result in a change in the interest rate that makes the amount of money avail-able willingly held.

The thought experiment that we have just con-ducted can be performed in reverse by supposing that the interest rate is 3 per cent. In this situation, people want to hold £600 billion even though only £500 billion is available. To acquire more money, peo-ple will sell securities. There will be an excess supply of securities, so their prices will fall. As the prices of securities fall, the yield on them – the interest rate –

rises. People will continue to try to sell securities and try to acquire money until the interest rate has risen to 5 per cent, where the amount of money available is the amount that they want to hold.

◆ ◆ ◆ ◆   In this chapter, we have studied the institutions that make up the banking and financial system in the United Kingdom. We've seen how cash and deposits held at banks and building societies comprise the means of payment – money. We've also seen how the banks and building societies expand their deposits and create money by making loans. Finally, we've seen how interest rates adjust to make the quantity of money that firms and households are willing to hold equal to the quantity of money that the banking system has created.   ◆ ◆   In the next chapter, we're going to see how the quantity of money is regulated and influenced by the actions of the Bank of England. We're also going to discover how, by its influence on the money supply, the Bank of England is able to influence interest rates, there-by affecting the level of aggregate demand. It is through its effects on the money supply and inter-est rates and their wider ramifications that the Bank of England is able to help steer the course of the economy.

S U M M A R Y

What is Money?

Money, the means of payment, has four functions: it is a medium of exchange, a unit of account, a standard of deferred payment and a store of value. The earliest forms of money were commodities and, later, convert-ible paper money. Today we use fiat money in the form of notes and coins and, more importantly, pri-vate debt money in the form of deposits at banks and building societies.

The official measure of money in the United Kingdom is M4 which includes notes and coin held by the public together with deposits at banks and build-ing societies. It does not exactly correspond to the assets that function as means of payment – money – because it includes long-term deposits that must be converted into cash or chequable deposits to be used

as a means of payment. But these other deposits included in M4 are highly liquid. Cheques and credit cards are not money. (pp. 722–728)

Types of Security

There are three main types of security: fixed inter-est securities, bills and equities. Fixed interest securities are issued by governments and compa-nies. They are usually sold initially for £100. Often they have a maturity date on which the original price paid will be repaid by the borrower, but some are undated. Interest is paid at a fixed percentage of the original purchase price throughout the secu-rity's life.

Bills represent short-term loans. They are issued by governments and companies. They have a maturity date on which the borrower will repay the lender a specified amount. People buy new bills at a discount, that is, for less than the repayment value. People who buy bills get no interest on them but get a reward because the maturity value exceeds the discounted price originally paid.

Equities – or ordinary shares – are issued only by companies and are never repaid by companies. The owners of shares in any company receive no interest but instead receive dividends which are paid out of the company's profits and reflect the profitability of the company. (pp. 728–729)

Financial Intermediaries

The financial intermediaries whose liabilities serve as money are banks and building societies. All of these institutions take in deposits, hold cash reserves to ensure that they can meet their depositors' demands for cash, hold some securities and make loans. Financial intermediaries make a profit by borrowing at a lower interest rate than that at which they lend. Financial intermediaries provide four main economic services: they minimize the cost of obtaining funds, minimize the cost of monitoring borrowers, pool risks and create liquidity. (pp. 729–733)

How Banks Create Money

Banks and building societies create money by making loans. When a loan is made to one person and the amount lent is spent, much of it ends up as someone else's deposit. The total quantity of deposits that can be supported by a given amount of reserves (the deposits multiplier) is equal to 1 divided by the desired reserve ratio. (pp. 733–736)

The Demand for Money

The quantity of money demanded is the amount of cash held by the public plus the amount of deposits they hold at banks and building societies. The quantity of real money demanded depends on the interest rate and real GDP. A higher level of real GDP increases the quantity of real money demanded. A higher interest rate reduces the quantity of real money demanded. The quantity of nominal money demanded depends on real GDP, interest rates and the price level. The quantity of money demanded is sometimes changed by financial innovation. (pp. 736–744)

Interest Rate Determination

Changes in interest rate levels achieve equilibrium in the markets for money and securities. There is an inverse relationship between the interest rate level and the price of a security. The higher the interest rate, the lower is the price of a security. Money market equilibrium achieves an interest rate level and a security price level that make the quantity of real money available willingly held. (pp. 744–746)

KEY ELEMENTS

Key Terms

Key Figures and Table

REVIEW QUESTIONS

1 What is money? What are its functions?

2 What are the different forms of money?

3 What is the official measure of money in the United Kingdom? How closely does this measure correspond to the economic definition of money?

4 Are cheques and credit cards money? Explain your answer.

5 What is a financial intermediary? What are their economic functions?

6 What are the main deposit-taking financial inter- mediaries in the United Kingdom?

7 What are the main items in the balance sheet of a bank?

8 In what respects do building societies resemble banks and in what respects do they differ from banks?

9 How do banks create money?

10 Define the deposits multiplier. Explain why it equals 1 divided by the reserve ratio.

11 Distinguish between nominal money and real money.

12 What do we mean by the demand for money?

13 What determines the demand for real money?

14 What is the opportunity cost of holding money?

15 What happens to the interest rate on a fixed interest security if the price of the security increases?

16 How does equilibrium come about in the money market?

PROBLEMS

1 Which of the following are included in M4?
   a Bank notes in a cash dispenser.
   b Coins in a pay-telephone money box.
   c Your credit card.
   d The loan the bank has just credited to your deposit.
   e The cheque you have just written out for your rent.

2 You take £20 out of your bank from its cash dispenser. What happens to M4?

3 On the island of Sodor the banks have deposit liabilities of £2,000 billion, reserves of £250 bil- lion, loans of £1,000 billion and total assets of £2,500 billion.
   a Using Table 26.4 as a guide, set out the bal- ance sheet of the banks. If there are any missing assets, call them 'other assets' and if there are any missing liabilities, call them 'other liabilities'.
   b What is the banks' reserve ratio?
   c What is the deposits multiplier?

4 An immigrant arrives in Sparta with £1,000 which is put into a bank deposit. All the banks in Sparta have a desired reserve ratio of 10 per cent.
   a What is the initial increase in the quantity of bank deposits when the immigrant arrives?
   b How much does the immigrant's bank lend out?

   c Using a format similar to that in Table 26.6, calculate the amount lent and the amount of deposits created at each 'round', assuming like that table that there is no cash drain.
   d By how much has the quantity of money increased after 20 rounds of lending?
   e What is the ultimate increase in the quantity of money, in bank loans, and in bank deposits?

5 You are given the following information about the economy of Thrace. At present, real GDP is £4,000, the interest rate is 5 per cent and the quantity of real money demanded is £2,000. For each £1 increase in real GDP, the demand for real money increases 50 pence, other things remaining the same. Also, if the interest rate increases by 1 percentage point (for example, from 5 per cent to 6 per cent), the quantity of real money demanded falls by £50.
   a How much real money is demanded at an interest rate of 10 per cent?
   b How high would interest rates have to be for no money to be demanded?
   c Draw a graph showing the demand curve for real money when real GDP is £4,000.
   d Draw a graph showing the demand curve for real money when real GDP is £5,000.

CHAPTER 27

CENTRAL BANKING AND MONETARY POLICY

After studying this chapter you will be able to:

◆ Describe the role of the Bank of England

◆ Describe the tools used by the Bank of England to influence the money supply and interest rates

◆ Explain what an open market operation is and how it works

◆ Explain how an open market operation changes the money supply

◆ Explain how the Bank of England influences interest rates and the value of the pound

◆ Explain how the Bank of England influences real GDP and the price level

◆ Explain the quantity theory of money

IN 1983, A YOUNG COUPLE PLANNING TO BUY A FIRST HOME HAS FOUND THE PERFECT place. But mortgage rates are 15 per cent a year. Amid much distress, they put off their purchase until interest rates fall, making a mortgage affordable. What determines interest rates? Are they determined by forces of nature? Or is somebody pushing the buttons somewhere? ◆ ◆ You suspect that someone is indeed pushing the buttons. For you've just read in your newspaper: 'The Bank of England is prepared to reduce interest rates to stimulate aggregate demand.' And a few months earlier, you read: 'The Bank of England doesn't plan to cut interest rates unless inflation starts to fall.' What is the Bank of England? Why would it want to change interest rates? And how can it influence interest rates? ◆ ◆ During the 1970s, the quantity of money in the United Kingdom (and in many other countries)

Pushing the Buttons

increased quickly, but during the 1980s it increased at a slower pace. During the early 1990s, in Russia and Brazil, the quantity of money increased very rapidly. In Switzerland and Germany, the quantity of money has increased slowly. Does the rate of increase in the quantity of money matter? What are the effects of changes in the rate of increase in the quantity of money on the economy?

◆ ◆ ◆ ◆ In this chapter, we extend our study of banking to bring the central bank into the picture. We learn about the instruments available to a central bank that are used to manipulate the quantity of money and the interest rate.

The Bank of England

The Bank of England is the United Kingdom's central bank. A **central bank** is a public authority which has various functions. From an economic point of view, the Bank of England's most important function is to implement the monetary policy demanded by the government of the day. *Monetary policy* is the attempt to control the economy by changing the quantity of money in circulation and adjusting interest rates. Monetary policy is particularly concerned with controlling the rate of inflation, influencing the foreign exchange value of the currency and moderating business cycles. Later in this chapter we will study the tools available to the Bank of England in its conduct of monetary policy and we will work out the effects of the Bank of England's actions on interest rates. But first we'll examine the origins and functions of the Bank of England.

The Origins and Functions of the Bank of England

The Bank of England was established in 1694. At first, the Bank of England was much like any other bank, but later in 1694 it lent £1.2 million to the government and it soon developed a close and favourable relationship with the government. Over the following three centuries it gradually acquired its central banking functions and became very different from the other banks. These functions are:

◆ Banker to the government
◆ Sole effective issuer of bank notes
◆ Banker to other banks
◆ Lender of last resort

Let's look briefly at each of these functions.

Banker to the Government   The Bank of England's role as banker to the government means that the government's own bank deposits – called public deposits – are held there. It also means that the Bank of England manages the government's borrowing requirements. In principle, there are two ways in which the government can borrow, either from the Bank of England directly – taking a loan or overdraft like a business does – or by selling bonds. Except for those early days when the Bank did make a loan to the government, direct lending has been frowned on.

Instead of making direct loans to the government, the Bank of England manages the government's borrowing through the sale of securities. Some of these government securities are sold to the public, and some are bought by the Bank of England itself. This function of the Bank of England gives it a powerful place in the market for government securities, a power that it uses, as you will see later in this chapter, in its conduct of monetary policy.

Sole Effective Issuer of Bank Notes   As early as 1742, the Bank of England became the only large bank (that is, a bank with more than six owners) allowed to issue notes in England. But surprisingly, perhaps, it was not until 1921 that small English banks finally ceased issuing notes. Today, the Bank's monopoly on note issue is effectively complete since the banks in Scotland and Northern Ireland that issue their own notes must back their issue fully with Bank of England notes. That is, they must hold Bank of England notes of a total value that equals their own note issue.

Banker to Other Banks   The Bank of England's role as banker to the other banks means that the banks keep some money there, in deposits called bankers' deposits. It also means that the Bank of England helps the banks when they are short of funds. Recall from Chapter 26 that the banks have deposit liabilities that far exceed their cash reserves. So each bank runs the risk that it might not be able to honour its obligations to its depositors. If such a situation arises, the Bank of England is able to step in and provide assistance. But when it does so, it is exercising its function as lender of last resort. Let's look more closely at this function.

Lender of Last Resort   The Bank of England acts as a **lender of last resort** to the financial system. It provides loans when the system is short of reserves. But the Bank of England does not make loans directly to banks. Instead, it lends to *discount houses*. Discount houses are almost unique to the UK financial system, and their position in it is shown in Fig. 27.1[1]. They make a profit by borrowing from banks and by buying bills – commercial bills, local authority bills and

---

[1]The only other financial system that has discount houses is that of South Africa.

FIGURE 27.1

The Discount Houses and the Financial System

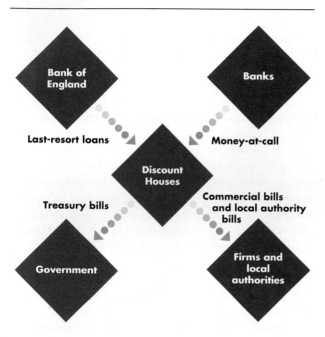

The discount houses occupy a central position in the financial system of the United Kingdom. They take very short-term loans from the banks — money-at-call — and when they are short of funds, take last-resort loans from the Bank of England. They use the funds they borrow to buy Treasury bills, commercial bills and local authority bills.

Treasury bills – and holding short-term bonds. The discount houses' borrowing is extremely short-term. Their main borrowing, known as *money-at-call*, is very short-term borrowing from banks, usually repayable within 24 hours. Their lending is also short-term, mainly for less than three months.

Only the discount house have access to *last-resort loans* from the Bank of England. To see how last resort loans work, imagine what happens when all the banks are short of reserves. The first line of defence for the banks is to recall the loans they have made to the discount houses. Now the problem has been passed on to the discount houses. They are short of money. If they remain short of money at the end of the banking day, the discount houses take a last-resort loan from the Bank of England. This loan costs the discount houses a higher interest rate than

they earn on their assets, so they take steps over the next few days to sell off other assets and repay the Bank of England.

The Balance Sheet of the Bank of England

The functions of the Bank of England are reflected in its balance sheet shown in Table 27.1[2]. The assets on the left side are what the Bank of England owns and the liabilities on the right side are what it owes. Most of the Bank of England's assets are UK government securities. The most significant aspect of the Bank of England's balance sheet is on the liabilities side.

The largest liability of the Bank of England is notes in circulation. These are the bank notes that are used in daily transactions. Some of these bank notes are in circulation with the public and others are in the tills and vaults of banks and other financial institutions.

You may wonder why Bank of England notes are considered a liability of the Bank. Notes are considered a liability of the bank that issues them because, when notes were invented, they gave their owner a claim on the coin reserves of the issuing bank. Such notes are convertible paper money. The holder of such a note could convert the note on demand into gold or coins at a guaranteed price. So when a bank issued a note, it held itself liable to convert that note into coins. Modern bank notes are non-convertible. A non-convertible note is a bank note that is not convertible into any coins or any other commodity and that obtains its value by government fiat – hence the term fiat money. Such bank notes are considered the legal liability of the bank that issues them. However, they are backed by holdings of securities and loans, not by reserves of commodities or coins. Bank of England notes are backed by the Bank's holdings of government securities.

The other significant liability of the Bank of England is the deposits held there by the banks. We saw these deposits as an asset in the balance sheets of the banks. The remaining liability of the Bank of

---

[2] The Bank of England publishes its balance sheet in two parts, one for what is known as the Banking Department and one for the Issue Department. But this division has no economic significance and the table shows the consolidated balance sheet for the Bank.

TABLE 27.1

Bank of England Balance Sheet for 29 September, 1993

Assets (billions of pounds)		Liabilities (billions of pounds)	
Government securities	8,319	Notes in circulation	17,120
Other securities	10,030	Public deposits	1,271
Other assets	4,888	Bankers' deposits	1,638
		Other liabilities	3,208
Total	23,237	Total	23,237

Source: *Bank of England Quarterly Bulletin*, November 1993, Table 1 and our calculations.

England consists of items such as government deposits (public deposits) and accounts held by foreign central banks (such as the German Bundesbank and the US Federal Reserve Board).

The two largest items on the liability side of the Bank of England's balance sheet make up most of the monetary base. The **monetary base** is the sum of notes in circulation, bankers' deposits and coin in circulation. The monetary base is also known as **M0**. (Coins, incidentally, are made by the Royal Mint, unlike bank notes which are printed by the Bank of England, so there is no entry for coins on the Bank of England's balance sheet.) Later in this chapter, we'll see how the Bank of England can change the monetary base and, as a result, change the quantity of money and interest rates.

We've now described the key functions of the Bank of England and studied its balance sheet. The key function of the Bank is to make monetary policy. But in this activity, the Bank is constrained in various ways. Its actions are limited by:

◆ Political constraints
◆ International constraints

Political Constraints

The political constraints on a central bank depend to a large degree on the law that established it and on the traditions that have grown up governing the relationship between the central bank and the government. There are two possible relationships between a country's central bank and its central government:

◆ Independence
◆ Subservience

Let's look at each case.

Independence An independent central bank is one that has complete autonomy to determine the nation's monetary policy. Government public servants and elected officials may comment on monetary policy but the governor of the bank is under no obligation to take into account the views of anyone other than his or her own staff and board of directors.

The argument for an independent central bank is that it enables monetary policy to be formulated with a long-term view of maintaining stable prices and prevents monetary policy from being used for short-term, political advantage. Countries that have independent central banks today are Germany, the United States and Switzerland. If, or when, the European Union eventually adopts a single currency, the new European central bank in control of that currency would undoubtedly be an independent central bank on the model of the German Bundesbank.

When the Bank of England was founded it was privately owned, but in an effort to retain the privileges granted to it by the government, it was always mindful of the wishes of the government, so it was never wholly independent in practice. Its independence ceased in principle in 1947 when it was bought by the government.

Subservience A subservient central bank is one that is subservient to its government which means that in the event of a difference of opinion between the central bank and government, it is the government that carries the day and, if necessary, the central bank governor must resign if he or she is unwilling to implement the policies dictated by the government. Most central banks are subservient central banks. Those advocating subservience of the central bank argue that monetary policy is essentially political in its effects and should therefore be subject to democratic control, just like fiscal policy and all other government policies.

Although, ultimately, the Chancellor of the Exchequer is responsible for the United Kingdom's monetary policy, this does not reduce the governor of the Bank of England to a position of impotence. Because of his expertise and authority in the field and because of the quality of the advice that he receives from the Bank's staff of senior economists and advisers, the governor has considerable power in both private and public discussions of monetary policy. Opinions would have to be sharply divided on a range of crucial matters before a government would be willing to run the risk of seeing the governor resign on a dispute over policy. Also, there are times when a government wants to pursue unpopular monetary policies and, at such times, it is very convenient for democratically elected ministers to hide behind the authority of the governor of the Bank of England.

Although a government can instruct a subservient central bank on its monetary policy, it cannot ask for policies that are impossible to pursue. The fact that each country is just one part of a larger international economy imposes some special constraints that we'll now examine.

International Constraints

The international constraints on a central bank arise from the nature of the country's foreign trade, investment and exchange rate policies. The monetary and financial system of the United Kingdom is closely integrated with the rest of the world and especially closely integrated with that of the rest of the European Union. These facts of financial life restrict the actions that the Bank of England might take.

First, the Bank cannot ignore interest rates in other countries. Second, it cannot ignore the effects of its own actions and events in the rest of the world on the value of the pound. That value is determined in a market – a worldwide market – for foreign exchange. There is one fundamental choice that must be made that has far-reaching implications for the monetary policy that the Bank can pursue. This is the choice between three possible foreign exchange regimes. They are:

◆ Fixed exchange rate
◆ Flexible exchange rate
◆ Managed exchange rate

A **fixed exchange rate** is an exchange rate whose value is fixed by the country's central bank. For example, the UK government could instruct the Bank of England to maintain a fixed exchange rate defining the pound to be worth, say, 2 US dollars. To keep this exchange rate for the pound, the Bank of England would have to be ready to buy pounds if sterling started to fall in value and sell them if it started to rise. As

it would be operating on behalf of the government, it would use up the government's official reserve holdings of foreign currencies when it bought pounds. When it sold pounds for foreign currencies, it would place the foreign currencies it acquired in the government's official reserves – called the exchange equalization account. To maintain a fixed exchange rate, the government would need large reserves of foreign currencies for the Bank to use to buy pounds in periods when its value seemed likely to fall.

A **flexible exchange rate** is an exchange rate whose value is determined by market forces in the absence of any central bank intervention.

A **managed exchange rate** is an exchange rate whose value is influenced by central bank intervention in the foreign exchange market. Under a managed exchange rate regime, the central bank's intervention does not seek to keep the exchange rate fixed at a pre-announced level but does seek to smooth out wild fluctuations in the exchange rate.

The exchange rate regime adopted by the United Kingdom has varied over the years. The main regimes have been:

◆ Pre-World War I (pre-1914) – fixed
◆ 1914–1925 – floating
◆ 1925–1931 – fixed
◆ 1931–1945 – floating
◆ 1945–1972 – fixed, adjustable peg
◆ 1972–1990 – managed
◆ 1990–1992 – fixed
◆ 1992 onwards – managed

For many years until 1914, the value of the pound was fixed against the US dollar at £1 = $4.87. The exchange rate then floated, apart from a brief period from 1925 to 1931, until the end of World War II. Following an agreement reached in 1944 at Bretton Woods in the United States, many Western countries adopted a system of fixed exchange rates, though occasional devaluations or revaluations were allowed causing the system to be called the *adjustable peg* system. The pound was devalued in 1949 and 1967.

Between 1972 and 1990, the pound again floated against other currencies, though the float was a managed one. Indeed, following massive oil price rises by the main oil exporting countries in the early 1970s, many countries suffered severe balance of payments problems and found themselves unable to stick to their old fixed exchange rates.

In 1990, the United Kingdom joined the exchange rate mechanism (ERM) of the European Monetary

System which had been set up some years earlier by the European Union (see Chapter 35). Under this system EU member countries try to maintain considerable stability between their own currencies. Although the exchange rates were not fixed, most members tried to keep their currencies within 2.25 per cent of an agreed value against each other member's currency and members tried to keep their currency stable in relation to the average of the other members' currencies. The United Kingdom joined the ERM later than most other members and sterling was allowed to fluctuate by as much as 6 per cent. This extra leeway was chiefly the result of the fact that the country had relatively high inflation before 1990 so that sterling was not very stable in relation to other currencies. Although the 6 per cent leeway meant sterling was not fixed, it was close to being fixed.

In September 1992, it proved impossible for the United Kingdom to prevent its currency falling more than 6 per cent against other ERM currencies so the pound was withdrawn from the ERM and is again on a managed float. Shortly afterwards, the Italian lira was also withdrawn. Further problems in 1993 meant that from 1 August that year the remaining members agreed to allow much wider 15 per cent limits.

Exchange Rate Regime and the Money Supply
The Bank of England is effectively a monopolist in the supply of pounds. It is true that other banks and building societies can create money, but the Bank of England can control how much can be created. So the Bank is in the same type of situation as a monopolist selling electricity to a town. The electricity monopolist can determine a price at which to sell electricity, leaving the market to decide how much to buy at that price, or it can decide on a production rate, leaving the market to determine the price at which that quantity will be sold. The monopolist cannot choose both the price of its output and the quantity that people will buy.

Similarly, if the Bank does choose the quantity of money that will be supplied, then it cannot also choose the price at which pounds exchange for other currencies (or for goods and services). Alternatively, if the Bank of England fixes the price at which pounds exchange for some other currency – or for a basket of currencies – then it cannot control the quantity of pounds outstanding. So, when a country fixes its exchange rate, its central bank has virtually no freedom of manoeuvre for determining an independent, national monetary policy.

By permitting the foreign currency value of the pound to fluctuate quite widely from 1972 to 1990 and since 1992, the Bank of England retained control over monetary policy in the United Kingdom, that is, over the UK money supply and interest rates. How the Bank exercised that control is discussed later in this chapter. How the foreign exchange markets work to determine the value of the pound and how the Bank's interest rate policies influence the pound are the subjects of Chapter 35.

We've now examined the origins and functions of the Bank of England, and the constitutional and international constraints it faces. Let's now look at the instruments it has available for its conduct of monetary policy.

Monetary Policy Tools

There are three main tools which a central bank can use to alter the money supply[3]:

◆ Asset requirements
◆ Interest rate on last-resort loans
◆ Open market operations

Asset Requirements We have seen that banks will use their experience to decide what level of reserves is prudent. But in many countries the central bank imposes controls over the minimum level of reserves to ensure that the banks behave in a way which it feels is reasonable. In the United Kingdom the only requirement at present is that each bank must keep at the Bank of England a deposit that is at least 0.35 per cent of its *eligible liabilities*. Eligible liabilities are a bank's total liabilities minus certain deductions, notably non-sterling deposits and long-term CDs. The deposits which banks keep at the Bank of England as a result of this 0.35 per cent rule are called *cash ratio deposits*. As these deposits have to be maintained, they cannot be withdrawn by the banks. The banks always try to keep a little extra at the Bank, and their extra deposits are called *operational deposits*.

If the Bank of England raised the level for cash ratio deposits, it would force the banks to contract their lending. To see why, suppose you are the

---

[3] In the past the Bank of England has also used credit ceilings which placed direct limits on the amount of money individual banks could create. Such ceilings are considered inferior to other methods of control, because they inhibit competition between banks, so they have not been used since 1972.

chairman of a bank which initially has eligible liabilities of £100 billion and a cash ratio deposit of £0.35 billion. And say the Bank of England raises the ratio for cash ratio deposits to 0.5 per cent of eligible liabilities. You now need £0.5 billion in your cash ratio deposit at the Bank so you need to find an extra £0.15 billion to place there. So you demand a repayment of £0.15 billion from the discount houses. They borrow £0.15 billion from the Bank of England which they then transfer to you, and you place this with your other deposit at the Bank. But now your loans to the discount houses are lower so that you have fewer highly liquid assets. In order to be prudent – and in order to persuade the Bank of England that you are prudent and deserve to keep your licence to operate as a bank – you must reduce your lending. So you end up with lending and liabilities at a much lower level than you started with.

If the Bank of England wants to increase bank lending it could take the opposite action and reduce the cash ratio deposits requirement imposed on the banks. But there would come a time when the imposed limits were as low as the banks deemed prudent. At that point any further lowering in the compulsory ratio would have no effect as the banks would not want to operate at the permitted new low ratios.

In the United Kingdom, changing the asset requirements of the banks was commonly used until the 1970s to alter the money supply. Since then the method has not been used but the Bank retains the right to use it if it wishes. The method is still used in many other countries, both in Europe and elsewhere.

Interest Rate on Last-resort Loans When the Bank of England makes a last-resort loan to the discount houses, it charges interest. For 270 years, between 1702 and 1972, the rate it charged was publicly announced by the Bank and was known as Bank Rate. After 1972 the name changed to minimum lending rate (MLR), but after 20 August, 1981 the Bank stopped announcing the rate it would charge on these loans. Instead it has allowed discount houses to find out the rate by asking when they actually want to borrow.

Last-resort lending is generally done at high 'penal' rates. In countries where the central bank makes last-resort loans directly to the banks, the effect of a rise in the interest rate on last-resort loans is simple. To decrease the likelihood of needing a last-resort loan, the banks will operate with higher reserves and will cut back on their lending. In the United Kingdom, where the Bank of England makes last-resort loans to the discount houses, the situation

is rather different. As the banks never take last-resort loans, a rise in the interest rate charged on last-resort loans has no direct effect on them. But a rise in the MLR does decrease bank lending. Let's see why.

Suppose you are the manager of a discount house and that you generally borrow from the banks at 5 per cent and lend your funds at 6 per cent. From time to time you have to repay your loans to the banks and instead borrow at a penal rate of 7 per cent from the Bank of England, so on these occasions you end up borrowing at 7 per cent and lending at 6 per cent. This is unpleasant but tolerable. However, suppose the Bank raises its penal rate to 8 per cent. You do not ever want to find yourself borrowing at 8 per cent and lending at 6 per cent. So you decide to prevent this happening by raising the interest rate on your own lending, say to 7 per cent.

An apparent danger of raising the rate on your lending is that people might not want to borrow from you any more. For if your lending rate rises and the lending rates of the banks do not, borrowers may switch from you to the banks. Curiously, this would not suit the banks, for if people stop borrowing from the discount houses, the discount houses will stop borrowing from the banks. And the banks need to lend money-at-call to the discount houses in order to have enough highly liquid assets. So the banks have to raise their interest rates in line with yours to keep you in business, because you will then borrow from them and enable them to have some highly liquid money-at-call. So their interest rates rise and the demand for loans from them falls. Their lending will therefore fall, but notice that their reserves have not fallen. They will have excess reserves but cannot cut their interest rates and lend any more.

If the Bank of England wishes to expand bank lending and the money supply, it can reduce the rate of interest on last-resort lending. This will encourage the discount houses to lend at lower rates. In turn, the banks will be able to lend at lower rates and encourage more people to borrow from them.

The interest rate on last-resort loans is rarely used on its own. It is usually part of an overall monetary policy action whose centrepiece is the quantity of monetary base. And this quantity is determined by the Bank of England's open market operations.

Open Market Operations An **open market operation** is the purchase or sale of UK government bills or bonds by the Bank of England. When the Bank of

England buys government securities, its payments for them put additional reserves in the hands of the banks and so loosen credit conditions. With extra reserves, the banks will increase their lending, the quantity of money increases and interest rates fall. When the Bank of England sells government securities, tighter monetary and credit conditions are created. With lower reserves, the banks decrease their lending, the money supply decreases and interest rates rise. This policy tool is the most important one, and we study it further in the next part of this chapter.

Controlling the Money Supply

The money supply is determined by the actions of the Bank of England. Let's see how. We begin by looking in some detail at what happens when the Bank of England conducts an open market operation.

How Open Market Operations Work

Open market operations affect the balance sheets of the Bank of England, the banks and the rest of the economy. Table 27.2 records the changes in these balance sheets. When the Bank of England buys securities, there are two possible sellers: the banks or other agents. Part (a) of the table works out what happens when banks sell the securities that the Bank of England buys.

When the Bank of England buys securities from the banks, it pays for them by crediting the banks' deposits at the Bank of England. The Bank of England's balance sheet changes. Its assets rise by £100 million – the additional securities bought – and its liabilities also rise by £100 million – the additional bankers' deposits. The banks' balance sheet also changes but their total assets remain constant. Their deposits at the Bank of England rise by £100 million and their securities fall by £100 million.

Part (b) of the table deals with the case in which the banks do not sell any securities and the Bank of England buys securities from agents other than the banks. The Bank of England's holdings of UK government securities increase by £100 million and other agents' holdings of government securities go down by £100 million. The Bank of England pays for these bills by giving cheques drawn on itself to the sellers. The

sellers take the cheques to their own banks where deposits rise by £100 million. The banks in turn present the cheques to the Bank of England which credits the banks' deposits there with the value of the cheques. Bankers' deposits at the Bank of England – which are part of their reserves – increase by £100 million.

In each case, then, an open market purchase of securities by the Bank of England raises the banks' deposits with itself and so increases the banks' reserves. If the Bank of England conducts an open market *sale* of securities, the events we have just traced occur in reverse. The Bank of England's assets and liabilities decrease in value as do the reserves of the banks.

The effects of an open market purchase that we traced in Table 27.2 are not the end of the story – they are just the beginning. With an increase in reserves, the banks can now make more loans. That has a big effect on the quantity of money for, as we saw in Chapter 26, by making loans banks themselves create money. Let's explore the next stage in the process.

Monetary Base and Bank Reserves

We've defined the *monetary base* as the sum of cash plus banks' deposits at the Bank of England. Some cash is held as reserves by banks. So the monetary base equals banks' reserves plus cash held by the public. When the monetary base rises, both bank reserves and cash held by the public tend to rise. But it is only the rise in reserves which can be used to enable the banks to create additional deposits and so create additional money. When the banks do get extra reserves and create extra deposits, they usually find that the public, who now have more deposits, also want more cash. So the public take some cash out of the banks and create a **cash drain** out of the banks. This cash drain reduces the banks' reserves and so reduces the amount of extra money they can create.

The **money multiplier** is the amount by which a change in the monetary base must be multiplied to determine the resulting change in the quantity of money. It differs from the simple money multiplier that we studied in Chapter 26. That simple money multiplier or *deposits multiplier* is the amount by which a change in bank reserves must be multiplied to determine the resulting change in deposits. Since the Bank of England can control the monetary base, but not the amount of it that is used as bank reserves, it is the money multiplier that is relevant in

TABLE 27.2

An Open Market Operation

(a) BANKS SELL SECURITIES TO THE BANK OF ENGLAND

Effects on the balance sheet of the Bank of England

Change in assets (millions of pounds)		Change in liabilities (millions of pounds)	
UK government securities	+100	Banks' deposits (reserves)	+100

Effects on the balance sheet of the banks

Change in assets (millions of pounds)		Change in liabilities (millions of pounds)	
Banks' deposits (reserves)	+100		
UK government securities	−100		

(b) OTHER AGENTS SELL SECURITIES TO THE BANK OF ENGLAND

Effects on the balance sheet of the Bank of England

Change in assets (millions of pounds)		Change in liabilities (millions of pounds)	
UK government securities	+100	Bank's deposits (reserves)	+100

Effects on the balance sheet of the banks

Change in assets(millions of pounds)		Change in liabilities (millions of pounds)	
Banks' deposits (reserves)	+100	Deposits	+100

Effects on the balance sheet of the other agents

Change in assets (millions of pounds)		Change in liabilities (millions of pounds)	
Deposits	+100	UK government securities	−100

determining the effects of the Bank's actions on the money supply. The key difference between the money multiplier and the simple money multiplier is that the money multiplier allows for the cash drain.

The Multiplier Effect of an Open Market Operation

We'll work out the multiplier effect of an open market operation for the case where the Bank of England buys securities from the banks. Because the purchases are made from the banks, they have no immediate effect on the quantity of money even though they do increase the banks' reserves. The banks hold more reserves and fewer securities. But the banks have *excess reserves*. When the banks have excess reserves, the sequence of events shown in Fig. 27.2 takes place. These events are:

◆ Banks lend their excess reserves.
◆ Deposits are created equal in value to the new loans.
◆ The money supply increases by the amount of the new deposits.
◆ The new deposits are used by the borrowers to make payments.
◆ Households and firms receive payments made by the borrowers.
◆ Part of the receipts are held as cash – a cash drain.
◆ Part of the receipts are retained in bank deposits
◆ Bank reserves fall by the amount of the cash drain.
◆ Desired reserves increase by a fraction – the desired reserve ratio – of the increase in deposits.
◆ Excess reserves fall partly because the cash drain reduces reserves and partly because desired reserves increase.
◆ Banks lend their excess reserves and the process just described repeats.

FIGURE 27.2

A Round in the Multiplier Process Following an Open Market Operation

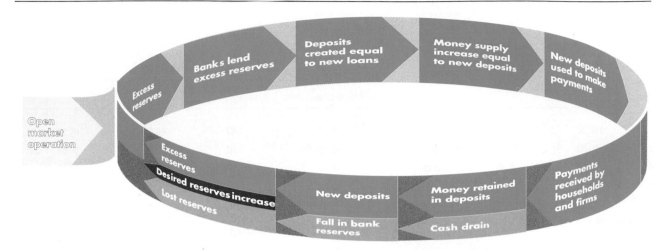

An open market purchase of government securities increases bank reserves and creates excess reserves. Banks make new loans and this lending increases the level of deposits and the money supply. New loans are spent, and the households and firms that receive these funds leave some in their bank deposits and take some as cash, so there is a cash drain from the banks. The cash drain reduces the level of bank deposits, though deposits are still higher than they were before the new loans were made. Because deposits are higher than at the start, banks need more reserves than they started with. The level of their excess reserves falls partly because they need more reserves and partly because of the cash drain. However, even at the end of the round banks still have some excess reserves, so they make more new loans and another round begins. The process repeats until excess reserves have been eliminated. The money supply increases for two reasons: the public hold more cash and more deposits.

The sequence just described is similar to that which we studied in Chapter 26 except that there we ignored the cash drain. The sequence repeats in a series of 'rounds' but each round begins with a smaller quantity of excess reserves than the previous one. The process continues until excess reserves have finally been eliminated.

Table 27.3 keeps track of the magnitudes of new loans, the cash drain, the increase in deposits and reserves, the increase in desired reserves and the change in excess reserves at each round of the multiplier process. It assumes that all banks want reserves of £1 for every £10 of deposits – these reserves will cover their cash ratio deposits at the Bank of England and a prudent level of cash in their branches. The table also assumes that the public want to hold £1 in cash for every £2 of deposits[4].

We'll focus on the first line of the table.

The initial open market operation increases the banks' reserves but, as deposits do not change, there is no change in desired reserves. So the banks have excess reserves of £100 million. They can now make new loans worth £100 million. To see why, suppose you are the manager of one bank which has reserves of £10 million and deposits of £100 million, and suppose you sell securities to the Bank of England for £1 million. You now have excess reserves of £1 million. You are keen to make new loans, but you know that when you lend money to your depositors they will spend it. If they spend it all by making cheques to people who bank at other banks, you will have to give reserves to those other banks. So you want to be sure that if all their spending *did* go to other banks, you would still end up with £1 of reserves for each £10 of deposits. You can be sure of this by making new loans for the amount of your excess reserves, that is for £1 million. Initially, deposits at your bank rise by £1 million to £101 million. The worst that can happen to your reserves is that the

---

[4]These numbers are chosen to illustrate the *principle* in the clearest possible way. We look later at the actual ratios and the money multiplier in the United Kingdom.

TABLE 27.3

The Expansionary Effect of an Open Market Operation

Round	Excess reserves at start of round	New loans = deposits created	Cash drain	Deposits created *not* withdrawn in cash	Change in desired reserves	Excess reserves at end of round	Increase in the money supply
				(millions of pounds)			
1	100.00	100.00	33.33	66.67	6.67	60.00	100.00
2	60.00	60.00	20.00	40.00	4.00	36.00	60.00
3	36.00	36.00	12.00	24.00	2.40	21.60	36.00
4	21.60	21.60	7.20	14.40	1.44	12.96	21.60
5	12.96	12.96	4.32	8.64	0.86	7.78	12.96
All other rounds		19.44	6.48	12.96	1.30	–	19.44
Total		250.00	83.33	166.67	16.67	–	250.00

borrowers spend this £1 million in favour of people who bank elsewhere. If they do, you must give reserves of £1 million to other banks and your reserves drop back to £10 million. At the same time, deposits at your bank fall by £1 million to £100 million as a result of spending by the borrowers, so you end up with your desired reserve ratio.

Let's return to Table 27.3 which looks at banks as a whole. They lend £100 million so deposits initially increase by this amount. When the money borrowed from the banks is spent, the people who receive it decide how much to keep in bank deposits and how much to withdraw in cash. When the public withdraw cash, bank reserves fall. If the recipients of the £100 million spent by the borrowers were to withdraw all £100 million in cash, the level of bank deposits and the level of bank reserves would both fall by £100 million to their original levels. The banks would have no excess reserves so there would be no further rounds of bank lending.

As it is, the recipients keep most of their receipts in their bank deposits. They take out £33.33 million of their receipts in cash and leave £66.67 million in deposits, for they like £1 in cash for every £2 in deposits. This cash drain reduces the reserves of the banks by £33.33 million. This fall in reserves is smaller than the level of new loans made by the banks – which was £100 million. Even the bank you manage

will probably find its reserves end up only about £0.33 million lower than they were when you made your extra £1 million worth of loans. Why is this, given that you have lent £1 million and given that most, if not all, of these loans may be spent in favour of people who bank elsewhere?

The answer is that when the Bank of England makes open market purchases, it persuades people to sell securities by offering high prices. So when you sold some of your banks' securities, other banks sold some of theirs. So they all had excess reserves and they all made new loans, and some of the borrowers at their banks spent money in favour of depositors with yours. You may well receive enough reserves from the other banks to offset the reserves you lose to them when your borrowers spend the new loans you give to them. The chief reason why you may actually end up with fewer reserves is that the depositors at your bank who have received payments from borrowers elsewhere will want to hold some of their extra money in cash form. So they will withdraw some cash from your bank. Taking the banks as a whole, reserves fall *only* because of the cash drain.

Looking at the top line of the table, we see that deposits initially increased by £100 million, the amount of the new loans. These new loans were spent by the borrowers and the people who received the money withdrew £33.33 million in cash, so the level of bank deposits fell back by £33.33 million, but it was still £66.67 million higher than it was before the loans were made. Because deposits were then £66.67 million higher than they were at the start of the round, the banks wanted £6.67 million more in reserves than they wanted at the start of the round. This reduced the level of excess reserves by £6.67 million. The level of excess reserves fell by a further £33.33 million as the banks lost this amount through cash withdrawals. So at the end of round one, the banks' excess reserves were £40 million less than they were immediately after the open market operations took place. Their excess reserves were then £100 million. They were £60 million at the end of the first round.

At this stage we have completed round 1. We have been around the circle shown in Fig. 27.2. The banks still have excess reserves but the level has fallen from £100 million at the beginning of the round to £60 million at the end of the round. Round 2 now begins. But before we look at round 2, let's see how much the money supply increased by in round 1. It increased by the increase in bank deposits – £66.67 million – plus the increase in cash held by the public – £33.33 million – which makes £100 million in all. This is, of course, equal to the £100 million created by the banks with their new loans.

Now look at round 2. With excess reserves of £60 million, the banks can make further new loans worth £60 million. The borrowers spend this and the recipients withdraw £20 million in a cash drain leaving £40 million in their deposits. As deposits are now £40 million more than they were at the end of the first round, the banks want £4 million more in reserves. The cash drain reduces excess reserves by £20 million while the banks' desire for extra reserves reduces excess reserves by £4 million. So excess reserves fall to £36 million. Notice in round 2 how the money supply increased by £60 million. You can work this out as the £40 million increase in bank deposits plus the increase of £20 million in the cash held by the public. Also, it equals the £60 million created by the banks with their round 2 loans.

The process that we've just described keeps on repeating. Table 27.3 shows the first five rounds in this process and collapses all the remaining ones into the next to last row of the table. At the end of the process, the quantity of money has increased by £250 million.

The accumulated increase in bank deposits, cash

FIGURE 27.3

The Multiplier Effect of an Open Market Operation

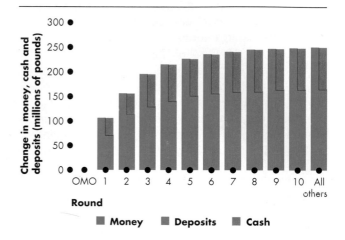

An open market operation (OMO) in which government securities are bought from the banks has no immediate effect on the money supply but creates excess reserves in the banking system. When loans are made with these reserves, the loans are used to buy goods and services. The recipients withdraw some of their receipts in the form of cash but keep the rest in bank deposits. In each round the money supply rises by the amount of the extra cash held by the recipients plus the extra deposits held by the recipients. The rising deposits cause the banks to want more reserves while the cash withdrawals reduce their reserves. So in each round the level of excess reserves falls. Banks continue to increase their lending until excess reserves have been eliminated.

and the quantity of money is illustrated in Fig. 27.3. As you can see, when the open market operation takes place (labelled OMO in the figure), there is no initial change in either the quantity of money or its components. Then, after the first round of bank lending, the quantity of money increases by £100 million – the size of the open market operation. In successive rounds, the quantity of money and its components continue to increase but by successively smaller amounts.

The Money Multiplier

Take another look at Table 27.3. In that example, the Bank of England bought £100 million worth of securities from the banks. The banks initially had £100 million more in their reserves. By the time the effects of the open market operation had worked through fully, there had been a cash drain to the public of £66.67 million. So by the end of the story, the banks had just £16.67 million more in their reserves than they had at the start while the public ended up with £83.33 million more in cash. We can see that the monetary base increased by just £100 million, the same amount as the value of securities purchased by the Bank of England.

However, while the monetary base increased by the value of the open market operation, the money supply increased by much more. It increased by £250 million. In other words it increased by a multiplied amount. The money multiplier is calculated as the ratio of the change in the quantity of money to the change in the monetary base. That is:

$$\text{Money multiplier} = \frac{\text{Change in quantity of money}}{\text{Change in monetary base}}.$$

In our example the value of the multiplier was 250/100 which is 2.5. What determines the value of the money multiplier in the United Kingdom?

You can see from Table 27.3 that the amount of money the banks can create in each round depends on how many excess reserves they have at the beginning of that round. They lose some excess reserves in each round, and the more they lose the less money they will be able to create in the next round. So the size of the money multiplier depends on how much excess reserves they lose in each round. This depends on two ratios. These ratios are:

◆ The cash holdings of households and firms as a fraction of total deposits
◆ The reserve holdings of banks as a fraction of total deposits

Table 27.4 shows how the money multiplier depends on these two ratios. It also provides numbers that illustrate the money multiplier for banks and building societies in the United Kingdom. Remember that M4 covers public holdings of cash (C) and all bank and building society deposits (D). The value of cash holdings of households and firms equals about 3.2 per cent of the value of their bank and building society deposits, so C/D is 0.032. The value of the reserve holdings of the banks and building societies (R) equals about 0.9 per cent of the value of bank deposits in M4, so R/D is 0.009. We can use these ratios to work out the value of the formula in the table and show that the money

---

TABLE 27.4

Calculating the Money Multiplier ◆

	In general	Numbers
1. THE VARIABLES		
Cash held by the public	C	
Reserves held by banks and building societies	R	
Monetary base	MB	
Retail deposits at banks and building societies	D	
Money supply	M	
Money multiplier	mm	
2. DEFINITIONS		
The monetary base is cash held by the public plus bank and building society reserves	$MB = C + R$	
The money supply (M4) is bank and building society deposits plus cash held by the public	$M = D + C$	
The money multiplier is the ratio of the change in the money supply to the change in the monetary base	$mm = \Delta M/\Delta MB$	
3. RATIOS		
Change in cash to change in deposits	$\Delta C/\Delta D$	0.032
Change in reserves to change in deposits	$\Delta R/\Delta D$	0.009
4. CALCULATIONS		
Begin with the definition	$mm = \Delta M/\Delta MB$	
Use the definitions of M and MB to give	$mm = \dfrac{\Delta D + \Delta C}{\Delta C + \Delta R}$	
Divide top and bottom by ΔD	$mm = \dfrac{1 + \Delta C/\Delta D}{\Delta C/\Delta D + \Delta R/\Delta D}$	$\dfrac{1 + 0.032}{0.032 + 0.009}$
		$= 25.2$

multiplier is 25.2. We used different values for the ratios in Table 27.3 where the multiplier was 2.5.

The monetary base is like the base of an inverted pyramid of money. The monetary base itself is divided into cash held by the public and bank reserves. Each pound of cash held by the public adds just £1 to the money supply. Each pound of reserves supports a multiple of itself as money. By changing the monetary base, the Bank of England changes reserves. The change in reserves has a multiplier or magnification effect on the quantity of money outstanding.

REVIEW

T he Bank of England is the United Kingdom's central bank. The Bank of England usually influences the money supply either by changing the interest rate on last-resort loans, or by open market operations. Open market operations not only change the excess reserves of the banking system but also set up a multiplier effect. When excess reserves encourage the banks to make loans and so create new deposits, some of the new deposits are with-drawn in cash causing a cash drain out of the banking system, but the remaining deposits stay in the system. As a result, the banks' demand for reserves rises as they have more deposits to support. The banks continue to lend until the cash drain and the increase in their desired reserves have eliminated all excess reserves. The multiplier effect of an open market operation depends on the scale of the cash drain and the size of the banks' desired reserve ratio. ◆

The Bank of England's objective in conducting open market operations or in taking other actions that influence the quantity of money in circulation is not simply to affect the money supply for its own sake. Its objective is to influence the course of the economy – especially the levels of output, employment and prices. But these effects are indi-rect. The Bank of England's immediate objective is to move interest rates up or down. To work out the effects of the Bank of England's actions on interest rates, we need to work out how and why interest

rates change when the quantity of money changes. We'll discover the answer to these questions by returning to the money market that we studied in Chapter 26.

The Money Supply and Interest Rates

I magine that GDP is hardly rising and that the Bank of England wants to increase aggregate demand and spending. To do so, it wants to reduce interest rates to encourage more borrowing and more investment. What does the Bank of England do? How does it push the buttons to achieve lower interest rates?

The Bank of England might undertake an open market operation, buying government securities from banks, households and firms. As a consequence, the monetary base increases, and banks start making additional loans. The money supply increases.

Suppose that the Bank of England undertakes sufficiently large open market operations to increase the money supply from £500 billion to £600 billion. As a consequence the supply curve of real money shifts to the right, as shown in Fig. 27.4(a), from MS_0 to MS_1. For a moment we have a situation where interest rates are 5 per cent and people want to hold £500 billion, yet they are actually holding £600 billion. The interest rate falls as individuals attempt to reduce their money holdings and buy additional securities. This raises security prices and reduces the interest rate on them. When the interest rate has fallen to 3 per cent, people will willingly holding the higher £600 billion quantity of real money that the banking system has now created.

Conversely, suppose that aggregate demand is ris-ing sharply and the Bank of England fears inflation. The Bank of England decides to take action to slow down spending and cuts the money supply. In this case, the Bank of England might undertake an open market sale of securities. As it does so, it reduces bank reserves and induces the banks to cut down the scale of their lending. What actually happens is that the value of the new bank loans made each day is lower than the value of existing loans that are repaid, so gradually the level of bank lending falls. This continues until the stock of loans outstanding

FIGURE 27.4

The Bank of England Changes the Interest Rate

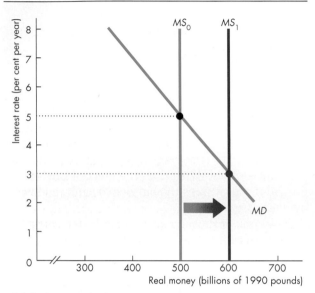

(a) An increase in the money supply

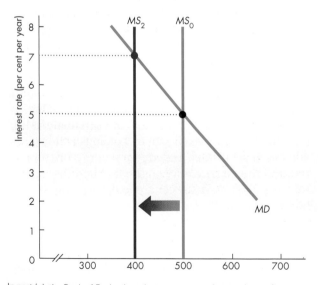

In part (a), the Bank of England conducts an open market purchase of securities, increasing the real money supply to £600 billion. The money supply curve shifts to the right. The new equilibrium interest rate is 3 per cent. In part (b), the Bank of England conducts an open market sale of securities, decreasing the real money supply to £400 billion. The money supply curve shifts to the left, and the interest rate rises to 7 per cent. By changing the money supply, at a given real GDP and price level, the Bank of England can adjust interest rates daily or weekly.

has fallen to a level consistent with the new lower level of reserves. Suppose that the Bank of England undertakes an open market sale of securities on a scale big enough to cut the real money supply to £400 billion. Then the supply of real money curve shifts to the left, as shown in Fig. 27.4(b), from MS_0 to MS_2. For a moment we have a situation where interest rates are 5 per cent and people want to hold £500 billion but are actually holding £400 billion. With less money available, people attempt to acquire additional money by selling securities. As they do so, security prices fall and interest rates rise. Equilibrium occurs when the interest rate has risen to 7 per cent, at which point the new lower real money stock of £400 billion is willingly held.

Discount Houses, Call-money and Last-resort Loans In our description of the events that follow an open market operation *sale* of securities designed to cut the quantity of money, we simplified the story by leaving out a piece of the adjustment process. When the banks are short of reserves, their first line of defence is to recall overnight loans (money-at-call) from the discount houses. The discount houses, now short of funds themselves, use their access to the Bank of England and take a last-resort loan. The banks now have the reserves they need and the open market operation has not decreased the monetary base at all. The Bank of England has provided funds through last-resort loans to replace what it removed with its open market sale.

In practice, though, the banks always do curtail their lending when the Bank makes open market sales of securities. For they know that if they don't, the Bank will simply undertake more and more open market sales. This will repeatedly cause the banks to lose reserves and so repeatedly cause them to force the discount houses to borrow at last resort. The discount houses will soon tire of paying high interest rates on these last-resort loans and will threaten to stop borrowing from the banks. Now a fall in lending by the banks to the discount houses means the banks have less money-at-call and so less of a highly liquid asset that is virtually as good as reserves. This in itself will cause them to cut back on their lending. The Bank may increase the pressure on the discount houses to encourage the banks to reduce their lending by increasing the interest rate on last-resort loans to the discount houses.

As all these actions take place, the monetary base gradually decreases and the effects of the open market operation are felt and have the ultimate outcome that we've already seen. Thus the discount houses slow down but do not change the final outcome of the effects of an open market operation. And by manipulating the last-resort lending rate, the Bank of England can fine-tune the timing of the effects of its open market operations.

The Bank of England in Action

All this discussion of pushing the buttons to alter interest rates sounds nice in theory, but does it really happen? Indeed it does. Let's look at the turbulent years of the late 1970s and the early 1980s and the fight against inflation.

The Bank of England in Action Before 1982   When inflation accelerated in the early 1970s, the Conservatives under Edward Heath and Labour under Harold Wilson and James Callaghan encouraged the Bank of England to use monetary policy in their fight against it. The Bank restrained the money supply to raise interest rates in an effort to reduce spending. If you look back to Fig. 26.4 you can see how interest rates increased between 1973 and 1976.

This tight money policy was eased a little after 1976 in an effort to boost spending. The reason for this desire to boost spending, despite its impact on the price level, was the rising tide of unemployment. But when Margaret Thatcher's government was elected in 1979 it made the fight against inflation its top priority. It was very difficult to restrain the real money supply at this time because the government sector had a deficit – it was spending more money than it received in income – and governments with deficits are always tempted to finance them, at least in part, by borrowing from the Bank of England. As soon as this borrowed money is spent, the reserves of the clearing banks rise and there is the prospect of a multiple expansion of the money supply. Nevertheless, despite this difficulty, interest rates did rise between 1979 and 1981 as you can see in Fig. 26.4. The only weapons used by the Bank to act directly on the money supply were open market operations and the interest rate on last-resort loans. These weapons were used to hold back the growth in the supply of bank loans and money, relative to the growth in their demand.

Let's relive the episode with the help of some economic analysis. As we saw in Fig. 27.4(b), to increase interest rates, the Bank of England has to cut the real money supply. In practice, because the economy is growing and because prices are rising, a slowdown in nominal money supply growth is enough to increase interest rates. It is not necessary actually to cut the nominal money supply. The growth rate of the money supply was cut, although by much less than the government wanted, and the rise in interest rates was thus less dramatic than it might have wished.

The Bank of England in Action After 1982   Interest rates were eased gradually between 1982 and 1988 as inflation was brought under control. A sudden surge in inflation in the late 1980s caused the Bank to raise interest rates again, and they were then held high to help maintain a rather high value for sterling after it joined the ERM in 1990. Once sterling left the ERM in 1992, when inflation was back at a low level, the Bank was able to reduce interest rates sharply in an effort to raise demand and help the economy move out of the 1991–1992 recession.

Profiting by Predicting the Bank of England

Day by day, even minute by minute, the Bank of England can influence interest rates and the money supply by its open market operations and by changing the interest rate on last-resort loans. By increasing the money supply, the Bank of England can cut interest rates; by reducing the money supply, the Bank of England can increase interest rates. Holders of securities know about these powers of the Bank of England. They also know about another relationship that we have worked out. They know that the higher the interest rate, the lower are the prices of securities, and that the lower the interest rate, the higher are the prices of securities. They can also put these two things together and know that, if they can predict changes in monetary policy, then they can predict future interest rates and future security prices. Predicting future financial asset prices is a potentially profitable activity. Predicting when interest rates will fall is the same as predicting when security prices will rise – and so is the same as predicting good times to buy securities. Predicting that interest rates will rise is the same as predicting that security prices will fall – and so is the same as predicting good times to sell securities.

Because predicting the Bank of England is profitable, a good deal of effort goes into that activity. But if people do anticipate the Bank of England's monetary policy changes, then security prices and interest rates will change as soon as the Bank of England's actions are foreseen. By the time the Bank of England actually takes its actions, these actions will have no effect. The effect will have occurred in anticipation of the Bank of England's actions. Only changes in the money supply that are not foreseen will change the interest rate level at the time that these changes occur.

Interest Rates and the Pound

We've seen that an increase in the money supply leads to lower interest rates and that a decrease in the money supply leads to higher interest rates. But a change in interest rates affects the exchange rate. Lower interest rates make the pound fall in value against other currencies, and higher interest rates make the pound rise in value against other currencies. These influences of interest rates on the foreign exchange value of the pound can limit the range of action of the Bank of England. In extreme situations, such as when there is a commitment to a fixed exchange rate, the Bank's hands are virtually tied by the exchange rate. It must move interest rates in whatever way is dictated by the prior commitment to defend the value of the pound. These matters are explained more fully in Chapter 35.

R E V I E W

At any given moment, the interest rate level is determined by the demand for and the supply of money. The interest rate makes the quantity of money demanded equal to the quantity of money supplied. Changes in the interest rate occur as a result of changes in the money supply. When the money supply change is unanticipated, interest rates will change at the same time as the change in the money supply. If a change in the money supply is anticipated, interest rates will start to change ahead of the change in the money supply. ◆

The money supply has a powerful effect on our economy. We've seen its influence on interest rates and the exchange rate. Our next task is to examine the effect of the money supply on real GDP and the price level.

Money, Real GDP and the Price Level

We now know how the Bank of England can influence the amount of money in the economy and how the quantity of money influences the interest rate. But does the quantity of money matter for the economy? What further effects does it have? Does it matter whether the quantity increases quickly or slowly?

We're going to address these questions first by using the aggregate demand–aggregate supply model. Then we're going to consider a special theory of money and prices – the quantity theory of money. Finally, we'll look at some historical and international evidence on the relationship between money and prices. Also, Our Advancing Knowledge on pp. 768–769 looks at the evolution of our understanding of the effects of changes in the quantity of money.

Money in the *AD–AS* Model

We've seen that the Bank of England uses monetary policy to steer the economy between unemployment on the one side and inflation on the other. Let's use the aggregate demand–aggregate supply model to work out the effects of the Bank's actions on real GDP and the price level.

Monetary Policy to Reduce Unemployment In Fig. 27.5, the economy is experiencing unemployment. Long-run aggregate supply along the *LAS* curve is £600 billion, but actual real GDP is only £550 billion, at the intersection of the aggregate demand curve AD_0 and the short-run aggregate supply curve is *SAS*. The price level is 125. With a large amount of unemployment, wages will eventually fall. As a result, the *SAS* curve will shift to the right, the price level will fall and real GDP will increase, restoring full employment. But this automatic adjustment process is extremely slow.

In an attempt to bring the economy to full employment more quickly, the Bank of England increases the quantity of money by conducting an open market operation. Banks, possessing excess reserves, make new loans and these loans create money. With a rise in the money supply comes a fall in interest rates. The combination of a fall in interest rates and more money in their bank accounts causes people to .

FIGURE 27.5

Monetary Policy to Reduce Unemployment

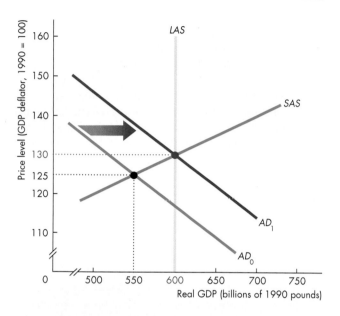

The economy is on aggregate demand curve AD_0 and short-run aggregate supply curve SAS. The price level is 125 and real GDP is £550 billion. Long-run aggregate supply is LAS and there is unemployment. An increase in the money supply shifts the aggregate demand curve to AD_1, the price level rises to 130 and real GDP increases to £600 billion, its full-employment level.

FIGURE 27.6

Monetary Policy to Lower Inflation

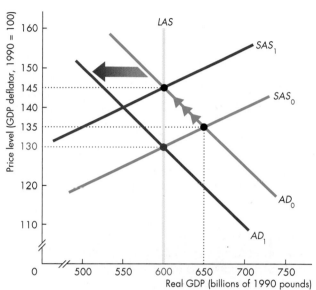

The economy is on aggregate demand curve AD_0 and short-run aggregate supply curve SAS_0. The price level is 135 and real GDP is £650 billion. Long-run aggregate supply is LAS, and there is above full employment. With no change in aggregate demand, wages increase, the short-run aggregate supply curve shifts to SAS_1, the price level rises to 145, and real GDP decreases to £600 billion. Before this adjustment occurs, a decrease in the quantity of money shifts the aggregate demand curve to AD_1. The price level falls to 130 and real GDP decreases to £600 billion.

increase their expenditure, so aggregate demand increases. The aggregate demand curve shifts to the right to become AD_1. The new equilibrium is at the intersection point of AD_1 and SAS. The price level rises to 130 and real GDP increases to £600 billion. The economy is now on its long-run aggregate supply curve and there is full employment.

To achieve this outcome, the Bank of England needs a combination of good judgement and good luck. A smaller increase in the money supply would not shift the aggregate demand curve as far to the right, and the economy would remain in an unemployment equilibrium. A larger increase in the money supply would shift the aggregate demand curve too far to the right and would create an inflation problem.

Let's see how the Bank of England can deal with an inflationary situation.

Monetary Policy to Lower Inflation In Fig. 27.6, the economy is overheated and is experiencing inflationary pressures. Long-run aggregate supply along the LAS curve is £600 billion. Initially, the short-run aggregate supply curve is SAS_0 and the aggregate demand curve is AD_0. Equilibrium occurs where the aggregate demand curve AD_0 intersects the short-run aggregate supply curve SAS_0. The price level is 135 and real GDP is £650 billion.

Even if the Bank of England takes no action, the economy will not remain at its current position. Because real GDP is above its long-run level, there is a shortage of labour and wages will begin to rise. As they do so, the SAS curve will shift to the left to

Understanding the Causes of Inflation

> '**Inflation is always**
> **and everywhere**
> **a monetary**
> **phenomenon.**'
>
> MILTON FRIEDMAN
> *The Counter-Revolution in*
> *Monetary Theory*

The combination of history and economics has taught us a great deal about the causes of inflation.

Severe inflation – hyperinflation – arises from a breakdown of the normal fiscal policy processes at times of war and political upheaval. Tax revenues fall short of government spending, and the gap between them is filled by printing money. As inflation increases, there is a *shortage* of money, so its rate of creation is increased yet further and prices rise even faster. Eventually, the monetary system collapses. Such was the experience of Germany in the 1920s, and Russia may be heading in this direction today.

In earlier times, when commodities were used as money, inflation resulted from the discovery of new sources of money. The most recent occurrence of this type of inflation was in the nineteenth century when gold, then used as money, was discovered in California and Australia.

In modern times, inflation has resulted from increases in the money supply that have accommodated increases in costs. The most dramatic such inflations occurred during the 1970s when oil price increases were accommodated by central banks around the world.

To avoid inflation, money supply growth must be held in check. But at times of severe cost pressure, central banks feel a strong tug in the direction of avoiding recession and accommodating the cost pressure. Yet some countries have avoided inflation more effectively than others. A key source of success is central bank independence. In low-inflation countries, such as Germany and Japan, the central bank decides how much money to create and at what level to set interest rates and does not take instructions from the government. In high-inflation countries, such as the United Kingdom in the 1970s and Italy, the central bank takes direct orders from the government about interest rates and money supply growth. This connection between central bank independence and inflation has been noticed by the architects of a new monetary system for the European Union who are modelling the European Central Bank on Germany's Bundesbank, not the Bank of England.

When inflation is especially rapid, as it was in Germany in 1923, money became almost worthless. In Germany at that time, bank notes were more valuable as kindling than as money, and the sight of people burning Reichmarks was a common one. Because no one wanted to hold money for too long, wages were paid and spent twice a day. Banks took deposits and made loans, but at interest rates that compensated depositors and the bank for the falling value of money – rates that could exceed 100 per cent a day. The price of a dinner might double during the course of an evening, making lingering over coffee a very expensive pastime.

Hyperinflation has never occurred in a computer-age economy. But imagine the scene if hyperinflation – an inflation rate of 50 per cent a month – did break out. ATMs would have to be refilled several times an hour, and the volume of paper (both money and receipts) they would spew out would grow to astronomical proportions. But most of us would try to avoid using money. Instead, we would buy as much as possible using credit cards. And we'd be eager to pay off our card balances quickly because the interest rate on unpaid balances would be 70 per cent a month. Only at such a high interest rate would it pay banks to lend to cardholders, since banks themselves would be paying interest rates of more than 50 per cent a month to induce people to deposit their money.

David Hume and the Quantity Theory of Money

DAVID HUME

Born in Edinburgh, Scotland, in 1711 and a close friend of Adam Smith, David Hume was a philosopher, historian, and economist of extraordinary breadth. His first book, by his own description, 'fell dead-born from the press'. But his essays – on topics ranging from love and marriage and the immortality of the soul to money, interest and the balance of payments – were widely read and earned him a considerable fortune.

Hume gave the first clear statement of the quantity theory of money – the theory that an increase in the quantity of money brings a proportional increase in the price level. And his account of the way in which an increase in the quantity of money brings an increase in prices anticipated the discovery, some 220 years later, of the Phillips curve and the Keynesian theory of aggregate demand.

SAS_1. The price level will rise to 145 and real GDP will decrease to its long-run level of £600 billion.

The Bank of England can help to prevent rising wages and rising prices by decreasing the quantity of money. By conducting an open market operation in which it sells securities, the Bank of England can decrease the money supply and shift the aggregate demand curve to the left to AD_1. If it takes this action before wages have increased, the new equilibrium is at the intersection point of AD_1 and SAS_0. The price level falls to 130 and real GDP decreases to £600 billion, its long-run level.

Again, to achieve its goal, the Bank of England needs a combination of good judgement and good luck. A smaller decrease in the money supply would not shift the aggregate demand curve as far to the left, and the economy would remain in an inflationary situation. A larger decrease in the money supply would shift the aggregate demand curve too far to the left and would create unemployment.

The aggregate demand–aggregate supply model tells us how real GDP and the price level respond to a change in the quantity of money. There is another model of money that is more limited than the AD–AS model that works in some situations. It is called the quantity theory of money.

The Quantity Theory of Money

The **quantity theory of money** is the proposition that an increase in the quantity of money leads to an equal percentage increase in the price level. The original basis of the quantity theory of money is a concept known as the velocity of circulation and an equation called the equation of exchange. The **velocity of circulation** is the average number of times a pound of money is used annually to buy the goods and services that make up GDP. GDP is equal to the price level (P) multiplied by real GDP (Y). That is:

$$\text{GDP} = PY.$$

Call the quantity of money M. The velocity of circulation, V, is determined by the equation:

$$V = PY/M.$$

For example, if GDP is £600 billion and if the quantity of money is £500 billion, the velocity of circulation is 1.2. On average, each pound of money circulates 1.2 times each year to purchase the final goods and services that make up GDP.

The **equation of exchange** states that the quantity of money (M) multiplied by the velocity of circulation (V) equals GDP, or:

$$MV = PY.$$

Given the definition of the velocity of circulation, this equation is always true – it is true by definition. With M equal to £500 billion and V equal to 1.2, MV is equal to £600 billion, the value of GDP.

The equation of exchange becomes the quantity theory of money by making two propositions:

◆ The velocity of circulation is a constant.
◆ Real GDP is not influenced by the quantity of money.

If these two propositions are true, the equation of exchange tells us that a given percentage change in the quantity of money brings about an equal percentage change in the price level. You can see why by solving the equation of exchange for the price level. Dividing both sides of the equation by real GDP (Y) gives:

$$P = (V/Y)M.$$

Because V and Y are constant, the relationship between the change in the price level (ΔP) and the change in the money supply (ΔM) is:

$$\Delta P = (V/Y)\Delta M.$$

Dividing this equation by the previous one gives the quantity theory proposition, namely that the percentage increase in the price level ($\Delta P/P$) equals the percentage increase in the money supply ($\Delta M/M$) that is:

$$\Delta P/P = \Delta M/M.$$

The Quantity Theory and the *AD–AS* Model

The quantity theory of money can be interpreted in terms of the aggregate demand–aggregate supply model. The aggregate demand curve is a relationship between the quantity of real GDP demanded (Y) and the price level (P), other things remaining constant. We can obtain such a relationship from the equation of exchange,

$$MV = PY.$$

Dividing both sides of this equation by real GDP (Y) gives:

$$P = MV/Y.$$

This equation may be interpreted as describing an aggregate demand curve by supposing that the money supply (M) and the velocity of circulation (V) are given. For then, the higher the price level (P), the lower is the quantity of real GDP demanded (Y).

In general, when the quantity of money changes, the velocity of circulation might also change. But the quantity theory asserts that velocity is a constant. If velocity is constant, an increase in the quantity of money increases aggregate demand and shifts the aggregate demand curve upward by the same amount as the percentage change in the quantity of money.

The quantity theory of money also asserts that real GDP is not affected by the money supply. This assertion is true only in the aggregate demand–aggregate supply model at full-employment equilibrium. As we saw in Fig. 27.4(a), starting out with unemployment, an increase in the quantity of money increases real GDP. And starting out at above full employment, a decrease in the quantity of money decreases real GDP. In these cases, the price level changes by a smaller percentage than the percentage change in aggregate demand and the money supply.

Figure 27.7 uses the AD–AS model to get the quantity theory result. Initially the economy is at full employment on the long-run aggregate supply curve LAS and at the intersection of the aggregate demand curve AD_0 and the short-run aggregate supply curve SAS_0. A 10 per cent increase in the quantity of money shifts the aggregate demand curve from AD_0 to AD_1. This shift, measured by the vertical distance between the two demand curves, is 10 per cent. With no change in wages, the economy moves to an above full-employment equilibrium. But as wages rise, the short-run aggregate supply curve shifts to the left to SAS_1 and a new full-employment equilibrium occurs at the intersection of AD_1 and SAS_1. Real GDP is back at its original level of £600 billion and the price level has increased to 143. The new price level is 10 per cent higher than the initial one (143 – 130 = 13 which is 10 per cent of 130).

So the aggregate demand–aggregate supply model predicts the same outcome as the quantity theory of money so long as the velocity of circulation is constant and so long as we compare two positions of full employment. In general the AD–AS model predicts a looser relationship between the quantity of money and the price level than that implied by the quantity theory.

FIGURE 27.7

Money Supply Growth at Full Employment

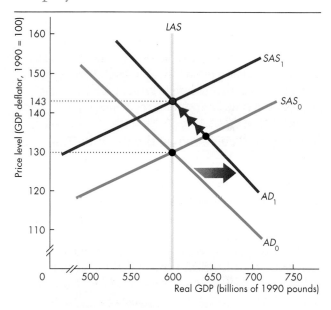

The economy is on aggregate demand curve AD_0 and short-run aggregate supply curve SAS_0. The price level is 130 and real GDP is £600 billion. Long-run aggregate supply is LAS, and there is full employment. A 10 per cent increase in the quantity of money shifts the aggregate demand curve to AD_1. Wages increase by 10 per cent and the short-run aggregate supply curve shifts to SAS_1. The price level rises to 143 – a 10 per cent increase – and real GDP remains at £600 billion. This outcome is the one predicted by the quantity theory of money.

Which theory of the relationship between the quantity of money and the price level is correct? Is the relationship as precise as implied by the quantity theory, or is it a looser relationship as implied by the aggregate demand–aggregate supply model? Let's look at the relationship between money and the price level, both historically and internationally.

Historical Evidence on the Quantity Theory of Money

The quantity theory of money can be tested by looking at data on the growth rate of the quantity of money and the inflation rate. Figure 27.8 shows the relationship between the growth rate of the quantity of M4 and the inflation rate in the United Kingdom for the 30 years between 1964 and 1993. Two things stand out in the figure. First, the two periods in which the inflation rate increased sharply – 1974–1975 and 1979–1980 – were preceded by large increases in the money supply growth rate – 1971–1973 and 1978. Second, there is only a loose relationship between these two variables. There are many movements in the inflation rate that are not at all closely related to changes in the money supply growth rate.

What does the international evidence tell us?

International Evidence on the Quantity Theory of Money

The international evidence on the quantity theory of money is summarized in Fig. 27.9, which shows the inflation rate and the money growth rate for 60 countries. There is an unmistakable tendency for high money growth to be associated with high inflation.

But like the historical evidence for the United Kingdom, these international data also tell us that money supply growth is not the only influence on inflation. Some countries have an inflation rate that exceeds the money supply growth rate, while others have an inflation rate that falls short of the money supply growth rate.

Correlation and Causation

The fact that money growth and inflation are correlated does not mean that we can determine, from that correlation, the direction of causation. Money growth might cause inflation; inflation might cause money growth; or some third variable might simultaneously cause inflation and money growth. In the quantity theory and in the aggregate demand–aggregate supply model, causation runs from money growth to inflation. But neither theory denies the possibility that at different times and places, causation might run in the other direction, or that some third factor, such as a government budget deficit, might be the root

---

FIGURE 27.8

Money Growth and Inflation in the United Kingdom

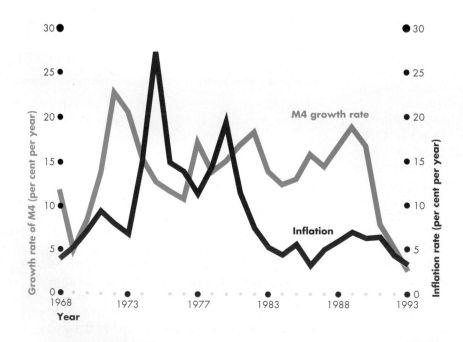

The increases in the inflation rate in 1974–1975 and 1979–1980 were preceded by large increases in the growth rate of M4. The money supply growth rate also increased in 1985–1989 while inflation increased again in 1987–1991. But there are many independent changes in the inflation rate, indicating that money growth is by no means the only cause of inflation.

Source: Central Statistical Office, *Economic Trends Annual Supplement 1994*, pp. 8 and 228–9.

FIGURE 27.9

Money Growth and Inflation in the World Economy

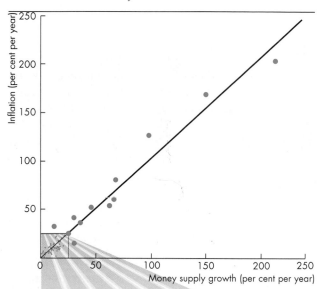

(a) All countries

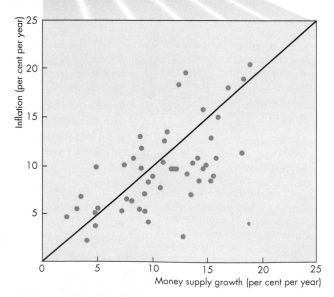

(b) Low-inflation countries

Inflation and money growth in 60 countries (in part a) and low-inflation countries (in part b) show that money growth is one influence, though not the only influence, on inflation.

Source: Federal Reserve Bank of St. Louis, *Review*, May/June, 1988, p. 15.

cause of both rapid money growth and inflation.

There are some occasions, however, that give us an opportunity to test our assumptions about causation. One of these is the 1970s. Rapid money supply growth during the late 1960s and early 1970s almost certainly caused the inflation outburst that occurred during the mid-1970s. It is hard to imagine the reverse causation – that the high inflation of 1975 caused rapid money growth in 1972.

R E V I E W

T he quantity of money exerts an influence on the price level. An increase in the quantity of money increases aggregate demand. In the short run, an increase in aggregate demand increases both the price level and real GDP. But on average, real GDP fluctuates around its full-employment level and increases in the quantity of money bring increases in the price level. Reading Between the Lines on pp. 774–775 also considers the relationship between the quantity theory of money and the price level. The quantity theory of money predicts that an increase in the quantity of money produces an equivalent percentage increase in the price level. The historical and international evidence on the relationship between the quantity of money and the price level provides broad support for the quantity theory of money as a proposition about long-run tendencies, but also reveals changes in the price level that occur independently of changes in the quantity of money.

◆ ◆ ◆ ◆ In this chapter, we've studied the determination of interest rates and discovered how the Bank of England can 'push the buttons' to influence interest rates by its open market operations that change the quantity of money. In Chapters 24 and 25 we discovered that the interest rate influences investment, aggregate expenditure and real GDP. In the next chapter, we're going to bring these two aspects of the macroeconomy together and study the wider effects of the Bank of England's actions – effects on investment and the level of aggregate demand.

Inflation, Broad Money and Narrow Money

The Essence of the Story

Broad definitions of the money supply have been used to account for asset price bubbles and debt deflation.

Narrow definitions of the money supply have been used to account for inflation.

The central banking system in the United States has recently been increasing the supply of dollars in the US economy, but without any major inflationary effect.

Much of the additional money base has gone to the commercial banks, which have put it into their own reserves.

In the United States, a new trend in saving has seen retired people take money out of low interest-rate bank accounts and put it into alternative funds with higher returns.

The main effect has been to increase the prices of these alternative assets.

THE TIMES, 14 SEPTEMBER 1993

Low inflation: the hidden blue rinse factor

Anthony Harris

WE do not hear very much from pure monetarists these days, but some still survive, and not just Professor Tim Congdon. He is a broad money man, which means that he has an excellent forecasting record in recent years. Broad money, which is heavily influenced by financial lending, has reliably told the story of asset price bubbles and debt deflation. That is perhaps why the Bundesbank, which used to practise narrow monetarism, has switched to the broader M3, with dire consequences for most of the rest of us.

The narrow money men, still to be found in the University of Chicago and a few of America's regional Federal Reserve Banks, would expect this trouble; they have always argued that broad money is as long as it is broad. But they are themselves in disarray. They believe that what matters is the monetary base – 'high powered money' in the text books, 'central bank money' in Germany. But they are faced with the most baffling story a theorist can confront: a clear cause, but no effect.

The Fed has been creating dollars at a reckless pace in its quest for low interest rates. In the past 12 months its own lending to the banking system has risen by 12.6 per cent, the US monetary base by 11.2 per cent and M1 by 12.4 per cent. This ought to be highly inflationary: but virtually no inflation has appeared....

Part of the story has been told in these columns. New money has been soaked up by the commercial banks, who have been happy to rebuild their own reserves, but have only recently become confident enough to lend to anyone else.... The rise in foreign dollar reserves reflects the US trade deficit which is potentially deflationary; but only a small part of it. What is missing, about $60 billion, is the rest of the trade deficit, not to mention capital flows, drugs and the rest: the dollars that are created then disappear....

America's retired used to live mainly on the interest from their savings accounts: their hero was Paul Volcker. They hate a low-rate policy – as do the British retired, as they showed at Christchurch. They have been switching on a huge scale out of savings accounts with the banks and savings institutions, and into various mutual funds promising higher income. So the Fed has caused inflation – the reinflation of asset prices, everywhere.

© The Times. Reprinted with permission.

Background and Analysis

When the central bank in a country undertakes open market operations (OMO) by purchasing securities from banks, the money raised forms excess reserves at the banks, which they lend to borrowers.

The lending of money creates new deposits which increase the money supply. These deposits are spent by the borrowers. Some of the money is put into established deposits by those receiving payment; the rest is kept as cash. This cycle goes on until the excess reserves are used up.

Inflation increases to the extent that this process increases total bank deposits and cash held by individuals (that is, it has increased total high-powered money holdings).

The phenomenon experienced in the United States, where the increase in high-powered money has not been inflationary, happened because the banks simply increased their own reserves.

Within total high-powered money, only that element spent by households and firms will be inflationary. That amount retained by banks, therefore not entering the circular flow of income, will not be inflationary.

The debate about broad or narrow money is partly a debate about which monetary aggregate is most closely linked to inflation. Most of the increase in high-powered money created by US Federal Reserve actions has gone into non-inflationary bank reserves.

Figure 1 shows how an increase in the money supply lowers the rate of interest.

Retired people in the United States have traditionally lived off the interest on their savings. In recent years, US interest rates have been cut to counter recession, but this has lowered the income from savings.

Banks have felt the need to restore reserves because the savings of retired people – a key source of funds for lending – have been withdrawn and placed in alternative investments with a higher return.

The main consequence of the Federal Reserve's actions has been to increase the price of these alternative investments by indirectly encouraging greater demand for them.

In Fig. 2, the initial increase in the money supply shifts AD_0 to AD_1. This induces higher input costs for firms, which shifts SAS_0 to SAS_1. These two forces work together to increase the price level.

The money multiplier is given as:

$$mm = \frac{1 + \Delta C/\Delta D}{\Delta R/\Delta D + \Delta C/\Delta D}$$

where D is total deposits, C is total currency, R is total reserves and Δ indicates 'change in'.

The ratio $\Delta R/\Delta D = 0.1$ and the ratio $\Delta C/\Delta D = 0.5$.

Thus

$$mm = \frac{(1 + 0.5)}{(0.1 + 0.5)}$$
$$= 2.5$$

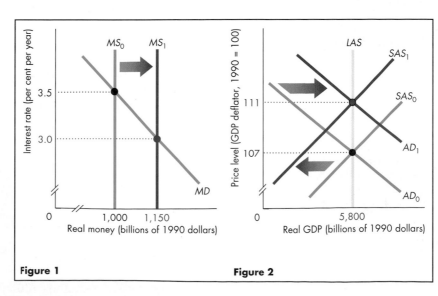

Figure 1

Figure 2

S U M M A R Y

The Bank of England

The Bank of England is the central bank of the United Kingdom. It acts as the government's bank and as a bank for bankers so that clearing between banks can be handled easily. The Bank also acts as a lender of last resort to the banks, though it only lends indirectly through the discount houses. (pp. 751–757)

Controlling the Money Supply

The Bank's main instruments for influencing the economy are changing the interest rate it charges on last-resort loans and open market operations. By buying government securities in the market – an open market purchase – the Bank is able to increase the monetary base and the reserves available to banks. As a result, there is an expansion of bank lending and a fall in interest rates. By selling government securities, the Bank of England is able to decrease the monetary base and the reserves of banks thereby curtailing loans and putting upward pressure on interest rates. The overall effect of a change in the monetary base on the money supply is determined by the money multiplier which, in turn, depends on the ratio of cash to deposits held by households and firms and on the ratio of reserves to deposits held by banks. (pp. 757–763)

The Money Supply and Interest Rates

If the quantity of real money is increased by the actions of the Bank of England, the interest rate falls and the prices of securities rise. People attempt to profit by predicting the actions of the Bank of England. To the extent that they can predict the Bank of England, interest rates and the prices of financial assets move in anticipation of the Bank's actions rather than in response to them. As a consequence, interest rates change when the Bank of England changes the money supply only if the Bank of England catches people by surprise. Anticipated changes in the money supply produce interest rate changes by themselves.

Interest rates affect the value of the pound against other currencies. That is, a change in the money supply leads to a change in interest rates and to a change in the foreign exchange value of the pound. (pp. 763–766)

Money, Real GDP and the Price Level

The quantity of money affects aggregate demand. An increase in the quantity of money increases aggregate demand and, in the short run, increases both the price level and real GDP. Over the long run, real GDP grows and fluctuates around its full-employment level, and increases in the quantity of money bring increases in the price level. The quantity theory of money predicts that an increase in the quantity of money increases the price level by the same percentage amount and leaves real GDP undisturbed. Both historical and international evidence suggest that the quantity theory of money is correct only in a broad average sense. The quantity of money does exert an influence on the price level but also on real GDP. There are other influences on the price level. Further, the correlation between money growth and inflation does not tell us the direction of causation. (pp. 766–773).

K E Y   E L E M E N T S

Key Terms

Key Figures and Table

R E V I E W   Q U E S T I O N S

1   Who are the main depositors at the Bank of England? Why do they hold deposits there?

2   What are the main policy tools of the Bank of England?

3   If the Bank of England wants to cut the quantity of money, does it buy or sell UK government securities in the open market?

4   Describe the events that take place when banks have excess reserves.

5   What is the money multiplier?

6   What is a cash drain? How does it affect the value of the money multiplier?

7   Explain why it pays people to try to predict the Bank of England's actions.

8   What happens to the interest rate if real GDP and the price level are constant and the money supply increases?

9   What does the aggregate demand–aggregate supply model predict about the effects of a change in the quantity of money on the price level and real GDP:
    a starting with unemployment?
    b starting with above full employment?
    c starting at full employment?

11   What is the equation of exchange and what is the velocity of circulation? What assumptions are necessary to make the equation of exchange the quantity theory of money?

12   What is the historical and international evidence on the quantity theory of money?

P R O B L E M S

1   You are given the following information about the economy of Atlantis. The banks have deposits of £300 million. Their reserves are £15 million, two-thirds of which is in deposits with the central bank. The public hold £30 million in cash.
    a What is the monetary base?
    b What is the money supply?
    c What is the money multiplier?

2   Suppose that the central bank in Atlantis undertakes an open market purchase of securities of £1 million. What happens to the money supply? Explain why the money supply changes by more than the change in the monetary base.

3   Quantecon is a country in which the quantity theory of money operates. The country has a constant population, capital stock and technology. In year 1, real GDP was £400 million, the price level was 200, and the velocity of circulation of money was 20. In year 2, the quantity of money was 20 per cent higher than in year 1.
    a What was the quantity of money in Quantecon in year 1?
    b What was the quantity of money in Quantecon in year 2?
    c What was the price level in Quantecon in year 2?
    d What was the level of real GDP in Quantecon in year 2?
    e What was the velocity of circulation in Quantecon in year 2?

PART 7
MACROECONOMIC PROBLEMS AND POLICIES

Talking

with

Wynne

Godley

After graduating at Oxford in politics, philosophy and economics, Professor Godley studied music and was a professional oboe player for a number of years. He worked for H. M. Treasury for fourteen years, from 1956 to 1970, and rose to the level of under-secretary, where he was in charge of conjuncture and forecasting. In 1970 he went to Cambridge as director of the Department of Applied Economics, a post he held for fifteen years. He has held various official positions: advisor to the Treasury Select Committee on public expenditure and more recently as one of the 'six wise men' – the Treasury's panel of independent forecasters.

What originally attracted you to the study of economics?

I was first drawn to economics as a member of the UK Treasury in the 1950s and 1960s although I had studied it, up to a point, as an undergraduate. I found it absorbingly interesting to follow the 'conjuncture' day by day and to be directly involved in strategic decision-taking. I have never been interested in economic theory for its own sake.

Which economist has had the greatest influence on you?

The answer has to be Nicholas Kaldor – the only economist I have known personally who was touched with genius; by which I mean that he possessed an in-exhaustible mechanism which drove him to respond creatively, and with complete originality, to any aspect of the subject with which he was confronted. He had, into the bargain, a remarkable sense of relative magnitudes and always seemed to know what was taking place throughout the world. Kaldor was profoundly at odds with the dominant modern (neo-classical) paradigm which he regarded as pernicious nonsense from beginning to end. In particular, he rejected the whole concept of 'equilibrium' as having any valid application to the evolution of real-world economic systems. And with equilibrium he rejected the assumption, underlying much contemporary political discussion, that, in one sense or another, market forces know best. I regret very much that Kaldor never attempted a comprehensive synthesis of his own ideas, as I believe he had it in him to change the subject in a radical way.

Can the study of economics provide enough knowledge to run a national economy?

If you mean economics as taught to students, or as revealed in the contents of the leading academic journals, my answer is an emphatic 'no'. To 'run a national economy' there are certain basic things you have to know which academic economists do not generally teach or think about very much. At the most basic level, you must have a thorough knowledge of how, in an accounting sense, everything fits together. It is insufficient, for instance, just to have a working knowledge of the national accounts. It is also necessary to understand how the flow variables which make up national income and expenditure are logically related to the stock variables which describe the financial system – this is a very intricate business which it is quite tedious to master. Then you need to build up a quantitative sense of how the various parts of the economic system, foreign as well as domestic, interact with one another as interdependent processes taking place in historical time. And you must

know a lot of institutional detail (for example how the tax system works) as well as knowing, in detail, about modern economic history (such as what kind of year 1973 was).

Academic econometrics has proved a great disappointment, hardly advancing knowledge at all. That is not surprising to me because reality is far too shifting and contingent to be encompassed by econometric techniques. The best one can do, faced with a forecasting or policy problem, is first inspect and analyse the current position quantitatively within a systematic framework, then identify the respects in which the present is the same as, or different from, earlier periods; in other words *pattern recognition* is the characteristic mode of cognition. To be a successful and practical policy maker or adviser, it is necessary to possess an expertise which cannot be taught or learned as an academic subject.

What are the realistic goals of macroeconomic performance?

I retain a very ambitious and even optimistic view about the realistic goals of economic policy. Don't forget, my system of ideas was largely formed during the period (say 1950–1970) when there was no unemployment to speak of and inflation was very low and not, whatever people now say, clearly accelerating. Those who take the opposite view must explain why it was that inflation in the United Kingdom fell from 10% to zero in the 1950s, although unemployment was under 2% for the whole decade. Moreover, although 'fine

tuning' has acquired a bad reputation, there was a pretty steady real growth rate for 25 years which was fast enough to entirely change the standard of living in the United Kingdom and some other countries.

I have never accepted that there has been some fundamental change which means that what was actually achieved during the first 25 years after the war suddenly became impossible to achieve thereafter. Don't forget that the halcyon postwar period was one in which 'rigidities', particularly in the labour market, were widespread and tyrannical.

I recognize that the increased internationalization of production and finance has made it much harder for any single country to pursue independent macroeconomic policies. However, this should lead not to scepticism about what policy can deliver, but to the search for active co-ordination of policies between countries. Unfortunately, governments do not, in general, seem ready for such coordination and I am afraid it will take a real crisis to force them into it.

What are the problems and what are the constraints of running an economy? Can the goal of achieving full employment be achieved?

The goals of macroeconomic policy are the same now as they always have been – rapid and stable growth with high employment and low inflation. I have found no reason to change the view which I held in the 1950s and 1960s that unemployment is caused by an insufficiency of aggregate

'**U**nemployment is caused by an insufficiency of aggregate demand, although I fully recognize, now as then, that the extent to which demand can be expanded is subject to binding constraints.'

demand, although I fully recognize, now as then, that the extent to which demand can be expanded is subject to binding constraints. I do not share the view which is predominant at the moment, notwithstanding the collapse of monetarism, that there is a natural level of unemployment which in the long run will come about spontaneously, and that governments *cannot* change output and unemployment except indirectly, by creating conditions under which market forces will work better. There is clearly a real danger that inflation will again become intolerable, but I think the really binding constraint on expansion is more likely to come from imbalances in international trade.

Is economic integration a good motor for increased economic growth?

Increased integration is a motor for growth for those countries that are relatively successful and a potential severe source of immiseration for those that are not. It is a well kept secret that

the theory of international trade is based on the assumption that (a) there is continuous full employment everywhere and (b) trade between countries is always balanced. Yet these are obviously assumptions which are counter-factual and tendentious – the very point at issue is whether the 'removal of trade barriers' is going to cause unemployment to rise in the weaker countries. It is no big deal to prove that if quantities of goods are given, people are better off exchanging them than not. Yet this, with its subtle variations, is what conventional trade theory does!

Will an integrated EU need a common currency to succeed?

There are great potential advantages to be derived from closer economic integration and the introduction of a common currency in Europe. But it is dangerous to proceed towards such a union unless appropriate political institutions are created which run the place in the interests of everyone. There has to be some kind of federal government which runs a federal fiscal as well as monetary

> ‘**M**arket forces cannot be counted on to do the job of equalization unaided or at all.’

policy, and promotes (as happens in any humane federation) the well-being of the relatively poor and relatively failing regions. Market forces cannot be counted on to do the job of equalization unaided or at all. The European Union budget is quite inadequate in size and scope to do a proper job; its main function has been to support European agriculture – a monstrous piece of protectionism of just the wrong kind.

Can unemployment be reduced by imposing trade barriers and encouraging import substitution policies?

While removal of trade barriers can be very dangerous for relatively weak or unsuccessful economies, I have never been a 'protectionist' in any ordinary sense and would never, for instance, support the use of trade barriers designed selectively to prop up an inefficient industry. We have to avoid a situation, which may already be overtaking us, in which endemic imbalances in trade generate unsustainable changes in the scale and structure of international assets and liabilities which eventually impart a new disinflationary impetus to the world economy. I believe that if the systemic problem were recognized for what it is, a way could be found to manage trade non-selectively which could head off the crisis, particularly if this were part of a wider scheme to coordinate macroeconomic policy more generally.

What advice would you give to anyone starting to study economics?

I would like to encourage students to develop a critical perspective on the subject right from the start by invariably enquiring exactly how the static models to be found in most text books are supposed to be informing us about dynamic processes. I would also beg them, before reaching any normative conclusions, such as that trade unions cause unemployment or that everyone benefits from free trade, to examine critically the precise assumptions on which these conclusions are based.

CHAPTER 28

FISCAL
AND
MONETARY
INFLUENCES
ON
AGGREGATE
DEMAND

After studying this chapter you will be able to:

◆ Explain how fiscal policy – a change in government purchases or taxes – influences interest rates and aggregate demand

◆ Explain how monetary policy – a change in the money supply – influences interest rates and aggregate demand

◆ Explain what determines the relative effectiveness of fiscal and monetary policy on aggregate demand

◆ Describe the Keynesian–monetarist controversy about the influence of fiscal and monetary policy on aggregate demand and explain how the controversy was settled

◆ Explain how the mix of fiscal and monetary policy influences the composition of aggregate expenditure

◆ Explain how fiscal and monetary policy influence real GDP and the price level in both the short run and the long run

EACH YEAR THE UK PARLIAMENT APPROVES A BUDGET PROPOSED BY THE government, with advice from the Treasury. In 1994, the budget put spending at £290 billion – close to 45 per cent of GDP – and taxes at £250 billion. How do taxes and government spending influence aggregate demand, interest rates and the exchange rate? ◆ ◆ Not far from the Houses of Parliament the Bank of England, in Threadneedle Street, pulls the nation's monetary policy levers. We've seen how the Bank of England influences interest rates and the exchange rate. But how do the effects of the Bank's actions ripple through to the rest of the economy? ◆ ◆ There are times when fiscal policy and monetary policy are in harmony with each other. And there are other times when they come into conflict. Do fiscal and monetary policies need to be coordinated? Are they equivalent to each other? Does it matter whether a recession is avoided by the Bank loosening up its monetary policy or by Parliament cutting taxes?

Parliament, the Treasury and the Bank of England

◆ ◆ ◆ ◆ We will answer these questions in this chapter. You already know that the effects of fiscal and monetary policy are determined by the interaction of aggregate demand and aggregate supply. And you know quite a lot about these two concepts. This chapter gives you a deeper understanding of aggregate demand and the way it is affected by the actions and interactions of the UK government and the Bank of England.

Money, Interest and Aggregate Demand

Our goal is to understand how fiscal and monetary policy influence real GDP and the price level (as well as unemployment and inflation). Real GDP and the price level are determined by the interaction of aggregate demand and aggregate supply, as described in Chapter 23. But the main effects of fiscal and monetary policy are on aggregate *demand*. Thus we focus our attention initially on these effects.

To study the effects of fiscal and monetary policy on aggregate demand we use the aggregate expenditure model of Chapters 24 and 25. This model determines equilibrium expenditure *at a given price level*. Such an equilibrium corresponds to a point on the aggregate demand curve (see Fig. 24.12). When equilibrium expenditure changes, the aggregate demand curve shifts by the amount of the change in equilibrium expenditure.

The aggregate expenditure model freezes the price level and asks questions about the directions and magnitudes of the shifts of the aggregate demand curve at a given price level. But the price level is not actually fixed. It is determined by aggregate demand and aggregate supply.

We begin our study of fiscal and monetary policy by discovering an interaction among aggregate expenditure decisions, the interest rate and the supply of money.

Spending Decisions, Interest and Money

We discovered in Chapter 24 that equilibrium expenditure depends on the level of autonomous expenditure. We also discovered that one of the components of autonomous expenditure – investment – varies with the interest rate[1]. The higher the interest rate, other things remaining the same, the lower is investment and hence the lower is autonomous expenditure and equilibrium expenditure. Therefore equilibrium expenditure and real GDP depend on the interest rate.

In Chapters 26 and 27, we saw how the interest rate is determined by equilibrium in the money market. We also saw that the demand for money depends on both real GDP and the interest rate. The higher the level of real GDP, other things remaining the same, the greater is the demand for money and the higher is the interest rate. Therefore the interest rate depends on real GDP.

We're now going to see how *both* real GDP and the interest rate are determined simultaneously. We'll then go on to see how the Bank's monetary policy and the government's fiscal policy affect both real GDP and the interest rate at a given price level.

Equilibrium Expenditure and the Interest Rate

Let's see how we can link together the money market, where the interest rate is determined, and the market for goods and services, where equilibrium expenditure is determined. Figure 28.1 illustrates the determination of equilibrium expenditure and the interest rate. The figure has three parts: part (a) illustrates the money market; part (b) shows investment demand; and part (c) shows aggregate planned expenditure and the determination of equilibrium expenditure. Let's begin with part (a).

The Money Market   The curve labelled *MD* is the demand for real money. The position of this curve depends on the level of real GDP. For a given level of real GDP, there is a given demand curve for real money. Suppose that the demand curve shown in the figure describes the demand for real money when real GDP is £600 billion. If real GDP is higher than £600 billion, the demand curve for real money is to the right of the one shown; if real GDP is below £600 billion, the demand curve for real money is to the left of the one shown.

The curve labelled *MS* is the supply curve of real money. Its position is determined by the monetary policy actions of the Bank of England, the behaviour of the banking system and the price level. At a given point in time, all these influences determine a quantity of money supplied that is independent of the interest rate. Hence the supply curve for real money is vertical.

The interest rate adjusts to achieve equilibrium in the money market – equality between the quantity of real money demanded and the quantity

---

[1] Actually, investment depends on the *real* interest rate. Here we assume there is no inflation and the real interest rate is equal to the *nominal* interest rate.

FIGURE 28.1

Equilibrium Interest Rate and Real GDP

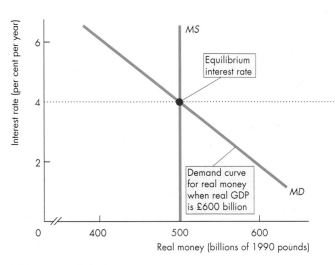

(a) Money and the interest rate

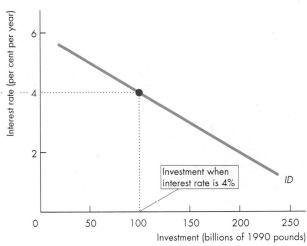

(b) Investment and the interest rate

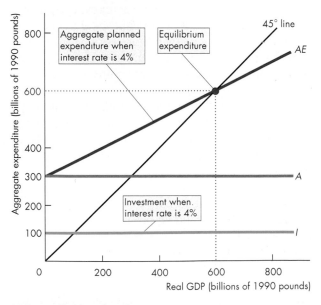

(c) Expenditure and real GDP

Equilibrium in the money market (part a) determines the interest rate. The money supply curve is *MS* and the demand curve for real money is *MD*. The position of the *MD* curve is determined by real GDP and the curve shown is for a real GDP of £600 billion. The investment demand curve (*ID*) in part (b) determines investment at the equilibrium interest rate determined in the money market. Investment is part of autonomous expenditure and its level determines the position of the aggregate expenditure curve (*AE*) shown in part (c). Equilibrium expenditure and real GDP are determined at the point at which the aggregate expenditure curve intersects the 45° line. In equilibrium, real GDP and the interest rate are such that the quantity of real money demanded equals the quantity of real money supplied and aggregate planned expenditure equals real GDP.

supplied. This equilibrium occurs at the point of intersection of the demand and supply curves of real money. In the economy illustrated in Fig. 28.1, the equilibrium interest rate is 4 per cent.

Investment and Interest Rate Next, let's look at part (b) where investment is determined. The investment demand curve is *ID*. The position of the investment demand curve is determined by profit expectations and, as those expectations change, the investment demand curve shifts. For given expectations, there is a given investment demand curve. This curve tells us the level of planned investment at each level of the interest rate. We already know the interest rate from equilibrium in the money market. When the investment demand curve is *ID* and the interest rate is 4 per cent, planned investment is £100 billion.

Equilibrium Expenditure   Part (c) shows the determination of equilibrium expenditure. This diagram is similar to the one that you studied in Chapter 24 (Fig. 24.11a). The aggregate expenditure curve (*AE*) tells us aggregate planned expenditure at each level of real GDP. Aggregate planned expenditure is made up of autonomous expenditure and induced expenditure. Investment is part of autonomous expenditure. In this example, investment is £100 billion and the other components of autonomous expenditure are £200 billion, so autonomous expenditure is £300 billion. These amounts of investment *I* and autonomous expenditure *A* are shown by the horizontal lines in part (c). Induced expenditure is the induced part of consumption expenditure minus imports. In this example, the marginal propensity to buy domestic goods and services is 0.5, therefore induced expenditure equals 0.5 multiplied by real GDP.

Equilibrium expenditure is determined at the point of intersection of the *AE* curve and the 45° line. Equilibrium expenditure occurs when aggregate planned expenditure and real GDP are each £600 billion. That is, the level of aggregate demand is £600 billion.

The Money Market Again   Recall that the demand curve *MD*, in part (a), is the demand curve for real money when real GDP is £600 billion. We've just determined in part (c) that when aggregate expenditure is at its equilibrium level, real GDP is £600 billion. What happens if the level of real GDP that we discover in part (c) is different from the value that we assumed when drawing the demand curve for real money in part (a)? Let's perform a thought experiment to answer this question.

Suppose, when drawing the demand curve for real money, we assume that real GDP is £500 billion. In this case, the demand curve for real money is to the left of the *MD* curve in part (a). The equilibrium interest rate is lower than 4 per cent. With

an interest rate below 4 per cent, investment is not £100 billion as determined in part (b), but a larger amount. If investment is larger than £100 billion, autonomous expenditure is larger and the *AE* curve lies above the one shown in part (c). If the aggregate expenditure curve is above the *AE* curve shown, equilibrium expenditure and real GDP are larger than £600 billion. Thus if we start with the demand curve for real money for a real GDP less than £600 billion, equilibrium expenditure occurs at a real GDP that is greater than £600 billion. There is an inconsistency. The real GDP assumed in drawing the demand curve for real money is too low.

Next, let's reverse the experiment. Assume a level of real GDP of £700 billion. In this case, the demand curve for real money lies to the right of the *MD* curve in part (a). The equilibrium interest rate is higher than 4 per cent. With an interest rate higher than 4 per cent, investment is less than £100 billion and the *AE* curve lies below the one shown in part (c). In this case, equilibrium expenditure occurs at a real GDP that is less than £600 billion. Again there is an inconsistency, but now the real GDP assumed in drawing the demand curve for real money is too high.

We've just seen that for a given money supply, money market equilibrium determines an interest rate that varies with real GDP. The higher the level of real GDP, the higher is the equilibrium interest rate. But the interest rate determines investment, which in turn determines equilibrium expenditure. The higher the interest rate, the lower is investment and equilibrium real GDP.

There is one particular level of both the interest rate and real GDP that simultaneously gives money market equilibrium and equilibrium expenditure. In the example we are studying, that interest rate is 4 per cent and real GDP is £600 billion. Only if we use a real GDP of £600 billion to determine the position of the demand curve for real money do we get a consistent story in the three parts of this figure. If the demand curve for real money is based on a real GDP of £600 billion, the interest rate determined (4 per cent) delivers investment of £100 billion that, in turn, generates equilibrium expenditure at the same level of real GDP that determines the position of the demand curve for real money.

Let's now study the effects of fiscal policy on aggregate demand.

Fiscal Policy and Aggregate Demand

Suppose that the economy is slowing down and that a recession looks likely. To head off the recession suppose that the government decides to stimulate aggregate demand by using fiscal policy, increasing its purchases of goods and services by £150 billion. A fiscal policy that increases aggregate demand is called an *expansionary fiscal policy*.

The effects of the government's actions are similar to those of throwing a pebble into a pond. There's an initial splash followed by a series of ever smaller ripples. The initial splash is the 'first round effect' of the fiscal policy action. The ripples are the 'second round effects'. Let's start by looking at the first round effects of the government's fiscal policy action.

First Round Effects of Fiscal Policy

The economy starts out in the situation shown in Fig. 28.1. The interest rate is 4 per cent, investment is £100 billion and real GDP is £600 billion. In this situation, the government increases its purchases of goods and services by £150 billion.

The first round effects of this action are shown in Fig. 28.2. The increase in government purchases increases autonomous expenditure. This increase is shown in Fig. 28.2 by the shift in the line A_0 to A_1. The increase in autonomous expenditure increases aggregate planned expenditure and shifts the AE curve upward from AE_0 to AE_1. Equilibrium expenditure increases to £900 billion. This increase in aggregate planned expenditure and equilibrium expenditure sets off a multiplier process that starts real GDP increasing. We described this process in Chapter 25. These are the first round effects of an expansionary fiscal policy and they are summarized in Fig. 28.3(a).

Second Round Effects of Fiscal Policy

At the end of the first round effect that we've just studied, real GDP is rising. The increase in real GDP increases the demand for money. The increase in the demand for money raises the interest rate. The rise in the interest rate decreases investment, and autonomous expenditure decreases. The decrease in autonomous expenditure decreases aggregate planned expenditure, which in turn decreases

FIGURE 28.2

First Round Effects of Expansionary Fiscal Policy

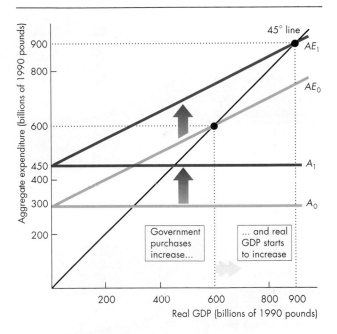

Initially, autonomous expenditure is A_0, the aggregate expenditure curve is AE_0, and real GDP is £600 billion. An increase in government purchases of goods and services increases autonomous expenditure to A_1. The aggregate expenditure curve shifts upward to AE_1 and equilibrium expenditure increases to £900 billion. A multiplier process is set off in which real GDP starts to increase. These are the first round effects of an expansionary fiscal policy.

equilibrium expenditure. These second round effects are summarized in Fig. 28.3(b). These effects go in the opposite direction to the first round effects, but they are smaller. They diminish the magnitude of the first round effects but do not change the direction of the outcome of the fiscal policy action. That outcome is an increase in real GDP, an increase in the interest rate and a decrease in investment.

When a new equilibrium is arrived at, the new higher real GDP and higher interest rate give simultaneous money market equilibrium and equilibrium expenditure similar to that in Fig. 28.1. This equilibrium is shown in Fig. 28.4. The demand for real money has increased to MD_1 and the interest rate has risen to 5 per cent in part (a). The higher interest rate has decreased investment in part (b). The increase in autonomous expenditure is £100 billion, which is

FIGURE 28.3

How the Economy Adjusts to an Expansionary Fiscal Policy

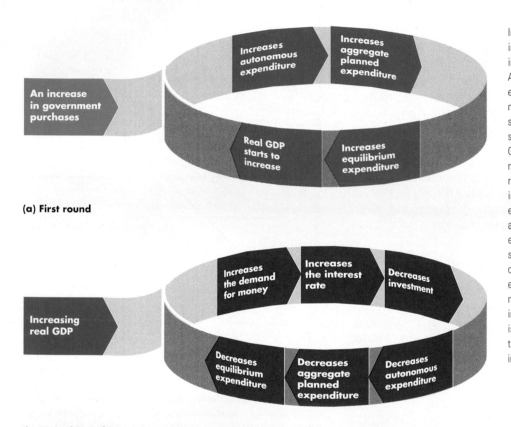

(a) First round

(b) Second round

In the first round (part a), an increase in government purchases increases autonomous expenditure. Aggregate planned expenditure and equilibrium expenditure increase. A multiplier process is set off that starts real GDP increasing. In the second round (part b), the rising real GDP increases the demand for money and interest rates rise. The rising interest rate decreases investment, decreases autonomous expenditure, and decreases aggregate planned expenditure and equilibrium expenditure. The second round effects work in the opposite direction to the first round effects and are smaller in magnitude. The outcome of an increase in government purchases is an increase in real GDP, a rise in the interest rate and a decrease in investment.

equal to the initial increase in government purchases of £150 billion minus the decrease in investment of £50 billion, shown in part (c). Finally, aggregate planned expenditure has increased to AE_1 and the new equilibrium expenditure is at a real GDP of £800 billion (also shown in part c).

Other Fiscal Policies A change in government purchases is only one possible fiscal policy action. Others are a change in transfer payments, such as an increase in job seekers' allowance or state pensions, and a change in taxes. All fiscal policy actions work by changing autonomous expenditure. The magnitude of the change in autonomous expenditure differs for different fiscal actions. But fiscal policy actions that change autonomous expenditure by a given amount

and in a given direction have similar effects on equilibrium real GDP and the interest rate regardless of whether they involve changes in purchases of goods and services, transfer payments, or taxes.

R E V I E W

An expansionary fiscal policy – an increase in government purchases of goods and services or an increase in transfer payments, or a decrease in taxes – affects aggregate demand by increasing autonomous expenditure.

FIGURE 28.4

The Effects of a Change in Government Purchases

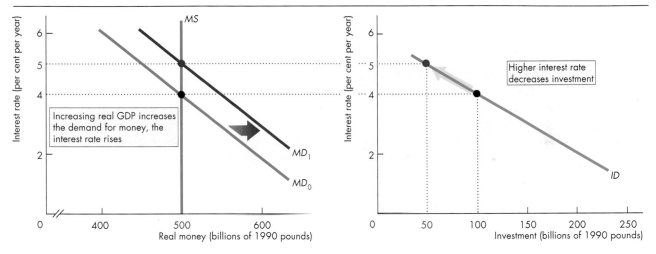

(a) Increase in the demand for money

(b) Decrease in investment

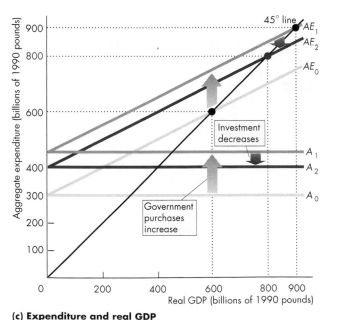

(c) Expenditure and real GDP

Initially, the demand curve for real money is MD_0, the real money supply is MS, and the interest rate is 4 per cent (part a). With an interest rate of 4 per cent investment is £100 billion on the investment demand curve ID (part b). The aggregate expenditure curve is AE_0, autonomous expenditure is A_0, and equilibrium expenditure and real GDP are £600 billion (part c). A £150 billion increase in government purchases increases autonomous expenditure (part c). Real GDP increases and increases the demand for money. The demand curve for real money shifts to the right to MD_1, raising the interest rate (part a). The higher interest rate decreases investment (part b). Autonomous expenditure increases to A_1 and aggregate planned expenditure increases to AE_1 (part c). These increases equal £100 billion – the initial increase in government purchases (£150 billion) minus the decrease in investment (£50 billion). The new equilibrium expenditure occurs at a real GDP of £800 billion.

◆ In the first round, aggregate planned expenditure increases, real GDP increases, the demand for money increases and the interest rate starts to rise.

◆ In the second round, the rising interest rate decreases investment, decreases autonomous expenditure, and decreases equilibrium expenditure and real GDP.

The second round effects go in the opposite direction to the first round effects but are smaller. An expansionary fiscal policy increases real GDP, increases the interest rate and decreases investment. ◆

We've seen that an expansionary fiscal policy raises interest rates and decreases investment. Let's take a closer look at this effect of fiscal policy.

Crowding Out and Crowding In

The tendency for an expansionary fiscal policy to increase interest rates and decrease investment is called **crowding out**. Crowding out may be partial or complete. Partial crowding out occurs when the decrease in investment is less than the increase in government purchases. This is the normal case – and the case we've just seen. Increased government purchases of goods and services increase real GDP, which increases the demand for real money and so interest rates rise. Higher interest rates decrease investment. But the effect on investment is smaller than the initial change in government purchases.

Complete crowding out occurs if the decrease in investment equals the initial increase in government purchases. For complete crowding out to occur, a small change in the demand for real money must lead to a large change in the interest rate, and the change in the interest rate must lead to a large change in investment.

Another influence of government purchases on investment that we've not considered so far works in the opposite direction to the crowding out effect and is called crowding in. **Crowding in** is the tendency for expansionary fiscal policy to *increase* investment. This effect works in three ways.

First, in a recession, an expansionary fiscal policy might create expectations of a more speedy recovery and bring an increase in expected future profits. With higher expected profits, the investment demand curve shifts to the right and investment increases despite higher interest rates.

The second source of crowding in is increased government purchases of capital. Such expenditure might increase the profitability of privately owned capital and lead to an increase in investment. For example, suppose the government increased its expenditure and built a new motorway that cut the cost of transporting a farmer's produce to a market that previously was too costly to serve. The farmer might now purchase a new truck to take advantage of the newly available profit opportunity.

The third source of crowding in is decreased taxes. If the expansionary fiscal policy cuts the taxes on business profits, firms' after-tax profits increase and additional investment might be undertaken.

As a practical matter, crowding out is probably more common than crowding in.

The Exchange Rate and International Crowding Out

We've seen that an expansionary fiscal policy leads to higher interest rates. But a change in interest rates also affects the exchange rate. Higher interest rates make the pound rise in value against other currencies. With interest rates higher in the United Kingdom than in the rest of the world, funds flow into the United Kingdom and people around the world demand more pounds. As the pound rises in value, foreigners find goods and services produced in the United Kingdom more expensive and people in the United Kingdom find imports less expensive. Exports fall and imports rise – net exports fall. The tendency for an expansionary fiscal policy to decrease net exports is called **international crowding out**. The decrease in net exports offsets to some degree the initial increase in aggregate expenditure brought about by an expansionary fiscal policy.

R E V I E W

C rowding out is the tendency for an expansionary fiscal policy to increase interest rates thereby reducing investment. Crowding out can be partial or complete. The normal case is partial crowding out – the decrease in investment is less than the initial increase in autonomous expenditure resulting from the fiscal action. ◆ ◆ Crowding in is the tendency for an expansionary fiscal policy to *increase* investment. Crowding in might occur in a recession if fiscal stimulation brings expectations of higher future profits, if the government purchases of capital hasten economic recovery, or if tax cuts stimulate investment. This issue is also considered in Reading Between the Lines on pps. 800–801. ◆ ◆ International crowding out is the tendency for an expansionary fiscal policy to decrease net exports. International crowding out occurs because fiscal expansion increases interest rates and makes the pound rise in value against other currencies. A stronger pound increases imports and decreases exports. ◆

Let's now study the effects of monetary policy on aggregate demand.

Monetary Policy and Aggregate Demand

The Bank of England is concerned that the economy is heading for a recession. To speed up the economy the Bank decides to increase aggregate demand by increasing the money supply. To work out the consequences of this monetary policy action, we divide its effects into first round and second round effects (just as we did with fiscal policy). Let's look at the first round effects of the Bank's monetary policy action.

First Round Effects of a Change in the Money Supply

The economy is in the situation that we studied in Fig. 28.1. The interest rate is 4 per cent, investment is £100 billion and real GDP is £600 billion. The Bank of England now increases the real money supply by £150 billion, from £500 billion to £650 billion. The first round effects of this action are shown in Fig. 28.5. The immediate effect is shown in part (a). The real money supply curve shifts to the right from MS_0 to MS_1, and the interest rate falls from 4 per cent to 1 per cent. The effect of the lower interest rate is shown in part (b). Investment increases from £100 billion to £250 billion – a movement along the investment demand curve. The effect of an increase in investment is shown in part (c). The increase in investment increases aggregate planned expenditure – an upward shift in the AE curve from AE_0 to AE_1. The increase in aggregate planned expenditure increases equilibrium expenditure, and real GDP starts to increase. That is, a multiplier process begins in which real GDP gradually increases towards its equilibrium level. We described such a process in Chapter 25.

We've just described the first round effects of an increase in the money supply: the interest rate falls, investment increases and real GDP starts to increase. These effects are illustrated in Fig. 28.6(a).

Second Round Effects of a Change in the Money Supply

At the end of the first round that we've just studied, real GDP is increasing. Increasing real GDP sets off the second round, which is illustrated in

Fig.28.6(b). A higher real GDP increases the demand for real money, and the interest rate rises. The higher interest rate brings a decrease in investment and a decrease in aggregate planned expenditure. With aggregate planned expenditure decreasing, equilibrium expenditure is also decreasing.

These second round effects go in the opposite direction to the first round effects, but they are smaller. They diminish the magnitude of the first round effects, but they do not change the direction of the outcome of the monetary policy action. That outcome is an increase in real GDP and a fall in the interest rate. When a new equilibrium is arrived at, the new higher real GDP and lower interest rate give simultaneous money market equilibrium and equilibrium expenditure similar to that in Fig. 28.1. This equilibrium is shown in Fig. 28.7. The demand for real money has increased to MD_1 and the interest rate has fallen to 2 per cent in part (a). The lower interest rate has increased investment in part (b). The increase in investment is £100 billion, which is equal to the initial increase of £150 billion minus a decrease of £50 billion, shown in part (c). Finally, aggregate planned expenditure has increased to AE_1 and the new equilibrium expenditure is at a real GDP of £800 billion (also shown in part c).

R E V I E W

A decrease in the money supply sets up the following sequence of events:

◆ In the first round, the interest rate increases, investment decreases and real GDP starts to decrease.

◆ In the second round, falling real GDP decreases the demand for money, lowers the interest rate, increases investment and increases equilibrium expenditure.

The second round effects go in the opposite direction to the first round effects but are smaller. A decrease in the money supply decreases real GDP and increases the interest rate. ◆

So far, we have looked at the effects of monetary policy on the interest rate and investment. There is another effect – on the foreign exchange rate and exports.

FIGURE 28.5

First Round Effects of an Increase in the Money Supply

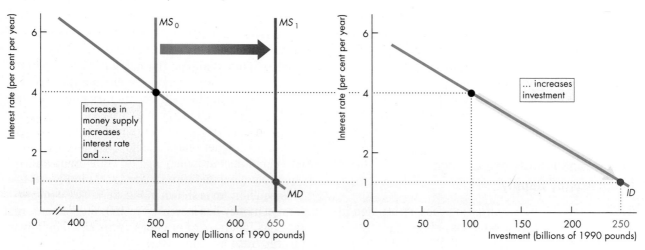

(a) Change in money supply

(b) Changes in investment

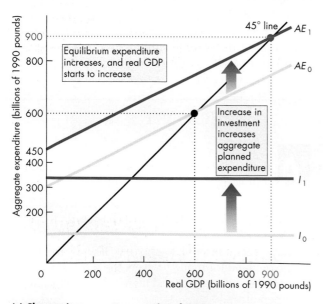

(c) Change in expenditure and real GDP

An increase in the money supply shifts the supply curve of real money from MS_0 to MS_1 (part a). Equilibrium in the money market is achieved by a fall in the interest rate from 4 per cent to 1 per cent. At the lower interest rate, investment increases (part b). The increase in investment increases both autonomous expenditure and aggregate planned expenditure (part c). The AE curve shifts upward from AE_0 to AE_1. Equilibrium real GDP increases from £600 billion to £900 billion. And a multiplier process is set up in which real GDP increases.

The Exchange Rate and Exports

An increase in the money supply decreases the interest rate. If the interest rate rises in the United Kingdom but does not fall in the United States, Japan and elsewhere in western Europe, international investors sell the now higher-yielding sterling assets and buy relatively lower-yielding foreign assets. As they undertake these transactions, they sell pounds and buy foreign currency. These actions decrease the

FIGURE 28.6

How the Economy Adjusts to an Increase in the Money Supply

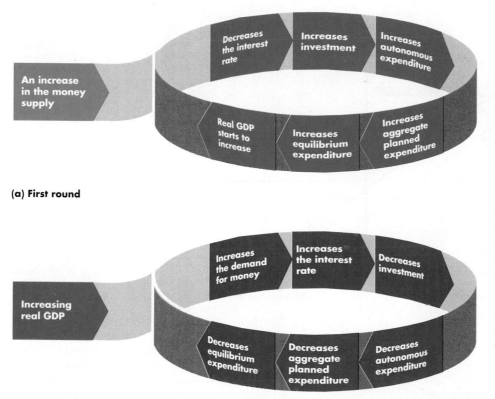

(a) First round

(b) Second round

In the first round (part a), an increase in the money supply decreases the interest rate, increases investment, autonomous expenditure, aggregate planned expenditure and equilibrium expenditure and makes real GDP start to increase. In the second round (part b), the increasing real GDP increases the demand for money, the interest rate rises and investment decreases. The decrease in investment decreases autonomous expenditure, aggregate planned expenditure and equilibrium expenditure. The second round effects work in the opposite direction to the first round effects but are smaller in magnitude. The outcome of an increase in the money supply is an increase in real GDP and a fall in the interest rate.

demand for pounds and increase the demand for foreign currencies. The result is a lower value of the pound against other currencies. (This mechanism is discussed in greater detail in Chapter 35.)

With the pound worth less, foreigners face lower prices for goods (in foreign currencies) and services produced in the United Kingdom and people in the United Kingdom face higher prices (in pounds) for foreign-produced goods and services. Exports from the United Kingdom increase, and imports into the United Kingdom decrease. The result is an increase in net exports from the United Kingdom. The effects of an increase in net exports are similar to the effects of an increase in investment that we've described above.

The Relative Effectiveness of Fiscal and Monetary Policy

We've now seen that equilibrium aggregate expenditure and real GDP are influenced by both fiscal and monetary policy. But which policy is the more potent? This question was once at the centre of a controversy among macro-economists, and later in this section we'll look at that controversy and see how it was settled. Let's begin by discovering what determines the relative effectiveness of fiscal and monetary policy.

FIGURE 28.7

The Effects of a Change in the Money Supply

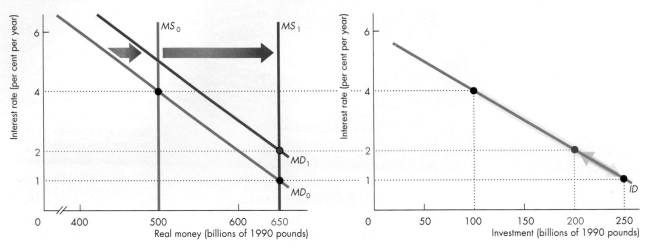

(a) Increase in the demand for money

(b) Decrease in investment

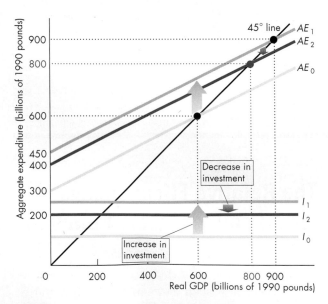

(c) Expenditure and real GDP

Initially, the demand curve for real money is MD_0, the real money supply is MS_0, and the interest rate is 4 per cent (part a). With an interest rate of 4 per cent investment is £100 billion on the investment demand curve ID (part b) and I_0 (part c). The aggregate expenditure curve is AE_0 and equilibrium expenditure and real GDP are £600 billion (part c). A £150 billion increase in the money supply shifts the money supply curve to the right to MS_1 (part a). The increased money supply lowers the interest rate to 1 per cent and investment increases to £250 billion (part b) and I_1 (part c). The increase in investment increases aggregate planned expenditure to AE_1 (in part c). Real GDP begins to increase. An increasing real GDP increases the demand for money. The demand curve for real money shifts rightward to MD_1, raising the interest rate (part a). The higher interest rate decreases investment (part b). The lower investment (shown as I_2 in part c) decreases aggregate planned expenditure to AE_2 (part c). The new equilibrium expenditure occurs at a real GDP of £800 billion with an interest rate of 2 per cent and investment of £200 billion.

The Effectiveness of Fiscal Policy

The effectiveness of fiscal policy is measured by the magnitude of the increase in equilibrium real GDP

resulting from a given increase in government purchases of goods and services (or decrease in taxes). The effectiveness of fiscal policy depends on the same two factors as the effectiveness of monetary policy:

◆ The sensitivity of investment demand to the interest rate
◆ The sensitivity of the demand for money to the interest rate

We're going to discover how these two factors influence the effectiveness of fiscal policy by studying Fig. 28.8.

Fiscal Policy Effectiveness and Investment Demand

Other things remaining the same, the more sensitive investment demand is to the interest rate, the smaller is the effect of a change in fiscal policy on equilibrium real GDP. Figure 28.8(a) shows why.

The figure shows two investment demand curves, ID_A and ID_B. Investment is more sensitive to a change in the interest rate along the demand curve ID_A than along the demand curve ID_B. An increase in government purchases increases real GDP and increases the demand for money. The demand curve for real money shifts from MD_0 to MD_1. This increase in the demand for money increases the interest rate from 4 per cent to 5 per cent. If the investment demand curve is ID_A, investment decreases from £100 billion to £50 billion. Contrast this outcome with what happens if the investment demand curve is ID_B. The same increase in the interest rate decreases investment from £100 billion to £75 billion.

The decrease in investment decreases autonomous expenditure, offsetting to some degree the increase in government purchases. Therefore the larger the decrease in investment, the smaller is the increase in equilibrium real GDP resulting from a given increase in government purchases. Thus fiscal policy is less effective with the investment demand curve ID_A than with the investment demand curve ID_B.

Fiscal Policy Effectiveness and the Demand for Money

Other things remaining the same, the more sensitive the demand for money is to the interest rate, the bigger is the effect of fiscal policy on equilibrium real GDP. Figure 28.8(b) shows why.

The figure shows two alternative initial (blue) demand curves for real money, MD_{A0} and MD_{B0}. The demand for money is less sensitive to a change in the interest rate along the demand curve MD_A than along the demand curve MD_B.

An increase in government purchases increases real GDP and increases the demand for money,

shifting the demand curve for real money to the right. If the initial curve is MD_{A0}, the new curve is MD_{A1}; if the initial curve is MD_{B0}, the new curve is MD_{B1}. Notice that the size of the shift to the right is the same in each case. In the case of MD_A, the increase in the demand for money increases the interest rate from 4 per cent to 5 per cent, and investment decreases from £100 billion to £50 billion. In the case of MD_B, the increase in the demand for money increases the interest rate from 4 per cent to 4.5 per cent, and investment decreases from £100 billion to £75 billion.

A decrease in investment decreases autonomous expenditure, offsetting to some degree the increase in government purchases. Therefore the smaller the decrease in investment, the larger is the increase in equilibrium real GDP resulting from a given increase in government purchases. Thus fiscal policy is less effective with the demand for real money curve MD_A than with the demand for real money curve MD_B.

The Effectiveness of Monetary Policy

The effectiveness of monetary policy is measured by the magnitude of the increase in equilibrium real GDP resulting from a given increase in the money supply. The effectiveness of monetary policy depends on two key factors:

◆ The sensitivity of investment demand to the interest rate
◆ The sensitivity of the demand for money to the interest rate

But other things remaining the same, the more effective is monetary policy, the less effective is fiscal policy. Let's see why by studying Fig. 28.9.

Monetary Policy Effectiveness and Investment Demand

Other things remaining the same, the more sensitive investment demand is to the interest rate, the bigger is the effect of a change in the money supply on equilibrium real GDP. Figure 28.9(a) shows why.

The figure shows two investment demand curves, ID_A and ID_B. Investment is more sensitive to a change in the interest rate along the demand curve ID_A than along the demand curve ID_B.

With the demand curve for real money MD, an increase in the money supply that shifts the real

FIGURE 28.8

The Effectiveness of Fiscal Policy

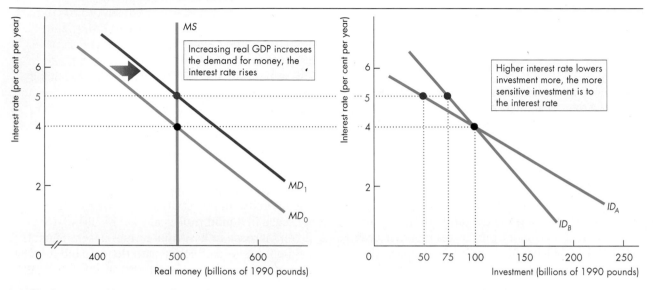

(a) Effectiveness and investment demand

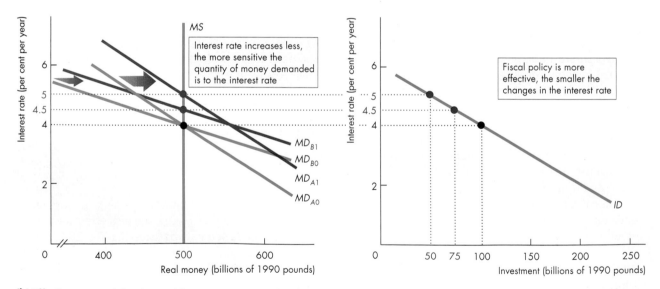

(b) Effectiveness and the demand for money

In part (a) the level of planned investment is more sensitive to a change in the interest rate along the investment demand curve ID_A than along the demand curve ID_B. An increase in government purchases increases real GDP and shifts the demand curve for real money from MD_0 to MD_1, raising the interest rate from 4 per cent to 5 per cent. With investment demand curve ID_A investment decreases from £100 billion to £50 billion, but with demand curve ID_B investment decreases to only £75 billion. The larger the decrease in investment, the smaller is the increase in equilibrium real GDP resulting from a given increase in government purchases. So fiscal policy is less effective with investment demand curve ID_A than with ID_B.

In part (b) the demand for money is less sensitive to a change in the interest rate along the demand curve for real money MD_A than along the demand curve MD_B. An increase in government purchases increases real GDP and the demand curve for real money shifts to the right – MD_{A0} shifts to MD_{A1} and MD_{B0} shifts to MD_{B1}. The size of the shift to the right is the same in each case. In the case of MD_A, the interest rate rises from 4 per cent to 5 per cent and investment decreases from £100 billion to £50 billion. In the case of MD_B, the interest rate rises to 4.5 per cent and investment decreases to only £75 billion. The smaller the decrease in investment, the larger is the increase in equilibrium real GDP resulting from a given increase in government purchases. So fiscal policy is less effective with the demand curve for real money MD_A than with MD_B.

FIGURE 28.9

The Effectiveness of Monetary Policy

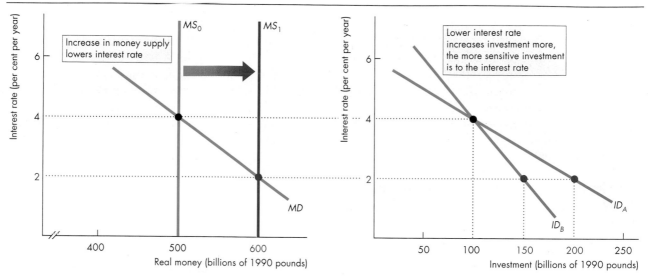

(a) Effectiveness and investment demand

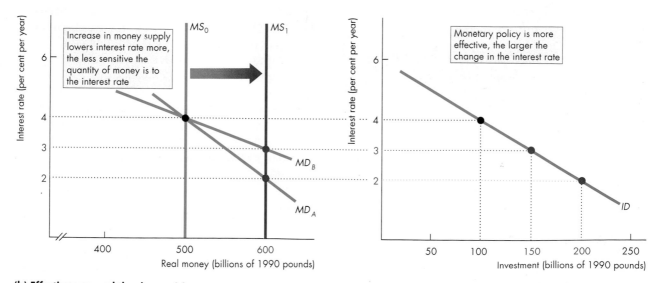

(b) Effectiveness and the demand for money

In part (a) planned investment is more sensitive to a change in the interest rate along the investment demand curve ID_A than along the demand curve ID_B. With the demand curve for real money MD, a shift in the real money supply curve from MS_0 to MS_1 lowers the interest rate from 4 per cent to 2 per cent. With investment demand curve ID_A investment increases from £100 billion to £200 billion, but with investment demand curve ID_B investment increases to only £150 billion. The larger the increase in investment, the larger is the resulting increase in equilibrium real GDP. So monetary policy is more effective with investment demand curve ID_A than with ID_B. In part (b) the demand for money is less

sensitive to a change in the interest rate along the demand curve for real money MD_A than along the demand curve MD_B. With the demand curve MD_A, an increase in the money supply that shifts the real money supply curve from MS_0 to MS_1 lowers the interest rate from 4 per cent to 2 per cent and increases investment from £100 billion to £200 billion. With demand curve MD_B the same increase in the money supply lowers the interest rate to only 3 per cent and increases investment to only £150 billion. The larger the increase in investment, the larger is the resulting increase in equilibrium real GDP. So monetary policy is more effective with demand curve MD_A than with MD_B.

money supply curve from MS_0 to MS_1 decreases the interest rate from 4 per cent to 2 per cent. If the investment demand curve is ID_A, investment increases from £100 billion to £200 billion. Contrast this outcome with what happens if the investment demand curve is ID_B. The same decrease in the interest rate increases investment from £100 billion to only £150 billion.

The larger the increase in investment, the larger is the resulting increase in equilibrium real GDP. Thus with the investment demand curve ID_A, monetary policy is more effective than with the investment demand curve ID_B.

Monetary Policy Effectiveness and the Demand for Money Other things remaining the same, the less sensitive the demand for money is to the interest rate, the bigger is the effect of a change in the money supply on equilibrium real GDP. Figure 28.9(b) shows why.

The figure shows two demand curves for real money, MD_A and MD_B. The demand for money is less sensitive to a change in the interest rate along the demand curve MD_A than along the demand curve MD_B.

If the demand curve for real money is MD_A, an increase in the money supply that shifts the real money supply curve from MS_0 to MS_1 decreases the interest rate from 4 per cent to 2 per cent. Investment increases from £100 billion to £200 billion. Contrast this outcome with what happens if the demand curve for real money is MD_B. In this case, the same increase in the money supply lowers the interest rate from 4 per cent to only 3 per cent and investment increases to only £150 billion.

The larger the increase in investment, the larger is the resulting increase in equilibrium real GDP. Thus with the demand curve for real money MD_A, monetary policy is more effective than with the demand curve for real money MD_B.

Interest Sensitivity of Investment Demand and the Demand for Money

What determines the degree of sensitivity of investment demand and the demand for money to interest rates? The answer is the degree of substitutability between capital and labour and the degree of substitutability between money and other financial assets.

Investment is the purchase of capital – of productive buildings, plant, vehicles and equipment. The

substitute for capital is labour, but it is an imperfect substitute. The amount of capital used, and the amount of investment undertaken, decreases as the interest rate increases. The degree to which a change in the interest rate brings a change in investment depends on how easily labour can be substituted for capital.

Money performs a unique function that other financial assets do not perform – it facilitates the exchange of goods and services. Therefore money and other financial assets are imperfect substitutes. Holding money has an opportunity cost, which is the interest forgone by not holding other financial assets. The amount of money that we hold decreases as its opportunity cost – the interest rate – increases. The degree to which a change in the interest rate brings a change in the quantity of money held depends on how easily other financial assets can be substituted for money.

The analysis that we have presented in this chapter of the effects of fiscal and monetary policy on aggregate expenditure was for several years in the 1950s and 1960s extremely controversial. It was at the heart of what was called the Keynesian– monetariest controversy. The Keynesian–monetarist controversy of today is different from that of the 1950s and 1960s and we'll consider that controversy – about how labour markets work – in Chapter 29. But that earlier Keynesian–monetarist controversy was an interesting episode in the development of modern macroeconomics. Let's take a look at the essentials of the dispute and see how it was resolved.

The Keynesian–Monetarist Controversy

The Keynesian–monetarist controversy is an ongoing dispute in macroeconomics between two broad groups of economists. Keynesians are macroeconomists whose views about the functioning of the economy represent an extension of the theories of John Maynard Keynes, published in Keynes' *General Theory* (see Our Advancing Knowledge, pp. 668–669). **Keynesians** regard the economy as being inherently unstable and as requiring active government intervention to achieve stability. They assign a low degree of importance to monetary policy and a high degree of importance to fiscal policy. **Monetarists** are macroeconomists who assign a high degree of importance to variations in the quantity of money as the main determinant of aggregate demand and who regard the economy as inherently stable. The founder of modern monetarism is Milton Friedman.

The nature of the Keynesian–monetarist debate has changed over the years. In the 1950s and 1960s, it was a debate about the relative effectiveness of fiscal policy and monetary policy in changing aggregate demand. We can see the essence of that debate by distinguishing three views:

◆ Extreme Keynesianism
◆ Extreme monetarism
◆ Intermediate position

Extreme Keynesianism The extreme Keynesian hypothesis was that a change in the money supply has no effect on the level of aggregate demand, and a change in government purchases of goods and services or in taxes has a large effect on aggregate demand.

There are two circumstances in which a change in the money supply has no effect on aggregate demand. They are:

◆ A vertical investment demand curve
◆ A horizontal demand curve for real money

If the investment demand curve is vertical, investment is completely insensitive to interest rates. In this situation, a change in the money supply changes interest rates, but those changes do not affect aggregate planned expenditure. Monetary policy is impotent.

A horizontal demand curve for real money means that people are willing to hold any amount of money at a given interest rate – a situation called a **liquidity trap**. With a liquidity trap, a change in the money supply affects only the amount of money held. It does not affect interest rates. With an unchanged interest rate investment remains constant. Monetary policy is impotent.

Extreme Keynesians assume that both of these conditions prevail. Notice that either one of these circumstances on its own is sufficient for monetary policy to be impotent, but extreme Keynesians suppose that both situations exist in reality.

Extreme Monetarism The extreme monetarist hypothesis was that a change in government purchases of goods and services or in taxes has no effect on aggregate demand and that a change in the money supply has a large effect on aggregate demand. There are two circumstances giving rise to

these predictions:

◆ A horizontal investment demand curve
◆ A vertical demand curve for real money

If an increase in government purchases of goods and services induces an increase in interest rates that is sufficiently large to reduce investment by the same amount as the initial increase in government purchases, then fiscal policy has no effect on aggregate demand. The outcome is complete crowding out, which we described earlier in this chapter. For this result to occur, either the demand curve for real money must be vertical – a fixed amount of money is held regardless of the interest rate – or the investment demand curve must be horizontal – any amount of investment will be undertaken at a given interest rate.

The Intermediate Position The intermediate position is that both fiscal and monetary policy affect aggregate demand. Crowding out is not complete, so fiscal policy does have an effect. There is no liquidity trap and investment responds to interest rates, so monetary policy does indeed affect aggregate demand. This position is the one that now appears to be correct and is the one that we've spent most of this chapter exploring. Let's see how economists came to this conclusion.

Sorting Out the Competing Claims The dispute between monetarists, Keynesians and those taking an intermediate position was essentially a disagreement about the magnitudes of two economic parameters:

◆ The sensitivity of investment demand to interest rates
◆ The sensitivity of the demand for real money to interest rates

If investment demand is highly sensitive to interest rates or the demand for real money is hardly sensitive at all, then monetary policy is powerful and fiscal policy relatively ineffective. In this case, the world looks similar to the claims of extreme monetarists. If investment demand is very insensitive to interest rates, or the demand for real money is highly sensitive, then fiscal policy is powerful and monetary policy is relatively ineffective. In this case, the world looks similar to the claims of the extreme Keynesians.

By using statistical methods to study the demand for real money and investment demand and by using

EU-wide Policies for Job Creation

FINANCIAL TIMES, 28 OCTOBER 1993

Case for EC-wide cuts in tax

Samuel Brittan

LET us consider a dynamic economy, such as Japan 20–30 years ago, or some of the east Asian 'tigers' today, whose trend growth rate is not far from 10 per cent a year. For such countries a growth rate of 5 per cent represents recession and one of zero a slump.

Although different numbers apply to the more sluggish European economies, the principles are the same. If the trend growth rate is about 3 per cent a year, then an achieved rate of, say, $1^1/_2$ per cent represents continued deterioration.

The main point is that an annual growth rate of 1.8 per cent is well below most estimates of the trend growth of UK productive capacity. What has been happening can be described as an incomplete recovery, a weak recovery or even a worsening depression. The best term is the American 'growth recession'. What this means is that output is rising modestly, but employment is still falling and the degree of slack increasing.

Much of the fashionable talk about growth in itself not bringing more jobs simply reflects the fact that growth is insufficient, even bearing in mind the need to prevent inflation from breaking out again.

Mr Jaques Delors, the EC president would like more public infrastructure spending to create jobs. Mr Clarke, the Chancellor, replies that is not governments' task to spend to create demand.

But it is their task, chancellor, it is – interpreting 'governments' broadly to include central banks as well as finance ministers. Demand management has been discredited because it was conducted in the past without regard to inflation.... Policies to raise demand need not involve increased government spending or increasing the state's role in the economy.

The basic Keynesian equations show that an increase in private spending is just as good as an increase in the government variety in promoting output and employment....

What this is leading up to is that a European-wide tax cut would be as good from the demand stimulation point of view as Mr Delors' infrastructure spending; and it would be better from the point of view of supply-side incentives and the signals it would send out.

© The Financial Times. Reprinted with permission.

Mr Kenneth Clarke, the UK Chancellor of the Exchequer, does not believe the government can spend money to create jobs.

Mr Jacques Delors, the president of the EU Commission, believes that governments can spend money to create jobs.

◆ Demand management policies were unsuccessful in the past because they did not allow for any effect on inflation.

◆ Tax cuts would stimulate private demand without the government needing to spend more itself.

◆ Tax cuts would generate growth which would create more jobs.

◆ Growth rates are below trend rates, so faster growth would increase inflation.

Expansionary demand management policies can be used to stimulate the economy, raising the rate of economic growth and encouraging the creation of new jobs.

Expansionary demand management policies include lowering tax rates and increasing government purchases.

Lower tax rates increase disposable income and increase aggregate expenditure.

If tax cuts are made across the European Union what one member state loses by importing from the other member states is cancelled out by other member states importing from it.

Growth rates are well below potential trend rates. This low growth, *ceteris paribus*, means a low level of job creation.

With actual growth rates below the potential rates, growth can rise without pressure on inflation. This growth gap indicates idle resources (such as unemployed labour) which can be employed without raising prices.

The lower tax rate raises firms' profit expectations. In part (a) of the figure the investment demand curve shifts to the right from ID_0 to ID_1.

In part (b) of the figure, autonomous expenditure rises by the increase in investment demand and the increase in autonomous consumption expenditure, from A_0 to A_1. The increase in consumption expenditure results from tax cuts.

Aggregate planned increases expenditure shifting the AE curve from AE_0 to AE_1.

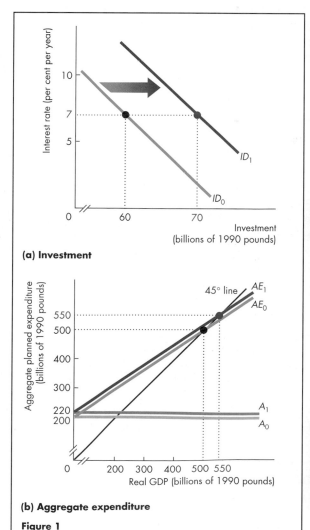

(a) Investment

(b) Aggregate expenditure

Figure 1

data from a wide variety of historical and national experiences, economists were able to settle this dispute. Neither extreme position turned out to be supported by the evidence and the intermediate position won. The demand curve for real money slopes downward. So does the investment demand curve. Neither curve is vertical or horizontal, so the extreme Keynesian and extreme monetarist hypotheses are rejected.

This particular controversy in macroeconomics is now behind us, but other controversies are still around. One concerns the relative magnitudes of the multiplier effects of fiscal and monetary policy. Another concerns the time lags of those effects. But the major unresolved issue that divides economists today concerns the working of the labour market, a controversy that we'll meet in the next chapter.

REVIEW

The relative effectiveness of fiscal and monetary policy depends on the sensitivity to interest rates of investment demand and the demand for money. Other things remaining the same, the more sensitive investment demand is to interest rates or the less sensitive the demand for money is, the smaller is the effect of a change in government purchases and the greater is the effect of a change in the money supply on equilibrium expenditure. The less sensitive investment demand is to interest rates or the more sensitive the demand for money, the larger is the effect of a change in government purchases and the smaller is the effect of a change in the money supply on equilibrium expenditure. ◆

Influencing the Composition of Aggregate Expenditure

Aggregate expenditure can be increased either by an expansionary fiscal policy or by an increase in the money supply. An expansionary fiscal policy increases aggregate expenditure and *raises* interest rates.

Increased expenditure increases income and consumption expenditure, but higher interest rates decrease investment. Hence if aggregate expenditure is increased by an expansionary fiscal policy, consumption expenditure increases and investment decreases. In contrast, an increase in the money supply increases aggregate expenditure and *lowers* interest rates. Again, increased expenditure increases income and consumption expenditure, but in this case lower interest rates increase investment. Hence if aggregate expenditure is increased by an increase in the money supply, both consumption expenditure and investment increase. Thus the method whereby aggregate expenditure is increased affects the *composition* of expenditure.

Politics of Fiscal and Monetary Policy The effects on the composition of aggregate expenditure resulting from different policies for changing aggregate expenditure are a source of tension between the various branches of government and influence the economy's long-term capacity for growth. Usually, the government does not want the Bank of England to tighten monetary policy, which increases interest rates. Instead it wants to see the Bank of England steadily expanding the money supply, keeping interest rates as low as possible.

The Bank of England, on the other hand, frequently points to the importance of keeping government purchases of goods and services under control and keeping taxes sufficiently high to pay for those goods and services. It argues that unless the government increases taxes or cuts its expenditure, then a more expansionary monetary policy cannot be pursued.

The choice of monetary or fiscal policy affects the long-term growth prospects of the United Kingdom because the long-term capacity of the economy to produce goods and services depends on the rate at which capital is accumulated – the level of investment. An expansionary fiscal policy that leads to a decrease in investment slows down the economy's long-term growth. But much government expenditure is on productive capital such as motorways and on education and health care that increases human capital. Increases in government purchases of goods and services such as these increase the economy's long-term growth.

Real GDP, the Price Level and Interest Rates

FIGURE 28.10

W e've now studied the effects of fiscal and
monetary policy on equilibrium expenditure
and real GDP at a given price level. But the effects
that we've worked out occur at each and every price
level. Thus the fiscal and monetary policy effects that
we've studied tell us about changes in aggregate
demand and shifts in the aggregate demand curve.

When aggregate demand changes both real GDP
and the price level change. To determine the
amounts by which each change, we need to look at
both aggregate demand and aggregate supply. Let's
now do this, starting with the short-run effects of
fiscal and monetary policy.

The Short-run Effects on Real GDP and the Price Level

When aggregate demand changes and the aggregate
demand curve shifts, there is a movement along the
short-run aggregate supply curve and both real GDP
and the price level change. Figure 28.10 illustrates
the change in real GDP and the price level that result
from an increase in aggregate demand. Initially, the
aggregate demand curve is AD_0, and the short-run
aggregate supply curve is *SAS*. Real GDP is £600 billion, and the GDP deflator is 130.

Now suppose that changes in fiscal and monetary
policy increase aggregate demand, shifting the aggregate demand curve to AD_1. At the initial price level
(GDP deflator equal to 130) the quantity of real GDP
demanded increases to £800 billion. This increase is
the one we studied earlier in this chapter. But real
GDP does not actually increase to this level. The
reason is that the price level increases, bringing a
decrease in the quantity of real GDP demanded. The
higher level of aggregate demand puts upward pressure on the prices of all goods and services, and the
GDP deflator rises to 135. At the higher price level,
the real money supply decreases.

The decrease in the real money supply increases
the interest rate, decreases investment, and decreases equilibrium expenditure and real GDP. The
increase in real GDP from £600 billion to £800 billion
is the result of the initial policy-induced increase in

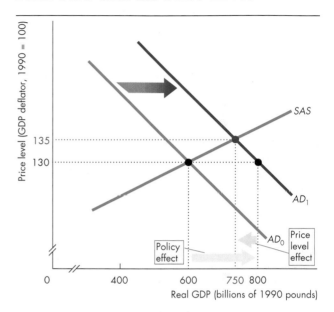

Policy-induced Changes in Real GDP and the Price Level

Initially aggregate demand is AD_0 and the short-run aggregate supply curve
is *SAS*. Real GDP is £600 billion and the GDP deflator is 130. Fiscal and
monetary policy changes shift the aggregate demand curve to AD_1. At the
initial price level (GDP deflator equal to 130) real GDP rises to £800 billion.
But the price level increases, bringing a decrease in the real money supply.
The decrease in the real money supply increases the interest rate, decreases
investment, and decreases equilibrium expenditure and real GDP. The
increase in real GDP from £600 billion to £800 billion is the result of the
initial policy-induced increase in aggregate demand at a given price level.
The decrease in real GDP from £800 billion to £750 billion is the result of the
decrease in the real money supply induced by the higher price level.

aggregate demand at a given price level; and the
decrease in real GDP from £800 billion to £750 billion
is the result of the decrease in the real money supply
induced by the higher price level.

The exercise that we've just conducted for an
increase in aggregate demand can be reversed to see
what happens when there is a policy-induced
decrease in aggregate demand. In this case, real GDP
decreases and the price level falls.

The effects that we've just worked out are short-
run effects. Let's now look at the long-run effects of
fiscal and monetary policy.

The Long-run Effects on Real GDP and the Price Level

The long-run effects of fiscal and monetary policy depend on the state of the economy when the policy action is taken. Again, we'll concentrate on the case of an *increase* in aggregate demand. If initially unemployment is above its natural rate and real GDP is below its long-run level, fiscal and monetary policy can be used to restore full employment. We can use the example in Fig. 28.10 to illustrate this case.

Suppose, in Fig. 28.10, that long-run aggregate supply is £600 billion. The increase in aggregate demand moves the economy from below full employment to full employment and that is the end of the story. The short-run and long-run adjustments are the same. For example, expansionary monetary policy was used in 1983 and 1984 to move the UK economy out of a serious recession into a period of sustained expansion.

But a policy-induced increase in aggregate demand might occur when the economy is already at full employment with real GDP at its long-run level. What then are the long-run effects?

We can see the answers in Fig. 28.11. The long-run aggregate supply curve is *LAS*. Initially, the aggregate demand curve is AD_0, and the short-run aggregate supply curve is SAS_0. Real GDP is £600 billion and the GDP deflator is 130.

Changes in fiscal and monetary policy increase aggregate demand, shifting the aggregate demand curve to AD_1. At the initial price level (GDP deflator equal to 130) the quantity of real GDP demanded increases to £800 billion – the increase we studied earlier in this chapter. But, as we've just seen, real GDP does not actually increase to this level. The higher price level decreases the real money supply and raises the interest rate. As a result investment, equilibrium expenditure and real GDP decrease. The new short-run equilibrium occurs at a real GDP of £750 billion and a GDP deflator of 135.

But real GDP is now above its long-run level and unemployment is below its natural rate. There is an inflationary gap. A shortage of labour puts upward pressure on wages. And as wages increase, the short-run aggregate supply curve begins to shift to the left. It keeps shifting until it reaches SAS_1. The GDP deflator increases to 145 and real GDP returns to its long-run level. Thus the long-run effect of an expansionary fiscal and monetary policy at full employment brings a rising price level but no change in real GDP.

FIGURE 28.11

The Long-run Effects of Policy-induced Changes in Real GDP and the Price Level

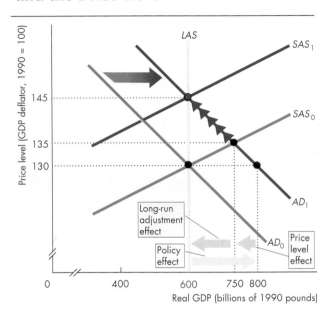

The long-run aggregate supply curve is *LAS* and initially the aggregate demand curve is AD_0 and the short-run aggregate supply curve is SAS_0. Real GDP is £600 billion and the GDP deflator is 130. Fiscal and monetary policy changes shift the aggregate demand curve to AD_1. At the new short-run equilibrium real GDP is £750 billion and the GDP deflator is 135. Because real GDP is above its long-run level wages increase and the short-run aggregate supply curve begins to shift to the left to SAS_1. At the new long-run equilibrium, the GDP deflator is 145 and real GDP is back at its original level.

REVIEW

A policy-induced change in aggregate demand changes both real GDP and the price level. The amount by which each changes depends on aggregate supply. In the short run, both real GDP and the price level increase, but the increase in real GDP is smaller than what would occur at a fixed price level. In the long run, the effects of fiscal and monetary policy depend on the state of the economy when the policy action is taken. Starting from a position below long-run real GDP, expansionary fiscal and monetary policy increases both real GDP and the price level and restores full employment. But starting from full employment, an expansionary fiscal and monetary policy brings a rise in the price level and no change in real GDP. ◆

◆ ◆ ◆ ◆ We have now studied the detailed effects of fiscal and monetary policy on real GDP, interest rates and the price level. We've seen what

determines the relative effectiveness of fiscal and monetary policy and how the mix of these policies can influence the composition of aggregate expenditure. But we've also seen that the ultimate effects of these policies on real GDP and the price level depend not only on the behaviour of aggregate demand but also on aggregate supply. Our next task is to turn to aggregate supply and study the determination of long-run and short-run aggregate supply, employment and unemployment.

S U M M A R Y

Money, Interest and Aggregate Demand

Real GDP and the price level are determined by the interaction of *aggregate demand* and *aggregate supply* (Chapter 23). Fiscal and monetary policy influence *aggregate demand*. To look at their effects we freeze the price level and study the magnitude of the shifts of the aggregate demand curve at a given price level. To do this we use the aggregate expenditure model (of Chapters 24 and 25). In this model, the aggregate expenditure curve tells us aggregate planned expenditure at a given price level and equilibrium expenditure corresponds to a point on the aggregate demand curve. Thus when equilibrium expenditure changes, the aggregate demand curve shifts.

Equilibrium expenditure depends on autonomous expenditure. But one component of autonomous expenditure, investment, varies with the interest rate. The higher the interest rate, other things remaining the same, the lower is investment, and hence the lower is autonomous expenditure and equilibrium expenditure. Therefore equilibrium expenditure and real GDP depend on the interest rate.

The interest rate is determined by equilibrium in the money market. The demand for real money depends on both real GDP and the interest rate. The higher real GDP, other things remaining the same, the greater is the demand for real money and the higher is the interest rate. Therefore the interest rate depends on real GDP.

Both real GDP and the interest rate are determined simultaneously. Equilibrium real GDP and the interest rate are such that the money market is in equilibrium and aggregate planned expenditure equals real GDP. (pp. 784–786)

Fiscal Policy and Aggregate Demand

A change in government purchases of goods and services or transfer payments or taxes influences aggregate demand by changing autonomous expenditure. An expansionary fiscal policy increases autonomous expenditure and increases aggregate planned expenditure. The increase in aggregate planned expenditure increases equilibrium expenditure and sets up a multiplier effect that increases real GDP. These are the first round effects. The rising real GDP sets up a second round. The increasing real GDP increases the demand for money, and the interest rate rises. With a rise in the interest rate, investment decreases. A decrease in investment decreases autonomous expenditure and decreases aggregate planned expenditure. These second round effects work in the opposite direction to the first round effects but are smaller in magnitude. The outcome of an increase in government purchases is an increase in real GDP, a rise in the interest rate and a decrease in investment.

The effect of higher interest rates on investment – the crowding out effect – might, in an extreme situation, be complete. That is, the decrease in investment might be sufficient to offset the initial increase in government purchases. In practice, complete crowding out does not occur. An opposing effect is crowding in, an increase in investment resulting from an increase in government purchases of goods and services. Such an effect may occur in a recession if fiscal stimulation brings expectations of economic recovery and higher future profits, if the government purchases capital that strengthens the economy, or if tax cuts stimulate investment.

Fiscal policy also influences aggregate demand through the foreign exchange rate. An increase in government purchases or a cut in taxes tends to increase interest rates and make the value of the pound rise against other currencies. When the pound strengthens, exports from the United Kingdom decrease and imports into the United Kingdom increase, so net exports from the United Kingdom decrease. (pp. 787–790)

Monetary Policy and Aggregate Demand

Monetary policy influences aggregate demand by changing the interest rate. An increase in the money supply lowers the interest rate. The lower interest rate increases investment, and higher investment increases aggregate planned expenditure. An increase in aggregate planned expenditure sets up a multiplier effect in which real GDP starts to increase. This is the first round effect. Increasing real GDP sets up a second round effect in which the demand for money increases and the interest rate rises. A rise in the interest rate decreases investment and decreases aggregate planned expenditure. The second round effect works in the opposite direction to the first round effect but is smaller in magnitude. The outcome of an increase in the money supply is an increase in real GDP and a fall in the interest rate. Monetary policy also influences aggregate demand through the foreign exchange rate. An increase in the money supply decreases the interest rate and makes the value of the pound fall against other currencies. When the pound weakens, imports into the United Kingdom decrease and exports from the United Kingdom increase, so net exports from the United Kingdom increase. (pp. 791–793)

The Relative Effectiveness of Fiscal and Monetary Policy

The relative effectiveness of fiscal and monetary policy on aggregate demand depends on two factors: the sensitivity of investment demand to the interest rate and the sensitivity of the demand for money to the interest rate. The more sensitive investment demand to the interest rate or the less sensitive the demand for money to the interest rate, the larger is the effect of a change in the money supply on aggregate demand. The less sensitive investment demand to the interest rate or the more sensitive the

demand for money to the interest rate, the larger is the effect of a fiscal policy change on aggregate demand.

The Keynesian–monetarist controversy concerns the relative effectiveness of fiscal and monetary actions in influencing aggregate demand. The extreme Keynesian position was that only fiscal policy affects aggregate demand and monetary policy is impotent. The extreme monetarist position is the converse – that only monetary policy affects aggregate demand and that fiscal policy is impotent. This controversy was the central one in macroeconomics in the 1950s and 1960s. As a result of statistical investigations, we now know that neither of these extreme positions is correct. The demand curve for real money and the investment demand curve both slope downward, and both fiscal and monetary policy influence aggregate demand.

The mix of fiscal and monetary policy influences the composition of aggregate demand. If aggregate demand increases as a result of an increase in the money supply, interest rates fall and investment increases. If aggregate demand increases as a result of an increase in government purchases of goods and services, interest rates rise and investment falls. These different effects of fiscal and monetary policy on aggregate demand create some political tensions. To keep aggregate demand in check and interest rates moderate, there must be a high enough level of taxes to support the level of government purchases. (pp. 793–803)

Real GDP, the Price Level and Interest Rates

When aggregate demand changes both real GDP and the price level change by amounts determined by both aggregate demand and aggregate supply. A policy-induced increase in aggregate demand shifts the aggregate demand curve to the right. The magnitude of the shift of the aggregate demand curve is equal to the effect of the policy change on aggregate demand at a given price level. In the short run, real GDP and the price level increase. The rise in the price level decreases the real money supply. The decrease in the real money supply increases the interest rate, decreases investment, and decreases real GDP.

The long-run effects of fiscal and monetary policy depend on the state of the economy when the policy action is taken. Starting out with unemployment above its natural rate and real GDP below its long-run level, expansionary fiscal and monetary policy increases real GDP and the price level and restores full employment. But starting out from full employment with real GDP at its long-run level, a policy-induced increase in aggregate demand increases the price level and leaves real GDP unchanged. (pp. 803–805)

K E Y   E L E M E N T S

Key Terms

Key Figures

R E V I E W   Q U E S T I O N S

1   Explain the link between the money market and the market for goods and services.

2   What are the first round effects of an increase in government purchases of goods and services?

3   What are the second round effects of an increase in government purchases of goods and services?

4   What is the outcome of an increase in government purchases of goods and services?

5   What role does the foreign exchange rate play in influencing aggregate demand when there is an expansionary fiscal policy?

6   What are crowding out, crowding in and international crowding out? Explain how each occurs.

7   What are the first round effects of an increase in the money supply?

8   What are the second round effects of an increase in the money supply?

9   What is the outcome of an increase in the money supply?

10   What role does the foreign exchange rate play in influencing aggregate demand when there is a change in the money supply?

11   What factors determine the effectiveness of fiscal policy and monetary policy?

12   Under what conditions is fiscal policy more effective than monetary policy in stimulating aggregate demand?

13   Distinguish between the hypotheses of extreme Keynesians and extreme monetarists.

14   Explain the Keynesian–monetarist controversy about the influence of monetary policy and fiscal policy on aggregate demand.

15   Explain how the Keynesian–monetarist controversy in Question 14 was settled.

16   Explain how fiscal policy and monetary policy influence the composition of aggregate demand.

17   Explain the effect of an increase in the money supply and expansionary fiscal policy on the price level and real GDP. Be careful to distinguish between the short-run and the long-run effect.

PROBLEMS

1 In the economy described in Fig. 28.1, suppose the government decreases its purchases of goods and services by £150 billion.

   a Work out the first round effects.

   b Explain how real GDP and the interest rate change.

   c Explain the second round effects that take the economy to a new equilibrium.

2 In the economy described in Fig. 28.1, suppose the Bank of England decreases the money supply by £150 billion.

   a Work out the first round effects.

   b Explain how real GDP and the interest rate change.

   c Explain the second round effects that take the economy to a new equilibrium.

3 The economies of two countries, Alpha and Beta, are identical in every way except the following: in Alpha, a change in the interest rate of 1 percentage point (for example, from 5 per cent to 6 per cent) results in a £1 billion change in the quantity of real money demanded. In Beta, a change in the interest rate of 1 percentage point results in a £0.1 billion change in the quantity of real money demanded.

   a In which economy does an increase in government purchases of goods and services

have a larger effect on real GDP?

   b In which economy is the crowding out effect weaker?

   c In which economy does a change in the money supply have a larger effect on equilibrium real GDP?

4 The economy is in a recession and the government wants to increase aggregate demand, stimulate exports and increase investment. It has three policy options: increase government purchases of goods and services, decrease taxes and increase the money supply.

   a Explain the mechanisms at work under each alternative policy.

   b What is the effect of each policy on the composition of aggregate demand?

   c What are the short-run effects of each policy on real GDP and the price level?

   d Which policy would you recommend that the government adopt?

5 The economy is at full employment, but the government is disappointed with the growth rate of real GDP. It wants to stimulate investment and at the same time avoid an increase in the price level. Suggest a combination of fiscal and monetary policies that will achieve the government's objective.

APPENDIX

To
Chapter 28

The
IS-LM
Model of
Aggregate
Demand

Equilibrium Expenditure and Real GDP

Aggregate planned expenditure depends on real GDP because consumption increases as real GDP increases. Aggregate planned expenditure also depends on the interest rate because the higher the interest rate, the lower is planned investment. These two influences on aggregate planned expenditure give rise to the *IS* curve.

The *IS* Curve

The *IS curve* shows combinations of real GDP and the interest rate at which aggregate expenditure is at its equilibrium level – aggregate planned expenditure equals real GDP.

Figure A28.1 derives the *IS* curve. Part (a) is similar to Fig. 25.2. The 45° line shows all the points at which aggregate planned expenditure equals real GDP. Curves AE_a, AE_b and AE_c are aggregate planned expenditure curves. Curve AE_a represents aggregate planned expenditure when the interest

rate is 5 per cent (row a of the table). Curve AE_b shows aggregate planned expenditure when the interest rate is 4 per cent (row b) and AE_c shows aggregate planned expenditure when the interest rate is 3 per cent (row c).

There is just one expenditure equilibrium on each of these three aggregate planned expenditure curves. On curve AE_a, the expenditure equilibrium is at point a, where real GDP is $400 billion. The expenditure equilibrium on curve AE_b occurs at point b, where real GDP is $600 billion. The expenditure equilibrium on AE_c occurs at point c, where real GDP is $800 billion.

Figure A28.1(b) shows each expenditure equilibrium again but highlights the relationship between the interest rate and real GDP at the expenditure equilibrium. Its horizontal axis, like Fig. A28.1(a), measures real GDP. Its vertical axis measures the interest rate. Point a in part (b) illustrates the expenditure equilibrium at point a in part (a) of the figure (or in row a of the table). It tells us that if the interest rate is 5 per cent, the expenditure equilibrium occurs at a real GDP of $400 billion. Points b and c in the figure illustrate the expenditure equilibrium at points b and c of part (a). The continuous line through these points is the *IS* curve.

Some relationships show 'cause' and 'effect'. For example, the investment demand curve tells us the level of investment (effect) at a particular interest

rate (cause). The *IS* curve is *not* a 'cause and effect' relationship. It can be read in two ways. It tells us that if the interest rate is 5 per cent, then aggregate planned expenditure equals real GDP only if real

FIGURE A28.1

Aggregate Planned Expenditure, Flow Equilibrium and the IS Curve

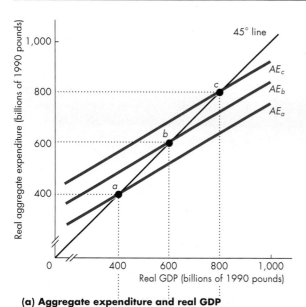

(a) Aggregate expenditure and real GDP

The table shows aggregate planned expenditure – the sum of autonomous expenditure and induced expenditure – that occurs at different combinations of the interest rate and real GDP. For example, if the interest rate is 5 per cent and real GDP is £800 billion, aggregate planned expenditure is £560 billion (top right-hand number). Flow equilibrium (equality of aggregate planned expenditure and real GDP) is shown by the green squares. Each of rows *a,b* and *c* represents an aggregate expenditure schedule, plotted as the aggregate expenditure curves AE_a, AE_b and AE_c, respectively, in part (a). Expenditure equilibrium positions are shown in part (a), where these *AE* curves intersect the 45° line and are marked *a*, *b* and *c*. Part (b) shows these same equilibrium positions but highlights the combinations of the interest rate and the real GDP at which they occur. The line connecting those points is the *IS* curve.

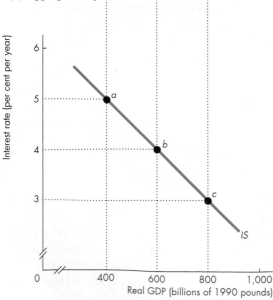

(b) The *IS* curve

	Interest rate (per cent per year)	Autonomous expenditure (billions of 1990 pounds)	Aggregate planned expenditure (billions of 1990 pounds)		
a	5	240	400	480	560
b	4	360	520	600	680
c	3	480	640	720	800

Induced expenditure	180	240	320
Real GDP (billions of 1990 pounds)	400	600	800

GDP is £400 billion. It also tells us that if real GDP is £400 billion, then the interest rate at which aggregate planned expenditure equals real GDP is 5 per cent.

The *IS* curve shows combinations of the interest rate and real GDP at which aggregate expenditure is at its equilibrium level. To determine the interest rate and real GDP, we need an additional relationship between those two variables. That second relationship between interest rates and real GDP comes from equilibrium in the money market.

Money Market Equilibrium

The quantity of money demanded depends on the price level, real GDP, and the interest rate. The quantity of money demanded is proportional to the price level. If the price level doubles, so does the quantity of money demanded. Real money is the ratio of the quantity of money to the price level. The quantity of real money demanded increases as real GDP increases and decreases as the interest rate increases.

The supply of money is determined by the actions of the Bank of England, the banks and other financial intermediaries. Given those actions, and given the price level, there is a given quantity of real money in existence. Money market equilibrium occurs when the quantity of real money supplied is equal to the quantity demanded. Equilibrium in the money market is a stock equilibrium. Figure A28.2 contains a numerical example that enables us to study money market equilibrium.

Suppose that the quantity of money supplied is £500 billion. Suppose also that the GDP deflator is 100 so that the quantity of real money supplied is also £500 billion. The real money supply is shown in the bottom part of the table. Money market equilibrium occurs when the quantity of real money demanded equals the quantity supplied – £500 billion. The quantity of real money demanded depends on real GDP and the interest rate. The table tells us about the demand for real money. Each row tells us how much real money is demanded at a given interest rate as real GDP varies and each column tells us how much is demanded at a given real GDP as the interest rate varies. For example, at an interest rate of 5 per cent and real GDP at £400 billion, the quantity

of real money demanded is £400 billion. Alternatively, at an interest rate of 4 per cent and real GDP at £600 billion, the quantity of real money demanded is £500 billion. The rest of the numbers in the table are read in a similar way.

Money market equilibrium occurs when the quantity of real money demanded equals the quantity supplied, £500 billion in this example. The green squares in the table indicate positions of money market equilibrium – combinations of interest rate and real GDP at which the quantity of money demanded is equal to the quantity supplied. For example, look at column *d*. Real GDP is £400 billion, and the quantity of real money demanded is £500 billion (equal to the quantity supplied) when the interest rate is 3 per cent. Thus at real GDP of £400 billion and an interest rate of 3 per cent, the money market is in equilibrium. At the other two green squares the interest rate is such that the quantity of real money demanded is £500 billion when real GDP is £600 billion and £800 billion respectively. That is, the green squares show combinations of the interest rate and real GDP at which the money market is in equilibrium.

The *LM* curve

The *LM curve* shows the combinations of real GDP and the interest rate at which the quantity of real money demanded equals the quantity of real money supplied. Figure A28.2 derives the *LM* curve. Part (a) shows the demand and supply curves for real money. The quantity supplied is fixed at £500 billion, so the supply curve *MS* is vertical. Each of the columns of the table labelled *d, e* and *f* is a demand schedule for real money – a schedule that tells us how the quantity of real money demanded rises as the interest rate falls. There is a different schedule for each level of real GDP. These three demand schedules for real money are graphed as demand curves for real money in part (a) of the figure as MD_d, MD_e and MD_f. For example, when real GDP is £400 billion, the demand curve for real money is MD_d. Money market equilibrium occurs at the intersection of the supply curve and the demand curves for real money at points *d, e* and *f* in part (a).

Figure A28.2(b) shows each money market equilibrium again but highlights the relationship between the interest rate and real GDP at which an equilibrium occurs. Points *d, e* and *f* in part (b) illustrate the money market equilibrium represented by the green squares in the table and by those similarly labelled points in part (a). The continuous line through these points is the *LM* curve. The *LM* curve shows the interest rate and real GDP at which money market equilibrium occurs when the real money supply is £500 billion.

Like the *IS* curve, the *LM* curve does not have a

'cause and effect' interpretation. The *LM* curve illustrated in Fig. A28.2(b) tells us that if the quantity of real money supplied is £500 billion and real GDP is £400 billion, then for money market equilibrium the interest rate is 3 per cent. It also tells us that if the quantity of real money supplied is £500 billion and the interest rate is 3 per cent, then for money market

---

FIGURE A28.2

The Money Market, Stock Equilibrium and the *LM* Curve

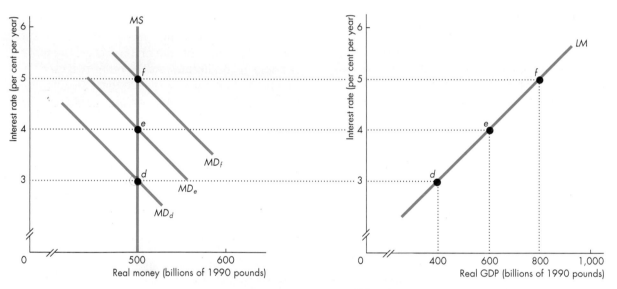

(a) Money market equilibrium

(b) The *LM* curve

The table shows the quantity of real money demanded at different combinations of the interest rate and real GDP. For example, if the interest rate is 5 per cent and real GDP is £400 billion, the quantity of real money demanded is £400 billion (top left number). Stock equilibrium – equality between the quantity of real money demanded and supplied – is shown by the green squares. Each of the columns *d*, *e* and *f* represents a demand schedule for real money, plotted as the demand curves for real money MD_d, MD_e and MD_f, respectively, in part (a). Money market equilibrium positions are shown in part (a), where these *MD* curves intersect the supply curve of real money *MS* and are marked *d*, *e* and *f*. Part (b) shows these same equilibrium positions but highlights the combinations of the interest rate and real GDP at which they occur. The line connecting those points is the *LM* curve.

Interest rate (per cent per year)	Quantity of real money demanded (billions of 1990 pounds)		
5	400	450	500
4	450	500	550
3	500	550	600
Real GDP	400	600	800

Real money supply (billions of 1990 pounds)	500	500	500
	d	*e*	*f*

equilibrium real GDP is £400 billion. That is, the *LM* curve shows combinations of the interest rate and real GDP at which there is money market equilibrium.

We now have two relationships between the interest rate and real GDP. The *IS* curve and the *LM* curve. Together, and at a given price level, these two relationships determine the interest rate or real GDP. They also enable us to derive the *aggregate demand curve*. Let's see how.

Equilibrium and the Aggregate Demand Curve

Equilibrium real GDP and the interest rate are shown in Fig. A28.3, which brings together the *IS* curve and the *LM* curve. This equilibrium is at the point of intersection of the *IS* curve and *LM* curve. Point *b* on the *IS* curve is a point of expenditure equilibrium. The interest rate and real GDP are such that aggregate planned expenditure equals real GDP. Point *e* on the *LM* curve is a point of money market equilibrium. The interest rate and real GDP are such that the quantity of real money demanded equals the quantity of real money supplied. At this intersection point, there is both flow equilibrium in the goods market and stock equilibrium in the money market. The equilibrium interest rate is 4 per cent and real GDP is £600 billion.

At all other points, there is either no expenditure equilibrium or the money market is not in equilibrium or both. At a point such as *a*, the economy is on its *IS* curve but off its *LM* curve. With real GDP at £400 billion and the interest rate at 5 per cent, the interest rate is too high or real GDP is too low for money market equilibrium. Interest rates adjust quickly and would fall to 3 per cent to bring about money market equilibrium, putting the economy at point *d*, a point on the *LM* curve. But point *d* is off the *IS* curve. At point *d*, with the interest rate at 3 per cent and real GDP at £400 billion, aggregate planned expenditure exceeds real GDP. By checking back to the table in Fig. A28.1, you can see that aggregate planned expenditure is £640 billion, which exceeds real GDP of £400 billion. With aggregate planned expenditure larger than real GDP, real GDP will increase. But as real GDP increases, so does the demand for real money and so does the interest rate.

FIGURE A28.3

IS–LM Equilibrium

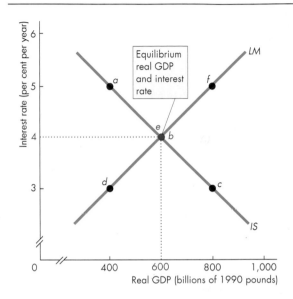

All points on the *IS* curve are points where aggregate planned expenditure equals real GDP. All points on the *LM* curve are points at which the quantity of real money demanded equals the quantity of real money supplied. The intersection of the *IS* curve on the *LM* curve determines the equilibrium interest rate and real GDP – 4 per cent and £600 billion. At this interest rate and real GDP, there is flow equilibrium in the goods market and stock equilibrium in the money market.

Real GDP and the interest rate would rise, and continue to do so, until the point of intersection of the *IS* and *LM* curves is reached.

The account that we have just given of what *would* happen if the economy was at a point like *a* or *d* tells us that the economy cannot be at such points. The forces that operate in such situations would be so strong that they would always push the economy to the intersection of the *IS* and *LM* curves.

The Effects of a Change in Price Level on the *LM* Curve

The price level enters the *IS–LM* model to determine the quantity of real money supplied. The Bank of England determines the money supply as a certain number of current pounds. The higher the price level, the lower is the real value of those pounds.

Because the price level affects the quantity of real money supplied, it also affects the *LM* curve. Let's see how.

Begin by asking what happens if the price level, instead of being 100, is 120–20 per cent higher than before. The money supply is £500 billion. With a GDP deflator of 100, the real money supply is also £500 billion. But if the GDP deflator is 120, the real money supply is £416.67 billion. (The real money supply is £500 billion divided by 1.2, which equals £416.67 billion.) For money market equilibrium we can see in the table of Fig. A28.2 what happens to the interest rate at a real GDP of £600 billion. With a GDP deflator of 120, the interest rate rises to 5 per cent in order to decrease the quantity of real money demanded to £416.67 billion – equal to the real money supply. Thus with a GDP deflator of 120, an interest rate of 5 per cent and real GDP of £600 billion become a point on the *LM* curve – point *g* in Fig. A28.4(a).

Next, suppose that the GDP deflator is lower than the original case – 86 instead of 100. Now the real money supply becomes £581.4 billion (the real money supply is £500 billion divided by 0.86, which equals £581.4 billion). Again for money market equilibrium we can see in the table of Fig. A28.2 what happens to the interest rate at a real GDP of £600 billion. With a GDP deflator of 86, the interest rate falls to 3 per cent in order to increase the quantity of real money demanded to £581.4 billion – equal to the real money supply. Thus with a GDP deflator of 86, an interest rate of 3 per cent and real GDP of £600 billion become a point on the *LM* curve – point *h* in Fig. A28.4(a).

The *LM* Curve Shift   The example that we have worked through tells us that there is a different *LM* curve for each price level. Figure A28.4(a) illustrates the *LM* curves for the three different price levels we have considered. The initial *LM* curve has the GDP deflator equal to 100. This curve has been relabelled as LM_0 in Fig. A28.4(a). When the GDP deflator is 120 and real GDP is £600 billion, the interest rate that achieves equilibrium in the money market is 5 per cent. This equilibrium is shown as point *g* on curve LM_1 in Fig. A28.4(a). The entire *LM* curve shifts left to LM_1 in order to pass through point *g*. When the GDP deflator is 86 and real GDP is £600 billion, the interest rate that achieves equilibrium in the money market is 3 per cent. This equilibrium is shown as point *h* on the curve LM_2 in

FIGURE A28.4

Deriving the Aggregate Demand Curve

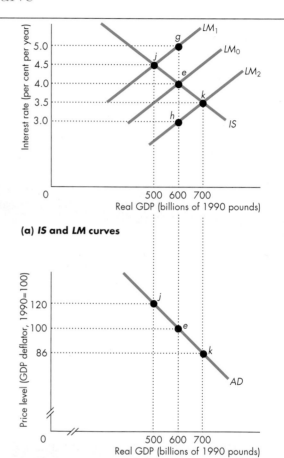

(a) *IS* and *LM* curves

(b) Aggregate demand curve

In part (a), if the GDP deflator is 100, the *LM* curve is LM_0. If the GDP deflator increases to 120, the *LM* curve shifts to the left to LM_1. A lower real money supply requires a higher interest rate at each level of real GDP for money market equilibrium. For example, if real GDP is £600 billion, the interest rate has to increase from 4 per cent to 5 per cent (point *g*). If the price level falls, the real money supply increases and the *LM* curve shifts to the right to LM_2 If real GDP is £600 billion, the interest rate falls to 3 per cent (point *h*) to maintain money market equilibrium. When the GDP deflator is 100, the *IS* and *LM* curves intersect at point *e* – real GDP of £600 billion. This equilibrium is shown in part (b) at point *e* on aggregate demand curve *AD*. This point tells us that when the GDP deflator is 100, the quantity of real GDP demanded is £600 billion. If the GDP deflator is 120, the *LM* curve is LM_1 and real GDP is £500 billion. A second point on the aggregate demand curve is found at *j*. If the GDP deflator is 86, the *LM* curve is LM_2 and real GDP is £700 billion. Another point on the aggregate demand curve is generated at point *k*. Joining points *j*, *e* and *k* gives the aggregate demand curve.

Fig. A28.4(a). Again, the entire *LM* curve shifts right to LM_2 in order to pass through point *h*.

Now that we have worked out the effects of a change in the price level on the position of the *LM* curve, we can derive the aggregate demand curve.

The Aggregate Demand Curve Derived

Figure A28.4 shows the derivation. Part (a) shows the *IS* curve and the three *LM* curves associated with the three different price levels (GDP deflators of 86, 100 and 120). When the GDP deflator is 100, the *LM* curve is LM_0. Equilibrium is at point *e* where real GDP is £600 billion and the equilibrium interest rate is 4 per cent. If the GDP deflator is 120, the *LM* curve is LM_1. Equilibrium is at point *j* where real GDP is £3.5 billion and the interest rate is 4.5 per cent. If the GDP deflator is 86, the *LM* curve is LM_2. Equilibrium is at point *k* where real GDP is £700 billion and the interest rate is 3.5 per cent. At each price level there is a different equilibrium real GDP and interest rate.

Part (b) traces the aggregate demand curve. The price level is measured on the vertical axis of part (b) and real GDP on the horizontal axis. When the GDP deflator is 100, equilibrium real GDP is £600 billion (point *e*). When the GDP deflator is 120, equilibrium real GDP is £500 billion (point *j*). And when the GDP deflator is 86, real GDP demanded is £700 billion (point *k*). Each of these points corresponds to the same point in part (a). The line joining these points in part (b) is the aggregate demand curve.

Now that we have derived the aggregate demand curve we can work out the effects of fiscal and monetary policy.

Fiscal Policy and Aggregate Demand

A change in government purchases or in taxes shifts the *IS* curve and the aggregate demand curve. In Chapter 25, we worked out the magnitude of the change in aggregate planned expenditure resulting from a change in government purchases or in taxes when the interest rate is constant. In terms of the *IS-LM* model, these multiplier effects tell us how far the *IS* curve shifts. But the change in aggregate planned expenditure at a given interest rate is not the same thing as a change in aggregate demand. For, when aggregate planned expenditure changes, the interest rate usually changes as well and that has further effects on expenditure plans.

Figure A28.5 illustrates three different effects of a change in fiscal policy. In all three parts of the figure, the same fiscal policy action takes place. There is either a rise in government purchases or a cut in autonomous taxes that shifts the *IS* curve from IS_0 to IS_1. In part (a), the normal case, the *LM* curve is upward sloping (LM_N). When the *IS* curve shifts, the interest rate increases and so does real GDP. But the increase in real GDP is smaller than the magnitude of the shift to the right in the *IS* curve. The reason is that the higher interest rate leads to a decrease in investment and that decrease in investment partially offsets the initial increased spending resulting from the fiscal policy action.

In part (b), the *LM* curve is horizontal (LM_H). The *LM* curve is horizontal only if there is a 'liquidity trap' – a situation in which people are willing to hold any quantity of money at a given interest rate. When the *IS* curve shifts to the right, real GDP increases by the same amount as the shift to the right of the *IS* curve. Interest rates stay constant. In this case, the multiplier effect of Chapter 25 still operates.

In part (c), the *LM* curve is vertical (LM_V). In this case, although the *IS* curve shifts to the right by exactly the same amount as in parts (a) and (b), real GDP stays constant. Here, the interest rate increases. The higher interest rate leads to a decrease in investment that exactly offsets the initial increase in expenditure resulting from the fiscal policy. There is complete crowding out. Complete crowding out occurs if the demand for real money is completely insensitive to interest rates. No matter what the interest rate, the quantity of real money demanded is a constant portion of real GDP.

Part (b) of the figure corresponds to the extreme Keynesian prediction, part (c) to the extreme monetarist prediction, and part (a) to the intermediate position.

Next, let's consider monetary policy.

Monetary Policy and Aggregate Demand

We saw earlier in this appendix that when the *LM* curve shifts because of a change in the price level, equilibrium real GDP changes and there is a movement along the aggregate demand curve. But a change in the money supply also shifts the *LM* curve. If the *LM* curve shifts because there is a change in the nominal money supply, then the aggregate demand curve shifts. The magnitude of

Fiscal Policy and Aggregate Demand

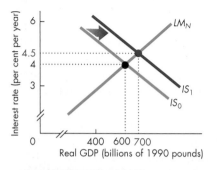

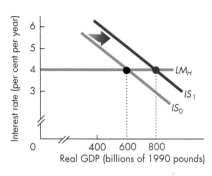

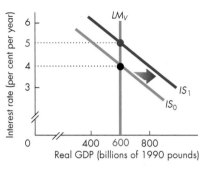

(a) Fiscal policy: normal case

(b) Fiscal policy: maximum effect on GDP

(c) Fiscal policy: no effect on GDP

An increase in government purchases or an autonomous tax cut shifts the *IS* curve to the right. The effects of fiscal policy on real GDP and the interest rate depend on the slope of the *LM* curve. In the normal case (part a), interest rates and real GDP rise. If there is a liquidity trap, the *LM* curve is horizontal (part b) and real GDP increases but interest rates stay constant. If the demand for money is insensitive to interest rates, the *LM* curve is vertical (part c) and interest rates rise but real GDP stays constant. In this case, there is complete 'crowding out'. The higher interest rate leads to a cut in investment that exactly offsets the initial fiscal policy action.

Monetary Policy and Aggregate Demand

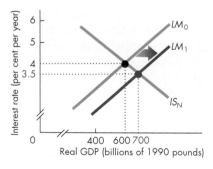

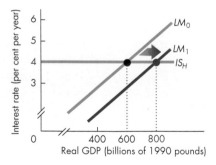

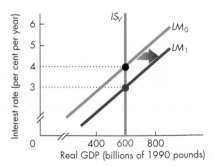

(a) Monetary policy: normal case

(b) Monetary policy: maximum effect on GDP

(c) Monetary policy: no effect on GDP

An increase in the money supply shifts the *LM* curve to the right. The effect of the monetary action on interest rates and real GDP depends on the slope of the *IS* curve. In the normal case (part a), interest rates fall and real GDP rises. The lower interest rates stimulate investment. In the special case (part b), the *IS* curve is horizontal. People don't care when they undertake their investment and will undertake any amount at an interest rate of 4 per cent. The change in the money supply changes real GDP but leaves the interest rate constant. If investment demand is completely insensitive to interest rates (part c), the *IS* curve is vertical and a change in the money supply lowers interest rates but leaves real GDP unchanged. In this case, the lower interest rate has no effect on investment, so there is no initial injection of additional expenditure.

the change in aggregate demand – the shift in the aggregate demand curve – depends on two factors: the size of the shift of the LM curve and the slope of the IS curve. Figure A28.6 shows three possible cases. In each case, the LM curve shifts to the right by the same amount, from LM_0 to LM_1. In part (a), the normal case, the IS curve is downward sloping (IS_N). When the money supply increases, the interest rate falls and real GDP rises. The rise in real GDP results from increased investment induced by the lower interest rate.

In part (b), the IS curve is horizontal (IS_H). This situation arises if people change the timing of their investment whenever the interest rate rises above or falls below 4 per cent. If the interest rate rises above 4 per cent, all investment stops; if the interest rate falls below 4 per cent, there is no limit to the amount of investment that people try to undertake.

At 4 per cent, any amount of investment will be undertaken. In this case, a change in the money supply shifts the LM curve and increases real GDP but leaves the interest rate unchanged.

In part (c), the IS curve is vertical (IS_V). This case arises if investment is completely insensitive to interest rates. People plan to undertake a given level of investment regardless of the interest cost involved. In this case, when the LM curve shifts, interest rates fall but the lower interest rate does not stimulate additional expenditure, so real GDP stays constant.

Part (c) corresponds to the views of extreme Keynesians. A change in the money supply has no effect on real GDP. Part (b) corresponds to the predictions of monetarists. A change in the money supply has a large and powerful effect on real GDP. Part (a) is the intermediate position.

CHAPTER 29

PRODUCTIVITY, WAGES AND UNEMPLOYMENT

After studying this chapter you will be able to:

◆ Explain why productivity and real GDP grow

◆ Explain how firms decide how much labour to employ

◆ Explain how households decide how much labour to supply

◆ Explain how wages and employment are determined

◆ Derive the long-run and short-run aggregate supply curves

◆ Explain what makes aggregate supply fluctuate

◆ Explain why unemployment exists and why its rate fluctuates

I N 1993, EACH HOUR OF WORK EARNED WORKERS IN THE UNITED KINGDOM 30 PER

CENT MORE than it did in 1983. And over the same period, the number of

people in the United Kingdom with jobs grew by more than 5 per cent.

What makes UK wages and the number of jobs grow over the years? ◆ ◆

As the economy grows, it ebbs and flows through the business cycle, with employ-

ment and real GDP marching in step with each other. Sometimes the UK economy

is in recession – real GDP has fallen. Such was the situation in 1991–1992 when

real GDP decreased by almost 3 per cent. What makes real GDP sometimes

decrease? ◆ ◆   In 1992–1993, British Rail shed 17,000 jobs, and in 1994

Granada Television announced that it would shed

200 senior managers. These are just two examples of

a general trend for firms in many industries to

streamline their labour forces. Because of this trend,

unemployment in the United Kingdom continued to

increase in 1992 and 1993. At the beginning of 1994, almost 11 per cent of the

labour force was unemployed. What causes unemployment? Why don't the unem-

ployed get jobs? And why is unemployment sometimes high as it was in 1993?

◆ ◆ ◆ ◆   In this chapter we'll look at productivity, wages and the labour market

in the United Kingdom. We'll discover what makes employment, productivity and

wages grow and why the unemployment rate is sometimes high. Our study com-

pletes a further block in the macroeconomic jigsaw puzzle – the aggregate supply

block. We'll return to the long-run and short-run aggregate supply curves that you

met in Chapter 23 and see how those curves are related to the labour market.

Incomes and Jobs

Productivity and Income Growth

When we talk about *productivity*, we usually mean labour productivity – although we can measure the productivity of any factor of production. **Labour productivity** is measured as total output per person employed. To study the growth of labour productivity and its effects on wages, employment and unemployment, we use the concept of the production function. A **production function** shows how output varies as the employment of inputs is varied. A **short-run production function** shows how output varies when the quantity of labour employed varies, holding constant the quantity of capital and the state of technology. Production functions exist for every kind of economic activity – building dams and roads or baking loaves of bread. But the production function that tells us about the relationship between *aggregate* employment and *aggregate* output is the short-run *aggregate* production function. The **short-run aggregate production function** shows how real GDP varies as the quantity of labour employed is varied, holding constant all other influences on production.

The table in Fig.29.1 records part of an economy's short-run aggregate production function. In that table, we look at the aggregate quantity of labour, measured in billions of hours a year, over the range 15 billion to 35 billion. Through that range of employment, real GDP varies between £400 billion and £700 billion a year (measured in 1990 pounds).

The short-run aggregate production function (*PF*) is illustrated in the graph in Fig. 29.1. The labour input is measured on the horizontal axis, and real GDP is measured on the vertical axis. The short-run production function slopes upward, showing that more labour input produces more real GDP.

The Marginal Product of Labour

The **marginal product of labour** is the additional real GDP produced by one additional hour of labour input, holding all other influences on production constant. We calculate the marginal product of labour as the change in real GDP divided by the change in the quantity of labour employed. Let's do such a calculation, using Fig. 29.1.

FIGURE 29.1

The Short-run Aggregate Production Function

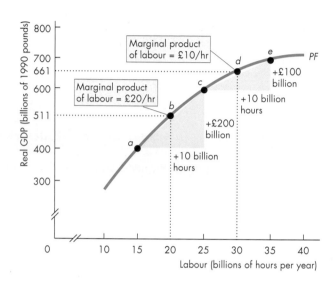

	Labour (billions of hours per year)	Real GDP (billions of 1990 pounds per year)
a	15	400
b	20	511
c	25	600
d	30	661
e	35	700

The short-run aggregate production function shows the level of real GDP at each quantity of labour input, holding all other inputs constant. The table lists five points on a short-run aggregate production function. Each row tells us the amount of real GDP that can be produced by a given labour input. Points *a* to *e* in the graph correspond to the rows in the table. The curve passing through these points traces the economy's short-run aggregate production function. The marginal product of labour is highlighted in the figure. As the labour input increases, real GDP increases but by successively smaller amounts. For example, a 10 billion hour increase in labour from 15 billion to 25 billion increases real GDP by £200 billion – a marginal product of £20 an hour. But a 10 billion hour increase in labour from 25 billion to 35 billion hours increases real GDP by only £100 billion – a marginal product of £10 an hour.

When the labour input increases from 15 to 25 million hours – an increase of 10 billion hours – real GDP increases from ₤400 billion to ₤600 billion – an increase of ₤200 billion. The marginal product of labour over this range is ₤20 an hour (₤200 billion divided by 10 billion hours). Next, look at what happens at a higher level of labour input. When the labour input increases by 10 billion hours from 25 billion to 35 billion hours, real GDP increases, but by less than in the previous case – by only ₤100 billion. Now the marginal product of labour is ₤10 an hour (₤100 billion divided by 10 billion hours).

The marginal product of labour is measured by the slope of the production function. Figure 29.1 highlights this fact. The slope of the production function at point b is ₤20 an hour. This slope is calculated as ₤200 billion – the change in real GDP from ₤400 billion to ₤600 billion – divided by 10 billion hours – the change in employment from 15 billion hours to 25 billion hours. Similarly, the slope of the production function at point d is ₤10 an hour.

Diminishing Marginal Product of Labour

The marginal product of labour declines as the labour input increases. This phenomenon, apparent from the calculations we've just made and visible in the figure, is called the diminishing marginal product of labour. The **diminishing marginal product of labour** is the tendency for the marginal product of labour to decline as the labour input increases, holding everything else constant.

Diminishing marginal product of labour arises because we are dealing with a *short-run* production function. As the quantity of labour employed is varied, all other inputs are held constant. Thus although more labour can produce more output, a larger labour force operates the same capital equipment – machines and tools – as does a smaller labour force. As more people are hired, the capital equipment is worked closer and closer to its physical limits, more breakdowns occur and bottlenecks arise. As a result, output does not increase in proportion to the amount of labour employed. The marginal product of labour declines as more labour is hired. This feature is present in almost all production processes and is also present in the relationship between aggregate employment and aggregate output – real GDP.

A change in the quantity of labour brings a movement along the production function. A change in any

other influence on production shifts the production function. Let's now look at these influences.

Economic Growth

Economic growth is the expansion of the economy's productive capacity. Economic growth results from two sources. They are:

◆ Capital accumulation
◆ Technological change

Capital Accumulation   Every year, some of the economy's resources are devoted to accumulating new capital. Much of this capital takes the form of machines, production lines and buildings. But a larger part takes the form of *human capital*. Human capital is acquired by attending university and by on-the-job experience. This last source of capital accumulation is now believed to be the largest single contributor to economic growth. Additional capital enables a given amount of labour to produce more output.

Technological Change   We also devote some of our resources to developing new technologies. Technological change has two stages, invention and innovation. **Invention** is the discovery of a new technique; **innovation** is the act of putting a new technique to work. Invention is the driving force behind technological change, but it is innovation that actually changes our productive capacity. Like capital accumulation, technological change also enables a given amount of labour to produce more output.

The Shifting Production Function   Because capital accumulation and technological change enable a given amount of labour to produce more output they shift the short-run aggregate production function upward. Figure 29.2 illustrates such a shift. The curve PF_{94} is the same as the production function in Fig. 29.1. During 1994 and 1995, new equipment is installed, labour becomes more skilful as a result of on-the-job experience, and new technologies are used. Some old, less productive capital wears out and is retired to the scrap heap. The net result is an increase in the productivity of the economy that results in an upward movement of the short-run aggregate production function to PF_{96}. When 25 billion hours of labour are employed, the economy can produce a real GDP of ₤600 billion in 1994 (point c).

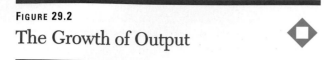

FIGURE 29.2

The Growth of Output

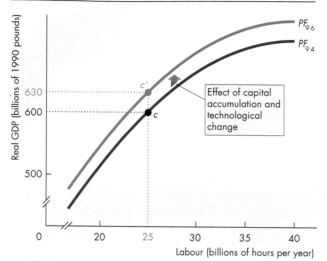

Output grows over time. The accumulation of capital and the adoption of more productive technologies makes it possible to achieve a higher level of real GDP for any given labour input. For example, between 1994 and 1996 the production function shifts upward from PF_{94} to PF_{96}. A labour input of 25 billion hours produces £600 billion of real GDP in 1994 (point c) and £630 billion in 1996 (point c').

By 1996, that same quantity of labour can produce £630 billion (point c'). Each level of labour input can produce more output in 1996 than in 1994.

Variable Growth Rates

Capital accumulation and technological change do not proceed at a constant pace. In some years, the level of investment is high and the capital stock grows quickly. In other years – recession years – investment decreases and the capital stock grows slowly. Also, there are fluctuations in the pace of technological innovation. These fluctuations in the pace of capital accumulation and innovation result in fluctuations in the magnitude of the upward shift in the short-run production function from one year to another. But usually it shifts upward.

Occasionally the short-run aggregate production function shifts downward – productivity decreases. Such a downward shift can be the result of a widespread drought, a disruption to international trade, an

outbreak of civil disorder, or a war. A serious disruption to international trade occurred in 1974 when the Organization of Petroleum Exporting Countries (OPEC) placed an embargo on oil exports. This action deprived the industrialized world of one of its crucial raw materials. Firms could not obtain all the fuel they needed, and as a result the labour force was not able to produce as much output as usual. As a consequence, the short-run aggregate production function shifted downward in 1974.

Let's take a look at the UK's short-run aggregate production function and see what it tells us about UK productivity growth.

Productivity Growth in the United Kingdom

We can examine productivity growth in the United Kingdom by looking at the UK's short-run aggregate production function shown in Fig. 29.3. Concentrate first on the blue dots in this figure. There is a dot for each year between 1985 and 1993, and each one represents the values of real GDP and aggregate employment for a particular year. For example, the dot for 1985 tells us that in 1985 real GDP was £468 billion and labour hours were 44.9 billion; in 1993, real GDP is £546 billion and labour hours are 42.4 billion.

These two dots together with the other dots in the figure do not all lie on the same short-run aggregate production function. Instead, they each lie on their own short-run aggregate production function. Each year the stock of capital equipment and the state of technology change so that the economy's productive potential usually is higher than in the year before. The production function for 1985 is PF_{85} and that for 1993 is PF_{93}.

The 1993 short-run production function is 20 per cent higher than the 1985 aggregate production function. This fact means that if employment in 1993 had been the same as it was in 1985, real GDP in 1993 would have been £564 billion. Equivalently, if employment in 1985 had been the same as it was in 1993, real GDP in 1985 would have been £453 billion.

REVIEW

A production function tells us how the output that can be produced varies as inputs are varied. A short-run production function tells us how the

FIGURE 29.3

Short-run Aggregate Production Function in the United Kingdom

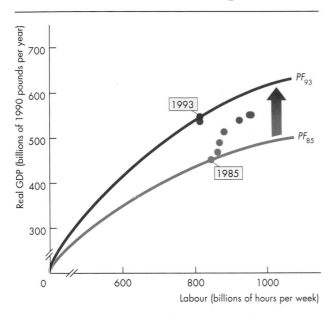

The dots in the figure show real GDP and aggregate hours of labour employed in the United Kingdom for each year between 1985 and 1993. For example, in 1985 labour input was 44.9 billion hours and real GDP was £468.1 billion. In 1993, labour input was 42.4 billion hours and real GDP was £545.8 billion. The dots do not lie on one short-run aggregate production function. Instead, the short-run aggregate production function shifts from year to year as capital accumulates and technologies change. The figure shows the short-run aggregate production functions for 1985 and 1993 – PF_{85} and PF_{93}. The 1993 production function is 20 per cent higher than that for 1985. For example, the 44.9 billion hours of labour that produced £468.1 billion of real GDP in 1985 would have produced £564 billion of real GDP in 1993. Similarly, the 42.4 billion hours of labour that produced £545.8 billion of real GDP in 1993 would have produced approximately £453 billion of real GDP in 1985.

Source: Central Statistical Office, *Economic Trends Annual Supplement, 1994 edition,* 23; *Economic Trends,* April 1994, T4; the Employment Department, *Employment Gazette,* May 1994, 10; and our calculations.

output that can be produced varies as the employment of labour varies, holding everything else constant. The short-run aggregate production function tells us how real GDP varies as total labour hours vary. The marginal product of labour – the increase in real GDP resulting from a one-hour increase of labour input – diminishes as the labour input increases. ◆ ◆ The short-run production function usually shifts upward from year to year but, on occasion, it shifts downward. Capital accumulation and technological advances shift the short-run aggregate production function upward. Shocks such as droughts, disruptions of international trade, or civil and political unrest shift the production function downward. The short-run aggregate production function in the United Kingdom shifted upward by 20 per cent between 1985 and 1993. ◆

We've seen that output in any year depends on the position of the short-run aggregate production function and on the quantity of labour employed. Even if the short-run aggregate production function shifts upward, it is still possible for output to fall because of a fall in employment. For example, in 1991 employment and real GDP fell as the economy went into recession. To determine the level of output, we need to understand not only the influences on the short-run aggregate production function but also those on the level of employment. And to determine the level of employment, we need to study the demand for and supply of labour and how the market allocates labour to jobs. We'll begin by studying the demand for labour.

The Demand for Labour

The **quantity of labour demanded** is the number of labour hours hired by all the firms in an economy. The **demand for labour** is the quantity of labour demanded at each real wage rate. The **real wage rate** is the wage per hour expressed in constant pounds – for example, the wage per hour expressed in 1990 pounds. The wage rate expressed in *current pounds* is called the **money wage rate**. A real wage rate expressed in 1990 pounds tells us what today's money wage rate would buy if prices today were the same as in 1990. We calculate the real wage rate by dividing the money wage rate by the GDP deflator and multiplying by 100. For example, if the money wage rate is £18 and the GDP deflator is 120, the real wage rate is £15 (£18 divided by 120 and multiplied by 100 equals £15).

We can represent the demand for labour as a schedule or a curve. The table in Fig. 29.4 sets out an example of a demand for labour schedule. Row *b* tells us that at a real wage rate of £20 an hour, 20 billion hours of labour (a year) are demanded. The other rows of the table are read in a similar way. The demand for labour schedule is graphed as the demand for labour curve (*LD*). Each point on the curve corresponds to the row identified by the same letter in the table.

Why is the quantity of labour demanded influenced by the *real* wage rate? Why isn't it the *money* wage rate that affects the quantity of labour demanded? Also, why does the quantity of labour demanded increase as the real wage rate decreases? That is, why does the demand for labour curve slope downward? Let's answer these questions.

Diminishing Marginal Product and the Demand for Labour

Firms are in business to maximize profits. Each worker that a firm hires adds to its costs and increases its output. Up to a point, the extra output produced by the worker is worth more to the firm than the wages the firm has to pay. But each additional hour of labour hired produces less output than the previous hour – the marginal product of labour diminishes. As the amount of labour employed increases and the capital equipment employed is constant, more workers have to use the same machines and the plant operates closer and closer to its physical limits. Output increases, but it does not increase in proportion to the increase in labour input. As the firm hires more workers, it eventually reaches the point where the revenue from selling the extra output produced by an additional hour of labour equals the hourly wage rate. If the firm hires even one more hour of labour, the extra cost incurred will exceed the revenue brought in from selling the extra output. The firm will not employ that additional hour of labour. It hires the quantity of labour such that the revenue brought in by the last hour of labour input equals the money wage rate.

To see why it is the *real* wage rate, rather than the money wage rate, that affects the quantity of labour demanded, let's consider an example.

The Demand for Labour in a Jam Factory

A jam factory employs 400 hours of labour. The additional output produced by the last hour hired is 11 pots of jam. That is, the marginal product of labour is 11 pots of jam an hour. Jam sells for £1 a pot, so the revenue brought in from selling these 11 pots is £11. The money wage rate is also £11 an

FIGURE 29.4

Demand for Labour

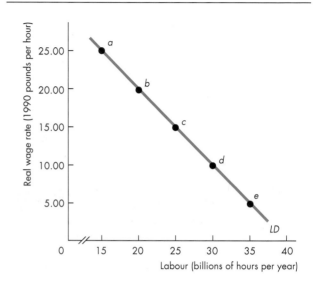

	Real wage rate (1990 pounds per hour)	Quantity of labour demanded (billions of hours per year)
a	25	15
b	20	20
c	15	25
d	10	30
e	5	35

The quantity of labour demanded increases as the real wage rate decreases, as illustrated by the labour demand schedule in the table and the demand for labour curve (*LD*). Each row in the table tells us the quantity of labour demanded at a given real wage rate and corresponds to a point on the labour demand curve. For example, when the real wage rate is £15 an hour, the quantity of labour demanded is 25 billion hours a year (point *c*). The demand for labour curve slopes downward because firms hire additional labour so long as its marginal product of labour is greater than or equal to the real wage rate. The lower the real wage rate, the larger is the number of workers whose marginal product exceeds that real wage rate.

hour. This last hour of labour hired brings in as much revenue as the wages paid out, so it just pays the firm to hire that hour of labour. The firm is paying a real wage rate that is exactly the same as the marginal product of labour – 11 pots of jam. That is, the firm's real wage rate is equal to the money wage rate of £11 an hour divided by the price of jam, £1 a pot.

A Change in the Real Wage Rate   Let's work out what happens when the real wage rate changes. Suppose the money wage rate increases to £22 an hour while the price of jam remains constant at £1 a pot. The real wage rate has now increased to 22 pots of jam – equal to the money wage of £22 an hour divided by £1 a pot, the price of a pot of jam. The last hour of labour hired now costs £22 but brings in only £11 of extra revenue. It does not pay the firm to hire this hour of labour. The firm decreases the quantity of labour employed until the marginal product of labour brings in £22 of revenue. This occurs when the marginal product of labour is 22 pots of jam – that is, 22 pots at £1 a pot sell for £22. The marginal product is again equal to the real wage rate. But to make the marginal product of labour equal to the real wage rate, the firm has to decrease the quantity of labour employed. Thus when the real wage rate increases, the quantity of labour demanded decreases.

In the example we've just worked through, the real wage rate increased because the money wage rate increased with a constant output price. But the same outcome occurs if the money wage rate remains constant and the output price decreases. For example, if the wage rate remains at £11 an hour while the price of jam falls to 50 pence a pot, the real wage rate is 22 pots of jam and the jam factory hires the amount of labour that makes the marginal product of labour equal to 22 pots.

A Change in the Money Wage Rate with a Constant Real Wage   To see why the money wage rate does not affect the quantity of labour demanded, suppose that the money wage rate and all prices double. The money wage rate increases to £22 an hour and the price of jam increases to £2 a pot. The jam factory is in the same real situation as before. It pays £22 for the last hour of labour employed and sells the output produced by that labour for £22. The money wage rate has doubled from £11 to £22 an hour, but nothing *real* has changed. The real wage rate is still 11 pots of jam. As far as the firm is concerned, 400 hours is still the right quantity of labour to hire. The money wage rate has changed, but the real wage rate and the quantity of labour demanded have remained constant.

The Demand for Labour in the Economy

The demand for labour in the economy as a whole is determined in the same way as in the jam factory. Thus the quantity of labour demanded depends on the real wage rate, not the money wage rate, and the higher the real wage rate, the smaller is the quantity of labour demanded.

We now know why the quantity of labour demanded depends on the real wage rate and why the demand for labour curve slopes downward, but what makes it shift?

Changes in the Demand for Labour

When the marginal product of each hour of labour changes, the demand for labour changes and the demand for labour curve shifts. The accumulation of capital and the development of new technologies are constantly increasing the marginal product of each hour of labour. We've already seen one effect of such changes. They shift the short-run aggregate production function upward, as shown in Fig. 29.2. At the same time, they make the short-run aggregate production function *steeper*. Anything that makes the short-run production function steeper increases the marginal product of each hour of labour – that is, it increases the extra output obtained from one additional hour of labour. At a given real wage rate, firms will increase the amount of labour they hire until the revenue brought in from selling the extra output produced by the last hour of labour input equals the hourly wage. Thus as the short-run aggregate production function shifts upward, the demand for labour curve shifts to the right.

In general, the demand for labour curve shifts to the right over time. But there are fluctuations in the pace at which the demand for labour curve shifts that match the fluctuations in the short-run aggregate production function. Let's look at the demand for labour in the United Kingdom and see how it has changed over the period since 1985.

The Demand for Labour in the United Kingdom

Figure 29.5 shows the average real wage rate and the quantity of labour employed in each year between 1985 and 1993. For example, in 1993 the real wage was £7.03 an hour (in 1990 pounds) and 42.4 billion hours of labour were employed.

FIGURE 29.5

Demand for Labour in the United Kingdom

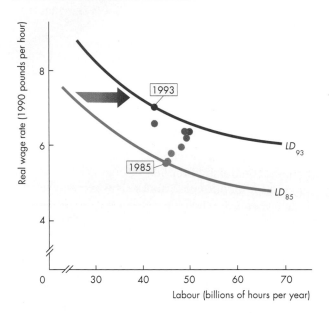

The figure shows the quantity of labour employed and the average real wage rate in the United Kingdom from 1985 to 1993. For example, in 1985 the real wage rate was £5.56 an hour and 44.9 billion hours of labour were employed. In 1993, the real wage rate was £7.03 an hour and 42.4 billion hours of labour were employed. These two points (and the dots for the years between them) do not lie on a single demand for labour curve. The demand for labour curve has shifted as a result of shifts in the short-run aggregate production function. The figure shows the demand curves for 1985 and 1993 – LD_{85} and LD_{93}. Over time, the demand for labour curve has shifted to the right.

Source: Central Statistical Office, *Economic Trends Annual Supplement, 1994 edition,* 23; *Economic Trends,* April 1994, T4; the Employment Department, *Employment Gazette,* May 1994, 10; and our calculations.

The figure shows two demand for labour curves, one for 1985 and the other for 1993. Between 1985 and 1993, the production function shifted upward and the marginal product of labour increased. If the quantity of labour employed in 1993 had been the same as in 1985, (44.9 billion hours) the real wage rate would have been £6.85 an hour. If the quantity of labour employed in 1985 had been the same as it was in 1993 (42.4 billion hours) the real wage rate in that year would only have been £5.70 an hour.

R E V I E W

The quantity of labour demanded is the quantity of labour hours hired by all firms in the economy. It depends on the real wage rate. For an individual firm, the real wage rate is the money wage rate paid to the worker divided by the price for which the firm's output sells. For the economy as a whole, the real wage rate is the money wage rate divided by the price level. The lower the real wage rate, the greater is the quantity of labour demanded. The demand for labour curve slopes downward. ◆ ◆ The demand for labour curve shifts because of shifts in the short-run aggregate production function. An increase in the capital stock or advances in technology embodied in the capital stock shift the short-run aggregate production function upward and increase the marginal product of labour. The demand for labour curve shifts to the right, but at an uneven pace. ◆

Let's now turn to the other side of the labour market and see how the supply of labour is determined.

The Supply of Labour

The **quantity of labour supplied** is the number of hours of labour services that households supply to firms. The **supply of labour** is the quantity of labour supplied at each real wage rate.

We can represent the supply of labour as a schedule or a curve. The table in Fig. 29.6 shows a supply of labour schedule. For example, row *b* tells us that at a real wage rate of £10 an hour, 20 billion hours of labour (a year) are supplied. The other rows of the table are read in a similar way.

The supply of labour schedule is graphed as the supply of labour curve (*LS*). Each point on the *LS* curve represents the row identified by the same letter in the table. As the real wage rate increases, the quantity of labour supplied increases. The supply of labour curve slopes upward.

But why does the quantity of labour supplied increase when the real wage rate increases? Because there is an increase in:

◆ Hours per worker
◆ The participation rate

Hours per Worker

In choosing how many hours to work, a household has to decide how to allocate its time between work and other activities. If a household chooses not to work for an hour, it does not get paid for that hour. The opportunity cost of not working an hour is what the household really gives up by not working. It is all the goods and services that the household could buy with the hourly money wage. So the opportunity cost of an hour of time spent not working is the real hourly wage rate.

What happens to people's willingness to work if the real wage rate increases? Such a change has two opposing effects:

◆ A substitution effect
◆ An income effect

Substitution Effect   The substitution effect of a change in the real wage rate works in exactly the same way as a change in the price of tapes affects the quantity of tapes demanded. Just as tapes have a price, so does time. As we've just noted, the real hourly wage rate is the opportunity cost of an hour spent not working. A higher real wage rate increases the opportunity cost of time and makes time itself a more valuable commodity. This higher opportunity cost of not working encourages people to reduce the time spent not working and increase the time spent working. Thus as the real wage rate increases, more hours of work are supplied.

Income Effect   But a higher real wage rate also increases people's incomes. As you know, the higher a person's income, the greater is their demand for all the different types of goods and services. One such 'good' is leisure – the time to do pleasurable things that don't generate an income. Thus a higher real wage rate also makes people want to

FIGURE 29.6

The Supply of Labour

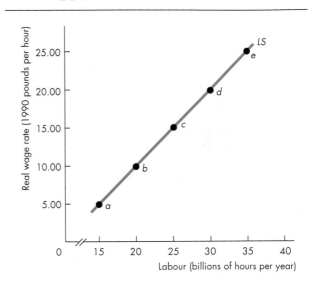

	Real wage rate (1990 pounds per hour)	Quantity of labour supplied (billions of hours per year)
a	5.00	15
b	10.00	20
c	15.00	25
d	20.00	30
e	25.00	35

The quantity of labour supplied increases as the real wage rate increases, as illustrated by the labour supply schedule in the table and the supply of labour curve (*LS*). Each row of the table tells us the quantity of labour supplied at a given real wage rate and corresponds to a point on the labour supply curve. For example, when the real wage rate is £15 an hour, the quantity of labour supplied is 25 billion hours a year (point *c*). The supply of labour curve slopes upward because households work longer hours, on average, at higher real wage rates and more households participate in the labour force. These responses are reinforced by intertemporal substitution – the retiming of work to take advantage of temporarily high wages.

enjoy longer leisure hours and supply fewer hours of work.

Which of these two effects dominates depends on each individual's attitude towards work and also on the real wage rate. Attitudes towards work, though varying across individuals, do not change much, on average, over time. But the real wage rate does change and brings changes in the quantity of labour supplied. At a very low real wage rate, the substitution effect is stronger than the income effect. That is, as the real wage rate increases, the inducement to substitute working time for leisure time is stronger than the inducement to spend part of a larger income on more leisure hours. As a consequence, as the real wage rate increases, the quantity of labour supplied increases.

At a high enough real wage rate, the income effect becomes stronger than the substitution effect. As the real wage increases, the inducement to spend more of the additional income on leisure time is stronger than the inducement to economize on leisure time.

Some people undoubtedly receive such a high real wage rate that a further increase would cause them to reduce their hours of work. But for most of us a higher real wage rate coaxes us to work more. Thus on average, the higher the real wage rate, the more hours each person works.

The Participation Rate

The **labour force participation rate** is the proportion of the working-age population that is either employed or unemployed (but seeking employment). For a variety of reasons, people differ in their willingness to work. Some people have more productive opportunities at home and so need a bigger inducement to quit those activities and work for someone else. Other individuals place a very high value on leisure, and they require a high real wage to induce them to do any work at all. These considerations suggest that each person has a reservation wage. A **reservation wage** is the lowest wage at which a person will supply any labour. Below that wage, a person will not work.

Those people who have a reservation wage below or equal to the actual real wage will be in the labour force, and those who have a reservation wage above the real wage will not be in the labour force. The higher the real wage rate, the larger is the number of people whose reservation wage falls below the real wage rate, and hence the larger is the labour force participation rate.

Reinforcing and strengthening the increase in hours worked per household and the labour force participation rate is an intertemporal substitution effect on the quantity of labour supplied.

Intertemporal Substitution

Households have to decide not only whether to work but also *when* to work. This decision is based not just on the current real wage but also on the current real wage relative to expected future real wages.

Suppose that the real wage rate is higher today than it is expected to be later on. How does this fact affect a person's labour supply decision? It encourages more work today and less in the future. Thus the higher today's real wage rate relative to what is expected in the future (other things being constant), the larger is the supply of labour.

Temporarily high real wages are similar to a high rate of return. If real wages are temporarily high, people can obtain a higher rate of return on their work effort by enjoying a smaller amount of leisure and supplying more labour in such a period. By investing in some work now and taking the return in more leisure time later, they can obtain a higher overall level of consumption of goods and services and of leisure.

R E V I E W

The opportunity cost of time is the real wage rate – the goods and services that can be bought with the income from an hour of work. An increase in the real wage rate, other things remaining the same, increases the supply of hours per worker and increases the labour force participation rate. A higher *current* real wage relative to the expected future real wage encourages people to supply more labour today and less in the future. ◆

We've now seen why, as the real wage rate increases, the quantity of labour supplied increases – why the supply of labour curve slopes upward. Next, we're going to bring the two sides of the labour market together and study the determination of wages and employment. But we are going to do this in two stages. First we'll see how the labour market works in the long run, and then we'll look at the short run.

Wages, Employment and Real GDP in the Long Run

We've discovered that as the real wage rate increases the quantity of labour demanded declines and the quantity of labour supplied increases. We now want to study how the two sides of the labour market interact to determine the real wage rate, employment and unemployment.

Given a long enough period of adjustment, the real wage rate will adjust to bring the quantity of labour demanded into equality with the quantity of labour supplied. Figure 29.7 illustrates the situation. The demand for labour curve is *LD* and the supply of labour curve is *LS*. This market determines an equilibrium real wage rate of £15 an hour and a quantity of labour employed of 25 billion hours. If the real wage rate is below its equilibrium level of £15 an hour, the quantity of labour demanded exceeds the quantity supplied. In such a situation, the real wage rate will rise since firms are willing to offer higher and higher wages in order to overcome their labour shortages. The real wage rate will continue to rise until it reaches £15 an hour, at which point there will be no shortage of labour.

If the real wage rate is higher than its equilibrium level of £15 an hour, the quantity of labour supplied exceeds the quantity demanded. In this situation, households are not able to get all the work they want and firms find it easy to hire labour. Firms will have an incentive to cut the wage and households will accept the lower wage to get a job. The real wage rate will fall until it reaches £15 an hour, at which point every household is satisfied with the quantity of labour it is supplying.

Changes in Wages and Employment

The effects of changes in demand and supply on wages and employment are identical to the effects

FIGURE 29.7

Equilibrium with Flexible Wages

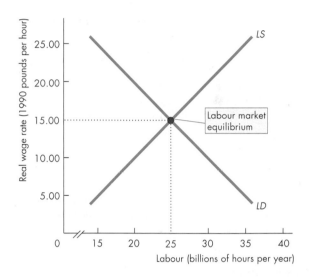

Equilibrium occurs when the real wage rate makes the quantity of labour demanded equal to the quantity supplied. This equilibrium occurs at a real wage rate of £15 an hour. At that real wage rate, 25 billion hours of labour are employed. At real wage rates below £15 an hour, the quantity of labour demanded exceeds the quantity supplied and the real wage rate rises. At real wage rates above £15 an hour, the quantity of labour supplied exceeds the quantity of labour demanded and the real wage rate falls.

of changes in demand and supply on the price and quantity of Walkmans that we studied in Chapter 4. An increase in the demand for labour shifts the demand for labour curve to the right and increases both the real wage rate and the quantity of labour employed. A decrease in the demand for labour shifts the demand for labour curve to the left and decreases both the real wage rate and the quantity of labour employed. An increase in the supply of labour shifts the supply of labour curve to the right, lowering the real wage rate and increasing employment. A decrease in the supply of labour shifts the supply of labour curve to the left, raising the real wage rate and decreasing employment.

Long-run Aggregate Supply

With what you have now learned about the labour market in the long run, you can derive the long-run aggregate supply curve, which you first met in Chapter 23. Recall that along the long-run aggregate supply curve, the quantity of real GDP supplied is independent of the price level – the long-run aggregate supply curve is vertical.

The reason is that as the price level changes, the *money wage rate* adjusts to keep the real wage rate at the level that makes the quantity of

FIGURE 29.8

Aggregate Supply with Flexible Wages

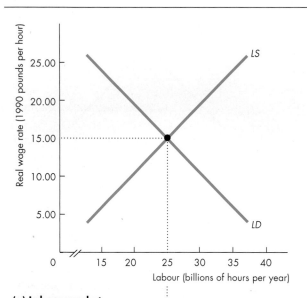

(a) Labour market

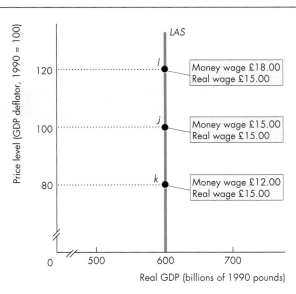

(c) Long-run aggregate supply curve

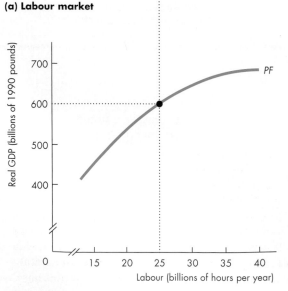

(b) Short-run aggregate production function

Labour market equilibrium determines the real wage rate and employment. The demand for labour curve (*LD*) intersects the supply of labour curve (*LS*) at a real wage rate of £15 an hour and 25 billion hours of employment (part a). The short-run aggregate production function (*PF*) and employment of 25 billion hours determine real GDP at £600 billion (part b). Real GDP supplied is £600 billion regardless of the price level. The long-run aggregate supply curve is the vertical line (*LAS*), in part (c). If the GDP deflator is 100, the economy is at point *j*. If the GDP deflator is 120, the money wage rate rises to keep the real wage rate constant at £15 an hour, employment remains at 25 billion hours and real GDP is £600 billion. The economy is at point *l*. If the GDP deflator is 80, the money wage rate falls to keep the real wage rate constant at £15 an hour, employment remains at 25 billion hours and real GDP is £600 billion. The economy is at point *k*.

labour demanded equal the quantity supplied.

Figure 29.8 illustrates the derivation of the long-run aggregate supply curve. Part (a) shows the aggregate labour market. The demand and supply curves shown are exactly the same as those in Fig. 29.7. The equilibrium, a real wage of £15 an hour and employment of 25 billion hours, is exactly the same equilibrium that was determined in that figure.

Figure 29.8(b) shows the short-run aggregate production function. This production function is the one shown in Fig. 29.1. We know from the labour market (part a) that 25 billion hours of labour are employed. Part (b) tells us that when 25 billion hours of labour are employed, real GDP is £600 billion.

Figure 29.8(c) shows the long-run aggregate supply curve. That curve tells us that real GDP is £600 billion regardless of the price level. To see why, look at what happens to real GDP when the price level changes.

Start with a GDP deflator of 100. In this case, the economy is at point *j* in part (c) of the figure. That is, the GDP deflator is 100 and real GDP is £600 billion. We've determined, in part (a), that the real wage rate is £15. With a GDP deflator of 100, the money wage rate (the wage rate in current pounds) is also £15 an hour.

What happens to real GDP if the GDP deflator falls from 100 to 80 (a 20 per cent decrease in the price level)? If the money wage rate remains at £15 an hour, the real wage rate rises and the quantity of labour supplied exceeds the quantity demanded. In such a situation, the money wage rate will fall. It falls to £12 an hour. With a money wage rate of £12 and a GDP deflator of 80, the real wage rate is still £15 (£12 divided by 80 and multiplied by 100 equals £15). With the lower money wage rate but a constant real wage rate, employment remains at 25 billion hours and real GDP remains at £600 billion. The economy is at point *k* in Fig. 29.8(c).

What happens to real GDP if the GDP deflator rises from 100 to 120 (a 20 percent increase in the price level)? If the money wage rate stays at £15 an hour, the real wage rate falls and the quantity of labour demanded exceeds the quantity supplied. In such a situation, the money wage rate rises. It will keep rising until it reaches £18 an hour. At that money wage rate, the real wage rate is £15 (£18 divided by 120 and multiplied by 100 equals £15) and the quantity of labour demanded equals the quantity supplied. Employment remains at 25 billion

hours and real GDP remains at £600 billion. The economy is at point *l* in Fig. 29.8(c).

Points *j*, *k* and *l* in part (c) all lie on the long-run aggregate supply curve. We have considered only three price levels. We could have considered any price level and we would have reached the same conclusion: a change in the price level generates a proportionate change in the money wage rate and leaves the real wage rate unchanged. Employment and real GDP are also unchanged. The long-run aggregate supply curve is vertical.

Economic Growth

The demand for labour increases over time because capital accumulation and technological change increase the marginal product of labour. The supply of labour increases over time because the working-age population steadily increases. The combined effect of these increases in both the demand for and the supply of labour is a steady increase in long-run aggregate supply – economic growth. Also, capital accumulation and technological change outpace the growth of population, so the demand for labour increases by more than the supply of labour – the shift to the right in the demand curve is larger than the shift in the supply curve – and not only do real GDP and the level of employment increase, but so also does the real wage rate. This issue is also considered in Reading Between the Lines on pp. 842–843.

REVIEW

I n the long run, the wage rate adjusts to make the quantity of labour demanded equal the quantity of labour supplied. The real wage rate, employment and real GDP are independent of the price level. The aggregate supply curve is vertical. Economic growth – rising real GDP and employment and rising real wages – occurs because of capital accumulation and technological change that outpace population growth. ◆

Let's now examine the labour market in the short run.

Wages, Employment and Real GDP in the Short Run

In the short run, the *money* wage rate is fixed. But the real wage rate is not fixed. Recall that the real wage rate equals the money wage rate divided by the price level. With a fixed money wage rate, the real wage rate changes when the price level changes.

The Real Wage Rate in the Short Run

With a fixed money wage rate, the real wage rate varies inversely with the price level – it rises when the price level falls and falls when the price level rises. You can see this relationship between the real wage rate and the price level in Fig. 29.9. The money wage rate is fixed at £15 an hour. When the GDP deflator is 100, the real wage rate is also £15 an hour, as shown at point *c*. If the GDP deflator falls to 75, the real wage rate rises to £20 an hour, as shown at point *b*, and if the GDP deflator rises to 150, the real wage rate falls to £10 an hour, as shown at point *d*.

Employment in the Short Run

As the real wage rate changes, so does the level of employment. It is usually assumed that the level of employment is determined by the quantity of labour demanded and that in the short run, households supply the labour that firms demand, even if to do so they are temporarily knocked off their supply curves.

In Fig. 29.9, the money wage rate is £15 an hour. If the GDP deflator is 100 and the real wage rate is £15 an hour, the level of employment, determined by the quantity of labour demanded, is 25 billion hours (point *c* in the figure). If the GDP deflator is 75 and the real wage rate is £20 an hour, the quantity of labour demanded and employed is 20 billion hours (point *b* in the figure). Households supply less labour than they would like to. If the GDP deflator is 150 and the real wage rate is £10 an hour, the quantity of labour demanded and employed is 30 billion hours (point *d* in the figure). In this case, households supply more labour than they would like to.

It is easy to understand why a household might supply less labour, but why would it supply *more* labour than it would like to? In the long run, it would not. But for the duration of the existing contract, the household might agree to supply whatever quantity of labour the firm demands in exchange for a job and a guaranteed money wage rate.

Short-run Aggregate Supply

With what you have now learned about the labour market in the short run, you can derive the short-run aggregate supply curve, which you first met in

---

FIGURE 29.9

A Labour Market with Sticky Money Wages

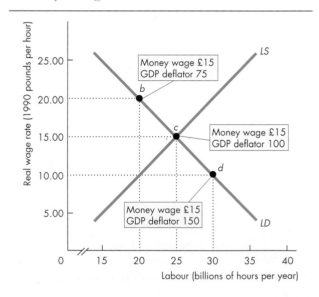

The labour demand curve is *LD* and the labour supply curve is *LS*. The money wage rate is set to achieve an expected balance between the quantity of labour demanded and the quantity supplied. If the GDP deflator is expected to be 100, the money wage rate is set at £15 an hour. The labour market is expected to be at point *c*. The quantity of labour employed is determined by the demand for labour. If the GDP deflator turns out to be 100, then the real wage rate is equal to £15 and the quantity of labour employed is 25 billion hours of labour. The economy operates at point *c*. If the GDP deflator turns out to be 75, then the real wage rate is £20 an hour and the quantity of labour employed falls to 20 billion hours. The economy operates at point *b*. If the GDP deflator is 150, then the real wage rate is £10 an hour and the quantity of labour employed increases to 30 billion hours. The economy operates at point *d*.

Chapter 23. Recall that along the short-run aggregate supply curve, the money wage rate is fixed and that the short-run aggregate supply curve slopes upward.

Figure 29.10 illustrates the derivation of the short-run aggregate supply curve and explains why it slopes upward. Start by looking at part (a) which describes the labour market. The three equilibrium levels of real wages and employment we discovered in Fig. 29.9 are shown again here. The money wage rate is fixed at £15 an hour. If the price level is 100, the real wage rate is also £15 an

---

FIGURE 29.10

Aggregate Supply with Sticky Wages

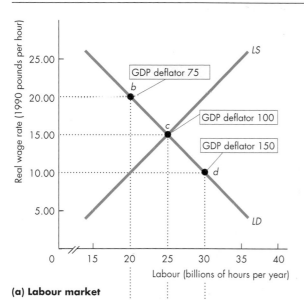

(a) Labour market

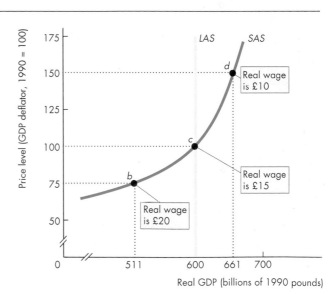

(c) Aggregate supply curve

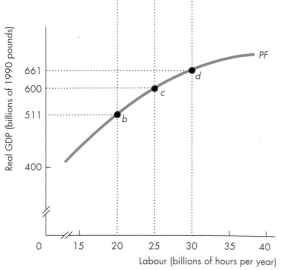

(b) Short-run aggregate production function

The money wage rate is fixed at £15 an hour. In part (a), the demand for labour curve (*LD*) intersects the supply of labour curve (*LS*) at a real wage rate of £15 an hour and 25 billion hours of employment. If the GDP deflator is 100, the economy operates at this point – *c*. In part (b), the short-run aggregate production function (*PF*) determines real GDP at £600 billion. This is long-run aggregate supply (*LAS*) in part (c). If the GDP deflator is 75, real wages are £20 an hour and the economy is at point *b* – employment is 20 billion hours (part a) and real GDP is £511 billion (part b). The economy is at point *b* on its short-run aggregate supply curve (*SAS*) in part (c). If the GDP deflator is 150, real wages are £10 an hour and the economy is at point *d* – employment is 30 billion hours (part a) and real GDP is £661 billion (part b). The economy is at point *d* on its short-run aggregate supply curve in part (c).

hour and 25 billion hours of labour are employed – point *c*. If the price level is 75, the real wage rate is $20 an hour and employment is 20 billion hours – point *b*. If the price level is 150, the real wage rate is $10 an hour and employment is 30 billion hours – point *d*.

Figure 29.10(b) shows the short-run aggregate production function. We know from the labour market (part a) that at different price levels, different quantities of labour are employed. Part (b) tells us how these employment levels translate into real GDP. For example, when employment is 20 billion hours, real GDP is $511 billion – point *b*. When employment is 25 billion hours, real GDP is $600 billion – point *c*, and when employment is 30 billion hours, real GDP is $661 billion – point *d*.

Figure 29.10(c) shows the aggregate supply curves. The long-run aggregate supply curve, *LAS*, is the one we've already derived in Fig. 29.8. The short-run aggregate supply curve, *SAS*, is derived from the labour market and production function we've just examined. To see why, first focus on point *b* in all three parts of the figure. At point *b*, the price level is 75. From the labour market (part a) we know that in this situation, the real wage is $20 an hour and 20 billion hours of labour are employed. At this employment level we know from the production function (part b) that real GDP is $511 billion. That's what point *b* in part (c) tells us – when the price level is 75, real GDP supplied is $511 billion. The other two points, *c* and *d*, are interpreted in the same way. At point *d*, the price level is 150 so the real wage rate is $20 an hour and 30 billion hours of labour are employed (part a). This employment level produces a real GDP of $661 billion. Points *b*, *c* and *d* are points on the short-run aggregate supply curve.

The short-run aggregate supply curve intersects the long-run aggregate supply curve at the expected price level – where the GDP deflator is 100. At price levels higher than that expected, the quantity of real GDP supplied exceeds its long-run level, and at price levels lower than that expected, the quantity of real GDP supplied falls short of its long-run level.

Notice that the short-run aggregate supply curve, like the one in Chapter 23, is *curved*. As the price level rises, real GDP increases but the increments in real GDP become successively smaller. The straight-line *SAS* curve we are using is an approximation to this curve.

REVIEW

In the short run, the money wage rate is fixed. The level of employment is determined by the demand for labour and the real wage rate. The higher the price level, the lower the real wage rate and the higher is the quantity of labour demanded. Changes in the price level bring changes in the real wage rate, changes in the level of employment and changes in the quantity of real GDP supplied – movements along the short-run aggregate supply curve. ◆

We have studied the determination of wages and employment in the long run when money wages are flexible and in the short run when money wages are fixed. But how long does it take to get to the long run – or, equivalently, how long is the short run? And why are wages fixed in the short run? Why don't they adjust continuously to keep the quantity of labour demanded equal to the quantity supplied at full employment? These are controversial issues in macroeconomics.

How Sticky Are Wages?

When there is an excess demand for labour – when the quantity demanded exceeds the quantity supplied – real wages must rise to restore full employment. When there is an excess supply of labour – when the quantity supplied exceeds the quantity demanded – real wages must fall to restore full employment. Real wages can change either because the price level changes or because the money wage rate changes. How quickly does the money wage rate change to help achieve full employment?

There is close to complete agreement that money wages rise quickly to restore full employment when there is an excess demand for labour. So the economy does not remain to the right of the long-run aggregate supply curve for long periods. But there is no general agreement about how quickly money wages fall to restore full employment when there is an excess supply of labour and unemployment is above the natural rate. Some economists believe that money wages fall quickly enough to keep the quantity of labour demanded equal to the quantity supplied. For these economists, the short run is very short and it takes almost no time to reach the long run. Other economists believe that money wages adjust very slowly and that the labour market remains in its short-run condition for a very long time. Let's look a bit more closely at these two views.

The Flexible Wage View

Most people's wages – *money wages* – are determined by wage contracts that run for at least one year and often for two or three years. Doesn't this fact mean that money wages are not flexible? Not necessarily. Money wage rates, even those that are fixed by wage contracts, can and do adjust upward or downward. For example, some workers receive bonus payments in good times and lose those bonuses in bad times. Some workers get overtime at high rates of pay in good times but only get work at the normal hourly wage rate in bad times. Workers often get unusually rapid promotion to jobs with a higher wage rate in good times and get stuck on a lower rung of the promotion ladder in bad times. Thus fluctuations in bonuses, overtime pay and the pace of promotion result in changes in the average wage rate even when wage rate schedules don't change.

The flexible wage view is that these sources of wage change are sufficient to achieve a continuous balance between the quantity of labour demanded and the quantity supplied.

Real Business Cycle Theory   In the flexible wage view of the labour market, the only source of the business cycle – of fluctuations in real GDP and other economic aggregates – is shifts in the aggregate supply curve. A change in aggregate demand – a shift in the aggregate demand curve – brings a change in the price level but no change in real GDP. The view that aggregate supply fluctuations alone are responsible for the business cycle is called the **real business cycle theory**.

According to real business cycle theory, random fluctuations in the pace of technological change cause fluctuations in the pace of capital accumulation, so the short-run aggregate production function shifts upward at an uneven pace. These changes in the short-run aggregate production function change the demand for labour, shifting the demand for labour

curve to the right, but again at an uneven pace. Population growth increases the supply of labour and the supply of labour curve shifts to the right. But the uneven pace of technological change brings fluctuations in the real wage rate that are anticipated, to some degree, and so lead to changes in the supply of labour from intertemporal substitution.

These changes in the production function, the demand for labour and the supply of labour change equilibrium employment, the real wage rate and real GDP. They do so by shifting the long-run aggregate supply curve.

The general trend from the ongoing process of technological change is an increase in long-run aggregate supply. The aggregate supply curve shifts to the right, and real GDP increases. But the pace at which the long-run aggregate supply curve shifts to the right varies, leading to fluctuations in the growth rate of real GDP. Occasionally, the short-run production function shifts downward. When it does so, the demand for labour curve shifts to the left, employment falls, and the long-run aggregate supply curve shifts to the left, decreasing real GDP.

The Sticky Wage View

Most economists, while recognizing the scope for flexibility in wages from bonuses and overtime wage rates, believe that these sources of flexibility are insufficient to keep the quantity of labour supplied equal to the quantity demanded. Basic money wage rates rarely adjust more frequently than once a year, so money wage rates are fairly rigid – sticky. Real wage rates change more frequently than money wage rates because of changes in the price level, but according to the sticky wage theory these adjustments do not make real wages sufficiently flexible to maintain full employment.

Several different models have been developed to explain why money wages might be sticky for relatively long periods. The main ones are:

◆ Implicit risk-sharing contracts
◆ Incomplete price level information
◆ Menu costs

Implicit Risk-sharing Contracts

People dislike risk and buy insurance that compensates them if an unwanted bad outcome arises. Insurance against the risk of fire, a car accident, theft and ill-health is commonplace. But one of the biggest risks we face is the loss of income from losing our job. And insurance companies don't offer policies that protect our incomes in the event of job loss.

But employers and employees can enter into implicit risk-sharing contracts that provide income insurance. An **implicit contract** is an informal arrangement that has the force of a formal written contract. An employment contract implicitly contains two transactions. The firm buys labour from the household and the household buys income insurance from the firm. The wage is 'sticky' to protect the worker against fluctuating economic conditions. The household 'pays' for income insurance in the form of a wage that is below what it would otherwise be in times of average or high demand. But the household benefits from the insurance by receiving a wage that is greater than what it otherwise would be in times of low demand.

This explanation of sticky wages is actually an explanation of sticky *real* wages, not sticky *money* wages. If the price level changes, firms and workers with an implicit contract can easily see that the money wage rate must be changed to preserve the original implicit agreement. With sticky real wages and flexible money wages, the labour market does not reach an equilibrium in which the quantity of labour demanded equals the quantity supplied. But it does reach an equilibrium that does not depend on the price level. The aggregate supply curve is vertical.

Incomplete Price Level Information

The supply of labour depends on the real wage rate – the money wage rate divided by the price level. But when people decide how much labour to supply, they know only the money wage rate being offered. They don't know the prices of the goods and services they will buy with their wages. They don't know the real wage rate. So, to make a labour supply decision, they forecast the price level and base their decision on the *expected* real wage rate. The expected real wage rate is the money wage rate divided by the expected price level. On the other side of the labour market, firms know the prices they are getting for the goods and services they are producing, so they know the *actual* real wages they are paying.

These features of the labour market form the basis of a theory of partly sticky money wages suggested by Robert E. Lucas Jr. (see Our Advancing

Knowledge, pp. 886–887. The theory is illustrated in Fig. 29.11. The labour market is shown in a figure in which the *money* wage rate is measured on the vertical axis. The demand for labour depends on the *real* wage rate, so, when graphed against the money wage rate, there is a different demand curve for each price level (P). If the price level is 100, the demand curve is LD_0. If the price level is 200, the demand curve is LD_1 and if the price level

FIGURE 29.11

Incomplete Price Level Information

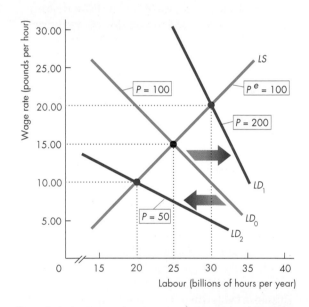

The vertical axis measures the *money* wage rate, so the position of the demand for labour curve depends on the price level (P). The demand for labour is LD_0 when the price level is 100, LD_1 when the price level is 200 and LD_2 when the price level is 50. The supply of labour depends on the expected real wage and the position of the supply curve depends on the expected price level (P^e). The supply curve LS is that for an expected price level of 100. Equilibrium is at the point of intersection of the demand and supply curve. When the price level is 100, employment is 25 billion hours and the real and nominal wage rate is £15 an hour. If the price level rises to 200, employment increases to 30 billion hours, the nominal wage rate rises to £20, the real wage rate falls and the expected real wage rate rises. If the price level falls to 50, employment decreases to 20 billion hours, the nominal wage rate falls to £10, the real wage rate rises and the expected real wage rate falls.

is 50, the demand curve is LD_2. (We're using big differences in the price level to make things as clear as possible.)

Notice that the demand curves LD_0, LD_1 and LD_2 are not parallel. That is because when the price level changes, the curve shifts by a fixed *percentage* amount. For example, if with a price level of 100 and a money wage rate of £15 an hour, the quantity of labour demanded is 25 billion hours a year, then that same quantity will be demanded at a price level of 200 and a money wage rate of £30 an hour, or a price level of 50 and a money wage rate of £7.70 an hour.

The supply of labour depends on the *expected real* wage rate. So the position of the supply curve depends on the *expected price level (P^e)*. The supply curve LS is that for an expected price level of 100. A change in the actual price level that is not perceived or expected does not change the supply of labour and does not shift the labour supply curve.

If the actual price level equals the expected price level, the labour market equilibrium is at an employment level of 25 billion hours and a real and nominal wage rate of £15 an hour, the same as in the flexible wage rate case. If the actual price level is 200, the money wage rate rises to £20 and employment increases to 30 billion hours. The *real* wage rate falls to £10 (£20 divided by 200 and multiplied by 100), and the expected real wage rate *rises* to £20. Because the actual real wage rate has fallen, the quantity of labour demanded increases and because the expected wage rate has risen, the quantity of labour supplied increases.

If the actual price level is 50, the money wage rate falls to £10 and employment decreases to 20 billion hours. But the actual real wage rate rises to £20 (£10 divided by 50 and multiplied by 100), and the expected real wage rate *falls* to £10.

So, with incomplete information about the price level, employment changes as the price level changes. Because employment changes, so does the quantity of real GDP supplied. The short-run aggregate supply curve is upward sloping.

Wages are sticky but not fixed. Wages change by a smaller percentage than the change in the price level. But the closer the expected price level is to the actual price level, the closer the predictions of this theory are to the flexible wage theory. With the Consumer Price Index being measured and widely publicized every month, this source of partial wage stickiness is not likely to play a major role in actual labour markets.

Menu Costs

When prices or wages are changed, some costs are incurred. The cost of changing a price or a wage rate is called a **menu cost**. The name comes from the simple fact that if a restaurant changes its prices, it must print a new menu and the cost of doing so is the cost of changing prices.

Menu costs in the labour market are large. They arise from the fact that most wages are determined as part of a contract that is negotiated collectively between a union and an employer and that each party to the negotiations must spend considerable resources researching the demand and supply conditions and preparing the best possible strategy for a bargaining process. Because of these costs, contracts are renegotiated at infrequent intervals and, in the intervening period, wages are fixed, or change along a pre-agreed path.

This explanation for sticky wages is the most convincing currently available, although an objection to it is that wage contracts could use cost-of-living adjustments at a small menu cost.

So far, we have been examining models of the labour market that determine employment and the wage rate. We have seen that in the sticky wage models, employment is not necessarily equal to the quantity of labour supplied. Such a situation looks like one of unemployment. But we have not explicitly studied unemployment. How is unemployment determined? This is our next question.

Unemployment

We discovered in Chapter 21 that unemployment is an ever present feature of economic life and that the unemployment rate sometimes rises to a level that poses a massive problem for millions of families (see pp. 581–586). Yet the labour market models we have just been studying seem to ignore this important phenomenon. They determine the real wage rate and aggregate hours of labour employed, but they don't say anything about *who* supplies the hours. Unemployment arises when some people in the labour force are working zero hours but are seeking work. Why does unemployment exist? Why does its rate vary?

There are four main explanations for unemployment:

◆ Job search
◆ Efficiency wages
◆ Insiders and outsiders
◆ Sticky wages

We'll examine the four explanations in turn.

Job Search

Suppose that a firm employs 400 hours of labour each week and has 10 workers, each working 40 hours. If the firm decides to cut back its production and reduce employment to 360 hours, it might either lay off one worker or cut the hours of each of its 10 workers to 36 hours a week. In most production processes, the profitable reaction for the firm is to lay off one worker and keep the remaining workers' hours constant. There is an optimum or efficient number of hours for each worker. Work hours in excess of the optimum level result in decreased output per hour as workers become tired. Employing a large number of workers for a small number of hours each also lowers output per hour since workers take time to start up and there are disruptions to the production process caused by workers leaving and arriving. It is for these reasons that labour is an economically indivisible factor of production. That is, taking account of the output produced per hour, firms hire labour in indivisible lumps. As a consequence, when the demand for labour changes, the number of people employed changes rather than the number of hours per worker.

Being dismissed or laid off would not matter if an equally good job could be found right away. But finding a job takes time and effort – it has an opportunity cost. Firms are not fully informed about the potential workers available to them and households are not fully informed about the potential jobs available to them. As a consequence, both firms and workers have to search for a profitable match. Let's examine this source of unemployment.

Labour Market Stocks and Flows Because households are incompletely informed about available jobs, they find it efficient to devote resources to searching for the best available job. Time spent searching for a job

is part of unemployment. Let's take a closer look at this source of unemployment by examining the decisions that lead to labour market flows. Figure 29.12 provides a schematic summary of this discussion.

The working-age population is divided into two groups: those in the labour force and those not in the labour force. Those not in the labour force are full-time students, homemakers and retired people. The labour force consists of two groups: the employed and the unemployed.

Decisions made by the demanders of labour and the suppliers of labour result in five types of flows that change the numbers of people employed and unemployed. The flows resulting from these decisions are shown by the arrows in the figure. Let's look at these decisions and see how the flows that result from them affect the amount of employment and unemployment.

1. There is a flow into the labour force as full-time students decide to leave school or university and homemakers decide to enter or re-enter the labour force. Initially, when such people enter the labour force, they are unemployed. These decisions result in an increase in the labour force and an increase in unemployment.

2. There is a flow from employment to unemployment resulting from employers deciding to lay off temporarily or dismiss workers and from workers deciding to leave their current job to find a better one. These decisions result in a decrease in employment and an increase in unemployment but no change in the labour force.

3. There is a flow from the labour force as employed people decide to leave their jobs to become homemakers, go back to school or university, or retire. These decisions result in a decrease in employment and a decrease in the labour force but no change in unemployment.

4. There is a flow from the labour force as unemployed people give up the search for a job. These people are *discouraged workers* whose job search efforts have been repeatedly unsuccessful. These decisions to leave the labour force result in a decrease in unemployment and a decrease in the labour force.

5. There is a flow from unemployment to employment as firms recall temporarily laid-off workers and hire new workers. These decisions result in an increase in employment, a decrease in unemployment and no change in the labour force.

FIGURE 29.12

Labour Market Flows

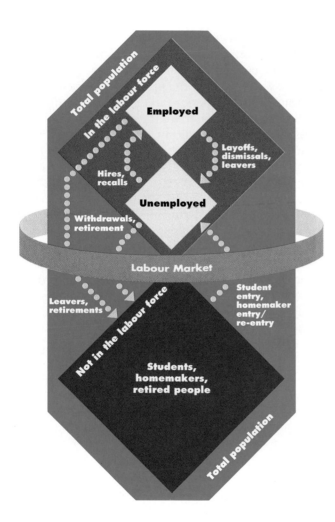

The working-age population is divided into two groups: those in the labour force and those not in the labour force. The labour force is composed of the employed and the unemployed. Flows into and out of the labour force and between employment and unemployment determine the number of people unemployed. New entrants from full-time schooling and re-entrants flow into unemployment. Flows from employment to unemployment result from dismissals, layoffs and leavers. Flows from unemployment to employment result from hires and recalls. Flows from the labour force occur as people decide to become homemakers, go back to school, or retire. Flows from the labour force also occur as unemployed people get discouraged by their failure to find a job.

At any one moment, there is a stock of employment and unemployment. Over any given period, there are flows into and out of the labour force and between employment and unemployment. In June 1994, for example, there were 27.9 million people in the labour force – 80 per cent of the working-age population. Of these, 2.6 million (9.3 per cent of the labour force) were unemployed and 25.3 million (90.7 per cent of the labour force) were employed.

Unemployment with Flexible Wages

According to the flexible wage model of the labour market, all the unemployment that exists arises from the sources we've just reviewed. The unemployment rate is always equal to the natural rate of unemployment. There is a balance between the quantity of labour demanded and the quantity of labour supplied. But the quantity of labour supplied is the number of hours available for work at a given moment without further search for a better job. And the quantity of labour demanded is the number of hours that firms wish to hire at a given moment in time, given their knowledge of the individual skills and talents available. In addition to supplying hours for work, households also supply time for job search. Those people that devote no time to working and specialize in job search are the ones who are unemployed.

Figure 29.13 illustrates such a situation. The labour force – everyone who has a job and all those who are looking for one – is larger than the supply of labour. The supply curve of labour (LS) tells us about the quantity of labour available with no further job search. The labour force curve (LF) tells us about the quantity of labour available with no further job search plus the quantity of job search. In the figure, the quantity of labour supplied and the labour force increase as the real wage rate increases. But the quantity of job search, measured by the horizontal distance between the LS and LF curves is constant. (This is an assumption. In real labour markets, the supply of job search may also increase as the real wage rate increases.)

Equilibrium in the labour market occurs at the real wage rate that makes the quantity of labour demanded equal to the quantity of labour supplied, not the labour force. Unemployment arises from the fact that information about jobs and workers is costly and that it takes time for people without work to find an acceptable job. According to the flexible

FIGURE 29.13

Unemployment with Flexible Wages

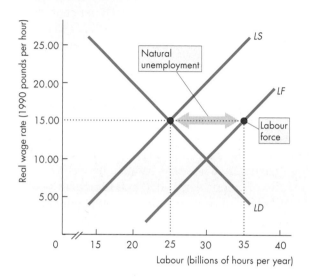

Some members of the labour force are immediately available for work at a given real wage rate and this amount determines the supply of labour (*LS*). Other members of the labour force are searching for the best available job. Adding this quantity to the supply of labour gives the labour force curve (*LF*). Equilibrium occurs at the real wage rate that makes the quantity of labour supplied equal to the quantity demanded. The economy is at full employment and unemployment is at its natural rate.

wage theory, fluctuations in unemployment are caused by changes in the labour market flows that change the supply of labour, the labour force and the demand for labour. These changes shift the *LS*, *LF*, and *LD* curves and change the natural rate of unemployment. The main influences are:

◆ Demographic change
◆ Unemployment benefits
◆ Technological change

Demographic Change   The supply side of the labour market is influenced by the age distribution of the population. A large increase in the proportion of the population of working age brings an increase in the rate of entry into the labour force and a corresponding increase in the unemployment rate as the new entrants take time to find the best available

jobs. Such a demographic change has influenced the labour market in the United Kingdom in recent years. A bulge in the birth rate occurred in the late 1940s and early 1950s, following World War II. This bulge resulted in an increase in the proportion of new entrants into the labour force during the 1970s. It resulted in a shift to the right in the *LS* curve, an even greater shift to the right in the *LF* curve, and an increase in the unemployment rate.

As the birth rate declined, the bulge moved to older age groups and the proportion of new entrants into the labour force declined during the 1980s. During this period, the shift in the *LS* curve was larger than the shift in the *LF* curve, and the unemployment rate declined.

Unemployment Benefits   One of the most significant supply side events influencing unemployment is the establishment of generous unemployment benefits. The length of time that an unemployed person is willing to spend searching for a job depends, in part, on the opportunity cost of that search. With no unemployment benefits and no income during a spell of unemployment, an unemployed person faces a high opportunity cost of job search. In this situation, search is likely to be short and an unattractive job is likely to be accepted as a better alternative to continuing a costly search process. With generous unemployment benefits, the opportunity cost of job search is low. In this situation, search is likely to be prolonged. An unemployed worker will hold out for the ideal job.

Over the years, the opportunity cost of job search has fallen as unemployment benefits have been increased. As a result, the amount of job-search unemployment has steadily increased.

Technological Change   Cycles in unemployment arise from the fact that the scale of hiring, dismissing and job leaving ebbs and flows with fluctuations in real GDP – with the business cycle. These labour market flows and the resulting unemployment are also strongly influenced by the pace and direction of technological change. When some firms and sectors of the economy are expanding quickly and others are contracting quickly, labour turnover increases. This means that flows between employment and unemployment and the pool of those temporarily unemployed increases at such a time. The relative decline of traditional industries, such as ship building in Scotland and coal mining in Wales and northern England, and the expansion of new industries, such as the computer industry in East Anglia and financial services in London and the south east of England, are a major source of flows of labour and of the rise in unemployment that occurred during the 1970s and early 1980s.

Job Creation and Job Destruction

The magnitude of changes in labour market flows can be seen by looking at some newly available data compiled by Steve Davis of the University of Chicago Business School and John Haltiwanger of the University of Maryland. Using data from individual plants in the manufacturing sector of the US economy, they have painted a remarkable picture of the changing job scene in the United States. (We don't have the equivalent data for the United Kingdom, but it would be surprising if the picture here is very different from that in the United States.) The picture is shown in Fig. 29.14.

Look first at part (a), which shows the amount of job creation and destruction. On average, about 5 per cent of all jobs in the United States disappear each year and a similar number of new jobs are created. Adding the jobs destroyed and created together gives a measure of the total amount of turnover in the US labour market arising from this process – shown as 'Sum' in the figure. Subtracting jobs destroyed from jobs created gives the change in the number of US jobs – shown as 'Net' in the figure. As you can see, the scale of US job turnover is not only large but it also fluctuates a great deal. Part (b) shows how the fluctuations in job creation and destruction correspond with fluctuations in the US unemployment rate.

Whether fluctuations in the job creation and job destruction rates cause fluctuations in the unemployment rate, or whether fluctuations in both the job creation and job destruction rate and the unemployment rate have a common cause is not known.

The next influences on the natural rate of unemployment that we'll examine arise from non-competitive features of the labour market.

Efficiency wages

A firm can increase its labour productivity by paying wages above the competitive wage rate. The higher wage attracts a higher quality of labour, encourages

FIGURE 29.14

Job Creation, Job Destruction and Unemployment

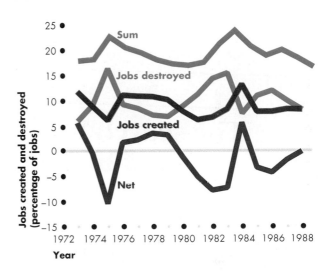

(a) Job creation and destruction rates

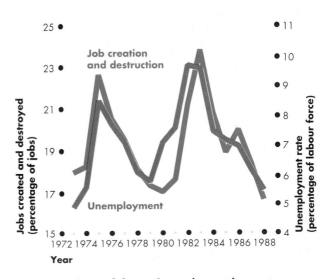

(b) Job creation and destruction and unemployment

On average 10 per cent of existing US jobs disappear each year (Jobs destroyed in part a) and a similar number of new jobs are created. The total amount of US job creation and destruction (Sum) and the rate of US job creation minus the rate of US job destruction (Net) fluctuate. Those fluctuations follow a similar cycle to that in the US unemployment rate (part b).

Source: Data kindly provided by Steve Davis and John Haltiwanger.

Job Creation: More and Better Jobs

FINANCIAL TIMES, 4 OCTOBER 1993

The search for both more and better jobs

Martin Wolf

IN 1993, ...unemployment in industrial countries is expected to surpass 32 m, 3 m more than in 1982, the trough of the previous recession. The social and economic costs of this are enormous....

Little wonder that the European Community, whose overall unemployment rate is projected by the IMF at close to 12 per cent in 1994, is engaged upon its own analysis of the obstacles to employment.

Yet we already know something about both the employment problem and the possible solutions. First, ...the growth of unemployment since the early 1970s, particularly in the EC can be explained neither by accelerated productivity growth nor by faster growth of trade with developing countries.

Second, the relationship between the growth of output and employment has varied enormously across the leading industrial countries. Third, those differences in labour absorption have, as could be predicted, been inversely related to growth of real wages. Last, differences in the performance of overall employment have not had equivalent effects on unemployment, still less on the non-employment, of unskilled males.

The trend growth of labour productivity has fallen from 5 per cent a year in the EC of 30 years ago to a little over 1 per cent a year now. Nevertheless, unemployment has risen almost continuously, from 2 per cent of the EC labour force in 1970....

Between 1972 and 1992, real gross domestic product rose by 61 per cent in the US, by almost exactly the same proportion in France and Germany, by a little more in Italy, and by a little less in the UK. Yet employment rose by 43 per cent in the US and by very little in France, Germany and Italy and the UK.

If output growth is the same, while employment growth is very different, increases in real wages will also differ.

The best possibility, however, would be to imitate the Japanese. Between 1972 and 1992, Japanese GDP rose by 119 per cent, Japanese employment by 25 per cent and Japanese real wages by 41 per cent, while unemployment remained negligible. The Japanese solution was the highest rate of formation of physical and human capital in the industrial world, combined with a labour market that gave new job opportunities to outsiders *and* job protection to insiders. This is the only route towards the magic trio of higher output, higher employment and better jobs.

© The Financial Times. Reprinted with permission.

Unemployment in the European Union is very high.

Countries in the European Union have rates of economic growth similar to the United States, but far fewer jobs are created.

This difference between growth rates and rates of job creation has led to different levels of real wages.

In the United States, real wages have fallen whereas in the EU countries they have risen.

In Japan, rising GDP, employment and real wages, along with low unemployment, have been achieved by very high rates of human and physical capital formation.

Economic growth by itself does not guarantee an expansion in the number of jobs.

A given growth rate can result in different employment intensities. That is, depending on how the growth is generated, employment can rise a lot or a little.

In the United States, growth has a high employment intensity. This is matched by a fall in real wages of 10 per cent between 1972 and 1992.

In the European Union, growth has a much lower employment intensity, but those in work saw real wages rise considerably. In essence, the European Union has been very bad at creating new jobs.

The Japanese model is seen as the best one in order to achieve all desirable aims. By investing in capital and people, Japan has generated high economic growth and higher employment and kept unemployment down, while at the same time granting workers higher real wages.

Figure 1 shows the effect of Japan's investment in physical and human terms. In part (a) the demand for labour curve shifts to the right and in part (b) the production curve shifts upward.

Employment, real wages and real GDP increase (Reading Between the Lines in Chapter 23, pages 658–659, considers deflation in Japan in more detail.)

Figure 2 shows the increase in real GDP as a shift of the LAS curve to the right.

The Japanese model of growth, like the US model, has high employment intensity. Unlike the US model, however, overall growth levels permit higher real wages to be paid.

If the European Union fails to invest so extensively in physical and human capital, the investment it does undertake will not increase employment or real GDP by as much as Japan.

Real wages in the EU will still rise, but employment and real GDP will not rise by as much as in Japan.

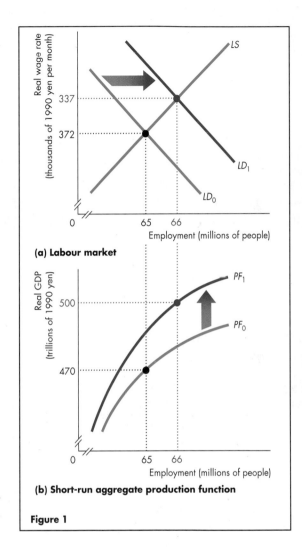

(a) Labour market

(b) Short-run aggregate production function

Figure 1

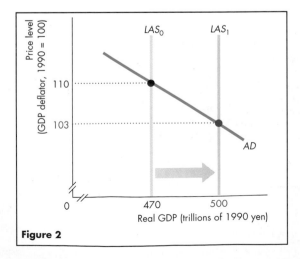

Figure 2

greater work effort, and cuts down on the firm's labour turnover rate and recruiting costs. But the higher wage also adds to the firm's costs. So a firm offers a wage rate that balances productivity gains and additional costs. The wage rate that maximizes profit is called the **efficiency wage**.

The efficiency wage will be higher than the competitive equilibrium wage. If the wage were lower than the competitive wage, competition for labour would bid the wage up. With an efficiency wage above the competitive wage, some labour is unemployed and the employed have an incentive to perform well to avoid being dismissed.

The efficiency wage theory is not a theory of sticky wages. It is a theory of flexible wages set at a level that creates a permanent gap between the quantity of labour demanded and the quantity supplied. The efficiency wage theory relies on the costly job-search mechanisms that we studied earlier in this chapter and can be viewed as one more reason why the natural rate of unemployment is not zero.

Insiders and Outsiders

Insider–outsider theory is an explanation of why firms don't hire new workers – outsiders – in a recession when unemployment is high. In particular, why don't they cut their wage costs by offering the unemployed a lower wage rate than that paid to their existing workers – insiders?

The explanation is that to be productive, new workers must receive on-the-job training from existing workers. If the existing workers provided such training to potential workers who are paid a lower wage, the insider's bargaining position would be weakened. So insiders will not train outsiders unless outsiders receive the same wage rate as insiders.

When bargaining for a wage contract, unions represent insiders only and so the wage agreed exceeds the competitive wage. And there are always some workers – outsiders – who are unable to find work. Like the efficiency wage theory, this theory is yet another reason why the natural rate of unemployment is positive.

According to the three theories of unemployment we have looked at, unemployment arises from the internal workings of the labour market. And fluctuations in the unemployment rate result

from demographic changes, policy and technological change.

In contrast to these theories, the sticky wage theory of the labour market emphasizes fluctuations in *aggregate demand* as sources of fluctuations in unemployment. Let's see why.

Unemployment with Sticky Wages

With sticky money wages, unemployment might rise above or fall below the natural rate. If the real wage rate is above its full-employment level, the quantity of labour employed is less than the quantity supplied and unemployment is above its natural rate. Such a

---

FIGURE 29.15

Unemployment with Sticky Money Wages

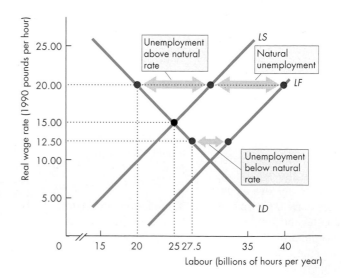

The money wage rate is £15 an hour. If the GDP deflator turns out to be 75, the real wage rate is £20 an hour. At this higher real wage rate, the quantity of labour demanded falls short of the quantity of labour supplied and unemployment is above its natural rate. If the GDP deflator turns out to be 120, the real wage rate is £12.50 an hour. At this lower real wage rate, the quantity of labour demanded exceeds the quantity of labour supplied and unemployment is below its natural rate. Fluctuations in the price level, with sticky money wages, cause fluctuations in the level of unemployment.

situation is shown in Fig. 29.15. The *LS* and *LF* curves are the same as those in Fig. 29.13 and the natural rate of unemployment is measured by the horizontal distance between those two curves.

The money wage rate is £15 an hour. If the GDP deflator is 75, the real wage rate is £20 an hour and the quantity of labour demanded is 20 billion hours. Unemployment is above its natural rate. If the GDP deflator is 120, the real wage rate is £12.50 an hour and the quantity of labour demanded is 27.5 billion hours. Unemployment is below its natural rate.

Fluctuations in aggregate demand bring fluctuations in the price level. These fluctuations move the economy (upward and downward) along its demand for labour curve. At the same time, unemployment fluctuates around its natural rate. According to the sticky wage theory, fluctuations in unemployment arise primarily from the mechanism just described. Changes in the real wage rate arising from a sticky money wage rate and a changing price level result in movements along the labour demand curve and movements along the short-run aggregate supply curve. The rates of job creation and job destruction also fluctuate (as shown in Fig. 29.14), but those fluctuations are the result of aggregate demand fluctuations.

Economists who emphasize the role of sticky wages in generating fluctuations in unemployment usually regard the natural rate of unemployment as constant – or slowly changing. Fluctuations in the actual unemployment rate are fluctuations around the natural rate. Notice that this interpretation of fluctuations in unemployment contrasts with that of the flexible wage theory. The flexible wage model predicts that *all* changes in unemployment are fluctuations in the natural rate of unemployment.

If most of the fluctuations in unemployment *do* arise from sticky wages, then aggregate demand management can moderate those fluctuations in unemployment. By keeping aggregate demand steady so that the price level stays close to its expected level, the economy can be kept close to full employment.

◆ ◆ ◆ ◆ We have now studied the labour market and the determination of long-run and short-run aggregate supply, employment, wages and unemployment. We've examined the forces that change aggregate supply, shifting the long-run and short-run aggregate supply curves. We've also examined the sources of productivity growth in the UK economy. Our next task is to bring together the aggregate demand and aggregate supply sides of the economy again and see how they interact to determine inflation and business cycles. We are going to pursue these tasks in the next two chapters.

SUMMARY

Productivity and Income Growth

The short-run aggregate production function tells us how real GDP varies as the aggregate quantity of labour employed varies with a given stock of capital equipment and a given state of technology. As the labour input increases, real GDP increases but by diminishing marginal amounts. Capital accumulation and technological change lead to productivity growth that causes the short-run aggregate production function to shift upward over time. Occasionally the production function shifts downward because of negative influences such as restrictions on international trade. The short-run aggregate production function in the United Kingdom shifted upward by 20 per cent between 1985 and 1993. (pp. 820–823)

The Demand for Labour

Firms choose how much labour to demand. The lower the real wage rate, the larger is the quantity of labour hours demanded. In choosing how much labour to hire, firms aim to maximize their profits. They achieve this objective by ensuring that the revenue brought in by an additional hour of labour equals the hourly wage rate. The more hours of labour that are employed, the lower is the revenue brought in by the last hour of labour. Firms can be induced to increase the quantity of labour hours demanded by either a decrease in the wage rate or an increase in the revenue brought in – by an increase in the price of output. Both a decrease in the wage rate and an increase in prices result in a lower real wage rate. Thus the lower the real wage rate, the greater is the quantity of labour demanded.

The relationship between the real wage rate and the quantity of labour demanded is summarized in the demand for labour curve, which slopes downward. The demand for labour curve shifts as a result of shifts in the short-run aggregate production function. (pp. 823–826)

The Supply of Labour

Households choose how much labour to supply. They also choose the timing of their labour supply. A higher real wage rate encourages the substitution of work for leisure – the substitution effect – and encourages the taking of more leisure – the income effect. The substitution effect dominates the income effect, so the higher the real wage rate, the more hours each worker supplies. Also, the higher the real wage rate, the higher is the labour force participation rate. A higher *current* wage relative to the expected future wage encourages more work in the present and less in the future – the intertemporal substitution effect. Taking all these forces together, the higher the real wage rate, the greater is the quantity of labour supplied.

The relationship between the real wage rate and the quantity of labour supplied is summarized in the supply of labour curve, which slopes upward. (pp. 826–828)

Wages, Employment and Real GDP in the Long Run

In the long run, money wages are flexible and the real wage rate, the level of employment and the quantity of real GDP supplied are independent of the price level. The long-run aggregate supply curve is vertical.

Capital accumulation and technological change increase the marginal product of labour and increase the demand for labour – shift the demand for labour curve to the right. Population growth increases the supply of labour – shifts the supply of labour curve to the right. But capital accumulation

and technological change outpace population growth. The combined effect of these changes is increasing employment, real wages and real GDP – economic growth. (pp. 829–831)

Wages, Employment and Real GDP in the Short Run

In the short run, money wages are fixed and real wages change only when the price level changes. The level of employment is determined by the demand for labour and, except at full employment, households are off their supply curves. Fluctuations in the price level generate fluctuations in the quantity of labour demanded and in employment and real GDP. The higher the price level, the lower the real wage rate, the greater the quantity of labour demanded and the greater is employment and real GDP. The short-run aggregate supply curve slopes upward. (pp. 832–834)

How Sticky Are Wages?

There are two views about wages. One – the flexible wage view – is that they adjust quickly to maintain full employment. The other – the sticky wage view – is that money wages *increase* quickly to restore full employment when there is an excess demand for labour but *decrease* very slowly when there is an excess supply of labour.

The three main explanations for sticky wages are implicit risk-sharing contracts, incomplete price level information and menu costs.

Implicit risk-sharing contracts arise as a method of providing income insurance. Firms benefit by being able to hire labour at a lower wage rate on average and households benefit by having a more certain income. This source of sticky wages explains sticky *real* wages but not sticky *money* wages.

With incomplete information about the price level, people base their labour supply decision on the *expected* real wage rate and the *expected price level*. A change in the price level brings a less than proportionate change in the money wage rate and a change in employment and output.

When prices or wages are changed, some costs – menu costs – are incurred. Menu costs in the labour market are large and result in infrequent changes in negotiated wage rates. (pp. 834–837)

Unemployment

The labour market is in a constant state of change or labour turnover. Labour turnover creates unemployment. New entrants to the labour force and workers re-entering after a period of household production take time to find a job. Some people leave an existing job to seek a better one. Some are laid off, and others are dismissed and forced to find another job. The pace of labour turnover is not constant. When technological change is expanding one sector and contracting another, labour turnover increases. Finding new jobs takes time and the process of adjustment may create overtime and unfilled vacancies in the expanding sector but unemployment in the contracting sector.

Even if wages are flexible, unemployment arising from labour-market turnover cannot be avoided. The unemployment rate arising from this source is the natural rate of unemployment. In labour markets with flexible wages, all fluctuations in unemployment are fluctuations in the natural rate arising from changes in the rate of labour turnover. The scale and cycles in the rates of job creation and job destruction are consistent with the flexible wage theory.

The natural rate includes unemployment arising from efficiency wages and insider–outsider relations. The efficiency wage is the wage that maximizes a firm's profit taking into account that a higher wage increases both cost and productivity. The efficiency wage exceeds the competitive market wage and results in unemployment. Those with jobs (insiders) are unwilling to train those without jobs (outsiders) unless the outsiders are paid the same wages as the insiders. And in negotiating their wages, the insiders take only their own interests into account. So they agree a wage at which some outsiders would like to become insiders and unemployment persists.

If wages are sticky, unemployment arises for the same reasons as in the case of flexible wages and for one additional reason. With sticky wages the real wage may not move quickly enough to keep the quantity of labour demanded equal to the quantity supplied. In such a case, an increase in the real wage rate can result in unemployment rising above its natural rate and a decrease in real wages can result in unemployment falling below its natural rate. (pp. 837–845)

K E Y   E L E M E N T S

Key Terms

Key Figures

REVIEW QUESTIONS

1 What is the relationship between output and labour input in the short run? Why does the marginal product of labour diminish?

2 If the short-run production function shifts from 1994 to 1996 by the amount shown in Fig. 29.2, what happens to the marginal product of labour between 1992 and 1993?

3 Explain why the demand for labour curve slopes downward.

4 Given your answer to Question 2, does the demand for labour curve shift between 1994 and 1996? If so, in what direction and by how much?

5 Why does the labour force participation rate rise as the real wage rate rises?

6 How is the quantity of labour currently supplied influenced by the wage rate today relative to those expected in the future?

7 Explain what happens in a labour market in the long run when technological change increases the marginal product of labour for each unit of labour input.

8 In Question 7, explain what happens to the long-run aggregate supply curve.

9 Explain what happens in a labour market in the short run when the price level changes.

10 In Question 9, explain whether there is a shift in or a movement along the short-run aggregate supply curve.

11 Explain how unemployment can arise if wages are flexible.

12 Describe the main facts about the rates of job creation and job destruction.

13 Explain how unemployment fluctuates above its natural rate.

PROBLEMS

Use the following information about an economy to answer Problems 1 to 7. The economy's short-run production function is:

Labour (millions of hours per year)	Real GDP (millions of 1990 pounds per year)
1	38
2	54
3	68
4	80
5	90
6	98
7	104
8	108

Its demand and supply schedules for labour are:

Real wage rate (1990 pounds per hour)	Quantity of labour demanded (millions of hours per year)	Quantity of labour supplied (millions of hours per year)
3	8	4
5	7	5
7	6	6
9	5	7
11	4	8
13	3	9
15	2	10
17	1	11

1 In the long run when wages are flexible, how much labour is employed and what is the real wage rate?

2 If in Problem 1 the GDP deflator is 120, what is the money wage rate?

3 Calculate the long-run aggregate supply curve in the economy described in Problem 1.

4 If money wages are fixed at £7 an hour and the GDP deflator is 100, what is the real wage rate and level of employment in this economy?

5 Find three points on the economy's short-run aggregate supply curve when the money wage rate is £7 an hour.

6 Calculate the real wage rate at each of the points you used in answering problem 5.

7 At what price level and level of employment do the short-run and long-run aggregate supply curves intersect?

8 There are two economies, each with *constant* unemployment rates but with a great deal of labour market turnover. In economy A, there is a rapid pace of technological change. Twenty per cent of the labour force is either dismissed or leaves its job every year and 20 per cent is hired every year. In economy B, only 5 per cent is dismissed or leaves and 5 per cent is hired. Which economy has the higher unemployment rate? Why?

9 There are two economies, Flexiland and Fixland. These economies are identical in every way except that in Flexiland, real wages are flexible and maintain equality between the quantities of labour demanded and supplied. In Fixland, wages are sticky but the money wage rate is set so that, *on average*, the quantity of labour demanded equals the quantity supplied.

a Explain which economy has the higher average unemployment rate.

b Explain which economy has the largest fluctuations in unemployment.

CHAPTER 30

INFLATION

I
N THE CLOSING YEARS OF THE ROMAN EMPIRE, EMPEROR DIOCLETIAN PRESIDED over a massive inflation. Prices increased at a rate of more than 300 per cent a year. In 1993, as Russia attempted to introduce a market economy, President Boris Yeltsin struggled to contain a similarly massive inflation. Rapid inflations are also occurring in other East European countries such as Ukraine and Poland as well as in many Latin American countries. The United Kingdom, too, has had a high inflation rate in its recent past – during the 1970s and early 1980s. But today the United Kingdom, along with most other rich industrial countries, has a low inflation rate. What causes inflation? Why does inflation sometimes become extremely rapid and at other times subside? ◆ ◆ To make good decisions we need good forecasts of inflation, and not just for next year but for many years into the future. How do people try to anticipate inflation? And how do expectations of inflation influence the economy? ◆ ◆ As the inflation rate rises and falls, the unemployment rate and interest rates also fluctuate. What is the connection between inflation and unemployment and between inflation and interest rates?

From Rome to Russia

◆ ◆ ◆ ◆ In this chapter, you will learn about the forces that generate inflation, the consequences of inflation, and the way that people try to forecast and therefore anticipate inflation. But first, let's remind ourselves of what inflation is and how its rate is measured.

Inflation and the Price Level

Inflation is the *process* of *rising prices*. It is not a one-time increase in the price level. If the price level is increasing by 10 per cent a year, the economy is experiencing inflation. If the price level rises by 10 per cent and then stabilizes, the economy has experienced a one-time jump in the price level.

The inflation rate is the percentage rise in the price level. That is,

$$\text{Inflation rate} = \frac{\text{Current year's price level} - \text{Last year's price level}}{\text{Last year's price level}} \times 100.$$

Let's write this equation in symbols. We'll call this year's price level P_1 and last year's price level P_0, so that,

$$\text{Inflation rate} = \frac{P_1 - P_0}{P_0} \times 100.$$

For example, if the price level this year is 143 and the price level last year was 130, the inflation rate is 10 per cent a year. That is,

$$\text{Inflation rate} = \frac{143 - 130}{130} \times 100$$

$$\text{Inflation rate} = \frac{13}{130} \times 100$$

$$= 10 \text{ per cent a year.}$$

This equation shows the connection between the *inflation rate* and the *price level*. For a given price level last year, the higher the price level in the current year, the higher is the inflation rate.

Keep the distinction between the price level and the inflation rate clear. If the price level is *rising*, the inflation rate is *positive*. If the price level is *falling*, the inflation rate is *negative*. If the price level rises at a *faster* rate, then the inflation rate *increases*. If the price level rises at a *slower* rate, then the inflation rate *decreases*.

We are going to study the forces that generate inflation and the consequences of inflation. First, we'll study the effects of inflation on real GDP, real wages and employment. Next, we'll examine the connection between inflation and unemployment. Finally, we'll look at the effects of inflation on interest rates. We'll discover that the effects of

inflation on all these variables depends on whether the inflation is anticipated or unanticipated. **Anticipated inflation** is inflation that is correctly foreseen. **Unanticipated inflation** is inflation that is not foreseen – that takes people by surprise.

We'll begin by using the aggregate demand–aggregate supply model to study the sources of inflation. In that model, inflation can result from either an increase in aggregate demand or a decrease in aggregate supply. The economy follows a different course depending on which source of inflation is at work. We'll begin by studying the effects on inflation of an increase in aggregate demand.

Demand–Pull Inflation

The inflation resulting from an increase in aggregate demand is called **demand–pull inflation**. Such an inflation may arise from any individual factor that increases aggregate demand. Although there are several such factors, the most important that generate *ongoing* increases in aggregate demand are:

◆ Increases in the money supply
◆ Increases in government purchases
◆ Increases in the price level in the rest of the world

When aggregate demand increases, the aggregate demand curve shifts to the right. Let's trace the effects of such an increase.

Inflation Effect of an Increase in Aggregate Demand

Suppose that last year the GDP deflator was 130 and real GDP was £600 billion. Long-run real GDP was also £600 billion. This situation is shown in Fig. 30.1(a). The aggregate demand curve is AD_0, the short-run aggregate supply curve is SAS_0, and the long-run aggregate supply curve is LAS.

In the current year, aggregate demand increases to AD_1. Such a situation arises if, for example, the Bank of England loosens its grip on the money supply or the government increases its purchases of goods and services. The economy moves to the point where the aggregate demand curve AD_1

FIGURE 30.1

Demand–Pull Inflation

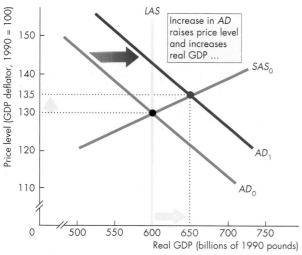

(a) Initial effect

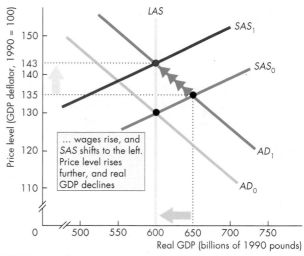

(b) Wages adjust

In part (a), the aggregate demand curve is AD_0, the short-run aggregate supply curve is SAS_0 and the long-run aggregate supply curve is LAS. The GDP deflator is 130 and real GDP is £600 billion, its long-run level. Aggregate demand increases to AD_1 (because the Bank of England increases the money supply or the government increases its purchases of goods and services). The new equi-

librium occurs where AD_1 intersects SAS_0. The economy experiences inflation (the GDP deflator rises to 135) and real GDP increases to £650 billion. In part (b), starting from above full employment, wages begin to rise and the short-run aggregate supply curve shifts to the left towards SAS_1. The price level rises further, and real GDP returns to its long-run level.

intersects the short-run aggregate supply curve SAS_0. The GDP deflator increases to 135, and real GDP increases to £650 billion. The economy experiences 3.8 per cent inflation (a GDP deflator of 135 compared with 130 in the previous year) and an increase in real GDP.

The situation that developed in the UK economy in the period 1971 to 1974 is a good example of the process we have just analysed. In those years, the main influence on aggregate demand in the United Kingdom was an expansionary monetary and fiscal policy pursued by the Conservative government of Prime Minister Edward Heath and his Chancellor of the Exchequer Anthony Barber. As a consequence, the aggregate demand curve shifted to the right, the price level increased quickly and real GDP moved above its long-run level.

The situation in Fig. 30.1(a) is not the end of the story. Let's see why not.

Wage Response

The economy cannot produce an above full-employment level forever. With unemployment below its natural rate, there is a shortage of labour. Wages begin to increase, and the short-run aggregate supply curve starts to shift to the left. Prices rise further, and real GDP begins to fall. With no further change in aggregate demand – the aggregate demand curve remains at AD_1 – this process comes to an end when the short-run aggregate demand curve has moved to SAS_1 in Fig. 30.1(b). At this time, the GDP deflator has increased to 143 and real GDP has returned to its long-run level, the level from which it started.

A Price–Wage Inflation Spiral

The inflation process we've just studied eventually comes to an end when, for a given increase in aggregate demand, wages have adjusted enough to restore the real wage rate to its full-employment level. But suppose that the initial increase in aggregate demand resulted from a large government budget deficit financed by creating more and more money. If such a policy remains in place, aggregate demand will continue to increase year after year. The aggregate demand curve will keep shifting to the right, putting continual upward pressure on the price level. The economy will experience perpetual demand–pull inflation.

Figure 30.2 illustrates a perpetual demand–pull inflation. The starting point is the same as that shown in Fig. 30.1. The aggregate demand curve is AD_0, the short-run aggregate supply curve is SAS_0, and the long-run aggregate supply curve is LAS. Real GDP is £600 billion and the GDP deflator is 130. Aggregate demand increases, shifting the aggregate demand curve to AD_1. Real GDP increases to £650 billion, and the GDP deflator rises to 135. The economy is at an above full-employment equilibrium. There is a shortage of labour and the wage rate rises, shifting the short-run aggregate supply curve to SAS_1. The GDP deflator increases to 143, and real GDP returns to its long-run level.

But the money supply increases again by the same percentage as before and aggregate demand continues to increase. The aggregate demand curve shifts to the right to AD_2. The GDP deflator increases further, real GDP exceeds its long-run level and the wage rate continues to rise. As the SAS curve shifts to SAS_2, the GDP deflator increases further to 157. As aggregate demand continues to increase, the price level rises continuously, generating a perpetual demand–pull inflation and a price–wage inflation spiral. Real GDP fluctuates between £600 billion and £650 billion.

In the price–wage inflation spiral that we've just described, aggregate demand increases and wage increases alternate – first aggregate demand increases, then wages, then aggregate demand, and so on. If, after the initial increase in aggregate demand that took real GDP to £650 billion, aggregate demand continues to increase *at the same time* as the wage rate increases, real GDP remains above its long-run level at £650 billion as the demand–pull inflation proceeds.

Demand–Pull Inflation in Essex You may better understand the inflation process that we've just described by considering what is going on in an individual part of the economy, such as an Essex jam factory. Initially when aggregate demand increases, the demand for jam increases and the price of jam rises. Faced with a

FIGURE 30.2

A Price–Wage Inflation Spiral

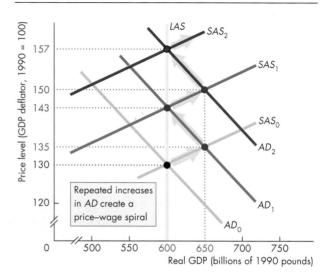

The aggregate demand curve is AD_0, the short-run aggregate supply curve is SAS_0 and the long-run aggregate supply curve is LAS. Real GDP is £600 billion, and the GDP deflator is 130. Aggregate demand increases, shifting the aggregate demand curve to AD_1. Real GDP increases to £650 billion and the GDP deflator rises to 135. With the economy operating above full employment, the wage rate begins to rise, shifting the short-run aggregate supply curve to the left to SAS_1. The GDP deflator increases to 143 and real GDP returns to its long-run level. As aggregate demand continues to increase, the aggregate demand curve shifts to AD_2. The GDP deflator increases further, real GDP exceeds its long-run level, and the wage rate continues to rise. As the short-run aggregate supply curve shifts to the left to SAS_2, the GDP deflator increases to 157. As aggregate demand continues to increase, the price level rises, generating a perpetual demand–pull inflation. Real GDP fluctuates between £600 billion and £650 billion. But if aggregate demand increases *at the same time* as wages increase, real GDP remains at £650 billion as the demand–pull inflation occurs.

higher price, the jam factory works overtime and increases production. Conditions are good for workers in Essex, and the jam factory finds it hard to hang on to its best people. To do so it has to offer higher wages. As wages increase, so do the costs of the jam factory.

What happens next depends on what happens to aggregate demand. If aggregate demand remains constant (as in Fig. 30.1b), the firm's costs are increasing, but the price of jam is not increasing as quickly as its costs. Production is scaled back. Eventually, wages and costs increase by the same amount as the price of jam. In real terms, the jam factory is in the same situation as initially – before the increase in aggregate demand. The jam factory produces the same amount of jam and employs the same amount of labour.

But if aggregate demand continues to increase, so does the demand for jam, and the price of jam rises at the same rate as wages. The jam factory continues to operate above full employment, and there is a persistent shortage of labour. Prices and wages chase each other upward in an unending price–wage spiral.

R E V I E W

Demand–pull inflation results from any initial factor that increases aggregate demand. The most important such factors are an increase in the money supply and an increase in government purchases of goods and services. Initially, the increase in aggregate demand increases the price level and real GDP. With the economy operating at above full employment, the wage rate rises, decreasing short-run aggregate supply. If aggregate demand remains constant at its new level, the price level rises further and real GDP returns to its long-run level. If aggregate demand continues to increase, wages chase prices in an unending price–wage inflation spiral. ◆

Next, let's look at how shocks to aggregate supply can create inflation.

Supply Inflation and Stagflation

Inflation can result from a decrease in aggregate supply. The two main sources of a decrease in aggregate supply are:

◆ An increase in wage rates
◆ An increase in the prices of key raw materials

These sources of a decrease in aggregate supply operate by increasing costs, and such an inflation is called **cost–push inflation**.

Other things remaining the same, the higher the cost of production, the smaller is the amount produced. At a given price level, rising wage rates, or rising prices of key raw materials such as oil, lead firms to decrease the quantity of labour employed and to cut production. This decrease in short-run aggregate supply shifts the short-run aggregate supply curve to the left. Let's see what that does to the price level.

Inflation Effect of a Decrease in Aggregate Supply

Suppose that last year the GDP deflator was 130 and real GDP was £600 billion. Long-run real GDP was also £600 billion. This situation is shown in Fig. 30.3. The aggregate demand curve was AD_0, the short-run aggregate supply curve was SAS_0, and the long-run aggregate supply curve was LAS.

FIGURE 30.3

Cost–Push Inflation

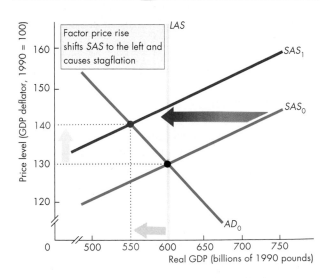

Initially the aggregate demand curve is AD_0, the short-run aggregate supply curve is SAS_0 and the long-run aggregate supply curve is LAS. A decrease in aggregate supply (for example, resulting from an increase in the world price of oil) shifts the short-run aggregate supply curve to SAS_1. The economy moves to the point where the short-run aggregate supply curve SAS_1 intersects the aggregate demand curve AD_0. The GDP deflator increases to 140, and real GDP decreases to £550 billion. The economy experiences inflation and a contraction of real GDP – *stagflation*.

In the current year, a sharp increase in world oil prices decreases short-run aggregate supply. The short-run aggregate supply curve shifts to the left to SAS_1. The GDP deflator increases to 140, and real GDP decreases to £550 billion. The economy experiences 7.7 per cent inflation (a GDP deflator of 140 compared with 130 in the previous year) and a contraction of real GDP – *stagflation*.

Aggregate Demand Response

When the economy is stuck at an unemployment equilibrium such as that shown in Fig. 30.3, there is often an outcry of concern and a call for action to restore full employment. Such action can include an increase in government purchases of goods and services or a tax cut, but the most likely is a response from the Bank of England that increases the money supply. If the Bank of England does respond in this way, aggregate demand increases and the aggregate demand curve shifts to the right. Figure 30.4 shows an increase in aggregate demand that shifts the aggregate demand curve to AD_1 and restores full employment. But this happens at the expense of a yet higher price level. The price level rises to 143, a 10 per cent increase over the original price level.

A Cost–Price Inflation Spiral

Suppose now that the oil producers, seeing the prices of everything they buy increase by 10 per cent, decide to increase the price of oil yet again. Figure 30.5 continues the story. The short-run aggregate supply curve now shifts to SAS_2, and another bout of stagflation ensues. The price level rises further to 154, and real GDP falls to £550 billion. Unemployment increases above its natural rate. If the Bank of England responds yet again with an increase in the money supply, aggregate demand increases and the aggregate demand curve shifts to AD_2. The price level rises even higher – to 157 – and full employment is again restored. A cost–price inflation spiral results. But if the Bank of England does not respond, the economy remains below full employment until the initial price increase that triggered the stagflation is reversed.

You can see that the Bank of England has a dilemma. If it increases the money supply to restore full employment, it invites another oil price hike that will call forth yet a further increase in the money supply. Inflation will rage along at a rate decided by the oil

FIGURE 30.4

Aggregate Demand Response to Cost Push

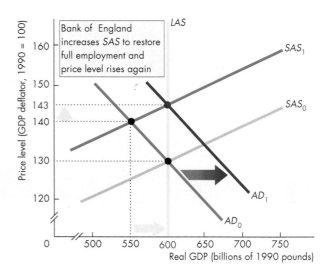

Initially the aggregate demand curve is AD_0, the short-run aggregate supply curve is SAS_0 and the long-run aggregate supply curve is LAS. A decrease in aggregate supply shifts the short-run aggregate supply curve to the left to SAS_1. The GDP deflator rises from 130 to 140 and real GDP decreases from £600 billion to £550 billion. The economy experiences stagflation. It is stuck at an unemployment equilibrium. If the Bank of England responds by increasing aggregate demand to restore full employment, the aggregate demand curve shifts to the right to AD_1. The economy returns to full employment, but at the expense of higher inflation. The price level rises to 143.

exporting nations. If the Bank of England keeps the lid on money supply growth, the economy operates with a high level of unemployment. The Bank of England faced such a dilemma in 1974 and the early 1980s when OPEC pushed oil prices higher. At first, the Bank accommodated these price increases and inflation exploded. But during the early 1980s, the Bank decided not to respond to the oil price hike with an increase in the money supply. The result was a massive recession, but also, eventually, a fall in inflation.

Cost–Push Inflation in Essex What is going on in the Essex jam factory when the economy is experiencing cost–push inflation? When the oil price

FIGURE 30.5

A Cost–Price Inflation Spiral

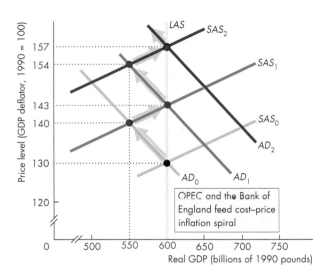

When a cost increase (for example, an increase in the world oil price) decreases short-run aggregate supply from SAS_0 to SAS_1, the GDP deflator rises to 140 and real GDP decreases to £550 billion. The Bank of England responds with an increase in the money supply that shifts the aggregate demand curve from AD_0 to AD_1. The GDP deflator rises again to 143 and real GDP returns to £600 billion. The cost increase is applied again shifting the short-run aggregate supply curve to SAS_2. Stagflation is repeated and the GDP deflator now rises to 154. The Bank of England responds again taking the aggregate demand curve to AD_2 and the cost–price inflation spiral continues as the price level rises to 157.

increases, so do the costs of making jam. These higher costs decrease the supply of jam, increasing its price and decreasing the quantity produced. The jam factory lays off some workers. This situation will persist until either the Bank of England increases aggregate demand or the price of oil falls. If the Bank of England increases aggregate demand, as it did in the mid-1970s, the demand for jam increases and so does its price. The higher price of jam brings higher profits and the jam factory increases its production. It rehires the laid-off workers. But if the Bank of England resists the pressure to increase aggregate demand, the price of oil eventually falls and jam production gradually increases.

Cost–push inflation results from any initial factor, such as an increase in the wage rate or an increase in the price of a key raw material that decreases aggregate supply. The initial effect of a decrease in aggregate supply is an increase in the price level and a decrease in real GDP – *stagflation*. If monetary or fiscal policy increases aggregate demand to restore full employment, the price level rises further. If aggregate demand remains constant, the economy stays below full employment until the initial price rise is reversed. If the response to stagflation is an increase in aggregate demand, a freewheeling cost–push inflation takes place at a rate determined by the speed with which costs are pushed upward. ◆

Anticipating Inflation

With demand–pull inflation, a persistent increase in the money supply increases aggregate demand and creates a price–wage inflation spiral. With cost–push inflation, a persistent increase in factor prices accommodated by persistent increases in the money supply creates a cost–price inflation spiral. Regardless of whether the inflation is demand pull or cost push, the failure to *anticipate* inflation correctly imposes costs on firms and workers. And these costs create an incentive for people to try to anticipate the inflation. Let's examine these consequences.

Labour Market Consequences of Unanticipated Inflation

Unanticipated inflation has two main consequences for the operation of the labour market. They are:

◆ Redistribution of income
◆ Departures from full employment

Redistribution of Income   Unanticipated inflation redistributes income between workers and employers. In some situations, workers gain at the expense of employers and, in other situations, employers gain at the expense of workers.

If an unexpected increase in aggregate demand increases the inflation rate, then wages will not have been set high enough. Profits will be higher than expected, and wages will buy fewer goods and services than expected. Employers gain at the expense of workers. But if aggregate demand is expected to increase at a rapid rate and it fails to do so, workers gain at the expense of employers. In this situation, the anticipated inflation rate is higher than the actual inflation rate. Wages will have been set too high and profits will be squeezed. Workers will be able to buy more with their income than was originally anticipated.

These redistributions between workers and employers create an incentive for both firms and workers to anticipate inflation correctly. Some other costs of unanticipated inflation fall on both workers and firms at the same time. These are the costs arising from departures from full employment.

Departures from Full Employment Unanticipated inflation results in departures from full employment. You can confirm this proposition by looking at Figs. 30.2 and 30.5. To see why departure from full employment imposes costs, let's return to the jam factory in Essex.

If the factory and its workers are not anticipating inflation, but an inflation actually occurs, wages will be set too low and employment will increase above the full employment level. The price of jam and of other goods and services increases but the wage rate doesn't change. The real wage rate falls and the factory increases production. Workers begin to leave the jam factory to look for jobs that pay a higher real wage rate, one closer to that prevailing before the outburst of inflation. This outcome imposes costs on both the firm and the workers. The firm operates its plant at a high output rate and incurs overtime costs and higher maintenance and parts replacement costs. The workers end up feeling cheated. They've worked overtime to produce the extra output and, when they come to spend their wages, they discover that prices have increased, so their wages buy a smaller quantity of goods and services than anticipated.

If the jam factory and its workers anticipate a high inflation rate that does not occur, wages will be set too high, and unemployment will increase. Those workers keeping their jobs gain, but those who

become unemployed lose. Also, the jam factory loses because output and profits fall.

So unanticipated inflation imposes costs regardless of whether the inflation forecast turns out to be wrong on the up side or the down side. The presence of these costs creates an incentive to forecast inflation as accurately as possible – to anticipate inflation correctly. Let's now see people make their forecasts of inflation.

How People Forecast Inflation

People devote different amounts of time and effort to forecasting inflation. Some people specialize in forecasting and make a living from it. They are economists who work for public and private forecasting agencies and firms.

Specialist forecasters stand to lose a great deal from wrong forecasts and have a strong incentive to make their forecasts as accurate as possible – minimizing the range of error and at least making them correct on average. Also, organizations that stand to lose by having wrong forecasts invest a good deal of effort in checking the forecasts made by the specialists. For example, banks, trade unions, government departments and most large private-sector producers of goods and services devote a lot of effort to making their own forecasts and comparing them with the forecasts of others. Specialist forecasters use vast amounts of data, which they analyse with the help of statistical models of the economy. The models they use are based on (but are more detailed than) the aggregate demand–aggregate supply model that you are studying in this book.

How Economists Predict People's Forecasts

Economics tries to predict the choices that people make. Since people's choices depend on their forecasts of phenomena such as inflation, we must predict their forecasts in order to predict their choices. How do economists go about that task?

They assume that people are as rational in their use of information when forming expectations as they are in all their other economic actions. Lacking crystal balls, they cannot be always right about the future. But they can use all the relevant information available to them to make their forecasting errors as small as possible. That is, they can make a rational expectation. A **rational expectation** is a forecast based on all the available relevant information. It has two features:

◆ The expected forecast error is zero.
◆ The range of the forecast error is as small as possible.

With an expected forecast error of zero, a rational expectation is right *on average*. But it is not an accurate forecast. It has the same chance of being too high as it has of being too low.

The assumption that people do not waste information when they make their forecasts does not tell us what information they actually use. So we make one further assumption. They use the *information that economic theory predicts is relevant*. For example, to predict people's expectations of the price of orange juice, we use the economic model of demand and supply, together with all the available information about the positions of the demand and supply curves for orange juice. To make a prediction about people's expectations of the price level and inflation, we use the economic model of aggregate demand and aggregate supply.

Let's see how we can use the aggregate demand and supply model to work out the rational expectation of the price level.

Rational Expectation of the Price Level

We use the aggregate demand–aggregate supply model to forecast the price level in the same way that the meteorologist uses a model of the atmosphere to forecast the weather. But there is a difference between the meteorologist's model of the atmosphere and the economist's model of the economy. In the meteorologist's model, tomorrow's weather does not depend on people's forecast of it. In the economist's model, next year's price level *does* depend on people's forecast of it. To work out the rational expectation of the price level, we must take account of this dependence of the actual price level on the forecasted price level.

We're going to work out the rational expectation of the price level, using Fig. 30.6 to guide our analysis. The aggregate demand–aggregate supply model predicts that the price level is at the point of intersection of the aggregate demand and short-run aggregate supply curves. To forecast the price level, therefore, we have to forecast the positions of these curves.

Let's begin with aggregate demand. To forecast the position of the aggregate demand curve we must forecast all the variables that influence aggregate demand. Suppose that we have done this and our forecast of aggregate demand is given by the curve *EAD*, the *expected* aggregate demand curve.

Our next task is to forecast the position of the short-run aggregate supply curve, but here we have a problem. We know that the position of the short-run aggregate supply curve is determined by two things:

◆ Long-run aggregate supply
◆ The money wage rate

The short-run aggregate supply curve intersects the long-run aggregate supply curve at the full-employment price level. So we need a forecast of the position of the long-run aggregate supply curve. To make such a forecast we must forecast all the factors that determine long-run aggregate supply. Suppose that we have made the best forecast we can of long-run real GDP and that we expect long-run aggregate supply to be $600 billion. The *expected* long-run aggregate supply curve is *ELAS* in Fig. 30.6.

The final ingredient we need is a forecast of the money wage rate. Armed with this information, we have a forecast of the point on the *ELAS* curve at which the short-run aggregate supply intersects it. The forecast of the money wage rate depends on the degree of wage flexibility, and we need to look at two cases:

◆ Sticky wages
◆ Flexible wages

Rational Expectation in the Short Run In the short run, money wages are already set, so forecasting money wages is easy. The forecast is equal to the current actual wage rate. Given that fixed wage rate and the expected long-run aggregate supply curve *ELAS*, there is an expected short-run aggregate supply curve. In Fig. 30.6(a), such a curve is $ESAS_0$.

The rational expectation of the price level is the point of intersection of *EAD* and $ESAS_0$, a price level of 120. The rational expectation of inflation is calculated as the percentage amount by which the forecasted future price level exceeds the current price level. For example, if the current price level is 110, and next year's forecasted price level is 120, the expected inflation rate over the year is 9.1 per cent.

There is also a rational expectation of real GDP. Given the wage rate and the expected short-run aggregate supply curve $ESAS_0$, the rational expectation is that real GDP will be $650 billion and the economy will be at an above full-employment equilibrium.

FIGURE 30.6

Rational Expectation of the Price Level

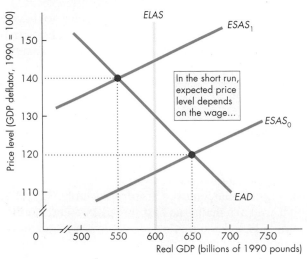

(a) The short run

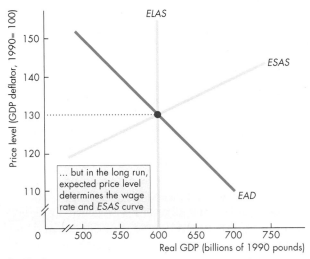

(b) The long run

The rational expectation of the price level is constructed by forecasting the expected aggregate demand curve (*EAD*) and the expected short-run aggregate supply curve (*ESAS*). The rational expectation of the price level occurs at the point of intersection of curves *EAD* and *ESAS*. To forecast the position of *ESAS*, forecasts of the long-run aggregate supply curve *ELAS* and the wage rate are needed. In the short run (part a), wages are sticky and do not respond to price level expectations, so the position of the expected short-run aggregate supply curve depends on *ELAS* and the fixed wage rate. With a low wage rate,

the expected short-run aggregate supply curve is $ESAS_0$ and the rational expectation of the price level is 120. With a high wage rate, the expected short-run aggregate supply curve is $ESAS_1$ and the rational expectation of the price level is 140.

In the long run (part b), wages are flexible and respond to the expected price level. The rational expectation of the price level is at the point of intersection of *EAD* and *ELAS*. The wage rate is determined by this expected price level, and the expected short-run aggregate supply curve is *ESAS*.

Figure 30.6(a) shows another case – one in which the expected short-run aggregate supply curve is $ESAS_1$. Here, the wage rate is higher. The rational expectation of the price level is determined at the point of intersection of *EAD* and $ESAS_1$, an expected price level of 140. With a current price level of 110, the expected inflation rate over the year is 27 per cent. The economy is expected to be at an unemployment equilibrium, with a real GDP of $550 billion.

Rational Expectation in the Long Run   In the long run, wages are flexible and to forecast the position of the short-run aggregate supply curve we must first forecast the money wage rate. But the money wage rate is set to make the expected real wage rate give full employment. So to set the money wage rate, people use a forecast – a rational expectation – of the price

level. There seems to be a problem here: we need a forecast of the wage rate; and to forecast the wage rate, we need a forecast of the price level.

The problem is solved by finding a forecast of both the price level and the money wage rate that are consistent with each other. There is only one such consistent forecast. It occurs when the forecasted wage rate makes the expected short-run aggregate supply curve *ESAS* pass through the intersection of the expected aggregate demand curve and the expected long-run aggregate supply curve. This case is shown in Fig. 30.6(b). The forecasted price level is 130, determined at the intersection of the *EAD* and the *ESAS* curves. Here, we forecast the position of the short-run aggregate supply curve and the price level at the same time, and the two forecasts are consistent with each other.

Model, Theory and Reality

The analysis we've just conducted shows how economists work out a rational expectation. But do real people form expectations of the price level by using that same analysis? We can imagine that graduates of economics might, but it seems unrealistic to attribute such calculations to most people. Does this make the whole idea of rational expectations invalid?

The answer is no. In performing our calculations, we have been building an economic model. That model does not seek to describe the thought processes of real people. Its goal is to make predictions about *choices*, not mental processes. The theory is that the forecasts people make, regardless of how they make them, are the same (on average) as the forecasts that an economist makes using the relevant economic theory.

We've seen how unanticipated changes in aggregate demand and aggregate supply create inflation and impose costs. We've also seen how people try to anticipate inflation and avoid those costs. Let's next see how things work out when forecasts are correct – when people are lucky and correctly anticipate the future.

Anticipated Inflation

If people could correctly anticipate the future course of inflation, they would always set the money wage rate at its full employment level.

Let's suppose that last year the GDP deflator was 130 and real GDP was £600 billion. Let's also suppose that the economy was at full employment and its long-run real GDP last year was £600 billion. Figure 30.7 illustrates the economy last year. The aggregate demand curve last year was AD_0, the aggregate supply curve was SAS_0 and the long-run aggregate supply curve was LAS. Since the economy was in equilibrium at long-run real GDP, the actual price level equalled the expected price level.

To simplify our analysis, let's suppose that at the end of last year long-run real GDP was not expected to change, so that this year's expected long-run aggregate supply is the same as last year's. Let's also suppose that aggregate demand was expected to increase, so that the expected aggregate demand curve for this year is AD_1. We can now calculate the rational expectation of the price level for this year. It is a GDP deflator of 132, the price level at which the new expected aggregate demand curve intersects the expected long-run aggregate supply curve.

The expected inflation rate is 10 per cent, the percentage change in the price level from 130 to 143.

Wages increase as a result of the expected inflation and the short-run aggregate supply curve also shifts to the left. In particular, given that expected inflation is 10 per cent, the short-run aggregate supply curve for next year (SAS_1) shifts upward by that same percentage amount (10 per cent) and passes through the long-run aggregate supply curve (LAS) at the expected price level.

If aggregate demand turns out to be the same as expected, the actual aggregate demand curve is AD_1. The intersection point of AD_1 and SAS_1 determines

---

FIGURE 30.7

Anticipated Inflation

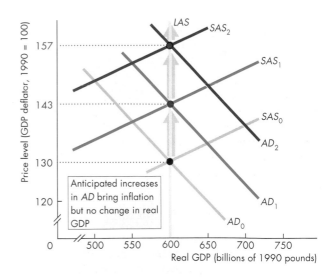

The actual and expected long-run aggregate supply curve (*LAS*) is at a real GDP of £600 billion. Last year, aggregate demand was AD_0, and the short-run aggregate supply curve was SAS_0. The actual price level was the same as that expected – a GDP deflator of 130. This year aggregate demand is expected to rise to AD_1. The rational expectation of the GDP deflator changes from 130 to 143. As a result, the short-run aggregate supply curve shifts left to SAS_1. If aggregate demand actually increases as expected, the actual aggregate demand curve AD_1 is the same as the expected aggregate demand curve. Equilibrium occurs at a real GDP of £600 billion and an actual GDP deflator of 143. The inflation is correctly anticipated.

Next year the process continues with aggregate demand increasing as expected to AD_2 and wages rising to shift the short-run aggregate supply curve to SAS_2. Again, real GDP remains at £600 billion and the GDP deflator rises, as anticipated, to 157.

the actual price level – where the GDP deflator is 143. Between last year and this year, the GDP deflator increased from 130 to 143 and the economy experienced an inflation rate of 10 per cent, the same as the anticipated inflation rate.

What caused the inflation? The immediate answer is the anticipated and actual increase in aggregate demand. Because aggregate demand was *expected* to increase from AD_0 to AD_1, the short-run aggregate supply curve shifted up from SAS_0 to SAS_1. Because aggregate demand actually did increase by the amount that was expected, the actual aggregate demand curve shifted from AD_0 to AD_1. The combination of the anticipated and actual shifts of the aggregate demand curve to the right produced an increase in the price level that was anticipated.

Only if aggregate demand growth is correctly forecasted does the economy follow the course described in Fig. 30.7. If the expected growth rate of aggregate demand is different from its actual growth rate, the expected aggregate demand curve shifts by an amount different from the actual aggregate demand curve. The inflation rate departs from its expected level and, to some extent, there is unanticipated inflation. It is this type of inflation that we studied in the first part of this chapter.

We've seen that when inflation is anticipated, the economy remains on its long-run aggregate supply curve. Does this mean that an anticipated inflation has no costs?

The Costs of Anticipated Inflation

An anticipated inflation at a moderate rate – a few per cent a year – probably has a very small cost. But an anticipated inflation at a rapid rate is extremely costly.

Recall that inflation is the pace at which money loses its value. If money loses value at an anticipated rapid rate, it does not function well as a medium of exchange. In such a situation people try to avoid holding money. They spend their incomes as soon as they receive them, and firms pay out incomes – wages and dividends – as soon as they receive revenue from their sales. During the 1920s, when inflation in Germany reached *hyperinflation* levels, rates in excess of 50 per cent a month, wages were paid and spent twice in a single day! Also, at high anticipated inflation rates, people seek alternatives to money as a means of payment (for example, cigarettes or foreign currency). During the 1980s when inflation in Israel reached 1,000 per cent a year, the US dollar started to replace the

worthless shekel. Also, in times of anticipated inflation, barter becomes more common.

The activities that are encouraged by a high anticipated inflation rate use valuable time and other resources. Instead of people concentrating on the activities at which they have a comparative advantage, they find it more profitable to search for ways of avoiding the losses that inflation inflicts.

In terms of the aggregate demand–aggregate supply model, a rapid anticipated inflation shifts the *LAS* curve to the left – it decreases long-run aggregate supply. The faster the anticipated inflation rate, the further to the left the *LAS* curve shifts.

There are many examples of costly anticipated inflations around the world, especially in South American countries such as Argentina, Bolivia and Brazil, and in Russia and other East European countries. The closest that the United Kingdom has come to such a situation was in the 1970s and again in the early 1980s when the inflation rate exceeded 15 per cent a year.

Stopping an Anticipated Inflation

An anticipated inflation can be very stubborn and hard to stop. The monetary and fiscal policies that create inflation also create expectations of inflation that reinforce the inflationary effects of the policy. Also, people don't like to have their expectations disappointed, so if they anticipate a high inflation rate, they want a high inflation rate. Such was the situation in the United Kingdom in the 1970s and early 1980s.

REVIEW

D ecisions to work and produce are based on forecasts of inflation, but the returns to firms and workers depend on actual inflation. Wrong inflation forecasts impose costs on firms and workers. To minimize these costs, people make forecasts that use all available information. Such a forecast is called a *rational expectation*. To predict people's forecasts of the future price level, we use the aggregate demand–aggregate supply model. ◆ ◆ If people correctly anticipate changes in aggregate demand and aggregate supply, the result is anticipated inflation. If the anticipated inflation rate is moderate, real GDP is unchanged. But a rapid anticipated inflation diverts productive resources and decreases long-run aggregate supply. ◆

Inflation over the Business Cycle: the Phillips Curve

We've seen that a speedup in aggregate demand growth that is not fully anticipated increases both inflation and real GDP growth. It also decreases unemployment. Similarly, a slowdown in the growth rate of aggregate demand that is not fully anticipated slows down both inflation and real GDP growth and increases unemployment. We've also seen that a fully anticipated change in the growth rate of aggregate demand changes the inflation rate and has no effect on real GDP or unemployment. Finally, we've seen that a decrease in aggregate supply increases inflation and decreases real GDP growth. In this case, unemployment increases.

The aggregate demand–aggregate supply model that we have used to obtain these results gives predictions about the level of real GDP and the price level. Given these predictions, we can work out how unemployment and inflation have changed. But the aggregate demand–aggregate supply model does not place inflation and unemployment at the centre of the stage.

An alternative way of studying inflation and unemployment focuses directly on their joint movements and uses a relationship called the Phillips curve. The Phillips curve is so named because it was popularized by New Zealand economist A. W. Phillips when working at the London School of Economics in the 1950s. A **Phillips curve** is a curve showing the relationship between inflation and unemployment. There are two time frames for Phillips curves:

◆ The short-run Phillips curve
◆ The long-run Phillips curve

The Short-run Phillips Curve

The **short-run Phillips curve** is a curve showing the relationship between inflation and unemployment, holding constant:

1. The expected inflation rate
2. The natural rate of unemployment

Figure 30.8 shows a short-run Phillips curve *SRPC*. Suppose that the expected inflation rate is 10 per cent a year and the natural rate of unemployment is 6 per cent, point *a* in the figure. The short-run Phillips curve passes through this point. If the unemployment rate falls below its natural rate, inflation rises above its expected rate. This joint movement in the inflation rate and the unemployment rate is illustrated as a movement up the short-run Phillips curve from point *a* to point *b* in the figure. Similarly, if unemployment rises above the natural rate, inflation falls below its expected rate. In this case, there is movement down the short-run Phillips curve from point *a* to point *c*.

FIGURE 30.8

The Short-run Phillips Curve

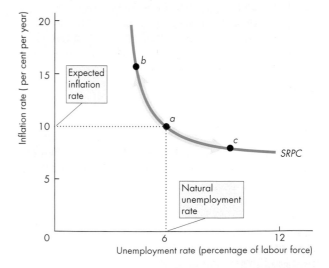

The short-run Phillips curve *SRPC* shows the relationship between inflation and unemployment at a given expected inflation rate and given natural unemployment. With an expected inflation rate of 10 per cent a year and a natural rate of unemployment of 6 per cent, the short-run Phillips curve passes through point *a*. An unanticipated increase in aggregate demand reduces unemployment and increases inflation – a movement up the short-run Phillips curve. An unanticipated decrease in aggregate demand increases unemployment and lowers inflation – a movement down the short-run Phillips curve.

This negative relationship between inflation and unemployment along the short-run Phillips curve is explained by the aggregate demand–aggregate supply model. Suppose that, initially, inflation is anticipated to be 10 per cent a year and unemployment is at its natural rate. This situation is illustrated by the aggregate demand–aggregate supply model in Fig. 30.7 and by the Phillips curve approach as point a in Fig. 30.8. Suppose that now an unanticipated increase in the growth of aggregate demand occurs. In Fig. 30.7 the aggregate demand curve shifts to the right more quickly than expected. Real GDP increases, the unemployment rate decreases, and the price level starts to increase at a rate faster than expected. The economy moves up the Phillips curve from point a to say point b in Fig. 30.8. If the unanticipated increase in aggregate demand is temporary, aggregate demand growth slows to its previous level. When it does so, the process is reversed and the economy moves back to point a in Fig. 30.8.

A similar story can be told to illustrate the effects of an unanticipated decrease in the growth of aggregate demand. In this case, an unanticipated slowdown in the growth of aggregate demand reduces inflation, slows real GDP growth and increases unemployment. The economy moves down the short-run Phillips curve from point a to say point c.

The Long-run Phillips Curve

The **long-run Phillips curve** is a curve showing the relationship between inflation and unemployment, when the actual inflation rate equals the expected inflation rate. The long-run Phillips curve is vertical at the natural rate of unemployment. It is shown in Fig. 30.9 as the vertical line *LRPC*.

If the expected inflation rate is 10 per cent a year, the short-run Phillips curve is $SRPC_0$. If the expected inflation rate falls to 8 per cent a year, the short-run Phillips curve shifts downward to $SRPC_1$. At points a and d, inflation is equal to its expected rate and unemployment is equal to its natural rate. The distance by which the short-run Phillips curve shifts downward when the expected inflation rate falls is equal to the change in the expected inflation rate. Points a and d lie on the long-run Phillips curve *LRPC*. This curve tells us that any inflation rate is possible at the natural rate of unemployment.

To see why the short-run Phillips curve shifts when the expected inflation rate changes let's do an experiment. The economy is at full employment and a fully anticipated inflation is raging at 10 per cent a year. The Bank of England and the government now begin a permanent attack on inflation by slowing money supply growth and cutting the government deficit. Aggregate demand growth slows down and the inflation rate falls to 8 per cent a year. At first, this decrease in inflation is unanticipated, so wages continue to rise at their original rate shifting the short-run aggregate supply curve to the left at the same pace as before. Real GDP falls and unemployment increases. In Fig. 30.9, the

FIGURE 30.9

The Short-run and Long-run Phillips Curves

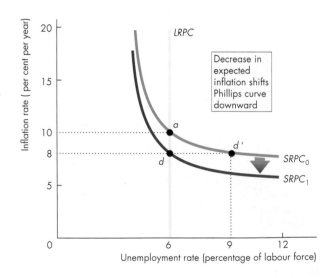

The long-run Phillips curve is *LRPC*, a vertical line at the natural rate of unemployment. A decrease in inflation expectations shifts the short-run Phillips curve down by the amount of the fall in the expected inflation rate. Here, when expected inflation falls from 10 per cent a year to 8 per cent a year, the short-run Phillips curve shifts from $SRPC_0$ to $SRPC_1$. The new short-run Phillips curve intersects the long-run Phillips curve at the new expected inflation rate at point d. With the original expected inflation rate (of 10 per cent), an inflation rate of 8 per cent a year would occur at an unemployment rate of 9 per cent, at point d'.

economy moves from point a to point d' on the short-run Phillips curve $SRPC_0$.

If the actual inflation rate remains steady at 8 per cent a year, eventually this rate will come to be expected. As this happens, wage growth slows down and the short-run aggregate supply curve shifts to the left less quickly. Eventually it shifts to the left at the same pace at which the aggregate demand curve is shifting to the right. The actual inflation rate equals the expected inflation rate and full employment is restored. Unemployment is back at its natural rate. In Fig. 30.9, the short-run Phillips curve has shifted from $SRPC_0$ to $SRPC_1$ and the economy is at point d.

Changes in the Natural Rate of Unemployment

The natural rate of unemployment changes for many reasons that are explained in Chapter 29 (pp. 837–845). A change in the natural rate of unemployment shifts both the short-run and the long-run Phillips curves. Such shifts are illustrated in Fig. 30.10. If the natural rate of unemployment increases from 6 per cent to 9 per cent, the long-run Phillips curve shifts from $LRPC_0$ to $LRPC_1$, and if expected inflation is constant at 10 per cent a year, the short-run Phillips curve shifts from $SRPC_0$ to $SRPC_1$. Because the expected inflation rate is constant, the short-run Phillips curve $SRPC_1$ intersects the long-run curve $LRPC_1$ (point e) at the same inflation rate as the short-run Phillips curve $SRPC_0$ intersects the long-run curve $LRPC_0$ (point a).

The Phillips Curve in the United Kingdom

Figure 30.11 shows the relationship between inflation and unemployment in the United Kingdom. Begin by looking at part (a), a scatter diagram of inflation and unemployment since 1968. Each dot in the figure represents the combination of inflation and unemployment for a particular year. As you can see, there does not appear to be any clear relationship between inflation and unemployment. We certainly cannot see a Phillips curve similar to that shown in Fig. 30.8.

But we can interpret the data in terms of a shifting short-run Phillips curve. Figure 30.11(b) provides such an interpretation. Two short-run Phillips curves appear in the figure.

During the late 1960s the natural rate of unem-

FIGURE 30.10

A Change in the Natural Rate of Unemployment

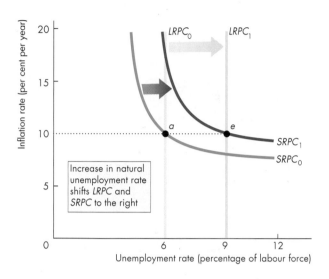

A change in the natural rate of unemployment shifts both the short-run and long-run Phillips curves. Here the natural rate of unemployment increases from 6 per cent to 9 per cent, and the two Phillips curves shift to the right to $SRPC_1$ and $LRPC_1$. The new long-run Phillips curve intersects the new short-run Phillips curve at the expected inflation rate – point e.

ployment was around 2 per cent and the expected inflation rate was about 4 per cent a year. The short-run Phillips curve of the late 1960s is not shown but it started to shift upward during the early 1970s and by 1974 it was $SRPC_0$. In this year, the natural unemployment rate was about 4 per cent and the expected inflation rate was 10 per cent a year. The short-run Phillips curve shifted upward in the late 1970s to $SRPC_1$ in 1980. Like 1974, these were years of extremely large oil price increases that had profound effects on both the natural rate of unemployment and the expected inflation rate. During the 1980s, the short-run Phillips curve shifted downward. By the early 1990s the Phillips curve had returned to $SRPC_0$. At this time, the expected inflation rate was similar to its early 1970s level, but the natural rate of unemployment remained high.

FIGURE 30.11

Phillips Curves in the United Kingdom

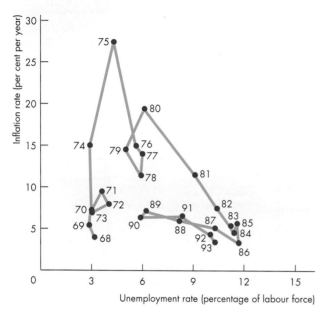

(a) The time sequence

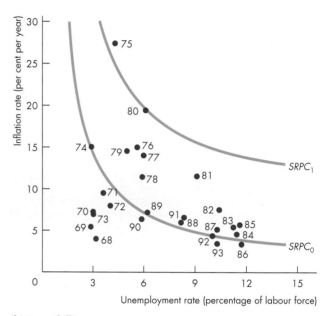

(b) Two Phillips curves

In part (a) each dot represents the combination of inflation and unemployment for a particular year in the United Kingdom. There is no clear relationship between the two variables. Part (b) interprets the data in terms of a shifting short-run Phillips curve. The short-run Phillips curve of the early 1970s to

$SRPC_0$. It shifted upward in the late 1970s and early 1980s to $SRPC_1$. The short-run Phillips curve shifts back down to $SRPC_0$. At this time, the expected inflation rate was similar to its early 1970s level but the natural rate of unemployment remained high.

REVIEW

An unanticipated increase in the inflation rate decreases unemployment and results in a movement up the short-run Phillips curve. An unanticipated decrease in the inflation rate increases unemployment and results in a movement down the short-run Phillips curve. A change in the expected inflation rate shifts the short-run Phillips curve (upward for an increase in inflation and downward for a decrease in inflation) by an amount equal to the change in the expected inflation rate. A change in the natural rate of unemployment shifts both the short-run and the long-run Phillips curve to the right for an increase in the natural rate and to the left for a decrease. The relationship between inflation and unemployment in the United Kingdom can be interpreted in terms of a shifting short-run Phillips curve. ◆

So far, we've studied the effects of inflation on real GDP, real wages, employment and unemployment. But inflation lowers the value of money and changes the real value of the amounts borrowed and repaid. As a result, interest rates are influenced by inflation. Let's see how.

Interest Rates and Inflation

There have been large fluctuations in interest rates in the United Kingdom in recent years. In the early 1960s, companies could raise long-term capital at interest rates of 5 per cent a year. By the end of the 1960s, that interest rate had climbed to 9 per cent a year. During the 1970s, the interest rates paid by firms for long-term loans fluctuated between 9 and 14 per cent a year. During the early 1980s, interest rates hit close to 15 per cent a year. They fell during the rest of the 1980s and by 1993 had returned to the levels of the late 1960s. Why have interest rates fluctuated so much and why were they so high during the late 1970s and early 1980s?

A major part of the answer to these questions is that the inflation rate also fluctuated and that interest rates fluctuated to compensate for the fall in the value of money. But the precise relationship between interest rates and inflation depends on whether inflation is anticipated or unanticipated. Let's begin by considering the effects of unanticipated inflation.

Interest Rates and Unanticipated Inflation

We'll work out the effects of inflation on interest rates by using Fig. 30.12. This figure is similar to Fig. 27.4 (p. 760) which explains the effects of the Bank of England's actions on interest rates.

Initially the economy is at full employment and there is no inflation and none is expected. The *real* quantity of money is £500 billion and the money supply curve is MS_0. The demand for money curve is MD_0 and the interest rate is 5 per cent a year. This interest rate is both the *nominal* interest rate and the *real* interest rate. To see why, recall that

Real interest rate = Nominal interest rate – Inflation rate.

Because the inflation rate is zero, the real and nominal interest rates are the same.

To get an inflation going, the Bank of England must increase the quantity of money. Suppose the Bank increases the quantity of money to £525 billion – a 5 per cent increase – so that the money supply curve shifts to the right to MS_1. The nominal interest rate falls to 4 per cent a year.

With a lower interest rate, aggregate planned expenditure increases and the aggregate demand

FIGURE 30.12

Money Growth, Inflation and the Interest Rate

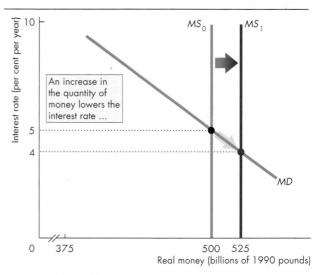

(a) Unanticipated increase in money

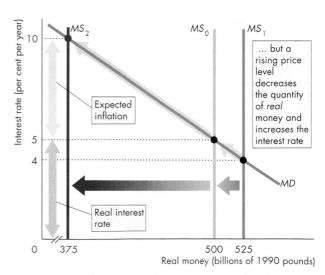

(b) Anticipated money growth

The demand for money curve is MD_0, the supply of money curve is MS_0 and the interest rate (*nominal* and *real*) is 5 per cent a year. The Bank of England increases the quantity of money and the money supply curve shifts to the right to MS_1. In part (a), the interest rate falls to 4 per cent. In part (b), as the price level rises, the quantity of real money decreases and the interest rate returns to its original level. If the Bank of England continues to increase the quantity of money and if people anticipate the resulting inflation, the price level continues to rise and the quantity of real money falls until the interest rate increases above its original level by an amount equal to the anticipated inflation rate.

curve shifts to the right. Both real GDP and the price level rise. The higher real GDP increases the demand for money (not shown in Fig. 30.12). The higher price level decreases the quantity of *real* money and the money supply curve shifts to the left. Both of these influences increase the interest rate.

With real GDP above its long-run level, wages begin to rise. As they do so, the short-run aggregate supply curve shifts to the left. The price level rises yet higher and real GDP decreases as the economy heads back towards full employment. When full employment is again restored, real GDP is back at its original level and the price level has increased by the same percentage as the money supply. Figure 30.12(b) shows the effects of these events in the money market. The quantity of real money is back at its original level of £500 billion and the interest rate is back at 5 per cent.

Interest Rates and Anticipated Inflation

If the Bank of England increases the quantity of money just once and then holds the quantity steady, the price level remains constant at its higher level and inflation returns to zero. But suppose the Bank continues to increase the quantity of money by 5 per cent a year and that people come to anticipate a resulting 5 per cent a year inflation. (To keep things simple, we are ignoring growing long-run aggregate supply.) In these circumstances, people are not willing to hold bonds at an interest rate of 5 per cent a year. Why not? Because the *real* interest rate has fallen.

People sell bonds and increase their demand for goods and services. As they do so, the price of bonds falls and the interest rate increases. At the same time, aggregate demand increases faster and the inflation rate speeds up to a rate that for a period exceeds the rate at which the quantity of money is increasing. The quantity of *real* money decreases further as the interest rate increases.

Only when interest rates have increased by enough to compensate bond holders for the antici-pated falling value of money is a long-run equilibrium restored. Such an equilibrium is shown in Fig. 30.12(b). When the real money supply has decreased to MS_2 and the interest rate has increased to 10 per cent, the *real* interest rate has returned to its original level of 5 per cent a year.

Thus an unanticipated increase in the money supply brings a fall in interest rates. An anticipated and ongoing increase in the money supply increas-es interest rates. The decrease in interest rates following an increase in the money supply is an immediate but temporary response. The increase in interest rates associated with an increase in the growth rate of the money supply is a long-run response.

The Effect of Unanticipated Inflation on Borrowers and Lenders

When inflation is unanticipated, the *real interest rate* falls and borrowers gain at the expense of lenders. You can appreciate this outcome by looking at the situation of Sue. Sue lends Joe £5,000 for one year at an interest rate of 5 per cent a year. After one year, Sue plans to buy a car that today costs £5,250. She will have the £5,250 she needs made up of the £250 of interest plus her original £5,000.

If there is no inflation, Sue can buy the car. But suppose that prices rise during the year and a car that cost £5,250 at the beginning of the year costs £5,500 at the end of the year. Sue can't afford to buy the car at that price. Actually, Sue is as far away from being able to buy the car as she was at the beginning of the year. She's got more money, but everything now costs more. Sue has *really* made no interest income at all; and the bank has *really* paid no interest. The *real interest rate* is zero.

Sue has lost £250 and Joe has profited by £250.

The Effect of Anticipated Inflation on Borrowers and Lenders

We've seen that when inflation is anticipated, the *nominal interest rate* increases by an amount equal to the inflation rate and the *real interest rate* remains constant. In this situation, inflation has no effect on borrowers and lenders. To see why, sup-pose that Sue (and all the other borrowers and lenders) anticipate that inflation is going to be 10 per cent a year.

If Sue anticipates a 5 per cent inflation rate, she will not be willing to lend Joe £5,000 at an interest rate of 5 per cent a year. In fact, if 5 per cent a year is the interest rate she (and other lenders) will accept when there is no inflation, then the interest rate they will accept when inflation is anticipated to be 5 per cent a year is 10 per cent a year. At the end of the year, Sue will have £5,000 and £500 in interest and so she has £5,500 with which to buy the car. Sue's interest of £500 can be thought of as a real interest of £250 and another £250 as compensation for the loss in the value of money. Sue *really* receives a 5 per cent interest rate, and that's what the borrower *really* pays. The *real interest rate* is unchanged and is 5 per cent, the same as with a zero (anticipated) inflation rate.

We've seen that an unanticipated inflation leads to a decrease in the real interest rate and that an anticipated inflation leads to an increase in the nominal interest rate and no change in the real interest rate. Therefore, the higher the anticipated inflation rate, the higher is the nominal interest rate. To the extent that inflation is in fact anticipated, interest rates and the inflation rate will move up and down together. Let's see if they do.

Inflation and Interest Rates in the United Kingdom

The relationship between nominal interest rates and the inflation rate in the United Kingdom is illustrated in Fig. 30.13. The interest rate measured on the vertical axis is that paid by the UK government on 3-month Treasury bills. Each point on the graph represents a year in recent macroeconomic history between 1968 and 1993. The blue line shows the relationship between the nominal interest rate and the inflation rate if the real interest rate is constant at 0.9 per cent a year, its actual average value in this period. As you can see, there is a positive relationship between the inflation rate and the interest rate, but it is not exact. As we have just seen, it is only *anticipated* inflation that influences interest rates. Thus only to the extent that a higher inflation rate is anticipated, does it result in higher interest rates.

In the late 1960s, both actual and expected inflation were moderate and so were nominal interest rates. In the early 1970s, inflation began to increase, but it was not expected to increase much and certainly not to persist. As a result, nominal interest rates did not rise very much at that time. From 1974 to 1976, there was a burst of unexpectedly high inflation. Interest rates increased somewhat but not by nearly as much as the inflation rate. During the

late 1970s and early 1980s, double-digit inflation came to be expected as an ongoing and highly persistent phenomenon. As a result, nominal interest rates increased to around 13 per cent a year. Then in 1982, 1983 and 1984, the inflation rate fell – at first unexpectedly. Interest rates began to fall but not nearly as quickly as the inflation rate. In the mid-1980s, interest rates remained high although inflation was moderate. They rose again in 1989 and 1990, mainly because the Bank of England was pursuing a disinflationary monetary policy, and then continued to fall into the 1990s.

The relationship between interest rates and the inflation rate is even more dramatically illustrated by international experience. For example, in recent years Chile has experienced an inflation rate of

---

FIGURE 30.13

Inflation and the Interest Rate

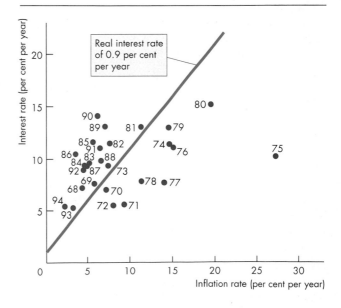

Other things remaining the same, the higher the expected inflation rate, the higher is the interest rate. A graph showing the relationship between interest rates and the actual inflation rate reveals that the influence of inflation on interest rates is a powerful one. Here, the interest rate is that paid by the government on 3-month Treasury bills. Each point represents a year between 1968 and 1993.

Source: Inflation rate: Fig. 22.1. Interest rate: *Bank of England Quarterly Review.*

Hyperinflation in Eastern Europe

FINANCIAL TIMES, 27 APRIL 1993

Hyperinflation threatens eastern European reform

George Graham

CENTRAL Europe and the former Soviet Union will need continued financial and technical help from the industrialised nations, if they are to stay on the path of economic reform, the IMF warns.

Most countries of central and eastern Europe have already adopted radical changes in economic policy, but the course of reform faces considerable strains from large government budget deficits and from the threat of hyperinflation.

'The risk of hyperinflation is now the major threat to continued reform in the former Soviet Union. High and accelerating inflation has already caused massive capital flight and, if unchecked, will eventually destroy the price system and make further economic reform virtually impossible,' the report warns.

The IMF's economists have revised their growth forecasts for both central Europe and the former Soviet Union sharply downwards since their last projections six months ago.

Even so, they see the severe economic contraction experienced in central Europe in 1991 and 1992 slowing down this year, with growth resuming in 1994.

Output is still expected to contract by 11.8 per cent in the former Soviet Union this year, and by 3.5 per cent in 1994.

'But, if macroeconomic stability can be achieved and if the economic reform programmes are followed through, most of the countries in the former Soviet Union could experience sharply falling inflation during 1993 and economic turnaround as early as the middle of the decade,' the report says.

The IMF warns that government budgets are still showing considerable strains in central Europe because of the dramatic decline in tax revenues. Albania, Bulgaria and the former Yugoslavia all showed budget deficits in excess of 10 per cent of gross domestic product last year.

In the former Soviet Union, the republics of Armenia, Georgia and Ukraine all ran government deficits in excess of 30 per cent of GDP.

Monetisation of these deficits, with excessive credit expansion by the central banks and the explosive growth of inter-enterprise arrears, are the main factors behind inflation, the report warns.

© The Financial Times. Reprinted with permission.

The countries of Central and Eastern Europe are implementing economic reforms to become market-based economies.

The future of these reforms is threatened by the possibility of hyperinflation.

This inflation has come from central banks expanding credit very quickly and from the large increase in government deficits.

These reforming countries have also experienced a significant fall in output.

If, however, the governments see the reform process through, inflation will fall and economic turnaround should come within the next two to three years.

Since the fall of communism in 1989, the new governments of the former Soviet bloc countries have undertaken major reforms of their economies.

These changes have led to a number of problems that have increased inflationary pressures.

Government budget deficits have deteriorated dramatically, principally because of a decline in tax revenues. The main sources of these revenues were various taxes on enterprises.

Governments have monetized, or funded, these deficits by such means as issuing bonds. This increases inflation by increasing the money supply.

Central banks have granted large amounts of credit. This has increased the money supply and hence inflation.

The granting of more credit has been a particular problem in Russia, where the politicians have tried to achieve macroeconomic stability by tight economic policies.

The governor of the Russian central bank, however, is independent of parliament and has chosen to make more credit available, which has undermined attempts to achieve economic stabilization.

Enterprises have increasingly needed to borrow from banks in order to remain in business because of delays in payment from other enterprises. This has also resulted in an increase in the money supply.

The fear of the International Monetary Fund (IMF) is that if this inflationary growth is allowed to continue, the reforms themselves could be threatened.

If budget deficits are allowed to build up, governments may be less inclined to restrain inflation. Inflation can act as a tax which could help offset the general decline in government tax revenues and reduce the value of the deficit.

Hyperinflation would result in a dramatic lowering of the value of financial assets and thus lead to capital flight, as asset holders would be inclined to move their assets to other countries with stable economies.

Although output in the economy has fallen, the government must maintain downward pressure on inflation in order to sustain and complete the reform process.

In the figure, increases in the money supply shift the *AD* curve to the right. Wage rises and a contraction of the economy's production function shift the *SAS* curve to the left.

The figures show how prices have risen and net material product (NMP – the variable East European countries used instead of GDP) has fallen from 1990 to 1992.

Growth in the money supply needs to be restrained in order to limit the rightward shift of the *AD* curve. This would help limit pressure on wage levels, hence the leftward shift of the *SAS* curve.

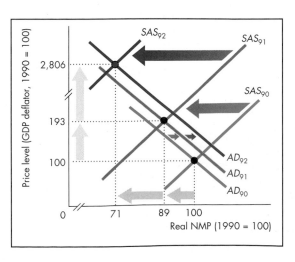

around 30 per cent a year with nominal interest rates of about 40 per cent a year. Brazil has experienced inflation rates of more than 200 per cent a year with nominal interest rates also above 200 per cent a year. At the other extreme, such countries as Japan and Belgium have low inflation and low nominal interest rates.

REVIEW

An unanticipated inflation results in a fall in the real interest rate. An anticipated inflation results in an increase in the nominal interest rate and no change in the real interest rate. If most changes in the inflation rate are anticipated, the inflation rate and interest rates will move up and down together. This relationship is present in the United Kingdom data. ◆

The Politics of Inflation

We noted at the beginning of this chapter that inflation has plagued nations over many centuries, from the Roman empire to modern Russia. (There are examples of inflation from even earlier times going back to the earliest civilizations.) What are the deeper sources of inflation that are common to all these vastly different societies? The answer lies in the political situation. There are three main political sources of inflation. They are:

◆ Inflation tax
◆ Contest for income shares
◆ Errors in forecasting the natural unemployment rate

Let's look at each of these sources.

Inflation Tax

Inflation is not a tax in the usual sense. Governments don't pass inflation tax laws like income tax and VAT laws. But inflation works just like a tax. One way in which a government can finance its expenditure is by selling bonds to the central bank. If the UK government sells bonds to the Bank of England, those bonds are paid for with new money – with an increase in the monetary base. When the government finances its expenditure in this way, the quantity of money increases. So the government gets resources from inflation just as if it had increased taxes. And the holders of money pay this tax to the government. They do so because the real value of their money holdings decrease at a rate equal to the inflation rate.

Inflation is not used as a major source of tax revenue in the United Kingdom. But in some countries it is. The closing years of the Roman empire and the transition years to a market economy in Russia and Eastern Europe are examples. In the case of the Roman empire, the empire had grown beyond its capacity to administer the collection of taxes on a scale sufficient to cover the expenditures of the government. In the case of Russia, the traditional source of government revenue was from state-owned enterprises. In the transition to a market economy, government revenue from these enterprises dried up but expenditure commitments did not decline in line with this loss of revenue. In both cases, the inflation was used to finance expenditures. Reading Between the Lines on pp. 870–871 considers further the situation in Russia.

As a general rule, the inflation tax is used when conventional revenue sources are insufficient to cover expenditures and the larger the revenue shortfall, the larger is the inflation tax and the inflation rate.

Contest for Income Shares

Another possible political source of inflation is a contest among various groups for an increased share of the Gross Domestic Product. Suppose that one group with increased monopoly power over some factor of production exercises its power by increasing the price of the factor. The group might be a large trade union or an international cartel that controls a natural resource.

The initial effect of the factor price increase is stagflation. If the central bank responds with an increase in the money supply, prices rise, the monopoly's gain disappears, and the economy returns to full employment but at a higher price level. If the monopoly repeats its action, inflation ensues.

Inflation from this source will arise when there is a lack of consensus about the appropriate distribution of income and when there are changes in the degree of monopoly power of the owners of factors of production. This source of inflation probably occurs only extremely rarely.

Errors in Forecasting the Natural Unemployment Rate

One objective of fiscal and monetary policy is to stabilize aggregate demand and keep the economy close to full employment. If demand increases too quickly, the economy overheats and inflation increases. If demand increases too slowly, recession occurs and inflation declines.

In judging the appropriate level of aggregate demand, the government and the Bank of England must make a judgement about long-run aggregate supply and the natural rate of unemployment. No one knows what the natural rate is, and its level must be estimated from the current state of the economy. When the natural rate of unemployment increases – and long-run aggregate supply grows at a slower rate – and when this change is not foreseen, aggregate demand grows too rapidly and the inflation rate increases. When the natural rate of unemployment decreases – and long-run aggregate supply grows at a faster rate – and when this change is not foreseen, aggregate demand grows too slowly and the inflation rate decreases.

This source of changes in the inflation rate possibly explains most of the *changes* in the inflation rate in the United Kingdom and other countries during the past 30 years.

R E V I E W

Inflation stems from the political situation. Inflation is a source of government revenue – inflation is a tax. When conventional tax sources are inadequate, the inflation tax is used. Inflation could also arise as the outcome of a contest for bigger income shares among groups with some monopoly power. But changes in inflation in the United Kingdom and other countries have possibly resulted from changes in the natural unemployment rate – and changes in long-run aggregate supply – that could not be foreseen and that resulted in fiscal and monetary policies that were seen after the event to be inappropriate. ◆

◆ ◆ ◆ ◆ We have now completed our study of inflation and the relationships between the inflation rate, the unemployment rate and the interest rate. Our next task, which we'll pursue in Chapter 31, is to see how the aggregate demand–aggregate supply model that we have used to study inflation also helps us to explore and interpret fluctuations in real GDP and explain recessions and depressions.

S U M M A R Y

Inflation and the Price Level

Inflation is a process of persistently rising prices. The price level rises when the inflation rate is positive and falls when the inflation rate is negative. The price level rises *more quickly* when the inflation rate *increases* and *more slowly* when the inflation rate *decreases*. Inflation can result from either rising aggregate demand or falling aggregate supply. The consequences of inflation depend on which of these sources it springs from and whether it is *anticipated* or *unanticipated*. (p. 852)

Demand–Pull Inflation

Demand–pull inflation arises from increasing aggregate demand. Its origin can be any of the factors that shift the aggregate demand curve to the right. The main such factors are an increasing money supply, increasing government purchases of goods and services, and rising prices in the rest of the world. When the aggregate demand curve shifts to the right, other things remaining the same, both real GDP and the GDP deflator increase and unemployment falls. With a shortage of labour, wages begin to increase and the short-run aggregate supply curve shifts to the left, raising the GDP deflator still more and decreasing real GDP.

If aggregate demand continues to increase, the aggregate demand curve keeps shifting to the right and the price level keeps on rising. Wages respond, aggregate demand increases again, and a price–wage inflation spiral ensues. (pp. 852–855)

Supply Inflation and Stagflation

Cost–push inflation can result from any factor that decreases aggregate supply, but the main such factors are increasing wage rates and increasing prices of key raw materials. These sources of a decreasing aggregate supply bring increasing costs that shift the short-run aggregate supply curve to the left. Firms decrease the quantity of labour employed and cut back production. Real GDP declines and the price level rises. If no action is taken to increase aggregate demand, the economy remains below full employment until the initial price increase that triggered the stagflation is reversed.

Action by the Bank of England or the government to restore full employment (an increase in the money supply or in government purchases of goods and services or a tax cut) increases aggregate demand and shifts the aggregate demand curve to the right, resulting in a yet higher price level and higher real GDP. If the original source of cost–push inflation is still present, costs rise again and the short-run aggregate supply curve shifts to the left again. If the Bank of England or the government respond again with a further increase in aggregate demand, the price level rises even higher. Inflation proceeds at a rate determined by the cost–push forces. (pp.855–857)

Anticipating Inflation

The decisions made by firms and households to produce and work are based on forecasts of inflation. But the actual levels of real GDP, real wage and employment depend on actual inflation. Errors in forecasting inflation are costly and people have an incentive to anticipate inflation as accurately as possible.

Forecasters use data and statistical models to generate expectations and economists predict people's forecasts by using the rational expectations hypothesis – the hypothesis that inflation forecasts are made by using the aggregate demand–aggregate supply model together with all the available information on the positions of the aggregate demand and aggregate supply curves.

When changes in aggregate demand are correctly anticipated, inflation is anticipated, and, if its rate is moderate, it does not affect real GDP, real wages, or employment. A rapid anticipated inflation decreases long-run aggregate supply, real wages, and employment. (pp. 857–863)

Inflation over the Business Cycle: the Phillips Curve

Phillips curves describe the relationships between inflation and unemployment. The short-run Phillips curve shows the relationship between inflation and unemployment, holding constant the expected inflation rate and the natural rate of unemployment. The long-run Phillips curve shows the relationship between inflation and unemployment when the actual inflation rate equals the expected inflation rate. The short-run Phillips curve slopes downward – the lower the unemployment rate, the higher is the inflation rate, other things remaining the same. The long-run Phillips curve is vertical at the natural rate of unemployment – the natural rate hypothesis.

Changes in aggregate demand, with a constant expected inflation rate and natural rate of unemployment, bring movements along the short-run Phillips curve. Changes in expected inflation bring shifts in the short-run Phillips curve. Changes in the natural rate of unemployment bring shifts in both the short-run and long-run Phillips curves.

There is no clear relationship between inflation and unemployment in the United Kingdom, but the joint movements in those variables can be interpreted in terms of a shifting short-run Phillips curve. (pp. 863–866)

Interest Rates and Inflation

Expectations of inflation affect nominal interest rates. The higher the expected inflation rate, the higher is the nominal interest rate. Borrowers will willingly pay more and lenders will successfully demand more, as the anticipated inflation rate rises. Borrowing and lending and asset-holding plans are made consistent with each other by adjustments in the real interest rate – the difference between the nominal interest rate and the expected inflation rate. (pp. 867–872)

The Politics of Inflation

Inflation is one source of revenue for the government – it is a tax – and its rate increases when the government has financial needs that exceed its ability to collect income taxes and sales taxes. Inflation can also arise from a contest for a bigger income share among groups with monopoly power. These sources of inflation are uncommon in the major industrial countries. A possible source of inflation in the United Kingdom and other countries in recent years is errors in forecasting the natural unemployment rate. No one knows the magnitude of the natural unemployment rate, and its level must be estimated from the current state of the economy. Unforeseen increases in the natural rate of unemployment bring an increase in the inflation rate when policy makers mistakenly try to lower unemployment by stimulating aggregate demand. There is some evidence that these mistakes of the 1970s and 1980s are leading to a tougher attitude towards inflation and a more relaxed attitude towards unemployment in the 1990s. (pp. 872–873)

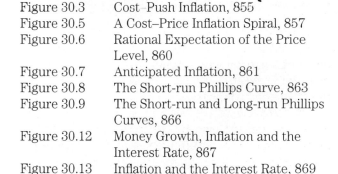

KEY ELEMENTS

REVIEW QUESTIONS

1   Distinguish between the price level and the inflation rate.

2   Distinguish between anticipated and unanticipated inflation.

3   Distinguish between demand–pull inflation and cost–push inflation.

4   Explain how a price–cost inflation spiral occurs.

5   Explain how a cost–price inflation spiral occurs.

6   Why are wrong inflation expectations costly? Suggest some of the losses that an individual would suffer in labour markets and in asset markets.

7   What is a rational expectation? Explain the two features of a rational expectation.

8   What is the rational expectation of the price in:
    a The short run?

    b The long run?

9   Explain how anticipated inflation arises.

10 What are the main factors leading to changes in aggregate demand that produce ongoing and persistent inflation?

11 How does a change in the quantity of money influence the interest rate:
    a When it changes once and is unanticipated?
    b When its change is ongoing and anticipated?

12 What is the connection between expected inflation and nominal interest rates?

13 What does the short-run Phillips curve show?

14 What does the long-run Phillips curve show?

15 What have been the main shifts in the short-run Phillips curve in the United Kingdom during the 1970s, 1980s and 1990s?

PROBLEMS

1 Work out the effects on the price level of the following unexpected events:
  a An increase in the money supply
  b An increase in government purchases of goods and services
  c An increase in income taxes
  d An increase in investment demand
  e An increase in the wage rate
  f An increase in labour productivity

2 Work out the effects on the price level of the same events listed in Problem 1 when they are correctly anticipated.

3 An economy's long-run aggregate supply is £400 billion, and it has the following expected aggregate demand and short-run aggregate supply curves:

Price level (GDP deflator)	Expected GDP demanded (billions of 1990 pounds)	Expected GDP supplied (billions of 1990 pounds)
80	5	1
100	4	3
130	3	5
150	2	7

  a What is the expected price level?
  b What is expected real GDP?
  c Are wages expected to be fixed?

4 In the economy of Problem 3, the expected price level increases to 130.
  a What is the new *SAS* curve in the short run when wages are fixed?
  b What is the new *SAS* curve in the long run when wages are flexible?
  c In parts (a) and (b) is real GDP expected to be above or below full employment?

5 In 1994, the expected aggregate demand schedule for 1995 is as follows:

Price level (GDP deflator)	Expected real GDP demanded (billions of 1990 pounds)
130	400
121	390
122	380
123	370
124	360

In 1994, the long-run real GDP is £380 billion

and the real GDP expected for 1995 is £390 billion. Calculate the 1994 rational expectation of the price level for 1995 if the money wage rate
  a Is not expected to change
  b Is expected to change to its long-run equilibrium level

6 The economy in Problem 3 has the following short-run aggregate supply schedule:

Price level (GDP deflator)	Real GDP supplied (billions of 1990 pounds)
130	320
121	350
122	380
123	410
124	440

  a Under what conditions is this short-run aggregate supply schedule consistent with your answer to Problem 3?
  b Calculate the actual and expected inflation rate if the aggregate demand curve is expected to shift upward by 10 per cent and if it actually does shift upward by that amount.

7 An economy has a natural rate of unemployment of 4 per cent when its expected inflation rate is 6 per cent. Its inflation and unemployment history is as follows:

Inflation rate (per cent per year)	Unemployment rate (percentage of the labour force)
10	2
8	3
6	4
4	5
2	6

  a Draw a diagram of this economy's short-run and long-run Phillips curves.
  b If the actual inflation rate rises from 6 per cent a year to 8 per cent a year, what is the change in the unemployment rate? Explain why it occurs.
  c If the natural rate of unemployment rises to 5 per cent, what is the change in the unemployment rate? Explain why it occurs.
  d Go back to part (a). If the expected inflation rate falls to 4 per cent a year, what is the change in the unemployment rate? Explain why it occurs.

CHAPTER 31

RECESSIONS
AND
DEPRESSIONS

After studying this chapter you will be able to:

◆ Describe the origins of the United Kingdom's 1980–1981 and 1991–1992 recessions

◆ Describe the course of interest rates and expenditure as the economy contracts

◆ Describe the labour market in a recession

◆ Compare and contrast the flexible and sticky wage theories of the labour market in a recession

◆ Describe the depressed UK economy of the 1920s and the Great Depression between 1929 and 1933

◆ Compare the economy of the 1930s with that of today and assess the likelihood of another major depression

I N OCTOBER 1929, ALMOST WITHOUT WARNING, CAME AN UNPRECEDENTED STOCK market crash. Overnight, the values of stocks and shares trading in New York, London, Paris and Berlin fell by up to 30 per cent. In the next four years, there followed the worst depression in recorded history. By 1933, world output had fallen to only two-thirds of its 1929 level. Compared with some countries the United Kingdom fared relatively well. Even so, output fell by 7 per cent before reaching the trough in 1931, and with this fall there came a rise in unemployment to over 20 per cent and a fall in prices of around 10 per cent. What caused the Great Depression? ◆ ◆ In October 1987, stock markets in the United Kingdom and throughout the world crashed. This severe and widespread stock market crash caused some commentators to draw parallels between 1987 and 1929. Are there similar forces at work today that might bring about a Great Depression like that of the 1930s? ◆ ◆ Although they

What Goes Up Must Come Down

were not in the same league as the Great Depression, the United Kingdom experienced severe recessions in 1980–1981 and 1991–1992. In 1981 real GDP was 3.2 per cent below the 1979 level and unemployment exceeded 8 per cent. Unemployment stayed high for a long time, peaking at over 11 per cent in 1986. In 1992 real GDP was 2.7 per cent below the 1990 level, and unemployment peaked in 1993 at 11 per cent. What caused the 1980–1981 and 1991–1992 recessions? Are all recessions triggered in the same way or is there a variety of causes?

◆ ◆ ◆ ◆ In this chapter we use the macroeconomic tools that we have studied in the previous chapters to explain economic contractions. We'll unravel some of the mysteries of recession and depression and assess the likelihood of a serious depression such as that of the 1930s occurring again.

Two Recent Recessions

The most severe post-war recessions in the United Kingdom occurred in 1980–1981 and 1991–1992. We'll begin by examining the forces that initiated these recessions. Then we'll examine the mechanisms at work during these episodes of macro-economic history, paying special attention to the labour market and to the central disagreement among economists about how the labour market works during an economic contraction.

The Origin of the 1980–1981 Recession

The UK economy had a fairly good year in 1979. Real GDP grew by almost 3 per cent and unemployment held steady at about 4 per cent. But there was a black cloud hanging over the economy. That cloud was the continuation of two-digit inflation. Indeed by 1979 inflation was running at nearly 17 per cent. The new government of Margaret Thatcher was very concerned about this inflation and in 1980 it introduced a policy package termed the 'medium term financial strategy' which was aimed at sharply reducing the rate of growth of the money supply and thereby sharply reducing the rate of inflation. But inflation had become so deeply ingrained that few people had confidence in the likely success of the anti-inflation war that started in 1980. What happened by 1981 as the anti-inflation policies of the government came into conflict with stubborn inflationary expectations?

The answer is that there was a recession. The origin of that recession and its magnitude are illustrated in Fig. 31.1. Aggregate demand and short-run aggregate supply in 1979 are shown by AD_{79} and SAS_{79}. Real GDP was £433 billion and the GDP deflator was 46. With a widespread expectation that inflation was going to continue at around 17 per cent a year, wages increased, shifting the short-run aggregate supply curve to the left to SAS_{81}. Over the two years to 1981, aggregate demand was expected to continue increasing at the same pace as it had in 1979, and the expected aggregate demand curve for 1981 was EAD_{81}. If expectations had been correct, the economy would have moved to the intersection of SAS_{81} and EAD_{81}, with real GDP continuing to grow at its trend rate and inflation remaining at around 17 per cent a year.

Events did not turn out as expected. Two things occurred which resulted in the actual level of

FIGURE 31.1

The 1980–1981 Recession in the United Kingdom

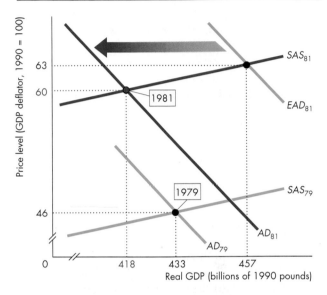

In 1979, the UK economy was on its aggregate demand curve AD_{79} and its short-run aggregate supply curve SAS_{79}, with real GDP at £433 billion (in 1990 pounds) and the GDP deflator at 46 (with 1990 = 100). Inflation was raging and wages were increasing rapidly to reflect the strong inflationary expectations. By 1981 the short-run aggregate supply curve shifted to SAS_{81}. If aggregate demand had increased steadily, as it was expected to do, the aggregate demand curve would have moved to EAD_{81} and the economy would have experienced an increase in real GDP and inflation at around 17 per cent a year. But demand increased by less than expected. The government slowed down money growth and forced interest rates up. Also the growth of North Sea oil output raised the value of sterling and so reduced the demand for exports and for import substitutes. So the aggregate demand curve shifted only to AD_{81}. This shift combined with the shift in aggregate supply to SAS_{81} to put the economy into recession. Real GDP fell and inflation moderated.

aggregate demand in 1981 being much lower than expected. First, the government applied a severe dose of monetary restraint. Interest rates were allowed to rise and this slowed down the pace of investment, which fell by 25 per cent between 1979 and 1981, and it also had some downward effect on the level of consumer spending. Second, the value of sterling rose sharply on the foreign exchange markets. There were two reasons for this rise. One reason was the high interest rates which put upward pressure on the exchange rate because they meant that the United Kingdom was an attractive place to hold money and securities. The other reason was the increasing output of North Sea oil which meant that the United Kingdom was importing far less oil. The increased value of sterling in foreign exchange markets had two effects. First, foreign citizens decided to buy fewer UK-made products, so demand for UK exports fell. Second, UK citizens decided to buy fewer home-produced products – such as Rovers – and instead buy more foreign products – such as BMWs – as these now cost fewer pounds to buy. So the demand for UK products which were in competition with imports fell.

These factors meant that the aggregate demand curve moved only to AD_{81} instead of shifting to EAD_{81}. Because aggregate demand increased more slowly than the pace at which short-run aggregate supply decreased, the economy moved into recession. Real GDP fell to £418 billion and the inflation rate began to slow down. The situation was really quite simple. The SAS curve shifted by an amount based on expectations of a continuation of high inflation. The AD curve shifted by much less than was expected. The result was a continuation of inflation, but at a lower pace than expected, together with a fall in aggregate output.

The Origin of the 1991–1992 Recession

One of the most striking aspects of the 1991–1992 recession was that it arose quite suddenly and was much more severe than anyone predicted at the start. Its origins may lie partly in memories of the 1980–1981 recession. Following that recession, unemployment peaked in mid-1986 at 11 per cent and stayed almost as high for three and a half years. It then fell very gradually until 1990 when it briefly dipped below 6 per cent.

Remember that a major contributory factor in the 1981 recession was the tight monetary policy designed to reduce inflation. Inflation actually started to fall quite quickly. Retail prices, for instance, had risen by 21 per cent between mid-1979 and mid-1980, but they rose by under 4 per cent between mid-1982 and mid-1983. However, prices then began to rise a little more quickly, just enough for the government to decide to maintain a fairly tight monetary policy. This helped reduce the rate at which the economy recovered in the mid-1980s.

FIGURE 31.2

The 1990–1992 Recession in the United Kingdom

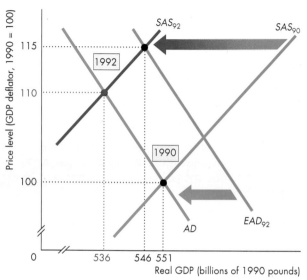

In 1990, the UK economy was on its aggregate demand curve AD and its short-run aggregate supply curve SAS_{90}, with real GDP at £551 billion (in 1990 pounds) and the GDP deflator at 100 (with 1990 = 100). Inflation was over 10 per cent and wages were increasing rapidly to reflect high inflationary expectations. The short-run aggregate supply curve shifted upward and by 1992 it was SAS_{92}. Aggregate demand was expected to rise moderately. If it had done so, the aggregate demand curve would have moved to EAD_{92} and the economy would have experienced a slight fall in real GDP and inflation at around 7 per cent per year. But demand did not increase. A modest rise in interest rates created a collapse in business confidence and investment fell sharply. This fall was offset by slight increases in the other components of aggregate demand so that aggregate demand stayed put at AD. The combination of continuing high inflation expectations, shifting the SAS curve to the left, and static aggregate demand put the economy into recession. Real GDP dropped back and inflation fell sharply.

By 1989 inflation had risen to around 8 per cent, and by 1990 it was back into double figures. This was a cruel blow for a Conservative government that was so proud of having curbed inflation once, so the government decided to have another dose of tight monetary policy. However, as interest rates were already high, the increase in interest rates was noticeably more moderate than it had been in the early 1980s, and indeed by 1991 interest rates were allowed to fall once again.

We can see what happened to output and prices between 1990 and 1992 by looking at Fig. 31.2. Aggregate demand and short-run aggregate supply in 1990 are shown by AD and SAS_{90}. Real GDP was £551 billion (in 1990 pounds) and the GDP deflator was 100 (with 1990 = 100). It seems that people expected inflation to continue at around 10 per cent so wages increased, shifting the short-run aggregate supply curve to the left to SAS_{92}. Over the two years to 1992, aggregate demand was expected to increase slightly, the general trend of increases in demand being more than enough to offset any small fall in investment resulting from the modest rise in interest rates. So the expected aggregate demand curve for 1992 was EAD_{92}. If expectations about aggregate demand had been correct, the economy would have moved to the intersection of SAS_{92} and EAD_{92} with real GDP around £546 billion, a little lower than in 1990, and the price level at around 115, indicating average inflation of around 7 per cent per year.

As it happened, investment fell sufficiently to match the increases in the other components of aggregate demand. So aggregate demand was static and the economy settled at the intersection of the new SAS_{92} curve and the original AD curves. Real GDP had fallen to £536 billion while the price level was 110, indicating inflation of under 5 per cent per year. What was surprising was that the modest rise in interest rates had

such a large impact on aggregate demand. This impact was felt almost entirely by investment which fell by over 13 per cent in 1991. It seems that businesses anticipated there would be another long period of high interest rates, restrained demand and low profits, and it was this expectation of low profits combined with a modest rise in interest rates that led to such a sharp downturn in investment.

Apart from the government's desire to beat inflation, there was another reason why by 1992 people expected a long period of high interest rates. In that year the government took sterling into the EU's Exchange Rate Mechanism (ERM). With high interest rates, sterling had a high value, and it would be difficult to maintain this value if interest rates were allowed to drop back, even though a rapid decline in inflation rates during 1992 made it less necessary to restrain aggregate demand. However, by 1993 sterling was taken out of the ERM, and inflation was below 5 per cent. This combination of events enabled interest rates to be brought down, so that gradually the economy moved out of recession and unemployment began to fall – see the cartoon.

While the causes of recessions vary a little from one to another, they all tend to have some common features. Let's take a closer look at them beginning with the behaviour of interest rates.

Money and Interest Rates in Recessions

The markets in which things begin to happen first and move fastest are the markets for money and securities. At the onset of a recession interest rates may rise or fall, but once the recession is under way, interest rates fall, and by the time real GDP has reached its trough, interest rates have often fallen to levels lower than those at the onset of the recession. Why do interest rates behave in this manner? To find out, let's study the money market in the 1991–1992 recession.

Figure 31.3 tells the story from 1990 to 1992. The supply of real money in 1990 was about £457 billion so the supply curve of real money was that labelled MS_{90}. The demand curve for real money in 1990 was MD_{90}. Interest rates in 1990 were determined at the intersection point of MD_{90} and MS_{90} and were about 15 per cent a year. Over the next two years, the worsening recession produced falls in real GDP and subsequent falls in the demand curve for real money to MD_{91} and then MD_{92}. The Bank of England exercised modest restraint on the growth of nominal M4

© Ron Tundberg

FIGURE 31.3

Interest Rates and Money in the 1991–1992 Recession

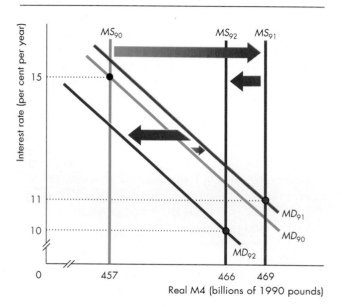

As the economy moves towards the trough of a recession, interest rates always fall. The chief reason for this is that as real GDP falls, so does the demand for money. The figure illustrates this for the 1991–1992 recession. In mid-1990, interest rates were 15 per cent – at the intersection of the MS_{90} and MD_{90} curves. In each of the following two years, the demand for money decreased as real GDP and incomes decreased. The new curves are shown by MD_{91} and MD_{92}. The real money supply rose quite sharply in 1991, to MS_{91}, as the Bank of England allowed the money supply to rise faster than prices, but the Bank exercised more restraint in 1992 and the supply of real money fell back to MS_{92}. Interest rates fell to 11 per cent in 1991 and 10 per cent in 1992.

between 1990 and 1991, and it grew more rapidly than prices which were already rising more slowly than in 1991. So the supply curve of real money shifted to the right to MS_{91}, which intersected MD_{91} at an interest rate of 11 per cent. Between 1991 and 1992, the supply of nominal money rose very little so that, allowing for only moderate inflation, there was a fall in the supply of real money and the supply curve of real money shifted to the left to MS_{92}, which intersected MD_{92} at an interest rate of 10 per cent. Reading Between the Lines on pp. 892–893 considers these effects for Germany.

Looking at Fig. 31.3, you can see that the supply of real money ended up higher than it was to begin with. But the demand for real money fell, owing to the fall in real GDP and real incomes, and it is this fall which ensured that interest rates ended up lower than they were at the onset of the recession. Changes in interest rates cause changes in aggregate expenditure. So let's look more closely at how aggregate expenditure changed in the 1991–1992 recession.

Expenditure in Recessions

When the economy is in a recession, real GDP falls. As real GDP equals real aggregate expenditure so real aggregate expenditure also falls. The main component of aggregate expenditure that falls is investment. Indeed we have already noted that investment dropped sharply in 1991. Why is there always a sharp drop in investment?

One reason why investment falls is that in the early stages of a recession there is usually an increase in real interest rates, that is (approximately) the difference between the nominal interest rate and the expected inflation rate, and this increase in real interest rates raises the opportunity cost of buying new capital equipment. We have said that nominal interest rates may rise or fall as an economy moves into recession, so why do real interest rates usually increase at such a time? The reason is that the inflation rate begins to fall as an economy moves into recession. If nominal interest rates rise while the inflation rate falls, then there will be a sharp rise in real interest rates. On the other hand, if nominal interest rates fall – as they did in 1991 – while the rate of inflation falls, then in principle real interest rates might rise, stay the same or fall. But in practice any fall in nominal interest rates is usually less than the fall in the inflation rate, so once again real interest rates still tend to rise, and this happened in 1991.

Another reason why the onset of a recession triggers a fall in investment is that expectations of falling output lead to a downward revision of profit expectations which dampens investment spending. We saw that this was specially important in the 1991–1992 recession.

A decrease in investment has two effects. First, it decreases aggregate expenditure and aggregate demand. Second, it slows down the growth of aggregate supply. The effects on aggregate supply occur partly because the slowdown in investment results in the capital stock growing less quickly and partly because the slowdown in investment reduces the pace of innovation of new technologies. But it is the effect of decreased investment on aggregate demand that dominates.

One of the main reasons people why fear a recession is because it is associated with a high unemployment rate. What happens in the labour market during a recession? Why does unemployment increase during a recession? Let's now examine these questions.

The Labour Market in Recession

For illustrative purposes, we'll examine the labour market in the 1980–1981 recession. We take this recession because it eventually led to the highest level of unemployment since the pre-World War II peak. Figure 31.4 provides a summary and analysis of the main events. The demand curve for labour in 1979 was LD_{79}. By 1981 the demand for labour had increased to LD_{81}. The main forces leading to this increased demand were the accumulation of capital and technological change.

While the demand for labour increased, there was a negligible change in the supply of labour because the population of working age was fairly constant. Thus the supply of labour stayed as shown by LS. But how were the actual levels of employment and wages determined in the labour market?

There is controversy about how the labour market works and about its ability to act as a coordination mechanism to bring about an equality between the quantities of labour demanded and supplied. Let's see how we can interpret the events occurring in the UK labour market in 1979–1981, using two theories of the labour market – the sticky wage theory and the flexible wage theory – and see why economists continue to be unable to agree on how the labour market functions.

The Sticky Wage Theory   The sticky wage theory of the labour market is illustrated directly in Fig. 31.4. In 1979, the labour market operated at the point of intersection of LS and LD_{79}. The quantity of labour supplied and demanded was 52 billion hours at a wage rate of £5.30 per hour (in 1990 pounds). This represents the situation that actually existed in 1979. Let's assume that the actual unemployment rate in 1979 was also the natural rate of unemployment.

By 1981, money wages increased at a pace consistent with expectations of inflation continuing at around 17 per cent a year. In the event, the inflation rate slowed down so real wages increased unexpectedly. They went up to about £5.60 an hour (still at 1990 pounds). With higher real wages, the quantity of labour demanded declined – there was a movement along the demand curve. But also, with higher real wages, the quantity of labour supplied increased – there was a movement along the supply curve. The difference between the quantity of labour supplied and the quantity demanded at

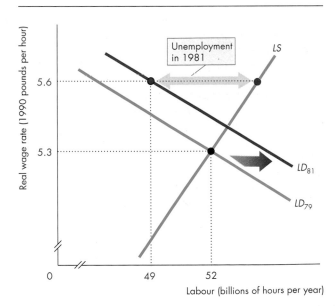

FIGURE 31.4

The Labour Market in Recession: Sticky Wage Theory

The supply of labour curve in both 1979 and 1981 was LS. The demand for labour was LD_{79} in 1979 and LD_{81} in 1981. Wages and employment in 1979 were at the intersection of LS and LD_{79} with a real wage rate of £5.30 an hour and 52 billion hours of labour being demanded and supplied. We'll assume that unemployment was at its natural rate. In 1981, higher money wages combined with lower than expected inflation increased the real wage rate to £5.60 an hour. Employment decreased to 49 billion hours. The difference between the quantity of labour demanded and the quantity supplied at the new wage is the unemployment gap – the extent to which unemployment exceeds its natural rate.

the higher real wage rate represents the unemployment gap – the extent to which unemployment exceeds its natural rate.

To secure full employment in 1979, with 52 billion hours of labour a year, the real wage rate would have needed to be much lower than it actually was. Because the real wage rate was sticky – that is because workers are reluctant to accept a fall in wages – the wage rate did not fall. So there was additional unemployment on top of natural unemployment.

Flexible Wage Theory   There is an alternative interpretation of the labour market in recession to the sticky wage theory we have just presented – the flexible wage theory. According to this theory, wages are flexible and do adjust to bring equality between the demand for labour and the supply of labour. So all fluctuations in unemployment are fluctuations in the natural rate of unemployment. To understand this theory, though, we need to appreciate that changes in economic aggregates such as total employment hours hide changes in the *structure* of the labour market. So we need to look at the markets for different types of labour.

The theory is illustrated with the model economy displayed in Fig. 31.5. We will keep the analysis simple by ignoring workers employed by governments and dividing workers employed by industry into two broad groups. One of these groups works in industries producing goods and the other group works in

---

FIGURE 31.5

The Labour Market in Recession: Flexible Wage Theory

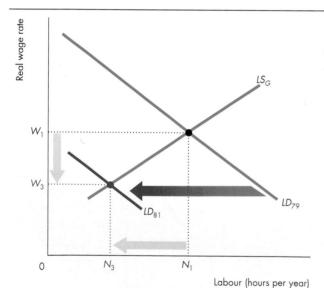

(a) Goods industries

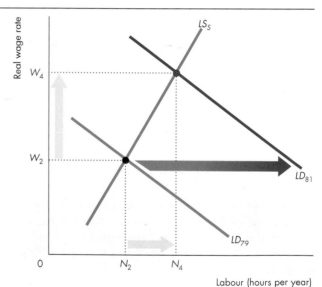

(b) Service industries

The two parts of the figure relate to workers in goods industries and workers in service industries. In part (a), the supply curve of workers in goods industries is LS_G and in part (b) the supply curve of workers in service industries is LS_S. The demand curves for both types of labour in 1979 and 1981 are LD_{79} and LD_{81}. In 1979, the wages of workers in goods industries are W_1 and the employment level is N_1 while the wages of workers in service industries are W_2 and the employment level is N_2. In 1981 there is a decrease in the demand for labour in goods industries and an increase in the demand for labour in service industries. Employment in goods industries falls to N_3 and wages fall to

W_3. Employment in service industries increases to N_4 and wages rise to W_4. Total employment in the two groups declines – the decrease in employment in the goods industries exceeds the increase in employment in the service industries. The average wage rate is a weighted average of the wage rates of the two groups. The average wage rate rises partly because the upward change in the wage rate of workers in service industries is greater than the downward change in the wage rate of workers in goods industries and partly because the proportion of jobs held by workers in service industries increases.

industries producing services. Incidentally, the goods industries tend to be concentrated in the northern part of the United Kingdom while the service industries tend to be concentrated in the southern part. It is hard for workers to shift from one group to another because doing so entails learning new skills and – very often – moving to another home. The market for labour in goods industries is shown in part (a) and the market for labour in service industries in part (b).

Focus first on the supply curves. The supply curve of labour in goods industries is LS_G and of labour in service industries is LS_S. Notice that we have made the two supply curves similar in shape. In practice there may be some differences – maybe people are less willing to work in one group than another and so a higher wage has to be paid to attract labour to the less popular group. But the flexible wage model we are about to present applies whether or not such differences exist, and we ignore them to keep the analysis simple. We will also assume that the two supply curves stayed put between 1979 and 1981.

The demand for labour curves in 1979 and 1981 are shown as LD_{81} in the two parts of the figure. Focus first on the situation prevailing in 1979. In the market for labour producing goods, the wage rate is W_1 and the level of employment N_1 – determined at the point of intersection of LS_G and LD_{79}. In the market for labour producing services, the wage rate is W_2 and the employment level N_2 – at the intersection point of LS_S and LD_{79}. There are similar numbers of workers in each group, and the wage rates in each group are also similar. Aggregate employment is the sum of the employment of the workers in each group. Average wages are an average of the wage rates in each group (W_1 and W_2) where the average is weighted by the exact proportions of the two kinds of labour.

What happens between 1979 and 1981? In this economy, the overall demand for labour decreases in those two years, but this overall decrease results from a large decrease in the demand for labour in goods industries and an increase in the demand for labour in the service industries. The wages of workers in goods industries decrease to W_3 and their employment level decreases to N_3. The wages of workers in service industries increase to W_4 and their employment increases to N_4. Aggregate employment decreases because the decrease in employment in goods industries exceeds the increase in the service industries. But the average wage rate rises partly because the rise in the wage rates of

workers in service industries is bigger than the fall in the wage rates of workers in goods industries and partly because the proportion of workers in service industries – where wage rates are now higher – has increased.

There is an increase in unemployment as the workers in goods industries whose labour demand declines become unemployed or start to look for a better job. But the change in employment is a change in the natural rate of unemployment. There is no gap between the quantity of labour supplied and the quantity demanded for either group. The labour market is in equilibrium and the plans of demanders and suppliers of labour are completely coordinated.

Which Theory of the Labour Market is Correct?   What exactly do economists disagree about concerning the labour market and why? The essence of the controversy is nicely summarized in Figs. 31.4 and 31.5. First, everyone agrees about the facts. Real wages in 1979 were about £5.30 an hour, on average. In 1981, they increased to £5.60, on average. Employment in 1979 was 52 billion hours and it fell to 49 billion hours in 1981.

In addition, there is not much disagreement about the demand for labour. Most economists agree that the quantity of labour actually employed is determined by the profit-maximizing decisions of firms. That quantity depends on the real wage. This means that the level of employment and the real wage in any particular year are at a point on the demand for labour curve. If we agree that the employment level and real wage are at a point on the demand for labour curve, we can work out where the demand for labour curve is and work out what makes it shift. So there is much agreement among economists about the slope and position of the demand for labour curve.

Where economists disagree is over the supply of labour and the forces at work in achieving a labour market equilibrium. Because a large amount of labour is supplied on long-term contracts, and on wages and other terms that remain fixed for the duration of the contract, most economists believe that households as a whole are not normally operating on the supply curve of labour. Sometimes they are, but much of the time they are not. In other words, they believe that the situation is often like that shown for 1981 in Fig. 31.3 – where the economy settled at some point other than where the

Understanding Business Cycles

> 'We don't want to manage the US economy. And we don't think anybody else should take the job either.'
>
> ROBERT E. LUCAS JR
> *Personal Interview*

Economic activity has fluctuated between boom and bust for as long as we've had records, and the range of fluctuations became especially pronounced during the nineteenth and early twentieth centuries. Understanding the sources of economic fluctuations has turned out to be difficult for two reasons.

First, there are no simple patterns. Every new episode of the business cycle is different from its predecessor in some important way. Some cycles are long and some short, some are mild and some severe. We never know with any certainty when the next turning point (down or up) is coming or what will cause it.

Second, resources are scarce even in a recession or a depression. But at such times, large quantities of scarce resources go unemployed. A satisfactory theory of the business cycle must explain this fact. Why don't scarce resources *always* get fully employed?

There are plenty of simple, but wrong, theories of the business cycle. And when these theories are used to justify policies, they can create severe problems. For example, during the 1960s, recessions were believed to result from insufficient aggregate demand. The solution: increase government spending, cut taxes and cut interest rates. Countries that pursued such policies most vigorously, such as the United Kingdom, found their economic growth rates sagging, unemployment rising and inflation accelerating.

Today's new theory – real business cycle theory – predicts that fluctuations in aggregate demand have *no* effect on output and employment and change only the price level and inflation rate. But

What happens to the economy when people lose confidence in banks? They withdraw their funds. These withdrawals feed on themselves, creating a snowball of withdrawals and, eventually, panic. Short of funds with which to repay depositors, banks call in loans, and previously sound businesses are faced with financial distress. They close down and lay off workers. Recession deepens and turns into depression. Bank failures and the resulting decline in the nation's supply of money and credit were a significant factor in deepening and prolonging the Great Depression. But they taught us the importance of stable financial institutions and gave rise to the establishment of federal deposit insurance to prevent such financial collapse.

How can it be that a building designed as a shop has no better use than to be boarded up and left empty? Not enough aggregate demand, say the Keynesians. Not so, say the real business cycle theorists. Technological change has reduced the building's current productivity as a shop to zero. But its expected future productivity is sufficiently high that it is not efficient to refit the building for some other purpose. All unemployment – whether of buildings or people – can be explained in a similar way. For example, how can it be that a person trained as a shop assistant is without work during a recession? Not enough aggregate demand is one answer. Another is that the current productivity of shop assistants is low, but their expected future productivity is sufficiently high that it does not pay an unemployed assistant to retrain for a job that is currently available.

this theory ignores the *real* effects of financial collapse of the type that occurred in the 1930s. If banks fail on a large scale and people lose their wealth, other firms also begin to fail and jobs are destroyed. Unemployed people cut their spending, and output falls yet further. Demand stimulation may not be called for, but action to ensure that sound banks survive certainly is.

Robert E. Lucas, Jr: Today's Macroeconomic Revolutionary

ROBERT E. LUCAS JR

Many economists, past and present, have advanced our understanding of business cycles. But one contemporary economist stands out. He is Robert E. Lucas, Jr of the University of Chicago. In 1970, as a 32-year-old professor at Carnegie-Mellon University, Lucas challenged the Keynesian theories of economic fluctuations and launched a macroeconomic revolution based on two principles: rational expectations and equilibrium. Like all scientific revolutions, the one touched off by Lucas was controversial. Twenty years later, rational expectations (whether right or wrong) is accepted by most economists. But the idea that the business cycle and unemployment can be understood as equilibria remains controversial and, for some economists, even distasteful. Lucas believes that we still know too little about the causes of the business cycle to be able to stabilize the economy.

demand and supply curves of labour intersect with substantial unemployment in excess of the natural level of unemployment.

Other economists believe that the combination of the real wage rate and the level of employment not only represents a point on the demand for labour curve but also a point on the supply of labour curve. In essence this means that the labour market settles at the point where the two curves intersect, but to rationalize the aggregate data it is really necessary to study a model economy at a disaggregate level distinguishing between various types of labour. Economists who regard the flexible wage model as being the appropriate one emphasize not only its ability to explain the facts about average wages and aggregate employment, but also its consistency with other evidence about the structure of the labour market.

For example, during the 1980–1981 recession, employment in service industries did increase slightly while employment in manufacturing industry declined very sharply. As indicated in Fig. 31.5, this is consistent with a flexible wage theory explanation of the overall changes in unemployment and wage increases during the recession. Note, however, that the fact that these changes in the composition of employment were consistent with that theory does not demonstrate that the flexible wage theory is correct. How can we test whether that theory is correct?

Unfortunately, there is a fundamental problem in that no one has yet suggested a test that is sufficiently clear for all economists to agree on. The controversy will be settled only when economists can agree on, and implement, a test of their competing views about whether wages are sticky or flexible. Once such a test has been implemented, we shall be able to put this controversy behind us. But until then, professional economists and students of the subject have to live with the fact that we remain ignorant about a large and important issue at the heart of macroeconomics. This controversy is featured in Our Advancing Knowledge on pp, 886–887.

Determining which of these two theories is correct is not just a matter of academic curiosity. It is a matter of enormous importance in designing an appropriate anti-recessionary policy. If the flexible wage theory is true, there is only one aggregate supply curve, the vertical long-run aggregate supply curve. This would

mean that any attempt to bring the economy out of recession by increasing aggregate demand – for example by increasing the money supply and lowering interest rates or by fiscal policy measures – is doomed to failure and can result only in a higher price level (more inflation). Conversely, if the sticky wage theory is correct, then the short-run aggregate supply curve slopes upward. This would mean that an increase in aggregate demand, although increasing the price level somewhat, would also increase real GDP and so bring the economy out of a recession.

Another Great Depression?

We have seen that there were serious recessions in 1980–1981 and 1991–1992. Neither of these was as serious as the Great Depression, but the question remains as to whether there could be another recession as serious as that. Some people thought there might be another huge recession after the 1987 stock market crash, recalling that the 1929 stock market crash played a large part in the Great Depression.

No one knows the answer to the question of whether there might one day be another Great Depression. But we can try to assess the likelihood of such an event. Let's begin by asking some questions. Why was the UK economy already depressed throughout the 1920s? Why was there a stock market crash and a Great Depression worldwide? How did these worldwide events affect the United Kingdom? Just how bad did things get in the United Kingdom in the early 1930s? Once we've finished discussing what happened in the 1930s, we'll consider the question of whether it could happen again and how likely such an event would be.

The UK Economy in the 1920s

The 1920s were a very difficult decade for the UK economy. People had grown used to the ups and downs in unemployment in the nineteenth century, but unemployment in the worst years had rarely exceeded 10 per cent. Moreover, in the first 14 years of the twentieth century, unemployment had never exceeded 8 per cent. And during those 14 years output and incomes had risen strongly in what was already an exceptionally rich country. However, the economic situation was not as rosy as it might have seemed. For a long time the United Kingdom had been the workshop of the world. But now more and more countries were industrializing rapidly, and even without the impact of a war it was inevitable that industry in the United Kingdom would face ever-stiffening competition. Some industries, at least, would be bound to contract in the face of this competition.

Of course no one would have been surprised if the aftermath of World War I caused difficulties. Four million servicemen were demobilized in 1919 alone, and this seemed likely to create substantial unemployment. Oddly, perhaps, mass unemployment did not arrive until 1921. In 1920, there was a very brief boom as the world undertook reconstruction and a replenishing of stocks. The decline which arrived in 1921 had several causes. One was that while the government had cut its expenditure, it had done little to cut taxes as it wanted to run a surplus to pay off the loans it had borrowed in the war. If the people who were repaid had spent their money in the United Kingdom, aggregate demand might not have been too badly affected, but many of them chose to use their money to invest abroad, often in countries belonging to the British Empire.

Another factor was increased foreign competition. The coal industry was badly affected. This was partly because the United Kingdom became industrialized before other countries and so was the first country to exhaust the seams which were easy to reach. By the 1920s, UK coal was more costly to dig up than Polish or German coal, and UK coal production halved between 1913 and 1929. The textile industry was also badly affected by foreign competition. It had benefited greatly from the new technologies of the industrial revolution, but it now faced severe competition from countries such as ·India, Japan and China. The number of workers employed in textiles more than halved between 1913 and 1937. There were similar problems in shipbuilding and iron and steel.

The problems were not helped by the return of sterling to the gold standard in 1925. This meant that the Bank of England would once again exchange sterling for gold at a fixed rate. Because other countries adopted similar procedures sterling was effectively on a fixed exchange rate. This might not have mattered too much if the rate had been set at a realistic level. Instead, it was set at the pre-war level of £1 = $4.86, and this represented a significant appreciation from a low 1924 level of £1 = $4.26. The reason for adopting the pre-war rate was only partly nostalgia. People in the City of London feared that adopting any lower rate would betray a weakness of sterling that might threaten London's position as a major financial centre. The rise in the value of sterling might seem relatively modest, but remember that unemployment had soared to over 14 per cent in 1922 and was still over 11 per cent in 1925. This was hardly the time to make UK products more costly for foreigners to buy.

It seemed the only way that many industries could remain competitive was to cut wages, and it was wage cuts in mining that led to the ill-fated general strike of 1926. In fact, however, aggregate demand picked up a little and for the next three years unemployment fell a little. One cause of increased demand was that taxes at last began to fall. Another was that world food prices fell so that demand for manufactured goods like those produced in the United Kingdom increased. So by 1929 there might have been some cautious optimism. But any hopes of recovery were shattered by the events of 1929.

The Wall Street Crash and the Great Depression

The most dramatic events of 1929 occurred in October when the stock market on Wall Street collapsed, losing more than one-third of its value in only two weeks. Let's consider why there was a crash in New York and why this was followed by the Great Depression. Then we'll see what effects this depression had on the United Kingdom.

In the United States, the late 1920s were years of economic boom. New housing was built on an unprecedented scale, new firms were created, and the capital stock of the nation expanded. But these were also years of increasing uncertainty. The main source of increased uncertainty was international. The world economy was going through tumultuous times. The patterns of world trade were changing. As we have seen, the United Kingdom had ceased to be the traditional economic powerhouse of the world and was having a very difficult time. New economic powers such as Germany and Japan began to emerge. The UK's currency may have been fixed, but fluctuations in the values of several other important currencies, together with the introduction of restrictive trade policies by many countries, further increased the uncertainty faced by firms. There was also domestic uncertainty arising from the fact that there had been such a strong boom in recent years, especially in the capital goods sector and housing. No one believed that the boom could continue but there was great uncertainty as to when it would end and how the pattern of demand would change.

This environment of uncertainty led to a slow-down in consumer spending, especially on new homes and consumer durables. By the autumn of 1929, the uncertainty had reached a critical level and contributed to the stock market crash. The stock market crash, in turn, heightened people's fears about economic prospects in the foreseeable future. Fear fed fear. Investment collapsed. The building industry almost disappeared. An industry that had been operating flat out just two years earlier was now building virtually no new houses. It was this drop in investment, and a drop in consumer spending on durables, that led to the initial decrease in aggregate demand.

At this stage, what became the Great Depression was no worse than many previous recessions the United States had been in. What distinguishes the Great Depression from previous recessions (and subsequent ones) are the events that followed between 1930 and 1933. But even to this day, American economists have not come to an agreement on how to interpret those events. Everyone agrees that there were many factors causing aggregate demand to decrease, but they disagree on which were the most important factors.

One view is that spending continued to fall chiefly because there was increasing pessimism and uncertainty which led to a dramatic drop in investment. Another view is that the continuation of the contraction was almost exclusively the result of the subsequent worsening of financial and monetary conditions, and in particular a severe cut in the money supply that lowered aggregate demand, prolonging the contraction and deepening the depression. Certainly there was a massive 20 per cent fall in the money supply between 1930 and 1933 which led to high nominal and high real interest rates and dampened investment.

Interestingly, the fall in the money supply was not a result of the monetary authorities reducing the monetary base – that is cash plus bank reserves – and indeed the monetary base hardly fell at all. Instead, many banks collapsed following unsound lending in the boom period, and this encouraged the surviving banks to operate with higher reserve ratios, so there was a huge drop in the bank deposit component of the money supply. This drop was exacerbated by the fact that many people, fearful of their own bank collapsing, withdrew their deposits in cash so that there was a large increase in publicly held cash and a large drop in bank reserves.

What role did the stock market crash of 1929 play in producing the Great Depression? It certainly created an atmosphere of fear and panic, and it probably contributed to the overall air of uncertainty that dampened investment spending. It also reduced the wealth of stockholders, encouraging them to cut back on their consumption spending. But the direct effect of the stock market crash on consumption, although a contributory factor to the Great Depression, was not the major source of the drop in aggregate demand. It was the collapse in investment arising from increased uncertainty that brought the 1930 decline in aggregate demand.

The stock market crash was, however, a predictor of severe recession. It reflected the expectations of stockholders concerning future profit prospects. As those expectations became pessimistic, the prices of stocks were bid lower and lower. That is, the behaviour of the stock market was a consequence of expectations about future profitability and those expectations were lowered as a result of increased uncertainty.

The four years that followed were years of monstrous economic depression – depression so severe that it came to be called the Great Depression. By 1933 real GDP in the United States had fallen by about 30 per cent of its 1929 value while prices had fallen by about 27 per cent.

The United Kingdom in 1929–1933

It was not only the United States which suffered a stock market crash in 1929. Similar falls occurred in London and in other financial centres around the world. There are several reasons why stock market crashes often occur simultaneously in many countries. One key reason is that if stock (share) prices fall suddenly in, say, New York, then people will be keener to buy cheap stocks there, so the demand for shares and share prices elsewhere fall too. Another reason why other stock markets fell in 1929 was that the fears which sparked off the Wall Street crash were, as we have seen, largely international fears about the future of international trade and prosperity. A further reason which applied in 1929 is that the United States is a very big country. If the uncertainty there sparked off a stock market crash, then it would doubtless lead – as it did – to a fall in investment and a rise in unemployment. This would cut imports by the United States which would in turn reduce output and incomes elsewhere, thereby causing further gloom.

So it was not surprising that the stock market crashes were followed by the widespread Great Depression. The international fears about trade and prosperity resulted from increased restrictions on trade and growing fluctuations in exchange rates which led to a widespread fall in investment. Investment fell sharply in the United Kingdom, but the fall was less dramatic than in most countries. For example, investment in the United Kingdom fell by about 11 per cent when the economy bottomed out in 1931. This fall was actually less than the fall of 25 per cent noted earlier for the 1979–1981 period and lower than the 13 per cent fall in 1991 alone. In contrast, the Canadian economy did not bottom out until 1933, and by then investment had fallen by a staggering 90 per cent. Probably the fall was less dramatic in the United Kingdom simply because investment was already low in 1929 as a result of the depressed 1920s. It was on the export front that the United Kingdom suffered most in the next few years. Between 1929 and 1931 the quantity of exports fell 32 per cent. There was nothing like this in the two most recent recessions. Between 1979 and 1981, exports fell by a mere 7 per cent, and between 1989 and 1991 exports actually rose.

The dimensions of the 1929–1931 depression can be seen graphically in Fig. 31.6. The figure shows the situation on the eve of the Great Depression in 1929 when the economy was on its aggregate demand curve (AD_{29}) and short-run aggregate supply curve (SAS_{29}). Real GDP was £143 billion (at 1990 pounds) and the GDP deflator was 3.3 (with 1990 = 100).

In the 1929–1931 period there was widespread expectation that prices would fall. In 1929 this

FIGURE 31.6

The 1929–1931 Depression

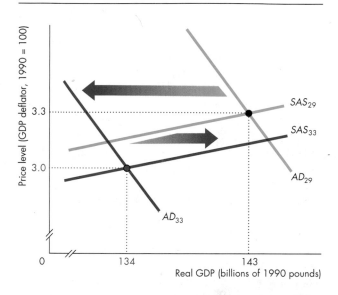

In 1929, real GDP was £143 billion (at 1990 pounds) and the GDP deflator was 3.3 (with 1990 = 100) at the intersection of AD_{29} and SAS_{29}. By 1931, the worldwide depression had led to a large drop in export demand, and increased pessimism and uncertainty also resulted in a drop in investment. So aggregate demand decreased to AD_{31}. To some degree, the decrease in aggregate demand was anticipated, so wages fell and the short-run aggregate supply curve moved to SAS_{31}. By 1931, real GDP had fallen to £134 billion (about 93 per cent of its 1929 level) and the GDP deflator had fallen to 3.0 (about 91 per cent of its 1929 level).

expectation would have been chiefly caused by the fact that prices had fallen quite a lot during the depressed years of the 1920s. In 1930 and 1931 the expectation would have been stimulated by decreasing demand. As a result of people expecting prices to fall, wages fell. With lower wages, the short-run aggregate supply curve shifted to SAS_{31}. But aggregate demand decreased by a larger amount than expected to AD_{31}. By 1931 the economy was in a much deeper recession than had been the case in 1929. Compared with 1929, real GDP fell by about 7 per cent to £134 billion and the price level fell by about 10 per cent to a GDP deflator of 3.0. When the price level is falling the economy is experiencing *deflation*.

Inflation and Interest Rates in Germany

FINANCIAL TIMES, 22 JULY 1994

Tietmeyer fuels hopes of German rate fall

Christopher Parkes, Frankfurt

Mr Hans Tietmeyer, the Bundesbank president, yesterday reinforced expectations that German interest rates could fall again in the autumn by saying that growth in money supply is lower than unadjusted figures suggest and that inflation is heading in the right direction.

Mr Tietmeyer, speaking after a mid-year review of the bank's M3 measure of money supply indicated that the German central bank was relying less than usual for policy guidance on its volatile M3 indicator. The distinction between money which could potentially fuel inflation (the normal M3 constituents) and funds invested for the long-term had become less clear, he said.

But the Bundesbank would not give up M3, he stressed. It was a part of Germany's 'stability culture'. Experience showed the link between the measure and future inflation to be intact, while yesterday's review of alternatives had shown them to be 'second-best solutions', he said.

A review of possible modifications to presentation and interpretation would continue until December when the 1995 M3 growth target was due to be fixed.

Meanwhile, trends in public spending policy, wage agreements and near-term inflation were important factors guiding policy, he suggested.

'As long as other sources make us confident that future price developments are moving in the right direction, deviations from the M3 target path can to some extent be tolerated', Mr Tietmeyer said.

The consumer price index, currently rising at 3 per cent, was on the right track, and there were signs of further flattening, he said. Recent increases in raw materials prices were being countered by the relative strength of the D-Mark against the US dollar, he added.

Although a statement from the bank warned that lingering excess liquidity in the M3 figure would cause concern, Mr Tietmeyer claimed the measure had been growing at an 'adjusted' annual rate of around 6 per cent for the last three months.

This is close to the bank's target range of 4–6 per cent, which has been exceeded so far this year. The unadjusted M3 growth rate for June, released earlier this week, was 11.3 per cent.

© The Financial Times. Reprinted with permission.

German inflation is falling.

Adjusted figures for growth in the money supply show a slower rate of growth than expected.

The president of the German Bundesbank therefore feels interest rates could fall within a few months.

The monetary aggregate M3 would continue to be used as a tool for predicting and controlling inflation, despite concerns about its use.

Factors other than growth in M3 would also be considered in determining policy.

The central focus of the policy of the German Bundesbank is the control of inflation.

The costs of German unification were increasing inflationary pressures within Germany. The Bundesbank responded by raising interest rates.

Given the dominance of the German currency, the Deutschmark, within the European Monetary System (EMS) and freedom of capital flows, interest rates in other European countries had to be raised to maintain exchange rates within the EMS.

High interest rates across Europe led to lower investment, lower consumer expenditure and an economic recession.

Recessionary pressures in European economies led to changes in the EMS, including some member countries withdrawing from the system. Interest rates were lowered to help investment and consumer spending pull economies out of recession.

As inflationary pressures have receded in Germany, so the Bundesbank has been able to reduce its interest rates, with the possibility of further cuts if downward inflationary trends are confirmed.

In the figure, the recession lowers real GDP and shifts the demand for money curve MD_0 to the left to MD_1. Although the nominal money supply increases, inflation leads to a fall in the real money supply. The real money supply curve shifts to the left from MS_0 to MS_1. The interest rate rises.

Continuing recession shifts the demand for real money curve further to the left to MD_2, but as the higher interest rate reduces inflation, so the rise in nominal money supply results also in an increase in real money supply. The real money supply curve shifts back to the right to MS_2.

Interest rates now fall. With inflation coming increasingly under control, the scope for further interest rate cuts is higher, since a lower growth in nominal money supply still translates into a fall in the growth rate of the real money supply.

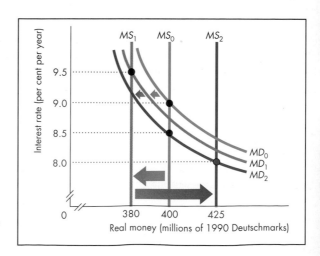

The Labour government of 1929–1931 did little to help the situation. It did not want to reduce the exchange rate as it thought it would be a breach of faith to people who had invested in sterling to lower its value. It did not want an expansionary monetary policy, partly for fear of sparking off the sort of inflation and, perhaps, hyperinflation that had occurred a few years earlier in Germany. And it not want an expansionary fiscal policy, with tax cuts or government expenditure increases, because the government already had a deficit with its expenditure running at a higher level than its tax receipts. Indeed the chancellor, Philip Snowden, wanted this government deficit to be eliminated with spending cuts.

In fact a coalition government was formed under Ramsay MacDonald in 1931 and this at once cut government spending by reducing the pay of the armed forces and most other government employees by 10 per cent and reducing the pay of teachers by 15 per cent. It also cut the very modest transfer payments to unemployed people by 10 per cent and ended all such benefits to anyone unemployed for more than 26 weeks unless they failed an exceptionally stringent means test; this policy caused a lasting abhorrence of means testing. Some sailors at Invergordon were so incensed by the pay cut that they refused to report for duty. Foreigners suspected a naval mutiny and rushed to sell sterling. This forced the government to abandon the gold standard and the pound soon fell to £1 = $3.80 which helped bring the economy round. It has been said by some cynics that the sailors of Invergordon accomplished more than most other naval operations!

Unemployment continued to rise for a while, peaking at over 22 per cent in 1932, but output rose after 1931 and employment soon rose too. Aside from the fall in the exchange rate, recovery was helped by a large fall in interest rates in 1932 and the reversal in 1934 of the cuts in government employees' pay. Also, tariffs were imposed on many imports, though not on produce from countries in the British Empire, and this reduced imports thus raising spending at home. Furthermore, confidence began to return so that investment began to pick up.

Can it Happen Again?

Since, even today, we have an incomplete understanding of the causes of the Great Depression, we are not able to predict such an event or to be sure that it cannot occur again. But there are some important differences between the economy of the 1990s and that of the 1930s that make a severe depression much less likely today than it was 60 years ago. The most important features of the economy that make severe depression less likely today are as follows:

◆ Bank deposit insurance in the United States
◆ The Bank of England's role as lender of last resort
◆ Taxes and government spending
◆ Multi-income families

Let's examine these in turn.

Bank Deposit Insurance As a result of the Great Depression, the US government set up in the 1930s the Federal Deposit Insurance Corporation (FDIC). The FDIC insures bank deposits up to $100,000 per depositor so most depositors need no longer fear bank failures. If a bank fails, as occasionally happens in the United States, the FDIC pays the depositors. With government-insured bank deposits, one of the key events that turned a fairly ordinary recession into the Great Depression is most unlikely to occur. It was the fear of bank failure that caused people to withdraw their deposits from banks. The aggregate consequence of these individually rational acts was to cause the very bank failures that were feared. With deposit insurance, most depositors have nothing to lose if a bank fails and so have no incentive to take actions that are likely to give rise to that failure.

Lender of Last Resort There is a limited amount of deposit insurance in the United Kingdom, but the main protection against bank failure is the system of lending at last resort operated by the Bank of England. If a single bank is short of reserves, it can borrow reserves from other banks or from the discount houses which will borrow them from the Bank of England. If the entire banking system is short of reserves, then all banks can borrow from the Bank of England via the discount houses. By making reserves available (at a suitable interest rate), the Bank can make the quantity of reserves in the banking system respond flexibly to the demand for those reserves. Bank failure can be prevented, or at least restricted, to cases where bad management practices are the source of the problem. Widespread failures of the type that occurred in the United States in the Great Depression can be prevented.

The Federal Reserve System in the United States – that is the central bank of the United States – also now acts as a lender of last resort if necessary. It is interesting to note that during the weeks following the October 1987 stock market crash, the chairman of the system used every opportunity available to remind the world banking and financial community of its ability and readiness to maintain calm financial conditions.

Taxes and Government Spending   The government sector was a much less important part of the economy in 1929 than it has become today. In 1929, government purchases of goods and services were 13 per cent of GDP. In contrast, today they are more than 24 per cent. Government transfer payments and subsidies were under 6 per cent of GDP in 1929. These items have grown to over 16 per cent of GDP today.

Larger levels of government purchases of goods and services and government subsidies mean that when recession hits, a large component of aggregate demand does not decrease. It is government transfer payments, however, that are the most important economic stabilizer. When the economy goes into recession and depression, more people qualify for job-seeker's allowances and other transfer payments. So, although disposable income falls, the extent of the fall is moderated. Consumers' expenditure, in turn, does not decline by as much as it would in the absence of such government programmes. But limited decline in consumers' expenditure limits the overall decrease in aggregate expenditure, thereby limiting the magnitude of an economic downturn.

Multi-income Families   At the time of the Great Depression, families with more than one wage earner were rather less common than they are today. In other words, the proportion of the people of working age who regard themselves as part of the labour force is higher now than it was then. So even if the unemployment rate increased to 22 per cent today, a larger percentage of the adult population would actually have jobs. Moreover, multi-income families have greater security than single-income families. The chance of both (or all) income earners in a family

losing their jobs simultaneously is much lower than the chance of a single earner losing work. With greater family income security, family consumption is likely to be less sensitive to fluctuations in family income that are seen as temporary. So when aggregate income falls, it may not cause a cut in consumption. For example, during the 1980–1981 recession, as real GDP fell by 3 per cent, personal consumption expenditure actually rose by 0.2 per cent.

For the four reasons we have just reviewed, it appears the economy has better shock-absorbing characteristics today than it had in the 1920s and 1930s. Even if there is a collapse of confidence leading to a fall in investment, the recession mechanism that is now in place will not translate that initial shock into the large and prolonged fall in real GDP and rise in unemployment that occurred 60 years ago.

Other economies are also more immune to severe recession than they were 60 years ago. It is interesting to contrast the reactions to the stock market crashes in Wall Street of 1929 and 1987. The crashes were of similar size. The 1929 crash led to a large fall in investment and a near collapse of spending on consumer durables. The 1987 crash had negligible effects on these components of spending. Because other countries are more immune to recession, so UK exports are less likely to experience the dramatic falls that were experienced in 1929–1931, and this too makes a severe recession less probable.

None of this means there could not possibly be another Great Depression. But it would certainly take a very severe shock to trigger one off.

◆ ◆ ◆ ◆   We have now completed our study of the working of the macroeconomy. We've studied the macroeconomic model of aggregate demand and aggregate supply and we've learned a great deal about the workings of the markets for goods and services, labour and money and securities. We have applied our knowledge to explaining and understanding the problems of unemployment, inflation and business cycle fluctuations.

In the next part of the book we will study two aspects of macroeconomic policy – the policies that governments can take to stabilize the economy and the problems imposed by the government sector's frequent budget deficits.

SUMMARY

Two Recent Recessions

The 1980–1981 recession resulted from a fall in the growth of aggregate demand, triggered by the government's monetary policy and an appreciation of sterling which resulted chiefly from high interest rates and from growth in the output of North Sea oil. Wages rose on the presumption that inflation would continue at 17 per cent a year, and those wage changes decreased the short-run aggregate supply curve. The decrease in the short-run aggregate supply curve was much larger than the increase in aggregate demand. As a consequence, real GDP declined but inflation moderated.

The 1991–1992 recession resulted from a sharp fall in investment. This fall was partly the result of a tightening of monetary policy and partly the result of a collapse in business confidence. Businesses feared that the war on inflation could be prolonged, and that interest rates might also have to remain high to maintain the value at which sterling was set when it was taken into the ERM in 1990. Wages increased on the presumption that inflation would continue at 10 per cent a year, and those wage changes shifted the short-run aggregate supply curve upward. While the short-run aggregate supply shifted to the left, aggregate demand remained roughly constant. The result was that real GDP fell and inflation moderated.

In a recession, interest rates may initially rise or fall, but eventually the fall in real GDP reduces the demand for money and interest rates fall. There is controversy about the behaviour of the labour market during a recession. According to the sticky wage interpretation of events, real wages do not adjust to bring equality between the quantities of labour demanded and supplied. When the economy goes into recession, the quantity of labour supplied exceeds the quantity demanded and unemployment exceeds its natural rate. According to the flexible wage interpretation of events, real wages do adjust to maintain continuous equality between the quantities of labour demanded and supplied. Changes in demand for different types of labour result in a change in the composition of those with jobs and a change in the average wage rate. The increase in unemployment that occurs during the recession arises from increased job-search activity associated with a high degree of labour turnover resulting from changes in the pattern of demand for different types of labour. Macroeconomists have not yet devised the acid test that enables them to resolve their dispute about the labour market mechanism in recession. (pp. 879–888)

Another Great Depression?

For the UK economy the 1920s were a decade of recession that was chiefly caused by growing competition for many industries from newly industrializing countries. The recession was aggravated by a 1925 decision to return sterling to its pre-World War I exchange rate. Just as things seemed to be improving, the economy was adversely affected by the worldwide Great Depression which followed the spectacular Wall Street crash in the autumn of 1929.

The Great Depression was more severe than any before it or since. It started in the United States with increased uncertainty and pessimism which brought a fall in investment (especially in housing) and purchases of consumer durables. They also brought on the stock market crash. The crash added to the pessimistic outlook and further spending cuts occurred. There then followed a near total collapse of the financial system. Banks failed and the money supply fell, resulting in a continued decrease in aggregate demand. Expectations of falling prices led to falling wages but the decrease in aggregate demand continued to exceed expectations and real GDP continued to decline.

The pessimism and uncertainty were not confined to the United States and they caused falls in investment in many other countries including the United Kingdom. Many countries were also affected indirectly by the falling output and income of the

United States, for these falls reduced its imports and so led to lower incomes and production elsewhere. The UK's exports suffered particularly badly. Combined with the fall in investment, the fall in exports created a fall in output of 7 per cent and sent unemployment up to over 22 per cent. The economy gradually recovered in the 1930s, helped by a fall in the value of the pound and a fall in interest rates.

The Great Depression itself produced some reforms in the United States that make a repeat of such a depression much less likely. The most important of these was the development of the Federal Reserve system as lender of last resort and the introduction of deposit insurance, for both of these reduced the risk of bank failure and financial collapse.

More generally, the risk of severe recession has been reduced in the United Kingdom and many other countries. Higher levels of government spending have given the economy greater resistance against depression. Also job-seekers' allowances are now much more generous, so that the incomes of those who are made redundant fall less severely. And the increased labour force participation rate provides a greater measure of security, especially for families with more than one wage earner. For these reasons an initial large change in either aggregate demand or aggregate supply is much less likely to translate into an accumulative depression than was the case in the early 1930s. Thus even a stock market crash as severe as the one that occurred in 1987 did not lead to a collapse in aggregate demand. (pp. 888–895)

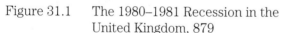

K E Y   E L E M E N T S

Key Figures

Figure 31.1 The 1980–1981 Recession in the United Kingdom, 879

Figure 31.2 The 1991–1992 Recession in the United Kingdom, 880

Figure 31.4 The Labour Market in Recession: Sticky Wage Theory, 883

Figure 31.5 The Labour Market in Recession: Flexible Wage Theory, 884

R E V I E W   Q U E S T I O N S

1 What triggered the 1980–1981 recession? What triggered the 1991–1992 recession?

2 What was the path of interest rates as the economy went through the recession?

3 Can the events of the 1980–1981 recession be explained by a flexible wage theory? Explain why or why not.

4 Describe the changes in employment and real wages in the 1980–1981 recession. With which theory of the labour market are these changes in real wages and unemployment consistent?

5 What factors helped the economy recover from the 1991–1992 recession?

6 Why did the economy suffer from high unemployment during the 1920s?

7 Describe the changes in real GDP, unemployment and the price level that occurred during the Great Depression years of 1929 to 1931.

8 What were the main causes of the onset of the Great Depression in 1929?

9 What features of today make it less likely than in 1929 that a Great Depression will occur?

PROBLEMS

1 Analyse the changes in the interest rate during the 1991–1992 recession by drawing a diagram of the money market showing shifts in the demand and supply curves for real money. What policy changes could have prevented the recession? What would the effects of such actions have been on real GDP and the price level?

2 During the 1980–1981 recession, real wages rose and employment fell. How can these events be explained by the sticky wage theory? Can they be explained by the flexible wage theory?

3 Compare and contrast the events that took place between 1929 and 1931 with those of 1990–1992.

4 List all of the features of the UK economy in 1995 that you can think of that are consistent with a pessimistic outlook for the rest of the 1990s.

5 List all of the features of the UK economy in 1995 that you can think of that are consistent with an optimistic outlook for the rest of the 1990s.

6 How do you think the United Kingdom economy is going to evolve over the next year or two? Explain your predictions, drawing on the pessimistic and optimistic factors that you have listed in the previous two questions and on your knowledge of macroeconomic theory.

CHAPTER 32

STABILIZING
THE
ECONOMY

After studying this chapter you will be able to:

◆ Describe the goals of macroeconomic stabilization policy

◆ Describe the main features of monetary and fiscal policy since 1968

◆ Distinguish between fixed rules and feedback rules for stabilization policy

◆ Explain how the economy reacts to demand and supply shocks under fixed-rule and feedback-rule policies

◆ Explain why lowering inflation usually brings recession

I N THE DEPTHS OF THE GREAT DEPRESSION, PEOPLE TURNED TO A COALITION government under Ramsay MacDonald to deliver them from that economic catastrophe. Almost 60 years later, when John Major arrived in Downing Street, the economy stood on the brink of another recession. Again people wanted the government to intervene. But who is in charge of the economy? When recession strikes or inflation soars, what can the government do about it? ◆ ◆ In 1979, the Labour party lost a general election to the Conservatives. Unemployment was 4 per cent which – at the time – was considered very high and inflation was around 15 per cent. When Margaret Thatcher was returned as prime minister in 1983 and 1987, and when John Major was returned in 1992, inflation had dropped to below 4 per cent, but unemployment was around 10 per cent. How important was the economy in determining these election outcomes? ◆ ◆ The second half of the 1980s was a period of fairly low inflation, falling unemployment and rising output. How was all this achieved? Then, towards 1990, prices rose quickly, and by the early 1990s the economy was in recession with rising unemployment and falling output and incomes. What can be done to recreate the success of the late 1980s?

Who's in Charge?

◆ ◆ ◆ ◆ In this chapter, we're going to study the problems of stabilizing the UK economy – of avoiding inflation, high unemployment and wildly fluctuating growth rates of real GDP. The chapter will give you a clearer and deeper understanding of the macroeconomic policy problems facing the United Kingdom today and of the political debate concerning those problems.

The Stabilization Problem

The stabilization problem is to deliver a macroeconomic performance that is as smooth and predictable as possible. Solving this problem involves specifying targets to be achieved and then devising policies that result in getting as close as possible to those targets. There are two main macroeconomic targets. They are:

◆ Steady growth in real GDP
◆ Low and predictable inflation

Real GDP Growth and Unemployment

You will remember from Chapter 1 that the fundamental economic problem is scarcity. Each year, the economy is capable of producing more goods and services than before. If the amount that is actually produced, real GDP, rises more slowly than the amount which could be produced, then output is lost. We could be squeezing more out of scarce resources. Keeping real GDP growth steady and equal to long-run aggregate supply growth avoids this.

Fluctuations in real GDP growth also bring fluctuations in unemployment. When unemployment rises above its natural rate, productive labour is wasted and there is a slowdown in the accumulation of human capital. If such unemployment persists, serious psychological and social problems arise for the unemployed workers and their families. When unemployment falls below its natural rate, expanding industries are held back by labour shortages. Keeping real GDP growth steady helps keep unemployment at its natural rate and avoids the waste and shortage of labour.

Fluctuations in real GDP growth contribute to fluctuations in the international trade balance. An international trade deficit enables a country's actions to purchase more goods and services than they have produced. But to do so they must borrow from the rest of the world and pay interest on their borrowing. An international trade surplus enables them to lend to the rest of the world and earn interest. But to do so they must purchase fewer goods and services than they have produced. Keeping real GDP growth steady helps keep the balance of trade with the rest of the world steady and enables them to consume what they have produced and avoid a build-up of debt interest.

Inflation

When inflation fluctuates unpredictably, money becomes less useful as a measuring rod for conducting transactions. Borrowers and lenders and employers and workers must take on extra risks. Keeping the inflation rate steady and predictable avoids these problems.

Keeping inflation steady also helps keep the value of the pound steady in relation to other currencies. Other things being equal, if the inflation rate goes up by 1 percentage point, the pound loses 1 per cent of its value against the currencies of other countries. Large and unpredictable fluctuations in the foreign exchange rate – the value of the pound against other currencies - make international trade and international borrowing and lending less profitable and limit the gains from international specialization and exchange. Keeping inflation low and predictable helps avoid such fluctuations in the exchange rate and enables international transactions to be undertaken at minimum risk and on the desired scale.

Policy performance, judged by the two policy targets – real GDP growth and inflation – is shown for the years 1968–1993 in Fig. 32.1. Here the red line shows real GDP growth and the green shaded area shows inflation. As you can see, performance has fallen far short of stabilizing the economy. Why has the economy been so unstable? And can policy do better, making the next 25 years more stable than the last 25? Answering these questions will occupy most of the rest of this chapter. Let's begin by identifying the key players and the policy actions they have taken.

Players and Policies

There are two key players that formulate and execute macroeconomic stabilization policy in the United Kingdom:

◆ The government
◆ The Bank of England

The UK Government

The UK government implements the nation's fiscal policy. This is summarized each year in the budget. The **budget** is a statement of the government's

FIGURE **32.1**

Macroeconomic Performance: Real GDP and Inflation

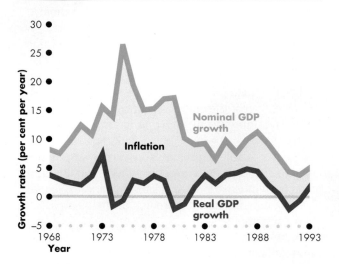

Real GDP growth and inflation have fluctuated a great deal during the years 1968–1993. In the 1970s inflation mushroomed, as shown by the green area. This macroeconomic performance falls far short of the goals of a stable real GDP growth rate and moderate and predictable inflation.

Sources: Central Statistical Office, *Economic Trends Annual Supplement 1992 Edition*, p.10, and *Economic Trends*, various issues.

financial plan. It itemizes spending programmes and their costs, tax revenues and the proposed deficit or surplus.

Fiscal policy has three elements:

◆ Spending plans
◆ Tax laws
◆ Deficit or surplus

Spending Plans The expenditure side of the budget is a list of programmes, together with the amount that the government plans to spend on each programme and a forecast of the total amount of government expenditure. For some items of expenditure, the amount to be spent can be directly controlled by government departments. These items include new hospitals and grants to universities. For other items of expenditure, the government may commit itself to particular programmes whose total costs depend on actions that the government can forecast but not

directly control. For example, National Insurance expenditure depends on the state of the economy and on how many people qualify for benefits.

Tax Laws Parliament makes decisions about government revenue by enacting tax laws. As in the case of some important items of government expenditure, the government cannot control with precision the amount of tax revenue that it will receive. Parliament makes the tax laws and fixes tax rates, but the amount of tax that is actually paid is determined by the actions of the millions of people and firms who make their own choices about how much to work and spend and save.

Deficit The difference between the total expenditure on government programmes and the total tax revenue received equals the central government deficit or surplus. We will discuss the deficit in detail in Chapter 33. Since 1972, the government spent more than it received in each year except 1988 and 1989.

There was a surplus in 1988 and 1989 principally because a growing output led to higher tax receipts while falling unemployment led to lower National Insurance benefits. The government could have taken more dramatic steps to reduce the deficits in other years by increasing its own revenue. But there are two competing views about how this objective might have been best achieved. One view is that tax reform and lower tax rates will increase revenue by stimulating economic activity, thus increasing the incomes on which taxes are paid by enough to ensure that lower tax rates, combined with higher incomes, bring in higher revenue. This view is associated with the 'supply side' views of former Prime Minister Margaret Thatcher and her close friend, the former US President Ronald Reagan. Margaret Thatcher's government did reduce income tax rates on a number of occasions. The other view is that revenue can be increased only by increasing tax rates and introducing new taxes.

Fiscal Policy A broad summary of fiscal policy since 1968 is given in Fig. 32.2. Here you can see the levels of government spending, taxes and the budget balance – each as a percentage of GDP. When spending is less than taxes, the budget balance is positive – the government has a surplus – and when spending exceeds taxes, the budget balance is negative – the

FIGURE 32.2

The Fiscal Policy Record: A Summary

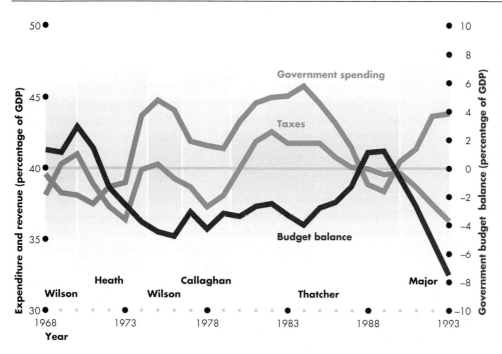

Fiscal policy is summarized here by the performance of government spending, taxes and the budget balance. Taxes have fluctuated between 36 and 43 per cent of GDP while spending has fluctuated between 37 and 46 per cent. The budget balance shows taxes minus government spending. The balance has fluctuated between +3 per cent of GDP and –8 per cent of GDP. It has usually been negative because taxes have usually been lower than spending.

Sources: Central Statistical Office, *National Income and Expenditure 1979 Edition*, pp. 62–3, *National Income and Expenditure 1982 Edition*, pp. 58–9, *The Blue Book: United Kingdom National Accounts, 1993 Edition*, p. 71, *Economic Trends Annual Supplement 1993 Edition*, p. 10, and *Economic Trends*, various issues.

government has a deficit. You can also see the names of the various prime ministers in this period.

Under Edward Heath's Conservative government, fiscal policy became more expansionary, and the subsequent Labour administrations of Harold Wilson and James Callaghan maintained this stance in the face of rising unemployment. Margaret Thatcher was committed to reducing government spending and taxes in order to promote incentives, but she also wanted to reduce the expansionary deficit as part of the war waged against inflation. She had little success in reducing the proportion of GDP taken by taxes, but she did manage to trim government spending. The spending cuts enabled the government to cut its expansionary deficit and even run a surplus in 1988 and 1989. But since then spending has soared and there is an expansionary deficit once again.

The Bank of England

The name of the *Bank of England* suggests that it is concerned with only one of the four nations that

make up the United Kingdom, but in fact it is the central bank for the whole of the United Kingdom. The main features of the Bank of England are described in Chapter 27. The Bank influences the economy chiefly by trading in markets in which it is one of the major participants. The two most important groups of these markets are those for government securities and foreign currencies. Its decisions to buy and sell in these markets influence interest rates, the value of sterling in terms of foreign currencies and the amount of money in the economy. These variables that the Bank of England can influence directly affect in turn the conditions on which the millions of firms and households in the economy undertake their own economic actions.

However, the Bank of England itself operates under severe constraints. These constraints come in two forms. First, there is an institutional constraint. The Bank is owned by the government and is required to try to implement monetary policies as laid down by the government. Although we shall talk in this chapter about the choices of policy available to the Bank, it is ultimately the government that decides which choice the Bank should select. Second, there is an economic constraint. The extent to which the Bank – or the government – can choose what monetary policy to pursue is constrained by the spending and taxing decisions made by the UK government.

Monetary Policy A broad measure of the influence of monetary policy is the growth rate of the money supply. Figure 32.3 shows the record since 1968. Here you can see the growth rate of M4. Once again you can also see the names of the various prime ministers in this period. No one urged the Bank to adopt an expansionary monetary policy more assiduously than Edward Heath who was confronted with unemployment rising to 3 per cent, a figure which was alarming as it had not been seen since just after World War II, and also with the shock of the first OPEC oil price rises. Monetary growth remained in double digits until as recently as 1991. But monetary policy was tighter in the early 1980s than it might seem from the graph because inflation was raging,

and the growth of real money was substantially less than the growth of nominal money.

We've now reviewed the targets of stabilization policy and seen that performance has been erratic. We've also described the key players in the policy-making game. Let's now turn our attention to the methods used for stabilizing the economy.

Alternative Stabilization Policies

How might the economy be stabilized? The answer is that there are many different monetary and fiscal policies that can be pursued. To understand the issues behind the choice of these policies, it is convenient to classify all possible policies into two broad categories:

◆ Fixed rules
◆ Feedback rules

Fixed Rules In the context of economic policy, a **fixed rule** specifies an action that must be pursued at all times irrespective of the state of the economy. In

---

FIGURE 32.3

The Monetary Policy Record: A Summary

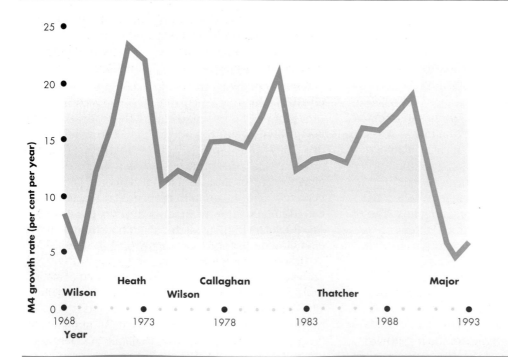

The monetary policy record is summarized here by the growth rate of M4. Monetary expansion was particularly rapid around 1972–1973, 1981 and 1990. Monetary expansion was particularly slow in 1992–1993.

Sources: Central Statistical Office, *Economic Trends Annual Supplement 1992 Edition*, pp. 161-2, and *Economic Trends*, various issues.

everyday life there are many examples of fixed rules. One example is the rule that motorists must stop when they come to a traffic light showing red, irrespective of the traffic flows at the time. The best known fixed rule for stabilization policy is one that has long been advocated by the American Nobel Prize winning economist Milton Friedman. He proposes setting the quantity of money growing at a constant rate year in and year out, regardless of the state of the economy. Inflation persists because continual increases in the money supply raise aggregate demand. Friedman proposes allowing the money supply to grow at a rate that would hold the *average* inflation rate at zero.

Feedback Rules In the context of economic policy, a **feedback rule** specifies how action must be adjusted to respond to varying circumstances. An everyday example of a feedback rule is a road sign instructing motorists to give way to traffic on a major road. Motorists may proceed if the major road is clear but must otherwise stop, so that they base their action on the present state of main road traffic. An example of a feedback rule for stabilization policy is one that specifies how changes in policy instruments such as the money supply, interest rates, or even taxes, should be changed in response to the present and forecast state of the economy. For example, the Bank of England would be pursuing a feedback rule if a fall in the value of sterling on the foreign exchange markets caused it to engage in an open market operation aimed at restraining the money supply growth rate and raising interest rates.

The key distinction between a fixed rule and a feedback rule is that with a fixed rule, policy instruments are set without regard to whether the economy is depressed, booming, or moving into recession or recovery, while with a feedback rule, policy instrument settings are changed in direct response to the state of the economy.

REVIEW

Stabilization policy seeks chiefly to ensure stable growth of real GDP, which should also secure unemployment at the natural rate, and stable low inflation. In practice neither real GDP growth nor inflation has been very stable. Stabilization poli-

cies are selected and implemented by the government and the Bank of England. Their policies can be divided into two groups according to whether they are based on fixed rules or feedback rules. ◆

Let's study the effects of a fixed rule and a feedback rule for the conduct of stabilization policy. We can do this by seeing how real GDP and inflation will behave under the two alternative rules. We will see what happens with both sorts of rule when there are aggregate demand shocks, and then what happens with them when there are aggregate supply shocks.

Stabilization Policy and Aggregate Demand Shocks

We'll study a model economy that starts out at full employment and has no inflation. Figure 32.4 illustrates this situation. The economy has the short-run aggregate supply curve *SAS*. The aggregate demand curve is initially AD_0. These two curves intersect at a point on the long-run aggregate supply curve *LAS*. The GDP deflator is 130 and real GDP is $600 billion. Now let's see what happens if there is a change in aggregate demand.

Suppose that there is an unexpected and temporary decrease in aggregate demand. Perhaps there is a wave of pessimism about the future that results in a decrease in investment demand, or perhaps there is a recession in the rest of the world that leads to a fall in exports. Regardless of the origin of the decrease in aggregate demand, the aggregate demand curve shifts to the left, to AD_1 in the figure. Because the decrease in aggregate demand is unanticipated, expected aggregate demand remains at AD_0, so the expected GDP deflator remains at 130. The short-run aggregate supply curve stays at *SAS*. Aggregate demand curve AD_1 intersects the short-run aggregate supply curve *SAS* at a GDP deflator of 125 and a real GDP of $550 billion. The economy is in a depressed state. Real GDP is below its long-run level and unemployment above its natural rate.

Recall that we are assuming that the decrease in aggregate demand from AD_0 to AD_1 is not permanent. So we assume that as time passes aggregate

FIGURE 32.4

A Decrease in Aggregate Demand

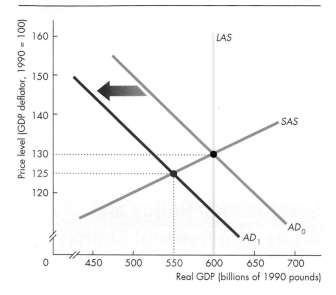

The economy starts out at full employment on aggregate demand curve AD_0 and short-run aggregate supply curve SAS, with the two curves intersecting on the long-run aggregate supply curve LAS. Real GDP is £600 billion and the GDP deflator is 130. A decrease in aggregate demand – perhaps due to pessimism about future profits – unexpectedly shifts the aggregate demand curve to AD_1. Real GDP falls to £550 billion, and the GDP deflator falls to 125. The economy is in a depressed state.

demand gradually increases back to its original level of AD_0. Maybe firms' investment picks up as confidence in the future improves, or maybe exports gradually rise as an economic recovery proceeds in the rest of the world. For some reason, then, the aggregate demand curve gradually returns to AD_0, but it takes a long time to do so.

We are going to work out how the economy would respond under two alternative policy packages during the period in which aggregate demand gradually increases to its original level. We'll look at a package of fixed-rule policies and a package of feedback-rule policies. Figure 32.5 illustrates the analysis.

Aggregate Demand Shock with Fixed Rules

The fixed rules we'll study here are ones which say that neither fiscal policy nor monetary policy should react to the state of real GDP or to changes in real

GDP. So when aggregate demand decreases, there will be no change in government spending plans and tax laws and no change in the money supply. The response of the economy under this package of fixed rules is shown in Fig. 32.5(a).

When aggregate demand decreases to AD_1, no policy measures are taken to bring the economy back to full employment. But recall that we are assuming that aggregate demand gradually increases because of other factors and eventually returns to AD_0. As it does so, real GDP and the GDP deflator gradually increase. The GDP deflator gradually returns to 130 and real GDP to its long-run level of £600 billion. Throughout this process, the economy experiences more rapid growth than usual but beginning from a state of excess capacity. Unemployment remains high until the aggregate demand curve has returned to AD_0.

Let's contrast this adjustment with what occurs under a feedback-rule monetary policy.

Aggregate Demand Shock with Feedback Rules

The feedback rules that we'll study here are ones which say that both fiscal policy and monetary policy should react in an expansionary way when real GDP falls below its long-run level. So when real GDP falls below its long-run level, there will be a rise in government spending plans and a fall in taxes – and so a rise in the government deficit – and there will also be a rise in the money supply. Conversely, both fiscal and monetary policy should react in a contractionary way when real GDP rises above its long-run level. The response of the economy under this package of feedback rules is shown in Fig. 32.5(b).

When aggregate demand decreases to AD_1, the increased government spending, lower taxes and rise in the money supply combine to shift the aggregate demand curve back to AD_0. Real GDP jumps back to its full-employment level and the GDP deflator jumps back to 130. As the other forces that increase aggregate demand come into play, the expansionary fiscal and monetary policies are gradually eased and eventually withdrawn, to hold the aggregate demand curve steady at AD_0.

The Two Policies Compared

Under a fixed-rule policy, the economy goes into a recession and stays there for as long as it takes the

FIGURE 32.5

Two Stabilization Policies: Aggregate Demand Shocks

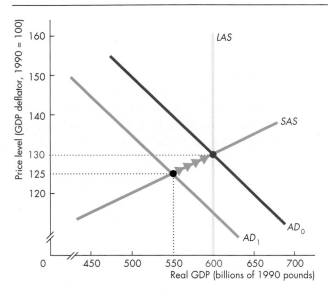

(a) Fixed rule

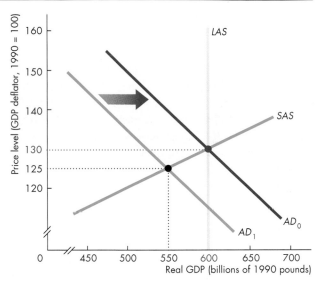

(b) Feedback rule

The economy is in a depressed state with a GDP deflator of 125 and real GDP of £550 billion. The short-run aggregate supply curve is *SAS*. Part (a) shows the effects of fixed-rule stabilization policies. These leave the aggregate demand initially at AD_1, so the GDP deflator remains at 125 and real GDP remains at £550 billion. As other influences on aggregate demand gradually increase, the aggregate demand curve shifts back to AD_0. As it does, real GDP rises back to £600 billion and the GDP deflator increases to 130. Part (b)

shows the effects of feedback-rule stabilization policies. These are expansionary and increase aggregate demand, shifting the aggregate demand curve from AD_1 to AD_0. Real GDP returns to £600 billion and the GDP deflator returns to 130. Fiscal and monetary policies then become gradually contractionary as the other influences on aggregate demand increase its level. As a result, the aggregate demand curve is kept steady at AD_0 and real GDP stays at £600 billion.

aggregate demand curve to return to its original position. Only gradually does the recession come to an end and aggregate demand return to its original level. But under a feedback-rule policy, the economy is pulled out of its recession quickly by the policy action. And the expansionary policies used to raise aggregate demand are gradually eased when other factors raise aggregate demand, so that real GDP is held back at its long-run level.

The price level and real GDP fall and rise by exactly the same amounts in the two cases, but real GDP stays below its long-run level for longer with a fixed rule than it does with a feedback rule.

So Feedback Rules Are Better?

Isn't it obvious that feedback rules are better than fixed rules? Can't the government and the Bank of England use feedback rules to keep the economy

close to full employment with a stable price level? Of course, unforecast changes – such as the decrease in aggregate demand in our example – will knock the economy from time to time. But by responding with appropriate changes in government spending, taxes and the quantity of money, can't the players minimize the damage from such a shock? It certainly appears to be so from our analysis.

Despite the apparent superiority of feedback rules, many economists remain convinced that fixed rules stabilize the economy more effectively than feedback rules. They make three assertions to justify their views. These assertions are:

◆ Full-employment real GDP is not known.
◆ Policy lags are longer than the forecast horizon.
◆ Feedback rules are less predictable than fixed rules.

Let's look at these assertions.

Knowledge of Full-employment Real GDP   To decide whether a feedback policy needs to stimulate aggregate demand or retard it, it is necessary to know whether the current level of real GDP is above or below the full-employment level. Unfortunately, the full-employment level of real GDP is not known with certainty. This means there may often be uncertainty about the *direction* in which a feedback policy should push the level of aggregate demand. One reason why the full-employment level of real GDP is not known for certain is that we are not sure what the natural level of unemployment is and hence are not sure what level of employment would occur when unemployment is at its natural rate. This, in turn, is because there is uncertainty and disagreement about how the labour market works.

Policy Lags and the Forecast Horizon   Even if the full-employment level of real GDP were known, there would still be problems with a feedback rule. Suppose that at present real GDP is below the full-employment level and a good estimate has been made of the increase in aggregate demand that is necessary to get real GDP to the full-employment level. Should the Bank of England react by increasing the rate of growth of the money supply and so reduce interest rates by enough to increase investment by firms and purchases of consumer durables by the appropriate amount? Or should the government reduce taxes and raise its spending by the appropriate amounts? Or maybe there could be a mix of monetary and fiscal expansion.

Unfortunately, these expansionary policies take up to two years to have their full effect on aggregate demand. By the time those two years are over, aggregate demand may have increased anyway. For instance, there might be a boom in foreign countries leading to a surge in exports, or a rise in business confidence leading to a surge in investment. So the result of implementing the 'appropriate' feedback policies will be to create a level of aggregate demand that is too high.

Of course, if the policy makers could accurately forecast the levels of exports and investment spending and the other components of aggregate demand over the next two years, they could allow for changes in them when preparing their feedback policies. But it is very difficult to make reasonably accurate forecasts even a year ahead. Moreover, it is not even possible to predict the precise timing and magnitude of the effects of the policies themselves. So feedback policies that react to today's economy may be inappropriate for the state of the economy at that uncertain future date when the effects are felt.

Let's see why monetary and fiscal policies operate with such a lag. Take monetary policy first. Suppose that today the economy is in recession. The Bank of England reacts with an increase in the money supply growth rate. When the Bank takes this action, the first reaction is a fall in interest rates. Some time later, lower interest rates produce an increase in investment and in purchases of consumer durable goods. Some time still later, this rise in expenditure increases income which in turn induces higher consumption expenditure. Later yet, the higher expenditure increases the demand for labour and eventually wages and prices rise. The sectors in which the spending increases occur vary and so does the impact on employment. It can take anywhere from nine months to two years for an initial action by the Bank to cause a change in real GDP, employment and the inflation rate.

You can see that to smooth the fluctuations in aggregate demand, the Bank of England needs to take actions today that are based on a forecast of what will be happening over a period stretching up to two years into the future. It is no use taking actions a year from today to influence the situation that prevails then, for it will be too late. And, because the Bank cannot accurately predict the shocks to aggregate demand that will occur during this period, it cannot be sure of taking the appropriate measures today. So the Bank cannot deliver the type of aggregate demand-smoothing performance that we assumed in the model economy we studied earlier in this chapter.

The problems for fiscal policy feedback rules are similar to those for monetary policy but are even more severe because of the lags in the implementation of fiscal policy. The Bank of England can take actions relatively quickly. But the government rarely changes tax rates or makes major changes in its spending levels except in its annual November budget. Even then, more months may elapse before the new tax rates and spending plans come into effect. So even before a fiscal policy action is implemented, the economy may have moved on to a new situation that calls for a different feedback from the one that is in the legislative pipeline.

Because monetary and fiscal policy take so long to have their full effects, it is clear that adopting feedback rules that react to the state of the economy at the time is risky. If the policy makers react to a recessed economy with expansionary monetary and fiscal policies, it is possible that when they take full effect aggregate demand will have increased anyway and the economy is overheated. So it is possible for feedback rules to aggravate the fluctuations in the economy rather than smooth them out. For this reason, UK governments in the 1980s and 1990s have been much less enthusiastic about feedback rules than their predecessors, though they have not adopted a fully fixed-rules stance either.

Predictability of Policies To make decisions about long-term contracts for employment (wage contracts) and for borrowing and lending, people have to anticipate the future course of prices – the future inflation rate. To make a forecast of inflation, it is necessary to forecast aggregate demand. Suppose that people anticipate that aggregate demand is going to increase less quickly next year than it has increased this year. In view of this anticipation, firms and workers agree to a slower rate of wage increase. The short-run aggregate supply curve shifts to the left less quickly as a result of the expectation of slower growth in aggregate demand. If aggregate demand *actually* slows down, as anticipated, inflation also slows but firms continue to produce at their capacity output levels and there is full employment. A correctly anticipated slowdown in the growth of aggregate demand has resulted in a slowdown in inflation but with no slowdown in output growth and no increase in unemployment.

Contrast this case with one in which there is an unanticipated slowdown in aggregate demand. Aggregate demand is anticipated to continue growing at its current rate but, in fact, it slows down. With this anticipation, firms and workers agree to keep money wages rising at their current rate. As a consequence, the short-run aggregate supply curve shifts to the left. When aggregate demand fails to increase at the expected rate, real GDP falls below its long-run level, unemployment rises above its natural rate, and there is a slowdown in inflation. The economy goes into recession because money wages have been set too high for the level of aggregate demand that has actually come about.

Why might aggregate demand growth slow down unexpectedly? There are many possible reasons but one is that the Bank of England may unexpectedly slow down the growth rate of the money supply,

forcing interest rates up and lowering investment. Such an action by the Bank of England would slow inflation but would also push real GDP below its long-run level and increase unemployment. If the Bank sticks to a rock-steady, fixed rule for increasing the money supply, then the Bank itself cannot be a contributor to unexpected fluctuations in aggregate demand. To the extent that the Bank of England's actions are unpredictable, they lead to unpredictable fluctuations in aggregate demand. These fluctuations, in turn, produce fluctuations in real GDP, employment and unemployment.

There is more scope for the Bank of England's actions to be unpredictable when it is pursuing a feedback rule rather than a fixed rule, for in such a situation it is necessary to predict the future values of the variables to which the Bank reacts. Consequently, the feedback rule for monetary policy can create more unpredictable fluctuations in aggregate demand than a fixed rule. Economists disagree about whether those bigger fluctuations offset the potential stabilizing influence of the predictable changes the Bank of England makes. No agreed measurements have been made to settle this dispute. Nevertheless, the unpredictability of the Bank's actions is an important fact of economic life.

There are at least two reasons why the Bank of England seeks to keep some of its actions behind a smokescreen. First, the Bank wants to maintain as much freedom of action as possible and so does not want to state with too great a precision the rules that it will follow in any given circumstances. Second, the Bank is part of a political process and, although it is not a government department like the Treasury, it is required to operate monetary policies laid down by the government. For such reasons, the Bank does not specify feedback rules that are as precise as the one that we have analysed in this chapter, and so cannot deliver an economic performance that has the stability that we generated in the model economy.

If it is difficult for the Bank of England to pursue a predictable, feedback monetary stabilization policy, it is probably impossible for the government to pursue a predictable, feedback fiscal stabilization policy. Since a fiscal stabilization policy is formulated in terms of spending programmes and tax laws and since these programmes and laws themselves are the outcome of a political process there can be no effective way in which a predictable feedback fiscal stabilization policy can be adhered to.

F ixed-rule policies keep fiscal and monetary policy set steady and independent of the state of the economy. Feedback policies cut taxes, increase spending and speed up money supply growth when the economy is in recession, and reverse these measures when the economy is overheating. Feedback rules apparently do a better job but we are not sure that is the case. Their successful use requires a good knowledge of the current state of the economy, an ability to forecast as far ahead as the policy actions have effects, and clarity and openness about the feedback rules being used. ◆

We have reviewed three reasons why feedback rules might not be more effective than fixed rules in controlling aggregate demand. The evolution of views about aggregate demand stabilization is featured in Our Advancing Knowledge on pp. 912–913. But there is a fourth reason why some economists prefer fixed rules. This is that not all shocks to the economy come from the demand side. Advocates of feedback rules believe that demand shocks are the dominant ones. Advocates of fixed rules believe that supply shocks are the dominant ones. Let's now see how aggregate supply fluctuations affect the economy under fixed rules and under feedback rules and see why those economists who believe that aggregate supply fluctuations are the dominant ones also favour fixed rules rather than feedback rules.

Stabilization Policy and Aggregate Supply Shocks

T here are two reasons why aggregate supply fluctuations can cause problems for a stabilization feedback rule:

◆ Cost–push inflation
◆ Slowdown in productivity growth

In either of these situations the economy experiences stagflation, in which real GDP stops growing or even declines while inflation accelerates. Let's study the effects of alternative policies to deal with this problem.

Cost–Push Inflation

Cost–push inflation is inflation that has its origins in cost increases. The two most important potential sources of cost increases are wage increases and rises in raw material prices, such as the massive rises in oil prices that occurred in the 1970s and early 1980s. To proceed, a wage–push inflation must be accommodated by an increase in the money supply – which in turn increases aggregate demand. Feedback rules make wage–push inflation possible. Fixed rules make such inflation impossible. Let's see why.

Consider the economy that is shown in Fig. 32.6. Aggregate demand is AD_0, short-run aggregate supply is SAS_0, and long-run aggregate supply is LAS. Real GDP equals its capacity level of £600 billion and the GDP deflator is 130.

Now suppose that a number of trade unions or key suppliers of raw materials try to gain a temporary advantage by increasing wages or the price of their materials. To make the exercise interesting, let's suppose that the people in question are concerned with a significant portion of the economy. As a consequence, when they increase the wage rate or the price of a raw material such as oil, the short-run aggregate supply curve shifts to the left from SAS_0 to SAS_1.

Fixed Rule Figure 32.6(a) shows what happens in a model economy if the government follows a fixed rule for fiscal policy and the Bank of England follows a fixed rule for monetary policy. Suppose that the fixed rules are no changes in government spending or taxes and no changes in the money supply – that is a zero money supply growth. With these fixed rules, the government and the Bank pay no attention to the fact that there has been an increase in wages or raw material prices. No policy actions are taken. The short-run aggregate supply curve will have shifted to the left to SAS_1 and aggregate demand will stay at AD_0. The price level will rise to a GDP deflator of 140, and real GDP will fall to £550 billion. The economy is experiencing stagflation.

The economy will remain depressed until such time as those responsible for increased wages or

FIGURE 32.6

Two Stabilization Policies: Short-run Aggregate Supply Shocks

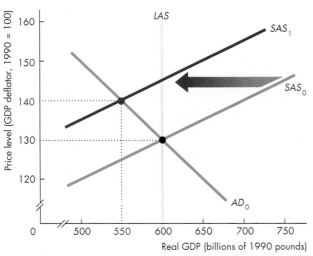

(a) Fixed rule

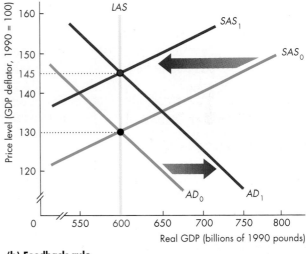

(b) Feedback rule

The economy starts out on AD_0 and SAS_0, with a GDP deflator of 130 and real GDP of £600 billion. Some trade unions, or suppliers of key raw materials, force up their wages or prices, shifting the short-run aggregate supply curve to SAS_1. Real GDP falls to £550 billion and the GDP deflator increases to 140. Part (a) shows the effect of fixed-rule stabilization policies in which the government and Bank of England make no changes to aggregate demand. The economy stays depressed until wages or raw material prices fall again, and

the economy returns to its original position. Part (b) shows the effect of feedback rules. With these, the government cuts taxes and/or raises its spending while the Bank of England raises the money supply. These policies raise aggregate demand to AD_1. Real GDP returns to the full-employment level, £600 billion, but the GDP deflator increases to 145. The economy is set for another round of cost–push inflation.

raw material prices reverse their action. This decrease in wages may take a long time to come about. Eventually, however, the low level of real GDP and associated high level of unemployment will bring about a lowering of the wages and prices whose increase caused the initial problem. The short-run aggregate supply curve will shift back to the right to SAS_0. The GDP deflator will fall to 130 and real GDP will increase to £600 billion.

Feedback Rule Figure 32.6(b) shows what happens if the government and the Bank of England operate feedback rules. The starting point is the same as before – the economy is on SAS_0 and AD_0 with a GDP deflator of 130 and real GDP of £600 billion. Wages or raw material prices are increased and the short-run aggregate supply curve shifts to the left to SAS_1. The economy goes into a recession

with real GDP falling to £550 billion and the price level increasing to 140. The Bank's monetary feedback rule is to increase the money supply growth rate when real GDP is below its long-run level. And the government's fiscal feedback rule is to cut taxes and raise spending when real GDP is below its long-run level. So, with real GDP at £550 billion, the Bank raises the money supply growth rate and the government raises its spending and cuts its taxes. The aggregate demand curve shifts to the right to AD_1. The price level increases to 130 and real GDP returns to £600 billion. The economy moves back to full employment but at a higher price level.

The union workers or raw material suppliers who saw a personal advantage in forcing up their wages or prices before, will see the same advantage once again. So the short-run aggregate supply

Evolving Approaches to Economic Stabilization

> 'You have to find a real crackpot to get an economist who doesn't accept the principle of government intervention in the business cycle.'
>
> KENNETH ARROW
> *Time, March 3, 1961*

When it comes to stabilizing the economy, people differ in their opinions about what's best. But there was a time when you would have been hard pressed to find an economist who did not believe that active measures taken by a well-informed government could make the market economy function more smoothly. That time was the mid-1960s, when Harold Wilson was Prime Minister.

Using the expenditure multiplier model (of Chapter 25), economists believed that setting the levels of government purchases and taxes at the appropriate levels would allow continuous full employment, and steady economic expansion could be maintained indefinitely.

The practice of active stabilization policy worked well until the mid-1960s, but then inflation began to creep upward. Advocates of activist policies blame greedy trade unions and fixed exchange rates. Opponents of activism blame the activist policies themselves, claiming that once an activist policy is anticipated, its effects on output are weak and its main effects are on inflation.

Whichever view is correct, activist policies came into official disrepute during the 1970s, when oil price hikes left no doubt that the main problem (at least for the time being) was not demand fluctuations, but supply shocks. Distrust of activist stabilization became particularly strong during Margaret Thatcher's premiership when the prevailing view was that government should set the rules of the game and leave the private sector to get on with the creation of jobs and wealth.

The recession of 1991 saw a return to a more pragmatic approach with attempts to stimulate demand by lowering interest rates, but not too aggressively, especially with such a large and persistent government and trade deficit. If and when the deficit subsides, there is likely to be renewed enthusiasm for more ambitious fiscal policies to stimulate demand during recessions.

The accumulation of economic data and the development of statistical models of the economy gave a strong boost of confidence to Harold Wilson's economic advisers, such as Nicholas Kaldor. Using their models and best judgements about where the economy was and where it was heading, Wilson's advisers devised policies to maintain low unemployment and improve growth but without increasing inflation.

Today, even in a recession, there is little talk of cutting taxes and increasing spending to lift the economy back to full employment. The fear is still that inflation will rise again. The president of the Bundesbank is a powerful voice in European macroeconomic policy as the framework he devises, particularly for interest rates, impinges on all other EU nations. Cutting interest rates may stimulate investment but it will also encourage increased consumption and a fall in the exchange rate of EU currencies, both of which may engender higher inflation. Simply cutting interest rates may solve short-run problems but in turn is believed to create more serious long-term problems.'

Milton Friedman Versus The Keynesians: The Rise and Fall of Fine-Tuning

From 1946 to 1983, Milton Friedman, now a Senior Fellow at the Hoover Institution at Stanford University, was one of the leading members of the Chicago School. This approach to economics was developed at the University of Chicago and based on the views that free markets allocate resources efficiently and that stable and low money supply growth delivers macroeconomic stability. In the early 1960s, these views were in a distinct minority, and many economists placed them in the 'crackpot' category. By reasoning from basic economic principles, Friedman predicted that persistent demand stimulation would not increase output but would cause inflation. When output growth slowed and inflation broke out in the 1970s, Friedman seemed like a prophet, and for a time, his policy prescription – known as monetarism – was embraced around the world.

MILTON FRIEDMAN

curve will shift to the left once more and the government and the Bank will chase it with an increase in aggregate demand. The economy will be in an inflationary spiral.

Incentives to Push Up Wages and Raw Material Prices

You can see that there are no checks on the incentives to push up wages or raw material prices if the government and the Bank of England pursue feedback rules of the type that we've just analysed. If some group sees a temporary gain from pushing up wages or prices and if the government and the Bank always react in a way that prevents unemployment and slack business conditions from emerging, then cost–push elements will face no constraints.

But when the government and the Bank pursue fixed rules, the incentive to attempt to steal a temporary advantage by increasing wages or prices is severely weakened. The cost of higher unemployment and lower output is a consequence that each group will have to face and recognize.

Thus fixed rules are capable of delivering a steady inflation rate (or even zero inflation) while feedback rules, in the face of cost–push pressures, will leave the inflation rate free to rise and fall at the whim of whichever group believes a temporary advantage to be available from pushing up its wage or price.

Slowdown in Productivity Growth

Some economists believe that fluctuations in real GDP (and in employment and unemployment) are caused not by fluctuations in aggregate demand or wages but by fluctuations in the growth rate of long-run aggregate supply. These economists have developed a new theory of aggregate fluctuations called the real business cycle theory. The **real business cycle theory** is a theory of aggregate fluctuations which assumes that wages are flexible and argues that the economy is disturbed by random shocks to its aggregate production function. The word 'real' draws attention to the idea that, according to this theory, the most important sources of aggregate fluctuations are real things – random shocks to the economy's real production possibilities – rather than nominal things – the money supply and its rate of growth.

According to the real business cycle theory, there is no useful distinction to be made between

the long-run aggregate supply curve and the short-run aggregate supply curve. Because wages are flexible, the labour market is always in equilibrium at the natural rate of unemployment. The vertical long-run aggregate supply curve is also the short-run aggregate supply curve. Fluctuations occur because of shifts in the long-run aggregate supply curve. Normally, the long-run aggregate supply curve shifts to the right – the economy expands. But the pace at which the long-run aggregate supply curve shifts to the right varies. Also, on occasion, the long-run aggregate supply curve shifts to the left, bringing a decrease in aggregate supply and a fall in real GDP.

An economic policy that influences the aggregate demand curve has no effect on real GDP. But it does affect the price level. However, if a feedback policy is used to increase aggregate demand every time real GDP falls, and if the real business cycle theory is correct, then the feedback monetary policy will make price level fluctuations more severe than they would be otherwise. To see why, consider Fig. 32.7.

Imagine that the economy starts out on aggregate demand curve AD_0 and long-run aggregate supply curve LAS_0 at a GDP deflator of 130 and with real GDP equal to £600 billion. Now suppose that long-run aggregate supply decreases to LAS_1. An actual decrease in long-run aggregate supply could occur as a result of a natural catastrophe or perhaps as the result of a disruption of international trade which might follow a tariff war between countries.

Fixed Rules

With fixed rules for fiscal and monetary policy, the decrease in long-run aggregate supply causes no response from the government or the Bank of England so there is no effect on aggregate demand. The aggregate demand curve remains AD_0. Real GDP falls to £550 billion and the GDP deflator increases to 140.

Feedback Rules

Now suppose that the government and the Bank of England use feedback rules. In particular, suppose that when real GDP falls, the government raises its spending and cuts its taxes while the Bank increases the money supply to increase aggregate demand. In this example, the fiscal and monetary feedback policies shift the aggregate demand curve to AD_1. The policy goal is to bring real GDP back to £600 billion. But the long-

FIGURE 32.7

Stabilization Policy: Long-run Aggregate Supply Shocks

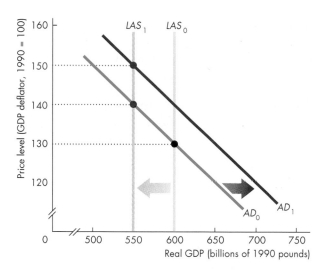

The economy starts out on AD_0 and LAS_0 with a GDP deflator of 130 and real GDP of £600 billion. A productivity slowdown shifts the long-run aggregate supply curve from LAS_0 to LAS_1. Real GDP falls to £550 billion and the GDP deflator rises to 140. With fixed-rule policies, there is no change in government spending, taxes or the money supply, so aggregate demand stays at AD_0 and that is the end of the matter. With feedback-rule policies, the government cuts taxes and/or raises its spending while the Bank of England raises the money supply. These policies raise aggregate demand to AD_1, intending to increase real GDP. But the result is an increase in the price level – the GDP deflator rises to 150 – with no change in real GDP.

run aggregate supply curve has shifted and so long-run GDP has fallen to £550 billion. The increase in aggregate demand cannot bring forth an increase in output if the economy does not have the capacity to produce that output. So real GDP stays at £550 billion, but the price level rises still further – the GDP deflator goes to 150. You can see that in this case the attempt to stabilize real GDP using a feedback rule for monetary policy has no effect on real GDP but generates a substantial price level increase.

We've now seen some of the shortcomings of using a feedback rule for monetary policy. Some economists believe that these shortcomings are serious and urge the government and the Bank to

implement fixed rules. Others, regarding the potential advantages of a feedback rule as greater than its costs, urge the Bank to continue to pursue such policies.

If EU countries succeed in their avowed aim of creating a common currency and a single central bank for the European Union, then it is very possible that such a central bank would be asked to adopt a fixed rule. This is partly because some advocates of European monetary integration are impressed by the arguments for fixed rules that we have just outlined. And it is partly because no EU central bank could behave as each member would like, since some members might want restraint while others might want expansion. In the complex negotiating world of the European Union it would be a lot easier politically to have fixed rules!

Nominal GDP Targeting

Attempting to keep the growth rate of nominal GDP steady is called **nominal GDP targeting**. James Tobin of Yale University and John Taylor of Stanford University have suggested that nominal GDP targeting is a useful operating goal for macroeconomic policy.

The nominal GDP growth equals the real GDP growth rate plus the inflation rate. When nominal GDP grows quickly, it is usually because the inflation rate is high. When nominal GDP grows slowly, it is usually because real GDP growth is negative – the economy is in recession. Thus by keeping nominal GDP growth steady, it is hoped to avoid excesses of inflation and recession.

Nominal GDP targeting uses feedback rules. Expansionary fiscal or monetary actions increase aggregate demand when nominal GDP is below target and contractionary fiscal or monetary actions decrease aggregate demand when nominal GDP is above target. The main problem with nominal GDP targeting is that there are long and variable time lags between the identification of a need to change aggregate demand and the effects of the policy actions taken.

Macroeconomists are still debating the merits of the alternative policies for achieving stability. But they are gradually arriving at a new consensus about what can be achieved. Reading Between the Lines on pp. 918–919 considers what is currently being achieved in the United Kingdom.

Taming Inflation

So far, we've concentrated on stabilizing real GDP either directly or indirectly and *avoiding* inflation. But often the problem is not to avoid inflation but to tame it. How can inflation, once it has set in, be cured? Let's look at some alternative ways.

A Surprise Inflation Reduction

To study the problem of reducing inflation, we'll use two equivalent approaches, the aggregate demand–aggregate supply model and the Phillips curve. You met the Phillips curve in Chapter 30 (pp. 863–866) and it enables us to keep track of what is happening to both inflation and unemployment.

The economy is shown in Fig. 32.8. In part (a) it is on aggregate demand curve AD_0 and short-run aggregate supply curve SAS_0 with real GDP at £600 billion and the GDP deflator at 130. With real GDP at its long-run level (on the LAS curve), there is full employment. Equivalently, in part (b), the economy is on its long-run Phillips curve, $LRPC$ and short-run Phillips curve $SRPC_0$. Inflation is raging at 10 per cent a year and unemployment is at its natural rate which we will take to be 6 per cent.

Next year, aggregate demand is *expected* to increase, shifting the aggregate demand curve in Fig. 32.8(a) to AD_1. Expecting this increase in aggregate demand, wages increase to shift the short-run aggregate supply curve to SAS_1. If expectations are fulfilled, the GDP deflator rises to 143 – a 10 per cent inflation – and real GDP remains at its long-run level. In part (b), the economy remains at its original position.

But suppose the Bank of England tries to slow down inflation to 4 per cent a year. If it simply slows down the growth of aggregate demand, the aggregate demand curve in part (a) shifts to AD_2. With no slowdown in the expected inflation rate, wage increases shift the short-run aggregate supply curve to SAS_1. Real GDP decreases to £550 billion and the GDP deflator rises to 140.4 – an inflation rate of 8 per cent a year. In Fig. 32.8(b), there is a movement along the short-run Phillips curve $SRPC_0$ as unemployment rises to 9 per cent and inflation falls to 8 per cent a year. The policy has succeeded in slowing inflation, but by less than desired and at a cost of recession. Real GDP is below its long-run level and unemployment is above its natural rate.

A Credible Announced Inflation Reduction

Suppose that instead of simply slowing down the growth of aggregate demand, the Bank of England announced its intention ahead of its action and in a credible and convincing way so that its announcement was believed. The lower level of aggregate demand becomes expected. In this case, wages increase at a pace consistent with the lower level of aggregate demand and the short-run aggregate supply curve in Fig. 32.8(a) shifts to SAS_2. When aggregate demand increases shifting the aggregate demand curve to AD_2, the GDP deflator rises to 136.5 – an inflation rate of 5 per cent a year – and real GDP remains at its full-employment level.

In Fig. 32.8(b), the lower expected inflation rate shifts the short-run Phillips curve downward to $SRPC_1$, and inflation falls to 5 per cent a year while unemployment remains at its natural rate.

Inflation Reduction in Practice

When the Bank of England in fact slowed down inflation in 1980, UK citizens paid a very high price. The Bank's monetary policy action was unpredicted. As a result, it occurred in the face of wages that had been set at too high a level to be consistent with the growth of aggregate demand that the Bank subsequently allowed. The consequence was recession – a decrease in real GDP and a rise in unemployment. Couldn't the Bank have lowered inflation without causing recession by telling people far enough ahead of time that it did indeed plan to slow down the growth rate of aggregate demand?

The answer appears to be no. The main reason is that people form their expectation of the Bank of England's actions (like they form expectations about anyone's actions) on the basis of actual behaviour, not on the basis of stated intentions. How many times have you told yourself that it is your firm intention to lose some weight or to keep within your income and put a few pounds away for a rainy day, only to discover that, despite your very best intentions, your old habits win out in the end?

Forming expectations about the Bank of England's behaviour is no different except, of course, it is more complex than forecasting your own behaviour. To form expectations of the Bank's actions, people look at the Bank's past *actions*, not its stated intentions. Based on such observations, they try to work out what the Bank's policy is, to

FIGURE 32.8

Lowering Inflation

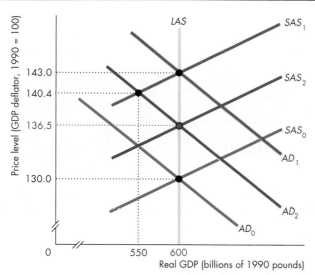

(a) Aggregate demand and aggregate supply

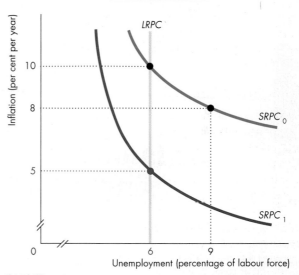

(b) Phillips curves

Initially, aggregate demand is AD_0 and short-run aggregate supply is SAS_0. Real GDP is £600 billion – its full-employment level on the long-run aggregate supply curve LAS. Inflation is running at 10 per cent a year. If it continues to do so, the aggregate demand curve will shift to AD_1 and the short-run aggregate supply curve to SAS_1. The GDP deflator will rise to 143. This same situation is shown in part (b) with the economy on the short-run Phillips curve $SRPC_0$.

With an unexpected slowdown in aggregate demand growth, the aggregate demand curve shown in part (a) shifts to AD_2, real GDP falls to £550

billion, and inflation slows to 8 per cent with the GDP deflator at 140.4. In part (b), unemployment rises to 9 per cent as the economy slides down $SRPC_0$.

If a credibly announced slowdown in aggregate demand growth occurs, the short-run aggregate supply curve shown in part (a) shifts to SAS_2, the short-run Phillips curve shown in part (b) shifts to $SRPC_1$, inflation slows to 5 per cent, real GDP remains at £600 billion and unemployment remains at its natural rate of 6 per cent.

---

forecast its future actions, and to forecast the effects of those actions on aggregate demand and inflation.

As the Bank had been reluctant to pursue tight monetary policies in the 1970s, people did not expect it to do so in 1980. The subsequent recession saw unemployment rising by 7 per cent from 4 per cent in early 1980 to 11 per cent by 1985. When inflation subsequently rose again in the late 1980s, people were a little less surprised that the Bank adopted a tight monetary policy. And unemployment rose a little more modestly by 5 per cent.

A Truly Independent Central Bank

One suggestion for dealing with inflation is to make the Bank of England more independent and to

charge it with the single responsibility of achieving and maintaining price level stability (see Chapter 27). Some central banks are much more independent than the Bank of England. The German and Swiss central banks are the best examples. Another example is the New Zealand central bank. All these central banks have the responsibility of stabilizing prices but not real GDP, and of doing so without interference from the government.

If an arrangement could be devised for making the Bank of England take a longer-term view that concentrated only on inflation, it is possible that inflation could be lowered and kept low at a low cost. But in the light of the possibility of monetary union within the European Union, the debate over the Bank of England has begun to seem a little academic. It is unlikely that UK citizens will feel the

The End of the Recession in the UK

The UK economy is coming out of recession and its growth rate is forecast to increase.

A rise in the value of the pound could hit exports, but this effect is offset by lower unit labour costs.

Inflation is set to rise towards 4 per cent.

The pound could be allowed to rise in order to lower import prices and help limit the rise in inflation.

Tax increases aimed at reducing the large budget deficit may restrict the recovery and are politically unpopular.

Faster economic growth does not, however, reduce the need for these tax rises as a budget deficit equal to 4 per cent of GDP would still remain.

THE ECONOMIST, 7 AUGUST 1993

Britain: The Chancellor sings in his bath

KENNETH Clarke can hardly believe his luck. He has inherited from Norman Lamont a surprisingly robust recovery. GDP rose by 0.5% in the second quarter, the fourth successive quarterly rise. The panel of forecasters which *The Economist* polls each month expect Britain's economy to grow by 1.6% this year... and by 2.6% next year....

Exports are booming. In the three months to June their volume to non-EC countries was 17% higher than a year earlier.... True, the latest survey of manufacturers by the Confederation of British Industry pointed to clouds on the horizon: exports would weaken in the coming months, it said, mainly because of depressed demand in continental Europe. But the new flexibility in the ERM could blow that worry away. The widened ERM bands should allow Britain's EC partners to cut interest rates to spur their economics.

British manufacturers fret that they could become less competitive if sterling continues to climb against other currencies. Yet some of the pound's recent rise has been offset by a fall in labour costs in Britain relative to those on the continent....

Speculation about a cut in British base rates, currently 6%, is rife. It is argued that Mr Clarke will have to cut rates to prevent the pound becoming overvalued against falling EC currencies....

The Treasury's advice to Mr Clarke is to accept an appreciation of sterling to dampen import prices....

In March Mr Lamont pre-announced £10 billion of tax increases to take effect in 1994 and 1995, to reduce a public-sector borrowing requirement running at £50 billion ($75 billion), or 8% of GDP. Mr Lamont's plans included extending value-added tax to domestic fuel, at a rate of 8% next April and the full 17.5% in 1995. Ministers are under fierce pressure from backbenchers to drop this hugely unpopular idea, or at least to limit the rate of VAT on fuel to 8%. After all, faster-than-expected recovery will help to trim the budget deficit. Surely Mr Clarke now needs a smaller tax increase?

This is where the chancellor stops singing in his bath. Even after the planned tax increases, and even if the economy started running at full steam, a deficit of around 4% of GDP would remain. That is still too big for comfort. Further tax increases or spending cuts equivalent to at least 1% of GDP, or £7 billion, will be required over the next couple of years.

© The Economist. Reprinted with permission.

In implementing its economic policy, the government can affect a number of economic variables.

The Chancellor of the Exchequer, Kenneth Clarke, is trying to move the economy out of recession by encouraging economic growth. He is also trying to reduce the very large government budget deficit and the large deficit on the balance of trade.

Policy measures, implemented under a feedback rule, include reducing labour costs to make exports more competitive and so improve the balance of trade and stimulate growth. Taxes are also being increased to cut the budget deficit.

At the same time, the Chancellor is trying to ensure that any policy enacted to achieve these aims does not lead to higher inflation.

Continued recession in other EU countries is leading to cuts in interest rates in these countries. This may lead to a rise in the pound, which would reduce UK exports.

The UK government could respond by cutting interest rates, another feedback rule, but it is feared that such cuts could result in higher inflation, making UK exports less competitive.

A change in exports will shift the aggregate demand curve *AD*. If they rise, the *AD* curve shifts to the right and if they fall, the *AD* curve shifts to the left.

A change in domestic taxes will also affect aggregate demand. If they rise, the *AD* curve shifts to the left.

As the United Kingdom move out of recession the *AD* curve shifts from AD_0 to AD_1 in the figure. The size of the recessionary gap becomes smaller.

The combined effect of lower demand for UK exports in the rest of the European Union, coupled with higher taxes in the United Kingdom, will hinder recovery.

In the figure, this means that the shift to the right of the *AD* curve will slow down. Worse, aggregate demand could remain at AD_1. Worse still, the *AD* curve could actually shift to the left towards AD_0, pushing the economy back into recession.

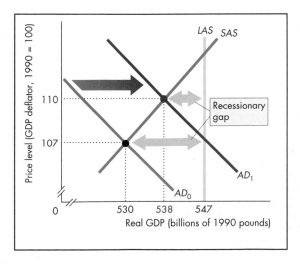

effects of an independent central bank unless or until sterling is replaced by a European currency in the hands of an independent central European bank.

Usually, when inflation is tamed, a recession results. The reason is that people form their expectation about policy on the basis of past policy actions. An independent central bank pursuing only price stability could possibly achieve price stability with greater credibility and at lower cost. ◆

◆ ◆ ◆ ◆ We've now examined the main issues of stabilization policy. We've looked at the goals of stabilization policy and at the lack of success of stabilization policy. We've seen how fixed and feedback rules operate under differing assumptions about the behaviour of the economy and why economists take different views on using these rules. We've also seen why lowering inflation usually is accompanied by recession. ◆ ◆ In the next chapter, we examine what many people believe is amost serious policy problem – the government's budget deficit.

S U M M A R Y

The Stabilization Problem

The stabilization problem is to keep the growth rate of real GDP steady, which also keeps unemployment at its natural rate, and to keep inflation low and predictable, which also avoids large fluctuations in the foreign exchange rate. (p. 901)

Players and Policies

foreign exchange rate.The key players and policies in the formulation and execution of macroeconomic policy are the UK government and the Bank of England. The government has ultimate control of both fiscal and monetary policy, but whereas it implements fiscal policy, the Bank implements monetary policy.

There are two broad types of stabilization policy: fixed rules and feedback rules. Fixed-rule policies are those that do not respond to the state of the economy, such as a constant growth rate of the money supply. Feedback-rule policies do respond to the state of the economy, stimulating activity in recession and holding activity in check in times of inflation. (pp. 901–905)

Stabilization Policy and Aggregate Demand Shocks

In the face of an aggregate demand shock, a fixed-rule policy takes no action to counter the shock. It permits aggregate demand to fluctuate as a result of all the independent forces that influence it. As a result, there are fluctuations in real GDP and the price level. A feedback-rule policy adjusts taxes, government purchases, or the money supply to offset the effects of other influences on aggregate demand. An ideal feedback rule keeps the economy at full employment, with stable prices.

Some economists argue that feedback rules make the economy less stable because they require greater knowledge of the state of the economy than we have, operate with time lags that extend beyond the forecast horizon, and introduce unpredictability about policy reactions. (pp. 905–910)

Stabilization Policy and Aggregate Supply Shocks

Two main aggregate supply shocks generate stabilization problems: cost–push inflation and a slowdown in productivity growth. A fixed rule minimizes the threat of and problems associated with cost–push inflation. A feedback rule validates cost–push inflation and leaves the price level and inflation rate free to move to wherever they are pushed. If productivity growth slows down, a fixed rule results in lower output (and higher unemployment) and a higher price level. A feedback rule that increases the money supply or cuts taxes to stimulate aggregate demand results in an even higher price level and higher inflation. Output and unemployment follow the same course as with a fixed rule. By using feedback policies aimed at keeping nominal GDP growth steady – nominal GDP targeting – it is hoped to avoid excessive increases in inflation and decreases in real GDP growth. (pp. 910–915)

Taming Inflation

Inflation can be tamed, and at little or no cost in terms of lost output or excessive unemployment, by slowing the growth of aggregate demand in a credible and predictable way. But usually, when inflation is slowed down, a recession occurs. The reason is that people form their expectation about policy on the basis of actual behaviour, by looking at past actions, not by believing announced intentions. If the Bank of England could be made more independent and pursue only a price stabilization goal, or if there were a common European currency under the control of an independent European central bank that pursued only a price stabilization goal, the cost of controlling inflation might be lower. (pp. 916–920)

K E Y   E L E M E N T S

Key Terms

Key Figures

R E V I E W   Q U E S T I O N S

1   What are the goals of macroeconomic stabilization policy?

2   Describe the key players that formulate and execute macroeconomic policy. Explain the interaction between these players.

3   What is the distinction between a fixed rule policy and a feedback rule policy?

4   Analyse the effects of a temporary decrease in aggregate demand if fixed rules apply.

5   Analyse the behaviour of output and the price level in the face of a permanent decrease in aggregate demand under:
   a   fixed rules
   b   feedback rules

6   Why do economists disagree with each other on the appropriateness of fixed and feedback rules?

7   Explain the main problems in using fiscal policy for stabilizing the economy.

8   Analye the effects of a rise in wages on real GDP and the price level if the Bank of England employs:
   a   a fixed monetary rule
   b   a feedback monetary rule

9   Explain nominal GDP targeting and why it reduces real GDP fluctuations and inflation.

10   Explain why the Bank of England's credibility affects the cost of lowering inflation.

PROBLEMS

1 The economy is experiencing 10 per cent inflation and 7 per cent unemployment. Set out economic policies that will lower both inflation and unemployment. Explain how and why your proposed policies will work.

2 The economy is booming and inflation is beginning to rise, but it is widely agreed that a massive recession is just around the corner. Weigh the advantages and disadvantages of the government and the Bank of England pursuing fixed-rules and feedback-rules policies.

3 The economy is in a recession and inflation is falling. It is widely agreed that a strong recovery is just around the corner. Weigh the advantages and disadvantages of the Bank of England pursuing a fixed- and a feedback-rule monetary policy.

CHAPTER 33

GOVERNMENT DEFICITS AND BORROWING REQUIREMENTS

After studying this chapter you will be able to:

◆ Explain why, in almost every year since 1972, governments in the United Kingdom spent more than they acquired from taxes and other revenues

◆ Distinguish between a government deficit, the public sector borrowing requirement and the national debt

◆ Distinguish between *nominal* and *real* borrowing requirements

◆ Explain why borrowing requirements appear to be larger than they really are

◆ Describe the different means available for financing borrowing requirements

◆ Explain why government borrowing can cause inflation

◆ Explain why government borrowing can be a burden on future generations

◆ Describe the measures that can be taken to eliminate deficits

E VERY YEAR BETWEEN 1972 AND 1986, AND EVERY YEAR SINCE 1990, THE government sector in the United Kingdom – that is the central government and local authorities taken together – spent more money than it received in revenue. In 1993, the deficit was nearly £50 billion, that is nearly £900 for every citizen in the country, and almost 8 per cent of GDP. Why has the government so often had a deficit? Were the deficits really as big as they seemed? How can we gauge the true scale of the deficits when there is so much inflation? ◆ ◆ Some countries, such as Bolivia, Chile, Brazil and Israel, have had large government deficits and runaway inflations. And following World War I, Germany suffered huge budget deficits which produced hyperinflation – price rises of more than 50 per cent a month. Do deficits mean the United Kingdom will eventually have rapid inflation? Do deficits make it harder, or even impossible, for the Bank of England to control the money supply and keep inflation in check? ◆ ◆ When we incur personal debts, we have to repay them some time in the future. When a government incurs debts the repayment may fall not only on its current taxpayers but also on their children and grandchildren. Do government deficits really create a burden for future generations? What are the future prospects for the deficit?

Government Spendthrifts

◆ ◆ ◆ ◆ In this chapter, we're going to study one of the biggest economic issues of the 1980s and 1990s. One of Margaret Thatcher's main objectives on coming to power in 1979 was to cut government spending and so remove the deficit. By 1987 it had disappeared, but by 1991 it was back. By the time you've read this chapter, you'll be able to explain what the deficit is all about.

The Meaning of Deficits and Surpluses

We'll begin by explaining three related concepts. These are:

◆ Government deficits and surpluses
◆ Government borrowing requirements
◆ Government debt

Government Surpluses and Deficits

The **government surplus** or **government deficit** is the difference between the government sector's total revenue and its total expenditure over a period of time (usually a year). Table 33.1 shows the main items of government revenue and expenditure in 1993. You can see that expenditure exceeded revenue by £49 billion so there was a government deficit of that amount. If revenue had exceeded expenditure, there would have been a government surplus.

The main source of government sector revenue is taxation. Table 33.1 shows that taxes on income – which include income tax and the corporation tax paid on company profits – accounted for under half the government's tax revenue. Taxes on expenditure – such as VAT and taxes on alcohol, tobacco and petrol – accounted for over half. A small amount of tax revenue arose from taxes on capital – these include inheritance tax which is levied on the estates of dead people and capital gains tax which is paid mostly by people who manage to sell shares at higher prices than they paid for them. Other sources of revenue include National Insurance contributions (discussed in Chapter 18), profits on government-owned businesses and interest on loans made by governments. Miscellaneous revenue includes many small items such as payments to the government by the European Union, passport fees and receipts from fines.

Another major source of government revenue in recent years has been the proceeds from sales of nationalized industries and council houses. The government does not include these proceeds on the revenue side of its accounts, so you may think that the deficit shown in the table is an over-estimate. But this is not so, because the figure shown for spending

on goods and services records actual spending on goods and services minus the proceeds from asset sales. In effect, selling a nationalized industry is regarded as a negative expenditure on goods and services. In fact, without these proceeds, the deficit in 1993 would have been larger than shown in the table.

TABLE 33.1

Government Sector Accounts for 1993

		Billions of pounds
Revenue:	Taxes on income	73
	Taxes on expenditure (including community charge)	99
	Taxes on capital	3
	National Insurance contributions	38
	Profits and interest	11
	Miscellaneous	4
	Total	227
Expenditure:	Spending on goods and services	149
	Transfer payments	88
	Subsidies and grants	16
	Grants paid abroad	5
	Debt interest	18
	Total	276
Balance	Government deficit	−49

This table shows the total revenue flowing into the government sector as a whole and the total spending by that sector. Note, though, that the proceeds from sales of nationalized industries and council houses are not included on the revenue side. But this does not mean that the government deficit figure shown is too large, because the figure shown for spending on goods and services shows actual spending minus receipts from sales of goods such as nationalized industries and council houses.

The table ignores payments between the central government and local authorities as these flows occur within the government sector. Most UK taxes are levied by the central government which pays large grants to local authorities to help them cover their spending.

Source: Central Statistical Office, *United Kingdom National Accounts 1994 Edition*, 1994, p. 74.

The government sector spends over half of its revenue on goods and services. The figure shown in the table includes purchases from government departments as well as purchases of new capital for use by those departments. The spending covers items such as defence and the police, universities and state schools, the national health service and social workers, motorways and fire services. The second most important type of spending is grants to the personal sector (transfer payments). These were discussed in Chapter 18 and include items such as state pensions, job-seeker's allowances, child benefit and student grants. The government sector also provides various subsidies – chiefly for agriculture, public transport and housing – and it gives occasional grants – chiefly to businesses with special needs. It also pays grants abroad – for instance to developing countries and the European Union – and it pays interest on money which it has borrowed.

The fact that the government sector has a deficit or a surplus does not mean that both the central government and local authorities have a deficit or a surplus. In 1993, for instance, local authorities had a surplus which was more than offset by a central government deficit to give an overall government deficit. The terms **budget deficit** and **budget surplus** are often used for the deficit or surplus of the central government alone. If the central government managed to make its expenditure precisely equal to its revenue, then it would have a **balanced budget**.

Borrowing Requirements

At first sight it may seem that if the government sector has a deficit of, say, £50 billion one year, then it must borrow £50 billion to cover this gap between its spending and its revenue. Certainly the size of the deficit is a major factor affecting how much the government sector needs to borrow, but the amount it has to borrow may not exactly equal its deficit. The difference arises because each year the government sector makes some new loans and each year some of its past loans are repaid. Suppose, for example, that one year the government sector has a deficit of £50 billion, that it lends £5 billion and is repaid £2 billion worth of loans it has made in the past. In that case the government sector will have a borrowing requirement of £53 billion (£50 billion plus £5 billion minus £2 billion). Of course the government sector does not always have to borrow. If it had a surplus of £20 billion, lent £5 billion and had £5 billion of past loans

repaid, its borrowing requirement would be –£20 billion which means it could repay £20 billion of loans it has borrowed in the past.

In the United Kingdom, people often refer to the **public sector borrowing requirement** which is the government sector borrowing requirement plus the borrowing requirement of the nationalized industries which are industries that are owned by the government. The government is concerned about borrowing by the nationalized industries as it is responsible for those industries, but in this chapter we will concentrate on the government sector alone.

Government Debt

We have seen that sometimes the government sector has to borrow and sometimes it can repay past loans. In 1988 and 1989 the UK's government sector repaid substantial amounts of past loans, but there is still a vast amount of past loans that have not been repaid. The term **government sector debt** refers to the total amount of loans which have been made to the government sector in the past and which have not been repaid. The government sector debt equals the central government's debt – which is called the **national debt** – and the total combined debt of all local authorities. The government sector debt is a stock. Every year when the government sector has a *positive* borrowing requirement – that is, every year when it needs to borrow – the government sector debt increases; and every year when the government sector has a *negative* borrowing requirement – that is, every year when it can repay some old loans – the government sector debt falls.

The Government Since 1968

The government sector's expenditure and revenue, measured as a percentage of GDP, are shown in Fig. 33.1 for the years 1968–1993. The figures for expenditure and revenue are presented in terms of percentages of GDP, rather than in billions of pounds, so that we can see their importance in relation to the scale of the economy. Because of economic growth and inflation, nominal GDP in 1993 was nearly 14 times what it was in 1968. When expenditure exceeds revenue, there is a deficit, shown by a red area, and when revenue exceeds expenditure, there is a surplus, shown by a green area.

As Fig. 33.1 illustrates, the government sector had a deficit between 1972 and 1987 and again from

FIGURE 33.1

Revenue, Expenditure and the Deficit

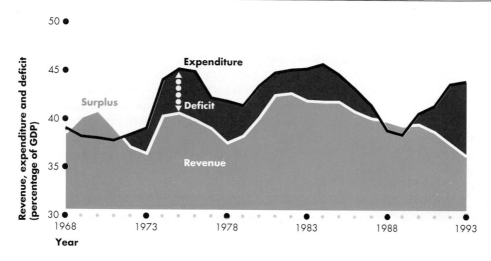

The figure records the government sector's revenue, expenditure, and deficit from 1968 to 1993. The deficit that first emerged in 1972 persisted until 1987. A deficit re-emerged in 1990.

Sources: Central Statistical Office, *National Income and Expenditure 1979 Edition*, pp. 62–3, *National Income and Expenditure 1982 Edition*, pp. 58–9, *The Blue Book: United Kingdom National Accounts, 1993 Edition*, p. 71, *Economic Trends Annual Supplement 1993 Edition*, p. 10, and *Economic Trends*, various issues.

1990. The deficit climbed fairly steadily to over 4 per cent of GDP in the mid-1970s and then dropped a little before rising to nearly 4 per cent again in 1984. It then declined quite quickly before disappearing rather dramatically in 1988 – only to reappear in 1990 and approach 8 per cent of GDP by 1993.

When the government has a deficit, it usually has a positive borrowing requirement, so its debt tends to rise. The opposite happens when there is a surplus. Changes in the size of the government sector debt are shown in Fig. 33.2. As you can see, however, the debt is shown here as a percentage of GDP rather than in money terms. It was over 90 per cent of GDP in 1968. During the 1970s it gradually declined to about 50 per cent. It hovered around the 50 per cent level for some years before falling sharply after 1987 to reach 35 per cent by 1992.

It is not surprising that the size of the debt fell in relation to GDP during the late 1980s when the government was running a small deficit or even a surplus. But why did it fall during the 1970s when the government sector had large deficits? The answer is that there was substantial inflation in the 1970s. As a result, the nominal value of GDP grew quickly. In contrast, the nominal value of past government loans stood still. So the value of past loans

fell in relation to GDP. It was only the need for substantial new loans which kept the value of the debt fairly constant in relation to GDP.

Why did the government sector have a large deficit for so long? Where did the deficit come from? The immediate source of the deficit can be seen by glancing at Fig. 33.1. In that figure, you can see that when the deficit first arose, in 1972–1973, its main origin was a decrease in the government's revenue at a time when expenditure was fairly stable. Revenue rose sharply in 1974, but expenditure rose even more sharply. Revenue and expenditure dipped a little in the late 1970s but rose again in the 1980s. You can also see that expenditure started to fall significantly from around 1984, and it was this fall which caused the deficit to turn into a surplus – for revenue too fell in the late 1980s, though only slightly. It was a rise in spending from 1990, combined with falling revenue, that caused a deficit to reappear.

Which sources of revenue fell in the early 1970s? Which elements of government revenue and expenditure increased most sharply in the mid-1970s? Which elements of government spending fell most rapidly from 1984? And which elements of spending rose again in 1990? Let's answer these questions by looking at the government sector's revenue and expenditure in a bit more detail.

FIGURE 33.2

The Government Sector's Debt

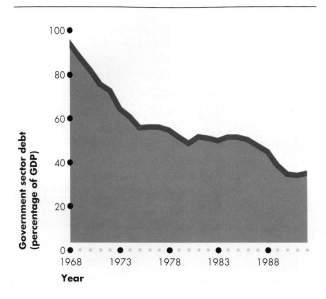

The government sector's debt is the total amount of money owed by the central government and local authorities to households and businesses at home or abroad. It represents the accumulation of all past borrowing by the government sector apart from loans that the government sector has already repaid. The debt fell in relation to GDP during the 1970s and the late 1980s.

Sources: Central Statistical Office, *Annual Abstract of Statistics 1980 Edition*, p. 375, *1981 Edition*, p. 376, *1993 Edition*, p. 266 and *1994 Edition*, p. 263.

Government Sector Revenue We saw the main sources of government sector revenue in Table 33.1. Let's divide them into four main groups:

◆ Taxes on income,
◆ Taxes on expenditure
◆ National Insurance contributions
◆ Other sources

The main taxes on income are personal income tax and corporation tax, though there are also some special taxes on profits from North Sea oil extraction. Taxes on expenditure include all the taxes on the goods and services that we buy. VAT has the highest yield, followed by taxes on petrol, tobacco and alcohol; these taxes also include the rates paid by businesses and the local taxes paid by households. National Insurance contributions are paid by workers to ensure entitlement to the various

National Insurance benefits described in Chapter 18. Other sources chiefly comprise interest on money lent by the government sector and the profits of businesses owned by the government sector.

Figure 33.3(a) shows the revenues from these sources of revenue as percentages of GDP. You can see that both taxes on income and taxes on expenditure fell in the early 1970s, when the deficit arose, and that it was taxes on income and National Insurance contributions which rose most markedly later in the 1970s. Taxes on expenditure rose sharply in 1979 to 1980, when Margaret Thatcher decided to switch some of the burden of taxation from taxes on income to taxes on expenditure. Taxes on income did not initially fall very much owing to rising North Sea oil revenues at that time, but North Sea oil revenues have fallen since the late 1980s as a result of falling oil prices, and income tax yields have fallen with them.

The government sector's other sources of revenue were fairly stable until 1982 since when they have declined quite sharply. This is largely because the government has made fewer loans to industry and has received less interest in return. Also, the sales of local authority housing and the sales of nationalized industries have given the government sector a smaller direct involvement with activities from which it can earn some profits.

Government Sector Expenditure We will examine government expenditure by dividing it into four categories:

◆ Expenditure on goods and services
◆ Subsidies
◆ Grants to the personal sector
◆ Debt interest

Expenditure on goods and services covers the cost of services provided by both the central government and local authorities. About 25 per cent of this is accounted for by the national health service, about 20 per cent by defence, and another 20 per cent by education. Roads, the police and personal social services – such as social welfare workers – each account for about 5 per cent. The remaining 20 per cent is accounted for by a wide range of small activities such as fire services and street lighting. Subsidies include occasional 'one-off' grants as well as ongoing subsidy programmes. The main categories have always been subsidies to agriculture and certain loss-making nationalized industries, chiefly

FIGURE 33.3

Government Sector Revenue and Expenditure

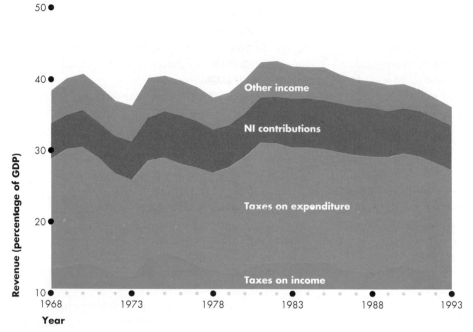

(a) Revenue

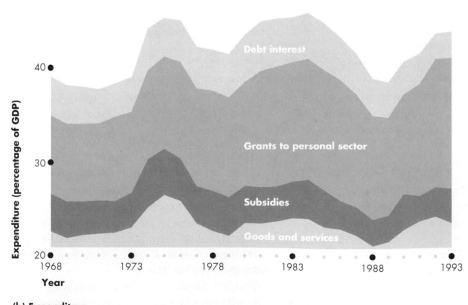

(b) Expenditure

Four categories of government sector revenue are shown in part (a): taxes on income, taxes on expenditure, National Insurance contributions and other income (chiefly profits and interest). Total government revenue accounted for much the same fraction of GDP in 1993 as in 1968. But National Insurance contributions grew slightly in importance while taxes on expenditure stayed roughly constant and the other sources fell. There were temporary falls in taxes on income and taxes on expenditure in the early 1970s. These falls were the main cause of the government sector deficit which emerged at that time.

Four categories of government sector expenditure are shown in part (b): expenditure on goods and services, subsidies, grants to the personal sector and debt interest. Expenditure on goods and services and subsidies fell slightly as a percentage of GDP after 1975 – but remember that the expenditure on these items is recorded after deducting receipts from sales of nationalized industries and council housing. Such receipts amounted to around 2 per cent of GDP in the period 1987–1990. Transfer payments have increased appreciably. The generally high levels of total expenditure after 1974 helped create a deficit in most of these years.

Sources: Central Statistical Office, *National Income and Expenditure 1979 Edition*, p. 63, *National Income and Expenditure 1982 Edition*, p. 58–9, *The Blue Book: United Kingdom National Accounts, 1993 Edition*, p. 71, *Economic Trends Annual Supplement 1993 Edition*, pp. 10 and 168, and *Economic Trends*, various issues.

British Coal and British Rail. Grants to the personal sector chiefly comprise the transfer payments that we looked at in Chapter 18. Thus they include National Insurance benefits along with child benefit, income support and family credits. Other transfer payments include housing benefit – which helps low income families with their rent and council tax payments – student grants and payments to parents whose children have assisted places at independent schools. Debt interest is the payment of interest by the government sector on its outstanding loans.

Figure 33.3(b) shows the expenditure under these four headings as percentages of GDP. Expenditure on goods and services increased substantially in the mid-1970s, thereby aiding the onset of the deficit. This spending was reduced a little in the late 1970s, and again in the late 1980s, thereby helping the deficit to end for a couple of years. But spending on goods and services rose again around 1990 to help restore a deficit once again.

The level of subsidies fell after 1984 following determined efforts to make the nationalized industries, especially British Coal and British Rail, cut their losses. There was a temporary rise in subsidies in 1990, chiefly as a result of large, one-off grants to the nationalized industries.

Grants to the personal sector grew in the early 1980s, a major factor being the increased transfers to unemployed people that were paid out when unemployment peaked at over 3 million people. The fall in unemployment in the late 1980s was a major reason why this category of expenditure fell, helping end the deficit, while the rise in unemployment around 1990 was a major reason why it subsequently rose once again and helped recreate the deficit.

The scale of debt interest payments by the government sector depends on the level of interest rates and the amount of past government borrowing. The rise in debt interest payments in relation to GDP in the early 1980s was caused by the high levels of interest rates at that time. Interest payments fell back in the late 1980s chiefly because the deficit turned into a surplus so that some past loans could be repaid and the level of outstanding debt in relation to GDP fell slightly.

Deficits, Surpluses and Business Cycles

There is an important relationship between the size of the government sector's deficits and surpluses and the business cycles through which the economy passes. Other things remaining the same, the deficit becomes larger, or the surplus becomes smaller, when the unemployment rate increases and the economy goes into recession. And other things remaining the same, the deficit falls, or the surplus increases, as unemployment falls and the economy recovers. Why is there this relationship between the budget and the economy? Part of the answer lies on the spending side and part on the taxes side of the government's account.

The scale of government spending and taxes depends on the state of the economy. The government passes tax laws defining the *rates* at which its taxes are imposed; it cannot decree the amount in *pounds* which people will pay. As a consequence, the taxes that the government collects depend on the level of income. If the economy is in a recovery phase of the business cycle, tax collections rise because with incomes rising and, in turn, with consumption rising, the government will collect more in taxes on income and expenditure. Conversely, if the economy is in a recession phase of the business cycle, then tax receipts fall.

Some of the government's spending programmes also react to the phases of the cycle. For example, when the economy is in a recession, so that unemployment is high, payments of job-seeker's allowance increase and so do payments of other income-related transfers. When the economy experiences boom conditions, transfer payments fall. We noted above that spending on transfers fell as the 1980–1981 recession faded and grew as the 1991–1992 recession appeared.

Coupled with changes in tax receipts, it is easy to see why, other things remaining the same, governments tend to have surpluses in good times and deficits in times of depression. However, other things are often not the same. This is clear from Fig. 33.4 which shows the government sector's deficit or surplus (as a percentage of GDP) and deviations in trend for GDP. As you can see, there is a fairly loose relationship between these two variables. The most striking relationship occurred between 1984 and 1988 when, as the economy's performance improved and then declined the deficit changed into a surplus and then back into a deficit.

What things were not the same at other periods? In the period from 1973 to 1974, unemployment rose to the highest level for many years – albeit a much lower level than it subsequently reached. The Conservative government was prepared to allow

FIGURE 33.4

The Deficit and the Business Cycle

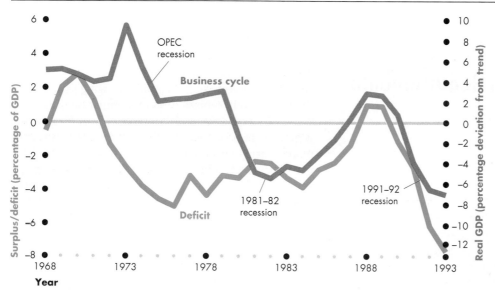

Other things remaining the same, the government sector deficit or surplus moves closely in line with fluctuations in real GDP. An expansion phase, as occurred from 1984 to 1988, leads to lower taxes and higher transfer payments and a lower deficit or even surplus. A contraction phase, as occurred after 1989, has the opposite effects. But when other things do not remain the same, the economy may expand while there is a move from surplus to deficit, as occurred between 1971 and 1973, or the economy may contract while the deficit falls, as occurred between 1979 and 1981.

Sources: Figures 21.6 and 33.1.

government spending to exceed tax revenues in an effort to curb unemployment. This policy actually had only a muted and short-lived effect on unemployment, but it took the government sector into deficit. The subsequent large rises in unemployment made later governments cautious about reducing the deficit until the 1980s, when renewed fears about inflation caused the government to seek to control the money supply which in turn made it try to reduce the government deficit. The privatization proceeds also helped reduce the deficit. But after 1985, as unemployment eventually began to fall, so the deficit fell even more quickly. And after 1990, as recession returned, so did a large deficit.

REVIEW

The government sector deficit emerged in 1972 because the government sector's tax receipts were reduced at a time when its expenditure was not falling. Thereafter both revenue and expenditure rose so that the deficit persisted. The deficit was transformed into a surplus in 1988 and 1989, even though revenue fell slightly, because spending fell more sharply; but from 1990 a rise in spending and falling income tax yields caused a large deficit to reappear.

◆ ◆   Other things remaining the same, deficits and surpluses are closely related to business cycles: the stronger the economy, the less likely there is to be a deficit and the more likely there is to be a surplus. Rising unemployment was a key factor causing rising government expenditure in the 1970s and the 1990s, and falling unemployment was the main cause of falling government expenditure in the late 1980s.   ◆

We've now seen where the deficit came from in 1972, why it changed into a surplus and then reappeared, and how deficits and surpluses relate to business cycles. We've also seen that some of the deficits were very large, and that large deficits tend to result in large borrowing requirements and large increases in the size of the government sector's debt. Indeed, the value of the government sector's debt rose about fivefold between 1968 and 1993. But were the borrowing requirements of the early 1980s and 1990s as high as they looked? Can it really be true that in 20 years the government borrowed four times more than had been borrowed in the entire previous history of the nation? These are important questions to which we'll now turn our attention.

Real Borrowing Requirements and Debts

Inflation distorts many things, not least of which is the size of government deficits, surpluses, borrowing requirements and debts. We will explore the effects of inflation on government borrowing requirements and debts. To remove the inflationary distortion from the measured values of government borrowing requirements, we need a concept of the real borrowing requirement. The **real borrowing requirement** is the change in the real value of the government sector's gross debt. The real value of the government sector's debt is equal to the market value of its debt adjusted for changes in the price level. We are going to see how we can calculate the real level of the borrowing requirements and we will see how such calculations change our views of the size of the government's borrowing requirements. But before we do that, let's consider things in more personal terms by examining the borrowing and debt of a family.

The Real Borrowing Requirement of a Family

In 1965, a young couple (perhaps your parents) had to borrow some money to buy a new house. Their borrowing took the form of a mortgage. The amount borrowed was £5,000. Today, the daughter and son-in-law of that couple are buying their first house. To do so, they also are borrowing. But they're borrowing £50,000 to buy their first house. Is the £50,000 deficit (mortgage) of the 1995 house-buyer really 10 times as big as the deficit (mortgage) of the 1965 house-buyer? In money terms, the 1995 borrowing is indeed 10 times as big as the 1965 borrowing. But in terms of what money will buy, that is in terms of the goods and services the two couples must forgo to repay their mortgages, these two debts are almost

equivalent to each other. Inflation in the years between 1965 and 1995 has raised the prices of most things to about 10 times what they were in 1965. So a loan of £50,000 in 1995 is really the same as a loan of £5,000 in 1965.

In the year when a family buys a new home and finances it with a mortgage, it has a positive borrowing requirement. But in all the following years, the family must arrange its affairs so that it can pay off some of the mortgage. So in all following years until the loan is fully repaid, the family must operate with a negative borrowing requirement. In each of these years, the family's outstanding debt is *reduced*. In money terms, or nominal terms, the amount by which its outstanding debt falls in a given year is, of course, equal to its repayment – or the money value of its negative borrowing requirement – in that year. However, inflation has an important effect here. Because inflation brings higher prices, it also brings a lower real value of outstanding debts. So the real value of the outstanding loan falls by the amount paid off each year plus the amount wiped out by inflation. Other things remaining the same, the higher the inflation rate, the faster is the mortgage really paid off, and the larger is the real value of the household's negative borrowing requirement.

The Government Sector's Real Borrowing Requirement

This line of reasoning applies with equal force to the government. Because of inflation, the government's borrowing requirement is not *really* as big as it appears. To see how we can measure the borrowing requirement and correct for the distortion of inflation, we'll work through a numerical example. For simplicity this will relate to a country where there is only a central government and where this government never lends and so never has any money repaid to it.

First, look at case A in Table 33.2 which shows what might happen one year if there is no inflation and has been none for many years. Government expenditure, excluding interest on its debt, is £50 billion. Government revenue is £55 billion. So if the government didn't have interest to pay, it would have a negative borrowing requirement of £5 billion and could repay £5 billion worth of loans. But the government starts the year with an outstanding debt of £100 billion and interest rates are running at 5 per cent a

TABLE 33.2

How Inflation Distorts the Borrowing Requirement

	Case A	Case B
Government spending (excluding debt interest)	£50 billion	£50 billion
Government revenue	£55 billion	£55 billion
Government debt at start of year	£100 billion	£100 billion
Inflation rate	0 per cent	10 per cent
Market interest rate	5 per cent	15 per cent
Real interest rate	5 per cent	5 per cent
Debt interest paid	£5 billion	£15 billion
Nominal borrowing requirement	£0 billion	£10 billion
Nominal value of debt at end of year	£100 billion	£110 billion
Real value of debt at end of year (value in beginning of year prices)	£100 billion	£100 billion
Real value of the borrowing requirement	£0 billion	£0 billion

Inflation distorts the measured deficit by distorting the debt interest payments made by the government. In this example, the real interest rate is 5 per cent a year and government debt is £100 billion, so debt interest in real terms is £5 billion. With no inflation, as in case A, the actual debt interest paid is also £5 billion. With 10 per cent inflation, as in case B, interest rates rise to around 15 per cent a year (in order to preserve a real interest rate of 5 per cent), and debt interest increases to £15 billion. The borrowing requirement increases by £10 billion from zero to £10 billion. It is true that in case B the government will actually borrow £10 billion, but this borrowing requirement is apparent, not real; for the real amount of outstanding debt at the end of the year is the same in each case! The real value of the outstanding debt does not rise in case B because the real value of the initial debt falls during the year, and thus the value of this fall offsets the amount of new borrowing done during the year.

year. So the government must pay £5 billion of debt interest (5 per cent on £100 billion). When we add the £5 billion of debt interest to the gov-

ernment's other spending, we see that the government's total expenditure is £55 billion, so the government has a balanced budget. We say that the government has a zero **nominal borrowing requirement** because this measures the nominal value of its borrowing requirement which is zero in this case. Notice that the government's debt stays constant at £100 billion. As there is no inflation, the real value of the debt is also constant. By definition, then, the real value of the borrowing requirement is zero.

Next, let's look at this same economy with exactly the same spending, taxes and initial debt but suppose that the inflation rate is 10 per cent a year and has been for many years – case B in Table 33.2. With 10 per cent inflation, the market interest rate will not be 5 per cent a year, but around 15 per cent. The reason why the interest rate is higher by around 10 percentage points is that the 10 per cent inflation causes the real value of outstanding debt to fall. Lenders – the households, firms and foreigners that have lent to the government in the past and that lend to it in the year covered by the table – know that the money they will eventually receive in repayment of any loans they made to the government will be worth less than the money they lent. The government also recognizes that the money it will use to repay its debts will have a lower value than the money it borrowed. So the government and the people from whom it borrows readily agree to a higher interest rate that compensates for these foreseen changes in the value of money. So, with a 15 per cent interest rate, the government has to pay £15 billion in debt interest – 15 per cent of £100 billion. When the £15 billion of debt interest is added to the government's other spending, total expenditure is £65 billion, £10 billion more than its revenue. So the government has a nominal borrowing requirement of £10 billion. At the end of the year, the government's total debt will have increased from £100 billion to £110 billion.

The difference between the two situations that we've just described is a 10 per cent inflation rate. Nothing else is different. What the government is actually spending and receiving is the same and the real interest rate is the same in the two cases. But in case A, government debt stays put at £100 billion while in case B it rises to £110 billion. However, the real debt stays the same in the two cases. To see why the real debt has stayed the same in case B, when the nominal value of its debt has risen to £110 billion, remember that in this case the prices of all things have increased by 10 per cent. If we deflate the increased government debt in case B to express the debt in constant pounds instead of current pounds, we see that real government debt has actually stayed put in case B too, for with 10 per cent inflation, you would need £110 billion at the end of the year to buy items which at the beginning would have cost £100 billion. So even in case B, the real situation is that the value of outstanding debt is the same at the end of the year as it was at the beginning. In effect, therefore, the government has not borrowed in real terms. It has certainly borrowed £10 billion, and on its own this borrowing increases the amount of debt it must repay. But against this, inflation has decreased the real value of the debt it started off with at the beginning of the year. Altogether, the real value of its debts has not risen in the year.

The numbers in Table 33.2 are hypothetical and deal with two imaginary situations. But the calculations we've just done provide us with a method of adjusting the government sector's nominal borrowing requirement to eliminate the effects of inflation and reveal the real borrowing requirement. How important is it to adjust the UK's borrowing requirement for inflation in order to obtain an inflation-free view?

The Real and Nominal Borrowing Requirements in the United Kingdom

Figure 33.5 provides an answer to the above question. The nominal and real borrowing requirements of the UK's government sector are plotted alongside each other. As you can see, the government sector had a positive nominal borrowing requirement in every year from 1970 to 1986, and also from 1991, yet its real borrowing requirement was actually negative (or zero) in every one of those years except 1975, 1977, 1981, 1983, 1984 and 1985.

The reason why all the positive nominal borrowing requirements seldom led to real borrowing requirements is that inflation was high during most of the years concerned. The few positive real borrowing requirements that did emerge resulted from particularly large nominal borrowing requirements.

Let's now go on to examine some of the effects of a deficit.

FIGURE 33.5

The Real and Nominal Borrowing Requirements

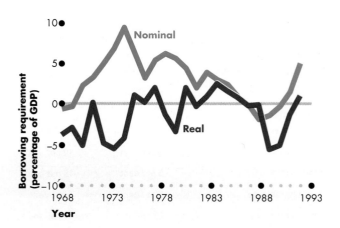

The real borrowing requirement removes the effects of inflation from interest rates and from the outstanding value of government debt. The real borrowing requirement and the nominal borrowing requirement follow a similar path, but the real borrowing requirement is generally lower than the nominal borrowing requirement. Indeed, in most years the real borrowing requirement has been negative even though the nominal one has been positive.

Sources: Nominal borrowing requirements from Central Statistical Office, *National Income and Expenditure 1979 Edition*, p. 103, *National Income and Expenditure 1982 Edition*, p. 99, and *The Blue Book: United Kingdom National Accounts, 1993 Edition*, p. 96; real borrowing requirements estimated by allowing for changes in value of debt, using debt figures from Fig. 33.2 and price changes from Fig. 21.4.

Government Borrowing and Inflation

Many people fear government borrowing because they believe that such borrowing leads to inflation. Does government borrowing cause inflation? That depends on who lends money to the government sector.

Financing a Borrowing Requirement

To meet a borrowing requirement, the government sector sells government securities called bonds. But the effects of bond sales depend on who buys the bonds. There are three main types of purchaser: the Bank of England, the clearing banks and households, firms and foreigners.

If the Bank of England buys the bonds, then it pays for them using new money (see Chapter 27, pp. 761–764). If the bonds are bought by the clearing banks, it is less certain whether the money supply will rise. It certainly will if the banks have ample excess reserves and create new money which they lend to the government and which it promptly spends. But if the banks have little or no excess reserves, they can buy government bonds only at the expense of holding fewer other securities or making fewer loans to other would-be borrowers, and in this case the money supply is not increased. As the banks generally do not have large excess reserves, the money supply does not usually rise if they buy bonds. If the bonds are bought by households or firms, then there is no change in the money supply: the public give money to the government for the bonds and the government gives the money back to the public as soon as it spends it – so money changes hands twice but the total money supply stays the same.

When the government finances its borrowing in a way that causes the money supply to rise, we say that it is indulging in money financing. **Money financing** is the financing of a government borrowing requirement by a sale of bonds to the Bank of England, which results in the creation of additional money. All other financing of government borrowing is called debt financing. **Debt financing** is the financing of a government borrowing requirement by a sale of bonds to anyone – whether household, firm or foreigner – except the Bank of England. In practice, bonds are issued by both the central government and by local authorities, but the Bank of England rarely buys new local authority bonds. So local authorities rely on debt finance while the central government has a choice between debt finance and money finance.

Let's look at the consequences of these two ways of financing the borrowing requirement, starting with debt financing.

Debt Financing　First, suppose the government borrows money by selling bonds to households and firms – or indeed to the clearing banks. To sell bonds, the government must offer the potential buyers a sufficiently attractive deal. In other words, the government must

offer a high enough rate of return to persuade people to lend their money. To keep the example simple, suppose that the government always repays its loans by buying back its bonds after one year. We may suppose that it finances each year's purchases by selling an appropriate amount of new bonds.

Let's suppose that the going interest rate is 10 per cent a year. To sell a bond worth £100, the government must promise not only to pay back the £100 at the end of the year but also to pay the interest of £10 accumulated on that debt. So in return for borrowing £100 today, the government must pay £110 a year from today. In one year's time, simply to stand still, the government would have to pay £110 to cover the cost of repaying, with interest, the bond that it sold a year earlier. Two years from today the government will have to pay £121 – the £110 borrowed plus 10 per cent interest (£11) on that £110. The process continues with the total amount of debt and total interest payments mushrooming year after year.

Money Financing　Next, consider what happens if instead of selling bonds to households and firms, the government sells bonds to the Bank of England. There are two important differences in this case compared with the case of debt financing. First, the government effectively pays no interest on these bonds; second, additional money gets created.

The government ends up paying no interest on the bonds bought by the Bank of England because the Bank is a public corporation – that is, it is a business that is owned by the government – whose profits are payable to the government. So other things remaining the same, if the Bank receives an extra million pounds from the government in interest payments on government bonds held by the Bank, the Bank's profits increase by that same million pounds and this extra profit flows back to the government.

When the Bank buys bonds from the government, it uses newly created money to do so – it simply writes a larger number against the deposit of the government. This newly created deposit money is then spent by the government, for it borrows only in order to finance spending that it cannot finance from its revenue. It is important to understand what happens when the government does spend its money. Suppose that it has sold bonds for £100 million to the Bank of England to buy a new destroyer. The Bank acquires the bonds and pays for them by raising the government's deposit by £100 million – it simply writes a larger number against the government's name. At that point in time the money supply has risen by only £100 million as the only change is the increased government deposit. But now the government spends the money and pays it to the owners of a shipyard. The government's deposit at the Bank of England falls by £100 million while the shipyard's deposit at, say, Barclays Bank, rises by £100 million, and this in itself causes no further rise in the money supply. However, Barclays Bank will ask the Bank of England for £100 million as every bank demands reserves when its customers receive money from depositors at other banks. The Bank of England will meet this request by raising Barclays' own deposit at the Bank of England by £100 million – the Bank of England simply writes £100 million more against Barclays' name and £100 million less against the government's name as soon as the government's cheque to the shipyard is processed. This means that Barclays now has larger reserves and can start creating more money itself by making additional loans. (See Chapters 26 and 27.)

As we studied in Chapter 23 and Chapter 30, an increase in the money supply causes an increase in aggregate demand. Higher aggregate demand eventually brings a higher price level. Persistent money financing leads to continuous increases in aggregate demand and to inflation.

Debt Financing Versus Money Financing In comparing these two methods of covering a borrowing requirement, it is clear that debt financing leaves the government with an ongoing obligation to pay interest. This obligation gets bigger each year unless the government manages to reduce its debt by running some surpluses. In contrast, interest payments do not worry the government at all when it uses money financing; certainly it pays interest to the Bank of England, but then the Bank pays profits to the government. So there is a clear advantage from the government's point of view in covering a borrowing requirement by money financing rather than by debt financing. Unfortunately, this solution causes inflationary problems for everybody else.

But the alternative, debt financing, is not problem free. Financing a borrowing requirement through bond sales to households, firms and foreigners causes a mushrooming scale of debt and interest payments. The larger the scale of debt and interest payments, the bigger the government's borrowing

problem becomes, and the greater is the temptation to end the process of debt financing and to begin to finance the borrowing requirement by selling bonds to the Bank of England – money financing. This ever-present temptation is what leads many to fear that borrowing requirements are inflationary even when they are not immediately money financed.

Unpleasant Arithmetic

Some economists have argued that debt financing can actually be even more inflationary than money financing. They point out that with debt financing, the debt will grow every year unless the government starts to run surpluses. Given the rarity of surpluses, the debt may simply grow and grow so that eventually it is reduced by creating a large amount of money with a resulting surge in prices. Rational people anticipate this and try to reduce the impact on their living standards by reducing their holdings of money and buying goods and services before prices rise. So inflation may begin even before any money financing occurs.

This argument was first advanced by Thomas Sargent (of the Hoover Institution at Stanford University) and Neil Wallace (of the University of Minnesota). They called their calculations 'unpleasant monetarist arithmetic'. It is *unpleasant* arithmetic because deferring the date at which a borrowing requirement is financed by money creation worsens the inflation that will ensue. It is unpleasant *monetarist* arithmetic because it forms an attack on the central proposition of monetarism. This proposition is that inflation is caused by an excessive growth rate of the money supply, which implies that inflation will not erupt if the money supply growth rate is contained. The unpleasant monetarist arithmetic calculations point out that the government's borrowing requirement must be sufficiently small to provide confidence in the ability and willingness of the government and the Bank of England to continue to keep money supply growth in line with the growth in the economy's capacity to produce goods and services. A borrowing requirement that is too large to reinforce that expectation will be inflationary, even if the government manages to rely wholly on debt finance in the early years.

But for a borrowing requirement to be the problem that Sargent and Wallace say it is, it must be a truly persistent phenomenon. A borrowing requirement that is large and that lasts even for a decade does not inevitably have to produce inflation. If expectations are widely held that the borrowing requirement is going to be brought under control at some reasonably near future date, then the unpleasant arithmetic, although correct, is not relevant.

International Evidence

We have a large amount of experience from a wide variety of countries on the relationship between inflation and borrowing requirements. What does that experience tell us? Are borrowing requirements, in fact, inflationary? To answer this question we must actually look at the relationship between government deficits and inflation because there is more widespread data available on government deficits than on borrowing requirements. But we know that deficits and borrowing requirements are closely related, even though they may not be identical.

Figure 33.6 contains data on inflation and deficits for 67 countries covering the 1980s. The countries are in three groups: Latin America (part a), the European Union (part b) and 47 others (part c). The 67 countries are the only ones for which there is data on both inflation and the deficit for most of the 1980s.

Notice, first, the tremendous range of experience. The highest inflation rate was almost 1,600 per cent per year – in Nicaragua (part a). The lowest inflation rate was less than 3 per cent – in the Netherlands (part b). The largest deficit was almost 20 per cent of GDP – again in Nicaragua. The smallest deficit (actually a surplus) was more than 2 per cent of GDP – in Luxembourg.

Second, look at the relationships between deficits and inflation. In the Latin American countries (part a), there is a clear tendency for these two variables to be correlated. The countries with the largest deficits (Nicaragua and Bolivia) have the highest inflation

Deficits and Inflation

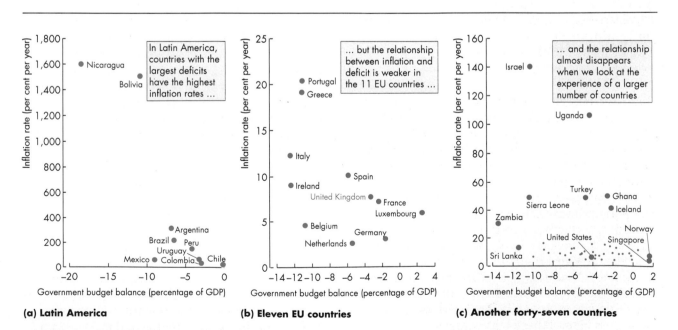

(a) Latin America

(b) Eleven EU countries

(c) Another forty-seven countries

The relationship between the deficit and inflation is shown for 9 Latin American countries (part a), 11 countries in the European Union (part b) and 47 other countries – including the United States (part c). There is a tendency for large deficit countries to be high inflation countries, but the correlation is weak.

Source: *International Financial Statistics Yearbook*, 1990. For each country, the dot shows its deficit (as a percentage of GDP) and inflation (GDP deflator) for the 1980s (or part of the decade where the full decade is not available).

rates. The countries with the smallest deficits (Chile, Columbia and Uruguay) have the lowest inflation rates. And countries with deficits between these have inflation rates that are intermediate as well (Argentina and Brazil). Only Mexico does not fit the pattern. Its inflation rate is lower than that in countries with much smaller deficits. In the European Union (part b), there is a similar, although somewhat weaker relationship between deficits and inflation. And the relationship, although still present, is very loose for the countries shown in part (c).

We have now reviewed the relationship between deficits and inflation. Deficits are not inevitably inflationary. But there is a correlation between deficits and inflation. And the larger the deficit and the longer it persists, the greater are the pressures and temptations to cover the deficit by creating money, thereby generating inflation.

Another common view about borrowing requirements is that they place a burden on future generations. Let's now examine that view.

A Burden on Future Generations?

It is sometimes said that 'we owe it to our children to reduce the government sector's outstanding debts'. Is this popular view correct? How could the government's debts burden future generations?

You may be tempted to answer this question as follows. You argue that somebody has to pay the interest on the huge government debt that its past borrowing has created and which it has not yet repaid, and someone must also repay that debt at maturity. The government will have to finance this interest and the repayment with money it takes from the people as taxes. So taxes will have to be higher than they would be if there were no government debt. Surely these higher taxes burden future generations?

Wait, though. The generation which pays the taxes also receives the interest and the repayment. So while the debt will be a burden to some members of the future generation – those people who pay the higher taxes but who have inherited few bonds or

none – it is also a benefit to others – those who pay the higher taxes but who have inherited many government bonds. In aggregate, the generation as a whole neither loses nor gains, although there will be some redistribution of income.

However, while the interest received in future equals the taxes paid in future, everyone will have to pay higher taxes. Should we worry about these higher taxes? This is a matter of opinion, but many people feel that whether we should worry depends on what the government did with the money which it borrowed to create the debt. If the government spent the money on, say, hosting the Olympic games or higher salaries for today's civil servants, the spending will be of no benefit to future taxpayers. So there does seem to be a case for concern that all future taxpayers must pay extra taxes when they are receiving no benefits. In contrast, if the government spent the money on assets from which future taxpayers will benefit – such as new hospitals and roads – there seems little need to worry that those future taxpayers must pay higher taxes.

We have seen that the extra future taxes resulting from government borrowing will be offset by future interest payments. However, there are still two ways in which government borrowing today can make future UK citizens as a whole worse off. First, many of the bonds will be bought by people living abroad, for instance in other EU countries, North America and Japan. So part of the future redistribution caused by the debt will be a redistribution from future UK citizens to future foreign holders of UK debt.

Second, government borrowing may slow down the pace of investment and reduce the stock of productive capital equipment available for future generations. This phenomenon is called crowding out.

Crowding Out

Crowding out is the tendency for an increase in government purchases of goods and services to cause a decrease in the total amount of capital goods accumulated by the country (see Chapter 28). If crowding out does occur, and if government purchases of goods and services are financed by government debt, the economy will have a larger stock of government debt and a smaller stock of capital – plant and equipment. In other words, unproductive government debt replaces productive capital.

Does crowding out occur? It *may not* occur if:

◆ There is unemployment.
◆ The government uses its loans to purchase capital on which the return equals (or exceeds) that on privately purchased capital.

Crowding out *does* occur if:

◆ There is full employment.
◆ The government uses its loans to pay for labour or raw materials or for capital on which the return is less than that on privately purchased capital.

The Level of Employment   If there is full employment, increased government purchases of goods and services (and an increased deficit) must result in a decrease in the purchases of other goods and services. But if there is unemployment, it is possible that an increase in government purchases (and an increased deficit) could result in a fall in unemployment and a rise in output. In such a case the deficit does not completely crowd out other expenditure. This possibility can occur only for short periods and when the economy is in recession.

Productive Government Purchases   Some government purchases – such as roads – are obviously devoted to productive capital. But there are some not-so-obvious examples. Education and health care are investments in productive human capital. Defence expenditure protects both our physical and human capital resources and is also productive capital expenditure. Suppose government borrowing was used to finance the purchase of assets like these. Even if the borrowing requirement led to a fall in investment by firms, it would not lead to a fall in the total accumulation of capital.

But suppose the government borrows to give money to government departments to pay the wages and salaries of people such as nurses or teachers, or to purchase raw materials such as medicines or chalk. The government purchases would not represent any accumulation of capital. So if the loans reduced investment by firms, accumulation of capital would fall and there would be crowding out. Let's see how investment by firms might fall.

How Crowding Out Occurs   For crowding out to occur, government borrowing must result in less investment, so that future generations have a smaller capital stock than they would otherwise have had. This drop in the capital stock means their incomes

will be lower than they would otherwise have been, so it is, in a sense, a burden to them.

The scale of investment depends on its opportunity cost. That opportunity cost is the real interest rate. Other things remaining the same, the higher the real interest rate, the less firms will want to invest in new plant and equipment. For government borrowing to crowd out investment, the borrowing itself must cause real interest rates to rise.

Some people believe that government borrowing does increase interest rates because the government's borrowing represents an increase in the demand for loans with no corresponding increase in the supply of loans. Figure 33.7 shows what happens in this case. Part (a) shows the demand and supply curves for loans. Initially, the demand for loans is D_0 and the supply of loans is S_0. The real interest rate is 3 per cent, and the quantity of loans made is £100 billion. Part (b) shows investment. At a real interest rate of 3 per cent, investment is £80 billion. Now suppose that the government runs a deficit and finances its deficit by borrowing. The demand for loans increases and the demand curve for loans shifts from D_0 to D_1. There is no change in the supply of loans, so the real interest rate increases to 4 per cent and the quantity of loans increases to £120 billion. Notice that the increase in the quantity of loans made is smaller than the increase in the demand for loans. That is, the demand curve shifts to the right by a larger amount than the increase in loans that actually occurs. The higher interest rate decreases investment and brings a smaller capital stock. Thus the increased stock of government debt crowds out some productive capital.

Does government borrowing make real interest rates rise as shown in Fig. 33.7? Many economists believe so, and they have some pretty strong evidence to point to. Certainly real interest rates in the United Kingdom have been high in many of the years when there has been a large real borrowing requirement, and there is a general tendency for real interest rates and the real borrowing requirement to fluctuate in sympathy with each other.

It is this relationship in the data that leads some economists to predict that a higher real borrowing requirement means higher real interest rates, lower investment and a smaller scale of capital accumulation. Because of its effects on real interest rates, government borrowing crowds out the accumulation of productive physical capital. As a consequence, future output will be lower than it

FIGURE 33.7

The Deficit, Borrowing and Crowding Out

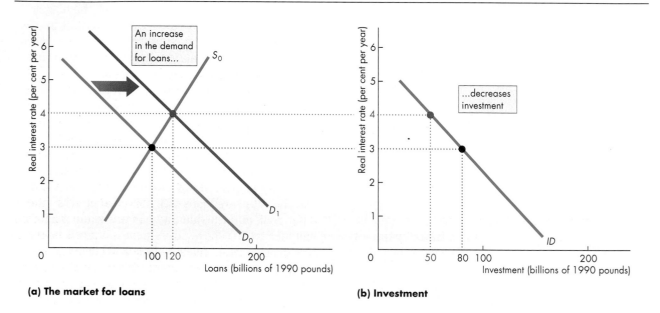

(a) The market for loans

(b) Investment

Part (a) shows the market for loans. The demand for loans is D_0 and the supply is S_0. The quantity of loans outstanding is £100 billion and the real interest rate is 3 per cent. Part (b) shows the determination of investment. At an interest rate of 3 per cent, investment is £80 billion per year. The government runs a deficit and finances the deficit by borrowing. The government's increase in

demand for loans shifts the demand curve to D_1. The interest rate rises to 4 per cent and the equilibrium quantity of loans increases to £120 billion. The higher interest rate leads to a decrease in investment in part (b). The government deficit crowds out capital accumulation.

otherwise would have been, and so the deficit burdens future generations.

Ricardian Equivalence

Some economists do not believe that government borrowing crowds out capital accumulation. On the contrary, they argue that debt financing and paying for government spending with taxes are equivalent. The level of government purchases of goods and services certainly matters, but not the way in which it is financed.

The first economist to advance this idea (known as Ricardian equivalence) was the great English economist David Ricardo. Recently, Ricardo's idea has been given a forceful restatement by Robert Barro of Harvard University in the United States. Barro argues as follows: if the government increases its purchases of goods and services by borrowing,

and so does not increase taxes, then people are clever enough to recognize that higher taxes are going to have to be paid later in order to cover the interest payments and repayment incurred on the debt that is being issued today. In recognition of having to pay higher taxes later, people will cut their consumption now and increase their saving, for in this way they will ensure that when the higher taxes finally are levied by the government, sufficient wealth has been accumulated to meet those tax liabilities without a further cut in consumption. The scale of increased saving matches the scale of increased government spending.

Figure 33.8 illustrates this case. Initially the demand for loans is D_0 and the supply of loans S_0. The real interest rate is 3 per cent and the quantity of loans outstanding is £100 billion. The government runs a deficit of £30 billion and finances that deficit by borrowing. The demand curve for loans shifts to the

FIGURE 33.8

Ricardian Equivalence

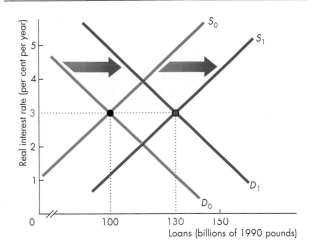

Initially, the demand for loans is D_0 and the supply of loans is S_0. The equilibrium quantity of loans is £100 billion and the real interest rate is 3 per cent. An increase in the government deficit, financed by borrowing, increases the demand for loans and shifts the demand curve to D_1. Households, recognizing that the increased government deficit will bring increased future taxes to pay the additional interest charges, cut their consumption and increase their saving. The supply curve of loans also shifts to the right to S_1. The equilibrium quantity of loans increases to £130 billion, but the real interest rate stays constant at 3 per cent. So there is no crowding out of investment.

right to D_1. At the same time, using the reasoning of Ricardo and Barro, there is a cut in consumption of £30 billion and an increase in the supply of loans. The supply curve shifts to the right to S_1. The quantity of loans increases from £100 to £130 billion and the real interest rate stays constant at 3 per cent. Citizens know that the interest they get on their extra lending will cover the extra taxes they will face to cover the interest on the government's extra borrowing. With no change in the real interest rate, there is no crowding out of investment.

Some economists argue that Ricardian equivalence breaks down because people take into account only future tax liabilities that will be borne by themselves and not by their children and their grandchildren. Proponents of the Ricardian equivalence proposition argue that it makes no difference whether future tax liabilities are going to be borne by those currently alive, or by their descendants. If the taxes are going to

be borne by children and grandchildren, the current generation takes account of those future taxes and adjusts its own consumption so that it can make bequests on a large enough scale to enable those taxes to be paid.

Laying out the assumptions necessary for Ricardian equivalence leaves most economists convinced that the proposition cannot be relevant. Yet there is a perhaps surprising amount of evidence in its support. In order to interpret the evidence, it is important to be clear that Ricardian equivalence does *not* imply that real interest rates are unaffected by the level of government purchases of goods and services. A high level of government purchases, other things remaining the same, brings a higher real interest rate. All that the Ricardian equivalence proposition implies is that the rise in real interest rates will not be affected by the way in which a given increase in government purchases is financed. When taxes are used, there is no rise in the supply of or demand for loans. When loans are used, the supply of and demand for loans rise equally. So real interest rates will be no higher with borrowing than they will be with taxes. So borrowing of itself does not cause crowding out.

Whether government borrowing does, in practice, affect real interest rates remains unproven. If people do take into account the future tax burdens of themselves, their children and their grandchildren, then saving will respond to offset the government borrowing and the borrowing will have little or no effect on real interest rates and capital accumulation. If people ignore the implications of the deficit for their own and their descendants' future consumption possibilities, the borrowing will indeed increase real interest rates. The jury remains out on this question.

Eliminating the Government Sector Deficit

How can the government sector reduce its borrowing requirement? As its borrowing requirement stems almost entirely from its deficit, it needs to reduce its deficit. There are just two ways of eliminating a deficit:

◆ Reducing expenditure
◆ Increasing revenue

Reducing Expenditure

Throughout modern history, government expenditure has tended to increase not only in total but as a percentage of GDP. Governments in the United Kingdom have done better than some other governments to contain the growth of government expenditure. In some European countries, governments spend close to 50 per cent of GDP. At its peak, that percentage increased to more than 53 per cent in the Netherlands in 1983.

Many elements of government expenditure have a built-in tendency to increase. Two of these are education and health care. As a country's total income rises, its citizens generally want to devote a larger share of that income to those items. If the government plays a significant role in the provision of these two services, it is inevitable that government purchases, expressed as a percentage of GDP, will gradually rise. Only by removing certain responsibilities from the domain of government can the government's share of GDP be effectively contained. Thus in many European countries the government is getting out of a wide variety of activities involving the provision of some services.

Since 1979, the UK government has toyed with various ways of doing this. For example, it has encouraged retired people to take out medical insurance; it has reduced the real level of maintenance grants paid to students and encouraged them to make up the difference with loans; and it has also looked at the possibility of private industry building toll roads where otherwise the government would have built roads out of its own revenues.

Nevertheless, it is not easy to privatize most of the government sector's programmes, and it is not easy to cut government spending significantly on the programmes that the government sector retains without cutting services to unacceptable levels. The government maintains a determination to cut out waste in public spending in an effort to ensure that services cost no more than the minimum, but detecting and cutting out waste is difficult – and there must be a finite amount of waste to eliminate. Reading Between the Lines on pp. 944–945 looks at cutting the budget deficit in the United Kingdom.

Perhaps the most promising way in which the government has tried to minimize the cost of providing some services is through what is called competitive tendering. **Competitive tendering** means allowing private firms to compete for con-

tracts to do work which was previously always handled by public employees. For example, cleaning hospitals and emptying dustbins used always to be done by health service employees and local authority employees respectively. But now tasks like these are open to whoever can do them most cheaply. The government departments which have traditionally done them generally make a bid for the work, but they will receive the contract only if no private firm undercuts their bid. It is very disappointing for the public employees if their bid fails for then they lose their jobs. Sometimes the people who lose their jobs get jobs with the successful private firm, but their pay may well be lower than it was before. Against this disappointment, the saving of the taxpayers' money should help keep taxes down or enable public services to improve.

Another big hope for cutting government expenditure in the 1990s is the so-called peace dividend. The **peace dividend** refers to the sharp cut that is being made to the defence budget following the disbanding of the Warsaw Pact and improved relations with Eastern Europe.

We can see, then, that there are various factors which may help keep public spending down. But against these factors there are demographic trends which mean the government will have to pay out more in state pensions to an increasing number of retired people. There will also be increased demands for health spending by young and old as new and more expensive treatments become available. So it is doubtful whether the percentage of GDP accounted for by government spending can be cut significantly.

Since 1979, the government has received much criticism for trying to remove the deficit by cutting government spending at all. Many people argued that it would have been better to eliminate the deficit by increasing government revenue. Let's examine that option.

Increasing Revenue

Two main approaches to increasing revenue have been proposed:

◆ Increase tax rates
◆ Decrease tax rates

Does this sound paradoxical? It isn't really paradoxical if you remember that what the government wants to do is to increase its *tax revenue*. Tax revenue is the product of the tax rate and the tax base. A **tax rate** is the percentage rate of tax levied on a particular activity. The **tax base** is the activity on which a tax is levied. For example, the tax base for personal income tax is earned income minus some specified allowances. The tax rates are 20 per cent, 25 per cent and 40 per cent (depending on income level).

There is ambiguity and disagreement about whether an increase in tax rates increases or decreases tax revenues. The source of the disagreement is something called the Laffer curve. The **Laffer curve** (named after Arthur Laffer, who first proposed it) is a curve that relates tax revenue to the tax rate. Figure 33.9 illustrates a Laffer curve for a hypothetical tax. Possible tax rates between 0 and 100 per cent are shown on the vertical axis. Tax revenue, measured in billions of pounds, is shown on the horizontal axis. If the tax rate is 0, then no tax revenue is raised. That is why the curve begins at the origin. As the tax rate increases, tax revenue also increases but only up to some maximum, m in the figure. In this example, once the tax rate has reached 40 per cent, the tax revenue is at its maximum. If the tax rate increases above 40 per cent, tax revenue falls. Why does this happen?

Revenue falls because there is a fall in the scale of the activity that is being taxed. Suppose that the item in question is petrol. With no tax, lots of people drive thirsty cars and consume millions of litres a week. If petrol is taxed, its price increases and the quantity bought declines. At first, the quantity bought falls by a smaller percentage than the percentage increase in the tax rate, and the tax revenue rises. But there comes a point at which the fall in the quantity demanded rises by a bigger percentage than the rise in the tax rate. At that point, tax revenue begins to decline. People sell their thirsty cars. Instead, they buy smaller cars, share car journeys and use public transport. The tax rate goes up but the tax base goes down and tax revenue declines.

You can now see that whether a cut in the *tax rate* increases or decreases *tax revenue* depends on where we are on the Laffer curve. If we're at a point such as a in Fig. 33.9, a decrease in the tax rate results in an increase in tax revenue. But if we're at point b, a decrease in the tax rate results in a decrease in tax revenue. To increase tax revenue from point b, we have to increase the tax rate.

Economists and other observers argue about where we are on the Laffer curve for each of the various taxes. Some people suspect that for the very

FIGURE 33.9

The Laffer Curve

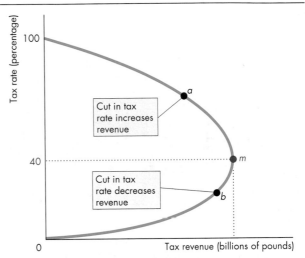

The Laffer curve shows the relationship between a tax rate and tax revenue. If the tax rate is 0 per cent, the government collects no tax revenue. As the tax rate increases, the government's tax revenue also increases, but up to some maximum (m). As the tax rate continues to increase, tax revenue declines. At a tax rate of 100 per cent, the government collects no revenue. Higher taxes act as a disincentive. The more heavily taxed is an activity, the less that activity is undertaken. When the percentage decrease in the activity is less than the percentage increase in the tax rate, we are at a point such as b and tax revenue rises. When the percentage decrease in the activity exceeds the percentage increase in the tax rate, we are at a point such as a and tax revenue decreases.

highly taxed commodities such as petrol, tobacco products and alcohol, we may be on the 'backward-bending' part of the Laffer curve, so that an increase in the tax rate would decrease tax revenue. But hardly anyone believes this to be the case for VAT which is the highest yielding tax on expenditure. The government thinks we may be on the backward-bending part of the Laffer curve for personal income tax, but many economists disagree.

Another approach to increasing revenue is to introduce new taxes on activities or items that were not previously taxed. The UK government has played cautiously here. Its most dramatic recent move, introduced in 1994, was to start taxing people on their use of electricity, gas and heating oil.

An alternative approach to raising government revenue is for the government to charge – or charge more – for some of the services it provides. The

Changing Attitudes on the Government Budget Deficit

THE INDEPENDENT II, 18 OCTOBER 1993

Clarke *vs* the Tory right on budgetary policy

Gavyn Davies

THE Tory right, which 12 years ago was absolutely determined to control 'fiscal profligacy' even at the expense of huge tax increases in 1981, is nowadays prone to argue that the budget deficit (though much larger now than it was then) is perfectly manageable. Meanwhile, the centre/left of the party, which opposed Mrs Thatcher's tax increases in 1981, now vociferously supports budgetary tightening.

…This game of intellectual musical chairs has mirrored a similar shift in thinking in the economics profession, where the classical economists are now the least persuaded of the need for tightening while the low church Keynesians tend to be more hawkish.

Financial crises

…The Keynesians have become more cautious about budgetary risks since 1981.…

The tendency for developed economics suddenly to encounter crises of government debt was a new phenomenon of the 1980s. Until the decline in global inflation really took hold a decade ago, it was usual for the rate of interest to be considerably below the growth rate of nominal gross domestic product in most countries. This… meant that debt tended to accumulate more slowly than GDP increased.

In the past 15 years, the decline in inflation, and the rise in real interest rates, has meant that governments must run a generally much tighter ship to ensure that the debt ratio remains under control.

This can be illustrated by a single example. In 1991, if the Treasury had then been performing 'debt sustainability' calculations, it would have been reasonable to suppose that the real rate of interest might stabilise at around 1 per cent, and that an ambitious inflation target would be about 8 per cent per annum. Based on these figures, the Government could stabilise its debt ratio at 50 per cent of GDP by running a *permanent* budget deficit of 5.0 per cent of GDP each year. In other words, because inflation was eating into the value of debt so rapidly, it was not difficult even for profligate governments to ensure that the real value of outstanding debt was kept under control.

Nowadays, the same calculation is much less reassuring. Real interest rates are close to 4 per cent, and the centre of the Government's inflation target is only 2.5 per cent. This means that the Exchequer can run a public sector borrowing requirement of only 2.5 per cent of GDP… if it wishes to stabilise the debt ratio at 50 per cent of GDP.

© The Independent. Reprinted with permission.

Throughout the 1980s, people on the right of the Conservative Party called for restraint in public spending.

People on the left of the Conservative Party are now the more concerned group when it comes to public expenditure, a shift in attitudes reflecting a more general shift in the broader economics profession.

The explanation given for this switch is the changes in real interest rates through the 1980s and their relative change against the rate of economic growth.

The real rate of interest reflects the nominal rate of interest and the rate of inflation. The rate of economic growth reflects the rate at which the country's ability to pay its debt rises (or falls) each year. If the country's ability to pay rises at least as fast as the debt, then this debt can readily be funded.

Through the 1980s, there were a number of differences in the trends of these variables. Average nominal interest rates were higher than earlier and inflation lower, leading to higher real interest rates, and therefore higher rates of increase in the total debt.

Over this same period, real GDP fluctuated dramatically. It fell in 1981, 1991 and 1992, but rose by about 4 per cent each year in the mid-1980s.

The higher inflation rate experienced prior to the 1980s meant that the real value of debt was eroded more rapidly (that is, inflation acted like a tax). This erosion of the real debt declined as control of inflation became the government's overriding aim.

The shift in attitude of the people on the right can partly be explained by their belief in the economic reforms carried out through the 1980s. Although there is now a narrower margin for error regarding debt sustainability, high rates of growth generated as the economy recovers should ensure this debt is sustainable and dealt with automatically.

The attitude of Keynesian economists can be explained as a lack of faith in the effectiveness of these reforms. In believing that they will not reduce unemployment significantly and will not produce high rates of economic growth, the way to ensure the debt is sustainable is to limit it by controlling public expenditure. This should be the approach until the recovery is clearly and strongly under way.

Figure 1 shows that interest rates were lower in 1970–1978 than in 1979–1992, with annual inflation higher in the earlier period than in the later period.

The government deficit of the 1990s was, by 1992, greater than for any year through the 1970s and 1980s and has come about much more quickly. Deficits occurred regularly between 1971 and 1986, but never reached the (nominal) magnitude of 1992's figure. This is shown in Fig. 2.

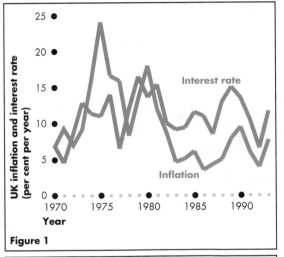

Figure 1

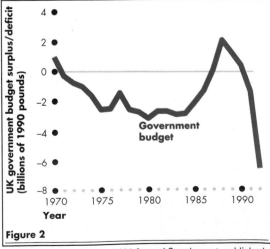

Figure 2

Source: Economic Trends 1994 Annual Supplement, published by the Central Statistical Office.

most widely known charges are probably those for medical prescriptions which have been raised several times since 1979. The government also wants to charge people for using motorways.

The pressure for higher government spending on improved government services will always be with us. In turn, the search for new sources of government revenue will also be a permanent feature of economic life.

◆ ◆ ◆ ◆   We have now completed our study of macroeconomics and of the challenges and problems of stabilizing the economy. In this study, our main focus has been the economy of the United Kingdom.

We have taken into account the linkages between the United Kingdom and the rest of the world, but international economic relations have not been our main concern. In the remaining chapters we are going to shift our focus and study some vital international issues. First, in Chapter 34, we examine the international exchange of goods and services. Second, in Chapter 35, we study the financing of international trade and the determination of the value of the pound in terms of other currencies. Third, in Chapter 36, we turn our attention to the problems of the poor developing countries and look at the momentous events taking place in Eastern Europe.

S U M M A R Y

The Meaning of Deficits and Surpluses

Since 1972, the expenditure of the government sector of the United Kingdom exceeded its revenue in every year except 1988 and 1989. The main cause of these deficits and surpluses is that government spending rose in the 1970s, dipped in 1988 and 1989, and then rose again. When the government sector has a deficit it generally has to borrow money – that is to say, it has a positive borrowing requirement. When it has a surplus it can generally repay some past loans – that is to say, it has a negative borrowing requirement. There is a link between the size of the government sector's deficit or surplus and business cycles. When the economy is in a recovery, taxes increase and transfer payments decrease as a percentage of GDP. The government sector tends to move from deficit to surplus. When the economy goes into recession, taxes decrease and transfer payments increase as a percentage of GDP, and so the government sector tends to go from surplus to deficit. (pp. 925–932)

Real Borrowing Requirements and Debts

Many of the deficits since 1972 have been large and led to the government sector needing to borrow large sums of money. Despite this, however, the real value of the government's debt fell almost every year. This is because inflation reduced the real value of the loans that had been previously made to the government sector. The real borrowing requirement

in a given year measures the real increase in the value of the government's debts and is found by subtracting from the new borrowing done in the year the fall in the real value of its previous borrowing. Adjusting the government's borrowing requirements for this fact and measuring the real borrowing requirement reveals that the real borrowing requirement has actually been negative in almost every one of the last 20 years. The cycles in the borrowing requirement remain the same, whether measured in terms of real or current pounds. (pp. 932–934)

Government Borrowing and Inflation

If borrowing requirements are money financed, they cause inflation. If they are debt financed, whether they cause inflation or not depends on how permanent they are. A temporary debt-financed borrowing requirement will have no inflationary effects. A permanent debt-financed borrowing requirement leads to inflation. It does so because the build-up of debt leads to a build-up of interest payments and a yet higher borrowing requirement. At some future date, the borrowing requirement will probably be money financed and the amount of money created will be larger, the longer the borrowing requirement persists and the more debt the government issues. Fear of future inflation leads to a demand here and now for less government debt and less money. So demand rises for other assets such as capital goods and consumer durables. As a consequence, inflation increases in anticipation of a future (and perhaps distant future) increase in money creation to finance the borrowing requirement. (pp. 934–938)

A Burden on Future Generations?

Whether government borrowing imposes a burden on future generations is a controversial issue. If the government borrows today, future citizens will have to pay taxes to meet the interest and repayment of that debt. But the interest and repayments will be paid to other future citizens, so the extra taxes create no loss of income for future generations as a whole. Instead there is a redistribution. Admittedly some of this redistribution will be to foreign citizens and will represent a transfer of income from the country with the debt to other countries.

However, some economists believe that government borrowing causes real interest rates to rise, so that borrowing lowers investment by firms. This means that – unless the government uses the loans to purchase productive assets of its own – the amount of capital we accumulate will be reduced. As a consequence, future output will be lower than it otherwise would have been and future generations will be 'burdened' with the effects of the government borrowing.

Other economists argue that if government spending is financed by borrowing, people will recognize that future taxes will have to increase to cover the interest payments on the extra debt and its repayment. And, in anticipation of those higher future taxes, saving will increase by as much as the government wants to borrow. So government borrowing has no more tendency to raise interest rates and crowd out investment than tax finance. (pp. 938–941)

Eliminating the Government Sector Deficit

When the government sector moved into surplus in 1988–1989, a start was made on repaying the government sector's debts. But the surplus was short lived. The future depends on the future of government expenditure and taxes. Reducing expenditure is very difficult and is unlikely to occur on a large scale. Any benefits from cuts in defence spending in the light of reduced tensions between Western and Eastern Europe are likely to be offset by an increased number of retired people who will receive state pensions and demand substantial health care. Increasing revenue could result from increasing some tax rates – those for taxes where we are on the upward-sloping part of the Laffer curve – and from decreasing other tax rates – those for taxes where we are on the backward-bending part of the Laffer curve. (pp. 941–946)

K E Y   E L E M E N T S

Key Terms

Balanced budget, 926
Budget deficit, 926
Budget surplus, 926
Competitive tendering, 942
Debt financing, 935
Government deficit, 925
Government sector debt, 926
Government surplus, 925
Laffer curve, 939
Money financing, 935
National debt, 926
Nominal borrowing requirement, 933
Peace dividend, 942

Public sector borrowing requirement, 926
Real borrowing requirement, 932
Tax base, 943
Tax rate, 943

Key Figures

Figure 33.1   Revenue, Expenditure and the Deficit, 927
Figure 33.4   The Deficit and the Business Cycle, 931
Figure 33.5   The Real and Nominal Borrowing Requirements, 934
Figure 33.9   The Laffer Curve, 943

R E V I E W   Q U E S T I O N S

1 What were the main changes in taxes and government spending associated with the emergence of the government sector deficit during the 1970s?

2 Trace the events since 1980 that resulted first in a continued government sector deficit, then produced a surplus, and then produced a deficit once again.

3 Distinguish between a government deficit and a positive borrowing requirement. Distinguish between a government surplus and a negative borrowing requirement.

4 Distinguish between the real borrowing requirement and the nominal borrowing requirement.

5 In calculating the real borrowing requirement, which of the following would you do:

a Value the interest payments in real terms and take into account the change in the real value of government debt?

b Calculate the interest payments in nominal terms and take into account the change in the real value of government debt?

c Calculate the interest payments in real terms but ignore the change in the real value of outstanding government debt?

6 Explain how, in a modern financial system, the government finances its deficit by creating money.

7 Review the ways in which the deficit can be a burden on future generations.

8 Why do some economists argue that taxes and government debt are equivalent to each other so that the deficit does not matter?

9 Why do some economists think that government revenue can be increased by cutting tax rates?

10 Why do some economists think that government revenue can be increased by reducing tax rates?

P R O B L E M S

1 You are given the following information about an economy. When unemployment is at its natural rate, which is 5.5 per cent, government spending and taxes are each 20 per cent of GDP. There is no inflation. For each 1 percentage point increase in the unemployment rate, government spending increases by 1 percentage point of GDP and taxes fall by 1 percentage point of GDP. Suppose that the economy experiences a cycle in which the unemployment rate takes the following values:

Year	1	2	3	4	5	6	7
Unemployment rate	5	6	7	6	5	4	5

a Calculate the actual deficit as a percentage of GDP for each year.

b Is the actual deficit related to the business cycle?

2 In one particular year in an imaginary economy, government expenditure, excluding debt interest, is £8.5 billion. Government revenue is

£10 billion. The government starts the year with a £25 billion outstanding debt. Interest rates are 24 per cent a year on all outstanding debt and there is a 20 per cent inflation rate. The government does not lend and receives no repayments of any loans it has made in the past. Calculate the following:

a The debt interest that the government pays.

b The government's nominal borrowing requirement.

c The value of the government debt outstanding at the end of the year.

d The government's real borrowing requirement.

e The real value of the government's debt outstanding at the end of the year (that is, the value expressed in terms of the beginning of the year prices).

3 Suppose the rate of return on private capital is 5 per cent. The government is planning an increase in health services at an annual cost of

£100 billion. These extra health services are expected to improve health and thus labour productivity resulting in an increase in GDP of £50 billion a year. There is full employment.

a What is the opportunity cost of the government programme?

b Does it make any difference to the opportunity cost if the programme is financed by current taxes, borrowing, or money creation?

c Will the programme be a burden or a benefit to future generations if it is financed by borrowing?

PART 8

GROWTH, DEVELOPMENT AND REFORM

Talking with Jeffrey Sachs

Jeffrey Sachs was born in Detroit and has spent his entire university career at Harvard, first as an undergraduate and eventually as a professor. Today, however, Professor Sachs spends most of his time on aeroplanes or in Eastern Europe. He first began advising foreign governments on economic policy by helping Bolivia with hyperinflation in 1985. His name burst before the public with his work on Poland, but now he is increasingly associated with the economic reforms of Boris Yeltsin and the Russian Federation.

How did you get drawn into the Eastern European reform area?

I started my work in Eastern Europe in Poland at the time that Solidarity was legalized in the spring of 1989. I had been invited by the Communist government to give advice to them about their financial troubles. Events obviously went very fast because soon after legalization there was an election, which Solidarity won overwhelmingly. From that point on, I became an economic advisor to believers in Solidarity and helped them draft an outline of a radical economic reform programme. Soon after that, a Solidarity government actually came to power, and I began to work on the implementation of economic reforms, which were widely viewed as the first and most comprehensive reforms in Eastern Europe. From there, I got to know reformers in all of the countries in the region and began to work closely with some Russian economists who are now senior members of the Yeltsin government. As democratization proceeded in Russia, these people invited me to help them develop their reform strategy.

Your name has been associated with the 'big bang' or 'cold turkey' approach to reform. Can you describe that approach and explain why you favour it over a more gradual and tentative one?

The basic idea is to start with the goal of the reform, such as to put in place a working capitalist system. Of course, it'll be a capitalist system that reflects the particular culture, history, tradition and resources of the country. It is an attempt not to find a so-called 'third way in' between the old system and the new system but to go fully towards the working capitalist model. In the case of Eastern Europe, the goal is even more explicit: to implement reforms that will make these countries harmonize with the economies of Western Europe so that in a short period of time – within a decade is their hope – they can actually become members of the European Union.

The essence of 'big bang' is that it's important to move comprehensively and quickly towards the goal of a working capitalist economy because various aspects of the market economy are all interrelated. If one does just a piece of the reform but leaves much of the old system intact, the conflicts of the old and the new are likely to make things considerably worse than better.

What are the major pieces of the radical reform strategy that you're recommending to governments in Eastern Europe?

The reform strategy comes down to four components. The first is macroeconomic stabilization, because usually these countries start out in a deep macroeconomic crisis characterized by high inflation and intense shortages. Second is economic liberalization, which means ending central planning,

trade quotas and other barriers that cut the country off from the world market. The third part of the reform is privatization, which is the transfer of state property back to private owners. Those private owners could be individuals or they could be, as in the West, financial intermediaries like mutual funds or banks or pension funds that are in turn owned by individuals. When I say privatization, I use the word 'transfer' rather than 'sell' because selling state property is only one way to privatize. There are other ways, such as giving away the state property to workers, managers, or the public. The Eastern European countries are privatizing through a mix of sales and direct giveaways. The fourth part of the radical reform is the introduction of social safety nets, which provide protection for the most vulnerable parts of society that are perhaps hardest hit by the reform or are already suffering even irrespective of the reform. That means putting in place unemployment benefits, an adequate retirement system and health care system, job training, public works spending and so forth. Those are the four main pillars.

It's called 'big bang' because you must move quickly on this. Probably the most dramatic part of all this is the stabilization and liberalization phase, where subsidies are cut very quickly and price controls are eliminated. The result is usually a very dramatic one-time jump in prices. That starts off the reform.

How long does the reform process generally take?

Certain things can be done quickly, and others take more time. Stabilization and liberalization can be accomplished fast, or most parts of them. Freeing price controls, eliminating trade barriers

and cutting subsidies, for example, can all be done on the first day of the programme, which is why it's sometimes called 'shock therapy' or 'cold turkey'. Privatization, though, takes much longer. Some aspects of the fourth component of the reform strategy, the social safety net, can be done quickly. For example, pensions of retirees can be protected through budgetary allocation. An unemployment insurance system was started up very quickly in Poland, and it has worked adequately. Other parts of the social safety net, for instance, real reform of the health care system, are very complex and take a considerable amount of time to effect.

Even if the reforms go very quickly, the process of change that those reforms set loose will take years or even decades to work themselves out. What do I mean? The socialist system wasn't just messed up in terms of the organization of production and the ways that prices were set. It was also systematically misusing resources by putting tremendous overemphasis on heavy industrial production while neglecting other important parts of the economy such as services and wholesale and retail trade. When you free up market forces, the market doesn't demand all the heavy industrial production that was built up in the past. This leads to unemployment, a drop in demand and people voluntarily quitting those industries to move into areas that were starved of people, resources and capital in the past. You get a great boom in retail trade, for example, with tens of thousands of new shops opening up. The reforms set loose that process, but the corresponding shift of resources could take five, ten, fifteen, even twenty years to adjust.

Even within a big bang approach, presumably you can't literally do everything at once. What are the highest priorities?

The highest priority is to avoid real financial chaos. Poland, Yugoslavia and Russia all fell into hyperinflation at the end of the Communist system. That meant that the new democratic government's highest priority was to end the underlying conditions that were feeding the hyperinflation. If you can accomplish the financial stability, then I think the next highest priority is to have the rudiments of the private property system in place, such as a commercial code and laws for corporate enterprises, contracts and protection of private property. Then the next priority is rapid privatization because until the enterprises are with real owners facing proper incentives, one has to be sceptical that they'll be managed in an efficient and sensible way.

Can the countries of Eastern Europe and the former Soviet Union evolve into democratic nations with market economies without economic aid from the West?

The whole history of radical economic change underscores the importance of financial assistance during the first critical years of reform. It takes many years for the real fruits of the reform to be widely evident in society. Certain costs of the reform, however, such as closing down old inefficient enterprises, can become evident very quickly. It's during that critical period between the introduction of the reforms and the time when they really are bearing fruit that lie the greatest dangers and also the greatest need for international assistance to help provide a cushion to living

standards and a bolstering of the reform effect until the reforms take hold.

The foreign assistance does not actually pay for the reconstruction of the country. It's never big enough. The Marshall Plan was not enough to really rebuild Europe, but what the Marshall Plan did was to give the new democratic postwar governments time to put in place market-based policies so that they could take hold.

Whether it's postwar Germany or Japan, Mexico's turnaround in the 1980s, or Poland at the beginning of the 1990s, countries on the path to economic and political reform need help at the beginning. For Russia and the other states of the Soviet Union, it will be the same. They will definitely need some years of Western and foreign help to keep their reforms on track and to make the living conditions tolerable.

What form will that aid take? Free-trading opportunities? Private investment? Government loans?

The form of aid has to be linked to the timetable of the reform process. At the beginning, say in the first year, the aid is inevitably of two sorts. First, humanitarian emergency assistance to make sure that food is getting to the table and that medical supplies are available. Second, stabilization assistance, or various kinds of financial support to help make the currency strong and to increase the flow of basic imports, which are needed just to keep the economy functioning. Russia has suffered a sharp decline in its own capacity to buy imports because its export earnings have fallen sharply over the past few years. They need help just to keep basic

imports going, and by doing that you help strengthen the currency.

In later years, you want to get away from that kind of emergency stabilization support and put much more attention on project financing to get new enterprises going. One hopes these will become the major engine of economic growth in the future. Private investment, of course, is to be desired, but it will take many years to attract. Private investors first want to know the market, and then they wait to see signs that the reforms are working and that political stability is being achieved. The official support from government has to come first. Then the private money will flow in.

What are the economic principles that you find most valuable in dealing with the acute problems of Russia today?

The starting point for me is to recognize that all of the successful economies in the world have a shared core set of institutions. There are, of course, major differences across countries, but all of the advanced industrial economies share certain features – such as a currency that trades, that can be used to buy goods without facing fixed prices or shortages, and that is convertible internationally; an open trading system in which, with some exceptions, goods can be bought and sold from abroad on normal market terms; an economy based on private ownership not state ownership; a legal infrastructure that supports private ownership so that property rights are clearly defined and defensible. Things like that. It's that core of institutions that is so important to put into place.

CHAPTER 34

TRADING WITH THE WORLD

After studying this chapter you will be able to:

- ◆ Describe the patterns and trends in international trade

- ◆ Explain comparative advantage

- ◆ Explain why all countries can gain from international trade

- ◆ Explain how prices adjust to bring about balanced trade

- ◆ Explain how economies of scale and diversity of taste lead to gains from international trade

- ◆ Explain why trade restrictions reduce the volume of imports and exports and why they reduce consumption possibilities

- ◆ Explain why countries adopt trade restrictions even though they reduce consumption possibilities

S INCE ANCIENT TIMES, PEOPLE HAVE TRIED TO TRADE AS FAR AS TECHNOLOGY allowed. The nations around the Mediterranean had a flourishing maritime trade 5,000 years ago. Today, container ships and jumbo jets carry billions of pounds worth of goods each year. Why do people go to such great lengths to trade with other nations? ◆ ◆ In recent years, many traditional UK industries, such as ship-building and coal-mining, have declined dramatically in the face of foreign competition. Do the benefits of international trade make up for the lost jobs in these industries? ◆ ◆ The wages of workers in the textiles and electronics factories of Taiwan and Hong Kong are low compared with UK wages. Can the United Kingdom compete with countries like that?

Marco Polo and Jumbo Jets

◆ ◆ During the Great Depression in the 1930s, most countries imposed tariffs – taxes on imports – and other import restrictions. Since 1945 these restrictions have been greatly eased. In 1973, for instance, the United Kingdom joined the European Union which prohibits trade barriers between members. And in 1993, new deals were struck with GATT (the General Agreement on Tariffs and Trade) that will lead to much freer trade between the European Union and other countries. What effect do tariffs have? Why don't we have completely free trade in the world?

◆ ◆ ◆ ◆ In this chapter, we're going to learn about international trade. We'll see how *all* nations, even those with high wages, can gain by specializing in producing the goods and services in which they have a comparative advantage and by trading with other countries. We'll also explain why, despite the benefits of international trade, many countries still restrict trade.

Patterns and Trends in International Trade

The goods and services that people in one country buy from people in other countries are called **imports**. The goods and services that people in one country sell to people in other countries are called **exports**. What are the most important things that the United Kingdom imports and exports? Most people would probably guess that a rich nation such as the United Kingdom exports goods such as machinery, road vehicles and chemicals, all of which require highly developed industries, and they would guess that it imports basic (or raw) materials, fuels and food. Let's look at the pattern of the UK's international trade in a recent year.

UK International Trade

Figure 34.1 provides a quick overview of the main goods and services that the United Kingdom exported and imported in 1992. We'll look at the trade in goods first, and then at the trade in services.

FIGURE 34.1

UK Exports and Imports, 1992

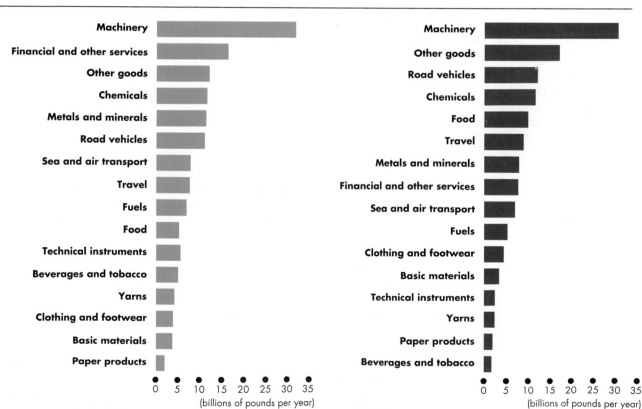

(a) Exports of goods and services

(b) Imports of goods and services

The figure divides the UK's exports and imports into a number of categories. The most important export categories are machinery, financial services and chemicals. Two of these – machinery and chemicals – are also among the main import categories. Other important import categories include road vehi- cles, food and sea and air transport. Financial services form the only category where exports greatly exceed imports.

Sources: Central Statistical Office, *The Pink Book 1993: United Kingdom Balance of Payments*, p. 31, and *Annual Abstract of Statistics, 1994 Edition*, pp. 85–88.

Trade in Goods You can see from Fig. 34.1 that the most important category of goods exported by the United Kingdom is indeed machinery – such as generating equipment, office machinery and electrical appliances. Exports of chemicals and road vehicles are also important, as are exports of metals and minerals. You can also see that food, fuels and basic materials are important imports.

But perhaps the most important feature of UK trade shown in the figure is that the patterns of exports and imports are remarkably similar. For example, machinery is the main import item as well as the main export item, with imports actually slightly exceeding exports, and there are also more imports than exports for road vehicles. This two-way trade in machinery and vehicles arises because, for example, the country exports generators and imports slightly different generators, and it exports Rovers and imports Fiats. Notice, too, that while imports of food, basic materials and fuels all exceed exports, the exports are sizeable and, in the case of fuel, almost equal imports.

Trade in Services On the services side, Fig. 34.1 shows that the main items are financial services (such as insurance and banking), sea and air transport, and travel. You can also see that exports of financial services were significantly higher than imports. You may be a little puzzled about international trade in services, for it does not involve moving goods in and out of the country as happens when a car is exported or imported. How are travel and other services exported and imported? Let's look at some examples.

Suppose that you decided to have a holiday in Germany, travelling there on a Lufthansa flight from Heathrow. What you buy from Lufthansa is not a good, but a transport service. Although the concept may sound odd at first, in economic terms you are importing that service from Germany. Since you pay a German company in exchange for a service, it doesn't matter that much of your flight time is over England. For that matter, the money you spend in Germany on items such as hotel bills and restaurant meals is also classified as the import of services. Similarly, the holiday taken by a German student in the United Kingdom counts as a UK export of services to Germany.

When UK citizens import televisions from South Korea, the owner of the ship that carries those tele-

visions might be Greek and the company that insures the cargo might be American. The payments that UK citizens make for the transport and insurance to the Greek and American companies are also payments for the import of services. Similarly, when a UK airline transports opals from Australia to Singapore, the transport cost is a UK export of a service to Singapore.

Geographical Patterns The United Kingdom is one of the world's five main trading nations and it has important trading links with almost every other country. Figure 34.2 gives a quick overview of the geographical pattern in UK international trade – though the figure covers only the exports and imports of goods which is known as **visible trade**. Over half of this visible trade takes place with other EU members, especially Germany, France, the Netherlands, Italy, Ireland and Belgium. However, the country which undertakes the most trade with the United Kingdom is the United States. There is also important trade with the non-EU countries of Western Europe and Japan.

Visible Balance The difference between the value of exports of goods and imports of goods is termed the **visible balance**. If the balance is positive, then the value of exports exceeds the value of imports and the United Kingdom is a **net exporter** of goods. But if the balance is negative, the value of imports exceeds the value of exports and the United Kingdom is a **net importer** of goods. Figure 34.2 shows that the United Kingdom is a net importer in the case of most of the countries listed, most notably the non-EU countries of Western Europe and Japan. However, the United Kingdom is a net exporter in a few cases, especially with the oil exporting countries.

The United Kingdom is usually a net importer of goods, so it is usual for it to be a net importer of goods from most individual countries. But the United Kingdom is also usually a net exporter of services, especially financial services, and we have already noted that this was true in 1992.

Trends in Net Exports International trade has become an increasingly important part of economic life. The United Kingdom now both exports and imports much larger quantities of almost all goods and services than it did even a decade ago. There

FIGURE 34.2

FIGURE 34.2

The Geographical Pattern of the UK's Visible International Trade, 1992

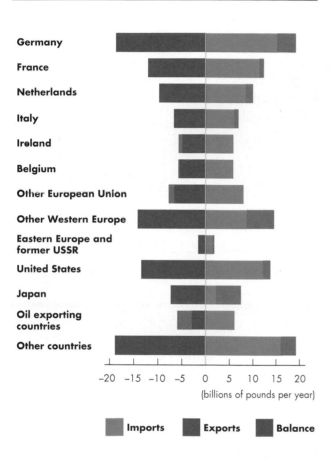

Germany
France
Netherlands
Italy
Ireland
Belgium
Other European Union
Other Western Europe
Eastern Europe and former USSR
United States
Japan
Oil exporting countries
Other countries

-20 -15 -10 -5 0 5 10 15 20
(billions of pounds per year)

Imports   Exports   Balance

The figure divides the UK's exports and imports of visibles – that is goods – into a number of countries and broader geographical areas. Well over half of UK visible trade is with the other members of the European Union. In 1992, the United Kingdom was a net importer from most other EU countries, and indeed it was also a net importer from most of the other countries and areas shown. But it was a net exporter in some cases, most notably the oil exporting countries.

Source: Central Statistical Office, *Annual Abstract of Statistics, 1994 Edition*, pp. 90–93.

the period between 1968 and 1993, that balance has often been negative – the United Kingdom has been a net importer of goods and services. But for three years from 1969 to 1972 it was a modest net exporter, and for seven years from 1977 to 1983 it was a substantial net exporter. The 1977–1983 period covers the years when North Sea oil output was very high so that oil exports were high. UK net exports have become seriously negative since 1987. A major factor in the recent trend has been a fall in the value of oil exports. This has been caused partly by a drop in North Sea oil production and partly by a fall in oil prices.

Net Exports and International Borrowing

When people buy more than they sell, they have to finance the difference by borrowing. When they sell more than they buy, they can use the surplus to make loans to others. This simple principle, which governs the income and expenditure and the borrowing and lending of individuals and firms, is also a feature of a country's net exports. If the United Kingdom imports more than it exports, it has to finance the difference by borrowing from the rest of the world. When the United Kingdom exports more than it imports, it makes loans to the rest of the world to enable them to buy products in excess of the value of the products they have sold to the United Kingdom.

This chapter does *not* cover the factors that determine net exports and the scale of international borrowing and lending which finance that balance. It is concerned with understanding the volume, pattern and directions of international trade rather than its balance. So that we can keep our focus on these topics, we'll build a model in which there is no international borrowing and lending – just international trade in goods and services. We'll find that we are able to understand what determines the volume, pattern and direction of international trade and also establish its benefits and the costs of trade restrictions within this framework. This model can be expanded to include international borrowing and lending, but such an extension does not change the conclusions that we'll reach here about the factors that determine the volume, pattern and directions of international trade.

Let's now begin to study those factors.

have also been important trends in the balance of UK international trade. Figure 34.3 shows net exports of goods and services. As you can see, in

---

FIGURE 34.3

UK Net Exports of Goods and Services, 1968–1993

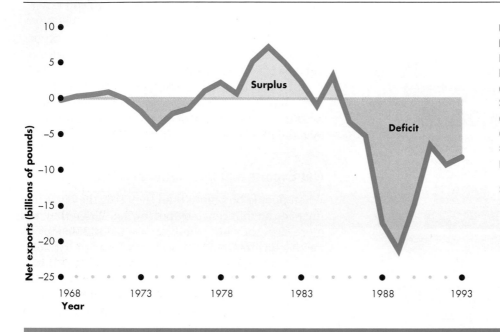

UK net exports fluctuate substantially but are usually negative as the United Kingdom is usually a net importer. However, the United Kingdom was a net exporter from 1977 to 1983, when North Sea oil production was high and oil exports and oil prices were high. Net exports have been seriously negative since 1987 when both North Sea oil output and oil prices fell.

Sources: Central Statistical Office, *Economic Trends Annual Supplement, 1992 Edition*, p. 138, and *The Pink Book 1993: United Kingdom Balance of Payments*, p. 15.

Opportunity Cost and Comparative Advantage

Let's apply the lessons that we learned in Chapter 3, about the gains from trade between Jane and Joe, to the trade between nations. We'll begin by recalling how we can use the production possibility frontier to measure opportunity cost.

Opportunity Cost in Utopia

Utopia – a fictitious country – can produce many products. We'll assume that it produces a constant amount of all goods and services except wheat and cars. Given its constant output of all other goods and services, it has only limited resources to devote to wheat and cars. The combinations of wheat and cars that it can produce are shown by the points along and inside the production possibility frontier shown in Fig. 34.4. The people of Utopia – the Utopians – are actually producing the combination of wheat and cars

shown by point *a* on the frontier, and they are consuming all the wheat and cars that they produce. So Utopia is producing and consuming 15 million tonnes of wheat and 8 million cars each year.

What is the opportunity cost of a car in Utopia? In other words, how much wheat production must be given up to produce one extra car? We can answer this question by calculating the slope of the production possibility frontier at point *a*. For, as we discovered in Chapter 3, the slope of the frontier measures the opportunity cost of one good in terms of the other. To measure the slope of the frontier at point *a*, place a straight line tangential to the frontier at point *a* and calculate the slope of that straight line. We have drawn a line touching *a* on the figure, and to help work out its slope we have made it part of a red triangle. Recall that to find the slope we move along the line and divide the change in the value of the variable measured on the *y*-axis by the change in the variable measured on the *x*-axis. Here, we measure tonnes of wheat on the *y*-axis and millions of cars on the *x*-axis. So the slope – the opportunity cost – is the change in the number of

FIGURE 34.4

Opportunity Cost in Utopia

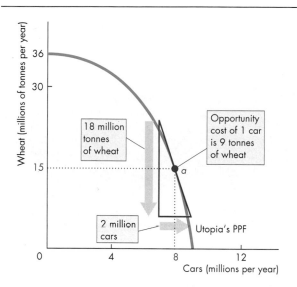

Utopia produces and consumes 15 million tonnes of wheat and 8 million cars a year. That is, it produces and consumes at point *a* on its production possibility frontier. Opportunity cost is measured as the slope of the production possibility frontier. We can calculate the slope at *a* by calculating the slope of a line which touches the frontier at *a*. Along this line, 2 million cars cost 18 million tonnes of wheat. Equivalently, 1 car costs 9 tonnes of wheat, or 9 tonnes of wheat cost 1 car.

tonnes of wheat divided by the change in the number of cars. As you can see from the red triangle in the figure, if the number of cars produced increases by 2 million, wheat production decreases by 18 million tonnes. So the slope is 18 million divided by 2 million, which equals 9. To get one more car, the Utopians must give up 9 tonnes of wheat. Thus the opportunity cost of 1 car is 9 tonnes of wheat. Equivalently, 9 tonnes of wheat cost 1 car.

Opportunity Cost in Erewhon

Now consider the production possibility frontier in Erewhon. This is another fictitious country and the only other country in our model world. Many goods and services are produced in Erewhon, but we will hold constant its output of all goods and services except wheat and cars. Figure 34.5 illustrates its production possibility frontier. Like the citizens of Utopia,

the citizens of Erewhon consume all the wheat and cars that they produce. Erewhon consumes 18 million tonnes of wheat a year and 4 million cars, at point *a*'.

We can do the same kind of calculation of opportunity cost for Erewhon as we have just done for Utopia. At point *a*', 1 car costs 1 tonne of wheat, or, equivalently, 1 tonne of wheat costs 1 car.

Comparative Advantage

Cars are cheaper in Erewhon than in Utopia. One car costs 9 tonnes of wheat in Utopia but only 1 tonne of wheat in Erewhon. But wheat is cheaper in Utopia than in Erewhon – 9 tonnes of wheat cost only 1 car in Utopia while that same amount of wheat costs 9 cars in Erewhon.

Erewhon has a comparative advantage in car production. Utopia has a comparative advantage in wheat production. A country has a **comparative advantage** in producing a good or service if it can produce that good or service at a lower opportunity cost than any other country. Let's see how opportunity cost differences and comparative advantage generate gains from international trade.

FIGURE 34.5

Opportunity Cost in Erewhon

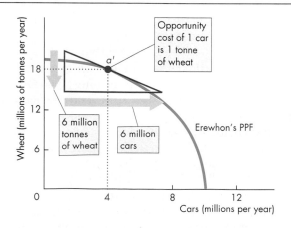

Erewhon produces and consumes 18 million tonnes of wheat and 4 million cars a year. That is, it produces and consumes at point *a*' on its production possibility frontier. Opportunity cost at *a*' is measured by the slope of the production possibility frontier at *a*'. Along the line touching the frontier at *a*', 6 million cars cost 6 million tonnes of wheat. Equivalently, 1 car costs 1 tonne of wheat, or 1 tonne of wheat costs 1 car.

The Gains from Trade

I f Erewhon bought wheat at the cost of wheat in Utopia, then Erewhon could buy 9 tonnes of wheat for 1 car. That is much lower than the cost of growing wheat in Erewhon, for there it costs 9 cars to produce 9 tonnes of wheat. If the Erewhon citizens – the Erewhonians – bought wheat at the low Utopia price, they could reap some gains.

If the Utopians bought cars at the cost of cars in Erewhon, they could obtain a car for 1 tonne of wheat. Since it costs 9 tonnes of wheat to produce a car in Utopia, the Utopians would gain from such an activity.

In this situation, it makes sense for Erewhonians to buy their wheat from Utopians and for Utopians to buy their cars from Erewhonians. Let's see how such profitable international trade comes about.

Reaping the Gains from Trade

We've seen that the Utopians would like to buy their cars from the Erewhonians and that the Erewhonians would like to buy their wheat from the Utopians. Let's see how the two groups do business with each other, concentrating attention on the international market for cars.

Figure 34.6 illustrates this market. On the horizontal axis we measure the quantity of cars traded internationally. On the vertical axis we measure the price of a car, but the price is expressed as its opportunity cost – the number of tonnes of wheat that a car costs. If no international trade takes place, that price in Utopia is 9 tonnes of wheat, indicated by point a in the figure. Again, if no trade takes place, that price is 1 tonne of wheat in Erewhon, indicated by point a' in the figure. The points a and a' in Fig. 34.6 correspond to the opportunity costs at the points identified by those same letters in Figs. 34.4 and 34.5. The lower the price of a car (in terms of wheat), the greater is the quantity of cars that the Utopians import from the Erewhonians. This fact is illustrated in the downward-sloping curve that shows Utopia's import demand for cars.

The Erewhonians respond in the opposite direction. The higher the price of cars (in terms of wheat), the greater is the quantity of cars that Erewhonians export to Utopians. This fact is reflected in Erewhon's export supply of cars – the upward-sloping line in the figure.

FIGURE 34.6

International Trade in Cars

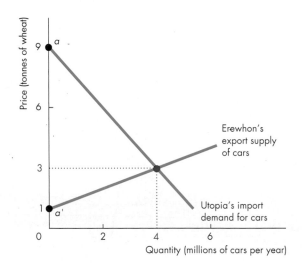

As the price of a car decreases, the quantity of imports demanded by Utopia increases – Utopia's import demand curve for cars is downward sloping. As the price of a car increases, the quantity of cars supplied by Erewhon for export increases – Erewhon's export supply curve of cars is upward sloping. Without international trade, the price of a car is 9 tonnes of wheat in Utopia (point a) and 1 tonne of wheat in Erewhon (point a'). With free international trade, the price of a car is determined where the export supply curve intersects the import demand curve – a price of 3 tonnes of wheat. At that price, 4 million cars a year are imported by Utopia and exported by Erewhon. The value of wheat exported by Utopia and imported by Erewhon is 12 million tonnes a year, the quantity required to pay for the cars imported.

The international market in cars determines the equilibrium price and quantity traded. This equilibrium occurs where the import demand curve intersects the export supply curve. In this case, the equilibrium price of a car is 3 tonnes of wheat. Four million cars a year are exported by Erewhon and imported by Utopia. Notice that the price at which cars are traded is lower than the initial price in Utopia but higher than the initial price in Erewhon.

Balanced Trade

Notice, too, that the number of cars exported by Erewhon – 4 million a year – is exactly equal to the number of cars imported by Utopia. How do the Utopians pay for the imported cars? By exporting wheat. How much wheat does Utopia export? You can find the answer by noticing that for 1 car Utopia has to pay 3 tonnes of wheat. So for 4 million cars it has to pay 12 million tonnes of wheat. Thus Utopia's exports of wheat are 12 million tonnes a year and Erewhon imports this same quantity of wheat.

Erewhon is exchanging 4 million cars for 12 million tonnes of wheat each year and Utopia is doing the opposite, exchanging 12 million tonnes of wheat for 4 million cars. Trade is balanced between these two countries. The value received from exports equals the value paid out for imports.

Changes in Production and Consumption

We've seen that international trade makes it possible for Utopians to buy cars at a lower price than they can produce them for themselves. It also enables Erewhonians to sell their cars abroad for a higher price than they could sell them at home, which is equivalent to saying that Erewhonians can buy wheat for a lower price in terms of cars. So everybody seems to gain. Erewhonians buy wheat at a lower price and Utopians buy cars at a lower price. How is it possible for everyone to gain? What are the changes in production and consumption that accompany these gains?

In an economy that does not trade with other economies, the production and consumption possibilities are identical. Without trade, the economy can consume only what it produces. So at best it can consume only at a point on its production possibility frontier. But with international trade an economy can consume different quantities of products from those that it produces. The production possibility frontier still describes the limit of what a country can produce, but it no longer describes the limits to what it can consume. Figure 34.7 will help you to see the distinction between production possibilities and consumption possibilities when two countries trade with each other.

Notice, first of all, that the figure has two parts, part (a) for Utopia and part (b) for Erewhon. The production possibility frontiers that you saw in Figs. 34.4 and 34.5 are reproduced here. Utopia chooses to produce and consume at point a while Erewhon chooses to produce and consume at a'. The slopes of the two black lines in the figure represent the opportunity costs in the two countries

when there is no international trade. Cars cost 9 tonnes of wheat in Utopia and 1 tonne of wheat in Erewhon. It is this difference in opportunity costs which makes the Utopians and Erewhonians want to start trading.

Changes in Production   We have seen that when Utopia and Erewhon start to trade, Utopians find that they want to buy cars from Erewhon while the Erewhonians want to buy wheat from Utopia. So when trade begins, we expect the Utopians to produce more wheat and fewer cars. We expect their production position to move up their production possibility frontier from a in part (a). At the same time, we expect the Erewhonians to produce more cars and less wheat, so we expect their production position to move down their production possibility frontier from a' in part (b). How far will the production positions move?

The production patterns will change until the countries settle at points like b in part (a) and b' in part (b). At these points, the slopes of the two production possibility frontiers are the same. So the opportunity cost of wheat in terms of cars is the same in each country and the opportunity cost of cars in terms of wheat is the same in each country. When the amount of trade each year is sufficient to make the opportunity costs in each country the same, there is no point in doing any more trade. So there is no incentive for any further specialization in production.

Why does production stop at b and b' rather than any other pair of points at which the two frontiers have the same slope? The answer is that we know from Fig. 34.6 that trade will settle down with the price of a car being 3 tonnes of wheat, and this is the price or opportunity cost that applies at b and b'. You can see that by looking at the slope of the red lines we have drawn as tangents at b and b'. If we move downwards along these red lines, we lose 3 tonnes of wheat for each car gained.

Changes in Consumption   Although Utopia ends up producing 5 million cars and 30 million tonnes of wheat, as shown by point b in Fig. 34.7(a), it does not consume these quantities. It can sell wheat and buy cars at the international price of 3 tonnes of wheat per car. This means it can buy cars and sell wheat to take its consumption to any point on the red line that touches its production possibility frontier at b. We know from Fig. 34.6 that it actually

FIGURE 34.7

Expanding Consumption Possibilities

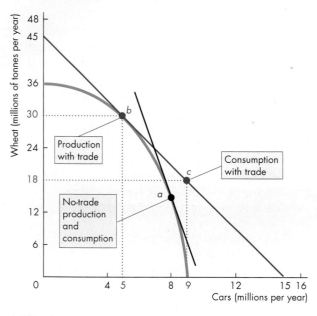

(a) Utopia

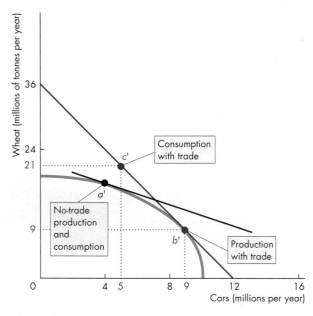

(b) Erewhon

With no international trade, the Utopians produce and consume at point *a* where the opportunity cost of a car is 9 tonnes of wheat (the slope of the black line in part a). Also, with no international trade, the Erewhonians produce and consume at point *a'* where the opportunity cost of 1 tonne of wheat is 1 car (the slope of the black line in part b). Goods can be exchanged internationally, at a price of 3 tonnes of wheat for 1 car, along the red line. In part (a), Utopia decreases its production of cars and increases its production of wheat, moving its production from *a* to *b*. It

exports wheat and imports cars, and it consumes at point *c*. The Utopians consume more of both cars and wheat than they would consume – at point *a* – if they did not trade. In part (b), Erewhon increases car production and decreases wheat production, moving its production from *a'* to *b'*. Erewhon exports cars and imports wheat, and it consumes at point *c'*. The Erewhonians consume more of both cars and wheat than they would consume – at point *a* – if they did not trade.

trades 4 million cars for 12 million tonnes of wheat. So we can mark on the red line in Fig. 34.7(a) the point, *c*, where it ends up consuming. It consumes 9 million cars – 4 million more than it produces – and it consumes 18 million tonnes of wheat – 12 million tonnes less than it produces.

Likewise, although Erewhon ends up producing 9 million cars and 9 million tonnes of wheat, as shown by point *b'* in Fig. 34.7(b), it does not consume these quantities. It can sell cars and buy wheat at the international price of 3 tonnes of wheat per car. This means it can buy cars and sell wheat to take its consumption to any point on the red line that touches its production possibility frontier at *b'*. We know from Fig. 34.6 that it actually trades 4 million cars for 12 million tonnes of wheat.

So we can mark on the red line in Fig. 34.7(b) the point, *c'*, where it ends up consuming. It consumes 5 million cars – 4 million fewer than it produces – and it consumes 21 million tonnes of wheat – 12 million tonnes more than it produces.

Calculating the Gains from Trade

You can now literally 'see' the gains from trade in Fig. 34.7. Without trade, Utopians produce and consume at *a* (part a) – a point on Utopia's production possibility frontier. With international trade, Utopians consume at point *c* (in part a) – a point *outside* the production possibility frontier. At point *c*, Utopians are consuming 3 million more tonnes of wheat a year and 1 million more cars a year than before. These increases in their consumption of cars and wheat, beyond the limits of the production possibility frontier, are the gains from international trade.

The Erewhonians also gain. Without trade, they consume at point a' (part b) – a point on Erewhon's production possibility frontier. With international trade, they consume at point c' – a point outside the production possibility frontier. With international trade, Erewhon consumes 3 million more tonnes of wheat a year and 1 million more cars a year than without trade. These are the gains from international trade for Erewhon.

Gains for All?

We have seen that if Utopia and Erewhon trade with each other, then the total consumption of each good can rise in each country. Gains in one country do not mean losses in the other. It is even possible that every individual in each country could at once be better off if trade started, but we cannot be certain of this. Who might lose? The most likely losers in Utopia are people who make cars, for the output of Utopian cars will result in fewer jobs in this industry. The most likely losers in Erewhon are the producers of wheat. We will look at these possible losers shortly, after completing our discussion of the factors that determine trade patterns.

Absolute Advantage

We have, so far, been studying comparative advantages. Now let's think about absolute advantages. A country has an **absolute advantage** over another in the production of some item if its output per unit of input is higher for that item. Let's suppose that the only input is labour and that in Erewhon fewer workers are needed to produce any given output of either wheat or cars than in Utopia. In this situation, Erewhon has an absolute advantage over Utopia in the production of both goods. With an absolute advantage in both goods, isn't it the case that Erewhon can outsell Utopia in all markets? If Erewhon can produce all goods using fewer factors of production than Utopia, why does it pay Erewhon to buy *anything* from Utopia?

The answer is that the cost of production in terms of the factors of production employed is irrelevant for determining the gains from trade. It does not matter how much labour (or land and capital) is required to produce 10 tonnes of wheat or a car.

What matters is how many cars must be given up to produce more wheat or how much wheat must be given up to produce more cars. That is, what matters is the opportunity cost of one good in terms of the other good. Erewhon may have an absolute advantage in the production of all goods and services, but it cannot have a comparative advantage in the production of all goods and services. The statement that the opportunity cost of cars in Erewhon is lower than in Utopia is identical to the statement that the opportunity cost of wheat is higher in Erewhon than in Utopia. Thus *whenever opportunity costs diverge, everyone has a comparative advantage in something*. All countries can potentially gain from international trade.

The story of the discovery of the logic of the gains from international trade is presented in Our Advancing Knowledge on pp. 968–969.

REVIEW

When countries have divergent opportunity costs, they can gain from international trade. Each country can buy goods and services from another country at a lower opportunity cost than it can produce them for itself. Gains arise when each country increases its production of those goods and services in which it has a comparative advantage – that is the goods and services which it can produce at an opportunity cost that is lower than that of other countries – and exchanges some of its production for that of other countries. All countries gain from international trade. Every country has a comparative advantage in something. ◆

Gains from Trade in Reality

The gains from trade that we have just studied between Utopia and Erewhon in wheat and cars are taking place in a model economy - in an economy that we have imagined. But these same phenomena occur every minute of every day in real-world economies. The United Kingdom buys cars and machinery from producers in other EU countries and sells chemicals, transport services and computers to consumers in those countries in return. The

United Kingdom buys shirts and fashion goods from the people of Hong Kong and sells them office equipment and machinery in return. It buys television sets and VCRs from South Korea and Taiwan and sells them financial and other services as well as manufactured goods in return.

Thus much of the international trade that we see in the real world takes precisely the form of the trade that we have studied in our model of the world economy. But much of the trade we observe does not seem the same as the trade in our model. For instance, the United Kingdom exports clothes to France *and* imports clothes from France. It exports cars to Germany *and* imports cars from Germany. Why do countries trade very similar manufactured products with each other? Can our model of international trade explain such exchange?

Trade in Similar Products

At first thought, it seems puzzling that countries would trade very similar goods. Consider, for example, UK trade in cars. Why does it make sense for the United Kingdom to produce cars for export and at the same time to import large quantities of cars from other members of the European Union and Japan? Wouldn't it make more sense for the United Kingdom to produce all the cars that people in the United Kingdom want to buy? After all, UK car producers have access to the best technology available for producing cars. The capital equipment, production lines, robots and so on used in the manufacture of cars are as available to UK car producers as they are to any other. This line of reasoning leaves a puzzle concerning the sources of international exchange of similar commodities produced by similar people using similar equipment. Why does it happen?

Diversity of Taste The first part of the answer to the puzzle is that people have a tremendous diversity of taste. Let's stick with the example of cars. Some people prefer sports cars, some prefer estate cars, some prefer medium-sized cars, and some prefer small cars. In addition to size and type of car, there are many other ways in which cars vary. Some have low fuel consumption, some have high performance, some are spacious and comfortable, some have four-wheel drive, some have front-wheel drive, some have automatic transmission, some are durable, some are flashy and some have a radiator

grill reminiscent of a Greek temple. People's preferences across these many features vary.

The tremendous diversity in tastes for cars means that people would be dissatisfied if they were forced to consume from a limited range of standardized cars. People value variety and demand it in the marketplace.

Economies of Scale The second part of the answer to the puzzle is economies of scale. *Economies of scale* are the tendency, present in many production processes, for the average cost of production to be lower, the larger the scale of production. In such situations, larger and larger production runs lead to ever lower average production costs. Many manufactured goods, including cars, experience economies of scale. For example, if a car producer makes only a few hundred – or perhaps a few thousand – cars of a particular type and design, it has to use production techniques that are much more labour-intensive and much less automated than those actually employed to make hundreds of thousands of cars of a particular model. With low production runs and labour-intensive production techniques, costs are high. With very large production runs and automated assembly lines, production costs are much lower. But to obtain lower costs, each automated assembly line has to produce a large number of identical or very similar cars.

It is the combination of diversity of taste and economies of scale that produces such a large amount of international trade in similar commodities. If every car bought in the United Kingdom today were made in the United Kingdom, and if the present wide range of cars were made available, production runs would be remarkably short. Car producers would not be able to reap many economies of scale. Although the current variety of cars could be made available, it would be at a very high price, and perhaps at a price that no one would be willing to pay.

But with international trade, each manufacturer of cars has the whole world market to serve. Each producer specializes in a limited range of products and then sells its output to the entire world market. This arrangement enables large production runs on the most popular cars and feasible production runs even on the most customized cars demanded by relatively few people. The situation in the market for cars is also present in many other industries, especially those producing specialized machinery and specialized machine tools. Thus international exchange of similar but slightly differentiated manufactured products is a highly profitable activity.

This type of trade can be understood with exactly the same model of international trade that we studied earlier. Although we normally think of cars as a single commodity, we simply have to think of sports cars and estate cars and so on as different goods. Different countries, by specializing in a few of these 'goods' are able to enjoy economies of scale and, therefore, a comparative advantage in their production.

The Gains from International Trade

You can see that comparative advantage and international trade bring gains regardless of the products being traded. When the rich countries of the European Union, Japan and the United States import raw materials from the developing countries and from Australia and Canada, the rich importing countries gain and so do the exporting countries. When we buy cheap television sets, VCRs, shirts and other goods from low wage countries, both we and the exporters gain from the exchange. It's true that if the United Kingdom increases its imports of coal and produces less coal itself, jobs in UK coal mines will disappear. So the redundant miners will certainly be worse off to begin with. But jobs in other sectors, sectors in which the United Kingdom has a comparative advantage and supplies to other nations, will expand. *After the adjustment is completed*, those whose jobs have been lost find employment in the expanding sectors and sometimes even at higher wages than they had previously. Also, they can buy items produced in other countries at even lower prices than those at which they were available before. So even they may well be better off eventually. The long-run gains from international trade are not generally gains for some at the expense of losses for others.

But it must be stressed that changes in comparative advantage lead to changes in international trade patterns which can take a long time to settle down. For example, an increase in coal imports and a corresponding relative decline in domestic mining will not immediately produce increased real income for displaced miners. Better jobs take time to find, and often people go through a period of prolonged search putting up with inferior jobs and

lower wages than they had before. It is only in the long run that every individual is likely to gain from international specialization and exchange. Short-run adjustment costs that can be large and relatively prolonged may be borne by groups that have lost their 0comparative advantage. Industrialists and trade unionists in the affected industries may well press the government to give their industry some protection.

Partly because of the costs of adjustment to changing international trade patterns, but partly also for other reasons, governments intervene in international trade restricting its volume. Let's examine what happens when governments restrict international trade. We'll contrast restricted trade with free trade. We'll see that free trade brings the greatest possible benefits. We'll also see why, in spite of the benefits of free trade, governments sometimes restrict trade.

Trade Restrictions

Governments restrict international trade in order to protect domestic industries from foreign competition. The restriction of international trade is called **protectionism**. There are two main protectionist methods employed by governments:

◆ Tariffs
◆ Non-tariff barriers

A **tariff** is a tax that is imposed by the importing country when a good crosses an international boundary. A **non-tariff barrier** is any action other than a tariff that restricts international trade. There are many types of non-tariff barrier. These include quantitative restrictions and licensing regulations limiting imports. We'll consider non-tariff barriers in more detail below. First, let's look at tariffs.

Tariff Imposition and Removal

The temptation for governments to impose tariffs is a strong one. First, tariffs provide revenue to the government. Second, they enable the government to satisfy special interest groups in import-competing industries. But, as we've seen, free international trade brings enormous benefits. Because free trade brings benefits and because the temptation to restrict trade is so great, many Western countries have entered into a multilateral agreement whose goal is the enhancement of free international trade – the General Agreement on Tariffs and Trade (GATT). The **General Agreement on Tariffs and Trade** is an international agreement designed to try to limit government intervention that restricts international trade. It was negotiated immediately following World War II and was signed in October 1947. Its goal is to liberalize trading activity and to provide an organization to administer more liberal trading arrangements. The GATT itself is a small organization located in Geneva, Switzerland.

Since the formation of the GATT, several rounds of negotiations have taken place and these have resulted in general tariff reductions. One of these, the Kennedy Round that began in the early 1960s, resulted in large tariff cuts. Yet further tariff cuts resulted from the Tokyo Round that took place between 1973 and 1979. The most recent GATT tariff round, the Uruguay Round, ended in a blaze of publicity late in 1993. It will lead to a dramatic reduction in trade restrictions, notably between the United States and the European Union. See also Reading Between the Lines on pp. 974–975 on this issue.

In addition to the multilateral agreements under the GATT, some other multilateral trade agreements are being put in place. The most important of these, from the point of view of the United Kingdom, is the European Union itself, which the United Kingdom joined in 1973. Internal tariffs in the European Union were largely eliminated as long ago as 1977. This is one reason why the United Kingdom does so much trade with other EU members.

How Tariffs Work

To see the effects of imposing tariffs and of removing them, we need to know how tariffs work. To analyse how tariffs work, let's return to the example of trade between Utopia and Erewhon. Suppose that these two countries are trading cars and wheat in exactly the same way that we analysed before. Erewhon exports cars and Utopia exports wheat. The volume of car imports into Utopia is 4 million a year and cars are selling on the world market for 3 tonnes of wheat. Let's suppose that wheat costs £1,000 a tonne so, equivalently, cars are selling for £3,000. Figure 34.8 illustrates this situation. The volume of trade in cars and their price are determined

at the point of intersection of Erewhon's export supply curve of cars and Utopia's import demand curve for cars.

Now suppose the government of Utopia, perhaps under pressure from car producers, decides to impose a tariff on imported cars. In particular, suppose a tariff of £4,000 per car is imposed. This is a huge tariff, but the car producers of Utopia are pretty fed up with competition from Erewhon! What happens?

The first part of the answer is obtained by studying the effects on the supply of cars in Utopia. Cars are no longer available at the Erewhon export supply price. The tariff of £4,000 must be added to that price – the amount paid to the government of Utopia on each car imported. So the supply curve in Utopia shifts in the manner shown in Fig. 34.8. The new supply curve becomes that labelled 'Erewhon's export supply of cars plus tariff'. The vertical distance

---

FIGURE 34.8

The Effects of a Tariff

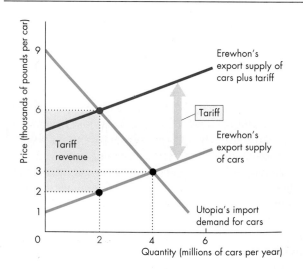

Utopia imposes a tariff on car imports from Erewhon. The tariff shifts the supply curve of cars in Utopia upward by the amount of the tariff. The price of cars in Utopia rises and the quantity of cars imported falls from 4 million to 2 million. The government of Utopia collects a tariff revenue of £4,000 on each of the 2 million cars imported – making a total tariff revenue of £8,000 million. Utopia's exports of wheat decrease as Erewhon now has a lower income from its exports of cars.

between Erewhon's export supply curve and the new supply curve is the tariff imposed by the government of Utopia.

The next part of the answer is found by determining the new equilibrium. Imposing a tariff has no effect on the demand for cars in Utopia and so has no effect on Utopia's import demand for cars. The new equilibrium occurs where the new supply curve intersects Utopia's import demand curve for cars. That equilibrium is at a price of £6,000 a car and with 2 million cars a year being imported. Imports fall from 4 million to 2 million cars a year. At the higher price of £6,000 a car, domestic car producers increase their production. Also, domestic wheat production decreases to free up the resources for the expanded car industry.

The Utopians' total spending on imported cars is £12,000 million, that is £6,000 a car multiplied by the 2 million cars imported. But not all of that money goes to the Erewhonians. They receive £2,000 a car or £4,000 million for the 2 million cars. The difference – £4,000 a car or a total of £8,000 million for the 2 million cars – is collected by the government of Utopia as tariff revenue.

Obviously, the government of Utopia is happy with this situation. It is now collecting £8,000 million that it didn't have before. But what about the Utopians? How do they view the new situation? The demand curve tells us the maximum price that a buyer is willing to pay for one more unit of a good. As you can see from Utopia's import demand curve for cars, if one more car could be imported, someone would be willing to pay almost £6,000 for it. Erewhon's export supply curve of cars tells us the minimum price at which additional cars are available. As you can see, one additional car would be supplied by Erewhon for a price only slightly over £2,000. So, as someone is willing to pay almost £6,000 for a car and someone else is willing to supply one for a little over £2,000, there is obviously a gain to be had from trading an extra car. In fact, there are gains to be had – willingness to pay exceeds the minimum supply price – all the way up to 4 million cars a year. Only when 4 million cars are being traded is the maximum price that a Utopian is willing to pay equal to the minimum price that is acceptable to an Erewhonian. Thus restricting international trade reduces the gains from international trade.

It is easy to see that the tariff has lowered Utopia's total import bill. With free trade, Utopia was paying £3,000 a car and buying 4 million cars a year

from Erewhon, so the total import bill was £12,000 million a year. With a tariff, Utopia's imports have been cut to 2 million cars a year and the price paid to Erewhon has also been cut to only £2,000 a car, so the import bill has been cut to £4,000 million a year. Doesn't this mean that Utopia's balance of trade has changed? Is Utopia now importing less than it is exporting?

To answer that question, we need to work out what's happening in Erewhon. We've just seen that the price that Erewhon receives for cars has fallen from £3,000 to £2,000 a car. So the price of cars in Erewhon has fallen. But because the price of cars has fallen, the price of wheat has increased. With free trade, the Erewhonians could buy 3 tonnes of wheat for 1 car. Now they can buy only 2 tonnes for 1 car. With a higher price of wheat, the quantity demanded by the Erewhonians decreases. As a result, Erewhon's imports of wheat fall, and so too do Utopia's exports of wheat. In fact, Utopia's wheat industry suffers for two reasons. First, there is a decrease in the quantity of wheat sold to Erewhon. Second, there is increased competition for inputs from the now expanded car industry. Thus the tariff leads to a contraction in Utopia's wheat industry.

It may seem paradoxical that a country imposing a tariff on cars would hurt its own export industry, reducing its exports of wheat. It may help to think of it this way: foreigners buy wheat with the money they make from exporting cars. If they export fewer cars, they cannot afford to buy as much wheat. In fact, in the absence of any international borrowing and lending, Erewhon has to cut its imports of wheat by exactly the same amount as the loss in revenue from its export of cars. Wheat imports into Erewhon will be cut back to a value of £4,000 million, the amount that can be paid for by the new lower revenue from Erewhon's car exports. Thus trade is still balanced in this post-tariff situation. Although the tariff has cut imports, it has also cut exports, and the cut in the value of exports is exactly equal to the cut in the value of imports. The tariff, therefore, has no effect on the visible trade balance – it reduces the volume of trade.

The result that we have just derived is perhaps one of the most misunderstood aspects of international economics. On countless occasions, politicians and others have called for tariffs in order to remove a visible trade deficit or have argued that reducing tariffs would produce a visible

Understanding the Gains from International Trade

> 'Free trade, one of the greatest blessings which a government can confer on a people, is in almost every country unpopular.'
>
> THOMAS MACAULAY
> *Essay on Mitford's History of Greece*

Until the mid-eighteenth century, it was generally believed that the purpose of international trade was to keep exports above imports and pile up gold. If gold was accumulated, it was believed, the nation would prosper; and if gold was lost through an international deficit, the nation would be drained of money and be impoverished. These beliefs are called *mercantilism*, and the *mercantilists* were pamphleteers who advocated with missionary fervour the pursuit of an international surplus. If exports did not exceed imports, the mercantilists wanted imports restricted.

In the 1740s, David Hume explained that as the quantity of money (gold) changes, so does the price level, and the nation's *real* wealth is unaffected. In the 1770s, Adam Smith explained that restricting imports lowers the gains from specialization and makes a nation poorer. Mercantilism was intellectually bankrupt.

Gradually, through the nineteenth century, the mercantilists' influence waned, and North America and Western Europe prospered in an environment of increasingly free international trade. But despite remarkable advances in economic understanding, mercantilism never quite died. It had a brief and devastating revival in the 1920s and 1930s, when tariff hikes brought about the collapse of international trade and accentuated the Great Depression. It subsided again after World War II with the establishment of the General Agreement on Tariffs and Trade (GATT).

In the eighteenth century, when mercantilists and economists were debating the pros and cons of free international exchange, the transportation technology available severely limited the gains from international trade. Sailing ships with tiny cargo holds took close to a month to cross the Atlantic Ocean. But the potential gains were large and so was the incentive to cut shipping costs. By the 1850s, the clipper ship had been developed, cutting the time for the journey from Liverpool to Boston to only 12.25 days. Half a century later, 10,000-ton steamships were sailing between the United Kingdom and the United States in just four days. As sailing times and costs declined, the gains from international trade increased and the volume of trade expanded.

The container ship and the Boeing 747 have revolutionized international trade and contributed to its contin- ued expansion. Today, most goods cross the oceans in containers – metal boxes – packed into and piled on top of ships like the one shown here. Container technology has cut the cost of ocean ship- ping by economizing on handling and by making cargoes harder to steal, which lowers insurance costs. It is unlikely that there would be much international trade in goods such as television sets and VCRs without this technol- ogy. High-value and perishable cargoes such as flowers and fresh food, as well as urgently needed itcms, travel by air. Every day, dozens of cargo-laden 747s fly between all major European cities and destinations across the Atlantic and Pacific Oceans.

But mercantilism lingers on. The often expressed view that the European Union should restrict Japanese imports is a modern manifestation of mercantilism. It would be interesting to have Hume and Smith commenting on these views. But we know what they would say – the same things that they said to the eighteenth-century mercantilists. And they would still be right.

From Smith and Ricardo to GATT

David Ricardo (1772–1832) was a highly successful 27-year-old stockbroker when he stumbled on a copy of Adam Smith's *Wealth of Nations* on a weekend visit to the country. He was immediately hooked and went on to become the most celebrated economist of his age and one of the greatest economists of all time. One of his many contributions was to develop the principle of comparative advantage, the foundation on which the modern theory of international trade is built. The example he used to illus- trate this principle was the trade between the United Kingdom and Portugal in cloth and wine.

The General Agreement on Tariffs and Trade (GATT) was established as a reaction against the devastation wrought by beggar-my-neighbour tariffs imposed during the 1920s. But it is also a triumph for the logic first worked out by Smith and Ricardo.

DAVID RICARDO

trade deficit. They reach this conclusion by failing to work out all the implications of a tariff. Because a tariff raises the price of imports and cuts imports, the easy conclusion is that the tariff strengthens the visible trade balance. But the tariff also changes the volume of *exports* as well. The equilibrium effects of a tariff are to reduce the volume of trade in both directions and by the same value on each side of the equation. The visible trade balance is left unaffected.

Learning the Hard Way   Although the analysis we have just worked through leads to the clear conclusion that tariffs cut both imports and exports and make all countries worse off than they otherwise would be, people have not found that conclusion easy to accept. Time and again individual countries have imposed high tariff barriers on international trade. Whenever tariff barriers are increased, the volume of trade falls. The most vivid historical example of this interaction of tariffs and trade occurred during the Great Depression years of the early 1930s when the world's largest trading nation, the United States, increased its tariffs, setting up a retaliatory round of tariff changes (beggar-thy-neighbour policies) in many countries. The consequence of very high tariffs in this period was that world trade almost ceased.

Let's now turn our attention to the other range of protectionist weapons – non-tariff barriers.

Non-tariff Barriers

We'll begin our discussion of non-tariff barriers by briefly describing five types:

◆ Quotas
◆ Voluntary export restraints
◆ Product standards regulations
◆ Public sector procurement bias
◆ Frontier delays and administrative burdens on international trade

A **quota** is a quantitative restriction on the import of a particular good. It specifies the maximum amount of the good that may be imported in a given period of time. Quotas are especially important in the textiles industry where there exists an international agreement, called the Multi-fibre Arrangement, which establishes quotas on a wide range of textile products. Agriculture is also subject to extensive quotas.

A **voluntary export restraint** (VER) is an agreement between two governments in which the government of the exporting country agrees to restrain the volume of its own exports. VERs are particularly important in regulating international trade in cars between Japan and North America and between Japan and Europe.

A **product standard regulation** is a legally defined standard of product design and quality content – usually based on health or safety considerations – that has an effect on the ease with which foreign goods can be sold in the domestic market.

When central or local governments buy domestically produced items in preference to cheaper or better imports they display what is termed **public sector procurement bias.** For example, many police forces around the world buy cars from a producer in their country as a matter of policy.

Frontier delays and administrative burdens can restrict trade by adding to the transport costs of international transactions. For example, EU countries set their own rates of value added tax and have often imposed border checks to prevent people importing items on which the tax has been paid in a low tax rate country.

Since World War II, non-tariff barriers have become important features of international trading arrangements, and there is general agreement that non-tariff barriers are now a more severe impediment to international trade than tariffs. The Eutropean Union abolished all remaining non-tariff barriers on 1 January, 1993 to create the single European market. The result is that the European Union is now the largest single integrated economy in the world, larger even than the United States.

Although it is difficult to quantify the effects of non-tariff barriers in a way that makes them easy to compare with tariffs, some studies have attempted to do just that. Such studies attempt to assess the tariff rate that would restrict trade by the same amount as the non-tariff barriers do. With such calculations, non-tariff barriers and tariffs can be added together to assess the total amount of protection. When we add non-tariff barriers to tariffs, the level of protection for the European Union as a whole increases. The United States is the least protectionist country in the world. Total protection is higher in the European Union, and higher still in other developed countries including Japan. The developing countries have the highest protection rates of all.

How Quotas and VERs Work

It is easy to see that non-tariff barriers will reduce the volume of trade. But it is useful to look at them a little more closely. We will focus here on the two most important types, quotas and VERs. To analyse them, we'll return to the example of trade between Utopia and Erewhon. Suppose that Utopia imposes a quota on car imports. Specifically, suppose that the quota restricts imports to no more than 2 million cars a year. What are the effects of this action?

The answer is found in Fig. 34.9. The quota is shown by the vertical red line at 2 million cars a year. Since it is illegal to import more than that number of cars, car importers buy only that quantity from Erewhon producers. They pay £2,000 a car to the Erewhon producer. But what do they sell their cars for? The answer is £6,000 each. As the import supply of cars is restricted to 2 million cars a year, importers with cars for sale will be able to get £6,000 each for them. The quantity of cars imported equals the quantity determined by the quota.

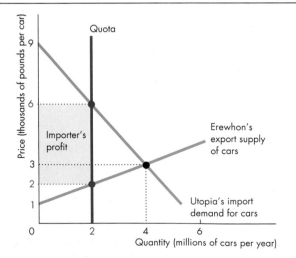

FIGURE 34.9

The Effects of a Quota

Utopia imposes a quota of 2 million cars a year on car imports from Erewhon. That quantity appears as the vertical line marked 'Quota'. As the quantity of cars supplied by Erewhon is restricted to 2 million, the price at which those cars will be traded rises to £6,000. Importing cars is highly profitable because Erewhon is willing to supply cars at £2,000 each. There is competition for import quotas – rent seeking.

Importing cars is now obviously a highly profitable business. An importer gets £6,000 for an item that costs only £2,000. So there is severe competition among car importers for the available quotas. Economists call the pursuit of the profits from quotas 'rent seeking'.

The value of imports – the amount paid to Erewhon – declines to £4,000 million, exactly as it did in the case of the tariff. So with lower incomes from car exports and with a higher price of wheat, Erewhonians cut back on their imports of wheat in exactly the same way they did under a tariff.

The key difference between a quota and a tariff lies in who gets the profit represented by the difference between the import supply price and the domestic selling price. In the case of a tariff, that difference goes to the government. In the case of a quota, that difference goes to the person who has the right to import under the import quota regulations.

A VER is like a quota arrangement where quotas are allocated to each exporting country. The effects of VERs are similar to those of quotas but differ from them in that the gap between the domestic price and the export price is not captured by domestic importers. Instead it is captured by the foreign exporter. The government of the exporting country has to establish procedures for allocating the restricted volume of exports among its producers.

REVIEW

When a country opens itself up to international trade and trades freely at world market prices, it expands its consumption possibilities. When trade is restricted, some of the gains from trade are lost. A country may be better off with restricted trade than with no trade, but not as well off as it could be if it engaged in free trade. A tariff reduces the volume of imports, but it also reduces the volume of exports. Under both free trade and restricted trade (and without international borrowing and lending), the value of imports equals the value of exports. With restricted trade, both the total value of exports and the total value of imports are lower than under free trade, but trade is still balanced. ◆

Why Quotas and VERs Might be Preferred to Tariffs

At first sight, it seems puzzling that countries would ever want to use quotas and even more puzzling that they would want to use VERs. We have seen that the same domestic price and the same quantity of imports can be achieved by using any of the three devices for restricting trade. However, a tariff provides the government with a source of revenue, whereas a quota provides domestic importers with a profit and a VER provides the foreign exporters with a profit. Why, then, would a country use a quota or a VER rather than a tariff?

There are two possible reasons why it might use a quota. First, a government has the right to allocate the quotas and it can use quotas to reward its political supporters. Remember that under a quota, licences to import become tremendously profitable. So the government can bestow riches on people by giving them licences to import. Second, quotas are more precise instruments for holding down imports. With quotas, as demand fluctuates, the domestic price of the good fluctuates widely as the quantity of imports is fixed. You can see this implication of a quota by going back to Fig. 34.9. Suppose that the demand for imports fluctuates. With a quota, these demand fluctuations may cause wide fluctuations in the domestic price of the import but they produce no change in the volume of imports. With a tariff, fluctuations in demand lead to smaller changes in the domestic price as they also result in changes   in the volume of imports. You will be able to see why both price and quantity change if you work out the effects of a change in demand in Fig. 34.8. So, if for some reason the government wants to control the quantity of imports but does not care about wide fluctuations in the domestic price, it will use a quota. A further point to note about quotas is that the government can sell them to importers instead of giving them away, and so actually transfer the importers' profits to itself.

Why would a government use VERs rather than a tariff or quota? The government may want to avoid a tariff or quota war with another country. If one country imposes a tariff or a quota, that might encourage another country to impose a similar tariff or quota on the exports of the first country. Such a tariff and quota war would result in a much smaller volume of trade and a much worse outcome for both countries. A VER can be viewed as a way of achieving trade restrictions to protect domestic industries but with some kind of compensation to encourage the foreign country to accept that situation and not retaliate with its own restrictions. Also, VERs are often the only form of trade restriction that can be entered into legally under the terms of the GATT.

Why would a government use any other form of non-tariff barrier? Product standard regulations – such as regulations on car safety or food additives – have the political advantage of offsetting the adverse effects of barriers on consumption possibilities by a real or apparent concern for consumer welfare. Public sector procurement bias may be concealed by suggestions that foreign goods were examined and merely found wanting, in the hope that they will not lead to retaliations. Frontier delays and administrative burdens may not be deliberately imposed to restrict trade – though they have this effect. The main reason for them in the European Union was to enable different countries to set different value added tax rates and prevent their citizens from going abroad if rates elsewhere are lower. Since 1993, all EU members have simply had to accept this. But maybe, in future, the value added tax rates set by different countries will gradually become more alike than they are at present.

Why is International Trade Restricted?

We've seen that international trade benefits a country by raising its consumption possibilities. Why do we restrict international trade when such restrictions lower our consumption possibilities? There are actually many reasons why international trade is restricted.

One reason that is suggested in some countries is to help domestic producers who have to compete with foreign firms that enjoy subsidies. Even in these cases, it does not obviously benefit a country to protect itself from cheap foreign imports.

Another argument for protection is the strategic one. In the event of a war, a country can find its trade seriously disrupted. This is particularly serious if it relies on imports for crucial goods such as food and weapons. To prevent such a situation, a country can protect its food and weapons industries – maybe, respectively, with tariffs and public sector procurement bias – in times of peace.

But perhaps the most common reason for continuing with protection arises from a point we have already noted. This is that while moves to free trade mean that consumption possibilities increase *on average*, initially, at least, not everyone shares in the gain and some people even lose. Free trade brings benefits to some and costs to others, with total benefits exceeding total costs. It is the uneven distribution of costs and benefits that is the principal impediment to achieving more liberal international trade.

To see this, let's return to our model world and the international trade in cars and wheat between Utopia and Erewhon. In Erewhon, for example, the benefits from opening up free trade accrue to all the producers of wheat and to those car producers who would not have to bear the costs of adjusting to a smaller car industry. The costs of free trade are borne by those car producers and their employees who have to move into the wheat industry. Now the number of people who gain will, in general, be enormous compared with the number who lose. However, the average gain per gainer may be rather small, while the average loss per loser may be quite large. If the loss that falls on those who lose is large, it will pay those people to incur considerable expense in order to lobby against free trade. They may see the loss from free trade as being so great that they will find it profitable to join a political organization that aims to prevent free trade. On the other hand, it may not pay those who gain to organize to achieve free trade. The gain from trade for any one gainer may be too small for that individual to want to spend much time or money on a political organization that aims for free trade. Each group is optimizing – weighing benefits against costs and choosing the best action for itself. The anti-free-trade group may, however, undertake a larger quantity of political lobbying than the pro-free-trade group.

Compensating Losers

If, in total, the gains from free international trade exceed the losses, why don't those who gain compensate those who lose so that everyone is in favour of free trade? To some degree, such compensation does take place, for example, through payments for people who are made redundant. But, as a rule, only limited attempts are made to compensate those who lose from free international trade. The main reason why full compensation is not attempted is that the costs of identifying the losers would be enormous. Also, it would never be clear whether or not a person who has fallen on hard times is suffering because of free trade or for other reasons, and perhaps reasons largely under the control of the individual. Furthermore, some people who look like losers at one point in time may, in fact, end up gaining. The young miner who loses his job in Nottinghamshire and becomes a building worker in Oxfordshire resents the loss of work and the need to move. But a year or two later, looking back on events, he counts himself fortunate. He's made a move that has increased his income and given him greater job security.

It is chiefly because the UK government – like other governments – does not, in general, compensate the losers from free international trade that protectionism is such a popular and permanent feature of economic and political life.

Political Outcome

The political outcome that emerges from this activity is one in which a modest amount of restriction on international trade occurs and is maintained. Politicians react to constituents pressing for protection and find it necessary, in order to get re-elected, to press for policies that protect these constituents. The producers of protected goods are far more vocal than the consumers of these goods. The political outcome, therefore, leans in the direction of maintaining protection.

◆ ◆ ◆ ◆ You've now seen how free international trade enables everyone to gain from increased specialization and exchange. By producing goods in which it has a comparative advantage and exchanging some of its own production for that of others, a country expands its consumption possibilities. Placing barriers on that international trade restricts the extent to which people can gain from specialization and exchange. By opening a country up to free international trade, the market for the things that it sells expands and the price rises. The market for the things that it buys also expands and the price falls. All countries gain from free international trade. As a consequence of price adjustments, and in the absence of international borrowing and lending, the value of imports adjusts to equal the value of exports. ◆ ◆ In the next chapter, we're going to study the ways in which international trade is financed and also learn why international borrowing and lending that permits unbalanced international trade arises. We'll discover the forces that determine the state of the UK balance of payments and the value of the pound in terms of foreign currencies.

The Gains from Trade Liberalization

FINANCIAL TIMES, 16 DECEMBER 1993

Doing good, despite themselves

Martin Wolf

What will the Uruguay Round trade deal mean to the world economy?

Official studies,... have estimated the increase in global economic welfare at between \$213bn and \$274bn in 1992 US dollars in 2002....

The estimate of \$213bn, which appeared in a joint study by the OECD and the World Bank published in May of this year, is based on the assumption of a 30 per cent across-the-board reduction of all tariffs (and input subsidies) on *all* commodities. The estimate of \$274bn comes from an OECD study published this autumn, which assumes a 36 per cent global reduction in tariffs and the trade-restricting effects of import barriers for both industrial and agricultural products. The results differ from the first study, mainly because the calculations made for the latter paper included cuts in industrial non-tariff barriers.

Somewhere in the middle comes a study by the Gatt Secretariat, published at the end of November 1993, which estimates an aggregate income gain of \$203bn by 2005....

The important puzzle, however, does not concern the size of the gains, but how difficult they are to achieve. In Gatt parlance, the trade liberalisation that is the source of the gain is a 'concession' to one's partners. The aim of clever negotiators is to minimise concessions, while maximising those from others. As a result, the more successful is a country in the negotiation game, the less it benefits.

The Uruguay Round deal is an excellent thing which will benefit almost all participants in the long run. But if only there were a less agonising way of persuading countries to abandon the protection that does them so much harm.

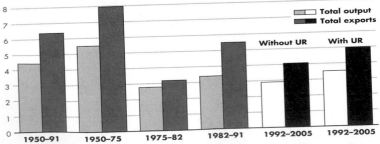

Annual average growth of world output and world exports (%)

Total output
Total exports

Without UR   With UR

1950–91   1950–75   1975–82   1982–91   1992–2005   1992–2005

Trade forecasts from Gatt Secretariat. Output forecasts derived on the assumption that the 1951–91 ratio of export to output growth continues between 1992 and 2005.

Source: Gatt, OECD 'Assessing the effects of the Uruguay Round'

© The Financial Times. Reprinted with permission.

The Essence of the Story

In December 1993, after seven years of negotiations, the Uruguay Round of multilateral trade negotiations was concluded.

Countries agreed to reduce trade barriers on a wide range of goods and services.

The gains from this agreement have been estimated at between \$213 billion and \$274 billion.

The gains have been hard to achieve because the main beneficiaries from trade liberalization were the most obstinate during the negotiations.

The biggest gains will be realized by the European Union, EFTA and Japan.

Most of these gains will come from liberalization in agriculture, the sector these countries have been most reluctant to liberalize.

Background and Analysis

Since its inception after World War II, the GATT has overseen a number of 'rounds' of multilateral trade liberalization talks.

Until the Uruguay Round, all trade liberalization concerned manufactured goods. The Uruguay Round included agriculture, services and intellectual property rights (such as patents).

Comparative advantage in manufactured goods has moved towards the countries of South East Asia.

These and other countries realized that lower trade barriers increase demand for their goods. Production rises and the volume traded increases, which stimulates domestic economic growth.

The European Union, Japan and EFTA have always had high levels of protection for many sectors, especially agriculture. Failure to reduce this protection previously has denied them considerable economic gains.

These countries are expected to gain the most because they have been forced to accept lower protection for agriculture.

Winners from negotiations are said to be those who reduce their protection the least while getting the most from others. These winners end up gaining the least from trade liberalization.

An exception is the Cairns Group of agricultural free traders. They can gain only by getting their trading partners to reduce protection unilaterally.

In the last 40 years, the volume of world trade has grown significantly more than world output (1,200 per cent compared with 600 per cent). In manufacturing, where most of the tariff reductions have been made, trade has risen 2,300 per cent while output has risen 800 per cent.

More recent estimates of gains in agricultural trade by some economists have suggested total gains may be below $100 billion. While less than the initial estimates, however, they are still considerable.

The figure compares the countries of Western Europe and the United States with the rest of the world. The production possibility frontiers are drawn assuming the rest of the world, which includes the countries of South East Asia, has a comparative advantage in manufactures.

Prior to the Uruguay Round, all countries are trading, and are therefore at point a or point a' outside their production possibility frontiers.

As trade liberalization lowers prices, the price ratio between manufactures (already considerably liberalized) and agriculture and services (only now being liberalized) changes. The countries move to points b and b', further outside their production possibility frontiers.

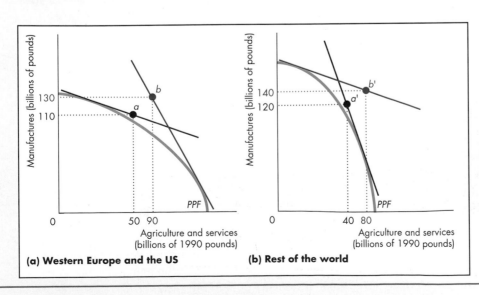

(a) Western Europe and the US

(b) Rest of the world

SUMMARY

Patterns and Trends in International Trade

Large flows of trade take place between countries. Resource-rich countries exchange natural resources for manufactures, and resource-poor countries import their resources in exchange for their own manufactures. However, by far the biggest volume of trade is in manufactured goods exchanged between the rich industrialized countries. The biggest single UK export item is machinery, which is also the UK's biggest import item. Trade in services is also important. The United Kingdom has a large surplus in its trade in financial services. Total trade has grown over the years. UK net exports fluctuate but are usually negative – the United Kingdom is usually a net importer. (pp. 955–957)

Opportunity Cost and Comparative Advantage

When opportunity costs differ between countries, the country with the lowest opportunity cost of producing a good or service is said to have a comparative advantage in it. Comparative advantage is the source of the gains from international trade. When a country can produce a unit of a good or service using fewer inputs, it is said to have an absolute advantage in it. A country could have an absolute advantage in the production of all goods or services, but it cannot have a comparative advantage in the production of all goods and services. Every country has a comparative advantage in something. (pp. 958–959)

The Gains from Trade

Countries can gain from trade if their opportunity costs differ. Through trade, each country can obtain goods or services at a lower opportunity cost than it could if it produced all goods or services at home. By specializing in producing the goods or services in which it has a comparative advantage and then trading some of those products for imports, a country can consume at points outside its production possibility frontier. Each country can consume at such a point.

In the absence of international borrowing and lending, trade is balanced as prices adjust to reflect the international supply and demand for goods and services. The world price is established at the level that balances the production and consumption plans of the trading parties. At the equilibrium price, trade is balanced and domestic consumption plans exactly match a combination of domestic production and international trade.

Comparative advantages explain the enormous volume and diversity of international trade that takes place in the world. But much trade effectively takes the form of exchanging similar goods for each other – one type of car for another. Such trade arises because of economies of scale in the face of diversified tastes. By specializing in producing a few goods, having long production runs, and then trading those goods internationally, consumers in all countries can enjoy greater diversity of goods at lower prices. (pp. 960–965)

Trade Restrictions

A country can restrict international trade by imposing tariffs or non-tariff barriers – such as quotas and voluntary export restraints (VERs). All trade restrictions raise the domestic price of imported goods, reduce the volume of imports and reduce the total value of imports. They also reduce the total value of exports by the same amount as the reduction in the value of imports.

Trade restrictions tend to create a gap between the domestic price and the foreign supply price of an import. In the case of a tariff, that gap is the tariff revenue collected by the government. But the government raises no revenue from a quota (unless it sells the import licences). Instead, domestic importers who have licences to import increase their profits. A voluntary export restraint resembles a quota except that a higher price is received by the foreign exporters.

Governments restrict trade because restrictions help the producers of the protected good or service and the workers employed by those producers. If their gain is sufficiently large and the loss per consumer is sufficiently small, the political equilibrium favours restricted trade. Politicians pay more attention to the vocal and active concerns of the few who stand to lose a lot than to the quieter and less strongly expressed views of the many who stand to gain little. (pp. 965–971)

R E V I E W   Q U E S T I O N S

1 What are the main exports and imports of the United Kingdom?

2 How are services traded internationally?

3 What is comparative advantage? Why does it lead to gains from international trade?

4 Explain why international trade brings gains to all countries.

5 Distinguish between comparative advantage and absolute advantage.

6 Explain why all countries have a comparative advantage in something.

7 Explain why the United Kingdom imports and exports such large quantities of certain similar goods – such as cars.

8 What are the main ways in which international trade is restricted?

9 What are the effects of a tariff?

10 What are the effects of a quota?

11 What are the effects of a voluntary export restraint?

12 Describe the main trends in tariffs and non-tariff barriers.

13 Which countries have the largest restrictions on their international trade?

14 Why do countries restrict international trade?

P R O B L E M S

1 Using Fig. 34.4, calculate the opportunity cost of cars in Utopia at the point on the production possibility frontier at which 2 million cars are produced.

2 Using Fig. 34.5, calculate the opportunity cost of a car in Erewhon when it produces 8 million cars.

3 Suppose that with no trade, Utopia produces 2 million cars and Erewhon produces 8 million cars. (These are different quantities from

those supposed in the chapter.) Which country has a comparative advantage in the production of cars?

4 If there is no trade between Utopia and Erewhon, how much wheat is consumed and how many cars are bought in each country?

5 Suppose that the two countries in Problems 1–4 trade freely.

  a Which country exports wheat?

  b What adjustments will be made to the

amount of each good produced by each country?

c What adjustment will be made to the amount of each good consumed by each country?

d What can you say about the price of a car and wheat under free trade?

6 Compare the total production of each good produced in Problems 4 and 5(b).

7 Compare the situation in Problems 1 and 2 with that analysed in this chapter. Why does Erewhon export cars in the chapter but import them in Problem 5?

8 The following figure depicts the international market for soy beans.

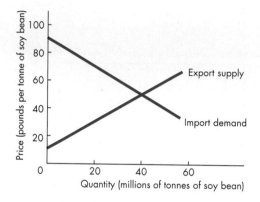

a What is the world price of soy beans if there is free trade between these countries?

b If the country that imports soy beans imposes a tariff of £20 a tonne, what is the world price of soy beans and what quantity of soy beans gets traded internationally? What is the price of soy beans in the importing country? Calculate the tariff revenue.

9 If the importing country in Problem 8(a) imposes a quota of 30 million tonnes, what is the price of soy beans in the importing country? What is the revenue from the quota and who gets this revenue?

10 If the exporting country in Problem 5(a) imposes a VER of 30 million tonnes of soy beans, what is the world price of soy beans? What is the revenue of soy bean growers in the exporting country? Which country gains from the VER?

11 Suppose that the exporting country in Problem 8(a) subsidizes production by paying its farmers £1 a tonne for soy beans harvested.

a What is the price of soy beans in the importing country?

b What action might soy bean growers in the importing country take? Why?

CHAPTER 35

THE BALANCE OF PAYMENTS AND THE POUND

After studying this chapter you will be able to:

- ◆ Explain how international trade is financed

- ◆ Describe a country's balance of payments accounts

- ◆ Explain what determines the amount of international borrowing and lending

- ◆ Explain why the United Kingdom is an international borrower

- ◆ Explain how the foreign exchange value of the pound is determined and why it fluctuates

- ◆ Explain why interest rates vary so much from one country to another

- ◆ Explain why a flexible exchange rate brings monetary independence

- ◆ Explain the moves towards exchange rate stability in the European Union

FOREIGN ENTREPRENEURS ARE BUYING UK ASSETS AT AN ASTONISHING rate. For example, in 1985, two Egyptians spent £615 million buying the House of Fraser chain of department stores, which includes Harrods, perhaps the best known UK shop, and in 1994, BMW bought Rover cars for £800 million. Why do foreigners find UK assets such attractive investments? ◆ ◆ The value of the pound against other currencies is reported daily. Why does the pound's value fluctuate? Can its value be stabilized? Why did the United Kingdom join the EU's exchange rate mechanism and then leave it? ◆ ◆ The world's capital markets are becoming ever more integrated. In October 1987, when Wall Street crashed, so also did the stock markets in London, Tokyo and elsewhere. Even so, interest rates in different countries vary widely. For example, in March 1994, the

The Global Economy

UK government was paying about 6.5 per cent per year on its medium-term (10-year) borrowing. At the same time, the French and German governments were each paying under 6 per cent while the Japanese government was paying around 3.5 per cent. Why don't people stop lending to low interest rate countries and pour all their money into countries where interest rates are high? Why aren't interest rates made the same everywhere by the force of such movements?

◆ ◆ ◆ ◆ In this chapter, we investigate the questions that have just been posed. We begin by reviewing the way in which international trade is financed and study the structure of the accounts in which international activities are recorded – the balance of payments accounts. We study the forces that determine the balance of international trade and the scale of international borrowing and lending.

Financing International Trade

When Dixons imports Toshiba television sets from Japan, Toshiba wants to receive Japanese yen, not pounds. When Tesco imports wine from France, the French wine producers want francs. And when British Airways buys Boeing 747 aircraft, Boeing wants dollars. So whenever we buy products from another country, we need to acquire the currency of that country in order to make the transaction. It doesn't make any difference what the item being traded is – it might be a consumer good or a capital good, a building, or even a firm.

We're going to study the markets in which transactions in money – in different types of currency – take place. But first we're going to look at the scale of international trading, and borrowing and lending, and at the way in which we keep records of these transactions. Such records are called the balance of payments accounts.

Balance of Payments Accounts

A country's **balance of payments accounts** give a record of its international transactions. In an ideal world, the statisticians who prepare the accounts would know about every international transaction and would take note of every one of them when they prepared the accounts. In practice, the statisticians do not know about every transaction, so their accounts do not give a complete record, but for the moment we will ignore the fact that there are omissions. They actually prepare two accounts for the balance of payments each year. The accounts have the following names:

◆ Current account
◆ Transactions in external assets and liabilities

Current Account   The **current account** records payments and receipts from four types of transaction:

◆ Exports and imports of goods
◆ Exports and imports of services
◆ Property income from abroad and paid abroad
◆ Current transfers from abroad and paid abroad

We studied exports and imports in Chapter 34 and in Chapter 24. Exports and imports of goods are often referred to as exports and imports of visibles. The balance of money from exports of goods and money spent on imports of goods is known as the

visible balance or the **balance of trade**. The term 'balance of trade' is rather misleading since it covers trade in goods alone and excludes trade in services. Often it is more useful to look at net exports which is the difference between the money received from exports of both goods and services and the money spent on both goods and services.

Property income is a term which covers payments of interest, profits and dividends. So property income from abroad refers to interest, profits and dividends paid to UK citizens as a result of their investments in foreign countries, while property income paid abroad refers to interest, profits and dividends paid to foreign citizens as a result of their investments in the United Kingdom.

Current transfers are gifts between people in different countries. They include gifts made directly by private individuals, such as a money Christmas present you might receive from an aunt in New Zealand, and gifts made indirectly, such as a donation to Rwanda which you might pay via a charity. Current transfers also include gifts made by governments, such as payments of aid to developing countries and payments between the UK government and international organizations, most notably the European Union.

We said that the visible balance refers to the balance of payments on exports and imports of goods. It is tempting to suppose that the invisible balance must refer to the balance of payments on exports and imports of services. In fact, the **invisible balance** refers to the balance on all items on the current account except for exports and imports of goods.

The largest items on the current account are exports and imports of goods. However, property income payments are also large. Payments for trade in services are much smaller than payments for trade in goods. Current transfers are very small in comparison with the other items.

Transactions in External Assets and Liabilities   The second balance of payments account is called **transactions in external assets and liabilities** and accounts for all purchases and sales of assets in other countries by UK citizens and all purchases and sales by foreign citizens of assets in the United Kingdom. The term 'citizens' covers households, businesses and governments.

The item **transactions in external assets** records the total value of assets in other countries bought by UK citizens minus the value of any assets in other countries that UK citizens have sold. In other words, it records the amount of foreign investment done by UK citizens. The assets concerned can take various forms. For example, UK citizens can acquire external assets in other countries by directly buying firms or land or buildings abroad. Alternatively they can acquire assets abroad by buying shares in foreign companies, or by lending money to foreign citizens or by placing money in foreign banks. Even buying foreign currencies is regarded as buying external assets.

The item **transactions in external liabilities** records the total value of UK assets acquired by foreign citizens minus the value of any assets in the United Kingdom that foreign citizens have sold. In other words, it records the amount of investment done in the United Kingdom by foreign citizens.

The UK's Balance of Payments Accounts

Table 35.1 shows the UK's balance of payments accounts for 1993. Notice that a minus sign is used for items where the United Kingdom spends money.

The UK Current Account   As you can see from the table, the United Kingdom had a current account deficit of £10.7 billion in 1993. That deficit arose chiefly from the fact that it had a deficit of £13.4 billion in visibles – it spent £134.3 billion on imported goods and received only £120.9 billion from exported goods. There was also a small deficit of £5.1 billion on current transfers – £10.5 billion minus £5.4 billion. Against these deficits there was a surplus of £5.1 billion on trade in services – £37.1 billion minus £32.0 billion – and a surplus of £2.7 billion in property income – £72.2 billion minus £69.5 billion. These surpluses were too small to outweigh the deficits.

How does the United Kingdom pay for its current account deficit? It can pay in two ways. One way is to dispose of some external assets. The other way is to borrow from abroad; this means that foreigners make loans to the United Kingdom which in turn means that the UK's external liabilities rise. To clarify this, let's take an analogy of an individual called Lorraine.

Individual Analogy   Lorraine can construct a current account for 1993 very similar to the current account we have looked at for the United Kingdom. She is a teacher and in 1993 earned £15,000. She has some

assets in the form of some shares and a bank deposit, and from these assets she received £1,000 in dividends and interest. She also received a gift of £2,000 from her parents. So her income on current account was £18,000. Against this, her current expenditure in 1993 was £500 in gifts and £18,500 in purchases of goods and services, making a total of £19,000. So Lorraine had a current deficit of £1,000, which is written as –£1,000 on her account as she spends more than her income.

TABLE 35.1

The UK's Balance of Payments Accounts in 1993

	(Billions of pounds)
CURRENT ACCOUNT	
Exports of goods	120.9
Imports of goods	−134.3
Exports of services	37.1
Imports of services	−32.0
Property income from abroad	72.2
Property income paid abroad	−69.5
Current transfers from abroad	5.4
Current transfers paid abroad	−10.5
Total	−10.7
TRANSACTIONS IN EXTERNAL ASSETS AND LIABILITIES	
Transactions in external assets	−162.8
Transactions in external liabilities	171.7
Balancing item	1.8
Total	10.7

The visible balance in 1993 was −£13.4 billion – the amount by which imports of goods exceeded exports of goods. The invisible balance was £2.7 billion – the net value of all the other items on the current account. The current balance of −£10.7 billion equals the visible balance plus the invisible balance.

Source: Central Statistical Office, *UK Economic Accounts*, The fourth quarter 1993, pp. 44, 45 and 59.

If Lorraine spends £1,000 more than her income, she must get hold of £1,000 from somewhere! There are two possibilities. One possibility is that she can reduce her assets: she can get hold of £1,000 by selling some of her shares or reducing her bank balance. If she does this, then there will be an entry of *plus* £1,000 under transactions in external assets. It is plus £1,000 to show that she has acquired £1,000 to spend. Of course she has acquired this £1,000 by reducing her stock of assets.

The other possibility is that Lorraine could borrow £1,000, perhaps from her bank. In this case she acquires a liability. There would be an entry of *plus* £1,000 under transactions in external liabilities to show that she had got hold of £1,000 to spend as a result of other people lending to her and giving her a liability.

UK Transactions in External Assets and Liabilities

Now let's return to the United Kingdom. We have seen that in 1993 its current balance was –£10.7 billion. This figure is negative to show that the United Kingdom spent more than it received on current account. It is analogous to Lorraine's current balance of –£1,000. The United Kingdom could have met some of this deficit by reducing its external assets, but it actually spent money acquiring some external assets. So it had to acquire large sums by means of an increase in its external liabilities. Much of these extra liabilities came in the form of foreigners acquiring assets here by lending the United Kingdom money, just as Lorraine's bank lent her money, but some liabilities arose when foreigners spent money in the United Kingdom acquiring assets such as businesses and shares.

Table 35.1 shows that in addition to a recorded current deficit of £10.7 billion the United Kingdom acquired external assets worth £162.8 billion (or rather it spent £162.8 billion more on acquiring new assets than it received by selling old ones). So it seems that it would need to balance the £10.7 billion and the £162.8 billion by acquiring extra external liabilities worth £173.5 billion. Instead, however, the recorded increase in external liabilities is only £171.7 billion which seems £1.8 billion too small.

This discrepancy arises because the figures in the table cover only those transactions known to the statisticians. If they knew about every single transaction, then they would find that the figure for transactions in external liabilities exactly offset the current deficit plus transactions in external assets.

But they don't know about every transaction. All they know is that the net value of all the omissions must be £1.8 billion as that is the difference between the figure of £171.7 billion – which shows the increase in external liabilities known to them – and the figure of £173.5 billion – which the other figures known to them suggest the increase in external liabilities ought to be. They write down this discrepancy under the heading **balancing item** which shows the net value of all omissions.

Among the external assets that can be acquired or sold are the official reserves. **Official reserves** are the central government's holdings of foreign currencies. The UK government keeps reserves of many foreign currencies. It generally holds them in central banks in the relevant countries.

The numbers in Table 35.1 give you a snapshot of the balance of payments accounts in 1993. In that year, the United Kingdom had a large current deficit. Was 1993 a typical year? This question is answered in Fig. 35.1 which shows the history of the UK balance of payments accounts from 1968. You can see that 1993 was not a typical year – it was the sixth year of very high current account deficits. The figure also shows changes in official reserves. These are usually smaller than the current balances but are occasionally much bigger, as in 1977 and 1987.

Borrowers and Lenders, Debtors and Creditors

Table 35.1 showed that in 1993 the United Kingdom acquired more external liabilities than external assets which means it borrowed more from the rest of the world than it lent to it. A country which borrows more from the rest of the world than it lends to it is termed a **net borrower**. A country which lends more to the rest of the world than it borrows from it is termed a **net lender**. When a country is a net borrower, it may just go deeper into debt or it may simply reduce the net assets it holds in the rest of the world.

To see whether a country is a net lender or a net borrower in a given year, we simply look at the changes in its external assets and external liabilities in that year. But sometimes we compare the total stock of a country's external assets and liabilities. A **debtor nation** is a country that during its entire history has acquired more external liabilities than external assets. The stock of claims held against it by the rest of the world exceeds the stock of its own claims on the rest of the world. A **creditor nation** is a country that has during its entire history

FIGURE 35.1

The Balance of Payments, 1968–1993

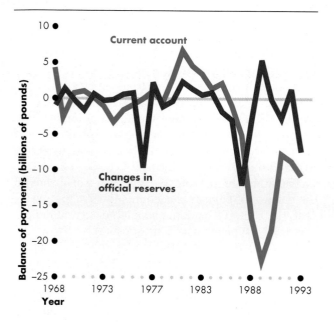

The current account balance was positive for most years in the 1970s. It moved into deficit in 1987 and into a record deficit in 1989. The figure also shows the changes in the country's official holdings of foreign currencies.

Sources: Central Statistical Office, *Economic Trends Annual Supplement, 1992 Edition*, pp. 138 and 154, and *The Pink Book 1993: United Kingdom Balance of Payments*, pp. 15 and 19.

acquired more external assets than external liabilities, so that it has more claims against the rest of the world than the rest of the world has against it.

The United Kingdom is a creditor nation. We can work this out from Table 35.1, which shows that the United Kingdom receives more property income than it pays. This means its citizens receive more interest, profits and dividends on their investments abroad than foreigners receive on their investments in the United Kingdom. This shows that the value of the investments held by UK citizens abroad must exceed the value of the investments held in the United Kingdom by foreign citizens.

There is an important distinction between being a net borrower and a debtor nation, and there's a

similar distinction between being a net lender and a creditor nation. At the heart of these distinctions is the one between flows and stocks. Borrowing and lending are flows. They are amounts borrowed or lent per unit of time. Debts are stocks. They are amounts owed at a point in time. The flows of borrowing and lending change the stock of debt. But the outstanding stock of debt depends mainly on past flows of borrowing and lending, not on the current period's flows. The current period's flows determine the *change* in the stock of debt outstanding.

We can deduce from the fact that the United Kingdom is a creditor nation that it has usually been a net lender. But in some years, such as those since 1986, it has been a net borrower. Of course it has not been the only net borrower. Indeed most countries are net borrowers. The largest net borrowers are the capital-hungry developing nations. The international debt of these developing countries grew from less than a third to more than a half of their gross domestic products during the 1980s, giving rise to what has been called the 'Third World debt crisis'. Against the numerous net borrowers are a small number of countries that are huge net lenders. These include oil-rich countries such as Kuwait and successful developed countries such as Germany and Japan.

Should the United Kingdom be concerned about being a net borrower? The answer depends on what is done with the borrowed money. If borrowing is financing investment that in turn is generating economic growth and higher income, borrowing is not a problem. If the borrowed money is being used to finance consumption, then higher interest payments are being incurred, and, as a consequence, reduced consumption will eventually be necessary. In practice, most of the money invested in the United Kingdom by foreigners *is* used to finance private sector investment in the pursuit of profits. UK citizens do the same, investing some of their saving abroad in the pursuit of profits there.

Current Account Balance

What determines the current account balance and the scale of a country's net foreign borrowing or lending?

To answer this question, we need to begin by recalling and using some of the things that we learned about the national income accounts. Table 35.2 will refresh your memory and summarize the necessary calculations for you. Part (a) lists the national income variables that are needed, with their symbols. Their values in the United Kingdom in 1993 are also shown. We have met all the symbols before except one – *NVPICT* – which shows the net value of the property income and current transfer flows on the balance of

payments accounts. We saw in our discussion of Table 35.1 that in 1993 the United Kingdom had a surplus of £2.7 billion in flows of property income and a deficit of £5.1 billion in flows of current transfers; taking the two together, there was a net deficit of £2.4 billion, or about £2 billion, as shown in Table 35.2. Some comment is also needed about the symbol *T*; as

TABLE 35.2

Surpluses, Deficits and the Financing of Investment

	Symbols and equations	UK values in 1993 (billions of pounds)
(a) VARIABLES		
Gross domestic product (GDP)	*Y*	627
Consumers' expenditure	*C*	405
Investment	*I*	82
Government purchases of goods and services	*G*	148
Exports of goods and services	*EX*	158
Imports of goods and services	*IM*	166
Saving	*S*	120
Taxes, net of transfer payments	*T*	100
Net value of property income and current transfers paid abroad	*NVPICT*	2
(b) DOMESTIC INCOME AND EXPENDITURE		
GDP (1)	$Y = C + I + G + EX - IM$	$627 = 405 + 82 + 148 + 158 - 166$
Uses of income (2)	$Y = C + S + T + NVPICT$	$627 = 405 + 120 + 100 + 2$
(c) SURPLUSES AND DEFICITS		
Subtract (2) from (1) (3)	$0 = I - S + G - T + EX - IM - NVPICT$	$0 = 82 - 120 + 148 - 100 + 158 - 166 - 2$
Rearrange (3) (4)	$(S - I) + (T - G) = EX - IM - NVPICT$	$(120 - 82) + (100 - 148) = (158 - 166 - 2)$
Private sector (5)	$S - I$	$120 - 82 = 38$
Government sector (6)	$T - G$	$100 - 148 = -48$
Current account (7)	$EX - IM - NVPICT$	$158 - 166 - 2 = -10$
(d) FINANCING INVESTMENT		
Investment is financed by the sum of:		
Private saving	*S*	120
Government saving	$T - G$	−48
Foreign saving	$NVPICT + IM - EX$	10
So (8)	$I = S + (T - G) + (IM - EX)$	$82 = 120 - 48 + 10$

Sources: Central Statistical Office, *Economic Trends*, April 1994, T66, and *Monthly Digest of Statistics*, April 1994, pp. 6 and 99.

in Chapter 22, this is the value of the government sector's revenue less transfers, subsidies and debt interest.

Part (b) presents two key national income equations. Equation (1) reminds us that gross domestic product is the sum of consumers' expenditure, investment, government purchases of goods and services, and net exports (the difference between exports and imports). What does equation (2) tell us?

We found in Chapter 22 that the value of the gross domestic product is equal to the income earned by the factors of production in the United Kingdom. And we said there that the households which own all the factors can allocate this income between consumers' expenditure, saving and taxes. However, we now know that people in the United Kingdom also use some of their income to pay property income and current transfers to people abroad, though in return people in the United Kingdom receive some property income and some current transfers from people abroad. The final outcome is that the income earned by the factors of production is allocated between consumers' expenditure, saving, taxes and net payments to foreigners of property income and current transfers. This is what equation (2) tells us.

We now move into part (c) where we examine surpluses and deficits. We start this in equation (3) which we find by subtracting equation (2) from equation (1). Then we rearrange equation (3) to form equation (4). This equation gives us an important result as it relates three balances, that is three surpluses or deficits. These surpluses and deficits are identified in equations (5), (6) and (7).

The first of these balances is the **private sector surplus or deficit** which is the difference between saving and investment $(S - I)$. If the private sector's saving exceeds its investment, it has a surplus, and if it is lower, it has a deficit. The other two balances are the government sector surplus or deficit $(T - G)$ and the surplus or deficit on the current account of the balance of payments $(EX - IM - NVPICT)$. You can see from the way equation (4) is written that the private sector surplus plus the government surplus equals the balance of payments current account surplus. In practice, one or more of these surpluses may be negative surpluses – or deficits. So a more general way of expressing equation (6) is to say that the private sector balance plus the government balance equal the current balance. You can see from

the numbers that in 1993 the private sector balance of £38 billion plus the government balance of –£48 billion equalled the current balance of –£10 billion.

Part (d) of Table 35.2 shows you how investment is financed. To increase investment, either private saving, the government surplus, or the current account deficit must increase.

The calculations that we've just performed are really nothing more than bookkeeping. We've simply manipulated the national income accounts and discovered that the current account balance equals the sum of the balances of the government and private sectors. But these calculations reveal a fundamental fact – the current balance can change only if either the government balance changes or the private sector balance changes. This fact is often lost sight of in popular discussions of the balance of payments.

We've seen that the current balance equals the sum of the government balance and the private sector balance. If, for example, the private sector had a constant balance, then the other two balances would move hand in hand. A rise in the government deficit would lead at once to a rise in the balance of payments deficit. Does an increase in the government deficit bring an increase in the current deficit?

The Three Balances

You can see whether an increase in the government deficit brings an increase in the balance of payments current account deficit by looking at Fig. 35.2. That figure shows the balances of the current account along with the balances of the government and private sectors. It covers the years 1968 to 1993. As you can see, up to 1974 the private sector had a small but fairly stable surplus, and its stability meant that the current account balance and the government balance moved in close sympathy with each other. They both moved from a small deficit to a small surplus and then back to a small deficit. But after 1974 the private sector moved gradually into a surplus, and this change meant that the other two balances no longer moved in close harmony. Instead, from 1975 until 1980, the government deficit grew while the current account was roughly in balance. Then from 1980 to 1984 the private sector balance remained roughly constant again, and so the other two balances moved in step. The current account moved from surplus to a balance while the government deficit increased. From 1985 to 1990, the private sector moved gradually from a surplus to a

FIGURE 35.2

The Three Balances

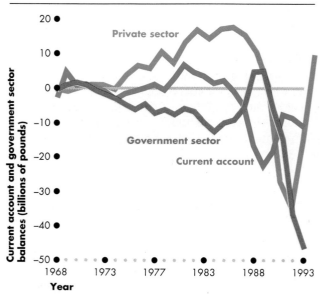

The balance of payments current account balance equals the sum of the private sector balance (saving minus investment) and the government sector balance (taxes minus government purchases). The relationship between these three balances is illustrated here. Up to 1974, the private sector balance was stable and the current account balance and the government balance moved in close harmony with each other. Between 1975 and 1985, a large private sector surplus emerged. At first, this surplus roughly offset the government deficit so the current account roughly balanced. But between 1979 and 1985, the private sector surplus was larger than the government deficit so the current balance was in surplus. Later in the 1980s the private sector moved into an enormous deficit while the government sector moved into a modest surplus from 1988 to 1990. The result was large deficits on the current balance. In the 1990s the private balance moved back into surplus, but the government sector moved back into deficit so that the current balance also remained in deficit.

Sources: Government sector balance from Central Statistical Office, *Economic Trends Annual Supplement 1994 Edition*, p. 234 and *Economic Trends*, April 1994, T66; current balance from Fig. 35.1.

deficit, so that the other two balances moved out of step once again, the current account moving from balance to deficit and the government moving from deficit to surplus. And from 1990 to 1993, the private sector moved back to surplus, again meaning that the other two balances moved out of step. This time the deficit on the current account shrank while the government deficit rose.

It is clear from Fig. 35.2 that the current account and government balances sometimes move in step

and sometimes move out of step. When they move independently, their independent variations are offset by variations in the private sector balance. Let's see why a change in the government balance can cause a change in the private sector balance.

Effects of Government Deficit on Private Surplus

As we've seen, the private sector surplus is saving minus investment. One of the main influences on the level of saving is disposable income. Anything that increases disposable income, other things remaining the same, increases saving and increases the private sector surplus. The main influences on investment are the interest rate and expectations of future profits. Other things remaining the same, anything that reduces interest rates or increases future profit expectations increases investment and decreases the private sector surplus.

Now the changes in taxes or government spending which change the budget deficit also influence income and interest rates. These changes, in turn, influence private sector saving and investment and so change the private sector balance. An increase in government purchases of goods and services or a tax cut – either of which will increase the government deficit – tend to increase both GDP and the interest rate. The higher GDP stimulates additional saving, but the higher interest rate dampens investment plans. So, to some extent, an increased government deficit induces an increased private sector surplus.

However, for an increase in the government deficit to lead to an increase in the private sector surplus, the government's actions must stimulate higher income or higher interest rates. There are two factors that can limit these channels of influence. First, if the economy is operating close to full employment, the higher government budget deficit does not produce a higher level of real GDP. Second, internationally mobile capital lessens the effect of increased government spending on interest rates. So the two mechanisms by which an increase in the government sector deficit can increase the private sector surplus can be relatively weak.

Effects of Government Deficit on Current Account Balance

If there is a change in the government deficit which does not influence the private sector balance, it must have its effect on the current account balance. But how does that effect come about? The easiest way of seeing the effect is to consider what happens when there is full employment. An increase in government purchases of goods and services or a tax cut lead to an increase in aggregate planned expenditure and an increase in aggregate demand. But with the economy at full employment there is no spare capacity to generate a comparable increase in output. Part of the increased demand for goods and services, therefore, spills over into the rest of the world and imports increase. Also, part of the domestic production going for export is diverted to satisfy domestic demand. Exports decrease. The rise in imports and the fall in exports increases the current account deficit. The excess of imports over exports leads to a net increase in borrowing from the rest of the world.

Of course, the economy does not always operate at full employment. Nor does foreign capital flow in at a fixed interest rate. Thus the link between government deficit and the current account deficit is not a mechanical one or a specially close one, as we saw in Fig. 35.2.

REVIEW

When UK citizens buy goods and services from the rest of the world, or invest in the rest of the world, they need foreign currency. When foreigners buy goods and services from the United Kingdom or invest in the United Kingdom, they need pounds. International transactions are recorded in the balance of payments accounts. The current account shows exports and imports of goods and services along with flows of property income and current transfers between the United Kingdom and the rest of the world. The account called transactions in external assets and liabilities shows how much the United Kingdom spends acquiring assets in other countries (minus the amount it receives by selling assets in other countries) and it also shows how much foreigners spend acquiring assets in the United Kingdom (minus the amount they receive by selling assets in the United Kingdom). Among the assets which the United Kingdom may buy (or sell)

are the official reserves of foreign currencies held by the government. In the late 1980s, the UK current account moved into a large deficit while the transactions in external assets and liabilities account moved into a correspondingly large surplus. The United Kingdom was a net borrower. The current account balance equals the government sector balance plus the private sector balance. During the late 1980s and early 1990s, the current account had a large deficit that was initially matched by a small government surplus combined with a large private sector deficit. It was later matched by a large government deficit and a smaller private sector surplus. ◆

The Pound and Net Exports

We have seen that when UK citizens buy foreign goods and services or invest in another country, the foreigners whom they pay want their country's currency, not sterling. And when foreigners buy goods and services made in the United Kingdom or invest in the United Kingdom, the UK citizens whom they pay want sterling rather than foreign currencies. The United Kingdom gets foreign currency and foreigners get sterling in the foreign exchange market. The **foreign exchange market** is the market in which the currencies of different countries are exchanged for one another. The foreign exchange market is not a place with market stalls. Instead it is made up of thousands of people all over the world – importers and exporters, banks and specialists in the buying and selling of foreign exchange called foreign exchange brokers. The foreign exchange market opens on Monday morning in Tokyo, when it is still midnight on Sunday in London. As the day advances, the foreign exchange market also opens in Zurich, Frankfurt, London, New York and finally in Vancouver and Los Angeles. Before these last two markets have closed, Tokyo is open again for the next day of business.

The price at which one currency exchanges for another is called a **foreign exchange rate**. For example, in December 1994, 1 pound bought 2.46 Deutschmarks. The exchange rate between the pound and the Deutschmark was 2.46 Deutschmarks per pound. Exchange rates can be expressed either way. We've just expressed the exchange rate between the pound and the Deutschmark as a number of Deutschmarks per pound. Equivalently, we could express the exchange rate in terms of pounds per Deutschmark. That exchange rate in November 1993 was $0.41 = DM1.00.

The actions of the foreign exchange brokers make the foreign exchange market highly efficient. Exchange rates are almost identical no matter where in the world the transaction is taking place. If Deutschmarks were cheap in London and expensive in Tokyo, soon someone would place an order to buy in London and an order to sell in Tokyo, thereby increasing demand in one place and increasing supply in another, moving the prices to equality.

Foreign Exchange Regimes

Foreign exchange rates are of critical importance to citizens of all countries. In the case of UK citizens they affect the costs of imported food and cars and the cost of foreign holidays. They affect the number of pounds that are earned from the whisky and clothes that are exported. Because of their importance, governments pay a great deal of attention to what is happening in the foreign exchange market and, more than that, take actions designed to achieve what they regard as desirable movements in exchange rates. As we noted in Chapter 27, there are three ways in which the government – or more precisely the Bank of England on behalf of the government – can operate in the foreign exchange market. So there are three possible foreign exchange market regimes. They are:

◆ Fixed exchange rate
◆ Flexible exchange rate
◆ Managed exchange rate

Under a **fixed exchange rate** regime, the value of the pound would be pegged by the Bank of England. Under a **flexible exchange rate** regime, the value of the pound would be determined by market forces with no intervention by the Bank of England. Under a **managed exchange rate** regime, the Bank of England would intervene in the foreign exchange market to smooth out fluctuations in the value of the pound but it would not seek to maintain the pound at an absolutely constant value for a long period of time. Also, under a managed exchange rate regime, the government would not announce the value of the pound that it wished the Bank of England to achieve at any particular moment.

Recent Exchange Rate History

In July 1944, at Bretton Woods in the United States, 44 major countries created the International Monetary Fund by signing its Articles of Agreement. The **International Monetary Fund** (IMF) is an international organization that monitors its members' balances of payments and exchange rate activities. It is located in Washington, DC. At the centrepiece of the articles of agreement was the establishment of a system of fixed exchange rates between members' currencies. The anchor for this fixed exchange rate system was gold. One ounce of gold was defined to be worth $35. All other members' currencies were pegged to the United States dollar at a fixed exchange rate. For example, the pound was set at $4.80 and the yen was set at ¥360 per $1.

Although the Articles of Agreement established fixed exchange rates, there was provision for countries to alter their exchange rates if the need arose. Thus exchange rates were adjustable. The pound was devalued twice. In September 1949 it was devalued to $2.80 and in November 1967 it was devalued to $2.40. In June 1972 the link with the dollar was abandoned and the pound was allowed to float. Between 1972 and 1990 there were times when fluctuations in the pound were almost completely freely determined by market forces but most of the time there was a managed exchange rate regime.

It was not only the United Kingdom that found problems with the fixed exchange rate regime of the international monetary system in the early 1970s. Although that system had served the world well during the 1950s and early 1960s, it came under increasing strain in the late 1960s and, by 1971, the system had almost collapsed. Since 1971, the world has operated a variety of flexible and managed exchange rate arrangements. Some currencies have increased in value, and others have declined. The pound is among the currencies that have declined. The Japanese yen is the currency that has had the most spectacular increase in value.

Figure 35.3(a) shows what has happened to the value of the pound in relation to five major currencies since 1968. Take the Italian lira first. In 1968 it cost 1,492 lira to buy 1 pound, but since then the value of the pound has risen against the lira. The red line shows how many pounds could be bought with 1,492 lira in each year since. There was no change in the era of fixed exchange rates and little change until 1978, but after that the pound gained rapidly in

FIGURE 35.3

Changes in Currency Values

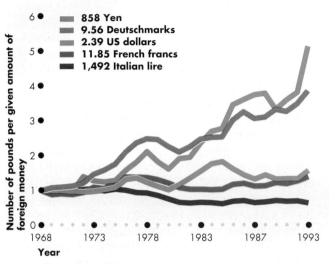

(a) Sterling value of foreign currency

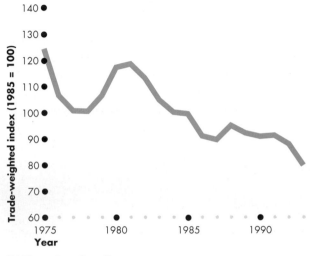

(b) The value of sterling

The relative values of currencies change over time. Part (a) shows how the yen, Deutschmark, dollar and franc have appreciated against the pound since 1968. The number of yen and Deutschmarks needed to buy £1 in 1968 would buy well over £3 in 1993. The dollar and franc have also appreciated against the pound but by smaller amounts. The lira has depreciated against the pound. The number of lira which were needed to buy £1 in 1968 would only buy 63 pence by 1993. So the exchange rate of the pound against the lira has risen since 1968 while the exchange rate of the pound against the other currencies

has fallen. Part (b) shows an index of the value of the pound against a basket of foreign currencies. This index series was calculated by the Bank of England which set the 1985 value at 100. The index fell from 124.8 in 1975 to 88.4 in 1993, a fall of over a quarter in 17 years. But notice that the pound did not fall in every year.

Source: Central Statistical Office, *Economic Trends Annual Supplement, 1992 Edition*, p. 157, and *Economic Trends*, January 1994, p. 60.

relation to the lira. By 1993, 1,492 lire would buy only £0.63. So the value of the lira in terms of pounds fell by over a third between 1968 and 1993. We say that the pound appreciated against the lira while the lira depreciated against the pound. **Currency appreciation** is the rise in the value of one currency against another while **currency depreciation** is the fall in the value of one currency in terms of another currency.

The lira was the only currency in the figure to depreciate against the pound. The yen and the Deutschmark had especially strong rises. In 1968 it cost 858 yen to buy 1 pound, but by 1993, 858 yen bought £5.13. And in 1968 it cost DM9.56 to buy 1 pound, but by 1993, DM9.56 bought £3.85. The figure also shows how the United States dollar and the

French franc have fared since 1968 when £1 cost respectively $2.39 and FFr11.85. These amounts of dollars and francs bought rather more pounds by 1993, but their appreciations were not so dramatic.

There are as many exchange rates for the pound as there are currencies for which it can be exchanged. The pound depreciated against some currencies, including the yen and the Deutschmark, and increased against others, such as the lira. To measure the average movement in the value of the pound, the Bank of England calculates the **trade-weighted index** which shows how the pound fares against a 'basket' of currencies. The basket contains the currencies of the countries with which the United Kingdom has its largest international transactions.

TABLE 35.3

Trade-weighted Index Calculation

Currency	Trade weight	Exchange rates (units of foreign currency per pound)		Contents of basket	Value of basket (pounds)	
		Year 1	Year 2		Year 1	Year 2
Deutschmark	0.40	5.40	3.10	DM216	40.00	69.70
US dollar	0.35	2.20	1.80	$77	35.00	42.80
French franc	0.25	9.50	10.60	FFr237.5	25.00	22.40
Total	1.00				100.00	134.90

Trade-weighted index:

Year 1   = 100.0

Year 2 (100 ÷ 134.90) × 100 = 74.13

An example of the calculation of the pound index is set out in Table 35.3. In this example, we suppose that the United Kingdom trades with only three countries: Germany, the United States and France. Forty per cent of the trade is with Germany, 35 per cent with the United States and 25 per cent with France. In year 1, the pound is worth DM5.4, $2.2, or FFr9.5.

Imagine putting these three foreign currencies into a basket worth £100, where 40 per cent of the value of the basket (£40 worth) is in Deutschmarks, 35 per cent (£35 worth) is in dollars, and 25 per cent (£25 worth) is in francs. The table lists the contents of the basket. There are DM216, $77 and FFr237.5. Converting these amounts of the three foreign currencies to pounds at the exchange rates prevailing in year 1 results in a basket worth £100. £40 worth of the basket are in Deutschmarks, £35 worth are in dollars and £25 worth are in francs. In year 1, the index number for the value of the basket is defined as 100.

To see whether the pound has appreciated or depreciated between years 1 and 2, we ask whether the basket of currencies – that is the basket of DM216, $77 and FFr237.5 – would cost more or fewer pounds in year 2 than it cost in year 1. Look at the last two columns of the table. The column headed year 1 reminds us that the three components of the basket cost £40, £35 and £25 respectively in year 1.

How much would the components cost in year 2? The answers are shown in the column headed year 2. Because the Deutschmark has appreciated, it now costs more than £40 to buy DM216 – in fact it costs £69.70. And because the dollar has appreciated it now costs more than £35 to buy $77 – in fact it costs £42.80. But because the franc has depreciated it now costs less than £25 to buy FFr237.5 – it costs £22.40. Altogether, the total number of pounds required to buy the basket that was worth £100 initially is now £134.90.

Because more pounds are now required to buy the basket of currency, the pound has decreased in value. To calculate the year 2 index for the pound, we take the value of the basket in the first year – £100 – divide it by the value of the basket in the second year – £134.90 – and multiply the result by 100. This calculation is set out in the table and, as you can see, the index in year 2 is 74.13. That is, the pound has depreciated, on average, against the other currencies in the basket, by about 26 per cent.

In the above calculations we supposed that the United Kingdom trades with just three countries. Figure 35.3(b) shows how the pound has actually fared since 1975. The value of the pound depreciated by about a quarter over the period 1975 to 1988 against the basket of currencies used by the Bank of England. But notice that the pound did not depreciate every year in this period. Since 1986 the pound has been fairly stable.

Exchange Rate Determination

What determines the foreign currency value of the pound? The foreign exchange value of sterling is a price and, like any other price, is determined by demand and supply. But what demand and what supply are relevant? What, exactly, is being demanded and supplied? There are various different ways of approaching this question.

We could, for instance, develop a model in which we examined the demand and supply of sterling cash. Or we could have a broader concept of the monetary base – that is bank reserves plus cash. Or we could broaden it again and look at the demand and supply of M4. Or we could take an even broader look and include some other assets denominated in sterling. In each case there is a demand and a supply, and in practice each market must eventually settle in equilibrium when sterling has its equilibrium foreign exchange value.

The Quantity of Sterling Assets   We shall select a slightly different definition of the quantity of sterling from any of those mentioned above. We shall define the **quantity of sterling** as a particular **quantity of sterling assets** that comprises the monetary base plus government debt held by the private sector – that is held by households and firms (other than the Bank of England). It is the quantity of sterling defined in this way whose supply and demand we will consider.

We have a particular reason for defining the quantity of sterling in this way. The quantity of it supplied depends on decisions made by the monetary authorities – the government and the Bank of England. And the quantity of it demanded depends on decisions made by the private sector – households and firms which hold these sterling assets. So we can readily isolate the effects of the monetary authorities and the private sector. Choices by the monetary authorities affect the supply while choices made by the private sector affect the demand.

There are two things about the quantity of sterling that need to be emphasized and explained a bit more fully. First, the quantity of sterling is a *stock*, not a *flow*. People make decisions about the quantity of sterling to hold, that is the stock they want. Admittedly people also make decisions about how much sterling to buy or sell, that is the flow changing hands in a period of time, but it is ultimately the decision about the stock people wish to hold that determines whether they wish to buy or sell sterling.

Second, the quantity of sterling is a stock *denominated in pounds*. The denomination of an asset defines the units in which a debt must be repaid. It is possible to make a loan using any currency of denomination. The UK government could borrow Japanese yen. If it did borrow in yen, it would issue a bond denominated in yen. Such a bond would be a promise to pay an agreed number of yen on an agreed date. It would not be a sterling debt and, even though issued by the UK government, it would not be part of the supply of sterling. Many governments actually do issue bonds in currencies other than their own.

Changes in the Quantity of Sterling Assets   There are two ways in which the quantity of sterling assets can change:

◆ The government has a deficit or surplus
◆ The Bank of England buys or sells assets denominated in a foreign currency

When the government has a deficit, it borrows by issuing bonds. These bonds, denominated in pounds, are held by households, firms, financial institutions, foreigners and the Bank of England. Bonds bought by the Bank of England are not part of the stock of sterling assets. Does this mean that when the Bank of England buys bonds from the public in a open market operation, the quantity of sterling assets falls? No, because when it makes such a purchase, it creates additional bank reserves – and hence adds to the monetary base – and this extra monetary base is part of the quantity of sterling assets. Thus when the Bank of England buys government debt, there is no change in the total quantity of sterling assets, just a change in its composition.

However, this does not mean that the Bank of England is unable to increase the quantity of sterling assets. It can do so by buying assets denominated in foreign currency. If the Bank of England buys some Deutschmarks in the foreign exchange market, the monetary base – and hence the quantity of sterling assets – increases by the amount paid for the marks.

We've now seen what sterling assets are and how their quantity can change. Let's study the demand for these assets.

The Demand for Sterling Assets

The law of demand applies to sterling assets just as it does to anything else that people value. The quantity of sterling assets demanded increases when the price of pounds in terms of foreign currency falls and decreases when the price of pounds in terms of foreign currency rises. There are two separate reasons why the law of demand applies to sterling assets.

First, there is a transactions demand. The lower the value of the pound, the larger is the demand for UK exports and the lower is the UK demand for imports. Hence the larger also is the amount of trade financed by pounds. Foreigners demand more pounds to buy UK exports and UK citizens demand less foreign currency and more pounds as they switch from importing to buying UK-made products.

Second, there is a demand arising from expected capital gains. Other things remaining the same, the lower the value of the pound today, the higher is its expected rate of appreciation (or the lower is its expected rate of depreciation). Hence the higher is the expected gain from holding sterling assets relative to the expected gain from holding foreign currency assets.

Suppose you expect the pound to be worth DM2 at the end of one year. If today the pound is worth DM2.5, you're expecting the pound to depreciate by DM0.5. Other things remaining the same, you will not plan to hold sterling assets in this situation. Instead, you will plan to hold Deutschmark assets. But if today's value of the pound is DM1.5, then you're expecting the pound to appreciate by DM0.5. In this situation, you will plan to hold sterling assets and take advantage of the expected rise in their value. Holding assets in a particular currency in anticipation of a gain in their value arising from a change in the exchange rate is one of the most important influences on the quantity demanded of sterling assets and of foreign currency assets. The more a currency is expected to appreciate, the greater is the quantity of assets in that currency that people want to hold.

Figure 35.4 shows the relationship between the foreign currency price of the pound and the quantity of sterling assets demanded – so it shows the demand curve for sterling assets. When the foreign exchange rate changes, other things remaining the same, there is a movement along the demand curve. You will see that we have measured the value of the pound by using its trade-weighted index.

Any other influence on the quantity of sterling assets that people want to hold results in a shift in the demand curve. Demand either increases or decreases. These other influences are:

◆ The volume of sterling-financed trade
◆ The interest rates on sterling assets
◆ The interest rates on foreign currency assets
◆ The expected future value of the pound

Table 35.4 summarizes the above discussion of the influences on the quantity of sterling assets that people demand.

The Supply of Sterling Assets

The supply of sterling assets is determined by the actions of the government and the Bank of England. We've seen that the quantity of sterling assets

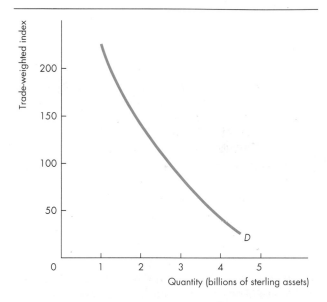

FIGURE 35.4

The Demand for Sterling Assets

The quantity of sterling assets that people demand, other things held constant, depends on the foreign exchange value of sterling. The lower the foreign exchange value of sterling (the lower its trade-weighted index), the larger is the quantity of sterling assets demanded. The increased quantity demanded arises partly from an increase in the volume of sterling trade, as foreigners buy more UK products and UK citizens buy fewer foreign products, and partly from an increase in the expected appreciation (or decrease in the expected depreciation) of sterling assets.

equals government debt plus the monetary base. Of these two items, the monetary base is by far the smaller. But it plays a crucial role in determining the supply of sterling assets. For the behaviour of the monetary base itself depends crucially on the foreign exchange rate regime in operation.

Under a fixed exchange rate regime, the supply curve of sterling assets is horizontal at the chosen exchange rate. The Bank of England stands ready to supply whatever quantity of sterling assets is demanded at the fixed exchange rate. Under a managed exchange rate regime, where the government wants to smooth fluctuations in the exchange rate, the supply curve of sterling assets is upward-sloping. The higher the foreign exchange rate, the larger is the quantity of sterling assets supplied. Under a flexible exchange rate regime, a fixed quantity of sterling assets is supplied, regardless of their

---

TABLE 35.4

The Demand for Sterling Assets

THE LAW OF DEMAND

The quantity of sterling assets demanded
Increases if:

◆ The foreign currency value
   of sterling falls

Decreases if:

◆ The foreign currency value
   of sterling rises

CHANGES IN DEMAND

The demand for sterling assets
Increases if:

◆ Sterling-financed trade
   increases

◆ Interest rates on sterling
   assets rise

◆ Interest rates on foreign
   currency assets fall

◆ The pound is expected
   to strengthen

Decreases if:

◆ Sterling-financed trade
   decreases

◆ Interest rates on sterling
   assets fall

◆ Interest rates on foreign
   currency assets rise

◆ The pound is expected
   to weaken

---

price. As a consequence, under a flexible exchange rate regime, the supply curve of sterling assets is vertical.

The supply of sterling assets changes over time as a result of the following:

◆ The government's budget
◆ The Bank of England's monetary policy

If the government has a budget deficit, the supply of sterling assets increases. If the government has a budget surplus, the supply of sterling assets decreases. The supply of sterling assets increases whenever the Bank of England increases the monetary base and decreases whenever the Bank of England reduces the monetary base.

The above discussion of the influences on the supply of sterling assets is summarized in Table 35.5.

The Market for Sterling Assets

Let's now bring the demand and supply sides of the market for sterling assets together and determine the exchange rate. Figure 35.5 illustrates the analysis.

Fixed Exchange Rate First, consider a fixed exchange rate regime such as that from 1944 to 1972. This case is illustrated in Fig. 35.5(a). During this period all the main currencies were fixed, mostly against the US dollar, and although individual currencies were occasionally devalued or revalued, in general the trade-weighted value of the pound was held constant. Part (a) shows it held constant at a base year level of 100. The supply curve of sterling assets is horizontal at the fixed index value of 100. If the demand curve is D_0, the quantity of sterling assets is Q_0. An increase in demand to D_1 results in an increase in the quantity of sterling assets from Q_0 to Q_1 but no change in the foreign currency value of sterling.

Flexible Exchange Rate Next look at Fig. 35.5(b), which shows what happens under a flexible

---

TABLE 35.5

The Supply of Sterling Assets

SUPPLY

Fixed exchange rate regime

The supply curve of sterling assets is horizontal at the fixed value for the pound.

Managed exchange rate regime

To smooth fluctuations in the foreign exchange value of sterling, the quantity of sterling assets supplied by the Bank of England increases if the foreign exchange value of the pound rises and decreases if the foreign exchange value of the pound falls. The supply curve of sterling assets is upward-sloping.

Flexible exchange rate regime

The supply curve of sterling assets is vertical.

CHANGES IN SUPPLY

The supply of sterling assets

Increases if:

◆ The UK government
   has a deficit

◆ The Bank of England
   increases the monetary base

Decreases if:

◆ The UK government
   has a surplus

◆ The Bank of England
   decreases the monetary base

FIGURE 35.5

Three Exchange Rate Regimes

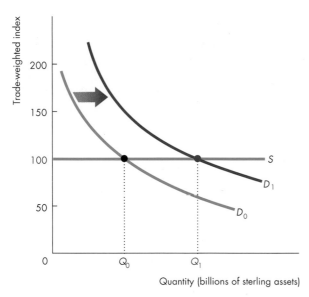

(a) Fixed exchange rate

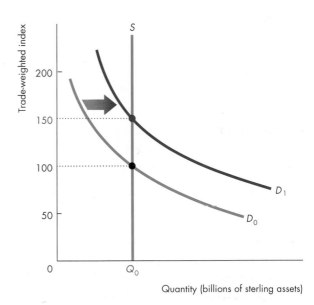

(b) Flexible exchange rate

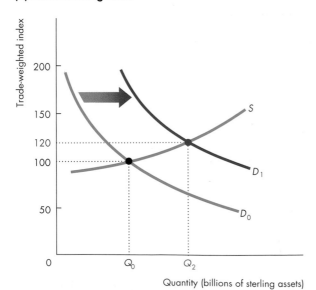

(c) Managed exchange rate

Under a fixed exchange rate regime (part a), the Bank of England would stand ready to supply sterling assets – by buying foreign currencies with sterling – or to take sterling assets off the market – by selling foreign currency for sterling – at a fixed value for the pound. The supply curve for sterling assets would be horizontal. Fluctuations in demand would lead to fluctuations in the quantity of sterling assets outstanding and to fluctuations in the nation's official holdings of foreign exchange. If demand increased from D_0 to D_1, the quantity of sterling assets would increase from Q_0 to Q_1. Under a flexible exchange rate regime (part b), the Bank of England would fix the quantity of sterling assets so that the supply curve of sterling assets was vertical. An increase in the demand for sterling assets from D_0 to D_1 would result only in an increase in the value of sterling – the trade-weighted index would rise from 100 to 150. The quantity of sterling assets would remain constant at Q_0. Under a managed exchange rate regime (part c), the supply curve of sterling assets is upward-sloping, so that if demand increased from D_0 to D_1, sterling appreciates but the quantity of sterling assets supplied also increases – from Q_0 to Q_2. The Bank of England moderates the rise in the value of sterling by increasing the quantity of sterling assets supplied, but it would not completely stop the value of sterling from rising as it would in the case of fixed exchange rates.

exchange rate regime. In this case, the quantity of sterling assets supplied is fixed at Q_0, so the supply curve of sterling assets is vertical. If the demand curve for sterling is D_0, the trade-weighted index for sterling would be 100. If the demand for

pounds increases from D_0 to D_1, the trade-weighted index increases to 150.

Managed Exchange Rate Now consider a managed exchange rate regime, as the United Kingdom has had since 1972 except between 1990 and 1992. This case appears in Fig. 35.5(c). Here, the supply curve is upward-sloping, though the slope may vary from time to time. When the demand curve is D_0, the trade-weighted index is 100. If demand increases to D_1, the index rises, but only to 120. Compared with the flexible exchange rate case, the same increase in demand results in a smaller increase in the exchange rate when it is managed. The reason for this is that the quantity supplied increases in the managed exchange rate case.

Exchange Rate Mechanism (ERM) Finally, what was the supply curve of sterling when the United Kingdom belonged to the EU's Exchange Rate Mechanism from 1990 to 1992? The answer is that the supply curve was very similar to the horizontal one shown in Fig. 35.5(a) because the government agreed to try to keep sterling at an agreed value expressed as an average of the other 11 EU countries' currencies. But sterling was allowed to move up or down by 6 per cent against this agreed value, so the Bank of England could manage the exchange rate a little. Thus the supply curve was not quite horizontal but sloped upward very slightly. The slopes for the most of the other currencies in the ERM were even flatter as their governments agreed to keep within narrow 2.25 per cent bands, but the slopes are now rather steeper as, since 1993, the bands have widened to 15 per cent.

The Exchange Rate Regime and the Official Reserves
There is an important connection between the foreign exchange rate regime and the country's official reserves. The UK government holds these official reserves of foreign currencies in bank accounts around the world. Mostly they are held in accounts at central banks in other countries. The government also holds sterling at the Bank of England. It splits its sterling at the Bank into two separate accounts, one which it uses itself for normal day-to-day purposes and the other, called the exchange equalization account (EEA), which it allows the Bank to use on its behalf to buy or sell official reserves.

Suppose the Bank tried to secure a completely fixed exchange rate as illustrated in Fig. 35.5(a), and suppose it found that the total demand by people around the world for sterling assets had increased. It could increase the quantity of sterling assets supplied very simply. It would use the money in the EEA to buy foreign currencies for the government. Whoever

sold foreign currencies to the Bank would be given cheques, and when the sellers presented these cheques to their own banks, those banks would demand a corresponding amount of extra reserves from the Bank of England. The Bank would therefore raise the deposits held at it by the other banks. This rise in reserves would increase the monetary base and hence the supply of sterling assets would rise. Notice that there would be no limit to how much the Bank could increase the supply of sterling assets in this way. If it used all the money in the EEA, it could simply increase the government's deposit there by writing a larger number against it – in other words by creating money by making a loan to the government, just as the Argent Bank and the other banks in Chapter 26 created money there.

In contrast, if the Bank finds that the total demand for sterling assets has fallen, it can reduce the quantity of sterling assets supplied by selling foreign currencies from the government's official reserves for sterling. Whoever buys the foreign currencies will be using cheques, and the Bank of England will then demand reserves from the buyers' banks. Thus reserves will fall, so that the monetary base and the supply of sterling assets fall too. Notice that there is a limit to how much the Bank can reduce the quantity of sterling assets supplied. The limit is the amount of official reserves there are available to sell.

We can see that with a fixed exchange rate, fluctuations in the demand for sterling assets result in fluctuations in official holdings of foreign exchange. What would happen if the Bank of England operated a flexible exchange rate regime? In this case, there would be no Bank of England intervention in the foreign exchange market. Regardless of what happened to the demand for sterling assets, no action would be taken to change the quantity of sterling assets supplied. Therefore there would be no changes in the country's official holdings of foreign exchange.

With a managed exchange rate, official holdings of foreign exchange have to be adjusted to meet fluctuations in the demand for sterling assets but in a less extreme manner than under fixed exchange rates. As a consequence, fluctuations in the official reserves are smaller under a managed exchange rate regime than under a fixed exchange rate regime.

Under the ERM of the European Union, the value of sterling was almost fixed. Thus there was a danger that fluctuations in official reserves would be almost as large as they would be with a rigidly fixed exchange rate. However, the countries which belong to the ERM agree to help each other maintain stable exchange rates. So if the demand for sterling assets fell, then the central banks of other members agreed to buy some sterling assets to ease the pressure on the UK's official reserves. However, the pressure became unsustainable in September 1992, which is why the United Kingdom then left the ERM.

Why is the Exchange Rate so Volatile?

During the days of sterling's managed float, from 1972 to 1990, and since 1992, there have been times when the value of the pound moved dramatically. On most of these occasions, the pound depreciated spectacularly, but on some occasions it appreciated quite strongly.

We have seen that, while it is subject to a managed float, the foreign exchange value of sterling fluctuates whenever there is change in the demand for or supply of sterling assets. The main reason for occasional sharp fluctuations is that changes in supply and demand sometimes interact. Sometimes a change in supply triggers a change in demand that reinforces the effects of the initial change in supply. Let's see how sharp fluctuations occurred in the value of sterling by looking closely at two episodes.

1978 to 1981   Between 1978 and 1981, the trade-weighted index of the pound rose by nearly 18 per cent. Figure 35.6(a) illustrates how this happened. In 1978 the trade-weighted index for the pound was 101 (with 1985 = 100) – where the supply curve S_{78} and

---

FIGURE 35.6

Why the Exchange Rate was so Volatile

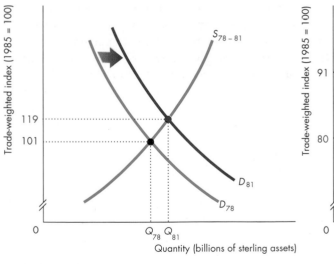

(a) 1978 to 1981

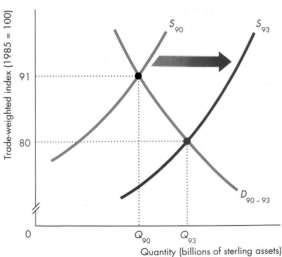

(b) 1990 to 1993

Since 1972 the Bank of England has mostly operated a managed float and at times the exchange rate has been very volatile. This volatility arises partly because there are many factors which affect the supply and demand curves for sterling assets. Sometimes several factors act together in the same direction. Between 1978 and 1981 (part a), the trade-weighted index for the pound (1985 = 100) rose from 101 to 119. This appreciation occurred because there was a large increase in the demand for sterling assets. This increase was partly caused by an increase in North Sea oil output which led to an increase in sterling financed trade. Also, there was a rise in world oil prices which caused the currencies of

many Western countries with large imports of oil to look shaky while sterling was appreciating – and this caused a further increase in the demand for sterling assets. Between 1990 and 1993 (in part b), the trade-weighted value of the pound fell from 91 to 80. This depreciation was due to a large increase in the supply of sterling assets. This increase occurred chiefly because the huge government deficit led to a huge increase in government borrowing and hence a huge increase in the stock of government bonds. The demand curve remained reasonably stable, any increase in demand caused by a rise in the volume of sterling financed trade being offset by a fall in UK interest rates.

the demand curve D_{78} intersect. You will see that over the next three years there was a large increase in the demand for sterling assets from D_{78} to D_{81} at a time when the supply was held more or less steady – it is shown steady as S_{78-81} in the figure. So the value of the pound rose to 119 in 1981.

Several factors have been suggested as contributing to the rise in demand. The growth in the output of oil from the North Sea was one of the most important factors. There was a demand for this oil from both UK citizens and foreign citizens, and as both wanted sterling to buy the oil, this led to an increase in the demand for sterling assets. Moreover, future growth in UK oil production was expected to lead to future appreciations of sterling, and this expectation itself increased the demand for sterling assets and added to the appreciation of sterling.

This rise in the demand for sterling assets would have led to only a modest rise in the value of sterling if the Bank of England and the government had greatly increased the supply of sterling assets. But at the time the Bank of England was trying to restrain the money supply while the government was trying to control its borrowing. Certainly the quantity of sterling assets supplied rose despite these efforts, but it is not unreasonable to depict this as simply the result of a movement along a stable upward-sloping supply curve.

1990 to 1993   Between 1990 and 1993, the trade-weighted index of the pound fell by about 12 per cent. Figure 35.6(b) illustrates how this happened. In 1990 the trade-weighted index for the pound was 91 – where the supply curve S_{90} and the demand curve D_{90} intersect. You will see that over the next three years there was a large increase in the supply of sterling assets from S_{90} to S_{93} at a time when the demand was more or less steady – it is shown as steady as D_{90-93} in the figure. So the value of the pound fell to 80 in 1993.

The increase in supply was caused partly by a rise in the monetary base which rose by 8 per cent over the period. But much more important was the rise in the issue of government bonds caused by the government's huge borrowing requirement which resulted from its huge deficits in 1991, 1992 and 1993 which we saw illustrated in Fig. 35.2. In contrast to the increase in supply, the demand for sterling assets was subjected to two influences which broadly offset each other to leave the demand curve where it was to begin with. Interest rates in

the United Kingdom fell, which reduced the demand for sterling assets, while the volume of sterling financed trade rose, which increased the demand for sterling assets.

REVIEW

T here are three possible foreign exchange rate regimes: fixed, flexible and managed. Under a fixed exchange rate regime, the Bank of England would peg the exchange rate but the official reserves of foreign currencies would have to carry the burden of holding the exchange rate constant. A decrease in the demand for sterling assets and an increase in the demand for foreign currency assets would have to be met by reducing the UK's official holdings of foreign currencies. Under a flexible exchange rate regime, the Bank of England would not intervene in the foreign exchange markets and the country's official holdings of foreign currencies would remain constant. With a managed exchange rate regime, the Bank of England would smooth exchange rate fluctuations to some extent but less strongly than under fixed exchange rates. Under a flexible or a managed exchange rate regime, the exchange rate is determined by the demand for and supply of sterling assets. Fluctuations in supply often induce reinforcing fluctuations in demand, bringing severe fluctuations in the exchange rate. There has been a managed exchange rate regime since 1992. ◆

Arbitrage, Prices and Interest Rates

A rbitrage is the activity of buying at a low price and selling at a high price in order to make a profit on the margin between the two prices. Arbitrage has important effects on exchange rates, prices and interest rates. An increase in the quantity of a commodity purchased forces its buying price up. An increase in the quantity of a commodity sold forces its selling price down. If the buying price of some commodity was lower than the selling price at one point in time, then arbitrage would occur. There would be an increase in the amount bought, forcing the buying price up, and an increase in the amount sold, forcing the selling price down. So arbitrage would cause the two prices to move until they were equal and no more arbitrage profit was available. An implication of arbitrage is the law of one price. The **law of one price** states that any given commodity will be available at a single price.

The law of one price has no respect for national borders or currencies. If the same commodity is being bought and sold on either side of the English Channel, it doesn't matter that one of these transactions is being undertaken in the United Kingdom and the other in France and that one is using pounds and the other francs. The forces of arbitrage bring about one price in the two countries. Let's see how.

Arbitrage

Consider the price of a floppy disk that can be bought in either the United Kingdom or France. We will ignore taxes and transport costs in order to keep the calculations simple, for these factors do not affect the fundamental issue.

Suppose that you can buy floppy disks in the United Kingdom for £5 a box. Suppose that this same box of disks is available in France for FFr50 a box. Where would it pay to buy disks – in France or in the United Kingdom? The answer depends on the relative costs of French and UK money. If £1 is worth FFr10, then it is clear that the price of the disks is the same in both countries. UK citizens can buy a box of disks in the United Kingdom for £5 or they can use £5 to buy FFr50 and then buy the disks in France. The cost will be the same either way. The same is true for the French. They can use FFr50 to buy a box of disks in France or they can use FFr50 to buy £5 and then buy the disks in the United Kingdom.

Suppose, however, that a pound is less valuable than in the above example. In particular, suppose that £1 is worth FFr9. In this case, it will be cheaper to buy the disks in the United Kingdom. The French can buy £5 for FFr45 and therefore can buy the disks in the United Kingdom for FFr45 a box compared with FFr50 in France. The same comparison holds for UK citizens. They can use £5 to buy FFr45 but that would not be enough to buy the disks in France since the disks cost FFr50 there. It therefore pays UK

citizens also to buy the disks in the United Kingdom.

If the situation described above did prevail, there would be an advantage in switching the purchases of disks from France to the United Kingdom. French citizens would cross the Channel to buy their disks in the United Kingdom, and they would keep on doing so until the fall in the demand for disks in France caused the price there to fall to FFr45. Once that had happened, the French would be indifferent between buying their disks in France and in the United Kingdom. Arbitrage would have eliminated the difference in prices in the two countries.

Perhaps you think this is an unrealistic example since, if there were a price difference, the French would not rush across the Channel to the United Kingdom every time they wanted to buy a box of floppy disks. But the fact that there is a profit to be made means that it would pay someone to organize the importing of disks into France from the United Kingdom thereby decreasing the demand for French disks and lowering their price. The incentive to undertake such a move would be present as long as disks were selling for a higher price in France than in the United Kingdom.

Purchasing Power Parity

Purchasing power parity occurs when money has equal value across countries. The word *parity* simply means equality. The phrase *purchasing power* refers to the *value of money*. Thus *purchasing power parity* directly translates to *equal value of money*.

Purchasing power parity is an implication of arbitrage and of the law of one price. In the floppy disk example, when £1 is worth FFr10, £5 will buy the same box of floppy disks that FFr50 will buy. The value of money, when converted to common prices, is the same in both countries. Purchasing power parity thus prevails in that situation.

Purchasing power parity theory predicts that purchasing power parity applies to all goods and to price indexes, not just to a single good such as the floppy disk that we considered above. For if any goods are cheaper in one country than in another, it will pay to convert money into the currency of that country, buy the goods in that country, and sell them in another. By such an arbitrage process, all prices are brought to equality.

One test of the purchasing power parity theory that has been proposed is to calculate the prices of goods in different countries converted to a common currency. One such good that has been used is the Big Mac, sold by McDonald's in all the major countries. It is claimed that if purchasing power parity holds, the Big Mac will cost the same everywhere. In fact, the Big Mac is more expensive in Stockholm than in London, and more expensive in London than in Buenos Aires. These facts have led some people to conclude that purchasing power parity does not hold.

There is an important problem with this test of purchasing power parity. Big Macs are not easily traded internationally. In fact, they are not even easily traded across cities within the United Kingdom. For example, it's lunch time in Liverpool, you are hungry and Big Macs are your thing. You don't have much choice but to buy your Big Mac right there. You can't take advantage of the fact that Big Macs are cheaper in Southampton and begin an arbitrage operation. Big Macs are examples of non-traded products. A **non-traded product** is a good or service that cannot be traded over long distances. Sometimes it is technically possible to undertake such a trade but prohibitively costly. In other cases, it is simply not possible to undertake the trade.

There are many examples of non-traded products. Many services provided are non-traded. You can't buy cheap haircuts or cheap street-sweeping services in Seoul and sell them at a profit in Birmingham. Location-specific goods, such as fast food, are also in this category. When goods cannot be traded over long distances, the goods are strictly different goods. A Big Mac in Liverpool is as different from a Big Mac in Southampton as it is from a pancake across the street.

Arbitrage operates to bring about equality in prices of identical goods, not different goods. It does not operate to bring about equality between prices of similar-looking goods in widely differing locations. For this reason, tests of the purchasing power parity theory based on the prices of non-traded products are faulty. Arbitrage does not only occur in markets for goods and services. It also occurs in markets for assets. As a result, it brings about another important equality or parity – interest rate parity.

Interest Rate Parity

Interest rate parity occurs when interest rates are equal across countries once the differences in risk are taken into account. Interest rate parity is a condition brought about by arbitrage in the markets for assets – markets in which borrowers and lenders operate.

At the beginning of this chapter, we noted some facts about interest rates in different countries. For example, in Japan, interest rates are lower than those in the United Kingdom. Suppose that it is possible to borrow in Tokyo at an interest rate of 3 per cent a year and lend in London at an interest rate of 6 per cent a year. Isn't it possible, in this situation, to make a huge profit on such a transaction? In fact it is not. Interest rates in Tokyo and London are actually equal – interest rate parity prevails.

The key to understanding why the interest rates are equal is to realize that if you borrow in Tokyo, you borrow *yen*, and if you lend money in London – by placing it on deposit in a bank – you are lending *pounds*. You will be repaid in *pounds* but you are obliged to repay in *yen*. The prices at which you do your currency conversions affect the interest rates that you pay and receive. How many pounds you need to pay for your yen depends on exchange rate when the loan is repaid. If the pound has depreciated, you'll need more pounds than you acquired in the first place.

The difference between the interest rates in Tokyo and London reflects the change in the exchange rate between the yen and the pound that, on average, people are expecting. In this example, the average expectation is that the pound will fall against the yen by 3 per cent a year. So when you sell pounds to repay your yen loan, you can expect to need 3 per cent more pounds than you received when you borrowed and converted the yen to begin with. This 3 per cent foreign exchange rate loss must be subtracted from the 6 per cent interest income you earn in London. So your return from lending in London, when you convert your money back into yen, is the same 3 per cent that you must pay for funds in Tokyo. Your profit is zero. Actually, you would incur a loss because you would pay a commission on your foreign exchange transaction.

In the situation that we've just described, interest rate parity prevails. The interest rate in Tokyo – when the expected fall in the value of the pound is taken into account – is almost identical to that in London. If interest rate parity did *not* prevail, it would be possible to profit, without risk, by borrowing at low rates and lending at high rates. Such *arbitrage* actions would increase the demand for loans in countries with low interest rates, and their interest rates would rise. And these actions would increase the supply of loans in countries with high interest rates, and their interest rates would fall. Such movements would restore the interest rate very quickly.

A World Market

Arbitrage in asset markets operates on a worldwide scale and keeps the world capital markets linked in a single global market. This market is an enormous one. It involves borrowing and lending through banks and on stock exchanges. The scale of this international business was estimated by Salomon Brothers, a US investment bank, at more than $1,000 billion in 1986. It is because of international arbitrage in asset markets that the fortunes of the stock markets around the world are so closely linked. A stock market crash in New York makes its new low-priced stocks look attractive compared with high-priced stocks in Tokyo, Frankfurt and London. So investors make plans to sell high in these other markets and buy low in New York. But before many such transactions can be put through, the prices in the other markets fall to match the fall in New York. Conversely, if the Tokyo market experiences rapid price increases and markets in the rest of the world stay constant, investors seek to sell high in Tokyo and buy low in the rest of the world. Again, these trading plans will induce movements in the prices in the other markets to bring them into line with the Tokyo market. The action of selling high in Tokyo reduces prices there and the action of buying low in Frankfurt, London and New York raises prices there.

What you have just learned about arbitrage and its effects on prices and interest rates has implications for a country's monetary and financial independence. Let's explore this issue.

Monetary Independence

Can the Bank of England insulate the UK economy from the rest of the world? The answer is that there is no perfect insulator. But there is a very effective way of securing an independent rate of inflation. This insulator is a flexible exchange rate.

Interdependence with a Flexible Exchange Rate By adopting a flexible exchange rate, UK monetary policy

can be geared towards UK economic objectives and does not respond to changes in monetary policy in other EU countries, the United States, Japan or elsewhere. Suppose, for example, that the Bundesbank – the central bank in Germany – reduces the money supply growth rate by 4 percentage points – for example from 6 per cent a year to 2 per cent a year. Eventually inflation in Germany decreases by 4 percentage points (see Chapter 30, p. 864, for an explanation of the influence of money supply growth on inflation and interest rates). At the same time the Bank of England makes no changes to its monetary policy. Consequently, the growth in the UK money supply is held steady and there is no change in the UK inflation rate.

In this situation, there will be some changes in the demand for pounds and Deutschmarks. These changes will occur because people will consider the effects of the German policy. They will work out that the Deutschmark is going to hold its value more than it did before the Bundesbank changed its monetary policy. So, compared with the pound, the Deutschmark has become relatively more attractive than it was. As a result, the demand for Deutschmarks will increase and the demand for pounds will decrease. The decrease in the demand for pounds results in a depreciation of sterling. This is not the end of the matter. Sterling will depreciate by the difference between the two inflation rates. Also, with an inflation rate difference that is plain for everyone to see, people will expect the depreciation of sterling to continue.

You can see, then, that with a flexible exchange rate, the rate of money supply growth and inflation in the United Kingdom is independent of what happens elsewhere. Interest rates in the United Kingdom may also be different from those in Germany. In the example we have just considered, UK interest rates will be higher than German interest rates by the expected depreciation rate of sterling.

Interdependence with a Fixed Exchange Rate
Suppose the UK government fixes the value of the pound against the Deutschmark. In this situation the forces of arbitrage will come into play and result in the UK inflation rate equalling that of Germany. This is because the forces of arbitrage keep the prices of traded goods in Germany and the United Kingdom the same.

Let's look at the situation more deeply. Suppose the Bundesbank reduces the German money supply growth rate from 6 per cent to 2 per cent a year and thus reduces the German rate of inflation by 4 per cent a year. With German prices initially rising more slowly than before, there is an increase in the demand for German-produced goods and services and a fall in demand for UK-produced goods and services. So there is a fall in the demand for sterling. To keep the exchange rate fixed, the Bank of England intervenes in the foreign exchange market to reduce the quantity of sterling supplied – it does this by buying up sterling with foreign currencies. Because of this shrinkage effect on the monetary base, the growth rate of the UK money supply is slowed down to a rate equal to the new rate at which the German money supply is growing. In turn, the UK inflation rate will be brought into line with the German inflation rate.

In effect, the UK inflation rate is no longer determined by the Bank of England but by the Bundesbank. To fix the value of sterling against the Deutschmark, the Bank of England must supply the quantity of pounds demanded at the price level fixed in Germany. In turn, because no depreciation of sterling is expected, UK interest rates will equal German interest rates. This means, in effect, that UK interest rates are determined by the Bundesbank.

Exchange Rates in Action   How do exchange rates work in practice? They work exactly like the theoretical description that you have just reviewed. During the 1960s, when the pound and other currencies were fixed in value against the dollar, and when, therefore, currencies were fixed in relation to each other, inflation rates were remarkably similar around the world. So also were interest rates. In recent times, most EU countries (including – from 1990 to 1992 – the United Kingdom) have joined the exchange rate mechanism (ERM) of the European Monetary System which until 1993 sought to keep its member countries' currencies fixed quite closely in relation to one another. The result was that these countries' inflation and interest rates came into close alignment.

In contrast, there is an enormous amount of evidence from the operation of floating exchange rates that they do indeed make financial independence possible. Countries such as Japan, Germany and Switzerland have persistently, year in and year out, achieved lower inflation rates and lower interest rates than any other countries. They have done so by keeping the growth rate of the money supply in their own economies close to the growth rate of real GDP. As a consequence, they have achieved low inflation. Their currencies have appreciated against other currencies and the expectation of continuing appreciation has kept their interest rates below those in other countries. However, while a managed float makes financial independence possible, it does not guarantee that the monetary authorities will grasp the opportunity. There are countries, such as the United Kingdom in the 1970s and much of the 1980s, that created money at a rapid pace – at an annual rate far in excess of the growth rate of real GDP. In these countries, a rapid rate of money supply growth brings a higher than average inflation rate and currency depreciation. The expectation of continuing depreciation results in interest rates being higher than those in other countries.

Exchange Rates in the European Union

We have now looked at the implications of fixed exchange rates and compared them with the implications of exchange rates that are not fixed – that is with flexible and managed exchange rates. The United Kingdom had a fixed exchange rate until 1972 and a conventional managed float until 1990. It then joined the exchange rate mechanism of the European Monetary System. It did so when Mrs Thatcher was still Prime Minister, but against her own instincts. The European Monetary System aims to have more or less fixed exchange rates between EU member countries. It is intended to lead to a situation where exchange rates will be permanently fixed. This will pave the way for full monetary union which means individual currencies in EU countries can be replaced by a single European currency. Let's look at monetary union, the European Monetary System and its exchange rate mechanism – and let's see why there is controversy about whether the United Kingdom should have joined that mechanism.

Monetary Union

The origin of the European Monetary System can be traced back to 1970 when the first – largely abandoned – plans were made for creating monetary and economic union within the European Union. **Monetary union** would involve the replacement of the currencies of the member countries by a single EU currency and also the creation of a European central bank to regulate the supply of this new European currency. Economic union would go far beyond monetary union and would involve the full harmonization of economic policies between individual EU countries. If economic union takes place, it will probably be best for all economic policies to be devised and implemented at the EU level. It is perhaps fair to say that those who are most enthusiastic about monetary and economic union are also those who are most keen for there to be full political union in the European Union with the creation of a federal government rather like the one in Washington, and with the EU member countries relegated virtually to the role of states. Thus the debate goes well beyond the economic issues discussed below.

Certainly there are economic arguments in favour of monetary union. Remember that the economic aim of the European Union is to eliminate all barriers to trade and to promote trade between countries, thereby promoting competition between firms for the benefit of the consumer. Life can be tough for firms in a competitive environment and firms are very anxious that the competition should be fair. So the firms in one country feel aggrieved if another country allows the value of its currency to depreciate so that its exports become cheaper. We have seen that any price differential is likely to be temporary, but this will not ease the grievance. We can see the grievance by returning to the example of floppy disks. We know that if the price is £5 a box in the United Kingdom and the exchange rate is £1 = FFr10, then the price will settle at FFr50 in France. And if the pound depreciates so that £1 = FFr9, then we know that demand for French disks will decrease and that disk prices in France will in time decrease to FFr45. But French disk manufacturers are hardly going to feel pleased about the depreciation of sterling and its consequences. So there is an understandable feeling among producers in each member country of the European Union that if they are to be exposed to fierce competitive forces, then at least they should be protected against depreciations in other member countries' currencies. A common currency would achieve such protection.

Another argument for monetary union claims that the existence of individual currencies is a hindrance to trade between member countries and therefore serves to reduce the benefits that consumers could gain from that trade. For example, inter-country transactions incur the costs of having to convert one currency into another, and banks always charge a fee for this service. Also, the fact that the relative values of different currencies can alter creates risks and uncertainty to those who undertake inter-country trade, and such risks and uncertainty are likely to result in less trade than would otherwise be the case.

The main argument against monetary union is that an individual EU country could not try to tackle unemployment by allowing its currency to depreciate in the hope of raising demand. Suppose, for example, that unemployment in the United Kingdom was high and the pound was depreciated. As we saw earlier in the case of floppy disks, people abroad would buy UK products in greater quantities, which would therefore mean that UK output would rise and hence there would be more jobs for the UK workforce.

What would happen if unemployment rose and there was a single European currency? One possibility is that wages and prices in the United Kingdom would fall in response to the low demand that caused the high unemployment, so that UK goods and services would become more competitive. Moreover, low wages would attract new investment which would create new jobs. However, relying on wage and price adjustments is not wholly satisfactory, partly because they might take place only slowly and partly because low wages would encourage some workers to emigrate. Quite apart from the social implications of widespread emigration, it would also further reduce demand in the United Kingdom. So if this objection to monetary union is to be overcome, the European Union needs to devise greatly improved policies for helping countries where unemployment is high. Actually, since unemployment rates tend also to vary within countries, the European Union would really want greatly improved regional policies for targeting help on particular regions where unemployment is very high. We saw in Chapter 20 that the European Union gives these areas a little help now. This chiefly involves support for measures designed to improve the infrastructure, such as new roads. But a stronger policy would surely be needed if monetary union takes place.

Will monetary union take place? At a meeting of EU countries in Maastricht in 1991, provisional agreement was reached on monetary union. It was agreed that monetary union would occur in 1997 provided at that least seven EU countries met specified 'convergence' conditions and provided that at least eight countries voted in favour. The United Kingdom would be allowed to opt out. In anticipation of success, an embryonic European central bank has been established in Germany.

But the convergence conditions may not be met. These include strict rules on government debt, which may not exceed 60 per cent of GDP, on government borrowing, which may not exceed 4 per cent of GDP, on exchange rate stability, as the country may not depreciate its currency, and on interest rates, which must not exceed the lowest elsewhere in the European Union by more than 1.5 per cent. In view of the turmoil in European exchange rates in 1993, it has to be said that the Maastricht timetable may be over-optimistic. If monetary union does occur, it may be much later than 1997. See also Reading Between the Lines pp. 1006–1007, on this issue.

The European Monetary System

As we noted earlier, the EU's interest in promoting stable exchange rates between members dates back to 1970. It may seem odd today that exchange rate fluctuations were thought to be a problem in 1970 as all exchange rates were then basically fixed. However, countries did periodically devalue – or occasionally revalue – their currencies. The 1970 concern was to try to get more stability between members' currencies than that offered by the old system of fixed exchange rates.

When the era of fixed exchange rates ended in the early 1970s, those people who wanted stability between EU currencies became even more anxious. Attempts were made to secure stability between a number of EU currencies, but these attempts foundered because there were huge increases in the price of oil which increased the value of each country's imports and put downward pressures, of varying amounts, on each country's currency. The European Monetary System was founded in 1979 as another more enduring effort to secure stable exchange rates within the European Union.

The **European Monetary System** (EMS) is an agreement on various provisions which reflect an attempt to promote exchange rate stability within the European Union. All the countries which were members of the European Union in 1979 – including the United Kingdom – joined the EMS at its inception, and all later EU members also belong. By seeking exchange rate stability, the EMS tries to prevent the sudden competitive advantages that depreciation can bring to individual countries and it hopes to reduce the risks and uncertainty attached to inter-country trade. It also aims to pave the way for full monetary union and, perhaps, economic union.

One of the provisions of the EMS is that EU members deposit one-fifth of their official reserves of gold and dollars with a body known as the European Monetary Cooperation Fund (EMCF). In return, each central bank is given some European Currency Units (ECUs). As explained in Chapter 26 (p. 725), the ECU is a composite currency composed of all 12 EU currencies. ECUs are used for transactions between central banks.

However, the key element of the EMS is the exchange rate mechanism. Some EU members opted out of this element initially and later joined in. The United Kingdom was one of the countries that opted out initially, and it waited until 1990 before joining. By 1992 all EU countries were members of the ERM except Greece.

The Exchange Rate Mechanism of the EMS

The **exchange rate mechanism** (ERM) is intended as a system of more or less fixed exchange rates between ERM members' currencies, though collectively the value of these currencies floats against the other currencies in the world. Thus the ERM aims for fixed exchange rates within the European Union but allows a float between these currencies and the rest of the world. But each ERM member seeks to keep its currency within a narrow band rather than at a precise level. Until 1993, most members tried to keep their currencies within 2.25 per cent of an agreed target level against other members. The United Kingdom was allowed a wider band of 6 per cent. A similar 6 per cent margin was also allowed for Italy and for Spain. But the United Kingdom and Italy withdrew in 1992, finding it impossible to maintain the values of their currencies, and there were more problems in 1993 when the remaining countries agreed to adopt much wider 15 per cent bands.

The formal arrangements are that each member's currency is given a 'central value' in terms of the ECU, and members try hard to keep within the agreed range of this central or target value. This is obviously much easier when they can move up or down by 15 per cent than it was when they could move up and down by only 2.25 per cent. If a member's currency diverges from its central value by more than three-quarters of the approved percentage range, it is supposed to take action to protect that level. For example, it might raise (or reduce) interest rates in an effort to increase (or reduce) the demand for assets denominated in its currency. Should this action fail, then other members would help.

The onus in these situations lies chiefly with the countries whose currencies are highest and lowest in relation to their central levels. These countries are meant to protect the level of the currency which is in danger of going outside the agreed limits. These countries can borrow from the EMCF if they need money to support a currency which is falling in value. Despite these procedures, realignments in target levels have occurred. Realignments have to be agreed between ERM members. There were many realignments in the early years, but there were relatively few between 1983 and 1993. Realignments have chiefly taken place when individual countries have had too much inflation to maintain their initial central values.

Why was the United Kingdom so reluctant to join the ERM? After all, by promoting exchange rate stability it goes some way towards providing the advantages of monetary union. Thus it should reduce the risks and uncertainties of trade between EU members and it should encourage acceptance of measures that promote competition if each member knows its producers cannot be damaged by regular depreciations in the currencies of other members. One reason for the delay in the UK's membership was that it was opposed by those who do not want monetary union. It is true that the main argument against a monetary union, that countries with high unemployment cannot reduce the value of their currencies, does not apply so strongly to the ERM since realignments are possible. But they are possible only with mutual consent. They cannot be undertaken at the sole discretion of individual countries at a time of their own choosing.

Another argument against the United Kingdom joining was that if sterling was fixed in relation to some other currencies, then – for reasons we have discussed earlier in this chapter – the United Kingdom would lose some of its monetary independence. Consequently, inflation rates in the United Kingdom would be likely to coincide with the inflation rates in the ERM member countries. Certainly inflation rates among those countries have converged a good deal since 1979. However, this argument for monetary independence became less appealing as time passed. This is because inflation rates in the ERM member countries converged at levels that were generally some way *below* the level in the United Kingdom. Why seek to be independent from a group which is enjoying lower rates of inflation? Indeed, this view of converging inflation rates was doubtless the main reason why Mrs Thatcher finally decided to join the ERM, for the UK inflation rate was rising in 1990 and there seemed something to be said for joining in the hope that it would reduce inflation rates. Indeed, the more firmly the government seemed committed to maintaining a fixed exchange rate, the more pressure UK firms were under to restrain costs in order to remain competitive with other EU countries.

Yet another argument put forward against the United Kingdom joining was that the value of sterling might prove more volatile than the value of other ERM member currencies. This would mean that it could be very difficult for the United Kingdom to stick within its agreed limits. One reason why it was thought that sterling might be very volatile is that its value is especially sensitive to changes in oil prices. Another possible cause of volatility was that the United Kingdom abandoned foreign exchange controls in 1979, long before most other EU countries. It was feared that the volatility of sterling would mean that there would be frequent occasions when the UK government would want sterling to be realigned, yet it might not always get approval for this from other members. Sterling certainly needed a major realignment in 1992, and at that time the government decided to leave the ERM altogether rather than risk more embarrassing realignments in the future.

Economic and Monetary Union

FINANCIAL TIMES, 7 MARCH 1994

EMU is still alive

Graham Bishop

MANY politicians and market participants alike have written off Economic and Monetary Union. That judgment may be too hasty.

Financial markets – liberalised by the Single European Market – have already created such convergence of long-term interest rates among a core group of EU members that no trend divergence in exchange rates is discounted: a de facto EMU of the few....

When the next Intergovernmental Conference (IGC) starts in 1996 there will be a formal constraint... will the Maastricht criteria to permit the start of EMU be satisfied?

The criteria were explicitly designed to promote price stability but there was an implicit strategic purpose: to minimise the risk that financial instability could spill over into the political arena.

Yet the opposite has happened. Policy and financial markets have become increasingly entwined. In 1992–93, financial markets – liberalised by the single market – demonstrated their power by shifting capital, prompting the upheavals in the ERM....

The two clear messages from the financial markets [are]:

☐ The remarkable convergence of long-term interest rates in some EU members since the ERM collapse implies that monetary union would run with the grain of markets.

☐ Nominal bond yields, that were recently close to post-war lows in many countries, imply that the purchasers of govern-ment debt do not feel that public deficits are excessive amid deep recession and with inflation heading for 30-year lows.

...If the capital flows of 1992–93 are any guide, the market will discipline states for whom EMU is unrealistic. Those states that are genuinely convergent will be presented with a de facto EMU.

Graham Bishop is Adviser on European Financial Affairs to Salomon Brothers, London

© The Financial Times. Reprinted with permission.

The European Union wants to create an Economic and Monetary Union (EMU) by the end of the century.

A prerequisite for EMU to occur is economic convergence, measured in terms of certain specified criteria, including interest rate convergence and the level of government deficits.

Many commentators have felt sufficient economic convergence would not happen.

The liberalization of financial markets is, however, leading to the convergence of long-term interest rates.

Nominal bond yields suggest that purchasers of government debt do not believe that government deficits are excessive and destabilizing.

These trends will ensure that a number of countries will form an EMU.

Background and Analysis

A move to EMU would mean exchange rates between the participating countries' currencies would be fixed as a prelude to a single currency.

In order to ensure this fixed exchange rate system is sustainable, convergence criteria have been established to assess which economies are suitable for membership of EMU.

These criteria are defined in terms of interest rate and inflation rate differentials, maximum permissible levels of public deficit and debt and exchange rate stability.

In particular, interest rate parity (IRP) is being brought about.

IRP implies a convergence of interest rates net of risk. As exchange rates within the European Union become more stable, IRP effectively means a convergence in the absolute levels of nominal interest rates.

The creation of a single financial market, allowing free capital movements, has helped to ensure that IRP comes about.

Where policies are implemented that go against convergence, capital movements will discipline policy makers. This helps explain the capital flows that caused the exchange rate mechanism (ERM) crises of 1992 and 1993.

Figure 1 shows the demand for and supply of pound assets. The exchange rate is the Deutschmarks per pound.

If Germany has higher interest rates than the United Kingdom, the supply of pounds will increase as people demand more Deutschmarks. The demand for pounds will decrease as people want to hold fewer pound assets.

If Germany has a lower inflation rate than the United Kingdom, the supply of pounds will increase as the price of imported German goods becomes relatively cheaper. The demand for pounds will fall as fewer people wish to buy UK goods, because UK exports become relatively more expensive over time.

The ERM aims to maintain the exchange rate within a narrow band. The effect of interest rate and inflation rate differentials described above pushes down the exchange rate.

In September 1992, the financial markets responded to policy makers trying to sustain too high an exchange rate by selling pounds, forcing the UK government to withdraw the pound from the ERM and letting it float down to a more realistic long-term level.

The Figure 2 shows the convergence in nominal long-term interest rates starting in 1979 when the ERM was created and ending in 1992–1993 when the two major crises occurred.

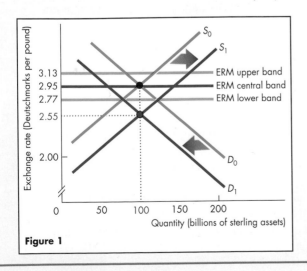

Figure 1

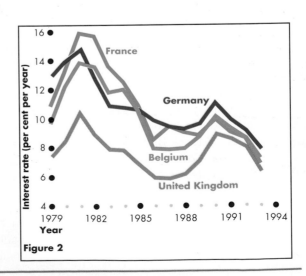

Figure 2

◆ ◆ ◆ ◆   You've now discovered what determines a country's current account balance and the foreign exchange value of its currency. The most important influences on the current account balance are the government sector deficit and the private sector deficit. A country where the government sector has a deficit will have a current account deficit too, unless its private sector has a large enough surplus. The value of a country's currency is determined by the demand and supply assets in that currency and is strongly influenced by monetary actions. A rapid increase in the supply of a currency will result in a decline in its value relative to other currencies.

You've also learned how international arbitrage links prices and interest rates together in different countries. International arbitrage does not occur in markets for non-traded products. But arbitrage operates in markets for traded goods and is especially powerful in markets for assets. Arbitrage in asset markets links interest rates around the world. Differences in national interest rates reflect the expectations of changes in exchange rates. Once these differences in expectations about exchange rates are taken into account, interest rates are equal across countries.   ◆ ◆   In the final chapter, we're going to look at some further global economic issues. We'll examine the problems faced by developing countries as they seek to grow and we'll look at the countries of Eastern Europe and China as they make the transition from planned economies to market economies.

S U M M A R Y

Financing International Trade

International trade, borrowing and lending are financed using foreign currency. A country's international transactions are recorded in its two balance of payments accounts. The first account – the current account – records receipts and expenditures connected with the sale and purchase of goods and services, as well as flows of property income (interest, profits and dividends) and current transfers (gifts). The second account records changes in external assets – that is, holdings by UK citizens of foreign assets – and changes in external liabilities – that is, holdings by foreign citizens of UK assets.

Historically, the United Kingdom has been a net lender to the rest of the world, but since the mid-1980s it has been a net borrower. Nevertheless, the stock of its external assets around the world still exceeds its external liabilities – that is the stock of foreign investment in the United Kingdom.

The current account balance is equal to the government sector balance plus the private sector balance. The current account balance fluctuates when the government sector and private sector balances fluctuate. In 1986 the current account was virtually in balance while a private sector surplus offset a government sector deficit. By 1993 the current account had a deficit which equalled the sum of a large government sector and a modest private sector surplus. (pp. 981–988)

The Pound and Net Exports

Foreign currency is obtained in exchange for domestic currency in the foreign exchange market. Central banks often intervene in foreign exchange markets. There are three types of foreign exchange rate regimes: fixed, flexible and managed. When the exchange rate is fixed, the government declares a value for the currency in terms of some other currency and the Bank of England takes actions to ensure that the price is maintained.

A flexible exchange rate is one in which the central bank takes no actions to influence the value of its currency in the foreign exchange market. The country's holdings of foreign currencies remain constant and fluctuations in demand and supply lead to fluctuations in the exchange rate.

A managed exchange rate is one in which the central bank takes actions to smooth fluctuations that would otherwise arise but does so less strongly than under a fixed exchange rate regime. (pp. 988–991)

Exchange Rate Determination

The foreign exchange rate is determined by the demand for and supply of sterling assets in the world economy. To fix the exchange rate, the Bank of England has to stand ready to sell pounds for foreign currencies or to buy pounds with foreign currencies. The country's official reserves of foreign currencies fluctuate to maintain the fixed exchange rate.

In a flexible or managed exchange rate regime, the exchange rate is determined by the demand for and supply of sterling. The demand for sterling depends on the volume of sterling-financed trade, the interest rates on sterling assets, the interest rates on foreign currency assets and expected changes in the value of the pound.

The supply of sterling depends on the exchange rate regime. Under fixed exchange rates, the supply curve is horizontal; under flexible exchange rates, the supply curve is vertical; under managed exchange rates, the supply curve is upward-sloping. The position of the supply curve depends on the government's budget and the Bank of England's monetary policy. The larger the budget deficit or the more rapidly the Bank of England permits the money supply to grow, the further to the right the supply curve moves. Fluctuations in the exchange rate occur because of fluctuations in demand and supply. Large fluctuations can arise from interlinked changes in demand and supply. A shift in the supply curve often produces an induced change in the demand curve that reinforces the effect on the exchange rate. (pp. 991–998)

Arbitrage, Prices and Interest Rates

Arbitrage – buying low and selling high – keeps the prices of goods and many services that are traded internationally close to equality across all countries. Arbitrage also keeps interest rates in line with each other.

Some goods and many services are not traded internationally – non-traded products. International arbitrage does not bring their prices into equality. For this reason, tests of purchasing power parity based on their prices are faulty.

Interest rates around the world look unequal, but the appearance arises from the fact that loans are contracted in different currencies in different countries. To compare interest rates across countries, we have to take into account changes in the values of currencies. Countries whose currencies are appreciating have low interest rates; countries whose currencies are depreciating have high interest rates. If the rate of currency depreciation is taken into account, interest rates are nearly equal. (pp. 998–1001)

Monetary Independence

With a fixed exchange rate, a country cannot use monetary policy to control its inflation rate and interest rates. A change in inflation in the rest of the world, other things remaining the same, changes inflation in the domestic economy. It also changes interest rates.

With a flexible exchange rate, a country can insulate itself from inflation and interest rate shocks coming from the rest of the world. If, in the face of a higher inflation rate in the rest of the world, domestic monetary policy is held steady, the domestic inflation rate stays constant. The currency appreciates and interest rates in the domestic economy stay below those in the rest of the world.

To achieve lower inflation and lower interest rates than other countries, the Bank of England needs to maintain a lower average growth rate of the UK money supply than the money supply growth rates that prevail in other countries. (pp. 1001–1002)

Exchange Rates in the European Union

The EU's exchange rate mechanism tries to secure virtually fixed exchange rates between members' currencies while allowing the whole bundle of currencies to float against those in the rest of the world. There are two reasons for wanting stability within the European Union. One is to promote fully free trade and fair competition between members, for exchange rate depreciations by one member make it harder for firms in other countries to compete, while exchange rate fluctuations create risks and uncertainty which reduce trade. The other is to pave the way for full monetary union with a single currency. The declared intention is to seek a single currency by 1997, with the United Kingdom perhaps opting out. But turmoil in the ERM in 1992 led to the United Kingdom and Italy withdrawing, and further turmoil in 1993 led to a loosening of links between the remaining members' currencies. These events seem likely to delay monetary union. (pp. 1002–1005)

KEY ELEMENTS

Key Terms

Arbitrage, 998
Balance of payments accounts, 981
Balance of trade, 981
Balancing item, 983
Creditor nation, 983
Currency appreciation, 990
Currency depreciation, 990
Current account, 981
Current transfers, 981
Debtor nation, 983
European Monetary System (EMS), 1004
Exchange Rate Mechanism (ERM), 1004
Fixed exchange rate, 989
Flexible exchange rate, 988
Foreign exchange market, 988
Foreign exchange rate, 988
Interest rate parity, 1000
International Monetary Fund (IMF), 989
Invisible balance, 981
Law of one price, 999
Managed exchange rate, 989
Monetary union, 1003

Net borrower, 983
Net lender, 983
Non-traded product,1000
Official reserves, 983
Private sector surplus or deficit, 986
Property income, 981
Purchasing power parity, 999
Quantity of sterling assets (quantity of sterling) 992
Trade-weighted index, 990
Transactions in external assets, 981
Transactions in external assets and liabilities, 981
Transactions in external liabilities, 982
Visible balance, 981

Key Figures and Tables

Figure 35.1	The Balance of Payments 1968–1993, 984
Figure 35.2	The Three Balances, 987
Figure 35.3	Changes in Currency Values, 990
Figure 35.5	Three Exchange Rate Regimes, 995
Table 35.2	Surpluses, Deficits and the Financing of Investment, 985
Table 35.4	The Demand for Sterling Assets, 994
Table 35.5	The Supply of Sterling Assets, 994

REVIEW QUESTIONS

1 What are the transactions recorded in a country's current account and in its transactions in external assets and liabilities account?

2 What is the relationship between the balances on the current account and the transactions in external assets and liabilities account?

3 Distinguish between a country that is a net borrower and one that is a creditor. Are net borrowers always creditors? Are creditors always net borrowers?

4 What is the connection between a country's current account balance and the government's budget deficit and the private sector deficit?

5 Why do fluctuations in the government budget balance lead to fluctuations in the current account balance?

6 Distinguish between the three exchange rate regimes: fixed, flexible and managed.

7 Review the main influences on the quantity of sterling assets that people demand.

8 Review the influences on the supply of sterling assets.

9 How does the supply curve of sterling assets differ under the three exchange rate regimes?

10 Why has the pound fluctuated so much?

11 What is arbitrage?

12 How does arbitrage lead to purchasing power parity?

13 What is interest rate parity?

14 How does interest rate parity come about?

15 How do fixed exchange rates limit independent monetary policy?

16 How do flexible exchange rates insulate an economy from changes in inflation in the rest of the world?

P R O B L E M S

1 The citizens of Gondwana, whose currency is the grain, conduct the following transactions in 1993:

	Billions of grains
Imports of goods and services	350
Exports·of goods and services	500
Borrowing from the rest of the world	60
Lending to the rest of the world	200
Increase in official holdings of foreign currency	10

a Set out the two balance of payments accounts for Gondwana.

b Does Godwana have a flexible exchange rate?

2 You are told the following about Ecoland, a country with a flexible exchange rate whose currency is the band:

	Billions of bands
GDP	100
Consumers' expenditure	60
Government purchases of goods and services	24
Investment	22
Exports of goods and services	20
Government budget deficit	4

Calculate the following for Ecoland:

a Imports of goods and services

b Current account balance

c Transactions in external assets and liabilities account balance

d Taxes (net of transfer payments, subsidies and debt interest)

e Private sector deficit/surplus

3 A country's currency appreciates and its official holdings of foreign currency increase. What can you say about the following?

a The exchange rate regime being pursued by the country

b The country's current account

c The country's transaction in external assets and liabilities account

4 The average annual interest rate in Japan is 3 per cent; in the United States it is 5 per cent; in the United Kingdom it is 7 per cent; and in France it is 9 per cent. What is the expected change over the coming year in each of the following?

a The pound against the Japanese yen

b The pound against the US dollar

c The pound against the French franc

d The Japanese yen against the French franc

CHAPTER 36

EMERGING
ECONOMIES

After studying this chapter you will be able to:

◆ Describe the international distribution of income

◆ Describe the fundamental economic problem that confronts all nations

◆ Describe the alternative systems that have been used to solve the economic problem

◆ Explain how the accumulation of capital and technological progress increase per capita incomes

◆ Describe the process of economic change in China

◆ Describe the economic problems confronting the former Soviet Union

◆ Describe the economic problems of other Eastern European countries

I<small>N 1946, AS</small> W<small>ORLD</small> W<small>AR</small> II <small>ENDED,</small> H<small>ONG</small> K<small>ONG EMERGED FROM</small> J<small>APANESE OCCU-</small> pation as a poor colony of the United Kingdom. Occupying a cluster of overcrowded rocky islands, Hong Kong, today, is a city of vibrant, hard-working and increasingly wealthy people. A similar story can be told of Singapore. Two and a half million people crowded into an island city nation have, by their dynamism, transformed their economy, increasing their average income more than sixfold since 1960. How do some countries manage to unshackle themselves from poverty? What do they have that other poor countries lack? Can their lessons be applied elsewhere? ◆ ◆ Extraordinary events have taken place. The People's Republic of China is undergoing massive economic change, gradually replacing its system of central planning with the market. Change is also taking place in Eastern Europe. The Berlin Wall

Economic Extremes

has fallen and Germany is reunited. East Germany's centrally planned economy has been replaced by a market economy. Poland, Hungary, the Czech Republic and Slovakia have all abandoned central planning. The Soviet Union has disintegrated and some of its former republics have abandoned the centrally planned economy and are moving towards a market economy. Why are so many countries abandoning central economic planning and jumping on the market bandwagon?

◆ ◆ ◆ ◆ This chapter brings you full circle and returns to the fundamental economic problem of scarcity and the alternative ways in which people cope with that problem. You've studied how Western European economies operate. You are now going to look at the bigger picture and examine the process of revolutionary change that is taking place in the world economy during the 1990s.

The International Distribution of Income

When we studied the distribution of income in the United Kingdom, we discovered that there is a great deal of inequality. As we will see, the differences in income within a country, large though they are, look insignificant when compared with the differences among the nations. Let's see how income is distributed among the nations of the world.

Poorest Countries

The poorest countries are sometimes called underdeveloped countries. An **underdeveloped country** is a country in which there is little industrialization, limited mechanization of the agricultural sector, very little capital equipment, and low income per person. In many underdeveloped countries, large numbers of people live on the edge of starvation. Such people devote their time to producing the meagre supplies of food and clothing required for themselves and their families. They have no surplus to trade with others or to invest in new tools and capital equipment. One of the most publicized of the poor countries is Ethiopia, where thousands of people spend their lives trekking across parched landscapes in search of meagre food supplies.

Just how poor are the poorest countries? Twenty-seven per cent of the world's population lives in countries whose per capita incomes range between 4 and 9 per cent of those in the United States. Although these countries contain 27 per cent of the world's people, they earn only 6 per cent of world income. These poorest of countries are located mainly in Africa.

Developing Countries

A **developing country** is one that is poor but is accumulating capital and developing an industrial and commercial base. The developing countries have a large and growing urban population and have steadily growing incomes. Income per person in such countries ranges between 10 and 30 per cent of that in the United States. These countries are located in all parts of the world but many are found in Asia, the Middle East and in Central America. Seventeen per cent of the world's people live in these countries and earn 11 per cent of world income.

Newly Industrialized Countries

Newly industrialized countries (often called NICs) are countries in which there is a rapidly developing broad industrial base and income per person is growing quickly. Today their incomes per person approach 50 per cent of those in the United States. Examples of such countries are Trinidad, Israel and South Korea. Three per cent of the world's people live in the newly industrialized countries and earn 3 per cent of world income.

Industrial Countries

Industrial countries are countries that have a large amount of capital equipment and in which people undertake highly specialized activities, enabling them to earn high incomes per person. These are the countries of Western Europe, Canada and the United States, Japan, and Australia and New Zealand. Seventeen per cent of the world's people live in these countries and they earn 49 per cent of world income.

Oil-rich Countries

A small number of oil-rich countries have very high incomes per person despite the fact that they are, in most other respects, similar to the poorest countries or developing countries. These countries have little industry, and indeed little of anything of value to sell to the world, except oil. Four per cent of the world's people live in these countries and they earn 4 per cent of world income. But that income is very unequally distributed within the countries. Most of the people in these countries have incomes similar to those in the poorest countries, but a small number of people are extremely rich – indeed, they are among the richest people in the world.

Communist and Former Communist Countries

Close to 33 per cent of the world's people live in communist countries or in countries that were formerly communist and are now making a transition towards capitalism. These countries earn 28 per cent of world income. A **communist country** is one in which there is limited private ownership of productive capital and of firms, limited reliance on the market as a means of allocating resources, and in which government agencies plan and direct the production and distribution of most goods and services. Rapid changes are taking place in many of these countries at the present time.

Per capita incomes in these countries vary enormously. In China, income per person is around 15 per cent of that in the United States. China is a developing country. Income per person in East Germany – now part of a reunited Germany – is almost 70 per cent of that of the United States. Other countries in this category include the Czech Republic and Slovakia, Poland, Hungary and the republics of the former Soviet Union. Some former communist countries, such as Romania, the states of the former Yugoslavia and Bulgaria, have incomes per person similar to those of the newly industrialized countries. Thus within the communist and former communist countries, there is a great deal of variety in income levels and the degree of economic development.

The World Lorenz Curve

A **Lorenz curve** plots the cumulative percentage of income against the cumulative percentage of population. If income is equally distributed, the Lorenz curve is a 45° line running from the origin. The degree of inequality is indicated by the extent to which the Lorenz curve departs from the 45° line of equality. Figure 36.1 shows two Lorenz curves: one curve depicts the distribution of income among households in the United Kingdom, and the other depicts the distribution of average income per person across countries.

As you can see, the distribution of income among countries is more unequal than the distribution of income among households within the United Kingdom. Forty per cent of the world's people live in countries whose incomes account for less than 10 per cent of the world's total. The richest 20 per cent of the people live in countries whose incomes account for 55 per cent of the world's total income. Inequality in income is even more severe than that apparent in Fig. 36.1, for the world Lorenz curve tells us only how unequal average incomes are among countries. Inequality within countries is not revealed by the world Lorenz curve.

Such numbers provide a statistical description of the enormity of the world's poverty problem. And they are *real* numbers. That is the effects of differences in prices have been removed. To appreciate the severity of the problem better, imagine that your

family has an income of 30 pence a day for each person. That 30 pence has to buy housing, food, clothing, transport and all the other things consumed. Such is the lot of more than a quarter of the world's people.

Although there are many poor people in the world, there are also many whose lives are undergoing dramatic change. They live in countries in which rapid economic growth is taking place. As a result of economic growth and development, millions of people now enjoy living standards undreamt of by their parents and inconceivable to their grandparents. Let's look at how different economic systems solve the economic problem.

FIGURE 36.1

The World Lorenz Curve: 1985

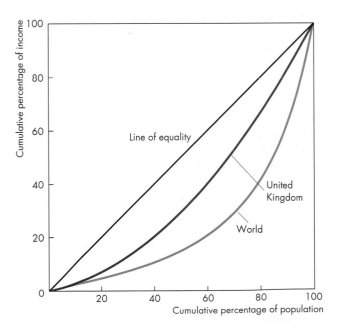

The cumulative percentage of income is plotted against the cumulative percentage of population. If income were distributed equally across countries, the Lorenz curve would be a straight diagonal line. The distribution of per capita income across countries is even more unequal than the distribution of income among households in the United Kingdom.

Sources: Robert Summers and Alan Heston, 'A New Set of International Comparisons of Real Product and Price Levels; Estimates for 130 Countries, 1950–1985,' *Review of Income and Wealth*, Series 34 (1988): 207–262; and *Current Population Reports, Consumer Income*, Series P-60, Nos. 167 and 168 (1990). US Department of Commerce, Bureau of the Census.

The Economic Problem and Its Alternative Solutions

The economic problem is the universal fact of scarcity – we want to consume more goods and services than the available resources make possible. The economic problem is illustrated in Fig. 36.2. People have preferences about the goods and services they would like to consume and about how they would like to use the factors of production that they own or control. Techniques of production – technologies – convert factors of production into goods and services. The economic problem is to choose the quantities of goods and services to produce – *what* – the ways to produce them – *how* – and the distribution of goods and services to each individual – *for whom*.

The production of goods and services is the objective of the economic system. But *what*, *how* and *for whom* goods and services are produced depends on the way the economy is organized – on who makes which decisions. Different systems deliver different outcomes. Let's look at the main alternatives that have been used.

Alternative Economic Systems

Economic systems vary in two dimensions:

◆ Ownership of capital and land
◆ Incentive structure

Ownership of Capital and Land   Capital and land may be owned entirely by individuals, entirely by the state, or by a mixture of the two. The private ownership of capital and land enables individuals to create and operate their own firms. It also enables them to buy and sell capital, land and firms freely at their going market prices. State ownership of capital and land enables individuals to control the use of these resources in state-owned firms but does not permit this control to be passed to others in a market transaction.

In practice, no economy has pure private ownership or pure and exclusive state ownership. For example, in an economy with widespread private ownership, the freedom to buy and sell firms is modified by laws on mergers. Also, national defence or the public interest may be invoked to limit private ownership. Such limitations operate to restrict the private ownership of beaches and areas of natural scenic beauty.

FIGURE 36.2

The Fundamental Economic Problem

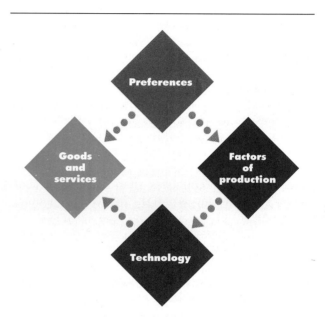

People have preferences about goods and services and the use of their factors of production. Technologies are available for transforming factors of production into goods and services. People want to consume more goods and services than can be produced with the available factors of production and technology. The fundamental economic problem is to choose *what* goods and services to produce, *how* to produce them and *for whom* to produce them. Different economic systems deliver different solutions to this problem.

In an economy that has predominantly state ownership, individuals sometimes own small plots of land and their homes. Also, in many economies, private ownership and state ownership exist side by side. In such cases, the state acts like a private individual and buys capital, land, or even a production enterprise from its existing owner.

Incentive Structure   An **incentive structure** is a set of arrangements that induce people to take certain actions. Incentives may be created by market prices, by administered prices and administrative sanctions, or by a mixture of the two.

An incentive system based on market prices is one in which people respond to the price signals they receive and the price signals themselves respond to people's actions. For example, suppose a severe frost in Spain wipes out the orange crop one year. The supply of orange juice falls. As a result, the price of orange juice rises. Faced with the higher price, people have an *incentive* to economize on orange juice and they decrease the quantity demanded. At the same time, the higher price of orange juice induces an increase in the demand for apple juice, a substitute for orange juice. As a result, the prices of apples and apple juice also rise. With higher prices for orange juice and apple juice, orange and apple growers in other countries have an *incentive* to increase the quantity supplied.

An incentive system based on administered prices is one in which administrators set prices to achieve their own objectives. For example, a government might want everyone to have access to cheap bread. As a result, bread might be priced at, say, a penny a loaf. Under these circumstances, people have an *incentive* to buy lots of bread. Poor children might even use stale loaves as footballs! (This use of bread apparently did actually occur in the former Soviet Union.) An incentive system based on administrative sanctions is one in which people are rewarded or punished in a variety of non-monetary ways to induce them to take particular actions. For example, a manager might reward a salesperson for achieving a sales goal with more rapid promotion, or with a bigger office.

Alternatively, a salesperson might be punished for failing to achieve a sales goal by being moved to a less desirable sales district. When an entire economy is operated on administrative incentives, everyone, from the highest political authority to the lowest rank of workers, faces non-monetary rewards and punishments from their immediate superiors.

Types of Economic System Economic systems differ in the ways in which they combine ownership and incentive arrangements. The range of alternatives is illustrated in Fig. 36.3. One type of economic system is **capitalism**, a system based on the private ownership of capital and land and on an incentive system based on market prices. Another type of economic system is **socialism,** a system based on state ownership of capital and land and on an incentive structure based on administered prices or sanctions arising from a central economic plan. **Central planning** is a method of allocating resources *by command*. A central plan for action is drawn up and the plan is

---

FIGURE 36.3

Alternative Economic Systems

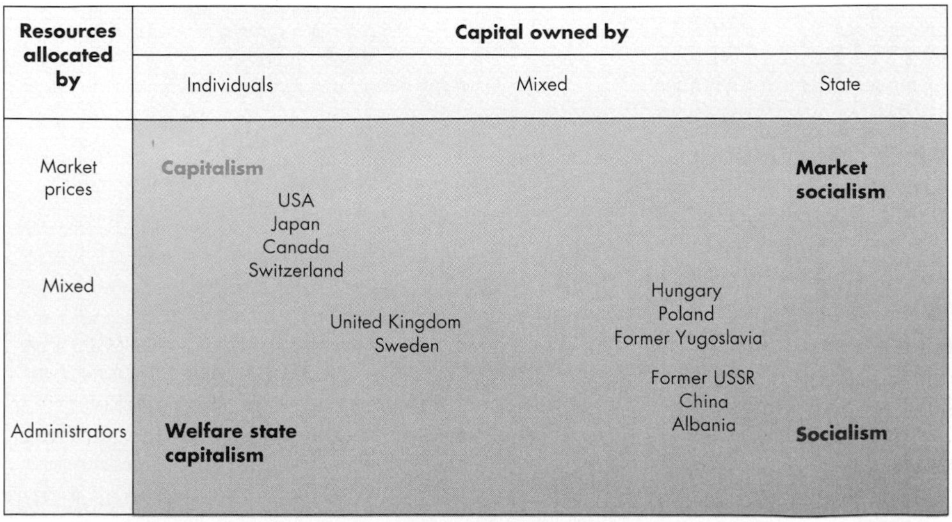

Resources allocated by	Capital owned by		
	Individuals	Mixed	State
Market prices	**Capitalism** USA Japan Canada Switzerland		**Market socialism**
Mixed		United Kingdom Sweden	Hungary Poland Former Yugoslavia
Administrators	**Welfare state capitalism**		Former USSR China Albania **Socialism**

Under capitalism, individuals own capital – farms and factories, plant and equipment – and resources are allocated by markets. Under socialism, the state owns capital and resources are allocated by a planning and command system. Market socialism combines state ownership of capital with a market allocation of resources. Welfare state capitalism combines private capital ownership with a high degree of state intervention in the allocation of resources.

implemented by creating a set of sanctions and rewards that ensure that the commands are carried out.

No country has used an economic system that precisely corresponds to one of these extreme types, but the United States, Japan and Switzerland come closest to being capitalist economies and Albania, the former Soviet Union and China before the 1980s came closest to being socialist economies. Socialism evolved from the ideas of Karl Marx (see Our Advancing Knowledge, pp. 1022–1023).

Some countries combine private ownership with state ownership and some combine market price incentives with administrative incentives and central planning. **Market socialism** (also called **decentralized planning**) is an economic system that combines state ownership of capital and land with incentives based on a mixture of market and administered prices. Hungary and the former Yugoslavia have had market socialist economies. In such economies, planners set the prices at which the various production and distribution organizations are able to buy and sell, and then leave those organizations free to choose the quantities of inputs and outputs. But the prices set by the planners respond to the forces of demand and supply.

Another combination is welfare state capitalism. **Welfare state capitalism** combines the private ownership of capital and land with state intervention in markets that modify the price signals to which people respond. Sweden, the United Kingdom and other West European countries are examples of such economies.

Alternative Systems Compared

Since all economic systems are made up of a combination of the two extreme special cases – capitalism and socialism – let's examine these two extreme types a bit more closely.

Capitalism Figure 36.4 shows how capitalism solves the economic problem of scarcity. Households own the factors of production and are free to use those factors, and the incomes they receive from the sale of their services, in any way they choose. These choices are governed by their preferences. The preferences of households are all-powerful in a capitalist economy.

Households choose the quantity of each factor of

FIGURE 36.4

Capitalism's Solution to the Economic Problem

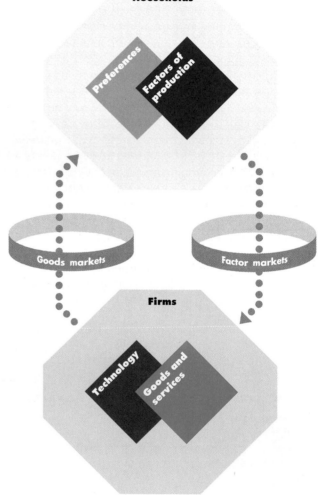

Under capitalism, the preferences of individual households dictate the choices that are made. Households own all the factors of production and sell the services of those factors in factor markets. Households decide which goods and services to consume and buy them in markets for goods and services. Firms decide which goods and services to produce and which factors of production to employ, selling their output and buying their inputs in the goods and factor markets. The markets find the prices that bring the quantities demanded and quantities supplied into equality for each factor of production and good or service. Capitalism economizes on information because households and firms need to know only the prices of various goods and factors that they buy and sell.

production to sell and firms that organize production choose the quantity of each factor to buy. These choices respond to the prices prevailing in the factor markets. An increase in a factor price gives households an incentive to increase the quantity supplied and gives firms an incentive to decrease the quantity demanded. Factor prices adjust to bring the quantity of each factor supplied into equality with the quantity of each factor demanded.

Households choose the quantity of each good or service to buy and firms choose the quantity of each to produce and sell. These choices respond to the prices confronting households and firms in the goods markets. An increase in the price of a good gives firms an incentive to increase the quantity supplied of that good and gives households an incentive to decrease the quantity demanded. Prices adjust to bring the quantity demanded and supplied into equality with each other.

Resources and goods and services flow in a clockwise direction from households to firms and back to households through the factor and goods markets. *What* is produced, *how* it is produced and *for whom* it is produced is determined by the preferences of the households, the resources that they own, and the technologies available to the firms.

Nobody *plans* the capitalist economy. Doctors perform nearly miraculous life-saving surgery by using sophisticated computer-controlled equipment. The equipment is designed by medical and electronic engineers, programmed by mathematicians, financed by insurance companies and banks, and bought and installed by hospital administrators. Each individual household and firm involved in this process allocates the resources that it controls in the way that seems best for it. The firms try to maximize profit and the households try to maximize utility. And these plans are coordinated in the markets for health care equipment, computers, engineers, computer programmers, insurance, hospital services, nurses, doctors, and hundreds of other markets for items that range from anaesthetic chemicals to apple juice.

When a surgeon performs an operation, an incredible amount of information is used. Yet no one possesses this information. It is not centralized in one place. The capitalist economic system economizes on information. Each household and firm needs to know very little about the other households and firms with which it does business. The reason is that *prices convey most of the information they need.* By comparing the prices of factors of produc-

tion, households choose the quantity of each factor to supply. And by comparing the prices of goods and services, they choose the quantity of each to buy. Similarly, by comparing the prices of factors of production, firms choose the quantity of each factor to use, and by comparing the prices of goods and services, they choose the quantity of each to supply.

Socialism Figure 36.5 shows how socialism solves the economic problem of scarcity. In this case the planners' preferences carry the most weight. Those preferences dictate the activities of the production enterprises. The planners control capital and natural resources, directing them to the uses that satisfy their priorities. The planners also decide what types of jobs will be available, and the state plays a large role in the allocation of the only factor of production owned by households – labour.

The central plan is communicated to state-owned enterprises which use the factors of production and the available technologies to produce goods and services. These goods and services are supplied to households in accordance with the central plan. The purchases by each individual household are determined by household preferences, but the total amount available is determined by the central planners.

A centrally planned economy has prices, but prices do not adjust to make the quantity demanded and supplied equal. Instead, they are set to achieve social objectives. For example, the prices of staple food products are set at low levels so that even the poorest families can afford an adequate basic diet. The effect of setting such prices at low levels is chronic shortages. The incentives that people respond to are the penalties and rewards that superiors can impose on and give to their subordinates.

REVIEW

The economic problem of *what*, *how* and *for whom* to produce the various goods and services is solved in different ways by different economic systems. Capitalism solves it by permitting households and firms to exchange factors of production and goods and services in markets. Firms produce the items that maximize their profits,

FIGURE 36.5

Socialism's Solution to the Economic Problem

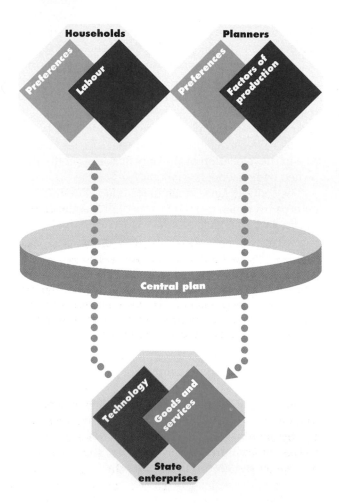

Under socialism, the preferences of the planners dictate the choices that are made. The planners control all the capital and natural resources owned by the state. They draw up plans and issue orders that determine how these resources will be used in the production of goods and services. Households decide which goods and services to consume and buy them in markets for goods and services. State enterprises produce the goods and services and employ the factors of production required by the central plan. The output of state enterprises is shipped to other enterprises in accordance with the plan or sold in the markets for goods and services. Prices are set by the planners to achieve social objectives and bear no relation to the quantities demanded and quantities supplied. Prices set at low levels for social reasons – as in the case of basic food products – result in chronic shortages.

households buy the goods that maximize their utility, and markets adjust prices to make buying and selling plans compatible. Socialism solves the economic problem by setting up a central planning system. The planners decide what will be produced and communicate their plans to state-owned enterprises. Incentives to fulfil the plan are created by a series of non-monetary rewards and sanctions. Each household decides what it wants to buy, but the total amount available is determined by the planners. Shortages, especially of basic staple food products, frequently arise. ◆

The rich countries of today attained their high living standards as a result of sustained economic growth. The poor countries of today will join the rich countries of tomorrow only if they can find ways of attaining and maintaining rapid growth. But what determines a country's economic growth rate? Let's turn to an examination of this crucial question.

Economic Growth

In aggregate, income equals the value of output. Thus to increase average income, a country has to increase its output. A country's output depends on its resources and the techniques it employs for transforming these resources into outputs. This relationship between resources and outputs is the *production function*. There are three types of resource:

◆ Land
◆ Labour
◆ Capital

Land includes all the natural, non-produced resources such as land itself, the minerals under it and all other non-produced inputs. The quantity of these resources is determined by nature and countries have no choice but to put up with whatever natural resources they happen to have. Countries cannot achieve rapid and sustained economic growth by increasing their stock of natural resources. But countries can and do experience fluctuations in income as a result of fluctuations in the prices of their natural resources. Furthermore, there are times at which those prices are rising quickly and such periods bring temporary income growth. The late 1970s is an example of a period in which resource-rich countries experienced rapid income growth as a result of rising commodity prices. But to achieve long-run, sustained income growth, countries have to look beyond their natural resources.

One such source of increased output is a sustained increase in *labour* resources. That is, a country can produce more output over the years simply because its population of workers grows. But for each successively larger generation of workers to have a higher income *per person* than the previous generation, output per person must increase. Population growth, on its own, does not lead to higher output per person.

The resource most responsible for rapid and sustained economic growth is capital. There are two broad types of capital – physical and human. *Physical capital* includes such things as roads and railways, dams and irrigation systems, tractors and ploughs, factories, lorries and cars, and buildings of all kinds. *Human capital* is the accumulated knowledge and skills of the working population. As individuals accumulate more capital, their incomes grow. Human capital accumulation is probably more important than physical capital in achieving a high rate of real income growth. As nations accumulate more capital per worker, labour productivity and output per capita grow.

To study the behaviour of per capita output, we use the per capita production function. The **per capita production function** shows how output per person varies as the per person stock of capital varies, in a given state of knowledge about alternative technologies. Figure 36.6 illustrates the production per person function. Output per person is measured on the vertical axis and the stock of capital per person on the horizontal axis. Curve *PF* shows how output per person varies as the amount of capital per person varies. A rich country such as the United Kingdom has a large amount of capital per person and a large output per person. A poor country such as Ethiopia has hardly any capital and very low output per person.

Capital Accumulation

By accumulating capital, a country can grow and move along its per capita production function. The greater the amount of capital (per person), the greater is output (per person). But the fundamental *law of diminishing returns* applies to the per

FIGURE 36.6

The Per Capita Production Function

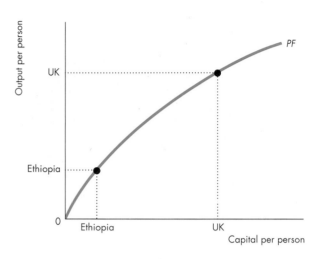

The per capita production function (*PF*) traces how output per person varies as the stock of capital per person varies. If two countries use the same technology, but one country has a larger capital stock, that country will also have a higher income per person. For example, suppose that Ethiopia and the United Kingdom each use the same technology. Ethiopia has a low capital stock per person and low level of output per person. The United Kingdom has a large capital stock per person and a large output rate per person.

capita production function. That is, as capital per person increases, output per person also increases but by decreasing increments. Thus there is a limit to the extent to which a country can grow merely by accumulating capital. Eventually, the country reaches the point at which the extra output from extra capital is simply not worth the effort of accumulating more capital. At such a point, it pays the country to consume rather than to increase its capital stock.

But no country has yet reached such a point because the per capita production function is constantly shifting upward as a result of improvements in technology. Let's see how technological change affects output and growth.

Technological Change

Although rich countries have much more capital per person than poor countries, that is not the only difference between them. Typically, rich countries use

Understanding the Limits of Central Planning

> 'The more complicated the whole, the more dependent we become on that division of knowledge between individuals whose separate efforts are coordinated by the impersonal... price system.'
>
> FRIEDRICH VON HAYEK
> *The Road to Serfdom*

Our economy is a highly planned one. But it is not centrally planned. The planning takes place inside corporations – some of them huge. Unilever, for example, is bigger than many countries. If it makes sense to plan Unilever's economy, why doesn't it make sense to plan a national economy?

This question has puzzled and divided economists for many years. The answer given by Friedrich von Hayek is that an economy produces billions of different goods and services, while a corporation, even a very large one, produces only a limited range of items. As a consequence, central planning requires the centralization of vast amounts of information that it is extremely costly to collect. The market economizes on this information. Each household or firm needs to know only the prices of the range of goods and services that it buys and sells. No household or firm needs to know every price. And none needs to know the technologies for producing anything beyond its area of specialization. Markets find the prices that make the plans of producers and consumers consistent.

But Hayek's answer leaves open another question. Why does Unilever plan? Why isn't the market used to allocate resources inside Unilever? This question was answered by Ronald H. Coase. Planning, he explained, economizes on transactions costs, while the market economizes on information costs. There is an optimal size of the planning unit (firm) and an optimal extent of the market for each activity.

Before 1978, the farms of China were operated as part of the national economic plan. The planners decided what would be produced and how the food would be distributed. Peasant farmers received an allocation of food, but their rewards were unrelated to their efforts. Food production and living standards were low. In 1978, Den Xiaoping reformed the farms. Families were permitted to take long-term leases on their land and to decide what to produce and where to sell it. The result was a massive increase in food production and a rapid increase in the standard of living. By 1984, the farms had become so productive that China became an *exporter* of grain.

Deng Xiaoping's 1978 economic reforms have had dramatic effects on China's large cities and urban population. New laws that permitted the creation of private firms resulted in massive numbers of new private enterprises springing up – manufacturing a wide range of consumer goods and providing employment for people who were no longer needed on the increasingly efficient farms. By 1990, real income per person had increased to 2.5 times its 1978 level. Between 1982 and 1988, real income per person grew at a staggering 9.7 per cent a year, almost doubling in six years. Many of the new private firms sell on world markets, and China's exports grew at a much faster rate than GDP during the 1980s. By 1990, they stood at 17 per cent of GDP.

The poor economic performance of the former Soviet Union, the communist countries of Eastern Europe and China before 1978 suggests that planning was taken too far in those countries and that the scope of the market was too restricted. These countries were run like big firms, but the firms were too big.

Karl Marx: An Alternative Economic Vision

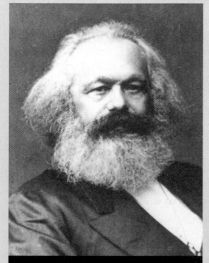

KARL MARX

Karl Marx (1818–1883) was a social scientist (political scientist, sociologist and economist) of extraordinary breadth and influence. Born in Germany, he spent most of his adult life in London, using the British Museum as his workplace. With little income, life was harsh for Marx and his wife (his childhood sweetheart to whom he was devoted). Marx's major work in economics was *Das Kapital*, in which he argued that capitalism was self-destructive and would be replaced by a system in which private property was abolished and a central plan replaced the market – a system he called 'communism'. Events have rejected Marx's theory, and his lasting contribution to modern economics is negligible. But his contribution to modern politics is substantial. Marxism, a political creed based on his ideas, thrives throughout much of the world today.

more productive technologies than do poor countries. That is, even if they have the same capital per person, the rich country produces more output than the poor country. For example, a farmer in a rich country might use a 10 horsepower tractor, whereas a farmer in a poor country might literally use 10 horses. Each has the same amount of 'horsepower' but the output achieved using the tractor is considerably more than that produced by using 10 horses. The combination of better technology and more capital per person accentuates still further the difference between the rich and poor countries.

Figure 36.7 illustrates the importance of the difference that technological advance makes. Imagine that the year is 1790 and both the United Kingdom and Ethiopia (then called Abyssinia) use the same techniques of production and have the same per capita production function, PF_{1790}. With a larger stock of capital per person, the United Kingdom pro-

duces a higher level of output per person in 1790 than does Ethiopia. By 1994, technological advances adopted in the United Kingdom, but not in Ethiopia, enable the United Kingdom to produce more output from given inputs. The per capita production function in the United Kingdom shifts upward to PF_{1994}. Output per person in the United Kingdom in 1994 is much higher than it was in 1790 for two reasons. First, the stock of capital equipment per person has increased dramatically; second, the techniques of production have improved, resulting in an upward shift in the production function.

The faster the pace of technological advance, the faster the production function shifts upward. The faster the pace of capital accumulation, the more quickly a country moves along its production function. Both of these forces lead to increased per capita output. A poor country becomes a rich country, partly by moving along its production function and partly by adopting better technology, thereby shifting its production function upward.

The importance of the connection between capital accumulation and output growth is illustrated in Fig. 36.8. Capital accumulation is measured by the percentage of output represented by investment. (Recall that investment is the purchase of new capital equipment.) The figure shows what has been happening to investment over time in developing countries and industrial countries and in the two extreme cases of developing countries – Singapore and Ethiopia. As you can see in part (a), the developing countries have been steadily increasing the percentage of income invested, while in industrial countries that percentage has declined slightly. Fast-growing Singapore invests more than 40 per cent of its income. Slow-growing Ethiopia invests less than 15 per cent of its income. The source of Singapore's dramatic growth and of Ethiopia's almost static income level can be seen in part (b).

FIGURE 36.7

Technological Change

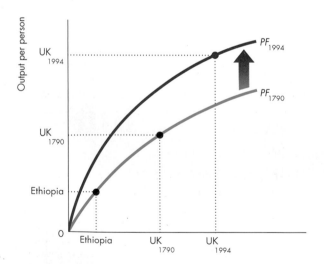

In 1790, the United Kingdom and Ethiopia have the same production function, PF_{1790}. By 1994, technological change has shifted the production function upward in the United Kingdom to PF_{1994}. Income per person in the United Kingdom has increased from UK_{1790} to UK_{1994}, partly because of an increase in the capital stock per person and partly because of an increase in productivity arising from the adoption of better technology.

R E V I E W

C ountries become rich by establishing and maintaining high rates of economic growth over prolonged periods. Economic growth results from the accumulation of capital and the adoption of

FIGURE 36.8

Investment Trends

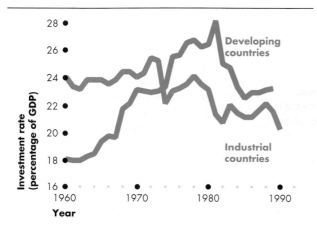

(a) Investment rates in industrial and developing countries

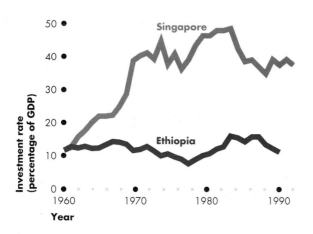

(b) Investment rates in Ethiopia and Singapore

The rate of investment in developing countries increased from 1960 to 1977 and subsequently decreased. Investment in industrial countries was steady during the 1960s and early 1970s but fell after 1974 (part a). Investment in Singapore has increased dramatically while that in Ethiopia has been almost constant (part b). High investment in Singapore has led to rapid growth, while low investment in Ethiopia has led to low growth.

Source: International Monetary Fund, *International Financial Statistics Yearbook*, 1992.

increasingly efficient technologies. The more rapid the accumulation of capital and the more rapid the pace of technological change, the faster is the rate of economic growth. Small changes in economic growth rates maintained over a long period of time make large differences to income levels. ◆

Since 1978 China has gradually introduced a market economic system. Let's look at how the transition to a market economy has dramatically changed China's growth rate.

Economic Transition in China

China is the world's largest nation. In 1994, its population was more than 1.2 billion – almost a quarter of the world's population. Chinese civilization is ancient and has a splendid history, but the modern nation – the People's Republic of China – dates only from 1949. A compact summary of key periods in the economic history of the People's Republic is presented in Table 36.1.

Modern China began when a revolutionary communist movement, led by Mao Zedong, captured control of China, forcing the country's previous leader, Chiang Kai-shek (Jiang Jie-shi) on to the island of Formosa – now Taiwan. China is a socialist country, which is largely non-industrialized. It is a developing country.

During the early years of the People's Republic, urban manufacturing industry was taken over and operated by the state and the farms were collectivized. Also primary emphasis was placed on the production of capital equipment.

The Great Leap Forward

In 1958, Mao Zedong set the Chinese economy on what he called the Great Leap Forward. The **Great Leap Forward** was an economic plan based on small-scale, labour-intensive production. The Great Leap Forward paid little or no attention to linking individual pay to individual effort. Instead, a revolutionary commitment to the success of collective plans was relied upon. The Great Leap Forward was an economic failure. Productivity increased, but so slowly that living standards hardly changed. In the agricultural sector, massive injections of modern, high-yield seeds, improved irrigation and chemical fertilizers were insufficient to enable China to feed its population. The country became the largest importer of grains, edible vegetable oils and even raw cotton.

TABLE 36.1

A Compact Summary of Key Periods in the Economic History of the People's Republic of China

Period	Main economic events/characteristics
1949	◆ People's Republic of China established under Mao Zedong
1949–1952	◆ Economy centralized under a new communist government
	◆ Emphasis on heavy industry and 'socialist transformation'
1952–1957	◆ First five-year plan
1958–1960	◆ The Great Leap Forward: an economic reform plan based on labour-intensive production methods
	◆ Massive failure
1966	◆ Cultural Revolution: revolutionary zealots
1976	◆ Death of Mao Zedong
1978	◆ Deng Xiaoping's reforms: liberalization of agriculture and introduction of individual incentives
	◆ Growth rates accelerated
1989	◆ Democracy movement; government crackdown

The popular explanation within China for poor performance, especially in agriculture, was that the country had reached the limits of its arable land and that its population explosion was so enormous that agriculture was being forced to use substandard areas for farming. The key problem was that the revolutionary and ideological motivation for the Great Leap Forward degenerated into what came to be called the Cultural Revolution. Revolutionary zealots denounced productive managers, engineers, scientists and scholars, and banished them to the life of the peasant. Schools and universities were closed and the accumulation of human capital was severely disrupted.

Deng Xiaoping's Reforms

In 1978, two years after the death of Mao Zedong, the new Chinese leader, Deng Xiaoping, proclaimed major economic reforms. Collectivized agriculture

was abolished. Agricultural land was distributed among households on long-term leases. In exchange for a lease, a household agreed to pay a fixed tax and contracted to sell part of its output to the state. But the household made its own decisions on cropping patterns, the quantity and types of fertilizers and other inputs to use, and also hired its own workers. Private farm markets were liberalized and farmers received a higher price for their produce. Also, the state increased the price that it paid to farmers, especially for cotton and other non-grain crops.

The results of Deng Xiaoping's reforms have been astounding. Annual growth rates of output of cotton and oil-bearing crops increased a staggering fourteen-fold. Soybean production, which had been declining at an annual rate of 1 per cent between 1957 and 1978, now started to grow at 4 per cent a year. Growth rates of yields per hectare also increased dramatically. By 1984, a country that six years earlier had been the world's largest importer of agricultural products became a food exporter!

The reforms not only produced massive expansion in the agricultural sector. Increased rural incomes brought an expanding rural industrial sector that, by the middle 1980s, was employing a fifth of the rural population.

China has gone even further and is encouraging foreign investment and joint ventures. In addition, it is experimenting with formal capital markets and now has a stock market.

Motivated partly by political considerations, China is proclaiming the virtues of what it calls the 'one country, two systems' approach to economic management. The political source of this movement is the existence of two capitalist enclaves in which China has a close interest: Taiwan and Hong Kong. China claims sovereignty over Taiwan. It therefore wants to create an atmosphere in which it becomes possible for China to be 'reunified' at some future date. Hong Kong, a UK crown colony, is currently leased by the United Kingdom from China. When the lease expires in 1997, Hong Kong will become part of China. Anxious not to damage the economic prosperity of Hong Kong, China is proposing to continue operating Hong Kong as a capitalist economy. With Hong Kong and Taiwan as part of the People's Republic of China, the stage will be set for the creation of other capitalist 'islands' in such dynamic cities as Shanghai.

The results of this move towards capitalism in China are dramatically summarized in the country's real GDP growth statistics. Between 1978 and 1990,

FIGURE 36.9

Economic Growth in China

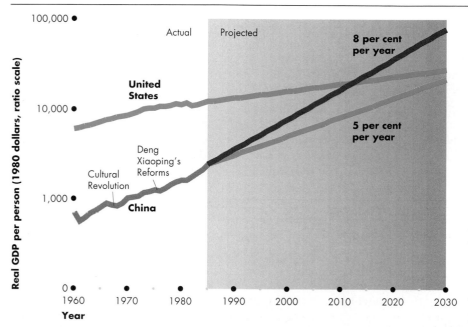

The growth of income per person in China is strongly influenced by the economic system. During the Cultural Revolution, income per person fell. Under a central planning and command mechanism in the early 1970s, income per person grew at a moderate pace. Under capitalist methods of production in agriculture following the 1978 reforms, growth of income per person increased dramatically. If China continues to grow at the pace it has achieved since 1978, and if the United States also maintains its post-1978 growth rate, China will catch up with the United States in 2010. Even if China slows to a 5 per cent growth rate, it will catch up with the United States in 2030.

Source: Alan Heston and Robert Summers, 'A New Set of International Comparisons of Real Product and Price Levels: Estimates for 130 Countries, 1950–1985,' *Review of Income and Wealth*, series 34, vol. 1, 1988, pp. 1–25, Appendix B.

real GDP per person grew at an average rate of 7.2 per cent a year – a 2.3-fold increase in income per person over the 12 year period. Between 1982 and 1988, real GDP per person grew at a staggering 9.7 per cent a year, almost doubling in a six year period. To see how staggering these growth rates are, look at Fig. 36.9. It shows the consequences of China and the United States maintaining their post-1978 average growth rates of real GDP per person. For the United States, that growth rate was a little over 1 per cent a year and for China it was almost 8 per cent a year. If it maintains these growth rates China catches up with the United States in a single generation by 2010. Even if China's growth slackens off to 5 per cent a year, with no change in the US growth rate, China catches up by 2030.

China is not only experiencing rapid growth of real income per person but is also increasing its international competitiveness. Its exports have grown during the 1980s at a much faster rate than GDP and, by 1990, stood at 17 per cent of GDP.

How has China achieved this dramatic success?

China's Success

China's success in achieving a high rate of economic growth has resulted from four features of its reforms.[1] They are:

◆ Massive rate of entry of new non-state firms
◆ Large increases in the productivity and profitability of state firms
◆ An efficient taxation system
◆ Gradual price deregulation

Entry of Non-state Firms The most rapidly growing sector of the Chinese economy during the 1980s was non-state industrial firms located typically in rural areas. This sector grew at an annual rate of 17.5 per cent between 1978 and 1990. In 1978, it produced

---

[1]This section is based on John McMillan and Barry Naughton, 'How to Reform a Planned Economy: Lessons from China', Graduate School of International Relations and Pacific Studies, University of California, San Diego, 1991.

22 per cent of the nation's industrial output. By 1990, it was producing 45 per cent of total industrial output. By contrast, the state-owned firms – the firms organized by the state under its national plan – shrank (relatively) from producing 78 per cent of total output in 1978 to 55 per cent in 1990.

The entry of new firms created a dramatic increase in competition both among the new firms and between the new firms and the state firms. This competition spurred both non-state and state firms into greater efficiency and productivity.

Increases in Productivity and Profitability of State Firms

China has not privatized its economy by selling off state firms. Instead, privatization has come from the entry of new firms. The state firms have continued to operate. But the government has a strong incentive to ensure that the state firms are profitable. If state firms make no profit, the government collects no taxes from them.

To achieve the greatest possible level of profit and tax revenue, the Chinese economic planners have changed the incentives faced by the managers of state enterprises to resemble those of the market incentives faced by the non-state sector. Managers of state-owned firms are paid according to the firm's performance – similar to managers in private firms.

The Chinese system gives incentives for managers of state enterprises to be extremely enterprising and productive. As a result of this new system the Chinese government is now able to auction off top management jobs. Potential managers bid for the right to be manager. The manager offering the best promise of performance, backed by a commitment of personal wealth, is the one that gets the job.

Efficient Taxation System

Firms (both private and state-owned) are taxed but the tax system is unusual and different from that in the UK economy. Firms are required to pay a fixed amount of profit in tax to the government. Once that fixed amount of tax has been paid, the firm keeps any additional profit it makes. In contrast, the tax system in the United Kingdom requires firms to pay a fixed percentage of their profits in tax. Thus in the United Kingdom, more profit means higher taxes while in China, taxes are set independently of a firm's profit level. The Chinese system creates much stronger incentives than does the UK system for firms to seek out and pursue profitable ventures.

Gradual Price Reform

China has not abandoned planning its prices. The socialist planning system keeps the prices of manufactured goods fairly high and keeps domestic prices higher than world prices. This pricing arrangement makes private enterprise production in China extremely profitable. In 1978, when the non-state sector was small, the profit rate in that sector was almost 40 per cent – for every pound invested 40 pence a year was earned. With such high profits there was a tremendous incentive for enterprising people to find niches and engage in creative and productive activity. The forces of competition have gradually lowered prices; rates of return, by 1990, had fallen to 10 per cent. But the price movements were gradual. There was no big bang adjustment of prices – no abandonment of the planning mechanism and rapid introduction of a free market system.

Growing Out of the Plan

As a result of the reforms adopted in the 1970s and pursued vigorously since then the Chinese economy has gradually become much more market-oriented and is, in effect, growing out of its central plan.[2] The proportion of the economy accounted for by private enterprise and market influenced prices has gradually increased and the proportion accounted for by state enterprises and planned and regulated prices has gradually decreased.

To sustain this process, changes in fiscal policy and monetary policy have been necessary. The reform of the economy has entailed the redesigning of the tax system. In a centrally planned economy the government's tax revenues come directly through its pricing policy. Also the government, as the controller of all financial institutions, receives all of the nation's saving. When the central planning system is replaced by the market, the government must establish a tax collection agency similar to the Inland Revenue in the United Kingdom. Also, it must establish financial markets so that the savings of households can be channelled into the growing private firms to finance their investment in new buildings, plant and equipment.

---

[2]Barry Naughton, *Growing Out of the Plan: Chinese Economic Reform, 1978–90*, Graduate School of International Relations and Pacific Studies, University of California, San Diego, 1992.

Despite the reform of its tax system, the government of China spends more than it receives in tax revenue and covers its deficit by the creation of money. The result is a steady rate of inflation. But the inflation in China is not out of control because the rapidly growing level of economic activity absorbs a great deal of the new money.

Whether China has found a way of making the transition from socialism to capitalism in a relatively painless way is a controversial issue. The violent suppression of the democracy movement in Tiananmen Square in the summer of 1989 suggests that China may have bought economic gains at the expense of political freedoms. But the experiment in comparative *economic* systems currently going on in China is one of the most exciting that the world has seen. Economists of all political shades of opinion will closely watch its outcome, and its lessons will be of enormous value for future generations – whatever those lessons turn out to be.

Let's now take a closer look at some other socialist economies. We'll begin with the country that invented central planning and 'exported' its system to the other socialist countries, the former Soviet Union.

Economic Change in the Former Soviet Union

The Soviet Union, or the Union of Soviet Socialist Republics (USSR), was founded in 1917 following the Bolshevik revolution led by Vladimir Ilyich Lenin. The union collapsed in 1991. The independent republics of the former Soviet Union are diverse and most are resource-rich. Their land area is three times that of the United States; their population is approaching 300 million, 20 per cent larger than the United States; they have vast reserves of coal, oil, iron ore, natural gas, timber and almost every other mineral resource. They are republics of enormous ethnic diversity with Russians making up 50 per cent of the population and many European, Asian and Arabic ethnic groups making up the other 50 per cent.

History of the Soviet Union

A compact economic history of the Soviet Union appears in Table 36.2. Although the nation was

founded in 1917, its economic management system was not put in place until the 1930s. The architect of this system was Joseph Stalin. The financial, manufacturing and transport sectors of the economy had been taken into state ownership and control by Lenin. Stalin added the farms to this list. He abolished the market and introduced a command planning mechanism, initiating a series of five-year plans that placed their major emphasis on setting and attaining goals for the production of capital goods. The production of consumer goods and services was given a secondary place and personal economic conditions were harsh. With emphasis on the production of capital goods, the Soviet economy grew quickly.

By the 1950s, after Stalin's death, steady economic growth continued, but the emphasis in economic planning gradually shifted away from capital goods towards consumer goods production. In the 1960s, the growth rate began to sag and by the 1970s and early 1980s, the Soviet economy was running into serious problems. Productivity was actually declining, especially in agriculture but also in industry. Growth slowed and, on some estimates, per capita income in the Soviet Union began to fall. It was in this situation that Mikhail Gorbachev came to power with plans to restructure the Soviet economy, based on the idea of increased individual accountability and rewards based on performance.

As a unified political entity, the Soviet Union effectively disintegrated following an unsuccessful coup to topple former President Mikhail Gorbachev in August 1991. Political freedoms began to be enjoyed in the late 1980s under President Gorbachev's programmes of *perestroika* (restructuring) and *glasnost* (openness). These political freedoms released nationalist and ethnic feelings that had been held in check for 50 years and created a virtual explosion of political activity. At the same time the economies of the now independent republics underwent tumultuous change.

We are going to look at that change. But you will better appreciate the severity and nature of the problems posed by economic change if we first look at the way the Soviet Union operated before it abandoned its central planning system.

Soviet-style Central Planning

Soviet-style central planning was a method of economic planning and control that had four key elements:

TABLE 36.2

A Compact Summary of Key Periods in the Economic History of the Soviet Union

Period	Main economic events/characteristics
1917–1921 (Lenin)	◆ Bolshevik Revolution
	◆ Nationalization of banking, industry and transport
	◆ Forced requisitioning of agricultural output
1921–1924 (Lenin)	◆ New Economic Policy, 1921
	◆ Market allocation of most resources
1928–1953 (Stalin)	◆ Abolition of market
	◆ Introduction of command planning and five-year plans
	◆ Collectivization of farms
	◆ Emphasis on capital goods and economic growth
	◆ Harsh conditions
1953–1970 (Khrushchev to Brezhnev)	◆ Steady growth
	◆ Increased emphasis on consumer goods
1970–1985 (Brezhnev to Chernenko)	◆ Deteriorating productivity in agriculture and industry
	◆ Slowdown in growth
1985–1991 (Gorbachev)	◆ *Perestroika* – reforms based on increased accountability
1991	◆ Break-up of the Soviet Union

◆ Administrative hierarchy
◆ Iterative planning process
◆ Legally binding commands
◆ Taut and inflexible plans

Administrative Hierarchy A large and complex hierarchy implemented and controlled the central economic plan that determined almost every aspect of economic activity. A **hierarchy** is an organization arranged in ranks, each rank being subordinate to the one above it. At the top was the highest *political* authority. Immediately below it was the economic planning ministry, the senior of a large number of ministries. Below the planning ministry were a large number of ministries that were responsible for the detailed aspects of production. For example, one ministry dealt with engineering production, another with fruit and vegetables, and another with rail transport. Responsibility for production processes was divided and subdivided yet further down to the level of the individual factories that carried out the production processes. For example, engineering was divided into light, heavy, electrical and civil divisions. Light engineering was divided into departments that dealt with individual product groups, such as ball bearings. And finally, ball bearings were manufactured in a number of factories. At each level of the hierarchy, there were superiors and subordinates. Superiors had absolute and arbitrary power over their subordinates.

Iterative Planning Process An iterative process is a repetitive series of calculations that get closer and closer to a solution. Central planning is iterative. A plan was proposed and adjustments were repeatedly made until all the elements of the plan were consistent with each other. But a plan was not arrived at as the result of a set of neat calculations performed on a computer. Rather, the process involved a repeated sequence of communications of proposals and reactions down and up the administrative hierarchy.

The process began with the issue of a big picture set of objectives or directives by the highest political authority. These directives were translated into targets by the planning ministry and retranslated into ever more detailed targets as they were passed down the hierarchy. Tens of millions of raw materials and intermediate goods featured in the detailed plans of the Soviet Union, which filled 70 volumes, or 12,000 pages, each year.

When the targets were specified as production plans for individual products, the factories reacted with their own assessments of what was feasible. Reactions as to feasibility were passed back up the hierarchy, and the central planning ministry made the targets and reports of feasibility consistent. A good deal of bargaining took place in this process, the superiors demanded the impossible and subordinates claimed requests to be infeasible.

Legally Binding Commands   Once a consistent (even if infeasible) plan had been determined by the planning ministry, the plan was given the force of law in a set of binding commands from the political authority. The commands were translated into increasing detail as they passed down the chain of command and were implemented by the production units in a way that most nearly satisfied the superiors of each level.

Taut and Inflexible Plans   In the former Soviet Union, the targets set by superiors for their subordinates were infeasible. The idea was that in the attempt to do the impossible, more would be achieved than if an easily attained task was set. The outcome of this planning process was a set of taut and inflexible plans. A taut plan is one that has no slack built into it. If one unit fails to meet its planned targets, all the other units that rely on the output of the first unit will fail to meet their targets also. An inflexible plan is one that has no capacity for reactions to changing circumstances.

Faced with impossible targets, factories produced a combination of goods and services that enabled their superiors to report plan fulfilment, but the individual items produced did not meet the needs of the other parts of the economy. No factory received exactly the quantity and types of inputs needed, and the economy was unable to respond to changes in circumstances. In practice, the plan for the current year was the outcome of the previous year plus a wished for but unattainable increment.

The Market Sector

A substantial amount of economic activity in the Soviet Union took place outside the central plan, in a market sector. Most of this activity was in agriculture. During the 1980s there were 35 million private plots worked by rural households in the USSR. Although these private plots were less than 3 per cent of the agricultural land of the Soviet Union they produced close to 25 per cent of total agricultural output and 33 per cent of all the meat and milk. Some estimates suggested that the productivity on private plots was 40 times that of state enterprise farms and collective farms. Other economic activities undertaken by Soviet citizens outside the planning system were illegal.

Money in the Soviet Union

Money played a minor role in the economy of the Soviet Union. It was used in the market sector and in the state sector to pay wages and buy consumer goods and services. But all the transactions among state enterprises and between state enterprises and government took place as part of the *physical* plan, and money was used only as a means of keeping records. International trade was undertaken by the direct exchange of goods for goods – barter.

Soviet Economic Decline

Table 36.3 illustrates the growth performance of the Soviet economy between 1928 and 1990. The economy performed extraordinarily well before 1970. Growth rates of output in excess of 5 per cent a year were achieved on average for the entire period between 1928 and 1970 bringing an eight-fold increase in aggregate output over these years. Then the growth rate began to fall. During the 1970s, output expanded by 3.2 per cent a year, and in the 1980s, growth collapsed to 2 per cent a year between 1980 and 1986 and then to only 1 per cent a year between 1986 and 1990. In 1990, the economy shrank by 4 per cent.

Why did the economy perform well before 1970 and then begin to deliver successively slower growth rates? And what brought the virtual collapse of the Soviet economy during the 1980s? The combination and interaction of three features were responsible. They are:

♦ Transition from investment to consumption economy
♦ External shocks
♦ Taut and inflexible plans

Transition from Investment to Consumption Economy

Before 1960, the Soviet economic planners concentrated on producing capital goods and maintaining a rapid rate of investment in new buildings, plant and equipment. They ran the Soviet economy like a large firm intent on rapid growth putting all its profits into yet more growth. The central planning system is at its best when implementing such a strategy. The planners know exactly which types of capital they need to remove or reduce bottlenecks and can achieve a high rate of growth.

During the 1960s the orientation of the Soviet economy began to change with a relative increase in

TABLE 36.3

Economic Growth Rates in the Soviet Union

Year	Growth rate (per cent per year)
1928–1937	5.4
1940–1960	5.7
1960–1970	5.1
1970–1979	3.2
1980–1986	2.0
1987	1.6
1988	4.4
1989	2.5
1990	–4.0

Economic growth in the Soviet Union was rapid between 1928 and 1970. During the 1970s, growth began to slow down and the growth rate became successively lower until the early 1990s, when the economy began to contract.

Sources: Paul R. Gregory and Robert C. Stuart, *Soviet Economic Structure and Performance*, 2nd edition (Harper & Row Publishers, Inc., New York, 1981); US Central Intelligence Agency, *USSR: Measures of Economic Growth and Development, 1950–1980*, US Congress, Joint Economic Committee (Washington, DC: US Government Printing Office, 1982); US Central Intelligence Agency, 'Gorbachev's Economic Program', Report to US Congress, Subcommittee on National Security Economics (13 April, 1989, Washington, DC: US Government Printing Office, 1989); and *The Economy of the USSR*, The World Bank, Washington, DC, 1990.

the production of consumer goods and services. By the 1970s and 1980s, this process had gone much further. A centrally planned economy is very bad at handling the complexities of producing a large variety of types, sizes, colours, designs and styles of consumer goods. The planners need to collect and take into account more information than their computers can handle.

As a result, the planners order the wrong goods to be produced, creating surpluses of some and chronic shortages of others. Easy-to-produce plain white bread is available in excessive quantities at give-away prices and hard-to-produce English muffins can't be found at any price. Surplus goods get wasted or used inefficiently, and increasing amounts of the resources that could be used to add to the economy's productive capital get diverted to

meeting ever more desperate consumer demands. Gradually, economic growth vanishes.

External Shocks The Soviet Union was the world's largest producer of crude oil and benefited enormously, during the 1970s, from the massive oil price increases. The extra revenue obtained from oil exports helped, during those years, to mask the problems just described. But the 1980s brought *falling* oil prices and sharply exposed the problems of the Soviet Union.

During the late 1980s, the countries of Eastern Europe that had been the Soviet Union's traditional trading partners embarked on their own transitions to market economies and began to look to the West for trading opportunities. As a consequence, the Soviet Union's sources of international trade collapsed.

Another major external shock was the escalation of the arms race. When the United States embarked on the 'Star Wars' programme, the implications for the Soviet defence programme were devastating. Mounting an equivalent programme would probably have been impossible, but even a smaller-scale response would have sapped the Soviet economy of its capacity to devote high-technology resources to meeting private consumption demands.

Taut and Inflexible Plans A flexible economic system might have been able to deal with the switch to consumption goods production and the consequences of a changing world economic environment. But the Soviet economy was not flexible. On the contrary, with its system of taut planning and its unresponsive command structure, it was only able to attempt to produce the same bundle of goods as it had produced in the previous year. With less revenue from oil and other raw material exports, fewer imported inputs could be obtained. Imbalances in the central plan rippled through the entire economy disrupting the production of all goods and putting the system itself under enormous strain.

Living Standards in the Late 1980s

The problems of the Soviet economy are put in sharp focus in Fig. 36.10. In this figure, the productivity and consumption levels of the former Soviet Union are compared with those of the United States, Western Europe (Germany, France and Italy), Japan and Portugal. As you can see from the

FIGURE 36.10

GDP and Consumption in the Soviet Union and Other Countries

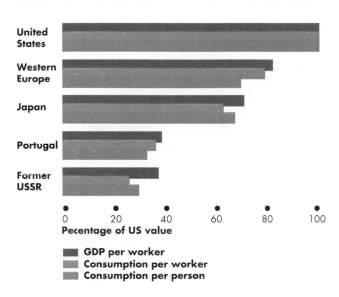

GDP per worker in the Soviet Union in the mid-1980s was less than 40 per cent of its level in the United States and similar to the levels in Portugal. Consumption per worker and consumption per person were even lower at less than 30 per cent of the US level. The Soviet Union lagged considerably behind Western Europe and Japan in GDP and consumption level.

Source: Abram Bergon, 'The USSR Before the Fall: How Poor and Why', *Journal of Economic Perspectives*. Volume 5, Fall, 1991, p. 44.

figure, average worker productivity in the Soviet Union, measured by GDP per worker, is less than 40 per cent of real GDP per worker in the United States and lags considerably behind the other West European countries and Japan. A similar picture is painted by comparing consumption per worker and consumption per person. The capitalist country whose level of productivity and consumption is most similar to that of the Soviet Union is Portugal.

Market Economy Reforms

By the end of the 1980s, there was widespread dissatisfaction throughout the Soviet Union with the economic planning system, and a process of transition towards the market economy began. This process had three main elements:

◆ Relaxing central plan enforcement
◆ Deregulating prices
◆ Permitting limited private ownership of firms

Relaxing Central Plan Enforcement   The transition in all three areas was one of gradual change. But the relaxation of central plan enforcement was the fastest and most far-reaching element of the transition. The idea was that by relaxing central control over the annual plan and permitting the managers of state enterprises greater freedom to act like the managers of private firms, enterprises would be able to respond to changing circumstances without having to wait for orders from the centre.

Deregulating Prices   Price deregulation was gradual and covered a limited range of products. Here, the idea was that by removing price controls the price mechanism would be able to allocate scarce resources to their highest-value uses. Shortages would disappear and be replaced by available but sometimes expensive goods and services. High prices would strengthen the inducement for producers to increase the quantities supplied.

Permitting Limited Private Ownership of Firms   The move towards the private ownership of firms was extremely gradual. The idea here was that enterprising individuals would able to move quickly to seize profit opportunities, responding to price signals much more rapidly than the replaced planning system could respond to shortages and bottlenecks. But the transition process ran into problems.

Transition Problems

There are three major problems confronting the republics of the former Soviet Union that complicate their transition to the capitalist market economic system. They are:

◆ Value and legal systems alien to capitalism
◆ Collapse of traditional trade flows
◆ Fiscal crisis

Value and Legal Systems   Seventy-five years of socialist dictatorship have left a legacy of values and memories alien to the rapid and successful establishment of a capitalist, market economy. The political leaders and people of the former Soviet Union have no personal memories of free political institutions and markets. And they have been educated, both formally and informally, to believe in a political creed in which traders and speculators are not just shady characters, but criminals. Unlearning these values will be a slow and perhaps painful process.

The legal system is also unsuited to the needs of a market economy in two ways. First, there are no well established property rights and methods of protecting those rights. Second, and more important, there is no tradition of government behaving like individuals and firms before the rule of law. In the Soviet system, the government *was* the law. Its economic plan and the arbitrary decisions made by superiors at each level in the hierarchy were the only law that counted. Rational, self-promoting actions taken outside the plan were illegal. It will take a long time to establish a legal system based on private property rights and the rule of law.

Collapse of Traditional Trade Flows   A centrally administered empire has collapsed and its constituent republics have decided to create a loose federation. Such a political reorganization can have devastating economic consequences. The most serious of these is the collapse of traditional trade flows. The Soviet Union was a highly interdependent grouping of republics organized on a wheel-hub basis with Moscow (and to a lesser degree Leningrad – now St Petersburg) at its centre. This view of the Soviet economy is shown in Fig. 36.11. The figure also shows the magnitude of the flows of goods from the republics through the Moscow hub.

The most heavily dependent republic, Belarus, delivered 70 per cent of its output to other republics and received a similar value of goods from the other republics. Even the least dependent republic, Kazakhstan, traded 30 per cent of its production with the other republics. The vast amount of inter-republic trade, managed by the central planners and channelled through the Moscow hub, means that individual enterprise managers had (and still have) little knowledge of where their products end up being used or of where their inputs originate.

With the collapse of the central plan, managers must search for supplies and for markets. Until they have built new networks of information, shortages of raw materials and other material inputs will be common and a lack of markets will stunt production. This problem can be solved by the activities of specialist traders and speculators, but the emergence of this

class of economic agent is likely to be slow because of political attitudes towards this type of activity.

The collapse of an economic empire does not inevitably lead to a collapse of traditional trade flows and an associated decline in production. But it usually has done so. The most similar collapse this century was that of the Austro-Hungarian Empire in 1919.

Like the Soviet Union, the Austro-Hungarian Empire was a centralized economic system organized with Vienna and Budapest as its hubs. There was a single currency and free trade. The empire was a great economic success, achieving rapid growth of living standards for its people. Following the collapse of the empire, tariffs were introduced, each country established its own currency, trade flows dried up and economic growth declined.

Fiscal Crisis   Under the central planning system of the Soviet Union, the central government collected taxes in an arbitrary way. One source of revenue was a tax on consumer goods, the rate of which was increased to eliminate shortages. With prices now being free to adjust to eliminate shortages, this source of government revenue has dried up. Another source (the major source) of revenue was the profits of the state enterprises. Since the state owned these enterprises, they also received the profits. With the collapse of central planning and the decentralization of control and privatization of state enterprises, this source of revenue has also declined.

Money played virtually no role in the Soviet Union's system of central planning. Workers received their wages in currency and used it to purchase consumer goods and services. But for the state enterprises and the government, money was just a unit for keeping records. With the collapse of central planning, money has become more important, especially for the government. With the loss of its traditional sources of revenue, and with no change in its spending, the government has a large budget deficit. It covers this deficit by printing money, and the result is inflation. The inflation rate during the final six months of the life of the Soviet Union – the first half of 1991 – reached close to 200 per cent and it was on a rising path.

Inflation is not an inevitable accompaniment of the collapse of an economic empire, but like the collapse of trade flows, it has happened before. The rate of growth of the newly created currencies of Austria, Hungary, Poland, Romania and Yugoslavia following the disintegration of the Austro-Hungarian

FIGURE 36.11

The Wheel-hub Economy of the Soviet Union

■ **Percentage of republic output exported to other republics**
■ **Percentage of republic output consumed within republic**

The Soviet economy was organized on a wheel-hub model. Vast amounts of goods and services were traded among the republics, but mainly through the Moscow hub. The percentages of production in each republic exported to other republics is shown along the spokes of the wheel.

Source: *The Economy of the USSR*, The World Bank, Washington, DC, 1990, p. 51.

Empire were extremely rapid and lead to hyperinflation in those countries. In Poland, the hyperinflation reached an annual rate of 250 million per cent.

R E V I E W

he Soviet Union's system of central economic planning and state ownership was established in the 1930s. Under this system, a hierarchical administrative structure engaged in an iterative planning process to arrive at a consistent economic plan. The plan was implemented by the political authority issuing legally binding commands that were translated into ever greater detail as they were passed down the chain of command. ◆ ◆ In practice, the plans were infeasible and inflexible and required that each production unit bettered its previous year's achievement by a target (but infeasible) amount. The system performed well before 1970 but became steadily less effective during the 1970s and 1980s. The system's inflexibility could not cope with the transition from an investment to a consumption economy and with a series of external shocks. As a result, its growth rate slowed and eventually output began to decrease. ◆ ◆ A market reform process was begun that deregulated prices, permitted limited private ownership of firms and relaxed the enforcement of the central plan. But the value and legal systems, the collapse of traditional trade flows, and a loss of tax revenue and inflation are making the transition extremely costly. ◆

Let's now examine economic transition in Eastern Europe.

Economic Transition in Eastern Europe

he formerly planned economies of Eastern Europe – Czechoslovakia, East Germany, Hungary and Poland – are also making transitions to market economies. The processes being followed and the problems faced are similar to those of the former Soviet Union. But their problems, although severe, take different forms from those of the Soviet Union. The major differences arise from political factors. Let's take a brief look at the transition process in these countries. See also Reading Between the Lines on pp. 1036–1037.

East Germany

For East Germany, the transition from a centrally planned economy has been the most dramatic and the most complete. On 3 October, 1990, East Germany united with West Germany. East Germany was a country with 16 million people, 26 per cent of the population of West Germany, and with a

Success and Failure in Eastern Europe

Hungary, the Czech Republic, and Poland are making economic reforms work.

Bulgaria, Romania, Slovakia and Ukraine might make reforms work but have not done so yet.

Russia and other ex-Soviet states are not taking the steps necessary to reform their economies.

Reform has succeeded where state enterprises have been privatized on a mass scale, and where large numbers of private businesses have sprung up offering new jobs.

The key to success is accepting that public-sector jobs must become private-sector jobs as quickly as possible and that, in the transition, production will fall and unemployment rise.

THE GLOBE AND MAIL, 20 FEBRUARY 1993

The competition to go capitalist

Peter Cook

THREE years after the fall of the Berlin Wall, Eastern Europe is dividing into two camps. The division is economic, and separates those countries that are making reforms work and those that have failed to make the transition to capitalism.

In the successful category are Hungary, the Czech Republic and Poland, together with two promising but still lagging reformers, Romania and Bulgaria. In the second category are Russia and other ex-Soviet states, though an exception can be made for Ukraine, which has suddenly become an avid reformer. Slovakia, newly divorced from the Czech Republic, is rated a borderline reformer that will probably slip backward in the months ahead....

...reforms succeed best at the local or micro-economic level.

Some ex-communist economies have turned the corner because so many private businesses have sprung up offering new, viable jobs to replace the old, non-viable ones. Reform has been a success where this has happened, a failure where it has not....

In the early days, (where reform has succeeded) a lot of emphasis was put on mass privatisation of existing big enterprises. Several countries, such as Poland and Hungary, have done better by liquidating or selling factories cheaply and quickly. The Czech Republic auctioned off some businesses, and is giving away others in a voucher scheme that is open to all its citizens.

However, it is not the old companies but the new ones that will give Poland its first taste of growth this year after four years of declining output; that have brought the unemployment rate in the Czech Republic below 3 per cent; and that has been responsible for Hungary's export boom to the West. For other countries following the model, the key is to accept that public-sector jobs must become private-sector jobs as quickly as possible and that, in the transition, production will fall and unemployment rise.

Reprinted by permission of the Globe and Mail, 1994. All rights reserved.

Background and Analysis

A planned, communist economy produces on its production possibility frontier, but at the wrong point. It produces too many defence-related goods and capital goods and too few consumer goods and services.

In the figure (parts a and b), the planned economy produces at point *a*. The production desired, and that which the market economy would give, is at point *c*.

An unattainable ideal would be to slide around the PPF from *a* to *c*. Such a transition would take resources from the state planned sector and put them immediately to work in the private market sector.

In real economies, the first step to reform is to privatise the state enterprises and to free people to run their own businesses. Initially, talented people are spending most of their efforts setting up and organizing businesses rather than producing goods.

The initial consequence of this reorganization is unemployment. Production and employment fall in the state planned sector *before* they rise in the private market sector.

But a successful reform has incentives in place for private firms to make profits and hire labour. And as the process proceeds, output eventually grows faster in the private market sector than it falls in the state planned sector, and the economy moves towards point *c*, as shown in part (a) of the figure.

Where the state planning system is not replaced by private enterprise, output falls in the state sector, but it does not increase (or does not increase very quickly) in the market sector. So the economy gets stuck at a point such as *b* in part (b).

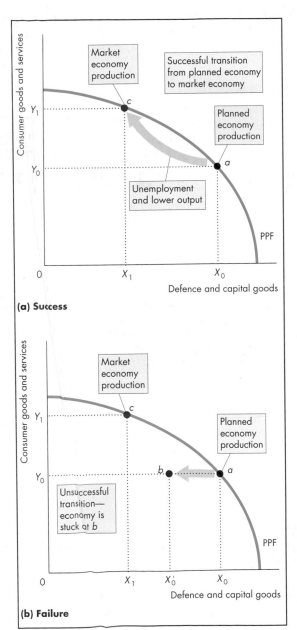

(a) **Success**

(b) **Failure**

GDP per person of less than 30 per cent of that of West Germany. Even before the formal reunification of the two parts of Germany, East Germany had begun to dismantle its Soviet-style planning system and replace it with a market economy.

The former East Germany adopted the monetary system of West Germany, deregulated its prices, and opened itself up to free trade with its western partner. State enterprises were permitted to fail in the competition with western private firms, private firms were permitted to open up in the former East Germany, and a massive sell-off of state enterprises was embarked upon.

The process of selling state enterprises began by the creation of a state corporation called Treuhamdanstalt (which roughly translates as 'Trust Corporation') that took over the assets of the almost 11,000 state enterprises. The idea was to then sell off these enterprises in an orderly way over a period of a few years. By November 1991, Treuhandanstalt had disposed of more than 4,000 firms. Most of these firms had been sold to the private sector but about 900 were closed down or merged with other firms.

The loss of jobs resulting from this rapid shake-out of state enterprises was large. Even by July 1990, before the two Germanies were reunited, unemployment in East Germany had reached one-third of the labour force. The unemployment rate in the east will remain high for some years, but the safety net of the West German social security system will cushion the blow to individual workers and their families.

East Germany has no fiscal policy crisis and no inflation problem. It has adopted the West German taxation and monetary systems and has assured financial stability. But the transition for East Germany will last for several years, even though it will be the most rapid transition imaginable.

Czech Republic, Slovakia, Hungary and Poland

The problems facing the Czech Republic, Slovakia, Hungary and Poland differ in important ways, but share some common features. And these common features are similar to some of the problems faced by the Soviet Union that we've already seen. The most severe of these are the collapse of traditional trade flows and the loss of traditional sources of government revenue.

Czech Republic and Slovakia Czechoslovakia removed its Communist government in what was called the 'Velvet Revolution' in November 1989 and almost immediately embarked on a programme of economic reforms aimed at replacing its centrally planned economy with a market system.

The first step in the transition was the freeing of wages, prices and interest rates. This step was accomplished quickly but the emergence of well-functioning markets did not immediately follow. Financial markets were especially nervous and a shortage of liquidity created a financial crisis.

The second step in the transition was privatization. Czechoslovakia pursued a so-called two-track policy of 'little privatization' and 'big privatization'. 'Little privatization' is the sale or, where possible, the return to their former owners, of small businesses and shops. 'Big privatization' is the sale of shares in the large industrial enterprises. One feature of this privatization process is the issue of vouchers to citizens that may be used to buy shares in former state enterprises.

Czechoslovakia's transition was slowed down by the decision of its people to divide into two parts and it has not yet reached the point of a positive economic payoff. Real GDP is growing, but very slowly, and unemployment is high.

Hungary Hungary has been in a long transition towards a capitalist, market economy. The process began in the 1960s when central planning was replaced by decentralized planning based on a price system. It has also established a taxation system similar to that in the market economies. But the privatization of large-scale industry only began in the 1990s and is proceeding slowly.

Because of its extreme gradualism, Hungary's transition is much less disruptive than those in the other countries. But it is feeling the repercussions of the economic restructuring of the other East European countries with which it has traditionally had the strongest trade links, so its rate of economic expansion has slowed substantially in recent years.

Poland Severe shortages, black markets and inflation were the starting point for Poland's journey towards a market economy. This journey began in September 1989 when a non-communist government that included members of the trade union Solidarity took office. The new government has deregulated prices and black markets have gone. It has also pursued a policy of extreme financial restraint, bringing the state budget and inflation under control.

Privatization has also been put on a fast track in Poland. In mid-1991, the government announced its Mass Privatization Scheme. Under this scheme, the shares of 400 state enterprises were to be transferred to a Privatization Fund, the shares in which were to be distributed freely to the entire adult population. This method of privatization is like creating a giant insurance company that owns most of the production enterprises and that is in turn owned by private shareholders.

◆ ◆ ◆ ◆   The transition to the market economy is changing Eastern Europe and the former Soviet Union. But the world has seen change of historical proportions before. The transformation of the economies of formerly war-torn Germany and Japan into the economic powerhouses of today is one example. Throughout all this change – past, present and future – our knowledge and understanding of the economic forces that produce the change and are unleashed by it have been gradually improving. There remains a great deal that we do not understand. But we have made a great deal of progress. The economic principles presented in this book summarize this progress and the current state of knowledge. As the world continues to change, you will need a compass to guide you into unknown terrain. The principles of economics are that compass!

S U M M A R Y

The International Distribution of Income

There is enormous inequality in the international distribution of income. The poorest countries have average per capita income levels of 4 per cent to 9 per cent of that in the United States. Half of the world's population earns only 15 per cent of world income and the richest 20 per cent of the world's population earns 55 per cent of income. (pp. 1014–1015)

The Economic Problem and its Alternative Solutions

The economic problem is the universal fact of scarcity. Different economic systems deliver different solutions to the economic problem determining *what*, *how* and *for whom* goods and services are produced. Alternative economic systems vary in two dimensions: ownership of capital and land and the incentives people face. Capital and land may be owned by individuals, by the state, or by a mixture of the two. Incentives may be created by market prices, by administered prices and administrative sanctions, or by a mixture of the two.

Economic systems differ in the ways in which they combine ownership and incentive arrangements. Capitalism is based on the private ownership of capital and land and on market price incentives.

Socialism is based on state ownership of capital and land and on administrative incentives and a central economic plan. Market socialism combines state ownership of capital and land with incentives based on a mixture of market and administered prices. Welfare state capitalism combines the private ownership of capital and land with state intervention in markets that change the price signals that people respond to. (pp. 1016–1020)

Economic Growth

Growth income per person results from the growth in capital per person and in technological change. The greater the fraction of income invested in new capital equipment and the faster the pace of technological change, the higher is the rate of economic growth. (pp. 1020–1025)

Economic Transition in China

Since the foundation of the People's Republic of China, economic management has been through turbulent changes. At first, China used the Soviet system of central planning. It then introduced the Great Leap Forward, which in turn degenerated into the Cultural Revolution. China at first grew quickly with heavy reliance on state planning and capital accumulation, but growth slowed and, at times, income per person actually fell. In 1978, China revolutionized its economic management, placing greater emphasis on private incentives and markets. As a consequence, productivity grew at a rapid rate and per capita income increased.

China's success in achieving a high rate of economic growth has resulted from four features of its reforms: a massive rate of entry of new non-state firms; large increases in the productivity and profitability of state firms; an efficient taxation system; and gradual price deregulation. Whether China has found a way of making the transition from socialism to capitalism in a relatively painless way is a controversial issue. But the experiment in comparative *economic* systems currently going on in China is one of the most exciting that the world has seen and economists of all political shades of opinion will closely watch its outcome, for its lessons will be of enormous value for future generations – whatever they turn out to be. (pp. 1025–1029)

Economic Change in the Former Soviet Union

The Soviet Union was founded in 1917 and collapsed in 1991. The economy of the Soviet Union was based on a system of central planning that had four key elements: an administrative hierarchy, an iterative planning process, legally binding commands, and taut and inflexible plans. The Soviet Union had a market sector in which a substantial amount of economic activity took place, especially in agriculture. Money played only a minor role in the economy of the Soviet Union.

The Soviet economy grew extraordinarily quickly before 1970 – in excess of 5 per cent a year – but during the 1970s, and more especially during the 1980s, output growth declined. By the early 1990s, the economy was shrinking. A combination of three features of the Soviet economy caused this deterioration in economic performance: the economy made a transition from being an investment economy to a consumption economy; the economy was hit by serious external shocks; and its taut and inflexible planning system was incapable of coping with these events.

By the end of the 1980s, the Soviet Union had begun a process of transition towards the market economy. This process had three main elements: the relaxation of central plan enforcement; the deregulation of prices; and the introduction of limited private ownership of firms. The transition was a process of gradual change but it ran into severe problems. The most important were: value and legal systems alien to capitalism; the collapse of traditional trade flows; and the emergence of a large state budget deficit and inflation. (pp. 1029–1035)

Economic Transition in Eastern Europe

The formerly planned economies of Czechoslovakia, East Germany, Hungary and Poland are also making transitions to market economies. East Germany's transition has been the most dramatic and the most complete. It has taken the form of a reunification of the two Germanies and the adoption by the former East Germany of West Germany's monetary and taxation system. Prices deregulation and privatization have been rapid. The Czech Republic and Slovakia have deregulated wages, prices and interest rates and are privatizing their industries by returning small businesses and shops to their former owners and by issuing vouchers to their citizens that may be used to buy shares in former state enterprises. Hungary began the process of moving towards a market economy during the 1960s when central planning was replaced by decentralized planning. Hungary has established a taxation system similar to that in the market economies. But the privatization of large-scale industry only began in the 1990s and is proceeding slowly. Poland has deregulated prices, pursued a policy of financial restraint that has brought inflation under control and put privatization on a fast track. (pp. 1035–1039)

KEY ELEMENTS

Key Terms

Capitalism, 1017
Central planning, 1017
Communist country, 1014
Decentralized planning, 1018
Developing country, 1014
Great Leap Forward, 1025
Hierarchy, 1030
Incentive structure, 1016
Industrial country, 1014
Lorenz curve, 1015
Market socialism, 1018
Per capita production function, 1021
Newly industrialized country, 1014
Socialism, 1017
Underdeveloped country, 1014
Welfare state capitalism, 1018

Key Figures and Tables

Figure 36.1   The World Lorenz Curve, 1985, 1015
Figure 36.2   The Fundamental Economic Problem, 1016
Figure 36.3   Alternative Economic Systems, 1017
Figure 36.4   Capitalism's Solution to the Economic Problem, 1018
Figure 36.5   Socialism's Solution to the Economic Problem, 1020
Figure 36.7   Technological Change, 1024
Figure 36.9   Economic Growth in China, 1027
Table 36.1   A Compact Summary of Key Periods in thc Economic History of the People's Republic of China, 1026
Table 36.2   A Compact Summary of Key Periods in the Economic History of the Soviet Union, 1030

REVIEW QUESTIONS

1 Describe the main differences between the richest and poorest countries.

2 Compare the distribution of income among families in the United Kingdom with the distribution of income among countries in the world. Which distribution is more unequal?

3 What is the fundamental economic problem that any economic system must solve?

4 What are the main economic systems? Set out the key features of each.

5 Give examples of countries that are capitalist, socialist, market socialist and welfare state capitalist. (Name some countries other than those in Fig. 36.3.)

6 How does capitalism solve the economic problem? What determines how much of each good to produce?

7 How does socialism solve the economic problem? What determines how much of each good to produce?

8 How does market socialism determine the price and quantity of each good?

9 What determines a country's per capita income level? What makes the per capita income level change?

10 Give an example of a country in which rapid economic growth has occurred and one in which slow economic growth has occurred. Which country has the higher investment rate?

11 Review the main episodes in China's economic management since 1949.

12 Compare the economic growth performance of the United States and China. What do we learn from this comparison?

13 What are the lessons of the economic experiment that is going on in China?

14 Why did the Soviet economy begin to fail in the 1980s?

15 What are the main features of the transition programme in the former Soviet Union?

16 What are the main problems faced by the republics of the former Soviet Union?

17 What are the problems faced by the other East European countries as they make the transition to a market economy?

P R O B L E M S

1 A poor country has 10 per cent of the income of a rich country. The poor country achieves a growth rate of 10 per cent per year. The rich country is growing at 5 per cent per year. How many years will it take income in the poor country to catch up with that of the rich country?

2 The per capita production function in Machecon is illustrated in the figure and in year 1, Machecon has 1 machine per person.

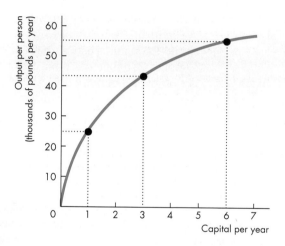

a What is output per person in Machecon?

b Machecon adds 1 machine per person to its capital stock during year 2. What is its new level of output and what is its economic growth rate in year 2?

c In year 3, Machecon adds 1 more machine per person to its capital stock. What now is its output and what is its economic growth rate in year 3?

d In year 4, Machecon adds no new machines to its capital stock, but a new technology becomes available that increases the productivity of each machine by 20 per cent. What is Machecon's output in year 4?

GLOSSARY

Above full-employment equilibrium   A situation in which macroeconomic equilibrium occurs at a level of real GDP above long-run aggregate supply.

Absolute advantage   A person has an absolute advantage in the production of a good or service if he or she is more productive than another person in its production. A country has an absolute advantage in the production of a good or service if its output per unit of inputs for that good or service is higher than that of another country.

Ad valorem **tax**   A tax on a good or service whose amount depends on the value of the good or service.

Adverse selection   The tendency for the people who accept contracts to be those with private information that they plan to use to their own advantage and to the disadvantage of the less informed party.

Agency relationship   The relationship between a firm and its owners, managers and workers and between a firm and other firms.

Agent   A person (or firm) hired by a firm (or another person) to do a specified job.

Aggregate demand   The entire relationship between the aggregate quantity of goods and services demanded – real GDP and demanded – and the price level – the GDP deflator – holding everything else constant.

Aggregate demand curve   A curve showing the quantity of real GDP demanded at each price level, holding everything else constant.

Aggregate expenditure curve   A graph of the aggregate expenditure schedule.

Allocative efficiency   The situation that occurs when no resources are wasted – when no one can be made better off without making someone else worse off.

Anticipated inflation   An inflation rate that has been, on average, correctly forecast.

Arbitrage   The activity of buying at a low price and selling at a high price in order to make a profit on the margin between the two prices.

Arc elasticity   The elasticity along an arc of a demand curve or supply curve.

Asset   Anything of value that a household, firm or government owns.

Assortative mating   Marrying within one's own socio-economic group.

Automatic stabilizer   A mechanism that decreases the size of fluctuations in aggregate expenditure that result from fluctuations in the components of aggregate expenditure.

Autonomous expenditure   The part of aggregate planned expenditure that is not influenced by real GDP.

Autonomous expenditure multiplier   The amount by which a change in autonomous expenditure must be multiplied to calculate the resulting change in equilibrium expenditure and real GDP.

Average cost pricing rule   A rule that sets the price equal to average total cost.

Average fixed cost   Total fixed cost per unit of output – total fixed cost divided by output.

Average product   Total product per unit of variable input – total product divided by the number of units of variable input.

Average propensity to consume   The ratio of consumption to disposable income.

Average propensity to save   The ratio of saving to disposable income.

Average revenue   Total revenue divided by the quantity sold. Average revenue also equals price.

Average revenue product   Total revenue resulting from the output which a factor helps to produce divided by the quantity of the factor used.

Average revenue product curve   A curve that shows the average revenue product of a factor at each quantity of the factor used.

Average total cost   Total variable cost per unit of output – total variable cost divided by output.

Balance of payments accounts   A record of a country's international transactions.

Balance of trade   The value of exports of goods minus the value of imports of goods.

Balance sheet   A list of assets and liabilities.

Balanced budget   A government budget that is in neither surplus nor deficit.

Balanced budget multiplier   The amount by which equal changes in government purchases and taxes must be multiplied to determine the change that they generate in equilibrium expenditure and real GDP.

Balancing item   The estimated net value of omissions from all other items recorded on the balance of payments accounts.

Bank   A financial intermediary that takes deposits, buys securities and makes loans.

Barriers to entry   Restrictions on the entry of new firms into an industry.

Barter   The direct exchange of goods for goods.

Bequest   A gift from one generation to the next.

Bilateral monopoly   A market structure in which a single buyer and a single seller confront each other.

Binding arbitration   A process in which a third party – an arbitrator – determines wages and other employment conditions.

Black market   An illegal trading arrangement in which buyers and sellers do business at a price higher than the legally imposed price ceiling.

Bond   A legally enforceable obligation to pay specified sums of money at specified future dates.

Break-even point   The output level at which total revenue equals total cost (and at which economic profit is zero).

Budget   The annual statement by the government of its financial plan; it itemizes spending programmes and their costs, tax revenues and the proposed deficit or surplus.

Budget equation   An equation that states the limits to consumption for a given income and given price.

Budget line   A line that graphs the limits to a household's consumption choices.

Budget stabilizers   Cumulative reductions in the level of tariffs on food imported into the European Union.

Budget surplus (or **budget deficit**)   The difference between government sector revenue and expenditure in a given period of time. If revenue exceeds expenditure, the government sector has a budget surplus. If expenditure exceeds revenue, the sector has a budget deficit.

Bureaucrats   Appointed officials who work at various levels in government departments.

Business cycle   The periodic but irregular up and down movement in economic activity measured by fluctuations in real GDP and other macroeconomic variables.

Capacity   The output rate at which a plant's average cost is at a minimum.

Capital   The real assets – the plant, buildings, vehicles and machinery used by a household, firm or government department.

Capital accumulation   The growth of capital resources.

Capital consumption   The reduction in the value of the capital stock that results from wear and tear and the passage of time.

Capital goods   Goods that can be used many times before they eventually wear out. Examples of capital goods are plant, buildings, vehicles and machinery.

Capital-intensive technique   A method of production that uses a relatively large amount of capital and a relatively small amount of labour to produce a given quantity of output.

Capital stock   The stock of plant, buildings, vehicles and machinery plus stocks of raw materials and unsold finished goods.

Capitalism   An economic system based on the private ownership of capital and land in production and on the market allocation of resources.

Capture theory of intervention   A theory that states that the interventions that exist are those that maximize producer surplus.

Cartel   A group of producers who enter a collusive agreement to restrict output in order to raise prices and profits.

Cash drain   The tendency for some of the funds lent by banks and building societies to remain outside the banking system and circulate as cash in the hands of the public.

Central bank   A public authority charged with regulating and controlling a country's monetary and financial institutions and markets.

Central planning   A method of allocating resources by command.

Ceteris paribus   Other things being equal, or other things remaining constant.

Change in demand   A shift of the entire demand curve for a good or service that occurs when some influence on buyers' plans, other than the price of the good or service, changes.

Change in supply   A shift in the entire supply curve for a good or service that occurs when some influence on producers' plans, other than the price of the good or service, changes.

Change in the quantity demanded   A movement along the demand curve for a good or service that results from a change in its price.

Change in the quantity supplied   A movement along the supply curve for a good or service that results from a change in its price.

Chequable deposit   A loan by a depositor to a bank or a building society, the ownership of which is transferable from one person to another by writing an instruction to the bank or the building society – a cheque – asking it to alter its records.

Choke price   The price at which it no longer pays to use a natural resource.

Closed economy   An economy that has no links with any other economy.

Closed shop   A plant or firm in which all the employees are required to join the trade union.

Closed union   A group of workers who have a similar range of skills but who may work for many different employers.

Collective bargaining   A process of negotiation between employers (or their representatives) and a union on wages and other employment conditions.

Collusive agreement   An agreement between two (or more) producers to restrict output in order to raise prices and profits.

Command economy   An economy that relies on a command mechanism.

Command mechanism   A method of determining *what, how,* and *for whom* goods and services are produced, based on the authority of a ruler or ruling body.

Common Agricultural Policy   The agricultural policy implemented by the European Union in member countries.

Communist country   A country in which there is limited private ownership of productive capital and of firms, limited reliance placed on the market as a means of allocating resources, and in which government agencies plan and direct the production and distribution of most goods and services.

Company   A firm owned by two or more shareholders.

Comparative advantage   A person has a comparative advantage in producing a good or service if he or she can produce it at a lower opportunity cost than anyone else. A country has a comparative advantage in producing a good or service if it can produce it at a lower opportunity cost than any other country.

Competitive tendering   Allowing private firms to compete for contracts to do work which was previously always done by public employees.

Complement   A good or service that is used in conjunction with another good or service.

Conglomerate merger   A merger between two firms whose outputs are little related.

Constant returns to scale   Technological conditions under which the percentage change in a firm's output is equal to the percentage change in its use of inputs.

Consumer equilibrium   A situation in which a consumer has allocated his or her income in a manner that maximizes total utility.

Consumer surplus   The difference between the value of a good or service and its price.

Consumers' expenditure   The term used in published UK statistics for consumption.

Consumption   The process of using up goods and services.

Consumption function   The relationship between consumption and disposable income.

Consumption goods   Goods that can be used just once. Examples are pickled onions and toothpaste.

Contraction   A business cycle phase in which there is a slow-down in the pace of economic activity.

Convertible shares   Shares whose holders receive fixed interest payments and who have the right to convert their convertible shares into ordinary shares at some future specified date.

Cooperative   A firm owned by a group of people who have a common objective and who collectively bear the risks of the enterprise and share in its profits.

Cooperative equilibrium   An equilibrium that results when each player in a game responds rationally to the credible threat of the other player to inflict heavy damage if the agreement is broken.

Coordinates   Lines on a graph running perpendicularly from a point to the axes.

Coordination mechanism   A mechanism that makes the choices of one individual compatible with the choices of others.

Corporation tax   A tax on company profits.

Cost–push inflation   Inflation that has its origin in cost increases.

Creditor nation   A country that during its entire history has invested more in the rest of the world than other countries have invested in it.

Cross elasticity of demand   The percentage change in the quantity demanded of a good or service divided by the percentage change in the price of a substitute or complement.

Cross-section graph   A graph that measures the value of an economic variable on one axis and the different members of a population (such as income groups) on the other.

Crowding in   The tendency for an expansionary fiscal policy to increase investment.

Crowding out   The tendency for an increase in government purchases of goods and services to increase interest rates, thereby reducing – or crowding out – investment expenditure.

Currency appreciation   The increase in the value of one currency in terms of another currency.

Currency depreciation   The fall in the value of one currency in terms of another currency.

Current account   A record of receipts from the sale of goods and services to foreigners, the payments for goods and services bought from foreigners, and property income and current transfers received from and paid to foreigners.

Current account balance   The net value of all the items on the current account.

Current transfers to and from abroad   Gifts between people in different countries.

Curve   Any relationship between two variables plotted on a graph, even a linear relationship.

Deadweight loss   A measure of allocative inefficiency – the reduction in consumer and producer surplus resulting from restricting output below its efficient level.

Debenture   A term often used in the United Kingdom for bonds issued by companies.

Debt financing   The financing of the government sector deficit by selling bonds to anyone (households, firms or foreigners) other than the Bank of England.

Debtor nation   A country that during its entire history has borrowed more money from the rest of the world than it has lent to it. It has a stock of outstanding debt to the rest of the world that exceeds the stock of its own claims on the rest of the world.

Decentralized planning   An economic system that combines socialism's state ownership of capital and land with capitalism's market allocation of resources.

Decreasing returns to scale   Technological conditions under which the percentage change in a firm's output is less than the percentage change in its use of inputs.

Deflation   A downward movement in the average level of prices.

Demand   The entire relationship between the quantity demanded of a good or service and its price.

Demand curve   A graph showing the relationship between the quantity demanded of a good or service and its price, holding everything else constant.

Demand for labour   The quantity of labour demanded at each level of the real wage rate, holding everything else constant.

Demand–pull inflation   Inflation that results from an increase in aggregate demand.

Demand schedule   A list of the quantities of a good or service demanded at different prices, holding everything else constant.

Depreciation   The fall in the value of capital or the value of a durable input resulting from its use and from the passage of time.

Depression   A deep business cycle trough.

Deregulation   The removal of rules that restrict prices, product standards and types and entry conditions in an industry.

Derived demand   Demand for an input not for its own sake but in order to use it in the production of goods and services.

Desired reserve ratio   The ratio of reserves to deposits that banks regard as necessary in order to be able to conduct their business.

Developing country   A country that is poor but is accumulating capital and developing an industrial and commercial base.

Diminishing marginal product of labour   The tendency for the marginal product of labour to decline as the labour input increases, holding everything else constant.

Diminishing marginal rate of substitution The general tendency for the marginal rate of substitution to diminish as the consumer moves along an indifference curve, increasing the consumption of good or service x and decreasing the consumption of y.

Diminishing marginal returns A situation in which the marginal producer of the last worker hired falls short of the marginal product of the second last worker hired.

Diminishing marginal utility The decline in marginal utility from a good or service that occurs as more and more of it is consumed.

Discounting The conversion of a future sum of money to its present value.

Discouraged workers People who do not have jobs and would like to work, but have stopped seeking work.

Diseconomies of scale Technological conditions under which the percentage increase in a firm's output is less than the percentage change in inputs; sometimes called decreasing returns to scale.

Disposable income Original income plus transfer payments minus taxes.

Dissaving Negative saving; a situation in which consumption exceeds disposable income.

Dividend yield The current dividend earned by a share as a percentage of its market price.

Dominant strategy A game strategy that is a player's unique best action regardless of the action taken by the other player.

Dominant strategy equilibrium A Nash equilibrium in which there is a dominant strategy for each player in the game.

Double counting Counting the expenditure on both the final good or service and the intermediate goods and services used in its production.

Duopoly A market structure in which two producers of a good or service compete with each other.

Durable input A factor of production that is not entirely used up in a single production period.

Economic depreciation The change in the market price of a durable input over a given period. Economic depreciation over a year is calculated as the market price of the input at the beginning of the year minus its market price at the end of the year.

Economic efficiency A state in which the cost of producing a given output is as low as possible.

Economic growth The persistent expansion of a country's production possibilities.

Economic information Data on prices, quantities and qualities of goods and services and factors of production.

Economic profit Total revenue minus total cost when the opportunity costs of production are included in cost.

Economic rent An income received by the owner of a factor over and above the amount required to induce that owner to offer the factor for its present use.

Economic theory A rule or principle that enables us to understand and predict economic choices.

Economics The study of how people use their limited resources to try to satisfy unlimited wants.

Economies of scale Technological conditions under which the percentage increase in a firm's output exceeds the percentage increase in its inputs; sometimes called increasing returns to scale.

Economies of scope Decreases in average total cost made possible by increasing the number of different goods or services produced.

Economizing Making the best use of scarce resources.

Economy A mechanism that allocates scarce resources among competing uses.

Efficient market A market in which the actual price embodies all currently available relevant information.

Elastic demand Demand with an elasticity greater than 1; the quantity demanded of a good or service drops by a larger percentage than its price rises.

Elasticity of demand The name used for price elasticity of demand when the minus sign is ignored

Elasticity of supply The percentage change in the quantity supplied of a good or service divided by the percentage change in its price.

End-state theory of distributive justice A theory of distributive justice that examines the fairness of the outcome of economic activity.

Entry The act of setting up a new firm in an industry.

Equal pay for work of equal value The payment of equal wages for different jobs that are judged to be of comparable worth.

Equation of exchange An equation that states that the quantity of money multiplied by the velocity of circulation of money equals the price level multiplied by real GDP.

Equilibrium A situation in which everyone has economized – that is, all individuals have made the best possible choices in the light of their own preferences and given their endowments and the available technologies – and in which those choices have been coordinated and made compatible with the choices of everyone else. Equilibrium is the solution or outcome of an economic model.

Equilibrium expenditure The level of aggregate planned expenditure that equals real GDP.

Equilibrium price The price at which the quantity demanded equals the quantity supplied. At this price, opposing forces exactly balance each other.

Equilibrium quantity The quantity bought and sold at the equilibrium price.

European currency unit (ECU) A composite currency that is used for limited purposes in the European Union; an ECU is defined as a 'basket' of the currencies of all twelve EU member currencies, the relative importance of each currency in the basket depending on the relative importance of that country's economy.

European monetary system (EMS) An agreement under which EU countries attempt to promote exchange rate stability within the European Union.

Excess capacity A state in which a firm's output is less than that at which average total cost is a minimum.

Excess reserves The difference between a bank's actual reserves and its desired reserves.

Exchange rate mechanism (ERM)   A system under which most EU countries regulate changes in the relative values of their currencies while allowing the average value of their currencies to float against those outside the European Union.

Exit   The act of closing down a firm and leaving an industry.

Expansion   A business cycle phase in which there is a speedup in the pace of economic activity.

Expected inflation rate   The rate at which people, on average, believe that the price level will rise.

Expected utility   The average utility arising from all possible outcomes.

Expenditure approach   A measure of GDP obtained by adding together consumption, investment, government purchases of goods and services, and net exports.

Exports   Goods and services sold by people in one country to people in other countries.

External benefits   Those benefits from a good or service accruing to people other than its buyer.

External costs   Those costs of a good or service borne by people other than its producer.

External diseconomies   Factors outside the control of a firm that raise its costs as industry output rises.

External economies   Factors beyond the control of a firm that lower its costs as industry output rises.

Externality   An effect of consumption or production which is not taken into account by the consumer or the producer and which affects the utility or costs of other consumers or producers.

Factor cost   The cost of all the factors of production used to produce a good or service.

Factor incomes approach   A measure of GDP obtained by adding together all the incomes paid by firms and government departments to households for the service of the factors of production they hire – wages, interest, rent and profits.

Factor market   A market in which factors of production are bought and sold.

Factors of production   The economy's productive resources – land, labour, and capital.

Feedback rule   A rule that states which policy instruments will be used and how each instrument will respond to the state of the economy.

Final goods and services   Goods and services that are not used as inputs in the production of other goods and services but are bought by their final users.

Financial asset   A paper claim of the holder against another household, firm or government.

Financial intermediary   A firm that takes deposits or loans from households and firms and makes loans to other households, firms and governments.

Firm   An institution that buys or hires factors of production and organizes them to produce and sell goods and services.

Fiscal policy   The government's attempt to vary its purchases of goods and services and its taxes to smooth the fluctuations in aggregate expenditure.

Five-firm concentration ratio   The percentage of the value of sales accounted for by the largest five firms in an industry.

Fixed cost   A cost that is independent of the output level.

Fixed exchange rate   An exchange rate which is pegged by the country's central bank.

Fixed inputs   Those inputs whose quantity used cannot be varied in the short run.

Fixed rule   A rule in place and maintained regardless of the state of the economy.

Flexible exchange rate   An exchange rate which is determined by market forces in the absence of central bank intervention.

Flow   A quantity measured over a period of time.

Foreign exchange market   The market in which the currencies of different countries are exchanged for one another.

Foreign exchange rate   The rate at which a country's currency exchanges for another's.

Forward market   A market in which a commitment is made at a price agreed here and now to exchange a specified quantity of a particular commodity at a specified future date.

Free rider   Someone who consumes a good or service without paying for it.

Free-rider problem   The tendency for the scale of provision of a public good to be too small – to be allocatively inefficient – if it is privately provided.

Frictional unemployment   Unemployment arising from new entrants into the labour market and from job turnover caused by technological change.

Full employment   A situation in which all unemployment is frictional.

Full employment equilibrium   A macroeconomic equilibrium at a point on the long-run aggregate supply curve.

Futures market   An organized market operated on a futures exchange in which large-scale contracts for the future delivery of goods can be exchanged.

Game theory   A method of analysing strategic behaviour.

GDP deflator   A price index that measures the average level of the prices of all the goods and services that make up GDP.

General Agreement on Tariffs and Trade (GATT)   An agreement that limits government taxes and other restrictions on international trade.

General government financial deficit   A term used on some published accounts for the government deficit.

Goods and services   All the valuable things that people produce. Goods are tangible and services are intangible.

Goods market   A market in which goods (or services) are bought and sold.

Government deficit   The total expenditure of the government sector less the total revenue of that sector in a given period.

Government purchases multiplier   The amount by which a change in government purchases of goods and services must be multiplied to determine the change in equilibrium expenditure that it generates.

Government sector debt   The total amount of loans which have been made to the government sector in the past which have not been repaid.

Government surplus or deficit   The difference between the government sector's total revenue and its total expenditure over a period of time.

Great Leap Forward   An economic plan for post-revolutionary China based on small-scale, labour-intensive production.

Gross domestic product (GDP)   The value of output produced in a country in a period of time.

Gross income   A household's original income plus the value of any transfer payments received.

Gross investment   The value of new capital equipment purchased in a given time period. It is the amount spent on replacing depreciated capital and on making net additions to the capital stock.

Gross national product (GNP)   GDP plus net property income from abroad.

Gross national disposable income (GNDI)   The income available for UK citizens to spend, calculated by deducting net payments of current transfers abroad from GNP.

Hidden economy   That part of the economy concerned with producing goods and services on which expenditure is not recorded in official statistics.

Historical cost   A cost that values a factor of production at the price actually paid for it.

Horizontal merger   A merger between firms with similar outputs.

Hotelling Principle   The proposition that the market for a stock of a natural resource is in equilibrium when the price of that resource is expected to rise at a rate equal to the interest rate.

Household production   The production of goods and services for consumption within the household.

Human capital   The accumulated skill and knowledge of human beings. It is the value of education and acquired skills.

Implicit rental rate   The rent that a firm implicitly pays to itself for the use of the durable inputs that it owns.

Imports   Goods and services bought by people in one country from people in other countries.

Imputed cost   An opportunity cost that does not involve an actual expenditure of money.

Income effect   The effect of a change in income on consumption.

Income elasticity of demand   The percentage change in the quantity demanded divided by the percentage change in income.

Increasing marginal returns   A situation in which the marginal product of the last worker hired exceeds the marginal product of the second last worker hired.

Increasing returns to scale   Technological conditions under which the percentage change in a firm's output exceeds the percentage change in its use of inputs.

Indexing   A technique that links payments made under a contract to the price level.

Indifference curve   A line showing all possible combinations of two goods or services among which a consumer is indifferent.

Indirect tax   A tax on the production or sale of a good or service. Indirect taxes are included in the price paid for the good or service by its final purchaser.

Individual demand   The relationship between the quantity of a good or service demanded by a single individual and the price of the good or service.

Induced expenditure   The sum of those components of aggregate planned expenditure that vary as real GDP varies.

Industrial country   A country that has a large amount of capital equipment and in which people undertake highly specialized activities, enabling them to earn high per capita incomes.

Inelastic demand   Demand with an elasticity between zero and 1; the quantity demanded of a good or service drops by a smaller percentage than its price rises.

Inferior good   A good (or service), the demand for which decreases when income increases.

Inflation   An upward movement in the average level of prices.

Inflation rate   The percentage change in the price level.

Information cost   The cost of acquiring information on prices, quantities and qualities of goods and services and factors of production – the opportunity cost of economic information received.

Injections   Expenditures that add to the circular flow of expenditure and income – investment, government purchases of goods and services, and exports.

Innovation   The act of putting a new technique into operation.

Intellectual property   The intangible product of creative effort, protected by copyrights and patents. This type of property includes books, music, computer programs and inventions of all kinds.

Interest rate parity   A situation in which interest rates are equal across all countries once differences in risk are taken into account.

Interest yield   The interest earned by a bond as a percentage of its market price.

Intermediate goods and services   Goods and services that are used as inputs into the production of another good or service.

International Monetary Fund (IMF)   An international organization that monitors members' balance of payments and exchange rate activities.

Invention   The discovery of a new technique.

Investment   The purchase of new plant, buildings, vehicles and machinery, and additions to stocks in a given time period.

Investment demand   The relationship between the level of investment and the real interest rate.

Investment demand curve   A curve showing the relationship between the real interest rate and the level of planned investment, holding everything else constant.

Invisible balance   The balance of all items on the current account of the balance of payments except for exports and imports of goods.

Joint unlimited liability   The liability of every partner for the full debts of a partnership.

Keynesian A macroeconomist whose beliefs about the functioning of the economy represent an extension of the theories of John Maynard Keynes. A Keynesian regards the economy as being inherently unstable, and as requiring active government intervention to achieve stability. A Keynesian assigns a low degree of importance to monetary policy and a high degree of importance to fiscal policy.

Labour The brain-power and muscle-power of human beings.

Labour force The total number of employed and unemployed workers.

Labour force participation rate The proportion of the working age population that is either employed or unemployed (but seeking employment).

Labour-intensive technique A method of production that uses a relatively large amount of labour and a relatively small amount of capital to produce a given quantity of output.

Labour subsidy A subsidy which is paid to help firms meet their labour costs.

Laffer curve A curve that relates the revenue from a tax to the tax rate.

Land Natural resources of all kinds.

Law of diminishing returns The general tendency for marginal product eventually to diminish as more of a single variable input is employed, holding the quantity of other inputs constant.

Law of one price A law stating that any given commodity will be available at a single price.

Leakages Income that is not spent on domestically produced goods and services – saving, taxes (net of transfer payments including debt interest), and imports.

Legal monopoly A monopoly that occurs when a law, licence, or patent restricts competition by preventing entry to the industry.

Lender of last resort The role of the central bank when it lends money to help the banks if they are short of reserves; most central banks lend directly to the banks, but the Bank of England lends indirectly via the discount houses.

Liability A debt – something that a household, firm or government owes.

Limited liability The limitation of liability of the firm's owners for its debts only up to the value of their financial investment.

Linear relationship The relationship between two variables depicted by a straight line on a graph.

Liquidity The degree to which an asset can be instantly converted into cash at a known price.

Liquidity trap A situation in which the demand curve for real money is horizontal at a given interest rate and people are willing to hold any amount of money at that interest rate.

Lobbying The activity of bringing pressure to bear upon government agencies or institutions through a variety of informal mechanisms.

Lockout The refusal by a firm to operate its plant and employ its workers.

Long run A period of time in which the quantities of all inputs can be varied.

Long-run aggregate supply The relationship between the aggregate quantity of final goods and services (real GDP) supplied and the price level (the GDP deflator) when there is full employment – that is when unemployment is at its natural rate.

Long-run average cost curve A curve that traces the relationship between the lowest attainable average cost and output when all inputs can be varied.

Long-run cost The cost of production when a firm uses the economically efficient plant size.

Long-run demand curve The demand curve that describes the change in the quantity demanded in response to a change in price after buyers have made all possible adjustments to their buying plans.

Long-run demand for labour The relationship between the wage rate and the quantity of labour demanded when all inputs can be varied.

Long-run elasticity of demand for labour The percentage change in the quantity of labour demanded divided by the percentage change in the wage rate when all inputs are varied.

Long-run Phillips curve Shows the relationship between inflation and unemployment when the actual inflation rate equals the expected inflation rate.

Long-run supply curve The supply curve that describes the response of the quantity supplied to a change in price after *all* technologically possible adjustments have been made.

Lorenz curve A curve that shows the cumulative percentage of income or wealth against the cumulative percentage of population.

Lump-sum subsidy A subsidy to a firm which involves occasional payments, often just once a year.

M0 Cash held outside the Bank of England by banks, building societies and the public plus banks' operational deposits at the Bank of England.

M4 Cash held by the public plus all sterling deposits at banks and building societies.

Macroeconomic equilibrium A situation in which the quantity of real GDP demanded equals the quantity of real GDP supplied.

Macroeconomics The branch of economics that studies the economy as a whole. It is concerned with aggregates and averages of behaviour rather than with detailed individual choices.

Managed exchange rate An exchange rate, the value of which is influenced by the central bank's intervention in the foreign exchange market.

Marginal benefit The change in total benefit resulting from a unit increase in output.

Marginal cost The change in total cost resulting from a unit increase in output.

Marginal cost pricing rule A rule that sets price equal to marginal cost. It maximizes total surplus in the regulated industry.

Marginal private cost The marginal cost directly incurred by the producer of a good or service.

Marginal product The change in total product resulting from a unit increase in a variable input, holding all other inputs constant.

Marginal product of capital   The change in total product resulting from a one-unit increase in the quantity of capital employed, holding the quantity of all other inputs constant.

Marginal product of labour   The change in total product (output) resulting from a one-unit increase in the quantity of labour employed, holding the quantity of all other inputs constant.

Marginal propensity to consume   The fraction of the last pound of disposable income that is spent on consumption.

Marginal propensity to import   The fraction of the last pound for real GDP spent on imports.

Marginal propensity to save   The fraction of the last pound of disposable income that is saved.

Marginal propensity to spend on domestic goods and services   The fraction of the last pound of real GDP spent on domestic goods and services.

Marginal rate of substitution   The rate at which a person will give up one good or service in order to get more of another and, at the same time, remain indifferent.

Marginal rate of transformation   Shows how much more of one good or service we can get if we reduce the production of another.

Marginal revenue   The change in total revenue resulting from a one-unit increase in the quantity sold.

Marginal revenue product   The change in total revenue resulting from employing one more unit of a factor.

Marginal revenue product curve   A curve that shows the marginal revenue product of a factor at each quantity of the factor hired.

Marginal social benefit   The pound value of the benefit from one additional unit of consumption, including the benefit to the buyer and any indirect benefits accruing to any other member of society.

Marginal social cost   The cost of producing one additional unit of output, including both the costs borne by the producer and any other costs indirectly incurred by any other member of society. It is the marginal cost incurred by the producer of a good, together with any marginal costs imposed as an externality on others.

Marginal tax rate   The fraction of the last pound of income paid to the government in taxes (net of any extra transfer payments received from the government).

Marginal utility   The change in total utility resulting from a one-unit increase in the quantity of a product consumed.

Marginal utility per pound spent   The marginal utility obtained from the last unit of a good or service consumed divided by its price.

Market   Any arrangement that facilitates buying and selling (trading) of a good, service, factor of production or future commitment.

Market activity   The supplying of labour through the market.

Market constraints   The conditions under which a firm can buy its inputs and sell its output.

Market demand   The relationship between the total quantity of a good or service demanded and its price.

Market economy   An economy that determines *what, how* and *for whom* goods and services are produced by coordinating individual choices through markets.

Market failure   The inability of an unregulated market to achieve allocative efficiency in all circumstances.

Market mechanism   A method of determining *what, how* and *for whom* goods and services are produced, based on individual choices coordinated through markets.

Market socialism   An economic system that combines socialism's state ownership of capital and land with capitalism's market allocation of resources.

Median voter theorem   The proposition that political parties will pursue policies that maximize the net benefit of the median voter.

Medium of exchange   Anything that is generally acceptable in exchange for goods and services.

Merger   The combining of the assets of two (or more) firms to form a single new firm.

Microeconomics   The branch of economics that studies the decisions of individual households and firms, and the way in which individual markets work. Microeconomics also studies the way in which taxes and government regulation affect people's economic choices.

Minimum wage law   A regulation making it illegal to hire labour below a specified wage.

Mixed economy   An economy that relies partly on the market mechanism and partly on a command mechanism to coordinate economic activity.

Mixed good   A good that lies between a private good and a public good.

Momentary supply curve   The supply curve that describes the immediate response of the quantity supplied to a change in price.

Monetarist   A macroeconomist who assigns a high degree of importance to variations in the quantity of money as the main determinant of aggregate demand and who regards the economy as inherently stable.

Monetary base   The level of bankers' deposits at the Bank of England plus cash held by the banks, building societies and the public.

Monetary exchange   A system in which some commodity or token serves as the medium of exchange.

Monetary policy   The attempt to control inflation and the foreign exchange value of the domestic currency and to moderate the business cycle by changing the quantity of money in circulation and adjusting interest rates.

Monetary union   The proposed replacement of the currencies of the EU member countries by a single EU currency, an arrangement which would require a European central bank to regulate the supply of the new European currency.

Money   A medium of exchange.

Money financing   The financing of the government sector deficit by the sale of bonds to the Bank of England which results in the creation of additional money.

Money multiplier   The amount by which a change in the monetary base must be multiplied to determine the resulting change in the quantity of money.

Money wage rate   The wage rate expressed in current pounds.

Monopolistic competition   A market type in which a large number of firms compete with each other by making similar but slightly different goods or services.

Monopoly   A market type in which there is a sole supplier of a good, service or resource that has no close substitutes and in which there is a barrier preventing the entry of new firms into the industry.

Monopsony   A market structure in which there is just a single buyer.

Moral hazard   When one of the parties to an agreement has an incentive, after the agreement is made, to act in a manner that brings additional benefits to himself or herself at the expense of the other party.

Multiplier   The change in equilibrium real GDP divided by the change in autonomous expenditure which caused GDP to change.

Nash equilibrium   The outcome of a game in which player A takes the best possible action given the action of player B, and player B takes the best possible action given the action of player A.

National debt   The central government's debt.

Nationalization   The act of placing a company under public ownership.

Nationalized industry   An industry owned and operated by a publicly owned authority directly responsible to a government.

Natural monopoly   A monopoly that occurs when there is a unique source of supply of raw material or when one large firm can supply the entire market at a lower price than two or more smaller firms can.

Natural rate of unemployment   The unemployment rate when the economy is at full employment and the only unemployment is frictional.

Natural resources   The non-produced factors of production with which we are endowed – all the gifts of nature, including land, water, air and all the minerals that they contain.

Negative relationship   A relationship between two variables that move in opposite directions.

Net benefit   Total benefit minus total cost.

Net borrower   A country that is borrowing more from the rest of the world than it is lending to it.

Net domestic product   GDP minus capital consumption.

Net export function   The relationship between a country's net exports and its real GDP, holding constant real GDP in the rest of the world, prices, and the exchange rate.

Net exporter   A country whose value of exports exceeds its value of imports – its balance of trade is positive.

Net exports   The expenditure by foreigners on UK-produced goods and services minus the expenditure by UK residents on foreign-produced goods and services.

Net financial assets   Financial assets minus financial liabilities.

Net importer   A country whose value of imports exceeds its value of exports – its balance of trade is negative.

Net investment   Net additions to the capital stock – gross investment minus depreciation.

Net lender   A country that is lending more to the rest of the world than it is borrowing from it.

Net national product   GNP minus capital consumption.

Net present value of an investment   The present value of a stream of marginal revenue products generated by the investment minus the cost of that investment.

Newly industrialized country   A country where there is a rapidly developing broad industrial base and where per capita income is growing quickly.

Nominal borrowing requirement   The nominal value of the government sector's borrowing requirement.

Nominal GDP   The output of final goods and services valued at current prices.

Non-market activity   Leisure and non-market production activities, including education and training.

Non-profit-making firm   An organization that chooses or is required to have equal costs and total revenue.

Non-renewable natural resources   Natural resources that can only be used once and that cannot be replaced once used.

Non-tariff barriers   Any action other than a tariff that restricts international trade.

Non-traded product   A good or service that cannot be traded over long distances.

Normal good   A good (or service) the demand for which increases when income increases.

Normative statement   A statement about what *ought* to be. An expression of an opinion that cannot be verified by observation.

Official reserves   The central government's holdings of foreign currencies.

Oligopoly   A market type in which small numbers of producers compete with each other.

Open economy   An economy that has economic links with other economies.

Open market operation   The purchase or sale of UK government securities by the Bank of England.

Open union   A group of workers who have a variety of skills and job types.

Opportunity cost   The best forgone alternative.

Optimizing   Balancing benefits against costs to do the best within the limits of what is possible.

Ordinary share   A title to the ownership of a fraction of a company.

Origin   The zero point that is common to both axes on a graph.

Original income   The income received by a household before allowing for any adjustments by the central government or local authorities.

Output approach   A measure of GDP obtained by summing the value added of each firm and government department in the economy.

Output quotas   Upper limits on output production by EU farmers, first introduced in 1984 for milk.

Overutilized capacity   When a plant produces more than the output at which average total cost is a minimum.

Partnership   A firm with two or more owners who have unlimited liability.

Patent   An exclusive right granted by the government to the inventor of a product or service.

Payoff   The score of each player in a game.

Payoff matrix   A table that shows the payoffs resulting from every possible action by each player for every possible action by each other player.

Peace dividend   The sharp cut that people hope will be made to the defence budget following improved relations with Eastern Europe and the collapse of communism.

Peak   The upper turning point of a business cycle – the point at which the economy is turning from expansion to contraction.

Per capita production function   A curve showing how per capita output varies as the per capita stock of capital varies, with a given technology.

Perfect competition   A state that occurs in markets in which the following conditions exist: a large number of firms sell an identical product; there are many buyers; there are no restrictions on entry; existing firms have no advantage over potential new entrants; and all firms and buyers are fully informed about the prices of each and every firm.

Perfect price discrimination   The practice of charging each consumer the maximum price that he or she is willing to pay for each unit bought.

Perfectly competitive firm's supply curve   A curve that shows how a perfectly competitive firm's output varies as the market price varies.

Perfectly elastic demand   Demand with an elasticity of infinity; the quantity demanded becomes zero if the price rises by the smallest amount and the quantity demanded becomes infinite if the price falls by the smallest amount.

Perfectly elastic supply   Elasticity of supply is infinite; the quantity supplied becomes zero if the price falls by the slightest amount, and the quantity supplied becomes infinite if the price rises by the slightest amount.

Perfectly inelastic demand   Demand with an elasticity of zero; the quantity demanded does not change as the price rises.

Perfectly inelastic supply   Elasticity of supply is zero; the quantity supplied does not change as the price changes.

Phillips curve   Shows the relationship between inflation and unemployment.

Physical assets   Plant, buildings, vehicles, machinery, stocks (of raw materials, work in progress and finished goods) and consumer durable goods. Physical assets are also called capital.

Physical limits   The maximum output that a plant can produce.

Point elasticity   The elasticity at a point on a demand curve or supply curve.

Politicians   Elected representatives in the EU, central and local government – from the prime minister, cabinet ministers and other ministers to ordinary MEPs, MPs and local councillors.

Portfolio choice   A choice concerning which assets and liabilities to hold.

Positive relationship   A relationship between two variables that move in the same direction.

Positive statement   A statement about what *is*. Something that can be verified by careful observation.

Poverty trap   A situation in which attempts to improve living standards by working harder have a negligible effect.

Preference share   A company share whose owner is usually entitled to fixed interest payments which must be paid before any dividends are paid to holders of ordinary shares.

Preferences   A ranking of likes and dislikes and the intensity of those likes and dislikes.

Present value   The value at the present time of a future sum of money. It is equal to the amount that, if invested today, will grow as large as that future sum, taking into account the interest that it will earn.

Price discrimination   The practice of charging a higher price to some customers than to others for an identical good or service, or of charging an individual customer a higher price on a small purchase than on a large one.

Price-earnings ratio   The current price of a share divided by the current profit per share.

Price effect   The effect of a change in the price of a good or service on the quantity consumed.

Price elasticity of demand   The percentage change in the quantity demanded of a good or service divided by the percentage change in its price.

Price index   A measure of the average level of prices in one period as a percentage of their level in an earlier period.

Price level   The average level of prices as measured by a price index.

Price stability   A situation in which the average level of prices is moving neither up nor down.

Price taker   A firm that cannot influence the price of its output.

Principal   A firm (or person) that hires a person (or firm) to undertake a specific job.

Principle of minimum differentiation   The tendency for competitors to make themselves almost identical in order to appeal to the maximum number of clients or voters.

Private enterprise   An economic system that permits individuals to decide on their own economic activities.

Private good   A good (or service), each unit of which is consumed by only one individual.

Private information   Information that is available to one person but is too costly for anyone else to obtain.

Private property right   Legally established title to the sole ownership of a scarce resource.

Private sector surplus or deficit   The difference between saving and investment. If saving exceeds investment, the private sector has a surplus. If investment exceeds saving, the private sector has a deficit.

Privatization   The process of selling a public corporation to private shareholders.

Process theory of distributive justice   A theory of distributive justice that examines the fairness of the *mechanism* or *process* that results in a given distribution.

Producer surplus   The difference between a producer's total revenue and the opportunity cost of production.

Product differentiation   Making a product slightly different from that of a competing firm.

Product standards regulations   Legally defined standards of product design, materials and ingredients, and quality, usually based on health or safety conditions, but having an effect on the ease with which foreign products can be sold in a domestic market.

Production   The conversion of natural, human and capital resources into goods and services.

Production function   A relationship showing how output varies as the employment of inputs is varied.

Production possibility frontier   The boundary between attainable and unattainable levels of production.

Productivity   The output per unit of input. For example, labour productivity can be measured as output per hour of labour.

Professional association   An organized group of professional workers, such as lawyers, dentists, or doctors, that seeks to influence their compensation and other labour market conditions affecting its members.

Profit maximization   Making the largest possible profit.

Progressive income tax   An income tax where the portion of income paid in tax is higher for people on high incomes than for people on low incomes.

Prohibition   Making the buying and selling of some particular good or service illegal.

Property   Anything of value.

Property income   Payments between countries of interest, profits and dividends.

Property rights   Social arrangements that govern the ownership, use and disposal of property.

Proportional income tax   An income tax where the portion of income paid in tax is the same for people on high incomes as it is for people on low incomes.

Protectionism   The restriction of international trade by governments.

Public choice theory   A theory predicting the behaviour of the government sector of the economy as the outcome of the individual choices made by voters, politicians and bureaucrats interacting in a political market-place.

Public corporation   A nationalized company.

Public interest theory   A theory predicting that government action will take place to eliminate waste and achieve an efficient allocation of resources.

Public interest theory of intervention   A theory that intervention is supplied to satisfy the demand of consumers and producers for the maximization of total surplus – or the attainment of allocative efficiency.

Public sector borrowing requirement (PSBR)   Refers to the government sector borrowing requirement plus the borrowing requirement of the nationalized industries.

Public sector procurement bias   A situation where central or local governments buy domestically produced goods or services in preference to cheaper or better ones produced abroad.

Purchasing power parity   A situation that occurs when money has equal value across countries.

Pure public good   A good or service, each unit of which is consumed by everyone and from which no one can be excluded.

Quantity demanded   The amount of a good or service that consumers plan to buy in a given period of time.

Quantity of labour demanded   The number of labour hours hired by all the firms in an economy.

Quantity of labour supplied   The number of hours of labour services that households supply to firms.

Quantity of sterling assets   The assets that comprise the monetary base plus government debt held by the private sector – that is, held by households and firms (other than the Bank of England).

Quantity supplied   The amount of a good or service that producers plan to sell in a given period of time.

Quantity theory of money   The proposition that an increase in the quantity of money leads to an equal percentage increase in the price level.

Quota   A restriction on the quantity of a good that a firm is permitted to sell or that a country is permitted to import.

Rate of return regulation   A regulation that sets the price at a level that enables the regulated firm to earn a specified target percentage return on its capital.

Rational choice   The best possible course of action from the point of view of the individual making the choice.

Rational expectation   A forecast that uses all of the relevant information available about past and present events and has the least possible error.

Rational ignorance   The decision not to acquire information, because the cost of doing so is greater than the benefit derived from having it.

Rawlsian theory of fairness   A theory of distributive justice that gives the biggest income possible to the least well-off.

Real borrowing requirement   The change in the real value of the government sector's gross debt in a given period.

Real business cycle theory   A theory of aggregate fluctuations based on the existence of flexible wages and random shocks to the economy's aggregate production function.

Real GDP   The output of final goods and services valued at prices prevailing in the base period.

Real income   Income expressed in units of goods or services. Real income in terms of a particular good or service is income divided by the price of that good or service.

Real interest rate   The interest rate minus the expected inflation rate.

Real money   The quantity of goods and services that a given amount of money will buy.

Real wage rate   The wage rate per hour expressed in constant pounds.

Recession   A contraction in the level of economic activity in which real GDP declines in two successive quarters.

Regional policy   A policy which seeks to reduce disparities – such as different unemployment rates – between different regions.

Regressive income tax   An income tax where the portion of income paid in tax is lower for people on high incomes than for people on low incomes.

Regulation   Rules enforced by a government agency to restrict economic activity by determining prices, product standards and types, and the conditions under which new firms may enter an industry.

Relative price   The ratio of the price of one good or service to the price of another. It is expressed as the number of units of one good or service that one unit of another will buy.

Renewable natural resources   Natural resources that can be used repeatedly without depleting what is available for future use.

Rent ceiling   A regulation making it illegal to charge a rent higher than a specified level.

Rent seeking   The activity of attempting to create a monopoly.

Resale price maintenance   A situation where a manufacturer supplies goods to retailers on the condition that they are sold to consumers at a specified price.

Reservation price   The highest price that a buyer is willing to pay for a good.

Reservation wage   The lowest wage rate at which a person and household will supply any labour to the market. Below that wage, a person will not work.

Reserve ratio   The fraction of a banks' total deposits that are held in reserves.

Reserves   Cash holdings in a bank's vault plus the bank's deposits with the Bank of England.

Residual claimant   The agent or agents who receive a firm's profits and are responsible for its losses.

Restrictive practice   An agreement between two firms not to compete in some respect such as price, output levels or quality.

Retail Price Index   Measures the average level of the prices of a basket of goods and services consumed by typical households.

Returns to scale   Increases in output that result from increasing all the inputs by the same percentage.

Risk   A state in which more than one outcome may occur and the probability of each possible outcome can be estimated.

Saving   Income minus consumption. Saving is measured in the national income accounts as disposable income minus consumers' expenditure.

Saving function   The relationship between saving and disposable income.

Scarcity   The universal state in which wants exceed the amount that available resources can produce.

Scatter diagram   A diagram which plots the value of one economic variable associated with the value of another.

Search activity   The time and effort spent in searching for someone with whom to do business.

Self-sufficiency   A state that occurs when each individual consumes only what he or she produces.

Set-aside   Payments to EU farmers to remove some of their land from agricultural production.

Short run   A period of time in which the quantities of some inputs are fixed while others can be varied.

Short-run aggregate production function   The relationship showing how real GDP varies as the quantity of labour employed varies, holding the capital stock and the state of technology constant.

Short-run aggregate supply   The relationship between the aggregate quantity of final goods and services (real GDP) supplied and the price level (the GDP deflator), holding everything else constant.

Short-run aggregate supply curve   A curve showing the relationship between the quantity of real GDP supplied and the price level, holding everything else constant.

Short-run demand curve   The demand curve that describes the initial response of buyers to a change in the price of a good or service.

Short-run demand for labour   The relationship between the wage rate and the quantity of labour demanded when the firm's capital input is fixed and labour is the only variable input.

Short-run elasticity of demand for labour   The percentage change in the quantity of labour demanded divided by the percentage change in the wage rate when labour is the only variable input.

Short-run industry supply curve   A curve that shows how the total quantity supplied in the short run by all the firms in an industry varies as the market price varies.

Short-run Phillips curve   Shows the relationship between inflation and unemployment, holding the expected inflation rate and the natural rate of unemployment constant.

Short-run production function   The relationship showing how output varies when the quantity of labour employed varies, holding constant the quantity of capital and the state of technology.

Short-run supply curve   The supply curve that describes the response of the quantity supplied to a change in price when only *some* of the technologically possible adjustments to the production process have been made.

Shutdown point   The level of output and price at which the firm is just covering its total variable cost.

Signal   An action taken outside a market that conveys information that can be used by that market.

Single-price monopoly   A monopoly that charges the same price for each unit of output.

Slope   The change in the value of the variable measured on the y-axis divided by the change in the value of the variable measured on the x-axis.

Socialism   An economic system based on state ownership of land and on a centrally planned allocation of resources.

Sole proprietorship   A firm with a single owner who has unlimited liability.

Specialization   The production of only one, or a few goods or services.

Specific tax   A tax on a good or service which is set as a fixed amount per unit of the good or service sold.

Standard of deferred payment   An agreed measure in which contracts for future receipts and payments are written.

Stock   A quantity measured at a point in time.

Stock exchange   An organized market for trading in securities.

Stocks   Holdings by firms of raw materials and finished goods.

Store of value   Any commodity that can be held and sold at a later time.

Strategic behaviour   Acting in a way that takes into account the expected behaviour of others and the mutual recognition of interdependence.

Strategies   All the possible actions of each player.

Strike   The refusal of a group of workers to work under the prevailing conditions.

Subsidy   A payment made by the government to producers of goods and services.

Subsidy on expenditure   A subsidy with which the government makes a payment to a firm for each unit of output supplied.

Substitutes   A good or service that may be used in place of another.

Substitution effect   The effect of a change in prices on the quantities consumed when the consumer remains indifferent between the original and the new combinations of consumed.

Sunk costs   The historical cost of buying plant and machinery that have no current resale value.

Supply   The entire relationship between the quantity supplied of a good or service and its price.

Supply curve   A graph showing the relationship between the quantity supplied and the price of a good or service, holding everything else constant.

Supply of labour   The quantity of labour supplied at each real wage rate.

Supply schedule   A list of quantities supplied at different prices, holding everything else constant.

Takeover   The purchase of one firm by another firm.

Targeting   Concentrating the payment of transfer payments on to the poorest households.

Tariff   A tax that is imposed by the importing country when a good crosses an international boundary.

Tax base   The activity on which a tax is levied.

Tax on expenditure   A tax on the production or the sale of a good or service.

Tax rate   The percentage rate at which a tax is levied on a particular activity.

Team production   A production process in which a group of individuals each specialize in mutually supportive tasks.

Technique   Any feasible way of converting inputs into output.

Technological efficiency   A state in which it is not possible to increase output without increasing inputs.

Technological progress   The development of new and better ways of producing goods and services.

Technology   The method for converting resources into goods and services.

Theory of distributive justice   A set of principles against which one can test whether a particular distribution of economic well-being is fair.

Time-series graph   A graph showing the value of a variable on the y-axis plotted against time on the x-axis.

Tit-for-tat strategy   A strategy in which a player cooperates in the current period if the other player cooperated in the previous period but cheats if the other player cheated in the previous period.

Total benefit   The total pound value that people place on a given level of provision of a public good.

Total cost   The sum of the costs of all the inputs used in production.

Total fixed cost   The cost of all the fixed inputs.

Total product   The total quantity produced by a firm in a given period of time.

Total product curve   A graph showing the maximum output attainable with a given amount of capital as the amount of labour employed is varied.

Total revenue   The amount received from the sale of a good or service. It equals the price of the good or service multiplied by the quantity sold.

Total surplus   The sum of consumer surplus and producer surplus.

Total utility   The total benefit or satisfaction that a person gets from the consumption of goods and services.

Total variable cost   The cost of variable inputs.

Trade union   A group of workers organized principally for the purpose of increasing wages and improving conditions.

Trade-weighted index   Shows the value of the pound against a basket of other currencies.

Transactions costs   The costs arising from finding a trading partner, negotiating an agreement about the price and other aspects of the exchange, and of ensuring that the terms of the agreement are fulfilled.

Transactions in external assets   The total value of assets in other countries bought by UK citizens minus the value of any other assets in other countries sold by UK citizens.

Transactions in external assets and liabilities   The account on the balance of payments which covers all purchases and sales of assets in other countries by UK citizens and all purchases and sales of assets in the United Kingdom by foreign citizens.

Transactions in external liabilities   The total value of UK assets acquired by foreign citizens minus the value of any UK assets that foreign citizens have sold.

Transfer earnings   The income required to induce the supply of a factor of production to its present use.

Transfer payment   A payment made by the government to households.

Transfer payments multiplier   The amount by which a change in transfer payments must be multiplied to determine the change that it generates in equilibrium expenditure and real GDP.

Trend   A general tendency for a variable to rise or fall.

Trigger strategy   A strategy in which a player cooperates if the other player cooperates but plays the Nash equilibrium strategy thereafter if the other player cheats.

Trough   The lower turning point of a business cycle the point at which the economy turns from contraction to expansion.

Two-part tariff   A pricing arrangement that results in consumers facing a bill with two parts.

Unanticipated inflation   Inflation that catches people by surprise.

Uncertainty   A state in which more than one event may occur but we don't know which one.

Underdeveloped country   A country in which there is little industrialization, limited mechanization of the agricultural sector, very little capital equipment, and low per capita income.

Unemployment   The number of adult workers who are not employed and who are seeking jobs.

Unemployment equilibrium   A situation in which macroeconomic equilibrium occurs at a level of real GDP below long-run aggregate supply.

Unemployment rate   Unemployment expressed as a percentage of the labour force.

Unit elastic demand   An elasticity of demand of 1; the quantity demanded of a good or service and its price change in equal proportions.

Unit elastic supply   An elasticity of supply of 1; the quantity supplied of a good or service and its price change in equal proportions.

Unit of account   An agreed measure for stating the prices of goods and services.

Unlimited liability   The legal responsibility for all debts incurred by a firm up to an amount equal to the entire wealth of its owner.

Utilitarian theory   The theory that the fairest outcome is the one that maximizes the sum of all individual utilities in society.

Utility   The benefit or satisfaction that a person obtains from the consumption of a good or service.

Utility maximization   The attainment of the greatest possible utility.

Utility of wealth   The utility that a person attaches to a given amount of wealth.

Value added   The value of a firm's output minus the value of the inputs bought from other firms.

Value of money   The amount of goods and services that can be bought with a given amount of money.

Variable cost   A cost that varies with the output level.

Variable inputs   Those inputs whose quantity used can be varied in the short run.

Velocity of circulation   The average number of times a pound is used annually to buy the goods and services that make up GDP.

Vertical merger   A merger between a firm and one of its suppliers or customers.

Visible balance   The balance of money received from exports of goods and money spent on the imports of goods.

Visible trade   The exports and imports of goods.

Voluntary export restraint (VER)   A self-imposed restriction by an exporting country on the volume of its exports of a particular good. Voluntary export restraints are often called VERs.

Voters   The consumers of the outcome of the political process.

Wants   The unlimited desires or wishes that people have for goods and services.

Wealth   The total assets of a household, firm or government minus its total liabilities.

Welfare   The overall well-being of a nation's citizens.

Welfare state capitalism   An economic system combining capitalism's private ownership of capital and land with a heavy degree of state intervention in the allocation of resources.

x-axis   The horizontal scale on a graph.

x-coordinate   A line running from a point horizontally to the y-axis. It is called the x-coordinate because its length is the same as the value marked off on the x-axis.

y-axis   The vertical scale on a graph.

y-coordinate   A line running from a point on a graph vertically to the x-axis. It is called the y-coordinate because its length is the same as the value marked off on the y-axis.

INDEX